ELEMENTS OF
Literature

INTRODUCTORY COURSE

ELEMENTS OF
Literature
INTRODUCTORY COURSE

In the joy of story,
in the power of story,
to create a world of power and joy
for all living beings.

—Floating Eagle Feather

HOLT, RINEHART AND WINSTON

A Harcourt Education Company

Austin • Orlando • Chicago • New York • Toronto • London • San Diego

Credits

EDITORIAL

Project Director: Kathleen Daniel

Managing Editors: Richard Sime, Bill Wahlgren

Project Editor: Robert Giannetto

Book Editors: Richard Kelso, Leslie Griffin, Hester Weeden

Editorial Staff: Steven Fechter, Julie Brye, Susan Kent Cakars, Dorothy M. Coe, Edward S. Cohen, Lanie Lee, Christine de Lignières, Ron Ottaviano, Jan Collins, Michael Zakhar, and Abigail Winograd; David Knaggs and Sharon Churchin; Vicky Aeschbacher, Jane Archer-Feinstein, Roger Boylan, James Decker, Eric Estlund, Peggy Ferrin, Emily Gavin, Mikki Gibson, Annie Hartnett, Sean Henry, Julie Hoover, Eileen Joyce, Marcia Kelley, Linda Miller, Chi Nguyen, Carla Robinson, Deanna Roy, Tressa Sanders, Errol Smith, Suzanne Thompson, and Stephen Wesson

Editorial Support Staff: Dan Hunter, Laurie Muir, David Smith, Leila Jamal, Elizabeth Butler, Ruth Hooker, Kelly Keeley, Marie Price, Margaret Sanchez

Permissions: Tamara Blanken, Sacha Frey, Mark Hughs

Research and Development: Joan Burditt

PRODUCTION AND DESIGN

Text Design: Preface, Inc.

Electronic Files: Preface, Inc., H&S Graphics, Inc.

Production and Manufacturing: Athena Blackorby

Marketing Design: Bob Bretz

COVER

Cover Artist: Greg Geisler

Photo Credits: Front cover: (leopard), Art Wolfe/Tony Stone Images; (goat), Dr. E. R. Degginger/Color-Pic, Inc.; (puppy), Reed/Barbara Lowe/Animals Animals; (parrot), Corbis Images/HRW; (spider), Larry West/FPG International. Back cover: (cat), Sam Dudgeon/HRW.

Quotation on Cover: Floating Eagle Feather (p. 570), courtesy of Linnet Books

Program Authors

Kylene Beers wrote the Reading Matters section of the book and developed the accompanying *Reading Skills and Strategies* component. A former middle school teacher, Dr. Beers has turned her commitment to helping readers having difficulty into the major focus of her research, writing, speaking, and teaching. A clinical associate professor at the University of Houston, Dr. Beers is also currently the editor of the National Council of Teachers of English journal *Voices from the Middle.* She is the author of *When Kids Can't Read: The Reading Handbook for Teachers 6–12* and co-editor of *Into Focus: Understanding and Creating Middle School Readers.* She has served on the review boards of the *English Journal* and *The Alan Review.* Dr. Beers is a recipient of the NCTE Richard W. Halle Award. She currently serves on the board of directors of the International Reading Association's Special Interest Group on Adolescent Literature.

Robert E. Probst established the pedagogical framework for the 1997, 2000, and the current editions of *Elements of Literature.* Dr. Probst is Professor of English Education at Georgia State University. He has taught English in Maryland and been Supervisor of English for the Norfolk, Virginia, Public Schools. He is the author of *Response and Analysis: Teaching Literature in Junior and Senior High School* and has contributed chapters to such books as *Literature Instruction: A Focus on Student Response; Reader Response in the Classroom; Handbook of Research on Teaching the English Language Arts; Transactions with Literature;* and *For Louise M. Rosenblatt.* Dr. Probst has worked on the National Council of Teachers of English Committee on Research, the Commission on Reading, and the Commission on Curriculum. He has also served on the board of directors of the Adolescent Literature Assembly and is a member of the National Conference on Research in Language and Literacy.

Robert Anderson wrote the Elements of Literature essay on drama. Mr. Anderson is a playwright, novelist, screenwriter, and teacher. His plays include *Tea and Sympathy; Silent Night, Lonely Night; You Know I Can't Hear You When the Water's Running;* and *I Never Sang for My Father.* His screenplays include *The Nun's Story* and *The Sand Pebbles.* Mr. Anderson has taught at the Writers' Workshop at the University of Iowa, the American Theater Wing Professional Training Program, and the Salzburg Seminar in American Studies. He is a past president of the Dramatists' Guild, a past vice president of the Authors' League of America, and a member of the Theater Hall of Fame.

John Leggett wrote the Elements of Literature essays on the short story and contributed to the instructional materials on short stories. Mr. Leggett is a novelist, biographer, and former teacher. He went to the Writers' Workshop at the University of Iowa in the spring of 1969, expecting to work there for a single semester. In 1970, he assumed temporary charge of the program, and for the next seventeen years he was its director. Mr. Leggett's novels include *Wilder Stone; The Gloucester Branch; Who Took the Gold Away?; Gulliver House;* and *Making Believe.* He also wrote the highly acclaimed biography *Ross and Tom: Two American Tragedies.*

John Malcolm Brinnin wrote the Elements of Literature essays on poetry and contributed to the instructional materials on poetry. Mr. Brinnin is the author of six volumes of poetry, which received many prizes and awards. He was a member of the American Academy and Institute of Arts and Letters. He was also a critic of poetry and a biographer of poets and was for a number of years director of New York's famous Poetry Center. His teaching career, begun at Vassar College, included long terms at the University of Connecticut and Boston University, where he succeeded Robert Lowell as Professor of Creative Writing and Contemporary Letters. Mr. Brinnin's books include *Dylan Thomas in America: An Intimate Journal* and *Sextet: T. S. Eliot & Truman Capote & Others.*

Judith L. Irvin established the conceptual basis for the vocabulary and reading strands and developed the Reading Skills and Strategies exercises for grades 6–8. Dr. Irvin teaches courses in curriculum, middle school education, and educational leadership at Florida State University. She was chair of the Research Committee of the National Middle School Association and was the editor of *Research in Middle Level Education* for five years. She taught middle school for eight years before seeking her doctorate in Reading-Language Arts. Dr. Irvin writes a column, "What Research Says to the Middle Level Practitioner," for the *Middle School Journal.* Her many books include *Reading and the Middle School Student: Strategies to Enhance Literacy* and *What Current Research Says to the Middle Level Practitioner.*

Special Contributors

Joseph Bruchac wrote the Elements of Literature essays on mythology and folk tales. Dr. Bruchac is a storyteller and writer whose poems, stories, and essays have appeared in more than four hundred magazines, from *National Geographic* to *American Poetry Review.* Author of sixty books, many of which reflect his Abenaki ancestry, he holds a Ph.D. in Comparative Literature and is the founder of the Greenfield Review Press. He lives in the house he was raised in by his grandparents in the Adirondack foothills. He frequently performs with his two grown sons, Jim and Jesse, who are also writers and storytellers.

Joann Leonard wrote the essay "From Page to Stage" and directed the students who appear in the photographs that illustrate *The Adventure of the Speckled Band* and *Rumpelstiltskin.* Ms. Leonard is the founder and director of MetaStages, a drama program for youth at the School of Theatre Arts at Pennsylvania State University. She is the author of *The Soup Has Many Eyes,* a historical memoir, and of *All the World's a Stage,* two collections of children's plays adapted from multicultural folk tales. Trained in theater at Northwestern University, Ms. Leonard studied mime in Paris and has appeared professionally as an actor throughout the United States and Europe.

Writers

The writers prepared instructional materials for the text under the supervision of Dr. Probst and the editorial staff.

Lynn Hovland
Former Teacher
Educational Writer and Editor
Berkeley, California

Erin Hurley
Former Faculty Member
Brown University
Providence, Rhode Island

Julith Jedamus
Educational Writer and Editor
Pacific Palisades, California

William Kaufman
Former Teacher
Educational Writer and Editor
Hempstead, New York

David Pence
Former Teacher
Educational Writer and Editor
Brooklyn, New York

Reviewers and Consultants

Reviewers assisted in choosing selections and evaluated instructional materials. Consultants assisted in securing student active-reading models and provided advice on current pedagogy.

Pat Berry
Western Middle School
Russiaville, Indiana

Regina Blais
North Cumberland Middle
  School
Cumberland, Rhode Island

Pamela Britts
Ladue Junior High School
St. Louis, Missouri

Lisa Brunelle
North Cumberland Middle
  School
Cumberland, Rhode Island

Toni Eyrich
Three Rivers Middle School
Cleves, Ohio

Ellen D. Foster
Albuquerque Public Schools
Albuquerque, New Mexico

Joyce Francis
Howard–Spring Street School
Bridgewater, Massachusetts

Sally Gaddis
Westview Middle School
Longmont, Colorado

Pamela Moore
Milford Junior High School
Milford, Ohio

Dr. Madeline Pan
East Orange School District
East Orange, New Jersey

Sharon Pope
Moody Middle School
Richmond, Virginia

Carol Roemer
Farnsworth Middle School
Guilderland, New York

Connie Sartori
Seminole Middle School
Seminole, Florida

Marilyn Walker
Waite Park School
Minneapolis, Minnesota

Susan Weaver
Maitland Middle School
Maitland, Florida

Jacqueline Yancy
JMF Center for Educational
  Services
Indianapolis, Indiana

Acknowledgments

For permission to reprint copyrighted material in the Annotated Teacher's Edition, grateful acknowledgment is made to the following sources:

American Library Association: From "Growing Up with Stories" by Mildred D. Taylor from *Booklist*, vol. 87, no. 7, December 1, 1990. Copyright © 1990 by the American Library Association.

Eliot Glazer for Tony Awards Online and Laurel Media, Inc.: Quote by Julie Taymor from an interview conducted by Chris Haines on December 6, 1996, from *Tony Awards Online.* Copyright © 1996 by Laurel Media, Inc. Available June 23, 1999, http://www.tonys.org /features/Taymor1.html.

The Gale Group: From "Virginia Hamilton" from *Contemporary Authors*, vol. 20, edited by Ann Evory and Linda Metzer. Copyright © 1984 by Gale Research Company. All rights reserved. Quote by Laura Ingram from *Dictionary of Literary Biography*, vol. 52, *American Writers for Children Since 1960: Fiction*, edited by Matthew J. Bruccoli. Copyright © 1986 by Gale Research Company. All rights reserved. From "Robert Cormier" from *Something About the Author*, vol. 45, edited by Anne Commire. Copyright © 1986 by Gale Research Company. All rights reserved. From "Ogden Nash" from *Something About the Author*, vol. 46, edited by Anne Commire. Copyright © 1987 by Gale Research Company. All rights reserved. From "Maya Angelou" from *Something About the Author*, vol. 49, edited by Anne Commire. Copyright © 1987 by Gale Research Company. All rights reserved. From "Bruce Coville" from *Something About the Author*, vol. 77, edited by Kevin S. Hile and Diane Telgen. Copyright © 1994 by Gale Research Inc. All rights reserved.

Green & Heaton Ltd.: From "In Mystery Stories, Rooms Furnished ..." by P. D. James (author of *A Certain Justice*) from *The New York Times*, August 25, 1983. Copyright © 1983 by P. D. James.

GuildAmerica® Books, an imprint of Doubleday Direct, Inc.: From Introduction by Joanna Cole from *Best-Loved Folktales of the World*, edited by Joanna Cole. Copyright © 1982 by Joanna Cole.

Harcourt, Inc.: From "Tentative (First Model) Definitions of Poetry" from *Good Morning, America* by Carl Sandburg. Copyright 1928 and renewed © 1956 by Carl Sandburg.

Patricia Lauber: From speech, "The Evolution of a Science Writer," by Patricia Lauber given at the National Council of Teachers of English Spring Conference, April 7, 1989, Charleston, South Carolina. Copyright © 1989 by Patricia Lauber.

Little, Brown and Company (Inc.): "The Cow," "The Eel," "The Fly" and "The Mules" from *Verses from 1929 On* by Ogden Nash. Copyright 1931, 1942, 1950 by Ogden Nash. "The Cow," "The Eel," and "The Mules" first appeared in *The New Yorker.* "The Fly" first appeared in *The Saturday Evening Post.*

Macmillan Library Reference USA, a division of Ahsuog, Inc.: From "Hans Christian Andersen" from *European Writers: The Romantic Century*, vol. 6, *Victor Hugo to Theodor Fontaine*, by Jacques Barzun, editor, and George Stade, editor-in-chief. Copyright © 1985 by Charles Scribner's Sons.

Carolyn L. Mazloomi: From "Artist's Statement" by Carolyn L. Mazloomi from *Carolyn Mazloomi.* Copyright © 1998 by Carolyn Mazloomi. Available April 22, 1999, http://www.mindspring.com /~mazloomi/statement.html.

National Council of Teachers of English: From "A Letter to Gabriela, a Young Writer" by Pat Mora from *English Journal*, September 1990. Copyright © 1990 by the National Council of Teachers of English.

James E. Person, Jr.: from "Ray Bradbury: 'A Poet of Affirmation'" from *The Detroit News*, August 30, 1995. Copyright © 1995 by James E. Person, Jr.

Publishers Weekly: Quote by Julius Lester from "Julius Lester," an interview by Barry List, from *Publishers Weekly*, February 12, 1988, pp. 67–68. Copyright © 1988 by Publishers Weekly.

Rizzoli International Publications, Inc.: From *Fabergé: Court Jeweler to the Tsars* by G. von Habsburg-Lothringen and A. von Solodkoff, translated by J. A. Underwood. Copyright © 1979 by Office du Livre, Fribourg, Switzerland.

Routledge: From Introduction from *Don't Bet on the Prince: Contemporary Feminist Fairy Tales in North America and England* by Jack Zipes. Copyright © 1986 by Jack Zipes.

Scholastic Inc.: From "Dr. Seuss" from *Meet the Authors and Illustrators*, edited by Deborah Kovacs and James Preller. Copyright © 1991 by Scholastic, Inc.

School Library Journal: From "School Visits: The Author's Viewpoint" by Avi with Betty Miles from *School Library Journal*, January 1987. Copyright © 1987 by School Library Journal.

Gary Soto: Autobiographical comment by Gary Soto. Copyright © 1997 by Gary Soto.

University of New Mexico Press: Quote by Pat Mora from *This Is About Vision: Interviews with Southwestern Writers*, edited by William Balassi, John F. Crawford, and Annie O. Eysturoy. Copyright © 1990 by University of New Mexico Press.

The H. W. Wilson Company: From "Jack Prelutsky" from *Fifth Book of Junior Authors & Illustrators*, edited by Sally Holmes Holtze. Copyright © 1983 by The H. W. Wilson Company. All rights reserved. From "Douglas Florian" and from "Lillian Morrison" from *Sixth Book of Junior Authors & Illustrators*, edited by Sally Holmes Holtze. Copyright © 1989 by The H. W. Wilson Company. All rights reserved.

SOURCES CITED

Quote by Lloyd Alexander from "Lloyd Alexander" from *Something About the Author*, vol. 49, edited by Anne Commire. Published by Gale Research Inc., Farmington Hills, MI, 1987.

From "Quotations from Ray Bradbury" from *The Ray Bradbury Page.* Available May 4, 1999, http://www.brookingsbook.com/bradbury /quotations.htm.

From "Ghosts and Voices: Writing from Obsession" by Sandra Cisneros from *Americas Review* 15, Spring 1987 (Houston, TX).

Quote by Robert Fulghum about Maya Angelou from *Washington Post Book World*, 1981.

From speech by Ann Petry from *Horn Book Magazine* (Boston, MA), April 1965, pp. 147–151.

From *By the Shores of Silver Lake* by Laura Ingalls Wilder. Published by HarperCollins Publishers, New York, NY, 1939.

Quote by Jane Yolen from "Jane Yolen" from *The Internet Public Library.* Available April 11, 1999, http://www.ipl.org/youth /AskAuthor/Yolen.html.

CONTENTS IN BRIEF

Collection 1: Moments of Truth

- **Elements of Literature:** Conflict
- **Reading Skills and Strategies**
  Dialogue with the Text
  Context Clues

LITERATURE and Connections
Read On: Independent Reading

COMMUNICATIONS WORKSHOPS
Writer's Workshop: Autobiographical Incident
Sentence Workshop: Sentence Fragments
Reading for Life: Using Text Organizers
Learning for Life: Decision Making

Collection 2: Unforgettable Personalities

- **Elements of Literature:** Autobiography and Biography
- **Reading Skills and Strategies**
  Dialogue with the Text
  Making Inferences

LITERATURE and Connections
Read On: Independent Reading

COMMUNICATIONS WORKSHOPS
Speaking and Listening Workshop: Interviewing
Writer's Workshop: Biographical Sketch
Sentence Workshop: Run-on Sentences
Reading for Life: Independent Reading
Learning for Life: Researching Media Personalities

Collection 3: Machine Mania: People and Technology

- **Elements of Literature:** Poetry
- **Reading Skills and Strategies**
  Dialogue with the Text
  Strategies for Reading Poetry

LITERATURE and Connections
Read On: Independent Reading

COMMUNICATIONS WORKSHOPS
Speaking and Listening Workshop: Oral Interpretation
Writer's Workshop: How-To Essay
Sentence Workshop: Stringy Sentences
Reading for Life: Reading a Manual
Learning for Life: Machines: A User's Guide

Collection 4: All Creatures Great and Small

- **Elements of Literature:** The Main Idea
- **Reading Skills and Strategies**
  Dialogue with the Text
  Organizers: Finding the Structure

LITERATURE and Connections
Read On: Independent Reading

COMMUNICATIONS WORKSHOPS
Writer's Workshop: Informative Report
Sentence Workshop: Wordy Sentences
Reading for Life: Searching the Internet
Learning for Life: Teaching People About Animals

Collection 5: Justice for All

- ■ **Elements of Literature: The Short Story**
- ■ **Reading Skills and Strategies**
  Dialogue with the Text
  Making and Adjusting Predictions

LITERATURE and Connections
Read On: Independent Reading

COMMUNICATIONS WORKSHOPS

Speaking and Listening Workshop: Social
  Interaction
Writer's Workshop: Supporting a Position
Sentence Workshop: Combining Sentences by
  Inserting Words
Reading for Life: Evaluating a Persuasive Message
Learning for Life: Persuading with Editorial
  Cartoons

Collection 6: Onstage!

- ■ **Elements of Literature: Drama**
- ■ **Reading Skills and Strategies**
  Forming Opinions

LITERATURE and Connections
Read On: Independent Reading

COMMUNICATIONS WORKSHOPS

Writer's Workshop: Persuasive Writing: Evaluation
Sentence Workshop: Combining Sentences by Using
  Groups of Words
Reading for Life: Understanding Induction and
  Deduction
Learning for Life: Settling Conflicts with Friends

Collection 7: Explaining Our World: Fact and Fiction

- ■ **Elements of Literature: Subjective and
  Objective Writing**
- ■ **Reading Skills and Strategies**
  Dialogue with the Text
  Reading for Varied Purposes

LITERATURE and Connections
Read On: Independent Reading

COMMUNICATIONS WORKSHOPS

Speaking and Listening Workshop: Speaking to
  Inform
Writer's Workshop: Observational Writing
Sentence Workshop: Combining Sentences by Using
  Connecting Words
Reading for Life: Reading a Science Book
Learning for Life: Scientific Research

Collection 8: Tell Me a Tale

- ■ **Elements of Literature:**
  Mythology
  Folk Tales
- ■ **Reading Skills and Strategies**
  Dialogue with the Text
  Using Word Parts to Build Meanings

LITERATURE and Connections
Read On: Independent Reading

COMMUNICATIONS WORKSHOPS

Writer's Workshop: Story
Sentence Workshop: Joining Sentences
Reading for Life: Reading a Map and a Time Line
Learning for Life: Making Oral Presentations

Resource Center

Handbook of Literary Terms
Communications Handbook
Language Handbook
Glossary

CONTENTS

Reading Matters . . . . 46 (xxx)
Test Smarts . . . . 56 (xl)

Collection One

Moments of Truth

**COLLECTION PLANNING
GUIDE T1A–T1D**

■ **Reading Skills and Strategies**
Dialogue with the Text

Thomas J. Dygard   **Just Once** . . . . SHORT STORY 2
Edwin A. Hoey   **Foul Shot** / Connections . . . . POEM 10

■ **Elements of Literature   Conflict**
It Makes a Story *by* John Leggett 14

Mary Whitebird   **Ta-Na-E-Ka** . . . . SHORT STORY . . .15
Robert Kyle   **Crow Poets** / Connections . . . . MAGAZINE ARTICLE . . .24

■ **Reading Skills and Strategies**
How to Own a Word: Context Clues 30

Lensey Namioka   **The All-American Slurp** . . . . SHORT STORY 31
Coming to America *by* James Cheung /
     Student to Student . . . . ESSAY 40

Gary Soto   **La Bamba** . . . . SHORT STORY 44

Robert Cormier   **President Cleveland, Where Are You?** . . . . SHORT STORY 53
Literature and Science / MVPs—Most Valuable Primates 63

Lloyd Alexander   **The Stone** . . . . SHORT STORY 69

■ **No Questions Asked**
Bill Cosby   **Lessons** . . . . ESSAY 82

Read On 85

Language /
Grammar Links

• Troublesome Verbs   **13**

• Subjects and Verbs—In
   Perfect Agreement   **29**

• Subject-Verb Agreement
   and the Search for the
   Subject   **43**

• Using Verb Tenses   **52**

• Style: Actions Speak Louder
   with Vivid Verbs   **68**

• Watch Your *Don'ts* and
   Doesn'ts   **81**

COMMUNICATIONS WORKSHOPS

Writer's Workshop   Narrative Writing: Autobiographical Incident   86

Sentence Workshop   Sentence Fragments   91

Reading for Life   Using Text Organizers   92

Learning for Life   Decision Making   93

Collection Two

Unforgettable Personalities

COLLECTION PLANNING GUIDE T93A–T93D

■ **Reading Skills and Strategies**
Dialogue with the Text

Gary Paulsen **Storm** *from* **Woodsong** . . . . AUTOBIOGRAPHY 96
Literature and Science / Call of the Wild 103

■ **Elements of Literature   Autobiography and Biography**
Personal Histories 108

Maya Angelou **Brother** *from* **I Know Why the Caged
Bird Sings** . . . . AUTOBIOGRAPHY 109
The Brother I Never Had *by* Gim George /
Student to Student . . . . ESSAY 114

Luci Tapahonso **Yes, It Was My Grandmother** . . . . POEM 117

Pat Mora **Petals / Los pétalos** *translated by* Nicolás Kanellos . . POEM 121

■ **Reading Skills and Strategies**
Making Inferences 125

Russell Freedman **The Mysterious Mr. Lincoln** . . . . BIOGRAPHY 126
Louis W. Koenig **Lincoln's Humor** / Connections . . . . ESSAY 132

Ann Petry **A Glory over Everything** *from* **Harriet Tubman:
Conductor on the Underground Railroad** . . BIOGRAPHY 136

■ **No Questions Asked**
Mark Twain *from* **The Adventures of Tom Sawyer** . . . . NOVEL 150

Read On 155

COMMUNICATIONS WORKSHOPS

Speaking and Listening Workshop Interviewing: Questions, Please   156

Writer's Workshop Expository Writing: Biographical Sketch   158

Sentence Workshop Run-on Sentences   163

Reading for Life Independent Reading   164

Learning for Life Researching Media Personalities   165

**Language /
Grammar Links**

• Using *Good* and *Well*
  Correctly **107**
• Style: Choosing Precise
  Words **116**
• Comparing with
  Adjectives **135**
• Don't Use *Bad* and *Badly*
  Badly **149**

Collection Three

Machine Mania: People and Technology

COLLECTION PLANNING
GUIDE T165A–T165D

■ **Reading Skills and Strategies**
Dialogue with the Text

Anonymous **John Henry** . . . . AFRICAN AMERICAN SONG 168
Literature and Social Studies / Hard Labor. 172
Gloria A. Harris **Working on the Railroad** / Connections . . . . . . .MAGAZINE ARTICLE . . 174

■ **Elements of Literature   Poetry**
Sound Effects *by* John Malcolm Brinnin. 178
from **The Pied Piper of Hamelin**
    by Robert Browning . . . . .POEM 178
Cynthia in the Snow *by* Gwendolyn Brooks . . . . .POEM 178
Good Hot Dogs *by* Sandra Cisneros . . . . .POEM 179

Jack Prelutsky **Ankylosaurus** . . . . .POEM 180

■ **Elements of Literature   Poetry**
Seeing Likenesses *by* John Malcolm Brinnin. 183
Your Poem, Man . . . *by* Edward Lueders . . . . . . .POEM 184

William Jay Smith **The Toaster** . . . . .POEM 186

Lillian Morrison **The Sidewalk Racer** *or* **On the Skateboard** . . .POEM 187

Bobbi Katz **Things to Do If You Are a Subway** . . . . .POEM 188
Literature and Real Life / Underground Poetry .189

Charles Malam   **Steam Shovel** . . . . POEM 190
The Lawn Mower *by* Taunya Woo /
   Student to Student . . . . POEM 192

■ **Reading Skills and Strategies**
Strategies for Reading Poetry 194

Douglas Florian   **The Hill Mynah** . . . . POEM 195
   The Hummingbird . . . . POEM 197

Shel Silverstein   **Jimmy Jet and His TV Set** . . . . POEM 199

Isaac Asimov   **The Fun They Had** . . . . SHORT STORY 204
Preston Gralla   **Netiquette** / Connections . . . . ESSAY 210

■ **No Questions Asked**
Hans Christian Andersen   **The Nightingale** *translated by* Anthea Bell . . . . FAIRY TALE 215

Read On 227

COMMUNICATIONS WORKSHOPS

Speaking and Listening Workshop   Oral Interpretation:
   Bringing a Poem to Life   **228**

Writer's Workshop   Expository Writing: How-To Essay   **230**

Sentence Workshop   Stringy Sentences   **235**

Reading for Life   Reading a Manual   **236**

Learning for Life   Machines: A User's Guide   **237**

**Language /
Grammar Link**

• End All End-Mark
   Errors   **214**

Collection Four

All Creatures Great and Small

**COLLECTION PLANNING
GUIDE T237A–T237D**

■ **Reading Skills and Strategies**
Dialogue with the Text

Isaac Bashevis Singer   **Zlateh the Goat** .... SHORT STORY 240

Cynthia Rylant   **Stray** .... SHORT STORY 250
Judith Viorst   **Mother Doesn't Want a Dog** / Connections ....POEM 255

Gary Soto   **Ode to Mi Gato** ....POEM 258
Meow *by* Suki Lehman-Becker / Student to Student ..POEM 260

■ **Reading Skills and Strategies**
Organizers: Finding the Structure 262

Ralph Helfer   **The Flood** *from* **The Beauty of the Beasts** ..... TRUE NARRATIVE 263
People Magazine   **Trial by Fire** / Connections .... MAGAZINE ARTICLE ..275

■ **Elements of Literature**   **The Main Idea**
What's It All About? 279

Huynh Quang Nhuong   *from* **The Land I Lost** ....ESSAY 280
Literature and Legends / Tall Tales 286

Robert Fulghum   *from* **All I Really Need to Know I Learned
in Kindergarten** ....ESSAY 291

■ **No Questions Asked**
Ogden Nash   **A Nash Menagerie** ....POEMS 299

Read On 301

COMMUNICATIONS WORKSHOPS

Writer's Workshop   Expository Writing: Informative Report   302

Sentence Workshop   Wordy Sentences   307

Reading for Life   Searching the Internet   308

Learning for Life   Teaching People About Animals   309

**Language /
Grammar Links**

• Making Pronouns and
Antecedents Agree   **249**

• Pronoun and Contraction
Mix-ups   **257**

• Clear Pronoun
References   **278**

• Pronouns as Objects of
Prepositions   **290**

• Style: Exaggeration Can Be
Funny   **298**

Collection Five

Justice for All

**COLLECTION PLANNING
GUIDE T309A–T309D**

■ **Reading Skills and Strategies**
Dialogue with the Text

Ray Bradbury   **All Summer in a Day** . . . . SHORT STORY 312

Lise Fisher   **Suit Helps Girl Enjoy Daylight** / Connections . . NEWS ARTICLE 321
Special Small World *by* Casie Anne Smith /
    Student to Student . . . . ESSAY 322

■ **Elements of Literature   The Short Story**
The Main Ingredient *by* John Leggett 326

Sandra Cisneros   **Eleven** / **Once** *translated by* Liliana Valenzuela . . . . . . SHORT STORY 327

■ **Reading Skills and Strategies**
Making and Adjusting Predictions 337

Mildred D. Taylor   **The Gold Cadillac** . . . . SHORT STORY 338
Literature and Social Studies / The South I Saw 346

Rosa Parks and Brian Lanker   **I Was Not Alone** *from* **I Dream a World** /
    Connections . . . . INTERVIEW 350

Yoshiko Uchida   **The Bracelet** . . . . SHORT STORY 356

Avi   **What Do Fish Have to Do with Anything?** . . . SHORT STORY 366

Dr. Seuss/Theodor Geisel   **The Sneetches** . . . . POEM 379

■ **No Questions Asked**

Judith Viorst   **The Southpaw** . . . . SHORT STORY 387

Read On 393

COMMUNICATIONS WORKSHOPS

Speaking and Listening Workshop Social Interaction	394
Writer's Workshop Persuasive Writing: Supporting a Position	396
Sentence Workshop Combining Sentences by Inserting Words	401
Reading for Life Evaluating a Persuasive Message	402
Learning for Life Persuading with Editorial Cartoons	403

**Language /
Grammar Links**

• Style: Figurative
  Language **325**

• Punctuating
  Dialogue **336**

• Style: Connotations **355**

• Look Who's Talking **365**

• Direct and Indirect
  Quotations **378**

Collection Six

Onstage!

COLLECTION PLANNING GUIDE T403A–T403D

■ **Elements of Literature Drama**
Before Our Eyes *by* Robert Anderson 406

■ **Reading Skills and Strategies**
Forming Opinions 407

Sir Arthur Conan Doyle **The Adventure of the Speckled Band**
dramatized by Mara Rockliff . . . . PLAY 408
Literature and Science / Cobra Copy 424
Bruce Coville **Duffy's Jacket** / Connections . . . . SHORT STORY 425
T. S. Eliot **Macavity: The Mystery Cat** / Connections . . . . . . POEM 429

■ **From Page to Stage** *by* Joann Leonard 434

Angel Vigil **Blanca Flor** . . . . PLAY 439
Literature and Dramatic Arts / Onstage
and Backstage: Theater Talk 444
Chris Krewson **Star Struck** / Connections . . . . NEWS ARTICLE 457
When I Was in *Oklahoma!* by Emily Goodridge /
Student to Student . . . . ESSAY 459

Jakob and Wilhelm Grimm **Rumpelstiltskin** *dramatized by* Mara Rockliff . . . . . . PLAY 462
Rosemarie Künzler **Rumpelstiltskin**
translated by Jack Zipes / Connections . . . . FAIRY TALE 471

■ **No Questions Asked**
Jack Manning **Stars of Stage, Screen . . . and**
Social Studies Class . . . . PHOTO ESSAY 476

Read On 479

COMMUNICATIONS WORKSHOPS

Writer's Workshop Persuasive Writing: Evaluation   480

Sentence Workshop Combining Sentences by Using Groups of Words   485

Reading for Life Understanding Induction and Deduction   486

Learning for Life Settling Conflicts with Friends   487

Collection Seven

Explaining Our World:
Fact and Fiction

COLLECTION PLANNING GUIDE T487A–T487D

■ **Reading Skills and Strategies**
Dialogue with the Text

Joseph Bruchac **Loo-Wit, the Fire-Keeper** . . . . NISQUALLY MYTH 490

Patricia Lauber *from* **Volcano** . . . . SCIENCE WRITING . . .498

■ **Elements of Literature   Subjective and Objective Writing**
Facts vs. Feelings 512

Louis Untermeyer **The Dog of Pompeii** . . . . SHORT STORY 513
Literature and Social Studies / A City Frozen in Time 520

Robert Silverberg **Pompeii** / Connections . . . . HISTORY 524

Cindy Chang **The Seventh Sister** .CHINESE FOLK TALE . . .528
Literature and Astronomy / Diamonds in the Sky .531
Why There Are Stars in the Sky *by* Morgan Faris Novak /
    Student to Student . . . . STORY 534

■ **Reading Skills and Strategies**
Reading for Varied Purposes: Narrative and Informative Texts 537

George Beshore **Scanning the Heavens** *from*
    Science in Ancient China . . . . SCIENCE WRITING . . .538

Zora Neale Hurston **How the Snake Got Poison** . . . . .AFRICAN AMERICAN FOLK TALE . . .545
Hilda Simon **Snakes: The Facts and the Folklore** /
    Connections . . . . SCIENCE ESSAY 550

■ **No Questions Asked**

Julius Lester **Why Dogs Chase Cats** . . . . .AFRICAN AMERICAN FOLK TALE . . .554

Read On 559

COMMUNICATIONS WORKSHOPS

Speaking and Listening Workshop Speaking to Inform   560

Writer's Workshop Descriptive Writing: Observational Writing   562

Sentence Workshop Combining Sentences Using Connecting Words   567

Reading for Life Reading a Science Book   568

Learning for Life Explaining Our World: Scientific Research   569

**Language /
Grammar Links**

• Forming the Plurals of
  Nouns **497**

• Style: Comparisons in
  Science Writing **511**

• Using Commas to
  Separate Adjectives
  in a Series **536**

• Using Commas to
  Separate Items in a
  Series **544**

• Style: Dialect—The Voice
  of the People **553**

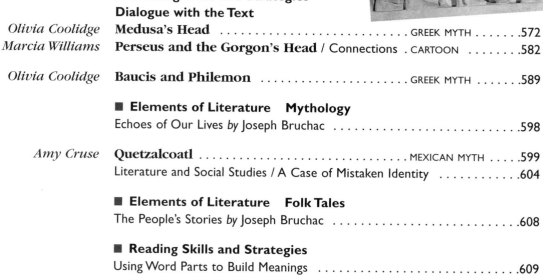

Collection Eight

Tell Me a Tale

COLLECTION PLANNING
GUIDE T569A–T569D

■ **Reading Skills and Strategies**
Dialogue with the Text

Olivia Coolidge **Medusa's Head** . . . . GREEK MYTH 572
Marcia Williams **Perseus and the Gorgon's Head** / Connections . CARTOON 582

Olivia Coolidge **Baucis and Philemon** . . . . GREEK MYTH 589

■ **Elements of Literature Mythology**
Echoes of Our Lives *by* Joseph Bruchac 598

Amy Cruse **Quetzalcoatl** . . . . MEXICAN MYTH 599
Literature and Social Studies / A Case of Mistaken Identity 604

■ **Elements of Literature Folk Tales**
The People's Stories *by* Joseph Bruchac 608

■ **Reading Skills and Strategies**
Using Word Parts to Build Meanings 609

Walter McVitty   **Ali Baba and the Forty Thieves** . . . . PERSIAN FOLK TALE . .610
Literature and Culture / To Be Continued 617
John, Sue, and the Talking Snake *by Sara Lesher* /
    Student to Student . . . . STORY 618

Hans Christian Andersen   **The Emperor's New Clothes** . . . . FAIRY TALE 623
Jane Yolen   **King Long Shanks** / Connections . . . . SHORT STORY 630

Virginia Hamilton   **He Lion, Bruh Bear, and**
    Bruh Rabbit . . . . AFRICAN AMERICAN FOLK TALE . . .639
Aesop   **The Fox and the Crow** *dramatized by* Mara Rockliff /
    Connections . . . . READER'S THEATER . .644
Aesop   **The Wolf and the House Dog**
    dramatized by Mara Rockliff / Connections . . . . READER'S THEATER . .645

■ **No Questions Asked**
John Gardner   **Dragon, Dragon** . . . . SHORT STORY 648

Read On 657

COMMUNICATIONS WORKSHOPS

Writer's Workshop Narrative Writing: Story		658
Sentence Workshop Joining Sentences		663
Reading for Life Reading a Map and a Time Line		664
Learning for Life Making Oral Presentations		665

**Language /
Grammar Links**

• Style: Words from
  Myths **588**

• The Homophones *Their,
  There,* and *They're* **597**

• *Effect* vs. *Affect* **607**

• Style: Words from
  Arabic **622**

• Style: Formal and
  Informal English **638**

• Proofreading:
  To, Too, and *Two* **647**

Resource Center

Handbook of Literary Terms   667

Communications Handbook   677

    Putting Together a Multimedia Presentation   677

      Scanning, Clipping, and Creating   678

      Making an Interactive Program   678

      Word Processing   679

    Research Strategies   680

      Using a Media Center or Library   680

      Using the Internet   680

      Evaluating Web Sources   681

      Listing Sources and Taking Notes   682

    Reading Strategies   684

      Using Word Parts   684

      Summarizing, Paraphrasing, and Outlining   685

    Study Skills   685

      Using a Thesaurus   685

      Using a Dictionary   686

      Reading Maps, Charts, and Graphs   687

    Strategies for Taking Tests   688

    Writing for Life   691

      Writing Business Letters   691

      Filling Out Forms   692

    Proofreaders' Marks   692

Language Handbook   693

    The Parts of Speech   693

    Agreement   703

    Using Verbs   706

    Using Pronouns   713

    Using Modifiers   717

    The Prepositional Phrase   721

    Sentences   724

    Complements   729

    Kinds of Sentences   733

    Writing Effective Sentences   736

    Capital Letters   743

    Punctuation   748, 754, 758

    Spelling   761

    Glossary of Usage   766

Glossary   773

Acknowledgments   781

Picture Credits   784

Index of Skills   785

    Literary Terms   785

    Reading and Critical Thinking   786

    Language (Grammar, Usage, and Mechanics)   787

    Vocabulary and Spelling   789

    Writing   790

    Speaking, Listening, and Viewing   791

    Research and Study   792

    Crossing the Curriculum   792

Index of Art   793

Index of Authors and Titles   795

Elements of Literature on the Internet

TO THE STUDENT

Discover more about the stories, poems, and essays in *Elements of Literature* by logging on to the Internet. At **go.hrw.com** we help you complete your homework assignments, learn more about your favorite writers, and find facts that support your ideas and inspire you with new ones. Here's how to log on:

1. Start your Web browser and enter **go.hrw.com** in the location field.

2. Note the keyword in your textbook.

go.hrw.com
LE0 6-1

3. In your Web browser, enter the keyword and click on GO.

LE0 6-1   go!
Enter keyword

Now that you've arrived, you can peek into the palaces and museums of the world, listen to stories of exploration and discovery, or view fires burning on the ocean floor. As you move through *Elements of Literature,* use the best online resources at **go.hrw.com.**

Elements of Literature

A Glory Over Everything
Anne Petry

More about the Writer

Ann Petry: Woman with a Calling
Writing may have been her calling, but Ann Petry didn't originally study to be a writer. Visit the Connecticut Women's Hall of Fame to find out about Petry's first career and other biographical facts.

The Power of the Word
What experiences in Ann Petry's life might have led her to write about Harriet Tubman? Visit Voices from the Gaps to find out how Ann Petry used her writing skills to fight prejudice.

Choices: Building Your Portfolio, page 148

Choices 2: At Journey's End
If you are writing an obituary summarizing Harriet Tubman's life, The Harriet Tubman Home Page might help. Find out how Harriet received a head injury when she was a child, follow her as she leads hundreds of slaves to freedom, or learn of her work during the Civil War.

Enjoy the Internet, but be critical of the information you find there. Always evaluate your sources for credibility, accuracy, timeliness, and possible bias.

Web sites accessed through **go.hrw.com** are reviewed regularly. However, online materials change continually and without notice. Holt, Rinehart and Winston cannot ensure the accuracy or appropriateness of materials other than our own. Students, teachers, and guardians should assume responsibility for checking all online materials. A full description of Terms of Use can be found at **go.hrw.com.**

SELECTIONS BY GENRE

Short Story

Just Once 2
Ta-Na-E-Ka 15
The All-American Slurp 31
La Bamba 44
President Cleveland, Where Are You? 53
The Stone 69
The Fun They Had 204
Zlateh the Goat 240
Stray 250
All Summer in a Day 312
Eleven/Once 327
The Gold Cadillac 338
The Bracelet 356
What Do Fish Have to Do with Anything? 366
The Southpaw 387
Duffy's Jacket 425
The Dog of Pompeii 513
King Long Shanks 630
Dragon, Dragon 648

Novel Excerpt

from The Adventures of Tom Sawyer 150

Nonfiction

Essay

Lessons 82
Lincoln's Humor 132
Netiquette 210
from The Land I Lost 280
from All I Really Need to Know I Learned
    in Kindergarten 291

Biography

The Mysterious Mr. Lincoln 126
A Glory over Everything: from Harriet Tubman:
    Conductor on the Underground Railroad 136

Autobiography

Storm from Woodsong 96
Brother from I Know Why the Caged Bird Sings . . . 109

True Narrative

The Flood from The Beauty of the Beasts 263

News and Magazine Article

Crow Poets 24
Working on the Railroad 174
Trial by Fire from People Magazine 275
Suit Helps Girl Enjoy Daylight 321
Star Struck 457

Interview

I Was Not Alone from I Dream a World 350

Science Writing

from Volcano 498
Scanning the Heavens from Science in
    Ancient China 539
Snakes: The Facts and the Folklore 550

History

Pompeii 524

Photo Essay

Stars of Stage, Screen . . . and Social
    Studies Class 476

Poetry

Foul Shot. 10
Yes, It Was My Grandmother 117
Petals/Los pétalos. 121
from The Pied Piper of Hamelin. 178
Cynthia in the Snow. 178
Good Hot Dogs. 179
Ankylosaurus 180
Your Poem, Man 184
The Toaster. 185
The Sidewalk Racer *or* On the Skateboard 187
Things to Do If You Are a Subway. 188
Steam Shovel. 190
The Hill Mynah 195
The Hummingbird 197
Jimmy Jet and His TV Set 199
Mother Doesn't Want a Dog 255
Ode to Mi Gato 258
A Nash Menagerie 299
The Sneetches 379
Macavity: The Mystery Cat. 429

Myth and Tale

Myth

Loo-Wit, the Fire-Keeper 490
Medusa's Head 572
Perseus and the Gorgon's Head 582
Baucis and Philemon 589
Quetzalcoatl. 599

Folk Tale and Fairy Tale

The Nightingale 215
Rumpelstiltskin. 471
The Seventh Sister 528
How the Snake Got Poison. 545
Why Dogs Chase Cats 554
Ali Baba and the Forty Thieves 610
The Emperor's New Clothes 623
He Lion, Bruh Bear, and Bruh Rabbit 639

Song

John Henry 168

Drama

Stage Play

The Adventure of the Speckled Band. 408
Blanca Flor 439
Rumpelstiltskin. 462

Reader's Theater

The Fox and the Crow 644
The Wolf and the House Dog. 645

FEATURES

Elements of Literature

Conflict: It Makes a Story 14
Autobiography and Biography. 108
Poetry: Sound Effects. 178
Poetry: Seeing Likenesses 183
The Main Idea: What's It All About? 279
The Short Story: The Main Ingredients. 326
Drama: Before Our Eyes 406
From Page to Stage 434
Subjective and Objective Writing. 512
Mythology: Echoes of Our Lives 598
Folk Tales: The People's Stories 608

Across the Curriculum

Literature and Science: Primates. 63
Literature and Science: Call of the Wild 103
Literature and Social Studies: Hard Labor 172
Literature and Real Life: Underground Poetry. . . 189
Literature and Legends: Tall Tales 286
Literature and Social Studies: The South I Saw. . . 346
Literature and Science: Cobra Copy. 424
Literature and Dramatic Arts: Theater Talk 444
Literature and Social Studies: Pompeii 520
Literature and Astronomy: The Milky Way 531
Literature and Social Studies: Quetzalcoatl 604
Literature and Culture: To Be Continued. 617

Student Models

Coming to America 40
The Brother I Never Had 114
The Lawn Mower. 192
Special Small World. 322
When I Was in *Oklahoma!* 459
Why There Are Stars in the Sky 534
John, Sue, and the Talking Snake. 618

No Questions Asked

Lessons 82
from The Adventures of Tom Sawyer 150

The Nightingale 215
A Nash Menagerie 299
The Southpaw 387
Stars of Stage, Screen . . . and Social
 Studies Class. 476
Why Dogs Chase Cats 554
Dragon, Dragon 648

Writer's Workshops

Narrative Writing: Autobiographical
 Incident 86
Expository Writing: Biographical Sketch 158
Expository Writing: How-To Essay. 230
Expository Writing: Informative Report 302
Persuasive Writing: Supporting a Position 396
Persuasive Writing: Evaluation 480
Descriptive Writing: Observational
 Writing 562
Narrative Writing: Story 658

Reading for Life

Using Text Organizers 92
Independent Reading. 164
Reading a Manual 236
Searching the Internet. 308
Evaluating a Persuasive Message 402
Understanding Induction and Deduction. 486
Reading a Science Book. 568
Reading a Map and a Time Line. 664

Learning for Life

Decision Making. 93
Researching Media Personalities. 165
Machines: A User's Guide 237
Teaching People About Animals 309
Persuading with Editorial Cartoons 403
Settling Conflicts with Friends 487
Explaining Our World: Scientific Research. 569
Making Oral Presentations 665

Connections

Foul Shot. 10
Crow Poets. 24
Lincoln's Humor. 132
Working on the Railroad. 174
Netiquette 210
Mother Doesn't Want a Dog 255
Trial by Fire. 275
Suit Helps Girl Enjoy Daylight. 321
I Was Not Alone 350

Duffy's Jacket 425
Macavity: The Mystery Cat. 429
Star Struck 457
Rumpelstiltskin. 471
Pompeii. 524
Snakes: The Facts and the Folklore 550
Perseus and the Gorgon's Head 582
King Long Shanks 630
The Fox and the Crow 644
The Wolf and the House Dog. 645

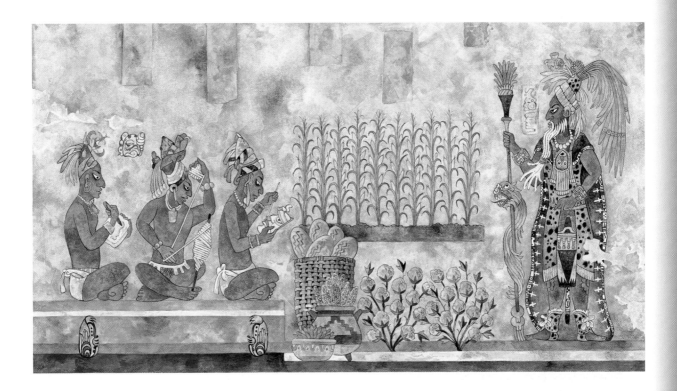

SKILLS

Reading Skills and Strategies

Reading Matters . . . . 46 (xxx)
Dialogue with the Text 2, 96, 168,
                         240, 312, 490, 572
Comparing and Contrasting Cultures 15, 589
Context Clues 30, 31
Making Predictions 44, 337, 338, 599
Summarizing 53, 280
Making Generalizations 69, 356
Finding the Main Idea 109, 291
Making Inferences 125, 250, 327
Using Prior Knowledge 126
Sequence 136
Strategies for Reading Poetry 194, 195
Cause and Effect 204, 439
Organizers: Finding the Structure 262
Chronological Order 263, 366
Forming Opinions 407, 408
Informative Writing 498
Comparing and Contrasting Texts 513, 545
Establishing Purposes for Reading 528
Reading for Varied Purposes 537, 538
Using Word Parts 609, 610

Literature Skills

Conflict 2, 15
Simile 44
Imagery 53, 121
Moral Lessons 69
Character 96, 366, 462
Description 109
Tone 117
Refrain 168
Onomatopoeia 181
Metaphors 185
Rhyme 199, 379
Irony 204
Foreshadowing and Suspense 240, 408
Theme 250, 356, 623
Ode 258
Humorous Essays 291
Setting 312
Point of View 327
Motifs 439
Origin Myths 490
Historical Fiction 513
How-and-Why Tales 528
Oral Tradition 545
Mythic Heroes 572
Metamorphosis 589
Golden-Age Myths 599
The Trickster 639

Language / Grammar Links

Troublesome Verbs 13
Subject-Verb Agreement 29, 43
Using Verb Tenses 52
Style: Vivid Verbs 68
Using *Don't* and *Doesn't* 81
Using *Good* and *Well* 107
Style: Choosing Precise Words 116
Comparing with Adjectives 135

Using *Bad* and *Badly* 149
End-Mark Errors 214
Making Pronouns and Antecedents Agree 249
Pronoun and Contraction Mix-ups 257
Clear Pronoun References 278
Pronouns as Objects of Prepositions 290
Style: Exaggeration 298
Style: Figurative Language 325
Punctuating Dialogue 336
Style: Connotations 355
Dialogue 365
Direct and Indirect Quotations 378
Forming the Plurals of Nouns 497
Style: Comparisons in Science Writing 511
Using Commas 536, 544
Style: Dialect 553
Style: Words from Myths 588
The Homophones *Their, There,* and *They're* 597
Effect vs. *Affect* 607
Style: Words from Arabic 622
Style: Formal and Informal English 638
Proofreading: *To, Too,* and *Two* 647

Vocabulary / Spelling Skills

Context Clues 13, 43
Acquisition Exercise 29, 68, 149, 249, 355,
                    365, 378, 511, 527, 544, 588, 607
Spelling Words with *ie* 52
Synonyms 81, 135, 290
Prefixes and Suffixes 107, 622
Using a Thesaurus 116
Greek Roots 214
Double Consonants 257
Concrete and Abstract Words 278
Compound Words 298
Semantic Mapping 325
Silent *E* 336
Analogies 433
Words from Other Languages 448
Spanish Words 461
Denotation and Connotations 475
American Indian Names 497

Silent Consonants 536
Homonyms: *Past* and *Passed* 553
Silent Letters 597
Interpreting Idioms 638
Using a Glossary 647

Speaking and Listening Workshops

Interviewing: Questions, Please 156
Oral Interpretation: Bringing a Poem to Life 228
Social Interaction 394
Speaking to Inform 560

Sentence Workshops

Sentence Fragments 91
Run-on Sentences 163
Stringy Sentences 235
Wordy Sentences 307
Combining Sentences 401
Combining Sentences 485
Combining Sentences 567
Joining Sentences 663

Assessment

Test Smarts . . . . 56 (xl)
Strategies for Taking Tests 688

ELEMENTS OF *Literature*

© 2003

Building a Foundation for Success in Literature and Reading

Time-tested and a favorite of teachers around the nation, **Elements of Literature** *has proven itself as the literature and language arts program that gets results and forges strong connections between students' lives and the literature teachers love to teach. Designed to get students actively involved in literature and learning, this unique program combines a student-centered approach to the study of literature with a sharp focus on the development of practical reading, writing, and life skills.*

GRAMMAR, LANGUAGE, AND WRITING RESOURCES

DAILY ORAL GRAMMAR TRANSPARENCIES AND WORKSHEETS
include exercises that review sentence construction, usage, and mechanics skills in the context of literary selections found in the *Student Edition.*

GRAMMAR AND LANGUAGE LINKS WORKSHEETS provide reinforcement,
practice, and extension of the grammar and language skills presented in the *Student Edition.*

AUTHENTIC AUTHORSHIP THAT SPEAKS TO STUDENTS

The success of *Elements of Literature* is due in large part to the team of authors that shaped it. Robert Anderson, John Malcolm Brinnan, and John Leggett, authors since the program's inception, have established the literary framework and have brought to the program a unique, motivational approach to instruction. Dr. Robert Probst has infused the program with a student-centered pedagogy, encouraging students to make the study of literature relevant to their lives and experiences. Renowned reading expert Dr. Kylene Beers has helped to integrate the reading strand in the *Student Edition* with creative, effective ways to reach struggling and reluctant readers. In addition, literacy expert Dr. Richard Vacca has helped to develop the conceptual framework of the reading strand, bringing to the program its strong emphasis on reading skills.

STUDENT EDITION THAT INVITES INVOLVEMENT

Frequent opportunities for skill building, personal and critical response, and writing practice prepare and motivate your students. Activities on **go.hrw.com** help students build literary and life skills. The **Test Smarts** section helps students prepare for standardized tests. The **Reading Matters** section, developed by reading expert Dr. Kylene Beers, helps students build a strong foundation in reading and master state and national standards.

ANNOTATED TEACHER'S EDITION THAT OPTIMIZES LESSONS

The *Annotated Teacher's Edition* helps you make the best use of the textbook with planning charts at point-of-use and references to the *One-Stop Planner® CD-ROM with Test Generator.* Helpful, creative suggestions for addressing the different kinds of learners in your classroom are annotated throughout the book.

ORGANIZATION THAT ENCOURAGES SUCCESS

- Grades 6, 7, and 8 are organized by genres centered around themes.
- Grades 9 and 10 include the study of genres in collections organized by theme.
- Grades 11 and 12 present selections chronologically and focus on themes emerging naturally from each literary period.
- Grade 11, *Literature of the United States with Literature of the Americas,* is available in two volumes.

LANGUAGE HANDBOOK WORKSHEETS
include tests at the end of each section that can be used either for assessment or for review.

WORKSHOP RESOURCES: TRANSPARENCIES AND WORKSHEETS
provide additional practice with the language skills presented in the **Writer's Workshop, Sentence Workshop,** and **Language Workshop** features of the *Student Edition.*

SPANISH RESOURCES

SPANISH RESOURCES help your Spanish-speaking students explore literature with translations of the **Before You Read** feature in the *Student Edition* and the *Graphic Organizers for Active Reading* teaching resource. This package also includes Spanish summaries of the literature selections, reading check questions in Spanish, and the *Visual Connections Videocassette Program* with Spanish soundtrack.

The Building Blocks of Solid Reading Skills

ELEMENTS OF

Literature *helps students become lifelong readers by building skills in reading comprehension, literary response and analysis, and vocabulary development. The cornerstone of the program, this strong emphasis on reading skills is integrated throughout the* **Student Edition** *and in highly effective resource and technology materials.*

READING SUPPORT

Every secondary classroom has students who haven't mastered the skills they need to be competent readers. The resources within the *Elements of Literature* program offer a multitude of means—strategies, skill-building exercises, MiniReads,™ graphic organizers, vocabulary and test practice to help students acquire the skills they need to be lifelong readers. Consumable worktexts make the lessons hands-on and easily accessible. Also available on CD-ROM.

HRW LIBRARY

This diverse collection of award-winning **HRW Library** titles builds students' independence and confidence as they become life-long readers. Each full-length work includes **Connections,** related readings such as poems, short stories, essays, memoirs, and interviews that extend themes into other genres, places, and times.

STUDY GUIDES

• background information and historical, cultural, and literary context

• reproducible masters for reading skills, vocabulary activities, and literary elements study

• more information at **www.hrw.com**

CONTENT AREA READERS

• reading selections in the context of the social sciences, science, and mathematics

• informational materials such as newspaper articles, biographies, and excerpts from nonfiction books

ADDITIONAL READING SUPPORT

AUDIO CD LIBRARY

helps struggling readers and auditory learners build comprehension skills with dramatic readings of the literary selections in *Elements of Literature.* In this extensive collection of audio CDs, professional actors read poems, plays, short stories, and essays.

WORDS TO OWN WORKSHEETS build

vocabulary skill and help students make words their own.

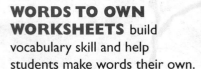

GRAPHIC ORGANIZERS FOR ACTIVE READING allow

students to respond to literature visually while mastering program content.

LITERARY ELEMENTS TRANSPARENCIES AND WORKSHEETS

include graphic organizers that help students identify and learn the literary terms presented in the *Student Editions*.

SPELLING AND DECODING WORKSHEETS

(GRADES 6–8) allow students to practice spelling (using words taken from literary selections) and explore sound correspondences and structure patterns.

Solidify Instruction with Planning and Assessment Resources

TEST PREP TOOL KIT

Comprehensive and flexible, the **Test Prep Tool Kit** features high-interest activities that keep students involved. The kit consists of 39 activity cards, correlated to state standards, that address the reading and writing objectives typically measured by standardized tests. The cards let students work at their own pace, allowing them to monitor their performance as they work to master a variety of reading and writing skills.

ONE-STOP PLANNER® CD-ROM WITH TEST GENERATOR

With editable lesson plans and an easy-to-use test generator, this convenient planning tool includes all the teaching resources for **Elements of Literature**. Also included are previews of all teaching resources, of the **Visual Connections Videocassette Program,** and of transparencies and worksheets linked to features in the **Student Edition.** Point-and-click menu formats make accessing information on the **One-Stop Planner** fast and easy in both Macintosh® and Windows® platforms.

MORE FOR PLANNING

LESSON PLANS, INCLUDING STRATEGIES FOR ENGLISH-LANGUAGE LEARNERS include resource checklists, ideas for teaching literature selections, and strategies for motivating students who are developing English proficiency.

CROSS-CURRICULAR ACTIVITIES engage students with lessons that encompass literature, science, music, history, geography, and technology.

BLOCK SCHEDULING LESSON PLANS WITH PACING GUIDE help you manage and pace block-scheduling instruction and activities.

MORE FOR ASSESSMENT

FORMAL ASSESSMENT includes literary-element tests, reading-application tests, genre tests, and English-language tests.

PORTFOLIO MANAGEMENT SYSTEM offers ideas for implementing portfolios in the classroom and blackline masters for assessing portfolios and performance on activities from the **Student Edition.**

STANDARDIZED TEST PREPARATION includes practice tests for reading along with blackline masters and transparencies for four writing modes.

PREPARATION FOR COLLEGE ADMISSION EXAMS prepares high school juniors and seniors for college admission exams with a collection of practice tests.

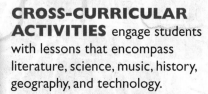

Reinforce Learning with Internet Resources

ONLINE RESOURCES

GO.HRW.COM

Internet references throughout the *Student Edition* direct you and your students to a Web site dedicated exclusively to content in *Elements of Literature.* From biographical information about authors to help with textbook activities and writing assignments, from historical background to cross-curricular support, this Web site allows your students to link instantly to well-researched resources that support the selections they are studying.

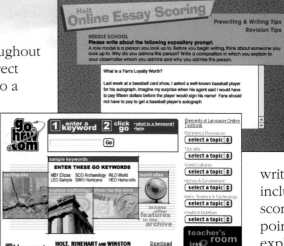

HOLT ONLINE ESSAY SCORING

Help your students improve their writing skills and give them practice with the kinds of prompts typically seen on state writing assessments. The site includes writing prompts, scores based on a four- or six-point holistic scale, and explanations of the scoring criteria.

MORE TECHNOLOGY

AUDIO CD LIBRARY helps struggling readers and auditory learners build comprehension skills with dramatic readings of the literary selections in *Elements of Literature.* In this extensive collection of audio CDs, professional actors read poems, plays, short stories, and essays.

VISUAL CONNECTIONS VIDEOCASSETTE PROGRAM features biographies, interviews, historical summaries, and cross-curricular connections that enrich and extend instruction. Available with Spanish and English soundtracks.

THE HOLT READER: AN INTERACTIVE WORKTEXT CD-ROM includes literary and informational selections and graphic organizers that guide students to participate actively in reading. This CD-ROM is a convenient alternative to *The Holt Reader: An Interactive WorkText* booklet.

WRITER'S WORKSHOP I AND 2 INTERACTIVE MULTIMEDIA CD-ROMS include a variety of writing assignments featuring step-by-step guidance—from prewriting to publishing—and the ability to share work online. These interactive CD-ROMs also include built-in word processing, a spell checker, and advanced writing tools.

LANGUAGE WORKSHOP INTERACTIVE MULTIMEDIA CD-ROM SOFTWARE reinforces and extends the grammar and writing lessons in *Elements of Literature* with a complete, interactive course in grammar, usage, and mechanics. (Grades 6–12)

Literature

AN INVITATION TO A DIALOGUE

Dr. Robert Probst, *Georgia State University*

The classroom is the place for students to learn to read and reflect on visions of human possibilities offered them by the great literature and to begin to tell their own visions and stories.

LITERATURE AND LIFE

Surely, of all the arts, literature is most immediately implicated with life itself. The very medium through which the author shapes the text—language—is grounded in the shared lives of human beings. Language is the bloodstream of a common culture, a common history.

— LOUISE ROSENBLATT

Mathematicians, scientists, and engineers build bridges and send people to the moon, statisticians calculate our insurance premiums and life expectancies, and accountants figure our taxes and amortize our house payments, but the poets, dramatists, novelists, and story-writers have nonetheless remained at the center of life. They bind us together as a society, and they define us as individuals within that society.

When we're very young we need stories almost as much as we need food and protection. Stories entertain us and help us sleep, but they also teach us how to get through the world. They tell us there are pots of gold waiting for us at the end of the rainbow, and they warn us about the trolls hiding under the bridges. They teach us about hope, fear, courage, and all the other elements of our lives. As we grow out of childhood, the great stories, poems, and plays of the world's literature encourage us to reflect on the issues that have intrigued men and women for centuries, inviting us into a continuing dialogue about human experience. When we're older, our own stories represent what we've done, capturing for us what we've made of our lives. Some we'll tell happily, some we'll tell with great pain, and some we may not tell at all, but they're all important because they are a way of making sense of our lives.

If literature is the ongoing dialogue about what it means to be human, then the language arts classroom is society's invitation to students to join that conversation. The texts we use represent the reflections of the world's cultures on the nature of human experience, and the writings we elicit from our students are their first efforts to join in that reflection. The classroom is the place for students to learn to read and reflect on visions of human possibilities offered them by the great literature and to begin to tell their own stories.

Literature offers an invitation to reflect, but it doesn't offer formulas to memorize or answers to write dutifully in notes so that later on, when life presents us with problems, we can pull out our tattered old notebooks and find our path sketched out for us. Literature is an invitation to a dialogue.

That, perhaps more than any other reason, is why it's so important that we teach literature and writing well. It's too easy to avoid the responsible thought demanded by the significant issues, too tempting to accept someone else's formulation of the truth. "Life imitates art," Richard Peck said in a speech in New Orleans in 1974, "especially bad art." By that he meant, I think, that we may too often give in to tempting laziness and allow our lives to be governed by visions of human possibilities that we take from film, television, or graffiti. The problem for teachers, of course, is to lead students not simply to absorb unthinkingly what art offers, but to reflect on it.

This textbook series tries to support teachers' efforts to lead students to think, to feel, and to take responsibility for themselves. It will have much in common with other textbooks. After all, we'd miss "The Raven" if he didn't land croaking on our windowsill one morning just before homeroom, and twelfth grade wouldn't be the same without an evening or two around the hearth with Beowulf. But if this series has much in common with other textbooks, it will also have much that differs—including new authors, perhaps authors we haven't met before, exploring lives and circumstances that previously may not have been well represented in the pages of school texts. Similarly, there will be familiar approaches to teaching—perhaps specific activities—that we've all come to rely upon, but there will be other suggestions that emphasize aspects of literary experience, writing, and discussion that may not have been prominent in other books.

PRINCIPLES OF THE PROGRAM

❶ First among the principles of the program is that *the subject matter of the language arts classroom is human experience comprehended and expressed in language.* The classroom invites the student into the dialogue about the big issues of human experience. The content of literature is the content of our days, and we think and feel about these issues before we enter the classroom and open the text.

When we do finally come to the text, it offers students an opportunity to begin to make sense of experience and to see it captured in the literature.

❷ Implicit in this vision of the language arts is a second principle, that *learning in the English classroom is a creative act,* requiring students to make things with language. Reading literature is a process of engaging the text, weighing it against the experiences readers bring to it.

Similarly, writing isn't simply a matter of learning and applying the rules of grammar and usage or of memorizing the structure and strategies of narratives, descriptions, and arguments.

> **Literature offers us access to hidden experiences and perceptions.**

❸ The third principle focuses on *the encounter between student and content.* It doesn't focus exclusively on the information and skills that have at times provided the framework for our instruction.

Nor, on the other hand, is teaching planned with thought only for the student's interests, needs, and desires, and thus organized around whatever concerns happen to predominate at the moment. It is, to borrow Rosenblatt's term, transactional.

❹ For this series, *the integration of the several aspects of the English language arts program* is the fourth governing principle. Literature can't be taught effectively without work in composition. Writing, without the inspiration offered by good literature, remains shallow and undeveloped. Oral language has to be acquired in the context of groups working collaboratively. These texts will suggest ways of interrelating instruction in literature, writing, and language.

WORKING WITH THE SERIES

You will find, as you work with selections in this textbook, that students have immediate responses to what they've read. That may be the place to start. The students' responses are very likely to lead you back to the issues you would have wanted to discuss anyway, and so the questions we've suggested might be addressed naturally during the flow of the discussion. Look for the potential in students' reactions and their questions even before turning to the questions in the "First Thoughts" section. Then, the questions in the text can extend or expand the discussion.

The same might be said about the writing. The series has been designed so that experiences with literature, with writing, and with group processes will often be interconnected. We hope that the literature will inspire and shape the students' writing, that their writing will lead back to further reading, and that the discussions and group activities suggested will build a supportive community in which all this work can take place.

The objective in all of this is for students to be able to draw upon their literary heritage and their developing skill with written and spoken language so that, as humane and reasoning people, they may be responsibly engaged with the world around them. If the language arts class helps to achieve that goal, we should be well satisfied with our labors.

> **The subject matter of the language arts classroom is human experience comprehended and expressed in language.**

Becoming a Strategic Reader

Dr. Judith Irvin, *Florida State University*

In the past, reading was viewed as a simple task of decoding words. Educators generally emphasized the strategies of sounding out words, recognizing words out of context by sight, and reproducing content by answering comprehension questions. Research has led to a new conceptualization of the reading process—that reading is a complex learning process. In this new view, readers construct meaning from a text, not simply by decoding words but by using reading strategies that incorporate and expand their prior knowledge. Prior knowledge includes not only readers' knowledge of the definition of a word, but also their responses to the context of the word—the entire text. Careful reading of a text using strategies like those explained in the following pages will allow readers to use their prior knowledge to create meaning and to extend their understanding of a text. As students become more involved in developing and reflecting on their reading and learning processes, meaning may now be defined as "something that is actively created rather than passively received" (Buehl, 1995, p. 8).

As will be explained, the process of constructing meaning is not linear, but recursive and interactive and helps to create a richer, more productive reading experience.

THE READER

Former models of reading focused on whether or not students had acquired specific skills. Recent models of reading allow that students come to learning with previous information about particular topics, with definite attitudes about reading, writing, and school in general, and with varying motivations for reading and learning. It is the interaction of what is in readers' minds with what is on the page within a particular context that helps them to comprehend what they read.

SCHEMA THEORY

It is impossible for readers to learn anything new without making connections to their prior knowledge or schemata. The schemata are like the components of an elaborate filing system inside every reader's head. If the reader's mind is the filing system, the schemata, then, are the ideas contained in the file folders within the system. For example, you probably have a schema for a computer, a mental picture of what a computer is and what it does. You probably also bring to that basic picture many other associations, ideas, and feelings. If you use computers regularly, your schema may include positive feelings about their limitless applications. If the computer revolution has left you yearning for the days of yellow note pads and typewriters, then you may have feelings of anxiety as you approach a computer manual. For teachers, it is important to remember that readers encountering new ideas must often be shown how the new material fits into their existing filing system.

THE TEXT

The content, format, and organization of a text are factors that make a text easy or difficult for students to understand. If students' schemata tell them that a particular assignment will be difficult or unrelated to their personal experiences, they will probably be reluctant to read it and will most likely not make much meaning of it. The students know with one look that they will read and respond to a poem differently from the way they will respond to a chapter in a science book. Proficient readers recognize a variety of types of texts and adjust their reading accordingly.

> It is the interaction of what is in readers' minds with what is on the page . . . that helps them to comprehend what they read.

THE CONTEXT

Readers approach texts differently, and they also vary their reading according to their purposes. If they are reading for pleasure, students may skip over a difficult word or read an exciting passage more than once. But if they are reading for class, skipping a word might mean not understanding an important concept needed in class the next day. A reader's purpose for reading also dictates how attentive he or she is to details and how much effort will be put into remembering what is read. Similarly, when and where the reading is done affects the reading process. Readers will make less meaning from texts they read on the bus or with thoughts of a sick relative in the backs of their minds than they might make if they had a quiet space and clear thoughts.

STRATEGIC LEARNING

Suppose that during a racquetball game you hit a straight shot down the right side of the court, and your opponent misses the ball. The point is yours. This well-placed shot may have been a lucky one, or it may have been the result of a strategy. Before you hit the ball, you may have noticed that your opponent was standing in the middle of the court, and you remembered that she is left-handed with a weak backhand. You hit the ball to exactly the right spot deliberately and strategically. The analogy of planning your shots in a game can be applied to learning.

Strategic learning involves analyzing the reading task, establishing a purpose for reading, and then selecting strategies for making meaning. A strategy is a conscious effort by the reader to attend to comprehension while reading. Weinstein explains that "learning strategies include any thoughts or behaviors that help us to acquire new information in such a way that the new information is integrated with our existing knowledge" (Weinstein, p. 590). Strategies occur before reading when readers activate prior knowledge by thinking and discussing the title and topic and by identifying a purpose for reading. They also occur during reading as readers use context to figure out unknown words and monitor their understanding, and beyond the reading when readers summarize or evaluate the main ideas of the text.

METACOGNITION

Reading is often referred to as a cognitive event. It is also a metacognitive event. Cognition refers to a person's using the knowledge and skills he or she possesses; metacognition refers to a person's awareness and understanding of that knowledge and conscious control over those skills. It is, essentially, thinking about one's way of thinking. Metacognition, then, is knowing how and when to use strategies to solve problems in understanding. It develops as a reader matures, usually during adolescence, but it can be taught and strengthened by explicit instruction and practice.

Becoming a proficient reader and writer is a lifelong process. Accepting the premise that meaning is constructed in the mind of the learner implies that metacognitive abilities must be operational for learning to occur. Young adolescents are just beginning to be able to consider their own thinking in relation to the thoughts of others. The middle level years are an ideal time to develop the metacognitive abilities that will serve them throughout life.

STRATEGIC READING IN THIS PROGRAM

Good readers are strategic, and being strategic involves the metacognitive abilities to think, plan, and evaluate their understanding of a text.

Early adolescence is partially characterized by a new capacity for thought. Students are moving from the concrete stage (able to think logically about real experiences) to the formal stage (able to consider "what if's," think reflectively, and reason abstractly). This intellectual change is gradual and may occur in different contexts at different times for different students.

Because formal thinking is just developing during the middle school years, concrete examples and step-by-step modeling are necessary to move students to the more abstract metacognitive thinking. The full-page Reading Skills and Strategies feature in *Elements of Literature* (Introductory, First, and Second Courses) helps students and teachers focus on reading strategies by addressing the following concepts:

- activating schema (prior knowledge) and building background information
- predicting and confirming
- organizing information
- drawing conclusions
- making inferences
- text differences
- retelling/summarizing

Before students read, they are invited to use their prior knowledge by making predictions about the content of a selection, to establish a clear purpose for reading, and to think about reading strategies they might use as they read. During the reading process, students are guided to use context, to connect what they are reading with what they already know, and to continue to monitor and evaluate their comprehension. And, after completing their reading, students have opportunities to review their reading through peer discussion, class discussion, review of reading notes, and use of graphic organizers.

New research and practice in literacy learning reflect a more holistic view of understanding text. *Elements of Literature* provides students with opportunities to apply reading strategies to a variety of texts in a meaningful manner.

REFERENCES

Buehl, D. *Classroom Strategies for Interactive Learning.* Schofield, WI: Wisconsin State Reading Association, 1995.
Weinstein, C. E. "Fostering Learning Autonomy Through the Use of Learning Strategies." *Journal of Reading* 30 (1987): 590–595.

Reaching Struggling Readers

AN INTERVIEW WITH DR. KYLENE BEERS

Dr. Kylene Beers

from the Editor's Desk

As we have listened to teachers over the past few years, one dominant issue has emerged: How do we teach literature to struggling readers? In our search for an answer, we read the research, attended workshops, and interviewed teachers and students. It was obvious that fill-in-the-blank drill worksheets weren't the answer. It was time for a change, but nothing we encountered seemed to offer a real solution to the problem of teaching literature to struggling readers.

Finally, one day Dr. Robert Probst suggested we contact Dr. Kylene Beers. He told us she knew a great deal about reading and might be the person with the answers. During our first meeting with Dr. Beers, she explained the link between reading skills and strategies and discussed the difference she had seen strategies make in the lives of struggling readers. She made a lot of sense to those of us who can recite whole sections of the *Iliad* but had never heard the words *reading* and *strategy* in the same sentence. A year and a half later we see the results of that first meeting: the *Reading Skills and Strategies: Reaching Struggling Readers* binder. This wasn't the easiest project in the history of publishing. Drill worksheets would have been easier to produce, but it was time for a change—time to turn struggling readers into successful ones.

Here are some of the questions we asked Dr. Beers during the course of this project.

The curriculum demands on English teachers are enormous. Teachers often ask us why they should add reading skills and strategies to an already loaded course.

66 I used to ask myself the same thing. Twenty years ago, when I began teaching, I expected that I'd carefully guide excited students through the prose and poetry of literary giants like Whitman, Emerson, Dickinson, Thoreau, Kipling, Joyce, Márquez, Angelou, and well, you know the names. I expected that students would arrive early for literature class and leave late for their next class. I expected I'd never have to worry about teaching someone to read—that was for the elementary teachers. I was going to teach *Literature.* Those expectations changed quickly. First, I didn't have students who loved literature. Most of my students didn't even like literature. Second, I didn't have students who could already read. When I didn't get the students I expected, I didn't know what to do.

Twenty years later, I'm still not getting what I expected when it comes to teaching. But I've learned that if I understand students' strengths and have some ideas about how to address their weaknesses, then they'll often give me more than I ever expected.

I've spent the past twenty years learning how to help these secondary students who can't read and don't like to read become better readers. I've worked with students at all grade levels and all ability levels. I've gone back to school to study how to teach reading and now I see myself as a reading/literature teacher. The teaching of literature and the teaching of reading are integral to one another, so interconnected that separating them seems an abomination. 99

How can a teacher use a literature anthology with the increasing number of students who have serious difficulty reading any text?

66 After many years of working with all types of readers, but especially struggling and reluctant readers, I've learned some things that have helped me reach those students. I've found that struggling readers have difficulty reading for a myriad of reasons. Often they don't know a lot of words, so limited vocabulary keeps them from understanding what they've read. Sometimes they lack decoding ability, so they don't know how to get through big words. Other times, they can recall words well, but they don't know how to make sense of what they've read. And sometimes, their distaste for reading makes them think reading is meaningless, so they see no reason for putting any effort into it. As I work with students and address those issues, I keep what I call the ABCDE rules in mind. A look at the diagram below will quickly show you what these rules are. 99

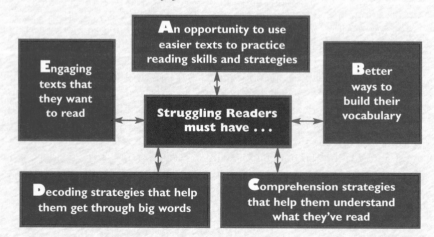

An opportunity to use easier texts to practice reading skills and strategies

Engaging texts that they want to read

Struggling Readers must have . . .

Better ways to build their vocabulary

Decoding strategies that help them get through big words

Comprehension strategies that help them understand what they've read

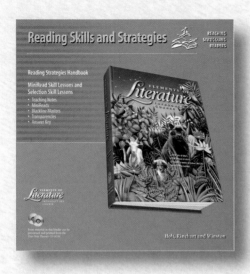

To help provide this **ABCDE** rule for struggling readers, what should a literature program include?

" A literature program should help teachers with each of those areas, particularly A, B, C, and E. If publishers want to help, they will have to develop specialized materials that complement the basal text. Here's what we did with the *Reading Skills and Strategies* binder for *Elements of Literature:*

❶ Easier selections provide practice for skills and strategies.

We hired a group of professional writers to write easy fiction and nonfiction pieces. These short selections, or MiniReads®, are written at an easier level than the selections in the literature book. The purpose of the MiniReads is to give students the opportunity to practice decoding skills, comprehension strategies, and vocabulary strategies with a text that is not only easier but engaging as well.

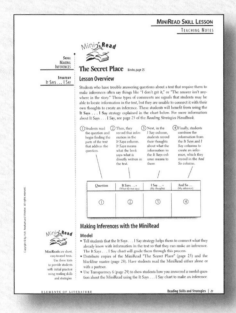

❷ Our MiniRead lessons include modeling.

Each MiniRead includes a complete lesson plan that provides modeling of the skill and strategy. Transparencies help teachers focus students on the strategies. Blackline masters give students a chance to practice the strategies before applying them to selections in the *Student Edition.*

❸ Reading skills and strategies are connected to the selections in *Elements of Literature.*

All skills and strategies are *applied* to selections in the anthology. The detailed lesson plans can be used not only with struggling readers but with all readers.

❹ The *Handbook* provides a thorough explanation of the research.

Without research to back them up, the lessons would have no foundation. The *Reading Strategies Handbook* includes transcripts from classrooms in which the strategies have been tested with struggling readers. The handbook *shows* rather than just *tells* how to initiate specific strategies, what pitfalls to avoid, and how to document progress. Articles about each of the strategies help teachers become more comfortable with using the strategies with any selection. "

Young Adolescent Learning

Dr. Judith Irvin, *Florida State University*

Young adolescents (ages 10–14) experience more changes physically, emotionally, socially, and cognitively during this period than during any other time of life. Children of all ages deserve "developmentally appropriate" school programs and practices; early adolescence, however, is a time when values are formed, self-esteem is enhanced or denied, and decisions with long-term implications are made. For many youth "early adolescence offers opportunities to choose a path toward a productive and fulfilling life. For many others, it represents their last best chance to avoid a diminished future" (Carnegie Council on Adolescent Development, p. 8).

Physically, young adolescents experience growth spurts in which there is a marked increase in height, weight, heart rate, lung capacity, and muscular strength. Bone grows faster than muscle, which may leave bones unprotected by muscles and tendons. Middle level students often have problems with coordination as a result of this rapid growth; thus, they are often characterized as awkward. Although all young adolescents experience this growth spurt, girls (10–11) tend to undergo these changes approximately two years earlier than boys (12–13). Being "off-time" with respect to maturation is what generally causes concern for young adolescents (Rice, 1990).

Socially, peers and social relationships are extremely important to young adolescents. Friendships are vital at this age, especially same-sex relationships. Feeling comfortable and secure with peers of the same sex at ages 10 to 12 helps young adolescents progress toward opposite sex relationships which come later. Because rejection by peers represents a major crisis, students at this age spend much of their time trying to figure out ways to win acceptance by their peers. The trying out of social situations is all a part of social learning and facilitates cognitive development. Some experiences are fleeting, some agonizing, and some thoughtful.

Emotionally, young adolescents begin the important task of forming a positive self-identity, which naturally brings on behavior characteristic of "trying things out." Some experts view early adolescence as a time of emotional turbulence and disruption, but it seems that the small percentage of students who exhibit signs of serious disturbance cause some adults to conclude that this period is one of turmoil and stress for all (Scales, 1991).

Emotions, both happy and sad, run high at this age. A teacher may observe the same girl happy and giggling at one minute, and sad and tearful the next minute. These extremes in emotion are normal experiences and are heightened by young adolescents' feelings of confusion about the changes within themselves and about their place within the social group.

Cognitive development is the least noticed but most profound. This age is characterized by a new capacity for thought. Students are moving from the concrete stage (able to think logically about real experiences) to the formal stage (able to consider "what if's," think reflectively, and reason abstractly). This intellectual change is gradual and may occur in different contexts at different times for different students.

The emerging formal thinker is able to consider the thoughts of others for the first time. Social interaction with peers helps young adolescents move beyond egocentrism. As students discuss issues that are important to them and resolve conflicting viewpoints, they are forced to re-examine their own views in light of the views of others. This process of social interaction enables young adolescents to mature both socially and intellectually.

The ability to think at an abstract level is related to social competence. "The ability to see another's point of view, to empathize, and to put oneself in the other person's shoes is characteristic of abstract thinking" (Milgram, p. 24). Young adolescents do not arrive at formal thought; they experiment with it, vacillating back and forth until they reason formally most of the time. It is important to remember, though, that some adults never reach an abstract level of thinking and some students consistently think on a concrete level. Adults can help young adolescents pass to formal thinking with their self-esteem intact by providing success-oriented opportunities to practice formal thinking.

IMPLICATIONS FOR THE CLASSROOM

Physically, middle level students need to move and change activities frequently. Socially, learning must include positive social interaction with peers and adults. Students must come to realize that others may think differently or hold differing points of view. A positive learning environment, one of acceptance on the part of the teacher and other students, is essential. Emotionally, students need to feel competent, and they need to achieve. They need to participate in school and classroom decisions, but they also require structure and clear limits. A positive self-identity is formed by meaningful interactions with learning activities and positive relationships with peers and adults.

Curriculum and instruction for young adolescents must be different from that of younger or older students. The middle level years are a time when students need to learn and experiment with learning how to learn and learning how to think. During this time of transition, material should be presented concretely, yet opportunities should be provided for progression to more abstract thought. Students need an opportunity to experiment with formal reasoning in a gradual and success-oriented way.

Efforts in middle level schools to break down the subject matter barriers, encourage student choice, minimize the comparison of students on the basis of ability, and provide more authentic assessment are consistent with enhancing cognitive, social, and emotional growth for young adolescents. In addition, efforts to integrate the language arts and integrate the content areas around themes are further attempts to design a curriculum that is responsive to the nature and needs of students in the middle grades.

An understanding of the developmental tasks of young adolescence is prerequisite to making informed decisions about appropriate school environments and learning experiences. Behaviors such as defiance signal a move toward autonomy, and egocentrism signals more abstract thinking. While these behaviors are not inherently desirable, they are indicative of normal growth and development. The more middle level educators understand and facilitate the developmental tasks of early adolescence, the better they can design a curriculum that meets the needs of their students.

Physically, young adolescents need

- opportunities to move and change activities
- flexibility of space, which may vary in size
- sturdy things, since adolescents are awkward and clumsy
- times of quiet and rest
- opportunities to test the limits of their physical ability
- an environment that downplays the differences in size and ability
- healthy food and especially healthy snacks as they need them
- adults to understand the changes they face
- sex education, information about growth and development

Socially, young adolescents need

- the opportunity to work in same- and opposite-sex groups
- an opportunity to relate to a close group of peers and a larger group of peers
- social activities—fun nights, carnivals they can work on
- free time to socialize
- opportunities to learn and practice social skills
- opportunities to explore values and beliefs

Emotionally, young adolescents therefore need

- an emotionally safe, supportive environment where students are free to risk and learn from failure as well as success
- successful experiences, which help students feel better about themselves as learners
- tolerance for mood swings

- help in understanding their bodies and emotional ups and downs
- an environment that fosters security and affection, a sense of belonging, self-confidence, and self-competence
- recognition and reward
- fun and adventure (educational and recreational)
- participation in school and classroom decisions
- structure and clear limits

Cognitively, young adolescents need

- a vehicle for connecting new information to what is already known, thus helping students to feel more confident about learning new material
- experiences in abstract thinking that may help students move gradually from the concrete to the abstract levels of reasoning
- opportunities to experiment with formal thought such as in cooperative learning groups
- discussions, debates
- learning strategies that help students develop their metacognitive abilities
- learning strategies that help students build background knowledge, activate what they know, and organize information
- time, discussion, prodding

REFERENCES

Carnegie Council on Adolescent Development. *Turning Points; Preparing Youth for the 21st Century.* Washington, DC: Author, 1989.

Milgram, J. "A Portrait of Diversity: The Middle Level Student." *Transforming Middle Level Education: Prospectives and Possibilities.* Ed. J. L. Irvin. Boston: Allyn and Bacon, 1992.

Rice, F. P. *The Adolescent: Development, Relationships, and Culture.* 6th ed. Boston: Allyn and Bacon, 1990.

Scales, P. A *Portrait of Young Adolescents in the 1900s.* Carrboro, NC: Center for Early Adolescence, 1991.

The Integration of Assessment and Instruction

Dr. Roger Farr, *Indiana University*

Assessment of student reading and writing has been important to educators and the public at large since the beginning of this century. Educators have needed some way to determine whether they are meeting their goals and objectives, and the public has wanted some means of making schools accountable for the considerable investment needed to maintain them. The development of large, standardized, very-short-answer tests has been one answer to these demands. They report normed scores that can be compared to a large national sample of students. Similar tests have been developed in most states as criterion-referenced measures that require a student to respond to an arbitrated number of particular educational objectives.

However, at the same time, emerging theory has persuasively described how language abilities actually develop, leading to new emphasis on teaching and measuring language performance as a process—not with the short-answer response typical of most tests used as accountability measures.

Writing tests have been around since 1915 and are now used in at least 35 states. There is new emphasis on writing in college entrance exams. Across all grades reading, writing, and thinking are being integrated in classroom instruction as a combined process.

Teachers have not defensively closed their ears to the critics' and general public's concern for accountabil-ity in the schools, however. They have been the primary constructors of city and state criterion-referenced measures attempting to measure and reflect the curricula they also helped structure. Through these tests, they have sought to raise their students' performances and scores on standardized tests and have analyzed the results for their implications for teaching.

What could more solidly assure that assessment reflect and measure instructional goals than to make it a part of instruction?

Meanwhile, teachers have continued to use a variety of daily classroom assessments to inform their teaching. These include observation and a host of other informal techniques and assessments accompanying the texts they use. Teachers have tended to react to the increased instructional time that testing consumes by making their classroom assessment a valid learning experience for the student and an instructional opportunity. What could more solidly assure that assessment reflect and measure instructional goals than to make it a part of instruction?

This dynamic trend in school assessment goes far beyond merely using test results as indicators of what needs to be taught or retaught. It assesses student progress on an ongoing basis as youngsters use language to construct meaning by reading, writing, and thinking every day! The teacher assesses both by observing the process and by analyzing the product.

Often this effort involves having the students keep portfolios that include many types of writing. Much of this writing reacts to and applies information from different texts that the students have read. Frequently included, too, in student portfolios are one or more of a variety of journals. These portfolios are of two general types:

- The *working portfolio* contains all the drafts of a particular piece of writing and ideas for future writing and intentions for future reading. It has records (logs) of reading and writing and journal entries or brief descriptions, observations, or sketches that can be expanded or used in other ways. It is like an artist's studio full of works in progress and works finished.

- The *show portfolio* can be designed to serve numerous purposes: It can be a selection of pieces to demonstrate to parents and/or administrators how a student's language use is developing. It can introduce a student to a new teacher or school. It is like a show that an artist mounts from the works kept in his or her studio.

Teachers are learning that there is a host of ways that portfolios and publishing efforts can be analyzed to assess their students' progress as language users. Most of these projects involve rewriting and provide drafts leading to the more finished product, a set that reveals both language product and the process that leads to it.

Language-processing experiences can culminate in some sort of publishing to communicate with peers and other audiences. Classroom newsletters, creative writing magazines, and other publications develop audience awareness and a keen sense of purpose for writing. Frequently these experiences involve the interaction of students reacting to and editing each other's work as ongoing and interactive assessment. Since all this hinges on the belief that the best way to learn to read, write, and think is to do as much of it as possible, just noting the quantity and fluency of student production is highly revealing.

There are many other observations and analyses that teachers can make that systemize this kind of assessment to a degree that supports its use in reporting progress to parents and other educators. Almost all portfolios include logs of what students read. Teachers are now encouraged to set up opportunities for their students to keep such records. These include notes on their reaction to numerous texts, and writing/thinking efforts in which they apply the meaning they have constructed by reading. This basic language/thinking process often involves both synthesis of texts and critical reaction to them. More often than not, it promotes an appreciation of and critical reaction to literature as well as the use of good writing as a model and as the ignition to an original student effort.

Of course, good teachers have long used these kinds of activities. What is new, it appears, is the emphasis on integrating language/thinking processing and on assessing while instructing!

Publishers have come to a similar understanding about language use and assessment. They have developed interactive performance assessments that use texts as prompts for student writing. These are usually presented with a prescribed writing task that identifies a believable audience and that is designed to seem highly valid to the student. Most often these prompts present several pieces of writing that may represent several genres. The student's thinking abilities are engaged by a task that calls for synthesis of and critical reaction to the texts in order to recommend some solution to an authentic problem.

In order to help the teacher analyze the student's performance on these interactive performance assessments, they are accompanied by a rubric that describes several ranks (or scores) for student responses for each of several key factors. For example, a student's response may be ranked from 3 (high) to 1 (low) on its indication (a) of how well the student has comprehended the text or texts, (b) of how well the student has written the response, and (c) of how well comprehension and writing have been integrated to accomplish the assigned task. Each rank for each factor may be described according to several subfactors: In writing, for example, the response may be ranked after consideration of organization, diction, and mechanics.

A second guide to scoring is even more helpful than the rubric. These assessments are given to a large and varied sample of students at the grade level for which each is created. Then a team of teachers or other specialists selects several sample or anchor papers to demonstrate each score of the ranking system for each factor. These are presented with analytical comments in a booklet with the rubric and are made available to teachers who use the assessment.

Some teachers and groups of teachers are developing these integrated performance assessments on their own. Some of them use published assessments as their models. Although the process is not easy, teachers who have done it remark on how much the experience teaches them about their instructional values and goals.

The ranked results of performance assessments can be reported to parents, administrators, critics of education, and the public at large. The model or anchor papers and rubrics stand as a clear and revealing explication of what the ranks mean if those who would rely on them make the effort to understand the data being used. Thus, integrated performance assessment can serve to inform accountability interests along with scores from standardized and criterion-referenced assessment.

Most important, portfolios and performance assessment develop the habit of self-assessing so that students go through life interested in personal development as readers, writers, and thinkers. This awareness can occur only when the student believes that the goals and objectives against which progress is being measured are real, interesting, and empowering.

Portfolios do that in the extreme if the student is allowed to maintain an important degree of control over the collection. Equally important to the success of the portfolio in developing self-assessment is regular student-teacher conferencing to discuss the portfolio contents, analyze progress, and set new goals.

Integrated performance assessments can achieve this if they are built around interesting prompts and if the tasks seem valid. The results of these student efforts, which usually include drafts that can be analyzed for process, can be studied and discussed by the student and the teacher in conference; and their appropriateness for student self-analysis is emphasized when a student is encouraged to include the set in his or her portfolio.

While legislators and educators together struggle with attempts to create assessments that can report on educational progress and accountability, teachers have been demonstrating dynamic new emphases in integrating language and thinking processes while turning assessment into highly effective instruction.

Reading Matters consists of five Strategy Lessons. The lessons have been designed specifically because "reading *does* matter." Here you'll find strategies that students can use to help them master reading informational and literary texts. The final Strategy Lesson (Lesson 5) focuses on reading fluency and can (and should) be used throughout the year. Each lesson offers a particular strategy that you can use as a preteaching, reteaching, or review tool.

Students should view the information in Reading Matters much as they would view the information in a handbook; it can be accessed at any point, read in any order, and revisited as many times as needed. That's the underlying philosophy of Reading Matters. As you look through these lessons, you'll find that strategies presented in each lesson can be used with various stories in *Elements of Literature*. Furthermore, these lessons can help students read various materials, not only the materials in this book.

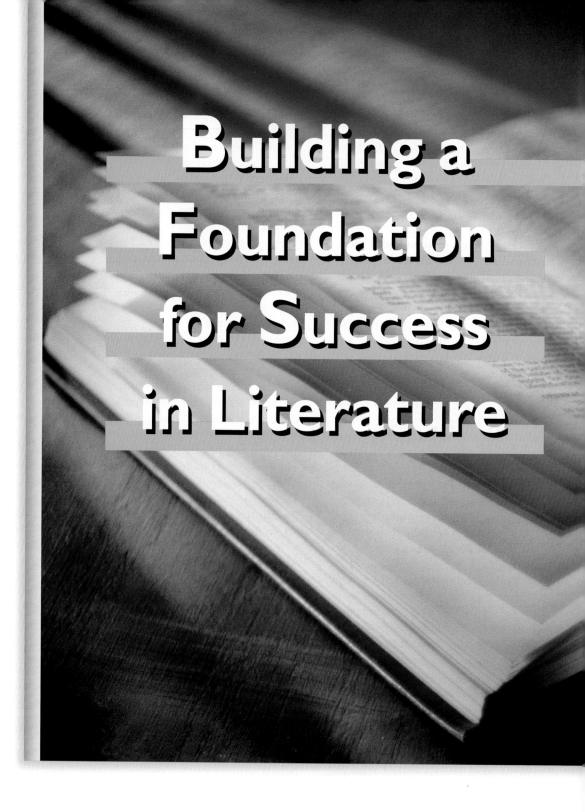

Building a Foundation for Success in Literature

A Foundation for Reading

Reading Matters *By Dr. Kylene Beers*

Strategy Lesson 1
   Identifying the Impact of Setting

Strategy Lesson 2
   How Character Affects Plot

Strategy Lesson 3
   Identifying Theme

Strategy Lesson 4
   Looking at Text Structures

Strategy Lesson 5
   Improving Fluency and Reading Rate

A Foundation for Test Taking

Test Smarts

Strategies for Taking Multiple-Choice Tests

Reading Comprehension

Strategies for Taking Writing Tests
   Writing a Fictional or Autobiographical Narrative
   Writing a Summary
   Writing a Response to Literature
   Writing a Persuasive Essay

TEST SMARTS

Preparing for Multiple-Choice Tests

Use the sample test items to help students prepare for multiple-choice tests. The items test students' ability to decipher unknown words using the context of the passage and to select the correct definition of a word with multiple meanings. The items also emphasize identification of explicitly stated facts and literal meaning, important skills for reading and applying complex, multistep instructions. Students are also asked to infer the main idea by distinguishing between supporting details and the major focus of the reading passage.

Preparing for Writing Tests

The writing lessons help prepare students for taking a variety of writing tests. Each lesson provides a writing prompt and sample responses based on that prompt. The strategies presented in each lesson can also be used to help students complete various Writer's Workshops in *Elements of Literature*.

USING READING MATTERS WITH THE STUDENT EDITION

As you look through Reading Matters, note that each lesson is addressed directly to your students. Students can turn to this section on an as-needed basis. That means you should

- preview Reading Matters with students early in the year
- make sure students understand that part of being a proficient reader means knowing how to get through difficult reading on their own
- remind students to refer to the Fluency Chart and Reading Rate Chart on *Student Edition* pages xxxviii and xxxix, and have them assess their fluency and reading rates throughout the year
- remind students often that these lessons can help them with all types of texts, informational texts as well as literary texts

Strategy Lesson 1

Identifying the Impact of Setting
Somebody Wanted But So

I asked my students to think about how the folk tale "Goldilocks and the Three Bears" would be different if it had taken place underwater instead of in the forest. One student said, "They'd all get wet." Someone else said that the bears would be fish. Another said that Goldilocks would be a mermaid. Then someone said, "The bears, which would be fish, wouldn't have gone out for a walk but instead would have gone to school!" She paused, then asked, "Get it? School . . . fish . . . fish travel in schools!" Everyone moaned, but they got it. Then they came up with all sorts of other ways in which the story would be different if it were set underwater (beds would be clam beds; porridge would be seaweed soup; fish wouldn't walk to school but would ride seahorses).

Change Setting, Change Story

Those students understood that changing the **setting**—when and where the story takes place—affects other elements of the story.

Characters, action, even the story's resolution can be affected by the story's setting. In fact, writers often make events happen *where* they happen and *when* they happen for specific reasons. Try this:

Think about . . .	and change the setting . . .
the Narnia books	from England to the United States
The Watsons Go to Birmingham—1963	from 1963 to 1863 and then to 1993
The Flintstones	from prehistoric times to the year 2000

Somebody Wanted But So . . .

Just how much of an impact does setting have on a story's problem and its resolution? To figure this out, you can use a strategy called **Somebody Wanted But So** (SWBS). Jot down those words on your paper, like this:

Somebody	Wanted	But	So

PRACTICE I

Think of an old story you are familiar with. Under "Somebody," name the "somebody" in the story. Under "Wanted," state what he or she wanted. In the "But" column, describe the problem that arose. Finally, under "So," explain how the problem was resolved. When you're done, your SWBS chart will look something like this:

Somebody	Wanted	But	So
Goldilocks	food and a place to rest in the forest since night was coming on,	there was no one in the lonely house she found,	she entered and ate the food on the table and ruined some things, then got scared when the bears came home from work.

1. What happens in the "Wanted" column if the location of the story changes? (Set the story in a place other than the forest, and see what happens.)

2. What happens in the "Wanted" column if the time of the story is changed (to early morning, for example)?

3. How might changing that column affect the "But" and "So" columns?

4. How much of a difference do the changes in setting make to the outcome of the story?

PRACTICE 2

In the story "The Stone" (page 69), setting is important. Make an SWBS chart for several of the characters in that story. Next, think about what changes would occur in the "Wanted," "But," and "So" columns if the story were set in the present in a city rather than in the past in the country. Are the changes in the outcome column—the "So" column—significant?

PRACTICE I
Possible Answers

1.

Wanted

a comfortable hotel room in a big city, since night was coming on,

2.

Wanted

a big breakfast and a tooth-brush since it was early morning,

3. *Changing the location to a big city:*

But	So
she didn't have money for a hotel room,	so she stayed at a youth hostel and met a group of teenagers from Spain.

Changing the time of the story to early morning:

But	So
there was no one in the lonely house she found,	she entered, ate the breakfast on the table, ruined some things, and then got scared when the bears came home from work.

4. Possible response (based on the sample answers above): Changing the location to a big city might result in a completely different ending, while changing the time of the story to early morning might not change the ending at all.

PRACTICE 2
Possible Answers

Somebody	Wanted	But	So
Maibon	never to get old, so he took a rock from a dwarf,	his crops didn't grow, his eggs didn't hatch, and his cow didn't calve,	he decided to grow old gracefully and got rid of the rock.
Modrona	her husband to take care of the family first,	he wanted only to be young,	she made him get rid of the rock.

Somebody	Wanted	But	So
Maibon	never to get old, so he took a rock from a dwarf,	his job was the same every day, and he got bored,	he decided to grow old gracefully and got rid of the rock.
Modrona	her husband to take care of the family business,	he wanted only to be young,	she made him get rid of the rock.

Strategy Lesson 2

How Character Affects Plot

If . . .Then . . .

Take a Close Look!

Is the runner in this picture
- confident or fearful?
- strong or weak?

The outcome of this runner's leap depends on how you interpret the drawing. Without any information about the character, it's hard to know what he is going to do. In the same way, knowing something about a character helps you understand the development of a story's plot and the resolution of the conflict.

Remember

Plot is the series of related events that make up a story.

Conflicts are the problems faced by the characters.

The **resolution** is the final part of the story, in which the conflicts are resolved and the story ends.

Characters are the people or animals that are the actors in the plot.

If–Then . . .

It's not difficult to identify the characters in a story or describe the events of the plot, but sometimes it's hard to explain how a character's qualities affect the outcome of the plot. To do this, use the **If . . . Then . . .** strategy.

If–Then at Work: "Three Little Pigs"

If Pig Number Three is smart and hardworking, *then* he'll live in a brick house, outwit the wolf when the wolf comes knocking at his door, and live happily ever after. But *if* Pig Number Three is as careless and lazy as his brothers, *then* he'll live in a house made of flimsy materials, be outwitted by the wolf, and find himself the wolf's next meal.

PRACTICE 1

Sometimes characters surprise us. A weak character who is put to the test becomes extraordinarily brave. An honest character who faces a difficult situation cheats. That is one of the joys of reading: In a well-written story, people can surprise us—just as they do in real life.

The "If" column of the chart below presents three versions of a character named Sam. Complete the "Then" column by writing a few lines describing what would happen if each "Sam" were faced with the following situation:

Sam has just found a wallet with two hundred dollars inside. There is no identification in the wallet. What will Sam do?

If	Then
Sam is stingy but honest	
Sam is generous but lazy	
Sam is ambitious but unfriendly	

PRACTICE 2

After you read "Ta-Na-E-Ka" (page 15), think about the main character, Mary. Look at the list of character traits on the right, and find the four qualities that best describe Mary.

Then, think about how the story would be different if Mary had the opposite qualities. How would the plot be different? How would the conflict be resolved? How would the story end?

Set up your exercise like this:

If	Then
Mary had been...	[this would probably have happened]

Character Traits

bold/shy
brave/cowardly
careful/careless
eager/reluctant
expert/unskilled
fair/unfair
faithful/disloyal
friendly/unfriendly
gentle/fierce
genuine/fake
happy/sad
hardworking/lazy
honest/sneaky
kind/cruel
obedient/disobedient
patient/impatient
powerful/weak
reliable/unreliable
respectful/rude
wise/foolish

PRACTICE 1
Possible Answers

If	Then
Sam is stingy but honest,	he will probably put up posters to find the owner, but he may request a reward for his efforts.
Sam is generous but lazy,	he will probably mean to put up posters but never get around to it.
Sam is ambitious but unfriendly,	he will probably keep the money and buy something for himself.

PRACTICE 2
Possible Answers

If	Then
Mary had been shy,	she would probably have been afraid of Ernie.
Mary had been lazy,	she probably wouldn't have offered to babysit to repay the money she borrowed.
Mary had been foolish,	she probably wouldn't have come up with such a good plan to survive Ta-Na-E-Ka.

Identifying Theme
Most Important Word

If finding the **theme** of a story or novel is as difficult for you as finding a needle in a haystack, read on!

Theme Isn't Topic or Plot

Theme—what a story reveals about life—emerges as you read the story or novel. Don't confuse theme with topic or plot.

- The **topic** of the poem "Casey at the Bat" is a baseball game.
- The **plot** involves a mighty baseball player who tries to save a game but instead strikes out.
- Some might say the **theme** shows us that in life many things are uncertain; others might say the theme shows us that even the mightiest sometimes meet with failure.

In other words, the same story or novel might reveal different themes to different people.

Most Important Word

To find the theme of a piece of literature, try a strategy called **Most Important Word.** Ask yourself what the most important word in a story is, and *why* that word is so important. Thinking about these questions will help you focus on the theme of the work. After you decide on the word, consider how it relates to the setting, characters, plot, and conflict of the story.

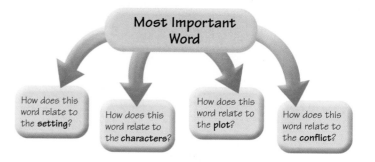

Most Important Word

How does this word relate to the **setting**?

How does this word relate to the **characters**?

How does this word relate to the **plot**?

How does this word relate to the **conflict**?

PRACTICE I

After reading "The All-American Slurp" (page 31), one student stated the theme as "Embarrassing things sometimes happen to all people." She decided that that was the theme after choosing *embarrassed* as the most important word and thinking about how the idea of being embarrassed related to the characters, plot, setting, and conflict of the story.

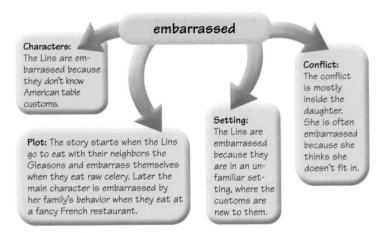

How would the information in these boxes change if you thought the most important word in "The All-American Slurp" was *family* or *American* or even *slurp?*

PRACTICE 2

After you read "Just Once" (page 2), choose the most important word or phrase from the three choices listed just below (or choose a word of your own). Then, complete the chart. Use the information in the chart to figure out the story's theme. (You can usually state a story's theme in one sentence.)

glory   hang-up   just once

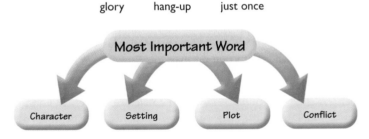

Possible Answers

Most important word: *family*
Characters: The narrator is a member of the Lin family, and her friend Meg is a member of the Gleason family.
Plot: The narrator feels embarrassed because she and her family appear foolish, as they do not know American table customs. Later, she realizes that the Gleason family look just as foolish eating a Chinese dinner, because they do not know Chinese table customs.
Setting: Each family experiences being in an unfamiliar setting, where customs are new to them.
Conflict: The conflict is inside the narrator, who is embarrassed because she thinks that she and her family don't fit in. She realizes, though, that her family is really no different from the Gleasons.

PRACTICE 2
Possible Answers

Most important word: *glory*
Characters: Bryan "the Moose" wants to feel the glory of carrying the ball.
Plot: The Moose wishes he could get to carry the ball just once. His wish comes true, but he realizes that the glory isn't worth the pain of being tackled.
Setting: Football fields give players, especially fullbacks, an opportunity for glory.
Conflict: The conflict is inside the Moose, who thinks he wants the glory of running the ball. He learns, however, that he prefers the anonymous glory of being a lineman.
Theme: Not everyone is suited for the glory of running the ball; for some, the anonymous glory of being a lineman is best.

4 Looking at Text Structures

Comparison and Contrast

When writers point out ways in which things are alike, they are making a **comparison**. When they point out ways in which things are different, they are making a **contrast**. Here are some words and phrases that signal comparisons and contrasts:

Comparison	Contrast
additionally, also, by the same token, equally, in the same manner, just as, like, likewise, similarly, too	although, but, by contrast, different from, however, in spite of, nevertheless, on the contrary, on the other hand, though, unlike, yet

Writers of informational texts often use comparison and contrast.

Sequencing and Chronological Order

Writers use a **sequence structure** when the order of events is important. *Sequence* refers to the order in which events occur. **Chronological order,** the time order in which events occur, is one kind of sequence structure.

Which of these would you write using a sequence structure?

1. a description of what you did at school yesterday

2. an essay explaining why you believe the age for getting a driver's license should be lowered or raised

3. instructions for dealing with a flash fire in your area

4. instructions for making pizza at home

If you aren't sure which of these require a sequence structure, try discussing each topic without using words like *first, second, third, next, later, after, then,* and *finally.* If you find that you don't need these words, the sequence, or order of events, probably isn't important.

Informational texts in which sequencing is often used include science articles, history texts, and instruction manuals.

Cause and Effect

Another text structure writers use is called **cause and effect**. This structure is often used in informational texts, such as social studies books, which focus on the causes and effects of wars or discoveries or political movements. The following sentences illustrate the cause-and-effect structure:

1. Because the temperature fell below thirty-two degrees, the water froze.

2. Jonas stopped smiling when he got braces on his teeth.

3. Scientists theorized that the dinosaurs were wiped out when a huge meteorite smashed into the earth.

4. The wind from the volcanic eruption carried rocks that flattened whole forests of 180-foot trees.

Here's how that information might be presented in a cause-and-effect chart:

Cause	Effect
Temperature fell below thirty-two degrees.	The water froze.
Jonas got braces.	Jonas stopped smiling.
Meteorite smashed into the earth.	Dinosaurs disappeared.
Wind carried rocks.	Rocks flattened forests.

When you read a text that discusses cause and effect, keep track of **causal relationships** (causes and effects) by making a chart like the one above. As you read, ask yourself what caused various outcomes.

PRACTICE

What text structure (**comparison and contrast, sequencing,** or **cause and effect**) is used in each of the following sentences?

1. Blood that travels to the heart through veins carries carbon dioxide; blood that travels from the heart through arteries carries oxygen.

2. After blood passes through the lungs, it returns to the heart through the pulmonary veins.

3. If the heart's mitral valve is blocked, blood can't flow from the upper left chamber of the heart to the lower left chamber. If it can't flow to that chamber, it can't get to the aorta, and problems arise.

4. Exercise helps strengthen the heart.

PRACTICE I
1. comparison and contrast
2. chronological
3. cause and effect
4. cause and effect

5 Improving Fluency and Reading Rate

Did you know that people sometimes get tickets for driving too *slowly*?

It's also possible to read too slowly. If people read too quickly, they may miss important information; if they read too slowly, they may have trouble making sense of what they're reading.

How Can I Improve?

Reading fluency (how easily and well you read) and **reading rate** (how fast you read) are related. If you are a fluent reader, you

- read with expression
- know when to pause
- read by phrases or thought groups instead of word by word
- know when you don't understand what you've read
- know how to adjust your rate to what you are reading

Name		
Date		
Listener's Name		

Oral Fluency	Often 5 points	Some- times 3 points	Never 0 points
Reads word by word			
Stops and starts			
Re-reads words or sentences			
Ignores			
• periods			
• commas			
• question marks			
• quotation marks			
Reads too fast			
Reads too slowly			
Slurs words			
Reads too loudly			
Reads too softly			
Guesses at pronunciations			
Seems nervous			
Loses place in text			

Final Score: _____

If you think you need to improve your fluency, practice reading aloud, either alone (use a tape recorder so that you can listen to yourself) or with a buddy.

Choose a passage or paragraph that's 150–200 words long. Read it to yourself silently a few times; then, read it aloud. Afterward, fill out the checklist above.

Keep practicing; you'll soon see that your score is going down—which means that your fluency is going up.

What's My Reading Rate?

If fluency is tied to reading rate, then what rate is right? Remember that different rates are right for different kinds of texts. You might zip through a comic book, but you need to move more slowly through your social studies textbook. In other words, your reading rate depends on what you're reading and why you're reading it.

If you think you read too slowly all the time, you can improve your reading rate. Follow these steps:

1. Choose something you want to read. (Don't choose something that's too easy.)
2. Ask a friend to time you as you read aloud for one minute.
3. Count the words you read in that one minute.
4. Repeat this process two more times, with different passages.
5. Add the three numbers, and divide the total by three.

That number is your oral reading rate.

The chart at the right shows average reading rates for students in grades 3–6.

Grade Level	Average Words per Minute
3	110
4	140
5	160
6	180

If you think your rate is too slow, practice reading aloud every week or so, having someone time you as you read for one minute. Use the *same* passages to practice fluency. Use *new* passages to check your reading rate.

Don't Forget . . .

If you don't understand what you read, you aren't reading fluently. As you read, keep asking yourself if what you're reading makes sense. If you get confused at any point, stop and re-read. From time to time, pause and think about what you've read. Sum up the main events or ideas. Be sure you understand what causes events to happen. Compare what actually happens with what you expected. If you still don't understand what you're reading, try reading more slowly.

Test Smarts

Strategies for Taking Multiple-Choice Tests

If you have ever watched a quiz show on TV, you know how multiple-choice tests work. You get a question and (usually) four choices. Your job is to pick the correct one. Taking multiple-choice tests will get much easier when you apply these Test Smarts:

T rack your time.

E xpect success.

S tudy the directions.

T ake it all in.

S pot those numbers.

M aster the questions.

A nticipate the answers.

R ely on 50/50.

T ry. Try. Try.

S earch for skips and smudges.

Track Your Time

You race through a test for fear you won't finish, or you realize you have only five minutes left to complete eleven zillion questions. Sound familiar? You can avoid both problems if you take a few minutes before you start to estimate how much time you have for each question. Using all the time you are given can help you avoid making errors. Follow these tips to set **checkpoints:**

- How many questions should be completed when one quarter of the time is gone?
- What should the clock read when you are halfway through the questions?
- If you find yourself behind your checkpoints, you can speed up.
- If you are ahead, you can—and should—slow down.

Expect Success

Top athletes know that attitude affects performance. They learn to deal with their negative thoughts. So can you! Do you compare yourself with others? Most top athletes will tell you that they compete against only one person: themselves. They know they cannot change another person's performance. Instead, they study their own performance and find ways to improve it. That makes sense for you, too. Review your last scores. Figure out just what you need to do to top them. You can!

What if you get anxious? It's OK if you do. A little nervousness will help you focus. Of course, if you're so nervous that you think you might get sick or faint, take time to relax for a few minutes. Calm bodies breathe slowly. You can fool yours into feeling calmer and thinking more clearly by taking a few deep breaths—five slow counts in, five out.

Study the Directions

You're ready to go, go, go, but first it's wait, wait, wait. Pencils. Paper. Answer sheets. Lots of directions. Listen! In order to follow directions, you have to know them. Read all test directions as if they contained the key to lifetime happiness and several years' allowance. Then, read them again. Study the answer sheet. Does it look like this?

1

2

3

4

or like this?

1   2   3   4

What about answer choices? Are they arranged

A   B   C   D

or

A   B   A   C
         or
C   D   B   D

Directions count. Be very, very sure you know exactly what to do and how to do it before you make your first mark.

Take It All In

When you finally hear the words "You may begin," briefly **preview the test** to get a mental map of your tasks:

- Know how many questions you have to complete.
- Know where to stop.
- Set your time checkpoints.
- Do the easy sections first; easy questions are worth just as many points as hard ones.

Spot Those Numbers

"I got off by one and spent all my time trying to fix my answer sheet." *Oops.* Make it a habit to

- match the number of each question to the numbered space on the answer sheet every time
- leave the answer space blank if you skip a question
- keep a list of your blank spaces on scratch paper or somewhere else—but *not* on your answer sheet. The less you have to erase on your answer sheet, the better.

Master the Questions

Be sure—very sure—that you **know what a question is asking you.** Read the question at least twice before reading the answer choices. Approach it as you would a mystery story or a riddle. Look for clues. Watch especially for words like *not* and *except*—they tell you to look for the choice that is false or different from the other choices or opposite in some way. For a reading-comprehension test, read the selection, master all the questions, and then reread the selection. The answers will be likely to pop out the second time around. Remember: A test isn't trying to trick you; it's trying to test your knowledge and your ability to think clearly.

Anticipate the Answers

Before you read the answer choices, **answer the question yourself. Then, read the choices.** If the answer you gave is among the choices listed, it is probably correct.

Rely on 50/50

"I . . . have . . . no . . . clue." You understand the question. You have an answer, but your answer is not listed, or perhaps you drew a complete blank. It happens. Time to **make an educated guess**—not a *wild* guess, but an *educated* guess. Think about quiz shows again, and you'll know the value of the 50/50 play. When two answers are eliminated, the contestant has a 50/50 chance of choosing the correct one. You can use elimination, too.

Always read every choice carefully. **Watch out for distracters**—choices that may be true but are too broad, too narrow, or not relevant to the question. Eliminate the least likely choice. Then, eliminate the next, and so on until you find the best one. If two choices seem equally correct, look to see if "All of the above" is an option. If it is, that might be your choice. If no choice seems correct, look for "None of the above."

Try. Try. Try.

Don't give up. You might be surprised by how many students do give up. Think of tests as a kind of marathon. Just as in any marathon, people get bored, tired, hungry, thirsty, hot, discouraged. They may begin to feel sick or develop aches and pains. They decide the test doesn't matter.

Remember: The last question is worth just as much as the first question, and the questions on a test don't always get harder as you go. If the question you just finished was really hard, an easier one is probably coming up. Take a deep breath, and give it your all, all the way to the finish.

Search for Skips and Smudges

"Hey! I got that one right, and the machine marked it wrong!" If you have ever—ever—had this experience, pay attention! When this happens in class, your teacher can give you the extra point. On a machine-scored test, however, you would lose the point and never know why. So, listen up: All machine-scored answer sheets have a series of lines marching down the side. The machine stops at the first line and scans across it for your answer, stops at the second line, scans, stops at the third line, scans, and so on, all the way to the end. The machine is looking for a dark, heavy mark. If it finds one where it should be, you get the point. If you leave a question blank or accidentally mark two answers instead of one, you lose a point. If your marks are not very dark, the machine sees blank spaces, and you'll lose more points.

To avoid losing points, take time at the end of the test to make sure you

- did not skip any answers
- gave one answer for each question
- made the marks heavy and dark and within the lines

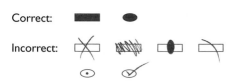

Get rid of smudges. Make sure there are no stray pencil marks on your answer sheet. Cleanly erase those places where you changed your mind. Check for little stray marks from pencil tapping.

Reading Comprehension

Many tests have a section called **reading comprehension.** Taking a reading-comprehension test is a bit like playing ball. You don't know where the ball will land, so you have to stay alert to all possibilities. However, just as the ball can come at you in only a few ways, there are only a few kinds of questions that can be used on reading-comprehension tests. This discussion will help you identify the most common ones.

The purpose of the reading-comprehension section is to test your understanding of a reading passage. Be sure to keep these suggestions in mind when you read a selection on a test:

- **Read the passage once** to get a general overview of the topic.
- If you don't understand the passage at first, keep reading. **Try to find the main idea.**
- Then, **read the questions** so that you'll know what information to look for when you reread the passage.

Two kinds of texts are used here. The first one is an informational text. The second is an updated fairy tale.

DIRECTIONS: Read the following selection. Then, choose the *best* answer for each question. Mark each answer on your answer sheet in the square provided.

Call of the Wild

Baffin Island, a remote, wild region of Canada, is home to a group of canids that survive on their own, obeying no master but their ancient instincts. (*Canid* is a term that covers all dog-like creatures, including dogs, wolves, jackals, foxes, and coyotes.) Scientists went to Baffin Island to observe a group of five adult wolves that functioned as a family. The group included a litter of seven young wolves whose parents were the leaders of the clan.

The group occupied a series of five dens (shelters the wolves dig in the earth) on hills near a river. The dens were just about halfway between the summer and winter ground of the wolves' main prey, caribou, large deer that live in tundra regions like Baffin.

Like humans, the wolves use division of labor to provide for the needs of the group. While one wolf goes out on a long, wearying search for food, another stays behind to guard the pups. When the designated hunter returns, giving out meat to the hungry pups and preparing for a long nap—sometimes up to eighteen hours—the "baby sitter" sets out on the long journey across the tundra in search of more caribou meat.

ITEM 1 asks for vocabulary knowledge.

1. In the first sentence of the passage, the word <u>remote</u> means —

   A tiny   **C** bustling

   B filthy   **D** distant

Answer: Look at the surrounding sentences, or **context,** to see which definition fits.

A is incorrect. If the area is wild, it is unlikely to be tiny.

B is incorrect. Wild areas are not likely to be filthy.

C is incorrect. Wild areas are not bustling. *Bustling* is a word usually applied to a place where there are crowds of people.

D is the best answer. Wild regions are usually distant from towns and cities.

ITEM 2 asks you to use context clues to determine the meaning of a word.

2. What is the meaning of the italicized word *canids*? Look for a context clue.

   F It is a term that covers all doglike creatures.

   G It is a word for animals that live in Canada.

   H It is another word for a dog.

   J It is another word for a wolf.

Answer: Look at the context to see which answer makes sense.

F is correct. The definition of *canids* is given in parentheses in the next sentence.

G is incorrect. This definition is not close.

H is incorrect. *Canid* refers to animals other than just dogs.

J is incorrect. *Canid* refers to animals other than just wolves.

ITEM 3 asks you to identify the meaning of a word with multiple meanings.

3. In the phrase "a litter of seven young wolves," the word *litter* means —

   A scatter bits of trash

   B a stretcher

   C bits of trash

   D a family of baby animals

Answer: Try out each meaning in the context of the sentence.

A is incorrect. Although the word *litter* can be a verb meaning "scatter bits of trash," as in "litter halls with garbage," this meaning does not fit the context.

B is incorrect. Although the word *litter* can mean "a stretcher," as in "an injured person lay on a litter," this meaning does not fit the context of the sentence.

C is incorrect. Although the word *litter* can be a noun meaning "bits of trash," as in "streets full of litter," this meaning does not fit the context of the passage.

D is correct. In references to mammals, a *litter* is "a family of young animals," as in "a litter of seven young wolves" in this passage.

ITEM 4 asks for close reading. Read carefully to see if the answer is stated directly in the text.

4. Why did these scientists go to Baffin Island?

   F To rescue a litter of wolves threatened by the cold

   G To observe a group of five adult wolves that functioned as a family

   H To prove that wolves are just like dogs

   J To follow the wolves for a year

Answer: Read the passage carefully to see if the answer is directly stated.

G is the correct answer. It is a direct quote from the passage. Once you find this, you know that **F, H,** and **J** are incorrect.

ITEM 5 asks for close reading. Read carefully to see if the answer is stated directly in the text.

5. How are the wolves like humans?

   A They use division of labor.

   B They take good care of their young.

   C They gather more food than they need.

   D They use baby sitters while searching for food.

Answer: Read the passage carefully to see if the answer is directly stated.

A is the correct answer. It is cited in the text. Now you know you can eliminate all the other answer choices.

ITEM 6 asks for an inference.

6. What statement *best* sums up the main point of this passage?

    F Baffin Island is a remote, wild region in Canada.

    G Canids obey no master.

    H The wolves' main prey is caribou.

    J Wolves work together to provide for the needs of the group.

Answer: Ask yourself which statement covers the passage as a whole.

F is incorrect. It is only one detail in the passage.

G is incorrect. It also is only one of many details in the passage.

H is incorrect. It also is only one of many details in the passage.

J is the best answer. It covers almost all the details in the passage.

DIRECTIONS: Read the following selection. Then, choose the *best* answer for each question. Mark each answer on your answer sheet in the space provided.

Technologically Correct Fairy Tales: Little Red Riding Hood

One summer morning, Little Red Riding Hood was on her way to her grandmother's house when, on the path through the woods, she met Mr. Canis Lupus. Her mother had warned her not to speak to anyone, but this wolf looked friendly.

"Where are you going, little girl?" quizzed Mr. Lupus, otherwise known as Gray Wolf. He squinted his shifty eyes. He was a hungry wolf.

"I'm taking some fresh rolls and butter to my grandmother," Little Red Riding Hood answered.

"I know who your grandmother is," cried Mr. Lupus, and off he ran without so much as a catch-you-later.

Reaching Grandmother's cottage first, Wolf tied up Grams and put her in the closet. Then he changed into one of her outfits, pulled out his new laptop, and started a game of hearts.

When Little Red Riding Hood arrived, she said, "Why, Grams, what a big scanner you have."

"All the better to digitize you with, my dear," said Wolf in a high-pitched voice.

"Why, Grams, how many chips you have!" exclaimed Little Red Riding Hood.

"All the better to remember you with, my dear," snorted Wolf.

"Why, Grams, what a lot of mega-hertz you have," cried Little Red Riding Hood.

"All the better to process you with, my dear," hooted Wolf, and he sprang at Little Red Riding Hood, ready to have her for dinner.

Just then a Webmaster appeared in the doorway. Seeing disaster about to happen, the techie deleted Wolf's program and refused to let him boot up again until he had released Red Riding Hood, untied Grams, and traded in his hearts for a heart.

ITEM 1 is a vocabulary question.

1. In the selection, the underlined words <u>Canis Lupus</u> mean —

   A character

   B gray wolf

   C fox

   D dog

Consider the surrounding sentences, or context, to identify the best definition.

A is incorrect. Mr. Canis Lupus *is* a character in the story, but that is not what the term means.

B is the best answer. The story states that Mr. Canis Lupus was also called Gray Wolf.

C is incorrect. A fox is not a character in the story.

D is incorrect. A dog is not a character in the story.

Now, try ITEM 2 on your own. It is another vocabulary question.

2. In the selection, the word *chips* means —

   F memory capacity in a computer

   G salty snack made of potatoes

   H places where small pieces have been broken off

   J wooden shavings from a block

F is the best answer. G, H, and **J** are all definitions of *chips,* but not as the word is used in this story.

ITEM 3 asks you a factual question.

3. Where does Little Red Riding Hood meet Mr. Lupus?

   A Far, far from home

   B On her way to Grandfather's

   C Under the birches

   D On the path through the woods

A is incorrect. The story never says that Little Red Riding Hood is far, far from home.

B is incorrect. There is no grandfather character.

C is incorrect. There are woods, but the type of tree is not identified.

D is the best answer. This is where Little Red Riding Hood meets the wolf.

Now, try ITEM 4 on your own. This factual item asks you to fill in the blank.

4. Little Red Riding Hood is bringing her grandmother —

   F her cloak to repair

   G a basket of cookies

   H an apple pie

   J rolls and butter

J is the best answer. None of the other choices are mentioned in the story.

ITEM 5 is another factual question, but you may have to look a little harder to find the answer.

5. What words or phrases does the writer use to give a glimpse of the wolf's character?

   A grim, sneaky, evil

   B shifty eyes

   C grand, decisive, heroic

   D little, meek, polite

A is incorrect. Although you may think of the wolf as having a grim, sneaky, and evil character from other versions of the story you know, the question asks for words the writer uses. These words are not used in the story.

B is the best answer. These words are used to describe the wolf's eyes. Shifty eyes suggest deceit.

C is incorrect. These words are not in the story.

D is incorrect. These words are not in the story.

Now, try **ITEM 6** on your own. This is an interpretation question, so you'll have to think about it.

6. The wolf puts on one of Grandmother's outfits because he —

    F is cold

    G wants a disguise

    H is having a bad hair day

    J is afraid of the Webmaster

G is the best answer. The wolf is pretending to be Little Red Riding Hood's grandmother. The other answers do not fit the plot of the story.

ITEM 7 is another interpretation question.

7. Which character's actions determine what happens at the end of the story?

    A The Webmaster's

    B The grandmother's

    C The wolf's

    D Little Red Riding Hood's

A is the best answer. The Webmaster prevents further disaster from happening and makes the wolf change his ways.

B is incorrect. The grandmother is present but is tied up in the closet.

C is incorrect. The wolf would not have ruined his own plans.

D is incorrect. Little Red Riding Hood is present but doesn't say or do anything at the end of the story.

ITEM 8 asks a vocabulary question.

8. Which statement about the word *megahertz* is *most* accurate?

    F It has to do with wolves.

    G It means "courage."

    H It refers to food.

    J It has to do with computers.

J is correct. The story uses other computer terms in this dialogue: *scanner, digitize,* and *chips.* Little Red Riding Hood's third remark to the wolf-grandmother also has to do with computers. The other choices don't make sense.

ITEM 9 is another interpretation question.

9. Which is the *best* statement of the story's main message?

    A Computers are dangerous.

    B All wolves are evil.

    C Children should obey their elders.

    D Old people should not live alone.

C is the best answer. None of the other choices are even suggested in the story.

Strategies for Taking Writing Tests
Writing a Fictional or Autobiographical Narrative

Sometimes a prompt on a writing test asks you to write a narrative, or story. The following steps will help you write a **fictional** or **autobiographical** narrative. The responses are based on this prompt.

> **Prompt**
> Describe an experience you had that changed your perspective—made you see the world or yourself differently.

Thinking It Through: Writing a Fictional or Autobiographical Narrative

■ **STEP 1 Read the prompt carefully.**
Does the prompt ask you to write a fictional story (a story that is made up) or an autobiographical story (a story of something that really happened to you)?

The prompt asks me to write about my own experience.

STEP 2 Outline the plot of your narrative. What is the sequence of events that makes up your story?

1. *Some kids in my class were teasing Joel.*
2. *Suddenly, I found myself walking up to one of the bullies and yelling, "Stop!"*
3. *It got really quiet.*
4. *The bullies left, looking embarrassed.*
5. *Joel left, too, but later thanked me. I realized I was stronger than I thought.*

STEP 3 Identify the major and minor characters. What do they look and act like? How do they sound when they speak?

Joel is tall but very gentle. He is also quiet. The ringleader of the bullies is small but mean. He yells at people a lot. I am shy and not that tall. I don't consider myself brave.

STEP 4 Identify the setting of your narrative. Where and when does your story take place?

—on the soccer field
—near the bleachers
—right after school
—in the month of May

STEP 5 Draft your narrative, adding dialogue, suspense, and sensory details. Dialogue, the actual words characters or people say, will add interest to your story; suspense will hold readers' attention; sensory details will bring your story to life.

"Thanks for helping me before."
"That's okay, Joel."

STEP 6 Revise and proofread your narrative. Make sure the events in your story are presented in a logical order. To show the sequence of events, use transitions, such as *first, then, next, before,* and *later.*

Writing a Summary

As you progress through school, you may take tests that ask you to write a **summary.** In summary writing, you read a passage and then rewrite in your own words its main idea and significant details. How would you answer the prompt to the right?

The following steps will help you write a summary in response to such a prompt. The student responses are based on only five

> **Prompt**
> Summarize the article "Working on the Railroad" by Gloria A. Harris.

paragraphs in the selection "Working on the Railroad" on pages 174–175. On a test, though, you would summarize the entire selection.

Thinking It Through: Writing a Summary

■ STEP 1 **Read the passage carefully. Identify the main idea, and restate it in your own words.** If the main idea is not directly stated, look at all the details and decide what point the writer is making about the general topic of the passage.

Many railroad workers invented equipment to make their jobs safer and less difficult.

STEP 2 **Identify important details to include in the summary.** Which details directly support the main idea of the selection? Look for at least one key idea or detail in each paragraph.

—inventions replaced dangerous jobs

—dangerous job: coupling cars

—Andrew Beard invented automatic coupler

—dangerous job: oiling engines

—Elijah McCoy invented self-lubricating cup

STEP 3 **Write the main idea and most important details in a paragraph, using your own words.** Give details in the order in which they are presented in the passage, and use transitions between the ideas.

Railroad jobs were dangerous and exhausting, so many railroad workers invented equipment to make their jobs easier and safer. Two particularly dangerous jobs were coupling cars and oiling engines. These were replaced by the inventions of railroad workers. Andrew Beard, who lost his leg in a coupling accident, invented an automatic coupler, which joined railroad cars together automatically. Elijah McCoy invented a self-lubricating cup that dripped oil into a train's engine.

Moments of Truth

Theme

Age of Enlightenment *In literature, as in life, moments of truth often hit us after we have stretched ourselves in some way or undergone an ordeal that has changed us. Moments of truth can come after we have accomplished something wonderful— or have done something we wish we could go back and do over.*

Reading the Anthology

Reaching Struggling Readers

The *Reading Skills and Strategies: Reaching Struggling Readers* binder provides materials coordinated with the Pupil's Edition (see the Collection Planner, p. T1C) to help students who have difficulty reading and comprehending text, or students who are reluctant readers. The binder for sixth grade is organized around eleven individual skill areas and offers the following options:

- **Mini Read** MiniReads are short, easy texts that give students a chance to practice a particular skill and strategy before reading selections in the Pupil's Edition. Each MiniRead Skill Lesson can be taught independently or used in conjunction with a Selection Skill Lesson.

- **Selection Skill Lessons** Selection Skill Lessons allow students to apply skills introduced in the MiniReads. Each Selection Skill Lesson provides reading instruction and practice specific to a particular piece of literature in the Pupil's Edition.

Reading Beyond the Anthology

Read On

Collection One includes an annotated bibliography of books suitable for extended reading. The suggested books are related to works in this collection by theme, by author, or by subject. To preview the Read On for Collection One, please turn to p. T85.

HRW Library

The *HRW Library* offers novels, plays, and short-story collections for extended reading. Each book in the Library includes one or more major works and thematically or topically related Connections. A Study Guide provides teaching suggestions and worksheets. For Collection One, the following titles are recommended.

HATCHET
Gary Paulsen
The moment of truth for the young hero of this novel comes when his plane crashes and the boy finds himself all alone in the wilderness— with only a hatchet to help him.

THE TRUE CONFESSIONS OF CHARLOTTE DOYLE
Avi
For the heroine of this story, the moment of truth comes when the ship on which she is sailing from England to America is seized by a mutinous crew. The young lady soon learns what she is capable of.

Skills Focus

Selection or Feature	Reading Skills and Strategies	Elements of Literature	Language/ Grammar	Vocabulary/ Spelling	Writing	Listening/ Speaking	Viewing/ Representing
Just Once (p. 2) Thomas J. Dygard	Dialogue with the Text, pp. 2, 11 Retell a Story, p. 11 Summarize, p. 12 Context Clues, p. 13	Conflict, pp. 2, 11 Title, p. 11	Irregular Verbs, p. 13 • Past Tense • Past Participle	Use Context to Recognize Words, p. 13	Note Details of a Conflict, p. 12 Write a Sportscast, p. 12 Write an Explanation of a Life Map, p. 12 Retell a Poem, p. 12	Read a Sports-cast Aloud, p. 12	Draw a Life Map, p. 12
Elements of Literature: Conflict (p. 14)		Conflict, p. 14 • External • Internal					
Ta-Na-E-Ka (p. 15) Mary Whitebird	Compare and Contrast Cultures, pp. 15, 27	Conflict, pp. 15, 27 • External • Internal	Subject-Verb Agreement, p. 29 Compound Subject, p. 29	Use Words in Context, p. 29	Freewrite, p. 28 Describe Ta-Na-E-Ka or Write a Poem About Cultural Heritage, p. 28	Present Data on Rituals, p. 28 Debate Issues of Gender Equality, p. 28	Use a Chart to Organize Information, p. 27
Reading Skills and Strategies: How to Own a Word (p. 30)	Use Context Clues, p. 30 Use Reference Aids, p. 30						
The All-American Slurp (p. 31) Lensey Namioka	Use Context Clues, pp. 31, 43 Predict, p. 41 Identify Key Events, p. 41	Reader's Theater, p. 31 Message, p. 41	Subject-Verb Agreement, p. 43 Identify the Subject, p. 43	Use Words in Context, p. 43 Context Clues, p. 43	Script a Scene, p. 42 Write a Phrase Book, p. 42 Write Tips on What to Do in Your Town, p. 42	Perform a Scene, p. 42 Talk About Eating Customs, p. 42	Draw Diagrams of Eating Customs, p. 42 Make a Map of the School, p. 42
La Bamba (p. 44) Gary Soto	Make Predictions, pp. 44, 50	Simile, pp. 44, 50	Verb Tenses, p. 52	Spell Words Correctly: *ie* or *ei*, p. 52	Write Notes on a Performance, p. 51 Write a Brochure, p. 51 Write a Comparison-Contrast Paragraph, p. 51	Interview a Public Speaker, p. 51	Use a Venn Diagram, p. 51 Create a Poster for a Talent Show, p. 51
President Cleveland, Where Are You? (p. 53) Robert Cormier	Summarize, pp. 53, 67	Sensory Details, pp. 53, 67 Conflict, p. 66	Vivid Verbs, p. 68	Choose the Correct Word in Context, p. 68	Write About a Specific Event, p. 67 Write the Story from Another Point of View, p. 67	Role-Play Moments from the Story, p. 67	Make a Story-board, p. 67
The Stone (p. 69) Lloyd Alexander	Make Generalizations, pp. 69, 79 Make Predictions, p. 79	Moral Lessons, pp. 69, 79 Main Events, p. 79 Character, p. 79	*Don't* and *Doesn't*, p. 81	Synonyms, p. 81	Freewrite About Incidents, p. 80 Write a Short Short-Story, p. 80 List Vivid Words, p. 80	Report on Moral Lessons, p. 80	Make a Drawing, p. 80
No Questions Asked: Lessons (p. 82) Bill Cosby	The **No Questions Asked** feature provides students with an unstructured opportunity to practice reading strategies using a selection that extends the theme of the collection.						
Writer's Workshop: Autobiographical Incident (p. 86)		Sensory Details, p. 87			Write an Autobiographical Incident, pp. 86–90.		Make a Word Cluster, p. 87
Sentence Workshop: Sentence Fragments (p. 91)			Sentence Fragments, p. 91		Revise Sentence Fragments, p. 91		
Reading for Life: Using Text Organizers (p. 92)	Locate Information, p. 92 • Table of Contents • Headings • Graphic Features						
Learning for Life: Decision Making (p. 93)					Write an Advice Manual, p. 93 Write a Skit, p. 93 Write a Song, p. 93	Interview Adults, p. 93	

Collection One Moments of Truth

Resources for this Collection

Note: All resources for this collection are available for preview on the *One-Stop Planner CD-ROM 1 with Test Generator.* All worksheets and blackline masters may be printed from the CD-ROM.

Internet Resources
go.hrw.com LE0 6-1

Selection or Feature	Reading and Literary Skills	Language and Grammar

Just Once (p. 2)
Thomas J. Dygard
Connections: Foul Shot (p. 10)
Edwin A. Hoey
	• *Reading Skills and Strategies: Reaching Struggling Readers*
	  • MiniRead Skill Lesson, p. 1
	  • Selection Skill Lesson, p. 7
	• *Graphic Organizers for Active Reading,* Worksheet p. 1
		• *Grammar and Language Links:*
		  Troublesome Verbs, Worksheet p. 1
		• *Language Workshop CD-ROM,*
		  Irregular Verbs
		• *Daily Oral Grammar,*
		  Transparency 1

Elements of Literature: Conflict (p. 14)	• *Literary Elements,* Transparency 1	

Ta-Na-E-Ka (p. 15)
Mary Whitebird
Connections: Crow Poets (p. 24)
Robert Kyle
	• *Reading Skills and Strategies: Reaching Struggling Readers*
	  • MiniRead Skill Lesson, p. 19
	  • Selection Skill Lesson, p. 25
	• *Graphic Organizers for Active Reading,* Worksheet p. 2
	• *Literary Elements:*
	  Transparency 1; Worksheet p. 4
		• *Grammar and Language Links:*
		  Subjects and Verbs, Worksheet p. 3
		• *Language Workshop CD-ROM,*
		  Subject-Verb Agreement
		• *Daily Oral Grammar,*
		  Transparency 2

The All-American Slurp (p. 31)
Lensey Namioka
	• *Reading Skills and Strategies: Reaching Struggling Readers*
	  • MiniRead Skill Lesson, p. 37
	  • Selection Skill Lesson, p. 45
	• *Graphic Organizers for Active Reading,* Worksheet p. 3
		• *Grammar and Language Links:*
		  Subject-Verb Agreement, Worksheet p. 5
		• *Language Workshop CD-ROM,*
		  Subject-Verb Agreement
		• *Daily Oral Grammar,*
		  Transparency 3

La Bamba (p. 44)
Gary Soto
	• *Reading Skills and Strategies: Reaching Struggling Readers*
	  • MiniRead Skill Lesson, p. 55
	  • Selection Skill Lesson, p. 63
	• *Graphic Organizers for Active Reading,* Worksheet p. 4
		• *Grammar and Language Links:*
		  Using Verb Tenses, Worksheet p. 7
		• *Language Workshop CD-ROM,*
		  Verb Tenses
		• *Daily Oral Grammar,*
		  Transparency 4

President Cleveland, Where Are You? (p. 53)
Robert Cormier
	• *Reading Skills and Strategies: Reaching Struggling Readers*
	  • MiniRead Skill Lesson, p. 76
	  • Selection Skill Lesson, p. 82
	• *Graphic Organizers for Active Reading,* Worksheet p. 5
		• *Grammar and Language Links:*
		  Style: Vivid Verbs, Worksheet p. 9
		• *Daily Oral Grammar,*
		  Transparency 5

The Stone (p. 69)
Lloyd Alexander
	• *Reading Skills and Strategies: Reaching Struggling Readers*
	  • MiniRead Skill Lesson, p. 90
	  • Selection Skill Lesson, p. 97
	• *Graphic Organizers for Active Reading,* Worksheet p. 6
		• *Grammar and Language Links:*
		  Don'ts and Doesn'ts Worksheet p. 11
		• *Language Workshop CD-ROM,*
		  Subject-Verb Agreement
		• *Daily Oral Grammar,*
		  Transparency 6

No Questions Asked: Lessons (p. 82) Bill Cosby	The **No Questions Asked** feature provides students with an unstructured opportunity to practice reading strategies using a selection that extends the theme of the collection.	
Writer's Workshop: Autobiographical Incident (p. 86)		
Sentence Workshop: Sentence Fragments (p. 91)		• *Workshop Resources,* p. 37 • *Language Workshop CD-ROM,* Sentence Fragments
Learning for Life: Decision Making (p. 93)		

Collection Resources

- *Cross-Curricular Activities*, p. 1
- *Portfolio Management System:*
  Introduction to Portfolio Assessment, p. 1;
  Parent/Guardian Letters, p. 87

- *Formal Assessment,*
  Reading Application Test, p. 14
- *Test Generator,* Collection Test

Vocabulary, Spelling, and Decoding	Writing	Listening and Speaking, Viewing and Representing	Assessment
• *Words to Own,* Worksheet p. 1 • *Spelling and Decoding,* Worksheet p. 1	• *Portfolio Management System,* Rubrics for Choices, p. 105	• *Audio CD Library,* Disc 1, Track 2 • *Portfolio Management System,* Rubrics for Choices, p. 105	• *Formal Assessment,* Selection Test, p. 1 • *Standardized Test Preparation,* p. 10 • *Test Generator* (One-Stop Planner CD-ROM)
			• *Formal Assessment,* Literary Elements Test, p. 13
• *Words to Own,* Worksheet p. 2 • *Spelling and Decoding,* Worksheet p. 2	• *Portfolio Management System,* Rubrics for Choices, p. 106	• *Audio CD Library,* Disc 1, Track 3 • *Viewing and Representing:* Fine Art Transparency 1 Worksheet p. 4 • *Portfolio Management System,* Rubrics for Choices, p. 106	• *Formal Assessment,* Selection Test, p. 3 • *Standardized Test Preparation,* p. 12 • *Test Generator* (One-Stop Planner CD-ROM)
• *Words to Own,* Worksheet p. 3 • *Spelling and Decoding,* Worksheet p. 3	• *Portfolio Management System,* Rubrics for Choices, p. 107	• *Visual Connections,* Videocassette A, Segment 1 • *Audio CD Library,* Disc 1, Track 4 • *Portfolio Management System,* Rubrics for Choices, p. 107	• *Formal Assessment,* Selection Test, p. 5 • *Standardized Test Preparation,* p. 14 • *Test Generator* (One-Stop Planner CD-ROM)
• *Spelling and Decoding,* Worksheet p. 4	• *Portfolio Management System,* Rubrics for Choices, p. 108	• *Audio CD Library,* Disc 2, Track 2 • *Portfolio Management System,* Rubrics for Choices, p. 108	• *Formal Assessment,* Selection Test, p. 7 • *Standardized Test Preparation,* p. 16 • *Test Generator* (One-Stop Planner CD-ROM)
• *Words to Own,* Worksheet p. 4 • *Spelling and Decoding,* Worksheet p. 5	• *Portfolio Management System,* Rubrics for Choices, p. 109	• *Audio CD Library,* Disc 2, Track 3 • *Viewing and Representing:* Fine Art Transparency 2 Worksheet p. 8 • *Portfolio Management System,* Rubrics for Choices, p. 109	• *Formal Assessment,* Selection Test, p. 9 • *Standardized Test Preparation,* pp. 18, 20 • *Test Generator* (One-Stop Planner CD-ROM)
• *Words to Own,* Worksheet p. 5 • *Spelling and Decoding,* Worksheet p. 6	• *Portfolio Management System,* Rubrics for Choices, p. 110	• *Audio CD Library,* Disc 2, Track 4 • *Viewing and Representing:* Fine Art Transparency 3 Worksheet p. 12 • *Portfolio Management System,* Rubrics for Choices, p. 110	• *Formal Assessment,* Selection Test, p. 11 • *Test Generator* (One-Stop Planner CD-ROM)
		• *Audio CD Library,* Disc 2, Track 5	• *Standardized Test Preparation,* p. 22

	• *Workshop Resources,* p. 1
	• *Writer's Workshop 1 CD-ROM,* Autobiographical Incident
			• *Portfolio Management System*
			  • Prewriting, p. 111
			  • Peer Editing, p. 112
			  • Assessment Rubric, p. 113

		• *Viewing and Representing,* HRW Multimedia Presentation Maker	• *Portfolio Management System,* Rubrics, p. 114

 Transparency   CD-ROM   Video   Audio CD

Collection

One

*You must do the things
you think you cannot do.*
—*Eleanor Roosevelt*

OBJECTIVES

1. Read literature in a variety of genres on the theme "Moments of Truth"
2. Interpret literary elements used in the literature, with special emphasis on conflict
3. Apply a variety of reading strategies, particularly context clues
4. Respond to the literature in a variety of modes
5. Learn and use new words
6. Plan, draft, revise, edit, proof, and publish a narrative of an autobiographical incident
7. Demonstrate the ability to find information in a textbook
8. Explore through a variety of projects how decisions are made

Introducing the Theme

Ask students to recall a character from a book, movie, or television show who learned something important about himself or herself from an experience. Explain that the main characters in the stories in this collection all learn something important about themselves and, as a result, may be able to make wiser decisions about their future. Encourage students to think about their own experiences and what they have learned from them as they read.

Resources

Portfolio Management System
- Introduction to Portfolio Assessment, p. 1
- Parent/Guardian Letters, p. 87

Formal Assessment
- Reading Application Test, p. 14

Test Generator
- Collection Test

Cross-Curricular Activities
- Teaching Notes, p. 1

Writing Focus: Autobiographical Incident

The following **Work in Progress** assignments in this collection build to a culminating **Writer's Workshop** at the end of Collection 1.

• Just Once	Jot down details about a conflict (p. 12)
• Ta-Na-E-Ka	Freewrite about a life experience (p. 28)
• The All-American Slurp	Write about a friendship (p. 42)
• La Bamba	Jot down reactions to performing (p. 51)
• President Cleveland, Where Are You?	Use sensory details to describe an event (p. 67)
• The Stone	Freewrite about mixed feelings (p. 80)

Writer's Workshop: Narrative Writing / Autobiographical Incident (p. 86)

Moments of Truth

Responding to the Quotation

Ask students to explain this quotation in their own words. [Possible responses: Don't be limited or restrained by fear of failure; take risks to achieve your goals.]

RESPONDING TO THE ART

This photograph of the Toms River (N.J.) East American All-Stars, the 1998 Little League World Series Champions, depicts a gratifying moment of truth for the young athletes who competed against the world's best baseball players in their age group and prevailed. One of the few amateur sporting events to receive international media coverage, the tournament, held each year in Williamsport, Penn., is a pressure cooker of childhood triumphs and crushing defeats.

Writer's Notebook

WORK IN PROGRESS

Ask students to freewrite for two or three minutes about an experience that taught them or someone they know something important about themselves. Consider sharing an experience of your own to prompt their thinking. *Remind students to choose a situation they would not mind sharing with others.*

Selection Readability

This Annotated Teacher's Edition provides a summary of each selection in the student book. Following each Summary heading, you will find one, two, or three small icons. These icons indicate, in an approximate sense, the reading level of the selection.

■ One icon indicates that the selection is easy.
■ ■ Two icons indicate that the selection is at an intermediate reading level.
■ ■ ■ Three icons indicate that the selection is challenging.

OBJECTIVES

1. Read and interpret the story
2. Identify conflict
3. Monitor comprehension
4. Express understanding through creative and critical writing, speaking, and art
5. Identify and use irregular verbs correctly
6. Understand and use new words
7. Use context clues

SKILLS

Literary, Reading, Writing
- Identify conflict
- Monitor comprehension
- Collect ideas for an auto-biographical incident
- Create a sportscast
- Write a paragraph of explanation
- Retell a poem as a story or newscast

Speaking
- Tape a newscast

Grammar/Language
- Use irregular verbs correctly

Vocabulary
- Understand and use new words

Art
- Draw a life map

Viewing/Representing
- Compare the art to the title of a poem (ATE)

Planning

- **Block Schedule**
  Block Scheduling Lesson Plans with Pacing Guide
- **Traditional Schedule**
  Lesson Plans Including Strategies for English-Language Learners
- **One-Stop Planner**
  CD-ROM with Test Generator

Before You Read

JUST ONCE

Make the Connection

Front and Center

Have you ever dreamed of walking onstage to get an Oscar? Do you long to be a basketball star? Would you give anything to be the best dancer at your school? We aim for many different goals in life. One dream that many of us share is to hear the crowd cheering, just once, just for us. You may have to fight your way to that moment of glory. What are you willing to do—and not do—to be a star?

Elements of Literature

Conflict: Story Struggle

In this story, Bryan "the Moose" Crawford, a football player, wants to hear the crowd roar for him. His fight against the forces that oppose him creates **conflict.** That's the struggle that pulls us into a story and won't let go until we find out who (or what) wins.

> **C**onflict is a struggle or clash between opposing characters or forces.
>
> *For more on Conflict, see pages 14 and 326 and the Handbook of Literary Terms.*

2 MOMENTS OF TRUTH

Reading Skills and Strategies

Dialogue with the Text

When you read a story actively, a lot goes on in your head.

- You connect what you read with your own experience.
- You ask yourself questions and make predictions about what will happen next.
- You challenge the text.
- You reflect on its meaning.

As you read, you create your own meaning from the text. No two readers will read a text in exactly the same way.

Jotting down notes as you read will help you become aware of yourself as a reader. Try keeping a sheet of paper beside each page so that you can note your thoughts next to the passage you're responding to. One reader's comments appear on the first page of "Just Once" as an example.

Preteaching Vocabulary

Words to Own

Have students read the definitions of the Words to Own listed on the bottom of the selection pages. Then have them explain their answers to the following questions.

1. Which would be a more important news story, a **devastating** earthquake or a mild earthquake?
2. Does **nurturing** a garden help it or hurt it?
3. If you wrote a best-selling novel, would you want to be **anonymous**?
4. Do you like it when people are **tolerant** of your mistakes?
5. Would you make a serious decision quickly, or would you **ponder** it?

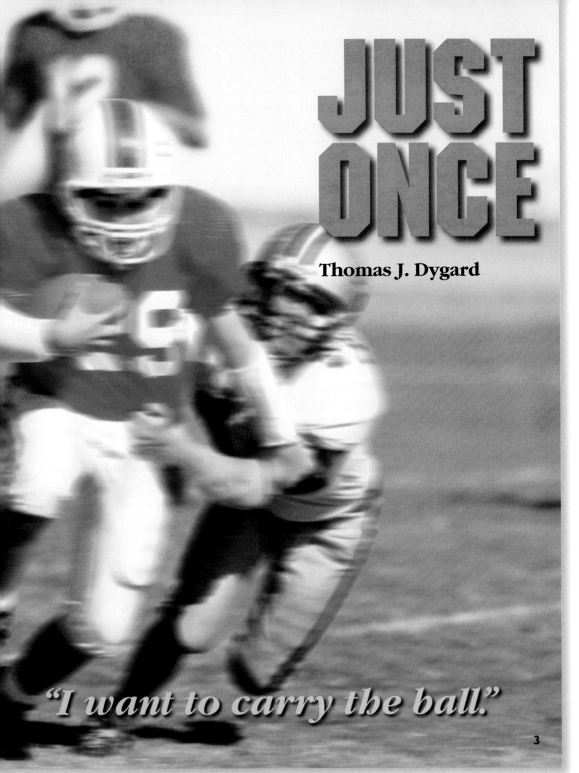

JUST ONCE

Thomas J. Dygard

"I want to carry the ball."

3

Summary ■ ■

Bryan Crawford, "The Moose," plays left tackle for the Bedford City Bears. His hangup is that he wants to change his role and carry the ball. He wants to hear the fans cheer for him as they do for runner Jerry Dixon. The coach good-naturedly denies the Moose's request, and the team's backs agree, but the Moose continues a campaign, and during a home game fans yell, "Give the Moose the ball!" Since the Bears lead 28–0 at halftime, the coach gives him a chance. Although the Moose scores and is cheered, he is disillusioned when confronted by the menacing wall of tacklers facing him and by the pummeling they give him as he makes the goal. After this enlightening experience about the reality of the role he coveted, he tells the coach, "Never again."

Resources ——

Listening
Audio CD Library
A recording of this story is provided in the *Audio CD Library*:
• Disc 1, Track 2

Selection Assessment
Formal Assessment
• Selection Test, p. 1
Test Generator
• Selection Test

  *Resources: Print and Media*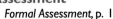

Reading
• *Reading Skills and Strategies*
    MiniRead Skill Lesson, p. 1
    Selection Skill Lesson, p. 7
• *Graphic Organizers for Active Reading*, p. 1
• *Words to Own*, p. 1
• *Spelling and Decoding*, p. 1
• *Audio CD Library*
    Disc 1, Track 2

Writing and Language
• *Daily Oral Grammar*
    Transparency 1
• *Grammar and Language Links*
    Worksheet, p. 1
• *Language Workshop CD-ROM*

Assessment
• *Formal Assessment*, p. 1
• *Portfolio Management System*, p. 105
• *Standardized Test Preparation*, p. 10
• *Test Generator (One-Stop Planner CD-ROM)*

Internet
• go.hrw.com (keyword: LE0 6-1)

❓ What do you suppose the main struggle, or conflict, in the story is going to be about? [The Moose secretly longs for the kind of recognition that goes with scoring a touchdown, yet that is not his job.]

Using the Glossary to Find Pronunciations

Words to Own are useful words from selections that will help students expand their vocabulary and knowledge base. Pronunciations for these words are often given with their definitions on the page where the word appears in the selection. If students have trouble pronouncing a particular word, they should turn to the guide to pronunciation symbols that appears at the bottom of p. 773, the first page of the Glossary. The guide contains words and symbols that will help students decode unfamiliar words.

Everybody liked the Moose. To his father and mother he was Bryan—as in Bryan Jefferson Crawford—but to everyone at Bedford City High he was the Moose. He was large and strong, as you might imagine from his nickname, and he was pretty fast on his feet—sort of nimble, you might say—considering his size. He didn't have a pretty face but he had a quick and easy smile—"sweet," some of the teachers called it; "nice," others said.

But on the football field, the Moose was neither sweet nor nice. He was just strong and fast and a little bit devastating as the left tackle of the Bedford City Bears. When the Moose blocked somebody, he stayed blocked. When the Moose was called on to open a hole in the line for one of the Bears' runners, the hole more often than not resembled an open garage door.

Now in his senior season, the Moose had twice been named to the all-conference team and was considered a cinch for all-state. He spent a lot of his spare time, when he wasn't in a classroom or on the football field, reading letters from colleges eager to have the Moose pursue higher education—and football—at their institution.

But the Moose had a hang-up.

He didn't go public with his hang-up until the sixth game of the season. But, looking back, most of his teammates agreed that probably the Moose had been nurturing the hang-up secretly for two years or more.

A The Moose wanted to carry the ball.

For sure, the Moose was not the first interior lineman in the history of football, or even the history of Bedford City High, who banged heads up front and wore bruises like badges of honor—and dreamed of racing down the field with the ball to the end zone[1] while everybody in the bleachers screamed his name.

But most linemen, it seems, are able to stifle the urge. The idea may pop into their minds from time to time, but

---

1. **end zone:** area between the goal line and the end line (the line marking the boundary of the playing area) at each end of a football field.

WORDS TO OWN
devastating (dev′əs·tāt′iŋ) v. used as adj.: causing great damage or destruction.
nurturing (nur′chər·iŋ) v.: promoting the growth of; nourishing.

4 MOMENTS OF TRUTH

Dialogue with the Text
Why did everyone like the Moose? The story will probably end up telling.

There are some difficult words, but the descriptive sentences help you understand.

If he is getting college applications, is he smart also?

This describes well what a sports player feels in that situation.

—John Kolar
Mountain Junior High School
Austin, Texas

Reaching All Students

Struggling Readers
Dialogue with the Text was introduced on p. 2. For a lesson directly tied to this story that teaches students to monitor comprehension by using a strategy called Think-Aloud, see the *Reading Skills and Strategies* binder:
• MiniRead Skill Lesson, p. 1
• Selection Skill Lesson, p. 7

English Language Learners
Enlist sports fans in the class to help English language learners understand basic football rules and terms. Similarities and differences between American football and soccer may be explored. For additional strategies to supplement instruction for these students, see
• *Lesson Plans Including Strategies for English-Language Learners*

Advanced Learners
As students read, and afterward, have them consider what they have learned about football and football players from the story and how it compares and contrasts with what they learn from (a) watching a sports event, (b) watching or reading a news report of a sports event. Ask students to arrange their ideas on a graphic organizer, such as a chart.

in their hearts they know they can't run fast enough, they know they can't do that fancy dancing to elude tacklers, they know they aren't trained to read blocks. They know that their strengths and talents are best utilized in the line. Football is, after all, a team sport, and everyone plays the position where he most helps the team. And so these linemen, or most of them, go back to banging heads without saying the first word about the dream that flickered through their minds.

Not so with the Moose.

That sixth game, when the Moose's hang-up first came into public view, had ended with the Moose truly in all his glory as the Bears' left tackle. Yes, glory—but uncheered and sort of <u>anonymous</u>. The Bears were trailing 21-17 and had the ball on Mitchell High's five-yard line, fourth down,[2] with time running out. The rule in such a situation is simple—the best back carries the ball behind the best blocker—and it is a rule seldom violated by those in control of their faculties.[3] The Bears, of course, followed the rule. That

---

2. **fourth down:** In football the team holding the ball is allowed four downs, or attempts to carry the ball forward at least ten yards.
3. **faculties:** mental powers.

---

meant Jerry Dixon running behind the Moose's blocking. With the snap of the ball, the Moose knocked down one lineman, bumped another one aside, and charged forward to flatten an approaching linebacker. Jerry did a little jig behind the Moose and then ran into the end zone, virtually untouched, to win the game.

After circling in the end zone a moment while the cheers echoed through the night, Jerry did run across and hug the Moose, that's true. Jerry knew who had made the touchdown possible.

But it wasn't the Moose's name that everybody was shouting. The fans in the bleachers were cheering Jerry Dixon.

It was probably at that precise moment that the Moose decided to go public.

In the dressing room, Coach Buford Williams was making his rounds among the cheering players and came to a halt in front of the Moose. "It was your great blocking that did it," he said.

"I want to carry the ball," the Moose said.

WORDS TO OWN

anonymous (ə·nän′ə·məs) *adj.*: nameless; done by an unidentified person.

JUST ONCE 5

B **Cultural Connections**
Football
Ask one or more knowledgeable volunteers to explain the basics of football for any students who might not be familiar with the game. Make sure all students grasp the main point: that the linemen perform the job of blocking, a secondary task that enables the seemingly more glamorous runners to score touchdowns.

C **Reading Skills and Strategies**
Dialogue with the Text
? Is it true in real life that linemen go unnoticed? [Possible responses: Yes, they have always received less fame and money than quarterbacks and receivers; no, knowledgeable fans are increasingly aware of their importance, and the best linemen are recognized and rewarded.]

Using Students' Strengths

Visual Learners
On the chalkboard, draw a large diagram of a football field, or have a knowledgeable student draw one. Include end zones, ten-yard markers, and Xs and Os for the positions. Label the following positions: left tackle, quarterback, running backs. At points in the story, you might ask a volunteer to diagram plays. To find another approach for visual learners, use the *Graphic Organizer for Active Reading,* p. 1.

Kinesthetic Learners
The story is full of physical action described in vivid terms. Encourage students to jot down specific words and phrases that clearly describe the action on the field or on the sidelines. Suggest that students take a moment to imagine the feeling of each action.

Interpersonal Learners
The central conflict of "Just Once" involves an athlete who wants to convince others to let him depart from his usual role on a team. Divide students into teams and have them discuss how the Moose goes about trying to get his way. Encourage critical thinking: What does the Moose do right? What, if anything, does he do wrong? How would students have acted in his situation? Ask groups to share their ideas with the class.

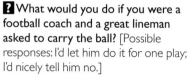

A Reading Skills and Strategies

Dialogue with the Text

❓ What would you do if you were a football coach and a great lineman asked to carry the ball? [Possible responses: I'd let him do it for one play; I'd nicely tell him no.]

B Elements of Literature

Conflict

❓ How does the Moose make his conflict more apparent? [He repeats his demand to the coach.] What effect does this have on the drama of the story? [The Moose is not going to let his desire to carry the ball be ignored.]

C Critical Thinking

Interpreting

❓ What do you think the coach is really thinking about? [Possible response: He is thinking about how to answer the Moose; he is trying to stay calm.]

D English Language Learners

Sports Jargon

Ask volunteers to explain what the quarterback does. [He passes the ball and, often, calls plays.]

E Elements of Literature

Conflict

❓ How is the conflict in the story growing? [What began as the Moose's private struggle is now a topic of discussion for the football team, the school, and even the town. Everyone seems to have an opinion.]

Coach Williams was already turning away and taking a step toward the next player due an accolade[4] when his brain registered the fact that the Moose had said something strange. He was expecting the Moose to say, "Aw, gee, thanks, Coach." That was what the Moose always said when the coach issued a compliment. But the Moose had said something else. The coach turned back to the Moose, a look of disbelief on his face. "What did you say?"

"I want to carry the ball."

Coach Williams was good at quick recoveries, as any high school football coach had better be. He gave a tolerant smile and a little nod and said, "You keep right on blocking, son."

This time Coach Williams made good on his turn and moved away from the Moose.

The following week's practice and the next Friday's game passed without further incident. After all, the game was a road game over at Cartwright High, thirty-five miles away. The Moose wanted to carry the ball in front of the Bedford City fans.

Then the Moose went to work.

He caught up with the coach on the way to the practice field on Wednesday. "Remember," he said, leaning forward and down a little to get his face in the coach's face, "I said I want to carry the ball."

Coach Williams must have been thinking about something else because it took him a minute to look up into the Moose's face, and even then he didn't say anything.

"I meant it," the Moose said.

"Meant what?"

"I want to run the ball."

"Oh," Coach Williams said. Yes, he remembered. "Son, you're a great left tackle, a great blocker. Let's leave it that way."

The Moose let the remaining days of the practice week and then the game on Friday night against Edgewood High pass while he reviewed strategies. The review led him to Dan Blevins, the Bears' quarterback. If the signal caller would join in, maybe Coach Williams would listen.

"Yeah, I heard," Dan said. "But, look, what about Joe Wright at guard, Bill Slocum at right tackle, even Herbie Watson at center. They might all want to carry the ball. What are we going to do—take turns? It doesn't work that way."

So much for Dan Blevins.

The Moose found that most of the players in the backfield agreed with Dan. They couldn't see any reason why the Moose should carry the ball, especially in place of themselves. Even Jerry Dixon, who owed a lot of his glory to the Moose's blocking, gaped in

4. **accolade** (ak′ə·lād′): something said or done to express praise.

WORDS TO OWN

tolerant (täl′ər·ənt) *adj.*: patient; showing acceptance of others.

6 MOMENTS OF TRUTH

Crossing the Curriculum

Sports

Give fans of other sports the opportunity to compare and contrast their favorites with football. Basic distinctions can be made between contact and noncontact sports, and between sports that have continuous play, such as soccer and basketball, and those with discontinuous play, such as football and baseball. Invite students to create a chart showing how closely or distantly various sports are related to each other.

Mathematics

Students who like both football and mathematics might enjoy creating a presentation on football statistics. The presentation should include a brief explanation of the most important statistics and a discussion of why statistics are useful in sports. Students may also discuss which statistics they find most (and least) meaningful; the effect of computers on sports statistics; and how sports statisticians earn a living.

disbelief at the Moose's idea. The Moose, however, got some support from his fellow linemen. Maybe they had dreams of their own, and saw value in a precedent.[5]

As the days went by, the word spread—not just on the practice field and in the corridors of Bedford City High, but all around town. The players by now were openly taking sides. Some thought it a jolly good idea that the Moose carry the ball. Others, like Dan Blevins, held to the purist[6] line—a left tackle plays left tackle, a ball carrier carries the ball, and that's it.

Around town, the vote wasn't even close. Everyone wanted the Moose to carry the ball.

"Look, son," Coach Williams said to the Moose on the practice field the Thursday before the Benton Heights game, "this has gone far enough. Fun is fun. A joke is a joke. But let's drop it."

"Just once," the Moose pleaded.

Coach Williams looked at the Moose and didn't answer.

The Moose didn't know what that meant.

The Benton Heights Tigers were duck soup for the Bears, as everyone knew they would be. The Bears scored in their first three possessions and led 28-0 at the half. The hapless[7] Tigers had yet to cross the fifty-yard line under their own steam.

All the Bears, of course, were enjoying the way the game was going, as were the Bedford City fans jamming the bleachers.

Coach Williams looked irritated when the crowd on a couple of occasions broke into a chant: "Give the Moose the ball! Give the Moose the ball!"

5. **precedent** (pres′ə·dənt): action or statement that can serve as an example.
6. **purist** (pyoor′ist): someone who insists that rules be followed strictly.
7. **hapless:** unlucky.

On the field, the Moose did not know whether to grin at hearing his name shouted by the crowd or to frown because the sound of his name was irritating the coach. Was the crowd going to talk Coach Williams into putting the Moose in the backfield? Probably not; Coach Williams didn't bow to that kind of pressure. Was the coach going to refuse to give the ball to the Moose just to show the crowd—and the Moose and the rest of the players—who was boss? The Moose feared so.

In his time on the sideline, when the defensive unit was on the field, the Moose, of course, said nothing to Coach Williams. He knew better than to break the coach's concentration during a game—even a runaway victory—with a comment on any subject at all, much less his desire to carry the ball. As a matter of fact, the Moose was careful to stay out of the coach's line of vision, especially when the crowd was chanting "Give the Moose the ball!"

By the end of the third quarter the Bears were leading 42-0.

Coach Williams had been feeding substitutes into the game since half time, but the Bears kept marching on. And now, in the opening minutes of the fourth quarter, the

JUST ONCE 7

F **Reading Skills and Strategies**
Dialogue with the Text
? What do you think the coach's look means? [Possible responses: "Get away and stop asking"; "What am I going to do about this kid?"; "Well, we'll see. . ."]

G **Vocabulary Note**
Using Context Clues
Encourage students to use the context—the Bears' easy victory—to guess the meaning of the expression *duck soup*. [something that is done easily, not a challenge]

H **Reading Skills and Strategies**
Dialogue with the Text
? What do you think the coach is going to do? [Possible responses: He's going to let the Moose carry the ball; he's going to make the Moose leave the game.]

I **Vocabulary Note**
Using Context Clues
Have students use context clues to guess the meaning of *runaway victory*. [an easy victory]

J **Critical Thinking**
Speculating
? Why does the Moose think that avoiding the coach will help his cause? [With the crowd chanting for him, the Moose wants to avoid angering the coach.]

Making the Connections

Connecting to the Theme: "Moments of Truth"

School athletics have traditionally been considered an area where young people learn about themselves and about life. In "Just Once," the Moose experiences several enlightening moments when he tries to become a runner rather than a blocker. He learns about expressing his wishes, about negotiating conflicts with peers and authorities, about accepting the consequences of getting his wishes, and about accepting himself. After students have read the story, ask them what they think the hero of the story specifically learns. Encourage them to connect his moments of truth with enlightening experiences of their own—possibly in settings very different from that of a football field.

A **Elements of Literature**

Conflict

? What part of his struggle has the Moose won? [He is being allowed to carry the ball.] What new conflict emerges now that the Moose has been given his chance? [how well he will perform in his new position]

B **Reading Skills and Strategies**

Dialogue with the Text

? Runners don't usually call their own plays; the quarterback or coach does. Why doesn't it matter now? [The Bears are so far ahead that the Moose's plays couldn't possibly lose the game for them.]

C **Struggling Readers**

Finding Details

? What does the Moose find surprising about his new position? [He's surprised at how many tacklers are running toward him—and at how dangerous it is to run with the football.]

D **Advanced Learners**

Cause and Effect

? How is the Moose himself the cause of five or six tacklers becoming free? [If he were blocking instead of running, he would have blocked some of the tacklers. With the Moose running, the blocking isn't as good.]

E **Critical Thinking**

Extending the Text

? What has the Moose learned about football—and about life—that makes him want to thank the blocker? [Possible response: About football, the Moose learned that blocking is important. About life, he learned that everyone's role is important and that people need each other to succeed.]

Moose and his teammates were standing on the Tigers' five-yard line, about to pile on another touchdown.

The Moose saw his substitute, Larry Hidden, getting a slap on the behind and then running onto the field. The Moose turned to leave.

Then he heard Larry tell the referee, "Hinden for Holbrook."

Holbrook? Chad Holbrook, the fullback?

Chad gave the coach a funny look and jogged off the field.

A Larry joined the huddle and said, "Coach says the Moose at fullback and give him the ball."

Dan Blevins said, "Really?"

"Really."

The Moose was giving his grin—"sweet," some of the teachers called it; "nice," others said.

B "I want to do an end run," the Moose said. Dan looked at the sky a moment, then said, "What does it matter?"

The quarterback took the snap from center, moved back and to his right while turning, and extended the ball to the Moose.

The Moose took the ball and cradled it in his right hand. So far, so good. He hadn't fumbled. Probably both Coach Williams and Dan were surprised.

8 MOMENTS OF TRUTH

He ran a couple of steps and looked out in front and said aloud, "Whoa!"

Where had all those tacklers come from?

C The whole world seemed to be peopled with players in red jerseys—the red of the Benton Heights Tigers. They all were looking straight at the Moose and advancing toward him. They looked very determined, and not friendly at all. And there were so many of **D** them. The Moose had faced tough guys in the line, but usually one at a time, or maybe two. But this—five or six. And all of them heading for him.

The Moose screeched to a halt, whirled, and ran the other way.

Dan Blevins blocked somebody in a red jer- **E** sey breaking through the middle of the line, and the Moose wanted to stop running and thank him. But he kept going.

His reverse had caught the Tigers' defenders going the wrong way, and the field in front of the Moose looked open. But his blockers were going the wrong way, too. Maybe that was why the field looked so open. What did it matter, though, with the field clear in front of him? This was going to be a cakewalk;[8] the Moose was going to score a touchdown.

Then, again—"Whoa!"

Players with red jerseys were beginning to fill the empty space—a lot of them. And they were all running toward the Moose. They were kind of low, with their arms spread, as if they wanted to hit him hard and then grab him.

8. **cakewalk:** easy task.

Assessing Learning

A picture of Jerry Dixon dancing his little jig and wriggling between tacklers flashed through the Moose's mind. How did Jerry do that? Well, no time to <u>ponder</u> that one right now. **F**

The Moose lowered his shoulder and thundered ahead, into the cloud of red jerseys. Something hit his left thigh. It hurt. Then something pounded his hip, then his shoulder. They both hurt. Somebody was hanging on to him and was a terrible drag. How could he run with somebody hanging on to him? He knew he was going down, but maybe he was across the goal. He hit the ground hard, with somebody coming down on top of him, right on the small of his back.

The Moose couldn't move. They had him pinned. Wasn't the referee supposed to get these guys off?

Finally the load was gone and the Moose, still holding the ball, got to his knees and one hand, then stood.

He heard the screaming of the crowd, and he saw the scoreboard blinking.

He had scored.

His teammates were slapping him on the shoulder pads and laughing and shouting.

The Moose grinned, but he had a strange and distant look in his eyes.

He jogged to the sideline, the roars of the crowd still ringing in his ears.

"OK, son?" Coach Williams asked. **G**

The Moose was puffing. He took a couple of deep breaths. He relived for a moment the first sight of a half dozen players in red jerseys, all with one target—him. He saw again the menacing horde of red jerseys that had risen up just when he'd thought he had clear sailing to the goal. They all zeroed in on him, the Moose, alone.

The Moose glanced at the coach, took another deep breath, and said, "Never again." **H**

WORDS TO OWN

ponder (pän'dər) v.: think deeply about.

MEET THE WRITER

"I'm Not a Writer. I'm a Rewriter."

For **Thomas Dygard** (1931–1996), writing and editing newspaper articles was a full-time job; writing novels was the hobby he loved most. Dygard wrote seventeen novels, all sports related, for young people. In spite of his years of working with words, he said he always considered writing a challenge.

66 My mistakes in my writing are so common that I'd bet I've thrown more pieces of paper in a wastebasket than any person alive. I'm not a writer. I'm a rewriter. As for having learned it all, I know that I haven't, and I also know that I never will. 99

F **Reading Skills and Strategies**

Dialogue with the Text

? Why does the Moose think of Jerry Dixon as he's running with the ball? [Sample responses: The Moose realizes that Jerry is good at what he does. Being smaller than the Moose, Jerry is able to elude tacklers; Jerry has more practice than the Moose at running with the ball.]

G **Elements of Literature**

Conflict

? How is the Moose's conflict resolved? [He gets the opportunity to run with the ball, and scores, but decides to go back to being a blocker.]

H **Critical Thinking**

Challenging the Text

? What parts of the ending seemed real or convincing to you, and what parts seemed unreal or unconvincing? [Possible responses: The touchdown is convincing because the Moose's inexperience led him to make "wrong" moves that confused the defense. It's unconvincing that after scoring on his first try he doesn't want to remain a runner; it's convincing that he realizes he is better at blocking than running; his reason for quitting—not wanting to get tackled—is unbelievable, since linemen get hit a lot too.]

BROWSING IN THE FILES

About the Author. A reporter and bureau chief for the Associated Press, Thomas Dygard published his first novel, *Running Scared*, in 1977. "I started writing young-adult fiction for the fun and satisfaction of it, and it's still fun and satisfying, and I think it always will be." He went on to publish a book a year until 1986. In 1993, he retired from the Associated Press and moved to Evansville, Indiana, where he continued writing young-adult fiction full-time.

Connections

Ⓐ Struggling Readers

Breaking Down Difficult Text

❓ What does "two 60's stuck on the scoreboard" mean? [The score is tied 60–60.]

Ⓑ Reading Skills and Strategies

Dialogue with the Text

❓ The poet captures the tension and the agonizing feeling of the last crucial seconds of a close basketball game. How does he do that? [Possible responses: He chooses vivid descriptive verbs like *breathes, crouches, lands, leans, and wobbles;* he spreads the action out into a long series of short lines to make the reader feel the suspense in every small movement.]

Ⓒ Appreciating Language

Invented Words

❓ What do you think *ROAR-UP* means? [The moment at which the crowd gets to its feet and cheers.]

RESPONDING TO THE ART

Carolyn L. Mazloomi is a fiber artist and historian recognized as one of the most inventive American quiltmakers working today. Much of her art contains references to African American life and its ancestral tradition. About her quilts, she says, "The spiritual and physical warmth of quilts has always excited me. . . . The quilts are made without the benefits of patterns, with colors and shapes put together intuitively. . . . The techniques I use consist of piecing, appliqué, painting, stamping, and quilting. It is my aim to let the viewer feel 'the spirit of the cloth.'"

Activity. Ask students to consider how the quilt reflects the "dreams" conveyed in the title. [Possible responses: The shooter hanging in the air and the glow from the center of the quilt make the action seem slow moving or suspended, as in a dream. The players' slender frames and tremendous height are dreams for would-be stars of the game.]

T10

Foul Shot

Edwin A. Hoey

Hoop Dreams (1997) by Carolyn L. Mazloomi. Quilt (4.5′ × 5′).

Ⓐ With two 60's stuck on the scoreboard
And two seconds hanging on the clock,
The solemn boy in the center of eyes,
Squeezed by silence,
5 Seeks out the line with his feet,
Soothes his hands along his uniform,
Gently drums the ball against the floor,
Then measures the waiting net,
Raises the ball on his right hand,
10 Balances it with his left,
Calms it with fingertips,
Breathes,
Crouches,
Waits,
And then through a stretching of stillness,
15 Nudges it upward.

The ball
Ⓑ Slides up and out,
Lands,
Leans,
20 Wobbles,
Wavers,
Hesitates,
Exasperates,
25 Plays it coy
Until every face begs with unsounding
      screams—
And then

            And then

                  And then,

30 Ⓒ Right before ROAR-UP,
Dives down and through.

Connecting Across Texts

Connecting with "Just Once"

Both "Foul Shot" and "Just Once" are about school athletes. Invite students to describe more specific similarities between the two selections, such as the "moment of truth" for the foul shooter and for the Moose. [Possible responses: For both boys, sports are a forum in which they test their abilities and their self-worth. Although the foul shooter's emotions aren't described, we can assume that winning the game in the last two seconds enhances his self-esteem and makes him feel he can meet challenges. The Moose's "moment of truth" occurs when he recognizes his strengths and weaknesses as a football player and comes to the realization that in a team effort, everyone's contribution is important.]

First Thoughts

[respond]

1. Respond to "Just Once" by completing one or more of these sentences.
   - If I were in the Moose's shoes, I'd . . .
   - I thought this story was . . .
   - I was confused by . . .

Shaping Interpretations

[analyze]

2. When do you think the Moose's "moment of truth" comes? What do you think he learns at that moment? Check your Dialogue with the Text notes for ideas.

[interpret]

3. Describe the Moose's **conflict** when the crowd chants "Give the Moose the ball!" (page 7). What does he want? What is keeping him from getting it?

[infer]

4. What do you think the Moose expects will happen when he carries the ball? How is his dream different from reality?

[connect]

5. Besides being about sports, what does "Foul Shot" (see *Connections* on page 10) have in common with "Just Once"?

Connecting with the Text

[speculate]

6. Imagine that you could be a star of anything you chose. What would you want to be? What **conflicts** do you think you would have to overcome in your climb to the top?

[connect]

7. One of Thomas Dygard's novels, *Winning Kicker,* is about a girl who tries out for a school football team. How do you feel about girls' playing on high school teams that are usually all male?

Challenging the Text

[interpret]

8. The **title** of this story could have been "Never Again." Come up with a third title for the story. Then, tell which title you like best and why.

[compare]

9. Is this a "boy's story," or does it appeal to both boys and girls? Do different stories appeal to boys and girls? Take a survey of your classmates to find out what they think.

> ### Reading Check
> Imagine that the Moose's girlfriend is out of town for his big game. As soon as he gets home, the Moose phones her. With a partner, retell **what happens** in the story in a phone conversation between the Moose and his girlfriend.

First Thoughts

1. Sample responses:
   - If I were in the Moose's shoes, I'd still want to run.
   - I thought this story was too predictable.
   - I was confused by why the Moose changed his mind at the end.

Shaping Interpretations

2. The Moose's "moment of truth" comes when he realizes that despite a successful run, he prefers to block rather than to be tackled.
3. He wants to get the ball, but the decision is the coach's.
4. He expects to enjoy running and to hear the crowd cheer for him, but he learns that he dislikes being the target of tacklers.
5. Possible response: Both explore the skills and tensions involved in scoring and the importance of an audience.

Connecting with the Text

6. Possible responses: I'd be a basketball star; I'd have to overcome not being very tall, and having to compete with many other talented players; I'd be a movie star; I'd have to overcome not liking to perform before a camera.
7. Possible responses: It's fine with me; I think boys and girls should have separate teams but equal opportunities to play.

Challenging the Text

8. Possible response: "Moose's Moment." I like that best because of the *m*'s and because it connects to the story's meaning.
9. Encourage a variety of responses. Recognize that more than one response may imply equality for boys and girls. Help students to see that their views on gender roles may reflect views in their community or in the culture at large.

Reading Check
Possible Response

"Jodi, you'll never guess what happened. Coach let me run the ball against Benton Heights."

"You're kidding?"

"No, it was the strangest thing. I finally asked Coach Williams after our game with Mitchell High and he just looked at me like I was crazy."

"Then what happened?"

"Well, first everybody on the team, then everybody at school, then practically the whole town started talking about it. When we were playing Benton Heights and creaming them, the fans started chanting, 'Give the Moose the ball!'"

"What did Coach Williams do?"

"Well, he didn't do anything at first, but then he put me in the game. Blevins handed off to me, and there I was, running the ball. First, I went one way, then I reversed, but all I could see were red jerseys coming at me. I was so scared, but I finally ran it across for a touchdown. After that, I told Coach Williams, 'Never again.'"

Grading Timesaver

Rubrics for each Choices assignment appear on p. 105 in the *Portfolio Management System*.

CHOICES: Building Your Portfolio

1. **Writer's Notebook** With each selection, a Writer's Notebook activity appears as the first option in the Choices section. These brief, work-in-progress assignments build toward the writing assignment presented in the Writer's Workshop at the end of the collection. If students save their work for their Writer's Notebook activities as they move through the collection, they should be able to use some of them as starting points for the Workshop.

2. **Creative Writing/Speaking** Students may work in pairs or individually. Remind students that a summary is a shortened version of events, which covers the main points and important details. Tell students that their delivery should be clear yet animated and enthusiastic.

3. **Critical Writing/Art** Students may work individually or in pairs. Pairs should discuss their responses together; one partner may then draw the map and the other write the paragraph, or both may write and draw together.

4. **Changing Genres** Advanced students may wish to work independently. Students may also work in small groups, prewriting by having volunteers reread the poem aloud, and then discussing how a story or newscast would focus on different details and show the action from a different point of view.

CHOICES: Building Your Portfolio

Writer's Notebook

1. Collecting Ideas for an Autobiographical Incident

Think of a time when, like the Moose, you faced a conflict between doing what you wanted and doing what was good for a group you belonged to. The group might be your family, friends, classmates, or team. If you have never faced that kind of conflict, think of a time when you struggled with something, such as another person, an animal, an ocean undertow, or a rainstorm. Jot down as many details of the experience as you can.

> The time my friends and I got lost on a camping trip: We fought the cold all night. We couldn't make a fire. It was too windy.

Creative Writing/Speaking

2. Now Hear This

Create a sportscast of the Bears-versus-Tigers game. First, write a **summary** of what happened. Use details in the story to answer *who, what, when, where, why,* and *how* questions. Give your report a snappy lead-in to capture your listeners' attention. Then, practice reading your report for a broadcast. Tape your sportscast, and play it for your classmates.

Critical Writing/Art

3. The Way to the Prize

As a high school senior, the Moose longs to hear the cheers of the crowd. People want different things at different times in their lives. Draw a life map as a kind of road or journey showing a person at one end and the prize or goal at the other end. Draw some of the forces that the person may have to overcome along the way. Then, write a paragraph explaining your map. (It does not have to be a map of the kind of life *you* want.)

Changing Genres

4. Foul Shot: The Story

Retell the *Connections* poem on page 10 as a story or a newscast. You may have to supply some details, such as descriptions of the main characters, and some background.

GRAMMAR LINK   MINI-LESSON

Troublesome Verbs

Language Handbook HELP

See Irregular Verbs, pages 707–709.

Technology HELP

See Language Workshop CD-ROM. *Key word entry: irregular verbs.*

Irregular verbs can keep you from scoring a touchdown in the game of speaking and writing correctly. To form the **past tense** and **past participle** of most verbs, you add *-d* or *-ed*, but irregular verbs change in sneaky ways. You just have to memorize them. (The past participle is the form you use with the helping verbs *has, have,* and *had.*)

Here are some irregular verbs from "Just Once."

Base Form	Past	Past Participle
rise	rose	(have) risen
say	said	(have) said
see	saw	(have) seen
take	took	(have) taken
think	thought	(have) thought

Try It Out

In the following sentences, find the incorrect verb forms and replace them with the correct forms.

1. The Moose rised from the field and seed a cloud of red jerseys.

2. The Moose thinked he wanted to hear the fans cheer for him.

3. Yesterday the Moose sayed to the coach, "I want to carry the ball."

VOCABULARY   HOW TO OWN A WORD

WORD BANK

devastating
nurturing
anonymous
tolerant
ponder

Using Context to Recognize Words

The **context** of a word—the words or sentences surrounding it—can help you figure out what the word means. In the paragraph below, each underlined word has at least one **context clue.** Copy the paragraph onto a piece of paper. Then, circle the clues that help you guess the words' meanings. (For more on context clues, see page 30.)

The coach read aloud the <u>anonymous</u> note, wondering who had written it. "Please take some time to <u>ponder</u> our request carefully. You may think that it would have a <u>devastating</u> effect, but we're sure it won't ruin the sports program. It's time to be <u>tolerant</u> and fair. After all, we've been <u>nurturing</u> our dream for months. It's a dream that our families encourage, too. Please let girls try out for the team."

JUST ONCE 13

Grammar Link Quick Check

The following irregular verbs appear in "Just Once." The base form of each is given below. For each verb, indicate the past and past participle forms.

1. have
2. spend
3. go
4. know
5. come
6. mean
7. do
8. run
9. make
10. catch

Answers:
1. had; (have) had
2. spent; (have) spent
3. went; (have) gone
4. knew; (have) known
5. came; (have) come
6. meant; (have) meant
7. did; (have) done
8. ran; (have) run
9. made; (have) made
10. caught; (have) caught

Resources ———

Elements of Literature
Conflict
For additional instruction on conflict, see *Literary Elements:*
• Transparency 1

Assessment
Formal Assessment
• Literary Elements Test, p. 13

Elements of Literature
This feature defines and presents examples of conflict, both internal and external.

Mini-Lesson:
Conflict
The two forms of conflict are a fundamental principle of narrative that students will encounter again and again. Use the following activity before students read the Elements of Literature essay, except as noted for the final step.

Applying the Element
• Have a volunteer read aloud the *Calvin and Hobbes* cartoon strip at the bottom of the essay.
• Discuss the question, "What conflict or conflicts is Calvin talking about?" [Possible responses: Imaginary conflict between numbers; his own conflict about whether to do the math homework.]
• Ask whether the conflicts are all within Calvin himself or between Calvin and the outside world. Use students' responses to introduce the concepts of internal and external conflict.
• After students have read the essay, invite them to brainstorm other possible conflicts Calvin might face, and to classify them as internal or external.

CONFLICT: It Makes a Story *by* John Leggett

Where does a story's energy come from? It comes from **conflict.** Conflict is a struggle between opposing forces. When a pinch hitter picks up a bat and starts toward the plate or when a doctor frowns at a lab report, a conflict has started. A story begins.

We all know about conflict. We deal with it every day from the moment we wake up in the morning. The conflict might be about guilt over the homework we didn't finish, or it might have to do with some big guy who bumps into us in the hall. If we don't overcome the conflict, we feel frustrated and angry. If we do overcome it, we feel great.

The Ins and Outs of Conflict
In everyday life and in stories, there are two basic types of conflict. **External conflict** is a struggle between a character and some outside force. It may take place when one person threatens another. An example might be a bully who waits for a smaller child on the way home. An external conflict may also take place between one person and a group. For instance, an outlaw in a Western story may struggle with a sheriff and his deputies. An external conflict also may take place when a person is challenged or threatened by nature. This kind of conflict might involve a mountain climber struggling to reach the peak of a steep, ice-covered mountain or teenagers struggling to survive on their own in the wilderness.

The second type of conflict takes place inside our minds or hearts. **Internal conflict** is a struggle between opposing desires or emotions inside a person. Suppose, for example, that a desire to pass a test tempts Miranda to glance at Alice's paper. At the same time, Miranda doesn't want to lose the respect of her teacher and classmates, who disapprove of cheating. As she decides whether or not to look at Alice's answer, Miranda is struggling with an internal conflict. This struggle between opposing desires or emotions can be the strongest conflict of all.

CALVIN AND HOBBES © Watterson. Reprinted with permission of UNIVERSAL PRESS SYNDICATE. All rights reserved.

14 MOMENTS OF TRUTH

Using Students' Strengths

Intrapersonal Learners
Have students freewrite about an internal conflict and an external conflict that they have dealt with in the past. What was it about? Who was involved? Why did it happen? How did they feel? How was it resolved?

Kinesthetic Learners
Have students improvise peaceful resolutions to the following situations:
• Both you and your brother or sister need the last stamp to mail a letter. [external]
• You want to watch TV, but you have a test to study for. [internal]

Before You Read

TA-NA-E-KA

Make the Connection

"When I Was Your Age . . ."
Rate each statement below with a number from 0 to 4.

disagree 0 1 2 3 4 agree

1. Most adults understand the problems of growing up.
2. Most adults expect too much of young people.
3. Most kids at least try to see problems from an adult's point of view.

Quickwrite

Respond to one of the three statements above. Explain why you feel as you do.

Elements of Literature

Conflicts: Inside and Out

If you had to survive on your own in the woods, how would you handle the **external conflict** with nature?

What would you do if your family expected you to keep up a tradition you weren't sure you believed in?

How would you deal with the **internal conflict** of feeling torn between family tradition and the modern world? In this selection, Mary faces both of these conflicts as she takes part in an ancient ritual called Ta-Na-E-Ka.

> **E**xternal conflict is a struggle between a character and some outside force. **Internal conflict** is a struggle between opposing desires or emotions inside a person.
>
> *For more on Conflict, see pages 14 and 326 and the Handbook of Literary Terms.*

Background

Literature and Social Studies

This story has to do with the traditions of the Native Americans known as the Kaw. The Kaw are also known as the Kansa; both names are forms of a word that means "people of the south wind." The Kaw originally lived along the Kansas River.

 go.hrw.com
LEO 6-1

Reading Skills and Strategies

Comparing and Contrasting Cultures: We Are the World

Culture is a people's way of life—their beliefs, customs, traditions, arts, language. As you read, you'll probably find yourself comparing and contrasting traditional Kaw culture with other cultures you know about, especially your own. After all, that's the one you know best. To **compare** cultures, look for things that they share. To **contrast** cultures, look for things that make them different.

TA-NA-E-KA 15

Preteaching Vocabulary

T15

Summary ■ ■

Mary Whitebird, a Kaw Native American, has reached the age of eleven, when "a boy could prove himself a warrior, and a girl took the first steps to womanhood." She and her cousin, Roger Deer Leg, face the traditional endurance ritual, which requires initiates to spend five days alone in the woods—barefoot, nearly naked, and living by their wits. Both Mary, who narrates the story, and Roger think the ritual is outdated. Their grandfather Amos Deer Leg, insists on continuing the rite of passage. To survive the ordeal, Roger adheres to the tradition, but Mary borrows money from her teacher and buys food at a restaurant. The restaurant's owner allows her to stay, provides her with clothing, and even teaches her to cook. When they return, Roger is hungry and blistered, while Mary looks clean and well-fed. Her moment of truth arrives when she confesses how she has spent the days of her Ta-Na-E-Ka. Initially Grandfather is disappointed, but he admits that Mary has passed the test in her own, more modern way.

Resources ──

Listening
Audio CD Library
A recording of this story is provided in the *Audio CD Library:*
• Disc 1, Track 3

Viewing and Representing
Fine Art Transparency
A fine art transparency of Kevin Warren Smith's *Cloak of Heritage* can be used after reading this story and "The All-American Slurp."
• Transparency 1
• Worksheet, p. 4

Ta-Na-E-Ka

Mary Whitebird

A s my birthday drew closer, I had awful nightmares about it. I was reaching the age at which all Kaw Indians had to participate in Ta-Na-E-Ka. Well, not all Kaws. Many of the younger families on the reservation were beginning to give up the old customs. But my grandfather, Amos Deer Leg, was devoted to tradition. He still wore handmade beaded moccasins instead of shoes and kept his iron-gray hair in tight braids. He could speak English, but he spoke it only with white men. With his family he used a Sioux dialect.[1]

Grandfather was one of the last living Indians (he died in 1953, when he was eighty-one) who actually fought against the U.S. Cavalry. Not only did he fight, he was wounded in a skirmish at Rose Creek—a famous encounter in which the celebrated Kaw chief Flat Nose lost his life. At the time, my grandfather was only eleven years old.

Eleven was a magic word among the Kaws. It was the time of Ta-Na-E-Ka, the "flowering of adulthood." It was the age, my grandfather informed us hundreds of times, "when a boy could prove himself to be a warrior and a girl took the first steps to womanhood."

"I don't want to be a warrior," my cousin, Roger Deer Leg, confided to me. "I'm going to become an accountant."

---

1. **Sioux** (s$\overline{oo}$) **dialect:** one of the languages spoken by the Plains Indians, including the Kaw.

Sitting Bull Returns at the Drive-In (1976) by Willard Midgette.

16 MOMENTS OF TRUTH

National Museum of American Art, Washington, D.C./Art Resource, New York.

Resources: Print and Media ──

Reading
• *Reading Skills and Strategies*
  MiniRead Skill Lesson, p. 19
  Selection Skill Lesson, p. 25
• *Graphic Organizers for Active Reading*, p. 2
• *Words to Own*, p. 2
• *Spelling and Decoding*
  Worksheet, p. 2
• *Audio CD Library*
  Disc 1, Track 3

Elements of Literature
• *Literary Elements*
  Transparency 1
  Worksheet, p. 4

Writing and Language
• *Daily Oral Grammar*
  Transparency 2
• *Grammar and Language Links*
  Worksheet, p. 3
• *Language Workshop CD-ROM*

Viewing and Representing
• *Viewing and Representing*
  Fine Art Transparency 1
  Fine Art Worksheet, p. 4

Assessment
• *Formal Assessment*, p. 3
• *Portfolio Management System*, p. 106
• *Standardized Test Preparation*, p. 12
• *Test Generator (One-Stop Planner CD-ROM)*

Internet
• go.hrw.com (keyword: LE0 6-1)

Eleven was the time of Ta-Na-E-Ka, "when a boy could prove himself a warrior and a girl took the first steps to womanhood."

A **Critical Thinking**

Making Judgments

? What is giving Mary nightmares? [Anxiety about the upcoming Ta-Na-E-Ka ritual.]

B **Reading Skills and Strategies**

Comparing and Contrasting Cultures

? What details of present-day and of older Kaw culture does the description give? [Traditional Kaw men wore moccasins and long, braided hair, and spoke a Sioux dialect; present-day Kaw wear shoes and speak English.]

C **Elements of Literature**

External and Internal Conflict

? What **internal conflict** do Mary and Roger share? [Neither wants to go through with the ritual.] **How is it also an external conflict?** [They are in conflict with their elders.]

RESPONDING TO THE ART

Willard Midgette (1937–1978) was born in New York City and spent most of his life there. He went west when he was appointed artist-in-residence at Reed College in Oregon. While working at the Roswell Museum and Art Center in New Mexico, he developed an interest in Native Americans, and his paintings of them are his best-known works. Later, Midgette returned to New York City to create environmental works based on urban life. **Activity.** Ask students to describe what is happening in the painting. [Native Americans at a drive-in theater are watching a movie about native Americans of the past.] Have students identify elements from both past and present cultures in the painting. [Possible responses: the traditional clothing and headdresses; the drive-in, cars, pick-up trucks, and work clothes.]

Reaching All Students

Struggling Readers

Comparing and Contrasting Cultures was introduced on p. 15. For a lesson directly tied to this selection that teaches students to compare and contrast by using a strategy called Anticipation Guides, see the *Reading Skills and Strategies* binder:
• MiniRead Skill Lesson, p. 19
• Selection Skill Lesson, p. 25

English Language Learners

Be sure that English language learners are familiar with the references to the history and culture of Native Americans. In particular, they should understand the meaning of the term "reservation" as used in the story. For additional strategies to supplement instruction for these students, see
• *Lesson Plans Including Strategies for English-Language Learners*

Comparing and Contrasting Cultures

? What are some other kinds of rituals that Mrs. Richardson may be referring to? [Possible responses: family traditions, religious rites, holiday celebrations, birthday parties, the Pledge of Allegiance.]

B Elements of Literature

Character

? What does this passage reveal about the narrator's character? [Possible responses: She is ambitious; her fantasies draw upon European rather than Native American images; she is independent.]

Historical Connections

The Sioux, or Dakota, are a confederation of seven tribes, some of whom migrated from the northeastern forests to Minnesota around the early 1600s, then spread through the upper Great Plains. In the 1860s and during the Black Hills gold rush of the 1870s, they fought the U.S. Cavalry under leaders including Sitting Bull, Red Cloud, and Crazy Horse. The Kaw, and their close relatives the Osage, speak a Siouan language but are not one of the seven tribes of the Sioux confederation. The Kaw may have lived in the Ohio Valley in prehistoric times and moved to the Kansas River early in the period of white settlement. Losing claim to much of their land in treaties with the U.S. government, they were forced to relocate to a reservation at Council Grove, Kansas, by 1847, then to a reservation in Oklahoma in 1873.

"None of the other tribes make girls go through the endurance ritual," I complained to my mother.

"It won't be as bad as you think, Mary," my mother said, ignoring my protests. "Once you've gone through it, you'll certainly never forget it. You'll be proud."

I even complained to my teacher, Mrs. Richardson, feeling that, as a white woman, she would side with me.

A She didn't. "All of us have rituals of one kind or another," Mrs. Richardson said. "And look at it this way: How many girls have the opportunity to compete on equal terms with boys? Don't look down on your heritage."

B Heritage, indeed! I had no intention of living on a reservation for the rest of my life. I was a good student. I loved school. My fantasies were about knights in armor and fair ladies in flowing gowns being saved from

dragons. It never once occurred to me that being an Indian was exciting.

But I've always thought that the Kaw were the originators of the women's liberation movement. No other Indian tribe—and I've spent half a lifetime researching the subject—treated women more "equally" than the Kaw. Unlike most of the subtribes of the Sioux Nation, the Kaw allowed men and women to eat together. And hundreds of years before we were "acculturated,"[2] a Kaw woman had the right to refuse a prospective husband even if her father arranged the match.

The wisest women (generally wisdom was equated with age) often sat in tribal councils. Furthermore, most Kaw legends revolve around "Good Woman," a kind of super-

2. **acculturated** (ə·kul′chər·āt′id): adapted to a new or different culture.

Using Students' Strengths

Visual Learners

If possible, show students a film or video about Plains Indian culture and traditions. Alternatively, show photographs and illustrations of Plains culture. If you live in an area that is rich with Native American history, a trip to the local museum may be fruitful. To find another approach for engaging visual learners in the selection, see the *Graphic Organizers for Active Reading*, p. 2.

Logical/Mathematical Learners

Have students consider the difference between what things cost in 1947 and what they cost today. Mary's first meal on her Ta-Na-E-Ka costs forty-five cents. Ask students to determine in small groups how much money a hamburger and a milkshake cost today and how much money they would need in order to eat for five days.

squaw, a Joan of Arc[3] of the high plains. Good Woman led Kaw warriors into battle after battle, from which they always seemed to emerge victorious.

And girls as well as boys were required to undergo Ta-Na-E-Ka.

The actual ceremony varied from tribe to tribe, but since the Indians' life on the plains was dedicated to survival, Ta-Na-E-Ka was a test of survival.

"Endurance is the loftiest virtue of the Indian," my grandfather explained. "To survive, we must endure. When I was a boy, Ta-Na-E-Ka was more than the mere symbol it is now. We were painted white with the juice of a sacred herb and sent naked into the wilderness without so much as a knife. We couldn't return until the white had worn off. It wouldn't wash off. It took almost eighteen days, and during that time we had to stay alive, trapping food, eating insects and roots and berries, and watching out for enemies. And we did have enemies—both the white soldiers and the Omaha warriors, who were always trying to capture Kaw boys and girls undergoing their endurance test. It was an exciting time."

"What happened if you couldn't make it?" Roger asked. He was born only three days after I was, and we were being trained for Ta-Na-E-Ka together. I was happy to know he was frightened, too.

"Many didn't return," Grandfather said. "Only the strongest and shrewdest. Mothers were not allowed to weep over those who didn't return. If a Kaw couldn't survive, he or she wasn't worth weeping over. It was our way."

3. **Joan of Arc** (1412–1431): French heroine who led her country's army to victory over the English at Orléans, France, in 1429.

"What a lot of hooey," Roger whispered. "I'd give anything to get out of it."

"I don't see how we have any choice," I replied.

Roger gave my arm a little squeeze. "Well, it's only five days."

Five days! Maybe it was better than being painted white and sent out naked for eighteen days. But not much better.

We were to be sent, barefoot and in bathing suits, into the woods. Even our very traditional parents put their foot down when Grandfather suggested we go naked. For five days we'd have to live off the land, keeping warm as best we could, getting food where we could. It was May, but on the northernmost reaches of the Missouri River, the days were still chilly and the nights were fiercely cold.

Grandfather was in charge of the month's training for Ta-Na-E-Ka. One day he caught a grasshopper and demonstrated how to pull its legs and wings off in one flick of the fingers and how to swallow it.

I felt sick, and Roger turned green. "It's a darn good thing it's 1947," I told Roger teasingly. "You'd make a terrible warrior." Roger just grimaced.

WORDS TO OWN
loftiest (lôf′tē·əst) *adj.*: noblest or highest.
shrewdest (shrōōd′əst) *adj.* used as *n.*: cleverest; sharpest.
grimaced (grim′ist) *v.*: twisted the face to express pain, anger, or disgust.

Getting Students Involved

Cooperative Learning
Surviving in the Wilderness. Divide the class into groups of four. Tell students to pretend that they and the members of their group are going on a five-day wilderness adventure. They need to decide what to take to keep their group alive for five days. Everything they select must fit into their backpacks. Have each student make a list of what to take for one of the following categories: food, clothing, equipment, and first aid.

Each group should go over its members' lists to eliminate unnecessary items. Have students report to the class and turn in their survival lists. As a class, discuss possible sources of food, water, shelter, and fuel in your wilderness region.

Brainstorming. To help students understand generational conflicts, divide the class into four groups and assign each group the discussion topic "How is our generation different from our parents' and grandparents' generations?" Ask them to consider tastes in clothing, music, interests, hobbies, and in any other ways their lives are different. Ask students to brainstorm a list of ways that the generations can get along and understand one another better. Have students report their ideas to the class.

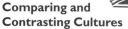
I knew one thing. This particular Kaw Indian girl wasn't going to swallow a grasshopper no matter how hungry she got. And then I had an idea. Why hadn't I thought of it before? It would have saved nights of bad dreams about squooshy grasshoppers.

I headed straight for my teacher's house. "Mrs. Richardson," I said, "would you lend me five dollars?"

"Five dollars!" she exclaimed. "What for?"

"You remember the ceremony I talked about?"

"Ta-Na-E-Ka. Of course. Your parents have written me and asked me to excuse you from school so you can participate in it."

"Well, I need some things for the ceremony," I replied, in a half-truth. "I don't want to ask my parents for the money."

"It's not a crime to borrow money, Mary. But how can you pay it back?"

"I'll baby-sit for you ten times."

"That's more than fair," she said, going to her purse and handing me a crisp, new five-dollar bill. I'd never had that much money at once.

"I'm happy to know the money's going to be put to a good use," Mrs. Richardson said.

A few days later the ritual began with a long speech from my grandfather about how we had reached the age of decision, how we now had to fend for ourselves and prove that we could survive the most horrendous of ordeals. All the friends and relatives who had gathered at our house for dinner made jokes about their own

Ta-Na-E-Ka experiences. They all advised us to fill up now, since for the next five days we'd be gorging ourselves on crickets. Neither Roger nor I was very hungry. "I'll probably laugh about this when I'm an accountant," Roger said, trembling.

"Are you trembling?" I asked.

"What do you think?"

"I'm happy to know boys tremble, too," I said.

At six the next morning, we kissed our parents and went off to the woods. "Which side do you want?" Roger asked. According to the rules, Roger and I would stake out "territories" in separate areas of the woods, and we weren't to communicate during the entire ordeal.

"I'll go toward the river, if it's OK with you," I said.

WORDS TO OWN
gorging (gôrj'iŋ) v.: filling up; stuffing.

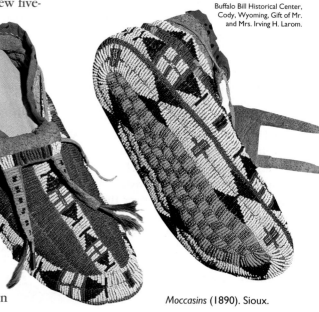

Buffalo Bill Historical Center, Cody, Wyoming, Gift of Mr. and Mrs. Irving H. Larom.

Moccasins (1890). Sioux.

"Sure," Roger answered. "What difference does it make?"

To me, it made a lot of difference. There was a marina a few miles up the river, and there were boats moored there. At least, I hoped so. I figured that a boat was a better place to sleep than under a pile of leaves.

"Why do you keep holding your head?" Roger asked.

"Oh, nothing. Just nervous," I told him. Actually, I was afraid I'd lose the five-dollar bill, which I had tucked into my hair with a bobby pin. As we came to a fork in the trail, Roger shook my hand. "Good luck, Mary."

"N'ko-n'ta," I said. It was the Kaw word for "courage."

The sun was shining and it was warm, but my bare feet began to hurt immediately. I spied one of the berry bushes Grandfather had told us about. "You're lucky," he had said. "The berries are ripe in the spring, and they are delicious and nourishing." They were orange and fat, and I popped one into my mouth.

Argh! I spat it out. It was awful and bitter, and even grasshoppers were probably better tasting, although I never intended to find out.

I sat down to rest my feet. A rabbit hopped out from under the berry bush. He nuzzled the berry I'd spat out and ate it. He picked another one and ate that, too. He liked them. He looked at me, twitching his nose. I watched a redheaded woodpecker bore into an elm **(E)** tree, and I caught a glimpse of a civet cat[4] waddling through some twigs. All of a sudden I realized I was no longer frightened. Ta-Na-E-Ka might be more fun than I'd anticipated. I got up and headed toward the marina.

"Not one boat," I said to myself dejectedly. But the restaurant on the shore, Ernie's

4. **civet** (siv′it) **cat:** furry spotted skunk.

Riverside, was open. I walked in, feeling silly in my bathing suit. The man at the counter was big and tough-looking. He wore a sweat shirt with the words "Fort Sheridan, 1944," and he had only three fingers on one of his hands. He asked me what I wanted. **(F)**

"A hamburger and a milkshake," I said, holding the five-dollar bill in my hand so he'd know I had money.

"That's a pretty heavy breakfast, honey," he murmured.

"That's what I always have for breakfast," I lied.

"Forty-five cents," he said, bringing me the food. (Back in 1947, hamburgers were twenty-five cents and milkshakes were twenty cents.)

"Delicious," I thought. "Better 'n grasshoppers—and Grandfather never once mentioned that I couldn't eat hamburgers."

While I was eating, I had a grand idea. Why not sleep in the restaurant? I went to the ladies' room and made sure the window was unlocked. Then I went back outside and played along the riverbank, watching the water birds and trying to identify each one. I planned to look for a beaver dam the next day.

The restaurant closed at sunset, and I watched the three-fingered man drive away. **(G)** Then I climbed in the unlocked window. There was a night light on, so I didn't turn on any lights. But there was a radio on the counter. I turned it on to a music program. It was warm in the restaurant, and I was hungry. I helped myself to a glass of milk and a piece of pie, intending to keep a list of what I'd eaten so I could leave money. I also planned to get up early, sneak out through the window, and head for the woods before the three-fingered man returned. I turned off the radio, wrapped myself in the man's

Crossing the Curriculum

Science

Although Mary does not adopt this diet, a menu of grasshoppers, berries, roots, and trapped animals is suggested by Grandfather. Have students research any native or naturally occurring plants or animals found in their communities that they could live on, such as fruit or nut trees or wild herbs, and rabbits or deer. Then have students present their findings in oral reports.

Geography

Have students use an atlas to look up the following locations: Kansas, the Kansas River, Oklahoma, and the Missouri River. This will give them a better idea of where the Kaw, or Kansa, lived previously and where they lived when they left Kansas. Obtain a map of Oklahoma that lists Kay County and the Kaw, or Kansa, Reservation. Have students identify the location of the reservation and mark it on a U.S. map that they construct themselves. Students might also find the locations of other tribal reservations in Oklahoma and in other states throughout the U.S. and mark them accordingly. Post the map in the classroom to accompany discussions.

A Critical Thinking

Making Judgments

❓ Do you agree with Ernie's view of Ta-Na-E-Ka or with Mary's? Why? [Possible responses: Ernie's, because the ceremony is dangerous; Mary's, because the ceremony is an important part of her heritage.]

B Advanced Learners

Analyzing

❓ What does Mary learn from her Ta-Na-E-Ka? [how to make friends; how to cook; that she knows and values her people's culture; that she can take care of herself] How is it different from what she expected to learn? [She expected to learn to survive in the wilderness; instead, she learned to survive in the everyday world.]

C Elements of Literature

External and Internal Conflict

❓ What worries Mary as she returns home? [She worries that Grandfather will discover that she didn't stay in the wilderness.] Is this an external or an internal conflict? [Possible responses: external because it is between her and her grandfather; internal because the worry is inside her own mind.]

D Critical Thinking

Speculating

❓ What do you think Roger's Ta-Na-E-Ka was like? [He did what he was expected to: he remained in the wilderness, cold, hungry, and frightened, for five days.]

apron, and in spite of the hardness of the floor, fell asleep.

"What the heck are you doing here, kid?"

It was the man's voice.

It was morning. I'd overslept. I was scared.

"Hold it, kid. I just wanna know what you're doing here. You lost? You must be from the reservation. Your folks must be worried sick about you. Do they have a phone?"

"Yes, yes," I answered. "But don't call them."

I was shivering. The man, who told me his name was Ernie, made me a cup of hot chocolate while I explained about Ta-Na-E-Ka.

"Darnedest thing I ever heard," he said, when I was through. "Lived next to the reservation all my life and this is the first I've heard of Ta-Na-whatever-you-call-it." He looked at me, all goose bumps in my bathing suit. "Pretty silly thing to do to a kid," he muttered.

That was just what I'd been thinking for months, but when Ernie said it, I became angry. "No, it isn't silly. It's a custom of the Kaw. We've been doing this for hundreds of years. My mother and my grandfather and everybody in my family went through this ceremony. It's why the Kaw are great warriors."

"OK, great warrior," Ernie chuckled, "suit yourself. And, if you want to stick around, it's OK with me." Ernie went to the broom closet and tossed me a bundle. "That's the lost-and-found closet," he said. "Stuff people left on boats. Maybe there's something to keep you warm."

The sweater fitted loosely, but it felt good. I felt good. And I'd found a new friend. Most important, I was surviving Ta-Na-E-Ka.

My grandfather had said the experience would be filled with adventure, and I was having my fill. And Grandfather had never said we couldn't accept hospitality.

I stayed at Ernie's Riverside for the entire

period. In the mornings I went into the woods and watched the animals and picked flowers for each of the tables in Ernie's. I had never felt better. I was up early enough to watch the sun rise on the Missouri, and I went to bed after it set. I ate everything I wanted—insisting that Ernie take all my money for the food. "I'll keep this in trust for you, Mary," Ernie promised, "in case you are ever desperate for five dollars." (He did, too, but that's another story.)

I was sorry when the five days were over. I'd enjoyed every minute with Ernie. He taught me how to make Western omelets and to make Chili Ernie Style (still one of my favorite dishes). And I told Ernie all about the legends of the Kaw. I hadn't realized I knew so much about my people.

But Ta-Na-E-Ka was over, and as I approached my house at about nine-thirty in the evening, I became nervous all over again. What if Grandfather asked me about the berries and the grasshoppers? And my feet were hardly cut. I hadn't lost a pound and my hair was combed.

"They'll be so happy to see me," I told myself hopefully, "that they won't ask too many questions."

I opened the door. My grandfather was in the front room. He was wearing the ceremonial beaded deerskin shirt which had belonged to *his* grandfather. "N'g'da'ma," he said. "Welcome back."

I embraced my parents warmly, letting go only when I saw my cousin Roger sprawled on the couch. His eyes were red and swollen. He'd lost weight. His feet were an unsightly mass of blood and blisters, and he was moaning: "I made it, see. I made it. I'm a warrior. A warrior."

My grandfather looked at me strangely. I

Making the Connections

Connecting to the Theme: "Moments of Truth"

For the Kaw people, the age of initiation into the community is eleven. This is the moment of truth at which young men and women are sent out alone to test their ability to survive a rigorous situation marking their passage into adulthood. Many cultures both past and present have had initiation ceremonies, or rites of passage, in which youngsters make the transition from childhood to adulthood at a specific, clearly

defined moment. In Jewish culture it is the *bar mitzvah* (for boys) and *bat mitzvah* (for girls) at age thirteen. Young women in Hispanic cultures practice a coming-of-age ceremony on their fifteenth birthday, in a lavish, often formal, birthday party called the *quinceañera*. A similar tradition among American girls has been the "sweet sixteen" birthday. Today in the United States, a young person is no longer considered a minor,

for various purposes, at ages eighteen and twenty-one. Ask students at what age they think they will become adults, and why, and whether they think adulthood is achieved at a specific moment, or gradually over many years. They may wish to talk to older siblings, parents, cousins, or other trusted mentors about coming of age. You may wish to share your own ideas and experiences.

was clean, obviously well-fed, and radiantly healthy. My parents got the message. My uncle and aunt gazed at me with hostility.

Finally my grandfather asked, "What did you eat to keep you so well?"

I sucked in my breath and blurted out the truth: "Hamburgers and milkshakes."

"Hamburgers!" my grandfather growled.

"Milkshakes!" Roger moaned.

"You didn't say we *had* to eat grasshoppers," I said sheepishly.

"Tell us all about your Ta-Na-E-Ka," my grandfather commanded.

I told them everything, from borrowing the five dollars, to Ernie's kindness, to observing the beaver.

"That's not what I trained you for," my grandfather said sadly.

I stood up. "Grandfather, I learned that Ta-Na-E-Ka *is* important. I didn't think so during training. I was scared stiff of it. I handled it my way. And I learned I had nothing to be afraid of. There's no reason in 1947 to eat grasshoppers when you can eat a hamburger."

I was inwardly shocked at my own <u>audacity</u>. But I liked it. "Grandfather, I'll bet you never ate one of those rotten berries yourself."

Grandfather laughed! He laughed aloud! My mother and father and aunt and uncle were all dumbfounded. Grandfather never laughed. Never.

"Those berries—they are terrible," Grandfather admitted. "I could never swallow them. I found a dead deer on the first day of my Ta-Na-E-Ka—shot by a soldier, probably—and he kept my belly full for the entire period of the test!"

Grandfather stopped laughing. "We should send you out again," he said.

I looked at Roger. "You're pretty smart, Mary," Roger groaned. "I'd never have thought of what you did."

"Accountants just have to be good at arithmetic," I said comfortingly. "I'm terrible at arithmetic."

Roger tried to smile but couldn't. My grandfather called me to him. "You should have done what your cousin did. But I think you are more alert to what is happening to our people today than we are. I think you would have passed the test under any circumstances, in any time. Somehow, you know how to exist in a world that wasn't made for Indians. I don't think you're going to have any trouble surviving."

Grandfather wasn't entirely right. But I'll tell about that another time.

WORDS TO OWN
audacity (ô·das′ə·tē) *n.*: bold courage; daring.

TA-NA-E-KA **23**

E Struggling Readers
Finding Details/Questioning
? Is Grandfather angry at Mary? [No, he is first described as sad, and then as amused.] **Why not?** [Possible responses: He wisely understands that Mary has passed the test in her own way; he himself used his wits to survive his Ta-Na-E-Ka.]

F Appreciating Language
Word Choice
? Have students look up the word *dumbfounded* in a dictionary. Why does it so aptly describe the reaction of Mary's family? [Mary's family was so confounded and astonished that Grandfather laughed that they were speechless for a moment.]

G Reading Skills and Strategies
Comparing and Contrasting Cultures
? What challenging experiences do young people in our culture undergo as they enter adulthood? [Possible responses: getting a job; going to college; getting one's own apartment; passing particular tests at school; learning to drive.]

Resources

Selection Assessment
Formal Assessment
• Selection Test, p. 3
Test Generator
• Selection Test

Assessing Learning

Check Test: True-False
1. The narrator is a boy named Roger. [False]
2. Ta-Na-E-Ka is a ritual that eleven-year-old Kaw children participate in. [True]
3. On her Ta-Na-E-Ka, Mary sleeps on a boat. [False]
4. Mary learns how to cook chili from her grandfather. [False]
5. Mary eats grasshoppers and berries on her Ta-Na-E-Ka. [False]

Self-Reflection
Ask students to write on a sheet of paper three things they learned about the Ta-Na-E-Ka ritual or the Kaw tribe. (Short answers are appropriate here.) Then ask them to write how the things they learned from the story may be applied to their own lives.

Standardized Test Preparation
For practice in proofreading and editing, see
• *Daily Oral Grammar,* Transparency 2

The article describes how eight young Native American poets became part of the Library of Congress Poetry and Literature Series organized by former U.S. poet laureate Rita Dove. It was the first time that a group of Native Americans participated in the series. Poems by two of the "Crow Poets" follow the article.

Ⓐ Reading Skills and Strategies

Responding to the Text

❓ How would you feel if you had to read a poem in front of a large group of people? [Possible responses: scared, nervous; excited.]

Resources ————

Assessment
• *Standardized Test Preparation,* p. 12

Crow Poets

Robert Kyle

They arrived at the Washington, D.C., airport on a drizzly March night as merely eight students from a faraway Montana reservation. Twenty-four hours later, they would be making history as "the Crow Poets," the first members of their tribe—or any Native American group—ever invited to participate in the prestigious[1] Library of Congress Poetry and Literature series.

1. **prestigious** (pres·tij′əs): famous; respected.

Adorned in resplendent traditional regalia, the students filed into a packed reading room on the sixth floor of the towering marble Madison Building adjacent to the Capitol. One by one they ascended the small stage and stood confidently behind the podium, staring into a cluster of curious, unfamiliar faces, bright lights, and cameras. It was an imposing scenario capable of rattling the most experienced orator, yet the students recited stories of their people, land, and heritage with poise and grace.

The eight students, all from the Pryor, Montana, area, included eighth-grader Mike Beaumont and seventh-grader Yolanda Old

Students pose for photographs before the reading. Back row (left to right): Mike Beaumont, Charles Yarlott, Scott Plain Bull, Mike LaForge, and Chuck Lance. Front row (left to right): Loretta Shane, Yolanda Old Dwarf, Mick Fedullo, Rita Dove, and Nalayna Blaine.

Photography by Robert Kyle.

24 MOMENTS OF TRUTH

Connecting Across Texts

Connecting with "Ta-Na-E-Ka"
In their poems, the Crow poets seem very proud of their heritage and their ancestors. Ask students to fill out a Venn diagram to generate ideas on how the Crow poets and Mary are alike and different.

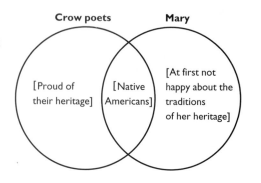

Crow poets   Mary

[Proud of their heritage]   [Native Americans]   [At first not happy about the traditions of her heritage]

Dwarf, both from St. Charles School; freshmen Mike LaForge and Chuck Lance, and seniors Scott Plain Bull and Loretta Shane, from Plenty Coups High School; and eighth-graders Nalayna Blaine and Charles Yarlott from Pretty Eagle School.

The event was made possible by the U.S. poet laureate,[2] Rita Dove. One of her responsibilities is to schedule readings by professional poets and authors. Determined to expand the program and to let other voices be heard, she remembered an old friend, Mick Fedullo, whom she knew was an advocate of developing the writing talent in students.

Earning Master of Fine Arts degrees at the same time in the University of Iowa's acclaimed Writer's Workshop, Dove and Fedullo both settled in the West. Dove taught English at Arizona State University from 1981 to 1989, while Fedullo had a calling to help Indian children.

"In the next few years, I witnessed the phenomenal effect Mick had on the Pima children at the Sacaton Middle School," Dove told the overflow audience during her introduction of him. "Mick followed his instincts and encouraged the children to use their own experiences as the basis for their writing. By believing that the children had something important to say, he was able to help them express themselves in that most rigorous of art forms, poetry."

Fedullo first visited the Crow Reservation in Montana in 1984, when he responded to an invitation from the state's Indian Education Association to present a workshop at its annual teacher's conference. Although

2. **U.S. poet laureate** (lôr′ē·it): official poet of the United States, chosen by the Library of Congress librarian, generally for a term of a year or two.

After the reading the Crow students changed from poets to tourists and enjoyed Washington, D.C.

Photography by Robert Kyle.

his two workshops attracted a combined total of only fifteen teachers, two came away convinced that their students and school, the Crow Agency Elementary, would benefit from Fedullo's poetry instruction.

He eventually spent a week at the school and later was asked to teach at other schools on the reservation. In 1989, he permanently relocated to Montana. He now resides in Pryor on the reservation and teaches part time at Plenty Coups High School while working as a language development specialist consultant at many reservations, including native villages in Alaska and Canada.

The process of selecting works for the March 1994 Washington, D.C., trip began a year earlier with poetry-writing contests at Plenty Coups High School and two other schools near the town of Pryor. The theme was "Keeping Our Heritage and Our Land."

(continued on next page)

TA-NA-E-KA 25

B **Critical Thinking**
Expressing an Opinion
❓ Do you think it is easier to write about something you have experienced or something you have not experienced? Why? [Possible responses: something you have experienced, because you know enough about it to describe it in exact detail; something you have not experienced, because your imagination is freer and you are not held back by worries or embarrassment.]

C **English Language Learners**
Vocabulary Development
Ask a volunteer to give a common synonym for *resides*. [lives]

Skill Link

Number and Agreement
Tell students that when a word refers to one person, place, thing, or idea, it is *singular* in number. When a word refers to more than one thing, it is *plural* in number. In a sentence, a verb should agree with its subject in number. Singular subjects take singular verbs. (Example: *The poet gives a reading of his work.*) Plural subjects take plural verbs. (Example: *The poets give a reading of their work.*) Some sentences have compound subjects. In a compound subject, two subjects are joined by *and, or,* or *nor* and may take a plural verb. (Example: *Rita Dove and Mick Fedullo love poetry.*) For more instruction on number and agreement, see the Language Handbook, pp. 703–706.

Activity
Identify each of the following subjects as singular, plural, or compound.

1. The poet laureate of the United States [singular]
2. Poetry lovers of America [plural]
3. Poets and their readers [compound]
4. Traditional or modern costumes [compound]
5. Neither the poets nor their listeners [compound]

T25

Ⓐ Reading Skills and Strategies
Responding to the Text
❓ What traditions does your family have, and what would you do if you started to forget them? [Possible responses: opening one present before Christmas; barbecuing in the backyard on Memorial Day; singing silly songs while driving on vacation. I'd ask someone to remind me, or record the tradition so as not to forget it.]

Ⓑ Elements of Literature
External and Internal Conflict
❓ What internal conflict do you think the speaker is facing? [Possible answers: the fear of losing his connection with his heritage; the struggle to maintain traditional ways in a modern world.]

Ⓒ Critical Thinking
Speculating
❓ What do you think the author means when she says her grandmother is close to her and far away at the same time? [Possible responses: They love each other, but the grandmother is ailing or lives far away; the grandmother may have died, but she is still close to the author's heart; they live near each other and love each other, but are from different eras.]

(continued from previous page)

Photography by Robert Kyle.

Here are two poems read by the Crow poets in Washington, D.C., that night.

Grandmother
Loretta Shane

Thinking of the days now past,
I see my grandmother young and beautiful.
She is like a flower ready to bloom,
Growing gracefully as the days go by,
Never knowing what the next day will bring.
Looking at her now, I see the beauty that was
  once before.
In a shell of long bitter years.
Ⓒ So close to me, and yet so far.
I admire my grandmother for who we are.

Vision
Mike LaForge

Ⓐ When I forget my traditions
I walk my land
Asking the Great Spirit's forgiveness.
Ⓑ I listen to the wind tell me stories about my
  ancestors,
5 Trying to regain my strength,
Keeping my weakness out, showing me
  how to succeed,
Keeping my heart to the beat of the drum,
Making my mind light as a feather,
Giving me great medicine.
Making my imagination gallop with the
10 horses.

The news article and poems on pages 24–26 are from the magazine *Native Peoples*.

Atsina Warriors (1908) by Edward S. Curtis.

Courtesy The San Diego Museum of Man, San Diego, California.

RESPONDING TO THE ART
Edward S. Curtis (1868–1952) was an American photographer who devoted most of his career to recording the vanishing traditional culture of Native American tribes. Living in the Seattle, Washington area, he took more than 40,000 photographs during this 35-year project.
Activity. Invite students to tell what they can learn from the photograph about the culture of these Native Americans.

Getting Students Involved

Enrichment Activity
Writing a Broadsheet Poem. Invite students to write free-verse (unrhymed, unmetered) poems beginning with either the first line of Loretta Shane's "Grandmother" or the first line of Mike LaForge's "Vision." Those lines, "Thinking of the days now past" and "When I forget my traditions," provide excellent prompts for a wide range of student thoughts and feelings about their earlier childhood, their cultural heritage, and older people they have known. Tell students that their poems can be any length, but that 8–12 lines is a suitable length for this activity. Encourage students to read their poems aloud. Then invite them to print their poems neatly on art paper. Post the results as broadsheets in class. A broadsheet may contain a small illustration, and some of its lettering—especially the first letter of the poem—may be ornamented.

MAKING MEANINGS

MAKING MEANINGS

First Thoughts

[respond]

1. How do you feel about the way Mary survives Ta-Na-E-Ka? Is it fair? Should she be sent out again?

Shaping Interpretations

[analyze]

2. Mary and Roger face an **external conflict** with the older generation about Ta-Na-E-Ka. What arguments do Mary's mother, grandfather, and teacher offer in support of the ritual? What arguments do Mary and Roger give against it? You may want to list their reasons in a chart like the one below. Whose side are you on?

For (Older Generation)	Against (Younger Generation)

[interpret]

3. What **internal conflict** does Mary feel when Ernie says that Ta-Na-E-Ka is silly?

[interpret]

4. Look at the statements you considered for the Quickwrite on page 15. How do you think Mary would have rated each statement before Ta-Na-E-Ka? How does Mary feel about her heritage and the older generation after the ritual?

[evaluate]

5. Do you agree with Grandfather that Mary could have passed the survival test "under any circumstances, in any time"? Explain.

Connecting with the Text

[connect]

6. What traditions does your family expect you to honor? Compare and contrast your feelings about these traditions with Mary's feelings about Kaw traditions.

Extending the Text

[synthesize]

7. Does this story teach a lesson about the role of tradition in today's society? What do you think that lesson might be?

[respond]

8. Mary's teacher says to her, "Don't look down on your heritage." Why do people sometimes "look down" on their heritage? What parts of your heritage do you value most?

TA-NA-E-KA 27

Reading Check

Imagine that you are Mary. Write three diary entries in which you describe your experiences and feelings (1) before Ta-Na-E-Ka, (2) during your time in the woods, and (3) after the ritual is over. Does Mary have a "moment of truth"?

Reading Check

Diary entries will vary but should include descriptions of feelings that Mary would have experienced, such as fear, acceptance, pride, and self-confidence. Mary does have a "moment of truth" when she discovers she can take care of herself and survive in a world that is different from her grandfather's.

First Thoughts

1. Some students may say that Mary should be sent out again because she did not follow instructions. Others may say that Mary should not be sent out again because she survived on her own, and that was the point of the ritual.

Shaping Interpretations

2. Possible answers: The older generation argues that surviving it will make you proud; it is a Kaw ritual; girls compete on equal terms with boys; endurance is a virtue. The younger generation argues that you do not need to be a warrior if you are going to work in an office; the test does not apply to the modern world; it is too dangerous.

3. She feels the need to defend her people's tradition to Ernie even though she really did not want to do Ta-Na-E-Ka.

4. Possible response: After the ritual, Mary respects her heritage and the older generation more than she did before.

5. Possible responses: Yes, because of her strong character, as shown throughout the story, she would have adapted to other circumstances. No, because although she was able to use her wits in a modern setting, in earlier times she would have been forced to survive in the wilderness, and would have needed different skills.

Connecting with the Text

6. Answers will vary. Encourage students to share their families' traditions with one another.

Extending the Text

7. Possible response: Traditions are worth keeping but may need to be altered to fit changing times.

8. Possible response: People can't always see how some of the rituals of their cultures apply to their own lives. Aspects of my heritage I value most are those that connect me to my family and make me feel part of something special.

Grading Timesaver

Rubrics for each Choices assignment appear on p. 106 in the *Portfolio Management System*.

CHOICES: Building Your Portfolio

1. Writer's Notebook Have students prepare for this activity by using a graphic organizer like this one:

Who	What	Why	Where	When

Remind students to save their work. They may use it as prewriting for the Writer's Workshop on pp. 86–90.

2. Creative Writing Have students use a map like this one to organize their thoughts before writing about their own Ta-Na-E-Ka.

Food — Shelter
First Night
Experiences — Feelings

3. Research/Cultural Diversity Have group members decide on individual responsibilities for their research. Have one member conduct interviews, another consult reference books, and another observe rituals in person or on video or film.

4. Debate Have students quickwrite on the questions in this section. Then have them determine which side of the argument they agree with. Create debate teams according to the results of the Quickwrite activity.

CHOICES: Building Your Portfolio

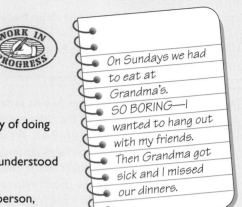

Writer's Notebook

1. Collecting Ideas for an Autobiographical Incident

Freewrite for five or ten minutes about a time in your life when you

- tried to convince someone that the old way of doing things didn't fit modern times
- learned the value of a tradition you hadn't understood before
- found a way to prove yourself to an older person, perhaps a teacher

On Sundays we had to eat at Grandma's. SO BORING—I wanted to hang out with my friends. Then Grandma got sick and I missed our dinners.

Creative Writing

2. Your Own Ta-Na-E-Ka

What would you do if you had to go on your own Ta-Na-E-Ka? How would you survive? What would you miss most? Imagine yourself in this situation, and write a description of your first day and night in the woods. You might prefer to follow the example of the Crow poets in the **Connections** beginning on page 24 and write a poem about your heritage. Try beginning your poem with this line, from one of the Crow poems:

"Thinking of the days now past."

Research/Cultural Diversity

3. Cultural Rituals

Many other cultures have coming-of-age rituals like Ta-Na-E-Ka. For example, you may have heard of the Jewish *bar mitzvah* or *bat mitzvah*, the Christian *confirmation*, the Sioux *vision quest*, or the *unoto ceremonies* of the Masai people of Africa. In a group, research one of these rituals or another one of your choice. Share your findings in a class presentation, using music, photographs, video, and food, as appropriate.

Debate

4. Equal Time

Do boys and girls have equal opportunities to prove themselves and gain recognition in your community? Do they face equal pressure from adults to be grown-up and responsible? Discuss these issues in your class, and then plan a class debate. One side should argue that girls and boys are treated equally, and the other side should argue that one group or the other gets special treatment.

Using Students' Strengths

Musical/Auditory Learners

For Choice 1 and for other freewriting or quickwriting activities in this book, have students record their thoughts on a tape recorder. Have them label each tape with their name, the selection title, the activity number, and the title "Freewrite" or "Quickwrite." This activity can also be used with visually impaired students.

Kinesthetic Learners

Ask students to choose a culture that interests them. Have them research that culture's coming-of-age ritual for Choice 3 and act out the most important aspects of the ritual for the class.

GRAMMAR LINK | MINI-LESSON

Subjects and Verbs—In Perfect Agreement

Language Handbook HELP

See Compound Subjects, page 705.

Technology HELP

See Language Workshop CD-ROM. Key word entry: subject-verb agreement.

In "Ta-Na-E-Ka" the generations disagree, but in correct sentences the subjects and the verbs always agree. This means that a singular subject needs a singular verb, and a plural subject needs a plural verb. Subject-verb agreement gets tricky when a sentence has a **compound subject**, that is, two subjects joined by *and, or,* or *nor.* To find the right verb, follow these rules:

1. Subjects joined by the word *and* take a plural verb.

   EXAMPLE   Mary and Roger <u>were</u> afraid.

2. Singular subjects joined by *or* or *nor* take a singular verb.

   EXAMPLE   Either Roger or Mary <u>reaches</u> the river.

3. When a singular subject and a plural subject are joined by *or* or *nor,* the verb agrees with the subject nearer the verb.

   EXAMPLES   Neither Mary's parents nor her *grandfather* <u>is</u> able to predict how Mary will survive.

   Neither Mary's grandfather nor her *parents* <u>are</u> able to predict how Mary will survive.

Try It Out

Try out your instincts for subject-verb agreement by choosing the right verb for each sentence below.

1. Either Mary's teacher or her grandfather <u>explains/ explain</u> that Kaw girls and boys compete on equal terms.

2. Both her mother and her teacher <u>says/say</u> that tradition is important.

3. Neither Mary's parents nor her grandfather <u>knows/know</u> that she has five dollars.

GRAMMAR LINK

Have students pick one or two excerpts from their portfolios. Then ask them to underline all compound subjects (subjects joined by *and, or,* or *nor*) and to circle each verb. Students should work with a partner to make sure each verb agrees with the subject.

Try It Out
Answers
1. explains
2. say
3. knows

VOCABULARY
Possible Answers
1. The highest virtue anyone can have is [honesty, love, compassion, mercy]
2. The most clever way to deal with conflict is [to avoid it; to use reason]
3. I would [make a face back at the person; walk away; ignore it]
4. In our culture, stuffing yourself is considered rude; in some other cultures, it is a compliment to the host.
5. I [do/do not] have the courage to try to survive in the woods.

Resources ———

Grammar
• *Grammar and Language Links,* p. 3

Vocabulary
• *Words to Own,* p. 2

Spelling
For related instruction, see
• *Spelling and Decoding,* p. 2

VOCABULARY | HOW TO OWN A WORD

WORD BANK
loftiest
shrewdest
grimaced
gorging
audacity

Personality Profile

Write your answers to these questions.

1. In your opinion, what is the <u>loftiest</u> virtue people can have?
2. What is the <u>shrewdest</u> way you'd deal with a conflict?
3. What would you do if someone <u>grimaced</u> at you?
4. Is <u>gorging</u> yourself acceptable behavior, or is it rude? Explain.
5. Do you have the <u>audacity</u> to try to survive in the woods alone? Explain.

TA-NA-E-KA 29

Grammar Link Quick Check

Identify the verb that agrees with the compound subject in the following sentences.

1. Mary or Roger <u>is/are</u> nervous about the Ta-Na-E-Ka. [is]
2. Mary's teacher or her parents <u>gives/give</u> her a five-dollar bill. [give]
3. Mary and her parents <u>respects/respect</u> Grandfather's point of view. [respect]

4. Roger or Mary's parents <u>admires/admire</u> Mary's approach to Ta-Na-E-Ka. [admire]
5. Mary's grandfather and her mother <u>thinks/think</u> Mary is clever to do a modernized Ta-Na-E-Ka. [think]

T29

Reading Skills and Strategies

Reading Skills and Strategies

This feature focuses on a specific reading strategy, which is applied in the selection that follows. Students will have the opportunity to practice each strategy using new material.

Mini-Lesson: Context Clues

- After students have read the pupil's page, present to them a nonsense word to illustrate the process of understanding a word through its context. For example, ask students if they know what the nonsense word *splange* means. Then ask them to define it after hearing it in the following sentence: "Harry got so excited he jumped up from the couch, upsetting his cup and saucer and spilling his splange all over Mrs. Peabody, who tried to wriggle out from under the hot liquid." From the context, it seems that splange could be tea or coffee or some other hot drink served in a cup and saucer.
- Have students identify the clues in the sentence that helped them determine the meaning of *splange*. [cup and saucer; spilling hot liquid]

HOW TO OWN A WORD: CONTEXT CLUES

We All Give Clues

Angie goes to the store with four-year-old Harry.

"Now, Harry," she says, "don't wander off. Stay close. I want you to stay in this *vicinity,* near me."

Although Harry is dying to crawl under the counters and untie people's shoelaces, he stays close to Angie. Would a four-year-old know the meaning of *vicinity*? Harry does seem to know what to do. He uses **context clues.**

Guessing Isn't So Bad

Harry could tell what Angie wanted even though he didn't know the meaning of *vicinity*. She gave him plenty of clues, like "don't wander off," "stay close," and "near me." When you're reading, you can sometimes guess the meaning of a word from two sources: (1) your own knowledge and experience and (2) **context,** or all the information surrounding the word. An example is shown in the chart below.

If You Can't Figure It Out

If the context doesn't tell you the meaning of a word in this book, do this:

- See if the word is underlined. If so, a definition appears at the bottom of the page.
- See if there is a number after the word. This indicates a footnote that will appear at the bottom of the page, explaining the word or phrase.
- Check the Glossary in the back of the book.

Puzzling Word from "The All-American Slurp"	Using Context Clues
"The Lakeview was an expensive restaurant, one of those places where a headwaiter <u>conducted</u> you to your seat. . . ."	**Conducted?** You can tell from the sentence that the waiter led people to their seats. Besides, I know that a conductor is someone who *leads* an orchestra. <u>Conducted</u> probably means "led."

Apply the strategy on the next page. ▶

Using Students' Strengths

Visual Learners

After students have finished this collection, give them additional practice with using context clues by asking them to locate the words they do not know from any one of the stories in this collection, to identify the context clues, and to create a chart like the one on the student's page with the example from "The All-American Slurp" (above).

Linguistic Learners

Divide the class into groups of three or four and have linguistic learners choose difficult words they know or from the dictionary and use them in sentences that include at least two context clues. Groups might also be engaged in a friendly competition using this activity to see who can be the first to guess the meaning.

Before You Read

THE ALL-AMERICAN SLURP

Make the Connection

Culture Shock

This comical short story is told by a young Chinese American girl. Her story is divided into six parts. As you read, don't be surprised if you feel the sudden urge to run into the kitchen for something to eat.

Reader's theater: getting ready.

After you read this story, you might work with a group and present parts of the story to the class. As you read, think about which of the six parts you'd like to present with a group. (Each part is numbered, as you'll see when you start reading.) Also, practice saying the word *slurp* or imitating the sound of people eating celery or pulling the threads off celery. How will you say *shloop*, which is the sound of a slurp in any language?

As you read, jot down notes on each section to help you decide which part of the story you'd like to perform and which character you'd like to play.

Reading Skills and Strategies

Using Context Clues

Reading this story will give you a chance to try the strategies for figuring out words shown on page 30. Remember to search around an unfamiliar word to find clues to its meaning. Don't worry if you don't know the exact meaning. The main thing is to understand and *enjoy* the story.

As any respectable Chinese knows, the correct way to eat your soup is to slurp.

go.hrw.com
LE0 6-1

THE ALL-AMERICAN SLURP 31

Planning

• **Block Schedule**
  Block Scheduling Lesson Plans with Pacing Guide

• **Traditional Schedule**
  Lesson Plans Including Strategies for English-Language Learners

• **One-Stop Planner**
  CD-ROM with Test Generator

Preteaching Vocabulary

Words to Own

Begin by inviting students to find the four Words to Own and their definitions at the bottom of pp. 33–34. Then have students work in pairs to compose one sentence for each word. If time allows, turn this activity into a game for doubled pairs. Tell pairs to replace the word in each of their sentences with a blank. Then have each pair read its sentences aloud to the other pair as a set of four fill-in-the-blank questions. How many of the blanks can each pair fill in correctly?

Summary ..

Having recently emigrated from China, the Lin family faces adjustment to American table customs. The daughter, who narrates the story, tells how her family is embarrassed when trying to eat unfamiliar foods such as raw celery served to them at their neighbor's home. The cultural conflict continues with humorous exaggeration as the family becomes more acculturated. Dining in an elegant restaurant to celebrate Mr. Lin's promotion as an engineer, the Lins show their appreciation of the soup by eating it in traditional Chinese fashion—by slurping—while the other diners stare. After three months, feeling more Americanized, the Lins host their own dinner party. They are amused to see their guests befuddled in an encounter with traditional Chinese food. After dinner, the narrator and her friend Meg slip off for chocolate milkshakes, which Meg slurps as she reaches the bottom of her glass. A moment of truth arrives when Meg confides the ironic message that "all Americans slurp."

Resources

Viewing and Representing
• Videocassette A, Segment 1
The Visual Connections segment "Americans All" provides a link to "Coming to America" by James Cheung, the Student to Student piece that accompanies "The All-American Slurp."

Listening
Audio CD Library
A recording of this story is provided in the *Audio CD Library:*
• Disc 1, Track 4

The All-American Slurp

Lensey Namioka

The first time our family was invited out to dinner in America, we disgraced ourselves while eating celery. We had immigrated to this country from China, and during our early days here we had a hard time with American table manners.

In China we never ate celery raw, or any other kind of vegetable raw. We always had to disinfect the vegetables in boiling water first. When we were presented with our first relish tray, the raw celery caught us unprepared.

We had been invited to dinner by our neighbors, the Gleasons. After arriving at the house, we shook hands with our hosts and packed ourselves into a sofa. As our family of four sat stiffly in a row, my younger brother and I stole glances at our parents for a clue as to what to do next.

Mrs. Gleason offered the relish tray to Mother. The tray looked pretty, with its tiny red radishes, curly sticks of carrots, and long, slender stalks of pale-green celery. "Do try

> I pulled the strings out of my stalk. Z-z-zip, z-z-zip.

Resources: Print and Media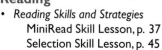

Reading
• *Reading Skills and Strategies*
    MiniRead Skill Lesson, p. 37
    Selection Skill Lesson, p. 45
• *Graphic Organizers for Active Reading,* p. 3
• *Words to Own,* p. 3
• *Spelling and Decoding*
    Worksheet, p. 3
• *Audio CD Library*
    Disc 1, Track 4

Writing and Language
• *Daily Oral Grammar*
    Transparency 3
• *Grammar and Language Links*
    Worksheet, p. 5
• *Language Workshop CD-ROM*

Viewing and Representing
• *Visual Connections*
    Videocassette A, Segment 1

Assessment
• *Formal Assessment,* p. 5
• *Portfolio Management System,* p. 107
• *Standardized Test Preparation,* p. 14
• *Test Generator (One-Stop Planner CD-ROM)*

Internet
• go.hrw.com (keyword: LE0 6-1)

some of the celery, Mrs. Lin," she said. "It's from a local farmer, and it's sweet."

Mother picked up one of the green stalks, and Father followed suit. Then I picked up a stalk, and my brother did too. So there we sat, each with a stalk of celery in our right hand.

Mrs. Gleason kept smiling. "Would you like to try some of the dip, Mrs. Lin? It's my own recipe: sour cream and onion flakes, with a dash of Tabasco sauce."

Most Chinese don't care for dairy products, and in those days I wasn't even ready to drink fresh milk. Sour cream sounded perfectly revolting. Our family shook our heads in unison.

Mrs. Gleason went off with the relish tray to the other guests, and we carefully watched to see what they did. Everyone seemed to eat the raw vegetables quite happily.

Mother took a bite of her celery. *Crunch.* "It's not bad!" she whispered.

Father took a bite of his celery. *Crunch.* "Yes, it *is* good," he said, looking surprised.

I took a bite, and then my brother. *Crunch, crunch.* It was more than good; it was delicious. Raw celery has a slight sparkle, a zingy taste that you don't get in cooked celery. When Mrs. Gleason came around with the relish tray, we each took another stalk of celery, except my brother. He took two.

There was only one problem: Long strings ran through the length of the stalk, and they got caught in my teeth. When I help my mother in the kitchen, I always pull the strings out before slicing celery.

I pulled the strings out of my stalk. *Z-z-zip, z-z-zip.* My brother followed suit. *Z-z-zip, z-z-zip, z-z-zip.* To my left, my parents were taking care of their own stalks. *Z-z-zip, z-z-zip, z-z-zip.*

Suddenly I realized that there was dead silence except for our zipping. Looking up, I saw that the eyes of everyone in the room were on our family. Mr. and Mrs. Gleason, their daughter Meg, who was my friend, and their neighbors the Badels—they were all staring at us as we busily pulled the strings of our celery.

That wasn't the end of it. Mrs. Gleason announced that dinner was served and invited us to the dining table. It was lavishly covered with platters of food, but we couldn't see any chairs around the table. So we helpfully carried over some dining chairs and sat down. All the other guests just stood there.

Mrs. Gleason bent down and whispered to us, "This is a buffet dinner. You help yourselves to some food and eat it in the living room."

Our family beat a retreat back to the sofa as if chased by enemy soldiers. For the rest of the evening, too mortified to go back to the dining table, I nursed a bit of potato salad on my plate.

Next day, Meg and I got on the school bus together. I wasn't sure how she would feel about me after the spectacle our family made at the party. But she was just the same as usual, and the only reference she made to the party was, "Hope you and your folks got enough to eat last night. You certainly didn't take very much. Mom never tries to figure out how much food to prepare. She just puts everything on the table and hopes for the best."

I began to relax. The Gleasons' dinner

WORDS TO OWN

lavishly (lav′ish·lē) *adv.*: abundantly; plentifully.
mortified (môrt′ə·fīd′) *v.* used as *adj.*: ashamed; embarrassed.
spectacle (spek′tə·kəl) *n.*: strange or remarkable sight.

THE ALL-AMERICAN SLURP **33**

A **English Language Learners**
   Idioms
Ask English language learners if they are familiar with the expression "to follow suit." If they are not, have one of your English proficient students offer an explanation. [to copy an action; to do something that someone else has done]

B **Cultural Connections**
Many peoples throughout the world have a lactose intolerance: they cannot digest milk products completely. Lactose intolerance is especially common among Asian and African peoples, and can be found in people of European ancestry as well.

C **Reading Skills and Strategies**
   Using Context Clues
Have students use context clues to infer the meaning of the phrase *in unison.* [clues—*our family, our heads*; meaning—"at the same time"]

D **Elements of Literature**
   Simile
? The narrator and her family left the dining table in embarrassment. To what does the narrator compare their action? [to that of soldiers retreating from enemies]

E **Critical Thinking**
   Hypothesizing
? What reasons might Meg have for her friendly comment about the party? [Possible responses: Her family might have been worried that the Lins didn't have a good time; her mother may have told her to say something nice about it.]

Reaching All Students

Struggling Readers
Using Context Clues was introduced on p. 31. For a lesson directly tied to this selection that teaches students to use context clues, see the *Reading Skills and Strategies* binder:
• MiniRead, Skill Lesson, p. 37
• Selection Skill Lesson, p. 45

English Language Learners
After students have read the story, have them write a question about something in it that they did not understand. Then have students work in groups to answer their questions. For additional strategies to supplement instruction for these students, see
• *Lesson Plans Including Strategies for English-Language Learners*

Advanced Learners
As students read, invite them to discuss or write about the questions, "What are good manners?" or "How should we act when we are hosts or guests so as not to offend others?"

A Elements of Literature
Theme
Here the narrator states one of the themes of the story. No matter how great are the cultural differences between us, there are similarities as well.

B Cultural Connections
Inform students that when people learn a second language in adulthood, it is very hard for them to lose the accent of their first language. It is much easier when the second language is learned in childhood.

C Reading Skills and Strategies

Using Context Clues
❓ What clues help you figure out the meaning of the word *blurted*? [the word *hurriedly* and the situation: Mrs. Lin was flustered and had no time to think about what she was supposed to say.]

A party wasn't so different from a Chinese meal after all. My mother also puts everything on the table and hopes for the best.

2 Meg was the first friend I had made after we came to America. I eventually got acquainted with a few other kids in school, but Meg was still the only real friend I had.

My brother didn't have any problems making friends. He spent all his time with some boys who were teaching him baseball, and in no time he could speak English much faster than I could—not better, but faster.

I worried more about making mistakes, and I spoke carefully, making sure I could say everything right before opening my mouth. **B** At least I had a better accent than my parents, who never really got rid of their Chinese accent, even years later. My parents had both studied English in school before coming to America, but what they had studied was mostly written English, not spoken.

Father's approach to English was a scientific one. Since Chinese verbs have no tense, he was fascinated by the way English verbs changed form according to whether they were in the present, past, perfect, pluperfect, future, or future perfect tense. He was always making diagrams of verbs and their inflections, and he looked for opportunities to show off his mastery of the pluperfect and future perfect tenses, his two favorites. "I shall have finished my project by Monday," he would say smugly.

Mother's approach was to memorize lists of polite phrases that would cover all possible social situations. She was constantly muttering things like "I'm fine, thank you. And you?" Once she accidentally stepped on **C** someone's foot and hurriedly blurted, "Oh, that's quite all right!" Embarrassed by her

slip, she resolved to do better next time. So when someone stepped on *her* foot, she cried, "You're welcome!"

In our own different ways, we made progress in learning English. But I had another worry, and that was my appearance. My brother didn't have to worry, since Mother bought him bluejeans for school, and he dressed like all the other boys. But she insisted that girls had to wear skirts. By the time she saw that Meg and the other girls were wearing jeans, it was too late. My school clothes were bought already, and we didn't have money left to buy new outfits for me. We had too many other things to buy first, like furniture, pots, and pans.

The first time I visited Meg's house, she took me upstairs to her room, and I wound up trying on her clothes. We were pretty much the same size since Meg was shorter and thinner than average. Maybe that's how we became friends in the first place. Wearing Meg's jeans and T-shirt, I looked at myself in the mirror. I could almost pass for an American—from the back, anyway. At least the kids in school wouldn't stop and stare at me in the hallways, which was what they did when they saw me in my white blouse and navy-blue skirt that went a couple of inches below the knees.

When Meg came to my house, I invited her to try on my Chinese dresses, the ones with a high collar and slits up the sides. Meg's eyes were bright as she looked at herself in the mirror. She struck several <u>sultry</u> poses, and we nearly fell over laughing.

WORDS TO OWN
sultry (sul′trē) *adj.*: sexy. *Sultry* also means "hot and humid" (said of weather).

Crossing the Curriculum

Geography
Ask students to locate China on a map or globe and to speculate on what method of transportation the narrator's family may have used to travel to the United States. Have them keep in mind that the family is not wealthy. Also have them locate San Francisco, New York City, and Vancouver, B.C., Canada, three major landing points for Chinese immigrants.

Fine Arts
Hand-painting bamboo fans is a traditional handicraft in China. Encourage interested students to obtain or make paper fans, and to paint pictures on them that represent events from the story.

3 The dinner party at the Gleasons' didn't stop my growing friendship with Meg. Things were getting better for me in other ways too. Mother finally bought me some jeans at the end of the month, when Father got his paycheck. She wasn't in any hurry about buying them at first, until I worked on her. This is what I did. Since we didn't have a car in those days, I often ran down to the neighborhood store to pick up things for her. The groceries cost less at a big supermarket, but the closest one was many blocks away. One day, when she ran out of flour, I offered to borrow a bike from our neighbor's son and buy a ten-pound bag of flour at the big supermarket. I mounted the boy's bike and waved to Mother. "I'll be back in five minutes!"

Before I started pedaling, I heard her voice behind me. "You can't go out in public like that! People can see all the way up to your thighs!"

"I'm sorry," I said innocently. "I thought you were in a hurry to get the flour." For dinner we were going to have pot stickers (fried Chinese dumplings), and we needed a lot of flour.

"Couldn't you borrow a girl's bicycle?" complained Mother. "That way your skirt won't be pushed up."

"There aren't too many of those around," I said. "Almost all the girls wear jeans while riding a bike, so they don't see any point buying a girl's bike."

We didn't eat pot stickers that evening, and Mother was thoughtful. Next day we took the bus downtown and she bought me a pair of jeans. In the same week, my brother made the baseball team of his junior high school, Father started taking driving lessons, and Mother discovered rummage sales. We soon got all the furniture we needed, plus a dartboard and a 1,000-piece jigsaw puzzle.

(Fourteen hours later, we discovered that it was a 999-piece jigsaw puzzle.) There was hope that the Lins might become a normal American family after all.

4 Then came our dinner at the Lakeview restaurant. The Lakeview was an expensive restaurant, one of those places where a headwaiter dressed in tails conducted you to your seat, and the only light came from candles and flaming desserts. In one corner of the room a lady harpist played tinkling melodies.

Father wanted to celebrate because he had just been promoted. He worked for an electronics company, and after his English started improving, his superiors decided to appoint him to a position more suited to his training. The promotion not only brought a higher salary but was also a tremendous boost to his pride.

Up to then we had eaten only in Chinese restaurants. Although my brother and I were becoming fond of hamburgers, my parents didn't care much for Western food, other than chow mein.

But this was a special occasion, and Father asked his co-workers to recommend a really elegant restaurant. So there we were at the Lakeview, stumbling after the headwaiter in the murky dining room.

D **Advanced Learners**
Interpreting
❓How has the incident with the bicycle affected Mrs. Lin's attitude toward Americanization? [Possible responses: She has a better understanding of certain aspects of American culture; she is more willing to adapt to that culture.]

E **Critical Thinking**
Making Predictions
❓What do you think will happen at the restaurant? [Possible response: The Lin family will find themselves in another embarrassing situation.]

F **Cultural Connections**
Point out that while most Americans consider chow mein to be Chinese food, it is actually a dish invented by Chinese immigrant chefs for their non-Chinese customers.

Speaking and Listening: Appreciating Spoken Language and Analyzing Oral Interpretation
Play the recording of this contemporary story (Disc 1, Track 4, in the *Audio CD Library*). After students have listened to the reader's interpretation, ask them what effect this oral reading had on them as listeners. Have them consider, for example, if the reader's pace, tone, and emphasis affected their emotional reaction to the story.

Getting Students Involved

Enrichment Activities
Random Reading. Have students conduct a Random Reading of the story. First, ask them to read the story silently, taking notes on the words, phrases, or sentences that create a vivid mental picture. Next, let students read aloud in random order the parts of the story they have marked. Then ask them to explain why they chose the passages they did.

Character Letter. Ask students to pretend that they are the narrator of the story, Lensey Namioka. Have them write a letter to Mary (of "Ta-Na-E-Ka") describing Lensey's moment of truth and comparing it to Mary's. Then ask students to exchange letters and to write a reply to Lensey in the voice of Mary.
Tableau. Assign students to groups to interpret the story through a tableau activity. Ask students to choose a favorite scene from the

story and to read it aloud together. Next, have a group leader tap one student in the group who will choose one character from the scene and speak as if he or she were the character, telling the character's feelings and thoughts. The leader taps the student again to stop him or her and then chooses another student to speak as a different character from the scene. This should continue until each "character" gets to speak.

A Reading Skills and Strategies
Connecting with the Text
Father seems to be prepared for any situation. Ask students if they know anyone like Father. Have them write a few sentences about that person in their Writer's Notebook—or they can make up a fictitious character with that trait and describe him or her briefly.

B Reading Skills and Strategies

Using Context Clues
❓ Based on the context, what might *at random* mean? [by chance; in no particular order]

C Reading Skills and Strategies

Using Context Clues
❓ Based on the context, what do you think the *consumption* of soup is? [drinking or eating it]

D Struggling Readers
Questioning
❓ Why does the narrator suddenly leave the table? [She is embarrassed when people in the restaurant notice how loudly her family is slurping their soup.]

E Elements of Literature
External and Internal Conflict
❓ What conflict is the narrator facing? [Possible response: external—the struggle to adjust to a new culture; internal—dealing with the painful feeling of being embarrassed by her family.]

At our table we were handed our menus, and they were so big that to read mine, I almost had to stand up again. But why bother? It was mostly in French, anyway.

Father, being an engineer, was always systematic. He took out a pocket French dictionary. "They told me that most of the items would be in French, so I came prepared." He even had a pocket flashlight the size of a marking pen. While Mother held the flashlight over the menu, he looked up the items that were in French.

"*Pâté en croûte,*" he muttered. "Let's see . . . *pâté* is paste . . . *croûte* is crust . . . hmmm . . . a paste in crust."

The waiter stood looking patient. I squirmed and died at least fifty times.

At long last Father gave up. "Why don't we just order four complete dinners at random?" he suggested.

"Isn't that risky?" asked Mother. "The French eat some rather peculiar things, I've heard."

"A Chinese can eat anything a Frenchman can eat," Father declared.

The soup arrived in a plate. How do you get soup up from a plate? I glanced at the other diners, but the ones at the nearby tables were not on their soup course, while the more distant ones were invisible in the darkness.

Fortunately my parents had studied books on Western etiquette before they came to America. "Tilt your plate," whispered my mother. "It's easier to spoon the soup up that way."

She was right. Tilting the plate did the trick. But the etiquette book didn't say anything about what you did after the soup reached your lips. As any respectable Chinese knows, the correct way to eat your soup is to slurp. This helps to cool the liquid and prevent you from burning your lips. It also shows your appreciation.

We showed our appreciation. *Shloop,* went my father. *Shloop,* went my mother. *Shloop, shloop,* went my brother, who was the hungriest.

The lady harpist stopped playing to take a rest. And in the silence, our family's consumption of soup suddenly seemed unnaturally loud. You know how it sounds on a rocky beach when the tide goes out and the water drains from all those little pools? They go *shloop, shloop, shloop.* That was the Lin family eating soup.

At the next table a waiter was pouring wine. When a large *shloop* reached him, he froze. The bottle continued to pour, and red wine flooded the table top and into the lap of a customer. Even the customer didn't notice anything at first, being also hypnotized by the *shloop, shloop, shloop.*

It was too much. "I need to go to the toilet," I mumbled, jumping to my feet. A waiter, sensing my urgency, quickly directed me to the ladies' room.

I splashed cold water on my burning face, and as I dried myself with a paper towel, I stared into the mirror. In this perfumed ladies' room, with its pink-and-silver wallpaper and marbled sinks, I looked completely out of place. What was I doing here? What was our family doing in the Lakeview restaurant? In America?

The door to the ladies' room opened. A woman came in and glanced curiously at me. I retreated into one of the toilet cubicles and latched the door.

Time passed—maybe half an hour, maybe an hour. Then I heard the door open again, and my mother's voice. "Are you in there? You're not sick, are you?"

Getting Students Involved

Cooperative Learning

A Dinner Party. Have students work in groups of three to plan a dinner party for some friends from another country. Ask them to decide what food and drink they will serve to make things easier for the guests; students may have to research the food and drink of their guests' culture to learn what will make the guests comfortable. One member of the group should design an invitation, one should write the menu, and one should write "how to eat" cards, explaining how Americans eat each food.

Cooperative Groups. To ensure that students work cooperatively, specify behaviors that are appropriate in learning groups. Ask students in each group to concentrate on one or two of the expected behaviors that follow.

- Encourage everyone to participate.
- Praise good ideas.
- Offer new ideas and ways to improve old ones.
- Listen attentively to others.
- Ask for help from others.

There was real concern in her voice. A girl can't leave her family just because they slurp their soup. Besides, the toilet cubicle had a few drawbacks as a permanent residence. **F** "I'm all right," I said, undoing the latch.

Mother didn't tell me how the rest of the dinner went, and I didn't want to know. In the weeks following, I managed to push the whole thing into the back of my mind, where it jumped out at me only a few times a day. Even now, I turn hot all over when I think of the Lakeview restaurant.

5 But by the time we had been in this country for three months, our family was definitely making progress toward becoming Americanized. I remember my parents' first PTA meeting. Father wore a neat suit and tie, and Mother put on her first pair of high heels. She stumbled only once. They met my homeroom teacher and beamed as she told them that I would make honor roll soon at

the rate I was going. Of course Chinese etiquette forced Father to say that I was a very stupid girl and Mother to protest that the **G** teacher was showing favoritism toward me. But I could tell they were both very proud.

6 The day came when my parents announced that they wanted to give a dinner party. We had invited Chinese friends to eat with us before, but this dinner was going to be different. In addition to a Chinese American family, we were going to invite the Gleasons.

"Gee, I can hardly wait to have dinner at **H** your house," Meg said to me. "I just *love* Chinese food."

That was a relief. Mother was a good cook, but I wasn't sure if people who ate sour cream would also eat chicken gizzards stewed in soy sauce.

Mother decided not to take a chance with chicken gizzards. Since we had Western guests, she set the table with large dinner

F Reading Skills and Strategies
Using Context Clues
? Judging from the context, what do you think a *drawback* is? [a negative aspect; a disadvantage]

G Cultural Connections
Etiquette
Traditional Chinese etiquette requires that people respond to compliments by showing modesty, as Mr. and Mrs. Lin do here.

H Reading Skills and Strategies
Making Predictions
? What do you think will happen when the Gleasons go to dinner at the Lins'? [Possible responses: The Gleasons will be as embarrassed as the Lins were when they ate dinner at the Gleasons' home; everything will go fine.]

Mother decided not to take a chance with chicken gizzards.

Skill Link

Subjects and Verbs
Tell students that the **subject** of a sentence is the noun or pronoun that the sentence is about. A **simple subject** consists of a single noun or pronoun (Henry; I; Restaurants; They). A **compound subject** contains more than one word linked by *and, or,* or *nor* (Henry and I; Henry or June; Neither Henry nor June). A **verb** is a word that shows an action or a state of being.

To make sure that a sentence is grammatically correct, it is helpful to be able to identify the subject and the main verb.

Activity
Write the following sentences on the chalkboard or copy them on a handout. Have students underline the subject and circle the verb in each sentence.

1. Mr. and Mrs. Lin traveled from China. [Mr. and Mrs. Lin; traveled]
2. The narrator felt embarrassed. [narrator; felt]
3. The narrator's best friend was Meg. [friend; was]
4. New foods sometimes taste strange at first. [foods; taste]
5. I decided not to cook gizzards. [I; decided]

Ⓐ Cultural Connection

Students may be interested in learning that the food served in many Chinese restaurants in North America is a hybrid form of Chinese cooking adapted to American tastes and dining customs. If there are Chinese American students in your class, they may be able to describe the differences between authentic Chinese food and Chinese American food.

Ⓑ Struggling Readers

Finding Details

❓ Are the Gleasons eating in the proper Chinese way? [no] How can you tell? [The narrator compares Mrs. Gleason's mixing of foods to mixing concrete, and she is very surprised by Mr. Gleason's using his fingers to eat instead of using his chopsticks.]

Ⓒ Reading Skills and Strategies

Using Context Clues

❓ Judging from the context, what does *coping* mean? [managing the best you can; handling a problem reasonably well]

Ⓓ Appreciating Language

Wordplay

Bring to students' attention the author's play on words that relates back to the title: "All Americans slurp" recalls "The All-American Slurp."

Resources ⎯⎯⎯⎯⎯ ◎

Formal Assessment
• Selection Test, p. 5
Test Generator
• Selection Test

---

plates, which we never used in Chinese meals. In fact we didn't use individual plates at all, but picked up food from the platters in the middle of the table and brought it directly to our rice bowls. Following the practice of Chinese American restaurants, Ⓐ Mother also placed large serving spoons on the platters.

The dinner started well. Mrs. Gleason exclaimed at the beautifully arranged dishes of food: the colorful candied fruit in the sweet-and-sour pork dish, the noodle-thin shreds of chicken meat stir-fried with tiny peas, and the glistening pink prawns° in a ginger sauce.

At first I was too busy enjoying my food to notice how the guests were doing. But soon I remembered my duties. Sometimes guests were too polite to help themselves and you had to serve them with more food.

I glanced at Meg to see if she needed more food, and my eyes nearly popped out at the sight of her plate. It was piled with food: The sweet-and-sour meat pushed right against the chicken shreds, and the chicken sauce ran into the prawns. She had been taking food from a second dish before she finished eating her helping from the first!

Ⓑ Horrified, I turned to look at Mrs. Gleason. She was dumping rice out of her bowl and putting it on her dinner plate. Then she ladled prawns and gravy on top of the rice and mixed everything together, the way you mix sand, gravel, and cement to make concrete.

I couldn't bear to look any longer, and I turned to Mr. Gleason. He was chasing a pea around his plate. Several times he got it to

°**prawns:** large shrimps.

---

the edge, but when he tried to pick it up with his chopsticks, it rolled back toward the center of the plate again. Finally he put down his chopsticks and picked up the pea with his fingers. He really did! A grown man!

All of us, our family and the Chinese guests, stopped eating to watch the activities of the Gleasons. I wanted to giggle. Then I caught my mother's eyes on me. She frowned and shook her head slightly, and I understood the message: The Gleasons were not used to Chinese ways, and they were just Ⓒ coping the best they could. For some reason I thought of celery strings.

When the main courses were finished, Mother brought out a platter of fruit. "I hope you weren't expecting a sweet dessert," she said. "Since the Chinese don't eat dessert, I didn't think to prepare any."

"Oh, I couldn't possibly eat dessert!" cried Mrs. Gleason. "I'm simply stuffed!"

Meg had different ideas. When the table was cleared, she announced that she and I were going for a walk. "I don't know about you, but I feel like dessert," she told me, when we were outside. "Come on, there's a Dairy Queen down the street. I could use a big chocolate milkshake!"

Although I didn't really want anything more to eat, I insisted on paying for the milkshakes. After all, I was still hostess.

Meg got her large chocolate milkshake and I had a small one. Even so, she was finishing hers while I was only half done. Toward the end she pulled hard on her straws and went *shloop, shloop.*

Ⓓ "Do you always slurp when you eat a milkshake?" I asked, before I could stop myself.

Meg grinned. "Sure. All Americans slurp."

---

38 MOMENTS OF TRUTH

Making the Connections

Connecting to the Theme: "Moments of Truth"

Ask students to discuss the question, "What is the moment of truth in this story?" [Possible response: the ending, when the narrator discovers that Americans as well as Chinese slurp—in other words, that people aren't as different as she had supposed.] Encourage students to offer a variety of answers. Help them realize that a good story may contain more than one meaning and that there is often no single right answer to a question about a story's theme.

T38

BROWSING IN THE FILES

About the Author. Lensey Namioka was born on June 14, 1929, in China, but immigrated to the United States with her parents, a linguist and a physician-writer. She has taught mathematics, monitored broadcasting for Japan Broadcasting Corporation, and has done translations for the American Mathematical Society. She enjoys music and lives with her husband and two daughters, Aki and Michi, in Seattle, Washington.

MEET THE WRITER

A Life on the Move

It's only natural for **Lensey Namioka** (1929–   ) to write about young people trying to cope with the strange ways of a new culture. She's spent much of her own life adjusting to new people and places. Namioka was born in China, where her family moved around a lot when she was young. "Being on the move meant that I grew up with almost no toys," she says. "To amuse ourselves, my sisters and I made up stories."

When she was a teenager, her family immigrated to the United States, where they continued to move from place to place.

In addition to realistic stories about teenagers of today, Namioka writes adventure novels set in long-ago Japan.

More About Coming to America

If you liked "The All-American Slurp," you might "shloop" up Lensey Namioka's novel *Yang the Youngest and His Terrible Ear* (Little, Brown). Yang is the only member of his family who has a "terrible ear" for music.

THE ALL-AMERICAN SLURP 39

Assessing Learning

Check Test: Short Answers

1. What two mistakes do the Lins make at the Gleasons'? [pulling strings from the celery and placing chairs at the buffet table]
2. Why does the narrator want a pair of jeans? [so she will look like all the other kids at school]
3. What is the narrator's friend's name? [Meg]
4. What type of food does the Lakeview restaurant serve? [French]

Informal Assessment

Reading. To check students' reading comprehension and encourage reflective reading, have them respond to one of the following questions.

- Are you like any character in this story? How?
- Does anyone in the story remind you of someone you know? In what way?
- What do you feel is the most important word, phrase, or passage? Why?
- Were any parts of this story confusing to you? Which parts, and why?

Standardized Test Preparation

For practice in proofreading and editing, see
- *Daily Oral Grammar,* Transparency 3

In this brief memoir, a young Chinese boy discusses what he left behind when immigrating to America. Later, he comes to realize what he has gained.

A Reading Skills and Strategies

Using Context Clues

❓ Television programs have *sponsors* who keep the programs on by paying for them. In the context of immigration, what might *sponsoring* mean? [Possible responses: supporting, encouraging, financing]

B Struggling Readers

Finding Details

❓ What job did the narrator's father hold in Hong Kong? [He was a police officer or detective.]

C Critical Thinking

Making Judgments

❓ Judging from the details of the narrator's life in Hong Kong, are there similarities between life there and life in the United States? [Possible response: Yes, people in Hong Kong also have nice cars, rugs in their houses, report cards, birthday cards, and yo-yos.]

D Critical Thinking

Extending the Text

❓ Why is it important to have friends? [Possible responses: to have someone to do things with; to have someone to confide in; to have someone to give you help when you need it.]

Resources

Assessment

• *Standardized Test Preparation,* p. 14

Coming to America

When I first heard that we were coming to America, I felt very happy. I wanted to know how different people lived. Do they have rugs in their houses in America? I wanted to see if they had a lot of nice cars, because in Hong Kong they have nice cars.

I asked my father and mother, "How come we have to go to America?" They told me that they had waited for thirteen years and they did not want to lose this opportunity because my mother's family was in America. My aunt was sponsoring us to come to America.

When I was eight years old, I quit school in the second grade. I packed pictures of my friends, cards that my friends had made, and all of my other going-away gifts. My mother packed Taoist° statues and some clothing. My father packed some police things, like important papers, and took retirement money with him. We cleaned out our apartment and we were ready to leave. When we closed our apartment door for the last time, I thought about the memories I had there, like when I got my report card, my first birthday party, and my first yo-yo.

I also felt very sad the day I left Hong Kong, because I had to leave my friends, family, and school. Right at that moment, when I was on the plane, I felt a tear escape from my eye.

After two days of flying on the airplane, we

° **Taoist** (dou′ist): relating to Taoism, a Chinese philosophy and religion.

finally landed in Boston. My aunt picked us up and took us out to eat in Chinatown. I asked my aunt, "Is this Chinatown?" It was dirty and people were throwing cigarette butts on the sidewalk. Dirty things left over from the Chinese restaurants were thrown into the street and plastic bags were blowing down the street. Homeless people were hanging around the T Station. I thought it was so gross! I had thought Chinatown would be clean!

Then we went to my aunt's house. I was fascinated because she had a big beautiful house. It was decorated and designed really well, and everything matched. She had a black leather sofa and a very nice stereo. We ended up living with my aunt for about a year.

Three days after we arrived in America I entered the Josiah Quincy School. On my first day I felt very nervous and uncomfortable. I wondered if the students would like me or not. Was the teacher mean or not? After a few weeks, I didn't feel so nervous or uncomfortable anymore. My new friends were nice to me and the teacher was not very mean. I was happy because I was one of them now.

After a few years we moved to North Quincy, and that's when we started on our own. We brought furniture, a car, a TV, tables, and telephones from my aunt's house. I have been living in this house for almost five years now and I like it a lot.

When I moved to Quincy, I met new friends such as Man Lok, Alex, Vincent, Sheldon, Jennifer, Jeff, John, and Eric. I had a new school and a new teacher. I feel very happy here because I now have what I lost when I moved to America.

— James Cheung
Atlantic Middle School
North Quincy, Massachusetts

Connecting Across Texts

Connecting with "The All-American Slurp"

The narrators of "The All-American Slurp" and "Coming to America" experience some of the same feelings and emotions as they try to fit in in the United States. Have students fill out a chart like the following one to identify when the narrators from each selection experienced the feelings and emotions listed.

	"All-American Slurp" narrator	"Coming to America" narrator
Happy		
Sad		
Surprised		

First Thoughts

[respond]

1. What scene in this story do you remember most? Why?

Shaping Interpretations

[analyze]

2. What American customs confuse the Lins when they eat at the Gleasons'? What mistakes do the Gleasons make when they eat at the Lins'?

[predict]

3. List some of the steps the Lins take to adapt to their new surroundings. Then, make a **prediction** about how they will eventually fit into American life.

[interpret]

4. Meg's comment that "all Americans slurp" might make you smile, but it also hints at the **message** of the story. What do you think that message is?

[synthesize]

5. How does finding new friends help both the narrator of "Coming to America" (page 40) and the narrator of "The All-American Slurp"?

Connecting with the Text

[connect]

6. Did Namioka's story make you see any of your own customs in a new light? Explain.

Extending the Text

[evaluate]

7. Lensey Namioka says she tries to make her writing as entertaining as possible. Did the conflicts in culture in this story make you laugh? Do you think using humor is a good way for people to deal with such conflicts? Give reasons for your opinion.

Reading Check

Sum up what happens in each of the story's six episodes:

1. [ ]
2. [ ]
3. [ ]

and so on.
In which episode does the narrator experience a "moment of truth"? Put a star in that box.

THE ALL-AMERICAN SLURP 41

First Thoughts

1. Possible responses: the scene at the buffet, because the Lins didn't know what a buffet was; the dinner scene at the Lins' house, because the Gleasons were as clumsy with Chinese customs as the Lins were with American customs.

Shaping Interpretations

2. The Lins are confused by the raw vegetables and the buffet dinner arrangement. The Gleasons have trouble with chopsticks, and they pile all their food onto their plates at once.

3. The narrator gets a pair of jeans, Father gets a promotion, Mother wears high heels, and the narrator's brother learns to play baseball. Answers will vary, but the details seem to imply that the Lins will adjust well to American life.

4. Possible response: Different cultures are not so different after all; people can usually find similarities underneath the surface differences.

5. For both narrators, having friends gives them confidence and a feeling of belonging. They learn American customs from their American friends.

Connecting with the Text

6. Possible responses: Yes, I learned that the customs of my culture are unique and interesting; I now appreciate how difficult it might be for someone to learn the customs of my culture.

Extending the Text

7. Responses will vary. Encourage students to use anecdotes from their own lives as well as examples from the story to support their opinions.

Reading Check

1. The Lins go to dinner at the Gleasons' and are not used to eating raw vegetables.

2. Meg and the narrator have fun trying on each other's clothes.

3. The narrator convinces her mother to buy her a pair of jeans.

4. The Lins have dinner at the Lakeview Restaurant and the narrator is embarrassed by her family's slurping.

5. The narrator's parents attend a PTA meeting.

6. The Gleasons have dinner at the Lins' and make mistakes like mixing their food together.*

CHOICES: Building Your Portfolio

1. **Writer's Notebook** Remind students to save their work. They may use it as prewriting for the Writer's Workshop on pp. 86–90.
2. **Creative Writing/Reader's Theater** Assign a role to each student in the group. Ask one student to write or type a final copy of the script and to make copies for everyone in the group. Ask another student to be in charge of gathering the props and another to direct the rehearsals.
3. **Cultural Diversity/Speaking** Have students work in small groups to conduct interviews with owners of restaurants featuring foods from various parts of the world. Suggest that they prepare a meal or dish to share with the class, using the utensils and table manners appropriate to the culture.
4. **Community Service** Have the class brainstorm a list of American expressions to use in the phrase book. Then divide the class into groups to create the phrase book and the school map. Have students put these items together with other suggestions they may think of to create a welcoming kit for newcomers.

CHOICES: Building Your Portfolio

Writer's Notebook

1. Collecting Ideas for an Autobiographical Incident

In "The All-American Slurp" the narrator and Meg become friends by doing things together, like trying on each other's clothes. Think of a time when you made a new friend. What drew the two of you together? What made the friendship grow? Write some notes about your friendship.

> *Sunita and I play on the same softball team. When she got sick, I brought her her homework. Later she lent me her skates. Now— best friends!*

Creative Writing/ Reader's Theater

2. All-American Scenes

Using the notes you took as you read, work together with some friends to prepare a reading of one of the scenes in this story. Each of you could read the lines of a different character. A narrator could read the descriptive and explanatory material. Write a script for the scene, including lines of dialogue and narration. You may want to make a list of props (like celery) to use in your performance. Rehearse your scene at least twice before you perform it for the class.

Cultural Diversity/ Speaking

3. Dinnertime Around the World

It's a Chinese custom to eat with chopsticks. It's an American custom to use a fork. In every culture, people have their own special ways of eating. Research the eating utensils, favorite foods, and table manners of a culture other than your own. Then, give a talk on what you found out. You might demonstrate some eating customs or draw diagrams or pictures to show certain dishes and table settings.

Community Service

4. Helping Hands

What could you do to help a newcomer from another culture feel welcome in your school? Form a welcoming committee, and list things you could do to help someone new. For example, make or collect

- a phrase book of slang expressions
- a map of your school
- tips on where to go and what to do in your town

Each member should pick a project to work on. When a newcomer arrives, you'll be ready to lend a helping hand.

42 MOMENTS OF TRUTH

Using Students' Strengths

Visual Learners
For Choice 1, allow students to prompt their memories by drawing pictures of their meetings with new friends.

Kinesthetic Learners
For Choice 3, have students use two pencils as if they were chopsticks to practice picking up crumpled paper. Provide each student with a set of chopsticks to try out at home, if they do not already own chopsticks. Have students report back to the class on their progress in learning this traditional Asian skill, which is increasingly part of Americans' repertoire.

Visual/Musical/Auditory Learners
If time and interest permit, let students create a "Welcome to Our School" video for Choice 4. It could include a tour of the school and introduce faculty members and other key people in the school.

GRAMMAR LINK

Subject-Verb Agreement and the Search for the Subject

Language Handbook HELP

See Problems in Agreement, pages 704 and 705.

Technology HELP

See Language Workshop CD-ROM. Key word entry: subject-verb agreement.

Finding the subject of a sentence can sometimes be tricky. With certain sentences you may have to play detective to be sure you've identified the right subject. Once you've got the subject, you can decide whether you need a singular or a plural verb. Here are some tips to help you:

Tip 1: In a question the subject often comes *after* the verb. To find the subject, change the question to a statement.

EXAMPLE What was/were the narrator's most embarrassing moments?

The narrator's most embarrassing moments were . . .

Tip 2: The subject of a sentence is *never* part of a prepositional phrase. Cross out any prepositional phrases before looking for the subject.

EXAMPLE A tray ~~of vegetables~~ was passed ~~to the Lins.~~

Try It Out

➤ Find the subject of each sentence and then choose the correct verb.

1. The strings of celery bothers/bother the Lins.

2. Where does/do Meg and the narrator go after dinner?

3. What does/do Meg say about slurping?

4. The goal of both families is/are to make their guests feel welcome.

➤ Whenever you see a question mark in your writing, go back and check that sentence for subject-verb agreement. Remember: The words *where* and *how* are never subjects.

GRAMMAR LINK

Students should choose an excerpt from their portfolios. Have them highlight the subjects in each sentence; if the sentence is a question, have them change the question to a statement. If the sentence is a statement, have them cross out the prepositional phrases. Then have students circle all the singular subjects and put a box around the plural subjects to check agreement.

Try It Out
Answers
1. bother
2. do
3. does
4. is

VOCABULARY
Possible Answers
1. Don't spread butter so lavishly, or there won't be any left.
2. When my mother kissed me in front of my friends, I was mortified!
3. Don't lick your fingers in a fancy restaurant unless you want to make a spectacle of yourself.
4. The fashion model's hips swayed as she took a sultry walk across the floor.

Resources

Grammar
• *Grammar and Language Links,* p. 5

Vocabulary
• *Words to Own,* p. 3

Spelling
For related instruction, see
• *Spelling and Decoding,* p. 3

VOCABULARY HOW TO OWN A WORD

| **WORD BANK** |
| lavishly |
| mortified |
| spectacle |
| sultry |

Using Words in Context

Write four sentences about the story, using the words in the Word Bank. In your sentences, give **context clues** that will help someone figure out the meanings of the words. (If you know any younger students, try your sentences out on them. Do your context clues get the meaning across?) Here is a good example of context clues from a sentence in the story (page 33). What clues tell you what a *buffet* is? (For more on context clues, see page 30.)

" 'This is a buffet dinner. You help yourselves to some food and eat it in the living room.' "

THE ALL-AMERICAN SLURP 43

Grammar Link Quick Check

Identify the correct verb in the following sentences.

1. What was/were the flavor of the milkshakes Meg and the narrator bought? [was]
2. Mistakes in table manners is/are often made by people learning to live in a new culture. [are]

3. Is/Are fashionable clothes important for people adjusting to a new culture? [Are]
4. Certain kinds of misunderstanding arises/arise when two cultures come together. [arise]
5. Is/Are your relatives moving to the United States? [Are]

OBJECTIVES

1. Read and interpret the story
2. Identify and analyze simile
3. Make predictions
4. Express understanding through writing, speaking, or art
5. Identify verb tenses and use verb tenses in a consistent manner in writing
6. Understand and use new words

SKILLS

Literary, Reading, Writing
- Identify and analyze simile
- Make predictions
- Collect ideas for an autobiographical incident
- Plan a brochure
- Write a comparison and contrast paragraph
- Create a poster

Speaking/Listening
- Conduct an interview

Grammar/Language
- Identify verb tenses and use verb tenses in a consistent manner in writing

Vocabulary
- Use new words
- Write a conversation spelling *ie* and *ei* words correctly

Art
- Create a poster

Planning

- **Traditional Schedule**
  Lesson Plans Including Strategies for English-Language Learners
- **One-Stop Planner**
  CD-ROM with Test Generator

Before You Read

LA BAMBA

Make the Connection

Starstruck

This story is about Manuel, a boy who wants to feel special. He gets up the nerve to perform in a talent show before the entire school. If his act is a hit, he'll impress his family and friends—especially the girls.

Nearly everyone wants to be the center of attention, at least once in a while. Do you ever yearn to be in the limelight? Has that limelight ever suddenly shone on you—with horrible results?

Quickwrite

Jot down a few notes about a time when you had to perform or make a presentation in front of a crowd. What do you remember about the experience? List some of the things that went through your mind. Did your mouth go dry, did your voice shake, did you forget your lines, did the piano keys all look the same?

go.hrw.com
LE0 6-1

Elements of Literature

Simile: Seeing Similarities

Manuel wants to hear "applause as loud as a thunderstorm" when he finishes his act. Thunder and applause are very different things, but the **simile** works. By comparing these two noises, the author helps us imagine exactly the kind of clapping Manuel longs to hear. Watch for other similes in this story. See if they help you see something especially vividly or hear it, smell it, feel it, taste it.

> **A simile** is a comparison between two unlike things that uses the word *like* or *as* or *resembles*.
>
> *For more on Simile and other Figures of Speech, see pages 183–184 and the Handbook of Literary Terms.*

Reading Skills and Strategies

Making Predictions: Thinking of What Happens Next

Making predictions means forecasting what will happen

next. To make predictions as you read "La Bamba," follow these steps:

- Keep asking questions as you read, and keep hunting for clues to the answers.
- Use your knowledge of what usually happens in stories.
- Think about how the characters might act, using what you know about them and about people in real life.

Stop when you get to the end of the second column on page 46. Jot down your prediction about what will happen to Manuel at the show.

Background

Literature and Music

Ritchie Valens (1941–1959), the professional singer mentioned in the story, was the first Mexican American rock star. He recorded hits such as "La Bamba." In 1959, when he was only seventeen, he was killed in a plane crash—a crash that killed two other rock-and-roll legends, Buddy Holly and the Big Bopper.

 *Resources: Print and Media*

Reading
- *Reading Skills and Strategies*
  MiniRead Skill Lesson, p. 55
  Selection Skill Lesson, p. 63
- *Graphic Organizers for Active Reading*, p. 4
- *Spelling and Decoding*, Worksheet p. 4
- *Audio CD Library*, Disc 2, Track 2

Writing and Language
- *Daily Oral Grammar*, Transparency 4

- *Grammar and Language Links*
  Worksheet, p. 7
- *Language Workshop CD-ROM*

Assessment
- *Formal Assessment*, p. 7
- *Portfolio Management System*, p. 108
- *Standardized Test Preparation*, p. 16
- *Test Generator (One-Stop Planner CD-ROM)*

Internet
- go.hrw.com (keyword: LE0 6-1)

LA BAMBA
Gary Soto

Manuel was going to pretend to sing Ritchie Valens's "La Bamba" before the entire school.

anuel was the fourth of seven children and looked like a lot of kids in his neighborhood: black hair, brown face, and skinny legs scuffed from summer play. But summer was giving way to fall: The trees were turning red, the lawns brown, and the pomegranate trees were heavy with fruit. Manuel walked to school in the frosty morning, kicking leaves and thinking of tomorrow's talent show. He was still amazed that he had volunteered. He was going to pretend to sing Ritchie Valens's "La Bamba" before the entire school.

Why did I raise my hand? he asked himself, but in his heart he knew the answer. He yearned for the limelight. He wanted applause as loud as a thunderstorm and to hear his friends say, "Man, that was bad!" And he wanted to impress the girls, especially Petra Lopez, the second-prettiest girl in his class. The prettiest was already taken by his friend Ernie. Manuel knew he should be reasonable since he himself was not great-looking, just average.

Manuel kicked through the fresh-fallen leaves. When he got to school, he realized he had forgotten his math workbook. If the teacher found out, he would have to stay after school and miss practice for the talent show. But fortunately for him, they did drills that morning.

During lunch Manuel hung around with Benny, who was also in the talent show. Benny was going to play the trumpet in spite of the fat lip he had gotten playing football.

"How do I look?" Manuel asked. He cleared his throat and started moving his lips in pantomime. No words came out, just a hiss that sounded like a snake. Manuel tried to look emotional, flailing his arms on the high notes and opening his eyes and mouth as wide as he could when he came to "Para bailar la baaaaammmba."[1]

After Manuel finished, Benny said it looked all right but suggested Manuel dance while he sang. Manuel thought for a moment and decided it was a good idea.

"Yeah, just think you're like Michael Jackson or someone like that," Benny suggested. "But don't get carried away."

During rehearsal, Mr. Roybal, nervous about his debut as the school's talent coordinator, cursed under his breath when

1. **para bailar la bamba** (pä′rä bï′lär lä bäm′bä): Spanish for "to dance the bamba."

LA BAMBA **45**

Summary ■ ■

For his school talent show, Manuel decides to pantomime a recording of Ritchie Valens's "La Bamba." During the rehearsal, however, the record is damaged, and Manuel doesn't realize it. Coping with stage fright at the talent show, Manuel goes onstage and begins his act. When the record sticks, Manuel reacts by pantomiming the same words over and over, while the audience laughs and applauds. On the verge of tears, Manuel is surprised that his friends congratulate him on being so clever and funny. Now, in the coveted limelight, he realizes that he has risen to the occasion. In bed that night, Manuel ironically reveals a small change in his character by thinking that next year, he won't volunteer for the show—probably.

Background

The closing years of the 1950s were devastating for rock-and-roll. In addition to the plane crash that killed Valens, Holly, and the Big Bopper, Elvis Presley was drafted into the Army in 1958, and Chuck Berry and Jerry Lee Lewis were involved in scandals. In the resulting vacuum, a smoother, "doo-wop" style, sung by crooning teen idols such as Fabian and Frankie Avalon, took hold. In the early 1960s, the Motown sound and the surfing sound of the Beach Boys brought some renewed vitality to the music. In 1963, the British invasion, led by the Beatles, marked a return to the guitar-based energy of Berry and Presley.

Resources

Listening
Audio CD Library
A recording of this story is provided in the *Audio CD Library*:
• Disc 2, Track 2

Selection Assessment
Formal Assessment
• Selection Test, p. 7
Test Generator
• Selection Test

Ⓐ **Elements of Literature**
Simile
❓ What is being compared? [Manuel's vocal hiss and the sound of a snake]

Reaching All Students

Struggling Readers
Making Predictions was introduced on p. 44. For a lesson directly tied to this story that teaches students to make predictions by using a strategy called Anticipation Guide, see the *Reading Skills and Strategies* binder:
• MiniRead Skill Lesson, p. 55
• Selection Skill Lesson, p. 63

English Language Learners
After students read the story, draw an outline of a boy on the chalkboard and label it Manuel. Have each student think of a word or phrase that describes Manuel—how he looks, how he sounds, how he feels, what his thoughts are. Write the words and phrases inside the outline. For additional strategies to supplement instruction for these students, see
• *Lesson Plans Including Strategies for English-Language Learners*

A **Reading Skills and Strategies**

Making Predictions

❓ Based on what happens here, what do you think will happen during the actual show? [Possible responses: The record player will break. Something will go wrong.]

B **Struggling Readers**

Varying Your Reading Rate

❓ Sometimes it's necessary to reread a passage slowly to find a crucial detail in the plot of the story. What is the crucial detail in this passage? [Manuel drops the record.]

C **Critical Thinking**

Making Judgements

❓ What do you think Manuel's parents are like, based on what you have read in this paragraph? [Possible responses: They care about their son; they are involved in Manuel's life.]

A the lever that controlled the speed on the record player jammed.

"Darn," he growled, trying to force the lever. "What's wrong with you?"

"Is it broken?" Manuel asked, bending over for a closer look. It looked all right to him.

Mr. Roybal assured Manuel that he would have a good record player at the talent show, even if it meant bringing his own stereo from home.

Manuel sat in a folding chair, twirling his record on his thumb. He watched a skit about personal hygiene, a mother-and-daughter violin duo, five first-grade girls jumping rope, a karate kid breaking boards, three girls singing "Like a Virgin," and a skit about the pilgrims. If the record player hadn't been broken, he would have gone after the karate kid, an easy act to follow, he told himself.

As he twirled his forty-five record, Manuel thought they had a great talent show. The entire school would be amazed. His mother and father would be proud, and his brothers and sisters would be jealous and pout. It would be a night to remember.

B Benny walked onto the stage, raised his trumpet to his mouth, and waited for his cue. Mr. Roybal raised his hand like a symphony conductor and let it fall dramatically. Benny inhaled and blew so loud that Manuel dropped his record, which rolled across the cafeteria floor until it hit a wall. Manuel raced after it, picked it up, and wiped it clean.

"Boy, I'm glad it didn't break," he said with a sigh.

That night Manuel had to do the dishes and a lot of homework, so he could only practice in the shower. In bed he prayed that he

wouldn't mess up. He prayed that it wouldn't be like when he was a first-grader. For Science Week he had wired together a C battery and a bulb and told everyone he had discovered how a flashlight worked. He was so pleased with himself that he practiced for hours pressing the wire to the battery, making the bulb wink a dim, orangish light. He showed it to so many kids in his neighborhood that when it was time to show his class how a flashlight worked, the battery was dead. He pressed the wire to the battery, but the bulb didn't respond. He pressed until his thumb hurt and some kids in the back started snickering.

But Manuel fell asleep confident that nothing would go wrong this time.

The next morning his father and mother beamed at him. They were proud that he was going to be in the talent show.

C "I wish you would tell us what you're doing," his mother said. His father, a pharmacist who wore a blue smock with his name on a plastic rectangle, looked up from the newspaper and sided with his wife. "Yes, what are you doing in the talent show?"

"You'll see," Manuel said, with his mouth full of Cheerios.

The day whizzed by, and so did his afternoon chores and dinner. Suddenly he was dressed in his best clothes and standing next to Benny backstage, listening to the commotion as the cafeteria filled with school kids and parents. The lights dimmed, and Mr. Roybal, sweaty in a tight suit and a necktie with a large knot, wet his lips and parted the stage curtains.

"Good evening, everyone," the kids behind the curtain heard him say. "Good evening to

46 MOMENTS OF TRUTH

Listening to Music

"La Bamba" (Traditional) performed by Ritchie Valens (available on CD from WEA/Atlantic/Rhino)

Rock-and-roll pioneer Ritchie Valens (1941–1959) recorded his first hit song, "Come On, Let's Go," when he was only seventeen years old. Soon afterwards, he had an even bigger hit with "Donna," a love ballad dedicated to his girlfriend. A California native, Valens adopted a stage name that shortened his real last name of

Valenzuela. His Chicano background prompted his most influential song, a rock version of the Mexican folk song "La Bamba," which became a Latin party staple. Almost thirty years after Valens perished in the tragic plane crash that also claimed the lives of his fellow rockers Buddy Holly and the Big Bopper, the popular LA-based Latin rock group Los Lobos did a new hit version of "La Bamba" for a film biography of Valens's life.

Activity

Play students the song "La Bamba" after they have read the story. Explain that the song is about a folk dance. If necessary clarify that the line *Para bailar la bamba,* which appears in the story, means "to dance the bamba." Then have students discuss the songs that they might choose if they were going to dance at a school talent show. Encourage interested students to put on such a show for classmates.

T46

you," some of the smart-alecky kids said back to him.

"Tonight we bring you the best John Burroughs Elementary has to offer, and I'm sure that you'll be both pleased and amazed that our little school houses so much talent. And now, without further ado, let's get on with the show." He turned and, with a swish of his hand, commanded, "Part the curtain." The curtains parted in jerks. A girl dressed as a toothbrush and a boy dressed as a dirty gray tooth walked onto the stage and sang:

Brush, brush, brush
Floss, floss, floss
Gargle the germs away—hey! hey! hey!

After they finished singing, they turned to Mr. Roybal, who dropped his hand. The toothbrush dashed around the stage after the dirty tooth, which was laughing and having a great time until it slipped and nearly rolled off the stage.

Mr. Roybal jumped out and caught it just in time. "Are you OK?"

The dirty tooth answered, "Ask my dentist," which drew laughter and applause from the audience.

The violin duo played next, and except for one time when the girl got lost, they sounded fine. People applauded, and some even stood up. Then the first-grade girls maneuvered onto the stage while jumping rope. They were all smiles and bouncing ponytails as a hundred cameras flashed at once. Mothers "awed" and fathers sat up proudly.

The karate kid was next. He did a few kicks, yells, and chops, and finally, when his father held up a board, punched it in two.

The audience clapped and looked at each other, wide-eyed with respect. The boy bowed to the audience, and father and son ran off the stage.

Manuel remained behind the stage, shivering with fear. He mouthed the words to "La Bamba" and swayed left to right. Why did he raise his hand and volunteer? Why couldn't he have just sat there like the rest of the kids and not said anything? While the karate kid was onstage, Mr. Roybal, more sweaty than before, took Manuel's forty-five record and placed it on a new record player.

"You ready?" Mr. Roybal asked.

"Yeah . . ."

Mr. Roybal walked back on stage and announced that Manuel Gomez, a fifth-grader in Mrs. Knight's class, was going to pantomime Ritchie Valens's classic hit "La Bamba."

The cafeteria roared with applause. Manuel was nervous but loved the noisy crowd. He pictured his mother and father applauding loudly and his brothers and sister also clapping, though not as energetically.

Manuel walked on stage and the song started immediately. Glassy-eyed from the shock of being in front of so many people, Manuel moved his lips and swayed in a made-up dance step. He couldn't see his parents, but he could see his brother Mario, who was a year younger, thumb-wrestling with a friend. Mario was wearing Manuel's favorite shirt; he would deal with Mario later. He saw some other kids get up and head for the drinking fountain, and a baby sitting in the middle of an aisle sucking her thumb and watching him intently.

What am I doing here? thought Manuel.

La Bamba 47

D English Language Learners
Multiple Meanings
❓ The word *part*, in this context, is a verb that means "to separate." What is another meaning for the word *part*? [a portion of something, not the whole thing]

E Appreciating Language
Word Choice
❓ The author is using figurative language here. Why do you think he chose the word *roared* to describe the audience's response? [Possible response: He wants to indicate how enthusiastic the audience is.] What other words could the author have used? [Possible responses: *yelled, screamed, shouted, blared, thundered.*]

F Critical Thinking
Speculating
❓ How do you think Manuel feels as he notices his brother thumb-wrestling and other kids walking toward the drinking fountain? [Possible responses: nervous, discouraged, dismayed, insulted.]

Crossing the Curriculum

Getting Students Involved

Art
Discussing Manuel's experiences may bring up the subject of students' own talents. Have students raise their hands in response to these questions: "Who plays a musical instrument?" "Who sings?" "Who dances?" "Who draws or paints or works with clay?" "Who likes to act?" Hold a mini-talent show to give students a chance to perform for their peers. Each act should last no longer than two minutes.

Music/Social Studies
Ask students to find other songs with interesting histories. Students should find songs that were associated with specific moments in history and that have become part of our cultural heritage. Obtain the songs and play them for the class. Then have students rate the songs and explain their responses. [Examples: "Tum, tum, tum"—the anti-war movement; "We Shall Overcome"—the civil rights movement; "Rock Around the Clock"—the popular beginning of rock-and-roll.]

Enrichment Activity
Character Letter. Have students imagine that they are sitting in the audience when Manuel performs at the talent show. Have them write a letter telling Manuel what they liked or didn't like about his performance. Ask volunteers to read their letters aloud to the class. Then have students pretend to be Manuel, and ask them to write letters back to his fans.

This is no fun at all. Everyone was just sitting there. Some people were moving to the beat, but most were just watching him, like they would a monkey at the zoo.

But when Manuel did a fancy dance step, there was a burst of applause and some girls screamed. Manuel tried another dance step. He heard more applause and screams and started getting into the groove as he shivered and snaked like Michael Jackson around the stage. But the record got stuck, and he had to sing

Para bailar la bamba
Para bailar la bamba
Para bailar la bamba
Para bailar la bamba

again and again.

Manuel couldn't believe his bad luck. The audience began to laugh and stand up in their chairs. Manuel remembered how the forty-five record had dropped from his hand and rolled across the cafeteria floor. It probably got scratched, he thought, and now it was stuck, and he was stuck dancing and moving his lips to the same words over and over. He had never been so embarrassed. He would have to ask his parents to move the family out of town.

After Mr. Roybal ripped the needle across the record, Manuel slowed his dance steps to a halt. He didn't know what to do except bow to the audience, which applauded wildly, and scoot off the stage, on the verge of tears. This was worse than the homemade flashlight. At least no one laughed then; they just snickered.

Manuel stood alone, trying hard to hold back the tears as Benny, center stage, played his trumpet. Manuel was jealous because he sounded great, then mad as he recalled that it was Benny's loud trumpet playing that made the forty-five record fly out of his hands. But

when the entire cast lined up for a curtain call, Manuel received a burst of applause that was so loud it shook the walls of the cafeteria. Later, as he mingled with the kids and parents, everyone patted him on the shoulder and told him, "Way to go. You were really funny."

Funny? Manuel thought. Did he do something funny?

Funny. Crazy. Hilarious. These were the words people said to him. He was confused but beyond caring. All he knew was that people were paying attention to him, and his brother and sisters looked at him with a mixture of jealousy and awe. He was going to pull Mario aside and punch him in the arm for wearing his shirt, but he cooled it. He was enjoying the limelight. A teacher brought him cookies and punch, and the popular kids who had never before given him the time of day now clustered around him. Ricardo, the editor of the school bulletin, asked him how he made the needle stick.

"It just happened," Manuel said, crunching on a star-shaped cookie.

At home that night his father, eager to undo the buttons on his shirt and ease into his La-Z-Boy recliner, asked Manuel the same thing, how he managed to make the song stick on the words "Para bailar la bamba."

Manuel thought quickly and reached for scientific jargon he had read in magazines. "Easy, Dad. I used laser tracking with high optics and low functional decibels per channel." His proud but confused father told him to be quiet and go to bed.

"Ah, que niños tan truchas,"[2] he said as he walked to the kitchen for a glass of milk. "I don't know how you kids nowadays get so smart."

2. **que niños tan truchas** (kā nēn′yōs tän troo′chäs): Spanish for "what smart kids."

Making the Connections

Connecting to the Theme: "Moments of Truth"

Remind students of the collection theme, "Moments of Truth," and its focus: learning something new that changes your understanding of yourself or your world. Use the following questions to prompt discussion of the story's connection to the collection theme:

• What is Manuel's moment of truth?
• In what way is his experience more challenging than he expected?

• How well does he meet the challenge?
• What enlightenment, or new understanding, comes to Manuel as a result?
• How might this new understanding affect his later life?

Manuel, feeling happy, went to his bedroom, undressed, and slipped into his pajamas. He looked in the mirror and began to pantomime "La Bamba," but stopped because he was tired of the song. He crawled into bed. The sheets were as cold as the moon that stood over the peach tree in their back yard.

He was relieved that the day was over. Next year, when they asked for volunteers for the talent show, he wouldn't raise his hand. Probably.

E

MEET THE WRITER

"My Friends . . . Jump Up and Down on the Page."

Like Manuel in "La Bamba," **Gary Soto** (1952–   ) grew up in a Mexican American family in California's San Joaquin Valley. He remembers himself as being competitive. He recalls:

66 I was a playground kid. I jumped at every chance to play. The game didn't matter. It could be kickball or baseball, or chess or Chinese checkers—anything that allowed me to compete. 99

He also says that he was not a very good student until he went to college and discovered poetry. Soon he yearned to be a writer himself—to win recognition by recapturing the world of his childhood in words. Of his early days as a writer, Soto remembers this:

66 I was a poet before I was a prose writer. As a poet, I needed only a sheaf of paper, a pen, a table, some quiet, and, of course, a narrative and spurts of image. I liked those years because the writing life was tidy. When I first started writing recollections

Gary Soto with his daughter Mariko and cat Corky.

and short stories, however, I needed more. I needed full-fledged stories and the patience of a monk. I needed to recall the narrative, characters, small moments, dates, places, etc. I was responsible for my writing, and, thus, it was tremendous work to keep it all in order. When I was writing *Living up the Street*, I clacked away on my typewriter with a bottle of white-out within view. I wrote, rewrote, and rewrote the rewrite, so that my friends would jump up and down on the page. 99

More by Gary Soto

To meet more of Gary Soto's lively friends, check out *Baseball in April* (Harcourt Brace) and *Local News* (Scholastic).

LA BAMBA 49

E Critical Thinking

Challenging the Text

? Do you like this ending for the story? Why or why not? [Sample responses: Yes, because it gives a last look at Manuel's personality; no, because it leaves too many open questions about what happens next.]

BROWSING IN THE FILES

About the Author. Gary Soto was born in Fresno, California, and now lives in Berkeley, California, where he teaches English and Chicano Studies at the University of California at Berkeley. His books are often about the experiences and feelings of youngsters growing up as Mexican Americans. He has written fiction, poetry, essays, and autobiographical recollections, and has produced short films for Spanish-speaking children.

A Critic's Comment. Reviewing Soto's book of young-adult stories, *Baseball in April*, for *The New York Times Book Review*, Roberto Gonzalez Echevarria wrote: "Because he stays within the teenagers' universe . . . he manages to convey all the social change and stress without bathos or didacticism. In fact, his stories are moving, yet humorous and entertaining."

FROM THE EDITOR'S DESK

We admit it—one reason we like this story is because we like the song! Seriously, though, Gary Soto has presented, through Manuel's fortunate ability to think on his feet, a universal conflict and triumphant resolution: the fear of performing in public, and the discovery that one can make mistakes and still prevail.

Assessing Learning

Check Test: Short Answers

1. Who is the main character in this story? [Manuel, a fifth grader]
2. Why does Manuel volunteer for the talent show? [to get attention and to impress a girl]
3. What does Manuel plan to do in the talent show? [He plans to lip-synch to a record of the song "La Bamba."]
4. Name three other acts that are in the talent show. [a skit about brushing teeth, a mother-and-daughter violin act, and a karate demon-stration]
5. Why does Manuel nearly start crying? [The record gets stuck, and he has to sing the same line again and again. He is embarrassed.]

Standardized Test Preparation

For practice with standardized test format specific to this selection, see
• *Standardized Test Preparation*, p. 16
For practice in proofreading and editing, see
• *Daily Oral Grammar*, Transparency 4

MAKING MEANINGS

First Thoughts

1. Possible responses: If I were Manuel, I would not forget to take a big bow; "La Bamba" is realistic because people often perform better than they expect in high-pressure situations; it is not realistic because in real life, mistakes usually don't work out in our favor.

Shaping Interpretations

2. Sample response: I predicted that something would go wrong at the performance, because something would have to go wrong to make it an interesting story, and also because Manuel is worried about performing. I didn't predict exactly what would go wrong or that it would turn out to help Manuel.

3. Manuel says the audience looks at him the way people look at a monkey in a zoo. He thought it would be fun, but instead it is embarrassing.

4. Possible responses: No, they love the performance because they think he's being funny on purpose. He might volunteer next year because he likes the positive attention. He might not volunteer again because his success came from an unpredictable mishap, which he wouldn't be able to repeat.

Connecting with the Text

5. Possible responses: It was funny. Humorous examples are the experience with the light bulb, and Manuel's onstage response to the stuck record. It was not funny because I felt too sorry for Manuel to laugh.

Extending the Text

6. Possible responses: A successful performance makes people proud and self-confident; it makes people more willing to face future challenges.

MAKING MEANINGS

First Thoughts

[respond]

1. How would you complete these sentences?
   - If I were Manuel, I would not . . .
   - "La Bamba" is realistic/unrealistic because . . .

Shaping Interpretations

[predict]

2. Think about the **prediction** you made about Manuel at the end of page 46. What did you base your prediction on? How well did you forecast what would happen?

[identify]

3. While he's onstage, what **simile** does Manuel use to describe the people watching him? How are Manuel's moments onstage different from what he imagined they would be?

[evaluate]

4. Does the audience agree with Manuel that his performance is a disaster? Explain why, in your opinion, Manuel will or won't volunteer for the talent show next year.

Connecting with the Text

[respond]

5. Do you think Gary Soto's descriptions of Manuel's experiences and of the talent show are funny? If so, tell which moments or descriptions struck you as humorous. If not, tell why you didn't laugh.

Extending the Text

[connect]

6. Performances like Manuel's create a lot of anxiety, but they give you something in return. What could a trial-by-fire performance like Manuel's do for you?

Reading Check

Imagine that Ricardo, the editor of the school bulletin, is interviewing Manuel for an article on his role in the talent show. What information does Manuel give him about volunteering for the show, rehearsing, and the actual performance? According to Manuel, what did he discover in his "moment of truth"?

Reading Check

Because of Manuel's external and internal conflicts about his performance, and because of the public nature that his comments would take in the school bulletin, he might make up a story about his participation in the talent show—a story that included only some of the facts. For example, he might tell Ricardo that he entered the show because he loves Ritchie Valens's song and because he wanted to hear the audience cheer him. He might say that he rehearsed often and that he was anxious when he went onstage; when he heard the record skip, he knew he had to do something, so he improvised and made the best of what could have been a disaster. In his moment of truth, he learned that he could be funny and could perform, or, in a larger sense, that he could adapt to challenges and that he is likable. You may wish to have pairs of students do the interview as a dramatic skit.

CHOICES: Building Your Portfolio

Writer's Notebook

1. Collecting Ideas for an Autobiographical Incident

Look back at your notes for the Quickwrite on page 44. What did you learn about yourself when you got up and performed? What did you like—or hate—about being in front of a crowd? Why would—or wouldn't—you do it again? Jot down some notes about your experience.

I learned that when I'm not actually speaking, I get very nervous and scared. Once I'm onstage, I get better, but I can't think about what I'm doing. I just do it.

Writing a Brochure/Speaking

2. The Show Must Go On

Many actors suffer from "butterflies in the stomach," or stage fright, before "going on." What do they do about it? Plan to write a brochure entitled "How to Deal with Stage Fright." Find an article or a book on public speaking. Then, interview someone who does a lot of speaking or performing (maybe the PTA president or a soloist in a choir). Collect all the tips you can.

Comparing and Contrasting

3. M and M

Both the Moose in "Just Once" (page 3) and Manuel in "La Bamba" find themselves in front of a roaring crowd. In what other ways are the two boys alike? Write a paragraph or two comparing and contrasting the Moose and Manuel. Focus on the problems and feelings they experienced. In what important way are they different? (Hint: Think about the way each story ends.) Before you write, use a Venn diagram like this one to organize your ideas:

The Moose   Manuel
different (alike) different

Writing/Art

4. Coming Soon to an Auditorium Near You!

You're on the publicity committee for your school talent show, and you're in charge of creating posters to advertise the show. Work alone or, if you prefer, with several classmates to make a poster. Use scenes and characters from "La Bamba" as the inspiration for your illustrations. You may want to invent a title for your talent show and include it, along with the times and dates of performances, on your poster.

Grading Timesaver

Rubrics for each Choices assignment appear on p. 108 in the *Portfolio Management System*.

CHOICES: Building Your Portfolio

1. **Writer's Notebook** Remind students to save their work. They may use it as prewriting for the Writer's Workshop on pp. 86–91. Have students use a graphic organizer like the following one to relate the events to their feelings.

Event	Feeling
[Waiting to go onstage]	[Nervous]
[Missed my entrance]	[Embarrassed]
[Got a standing ovation]	[Joyful!]

2. **Writing a Brochure/Speaking** Have students create their brochures using a desktop publishing program. Many of these programs have templates that can assist students in designing their brochures. Ask students to include charts and visual images using graphics programs if available.

3. **Comparing and Contrasting** Students might work in pairs. Initially, one partner should think of similarities and the other should think of differences. Then students may offer feedback and additional ideas in their partner's category as well as in their own.

4. **Writing/Art** Discuss with students the main events in the story. Have each group choose a different event to illustrate on its poster. Hang the completed posters in the classroom in the order the events occurred to form a storyboard.

Reaching All Students

Struggling Readers

Allow students who have difficulty writing to make a video on stage fright, rather than a brochure, for Choice 2. If they appear in their own video, have them incorporate their feelings of stage fright into the production. Encourage them to find ways to make the presentation lively, dramatic, and fun.

English Language Learners

Choice 4 is a good exercise for these students. Depending on their level of fluency, they may be able to suggest a title for the poster, write the times and dates of performances, and perhaps participate in the preliminary discussion of the main events. Those who are artistically talented will enjoy the chance to shine by drawing the illustration.

GRAMMAR LINK

Have students choose a piece from their portfolios. Have them determine whether the piece is written primarily in the past tense or the present tense. Ask them to circle all the verbs and to determine if each verb is in the correct tense. Let students work with a partner to check each other's work. In case of shifts in tense that are not mistakes, students should be able to explain the reason for the shift (e.g., tense may shift in dialogue and in flashbacks).

Try It Out
Answers

Manuel is the fourth of seven children and looks like a lot of kids in his neighborhood: black hair, brown face, and skinny legs scuffed from summer play. But summer is giving way to fall: The trees are turning red, the lawns brown, and the pomegranate trees are heavy with fruit. Manuel walks to school in the frosty morning, kicking leaves and thinking of tomorrow's talent show. Possible response: I like the present tense better in this description, but the past tense works better as the beginning of a story.

SPELLING

Ask the class to repeat the spelling jingle at least twice from memory before doing the activity. They may also consult it on this page. After students have checked each other's spelling in their written conversations, you might do a double-check.

Resources ───────

Grammar
• *Grammar and Language Links*, p. 7
Spelling
For related instruction, see
• *Spelling and Decoding*, p. 4

GRAMMAR LINK `MINI-LESSON`

Using Verb Tenses

Language Handbook HELP

See Verb Tense, pages 709-711.

Technology HELP

See Language Workshop CD-ROM. Key word entry: verb tenses.

Like most writers, Soto uses the past tense to tell a story. He writes about Manuel and the talent show as though the events have already happened:

> "Why did I raise my hand? he asked himself, but in his heart he knew the answer. He yearned for the limelight."

When writers want readers to feel that the events of a story are happening right now, they tell the story in the present tense:

> Why am I raising my hand? he asks himself, but in his heart he knows the answer. He yearns for the limelight.

No matter which tense you use, use it consistently. Be sure not to switch unnecessarily from the past tense to the present tense. (The past tense shows what has already happened. The present tense shows what is happening now.)

TENSES SWITCHED	Benny walked onto the stage, raised his trumpet . . . , and waits for his cue.
TENSES USED CONSISTENTLY	"Benny walked onto the stage, raised his trumpet . . . , and waited for his cue."

Try It Out

➤ Rewrite the first three sentences of "La Bamba," changing all past-tense verbs to present tense. (Do you like one version better than the other?)

➤ Take out a story you've written. Underline all present-tense verbs in one color and all past-tense verbs in another color. If you switched tenses incorrectly, decide which tense to keep, and revise your story.

SPELLING `HOW TO OWN A WORD`

Language Handbook HELP

See Spelling Rules, page 762.

The rhyme at the right will help you spell most words with the letters *ie* or *ei*. As with any rule, there are exceptions: *either, neither, weird.*

> *I* before *e*,
> Except after *c*,
> Or when sounded like *a*,
> As in *neighbor* and *weigh*.

Words to Summarize a Story

Write a conversation between Manuel and Benny that takes place the day after the talent show. Use these words, and be sure to spell them correctly: *believe, relieved, receive, friend, neighborhood, either, neither.* Add two or three more *ie* and *ei* words to the dialogue. Exchange papers, and check your classmate's *i*'s and *e*'s.

Grammar Link Quick Check

Rewrite the following sentences to make the verb tenses consistent.

1. Manuel's record was scratched and sticks when it was played. [Manuel's record was scratched and stuck when it was played, *or* . . . is scratched and sticks. . . .]
2. The audience applauds and thought Manuel was great. [The audience applauds and thinks Manuel is great; The audience applauds and thinks Manuel was great; The audience applauded and thought Manuel was great.]
3. Do you think Petra Lopez will be impressed when Manuel sang? [Do you think Petra Lopez will be impressed when Manuel sings?; Do you think Petra Lopez was impressed when Manuel sang?]
4. Manuel may perform in next year's talent show, if he had the courage. [Manuel may perform in next year's talent show, if he has the courage.]

Before You Read

PRESIDENT CLEVELAND, WHERE ARE YOU?

Make the Connection

Wanted: A Case of the "Wants"

This story is about eleven-year-old Jerry, who wants something so much that he's "half sick with longing" for it.

Quickwrite

What have you ever wanted so much that you couldn't get it out of your mind? Tell about a time when you wanted something so badly it hurt.

Elements of Literature

Sensory Details: The Uses of Description

Description is a kind of writing in which words are used to create pictures. To describe Jerry and his 1930s world, Robert Cormier uses

sensory details. Notice how he helps you see and even taste that five-cent package of gum: "pink sticks, three together, covered with a sweet white powder." On page 65, Cormier talks about how he learned to write description to "evoke scene and event and emotion."

Reading Skills and Strategies

Summarizing: Restating Important Events

Good readers stop from time to time as they read to summarize *what* has happened or to think about *why* something has happened. At three points in the story, you'll find this little picture: . When you come to these points, stop and sum up what has just happened. To summarize, follow these steps:

- Retell the major events in the order in which they happened.
- Sum up how each major event leads to the next.
- Sum up your understanding of *why* the characters behave as they do.

> **S**ensory details are details that appeal to one or more of the senses: sight, hearing, taste, smell, and touch.
>
> *For more on Description, see the Handbook of Literary Terms.*

Background

Literature and Social Studies

After the stock market crash of 1929, the United States plunged into the worst depression in its history. Banks closed, and industries stopped production. Millions of people found themselves jobless. In those days few government programs existed to help the needy. People depended on friends, relatives, or private charities for food and shelter.

In the 1930s, life was different in small ways as well. Boys and girls collected cowboy cards. Cowboys in the movies were big heroes then, just as sports stars and action figures are today.

go.hrw.com
LEO 6-1

PRESIDENT CLEVELAND, WHERE ARE YOU? **53**

OBJECTIVES

1. Read and interpret the story
2. Identify sensory details
3. Summarize the story
4. Express understanding through writing, speaking/listening
5. Identify vivid verbs and use such verbs in writing
6. Understand and use new words

SKILLS

Literary
- Identify sensory details

Reading
- Summarize the story

Writing
- Collect ideas for an auto-biographical incident
- Write from a different point of view

Speaking/Listening
- Role-play a moment from the story

Grammar/Language
- Use vivid verbs

Vocabulary
- Learn and use new words

Summarize
- Make a storyboard

Viewing/Representing (ATE)
- Discuss the time period depicted in a painting
- Compare the subjects of a painting with people of today

Planning

- **Block Schedule**
  Block Scheduling Lesson Plans with Pacing Guide
- **Traditional Schedule**
  Lesson Plans Including Strategies for English-Language Learners
- **One-Stop Planner**
  CD-ROM with Test Generator

Preteaching Vocabulary

Words to Own

Direct students' attention to the Words to Own and their definitions at the bottom of the story pages. Pronounce each word for the class as you point out its location. Because some of the words are relatively difficult to pronounce at first sight, you might want to take a few minutes to study the pronunciation keys in parentheses next to each word. Have volunteers read the words and their definitions aloud. Then divide students into groups of three or four and ask each group to brainstorm a story idea using any five (or more) of the vocabulary words. Their stories need not be fully plotted or characterized; accept any sketch of an idea for which the chosen vocabulary words make sense.

Summary ▪ ▪

For Jerry and his friends, who are growing up in a small town during the Great Depression of the 1930s, trading cowboy cards is serious business. When gum manufacturers suddenly switch to cards of the United States presidents, the boys change their focus, enticed by the prize of a free baseball glove for a complete set. Soon, Grover Cleveland is the only president missing from their collections. Jerry notices that his brother Armand is facing a different conflict: the older boy has fallen in love with a girl from the North Side, but he has no money to take her to the school dance. When Armand informs Jerry that on the North Side, Cleveland cards are abundant and Harding cards are in demand, Jerry sets off to capture the coveted Grover Cleveland. In the scene that follows, Armand has left for the dance, corsage under his arm and new shoes on his feet. Jerry has sacrificed the precious card—and risked losing favor with his friends—by selling the card to the unpopular spoiled rich boy in order to help out his brother. Ironically, although Jerry has faced a moment of truth and done the right thing, at the story's end he is still waiting to feel good about his deed.

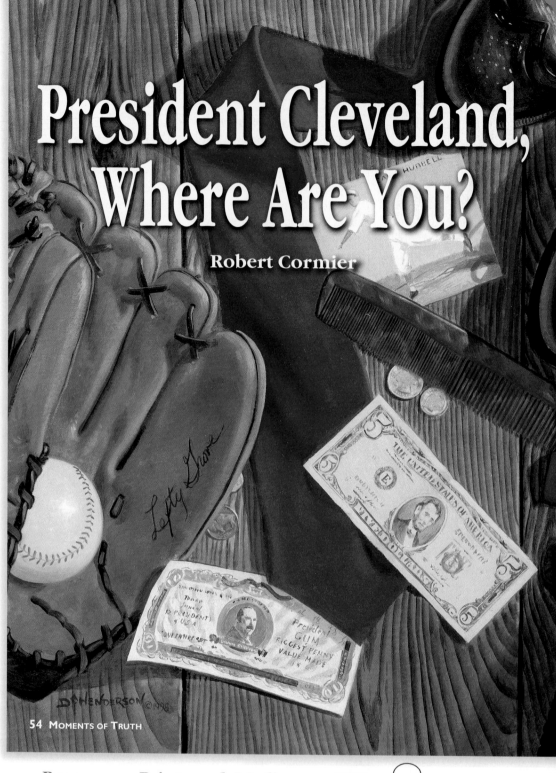

President Cleveland, Where Are You?

Robert Cormier

54 MOMENTS OF TRUTH

Resources

Listening
Audio CD Library
A recording of this story is provided in the *Audio CD Library:*
• Disc 2, Track 3

Selection Assessment
Formal Assessment
• Selection Test, p. 9
Test Generator
• Selection Test

Resources: Print and Media

Reading
• *Reading Skills and Strategies*
    MiniRead Skill Lesson, p. 76
    Selection Skill Lesson, p. 82
• *Graphic Organizers for Active Reading*, p. 5
• *Words to Own*, p. 4
• *Spelling and Decoding*, p. 5
• *Audio CD Library*
    Disc 2, Track 3

Writing and Language
• *Daily Oral Grammar*
    Transparency 5
• *Grammar and Language Links*
    Worksheet, p. 9

Viewing and Representing
• *Viewing and Representing*
    Fine Art Transparency 2
    Fine Art Worksheet, p. 8

Assessment
• *Formal Assessment*, p. 9
• *Portfolio Management System*, p. 109
• *Standardized Test Preparation*, pp. 18, 20
• *Test Generator (One-Stop Planner CD-ROM)*

Internet
• go.hrw.com (keyword: LE0 6-1)

You could almost hate Rollie Tremaine.

That was the autumn of the cowboy cards—Buck Jones and Tom Tyler and Hoot Gibson and especially Ken Maynard. The cards were available in those five-cent packages of gum: pink sticks, three together, covered with a sweet white powder. You couldn't blow bubbles with that particular gum, but it couldn't have mattered less. The cowboy cards were important—the pictures of those rock-faced men with eyes of blue steel.

On those wind-swept, leaf-tumbling afternoons, we gathered after school on the sidewalk in front of Lemire's Drugstore, across from St. Jude's Parochial School, and we swapped and bargained and matched for the cards. Because a Ken Maynard serial was playing at the Globe every Saturday afternoon, he was the most popular cowboy of all, and one of his cards was worth at least ten of any other kind. Rollie Tremaine had a treasure of thirty or so, and he guarded them jealously. He'd match you for the other cards, but he risked his Ken Maynards only when the other kids threatened to leave him out of the competition altogether.

You could almost hate Rollie Tremaine. In the first place, he was the only son of Auguste Tremaine, who operated the Uptown Dry Goods Store, and he did not live in a tenement but in a big white birthday cake of a house on Laurel Street. He was too fat to be effective in the football games between the Frenchtown Tigers and the North Side Knights, and he made us constantly aware of the jingle of coins in his pockets. He was able to stroll into Lemire's and casually select a quarter's worth of cowboy cards while the rest of us watched, aching with envy.

Once in a while I earned a nickel or dime

PRESIDENT CLEVELAND, WHERE ARE YOU? **55**

Background

Among the many differences students will notice between the 1930s and the present are differences in prices. In the story, it costs only ten cents to see a movie and only five cents to buy a candy bar. But because wages as well as prices were much lower during the Depression than they are today, a nickel or a dime might have made more of a dent in the family budget than the price of a movie or candy bar would today.

Ⓐ Elements of Literature
Metaphor
? Remind students that a metaphor is a comparison between two unlike things. In this case what is Rollie's house compared to? [a "big white birthday cake"] What does the house probably look like? [Possible responses: It is big; it has more than one or two stories; it is pretty to look at.]

Ⓑ Elements of Literature
Sensory Details
? What sense does the "jingle of coins" appeal to? [hearing]

Reaching All Students

Struggling Readers
Summarizing was introduced on p. 53. For a lesson directly tied to this story that teaches students to summarize by using a strategy called Somebody Wanted But So, see the *Reading Skills and Strategies* binder:
• MiniRead Skill Lesson, p. 76
• Selection Skill Lesson, p. 82

English Language Learners
Give students a summary of the story before they read. Then assign them short sections to read in full. For additional strategies for these students, see
• *Lesson Plans Including Strategies for English-Language Learners*

Advanced Learners
Encourage students to use the story as a springboard for research into aspects of the Depression era that intrigue them. For example, students may want to examine the economic factors that led to the Great Depression. They may want to know what life was like at its worst, or they may wish to find out what brought the greatest economic downturn in U.S. history to an end.

A **Struggling Readers**
Interpreting Idioms
"A millionaire, of sorts" is a relatively wealthy person; a person who is rich by certain standards. In this case, Jerry is rich only in comparison to his friends, and only in terms of cowboy cards.

B **English Language Learners**
Colloquialisms
This is a good opportunity to make sure students understand the basic colloquialisms for American coins: nickel, dime, and quarter, for five, ten, and twenty-five cents, respectively. You might have students solve a few change-making problems geared to their fluency levels. For example, "Louis buys forty cents' worth of candy. He gives the cashier two quarters. He gets one coin back. What is the coin?" [a dime]

C **Appreciating Language**
Vivid Verbs
❓ What verbs in this paragraph make you see and hear the action more vividly? [rushed, burst, slam]

D **Struggling Readers**
Finding Details
❓ Find the passage where the narrator's name is revealed. What is the narrator's name? [Jerry]

by running errands or washing windows for blind old Mrs. Belander, or by finding pieces of copper, brass, and other valuable metals at the dump and selling them to the junkman. The coins clutched in my hand, I would race to Lemire's to buy a cowboy card or two, hoping that Ken Maynard would stare boldly out at me as I opened the pack. At one time, before a disastrous matching session with Roger Lussier (my best friend, except where the cards were involved), I owned five Ken **A** Maynards and considered myself a millionaire, of sorts.

One week I was particularly lucky; I had spent two afternoons washing floors for Mrs. **B** Belander and received a quarter. Because my

father had worked a full week at the shop, where a rush order for fancy combs had been received, he <u>allotted</u> my brothers and sisters and me an extra dime along with the usual ten cents for the Saturday-afternoon movie. Setting aside the movie fare, I found myself with a bonus of thirty-five cents, and I then planned to put Rollie Tremaine to shame the following Monday afternoon.

Monday was the best day to buy the cards because the candy man stopped at Lemire's every Monday morning to deliver the new assortments. There was nothing more exciting in the world than a fresh batch of card boxes. I rushed home from school that day and hurriedly changed my clothes, eager to set off **C** for the store. As I burst through the doorway, letting the screen door slam behind me, my brother Armand blocked my way.

He was fourteen, three years older than I, and a freshman at Monument High School. He had recently become a stranger to me in many ways—<u>indifferent</u> to such matters as cowboy cards and the Frenchtown Tigers— and he carried himself with a mysterious dignity that was fractured now and then when his voice began shooting off in all directions like some kind of vocal fireworks.[1]

"Wait a minute, Jerry," he said. "I want to talk to you." He motioned me out of earshot **D** of my mother, who was busy supervising the usual after-school skirmish in the kitchen.

---

1. **vocal fireworks:** changing levels of sound—deep one minute, high the next. (Armand's voice is changing.)

WORDS TO OWN
allotted (ə·lät′id) v.: distributed to; gave as a share.
indifferent (in·dif′ər·ənt) adj.: having or showing no interest.

Using Students' Strengths

Visual Learners
Encourage students to use sensory details in the text as prompts for visualization. When they find such a detail, ask them to take the following steps: (1) close your eyes and take a few seconds to see the detail in your mind, (2) jot down the detail on paper, (3) tell classmates about the detail. Visual learners may also enjoy filling in the graphic organizer in *Graphic Organizers for Active Reading*, p. 5.

Kinesthetic Learners
Divide several decks of ordinary playing cards among students. Tell them to arrange one suit of cards in order from highest to lowest. After they examine their cards and decide on their suit, they should go around the room trading cards they do not need for ones they do. You may want to establish a prize or privilege for completing their suit so they learn how Jerry must have felt.

Interpersonal Learners
Have students work in groups of three or four to create a list of unfamiliar words (including the Words to Own). Each student should specialize in one portion of the story for this purpose. The group members then work together to define the words and assemble an alphabetical glossary for the story. Students who think they know the meaning of an unfamiliar word should suggest it; other students should check the meaning in a dictionary.

I sighed with impatience. In recent months Armand had become a figure of authority, siding with my father and mother occasionally. As the oldest son, he sometimes took advantage of his age and experience to issue rules and regulations.

"How much money have you got?" he whispered.

"You in some kind of trouble?" I asked, excitement rising in me as I remembered the blackmail plot of a movie at the Globe a month before.

He shook his head in annoyance. "Look," he said, "it's Pa's birthday tomorrow. I think we ought to chip in and buy him something. . . ."

I reached into my pocket and caressed the coins. "Here," I said carefully, pulling out a nickel. "If we all give a nickel, we should have enough to buy him something pretty nice."

He regarded me with contempt. "Rita already gave me fifteen cents, and I'm throwing in a quarter. Albert handed over a dime—all that's left of his birthday money. Is that all you can do—a nickel?"

"Aw, come on," I protested. "I haven't got a single Ken Maynard left, and I was going to buy some cards this afternoon."

"Ken Maynard!" he snorted. "Who's more important—him or your father?"

His question was unfair because he knew that there was no possible choice—"my father" had to be the only answer. My father was a huge man who believed in the things of the spirit. . . . He had worked at the Monument Comb Shop since the age of fourteen; his booming laugh—or grumble—greeted us each night when he returned from the factory.

A steady worker when the shop had enough work, he quickened with gaiety on Friday nights and weekends, . . . and he was fond of making long speeches about the good things in life. In the middle of the Depression, for instance, he paid cash for a piano, of all things, and insisted that my twin sisters, Yolande and Yvette, take lessons once a week.

I took a dime from my pocket and handed it to Armand.

"Thanks, Jerry," he said. "I hate to take your last cent."

"That's all right," I replied, turning away and consoling myself with the thought that twenty cents was better than nothing at all.

When I arrived at Lemire's, I sensed disaster in the air. Roger Lussier was kicking disconsolately at a tin can in the gutter, and Rollie Tremaine sat sullenly on the steps in front of the store.

"Save your money," Roger said. He had known about my plans to splurge on the cards.

"What's the matter?" I asked.

"There's no more cowboy cards," Rollie Tremaine said. "The company's not making any more."

"They're going to have President cards," Roger said, his face twisting with disgust. He pointed to the store window. "Look!"

A placard in the window announced: "Attention, Boys. Watch for the New Series. Presidents of the United States. Free in Each 5-Cent Package of Caramel Chew."

"President cards?" I asked, dismayed.

I read on: "Collect a Complete Set and Receive an Official Imitation Major League Baseball Glove, Embossed with Lefty Grove's Autograph."

Glove or no glove, who could become excited about Presidents, of all things?

E Elements of Literature
Conflict
What is Jerry's conflict, or problem, here? [He must choose between buying baseball cards and chipping in for his father's gift.]

F Critical Thinking
Hypothesizing
What might Jerry mean by "the things of the spirit?" [Possible responses: religion; hard work and sacrifice; the nonmaterial good things of life, such as family and friends, as opposed to money and possessions.]

G Elements of Literature
Sensory Details
What sensory details tell Jerry that there is "disaster in the air?" [Roger was kicking a tin can; Rollie sat sullenly on the steps.]

H Critical Thinking
Interpreting
What is the "disaster" that Jerry sensed when he sees his friends appearing so dejected? [The company has stopped making cowboy cards and has started making president cards; the boys are not excited about the president cards.] Do you think the subjects of the cards actually matter? [Yes, cowboys were heroes then, so they are the figures the boys admire most; no, trading cards is simply a diversion, so it doesn't matter who is printed on the front.]

I Cultural Connections
Trading cards became popular in the mid-1930s when gum companies began producing a waxed-paper package containing three sticks of bubble gum and a trading card. The cards featured sports figures; superheroes such as Superman; and, later, radio and television personalities.

Crossing the Curriculum

Social Studies
Provide each student with a list of the presidents in chronological order. Ask each student to find two facts about any five presidents. Place sheets of paper with each president's name around the room, and encourage students to fill in the sheets with the facts they researched. If students' facts already appear on the sheets, have them place a star next to that fact on the sheet. Afterward, assemble and display all the fact sheets.

Art
You might do this activity in conjunction with the preceding Social Studies activity. Have each student choose a president to research and draw. Students should work on large paper and then use a photocopier to reduce their drawings to the size of collectors' cards (about 2" X 3"). On the backs of the cards, ask students to write pertinent facts about the presidents.

Mathematics/Economics
Point out the amounts of money that Armand collects from his siblings to buy his father a birthday present. Then have students look in an encyclopedia or book on the Depression to find the prices of common objects such as shoes, toothbrushes, books, or food. Ask students to create a catalog showing a few items and their prices then and now. Catalogs may be simple lists, or may include illustrations and words.

School, This Year Means More Than Ever Before (Boys on Bicycles) (1921) by Norman Rockwell. Oil on canvas (26″ x 22″).

Rollie Tremaine stared at the sign. "Benjamin Harrison,[2] for crying out loud," he said. "Why would I want Benjamin Harrison when I've got twenty-two Ken Maynards?"

I felt the warmth of guilt creep over me. I jingled the coins in my pocket, but the sound was hollow. No more Ken Maynards to buy.

"I'm going to buy a Mr. Goodbar," Rollie Tremaine decided.

I was without appetite, indifferent even to a Baby Ruth, which was my favorite. I thought of how I had betrayed Armand and, worst of all, my father.

"I'll see you after supper," I called over my shoulder to Roger as I hurried away toward home. I took the shortcut behind the church, although it involved leaping over a tall

---

2. **Benjamin Harrison** (1833–1901): twenty-third president of the United States.

wooden fence, and I zigzagged recklessly through Mr. Thibodeau's garden, trying to outrace my guilt. I pounded up the steps and into the house, only to learn that Armand had already taken Yolande and Yvette uptown to shop for the birthday present.

Ⓐ I pedaled my bike furiously through the streets, ignoring the <u>indignant</u> horns of automobiles as I sliced through the traffic. Finally I saw Armand and my sisters emerge from the Monument Men's Shop. My heart sank when I spied the long, slim package that Armand was holding.

"Did you buy the present yet?" I asked, although I knew it was too late.

"Just now. A blue tie," Armand said. "What's the matter?"

"Nothing," I replied, my chest hurting.

He looked at me for a long moment. At first his eyes were hard, but then they softened. He smiled at me, almost sadly, and touched my arm. I turned away from him because I felt naked and exposed.

"It's all right," he said gently. "Maybe you've learned something." The words were gentle, but they held a curious dignity, the dignity remaining even when his voice suddenly cracked on the last syllable.

Ⓑ I wondered what was happening to me, because I did not know whether to laugh or cry.

Sister Angela was amazed when, a week before Christmas vacation, everybody in the class submitted a history essay worthy of a high mark—in some cases as high as A minus. (Sister Angela did not believe that

WORDS TO OWN
indignant (in·dig′nənt) *adj.*: angry because of something thought to be not right or unfair.

Photograph Courtesy of American Illustrators Gallery, New York, New York.

anyone in the world ever deserved an A.) She never learned—or at least she never let on that she knew—we all had become experts on the Presidents because of the cards we purchased at Lemire's. Each card contained a picture of a President and, on the reverse side, a summary of his career. We looked at those cards so often that the biographies imprinted themselves on our minds without effort. Even our street-corner conversations were filled with such information as the fact that James Madison was called "The Father of the Constitution," or that John Adams had intended to become a minister.

The President cards were a roaring success, and the cowboy cards were quickly forgotten. In the first place, we did not receive gum with the cards, but a kind of chewy caramel. The caramel could be tucked into a corner of your mouth, bulging your cheek in much the same manner as wads of tobacco bulged the mouths of baseball stars. In the second place, the competition for collecting the cards was fierce and frustrating—fierce because everyone was intent on being the first to send away for a baseball glove and frustrating because although there were only thirty-two Presidents, including Franklin Delano Roosevelt,[3] the variety at Lemire's was at a minimum. When the deliveryman left the boxes of cards at the store each Monday, we often discovered that one entire box was devoted to a single President—two weeks in a row the boxes contained nothing but Abraham Lincolns. One week Roger Lussier and I were the heroes of Frenchtown. We journeyed on our bicycles to the North Side, engaged three boys in a matching bout, and returned with five

3. **Franklin Delano Roosevelt** (1882–1945): Roosevelt was president at the time of this story.

new Presidents, including Chester Alan Arthur, who up to that time had been missing.

Perhaps to sharpen our desire, the card company sent a sample glove to Mr. Lemire, and it dangled, orange and sleek, in the window. I was half sick with longing, thinking of my old glove at home, which I had inherited from Armand. But Rollie Tremaine's desire for the glove outdistanced my own. He even got Mr. Lemire to agree to give the glove in the window to the first person to get a complete set of cards, so that precious time wouldn't be wasted waiting for the postman.

We were delighted at Rollie Tremaine's frustration, especially since he was only a substitute player for the Tigers. Once, after spending fifty cents on cards—all of which turned out to be Calvin Coolidge—he threw them to the ground, pulled some dollar bills out of his pocket, and said, "The heck with it. I'm going to buy a glove!"

"Not that glove," Roger Lussier said. "Not a glove with Lefty Grove's autograph. Look what it says at the bottom of the sign."

We all looked, although we knew the words by heart: "This Glove Is Not For Sale Anywhere."

Rollie Tremaine scrambled to pick up the cards from the sidewalk, pouting more than ever. After that he was quietly obsessed with the Presidents, hugging the cards close to his chest and refusing to tell us how many more he needed to complete his set.

I too was obsessed with the cards, because they had become things of comfort in a world that had suddenly grown dismal. After Christmas, a layoff at the shop had thrown

WORDS TO OWN

obsessed (əb·sest′) v. used as adj.: thinking about too much.

PRESIDENT CLEVELAND, WHERE ARE YOU? **59**

C **Struggling Readers**
Finding Details

❓ Why are the new cards a success? [They contain caramel that makes the boys look like baseball players chewing tobacco, the prize for collecting a complete set is a new baseball glove, and the competition is fierce because of the limited supply.]

D **Elements of Literature**
Sensory Details

❓ What words and phrases make the description of the glove in the window memorable? ["it dangled, orange and sleek"] What sense does the description appeal to? [sight]

E **Advanced Learners**
Interpreting

❓ Why is Rollie Tremaine's desire for the glove so strong? [Possible responses: as a form of revenge, since he probably knows the other boys do not like him; because he is spoiled and used to getting what he wants.]

Resources ————

Viewing and Representing
Fine Art Transparency
Have students apply what they have learned about conflict and "Moments of Truth" to the interpretation of *Afternoon Shadows* by Robert Vickery.
• Transparency 2
• Worksheet, p. 8

Getting Students Involved

Enrichment Activities

Strategic Reading. Have students work with partners in a Reciprocal-Teaching exercise. Divide the text into manageable sections, and ask students to take turns reading aloud to their partners. At the end of each section, the listener asks the reader questions about the portion just read. The reader tries to answer the questions. When questions cannot be answered

by either student, have students jot down the questions to ask during class discussion. After each section is read, partners switch roles of reader and listener. You may wish to model this exercise for students before they begin.

Found Poem. Have students work in groups of three to create a Found Poem about the story. Invite each student to find in the text at least

five sensory details, images, or vivid words that were memorable. Then have each group choose and list five of its members' choices. When the groups have finished choosing and listing, have them take turns reading aloud a line at a time from its lists. Record the reading and play it back to the class after each group has read all of its lines.

Across the Strip (1929) by John Kane.

The Phillips Collection, Washington, D.C.

RESPONDING TO THE ART

John Kane, a Scottish American regionalist painter, painted this scene of a section of Pittsburgh, the subject of many of his works in the 1920s and 1930s, showing tenement buildings, factories, a bridge, and the less crowded hills beyond.

Activities

1. Think of words that describe the city in the picture. [Possible responses: cramped, smoggy, small, industrial.]

2. How is this city similar to or different from your town or city? [Answers will vary.]

3. Does this city look like the town you imagined in the story? Why or why not? [Possible responses: Yes, because it is from the same era; no, I pictured a smaller town.]

A Elements of Literature

Characterization

? How would you describe Jerry's father, on the basis of what Jerry says about him? [Possible responses: He is hard-working, proud; responsible.]

my father out of work. He received no paycheck for four weeks, and the only income we had was from Armand's after-school job at the Blue and White Grocery Store—a job he lost finally when business dwindled as the layoff continued.

Although we had enough food and clothing—my father's credit had always been good, a matter of pride with him—the inactivity made my father restless and irritable. . . . The twins fell sick and went to the hospital to have their tonsils removed. My fa-

ther was confident that he would return to work eventually and pay off his debts, but he seemed to age before our eyes.

When orders again were received at the comb shop and he returned to work, another disaster occurred, although I was the only one aware of it. Armand fell in love.

I discovered his situation by accident,

WORDS TO OWN

dwindled (dwin'dəld) *v.*: steadily shrank; became less and less or smaller and smaller.

60 MOMENTS OF TRUTH

Skill Link

Identifying Verbs

Ask students what the following words have in common: *sell, give, throw, collect, chew.* [All express physical actions.] Then ask what the following words have in common: *think, feel, imagine, dream, remember.* [All express mental actions.] Explain that all ten of those words are verbs. Verbs can express physical or mental actions. Verbs can also express states of being. The verbs *be* and *become* are state-of-being verbs. Some verbs can be used as either action verbs

or as state-of-being verbs. For example:

Armand **looked** for a present for his father. [action]

Armand **looked** angry. [being]

Some words can be used as verbs or as other parts of speech. For example:

Jerry is going to **trade** a Warren G. Harding card for a Grover Cleveland card. [verb]

Exchanging a Harding card for a Cleveland card was a good **trade.** [noun]

Activity

Write the following sentences on the chalkboard or read them aloud twice, slowly. Have students identify the verb or verbs in each.

1. Jerry loved cowboy cards. [loved]

2. Jerry loved to collect cowboy cards. [loved; collect]

3. The company began to make president cards. [began; make]

4. Jerry suggested a trade. [suggested]

T60

when I happened to pick up a piece of paper that had fallen to the floor in the bedroom he and I shared. I frowned at the paper, puzzled.

"Dear Sally, When I look into your eyes the world stands still . . ."

The letter was snatched from my hands before I finished reading it.

"What's the big idea, snooping around?" Armand asked, his face crimson. "Can't a guy have any privacy?"

He had never mentioned privacy before. "It was on the floor," I said. "I didn't know it was a letter. Who's Sally?"

He flung himself across the bed. "You tell anybody and I'll muckalize you," he threatened. "Sally Knowlton."

> ### Another disaster occurred, although I was the only one aware of it. Armand fell in love.

Nobody in Frenchtown had a name like Knowlton.

"A girl from the North Side?" I asked, incredulous.

He rolled over and faced me, anger in his eyes, and a kind of despair, too.

"What's the matter with that? Think she's too good for me?" he asked. "I'm warning you, Jerry, if you tell anybody . . ."

"Don't worry," I said. Love had no particular place in my life; it seemed an unnecessary waste of time. And a girl from the North Side was so remote that for all practical purposes she did not exist. But I was curious. "What are you writing her a letter for? Did she leave town or something?"

"She hasn't left town," he answered. "I wasn't going to send it. I just felt like writing to her."

I was glad that I had never become involved with love—love that brought desperation to your eyes, that caused you to write letters you did not plan to send. Shrugging with indifference, I began to search in the closet for the old baseball glove. I found it on the shelf, under some old sneakers. The webbing was torn and the padding gone. I thought of the sting I would feel when a sharp grounder slapped into the glove, and I winced.

"You tell anybody about me and Sally and I'll——"

"I know. You'll muckalize me."

I did not divulge his secret and often shared his agony, particularly when he sat at the supper table and left my mother's special butterscotch pie untouched. I had never realized before how terrible love could be. But my compassion was short-lived, because I had other things to worry about: report cards due at Eastertime; the loss of income from old Mrs. Belander, who had gone to live with a daughter in Boston; and, of course, the Presidents.

Because a stalemate had been reached, the President cards were the dominant force in our lives—mine, Roger Lussier's, and Rollie Tremaine's. For three weeks, as the baseball season approached, each of us had a complete set—complete except for one President, Grover Cleveland. Each time a box of cards arrived at the store, we hurriedly

---

WORDS TO OWN

incredulous (in·krej'oo·ləs) *adj.*: unbelieving.
divulge (də·vulj') *v.*: reveal.
stalemate (stāl'māt') *n.*: situation in which no side can win; a draw.

PRESIDENT CLEVELAND, WHERE ARE YOU? **61**

Making the Connections

Cultural Connections: "Parochial Schools"

If you teach in a public school, some of your students may not know that a parochial school is a private elementary or secondary school that is funded and maintained by members of a particular religious group. Students and faculty at a parochial school are usually, but not always, members of the religious denomination that supports the school. In the United States, most parochial schools are maintained by the Roman Catholic church. The word *parochial* is the adjective form of the noun *parish* and derives its meaning from the fact that Catholic churches are organized into local parishes. Many Protestant denominations also maintain private schools, as do other religions. Jewish private schools are called *yeshivas* or, in Hebrew, *yeshivot*. Parochial school students are instructed in religion and in other subjects.

A Historical Connections

Grover Cleveland is the only U.S. president to be elected for two nonconsecutive terms. He was first elected president in 1884. In his 1888 bid for a second term, Cleveland lost the electoral vote to Benjamin Harrison even though he had won the popular vote. After a brief retirement, Cleveland ran again in 1892 and defeated Harrison.

B Appreciating Language
Vivid Verbs

? What vivid verbs make the action in this paragraph more dramatic? [*stormed, protested, vowed, muttering*]

C Elements of Literature
Sensory Details

? Here's an opportunity for you to supply a sensory detail the author did not include. What detail appealing to the sense of hearing might accompany the description of the tobacco tin being thrown? [its clatter against the pavement]

D Reading Skills and Strategies
Summarizing

Have students summarize the events that have just occurred. Summaries should mention that while Jerry and his friends lack Grover Cleveland cards, a nearby neighborhood lacks Warren G. Harding cards, thus setting up a possibility for a trade. Summaries may also include Armand's dejection over lacking the money to take Sally to a dance and Armand's helping Jerry fix a flat bicycle tire.

---

bought them (as hurriedly as our funds allowed) and tore off the wrappers, only to be confronted by James Monroe or Martin Van Buren or someone else. But never Grover Cleveland, never the man who had been the twenty-second *and* the twenty-fourth President of the United States. We argued about Grover Cleveland. Should he be placed between Chester Alan Arthur and Benjamin

> **A** *"Pa's got too many worries now to buy me new shoes or give me money for flowers for a girl."*

Harrison as the twenty-second President, or did he belong between Benjamin Harrison and William McKinley as the twenty-fourth President? Was the card company playing fair? Roger Lussier brought up a horrifying possibility—did we need *two* Grover Clevelands to complete the set?

B Indignant, we stormed Lemire's and protested to the harassed store owner, who had long since vowed never to stock a new series. Muttering angrily, he searched his bills and receipts for a list of rules.

"All right," he announced. "Says here you only need one Grover Cleveland to finish the set. Now get out, all of you, unless you've got money to spend."

C Outside the store, Rollie Tremaine picked up an empty tobacco tin and scaled it across the street. "Boy," he said. "I'd give five dollars for a Grover Cleveland."

When I returned home, I found Armand sitting on the piazza[4] steps, his chin in his hands. His mood of dejection mirrored my own, and I sat down beside him. We did not say anything for a while.

4. **piazza** (pē·az′ə): large, covered porch.

62 MOMENTS OF TRUTH

"Want to throw the ball around?" I asked.

He sighed, not bothering to answer.

"You sick?" I asked.

He stood up and hitched up his trousers, pulled at his ear, and finally told me what the matter was—there was a big dance next week at the high school, the Spring Promenade, and Sally had asked him to be her escort.

I shook my head at the folly of love. "Well, what's so bad about that?"

"How can I take Sally to a fancy dance?" he asked desperately. "I'd have to buy her a corsage. . . . And my shoes are practically falling apart. Pa's got too many worries now to buy me new shoes or give me money for flowers for a girl."

I nodded in sympathy. "Yeah," I said. "Look at me. Baseball time is almost here, and all I've got is that old glove. And no Grover Cleveland card yet . . ."

"Grover Cleveland?" he asked. "They've got some of those up on the North Side. Some kid was telling me there's a store that's got them. He says they're looking for Warren G. Harding."

"Holy smoke!" I said. "I've got an extra Warren G. Harding!" Pure joy sang in my veins. I ran to my bicycle, swung into the seat—and found that the front tire was flat.

"I'll help you fix it," Armand said.

Within half an hour I was at the North Side Drugstore, where several boys were matching **D** cards on the sidewalk. Silently but blissfully I shouted: President Grover Cleveland, here I come!

Taking a Second Look

Review: Comparing and Contrasting Cultures

Remind students that to compare two things is to find similarities between them, and to contrast two things is to find differences between them. If students read "Ta-Na-E-Ka" (pp. 15–29), they practiced comparing and contrasting Kaw and mainstream U.S. cultures. They also compared and contrasted cultures over time, by examining twentieth-century Kaw culture in relation to traditional Kaw culture.

Activity

1. Have students compare their own present-day culture and the small-town American culture of the Depression era.

2. Ask students to brainstorm differences and similarities they find between Jerry's world and their own. Have a volunteer keep a record of students' ideas.

MVPs—Most Valuable Primates

What connection could apes possibly have with trading cards? If you've ever visited Zoo Atlanta, you might know. Like baseball players and presidents in "President Cleveland, Where Are You?," the gorillas at Zoo Atlanta are featured on trading cards. Gorilla Trading Cards were created by Zoo Atlanta with the help of *The Atlanta Journal & Constitution.*

The aim of the cards is to help people appreciate this majestic endangered species. Most cards show a single member of the zoo's large collection of lowland gorillas. Listed on the back of each card are facts about the life and history of the gorilla, much like the statistics on the back of a baseball card. The cards introduce collectors to gorillas like Willie B., six feet tall and 415 pounds, and his daughter Kudzoo, who was born at the zoo in 1994.

Collecting gorilla cards is more than just fun. By increasing our knowledge and awareness of gorillas, the cards give the threatened species a better chance of survival.

Zoo Atlanta

Willie B.

Kudzoo

LITERATURE AND SCIENCE

Encourage students to look up basic facts about gorillas, such as their body size, habits, diet, habitat, and the causes of their endangerment. You might also invite volunteers to perform similar research for the other great apes (chimpanzees, bonobos, orangutans, and gibbons) and for other endangered species that interest them. Then have students discuss the following questions.

1. How do you think Gorilla Trading Cards will help save the endangered species? [Possible responses: They will make the public aware that something must be done to preserve the gorillas; by presenting gorillas as individuals, people may come to care about them more and therefore do more to help them.]

2. What other endangered species would you put on trading cards if you could? [Possible responses: wolves, whales, pandas, tigers, eagles.]

3. Suppose there are endangered species that aren't as popular as gorillas or as the other species you've named, because they aren't as cute or exciting. What should be done to help them? [Possible responses: educate the public; donate money to wildlife preservation.]

Resources

Assessment

• *Standardized Test Preparation*, p. 18

Making the Connections

Connecting to the Theme: "Moments of Truth"

Ask students to think about this story and to discuss why it is included in a collection called "Moments of Truth." [Possible response: Jerry has to face the truth about himself—that he has not been as generous with his family as he could have been, and that his preoccupation with trading cards is childish in comparison to his obligations to his loved ones. Jerry's father and brother have to face the truth about their loss of jobs and income. And in the end, Jerry has to face other truths: that you can't always get what you want; that you sometimes have to choose between two wishes, and that making the right choice doesn't necessarily make you happy.]

T63

After Armand had left for the dance, all dressed up as if it were Sunday, the small green box containing the corsage under his arm, I sat on the railing of the piazza, letting my feet dangle. The neighborhood was quiet because the Frenchtown Tigers were at Daggett's Field, practicing for the first baseball game of the season.

I thought of Armand and the ridiculous expression on his face when he'd stood before the mirror in the bedroom. I'd avoided looking at his new black shoes. "Love," I muttered.

Spring had arrived in a sudden stampede of apple blossoms and fragrant breezes. Windows had been thrown open and dust mops had banged on the sills all day long as the women busied themselves with housecleaning. I was puzzled by my lethargy. Wasn't spring supposed to make everything bright and gay?

I turned at the sound of footsteps on the stairs. Roger Lussier greeted me with a sour face.

"I thought you were practicing with the Tigers," I said.

"Rollie Tremaine," he said. "I just couldn't stand him." He slammed his fist against the railing. "Jeez, why did *he* have to be the one to get a Grover Cleveland? You should see him showing off. He won't let anybody even touch that glove. . . ."

I felt like Benedict Arnold[5] and knew that I had to confess what I had done.

"Roger," I said, "I got a Grover Cleveland card up on the North Side. I sold it to Rollie Tremaine for five dollars."

"Are you crazy?" he asked.

---

5. **Benedict Arnold** (1741-1801): American Revolutionary War general famous for becoming a traitor.

64 MOMENTS OF TRUTH

"I needed that five dollars. It was an—an emergency."

"Boy!" he said, looking down at the ground and shaking his head. "What did you have to do a thing like that for?"

I watched him as he turned away and began walking down the stairs.

"Hey, Roger!" I called.

He squinted up at me as if I were a stranger, someone he'd never seen before.

"What?" he asked, his voice flat.

"I had to do it," I said. "Honest."

He didn't answer. He headed toward the fence, searching for the board we had loosened to give us a secret passage.

I thought of my father and Armand and Rollie Tremaine and Grover Cleveland and wished that I could go away someplace far away. But there was no place to go.

Roger found the loose slat in the fence and slipped through. I felt betrayed: Weren't you supposed to feel good when you did something fine and noble?

A moment later, two hands gripped the top of the fence and Roger's face appeared. "Was it a real emergency?" he yelled.

"A real one!" I called. "Something important!"

His face dropped from sight and his voice reached me across the yard: "All right."

"See you tomorrow!" I yelled.

I swung my legs over the railing again. The gathering dusk began to soften the sharp edges of the fence, the rooftops, the distant church steeple. I sat there a long time, waiting for the good feeling to come.

WORDS TO OWN

lethargy (leth′ər·jē) *n.*: feeling of dullness and tiredness.

Skill Link

MEET THE WRITER

A Marvelous Moment

Like his character Jerry, **Robert Cormier** (1925–2000) grew up in a small town during the Great Depression. Also like Jerry, Cormier was part of a big French American family, and his father worked in a comb and brush factory. About his writing, Cormier said:

66 There's a sentence in 'President Cleveland, Where Are You?' which is probably the most significant I have written in terms of my development as a writer. The sentence echoes back to a lost and half-forgotten story I wrote in the days when I was scribbling stories in pencil at the kitchen table. The story was about a boy from the poorer section of town who falls desperately in love with a girl from the other side of town, where the people live—or so he thinks—grandly and affluently. The story was told in the first person, the story's narrator was a twelve-year-old boy.

The problem concerned description. The narrator (and I, the writer) faced the problem of describing the girl's house, a thing of grandeur and beauty, white and shining, alien to the three-story tenement building in which the boy lived. How to describe such a house? I knew little about architecture, next to nothing at all. 99

After much thought, Cormier hit on the solution:

66 Forget architecture—what did the house look like? Not what did it *really* look like, but what did it look like to this twelve-year-old boy? 99

Yes, that was the key—the viewpoint of the boy and not the writer. And from somewhere the description came. It looked like a big white birthday cake of a house! I knew this was exactly the kind of image I had sought. I felt the way Columbus must have felt when he sighted land.

In that moment, I had discovered simile and metaphor, had learned that words were truly tools, that figures of speech were not just something fancy to dress up a piece of prose but words that could evoke scene and event and emotion. Until that discovery at the kitchen table I had been intimidated [frightened] by much of what I encountered in books of grammar, including the definitions of similes and metaphors. Suddenly, the definitions didn't matter. What mattered was using them to enrich my stories—not in a 'Look, Ma, how clever I am' way, but to sharpen images, pin down emotions, create shocks of recognition in the reader.

At any rate, the story of the boy and the birthday cake of a house has been lost through the years. I doubt if it was ever published. In 'President Cleveland, Where Are You?' I resurrected the description. It occurs in the second sentence of the third paragraph, a tribute to a marvelous moment in my hesitant journey toward becoming a writer. 99

More Marvelous Moments

Cormier is famous for his novels about young adults struggling with difficult problems. Two of his award-winning novels are *The Chocolate War* and *I Am the Cheese* (both Dell).

PRESIDENT CLEVELAND, WHERE ARE YOU? 65

BROWSING IN THE FILES

About the Author. Robert Cormier said he never got chosen for a baseball team as a boy because he was usually out under a tree reading. Cormier began his career at a radio station writing commercials, and later he worked as a journalist. After several years writing news, he began to write books and stories for young people and adults. His books have been translated into many languages, consistently winning awards and appearing on lists of the best books for young adults. In 1983, his novel *I Am the Cheese* was made into a movie, and Cormier played the small role of a journalist.

Writers on Writing. Cormier thought of himself as a rewriter rather than a writer: "With each novel, I fill a shopping bag of material that has been rewritten. I think for every page that appears finally in the finished product there are probably three to four pages that don't."

He found that writing had many rewards, including getting letters from his readers. They asked many questions, a fact that showed him that his work had affected their lives.

Assessing Learning

Check Test: Short Answers

1. What is Jerry's best friend's name? [Roger]
2. What are the boys in this story collecting? [cowboy cards and president cards]
3. What is the prize for collecting a complete set of president cards? [a baseball glove]
4. What does Armand need before he can go to the dance at the high school? [money to buy a corsage for Sally and new shoes for himself]
5. How does Armand get the money? [Jerry sells his prize-winning Grover Cleveland card to Rollie and gives the money to Armand.]

Standardized Test Preparation

For practice with standardized test format specific to this selection, see
• *Standardized Test Preparation*, p. 20
For practice in proofreading and editing, see
• *Daily Oral Grammar*, Transparency 5

MAKING MEANINGS

First Thoughts

1. Possible responses: Yes, because I value my family most of all and I wouldn't care about trading cards; no, because in my family we learn to rely on ourselves and not ask others for help.

Shaping Interpretations

2. He feels guilty for not giving all his money to Armand to help buy their father a birthday gift.

3. Possible response: If you do something selfish, you may feel bad about it later.

4. Armand wants to have new shoes and to be able to buy flowers for Sally, but he has no money, and he doesn't want to ask his father for money.

5. Jerry wants the Grover Cleveland card to complete the set that would win him the prize baseball glove. When he gets the card, he is happy but has mixed feelings because he realizes he ought to sell it rather than take the prize. He sells it to someone he doesn't like because that person, Rollie Tremaine, has the money to buy it, and helping Armand with the money has become more important to him.

6. Jerry wanted the glove so much that, when he doesn't get it, he is very disappointed. Opinions on whether he will ever feel good about it will vary; some students may suggest that he will feel good about it as an adult.

Connecting with the Text

7. Possible response: The prices of goods are out of date, but baseball and other cards are traded today; falling in love and being loyal to your family are universal. Envy, wanting something badly, making a sacrifice, disappointment—these could all be part of someone's life today.

8. Possible responses: I would have reacted in the same way as Roger, who was unaware of the reason for Jerry's action; I would have reacted differently, since the card belonged to Jerry and what to do with it was his choice alone.

T66

MAKING MEANINGS

First Thoughts

[respond]

1. If you were Jerry, would you have made the same sacrifice for Armand? Why or why not?

Shaping Interpretations

[interpret]

2. When Jerry learns that Lemire's store will sell president cards rather than cowboy cards, he says, "I felt the warmth of guilt creep over me." Why do you think Jerry feels guilty?

[analyze]

3. When Jerry finds that his brother and sisters have already bought their father's gift, Armand says, "Maybe you've learned something." What do you think Jerry might have learned in this moment of truth?

[identify]

4. Describe the **conflict** Armand experiences when Sally asks him to the spring dance. (What does he want? What is keeping him from getting it?)

[analyze]

5. What does Jerry want more than anything else? How does he feel when he gets it? Why does he sell it to someone he doesn't even like?

[speculate]

6. At the end Jerry says, "I sat there a long time, waiting for the good feeling to come." Why doesn't he feel good right away? Do you think Jerry ever *will* feel good about what he did?

Connecting with the Text

[connect]

7. Are any of the events and details in the story too old-fashioned to appear in a story written today? Could any of them appear in any place and at any time? Which events and details could be part of your life today?

[respond]

8. If you were Jerry's best friend, Roger, how would you react to the news that Jerry sold the Grover Cleveland card to Rollie Tremaine? What would you say to Jerry?

Challenging the Text

[evaluate]

9. In this story, Jerry makes a great sacrifice for his brother. Did you find his action believable? Does Armand deserve this good turn?

Reading Check

a. Why does Jerry say "You could almost hate Rollie Tremaine"?

b. What is the topic of the essays that amaze Sister Angela?

c. What two disasters occur while Jerry is collecting president cards?

d. What does Jerry finally do with the president card he has so longed for?

Challenging the Text

9. Possible responses: Yes, it's believable because Jerry is at an age when he is starting to think about things in a more mature way; no, it's not believable, because brothers are often antagonistic. Armand deserves it because he demonstrated generosity and self-sacrifice when purchasing their father's birthday gift and his income supported the family when the father was laid off.

Reading Check

a. Rollie has more money than the other boys.
b. U.S. presidents
c. Jerry's father loses his job and Armand falls in love.
d. He sells it to Rollie Tremaine for five dollars in order to help his brother go to the dance with Sally.

CHOICES: Building Your Portfolio

Writer's Notebook

1. Collecting Ideas for an Autobiographical Incident

Write briefly about one of the following events or a related event. Why was this event important to you? You might want to include **sensory details:** What sights, sounds, tastes, smells, or textures do you connect with this occasion? Check your Quickwrite notes for ideas.

- a time when a friend or family member proved his or her love in a special way

- a time when you were very scared, happy, or angry

The time I didn't stick up for my little sister when a popular girl from my class was making fun of her
Later—felt angry with myself, cowardly

Summarizing

2. What Happened? Why Did It Happen?

As you read, you may have stopped at key points to sum up what has just happened and to explain why characters behave the way they do. Now, skim the story, and review your notes. With a partner, make a storyboard showing what happens in *one* of the three main parts of the story (each part ends with a little picture of an open book). A **storyboard** is a series of pictures (they do not have to be perfect pictures— stick figures are fine) showing what happens in a narrative. For your storyboard, write three or four sentences summarizing what has happened in that part of the story. Be sure to explain why you think things happened the way they did.

Creative Writing

3. My Side of the Story

This story is told by Jerry. He is the "I" of the story. Now, let Armand tell his side of the story. Armand will be the "I." You might begin when Armand looks at himself in the mirror before he goes to the dance (page 64). Be sure to let Armand reveal his feelings about both Sally and Jerry.

Speaking and Listening

4. What Really Happened?

Two important moments in the story are never described. What happens when Jerry offers to sell the President Cleveland card to Rollie Tremaine? What happens when Jerry offers the money from the trade to Armand? You decide. With a partner, choose one of the moments, and role-play what the two characters might have said to each other. Practice your role-playing until you feel ready to perform for the class.

Rubrics for each Choices assignment appear on p. 109 in the *Portfolio Management System.*

CHOICES: Building Your Portfolio

1. **Writer's Notebook**   Have students work on this activity independently, taking two to five minutes to prepare by jotting down any sensory details they can remember. Remind students to save their work. They may use it as prewriting for the Writer's Workshop on pp. 86–90.

2. **Summarizing**   A natural way for pairs to divide their labor is for one partner to draw the pictures and for the other to write the sentences. However, if partners feel comfortable with both skills, they may prefer to alternate tasks.

3. **Creative Writing**   Have students organize their thoughts by jotting down the main events in the order Armand might retell them. Have students include Armand's feelings about each event. Students may wish to use a two-column chart like the one below.

Event	Armand's Feelings

4. **Speaking and Listening**   Suggest that students work in pairs to write a short script of the dialogue they imagine occurred between the two characters in the scene. Have students use the script to rehearse the role-playing that they will perform in front of the class. Students need not memorize the script.

Using Students' Strengths

Kinesthetic Learners

Before students write Armand's story from his point of view for Choice 3, have them act out the scenes they will write about. Assign each student a part in one of the scenes to make sure that everyone participates.

Intrapersonal Learners

Students who have difficulty role-playing in a group may wish to write a scene showing one of the crucial moments. As a means of overcoming students' shyness, encourage them to read their scenes aloud, or offer to read the scene aloud for them.

LANGUAGE LINK

Ask students to underline all the verbs in an excerpt from their portfolio and then to revise the excerpt, choosing vivid verbs wherever appropriate. Remind students that although vivid verbs are more specific, sometimes a general verb is more appropriate. Students will not need to change every verb.

Try It Out
Possible Answers

1. Jerry <u>dragged</u> himself up the steps.
2. Jerry <u>zoomed</u> home from school.
3. Jerry <u>ached</u> for a President Cleveland card.
4. Rollie <u>clutched</u> the cards close to his chest.

Additional verbs Cormier uses include *burst, protested, insisted, stared,* and *journeyed.*

VOCABULARY
Possible Answers

1. I would be indignant because I would not be able to get my work done.
2. Yes, people are preoccupied with money.
3. It is only right to tell a friend's secret if someone's safety is involved.
4. If friends get stuck in an argument, they should ask someone else to help them.
5. "Come on! Don't slow down now!"
6. I was not surprised that he would look down on his younger brother.

Resources ————

Language
* *Grammar and Language Links,* p. 9

Vocabulary
* *Words to Own,* p. 4

Spelling
For related instruction, see
* *Spelling and Decoding,* p. 5

LANGUAGE LINK   MINI-LESSON

Style: Actions Speak Louder with Vivid Verbs

Language Handbook HELP

See Using Vivid Verbs, page 699.

SOME OF CORMIER'S VERBS
allotted
betrayed
imprinted
creep
dwindled
squinted

In "President Cleveland, Where Are You?" the boys didn't *trade* cards—they "*swapped* and *bargained* and *matched* for the cards." Jerry didn't *go* to the store—he *raced* to the store. The boys didn't *feel* envy for Rollie—they *ached* with envy. Vivid verbs are lively, specific action words that help readers picture the action clearly. Compare the two sets of examples below:

VAGUE	I <u>put</u> my hand into my pocket and <u>touched</u> the coins.
VIVID	"I <u>reached</u> into my pocket and <u>caressed</u> the coins."
VAGUE	As I <u>came</u> through the doorway, letting the screen door <u>close</u> behind me, my brother <u>was</u> in my way.
VIVID	"As I <u>burst</u> through the doorway, letting the screen door <u>slam</u> behind me, my brother Armand <u>blocked</u> my way."

Try It Out
➤ Paint a vivid picture by replacing the vague verbs in the following sentences with vivid verbs. Discuss your rewrites with classmates to see all the possibilities you have in verb choices.

1. Jerry <u>walked</u> up the steps.
2. Jerry <u>came</u> home from school.
3. Jerry <u>wanted</u> a President Cleveland card.
4. Rollie <u>held</u> the cards close to his chest.

➤ Go back to Cormier's story, and find verbs to add to the opposite list. Keep a verb bank in your notebook for reference as you revise your writing.

VOCABULARY   HOW TO OWN A WORD

WORD BANK
allotted
indifferent
contempt
indignant
obsessed
dwindled
incredulous
divulge
stalemate
lethargy

Opinion Poll

1. Would you be <u>indifferent</u> or <u>indignant</u> if you were not <u>allotted</u> your fair share of computer time? Why?
2. Do ads make people <u>obsessed</u> with expensive things? Explain.
3. Is it ever right to <u>divulge</u> a secret of a friend? Why?
4. What should friends do when they reach a <u>stalemate</u> in an argument?
5. What would the coach say if a feeling of <u>lethargy</u> overcame your team and your energy <u>dwindled</u>?
6. When Armand showed <u>contempt</u> for Jerry, were you <u>incredulous</u>? Why or why not?

68 MOMENTS OF TRUTH

Language Link Quick Check

Underline the verbs in the following sentences and replace them with vivid verbs.

1. Jerry <u>went</u> to his bike and <u>got</u> onto it. [Jerry <u>flew</u> to his bike and <u>jumped</u> onto it.]
2. Armand <u>watched</u> himself in the mirror. [Armand <u>admired</u> himself in the mirror.]
3. Rollie Tremaine <u>put</u> the caramel chew into his mouth. [Rollie Tremaine <u>tossed</u> the caramel chew into his mouth.]

4. Roger <u>walked</u> away from Jerry. [Roger <u>stomped</u> away from Jerry.]
5. Father <u>gave</u> each of us an extra dime that week. [Father <u>allowed</u> each of us an extra dime that week.]

Before You Read

THE STONE

Make the Connection

Wish List

Have you ever asked yourself, "If I were granted one wish, what would it be?" It's a question that could keep you thinking for hours. As you'll see, the next story starts normally enough, until the main character has a chance to change his life with a wish.

Quickwrite

Write a brief response to this question: Would you like to remain forever at the age you are now? Think about the pros and cons of always being twelve years old (or eleven, or any other age).

Elements of Literature

Moral Lessons: Advice for Living

In "The Stone" the main character, Maibon, learns an important lesson about life. The old fables and fairy tales were meant to teach children (and others) useful lessons about the right and wrong ways to behave. In this story a famous fantasy writer adopts the style and purpose of those old fairy tales.

> **A** **moral lesson** is a lesson about the right and wrong ways to behave.

Reading Skills and Strategies

Making Generalizations: Stating Lessons

When you read a story like "The Stone" and state its moral lesson, you are making a **generalization**. Making a generalization is like doing detective work. First you look for specific evidence—what happens in the story and what the characters learn. Then you consider this evidence and make a general statement about the lesson the story teaches.

go.hrw.com
LE0 6-1

THE STONE **69**

Preteaching Vocabulary

Words to Own

Have students find the vocabulary words and their definitions at the bottom of the selection pages. Ask them to check the abbreviations in the vocabulary entries to find out which words are verbs. [*delved, gaped, obliged, rue, mired*] Then have students identify the parts of speech of the other words. [*Jubilation* and *plight* are nouns; *fallow* is an adjective.] Divide students into small groups and direct each group to act out as many of the words as it can. Ask groups to report to you on how many of the words they felt they acted out well enough for an audience to guess. Have groups act out for the class the words they felt were interpreted best.

OBJECTIVES

1. Read and interpret the story
2. Identify and analyze the moral lesson of the story
3. Make generalizations
4. Express understanding through writing, art, or research/speaking
5. Identify the correct usage of *don't* and *doesn't* and use the words in writing
6. Understand and use new words
7. Understand and use synonyms

SKILLS

Literary
- Identify and analyze moral lessons

Reading
- Make generalizations

Writing
- Collect ideas for an autobiographical incident
- Write a short short story

Research/Speaking
- Report on moral lessons found in a work of fiction

Grammar/Language
- Use *don't* and *doesn't* correctly

Vocabulary
- Understand and use synonyms

Viewing/Representing
- Respond to details in an illustration (ATE)
- Describe a character in an illustration (ATE)

Planning

- **Traditional Schedule**
  Lesson Plans Including Strategies for English-Language Learners
- **One-Stop Planner**
  CD-ROM with Test Generator

T69

RESPONDING TO THE ART

Point out to students that illustrations and paintings contain numerous details that help convey the artist's point of view. **Activity.** What things in the illustration look old or tired? [Possible responses: the sagging roof on the house, the horse with its head hanging, the cart with its wheels bowed, the man's face.]

"*I've heard tell that you Fair Folk have magic stones that can keep a man young forever. That's what I want.*"

70 MOMENTS OF TRUTH

Resources: Print and Media

Reading
- *Reading Skills and Strategies*
  MiniRead Skill Lesson, p. 90
  Selection Skill Lesson, p. 97
- *Graphic Organizers for Active Reading*, p. 6
- *Words to Own*, p. 5
- *Spelling and Decoding*, p. 6
- *Audio CD Library*
  Disc 2, Track 4

Writing and Language
- *Daily Oral Grammar*
  Transparency 6
- *Grammar and Language Links*
  Worksheet, p. 11
- *Language Workshop CD-ROM*

Viewing and Representing
- *Viewing and Representing*
  Fine Art Transparency 3
  Fine Art Worksheet, p. 12

Assessment
- *Formal Assessment*, p. 11
- *Portfolio Management System*, p. 110
- *Test Generator (One-Stop Planner CD-ROM)*

Internet
- go.hrw.com (keyword: LE0 6-1)

THE STONE

Lloyd Alexander

There was a cottager named Maibon, and one day he was driving down the road in his horse and cart when he saw an old man hobbling along, so frail and feeble he doubted the poor soul could go many more steps. Though Maibon offered to take him in the cart, the old man refused; and Maibon went his way home, shaking his head over such a pitiful sight, and said to his wife, Modrona:

"Ah, ah, what a sorry thing it is to have your bones creaking and cracking, and dim eyes, and dull wits. When I think this might come to me, too! A fine, strong-armed, sturdy-legged fellow like me? One day to go tottering and have his teeth rattling in his head and live on porridge like a baby? There's no fate worse in all the world."

"There is," answered Modrona, "and that would be to have neither teeth nor porridge.

THE STONE 71

Summary ▪▪

In the fairy tale, Maibon, a simple cottager, encounters a red-haired dwarf named Doli who is trapped under a log. Maibon frees Doli and demands in return a magic stone to keep him from aging. After warning Maibon against the stone, Doli grants the wish, and Maibon goes home, where his practical wife scolds him for his foolishness. The stone works its magic, and Maibon does not grow older; however, nothing else in his household does, either. His cow won't calf, his hens' eggs won't hatch, his crops do not grow, and his baby's teething is halted. Realizing his folly, Maibon tries to get rid of the stone, but it keeps reappearing because he is conflicted about discarding it. Encountering Doli again, Maibon begs him to take back the stone. Convinced finally that his desire to remain young was a mistake, Maibon abandons the stone and returns home to find his fields growing and his animals and family back to normal.

Resources

Listening
Audio CD Library
A recording of this story is provided in the *Audio CD Library*:
• Disc 2, Track 4

Viewing and Representing
Fine Art Transparency
The painting *Mary,* which shows a girl looking at a stone, can be linked to Maibon's looking at the stone in the story.
• Transparency 3
• Worksheet, p. 12

Reaching All Students

Struggling Readers
Making Generalizations was introduced on p. 69. For a lesson directly tied to this selection that teaches students to make generalizations by using a strategy called It Says . . . I Say, see the *Reading Skills and Strategies* binder:
• MiniRead Skill Lesson, p. 90
• Selection Skill Lesson, p. 97

English Language Learners
Help students find contemporary American equivalents for the tale's colloquialisms, which have a deliberately Welsh ring to them. For additional strategies to supplement instruction for these students, see
• *Lesson Plans Including Strategies for English-Language Learners*

Advanced Learners
Encourage students to make generalizations and hypotheses about the need and value of fairy tales. Prompt them to ask and answer questions such as: What can we learn from stories that use magic or some other supernatural phenomenon to prove a point? How can exaggeration be useful in helping us see situations more clearly? Suggest that students read more of Lloyd Alexander's *Prydain* stories to find further evidence to support their opinions.

A Elements of Literature

Moral Lessons

The line, "Hoe your field or you'll have no crop to harvest . . ." implies a moral lesson. Ask students to state the lesson in their own words. [Possible response: You have to work to get what you want.] You may wish to repeat the line aloud slowly or write it on the chalkboard to help students arrive at the moral lesson.

B Reading Skills and Strategies

Making Generalizations

❓ This passage lists many specific examples of a general process. What is that process? [aging] What general idea does Maibon have about aging? [It brings decline; there is nothing good about it.]

C Critical Thinking

Classifying

❓ Based on what the dwarf says about his family's powers, what kind of story is this? [fantasy]

Get on with you, Maibon, and stop borrowing trouble. Hoe your field or you'll have no **A** crop to harvest, and no food for you, or me, or the little ones."

Sighing and grumbling, Maibon did as his wife bade him. Although the day was fair and cloudless, he took no pleasure in it. His ax blade was notched, the wooden handle splintery; his saw had lost its edge; and his hoe, once shining new, had begun to rust. None of his tools, it seemed to him, cut or chopped or delved as well as they once had done.

"They're as worn-out as that old codger[1] I saw on the road," Maibon said to himself. He squinted up at the sky. "Even the sun isn't as bright as it used to be and doesn't warm me half as well. It's gone threadbare as my cloak. **B** And no wonder, for it's been there longer than I can remember. Come to think of it, the moon's been looking a little wilted around the edges, too.

"As for me," went on Maibon, in dismay, "I'm in even a worse state. My appetite's faded, especially after meals. Mornings, when I wake, I can hardly keep myself from yawning. And at night, when I go to bed, my eyes are so heavy I can't hold them open. If that's the way things are now, the older I grow, the worse it will be!"

In the midst of his complaining, Maibon glimpsed something bouncing and tossing back and forth beside a fallen tree in a corner of the field. Wondering if one of his piglets had squeezed out of the sty and gone rooting for acorns, Maibon hurried across the turf. Then he dropped his ax and gaped in astonishment.

There, struggling to free his leg, which had been caught under the log, lay a short, thickset

---

1. **codger:** informal term meaning "elderly man."

---

figure: a dwarf with red hair bristling in all directions beneath his round, close-fitting leather cap. At the sight of Maibon, the dwarf squeezed shut his bright red eyes and began holding his breath. After a moment the dwarf's face went redder than his hair; his cheeks puffed out and soon turned purple. Then he opened one eye and blinked rapidly at Maibon, who was staring at him, speechless.

"What," snapped the dwarf, "you can still see me?"

"That I can," replied Maibon, more than ever puzzled, "and I can see very well you've got yourself tight as a wedge under that log, and all your kicking only makes it worse."

At this the dwarf blew out his breath and shook his fists. "I can't do it!" he shouted. "No matter how I try! I can't make myself

C invisible! Everyone in my family can disappear—poof! Gone! Vanished! But not me! Not Doli! Believe me, if I could have done, you never would have found me in such a plight. Worse luck! Well, come on. Don't stand there goggling like an idiot. Help me get loose!"

At this sharp command Maibon began tugging and heaving at the log. Then he

---

WORDS TO OWN

delved (delvd) v.: dug. Delved also means "searched."
gaped (gāpt) v.: stared with the mouth open, as in wonder or surprise.
plight (plīt) n.: bad situation.

---

72 MOMENTS OF TRUTH

Using Students' Strengths

Visual Learners

Encourage students to look through the illustrations before reading the story, to give them a sense of the setting and characters. As students read, encourage them to make sketches of the characters and events in their own styles. Visual learners may also benefit by filling in the graphic organizer on p. 6 of the *Graphic Organizers for Active Reading*.

Auditory Learners

Before reading "The Stone," read aloud one of Aesop's shorter fables, such as "The Fox and the Grapes," or tell students a proverb, such as "A bird in the hand is worth two in the bush." Use the example as an introduction to the concept of a moral. Explain that a story with a moral tries to teach the readers something about how they should behave or think, often by using animals or people with special powers.

Logical/Mathematical Learners

After students have read the story and arrived at a moral lesson (e.g., "It's better to age naturally than to try to stay young forever"; "Be careful what you wish for; it may backfire"), ask them to think of reasons why the moral both is and isn't convincing. Students, individually or in pairs, should write the reasons in a two-column chart. Then they may form a group to stage an informal debate for the class.

T72

of it with you ham-handed, heavy-footed oafs. Time was, you humans got along well with us. But nowadays you no sooner see a Fair Folk than it's grab, grab, grab! Gobble, gobble, gobble! Grant my wish! Give me this, give me that! As if we had nothing better to do!

"Yes, I'll give you a favor," Doli went on. "That's the rule; I'm <u>obliged</u> to. Now, get on with it."

Hearing this, Maibon pulled and pried and chopped away at the log as fast as he could and soon freed the dwarf.

Doli heaved a sigh of relief, rubbed his shin, and cocked a red eye at Maibon, saying:

"All right. You've done your work; you'll have your reward. What do you want? Gold, I suppose. That's the usual. Jewels? Fine clothes? Take my advice, go for something practical. A hazelwood twig to help you find water if your well ever goes dry? An ax that never needs sharpening? A cook pot always brimming with food?"

"None of those!" cried Maibon. He bent down to the dwarf and whispered eagerly, "But I've heard tell that you Fair Folk have magic stones that can keep a man young forever. That's what I want. I claim one for my reward."

Doli snorted. "I might have known you'd pick something like that. As to be expected, you humans have it all muddled. There's nothing can make a man young again. That's even beyond the best of our skills. Those stones you're babbling about? Well, yes, there are such things. But greatly overrated. All they'll do is keep you from growing any older."

"Just as good!" Maibon exclaimed. "I want no more than that!"

stopped, wrinkled his brow, and scratched his head, saying:

"Well, now, just a moment, friend. The way you look, and all your talk about turning yourself invisible—I'm thinking you might be one of the Fair Folk."

"Oh, clever!" Doli retorted. "Oh, brilliant! Great clodhopper! Giant beanpole! Of course I am! What else! Enough gabbling. Get a move on. My leg's going to sleep."

"If a man does the Fair Folk a good turn," cried Maibon, his excitement growing, "it's told they must do one for him."

"I knew sooner or later you'd come round to that," grumbled the dwarf. "That's the way

Words to Own
obliged (ə·blījd′) v.: forced.

THE STONE **73**

Getting Students Involved

A Critical Thinking

Making Judgments

❓ Do you trust Doli's advice? Why or why not? [Possible responses: Yes, because he knows more about the stones than Maibon does; no, because he may want to keep the stones for himself.]

B Advanced Learners

Speculating

❓ What problems might a person have if he or she stayed the same age forever? [Possible responses: outliving all his or her loved ones; not getting along with his or her friends because their ages would change and his or hers wouldn't.]

C Struggling Readers

Rereading

Have students reread this passage, and then help them understand what it reveals about Maibon's perception: Although Modrona has pointed out the foolishness and selfishness of his wish, Maibon's concern remains centered on the stone.

D Reading Skills and Strategies

Making Generalizations

❓ What generalization does Maibon make about Doli? [that Doli is dishonest] What evidence does Maibon have? [Maibon doesn't feel different in the evening from the way he did in the morning.] How valid is this evidence, and why? [It is not strong evidence about aging, for aging isn't noticeable during the course of one day.]

Doli hesitated and frowned. "Ah—between the two of us, take the cook pot. Better all around. Those stones—we'd sooner not give them away. There's a difficulty——"

A "Because you'd rather keep them for yourselves," Maibon broke in. "No, no, you shan't cheat me of my due. Don't put me off with excuses. I told you what I want, and that's what I'll have. Come, hand it over and not another word."

Doli shrugged and opened a leather pouch that hung from his belt. He spilled a number of brightly colored pebbles into his palm, picked out one of the larger stones, and handed it to Maibon. The dwarf then jumped up, took to his heels, raced across the field, and disappeared into a thicket.

Laughing and crowing over his good fortune and his cleverness, Maibon hurried back to the cottage. There he told his wife what had happened and showed her the stone he had claimed from the Fair Folk.

B "As I am now, so I'll always be!" Maibon declared, flexing his arms and thumping his chest. "A fine figure of a man! Oho, no gray beard and wrinkled brow for me!"

Instead of sharing her husband's jubilation, Modrona flung up her hands and burst out:

C "Maibon, you're a greater fool than ever I supposed! And selfish into the bargain! You've turned down treasures! You didn't even ask that dwarf for so much as new jackets for the children! Nor a new apron for me!

You could have had the roof mended. Or the walls plastered. No, a stone is what you ask for! A bit of rock no better than you'll dig up in the cow pasture!"

Crestfallen[2] and sheepish, Maibon began thinking his wife was right and the dwarf had indeed given him no more than a common field stone.

D "Eh, well, it's true," he stammered; "I feel no different than I did this morning, no better or worse, but every way the same. That red-headed little wretch! He'll rue the day if I ever find him again!"

So saying, Maibon threw the stone into the fireplace. That night he grumbled his way to bed, dreaming revenge on the dishonest dwarf.

Next morning, after a restless night, he yawned, rubbed his eyes, and scratched his chin. Then he sat bolt upright in bed, patting his cheeks in amazement.

"My beard!" he cried, tumbling out and hurrying to tell his wife. "It hasn't grown! Not by a hair! Can it be the dwarf didn't cheat me after all?"

"Don't talk to me about beards," declared his wife as Maibon went to the fireplace, picked out the stone, and clutched it safely in both hands. "There's trouble enough in the

---

2. **crestfallen:** discouraged.

WORDS TO OWN

jubilation (jōō'bə·lā'shən) n.: rejoicing; great joy.
rue (rōō) v.: feel sorrow or regret for.

---

74 MOMENTS OF TRUTH

Getting Students Involved

Cooperative Learning

Writing Fairy Tales. Have students work together in groups of three to brainstorm ideas for their own fairy tales to share with younger students. Suggest that they consult sources such as *Grimm's Fairy Tales* and *Andersen's Fairy Tales* to help them. Ask students to discuss and write the tales together. When a tale is completed, have one student in the group type or rewrite it neatly, have another design a cover, and have the third student illustrate the story.

Story Pyramid. Have students work in groups to create a story pyramid for "The Stone." Ask them to create their pyramid according to the following formula or another that they choose.

(1) _____

(2) _____ _____

(3) _____ _____ _____

1) Character's name; (2) Two words describing the **character;** (3) Three words describing **setting;** (4) Four words stating the problem or **conflict;** (5) Five words describing one event; (6) Six words describing another event; (7) Seven words describing a third event; (8) Eight words describing the **resolution,** or ending. Have one member of each group present the completed pyramid to the class.

chicken roost. Those eggs should have hatched by now, but the hen is still brooding Ⓔ on her nest."

"Let the chickens worry about that," answered Maibon. "Wife, don't you see what a grand thing's happened to me? I'm not a minute older than I was yesterday. Bless that generous-hearted dwarf!"

"Let me lay hands on him and I'll bless him," retorted Modrona. "That's all well and good for you. But what of me? You'll stay as you are, but I'll turn old and gray, and worn and wrinkled, and go doddering into my grave! And what of our little ones? They'll grow up and have children of their own. And grandchildren, and great-grandchildren. And you, younger than any of them. What a foolish sight you'll be!"

But Maibon, gleeful over his good luck, paid his wife no heed and only tucked the stone deeper into his pocket. Next day, however, the eggs had still not hatched. Ⓕ

"And the cow!" Modrona cried. "She's long past due to calve, and no sign of a young one ready to be born!"

"Don't bother me with cows and chickens," replied Maibon. "They'll all come right, in time. As for time, I've got all the time in the world!"

Having no appetite for breakfast, Maibon went out into his field. Of all the seeds he had sown there, however, he was surprised to see not one had sprouted. The field, which by now should have been covered with green shoots, lay bare and empty.

"Eh, things do seem a little late these days," Maibon said to himself. "Well, no hurry. It's that much less for me to do. The wheat isn't growing, but neither are the weeds."

Some days went by and still the eggs had not hatched, the cow had not calved, the wheat had not sprouted. And now Maibon saw that his apple tree showed no sign of even the smallest, greenest fruit.

"Maibon, it's the fault of that stone!" wailed his wife. "Get rid of the thing!"

"Nonsense," replied Maibon. "The season's slow, that's all."

Nevertheless, his wife kept at him and kept at him Ⓖ so much that Maibon at last, and very reluctantly, threw the stone out the cottage window. Not too far, though, for he had it in the back of his mind to go later and find it again.

Next morning he had no need to go looking for it, for there was the stone, sitting on the window ledge. Ⓗ

"You see?" said Maibon to his wife. "Here it is, back again. So it's a gift meant for me to keep."

"Maibon!" cried his wife. "Will you get rid of it! We've had nothing but trouble since you brought it into the house. Now the baby's fretting and fuming. Teething, poor little thing. But not a tooth to be seen! Maibon, that stone's bad luck and I want no part of it!"

Protesting it was none of his doing that the stone had come back, Maibon carried it into the vegetable patch. He dug a hole, not a very deep one, and put the stone into it.

THE STONE **75**

Ⓔ **Vocabulary Note**
Multiple Meanings
A bird is *brooding* when she sits on her eggs to warm them so they can hatch a *brood* of young. A person is *brooding* when he or she is thinking moodily for a long time.

Ⓕ **Elements of Literature**
Moral Lessons
❓ What moral lesson has Maibon not yet learned? [Possible responses: to listen to his wise wife; to think ahead; to be less self-centered.]

Ⓖ **Elements of Literature**
Character
❓ Maibon intends to retrieve the stone even though it seems to be having a bad effect on his home and family. What does this suggest about the kind of person Maibon is? [Possible responses: stubborn, because he will not listen to his wife's advice; selfish, because he wants to stay young even though it is hurting his family; deceitful, because he only gives the appearance of getting rid of the stone.]

Ⓗ **Critical Thinking**
Hypothesizing
❓ Why do you think the stone turned up again on the window ledge? [Possible responses: The stone is magically linked to Maibon because it was Doli's gift to him; it is magically linked to Maibon because he still believes it will be good for him; Doli is deliberately making mischief with Maibon.]

Crossing the Curriculum

Science
Have students perform a classroom experiment that shows how crystals—one form of rock, possibly the kind Doli possesses—are formed. Fill a small jar with a saturated solution of table salt and water. Attach a string to the lid of the jar, letting the string dangle into the solution. Put the jar on a shelf where it will not be disturbed. Salt crystals will form on the string. Ask students to keep an observation sheet to record the changes they see in the rock each day.

Art
Divide the class into groups, and have them draw a large circle on poster board to represent the stone in the story. Ask them to divide the stone into four sections and to draw in each section a picture that represents an event or character in the story. For example, students may choose to draw in one section an unhappy hen who cannot hatch eggs. Ask students to color or paint the pictures and to create a title for their work. Display the finished products.

A Reading Skills and Strategies

Making Generalizations

? Maibon finally realizes his mistake and understands the lesson of the stone. In expressing what he has learned he makes a generalization about the nature of life and change. What generalization does Maibon make? [Possible responses: Without change there is nothing to look forward to.]

B Critical Thinking

Interpreting

? How do you think Doli feels about Maibon? [Possible responses: Doli is angry with Maibon for not heeding his warning; he may feel sorry for Maibon because he thinks humans are ignorant; he doesn't feel sorry for Maibon because he thinks Maibon is selfish.]

C Elements of Literature

Moral Lessons

Maibon's statement expresses one possible moral lesson of his experience with the stone. Have students paraphrase the idea in their own words. [Possible responses: You can't fight fate; you have to take the good with the bad; change is good; whatever will be, will be.]

Next day, there was the stone, above ground, winking and glittering.

"Maibon!" cried his wife. "Once and for all, if you care for your family, get rid of that cursed thing!"

Seeing no other way to keep peace in the household, Maibon regretfully and unwillingly took the stone and threw it down the well, where it splashed into the water and sank from sight.

But that night, while he was trying vainly to sleep, there came such a rattling and clattering that Maibon clapped his hands over his ears, jumped out of bed, and went stumbling into the yard. At the well the bucket was jiggling back and forth and up and down at the end of the rope, and in the bottom of the bucket was the stone.

Now Maibon began to be truly distressed, not only for the toothless baby, the calfless cow, the fruitless tree, and the hen sitting desperately on her eggs, but for himself as well.

"Nothing's moving along as it should," he groaned. "I can't tell one day from another. Nothing changes, there's nothing to look forward to, nothing to show for my work. Why sow if the seeds don't sprout? Why plant if there's never a harvest? Why eat if I don't get hungry? Why go to bed at night, or get up in the morning, or do anything at all? And the way it looks, so it will stay for ever and ever! I'll shrivel from boredom if nothing else!"

"Maibon," pleaded his wife, "for all our sakes, destroy the dreadful thing!"

Maibon tried now to pound the stone to dust with his heaviest mallet, but he could not so much as knock a chip from it. He put it against his grindstone without so much as scratching it. He set it on his anvil and belabored it with hammer and tongs, all to no avail.

At last he decided to bury the stone again, this time deeper than before. Picking up his shovel, he hurried to the field. But he suddenly halted and the shovel dropped from his hands. There, sitting cross-legged on a stump, was the dwarf.

"You!" shouted Maibon, shaking his fist. "Cheat! Villain! Trickster! I did you a good turn, and see how you've repaid it!"

The dwarf blinked at the furious Maibon. "You mortals are an ungrateful crew. I gave you what you wanted."

"You should have warned me!" burst out Maibon.

"I did," Doli snapped back. "You wouldn't listen. No, you yapped and yammered, bound to have your way. I told you we didn't like to give away those stones. When you mortals get hold of one, you stay just as you are—but so does everything around you. Before you know it, you're <u>mired</u> in time like a rock in the mud. You take my advice. Get rid of that stone as fast as you can."

"What do you think I've been trying to do?" blurted Maibon. "I've buried it, thrown it down the well, pounded it with a hammer—it keeps coming back to me!"

"That's because you really didn't want to give it up," Doli said. "In the back of your mind and the bottom of your heart, you didn't want to change along with the rest of the world. So long as you feel that way, the stone is yours."

"No, no!" cried Maibon. "I want no more of it. Whatever may happen, let it happen. That's better than nothing happening at all. I've had my share of being young; I'll take my

---

WORDS TO OWN

mired (mīrd) v.: sunk or stuck, as if in mud.

Making the Connections

Cultural Connections

Many cultures have tales of imaginary beings in their folklore. The appearance and behavior of the creatures varies widely. Whereas Irish leprechauns are ugly little men, the Lorelei of Germanic legend is a beautiful enchantress. Ogres are giants who eat human beings. Germanic elves are tiny beings who live in the air and under the sea as well as on land. Scandinavian trolls are dwellers in caves and hills. Typically, fairies inhabit their own kingdom ruled by a king and queen, and are often mischievous. However, the familiar "fairy godmother" is beneficent. Arabian jinn can change size and shape and, although mostly destructive, are obliged to do the bidding of a human who has trapped them.

Ask students why they think so many cultures have imaginary beings such as these as part of their folklore, and why stories of this sort so often end in moral lessons. Invite students to read aloud fairy tales from other cultures. Then discuss as a class the similarities and differences among the tales.

share of being old. And when I come to the end of my days, at least I can say I've lived each one of them."

"If you mean that," answered Doli, "toss the stone onto the ground right there at the stump. Then get home and be about your business."

Maibon flung down the stone, spun around, and set off as fast as he could. When he dared at last to glance back over his shoulder, fearful the stone might be bouncing along at his heels, he saw no sign of it, or of the redheaded dwarf.

Maibon gave a joyful cry, for at that same instant the <u>fallow</u> field was covered with green blades of wheat, the branches of the apple tree bent to the ground, so laden they were with fruit. He ran to the cottage, threw his arms around his wife and children, and told them the good news. The hen hatched her chicks; the cow bore her calf. And Maibon laughed with glee when he saw the first tooth in the baby's mouth.

Never again did Maibon meet any of the Fair Folk, and he was just as glad of it. He and his wife and children and grandchildren lived many years, and Maibon was proud of his white hair and long beard as he had been of his sturdy arms and legs.

"Stones are all right in their way," said Maibon. "But the trouble with them is, they don't grow."

WORDS TO OWN
fallow (fal′ō) *adj.:* left unplanted.

THE STONE **77**

D Critical Thinking
Interpreting
❓ What does it mean to "live each one" of your days? [Possible responses: to live fully, using all your time productively and interestingly; to be excited by life, not bored by it; to live attentively and appreciatively, not letting your life slip by.]

E Elements of Literature
Moral Lessons
Have students share their responses to the moral of the story. [Possible responses: I agree that it's important to change and grow; I disagree because I would like to be young forever, even if it did bring problems.]

RESPONDING TO THE ART
What part of the story does this illustration portray, and what do the characters' expressions and body language suggest? [Possible responses: It is the scene where Maibon returns the stone. They both seem upset and argumentative, Maibon pointing to the stone, while Doli holds his hand up to silence him.]

Resources
Selection Assessment
Formal Assessment
• Selection Test, p. 11
Test Generator
• Selection Test

Making the Connections

Connecting to the Theme: "Moments of Truth"
Ask students why they think a character such as Maibon is included in a collection with this theme. [Possible response: Maibon was foolish and selfish at the beginning of the story, but he experienced a moment of truth when he learned how important it is to grow and change.]

Getting Students Involved

Enrichment Activity
Role-playing. Ask students to do some impromptu role-playing. Have pairs act out exchanges between Maibon and Modrona and between Maibon and Doli. They can use the exact words of the story or they can paraphrase. Encourage students to use the tone of voice they think would be appropriate for the character they are portraying.

MEET THE WRITER

A Hungry Reader

Even as a child, **Lloyd Alexander** (1924–   ), the prize-winning fantasy writer, loved books.

66 I was always a hungry reader—in more ways than one. I gobbled up stories and never had my fill. At the same time, I wanted a real taste of whatever food the people in the stories were eating. Reading about the Mad Tea Party in *Alice in Wonderland*, I pleaded for a cup of tea, bread and butter, and treacle. (Treacle, I guessed, was something like pancake syrup.) My poor mother! How did she ever find patience to put up with her son's reading-and-eating habits?

In *Treasure Island* . . . bloodthirsty pirates nearly find young Jim Hawkins hiding in an apple barrel. So, of course, I had to munch an apple. However, when Robin Hood and his Merry Men dined on venison washed down with flagons of brown October ale, I could only make believe with a hamburger and a glass of root beer. A dish of cornmeal mush took the place of Indian maize when, sitting cross-legged under our living-room lamp, I devoured *The Song of Hiawatha*. Our neighborhood grocer never sold—nor had we money to buy—anything like the rich feasts at *King Arthur's Round Table*. Instead of the roast goose of *A Christmas Carol*, I gnawed a chicken leg. The pages of *Winnie-the-Pooh*, along with my fingers, got sticky with honey. My mother's cookbook held no recipe for the nectar and ambrosia of Greek mythology; I settled for cornflakes and grape juice. Zeus must have smiled at that.

In time, to sighs of relief from my parents, I lost the habit of eating what I read about, but never my hunger for reading. I think the stories we love as children stay with us, somewhere in our hearts, to feed our imaginations. We never outgrow our need for them, any more than we outgrow our need for food. But, to me, the books I love are better than a feast. 99

More to Feast On

"The Stone" is just one of the stories you can find in Lloyd Alexander's book *The Foundling and Other Tales of Prydain* (Dell). In addition, Alexander has written about the fantasy world of Prydain in a whole series of books called the *Prydain Chronicles*. One book in this series, *The High King* (Dell), won a Newbery Award.

78

Assessing Learning

Check Test: True-False

Change the false statements to make them true, and write "True" next to the ones that are already true.

1. Maibon's wife Modrona is lazy. [Maibon's wife Modrona is practical and realistic.]
2. Maibon meets a genie with red hair and red eyes. [Maibon meets a dwarf.]
3. The stone makes Maibon stop aging. [True]
4. Modrona thinks her husband is foolish for keeping the stone for so long. [True]
5. Maibon's chickens lay golden eggs after he gets the stone. [Maibon's chickens are unable to hatch their eggs after he gets the stone.]

Standardized Test Preparation

For practice in proofreading and editing, see
• *Daily Oral Grammar*, Transparency 6

MAKING MEANINGS

First Thoughts

[respond]

 1. Look back at your notes for the Quickwrite on page 69. Did reading this story change your opinion? Why or why not?

Shaping Interpretations

[interpret]

2. Maibon's troubles start when he sees an old man. Do you agree that Maibon "borrows trouble," as his wife says? Why or why not?

[analyze]

3. When did you begin to suspect that Maibon's wish wasn't going to turn out the way he expected? Make a list of the clues that helped you **predict** that Maibon's wish would be a mistake.

[contrast]

4. What differences do you see between Maibon's **character** and his wife's? List some adjectives that contrast their characters. For example, you might continue the following chart:

Maibon	Modrona
stupid lazy	wise

[speculate]

5. Doli makes some guesses about Maibon's wish. What does Doli think about human values, or at least the values of Maibon's society? How would Doli have been surprised if Modrona had rescued him and had asked that a wish be granted?

[identify]

6. What **conflict,** or mixed feelings, does Maibon have about getting rid of the stone? When does his "moment of truth" come, and why is he finally able to toss the stone away?

[evaluate]

 7. At the end, Maibon says, "Stones are all right in their way. But the trouble with them is, they don't grow." What lesson has Maibon learned? How would you express the **moral lesson** of this story?

Challenging the Text

[evaluate]

8. How well do you think the story succeeds in teaching readers a lesson about how to behave? What value do you see in moral tales?

THE STONE 79

Reading Check

Draw a comic strip of four or five panels to show the **main events** in this story. Compare your comic-strip version of events with a partner's. Did you choose the same events?

Reading Check

The main events of the story are as follows:

1. Maibon sees the elderly peasant and becomes worried about aging.
2. Maibon frees Doli, who then grants him a wish.
3. Maibon is berated by his wife for appearing foolish and self-centered.
4. Nothing on Maibon's farm changes or grows.
5. Maibon tries to get rid of the stone, but it keeps returning to him.
6. Maibon returns to Doli to have the wish undone.

MAKING MEANINGS

First Thoughts

1. Possible responses: It changed my opinion, because I saw that being young forever would be a problem; it didn't change my opinion, because being young forever in real life would be more fun than the way it's presented in this story.

Shaping Interpretations

2. Possible responses: Yes, because he becomes overly concerned with old age while in his prime; yes, because strange things happen to Maibon when the dwarf gives him the stone.
3. Possible responses: The hens' eggs don't hatch; the cow doesn't give birth; the baby's teeth don't come in; and the wheat doesn't grow.
4. Maibon: stubborn, lazy, foolish, selfish; Modrona: wise, caring, unselfish, practical.
5. Doli thinks humans are foolish and selfish. Modrona probably would have wished for something more practical and less selfish.
6. Maibon tries to get rid of the stone because his wife tells him to, but he still doesn't want to grow old and he believes the stone can grant him that. When he realizes that life is boring and frustrating without change, he is able to throw the stone away.
7. Maibon learns that growth is an essential part of life. The moral lesson is that growth and change are a natural part of life.

Challenging the Text

8. Possible responses: It succeeds because it shows readers that there are unexpected consequences to making single-minded decisions; it doesn't succeed because what happened to Maibon couldn't happen in real life. Some people probably do learn something from moral tales; the tales provide a good way to teach moral values to children.

Grading Timesaver

Rubrics for each Choices assignment appear on p. 110 in the *Portfolio Management System*.

CHOICES:
Building Your Portfolio

1. **Writer's Notebook** *Remind students to choose a situation they would not mind sharing with others.* Ask students to save their work. They may use it as prewriting for the Writer's Workshop on pp. 86–90.

2. **Creative Writing** Have students prepare for this activity by filling out a graphic organizer like this one:

Wish	Problems with Wish
Money	Poor people beg him for money.
Jewelry	People try to steal it.

3. **Art** Students may work in pairs to take turns modeling a pose of Doli as he is described in the passage. Have them draw a quick sketch of the student model to use in creating their drawing, clay model, or puppet.

4. **Research/Speaking** Have students who have read the same story present a panel discussion. Different members of a team should summarize the story, state the moral, describe the characters, and compare the story they have read to "The Stone." Have the class ask questions of the panel, and ask panel members to answer the questions as if they were characters in the story they have read.

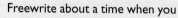

CHOICES: Building Your Portfolio

Writer's Notebook

1. Collecting Ideas for an Autobiographical Incident

Freewrite about a time when you

- had mixed feelings about growing up *or*
- had mixed feelings about keeping something or getting rid of it *or*
- found some good advice hard to accept

Jot down what you recall about the incident. Why was it so memorable for you?

> Mixed feelings about selling old toys:
> **Pro**
> —Earned money
> —Didn't play with them
> **Con**
> —Felt I was giving up old friends

Creative Writing

2. Wishes That Go Wrong

Doli advises Maibon to wish for something practical and then gives him several suggestions. Choose one of Doli's suggestions and write a short short story about how that wish could go wrong. (For instance, would the hazelwood twig find water *only* when Maibon needed it?) You can use Maibon and his wife as characters or invent new ones if you prefer.

Art

3. What a Sight!

List the vivid words the writer uses to describe Doli in the passage beginning with "There, struggling to free his leg" and ending with "'Help me get loose!'" (page 72). Then, make a colorful drawing, clay model, or fabric puppet of Doli to match the description. (Don't forget his purple face.)

Research/Speaking

4. Wishful Thinking

People have always told stories about what happens when wishes come true. If you like stories about wishes, go to your library and read one or more of the following stories. Report to the class on the moral lessons you uncover. (If you've already read some of these stories, review the texts to be sure you remember the main events.)

- *Tuck Everlasting*, a novel by Natalie Babbit (Farrar, Straus & Giroux)
- "The Monkey's Paw," a story by W. W. Jacobs, found in many short-story collections
- "The Fisherman and His Wife," a fairy tale by the Grimm brothers
- the story of King Midas, found in many collections of Greek mythology
- "The Stonecutter," a Japanese folk tale, found in *Best-Loved Folktales of the World*, selected by Joanna Cole (Doubleday)

Using Students' Strengths

Intrapersonal Learners
Encourage students to be honest with themselves in Choice 1. They may also explore in writing deep wishes they've had, the results, and what they learned about moderating their desires.

Kinesthetic Learners
Help students develop their image of Doli for Choice 3 by having them pantomime Doli as he tries to free his leg from under the tree.

Reaching All Students

English Language Learners
Use Choice 4 to give students an opportunity to practice their oral English skills. After students have read one of the recommended texts or any folk tale, have a storytelling day in class. Ask students to form small groups and to summarize the stories they have read. Remind students that they should not read the story aloud, but should tell it to the others. Model this activity by retelling the story of "The Stone."

GRAMMAR LINK   MINI-LESSON

Watch Your *Don'ts* and *Doesn'ts*

Language Handbook HELP

See Problems in Agreement, page 705.

Technology HELP

See Language Workshop CD-ROM. Key word entry: subject-verb agreement.

When Maibon has the stone, his beard <u>doesn't</u> grow and the hen's eggs <u>don't</u> hatch; his baby's tooth <u>doesn't</u> come in and the seeds <u>don't</u> sprout. The words *don't* and *doesn't* are contractions of *do not* and *does not*. Use *don't* with all plural subjects and with the pronouns *I* and *you*.

EXAMPLES   I <u>don't</u> [do not] make silly wishes.

You <u>don't</u> [do not] make silly wishes.

Most wishes <u>don't</u> [do not] come true.

Use *doesn't* with all singular subjects except *I* and *you*.

EXAMPLES   Maibon <u>doesn't</u> [does not] want to grow old.

He <u>doesn't</u> [does not] appreciate his life.

It <u>doesn't</u> [does not] make him happy anymore.

Try It Out

Choose the correct verb for each sentence.

1. Maibon <u>doesn't/don't</u> like growing old.
2. When he makes his wish, the seeds <u>doesn't/don't</u> grow anymore.
3. At first, he <u>doesn't/don't</u> understand why.
4. His wife <u>doesn't/don't</u> want him to keep the stone.
5. The trouble with the stone is it <u>doesn't/don't</u> grow.

VOCABULARY   HOW TO OWN A WORD

Making Sense of Synonyms

WORD BANK

delved
gaped
plight
obliged
jubilation
rue
mired
fallow

Synonyms are words with the same or nearly the same meanings. For example, *stone* and *rock* are synonyms. Synonyms are not always interchangeable, though. Fill out a chart like the one opposite for each word in the Word Bank. Go back to the story and locate the sentence where the word is used. See if a synonym could be used in the story in place of the word the writer chose.

Word
delved

Synonyms
dug, searched

Could synonym be used?
Dug is OK. Searched is not.

Sentence
None of his tools delved as well as they once had.

THE STONE 81

GRAMMAR LINK

Have students choose a selection in their portfolios to proofread for correct use of *don't* and *doesn't*. Ask them to circle the plural subject or pronoun of each sentence containing *don't* or *doesn't* and to put a box around the singular subject or pronoun of each sentence containing *don't* or *doesn't*. Have students confirm that they have used the correct contraction each time.

Try It Out
Answers
1. doesn't
2. don't
3. doesn't
4. doesn't
5. doesn't

VOCABULARY
Possible Answers
delved [dug; searched]
gaped [stared; hung open]
plight [predicament; condition]
obliged [required; helped]
jubilation [joy; celebration]
rue [regret; medicinal herb]
mired [stuck; delayed]
fallow [uncultivated; inactive]

Student sentences and the appropriate use of synonyms will vary.

Resources

Grammar
• *Grammar and Language Links*, p. 11
Vocabulary
• *Words to Own*, p. 5
Spelling
For related instruction, see
• *Spelling and Decoding*, p. 6

Grammar Link Quick Check

Choose the correct contraction, *don't* or *doesn't*.
1. In the end, Maibon <u>don't/doesn't</u> want to be young forever. [doesn't]
2. After Maibon gets the stone, the hen's eggs <u>don't/doesn't</u> hatch. [don't]
3. Doli <u>don't/doesn't</u> want to give Maibon the stone. [doesn't]
4. Modrona and Maibon <u>don't/doesn't</u> agree about the value of the stone. [don't]
5. Maibon and Doli <u>don't/doesn't</u> agree on what Maibon should wish for. [don't]

OBJECTIVES
1. Read and enjoy the story
2. Connect the selection to the collection theme

No Questions Asked

The literature in No Questions Asked gives students the chance to read a selection for enjoyment and enrichment as they further explore the collection theme. Annotated questions in the margins of the Teacher's Edition should be considered optional. No follow-up questions will appear after the selection.

The moments of truth cut both ways in this personal essay, as comedian Bill Cosby and his children realize they have a lot to learn from each other. With characteristic humor, Cosby confronts one daughter's substandard performance on a test and another's unorthodox study habits with gentle prodding intended to illuminate rather than control. Instead of becoming angry, Cosby recognizes that when addressed with respect, humor, patience, and love, children are more likely to learn from their mistakes.

Ⓐ Reading Skills and Strategies
Responding to the Text

❷ The daughter is turning her father's own words back on him. Is that fair? [Possible responses: Yes, because it shows that she's been listening to and thinking about what he said; no, because she's twisting what he really meant: he never meant that he didn't care about her marks.]

Resources 🎧

Listening

Audio CD Library
For a recording of this selection see the *Audio CD Library:*
• Disc 2, Track 5

No
Questions
ASKED

Lessons

Bill Cosby

The best that a parent can do today is be semi-involved in the schoolwork of a child.

"Sign this test, Dad," said my youngest daughter one evening, her left hand casually draped across the top two inches of the front page.

"May I see the mark first?" I replied.

Ⓐ "It's not important. You and Mom always say it's learning, not marks, that counts."

"Right, and I'd like to learn about your mark."

Bill Cosby as Cliff Huxtable with his TV children in scenes from his hit, *The Cosby Show.*

82 MOMENTS OF TRUTH

Reaching All Students

Struggling Readers

Although the abundance of dialogue makes this article readable for most students, some readers may lose track of who is talking. Advise students to look back to find the most recent line accompanied by an identifying speech tag such as, "I said." Then they will be able to go forward, counting speeches until they can identify the speaker of the line in question.

English Language Learners

Humor is often hard to appreciate in a second language, especially when it depends on word-play. Help students by explaining multiple meanings in passages such as, "I don't care if she should have marked it on a *ramp*." (p. 83). For additional strategies to engage these students with the literature, see
• *Lesson Plans Including Strategies for English-Language Learners*

Advanced Learners

In the form of light humor, the article delves into a number of serious issues concerning family relationships, growing up, and education, which should provide material for lively discussion. Encourage students to locate and critique the serious points Cosby is making, such as that students should be more focused on their studies. Also, invite students to evaluate Cosby's interaction with his daughters.

"Trust me, I got one."

"I appreciate your sharing that with me. And now I'd like to see it."

"You mean you'll only sign for a high one? I thought you were an equal-opportunity father."

"Is it lower than a D?"

"Dad, you have to remember that a mark is merely the teacher's opinion."

"Is it lower than an F? Have you gotten the world's first G?"

"The thing is, she should have marked this test on a curve."

"I don't care if she should have marked it on a *ramp*. If you don't move your hand, I don't move mine."

Slowly, she lifted her hand to reveal a bright red D.

"But this doesn't mean what you think," she said.

"Oh," I said, "it stands for *delightful*?"

"No, it's a *high* D."

"Good. You'll have no trouble getting into a barber college. Tell me, did you study for this test?"

"Oh, absolutely. I really did."

"Then how could you have gotten a D?"

"Because I studied the wrong things. But Dad, isn't it better to study the wrong things than not to study the right ones?"

And one of the wrong things to study is a child, for only a child can make you think that F is her teacher's initial.

And only a child can make you think that the best place for homework is an entertainment complex.

Perhaps the basic problem that children have today is not their concentration span, which is roughly as long as the life of a smoke ring, but their stereophonic approach to studying.

Another scene from *The Cosby Show*, which was based on Bill Cosby's real-life experiences.

One afternoon last year, I found one of my daughters doing her homework to the accompaniment of Oprah Winfrey, who was probing a question that had confounded Socrates:[1] Why Do Women Marry Jerks?

"You're doing a report on women who marry jerks?" I asked my daughter. "Don't forget to talk to your aunt."

"No, that's not my homework," she replied.

"Then what is your homework?"

"Biology, I think."

"Well, how can you figure anything out while watching TV?"

"Dad, can't you see I'm not *watching* TV? I'm trying to do this drawing. Do you happen to know what a leaf looks like?"

"I might be able to help you with that because I once passed through Vermont, but first, I want you to tell me: If you're not watching TV, why is it on?"

1. **Socrates** (säk′rə·tēz′) (c. 470–399 B.C.): Greek philosopher.

LESSONS 83

B **Critical Thinking**
Drawing Inferences
❓ Based on their way of conversing, what kind of relationship do you think this father and daughter have? [Possible response: close, friendly, open, caring, with the daughter allowed to express herself, but the father clearly in authority.]

C **Critical Thinking**
Evaluating
❓ Based on what you've seen of her, does the daughter's D on her test mean that she isn't a smart person? [No, she is obviously bright, witty, and responsive.]

D **Appreciating Language**
Figurative Language
❓ Remind students that comedians come up with imaginative ways to describe common things. Why does Cosby compare a young person's attention span to a smoke ring? [a smoke ring disappears in a few seconds] What does he mean by "stereophonic approach to studying"? [studying while doing something else at the same time; listening to the stereo while studying]

E **Critical Thinking**
Drawing Inferences
❓ Does the daughter seem to be focusing closely on her homework? [No; her comment, "Biology, I think," shows that she barely knows what subject she's studying.] Could her response be ironic? Why would Cosby include it? [Yes—he included it because it's funny; no—he included it to make his point that she was not fully concentrating on her studies.]

Resources ———

Assessment
• *Standardized Test Preparation*, p. 22

Using Students' Strengths

Visual Learners
Encourage students to visualize the setting in which the father and daughters live. Although there is little direct physical description of the setting in the article, not much is needed: It is a typical American household. Encourage students to visualize details that are left undescribed in the article, such as the furnishings of the house and the faces of the two characters.

Intrapersonal Learners
After students have read the scene, invite them to write one journal entry in the voice of the father and one in the voice of one of the daughters. In each entry, the character should comment on the conversation described in the article. At the end of each entry, have the student, writing in character, answer the questions, "Would you like your (father/daughter) to read this? Why or why not?"

"Dad, everyone has the TV on. You don't have to watch it—except your show, of course."

"Neurosurgeons like my show in the background. At least, that's what Nielsen[2] tells me."

Turning off the set, I said, "OK, let's see if we can remember what a leaf looks like."

Staring at me uneasily, she said, "It's so *quiet.* How can I work when it's so quiet?"

"I wonder why libraries don't have rumba bands."

Ⓐ "Libraries are different: You can hang out with your friends. The books are around in case nobody shows up."

"Honey, just listen for a moment: What you're hearing now is called silence. There used to be a lot of it in the world until about 1973, when most of it went right out the ozone hole. But if you can find any of the little that's left, it's still the best accompaniment for work. Thomas Jefferson had it when he wrote the Declaration of Independence. If he'd been watching *Dance Party,* he might have written, *All men are created awful.*"

"Can I at least phone someone?"

"You think Lincoln wrote the Gettysburg Address while he was on hold?"

"Dad, those were the olden days, when you were a kid. Things are much better now: Lincoln could *fax* that address to Gettysburg."

Mindlessly, she reached over and flipped on her stereo; and suddenly, she came alive, as if sniffing oxygen.

"Yes! Whitney, let's work!"

"When Whitney Houston makes a record," I said, "is she also listening to a tape of you?"

2. **Nielsen:** A.C. Nielsen Company, which rates the popularity of television programs.

84 MOMENTS OF TRUTH

"Dad, are you trying to make some point?"

"Yes: It's best to do one thing at a time. Can't you see that now?"

Ⓑ She would have seen had she been listening to me, but she was lost in the music. At least I had the comfort of knowing that her homework would be background for it—her homework and perhaps a soccer match.

MEET THE WRITER

Bill Cosby (1937–) was born and grew up in Philadelphia. When Cosby was twenty-three, he enrolled in Temple University in Philadelphia on an athletic scholarship (he had dropped out of high school in tenth grade). Cosby majored in physical education and played halfback on Temple's football team, but he chose comedy over sports as a career.

In 1984 *The Cosby Show,* a weekly comedy about Dr. Heathcliff Huxtable, his lawyer-wife, and their five children, made its first appearance on TV. For many years Cosby's show was one of the most successful comedies on television. Another measure of Cosby's success is the millions of dollars he and his wife, Camille, have donated to higher education.

READ ON

A Shock of Recognition

The Summer of the Swans (Puffin) by Betsy Byars is the story of a day in the life of fourteen-year-old Sara Godfrey. In just a little more than twenty-four hours, Sara's feelings about herself and her whole outlook on life change. It all begins when her younger brother Charlie disappears.

Out of Africa

Fourteen-year-old Chris can't wait to begin the adventure of a lifetime: a three-year stay with his father on Africa's Serengeti plain. In Eric Campbell's *The Place of Lions* (Harcourt Brace), a plane disaster is more adventure than Chris bargained for, and now he must find a way to save his father and the pilot. In this tale of heroism, Chris's ally in survival is an elderly lion.

Sailorman

In Armstrong Sperry's *Call It Courage* (Macmillan), ten-year-old Mafatu can't forget the terrible ocean tragedy that happened when he was a baby. He is deathly afraid of the ocean surrounding the South Sea island where he lives. Family and friends tease him until the day he decides to confront his fear.

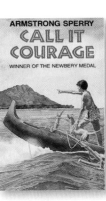

Other Picks

- Jackie French Koller, *If I Had One Wish* (Little, Brown). Alec fervently wishes that his little brother would disappear. Then he learns that wishes are sometimes best left unanswered.

- Patricia Beatty, *Lupita Mañana* (Beech Tree Books). When Lupita and her brother are sent from Mexico to California to look for work, they face unexpected obstacles. (This title is available in the HRW Library.)

- Scott O'Dell, *Island of the Blue Dolphins* (Yearling). Stranded on an island, a twelve-year-old Native American girl named Karana learns how to survive on her own.

Sustained Silent Reading

These titles can be used by students of various levels of ability and interest for sustained silent reading. Based on the Bornmuth formula, *The Summer of the Swans* scores at the lowest reading level, and *The Place of Lions* at the highest. For reluctant readers with an appetite for action and adventure, *Islands of the Blue Dolphins* may be the best choice.

Students need time to practice sustained silent reading. Their aims should be the following: (1) to learn to read phrases rather than one word at a time; (2) to gain automaticity and fluency; and (3) to self-monitor for comprehension.

To help students achieve these objectives, try these strategies: (1) Have students read for a specified amount of time over a period of several weeks (five minutes per class period or fifteen minutes twice a week, for example). (2) Give students a chart on which they can record the amount of text they read at each sitting. (3) Have students use a notebook to monitor their reading comprehension.

Writer's Workshop

Technology HELP

See Writer's Workshop 1 CD-ROM. *Assignment: Autobiographical Incident.*

ASSIGNMENT

Write a narrative about an experience you've had.

AIM

To write about an incident in your life; to express your feelings.

AUDIENCE

Your teacher, classmates, friends, or family or people who were involved in the incident.

NARRATIVE WRITING

AUTOBIOGRAPHICAL INCIDENT

When you write an **autobiographical incident,** you bring an experience or memory to life as you share a true story about yourself.

Professional Model

Because of my father's job, my family moved a great deal. I was *always* (at least it felt like always!) the "new kid" in school.

The beginning catches our attention.

I remember that when I was eleven years old, I was once again entering a brand-new school. And school had already begun. The kids had already gotten to know each other, had made friends. . . .

I arrived in the middle of the day, feeling very awkward and shy. I had had my hair cut the day before; it had been very long, and now it was very short, so I didn't even feel like myself. My mother took me to the school office, and they did the necessary paperwork to enroll me, and then she left me there. Someone took me to the classroom where I was supposed to be.

The writer describes her feelings— and her new haircut.

Action details are presented in time order.

Everyone stared at me, of course, when I entered the room. One of the students—reacting to my very short hair, I suppose—called out, "Is it a boy or a girl?"

Dialogue makes the incident vivid.

86 MOMENTS OF TRUTH

  *Resources: Print and Media*

Writing and Language
- *Portfolio Management System*
  Prewriting, p. 111
  Peer Editing, p. 112
  Assessment Rubric, p. 113
- *Workshop Resources*
  Revision Strategy Teaching Notes, p. 1
  Revision Strategy Transparencies 1, 2

- *Writer's Workshop 1 CD-ROM*
  Autobiographical Incident

The history
of the written
word is rich and...

Page 1

(continued)

> Do you know, that was *forty-four* years ago, that moment—yet I still remember how humiliating it felt.
>
> But guess what. I still wear my hair very short. I think it's my way, now, of saying, "Nyah, nyah. I don't care *what* you think."
>
> —from "Who's the New Kid?" by Lois Lowry

The writer tells how she feels about the incident today.

Prewriting

1. Writer's Notebook

If you have Writer's Notebook entries for this collection, review them to see if you want to develop one further. If not, use the ideas that follow to spark memories of your life.

2. Clustering and Freewriting

a. Some words spark memories. Try making clusters based on words that name feelings, such as *anger, joy, pride, fear, surprise,* and *kindness.* Around each word, jot notes about personal experiences that gave you that feeling.

b. Memories often hide from us until something triggers them. Try luring some of them out of hiding by sketching a time line of your life. Draw a line, and label the left end *birth* and the right end *now.* Above the line, write the major events of your life—perhaps the birth of a brother or sister or a move from one city to another. One of these may become your autobiographical incident.

3. Choosing Your Topic

From your ideas, pick a topic that meets these guidelines:

I found out Grandpa used to play in a jazz band.

For my birthday my friend gave me a mouse!

Surprise

The newspaper printed a letter that my friend and I wrote.

Mom says she's going to run for mayor.

Strategies for Elaboration

Sensory details show your readers what you saw, heard, touched, smelled, and tasted.

Imagine yourself back in the place and time of your incident. What sights stand out? What colors and shapes do you notice? Make notes about sights, sounds, smells, tastes, and textures—the way things feel when you touch them.

WRITER'S WORKSHOP **87**

Introducing the Writer's Workshop

- Read aloud the Professional Model on pp. 86–87 or have a female volunteer read it as students follow along. Encourage students to visualize the eleven-year-old girl in the narrative as well as the grown woman telling the story.
- Call students' attention to the comments in the margin, and ask them to point out specific passages in Lois Lowry's narrative in which the use of details and the expression of feelings enhance the narrative.
- With students, brainstorm some qualities that you and they think make for a good autobiographical narrative, such as:
  1. a story line in which events proceed clearly from one to another
  2. vivid, convincing details
  3. interesting characters
  4. the feeling that the writer is being honest
- Review the purpose of this assignment: to describe an incident from life and tell the reader how the writer felt about it. *Remind students to choose a situation they will not mind sharing with others.*

Teaching the Writer's Workshop

Prewriting

Have students use the techniques suggested on pp. 87–88 (or any others that may be helpful to them) to come up with ideas.

Reaching All Students

Struggling Writers

Finding a topic and recalling its details may be an initial stumbling block for some. Suggest that students begin by closing their eyes for a minute or two and "seeing" whatever scenes from their lives begin coming to life. Have students make clusters for one or more such incidents. See Strategies for Elaboration on p. 87 for further suggestions about returning mentally to a past incident.

English Language Learners

If these students feel insecure about writing a narrative in English, let them know that their experiences would probably be unfamiliar to most American students, and therefore extremely interesting. Allow students to write with a more fluent partner. Allow the student to draft the incident in his or her first language and then translate it into English with the help of the partner.

Drafting

- If you have not already taught the Student Model, do so before students begin their drafts.
- Remind students to double space when they write their drafts. They should also leave extra space in the right margin, for comments and editing marks.
- Reassure students that the recommended drafting and revising process is fluid and that each writer develops his or her own variation of the process. For example, the activities listed under Show, Don't Tell can be used before writing the first draft, or continuously during later drafts—they aren't for use only between the first and second drafts.

> **Framework for an Autobiographical Incident**
>
> **Significance:**
> _____
> _____
>
> **Introduction** (statement, description, or dialogue that catches readers' attention):
> _____
> _____
>
> **Order of events:**
> 1. _____
>   Details: _____
> 2. _____
>   Details: _____
> 3. _____
>   Details: _____
>
> **Conclusion** (refers to the meaning or importance of the incident):
> _____

Language/Grammar Link
H E L P

Irregular verbs: page 13.
Subject-verb agreement: pages 29, 43, and 81.
Verb tenses: page 52.
Vivid verbs: page 68.

Sentence Workshop
H E L P

Sentence fragments: page 91.

- I'm willing to share this incident with others.
- I remember a lot about this incident.
- This incident means something important to me.

4. What Does It Mean to Me?

An incident that you remember clearly, especially one from long ago, is important to you. For the moment, however, don't worry too much about what it means. If you wish, jot down a few notes on why you recall this particular incident. File those notes away somewhere, and pull them out later, after you've written about the incident. See if you would change your notes at that point.

Drafting

1. Writing Your First Draft

You'll discover new things about your incident as you write your draft. To start, quickly write down the basics: Where were you? What happened? When did it happen? Who was involved?

2. Show, Don't Tell

Once you've written the basic story, you can start gathering details about your incident that bring it to life.

a. Replay your incident in your mind. Recall names of people and places as well as bits of dialogue (people's spoken words). Recall how the people—including you—looked, sounded, and moved. Record these actions and sensory details.

b. How did you feel during the incident? Try acting it out.

c. Talk to others who were involved in the incident. See if their memories help you recall more details.

d. Examine objects that relate to your incident, such as souvenirs or photos. What memories do they help you recall?

If you've tried even a few of these strategies, you'll probably have lots of ideas about your incident. Read through your notes. Circle the details that seem interesting or important.

88 MOMENTS OF TRUTH

Using Students' Strengths

Logical/Mathematical Learners

These students may work better with prewriting methods that are more structured than clustering or freewriting. Suggest that after students have thought of one or more possible incidents from their pasts, they construct a 5W-H? chart like this one to develop details. They may wish to think of the incident as a case, and themselves as detectives piecing together what happened and what its effects were.

Who was there?	
What happened?	
Where did it happen?	
When did it happen?	
Why did it happen?	
How did it happen?	

3. Writing Your Second Draft

In your second draft you can expand your quick sketch by using some of the specific details you've recalled. If you wrote about why you recall this incident, reread those notes now. Do the details help you see the incident more clearly? The following excerpt is from the second draft of an autobiographical incident. Notice details that show what the writer feels.

Communications Handbook
H E L P

See Proofreaders' Marks.

Using the Model

As class members read the Student Model, be sure they understand the side notes. You can extend discussion by having students focus on questions like these:

? Where does the writer include specific sensory details to help you see and hear the incident? In writing your incident, what details would be most important to help the reader see and hear?

? Where does the writer state or imply her feelings? What was her main feeling? What other feelings did she have?

? This writer chose to write about a victory. Do victories make the most interesting stories? Why or why not?

Student Model

THE SWIM OF MY LIFE

It was a typical Houston day in the summer, hot and humid. The insects kept buzzing in my ears and sweat dripped down my forehead like ice cream melting and running down a cone. I got to splash into the water, but, although it felt good, I couldn't swim for fun. This was the Meet of Champions and I had to show my opponents what I was made of. I had six chances to place and swim for a medal. Every time I jumped into the water, I had to swim to my fullest extent. Stroke after stroke was stronger and stronger. It was a race against the clock.

After a swim I would jump out of the water soaking wet, look around, and check with my coach to see if I had placed. Two out of six times I had placed. I was so excited I could barely hold it all in.

I was sitting on the ready bench waiting nervously to swim. I would be swimming the stroke that was my natural stroke, breast stroke. I had so many butterflies in my stomach I thought they were having a family reunion!

"All thirteen–fourteen girl breast strokers to the edge of the pool!" the monotonous voice of the intercom spoke out. I was shaking from nervousness.

"Down and ready," the gunsman yelled, and then the shot was fired. In I jumped. I swam the fastest swim of my life. I was a dolphin and the water was my home. I touched the wall third and had broken my record!

Victory at last!

— Lacey Clayton
West Memorial Junior High School
Katy, Texas

Specific sensory details grab our attention.

The writer gives background information about the incident.

She presents details in time order.

She describes her feelings of excitement and, later, of nervousness.

Details of the incident, including exact words that were spoken, make us feel as if we were at the scene.

She tells why the incident was so important to her.

WRITER'S WORKSHOP 89

Using Students' Strengths

Musical/Auditory Learners
Ask students to reread "The Swim of My Life" slowly, imagining and inserting auditory details that were not included, such as splashes, crowd noise, and the narrator's breathing and heartbeat. Encourage students to use this same technique to incorporate sensory details into their own narratives.

Kinesthetic Learners
Ask students to reread "The Swim of My Life" slowly, imagining how their bodies would have felt at each stage of the incident. Encourage students to use this same technique to find sensory details for their own narratives.

Interpersonal Learners
These learners may benefit from beginning their topic searches by recalling a character. Encourage students to think of the people who have meant the most to them: childhood friends, siblings, and so on. Then ask students to cluster or freewrite about things they remember doing with their chosen character.

Evaluating and Revising

Have students use the Evaluation Criteria provided here to review their drafts and determine needed revisions.

Proofreading

Have students proofread their own papers first and then exchange them with another student. For this assignment, remind students to be particularly careful of subject-verb agreement and verb tense consistency. If time permits, the final copy should be put aside for at least a day before it is proofread for the final time by the author.

Remind students that they must spell accurately in final drafts. Suggest that they use a spelling checker if they are using a computer that has one. Make sure students understand that a spelling checker will not alert them to usage errors such as the misuse of *it's* for *its*.

Publishing

Students who don't mind sharing their autobiographical incident with a wider audience should look to the school literary magazine or another appropriate venue, such as the school's newspaper or web site, for publication.

Reflecting

Students might prepare a brief reflection on what they learned from the process of writing an autobiographical incident. Invite them to answer these two major questions:
• What did you learn about your life from this exercise?
• What did you learn about the process of writing?
To focus students' thinking about their writing process, have them review the evaluation criteria for an autobiographical narrative.

Resources

Peer Editing Forms and Rubrics
• *Portfolio Management System*, p. 112

Revision Strategy Transparencies
• *Workshop Resources*, p. 1

Grading Timesaver

Rubrics for this Writer's Workshop assignment appear on p. 113 of the *Portfolio Management System*.

Many writers, including the writer of the Student Model, use chronological order when they write a personal narrative. Using **chronological order** means telling about events in the order in which they happened.

An alternative is to use **comparison and contrast.** For instance, you may want to compare and contrast the good and bad parts of your experience.

Good	Bad

■ *Evaluation Criteria*

A good autobiographical incident

1. focuses on one experience

2. has a beginning that grabs readers' attention

3. includes action details in time order or as a series of "good" and "bad" events

4. includes sensory details to bring descriptions to life

5. tells what the incident means to the writer

---

4. Organizing Your Second Draft

When you're retelling an incident, you'll almost automatically put events in chronological order, just as they happened. You might sharpen your story, however, by looking closely at each event to see how it moves the story along. Ask yourself, "What does this event do for the story—does it give background, build suspense, answer a question?" Then, study your draft. Can you think of ways to make each section do its job better?

Evaluating and Revising

1. Peer Review

After you finish your second draft, exchange papers with a partner. Ask your partner to do the following:

• Highlight in color the sentences and phrases that seem especially good.

• Retell the story of your incident. (Listen carefully. If your partner mixes up the order of events, you may need to make your time order clearer.)

• Identify the most important parts of the incident. (Again, listen carefully. If your partner leaves out important parts, you may need to add details to make those parts more vivid.)

• Suggest ideas for revision.

Then, do the same for your partner's paper.

2. Revising

A good thing to check when revising your autobiography is the number of times you have used the pronoun *I*. You might want to eliminate half of them by rephrasing.

Also, think about your partner's comments and your self-evaluation. Then, decide how you want to revise your incident.

Sentence Workshop

SENTENCE FRAGMENTS

A **sentence** is a group of words that expresses a complete thought. When a group of words looks like a sentence but does not express a complete thought, it is a **sentence fragment.**

FRAGMENT   Already have one. [The sentence's subject is missing. *Who* already has one?]

SENTENCE   I already have one. [The subject *I* completes the sentence.]

FRAGMENT   Water down my back. [The sentence's verb is missing.]

SENTENCE   Water trickled down my back. [With the verb *trickled,* a complete thought is expressed.]

FRAGMENT   As the birthday grew closer. [Even with a subject and verb, this group of words does not express a complete thought.]

SENTENCE   As the birthday grew closer, I had awful nightmares about it.

Writer's Workshop Follow-up: Revision

Take out your autobiographical incident, and exchange papers with a classmate. Check your partner's paper for fragments, and suggest a revision for each one that you find. (There's one place where fragments are acceptable: You'll want to use fragments in the dialogue you write, because people often speak in fragments.) Exchange papers again, and revise any fragments your classmate found.

PEANUTS reprinted by permission of United Feature Syndicate, Inc.

Language Handbook
H E L P

See Sentence or Sentence Fragment?, pages 724–725; Sentence Fragments, page 737.

Technology
H E L P

See Language Workshop CD-ROM. Key word entry: sentence fragments.

Try It Out

Copy the following paragraph onto a separate sheet of paper, and edit it, correcting any sentence fragments.

Gary Soto has written five collections of poetry and several books. Including poetry, short fiction, and autobiographical recollections. Soto started out as a poet. But soon turned to stories. His characters are often teenagers. Who talk like real kids. Soto probably keeps a notebook handy. Even at the supermarket.

Resources ──────
Workshop Resources
• Worksheet, p. 37
Language Workshop CD-ROM
• Sentence Fragments

Try It Out
Answer
Gary Soto has written five collections of poetry and several books, including poetry, short fiction, and autobiographical recollections. Soto started out as a poet but soon turned to stories. His characters are often teenagers who talk like real kids. Soto probably keeps a notebook handy, even at the supermarket.

Assessing Learning

Quick Check: Sentence Fragments
Change the following fragments into complete sentences by adding a subject, adding a verb, completing the thought, or combining the fragment with the sentence before or after it.

1. Ate at Ernie's Riverside Restaurant. [Mary ate at Ernie's Riverside Restaurant.]
2. Jerry pedaled furiously to the drugstore. Because he wanted to buy more trading cards. [Jerry pedaled furiously to the drugstore because he wanted to buy more trading cards.]
3. Because she wore skirts. [Because she wore skirts, she felt out of place at school.]
4. Manuel practiced. Singing in the shower. [Manuel practiced singing in the shower.]
5. Modrona the practical one in the family. [Modrona was the practical one in the family.]

T91

OBJECTIVES
1. Learn techniques for finding information in a textbook
2. Use text organizers to locate information

Teaching the Lesson

Ask a volunteer to describe the table of contents of a book and its purpose. Emphasize the usefulness of a table of contents to find specific information in a book. Have students find the table of contents in their edition of *Elements of Literature*. Ask volunteers to identify the location of specific features, stories, and stories by specific authors.

Using the Strategies

Answers
1. Moments of Truth
2. Page 14
3. 1) Reading Skills and Strategies
   2) Elements of Literature
4. In the Reading Skills and Strategies feature

Reading for Life

Using Text Organizers

Situation

Another school year is beginning. You've just been handed this literature textbook. Use the following strategies to find out how the book is organized and how to **locate specific information** in it.

Strategies

Use the table of contents.

- You'll find the **table of contents** (TOC) near the front of the book. It lists the writers, selections, and special features in the order in which they appear in the book.

Look for headings.

- A **heading** is a kind of title for the information that follows it. The size or color of a heading sets it off from the rest of the text, so that it seems to jump out at you.

- Look for repeated headings like *Before You Read*. A particular repeated heading is always followed by the same kind of material.

Use graphic features.

- **Graphic features** like

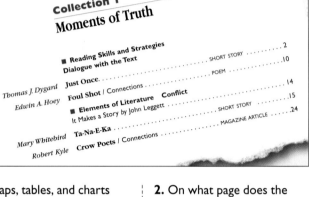

CONTENTS

Collection 1
Moments of Truth

■ Reading Skills and Strategies
Dialogue with the Text .... SHORT STORY 2

Thomas J. Dygard   Just Once .... POEM 10

Edwin A. Hoey   Foul Shot / Connections 14

■ Elements of Literature   Conflict
It Makes a Story by John Leggett .... SHORT STORY 15

Mary Whitebird   Ta-Na-E-Ka .... MAGAZINE ARTICLE 24
Robert Kyle   Crow Poets / Connections

maps, tables, and charts present information visually, in a combination of words and lines. Graphic features like boldface words, colors, and logos (tiny pictures that look like computer icons) help you locate specific kinds of information. For instance, an open-book logo like the one on page 2 appears with every reading activity, question, or lesson.

Using the Strategies

1. What is the collection title in the TOC above?

2. On what page does the lesson on conflict begin?

3. This TOC lists titles of literature selections (with authors' names at the left) and special features. What special features are listed here?

4. If you needed help in reading, where could you find it in this book?

Extending the Strategies

Give someone at home a guided tour of this textbook. Show how the table of contents, headings, and graphic features help you locate information.

Reaching All Students

Struggling Readers

Emphasize that part of finding information in a book consists of figuring out what you *don't* have to read. Text headings—including chapter headings, subheads, and captions—can help students find information quickly; so can tables of contents, graphics, and indexes. Have students use these tools to make up trivia-game questions and answers based on information in a specific collection in their book.

Advanced Learners

Have students imagine that they are in seventh grade. Ask them, "If you could learn about anything you wanted to in seventh grade, what would it be?" (This is their chance to develop a dream curriculum!) Then ask them to do preliminary research on their chosen topic, finding information about it in one or more books.

Learning for Life
Decision Making

OBJECTIVES
1. Understand the decision making process through reflection and interviews
2. Choose a method of presenting what has been learned—writing an advice manual, humorous skit, or song

Problem

The characters in this collection all made decisions, some good and some not so good. Making decisions can be tough because the right choice doesn't always jump up and down in front of you. How can people make good decisions in a world where there are so many choices?

Project

Analyze ways of making decisions, and present your findings.

Preparation

1. Either individually or with a group, write a list of decisions you've made—big or small—throughout your life.

2. Pick three of the decisions you listed, and write down the positive and negative things that happened as a result of each one.

3. Circle any decision you wish you had made differently. Explain why you feel this way. Think about how you make decisions.

Procedure

1. Interview two adults outside class. Find out how they make decisions and what they think about when deciding things. Here are some questions you could ask:

   • What are two of the most important decisions you've made?

   • How did you make the decisions?

   • What did you think about when making the decisions? Did you consider the positive and negative effects for yourself and others?

   • What do you do when you feel you've made the wrong decision?

   • What advice do you have for students learning to make decisions?

2. Make notes on the interview.

Presentation

Use one of these formats to present what you've learned:

1. Advice Manual

Write an advice manual for people of all ages who have difficulty making decisions. Include specific examples.

2. Humorous Skit

Write a humorous skit about a character who makes disastrous decisions and a wise friend who shows him or her how to make better decisions.

3. Song

Write a song about decision making. Use whatever style of music you prefer: rock, rap, blues, folk. Give your song a catchy title—for example, "It Sure Seemed Like a Good Idea at the Time."

Processing

Complete this sentence: The next time I have an important decision to make, I'll be sure to . . . .

Resources

Viewing and Representing
*HRW Multimedia
Presentation Maker*
Students may wish to use the *Multimedia Presentation Maker* to create an illustrated advice manual.

Grading Timesaver

Rubrics for this Learning for Life project appear on p. 114 of the *Portfolio Management System*.

Developing Workplace Competencies

Preparation	Procedure	Presentation
• Working on teams • Determining cause and effect • Thinking creatively	• Working with people from diverse backgrounds • Acquiring data • Processing information	• Teaching others • Communicating ideas and information • Exhibiting self-esteem

Collection Two

Unforgettable Personalities

Theme

One of a Kind   *In stories and in life, characters are what interest us most. Some of the characters we love are human, perhaps our parents or sisters or brothers; but some of the best-loved characters in literature and in life are animals.*

Reading the Anthology

Reaching Struggling Readers

The Reading Skills and Strategies: Reaching Struggling Readers binder provides materials coordinated with the Pupil's Edition (see the Collection Planner, p. T93C) to help students who have difficulty reading and comprehending text, or students who are reluctant readers. The binder for sixth grade is organized around eleven individual skill areas and offers the following options:

- **Mini Read** MiniReads are short, easy texts that give students a chance to practice a particular skill and strategy before reading selections in the Pupil's Edition. Each MiniRead Skill Lesson can be taught independently or used in conjunction with a Selection Skill Lesson.

- **Selection Skill Lessons** Selection Skill Lessons allow students to apply skills introduced in the MiniReads. Each Selection Skill Lesson provides reading instruction and practice specific to a particular piece of literature in the Pupil's Edition.

Reading Beyond the Anthology

Read On

Collection Two includes an annotated bibliography of books suitable for extended reading. The suggested books are related to works in this collection by theme, by author, or by subject. To preview the Read On for Collection Two, please turn to p. T155.

HRW Library

The *HRW Library* offers novels, plays, and short-story collections for extended reading. Each book in the Library includes one or more major works and thematically or topically related Connections. A Study Guide provides teaching suggestions and worksheets. For Collection Two, the following titles are recommended.

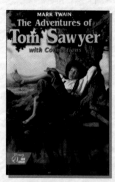

THE ADVENTURES OF TOM SAWYER
Mark Twain
Perhaps the most famous boy character in American literature, Tom Sawyer lives along the Mississippi River around 1840. Tom and his friends have many adventures—including a terrifying encounter with a murderer.

M. C. HIGGINS THE GREAT
Virginia Hamilton
M. C. Higgins is a boy readers won't forget. At first all he wants to do is get off the mountain where his family has lived for generations. When two strangers appear, M. C.'s world begins to change—forever.

Skills Focus

Selection or Feature	Reading Skills and Strategies	Elements of Literature	Language/ Grammar	Vocabulary/ Spelling	Writing	Listening/ Speaking	Viewing/ Representing
Storm (p. 96) Gary Paulsen	Dialogue with the Text, pp. 96, 105 Chart Character Traits, pp. 96, 105	Character, pp. 96, 105 Character Traits, p. 105 Anecdotes, p. 106	*Good* and *Well*, p. 107	Prefixes, p. 107	Write an Anecdote, p. 106 Retell the Story, p. 106 Write a Pawbook, p. 106		Draw Pictures for a Pawbook, p. 106
Elements of Literature: Autobiography and Biography		Autobiography, p. 108 Biography, p. 108					
Brother (p. 109) Maya Angelou	Find the Main Idea, pp. 109, 115 Infer, p. 109 Summarize, p. 115	Description, pp. 109, 115 Main Idea, p. 115	Precise Words, p. 116 Modifiers, p. 116	Synonyms, p. 116 • Use a Dictionary • Use a Thesaurus	List Details About a Person, p. 115 Restate the Main Idea, p. 115	Describe an Outdoor Game, p. 115	Chart Responses to Angelou's Description, p. 115
Yes, It Was My Grandmother (p. 117) Luci Tapahonso	Use a Diagram to Connect with the Text, pp. 117, 120	Tone, pp. 117, 120			Write a List of Questions, p. 120 Write a Poem, p. 120	Interview a Special Person, p. 120 Hold a Poetry Reading, p. 120 Reader's Theater, p. 120	
Petals/Los Pétalos (p. 121) Pat Mora		Imagery, pp. 121, 124			Take Notes on Someone's Appearance, p. 124 Write a Potluck Poem, p. 124		Make a Collage, p. 124
Reading Skills and Strategies: Making Inferences (p. 125)	Make Inferences, p. 125 • Prior Knowledge • Text Evidence						Make an Inference Chart, p. 125
The Mysterious Mr. Lincoln (p. 126) Russell Freedman	Use Prior Knowledge, p. 126 Make Inferences, pp. 126, 133 Use a KWL Chart, pp. 127, 133	Character, pp. 126, 133 Character Traits, p. 134	Adjectives, p. 135	Synonyms, p. 135	List Contrasting Character Traits, p. 134 Create a Biographical Sketch, p. 134	Discuss Two Books, p. 134 Present Scenes from Lincoln's Life, p. 134	Make a Character Graph, p. 134
A Glory Over Everything (p. 136) Ann Petry	Identify Sequence, pp. 136, 147 Infer, p. 147 Summarize, p. 148	Biography, p. 136 Character Traits, p. 147	*Bad* and *Badly*, p. 149	Vocabulary for the Workplace, p. 149	Take Notes About a Historical Event, p. 148 Write an Obituary, p. 148	Make a Tape Recording of Spirituals, p. 148	Use a Sequence Chart, p. 147 Paint a Mural, p. 148
No Questions Asked: *from* **The Adventures of Tom Sawyer** (p. 150) Mark Twain		The **No Questions Asked** feature provides students with an unstructured opportunity to practice reading strategies using a selection that extends the theme of the collection.					
Speaking and Listening Workshop: Interviewing (p. 156)	Summarize Information, p. 157					Interview an Expert, pp. 156–157	
Writer's Workshop: Biographical Sketch (p. 158)		Biography, p. 158 Chronological Order, p. 161			Write a Biographical Sketch, pp. 158–162		Make a Folding Diagram on Your Subject, p. 160
Sentence Workshop: Run-on Sentences (p. 163)			Run-on Sentences, p. 163		Revise Run-on Sentences, p. 163		
Reading for Life: Independent Reading (p. 164)	Adjust Reading Rate, p. 164	Infer, p. 164					
Learning for Life: Researching Media Personalities (p. 165)					Write Copy for a Newscast, p. 165	Create a Skit on a Celebrity Interview, p. 165	Make a Celebrity Collage, p. 165

Resources for this Collection

Note: All resources for this collection are available for preview on the *One-Stop Planner CD-ROM 1 with Test Generator*. All worksheets and blackline masters may be printed from the CD-ROM.

Internet Resources
go.hrw.com (Keyword: LE0 6-2)

Selection or Feature	Reading and Literary Skills	Language and Grammar

Storm *from* **Woodsong** (p. 96)
Gary Paulsen
	• *Reading Skills and Strategies: Reaching Struggling Readers*
	  • Selection Skill Lesson, p. 11
	• *Graphic Organizers for Active Reading*, Worksheet p. 7
		• *Grammar and Language Links:*
		  Using *Good* and *Well* Correctly, Worksheet p. 13
		• *Language Workshop CD-ROM*,
		  Good and *Well*
		• *Daily Oral Grammar,*
		  Transparency 7

Elements of Literature: **Autobiography and Biography** (p. 108)	• *Literary Elements,* Transparency 2	

Brother *from* **I Know Why the Caged Bird Sings** (p. 109)
Maya Angelou
	• *Reading Skills and Strategies: Reaching Struggling Readers*
	  • MiniRead Skill Lesson, p. 110
	  • Selection Skill Lesson, p. 116
	• *Graphic Organizers for Active Reading*, Worksheet p. 8
	• *Literary Elements:*
	  Transparency 2; Worksheet p. 7
		• *Grammar and Language Links:*
		  Choosing Precise Words, Worksheet p. 15
		• *Language Workshop CD-ROM*,
		  Modifiers
		• *Daily Oral Grammar,*
		  Transparency 8

Yes, It Was My Grandmother (p. 117) Luci Tapahonso	• *Graphic Organizers for Active Reading*, Worksheet p. 9	
Petals/Los Pétalos (p. 121) Pat Mora *translated by Nicolás Kanellos*	• *Graphic Organizers for Active Reading*, Worksheet p. 10	

The Mysterious Mr. Lincoln
(p. 126)
Russell Freedman
Connections: Lincoln's Humor
(p. 132)
Louis W. Koenig
	• *Graphic Organizers for Active Reading*, Worksheet p. 11	• *Grammar and Language Links:*
		  Comparing with Adjectives, Worksheet p. 17
		• *Language Workshop CD-ROM*,
		  Degrees of Comparison
		• *Daily Oral Grammar,*
		  Transparency 9

A Glory over Everything *from* **Harriet Tubman: Conductor on the Underground Railroad** (p. 136)
Ann Petry
	• *Reading Skills and Strategies: Reaching Struggling Readers*
	  • MiniRead Skill Lesson, p. 125
	  • Selection Skill Lesson, p. 131
	• *Graphic Organizers for Active Reading*, Worksheet p. 12
		• *Grammar and Language Links:*
		  Don't Use *Bad* and *Badly* Badly, Worksheet p. 19
		• *Language Workshop CD-ROM*,
		  Bad, Badly
		• *Daily Oral Grammar,*
		  Transparency 10

No Questions Asked: *from* **The Adventures of Tom Sawyer** (p. 150) Mark Twain	The **No Questions Asked** feature provides students with an unstructured opportunity to practice reading strategies using a selection that extends the theme of the collection.	
Speaking and Listening Workshop: **Interviewing: Questions, Please** (p. 156)		
Writer's Workshop: Biographical Sketch (p. 158)		
Sentence Workshop: Run-on Sentences (p. 163)		• *Workshop Resources*, p. 39 • *Language Workshop CD-ROM*, Run-on Sentences
Learning for Life: Researching Media Personalities (p. 165)		

Collection Planner

Collection Resources

- *Cross-Curricular Activities*, p. 13
- *Portfolio Management System:*
  Introduction to Portfolio Assessment, p. 1;
  Parent/Guardian Letters, p. 89
- *Formal Assessment*,
  Reading Application Test, p. 30
- *Test Generator*, Collection Test

Vocabulary, Spelling, and Decoding	Writing	Listening and Speaking, Viewing and Representing	Assessment
• *Words to Own*, Worksheet p. 6 • *Spelling and Decoding*, Worksheet p. 7	• *Portfolio Management System*, Rubrics for Choices, p. 115	• *Audio CD Library*, Disc 3, Track 2 🎧 • *Portfolio Management System*, Rubrics for Choices, p. 115	• *Formal Assessment*, Selection Test, p. 19 • *Standardized Test Preparation*, p. 24 • *Test Generator* (One-Stop Planner CD-ROM) 💿
			• *Formal Assessment*, Literary Elements Test, p. 29
• *Words to Own*, Worksheet p. 7	• *Portfolio Management System*, Rubrics for Choices, p. 116	• *Audio CD Library*, Disc 3, Track 3 🎧 • *Viewing and Representing:* Fine Art Transparency 4; Worksheet p. 16 • *Portfolio Management System*, Rubrics for Choices, p. 116	• *Formal Assessment*, Selection Test, p. 21 • *Standardized Test Preparation*, p. 26 • *Test Generator* (One-Stop Planner CD-ROM) 💿
	• *Portfolio Management System*, Rubrics for Choices, p. 117	• *Audio CD Library*, Disc 3, Track 4 🎧 • *Viewing and Representing:* Fine Art Transparency 5; Worksheet p. 20 • *Portfolio Management System*, Rubrics for Choices, p. 117	• *Formal Assessment*, Selection Test, p. 23 • *Test Generator* (One-Stop Planner CD-ROM) 💿
	• *Portfolio Management System*, Rubrics for Choices, p. 118	• *Audio CD Library*, Disc 3, Tracks 5, 6 🎧 • *Portfolio Management System*, Rubrics for Choices, p. 118	• *Formal Assessment*, Selection Test, p. 24 • *Test Generator* (One-Stop Planner CD-ROM) 💿
• *Words to Own*, Worksheet p. 8 • *Spelling and Decoding*, Worksheet p. 8	• *Portfolio Management System*, Rubrics for Choices, p. 119	• *Visual Connections*, Videocassette A, Segment 2 📼 • *Audio CD Library*, Disc 3, Track 7 🎧 • *Portfolio Management System*, Rubrics for Choices, p. 119	• *Formal Assessment*, Selection Test, p. 25 • *Standardized Test Preparation*, p. 28 • *Test Generator* (One-Stop Planner CD-ROM) 💿
• *Words to Own*, Worksheet p. 9 • *Spelling and Decoding*, Worksheet p. 9	• *Portfolio Management System*, Rubrics for Choices, p. 120	• *Visual Connections*, Videocassette A, Segment 3 📼 • *Audio CD Library*, Disc 3, Track 8 🎧 • *Viewing and Representing:* Fine Art Transparency 6; Worksheet p. 24 • *Portfolio Management System*, Rubrics for Choices, p. 120	• *Formal Assessment*, Selection Test, p. 27 • *Standardized Test Preparation*, pp. 30, 32 • *Test Generator* (One-Stop Planner CD-ROM) 💿
		• *Audio CD Library*, Disc 3, Track 9 🎧	
			• *Portfolio Management System*, p. 121

	• *Workshop Resources*, p. 5
	• *Writer's Workshop 1 CD-ROM*, Firsthand Biography 💿
			• *Portfolio Management System*
			  • Prewriting, p. 122
			  • Peer Editing, p. 123
			  • Assessment Rubric, p. 124

		• *Viewing and Representing*, HRW Multimedia Presentation Maker	• *Portfolio Management System*, Rubrics, p. 125

 Transparency 💿 CD-ROM 📼 Video 🎧 Audio CD

Collection Planner

T93D

OBJECTIVES

1. Read literature in different genres on the theme "Unforgettable Personalities"
2. Interpret literary elements used in the literature with special emphasis on autobiography and biography
3. Apply a variety of reading strategies, particularly making inferences
4. Respond to the literature in a variety of modes
5. Learn and use new words
6. Develop skill in interviewing
7. Plan, draft, revise, proof, and publish a biographical sketch
8. Identify and revise run-on sentences
9. Demonstrate the ability to select and read a book for independent reading
10. Explore through a variety of projects how the media affect our perception of celebrities and their influence on us

Introducing the Theme

Show students pictures of famous people that they are likely to know by sight. Ask students to explain what makes each person unforgettable. Explain to the class that each of the biographies, poems, and stories in this collection is about an unusual animal or person who leaves a deep and lasting impression on others—including on the reader. As they read the selections, remind students to look for qualities that make each of the main characters in the collection hard to forget.

Unforgettable Personalities

Writing Focus: Biographical Sketch

The following **Work in Progress** assignments in this collection build to a culminating **Writer's Workshop** at the end of Collection 2.

• Storm	Write an anecdote that illustrates a trait (p. 106)
• Brother	Describe a typical action of a great person (p. 115)
• Yes, It Was My Grandmother	Interview someone special (p. 120)
• Petals / Los pétalos	Detail the appearance of an older person (p. 124)
• The Mysterious Mr. Lincoln	Note contrasting character traits (p. 134)
• A Glory over Everything	Note an event in the life of a historical figure (p. 148)

Writer's Workshop: Expository Writing / Biographical Sketch (p. 158)

Collection

Two

Some are born great, some achieve greatness, and some have greatness thrust upon them.

—*William Shakespeare*

95

Responding to the Quotation

First, make sure students understand the three categories of greatness described in the quotation. You might paraphrase "some have greatness thrust upon them" as "some people become great through circumstances—perhaps by being in a certain place at a certain time, or perhaps by being looked upon as great by others." Ask students to name people or types of people who fit into each of the categories. [Possible responses: musical or mathematical prodigies are born great; George Washington, the first President of the United States, achieved greatness; sports heroes sometimes have greatness thrust upon them by their fans.]

RESPONDING TO THE ART

Activity. Ask students to describe experiences that might help each child achieve greatness. On the other hand, what experiences might *deny* them chances to be great?

Writer's Notebook

Ask students to freewrite about a person or animal in their lives that will always be unforgettable to them. Ask them to explain what makes this person or animal so special. *Remind students to choose a situation they would not mind sharing with others.*

Resources

Portfolio Management System
- Introduction to Portfolio Assessment, p. 1
- Parent/Guardian Letters, p. 89

Formal Assessment
- Reading Application Test, p. 30

Test Generator
- Collection Test

Cross-Curricular Activities
- Teaching Notes, p. 13

Selection Readability

This Annotated Teacher's Edition provides a summary of each selection in the student book. Following each Summary heading, you will find one, two, or three small icons. These icons indicate, in an approximate sense, the reading level of the selection.

■ One icon indicates that the selection is easy.

■ ■ Two icons indicate that the selection is on an intermediate reading level.

■ ■ ■ Three icons indicate that the selection is challenging.

OBJECTIVES

1. Read and interpret the story
2. Analyze character
3. Monitor comprehension
4. Express understanding through writing, research, or art
5. Identify the correct usage of *good* and *well,* and use these words correctly in writing
6. Learn and use new words
7. Use prefixes to understand the meanings of words

SKILLS

Literary, Reading, Writing
- Analyze character
- Monitor comprehension
- Write an anecdote
- Retell a story from a dog's point of view
- Write a handbook

Grammar/Language
- Use *good* and *well* correctly

Vocabulary
- Use new words
- Understand prefixes

Art
- Draw pictures

Viewing/Representing
- Identify the techniques a painter uses to create feelings (ATE)
- Identify similarities between art and text (ATE)

Planning

- **Block Schedule**
  Block Scheduling Lesson Plans with Pacing Guide
- **Traditional Schedule**
  Lesson Plans Including Strategies for English-Language Learners
- **One-Stop Planner**
  CD-ROM with Test Generator

Before You Read

STORM

Make the Connection

Animal Talk

- Two dogs meet and one immediately flops over on his back.

- A dog holds the muzzle of another dog in his mouth.

What are these dogs trying to communicate by their actions? What can we learn about a pet or wild animal from the animal's action?

Think-pair-share. Make a two-column chart like the one on this page. In the first column, list actions you have observed in different animals. In the second column, write what you think each action shows about the animal. Then, share your chart with a partner.

The Animal's Actions	What They Tell Me
My large dog lies down when a little dog comes near.	My dog's showing he's friendly and gentle.
Blue jays dive-bomb my cat when she's in the yard.	A really bold bird wants to protect its territory.

96 UNFORGETTABLE PERSONALITIES

Reading Skills and Strategies

Dialogue with the Text

As you read "Storm," keep a sheet of paper next to each page so that you can jot down your thoughts and feelings about Paulsen's dog story. One student's comments appear on the first page as an example.

Elements of Literature

Character: Pet Persona

You're about to meet an unforgettable personality—a dog named Storm. You'll get to know Storm by learning what he does, how he looks, and what his owner, Gary Paulsen, thinks and says about him. As you read, look for the traits that make Storm a **character** to love and remember.

> **A** **character** is a person or an animal in a story, play, or other literary work.
>
> *For more on Character, see the Handbook of Literary Terms.*

 go.hrw.com
LE0 6-2

Background

Literature and Real Life

"Storm" is part of the true story of Gary Paulsen's adventures in snowy northern Minnesota. There, his fascination with sled dogs gave him a close-up view of the wilderness. His growing obsession with dog sledding finally led him to enter the Iditarod (i·dit′ə·räd), a grueling 1,049-mile sled race across Alaska.

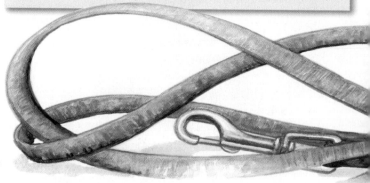

Preteaching Vocabulary

Words to Own

Have students locate the Words to Own and their definitions at the bottom of the story pages. Tell students that all three words are the same part of speech and ask them to identify it. [verb] Call on a volunteer to explain what verbs like these do in a sentence. [They express action.] Invite students to work with partners to show the actions of these three verbs. You might suggest the following possibilities or have students come up with their own.

1. Link arms with your partner. Now show how you can **disengage.**
2. For a moment stand on one foot. Did you nearly lose your balance? Show what you can do to **regain** your balance.
3. Suppose you want to **emit** the sound of a train, a machine, or a bird. Show how you would do it.

from **Woodsong**

STORM

Gary Paulsen

Siberian Husky by Scott Kennedy.

© 1994 Scott Kennedy. © The Greenwich Workshop®, Inc.
Courtesy of The Greenwich Workshop, Inc.
Shelton, Connecticut.

I t is always possible to learn from dogs, and in fact the longer I'm with them, the more I understand how little I know. But there was one dog who taught me the most. Just one dog.

Storm.

First dog. . . .

Joy, loyalty, toughness, peacefulness—all of these were part of Storm. Lessons about life and, finally, lessons about death came from him.

> **There was one dog who taught me the most. Just one dog. Storm.**

He had a bear's ears. He was brindle colored[1] and built like a truck, and his ears were rounded when we got him, so that they looked like bear cub ears. They gave him a comical look when he was young that somehow hung on to him even when he grew old. He had a sense of humor to match his ears, and when he grew truly old, he somehow resembled George Burns.[2]

---

1. **brindle colored:** gray or brown and streaked or spotted with a darker color.
2. **George Burns** (1896–1996): American comedian and actor with large ears.

Dialogue with the Text

You may think you're smart, but from a dog's point of view you're not as smart as you think you are.

It seems to me that Storm was more than a friend, more like a teacher.

Why do you say first dog?

This dog must have been raised by good owners if he was loyal, joyful, tough, and peaceful.

I like how you describe Storm, especially about his ears!

Even dogs have personalities, and Storm's was amiable.

Rana Jaber

— Rana Jaber
Southwest Middle School
Orlando, Florida

STORM 97

Summary ■■

This true story reveals the character traits of Storm, a powerful sled dog who taught his owner, writer Gary Paulsen, lessons about life. Storm shows his sense of humor by playing tricks and reveals his intelligence by finding ways to communicate with Paulsen. For example, Storm watches "with scale eyes" each time the sled is loaded and indicates his disapproval if the weight seems too heavy for the dogs to pull. Storm also communicates with a stick that he breaks off and keeps in his mouth. As long as he holds onto the stick, he is signaling his owner that everything is okay. When he pointedly drops the stick, however, it means that the owner is pushing the team too hard and it's time for a stop. Storm's personality makes him a one-of-a-kind dog.

Background

Dogsledding was once a principal mode of transportation for the Inuit, or Eskimo. Sled dogs are usually Eskimo dogs, Siberian huskies, Samoyeds, or Malamutes. They run in teams and can pull a sled and driver, called a musher, an average of twenty-five miles per day.

Resources

Listening
Audio CD Library
A recording of this story is provided in the *Audio CD Library:*
• Disc 3, Track 2

Resources: Print and Media

Reading
• *Reading Skills and Strategies*
  Selection Skill Lesson, p. 11
• *Graphic Organizers for Active Reading,* p. 7
• *Words to Own,* p. 6
• *Spelling and Decoding,*
  Worksheet, p. 7
• *Audio CD Library,* Disc 3, Track 2

Writing and Language
• *Daily Oral Grammar*
  Transparency 7
• *Grammar and Language Links,*
  Worksheet, p. 13
• *Language Workshop CD-ROM*

Assessment
• *Formal Assessment,* p. 19
• *Portfolio Management System,* p. 115
• *Standardized Test Preparation,* p. 24
• *Test Generator (One-Stop Planner CD-ROM)*

Internet
• go.hrw.com (keyword: LE0 6-2)

Ⓐ Elements of Literature

Character

❓ What does Storm do that makes him seem almost human? [He shows a sense of humor; he chuckles and plays tricks.]

Ⓑ Struggling Readers

Supplying Missing Words

Have students turn the fragment *Small jokes* into a sentence that fits the context. [Sample responses: He liked to play small jokes. He was always playing small jokes.]

Eager to Run by Scott Kennedy.

At peak, he was a mighty dog. He pulled like a machine. Until we retired him and used him only for training puppies, until we let him loose to enjoy his age, he pulled, his back over in the power curve, so that nothing could stop the sled.

Ⓐ In his fourth or fifth year as a puller, he started doing tricks. First he would play jokes on the dog pulling next to him. On long runs he would become bored, and when we least expected it, he would reach across the gang line and snort wind into the ear of the dog next to him. I ran him with many different dogs and he did it to all of them—chuckling when the dog jumped and shook his or her head—but I never saw a single dog get mad at him for it. Oh, there was once a dog named Fonzie who nearly took his head off, but Fonzie wasn't really mad at him so much as surprised. Fonzie

> *He raised his head, opened one eye, did a perfect double take—both eyes opening wide—and sat up.*

once nailed me through the wrist for waking him up too suddenly when he was sleeping. I'd reached down and touched him before whispering his name.

Ⓑ Small jokes. Gentle jokes, Storm played. He took to hiding things from me. At first I couldn't understand where things were going. I would put a bootie down while working on a dog, and it would disappear. I lost a small ladle[3] I used for watering each dog, a cloth glove liner I took off while working on a dog's feet, a roll of tape, and finally, a hat.

He was so clever.

When I lost the hat, it was a hot day and I had taken the hat off while I worked on a dog's harness. The dog was just ahead of

3. **ladle:** cup-shaped spoon with a long handle for dipping out liquids.

98 Unforgettable Personalities

Reaching All Students

Struggling Readers

Dialogue with the Text was introduced on p. 96. For a lesson directly tied to this selection that teaches students to monitor comprehension by using a strategy called Think–Aloud, see the *Reading Skills and Strategies* binder:
• Selection Skill Lesson, p. 11

English Language Learners

Use this story to introduce the names of various animals. Show pictures of several kinds of animals, writing and saying their names as you tape the pictures inside a circle on the chalkboard that is labeled "Animals." For additional strategies to supplement instruction for these students, see
• *Lesson Plans Including Strategies for English-Language Learners*

Advanced Learners

Invite students to meet in small groups to discuss the nature of intelligence and to come up with their own definition of the word. Have them discuss questions like these: In what different ways are human beings intelligent? Can nonhuman animals be considered intelligent? Are there situations in which an animal, such as a dog, might be more intelligent than a person? What do dogs "know" that humans do not?

© 1987 Scott Kennedy, © The Greenwich Workshop®, Inc. Courtesy of The Greenwich Workshop, Inc., Shelton, Connecticut.

Storm, and when I knelt to work on the harness—he'd chewed almost through the side of it while running—I put the hat down on the snow near Storm.

Or thought I had. When I had changed the dog's harness, I turned and the hat was gone. I looked around, moved the dogs, looked under them, then shrugged. At first I was sure I'd put the hat down; then, when I couldn't find it, I became less sure, and at last I thought perhaps I had left it at home or dropped it somewhere on the run.

Storm sat quietly, looking ahead down the trail, not showing anything at all.

I went back to the sled, reached down to disengage the hook, and when I did, the dogs exploded forward. I was not quite on the sled when they took off, so I was knocked slightly off balance. I leaned over to the right to regain myself, and when I did, I accidentally dragged the hook through the snow.

And pulled up my hat.

It had been buried off to the side of the trail in the snow, buried neatly with the snow smoothed over the top, so that it was com-

pletely hidden. Had the snow hook not scraped down four or five inches, I never would have found it.

I stopped the sled and set the hook once more. While knocking the snow out of the hat and putting it back on my head, I studied where it had happened.

Right next to Storm.

He had taken the hat, quickly dug a hole, buried the hat and smoothed the snow over it, then gone back to sitting, staring ahead, looking completely innocent.

When I stopped the sled and picked up the hat, he looked back, saw me put the hat on my head, and—I swear—smiled. Then he shook his head once and went back to work pulling.

Along with the jokes, Storm had scale eyes. He watched as the sled was loaded, carefully calculated the weight of each item, and let his disapproval be known if it went too far.

One winter a friend gave us a parlor stove with nickel trim. It was not an enormous stove, but it had some weight to it and some bulk. This friend lived twelve miles away—twelve miles over two fair hills followed by about eight miles on an old, abandoned railroad grade.[4] We needed the stove badly (our old barrel stove had started to burn through), so I took off with the team to pick it up. I left early in the morning because I wanted to get back that same day. It had snowed four or five inches, so the dogs would have to break trail. By the time we had done the hills and the railroad grade, pushing

---

4. **railroad grade:** rise or elevation in a railroad track.

WORDS TO OWN
disengage (dis'in·gāj') v.: unfasten.
regain (ri·gān') v.: recover.

STORM **99**

Skill Link

T99

A Elements of Literature

Character

? What character traits does Storm reveal by what he does? [Possible responses: He shows his intelligence—his stance shows he has figured out that the stove is very heavy; he shows his independence from the team—unlike the other dogs, he sits facing the sled and does not move when they do; he displays directness—he shows his anger by growling at the stove; he reveals his loyalty—despite his disapproval, he helps to pull the sled for the owner.]

B Reading Skills and Strategies

Dialogue with the Text

? Paulsen sets off sentence fragments as if they were paragraphs:
The enemy.
The weight on the sled.
How does this special treatment help you understand Storm's feelings? [Sample responses: By isolating these phrases, Paulsen shows that, in Storm's eyes, the stove is his opponent. Paulsen's isolating these phrases gives them weight, or significance, and this shows Storm's feelings about the weight, or heaviness, of the stove.]

C Critical Thinking

Speculating

? Why might Paulsen believe that a dog knows more about him than his own family does? [Sample responses: Because the dog and he are working closely together and communicating without words; because dogs are keen observers of their owners and respond to them in ways that humans do not; perhaps because Storm shares a very important part of Paulsen's life that his family knows little about.]

D Cultural Connection

The Iditarod

The Iditarod is a dogsled race from Anchorage to Nome, Alaska, held in mid-March each year. Dog teams cross almost 1,200 miles of snow and ice. To see the route, have students locate Anchorage and Nome on a map.

T100

---

in new snow all the time, they were ready for a rest. I ran them the last two miles to where the stove was and unhooked their tugs so they could rest while I had coffee.

We stopped for an hour at least, the dogs sleeping quietly. When it was time to go, my friend and I carried the stove outside and put it in the sled. The dogs didn't move.

Except for Storm.

He raised his head, opened one eye, did a perfect double take—both eyes opening wide—and sat up. He had been facing the front. Now he turned around to face the sled—so he was facing away from the direction we had to travel when we left—and watched us load the sled.

It took some time, as the stove barely fit on the sled and had to be jiggled and shuffled around to get it down between the side rails.

A Through it all, Storm sat and watched us, his face a study in interest. He did not get up but sat on his back end, and when I was done and ready to go, I hooked all the dogs back in harness—which involved hooking the tugs to the rear ties on their harnesses. The dogs knew this meant we were going to head home, so they got up and started slamming against the tugs, trying to get the sled to move.

All of them, that is, but Storm.

Storm sat backward, the tug hooked up but hanging down. The other dogs were screaming to run, but Storm sat and stared at the stove.

Not at me, not at the sled, but at the stove itself. Then he raised his lips, bared his teeth, and growled at the stove.

When he was finished growling, he snorted twice, stood, turned away from the stove, and started to pull. But each time we stopped at the tops of the hills to let the dogs catch their breath after pulling the sled and

Never Alone (detail) by Scott Kennedy.

stove up the steep incline, Storm turned and growled at the stove.

B The enemy.
The weight on the sled.

C I do not know how many miles Storm and I ran together. Eight, ten, perhaps twelve thousand miles. He was one of the first dogs and taught me the most, and as we worked together, he came to know me better than perhaps even my own family. He could look once at my shoulders and tell how I was feeling, tell how far we were to run, how fast we had to run—knew it all.

D When I started to run long, moved from running a work team, a trap line team, to training for the Iditarod, Storm took it in stride, changed the pace down to the long trot, matched what was needed, and settled in for the long haul.

He did get bored, however, and one day while we were running a long run, he started

---

Using Students' Strengths

Verbal Learners

The dogs "*slammed* against the tugs." One dog "*nailed*" the narrator "through the wrist." Ask students to look through the story and list vivid action verbs like these that help readers "picture" the dogs and events of the story, particularly through the senses of sight, touch, and hearing. Then have students study a pet animal and choose vivid action verbs to describe its behavior. Ask students to use these verbs in sentences about the pet.

Kinesthetic Learners

Storm uses body language and actions to communicate with his owner and to express such feelings as boredom on a long run, anger at a heavy weight, and approval or disapproval of the owner's handling of the team. Invite students to think about how they themselves communicate feelings like these without using words. Have students take turns pantomiming a feeling while other students guess the feeling that is being expressed.

© 1993 Scott Kennedy, © The Greenwich Workshop®, Inc. Courtesy of The Greenwich Workshop, Inc., Shelton, Connecticut.

doing a thing that would stay with him—with us—until the end. We had gone forty or fifty miles on a calm, even day with no bad wind. The temperature was a perfect ten below zero. The sun was bright, everything was moving well, and the dogs had settled into the rhythm that could take them a hundred or a thousand miles. **E**

And Storm got bored.

At a curve in the trail, a small branch came out over the path we were running, and as Storm passed beneath the limb, he jumped up and grabbed it, broke a short piece off—about a foot long—and kept it in his mouth.

All day.

And into the night. He ran, carrying the stick like a toy, and when we stopped to feed or rest, he would put the stick down, eat, then pick it up again. He would put the stick down carefully in front of him, or across his paws, and sleep, and when he awakened, he would pick up the stick, and it soon became a thing between us, the stick.

He would show it to me, making a contact, a connection between us, each time we stopped. I would pet him on top of the head and take the stick from him—he would emit a low, gentle growl when I took the stick. I'd "examine" it closely, nod and seem to approve of it, and hand it back to him. **F**

Each day we ran, he would pick a different stick. And each time I would have to approve of it, and after a time, after weeks and months, I realized that he was using the sticks as a way to communicate with me, to tell me that everything was all right, that I was doing the right thing. **G**

Once, when I pushed them too hard during a pre-Iitarod race—when I thought it

---

WORDS TO OWN
emit (ē·mit′) v.: give out.

E **Appreciating Language**
Word Choice
❓ Though most people would see the day as bitterly cold, Paulsen describes it using such words as "calm, even," "a perfect ten below zero," and "bright" sun. He uses the phrases "moving well" and "dogs had settled into the rhythm" to describe the difficult training for the Iditarod. What do these word choices suggest about Paulsen's feelings for the weather and task? [Possible responses: He sees conditions as ideal; he feels everything is going well; he is used to very low temperatures; he is contented.]

F **Reading Skills and Strategies**
Dialogue with the Text
❓ What do you learn from the fact that "examine" is enclosed in quotation marks? [The quotation marks show that Paulsen is pretending to examine the stick for the dog's benefit; he's joining the dog's game.]

G **Critical Thinking**
Expressing an Opinion
❓ Do you believe that Storm is using the sticks to communicate this message to the narrator? Why or why not? [Possible responses: Yes, because Storm seems very smart and clearly has a purpose in using the sticks; no, the dog may have a purpose, but it's not necessarily the one his owner thinks it is.]

Getting Students Involved

Cooperative Learning
Dog Wanted. Divide the class into groups of four. Have each group member take primary responsibility for one of these roles: recorder of ideas, writer of the ad, questioner or motivator of the group, and evaluator of the group's functioning. Provide each group with samples of help-wanted ads. Have groups brainstorm ideas for a help-wanted ad for a lead dog on a dogsledding team. Ads should include skills and personality needed in a sled dog, and particularly in a lead dog. Suggest that students list the skills and personality traits in a chart like the following to help them organize their thoughts before writing.

Skills	Personality Traits
Listens	Cooperative

Progressive Poem. Have students work together to write a Progressive Poem about Storm. Divide students into three groups, and assign each group an aspect of Storm's character to write about: appearance, temperament, or talents. Have each group write three lines of the poem. Ask the groups to combine the lines in an order that they agree on, to make revisions, and to share the poem with the class.

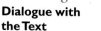

RESPONDING TO
THE ART

Activity. Have students discuss
why the man is holding the dog
and in what way the relationship
between the man and the dog in
the picture is like that of Paulsen
and Storm.

A Reading Skills
and Strategies

**Dialogue with
the Text**

? The narrator stated at the beginning
of the story that Storm taught him
lessons about life. What lesson is
Storm teaching the narrator here?
[Possible responses: That winning is not
always the most important thing; that a
musher should try to conserve a team's
energy.] How do you know what the
lesson is? [Possible responses: Through
Paulsen's action—resting the dogs and
letting other teams go by; through
Storm's readiness to pick up the stick
after the rest.]

B Elements of Literature

Character

? What does Storm's picking up and
dropping the stick show? [whether he
agrees with the driver's actions] What
do these actions reveal about Storm?
[Sample answers: his intelligence in creating his own means of communication;
his understanding of the dog team's
ability.]

Resources ───────

Selection Assessment
Formal Assessment
• Selection Test, p. 19
Test Generator
• Selection Test

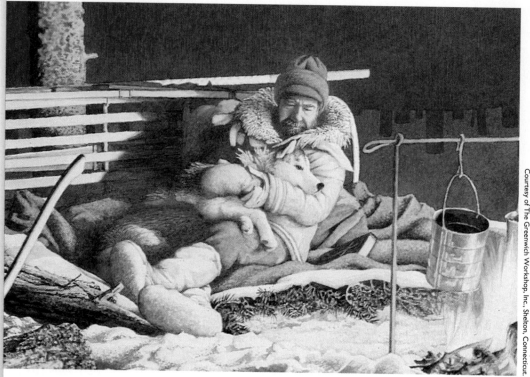

Never Alone (detail) by Scott Kennedy.

© 1993 Scott Kennedy. © The Greenwich Workshop, Inc.
Courtesy of The Greenwich Workshop, Inc., Shelton, Connecticut.

A was important to compete and win (a feeling
that didn't last long)—I walked up to Storm,
and as I came close to him, he pointedly
dropped the stick. I picked it up and held it
out, but he wouldn't take it. He turned his
face away. I put the stick against his lips and
tried to make him take it, but he let it fall to
the ground. When I realized what he was
doing, I stopped and fed and rested the team,
sat on the sled, and thought about what I was
doing wrong. After four hours or so of sitting—watching other teams pass me—I fed

them another snack, got ready to go, and was
gratified to see Storm pick up the stick. From
that time forward I looked for the stick always, knew when I saw it out to the sides of
his head that I was doing the right thing. And
it was always there.

Through storms and cold weather, on the
long runs, the long, long runs where there
isn't an end to it, where only the sled and the
winter around the sled and the wind are
there, Storm had the stick to tell me it was
B right, all things were right.

Making the Connections

**Connecting to the Theme:
"Unforgettable Personalities"**
Ask students, "Who is the unforgettable personality in this story?" Most students will agree
that it is Storm. Although Storm is a dog, he is
the title character and the most vivid personality in the piece. Ask students to describe the
qualities that make Storm memorable. [Sample
responses: his sense of humor—playing tricks,
hiding things; his intelligence—his ability to measure the weights of objects by observing with his

"scale eyes"; his communicating with a stick; his
teaching his owner lessons; his loyalty.] Then
invite students to share in discussion anecdotes
and descriptions of unforgettable animal personalities they have known. Students might
wish to write down some of their knowledge
of animals as raw material for Choice 1,
Writer's Notebook, on p. 106.

LITERATURE AND SCIENCE

Call of the Wild

You've seen the endearing behavior that makes dogs a favorite pet: loyalty, playfulness, and boundless affection. You've probably heard of the amazing talents of working dogs: the sheep dog that can outorganize a company president, the guard dog that can outfight a trained soldier, the bloodhound that can outsmart the cleverest detective. But what about the dogs that still live in the wild, as all dogs once did?

Baffin Island, a remote, wild region of Canada, is home to one such group of canids that survive on their own, obeying no master but their ancient instincts. (*Canid* is a term that covers all doglike creatures, including dogs, wolves, jackals, foxes, and coyotes.) Scientists went to Baffin to observe a group of five adult wolves that functioned as a family. The group included a litter of seven young wolves, whose parents were the leaders of the clan. It occupied a series of five dens (shelters the wolves dig into the earth) on hills near a river. The dens were just about halfway between the summer and winter ground of the wolves' main prey, the caribou, large deer that live in tundra regions like Baffin.

Like humans, the wolves use division of labor to provide for the needs of the group. While one wolf goes out on the long, wearying search for food, another stays behind to guard the pups. When the "designated hunter" returns, doling out meat to the hungry pups and preparing for a long nap—sometimes up to eighteen hours—the baby sitter sets out on the long journey across the tundra in search of more caribou meat.

This cycle, which has repeated itself generation after generation, shows us that canids forged a remarkably successful life long before they became our best friend.

Baffin Island, which measures 183,810 square miles, is the world's fifth largest island. It is located in northeastern Canada, and its geography is mostly tundra, or treeless land with permanently frozen subsoil. The subsoil, called *permafrost,* stays frozen because the temperature in the tundra is usually below the freezing point. Call students' attention to the scientific word *permafrost* and ask them to break it into two parts. [*perma* and *frost*] Students know what *frost* means. But what does *perma* mean? To find the answer, ask students to think of another word they know that starts with *perma* and to tell what it means. [*permanent,* "lasting, enduring, not changing"] Students can infer that the meaning of *permafrost* is "permanent frost."

Crossing the Curriculum

Mathematics
Remind students that a dogsled team covers an average of twenty-five miles per day. Give students the distances between specific places in Alaska where dogsledding is still used as transportation, or have students use the map legend to find the distance between two towns in northern Alaska. Have them figure how long it would take a dog team to travel that distance.

Science
Ask students to learn more about the sled dogs and their environment. Students should consider such topics as the climate and terrain in which the dogs work, the traits of certain breeds that make them effective sled dogs, how the dogs work as a team, their diet, and their remarkable accomplishments. Encourage students to locate photographs of the dogs and their environment for display.

Using Students' Strengths

Interpersonal Learners
Storm solves his problem of how to communicate with his owner by using the approval sticks. Have students brainstorm methods they might use in communicating to a parent, teacher, or friend their feelings about a problem. Invite students to meet in a small group, first to identify a problem that is common among people their age and second to suggest effective ways of communicating that could lead to a solution of the problem.

MEET THE WRITER

Good Cooking

As the son of an army officer who moved his family with each new assignment, **Gary Paulsen** (1939–   ) lived all over the United States when he was a boy. Because he was always moving, Paulsen had no real friends when he was growing up. One winter day he wandered into a public library to keep warm, and the librarian offered him a library card. He remembers:

66 When she handed me the card, she handed me the world. . . . It was as though I had been dying of thirst and the librarian had handed me a five-gallon bucket of water. I drank and drank. 99

This passion for reading eventually led to an interest in writing. Paulsen left his engineering job and became editor of a magazine, an experience he has called "the best of all possible ways to learn about writing." His first book was a collection of interviews with Vietnam War veterans. Since then he has written more than forty books, along with hundreds of magazine articles and short stories. Writing means the world to him:

66 I have not done anything else in my life that gives me the personal satisfaction that writing does. It pleases me to write—in the very literal sense of the word. When I have done well with it, and 'cooked' for a day so that it felt good when I put it down—it flowed and worked right. When all that is right, I go to sleep with an immense feeling of personal satisfaction. 99

More Good Cooking by Gary Paulsen

Paulsen has cooked up a feast of adventure stories for young adults. If you're interested in wilderness-survival tales, try the novels *Dogsong* and *Hatchet* (both published by Bradbury). Both were named Newbery Award Honor Books by the American Library Association. If you prefer true stories, explore *Woodsong* (Bradbury), from which "Storm" is taken. You might also enjoy *Father Water, Mother Woods* (Delacorte), in which Paulsen reflects on his hunting and fishing experiences in the north woods.

104

Assessing Learning

Check Test: True-False

1. Paulsen says that he has learned as much from his other dogs as from Storm. [False]
2. Storm is a strong, mighty dog with ears like a bear cub's. [True]
3. Storm's sense of humor leads him to play jokes on his owner and his teammates. [True]
4. Storm is happy to pull the heavy stove. [False]
5. Storm drags a stick through the snow to communicate with the narrator. [False]

Standardized Test Preparation

For practice with standardized test format specific to this selection, see
• *Standardized Test Preparation*, p. 24
For practice in proofreading and editing, see
• *Daily Oral Grammar*, Transparency 7

MAKING MEANINGS

First Thoughts

[respond]

1. Using your reading notes to re-fresh your memory, complete two of the following sentences:

   - I never realized before that dogs . . .

   - My favorite part of the story was . . .

   - If Storm belonged to me . . .

Shaping Interpretations

[analyze]

2. Describe Storm's **character**. List your ideas in a chart like this:

Storm's Actions	Storm's Character Traits
plays tricks on other dogs	sense of humor

[analyze]

3. When Paulsen describes Storm, he also gives clues about his own per-sonality. What kind of person do you think Paulsen is?

[infer]

4. In your opinion, what is the most important lesson about life that Paulsen learns from Storm?

Connecting with the Text

[connect]

5. Gary Paulsen describes Storm as the "dog who taught me the most." Think of something you have learned from an animal—either from simply watching the animal or from building a relationship with it. Com-pare what you learned with what Paulsen learns from Storm.

Extending the Text

[connect]

6. Why do you think some people become so attached to their pets? How do the people and the animals benefit from their friendship?

Challenging the Text

[interpret]

7. Do you think Paulsen's interpretations of Storm's jokes and tricks are accurate? To find out, what questions might you ask Paulsen? What other questions would you like to ask Paulsen about Storm?

Reading Check

Skim back through the story to find passages in "Storm" that create vivid mental pic-tures for you. Then, in a small group, read your favorite sec-tions aloud. As you do this oral reading, try to re-create a picture of Paulsen's unfor-gettable Storm.

Reading Check

Students may choose almost any passage from the text, including the description of Storm on p. 97 or the anecdotes about the hat trick, the stove, or the stick. Try to group students who have chosen different sections as their favorite passage.

MAKING MEANINGS

First Thoughts

1. Possible responses: I never realized before that dogs were so clever. My favorite part of the story was when Storm growled at the stove. If Storm belonged to me, I would want to spend all my time with him.

Shaping Interpretations

2. Sample responses:

Actions	Traits
hides hat	cleverness, playfulness
stares and growls at stove	independence
pulls heavy stove	loyalty
refuses to take stick	intelligence

3. Possible responses: dedicated, car-ing, humorous, observant, tough yet gentle.

4. Possible responses: Respecting oth-ers is more important than winning; a friend will tell you when you're wrong; it's important to play and enjoy life even when you're working; communicating can help to solve problems; teamwork requires loyalty and trust.

Connecting with the Text

5. Sample responses: When my dog was lame, she refused to move after she couldn't negotiate a slippery floor; in much the same way that Storm told Paulsen he was pushing the team, my dog told me not to expect the impossible. Our cat was a stray who kept coming around until we finally took her in; I learned to keep trying from her example, much as Paulsen learned to be play-ful from observing Storm.

Extending the Text

6. Possible answers: Because they are lonely or because their pets give them unquestioning love. People get companionship and love, and the pets get someone to take care of them.

Challenging the Text

7. Sample answers: Yes, because he seems to know his dog very well; no, he is exaggerating to make the story interesting. Sample questions: How are you so sure that Storm's actions mean what you think they mean? What other evidence do you have that Storm has a sense of humor?

Grading Timesaver

Rubrics for each Choices assignment are provided on p. 115 in the *Portfolio Management System*.

CHOICES: Building Your Portfolio

1. Writer's Notebook Encourage students to make a first draft of their anecdote without pausing to correct or polish it. If students revise the draft, they might try to improve its chronological order and degree of detail. Remind students to save their work. They may use it as prewriting for the Writer's Workshop on pp. 158–163.

2. Creative Writing You might read an excerpt from *Ben and Me* or *Mr. Revere and I* to help students see the possibilities of having an animal as the narrator of a story about a human.

3. Writing/Research/Art Provide students with books on a variety of animals, or have them find such books in the school library. If time permits, suggest that students interview pet owners they know, veterinarians, animal trainers, or kennel owners. *Before students conduct interviews, it is advisable to request parental or guardian permission.*

CHOICES: Building Your Portfolio

Writer's Notebook

1. Collecting Ideas for a Biographical Sketch

Paulsen makes Storm come alive by telling brief stories, or **anecdotes.** For example, Paulsen says that Storm likes to play jokes. To give an example of this unusual talent, Paulsen tells an anecdote about Storm burying his hat. Think about a person or an animal you'd like to write about. What special character trait immediately comes to your mind? Write an anecdote that illustrates this special characteristic.

> My cat thinks he's such a killer. I remember his first "prey"—an old potato chip bag. He batted it around as if it might put up a big fight.

Creative Writing

2. Straight from the Dog's Mouth

Imagine that Storm is so smart he wants to tell the world a few things about Paulsen. In fact, he's so smart he can write his own stories about his human pal. How would Storm tell the story of hauling the heavy stove? Use the personal pronoun *I* to retell the story from Storm's point of view.

Writing/Research/Art

3. Making Pawbooks

With a group, make one or two pawbooks (handbooks) for your classroom or library on the care and raising of dogs (or any other animal). First, decide together on a subject for each pawbook. Here are some ideas:

- *basic training*: tips on dog care, dog problems, and tricks for getting through the training period
- *picking a pooch*: information on how to match the right dog with the right person

- *dogspeak*: hints on how dogs use their bodies, their barks, and objects to communicate

Decide who will research, write, and draw pictures for each pawbook.

Siberian Husky by Scott Kennedy.
© 1994 Scott Kennedy, © The Greenwich Workshop®, Inc. Courtesy of The Greenwich Workshop, Inc., Shelton, Connecticut.

106 UNFORGETTABLE PERSONALITIES

Assessing Learning

Observation Assessment
Speaking and Listening. Use the following criteria to assess students' speaking and listening skills.

Criteria	Poor	Fair	Good
Volunteers ideas			
Considers ideas of others			
Communicates clearly			
Gives others the chance to speak			

GRAMMAR LINK MINI-LESSON

Using *Good* and *Well* Correctly

Language Handbook HELP

See Special Problems with Modifiers, page 719; Glossary of Usage: good, well, *page 768.*

Technology HELP

See Language Workshop CD-ROM. *Key word entry:* good *and* well.

The word *good* should be used to modify nouns and pronouns. The word *well* should generally be used to modify verbs.

EXAMPLES

> Storm's funny face always looked good to Paulsen. [*Good* modifies the noun *face.*]

> Storm pulled the heavy load well. [*Well* modifies the verb *pulled.*]

The word *good* should never modify a verb.

NONSTANDARD   Storm pulls good even when he is tired.

STANDARD   Storm pulls well even when he is tired.

Note: *Feel good* and *feel well* mean different things. *Feel good* means "to feel happy or pleased." *Feel well* means "to feel healthy."

EXAMPLES

> Even though he didn't feel well [healthy], Paulsen felt good [happy] when he saw Storm running toward him.

Try It Out

➤ Use the correct word in each underlined pair to complete the following sentences.

1. Storm ate good/well today.

2. The team looked good/well.

➤ Circle the words *good* and *well* whenever they appear in your writing. Then, draw an arrow from the circled word to the word it modifies. If the arrow points to a noun or a pronoun, be sure you've used an adjective. If the arrow points to a verb, an adjective, or an adverb, be sure you've used an adverb.

GRAMMAR LINK

Have students create a note card with the definitions of *good* and *well* to use as a reference tool. Then, ask students to look through the work in their portfolios to identify places where they have used the word *good* or *well*. Have them exchange papers with a partner to check that the words are used correctly.

Try It Out
Answers
1. well
2. good

VOCABULARY
Possible Responses

dis-	away, opposing	discount, disagree
re-	again	repeat, replace
e-	out	eject, elate

Resources

Grammar
• *Grammar and Language Links,* p. 13

Vocabulary
• *Words to Own,* p. 6

Spelling
For related instruction, see
• *Spelling and Decoding,* p. 7

VOCABULARY HOW TO OWN A WORD

WORD BANK

disengage
regain
emit

Prefixes

Each word in this Word Bank has a **prefix**—a letter or group of letters added to the beginning of a word or root to change its meaning. If you know what a few prefixes mean, you can figure out the meanings of many new words. Make a chart like the one that follows for the prefixes *dis-, re-,* and *e-.* Use each word in the Word Bank.

Prefix	Meaning	Examples:
anti-	"against"	antislavery antibiotic antifreeze

STORM 107

Grammar Link Quick Check

Choose between *good* and *well,* and underline the word that *good* or *well* modifies in the sentence.

1. Storm plays good/well tricks on the other dogs. [Storm plays *good* <u>tricks</u> on the other dogs.]

2. Sled dogs carry heavy loads good/well. [Sled dogs <u>carry</u> heavy loads *well.*]

3. To pull a heavy load over a long distance, sled dogs must feel strong and good/well. [To pull a heavy load over a long distance, sled <u>dogs</u> must feel strong and *well.*]

4. The narrator thinks Storm is a good/well dog. [The narrator thinks Storm is a *good* <u>dog.</u>]

5. Storm feels good/well when the narrator does the right thing. [<u>Storm</u> feels *good* when the narrator does the right thing.]

Resources

Elements of Literature
Autobiography and Biography
For additional instruction on nonfiction writing, see *Literary Elements:*
• Transparency 2

Assessment
Formal Assessment
• Literary Elements Test, p. 29

Elements of Literature

This feature focuses on autobiography and biography, two important forms of nonfiction writing.
Mini-Lesson:
Autobiography and Biography
• Review with students the difference between an autobiography and a biography. Ask them to name examples that they are familiar with.
• Ask students to create a list of facts about someone they know well, such as a relative or a best friend. The list should include items such as birth date and place, age, occupation, and interests. Have students use the fact list to develop a short biographical paragraph in the strictly factual style. Then have students rewrite the paragraph in the less strict style, adding details that are not facts but that could realistically have happened.
• Ask volunteers to read their selections aloud to illustrate the different biographical styles.

Applying the Element
As your class studies this collection, ask students to determine whether a given selection is autobiography or biography and whether or not it is strictly factual. Occasionally a selection may straddle categories: For instance, "Storm" is autobiographical about Gary Paulsen and biographical about his dog.

AUTOBIOGRAPHY AND BIOGRAPHY: Personal Histories

Nonfiction is "not fiction"—it is writing based on fact. The subjects of nonfiction are as varied as the world itself.

Autobiography: "Self-Written Life"

The most personal kind of nonfiction is autobiographical writing: writing about a person's life, written by that very person. *Autobiography* means, literally, "self" (*auto-*) "written life" (*bio-* + *-graphy*). In an **autobiography** we get "inside" the writer's mind. We share the writer's most personal thoughts, feelings, and ideas. Gary Paulsen's *Woodsong* (see page 97) is a good example of autobiographical writing.

Biography: "Written Life"

A **biography** is the story of a person's life, written by another person. Biographers research their subjects in depth. They interview people and read firsthand accounts, such as letters, journals, newspaper stories, and magazine articles. Many biographies include only events and conversations that really happened. A biography written in this strictly factual style might go as follows. (Elizabeth Blackwell was the first woman doctor in America.)

When Elizabeth Blackwell got to Geneva College in 1847, the faculty had admitted her, and the all-male student body had voted to accept her. But she was given no books. No one showed her where classes were held. She was even refused admittance to her anatomy class.

Other biographers add details that may not be factual but are historically possible. They make the biography read more like a novel. This kind of biographer might describe Blackwell's experience this way:

Elizabeth stood outside the door of the anatomy class clenching her hands. She was ready to explode from anger and humiliation. The faculty had admitted her to Geneva College in 1847. The all-male student body had even approved her coming. Still, here she was, ignored and snubbed. "A woman studying anatomy?" said the teacher to himself. "Shocking!"

A Writer on Biography

"The most difficult part of writing, whether it's biography or fiction, is deciding what to leave out. You want the reader to bring his or her own imagination to the piece. In biography, you are leaving out most things. Lincoln lived twenty-four hours a day for his whole life. It's the biographer's job to pick out the most significant details, the ones that tell something about the man or woman."
—Russell Freedman, author of "The Mysterious Mr. Lincoln" (page 127)

Reaching All Students

Struggling Readers
To help students understand the concept of the two genres, bring to class a biography and an autobiography about the same person. Ask volunteers to read the first paragraph of each book aloud. Have students compare the paragraphs, discussing the differences between the two.

Advanced Learners
Ask students to interview someone in the school or community and to write a chapter of the person's biography, using the style they choose—strictly factual or factual with possible details added. *Before assigning this activity, request parental or guardian permission.*

Before You Read

BROTHER

Make the Connection

"You're the Greatest"

In her autobiography, Maya Angelou says simply that her brother Bailey was "the greatest person in my world."

Quickwrite

Who is the greatest person in your world? Your choice could be someone you know or a public figure you admire. Write a few sentences telling who this person is and why he or she is "the greatest."

Elements of Literature

Description

Description is writing that uses words mainly to help us see. Angelou paints a portrait in words of her brother, Bailey. He's "small, graceful, and smooth," with "velvet-black skin" and "black curls." As you can tell from these details, description can also help us to *feel* something (the velvet skin). In addition, it can operate on our senses of smell, taste, and hearing.

Description is used in all kinds of writing—in fiction and poetry, of course, but also in history books, science books, newspapers, even personal letters and journals.

Description is writing intended to create a picture. Description can also help us smell, taste, hear, and feel something. Often description can reveal an emotion or an attitude.

For more on Description, see the Handbook of Literary Terms.

Reading Skills and Strategies

Finding the Main Idea: Check the Details

The **main idea** is the most important idea in a piece of writing. Main ideas are sometimes, but not always, stated directly. When a writer doesn't state the main idea, it's up to you to figure it out. You have to use details in the text to **infer,** or guess, what larger idea the writer is getting at. Listing key words and details as you read can help you find the main idea.

go.hrw.com
LE0 6-2

OBJECTIVES

1. Read and interpret the autobiography
2. Recognize description
3. Find the main idea
4. Express understanding through writing and speaking
5. Identify general and specific modifiers and use specific modifiers in writing
6. Learn and use new words
7. Locate synonyms by using a thesaurus

SKILLS

Literary, Reading, Writing
• Recognize description
• Find the main idea
• Describe a person
• State the main idea

Speaking/Performing
• Describe and demonstrate a game

Grammar/Language
• Choose precise words

Vocabulary
• Use new words
• Identify synonyms

Viewing/Representing
• Describe a portrait (ATE)
• Compare the subjects of a painting and a text (ATE)
• Discuss similarities between a painting and a text (ATE)

Bailey was the greatest person in my world.

Planning

• **Block Schedule**
  Block Scheduling Lesson Plans with Pacing Guide
• **Traditional Schedule**
  Lesson Plans Including Strategies for English-Language Learners
• **One-Stop Planner**
  CD-ROM with Test Generator

Preteaching Vocabulary

Words to Own

Invite students to locate the vocabulary words at the bottom of p. 110. Ask volunteers to say the words aloud and define them. Then have students say which of the words might be used in these situations: hearing chalk on the board [grating], honoring a teacher [lauded], seeing a disaster [aghast], taking a math test [precision], learning a skill [apt]. Finally, have students meet in small groups to answer these questions:

1. Identify sounds that you find **grating**.
2. Suppose your favorite musical group is **lauded** at an award ceremony. What might someone say?
3. Why do home builders have to measure with **precision**?
4. What recent news events have left people feeling **aghast**?
5. What sports or games were you **apt** at playing?

Summary ▪▪

Set in the 1930s in Arkansas, this is a loving sketch of Angelou's beloved only brother, Bailey. Angelou portrays him as graceful, mischievous, daring, clever, full of life, and protective of her. Descriptions of tricks and games he played reinforce this characterization.

Resources ————

Listening
Audio CD Library
A recording of the autobiographical excerpt is provided in the *Audio CD Library:*
• Disc 3, Track 3

Ⓐ Reading Skills and Strategies

Finding the Main Idea

❓ **What main idea is stated in the first paragraph?** [that Angelou loves and admires her brother; that he is the most important person in her world] **What details support the main idea?** [Angelou's gratitude for Bailey's being her only sibling; his beauty and grace; his love for her.]

Ⓑ Elements of Literature

Description

❓ **What details does the author use to describe her own appearance?** ["big, elbowy, and grating"; head "covered with black steel wool"] **What attitude about herself does the author reveal in this description?** [Sample responses: She feels she is awkward, large, unattractive; she feels she does not fit in.]

BROTHER

Maya Angelou

from I Know Why the Caged Bird Sings

Ⓐ
Ⓑ
Bailey was the greatest person in my world. And the fact that he was my brother, my only brother, and I had no sisters to share him with, was such good fortune that it made me want to live a Christian life just to show God that I was grateful. Where I was big, elbowy, and <u>grating</u>, he was small, graceful, and smooth. . . . He was <u>lauded</u> for his velvet-black skin. His hair fell down in black curls, and my head was covered with black steel wool. And yet he loved me.

When our elders said unkind things about my features (my family was handsome to a point of pain for me), Bailey would wink at me from across the room, and I knew that it was a matter of time before he would take revenge. He would allow the old ladies to finish wondering how on earth I came about, then he would ask, in a voice like cooling bacon grease, "Oh Mizeriz[1] Coleman, how is your son? I saw him the other day, and he looked sick enough to die."

<u>Aghast</u>, the ladies would ask, "Die? From what? He ain't sick."

And in a voice oilier than the one before, he'd answer with a straight face, "From the Uglies."

I would hold my laugh, bite my tongue, grit

1. **Mizeriz:** dialect term for "Mrs."

my teeth, and very seriously erase even the touch of a smile from my face. Later, behind the house by the black-walnut tree, we'd laugh and laugh and howl.

Bailey could count on very few punishments for his consistently outrageous behavior, for he was the pride of the Henderson/Johnson family.

His movements, as he was later to describe those of an acquaintance, were activated with oiled <u>precision</u>. He was also able to find more hours in the day than I thought existed. He finished chores, homework, read more books than I, and played the group games on the side of the hill with the best of them. He could even pray out loud in church and was <u>apt</u> at stealing pickles from the barrel that sat under the fruit counter and Uncle Willie's nose.

Once when the Store was full of lunchtime customers, he dipped the strainer, which we also used to sift weevils[2] from meal and flour,

2. **weevils:** small beetles that feed on grains, fruits, cotton, and so on.

WORDS TO OWN
grating (grāt'iŋ) *adj.*: irritating or annoying.
lauded (lôd'əd) *v.*: praised.
aghast (ə·gast') *adj.*: shocked or horrified.
precision (prē·sizh'ən) *n.*: correctness; accuracy.
apt *adj.*: quick to learn or understand.

110 UNFORGETTABLE PERSONALITIES

Resources: Print and Media

Reading
• *Reading Skills and Strategies*
   MiniRead Skill Lesson, p. 110
   Selection Skill Lesson, p. 116
• *Graphic Organizers for Active Reading*, p. 8
• *Words to Own*, p. 7
• *Audio CD Library*, Disc 3, Track 3

Elements of Literature
• *Literary Elements*
   Transparency 2
   Worksheet, p. 7

Writing and Language
• *Daily Oral Grammar*
   Transparency 8
• *Grammar and Language Links*
   Worksheet, p. 15
• *Language Workshop CD-ROM*

Viewing and Representing
• *Viewing and Representing*
   Fine Art Transparency 4
   Fine Art Worksheet, p. 16

Assessment
• *Formal Assessment*, p. 21
• *Portfolio Management System*, p. 116
• *Standardized Test Preparation*, p. 26
• *Test Generator (One-Stop Planner CD-ROM)*

Internet
• go.hrw.com (keyword: LE0 6-2)

Boy by the Sea (1995) by Jonathan Green, Naples, Florida.
Oil on canvas (18″ × 17″). Photograph by Tim Stamm.

Jonathan Green (1955–   ) was born in Gardens Corner, South Carolina, a coastal community near the state's Sea Islands. The Sea Islands of South Carolina and Georgia are the home of the Gullah culture, a unique African American subculture. While growing up in South Carolina, Jonathan Green absorbed the rich heritage of Gullah, and he portrays many aspects of that culture in his paintings. Though focusing on Gullah-inspired subjects, Green's paintings transcend the limits of a specific race or culture to embrace broad human themes of ordinary daily life and human dignity. A resident of Naples, Florida, Green has illustrated two children's books, *Father and Son* and *Noah*.

Activity. Ask students to compare and contrast the boy in the painting with Angelou's description of Bailey. [Possible response: The boy in the portrait seems to be older than Bailey in the experiences recalled by Angelou. (The boy in the portrait seems too old to play hide-and-seek, for example.) The boy in the portrait does not have long black curly hair, nor does he seem small. However, both boys are "graceful" and "smooth."]

Reaching All Students

Struggling Readers

Determining Main Idea was introduced on p. 109. For a lesson directly tied to this selection that teaches students to determine the main idea by using a strategy called Retelling, see the *Reading Skills and Strategies* binder:
- MiniRead Skill Lesson, p. 110
- Selection Skill Lesson, p. 116

English Language Learners

These students may not be familiar with the specific names of the children's games mentioned: hide-and-seek, follow the leader, and pop the whip. Ask others in the class to tell how these games are played and to chant the rhyme on p. 112. Then have English language learners describe similar games in their native countries. For additional strategies to supplement instruction for these students, see
- *Lesson Plans Including Strategies for English-Language Learners*

Advanced Learners

Ask these students to write diary entries from Bailey's point of view, in which he describes his own and his sister's activities on the days of the events that Angelou refers to. Encourage students to express Bailey's feelings about his sister and to use specific modifiers in the descriptions.

Description

? What senses do words in this description appeal to? [sight and touch: "clean streams down his ashy legs," "pockets full of loot"; sight: "laughing eyes"; smell: "like a vinegar barrel or a sour angel"] What attitude toward Bailey does this description express? [Sample responses: delight, admiration.]

B Reading Skills and Strategies

Finding the Main Idea

Ask students which sentence or sentences in the entire selection state the main idea. [the first and the last sentences] Have students restate the main idea in their own words and identify details that support it. [Possible restatement: Angelou's brother was her mainstay, the person who made her feel secure, protected, supported, and loved. Possible details: Bailey defended her when she was criticized; Bailey could do anything and was fearless; Bailey was a leader who loved to have fun.]

RESPONDING TO THE ART

This is another painting by **Jonathan Green**. For biographical information, see p. T111.
Activity. Ask students why they think this painting was chosen to accompany "Brother." [Sample response: In both, two children are playing together. The joyful, innocent mood of the painting echoes Maya Angelou's love for her brother.]

into the barrel and fished for two fat pickles. He caught them and hooked the strainer onto the side of the barrel, where they dripped until he was ready for them. When the last school bell rang, he picked the nearly dry pickles out of the strainer, jammed them into his pockets, and threw the strainer behind the oranges. We ran out of the Store. It was summer and his pants were short, so the **A** pickle juice made clean streams down his ashy legs, and he jumped with his pockets full of loot and his eyes laughing a "How about that?" He smelled like a vinegar barrel or a sour angel.

After our early chores were done, while Uncle Willie or Momma minded the Store, we were free to play the children's games as long **B** as we stayed within yelling distance. Play-ing hide-and-seek, his voice was easily identified, singing, "Last night, night before, twenty-four robbers at my door. Who all is hid? Ask me to let them in, hit 'em in the head with a rolling pin. Who all is hid?" In follow the leader, naturally he was the one who created the most daring and interesting things to do. And when he was on the tail of the pop the whip, he would twirl off the end like a top, spinning, falling, laughing, finally stopping just before my heart beat its last, and then he was back in the game, still laughing.

Of all the needs (there are none imaginary) a lonely child has, the one that must be satisfied, if there is going to be hope and a hope of wholeness, is the unshaking need for an unshakable God. My pretty black brother was my Kingdom Come.

Fishing on the Trail (1990) by Jonathan Green, Naples, Florida. Oil on canvas (47" × 79"). Photograph by Tim Stamm.

Taking a Second Look

Review: Making Generalizations
Remind students that a generalization is a broad statement that applies to many cases. To make a generalization, a reader combines the information in a text with information he or she already knows to make a judgment that extends beyond the text to the outside world.

Activities
1. Have students brainstorm a generalization based on evidence in "Brother." Help them begin by suggesting this example of evidence:

"When adults say unkind things about Maya, Bailey takes revenge." From this detail and from students' prior knowledge, have them make a generalization. [Possible response: Brothers and sisters often defend each other when an outsider criticizes one of them.]

2. Have student partners write another generalization based on "Brother." Invite them to explain their generalizations to the class.

MEET THE WRITER

"The Power of the Word"

When **Maya Angelou** (1928–) was three and her brother Bailey was four, their parents separated and sent them by train to live with their grandmother in the small, segregated town of Stamps, Arkansas. Momma (the children's name for their grandmother) ran a general store. This part of Angelou's life forms the background of "Brother."

Angelou's remarkable career has taken her far from that time in Stamps when she was Bailey's lonely, gawky sister. She worked hard—as a streetcar conductor, a waitress, a singer, a dancer, an actress, a civil rights worker, a college professor, a TV producer, and above all, a writer. In 1993, Maya Angelou read to the nation the poem President Clinton had asked her to compose and deliver at his inauguration.

In an interview Angelou talks about how she has triumphed, both as a person and as a writer, over obstacles in her path:

66 I believe all things are possible for a human being, and I don't think there's anything in the world I can't do. Of course, I can't be five feet four because I'm six feet tall. I can't be a man because I'm a woman. The physical gifts are given to me, just like having two arms is a gift. In my creative source, wherever that is, I don't see why I can't sculpt. Why shouldn't I? Human beings sculpt. I'm a human being. . . .

All my work, my life, everything is about survival. All my work is meant to say 'You may encounter many defeats, but you must not be defeated.' In fact, the encountering may be the very experience which creates the vitality and the power to endure.

My responsibility as a writer is to be as good as I can be at my craft. So I study my craft. I don't simply write what I feel, let it all hang out. That's baloney. That's no craft at all. Learning the craft, understanding what language can do, gaining control of the language, enables one to make people weep, make them laugh, even make them go to war. You can do this by learning how to harness the power of the word. 99

BROTHER 113

Making the Connections

Connecting to the Theme: "Unforgettable Personalities"

For Maya Angelou, her brother Bailey was an unforgettable personality. For thousands of her readers, Angelou herself is an unforgettable personality. Invite students to create character profiles of either Bailey or Maya Angelou by drawing the outline of a boy's or girl's head. Inside the shape, have students write vivid words or phrases that describe the character.

Assessing Learning

Check Test: Short Answers

1. How many brothers and sisters does the author have? [one brother]
2. What does Bailey look like? [He is small and graceful and has velvet-black skin and black curls.]
3. Why is Bailey seldom punished for his behavior? [because his family is so proud of him]
4. List three things Bailey is good at. [Possible responses: defending his sister, making use of his time, praying aloud, stealing pickles, playing group games.]
5. Name two games the children play. [Possible responses: hide–and–seek, pop the whip, follow the leader.]

Standardized Test Preparation

For practice with standardized test format, see
• *Standardized Test Preparation*, p. 26
For practice in proofreading and editing, see
• *Daily Oral Grammar,* Transparency 8

Student to Student

This short sketch reveals the narrator's appreciation of an older person's acceptance and love. The experience also helps influence his own behavior towards his two younger siblings.

Ⓐ Critical Thinking
Speculating
? Why might the author not want to talk? [Sample responses: He is enjoying himself just listening; he is too shy.]

Ⓑ Reading Skills and Strategies
Finding the Main Idea
Ask students to locate the author's statement of the main idea. [the third sentence in the fourth paragraph, beginning, "I never had an older brother. . . ."]

Ⓒ Critical Thinking
Expressing an Opinion
? Do you think the author is a good big brother? Why? [Possible responses: Yes, because he learned from Joe; yes, because he cares about his siblings.]

Resources

Viewing and Representing
Fine Art Transparency
The fine art transparency "Sing to the Stars" by Sandra Speidel can be used to enhance students' appreciation of "The Brother I Never Had."
• Transparency 4
• Worksheet, p. 16

Elements of Literature
For additional instruction on nonfiction writing, see *Literary Elements:*
• Transparency 2
• Worksheet, p. 7

The Brother I Never Had

That day stood clear in my mind. My cousin Joe and I were taking a stroll in the Jamaica area of New York. We had left my uncle's office at about three o'clock and walked to Mila's Diner down the street. I had always thought of Joe as my older brother, and today's experience reaffirmed it.

We walked into that neat little diner and ordered onion rings and Coke. Those onion rings were the best I had ever eaten. Joe introduced me to all the regulars at the diner, and then we sat with them for about an hour. They talked and I listened. They talked about college, work, girls, and life. My cousin kept trying to get me into the conversation, but I refused to speak.

After some time we walked over to the Jamaica Fish Market and looked at all the strange fish they had brought in that day. I tried to pick up a crab out of a basket full of crabs and got pinched. I tried to get some sympathy from Joe, but all he did was smile—not laugh, just smile.

We left the store and headed back to Mila's Diner. We hadn't talked much, just walked. I never had an older brother, and Joe was the only person that was like me and the only one I would consider as my older brother. I wanted to be just like him. He was strong, kind, and caring, and most of all, he loved me.

Now five years later I'm the older brother of two little people. I try to be the same person Joe was for me. He cared for me, as I care for my brothers. He watched out for me, as I watch out for my brothers. Joe is now in college and I guess we've gotten a bit farther apart. That's what getting older does to a person. Every once in a while, though, I think about that walk, and I always wonder if we can ever do it again.

—Gim George
Holy Spirit Regional School
Huntsville, Alabama

Connecting Across Texts

Connecting with "Brother"
Ask students to use information in "Brother" and "The Brother I Never Had" and experiences of their own to create a collage that characterizes what it means to be or to have a brother (or a sister). Provide old magazines from which students can cut words and pictures for this activity. At the bottom of their collage, ask students to complete the prompt: "A brother is . . ." Display their work in the classroom.

Assessing Learning

Observation Assessment
Use the following criteria to assess students' responses to literature.
A = Always   S = Sometimes   R = Rarely   N = Never

Criteria	Date	Rating
Understands the main idea of the literature		
Bases opinions on information from the literature		
Relates to the events and the characters		

MAKING MEANINGS

First Thoughts

[respond]

1. Divide a piece of paper into two columns. In the left-hand column, quote three or four **descriptions** from "Brother" that helped you "see" Bailey. In the right-hand column, write your response to each quotation.

Reading Check

Summarize this selection for a partner. Tell your partner who Bailey is and how Maya feels about him and about herself.

Shaping Interpretations

[interpret]

2. What words would *you* use to describe Bailey's personality? How did you feel about him?

[infer]

3. Did you feel surprised by anything in the last paragraph of "Brother"? What does this paragraph tell you about Angelou?

Connecting with the Text

[connect]

4. Angelou says that she was not as handsome as Bailey was. How important do you think physical appearance is in making someone lovable?

CHOICES: Building Your Portfolio

Writer's Notebook

1. Collecting Ideas for a Biographical Sketch

Go back to the notes you took for the Quickwrite on page 109. List more details that describe the greatest person in your world. Try to tell about some action that is typical of that person. The student essay on page 114 might give you ideas.

Finding the Main Idea

2. What Do You Think?

Check your reading notes, and write a few sentences telling what you think Angelou's **main idea** is. Sometimes the main idea of a passage is summed up in the first or last paragraph. What details in the first and last paragraphs help you understand what Angelou's brother means to her?

Speaking/Performing

3. Kid Capers

Angelou describes three outdoor games she and Bailey played as children. In a short talk, describe an outdoor game you played when you were younger. Tell how and where the game was played. Describe any special chants or rhymes that were part of the game. If possible, give a brief demonstration.

Reading Check

Sample Summary: Bailey is Maya Angelou's brother. She loves him, admires his physical appearance, grace, playfulness, and cleverness. Angelou feels lonely and insecure about her looks and appreciates Bailey's defending her against criticism.

MAKING MEANINGS
First Thoughts

1. Possible answers

Description	Response
"in a voice like cooling bacon grease"	He'd be a good defender—he's smooth.
"he jumped with his pockets full of loot and his eyes laughing"	He's very active and alive. He's fun to be with.
"he would twirl off the end like a top, spinning, falling, laughing"	He's a daredevil. He's athletic.

Shaping Interpretations

2. Possible answers: Loving, daring, clever, sly, energetic. Students may like Bailey because he is smart, fun, and a good leader; some may feel he is too fresh and bossy.
3. Possible surprises: that Angelou was a lonely child; that she says lonely children need a faith in an enduring God; that Bailey gave her the kind of security faith gives us. Possible response: The paragraph tells readers that Angelou is a wise and loving person.

Connecting with the Text

4. Sample responses: Appearance has little or nothing to do with being lovable; even a physically unattractive person can be lovable; a handsome person attracts attention and admiration and may seem easier to love.

Grading Timesaver

Rubrics for each Choices assignment appear on p. 116 in the *Portfolio Management System.*

CHOICES: Building Your Portfolio

1., 2., 3. Students should cite or describe as many relevant details as possible.

LANGUAGE LINK

Brainstorm with students a list of general and specific modifiers to help them distinguish the two types of modifiers and appreciate how specific modifiers create a picture. Then, ask students to underline all the modifiers in a work from their portfolios and to revise the work by replacing general modifiers with specific ones whenever appropriate.

Try It Out
Possible Responses
1. The baby was red and wrinkled.
2. Nora's hair is shiny black.
3. The store looked orderly and clean.

VOCABULARY

Possible Answers
Grating: abrasive, harsh, irritating, annoying
Lauded: praised, honored, extolled, complimented, commended
Precision: accuracy, correctness, exactness
Apt: clever, sharp, keenly intelligent

Resources

Language
- *Grammar and Language Links,* p. 15

Vocabulary
- *Words to Own,* p. 7

LANGUAGE LINK   MINI-LESSON

Style: Choosing Precise Words

Technology HELP

See Language Workshop CD-ROM. *Key word entry: modifiers.*

General modifiers are broad, vague adjectives and adverbs, like *nice, very,* and *cute.* They make writing boring because they don't give readers a clear picture of what you're describing.

Specific modifiers are definite, exact words, like *elbowy, consistently, outrageous,* and *velvet-black.* You can find specific modifiers in a thesaurus or a dictionary. Think of these two books as powerful resources at your command. They can help rescue you from boring modifiers.

Try It Out

Revise each sentence below, taking out the general modifiers and adding specific ones. Share your revised sentences in class.

1. The baby was very plain.
2. Nora's hair is really cute.
3. The store looked pretty good.

THE BORN LOSER reprinted by permission of Newspaper Enterprise Association, Inc.

VOCABULARY   HOW TO OWN A WORD

WORD BANK

grating
lauded
aghast
precision
apt

Thesaurus Rex to the Rescue

A **dictionary** tells you the meanings and pronunciations of words. A **thesaurus** (from a Greek word meaning "treasury" or "storehouse") contains lists of **synonyms** for certain words. If you look up *aghast* in a thesaurus, here are some synonyms you'll find: *surprised, taken aback, shocked, astonished.*

Use a thesaurus to look up the other words listed in the Word Bank, and make a list of the synonyms you find for each word. Then, go back to the text, and substitute some of your synonyms for Angelou's original choices. Do you prefer any of the synonyms you've found?

116 **UNFORGETTABLE PERSONALITIES**

Language Link Quick Check

Revise each sentence below, replacing the general modifiers with specific ones.
1. Angelou's story is <u>interesting</u>. [humorous, moving]
2. The illustrations are <u>pretty</u>. [realistic, expressive, well-drawn]
3. Bailey was <u>good</u> in group games. [creative, imaginative]
4. It would be <u>nice</u> to make people laugh like Bailey did. [fun, thrilling, sweet, enjoyable]
5. Angelou's brother is a <u>good</u> friend. [caring, protective, close, genuine, valuable, helpful]

Before You Read

YES, IT WAS MY GRANDMOTHER

Make the Connection

Unforgettable, That's What You Are

In this collection an unforgettable dog teaches Gary Paulsen important lessons, and a beloved brother proves himself to be "the greatest person" in Maya Angelou's world. How has someone special helped make you the person you are?

Quickwrite

Draw a gift diagram like the one below. Fill it with words, phrases, and memories that tell your special someone what he or she has done for you.

To Maxwell,
You taught
me . . .

Elements of Literature

Tone: It's an Attitude

You've probably heard people say "I don't like your tone of voice." **Tone** refers to the way a speaker is feeling. When you listen to people, you can tell from their voices and faces how they feel. You usually can tell if they are serious, happy, worried, or angry. When you read a poem or a story, however, you have to depend on words alone to learn how the speaker is feeling.

> **T**one is the attitude a writer takes toward an audience, a subject, or a character.
>
> *For more on Tone, see the Handbook of Literary Terms.*

YES, IT WAS MY GRANDMOTHER **117**

Planning

- **Block Schedule**
  Block Scheduling Lesson Plans with Pacing Guide
- **Traditional Schedule**
  Lesson Plans Including Strategies for English-Language Learners
- **One-Stop Planner**
  CD-ROM with Test Generator

OBJECTIVES

1. Read and interpret the poem
2. Analyze tone
3. Express understanding through writing or speaking and listening

SKILLS

Literary
- Analyze tone

Writing
- Write questions for an interview
- Write a poem

Speaking/Listening
- Interview a special person
- Perform a poem collaboratively

Viewing/Representing
- Compare the figure in a sculpture to the subject of a poem (ATE)

Resources: Print and Media

Reading
- *Graphic Organizers for Active Reading*, p. 9
- *Audio CD Library*, Disc 3, Track 4

Viewing and Representing
- *Viewing and Representing*
  Fine Art Transparency 5
  Fine Art Worksheet, p. 20

Assessment
- *Formal Assessment*, p. 23
- *Portfolio Management System*, p. 117
- *Test Generator (One-Stop Planner CD-ROM)*

Internet
- go.hrw.com (keyword: LE0 6-2)

Summary ■

The speaker remembers and admires her grandmother as a strong person who trained wild horses, worked hard, and disdained women's traditional role in the kitchen. The speaker is grateful to her grandmother for freeing her to choose her own way of life.

Resources ———

Listening

Audio CD Library

A vivid recording of this poem is provided in the *Audio CD Library:*
• Disc 3, Track 4

Viewing and Representing

Fine Arts Transparency

The fine arts transparency "My Mother's Kitchen" by Shonto Begay provides a provocative comparison and contrast to the attitude in the poem toward women in kitchens.
• Transparency 5
• Worksheet, p. 20

Ⓐ Elements of Literature

Character

❓What adjectives would describe the grandmother's character? [Sample responses: tough, alive, determined, skillful, liberated, hard-working.]

Ⓑ Elements of Literature

Tone

❓What is the speaker's attitude, or tone, toward the grandmother? [admiring] What words or phrases express that tone? [Students may mention that the speaker's descriptions of her grandmother's achievements express admiration; more specifically, ll. 18–19, "Oh, Grandmother, who freed me" express both admiration and gratitude.]

Ⓒ Critical Thinking

Interpreting

❓Notice what the speaker says about her grandmother in ll. 6–9 and about herself in ll. 18–25. In what ways are the two women alike? [Both are small. Both are free to cast off traditional roles and be themselves.] In what ways are they unlike? [Possible answers: Grandmother ties her hair "securely"; the speaker leaves her hair "wild." Grandmother tames wild horses, but the speaker does not even tame her own hair. Grandmother is disciplined, but the speaker is not.]

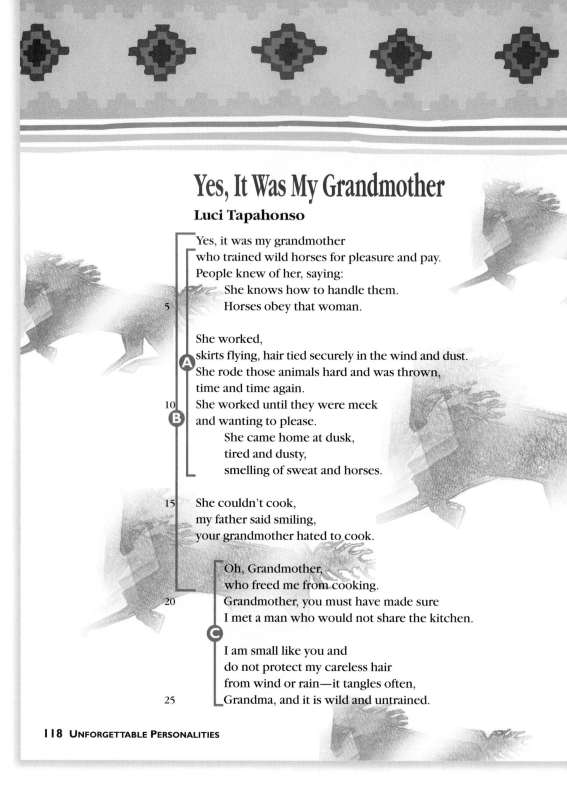

Yes, It Was My Grandmother

Luci Tapahonso

Yes, it was my grandmother
who trained wild horses for pleasure and pay.
People knew of her, saying:
    She knows how to handle them.
5   Horses obey that woman.

She worked,
skirts flying, hair tied securely in the wind and dust.
She rode those animals hard and was thrown,
time and time again.
10 She worked until they were meek
and wanting to please.
    She came home at dusk,
    tired and dusty,
    smelling of sweat and horses.

15 She couldn't cook,
my father said smiling,
your grandmother hated to cook.

Oh, Grandmother,
who freed me from cooking.
20 Grandmother, you must have made sure
I met a man who would not share the kitchen.

I am small like you and
do not protect my careless hair
from wind or rain—it tangles often,
25 Grandma, and it is wild and untrained.

Reaching All Students

Struggling Readers

Have partners create a dialogue with the poem by reading and responding to each line. Partners should take turns—one reads a line aloud, the other shares his or her immediate, spontaneous response.

English Language Learners

Help students recognize shifts in the speaker or the person addressed. In ll. 4–5, the community speaks; in ll. 15 and 17, the father speaks; in ll. 18–25, the speaker addresses Grandmother.

Advanced Learners

Suggest that students, independently or in a small group, create an illustrated verbal collage on art paper, showing how different characters might have viewed the grandmother. The characters should include the speaker, her father, the horses, and the grandmother herself. Words, phrases, and fictional quotations describing the grandmother may be hand-lettered or cut from periodicals.

MEET THE WRITER

Beautiful Talk

Luci Tapahonso (1953–   ), a member of the Navajo nation, was born and raised in Shiprock, New Mexico, within sight of the gigantic red-rock formation looming over the flat landscape that early explorers thought was a fantastic ship in the desert. Ever since she was a little girl, Tapahonso and her family have shared stories and songs. Tapahonso's family-storytelling tradition has been a rich source for her own writing.

66 There is such a love of stories among Navajo people that it seems each time a group of more than two gathers, the dialogue eventually evolves into sharing stories and memories, laughing, and teasing. . . . It is true that daily conversations strengthen us, as do the old stories of our ancestors that have been told since the beginning of the Navajo time. . . .

The combination of song, prayer, and poetry is a natural form of expression for many Navajo people. A person who is able to 'talk beautifully' is well thought of and considered wealthy. To know stories, remember stories, and to retell them well is to have been 'raised right'; the family of such an individual is also held in high esteem. . . . 99

Minnie Manygoats by Star Liana York.
Courtesy of the Zaplin-Lampert Gallery, Santa Fe, New Mexico.

YES, IT WAS MY GRANDMOTHER **119**

RESPONDING TO THE ART

Star Liana York (1952–   ) grew up in an artistic family in the Washington, D.C., area. Her ballerina mother and craftsman father inspired York to do woodworking and to cast miniature sculptures in a high-school jewelry-making class. When she got her own horse to ride in horse shows and rodeos, she became interested in the art and history of the West. York moved to New Mexico in 1985 and began sculpting figures of Native Americans, especially Navajo and Anasazi women. She works in an unusual fashion, neither sketching out an idea nor using live models before she begins shaping the clay.

Activity Tell students that this bronze sculpture is about 27 inches tall. Invite them to describe how the sculpture reflects the traditional Navajo saying "Walk in beauty." Then ask students to compare the three-dimensional figure with the grandmother in the poem. Note that one woman is associated with horses and one with goats. Both have "skirts flying" in the wind and both seem happy.

Making the Connections

Connecting to the Theme: "Unforgettable Personalities"

No one could forget a grandmother who trained wild horses. Invite students to close their eyes and visualize this character, then share oral descriptions of what they "remember" about her. Discuss how the poet has made sure that the grandmother will not be forgotten. [by writing about her; by using her as a role model]

Assessing Learning

Check Test: Short Answer

1. What was the grandmother's job? [training wild horses]
2. What work did she dislike? [cooking]
3. How does the speaker physically resemble her grandmother? [Both are small.]
4. What two things in the poem are identified as "wild and untrained"? [horses and the speaker's hair]

Making Meanings

First Thoughts

1. Possible responses: *Grandmother, yes, worked, freed, wild, untrained.*

Shaping Interpretations

2. Sample response: The poem says you can be free to be whatever you like, thanks to people who have gone before you.

3. The speaker's tone is admiring and celebratory. Qualities she admires in her grandmother and in herself include independence, individuality, and endurance.

Connecting with the Text

4. Students might say that the special person has helped them to have confidence in themselves, understand life, overcome obstacles and fears, be a kinder person, care about others, do better in school, or something similar.

Grading Timesaver

Rubrics for each Choices assignment appear on p. 117 in the *Portfolio Management System*.

CHOICES:
Building Your Portfolio

1. **Writer's Notebook** Have the class brainstorm types of questions that, without getting too personal, may reveal something unknown or surprising about the person.
2. **Creative Writing** Allow English language learners to write their poems in their first language, then translate them into English with the help of peer tutors.
3. **Reader's Theater** Encourage students to record and review a rehearsal of their reading, and to make revisions, before performing for the class.

Resources

Selection Assessment
Formal Assessment
• Selection Test, p. 23
Test Generator
• Selection Test

MAKING MEANINGS

First Thoughts

[respond]

1. What do you think is the most important word or expression in this poem?

Shaping Interpretations

[summarize]

2. In your own words, sum up what this poem says to you.

[analyze]

3. How would you describe the speaker's **tone**, or attitude? What qualities do you think she admires in her grandmother and is pleased to find in herself?

Connecting with the Text

[connect]

4. Think about the person you wrote about for the Quickwrite on page 117. How has he or she helped you to become the person you are? You may want to add new phrases and memories to your Quickwrite "gift box."

CHOICES: Building Your Portfolio

Writer's Notebook
1. Collecting Ideas for a Biographical Sketch

What *don't* you know about the people you know best? You may be surprised! Arrange to interview someone who is special to you, someone who has influenced you over the years. Before the interview, write at least three questions you want to ask.

Creative Writing
2. Yes, It Was My . . .

Write a poem about an unforgettable person. If it seems right for you, use the structure of the first stanza of Tapahonso's poem:

Yes, it was my . . .
who . . .
People knew of him/her,
  saying: . . .

Hold a poetry reading with classmates who also wrote about unforgettable personalities.

Reader's Theater
3. Tune In on Tone

With two or three classmates, perform this poem in a reader's theater. Take turns reading the poem aloud, and listen for places where the speaker's tone changes. Then, divide the poem into parts. Use your voice and facial expressions to bring out the tone in your section of the poem.

Before You Read

PETALS / LOS PÉTALOS

Make the Connection

Gems in the Shadows

Unforgettable personalities are not just the people who make jokes on TV or hang from cliffs in the movies or slam-dunk a basketball in a professional game. They're sometimes people who stay in the background, people we might just miss if we don't pay attention.

Quickwrite

Think of an older person you see often or know well. Imagine what this person looked like and what this person did years ago when he or she was young. Describe your subject as he or she was then and is now.

Elements of Literature

Imagery: An Appeal to Your Senses

Images are words that describe sights, sounds, smells, and tastes. They can also describe the way things feel. Poets try to create precise pictures of what they

experience. This means that they search for just the right words to create pictures in our minds.

Notice that in Mora's poem the title is the first line—and the first image—of the poem.

> **I**magery is language that appeals to the senses—sight, hearing, touch, taste, and smell.
> *For more on Imagery, see the Handbook of Literary Terms.*

Background

Literature and Social Studies

In Mexico and parts of the Southwest, tourists shop in open markets where the local people sell their handmade wares. Paper flowers, baskets, glassware, jewelry, and many other appealing items hang from walls and are heaped upon the tables. Tourists often bargain with sellers to try to get the lowest prices.

 go.hrw.com
LE0 6-2

go.hrw.com
LE0 6-2

Planning

  Resources: Print and Media

Mexican artist **Diego Rivera** (1886–1957) began studying art when he was ten years old. His early work was influenced by such European painters as Paul Cezanne and Pablo Picasso, but his later work was inspired by Mexican working people. A leader in the revival of mural painting, Rivera painted large frescoes on public buildings. These paintings, which often stirred controversy, illustrate Mexico's history and social problems. Following the artistic traditions of the indigenous people of Mexico, Rivera's work is bold and simple in design. His wife, the renowned painter Frida Kahlo, was also a major influence on him.

Activity. Explain that every artist has his or her own vision, or way of seeing the world. Pat Mora and Diego Rivera both depict Mexican women selling flowers. How are their two visions of this subject similar and different? Lead students to seek an answer in details of the poem and painting. For example, the woman in the poem is almost invisible to her customers, while the woman in the painting has a strong presence.

Flower Day by Diego Rivera (1886–1957), Mexico.

Los Angeles County Museum of Art, Los Angeles County Funds. Reproducción autorizada por el Instituto Nacional de Bellas Artes y Literatura.

Reaching All Students

Struggling Readers

Ask each student to read the poem aloud to a partner; each one then should write down one response he or she has to the poem. Readers should do this three times. When their readings are complete, discuss the responses in class. Did the responses change with subsequent readings?

English Language Learners

Ask Spanish-speaking students to read the Spanish translation aloud for the class. They can then compare the Spanish and English versions to make sure they understand all the English words.

Advanced Learners

Native speakers of English might try to understand the Spanish translation of "Petals," especially if they have already studied some Spanish. Point out the cognate word (a word that is similar to its English equivalent) *turqesa*, and invite students to find other examples. Have students guess the meanings of other words and check a Spanish dictionary for the actual definitions.

Petals
Pat Mora

have calloused her hands,
brightly colored crepe paper: turquoise,
yellow, magenta, which she shapes
into large blooms for bargain-hunting tourists
5 who see her flowers, her puppets, her baskets,
but not her—small, gray-haired woman
wearing a white apron, who hides behind
blossoms in her stall at the market,
who sits and remembers collecting wildflowers
10 as a girl, climbing rocky Mexican hills
to fill a straw hat with soft blooms
which she'd stroke gently, over and over again
with her smooth fingertips.

Los pétalos
translated by Nicolás Kanellos

le han causado callos en las manos,
crepé de colores brillantes: turquesa,
amarillo, rosado, que ella transforma
en pétalos grandes para turistas comprando a
lo barato
5 que al ver sus flores, títeres, canastas
no la ven a ella—canosa, diminuta,
en su delantal, escondiéndose detrás del
florecimiento en su puesto de mercado,
sentada recordando las florecitas silvestres que
colectaba
10 de niña, entre los cerros mexicanos
para llenar un sombrero de paja con flores
delicadas
que frotaba suavemente una y otra vez
con las puntitas tiernas de los dedos.

MEET THE WRITER
"In Words I Save Images"

Pat Mora
(1942–   ) is a
Mexican American
who grew up in
El Paso, Texas,
near the border
between the
United States and
Mexico. Much of
her poetry is
about the blending
of Hispanic cul-
ture into Ameri-
can society. "I write because I believe
that Hispanics need to take their rightful
place in American literature," she says.

In addition to several books of
poetry, she has written books for
children that are based on her own
childhood experiences.

Using imagery is Mora's way of
collecting her experiences and looking
them over again. She says:

> 66 Writing is a way of thinking about
> what I see and feel. In words I save
> images of people and scenes. Writing is
> not exactly like a picture album, though,
> because when I write I have to think
> about why I want to save those images,
> how I feel about them. 99

Summary ■ ■

An old woman sits in a Mexican market selling colorful flowers that she has
fashioned from crepe paper. Almost
invisible to her customers, she hides
behind the huge paper blossoms and
remembers collecting wildflowers in
the hills as a girl. This poem is a single
sentence and the title is its first word.

Resources ────

Listening
A recording of this poem is provided in
the *Audio CD Library*:
• Disc 3, Tracks 5, 6

A Struggling Readers
Breaking Down Difficult Text
Make students aware that the poem is
one long sentence. If students are having difficulty, invite them to work in
small groups to rewrite the poem,
breaking the one long sentence into
smaller sentences. You might ask a
reporter from each group to read its
revision to the class.

B Elements of Literature
Imagery
❓ What two senses do the images in ll.
1–9 appeal to? [sight and touch] Name
images that you can picture or sense
vividly. Tell what sense(s) each image
appeals to and name the precise words
that create the picture.

C Elements of Literature
Imagery
❓ Which images in ll. 11–13 bring to
mind the sense of touch? ["straw hat,"
"soft blooms," "stroke gently," "smooth
fingertips"]

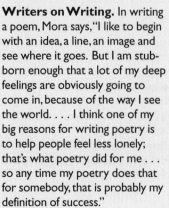

BROWSING IN THE FILES

Writers on Writing. In writing
a poem, Mora says, "I like to begin
with an idea, a line, an image and
see where it goes. But I am stubborn enough that a lot of my deep
feelings are obviously going to
come in, because of the way I see
the world. . . . I think one of my
big reasons for writing poetry is
to help people feel less lonely;
that's what poetry did for me . . .
so any time my poetry does that
for somebody, that is probably my
definition of success."

Making the Connections

**Connecting to the Theme:
"Unforgettable Personalities"**
Remind students of the collection theme, and
point out that for Pat Mora, the old flower
seller is unforgettable. Discuss why the woman
made such a lasting impression on Mora, despite
(or because of) the woman's being nearly invisible to the tourists. Then ask students what
images of the woman they themselves find most
memorable.

Assessing Learning

Check Test: Short Answers
1. The subject of this poem is an old woman
who sells _____. [paper flowers, puppets,
and baskets]
2. The woman's hands have been hardened by
_____. [petals]
3. The tourists do not see the
_____.[woman]
4. As a girl, the woman collected_____
in the hills. [wildflowers]

MAKING MEANINGS

First Thoughts

1. Possible responses: compassionate; sad; curious about the woman and her memories.

Shaping Interpretations

2. Possible responses: Turquoise, yellow, and magenta contrast with gray and white; large blooms contrast with small woman; selling contrasts with collecting; artificial paper flowers contrast with wildflowers; girl contrasts with woman; rocky hills contrast with soft blooms.

3. Possible responses: They do not see the woman because she is small and hides behind the huge, bright flowers; they do not see who the woman really is or who she was as a girl because they are only interested in what she sells.

Extending the Text

4. Possible responses: homeless people or people who work in little-recognized positions, such as street vendors or street cleaners.

Grading Timesaver

Rubrics for each Choices assignment appear on p. 118 in the *Portfolio Management System*.

CHOICES: Building Your Portfolio

1. **Writer's Notebook** Students may want to begin by creating a word web, with the word *appearance* in the inner circle and the words *face, hands, posture,* and *clothes* in surrounding circles.

2. **Creative Writing** Explain that potluck is a meal created from whatever is on hand, which can lead to a surprising combination of elements. You might form students into groups of three or four and have each member of a group create three images for each object. Invite groups to share their poems and objects with the class.

3. **Poetic Collage** Encourage students to title their collages in both English and Spanish.

T124

MAKING MEANINGS

First Thoughts

[respond]

1. How do you feel about the woman in this poem?

Shaping Interpretations

[contrast]

2. By using contrasting **images**, Mora makes her word pictures stand out. For instance, the woman's "calloused" hands contrast with the "smooth fingertips" of her youth. What other contrasting images can you find in the poem?

[interpret]

3. What is it that the "bargain-hunting tourists" don't see? Why don't they?

Extending the Text

[connect]

4. Can you think of other people like this flower seller, whose humanity is ignored by those who pass by? If so, who are they?

CHOICES: Building Your Portfolio

Writer's Notebook

1. Collecting Ideas for a Biographical Sketch

By looking at the way the woman in "Petals" is described, you can tell something about the kind of life she's had. Think of an older person you see often. Jot down some notes about that person's face, hands, posture, clothes, and overall appearance. What do you think that person was like when he or she was young? Look back at your notes for the Quickwrite on page 121 for ideas.

Creative Writing

2. Potluck Poem

Bring to class some object that you can experience with at least three of your five senses. Then, describe what you see, taste, smell, feel, or hear. After you've written your images, ask a classmate to come up with three other images to describe the same object. Keep adding images until you have a potluck poem, a kind of stew of images.

Art

3. Poetic Collage

Working alone or with a group of classmates, make a collage about the objects, people, and events you see in "Petals." A collage can be made up of pictures, objects, and words: photos from magazines, your own drawings, words from the Spanish version of the poem, even stones, flowers, cloth, and so on. What makes a collage interesting is how all these different images are put together.

Resources ——————

Selection Assessment
Formal Assessment
• Selection Test, p. 24
Test Generator
• Selection Test

Reading Skills and Strategies

Booking space on the Net:

OBJECTIVES
1. Understand how prior knowledge is used to make inferences
2. Understand how meaning is created by combining prior knowledge with evidence from a text

MAKING INFERENCES

At first glance this cartoon seems to be about a little dog carrying a large bone. If you look closer, though, you'll see a sign that gives you information that may change your mind. If you already know that a museum of natural history is likely to display large bones (your prior knowledge), you'll figure out that this dog has stolen a priceless display! You made an inference based on your prior knowledge and evidence from the cartoon.

What Is Prior Knowledge?

Good readers use their prior experiences and knowledge to make **inferences,** or educated guesses, about what is happening in a text. Here are some examples:

- Some prior knowledge is in our hearts. If you ever loved an animal the way Gary Paulsen loved Storm, you probably understood a great deal about Paulsen's feelings for his dog.

- Some prior knowledge is in our heads. If you live in Alaska and know about sled dogs, you brought prior knowledge to the story. If you don't, reading "Storm" added to your store of knowledge.

Using Evidence

Strategic readers make meaning from a text by combining their prior knowledge with evidence from the text. Making an inference chart like the one below is one way to illustrate this.

Inference Chart

Prior Knowledge	+	Evidence from the Text	=	My Inference
Natural history museums display skeletons of animals like dinosaurs.		There's a sign at the door.		The dog has swiped a bone from the museum, maybe a rare dinosaur bone.

Putting It Together

You probably already know a lot about the person in the next selection. You'll have a chance to draw from your prior knowledge, as well as to find new evidence, to help you make inferences about the mysterious Mr. Lincoln.

Apply the strategy on the next page. ➤

ZIGGY

Reading Skills and Strategies

This feature focuses on a specific reading strategy, making inferences by using evidence and prior knowledge. Students will have the opportunity to practice applying this strategy in the next selection, "The Mysterious Mr. Lincoln."

Mini-Lesson:
Making Inferences

- Remind students that *prior knowledge* means what they already know about something.

- Present a short piece of writing on a subject that most students will have some prior knowledge of, such as pets, plants, or games. Before students read the piece have them brainstorm information they already know about the subject.

- Have students read the selection and list new information they learned. Some of this new information should be based on inferences. Ask students to identify prior knowledge and new textual information that helped them make inferences.

- Advise students to recall relevant prior knowledge in order to understand new information whenever they read.

Reaching All Students

Struggling Readers
A good strategy to use with the skill Making Inferences is It Says...I Say. For information on using this strategy, see p. 25 of the *Reading Strategies Handbook* in the front of the *Reading Skills and Strategies* binder.

English Language Learners
These students' reasoning ability will often be far ahead of their ability to express their thoughts in English. Allowing students to reason in their first language and then translate their ideas into English will help them gain fluency in English. To accelerate this process, have English-fluent partners work with English language learners on paraphrasing or translating terms such as *prior knowledge, evidence from the text,* and *inference.*

Advanced Learners
Encourage these students to use the chart on this page and the KWL chart accompanying "The Mysterious Mr. Lincoln" in order to hone their skill in making inferences.

Before You Read

THE MYSTERIOUS MR. LINCOLN

Make the Connection

Face Value

"The Mysterious Mr. Lincoln" is the first chapter of a Newbery Medal–winning "photobiography" of Abraham Lincoln. The book is called a photobiography because it tells the story of Lincoln's life not just in words but with historical photographs, too.

Quickwrite

Look at the photograph of President Lincoln on page 130. What qualities do you see in his face? Write for a few moments about the **inferences** you can make about this man's character from looking at the photograph.

Reading Skills and Strategies

Using Prior Knowledge

Preview "The Mysterious Mr. Lincoln" by reading the opening quote and then

Preteaching Vocabulary

Words to Own

Write the words on the board and discuss their meanings. Then ask students to replace the underlined words with Words to Own.

1. Tired from work, Rosa Parks sought <u>rest</u> in a seat on the city bus and refused to get up for a white person. [repose]
2. Her action began a <u>struggle</u> for civil rights that became a <u>most important</u> event of the 1950s and the 1960s. [crusade, paramount]
3. African Americans no longer <u>were regular</u> <u>customers of</u> the Montgomery, Alabama, city buses. [patronized]
4. Never <u>reserved</u> about injustice, Martin Luther King, Jr.'s <u>face</u> filled with <u>life</u> as he spoke. [reticent, countenance, animation]
5. Even <u>awkward</u> teenagers joined the fight to <u>resist</u> unjust laws. [gawky, defy]
6. Threats against Dr. King were <u>signs</u> that he would not live long. [omens]

surveying the text with its photographs and captions. This process will help you recall what you already know about Lincoln and will suggest questions about what you would like to know. Record your recollections and questions about the man who, in 1861, became our sixteenth president. Use the K or W column of the KWL chart below.

K	W	L
What I Know	What I Want to Know	What I Learned
Lincoln was president during the Civil War.	Why was Lincoln "mysterious"?	

go.hrw.com
LE0 6-2

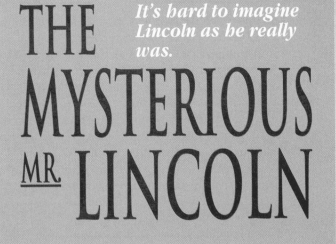

THE MYSTERIOUS MR. LINCOLN

It's hard to imagine Lincoln as he really was.

Russell Freedman

Abraham Lincoln wasn't the sort of man who could lose himself in a crowd. After all, he stood six feet four inches tall, and to top it off, he wore a high silk hat.

His height was mostly in his long, bony legs. When he sat in a chair, he seemed no taller than anyone else. It was only when he stood up that he towered above other men. **A**

At first glance most people thought he was homely. Lincoln thought so too, referring once to his "poor, lean, lank face." As a young man he was sensitive about his gawky looks, but in time, he learned to laugh at

WORDS TO OWN
gawky (gô'kē) *adj.*: awkward; lacking grace or elegance.

THE MYSTERIOUS MR. LINCOLN 127

Summary ▪ ▪

This first chapter of a Newbery Medal-winning photobiography presents details and anecdotes to personalize the familiar historical figure of Abraham Lincoln. Lincoln's gawky height, humor, homespun speech, superstitious beliefs, and folksy ways are contrasted with his ambition, sadness, reticence, skill in logical argument, and eloquence as a speaker and writer. The biographer points out that although Lincoln is known as the "Great Emancipator" who freed the slaves, his "paramount" objective in the Civil War was, at least at the beginning, to "save the Union." Initially critical of Lincoln, the great black leader Frederick Douglass came to admire the man for his accomplishments.

Resources

Viewing and Representing
Videocassette A, Segment 2
Entitled "Russell Freedman: Unforgettable Personalities," this segment presents the author responding to student questions.

Listening
Audio CD Library
A recording of the biographical excerpt is provided in the *Audio CD Library*:
• Disc 3, Track 7

A Reading Skills and Strategies
Using Prior Knowledge

? Because of his height, Lincoln physically "towered above other men." What else do you already know about him that shows he "towered above" others? In what other ways did Lincoln reach a great height? Write your answer in the K column of your chart.
[Possible responses: He rose above others to become president; he towers above most other presidents because he was a great leader who saved the Union and ended slavery.]

--- Resources: Print and Media ---

Reading
• *Graphic Organizers for Active Reading,* p. 11
• *Spelling and Decoding,* Worksheet, p. 8
• *Words to Own,* p. 8
• *Audio CD Library,* Disc 3, Track 7

Writing and Language
• *Daily Oral Grammar,* Transparency 9
• *Grammar and Language Links,* Worksheet p. 17
• *Language Workshop CD-ROM*

Viewing and Representing
• *Visual Connections,* Videocassette A, Segment 2

Assessment
• *Formal Assessment,* p. 25
• *Portfolio Management System,* p. 119
• *Standardized Test Preparation,* p. 28
• *Test Generator (One-Stop Planner CD-ROM)*

Internet
• go.hrw.com (keyword: LE0 6-2)

Ⓐ Elements of Literature

Character

Discuss how the author reveals Lincoln's quick wit, facility with language, and self-deprecating humor through this anecdote. First, make sure everyone understands the word *two-faced*. ["dishonest"; "double dealing"; "expressing two opposite views"] Then ask: What does Lincoln's response to his rival's accusation show about Lincoln? [Possible responses: that he is a fast thinker and is skilled at playing with words; that he has a keen sense of humor; that he is a masterly politician who deflects his opponent's criticism and makes his audience laugh.]

Ⓑ Cultural Connections

Tell students that two Frenchmen, painter Louis Daguerre and scientist Joseph Niépce, invented the daguerreotype, one of the earliest forms of photography, in the 1830s. Though this process required the subject to remain absolutely still for at least several minutes, it quickly became popular. Explain that the invention of photography changed people's ideas about privacy and their perceptions of themselves and the world. It allowed them for the first time to witness events and people many miles away. And it let them keep a pictorial record of their own lives. Invite students to speculate about how life today would be different if there were no cameras.

RESPONDING TO THE ART

Activity. Help students relate this picture of Lincoln's birthplace to the statement (p. 129): Lincoln "struggled hard to rise above his log-cabin origins." Ask students to tell what "log-cabin origins" suggests. [Possible answers: that his family was poor and uneducated, scratching out a living from the land; that Lincoln was a self-made, ambitious man.]

himself. When a rival called him "two-faced" during a political debate, Lincoln replied: "I leave it to my audience. If I had another face, do you think I'd wear this one?"

According to those who knew him, Lincoln was a man of many faces. In <u>repose</u> he often seemed sad and gloomy. But when he began to speak, his expression changed. "The dull, listless features dropped like a mask," said a Chicago newspaperman. "The eyes began to sparkle, the mouth to smile; the whole <u>countenance</u> was wreathed in <u>animation</u>, so that a stranger would have said, "Why, this man, so angular and solemn a moment ago, is really handsome!""

Lincoln was the most photographed man of his time, but his friends insisted that no photo ever did him justice. It's no wonder. Back then, cameras required long exposures. The person being photographed had to "freeze" as the seconds ticked by. If he blinked an eye, the picture would be blurred. That's why Lincoln looks so stiff and formal in his photos. We never see him laughing or joking.

Artists and writers tried to capture the "real" Lincoln that the camera missed, but something about the man always escaped

---

WORDS TO OWN

repose (ri·pōz′) *n.*: restful state.
countenance (koun′tə·nəns) *n.*: face or facial expression.
animation (an′i·mā′shən) *n.*: liveliness; life.

Log cabin: The Granger Collection, New York.

President Lincoln's first Home in Illinois.

128 UNFORGETTABLE PERSONALITIES

Reaching All Students

Struggling Readers

Using Prior Knowledge was introduced on p. 126 under Reading Skills and Strategies. The strategy Probable Passage helps students with this skill. For additional information on Probable Passage, see the *Reading Strategies Handbook* in the *Reaching Struggling Readers* binder, p. 43.

English Language Learners

For these students, you may want to preview such idioms as *do him justice*, meaning "to show to full advantage"; *phrases still running in our ears*, meaning "words that we long remember, that are famous"; *whistle down sadness*, meaning "attempting to keep up one's spirits by whistling." For additional strategies to supplement instruction for English language learners, see
• *Lesson Plans Including Strategies for English-Language Learners*

them. His changeable features, his tones, gestures, and expressions, seemed to <u>defy</u> description.

Today it's hard to imagine Lincoln as he really was. And he never cared to reveal much about himself. In company he was witty and talkative, but he rarely betrayed his inner feelings. According to William Herndon, his law partner, he was "the most secretive—<u>reticent</u>—shut-mouthed man that ever lived." **C**

In his own time, Lincoln was never fully understood even by his closest friends. Since then, his life story has been told and retold so many times he has become as much a legend as a flesh-and-blood human being. While the legend is based on truth, it is only partly true. And it hides the man behind it like a disguise.

The legendary Lincoln is known as Honest Abe, a humble man of the people who rose from a log cabin to the White House. There's no doubt that Lincoln was a poor boy who made good. And it's true that he carried his folksy manners and homespun speech to the White House with him. He said "howdy" to visitors and invited them to "stay a spell." He greeted diplomats while wearing carpet slippers, called his wife "mother" at receptions, and told bawdy[1] jokes at cabinet meetings. **D**

Lincoln may have seemed like a common man, but he wasn't. His friends agreed that he was one of the most ambitious people they had ever known. Lincoln struggled hard to rise above his log-cabin origins, and he was proud of his achievements. By the time he ran for president he was a wealthy man, earning a large income from his law practice and his many investments. As for the nickname Abe,

1. **bawdy:** humorous but crude.

he hated it. No one who knew him well ever called him Abe to his face. They addressed him as Lincoln or Mr. Lincoln.

Lincoln is often described as a sloppy dresser, careless about his appearance. In fact, he <u>patronized</u> the best tailor in Springfield, Illinois, buying two suits a year. That was at a time when many men lived, died, and were buried in the same suit.

It's true that Lincoln had little formal "eddication," as he would have pronounced it. **E** Almost everything he "larned" he taught himself. All his life he said "thar" for *there*, "git" for *get*, "kin" for *can*. Even so, he became an eloquent public speaker who could hold a vast audience spellbound and a great writer whose finest phrases still ring in our ears. He was known to sit up late into the night, discussing Shakespeare's plays with White House visitors.

He was certainly a humorous man, famous for his rollicking stories. But he was also moody and melancholy, tormented by long and frequent bouts of depression. Humor was his therapy. He relied on his yarns,[2] a friend observed, to "whistle down sadness."

He had a cool, logical mind, trained in the courtroom, and a practical, commonsense approach to problems. Yet he was deeply superstitious, a believer in dreams, <u>omens</u>, and visions. **F**

2. **yarns:** entertaining stories that rely on exaggeration for their humor. Storytellers like Lincoln could be said to "spin" yarns.

WORDS TO OWN
defy (dē·fī′) *v.:* resist completely.
reticent (ret′ə·sənt) *adj.:* reserved; choosing not to talk about what one thinks or feels.
patronized (pā′trən·īzd′) *v.:* was a regular customer of.
omens (ō′mənz) *n.:* events, objects, or situations that supposedly tell what will happen in the future.

THE MYSTERIOUS MR. LINCOLN **129**

C Elements of Literature
Character
? What do you learn about Lincoln's character in this paragraph? [He did not talk about his inner thoughts and feelings; he was reticent.] How does the author make this trait of Lincoln seem believable? [The author quotes Lincoln's law partner, who described Lincoln as "secretive" and "shut-mouthed."]

D English Language Learners
Regional Terms
Tell students that *howdy* is a greeting meaning "How do you do?" or "hello" and that *stay a spell* is a way of welcoming someone or inviting him or her to stay "for a short, indefinite period of time." Explain that these are regional terms, or expressions that people used in the area where Lincoln grew up. You might ask these students to share words used to greet visitors in their native language.

E Struggling Readers
Supplying Correct Pronunciation and Spelling
Point out that the correct spellings of "eddication" and "larned" are *education* and *learned* and that the "wrong" spelling imitates the way Lincoln would pronounce these words.

F Reading Skills and Strategies

Using Prior Knowledge
This is a good point to remind students to look back at their K-W-L chart, fill in new things they have learned, and write down additional things they would like to learn from the selection. Encourage students to share what they have learned by reading their chart entries aloud.

Taking a Second Look

Review: Using Context Clues
Remind students that when they read an unfamiliar word, they can make a guess about its meaning by finding clues in the context, or the material surrounding the word, and by using their prior knowledge. As an example, have students look at the word *melancholy* in the selection, in the next-to-last paragraph on p. 129. Ask them to guess the word's meaning and identify clues that suggest it. [Meaning: sad, gloomy, depressed. Possible clues: "depression"; "sadness"; the words "moody" and "But" suggest that *melancholy* means the opposite of *humorous* and *rollicking*.]

Activities
Have pairs of students list the words in this selection whose meanings they are unsure of. Then the partners should use context clues and their prior knowledge to make guesses about each word's meaning. Ask the partners to list each word, their guess of the word's meaning, and the context clues that helped them. Then call on a volunteer to find the word listed in either Words to Own, the footnotes, the glossary, or a dictionary. Have the student read the word's definition aloud.

We admire Lincoln today as an American folk hero. During the Civil War, however, he was the most unpopular president the nation had ever known. His critics called him a tyrant, a hick,[3] a stupid baboon who was unfit for his office. As commander in chief of the armed forces, he was denounced as a bungling amateur who meddled in military affairs he knew nothing about. But he also had his supporters. They praised him as a farsighted statesman, a military mastermind who engineered the Union victory.

Lincoln is best known as the Great Emancipator, the man who freed the slaves. Yet he did not enter the war with that idea in mind. "My paramount object in this struggle *is* to save the Union," he said in 1862, "and is *not* either to save or destroy slavery." As the war continued, Lincoln's attitude changed. Eventually he came to regard the conflict as a moral crusade to wipe out the sin of slavery.

No black leader was more critical of Lincoln than the fiery abolitionist[4] writer and editor Frederick Douglass. Douglass had grown up as a slave. He had won his freedom by escaping to the North. Early in the war, impatient with Lincoln's cautious leadership, Douglass called him "preeminently the white man's president, entirely devoted to the welfare of white

Copy of a fragment of a manuscript containing Lincoln's idea of democracy (about 1858). The original is missing.

As I would not be a slave, so I would not be a master. This expresses my idea of democracy—Whatever differs from this, to the extent of the difference, is no democracy—

A. Lincoln

Abraham Lincoln and his son Tad (1865).

---

3. **hick:** awkward, inexperienced person from the country.
4. **abolitionist:** anyone who wanted to end, or abolish, slavery in the United States.

WORDS TO OWN

paramount (par′ə·mount′) *adj.*: most important.
crusade (kroo·sād′) *n.*: struggle for a cause or belief.

Making the Connections

Connecting to the Theme: "Unforgettable Personalities"

Students almost certainly will have previously read something about Abraham Lincoln and have gathered some prior knowledge of his life and historical importance. They may, however, not have gathered an image of his remarkably complex personality until now. Have students work in groups of three or four to write a character profile of Abraham Lincoln on sheets of paper. Give students the following headings for the profile:

Name; Date of Birth; Place of Birth; Physical Appearance; Family History; Career; Greatest Achievements; Greatest Frustrations; Character Traits; Some Little-Known Facts About Lincoln; Date and Cause of Death. Students should be able to fill in much of the profile using this selection and prior knowledge. Interested students may do further research to complete the profile.

men." Later, Douglass changed his mind and came to admire Lincoln. Several years after the war, he said this about the sixteenth president:

"His greatest mission was to accomplish two things: first, to save his country from dismemberment[5] and ruin; and second, to free his country from the great crime of slavery. . . . Taking him for all in all, measuring the tremendous magnitude of the work before him, considering the necessary means to ends, and surveying the end from the beginning, infinite wisdom has seldom sent any man into the world better fitted for his mission than Abraham Lincoln."

5. **dismemberment:** separating into parts; dividing up.

C **Reading Skills and Strategies**
Summarizing
? How would you summarize what Frederick Douglass said about Lincoln? [Possible response: All things considered, Lincoln did a good job saving the Union and ending slavery, and he was the best man for the job.]

D **Reading Skills and Strategies**
Using Prior Knowledge
? What new knowledge do you have that will become prior knowledge the next time you read about Lincoln? [Possible responses: Lincoln was moody; he was called names by his critics; he was "folksy"; he was very ambitious.]

Resources
Selection Assessment
Formal Assessment
• Selection Test, p. 25
Test Generator
• Selection Test

MEET THE WRITER

"I Know Lincoln Better Than I Know Some of My Friends."

Russell Freedman (1929–) has written more than thirty nonfiction books for children and young adults. His book *Lincoln: A Photobiography*, which includes "The Mysterious Mr. Lincoln," won the Newbery Medal for the most distinguished contribution to children's literature in 1988. Freedman says he was thrilled and astonished when his book got the prize. It was the first time in thirty-two years that a nonfiction book had won the Newbery. Freedman had this to say about writing a biography of the famous sixteenth president:

66 The Lincoln I grew up with was a cardboard figure, too good to believe. As an adult, I read a couple of books that indicated he was just like everyone else—someone subject to depression, someone who had trouble making up his mind—and that intrigued me. When I had some inkling he was a complicated person in his own right, I decided I wanted to know more about him.

I got to know Lincoln the way I'd try to know anyone in real life. How do you understand people? You observe them, discover their memories, find out their thoughts, their ideas of right and wrong. Once you do that, they become somebody you know. I'd say I know Lincoln better than I know some of my friends because I've studied him more closely.

There are naturally many, many books written about Lincoln, but that didn't concern me. I thought I could write a biography that would say something special about Lincoln, about the Lincoln I had discovered for myself. 99

Russell Freedman's Hall of Fame

In other books Russell Freedman personally introduces you to many more personalities he has "discovered for himself." His other biographies include *Eleanor Roosevelt: A Life of Discovery; Franklin Delano Roosevelt* (both published by Clarion); *Jules Verne: Portrait of a Prophet; Teenagers Who Made History;* and *The Wright Brothers: How They Invented the Airplane* (all published by Holiday House).

THE MYSTERIOUS MR. LINCOLN **131**

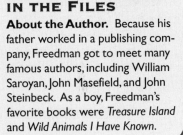

BROWSING IN THE FILES
About the Author. Because his father worked in a publishing company, Freedman got to meet many famous authors, including William Saroyan, John Masefield, and John Steinbeck. As a boy, Freedman's favorite books were *Treasure Island* and *Wild Animals I Have Known*.

Assessing Learning

Check Test: Short Answers

1. Lincoln is best known as the Great _____. [Emancipator]
2. Lincoln was the _____ president. (What number president was he?) [sixteenth]
3. Lincoln is famous for his humor, but he was also _____. [sad, melancholy]
4. At first, Lincoln's major objective in the Civil War was _____. [to save the Union]
5. _____ said that seldom has any man been "better fitted for his mission than Abraham Lincoln." [Frederick Douglass]

Standardized Test Preparation

For practice with standardized test format specific to this selection, see
• *Standardized Test Preparation,* p. 28
For practice in proofreading and editing, see
• *Daily Oral Grammar,* Transparency 9

Connections

A Critical Thinking

Interpreting

? Since cats cannot laugh, what do you think Lincoln's friend means? [Lincoln was so funny that he could make even someone who never laughs laugh.]

B Critical Thinking

Analyzing

? Lincoln's defense is funny, but does it make sense? [Possible answers: Yes, if the farmer should have used the other end of his weapon, then the dog should have used its other end too; no, the dog cannot use its other end as a weapon; no, Lincoln's argument is not meant to be sensible—he is ridiculing the other lawyer's notion that, while being attacked, the farmer should not have defended himself by using his weapon most effectively.]

C Reading Skills and Strategies

Using Prior Knowledge

At this point, encourage students to make additional entries to their K-W-L charts on what they learned about Lincoln as a result of reading this article.

Connections — AN ESSAY

Lincoln's Humor

Louis W. Koenig

A It is puzzling how Lincoln could laugh, joke, and tell stories, despite his terrible burdens as president during the Civil War. Lincoln was the first and the best humorist ever to occupy the White House. A friend said, "He could make a cat laugh."

Lincoln called laughter "the joyous, beautiful, universal evergreen of life." For Lincoln laughter relieved life's pressures and soothed its disappointments. Both as a lawyer and as a politician, he used amusing stories to make important points clear to his listeners. Storytelling put people at ease or nudged them from an unwanted topic or point of view. It also pleasantly brought an interview to a close and a visitor's welcome departure from the president's office.

Political opponents feared Lincoln's humorous jabs, which often destroyed their best arguments. Stephen A. Douglas, Lincoln's opponent in a Senate race, said, "Every one of his stories seems like a whack upon my back. . . . When he begins to tell a story, I feel that I am to be overmatched."

Lincoln's words got extra force from his facial expressions and gestures—a shrug of his shoulders, raised eyebrows, a turned-down mouth, a comically twisted face—which made his audiences roar with laughter.

Here is a sampling of Lincoln's humor and the uses he made of it:

• As a young lawyer, Lincoln once defended a farmer who had been attacked by his neighbor's dog. To fend off the dog, the farmer had poked it with a pitchfork, wounding it. The dog's owner then took the case to court to recover damages. His lawyer argued that the farmer should have struck the dog with the handle end of the pitchfork to avoid causing it serious harm. **B** In the farmer's defense, Lincoln exclaimed that the dog should have avoided frightening the farmer by approaching him with *its* other end.

• As president, Lincoln was besieged with visitors seeking jobs and favors. One day while a visitor was pressing his demands, Lincoln's doctor entered the room. Lincoln, holding out his hands, asked him, "Doctor, what are those blotches?" "They're a mild smallpox," the doctor replied. "They're all over me," said Lincoln. "It's contagious, I believe." "Very contagious," said the doctor as the visitor hastily departed. "There is one good thing about this," said Lincoln to his doctor after the caller had left. "I now have something I can give to everybody."

• **C** Impatient with his Civil War generals, who were slow to engage their forces in battle, Lincoln began requiring frequent reports of their progress. An irritated general sent this telegram to the White House: "We have just captured six cows. What shall we do with them?" Lincoln replied, "Milk them."

132 UNFORGETTABLE PERSONALITIES

Connecting Across Texts

Connecting with "The Mysterious Mr. Lincoln"

Ask students how reading "Lincoln's Humor" has enhanced the picture of Lincoln they formed from reading the main selection. Ask students to find specific passages in "The Mysterious Mr. Lincoln" that prepared them (served as prior knowledge) for "Lincoln's Humor." Strengthen the connection by having students include both pieces on one K-W-L chart.

Listening to Music

Lincoln Portrait by Aaron Copland, performed by the Los Angeles Philharmonic, Zubin Mehta (conductor), Gregory Peck (narrator)

Aaron Copland (kōp′lənd) (1900–1990), often called "the dean of American music," was a native of Brooklyn who nevertheless captured and celebrated the frontier spirit of America in compositions such as *Billy the Kid, Rodeo, John Henry,* and *Appalachian Spring.*

Activity

After students have read the selections, play all or part of the *Lincoln Portrait.* Then ask students how the music supports or adds to their impressions of Lincoln. Encourage students to write, paint, or sketch their own Lincoln portrait based on what they have heard and read.

T132

MAKING MEANINGS

First Thoughts

[respond]

 1. Look back at your notes for the Quickwrite on page 126. Does Freedman's portrait of Lincoln match up with your prior impressions? If not, how was Lincoln different from what you imagined?

Shaping Interpretations

[infer]

2. Why is Lincoln "mysterious"? What other **inferences** can you make about Lincoln's character from your reading of "Lincoln's Humor" (see *Connections* on page 132)?

[speculate]

3. How do you think Lincoln would have responded to this first chapter of his biography? Why?

Connecting with the Text

[analyze]

4. What was the most surprising thing you learned about Lincoln from this chapter? Why did it surprise you?

Extending the Text

[speculate]

5. If Lincoln could send a message to the American people today, what do you think he would say?

Challenging the Text

[interpret]

6. According to Freedman, Lincoln was a "man of many faces." What does this mean? In your opinion, how accurate is this description? Explain.

[evaluate]

7. What do you think of this chapter as an opening of a biography of Lincoln? Tell why it does or doesn't make you want to read the rest of the book.

Reading Check

Go back to your KWL chart on page 127, and in the first column, correct any statements that are inaccurate. Then, in the last column, list six new things you learned about Lincoln.

Long Abraham Lincoln a Little Longer.

The Granger Collection, New York.

THE MYSTERIOUS MR. LINCOLN **133**

Reading Check

Students' corrections will depend upon what they originally wrote in their chart. Possible new knowledge: Lincoln had very little formal education; he was a lawyer; he was sensitive about his looks when he was young; he hated his nickname; he didn't like to talk about himself; he had enemies on both sides during the Civil War.

MAKING MEANINGS

First Thoughts

1. Possible responses: Yes, it matches my prior impression of Lincoln as a great writer, speaker, and leader. No, I didn't realize he was so funny (and so sad).

Shaping Interpretations

2. Lincoln is mysterious because he didn't let even his closest friends know his inner thoughts and feelings; because his life has become shrouded in legend; because there were many contradictions about him—he could seem either homely or handsome; he was both humorous and sad; he had a clear logical mind yet believed in superstition. Possible inferences: Lincoln used humor to influence voters and jurors; Lincoln had common sense.

3. Possible responses: Lincoln would have enjoyed the humor, fairness, and honesty in the chapter because he valued humor, fairness, and honesty in life; Lincoln would have resented having his life and character pried into because he was secretive.

Connecting with the Text

4. Students may say that they were surprised that Lincoln got depressed, that he was so "folksy" in the White House and while campaigning, and that he was superstitious. Possible response: These facts are not part of his popular image.

Extending the Text

5. Possible responses: He would tell us to preserve democracy; to preserve a strong United States; to treat people of all kinds fairly; to see him as a human being, not a legend.

Challenging the Text

6. Possible meanings: Lincoln's facial expressions were varied; Lincoln had many sides or aspects to his personality. Possible responses: It is accurate because Lincoln was reticent, yet he was a great public speaker; depressive yet humorous; a common man but very ambitious and uncommonly successful; unschooled but brilliant.

7. Students may want to read more because the chapter makes Lincoln seem like a real person, someone they'd want to know. Some may feel that they've learned enough about Lincoln from this chapter in addition to their prior knowledge.

T133

Grading Timesaver

Rubrics for each Choices Assignment appear on p. 119 in the *Portfolio Management System.*

CHOICES: Building Your Portfolio

1. **Writer's Notebook**   Remind students to save their work. They may use it as prewriting for the Writer's Workshop on pp. 158–162.
2. **Creative Writing**   Inform students that if photographs are not available they can sketch their subject in a pose or situation that reveals the trait, or they can tell an anecdote that illustrates the trait. Students might present the sketch in a photo album into which they have inserted pictures with written captions.
3. **Speaking/Media**   Have students create a chart like the one following to use in comparing the books and in presenting their review to the class.

Strengths and Weaknesses	Rating	Reasons Recommended or Not
[Funny at times; makes you want to keep reading]	[4]	[Recommended because it is humorous and informative]

4. **Research/Performance**   Remind students that a tableau is a "frozen" scene. In one form of tableau, rather than a single narrator speaking, students take turns. First, the group leader taps one member on the shoulder, and that person speaks as Lincoln, telling what Lincoln is thinking at the moment. This student then taps another, and so on, with only one student at a time coming unfrozen.

T134

CHOICES: Building Your Portfolio

Writer's Notebook

1. Collecting Ideas for a Biographical Sketch

Freedman portrays Lincoln as a bundle of contradictions. For example, he tells us that Lincoln loved to tell jokes but that he was sometimes "moody and melancholy." Lincoln had little formal education, but his speeches "could hold a vast audience spellbound." Jot down some contrasting character traits in people you know (or know of). Then, pick one person from your notes whom you might like to write more about.

Janelle—looks clumsy, but great at volleyball.
Chris—always joking, but works hard after school.

Creative Writing

2. Get the Picture

Create a biographical sketch of someone, using many photographs. You might start your work by filling in a character graph like the one below. Use each "slice of the pie" to stand for one of your subject's traits. Make the size of the slices show how large a part each trait plays in your character's personality. In your sketch, include anecdotes or photographs that reveal your character's traits. Be sure to write a caption for each photograph.

Character Graph

Speaking/Media

3. "Picks and Pans"

Read two books on Lincoln—Russell Freedman's *Lincoln: A Photobiography* and one other. With a partner who has read the same two books, discuss the strengths and weaknesses of each. Then, present the books to the class as if you were a reviewer on TV. Explain why you would—or wouldn't—recommend each book to readers your age. Use a scale like the one below:
Forget it! 0 1 2 3 4 Read it!

Research/Performance

4. Lincoln Live

Do research on at least five key events in Lincoln's life. You might choose events such as growing up in a log cabin; delivering the Gettysburg Address; loving his sons; and ending slavery. You will have to decide how to present your scenes. One possibility is to do five tableaux, with a narrator describing what is happening in each.

134 UNFORGETTABLE PERSONALITIES

Skill Link

Writing: Comparing with Adjectives
Explain that adjectives have different forms or degrees that are used to compare people, places, and things. Show students this chart:

Degree	Use	Examples
Positive	to describe something	tall, ambitious
Comparative	to compare two people or things	taller, more ambitious
Superlative	to compare more than two	tallest, most ambitious

Point out that the comparative degree is formed by adding <u>either</u> *-er* or the word *more* to the adjective and that the superlative degree is formed by adding <u>either</u> *-est* or *most* to the adjective. (Explain that some forms are irregular. Example: *good, better, best.*)
Activity
Ask students to form the comparative and superlative degrees of these adjectives: *dull, formal, talkative, close, wealthy, sloppy, great, famous, moody,* and *critical.*

GRAMMAR LINK   MINI-LESSON

Language Handbook HELP

See Comparison of Modifiers, pages 717–719; Special Problems with Modifiers, pages 719–720.

Technology HELP

See Language Workshop CD-ROM. *Key word entry: degrees of comparison.*

Comparing with Adjectives

An adjective that compares two things is called a **comparative**. An adjective that compares three or more things is called a **superlative**. Watch out for these two common mistakes:

1. Don't use a superlative to compare only two people or things.

    EXAMPLES

                                        more
    Of his two main goals, saving the Union was ~~most~~ important to Lincoln.

                                        sharper
    Lincoln's rival was sharp, but Lincoln was ~~sharpest~~.

2. Don't use *more* and *-er* with the same word; don't use *most* and *-est* with the same word.

    EXAMPLES

    Many people thought Lincoln seemed ~~more~~ sadder in repose.

    During the Civil War, Lincoln was the most unpopular~~est~~ president ever.

> ### Try It Out
> Correct these comparisons:
> 1. Lincoln's most finest phrases are still heard today.
> 2. Some people say he was the most wittiest president.
> 3. In his debates with Stephen Douglas, Lincoln was the best speaker.

VOCABULARY   HOW TO OWN A WORD

WORD BANK

gawky
repose
countenance
animation
defy
reticent
patronized
omens
paramount
crusade

Synonyms: Making Mr. Lincoln Less Mysterious

Imagine that you're helping a third-grader research Abraham Lincoln. Your young friend wants to read "The Mysterious Mr. Lincoln," but some of the words are just too hard. Go back to the text and find each Word to Own. On a piece of paper, copy the sentence in which each word appears. Then, rewrite each sentence, substituting a simpler word or words for the Word to Own.

    Your substitutions are **synonyms,** or words that are similar in meaning. You can find synonyms in a **thesaurus** (a book of synonyms), in a **dictionary,** or in a reference book called a **synonym finder.** You can also check **reference software** or on-line libraries.

THE MYSTERIOUS MR. LINCOLN 135

GRAMMAR LINK

Ask students to choose a piece of writing from their portfolios and to underline all the comparative and superlative adjectives. Ask them to identify the adjectives they used incorrectly and to revise the selection. Have students exchange papers with a partner to check their corrections.

Try It Out
Answers
1. Lincoln's finest phrases are still heard today.
2. Some people say he was the wittiest president.
3. In his debates with Stephen Douglas, Lincoln was the better speaker.

VOCABULARY
Possible Responses

"As a young man he was sensitive about his [ugly] looks ...."
"[At rest] he often seemed sad and gloomy."
"... the whole [face] was wreathed in [liveliness] ..."
"His changeable features, his tones, gestures, and expressions, seemed to [resist] description."
"... he was 'the most secretive—[likely not to talk about himself]—shut-mouthed man that ever lived.'"
"In fact, he [was a regular customer of] the best tailor in Springfield ...."
"Yet he was deeply superstitious, a believer in dreams, [signs that seem to predict the future] and visions."
"'My [most important] object in this struggle *is* to save the Union ....'"
"... he came to regard the conflict as a moral [battle] ...."

Resources

Grammar
• *Grammar and Language Links,* p. 17

Vocabulary
• *Words to Own,* p. 8

Spelling
For related instruction, see
• *Spelling and Decoding,* p. 8

Grammar Link Quick Check

Correct the following comparisons.
1. Many people think that Lincoln was the <u>finer</u> of all our country's presidents. [finest]
2. He led our country at its <u>most dreadfullest</u> time. [most dreadful]
3. The Gettysburg Address may be Lincoln's <u>more famous</u> speech. [most famous]
4. The second anecdote about Lincoln is the <u>best</u> of the two. [better]
5. People debate whether Washington or Lincoln was a <u>more greater</u> president. [greater]

OBJECTIVES

1. Read and interpret the biography
2. Keep track of sequence
3. Express understanding through writing, art, or music
4. Identify the correct usage of *bad* and *badly*, and use these words in writing
5. Understand and use new words

SKILLS

Reading
- Keep track of sequence

Writing
- Collect ideas for a biographical report
- Write an obituary

Grammar/Language
- Use *bad* and *badly* correctly

Vocabulary
- Use new words

Art
- Paint a mural

Music
- Tape-record spirituals

Viewing/Representing
- Relate paintings to the events in a subject's life (ATE)
- Compare the styles of two painters (ATE)
- Imagine oneself in the landscape of a painting (ATE)
- Describe the personality in a portrait (ATE)

Planning

- **Block Schedule**
  Block Scheduling Lesson Plans with Pacing Guide
- **Traditional Schedule**
  Lesson Plans Including Strategies for English-Language Learners
- **One-Stop Planner**
  CD-ROM with Test Generator

Before You Read

A GLORY OVER EVERYTHING

Make the Connection

What Price Freedom?

This true story takes place during the mid-1800s, when most Southern states still allowed the practice of slavery. The horror of slavery began in the United States in 1619, when the first Africans arrived in the stinking holds of Dutch slave ships. Slavery was not abolished in the United States until 1865.

What would people feel who were held in slavery—owned body and soul by another person? What would they be unable to do? What sorrows would they face? What would they risk if they tried to escape?

Round robin. Share your thoughts with a small group of classmates. Then, choose a group member to summarize for the rest of the class the ideas your group talked about.

Quickwrite

Write about what you felt and learned during your group discussion. What questions do you have about slavery?

Reading Skills and Strategies

Sequence: It's What Happens When

Sequence is the order of events in a story. Writers often use time-order words or phrases, such as *first, next, then, now,* and *before,* to signal the order of events and the amount of time that has passed.

As you read about Harriet Tubman (or after you've finished reading, if you prefer), keep track of her journey to freedom by completing a sequence chart like the one shown below. Include the time-order words that signal the sequence of events.

Sequence Chart

| 1. **One day** a white woman asked Harriet what her name was. | → | 2. **After that** whenever she saw Harriet, she talked to her. | → | 3. **Then** she offered to help Harriet whenever Harriet needed help. |

Background

Literature and Social Studies

In 1849, when the following portion of Harriet Tubman's **biography** takes place, a runaway slave who crossed into a free state was considered free. By 1850, however, federal fugitive-slave laws decreed that runaway slaves were not safe until they reached Canada. People who hated slavery started the Underground Railroad to help runaways make their way to freedom. This was not a railroad, and neither was it underground. The Underground Railroad was made up of people from the North and South who offered shelter, food, and protection to those escaping to freedom in the North. To keep the route secret, the organization used railroad terms, such as

136 UNFORGETTABLE PERSONALITIES

Preteaching Vocabulary

Words to Own

Have volunteers locate the Words to Own and their definitions at the bottom of the selection pages and read them aloud. Tell students that four of the five words are the same part of speech and ask them to identify it. [adjective] Have students also identify the part of speech of the fifth word. [*elude*; a verb] Then have students choose the Word to Own that fits best in each of the sentences on the right.

1. In a game of hide-and-seek, the goal is to _____ your opponent. [elude]
2. The winning runner's legs were long and _____ . [sinewy]
3. I can't say why the best team lost; the reason is _____ . [inexplicable]
4. A player who is _____ and breaks the rules can be thrown out of a game. [defiant]
5. Everyone on the team had a _____ reason to be in the gym after school. [legitimate]

stations for the houses along the way and conductors for the people who offered help.

Harriet Tubman, who had escaped from slavery, became one of the most famous conductors on the railroad. She helped more than three hundred men, women, and children along the perilous road to freedom.

In this excerpt from her biography, we meet Harriet Tubman when she is a field hand at the Brodas Plantation in Maryland. As a young girl, Harriet had received a crushing blow when she refused to help tie up a runaway slave. The injury left a deep scar on her forehead; it also made her fall asleep quite suddenly and uncontrollably.

go.hrw.com
LE0 6-2

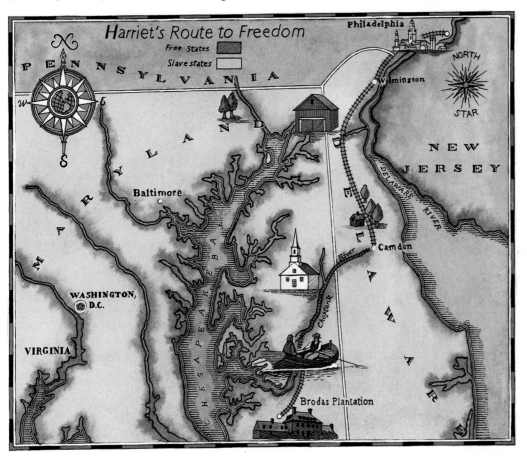

Harriet's Route to Freedom

Free States
Slave states

A GLORY OVER EVERYTHING 137

Summary ▪ ▪

On a plantation in Maryland, in 1849, Harriet Tubman persuades three of her brothers to run away with her to keep from being sold. This first attempt at freedom is thwarted by her brothers' fear, and the four siblings turn back. Soon afterward, however, Harriet starts out on her own, despite her vulnerability to sudden sleeping seizures. She sings a spiritual about "bound for the promised land" to let her sister know that she is leaving. A white woman who had previously offered help gives Harriet the names of two people on the Underground Railroad and tells her how to reach the first stop. With the aid of abolitionists who conceal her, feed her, and help transport her, Harriet travels 90 miles through rough country to reach Pennsylvania, where she is finally free. All the while, she is threatened by a handbill in which her former owner offers five hundred dollars reward for her return.

Background

Between 1840 and 1860, a few thousand people every year successfully escaped from slavery by using the Underground Railroad. Those who helped them included free blacks, white people, and slaves on plantations. The Railroad was not a centralized national organization but a loosely connected network of people who broke the law to help enslaved people reach freedom.

Resources: Print and Media

Reading
- *Reading Skills and Strategies*
    MiniRead Skill Lesson, p. 125
    Selection Skill Lesson, p. 131
- *Graphic Organizers for Active Reading*, p. 12
- *Words to Own*, p. 9
- *Spelling and Decoding*, Worksheet, p. 9
- *Audio CD Library*, Disc 3, Track 8

Writing and Language
- *Daily Oral Grammar*, Transparency 10
- *Grammar and Language Links*, Worksheet, p. 19
- *Language Workshop CD-ROM*

Viewing and Representing
- *Viewing and Representing*
    Fine Art Transparency 6
    Fine Art Worksheet, p. 24
- *Visual Connections*
    Videocassette A, Segment 3

Assessment
- *Formal Assessment*, p. 27
- *Portfolio Management System*, p. 120
- *Standardized Test Preparation*, pp. 30, 32
- *Test Generator (One-Stop Planner CD-ROM)*

Internet
- go.hrw.com (keyword: LE0 6-2)

When Harriet heard of the sale of her sisters, she knew that the time had finally come when she must leave the plantation.

A GLORY OVER EVERYTHING

Ann Petry

from **Harriet Tubman: Conductor on the Underground Railroad**

Ⓐ

One day in 1849, when Harriet was working in the fields near the edge of the road, a white woman wearing a faded sunbonnet went past, driving a wagon. She stopped the wagon and watched Harriet for a few minutes. Then she spoke to her, asked her what her name was, and how she had acquired the deep scar on her forehead.

Harriet told her the story of the blow she had received when she was a girl. After that, whenever the woman saw her in the fields, she stopped to talk to her. She told Harriet that she lived on a farm near Bucktown. Then one day she said, not looking at Harriet but looking instead at the overseer[1] far off at the edge of the fields, "If you ever need any help, Harriet, ever need any help, why, you let me know."

---
1. **overseer:** person who supervises workers; in this case, a slave driver.

138

Reaching All Students

Struggling Readers
Following sequence or chronology was introduced on p. 136. For a lesson directly tied to this selection that teaches students to follow chronology by using a strategy called Retellings, see the *Reading Skills and Strategies* binder:
• MiniRead Skill Lesson, p. 125
• Selection Skill Lesson, p. 131

English Language Learners
Use the terms *Underground Railroad* and *runaway* to introduce compound words. Point out that knowing the meanings of the small, simple words that form these terms can help readers define the compound terms. Ask students to try to find other compound words in the selection. For additional strategies to supplement instruction for these students, see
• *Lesson Plans Including Strategies for English-Language Learners*

That same year the young heir to the Brodas estate[2] died. Harriet mentioned the fact of his death to the white woman in the faded sunbonnet the next time she saw her. She told her of the panic-stricken talk in the quarter, told her that the slaves were afraid that the master, Dr. Thompson, would start selling them. She said that Doc Thompson no longer permitted any of them to hire their time.[3] The woman nodded her head, clucked to the horse, and drove off, murmuring, "If you ever need any help——"

The slaves were right about Dr. Thompson's intention. He began selling slaves almost immediately. Among the first ones sold were two of Harriet Tubman's sisters. They went south with the chain gang[4] on a Saturday.

When Harriet heard of the sale of her sisters, she knew that the time had finally come when she must leave the plantation. She was reluctant to attempt the long trip north alone, not because of John Tubman's threat to betray her[5] but because she was afraid she might fall asleep somewhere along the way and so would be caught immediately.

She persuaded three of her brothers to go with her. Having made certain that John was asleep, she left the cabin quietly and met her brothers at the edge of the plantation. They agreed that she was to lead the way, for she was more familiar with the woods than the others.

The three men followed her, crashing through the underbrush, frightening themselves, stopping constantly to say, "What was that?" or "Someone's coming."

She thought of Ben[6] and how he had said, "Any old body can go through a woods crashing and mashing things down like a cow." She said sharply, "Can't you boys go quieter? Watch where you're going!"

One of them grumbled, "Can't see in the dark. Ain't got cat's eyes like you."

"You don't need cat's eyes," she retorted. "On a night like this, with all the stars out, it's not black dark. Use your own eyes."

She supposed they were doing the best they could, but they moved very slowly. She kept getting so far ahead of them that she had to stop and wait for them to catch up with her, lest they lose their way. Their progress was slow, uncertain. Their feet got tangled in every vine. They tripped over fallen logs, and once one of them fell flat on his face. They jumped, startled, at the most ordinary sounds: the murmur of the wind in the branches of the trees, the twittering of a bird. They kept turning around, looking back.

They had not gone more than a mile when she became aware that they had stopped.

"On a night like this, with all the stars out, it's not black dark."

2. **Brodas estate:** Edward Brodas, the previous owner of the plantation, died in 1849 and left his property to his heir, who was not yet old enough to manage it. In the meantime the plantation was placed in the hands of the boy's guardian, Dr. Thompson.

3. **hire their time:** Some slaveholders allowed their slaves to hire themselves out for pay to other plantation owners who needed extra help. In such cases the slaves were permitted to keep their earnings.

4. **chain gang:** literally, a gang of people (slaves or prisoners) chained together.

5. Harriet's husband, John Tubman, was a free man who was content with his life. He violently disapproved of his wife's plan to escape and threatened to tell the master if she carried it out.

6. **Ben:** Harriet Tubman's father. Her mother is called Old Rit.

A GLORY OVER EVERYTHING **139**

Using Students' Strengths

Drawing Conclusions

? What kinds of dangers and obstacles did escaping slaves face? [Someone might recognize and report them. Handbills advertised that they were missing and encouraged people to capture them. Patrollers and bloodhounds searched for them. If they were returned to their master, they faced terrible punishment.]

B Reading Skills and Strategies

Finding Sequence

This is a good place to remind students to update their sequence charts. Invite two or more volunteers to read their sequence charts aloud.

C Reading Skills and Strategies

Making Predictions

? How do you think this news will affect Harriet? [Possible response: It will force her to escape immediately, without planning. It will cause her to run for freedom alone.]

She turned and went back to them. She could hear them whispering. One of them called out, "Hat!"

"What's the matter? We haven't got time to keep stopping like this."

"We're going back."

"No," she said firmly. "We've got a good start. If we move fast and move quiet——"

Then all three spoke at once. They said the same thing, over and over, in frantic hurried whispers, all talking at once:

A They told her that they had changed their minds. Running away was too dangerous. Someone would surely see them and recognize them. By morning the master would know they had "took off." Then the handbills advertising them would be posted all over Dorchester County. The patterollers[7] would search for them. Even if they were lucky enough to <u>elude</u> the patrol, they could not possibly hide from the bloodhounds. The hounds would be baying after them, snuffing through the swamps and the underbrush, zigzagging through the deepest woods. The bloodhounds would surely find them. And everyone knew what happened to a runaway who was caught and brought back alive.

She argued with them. Didn't they know that if they went back they would be sold, if not tomorrow, then the next day, or the next? Sold south. They had seen the chain gangs. Was that what they wanted? Were they going to be slaves for the rest of their lives? Didn't freedom mean anything to them?

"You're afraid," she said, trying to shame

7. **patterollers:** patrollers.

140 UNFORGETTABLE PERSONALITIES

them into action. "Go on back. I'm going north alone."

Instead of being ashamed, they became angry. They shouted at her, telling her that she was a fool and they would make her go back to the plantation with them. Suddenly they surrounded her, three men, her own brothers, jostling her, pushing her along, pinioning[8] her arms behind her. She fought against them, wasting her strength, exhausting herself in a furious struggle.

She was no match for three strong men. She said, panting, "All right. We'll go back. I'll go with you."

She led the way, moving slowly. Her thoughts were bitter. Not one of them was willing to take a small risk in order to be free. It had all seemed so perfect, so simple, to have her brothers go with her, sharing the dangers of the trip together, just as a family should. Now if she ever went north, she would have to go alone.

B

C Two days later, a slave working beside Harriet in the fields motioned to her. She bent toward him, listening. He said the water boy had just brought news to the field hands, and it had been passed from one to the other until it reached him. The news was that Harriet and her brothers had been sold to the Georgia trader and that they were to be sent south with the chain gang that very night.

8. **pinioning** (pin′yən·iŋ): binding or holding someone to make the person helpless.

WORDS TO OWN
elude (ē·lōōd′) *v.*: escape notice of.

> Harriet went on working but she knew a moment of panic.

Taking a Second Look

Review: Making Predictions

Remind students that when they make a prediction about a text, they are making an inference about what will happen next. They think about what has happened so far and what the characters are like. They also use their own general knowledge and previous reading experiences to infer what is likely to happen. As they read on and gather new information, they may revise their predictions.

Give students the example of a prediction a reader might make in the chart below when the brothers tell Harriet they are going back and she tries to persuade them to go on.

Activity
Ask students what they predicted when they read the last paragraph on p. 140 and on what they based their prediction. [Possible predictions: Harriet will escape immediately. Harriet will make a run for freedom alone. Possible bases for predictions: Harriet's character is strong, and she is determined to escape slavery.]

What Has Happened	What I Know	Prediction
The brothers scare themselves, are clumsy, and keep looking back.	It took great daring and courage to escape slavery.	The brothers will turn back.

Harriet went on working but she knew a moment of panic. She would have to go north alone. She would have to start as soon as it was dark. She could not go with the chain gang. She might die on the way because of those <u>inexplicable</u> sleeping seizures. But then she—how could she run away? She might fall asleep in plain view along the road.

But even if she fell asleep, she thought, the Lord would take care of her. She murmured a prayer, "Lord, I'm going to hold steady on to You, and You've got to see me through."

Afterward, she explained her decision to run the risk of going north alone in these words: "I had reasoned this out in my mind; there was one of two things I had a *right* to, liberty or death; if I could not have one, I would have the other; for no man should take me alive; I should fight for my liberty as long as my strength lasted, and when the time came for me to go, the Lord would let them take me."

At dusk, when the work in the fields was over, she started toward the Big House.[9] She had to let someone know that she was going north, someone she could trust. She no

9. **Big House:** plantation owner's house.

Hampton University Museum, Hampton, Virginia.

Harriet Tubman Series (1939–1940) No. 7 by Jacob Lawrence.
Harriet Tubman worked as water girl to field hands. She also worked at plowing, carting, and hauling logs.

longer trusted John Tubman and it gave her a lost, lonesome feeling. Her sister Mary worked in the Big House, and she planned to

WORDS TO OWN
inexplicable (in'ek·splik'ə·bəl) *adj*.: not explainable.

A GLORY OVER EVERYTHING 141

RESPONDING TO THE ART

Jacob Lawrence (1917–2000), an American painter and educator, lived with his family in the Harlem section of New York City, where he first showed his artistic talent in free art classes taught by Charles Alston (see p. 341). Lawrence later created several series of pictures, each focusing on historical figures or events important to African Americans. Abolitionists John Brown and Frederick Douglass are the subjects of two series. Another, *The Migration Series,* consists of sixty panels and tells the story of African Americans in great numbers moving to cities in the North from their rural homes in the South between the early 1900s and the 1940s. *The Harriet Tubman Series* consists of thirty-one panels and is among Lawrence's most famous works. **Activity.** Call students' attention to the fact that this selection is accompanied by only three of the thirty paintings in the series on Harriet Tubman. Invite them to look at the paintings, here and on pp. 143 and 145, and to speculate about events in Tubman's life that might be the subjects of other panels in the series.

Crossing the Curriculum

Social Studies
Have students work in pairs or small groups to prepare a presentation on one of the following related historical events and figures: Harriet Tubman's later accomplishments; Sojourner Truth; Frederick Douglass; the Dred Scott decision; the Emancipation Proclamation; the Montgomery, Alabama, bus boycott. Presentations should include the major facts, human interest stories, and pictures.

Fine Arts
Have students watch *The Autobiography of Miss Jane Pittman,* a film about an old woman who reflects on her life, including her years in slavery. Then have students create an artwork that depicts both Harriet Tubman and Jane Pittman, showing something that the two women have in common.

A Vocabulary Note

Context Clues

Ask students to try to figure out the meaning of the term *quarter*. [Possible answers: the area of the plantation reserved for field hands; the slaves' place of residence.] Have students identify clues in the context that suggest the meaning of *quarter*. [Harriet "turned aside" from the direction in which she had been headed, which was "toward the house," because Dr. Thompson saw her. As a "field hand," Harriet "had no legitimate reason" for going to the Big House, so when she turned and "went toward the quarter," she was going to a place where she belonged.]

B Critical Thinking

Interpreting

❓ What is Harriet's purpose in singing the song? [Possible responses: to tell her sister she is running away; to express defiance and anticipation of her freedom.]

C Cultural Connections

Ash cake was a kind of cake or bread that the slaves baked in the ashes of their fireplace. Salt was used to preserve meats and fish, such as herring.

D Critical Thinking

Speculating

❓ Why do you suppose Harriet took the quilt? [Possible responses: to keep warm at night; for its importance as a reminder of her past; because she worked too hard on it to abandon it.]

Cultural Connections

Recent research by Jacqueline L. Tobin and Raymond G. Dobard in *Hidden in Plain View* (Doubleday, 1999) suggests that the patterns in quilts created by slaves contained coded messages. The Monkey Wrench pattern, for example, one of ten patterns the authors identify as making up the "Underground Railroad Quilt Code"—signaled that slaves were to begin collecting items in preparation for escape.

---

tell Mary that she was going to run away, so someone would know.

A As she went toward the house, she saw the master, Doc Thompson, riding up the drive on his horse. She turned aside and went toward the quarter. A field hand had no legitimate reason for entering the kitchen of the Big House—and yet—there must be some way she could leave word so that afterward someone would think about it and know that she had left a message.

As she went toward the quarter, she began to sing. Dr. Thompson reined in his horse, turned around, and looked at her. It was not the beauty of her voice that made him turn and watch her, frowning; it was the words of the song that she was singing and something defiant in her manner that disturbed and puzzled him.

B
> *When that old chariot comes,*
> *I'm going to leave you,*
> *I'm bound for the promised land,*
> *Friends, I'm going to leave you.*
>
> *I'm sorry, friends, to leave you,*
> *Farewell! Oh, farewell!*
> *But I'll meet you in the morning,*
> *Farewell! Oh, farewell!*
>
> *I'll meet you in the morning,*
> *When I reach the promised land;*
> *On the other side of Jordan,*
> *For I'm bound for the promised land.*

C That night when John Tubman was asleep and the fire had died down in the cabin, she took the ash cake that had been baked for their breakfast and a good-sized piece of salt herring and tied them together in an old bandanna. By hoarding this small stock of food, she could make it last a long time, and with

the berries and edible roots she could find in the woods, she wouldn't starve.

D She decided that she would take the quilt[10] with her, too. Her hands lingered over it. It felt soft and warm to her touch. Even in the dark, she thought she could tell one color from another because she knew its pattern and design so well.

Then John stirred in his sleep, and she left the cabin quickly, carrying the quilt carefully folded under her arm.

Once she was off the plantation, she took to the woods, not following the North Star, not even looking for it, going instead toward Bucktown. She needed help. She was going to ask the white woman who had stopped to talk to her so often if she would help her. Perhaps she wouldn't. But she would soon find out.

When she came to the farmhouse where the woman lived, she approached it cautiously, circling around it. It was so quiet. There was no sound at all, not even a dog barking or the sound of voices. Nothing.

She tapped on the door, gently. A voice said, "Who's there?" She answered, "Harriet, from Dr. Thompson's place."

When the woman opened the door, she did not seem at all surprised to see her. She glanced at the little bundle that Harriet was carrying, at the quilt, and invited her in. Then she sat down at the kitchen table and wrote two names on a slip of paper and handed the paper to Harriet.

---

10. **the quilt:** Tubman had painstakingly stitched together a quilt before her wedding.

WORDS TO OWN

legitimate (lə·jit′ə·mət) *adj.*: reasonable; logically correct.
defiant (dē·fi′ənt) *adj.*: openly and boldly resisting.

---

142 UNFORGETTABLE PERSONALITIES

Listening to Music

African American spirituals performed by Paul Robeson

Arising in the days of slavery, African American spirituals had their roots in the complex rhythms and harmonies of African music. They expressed a deep faith in the Christianity that the slaves had adopted, but they also served as coded messages, as an indirect means for the slaves to communicate their discontent. The "promised land," for example, might be code for "freedom" or "the free states."

Activity

Have students listen to one or more spirituals after reading the selection. Examples: "Follow the Drinking Gourd," "Go Down, Moses," "Swing Low, Sweet Chariot." Remind students that the words of the song may present a coded message. Tell students to imagine that they are nineteenth-century slaves hearing the songs. Ask them to describe the performance in such a context. Then ask them to describe their emotional responses to the spirituals. Interested students may extend this project with Choice 4, p. 148.

She said that those were the next places where it was safe for Harriet to stop. The first place was a farm where there was a gate with big white posts and round knobs on top of them. The people there would feed her, and when they thought it was safe for her to go on, they would tell her how to get to the next house or take her there. For these were the first two stops on the Underground Railroad—going north, from the eastern shore of Maryland.

Thus Harriet learned that the Underground Railroad that ran straight to the North was not a railroad at all. Neither did it run underground. It was composed of a loosely organized group of people who offered food and shelter, or a place of concealment, to fugitives who had set out on the long road to the North and freedom.

Harriet wanted to pay this woman who had befriended her. But she had no money. She gave her the patchwork quilt, the only beautiful object she had ever owned.

That night she made her way through the woods, crouching in the underbrush whenever she heard the sound of horses' hoofs, staying there until the riders passed. Each time, she wondered if they were already hunting for her. It would be so easy to describe her, the deep scar on her forehead like

Hampton University Museum, Hampton, Virginia.

Harriet Tubman Series (1939–1940) No. 10 by Jacob Lawrence.

Harriet Tubman was between twenty and twenty-five years of age at the time of her escape. She was now alone. She turned her face toward the North, and fixing her eyes on the guiding star, she started on her long, lonely journey.

a dent, the old scars on the back of her neck, the husky speaking voice, the lack of height, scarcely five feet tall. The master would say

A GLORY OVER EVERYTHING 143

she was wearing rough clothes when she ran away, that she had a bandanna on her head, that she was muscular and strong.

She knew how accurately he would describe her. One of the slaves who could read used to tell the others what it said on those handbills that were nailed up on the trees along the edge of the roads. It was easy to recognize the handbills that advertised runaways because there was always a picture in one corner, a picture of a black man, a little running figure with a stick over his shoulder and a bundle tied on the end of the stick.

Whenever she thought of the handbills, she walked faster. Sometimes she stumbled over old grapevines, gnarled and twisted, thick as a man's wrist, or became entangled in the tough <u>sinewy</u> vine of the honeysuckle. But she kept going.

In the morning she came to the house where her friend had said she was to stop. She showed the slip of paper that she carried to the woman who answered her knock at the back door of the farmhouse. The woman fed her and then handed her a broom and told her to sweep the yard.

Harriet hesitated, suddenly suspicious. Then she decided that with a broom in her hand, working in the yard, she would look as though she belonged on the place; certainly no one would suspect that she was a runaway.

That night the woman's husband, a farmer, loaded a wagon with produce. Harriet climbed in. He threw some blankets over her, and the wagon started.

It was dark under the blankets and not ex-

She was surprised at her own lack of fear . . .

actly comfortable. But Harriet decided that riding was better than walking. She was surprised at her own lack of fear, wondered how it was that she so readily trusted these strangers who might betray her. For all she knew, the man driving the wagon might be taking her straight back to the master.

She thought of those other rides in wagons, when she was a child, the same clop-clop of the horses' feet, creak of the wagon, and the feeling of being lost because she did not know where she was going. She did not know her destination this time either, but she was not alarmed. She thought of John Tubman. By this time he must have told the master that she was gone. Then she thought of the plantation and how the land rolled gently down toward the river, thought of Ben and Old Rit, and that Old Rit would be inconsolable because her favorite daughter was missing. "Lord," she prayed, "I'm going to hold steady onto You. You've got to see me through." Then she went to sleep.

The next morning, when the stars were still visible in the sky, the farmer stopped the wagon. Harriet was instantly awake.

He told her to follow the river, to keep following it to reach the next place where people would take her in and feed her. He said that she must travel only at night and she must stay off the roads because the patrol would be hunting for her. Harriet climbed out of the wagon. "Thank you," she said simply, thinking how amazing it was that there should be

WORDS TO OWN

sinewy (sin′yo͞o·ē) *adj.:* strong; firm; tough.

Skill Link

Parts of Speech

Before you teach the Grammar Link on p. 149, review the definitions of *noun, pronoun, verb,* and *adjective*. In the following sentence, help students identify the nouns, pronoun, verbs, and adjectives and draw a line from each adjective to the noun it modifies.

       adj.   n. v. adj.   p.
• The courageous woman was alone when she
  v.   adj. n.   n.
escaped from the terrible state of slavery.

Activity

Have students label each noun, pronoun, verb, and adjective and draw a line from each adjective to the noun it modifies.

      adj. n.   v.
1. The frightened men quickly returned to the
  adj. n.   n.
  awful life on the plantation.

         n.   v.   adj.   p.
2. Though Harriet was afraid, she willingly

    v.   adj.   n   n.
risked great danger for freedom.
          adj.   n.   v.   n.   n.
3. When the white woman offered help, Harriet
   v.   p.
accepted it gratefully.

Harriet Tubman Series (1939–1940) No. 11 by Jacob Lawrence.

"$500 Reward! Runaway from subscriber of Thursday night, the 4th inst., from the neighborhood of Cambridge, my negro girl, Harriet, sometimes called Minty. Is dark chestnut color, rather stout build, but bright and handsome. Speaks rather deep and has a scar over the left temple. She wore a brown plaid shawl. I will give the above reward captured outside the county, and $300 if captured inside the county, in either case to be lodged in the Cambridge, Maryland, jail.
> (Signed) George Carter,
> Broadacres, near Cambridge, Maryland,
> September 24th, 1849"

white people who were willing to go to such lengths to help a slave get to the North.

When she finally arrived in Pennsylvania, she had traveled roughly ninety miles from Dorchester County. She had slept on the ground outdoors at night. She had been rowed for miles up the Choptank River by a man she had never seen before. She had been concealed in a haycock[11] and had, at one point, spent a week hidden in a potato hole in a cabin which belonged to a family of free Negroes. She had been hidden in the attic of the home of a Quaker. She had been befriended by stout German farmers, whose guttural[12] speech surprised her and whose well-kept farms astonished her. She had never before seen barns and fences, farmhouses and outbuildings, so carefully painted. The cattle and horses were so clean they looked as though they had been scrubbed.

When she crossed the line into the free state of Pennsylvania, the sun was coming up. She said, "I looked at my hands to see if I was the same person now I was free. There was such a glory over everything, the sun came like gold through the trees and over the fields, and I felt like I was in heaven."

11. **haycock:** pile of hay in a field.

12. **guttural:** harsh, rasping.

D **Struggling Readers**

Using Graphic Aids

On a map of the United States or its eastern region, have students trace the distance from Dorchester County, Maryland, to the Pennsylvania border— ninety miles, according to the text. Today this journey would take about an hour and a half by car, yet to Harriet Tubman it was a journey from one world to another.

E **Reading Skills and Strategies**

Finding Sequence

Invite volunteers to share their sequence charts for the entire selection. Ask students to suggest ways their peers' sequencing could be made more accurate or specific. You may wish to draw a master sequence chart on the chalkboard for students to compare with their own.

RESPONDING TO THE ART

Jacob Lawrence wrote and illustrated a 1968 children's book, *Harriet and the Promised Land,* which tells Harriet Tubman's story in verse.

Activity. Ask students to pretend that they are in the landscape of this Jacob Lawrence painting. Have them jot down their impressions of their surroundings and of the experience. Suggest that they use their notes to write a poem.

Professional Notes

Cultural Diversity

In pre–Civil War days, numerous Southern whites thought slavery was wrong. Many refused to own slaves. Some took their belief a step further and helped runaways. These included German and Czech immigrants who settled in central Texas. Invite students to research this topic in order to understand what motivated people from one culture to side with members of another culture.

Making the Connections

Connecting to the Theme: "Unforgettable Personalities"

Harriet Tubman will long be remembered for her strength and courage. On the chalkboard, begin a cluster diagram by putting the name Harriet Tubman in the center. Invite students to suggest words and phrases describing Tubman's character traits and accomplishments. Extend the discussion by asking, "What might Harriet be doing if she were alive today?"

MEET THE WRITER

"Remember Them"

Ann Petry (1908–1997) is best known for presenting the tragedy of African slavery in two biographies for young readers: one on Harriet Tubman and the other on Tituba, a young African woman from Barbados who was owned by a Salem family and tried for witchcraft in 1692.

In a speech at the New York Public Library, Petry tells of meeting a young reader who had just read her biography of Harriet Tubman. The meeting made Petry think about what she wanted the book to say to her readers:

66 As I was about to leave, a little girl came in to return a book of mine, a book I wrote about Harriet Tubman. She was carrying it hugged close to her chest. She laid it down on the table, and the librarian said to her, 'You know, this is Mrs. Petry, the author of the book you are returning.'

I must confess that I was dismayed; . . . though I have had children tell me they enjoyed something I had written, I had never had a face-to-face encounter with a young reader who was actually holding one of my books. The child looked at me, and I looked at her—and she didn't say anything and neither did I. I didn't know what to say. Neither did she. Finally she reached out and touched my arm, ever so gently, and then drew her hand back as though she were embarrassed. I copied her gesture, touching her gently on the arm, because I felt it would serve to indicate that I approved her gesture.

Then I left the library, but I left it thinking to myself: What have I said to this child in this book? . . . Of course, I have been saying: Let's take a look at slavery. I said it in *Harriet Tubman* and again in *Tituba of Salem Village.*

But what else was I saying? Over and over again, I have said: These are people. Look at them, listen to them, . . . remember them. Remember for what a long, long time black people have been in this country, have been a part of America: a sturdy, indestructible, wonderful part of America, woven into its heart and into its soul. 99

More of Ann Petry's People

To find out what happens to Harriet Tubman on her road to freedom, look for *Harriet Tubman: Conductor on the Underground Railroad.* You might also enjoy *Tituba of Salem Village* (both published by HarperCollins).

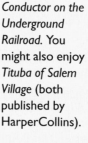

Assessing Learning

MAKING MEANINGS

First Thoughts

[respond] 1. Would you have tried to escape if you had been in Harriet Tubman's situation? Why or why not?

Shaping Interpretations

[analyze] 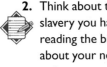 2. Think about the discussion of slavery you had before you began reading the biography, and think about your notes for the Quickwrite on page 136. Did any of your feelings or ideas change after you read this biography? Explain.

[infer] 3. What **inferences** can you make about the **character traits** that help Tubman find freedom? What makes her an unforgettable personality?

[interpret] 4. Many Africans held in slavery used songs to communicate forbidden messages. When Harriet Tubman sings about leaving on the chariot, what message is she giving to her sister? In the Bible the Israelites escaping slavery in Egypt eventually cross the Jordan River and enter the land they believe was promised to them by God. What is Tubman's Jordan? What is her Promised Land?

[compare] 5. Think back to "The Mysterious Mr. Lincoln." What did Abraham Lincoln and Harriet Tubman have in common? What did Lincoln have in common with the "conductors" on the Underground Railroad?

Extending the Text

[connect] 6. Tubman says that "there was one of two things I had a *right* to, liberty or death; if I could not have one, I would have the other; for no man should take me alive." What other people, in history or living today, risk death in order to be free?

Challenging the Text

[respond] 7. Ann Petry, the author of this biography, never knew Harriet Tubman personally, yet she describes Tubman's private thoughts and feelings during her escape. Explain why you think it is or isn't right for a biographer to add such details to someone's life story.

> ### Reading Check
>
> Imagine that you're a reporter for a secret newspaper put out by the Underground Railroad. Record information for a news story on Harriet's escape. Refer to your **sequence chart** to order the events. Use details in the story to answer *who, what, when, where, why,* and *how* questions.

Reading Check

The correct sequence includes Harriet's first attempt to escape with her brothers; their return to the plantation; the news of her impending sale; her immediate need to escape; her seeking help from the woman in Bucktown; her journey through the woods at night; her stopping at the farmhouse of a white couple; her night journey in the farmer's wagon; and her long and varied journey along the river to Pennsylvania. Possible questions: *"Who* helped her and who hindered her?" *"What* was the Underground Railroad?" *"When* did Harriet Tubman decide she had to escape?" *"Where* did Tubman end her journey to freedom?" *"Why* did some white people help runaway slaves?" *"How* did Tubman make her way to freedom?"

MAKING MEANINGS

First Thoughts

1. Students may say they would have been willing to risk death for freedom or that they would have been too afraid of being captured and brutalized to try to escape.

Shaping Interpretations

2. Students may say that the biography helped them better understand how the slaves actually felt; or that the biography increased their admiration of the daring, determined people who escaped slavery; or that the biography increased their respect for white people who took risks to help runaway slaves.

3. Possible responses: Tubman is determined, courageous, intelligent, agile, trusting, wary, honorable, and strong. She is unforgettable for her determination to be free and for her bravery in traveling alone despite great danger.

4. Her message to her sister is that she is going to try to escape to freedom. Tubman's Jordan is the border between Maryland and Pennsylvania, between the slave states and the free states. Her Promised Land is the free states.

5. Possible responses: Tubman and Lincoln both risked their lives (and Lincoln gave his) for ideals of freedom; both made difficult decisions requiring courage and fortitude. Both Lincoln and the conductors worked to help the slaves—Lincoln through political leadership, the conductors by physically guiding them toward freedom.

Extending the Text

6. Possible responses: soldiers, past and present, who risk their lives for their countries' freedom; volunteers in the civil rights movement in the 1950s and 1960s; Nelson Mandela; Martin Luther King, Jr.; the founders of the United States in the American Revolution; fighters in the Warsaw ghetto in 1943 and other anti-Nazi resistance fighters.

Challenging the Text

7. Possible responses: It is right if it makes the story more interesting without falsifying the historical facts. It is wrong because it is not a completely accurate representation of a person's life.

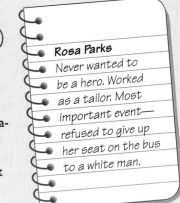

Grading Timesaver

Rubrics for each Choices assignment appear on p. 120 in the *Portfolio Management System*.

CHOICES: Building Your Portfolio

1. **Writer's Notebook** Students might decide what the most important event in the subject's life was by asking themselves, "What would (the subject) say was the highlight of his or her life?" Remind students to save their work. They may use it as prewriting for the Writer's Workshop on pp. 158–162.

2. **Creative Writing** Encourage students to use sequence notes, as they did for the selection, to keep track of the order of events. Tell students that obituaries often use chronological order, but that the beginning of an obituary is often either a general overview of the importance of the subject's life or a statement about the subject's death.

3. **Art/Mapping** One way to organize a mural is to place events in chronological order from left to right, like a time line—or like students' own sequence notes. Make sure students have a large flat surface to work on, where their mural can remain until dry.

Writer's Notebook

1. Collecting Ideas for a Biographical Sketch

Harriet Tubman's escape was probably the most important event in her life. Suppose you were writing a biography about a historical figure you admire. Use your history book, encyclopedia articles, and biographies to find out about events in the person's life. What do you think was the most important event or experience in that person's life? Make some notes about this event or experience. Why was it so important to your subject?

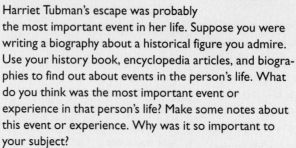

Rosa Parks
Never wanted to be a hero. Worked as a tailor. Most important event— refused to give up her seat on the bus to a white man.

Creative Writing

2. At Journey's End

Read part of a biography or an encyclopedia article to find out how Harriet Tubman lived the rest of her life after she arrived in the free state of Pennsylvania. Then, write an obituary that **summarizes** the highlights of her life.

Art/Mapping

3. The Big Picture

With others, paint a mural about Tubman's escape. Use a long strip of paper that you can post on the wall when you've finished. Decide together on three or four incidents that you want to picture. Decide also on the places you will want to show on your mural. Before you start painting, make sketches, decide on the materials and colors you'll use, and discuss how you'll make the painting interesting.

Music/Research

4. Catch the Spirit

Have you ever heard a spiritual, such as "Swing Low, Sweet Chariot"? Spirituals are a uniquely African American musical form. Most compare the singer's situation to a Biblical story or compare people to Biblical characters. Make a tape recording of spirituals that you especially like. Talk to musicians, or check the library or the Internet for background information. Add a commentary about the songs and the singers.

Harriet Tubman (1951) by Robert Savon Pious.

National Portrait Gallery, Smithsonian Institution, Washington, D.C./Art Resource, New York.

148 UNFORGETTABLE PERSONALITIES

4. **Music/Research** Before students begin Choice 4, play one or two spirituals for them. Discuss what the songs say to them and what they think the songs say to African Americans today. This will prepare students to complete the activity on their own.

GRAMMAR LINK · MINI-LESSON

Don't Use *Bad* and *Badly* Badly

Language Handbook HELP

See Glossary of Usage: bad, badly, *page 767.*

Technology HELP

See Language Workshop CD-ROM. *Key word entry:* bad, badly.

If you follow these rules, you'll never make another bad mistake using the words *bad* and *badly*. Use *bad* to modify a noun or pronoun. Use *badly* to modify an adjective or a verb.

EXAMPLES — Tubman worried that she would have a bad fall. [*Bad* modifies the noun *fall*.]

Tubman wanted her freedom badly. [*Badly* modifies the verb *wanted*.]

The word *bad* should never be used to modify a verb.

NONSTANDARD — Mr. Thompson treated runaways bad.

STANDARD — Mr. Thompson treated runaways badly.

Note: The expression *feel badly* has become acceptable, though it is ungrammatical, informal English.

INFORMAL — Tubman felt badly about leaving Old Rit.

FORMAL — Tubman felt bad about leaving Old Rit.

Try It Out

➤ Act as an editor. Which underlined word is grammatically correct?

1. Tubman felt bad/badly that her brothers gave up their attempt to escape.

2. The situation looked bad/badly to Tubman.

3. If Tubman were caught, she would be beaten bad/badly.

4. She wanted to escape from slavery bad/badly.

➤ Highlight the words *bad* and *badly* wherever they appear in your own writing. Then, draw an arrow from the highlighted word to the word it modifies. If the arrow points to a noun or pronoun, use *bad*. If the arrow points to a verb or an adjective, use *badly*.

VOCABULARY · HOW TO OWN A WORD

WORD BANK

elude
inexplicable
legitimate
defiant
sinewy

Vocabulary for the Workplace: A News Feature

Imagine that you're a newspaper reporter writing about Harriet Tubman.

1. Explain how Tubman managed to elude her pursuers.
2. Mention an inexplicable event that happened to Tubman.
3. Explain why Tubman had a legitimate reason to be defiant.
4. To illustrate your story, draw a picture of the sinewy vines Tubman encountered on her flight.

A GLORY OVER EVERYTHING 149

GRAMMAR LINK

Have students add the words *bad* and *badly* in appropriate places to a piece of writing from their portfolios. Have peer partners check whether students have used the words correctly.

Try It Out
Answers
1. bad
2. bad
3. badly
4. badly

VOCABULARY
Possible Responses
1. Harriet managed to elude her pursuers with the help of the Underground Railroad.
2. Harriet feared traveling alone because, for some inexplicable reason, she might suddenly fall asleep.
3. Harriet had a most legitimate reason to be defiant of her owner: no one has the right to enslave another human being.
4. Students' pictures should include thin but strong and tough vines.

Resources
Grammar
• *Grammar and Language Links*, p. 19
Vocabulary
• *Words to Own*, p. 9
Spelling
For related instruction, see
• *Spelling and Decoding*, p. 9

Grammar Link Quick Check

Choose the correct word in each underlined pair to complete the following sentences.

1. The brothers' decision to turn back is bad/badly made. [badly]
2. The brothers make a bad/badly decision. [bad]
3. Harriet's sleeping spells are the result of a bad/badly injury to her head. [bad]
4. Even if Harriet is bad/badly scared, she will travel on. [badly]
5. When Harriet enters Pennsylvania, her bad/badly times in slavery are in the past. [bad]

No Questions Asked

The literature in No Questions Asked gives students the chance to read a selection for enjoyment and enrichment as they further explore the collection theme. Annotated questions in the margins of the Teacher's Edition should be considered optional. No follow-up questions will appear after the selection.

In the first excerpt from *The Adventures of Tom Sawyer,* Tom decides to avoid school on a Monday morning by feigning illness. He wakes Sid with his moans and groans. Sid summons Aunt Polly, telling her that Tom must be dying. Discounting Tom's tale of a sore toe, Aunt Polly seizes on his complaint of a loose tooth. Although Tom loudly objects and announces that he no longer wants to miss school, Aunt Polly pulls the tooth, and Tom trudges off to school, mollified by his new ability to spit through the gap in his front teeth.

The second excerpt from *The Adventures of Tom Sawyer* introduces Huckleberry Finn, the town drunk's son, a "romantic outcast," and the idol of the more respectable boys in town. He wears discarded men's clothes and is unrestrained by the rules or conventions that apply to other boys. When Tom and Huck meet, Tom trades his recently pulled tooth for a tick that Huck has found in the woods.

One of the most famous personalities in all of American literature is a boy named Tom Sawyer. Tom is the hero of a novel by Mark Twain that takes place in a very small Mississippi River town called St. Petersburg. Tom Sawyer lives with his Aunt Polly, his half brother Sid, and his cousin Mary. Sid is always good; Tom is always in trouble. Aunt Polly is an unmarried lady who loves Tom dearly, but she often has difficulty understanding him. Tom's friend Huckleberry Finn is also a famous personality. He doesn't have to go to school or obey anyone. He is the envy of every boy in town.

from The Adventures of Tom Sawyer   Mark Twain

Dentistry

Monday morning found Tom Sawyer miserable. Monday morning always found him so—because it began another week's slow suffering in school. He generally began that day with wishing he had had no intervening holiday, it made the going into captivity and fetters again so much more odious.[1]

Tom lay thinking. Presently it occurred to him that he wished he was sick; then he could stay home from school. Here was a vague possibility. He canvassed his system. No ailment was found, and he investigated again. This time he thought he could detect colicky symptoms,[2] and he began to encourage them with considerable hope. But they soon grew feeble, and presently died wholly away. He reflected further. Suddenly he discovered something. One of his upper front teeth was loose. This was lucky; he was about to begin to groan, as a "starter," as he called it, when it occurred to him that if he came into court[3] with that argument, his aunt would pull it out, and that would hurt. So he thought he would hold the tooth in reserve for the present, and seek further. Nothing offered for some little time, and then he remembered hearing the doctor tell about a certain thing that laid up a patient for two or three weeks and threatened to make him lose a finger. So the boy eagerly drew his sore toe from under the sheet and held it up for inspection. But now he did not know the necessary symptoms. However, it seemed well worthwhile to chance it, so he fell to groaning with considerable spirit.

---

1. **odious** (ō′dē·əs): hateful, disgusting.
2. **colicky symptoms:** pains in the stomach.
3. **if he . . . court:** if he came before his aunt. (Twain is comparing Tom's aunt to a judge in court.)

Reaching All Students

Struggling Readers
Twain's vocabulary and syntax may pose difficulties for these students. Suggest that students read in pairs, stopping after each sentence to use context clues, footnotes, and if necessary a dictionary to obtain the meaning of unfamiliar words. Finally, suggest that students read each paragraph after they paraphrase, in order to clarify details and increase their understanding.

English Language Learners
Point out that the writing in the selection reflects two levels of southern dialect of the late nineteenth century: a slightly formal tone in the narration, and a very informal tone in the dialogue. You may want to match English language learners with English-fluent speakers for paired reading aloud. English language learners will also benefit from hearing a recording of the selection.

But Sid slept on unconscious.

Tom groaned louder and fancied that he began to feel pain in the toe.

No result from Sid.

Tom was panting with his exertions by this time. He took a rest and then swelled himself up and fetched a succession of admirable groans.

Sid snored on.

Tom was aggravated. He said, "Sid, Sid!" and shook him. This course worked well, and Tom began to groan again. Sid yawned, stretched, then brought himself up on his elbow with a snort, and began to stare at Tom. Tom went on groaning. Sid said:

"Tom! Say, Tom!" (No response.) "Here,

Pinch Bug in Church by Norman Rockwell, an illustration of one of Tom Sawyer's adventures.

THE ADVENTURES OF TOM SAWYER 151

Listening to Music

Portrait for Orchestra ("Mark Twain") by Jerome Kern, performed by the Boston Pops Orchestra, Keith Lockhart (conductor)

American composer Jerome Kern (1885–1945) helped turn the writing of popular songs into a respectable form of artistic expression. A native of New York, Kern worked in Tin Pan Alley, on 28th street, the area of the city that was then the heart of American popular songwriting. Among the enduring standards he composed are "The Last Time I Saw Paris," "Smoke Gets in Your Eyes," and "The Way You Look Tonight." Kern collaborated with lyricist Oscar Hammerstein II on the pioneering Broadway musical *Show Boat,* whose score is capped by the unforgettable "Ol' Man River."

Activity

Have students listen to Kern's musical portrait of Mark Twain after they read the selection and the Meet the Author feature. Discuss which of Twain's qualities the music captures. Then invite students to brainstorm ideas for musical portraits of some of the other personalities in this collection. For example, what would be the style and tempo of a musical portrait of Bailey, Maya Angelou's brother, and what instruments would play it? Musically gifted students may wish to create a musical portrait of one of the collection personalities.

Responding to the Text

To help students put themselves into the story, have them take on the roles of the characters. The scene in which Tom tries to enlist his brother Sid's sympathy is a good one for students to read aloud. So is the subsequent scene, in which Aunt Polly becomes involved and eventually pulls Tom's tooth. After students read each scene, encourage them to discuss their responses to each character.

B Appreciating Language

Word Choice

Mark Twain uses the word *mortified* here as it was originally used, to indicate death or decay. Tom is saying that his toe has gangrene. However, a much more common meaning of the word—"to experience shame or humiliation"—is the one that the reader thinks of, and that helps to make this sentence funny—Tom's toe is ashamed!

Tom! *Tom!* What is the matter, Tom?" And he shook him and looked in his face anxiously.

Tom moaned out:

"Oh don't, Sid. Don't joggle me."

"Why, what's the matter, Tom? I must call Auntie."

"No—never mind. It'll be over by and by, maybe. Don't call anybody."

"But I must! *Don't* groan so, Tom, it's awful. How long you been this way?"

"Hours. Ouch! Oh, don't stir so, Sid, you'll kill me."

A "Tom, why didn't you wake me sooner? Oh, Tom, *don't!* It makes my flesh crawl to hear you. Tom, what *is* the matter?"

"I forgive you everything, Sid. (Groan.) Everything you've ever done to me. When I'm gone——"

"Oh, Tom, you ain't dying, are you? Don't, Tom. Oh, don't. Maybe——"

"I forgive everybody, Sid. (Groan.) Tell 'em so, Sid. And Sid, you give my window sash and my cat with one eye to that new girl that's come to town, and tell her——"

But Sid had snatched his clothes and gone. Tom was suffering in reality, now, so handsomely was his imagination working, and so his groans had gathered quite a genuine tone.

Sid flew downstairs and said:

"Oh, Aunt Polly, come! Tom's dying!"

"Dying!"

"Yes'm. Don't wait—come quick!"

"Rubbage! I don't believe it!"

But she fled upstairs, nevertheless, with Sid and Mary at her heels. And her face grew white, too, and her lip trembled. When she reached the bedside she gasped out:

"You, Tom! Tom, what's the matter with you?"

"Oh, Auntie, I'm——"

"What's the matter with you—what *is* the matter with you, child?"

"Oh, Auntie, my sore toe's mortified!"

The old lady sank down into a chair and laughed a little, then cried a little, then did both together. This restored her and she said:

"Tom, what a turn you did give me. Now you shut up that nonsense and climb out of this."

The groans ceased and the pain vanished from the toe. The boy felt a little foolish, and he said:

B "Aunt Polly, it *seemed* mortified, and it hurt so I never minded my tooth at all."

"Your tooth indeed! What's the matter with your tooth?"

"One of them's loose, and it aches perfectly awful."

"There, there, now, don't begin that groaning again. Open your mouth. Well—your tooth *is* loose, but you're not going to die about that. Mary, get me a silk thread and a chunk of fire out of the kitchen."

Tom said:

"Oh, please, Auntie, don't pull it out. It don't hurt any more. I wish I may never stir if it does. Please don't, Auntie. *I* don't want to stay home from school."

"Oh, you don't, don't you? So all this row[4] was because you thought you'd get to stay home from school and go a-fishing? Tom, Tom, I love you so, and you seem to try every way you can to break my old heart with your outrageousness."

By this time the dental instruments were ready. The old lady made one end of the silk thread fast to Tom's tooth with a loop and tied the other to the bedpost. Then she seized the chunk of fire and suddenly thrust

4. **row** (rou): noise; commotion.

Using Students' Strengths

Interpersonal Learners

This classic tale of friendship cries out to be acted by a group of enthusiastic students—and although Tom and Huck are boys, it's perfectly okay if girls volunteer to play their roles as well. A group of four students can encompass Tom, Huck, Sid, and Aunt Polly. Encourage students to use Twain's dialogue, but allow them to invent additional dialogue in a similar spirit. Costumes and props—a tooth, a dead insect, a man's torn old suit—can add to the comic and dramatic effect. Give the group time to go over their lines and actions, either with or without writing a formal script, and to rehearse at least once. Then let the class enjoy the performance!

Intrapersonal Learners

It's easy, at this grade level, to see Tom and Huck as simple perpetrators of pranks. In high school, when they read *The Adventures of Huckleberry Finn,* students will see a more serious side of Huck. Give students an early glimpse of that side by asking, "If you were Huck Finn, what would your thoughts and feelings be?" Invite students to write their answers either in Huck's voice or in their own.

it almost into the boy's face. The tooth hung dangling by the bedpost now.

But all trials bring their compensations. As Tom wended[5] to school after breakfast, he was the envy of every boy he met because the gap in his upper row of teeth enabled him to expectorate[6] in a new and admirable way. He gathered quite a following of lads interested in the exhibition; and one that had cut his finger, and had been a center of fascination and homage up to this time, now found himself suddenly without an adherent,[7] and shorn of his glory. His heart was heavy, and he said with a disdain which he did not feel, that it wasn't anything to spit like Tom Sawyer. But another boy said, "Sour grapes!" and he wandered away a dismantled hero.

Huck Finn

Shortly, Tom came upon the juvenile pariah[8] of the village, Huckleberry Finn, son of the town drunkard. Huckleberry was cordially hated and dreaded by all the mothers of the town, because he was idle and lawless and vulgar and bad—and because all their children admired him so, and delighted in his forbidden society, and wished they dared to be like him. Tom was like the rest of the re-

spectable boys in that he envied Huckleberry his gaudy[9] outcast condition, and was under strict orders not to play with him. So he played with him every time he got a chance. Huckleberry was always dressed in the castoff clothes of full-grown men, and they were in perennial bloom and fluttering with rags. His hat was a vast ruin with a wide crescent lopped out of its brim; his coat, when he wore one, hung nearly to his heels and had the rearward buttons far down the back; but one suspender supported his trousers; the seat of the trousers bagged low and contained nothing; the fringed legs dragged in the dirt when not rolled up.

Huckleberry came and went at his own free will. He slept on doorsteps in fine weather and in empty hogsheads[10] in wet; he did not have to go to school or to church, or call any being master or obey anybody; he could go fishing or swimming when and where he chose, and stay as long as it suited him; nobody forbade him to fight; he could sit up as late as he pleased; he was always the first boy that went barefoot in the spring and the last to resume leather in the fall; he never had to wash, nor put on clean clothes; he could swear wonderfully. In a word, everything that goes to make life precious, that boy had. So thought every harassed, hampered, respectable boy in St. Petersburg.

Tom hailed the romantic outcast: "Hello, Huckleberry! . . . Say—what's that?"

"Nothing but a tick."

"Where'd you get him?"

"Out in the woods."

"What'll you take for him?"

"I don't know. I don't want to sell him."

5. **wended:** traveled.
6. **expectorate** (ek·spek′tə·rāt′): spit.
7. **adherent** (ad·hir′ənt): follower.
8. **pariah** (pə·rī′ə): outcast.

9. **gaudy** (gô′dē): flashy; showy and in poor taste.
10. **hogsheads:** very large barrels.

THE ADVENTURES OF TOM SAWYER 153

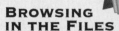
A "All right. It's a mighty small tick, anyway."

"Oh, anybody can run a tick down that don't belong to them. I'm satisfied with it. It's a good enough tick for me."

"Sho, there's ticks a-plenty. I could have a thousand of 'em if I wanted to."

"Well, why don't you? Becuz you know mighty well you can't. This is a pretty early tick, I reckon. It's the first one I've seen this year."

"Say, Huck—I'll give you my tooth for him."

"Less see it."

Tom got out a bit of paper and carefully unrolled it. Huckleberry viewed it wistfully. The temptation was very strong. At last he said, "Is it genuwyne?"

B Tom lifted his lip and showed the vacancy.

"Well, all right," said Huckleberry, "it's a trade."

Tom enclosed the tick in the percussion-cap box that had lately been the pinch bug's prison,[11] and the boys separated, each feeling wealthier than before.

11. Tom collects all sorts of things, including bugs and dead cats and teeth.

The Granger Collection, New York.

MEET THE WRITER

The Great Humorist

Mark Twain (1835–1910) is America's greatest comic writer and the author of two famous novels about growing up: *The Adventures of Tom Sawyer* (1876) and *The Adventures of Huckleberry Finn* (1884).

Twain was born Samuel Langhorne Clemens on the Missouri frontier, and he grew up in a town on the Mississippi River. As a boy he thrived on the teeming river traffic. As an adult he took his famous pen name from the cry the boatmen made when the water reached the safe depth of two fathoms: "Mark twain!" He later wrote *Life on the Mississippi,* a book about his experiences as a cub pilot on a Mississippi River steamboat.

More of Tom's Trials

To better know Tom Sawyer and his friends Jim, Becky, and Huck Finn, read *The Adventures of Tom Sawyer* (Signet). (This title is available in the HRW Library.)

Making the Connections

READ ON

No More Bore

A bored boy named Milo takes off on an adventure to the strange land of Dictionopolis. Once there, he gets some lessons about wasting time from the watchdog Tock and leads a search for Rhyme and Reason, two lost princesses. With the odd creatures he meets and the wild places he goes, Milo soon discovers, in Norton Juster's amazing fantasy *The Phantom Tollbooth* (Knopf), that there's plenty to do.

Sisters

Meg, Jo, Beth, and Amy March—four sisters—grow up in Massachusetts during the Civil War in Louisa May Alcott's *Little Women* (Penguin). This rich story of family love, a favorite of readers for over a century, has been made into four movies (most recently in 1994).

Not Your Average Family

The adventures of the family in William Sleator's *Oddballs* (Puffin) are simply hilarious. Wild ideas flow nonstop out of such kooky characters as Jack, the budding hypnotist; Vicky, who likes to dye herself purple; and Bill, mastermind of the odd "pituh-plays." Mischievous and witty, the characters in this collection of stories set a style of their own as they cope with growing up.

Other Picks

- Jean Craighead George, *My Side of the Mountain* (Dutton). Frustrated by his cramped life in the city, young Sam Gribley lives on his own for a year in the wilderness.

- Janusz Korczak, *King Matt the First* (Noonday). When the king dies, his young son Matt takes control and lets children trade places with adults to try to make a better world.

READ ON 155

Speaking and Listening Workshop

OBJECTIVES

1. Prepare and conduct an interview
2. Summarize the interview in writing
3. Share the interview with the class.
4. Observe and assess a television interview

Resources

Performance Rubric
• *Portfolio Management System*, p. 121

Introducing the Speaking and Listening Workshop

• Ask who in the class has interviewed someone or has been interviewed by someone. Invite students to share their experiences.
• Nearly all students will have seen, heard, or read interviews. Discuss these experiences. Ask questions such as: What kinds of people get interviewed? What are interviews about? What do you like about interviews you've seen? What don't you like about them? Then tell students that in this Workshop, they are going to learn to become interviewers.

Try It Out

Remind students to interview someone who wants to participate, and to choose an interviewee and a topic they would not mind sharing with an audience.

Try It Out

Interview a family member or friend about something important to that person: an issue or cause, a career, a hobby, or a trip. Follow the steps outlined in this lesson. Then, review your notes. Are they clear? Have you recorded facts and quotations accurately? Write a summary of your interview, and share it with the person you interviewed.

INTERVIEWING

QUESTIONS, PLEASE

Doctors ask about patients' health. Reporters grill sources. Talk-show hosts grill guests. All these people know how to *interview*—how to ask questions to learn more about a subject.

Preparing for the Interview

Some interviews focus on a topic, such as humpback whales or CD-ROMs. Others focus on the ideas and experiences of the person being interviewed. No matter what your focus, when you need firsthand information, you can use the following suggestions for conducting effective interviews:

1. Choose a topic. What do you hope to learn from your interview?

2. Choose a person to interview. Make a list of people who know about your topic. Then, narrow it down. Who has the best information? Who tells the best stories? Who has the most time for an interview?

3. Make an appointment. Call or write to the person you wish to interview. Describe the topics you hope to discuss. Then, arrange a time and place to conduct the interview. If necessary, you can interview the person by phone.

4. Make a list of questions to ask. Go to the library, and dig up some information about your subject. Use this background material to draw up a list of questions. Make sure your questions are brief and specific. Avoid questions that require simple yes or no answers.

Conducting the Interview

Remember that the person you are interviewing is the star

Reaching All Students

Struggling Readers
Some students may wish to do the Try It Out activity in groups of two or three. In that case, students should work together to choose the interviewee, make the appointment, and develop the list of questions. Students should divide the list of questions equally and take turns asking questions. Other struggling readers may gain self-esteem from doing the activity independently.

English Language Learners
These students may wish to interview an English-fluent classmate about an issue, such as tips for learning English and for adjusting to life in the United States. Alternatively, these students may enjoy interviewing a representative of their native culture. In that case, the interview my be conducted in the students' first language and translated into English, with the help of a classmate if necessary.

Advanced Learners
Have students polish their interviews and send them to magazines that focus on children's or teens' issues, on local topics, or on the specific topic covered in the interview. They will need to write a cover letter explaining who they are and the circumstances surrounding the interview. The current *Writer's Market* may help in choosing magazines.

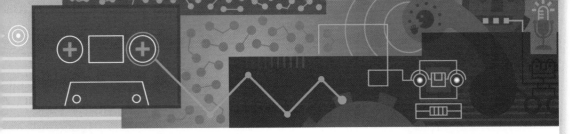

of the show, not you! Still, the more relaxed you are, the more comfortable your subject will be. Follow these guidelines:

1. Be on time for the interview.

2. Listen carefully. If you are confused by something, ask the person to explain it. Don't pretend to know more than you do. After all, you're there to learn.

3. Pace yourself. Rather than racing through your list of questions, stop and listen to what the person is saying. You may find that the remarks lead naturally to another question—something that might not be on your list.

4. Be courteous. Show respect for what the person has to say even if you disagree with the person's opinion.

5. Take notes. Even if you tape-record your interview, it's helpful to jot down important facts. You can also write down questions that occur to you as the person is speaking.

6. When you finish, thank the person for granting you the interview.

After the Interview

As soon as possible after the interview, follow these suggestions to make sure the information you have gathered is clear and complete:

1. Go over your notes to be sure they are clear.

2. If you tape-recorded the interview, listen to the tape and write down important facts and quotations.

3. Summarize the interview so you'll remember what was said.

4. If you need to check a fact or a quotation, call the person up.

5. If your interview is published, send a copy to the person you interviewed.

Try It Out

Pick out a news program on television, such as *Sixty Minutes* (CBS), *Meet the Press* (NBC), or *Larry King Live* (CNN). As you watch the hosts conduct their interview, ask yourself these questions: "Does the host seem well informed? Is the atmosphere relaxed? Does the interviewer allow time for complete and thoughtful answers? If a person's answer is unclear or incomplete, how does the interviewer respond?" Jot down your observations, and try to apply the lessons you learned to your own interviews.

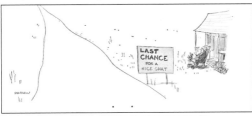

Drawing by Stevenson; © 1964, 1992. The New Yorker Magazine, Inc.

SPEAKING AND LISTENING WORKSHOP 157

- One way to help students select interviewees with whom they are comfortable is to have them interview each other. Have each student write on a piece of paper his or her name and a topic he or she knows something about. Put the papers in a container, and have each student draw one paper from the container.
- As additional preparation, have students write business letters or draft an over-the-phone request asking permission of the interviewee and suggesting a topic and time. You might give students a form that details the parts of a business letter.
- Students' should write at least five questions. Research can be done at the library or on-line.
- Before students interview their subject, remind them to ask questions in a slow but conversational voice, to take notes, and to summarize the interview from their notes.
- Provide students with examples of written interviews, both the narrative type and the transcript type, so they can see and hear what the finished product looks and sounds like.
- Guide students through this activity, answering questions as needed. Afterward, ask volunteers to share their summaries with the class, and encourage students to discuss what aspects of the interview they found (1) easy (2) hard (3) surprising.

Try It Out

As students watch television interviews, invite them to write down questions that were not asked that they would like to ask the subject. Some students may wish to invent answers to these questions. Also invite students to note occasions when, in their opinion, the subject gave an unsatisfactory answer. Have them speculate on what a satisfactory answer might have been.

Using Students' Strengths

Visual Learners

With the interviewee's consent, have students photograph or draw pictures of the interviewee to accompany the text of the interview. Suggest that students write captions for the pictures. Refer students to the *Meet the Writer* feature in this book as an example of an interview-and-picture layout.

Logical/Mathematical Learners

Interviewers can develop the ability to recognize and challenge illogical answers. One technique is to use follow-up questions, which may be prepared in advance or improvised. Another technique is to request a follow-up interview to clarify previous points. Skill and tact are required to challenge an interviewee in a friendly way. Have students interview each other with the goal of clarifying vague answers.

Writer's Workshop

Technology HELP

See Writer's Workshop 1 CD-ROM. *Assignment: Firsthand Biography.*

ASSIGNMENT
Write an essay about a real person.

AIM
To inform.

AUDIENCE
Your teacher, classmates, friends, or family. You might want to send your biography to your local newspaper if your subject is known in the community.

EXPOSITORY WRITING
BIOGRAPHICAL SKETCH

People we meet in school or in our community, people from the past, even people in our own homes have helped shape our lives. In your biographical sketch, you will create a portrait—a biography—of one of those people. Remember that a **biography** is the story of someone's life, told by another person.

Professional Model

It is difficult to describe Mother's purity and simplicity of character, and she will find it embarrassing that I speak of her in print. But I must. A great deal of what I am and what I achieved I owe to her. Not once can I recall, from my earliest recollections, hearing Mother lift her voice to us in anger. Even after my father's death, when she was grief-stricken and sorely troubled, she was not short with us. . . .

I cannot remember a single complaint from Mother. Though she toiled incessantly, she did not spend money on personal things. Her first concern was our needs. . . . I no longer reprove [scold] her when she lets someone take unfair advantage of her, as I might have when I was younger. She is what she is, bless her.

—from *My Lord, What a Morning*
by Marian Anderson

The writer tells why her mother is important to her.

She tells about her mother's actions and personality.

The end makes her feelings about her mother clear.

Resources: Print and Media

Writing and Language
- *Portfolio Management System*
  - Prewriting, p. 122
  - Peer Editing, p. 123
  - Assessment Rubric, p. 124

- *Workshop Resources*
  - Revision Strategy Teaching Notes, p. 5
  - Revision Strategy Transparencies 3, 4
- *Writer's Workshop 1 CD-ROM*
  - Firsthand Biography

The history of the written word is rich and...

Once upon a time

Page 1

Prewriting

1. Writer's Notebook

Review the entries you made in your Writer's Notebook for this collection. Then ask yourself these questions:

- Which of these people do I know well?
- Which of these people have shaped my life in some way?
- Which of these people would I enjoy writing about?

2. Freewriting

For more ideas, freewrite about one of the following:

- someone you love • someone you want to be like • someone who's earned a place in history • someone who helped you learn an important lesson

3. What a Time We Had!

Here is another idea to help you come up with a subject for your biography. On ten slips of paper, write down the most memorable times in your life. Briefly describe one incident on each slip of paper. Was someone with you at the time? What influence did that person have on you? Add this information to each slip of paper. See the chart on this page for an illustration of this idea. After you have completed all the slips of paper, pick the one involving the person you most want to write about.

4. Is Your Subject a Historical Figure?

If you decide to write a biographical sketch of a historical figure, you will need to gather some facts. As you research your subject, be sure to take detailed notes on your sources. If you quote something directly, you will have to document your source.

Memorable Time
proudest—the day I won the fifth-grade city swim meet

Person Involved
my coach, Ms. Ross

Person's Influence on Me
She taught me to believe in myself. She pushed me to do my best and never let me quit.

Communications Handbook
H E L P

See Listing Sources and Taking Notes.

Introducing the Writer's Workshop

- To motivate students, ask them to write a brief description of a famous person but not to name that person. Have students share their descriptions to see whether other students can identify the person. Discuss what elements created effective biographical descriptions, and why.
- Read aloud the Professional Model on p. 158 while students read it silently. Ask volunteers to identify the main idea of the model and the details that support the main idea.
- Point out the side notes that highlight the elements that make this model an effective biographical sketch.
- As students proceed through the steps of the writing process, guide them by modeling each step with your own writing.

Teaching the Writer's Workshop

Prewriting

Have students use the techniques suggested on pp. 159–160 (or any others that may be helpful to them) to come up with ideas.

Reaching All Students

Struggling Writers

You may need to guide students in limiting their descriptions so that they do not produce a jumble of unrelated details and arbitrary transitions. Suggest that students concentrate on one specific incident or behavior and a few details that show the importance of the person. They may use a cluster diagram like the following to organize their ideas.

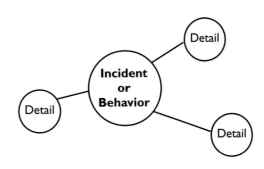

Drafting

- Encourage students to be selective when they choose details to include in their drafts. Suggest that when they write their descriptions they use very specific details to give readers an exact, vivid picture of the person. As an example, contrast "Uncle Bill wore a bright necktie" with "Uncle Bill wore a neon orange necktie with a pattern of lime-green lizards." Remind students that the descriptions of their subject must support and enhance their main points.
- Students might consider the following questions in determining the organization of their papers.
  - What is the main point I am trying to convey?
  - Should my biography focus on a single event or a series of events?
  - Have I included details about my subject's appearance and personality?
  - How is my subject like or unlike myself?

Outside

Appearance
black
small
schipperke
no tail
short ears

Actions
hyper
jumps a lot

Inside

Inner Qualities
affectionate
curious
likes to be active

Our Relationship
keeps me company
makes me laugh
I love him.

Strategies for Elaboration

Bringing Your Person to Life

To bring your person to life for your readers, try these strategies:

- Quote something the person says or has said that is funny or characteristic of him or her.
- Put the person in a setting that you associate with him or her. Describe the setting.
- Tell what other people think of the person.
- Tell what this person makes you think of. What do you associate with him or her—springtime, ballgames, walks in the park?

160 **Unforgettable Personalities**

Here are some techniques you might use to bring a historical figure to life:

- Include photos or pictures in your biography.
- Quote something the person said.
- Quote something that someone else said about the person.

5. What Your Subject Means to You

Look over your notes, and think about the questions below. Then, in a sentence or two, tell what your subject means to you—why did you choose this person as your subject?

- Have I learned something important from this person?
- How has my life changed because of this person?
- What would my life be like without this person?
- What would the world or our country be like without this person?

6. Fold It Up

To clarify some of the ideas you have gathered, try the following. Hold an 8½ X 11-inch piece of paper sideways. Fold it so that both ends meet in the middle, forming two side flaps. (See the diagrams on this page.) Label the left outside flap *Appearance,* and list physical details describing your subject. Label the right outside flap *Actions,* and list actions and behaviors of your subject. On the inside, label the top half *Inner Qualities,* and write what is important to your subject: interests, thoughts, and wishes. Label the bottom half *Our Relationship,* and tell why your subject is important to you. (Notice that the writer opposite chose an unusual subject.)

Drafting

1. Getting Started

Look over your Prewriting notes. Mark the sections you think are the most important. Be sure to include details of your subject's appearance and personality. If you're writing about a historical figure, you might want to tell about your subject's birthplace, education, and work.

Reaching All Students

English Language Learners

Remind students to watch their verb tenses. Their most important initial decision about tense will be whether to use the present or the past. This will, of course, depend largely on whether they are writing about a person they know or a historical person, and, for a living person, whether they are writing about the person's past or present activities. Tell students that they should use the same tense throughout unless there is a strong reason to change—for instance, if they are moving from the past time to the present. Allow students to consult English-fluent classmates as well as a dictionary in order to check verb tenses.

Advanced Learners

Use these ideas to extend the activity:

- Have students imagine and write their subject's response to the biography. What suggestions might he or she make?
- Suggest that students write the biography of a fictional character in a story they have read.
- Have them write a humorous fake biography of a real person—things he or she didn't, wouldn't, or couldn't do.

2. Shaping and Organizing

Look over your notes and decide which of the following would be the best way to organize your biography:

a. **Chronological order.** You can use chronological order, or time order, and tell the story of a single event, a single day, or a series of incidents in your subject's life.

b. **Features.** You can organize your description by different features of your subject's appearance and personality. Notice how Marian Anderson discusses details of her mother's personality on page 158. Notice also that the writer of the Student Model on page 162 first describes Sherman's appearance and then describes his personality.

c. **Comparison/contrast.** You can compare and contrast your subject with yourself or with other people, showing how your subject is unique. Look again at the Student Model. Notice that the writer compares Sherman with other dogs.

3. Crafting a Good Beginning and Ending

Catch your readers' interest right away with a strong beginning. Try one of the following ideas:

• Quote something meaningful your subject said.

• Mention an important fact or detail.

• Ask an interesting question about your subject.

A strong way to end your biography is with a clear statement of your subject's importance to you. Another way is to close with a memorable image of your subject.

Evaluating and Revising

Self-Evaluation

Reread your paper, and ask yourself:

• Where can I add specifics?

• How can I improve my introduction and conclusion?

• How can I make my feelings about my subject clearer?

Review your notes. Then, rewrite your paper, making the changes you have decided on.

Framework for a Biographical Sketch

Introduction (captures the reader's attention, shows the person in action, mentions an interesting biographical detail):

_____

_____

Body (describes the person's qualities; tells a story about the person; gives biographical details): _____

_____

_____

Conclusion (tells what the person means to you or presents a final word picture of your subject):

_____

_____

Language/Grammar Link
H E L P

Choosing precise words: page 116. Common usage problems: pages 107 and 149. Comparing with adjectives: page 135.

Evaluating and Revising

• Encourage each pair of peer reviewers to think of themselves as partners who are giving each other feedback and helping each other to improve the work.

• Have students use the Evaluation Criteria provided on p. 162 to review their own drafts and to determine needed revisions.

Choosing Reference Materials and Resources for Writing, Revising, and Editing

As students write, revise, and edit their biographical sketches, they should consult specific reference materials. For example, in writing their sketches, they might want to look in a book of synonyms, such as *Roget's International Thesaurus* or *Webster's New Dictionary of Synonyms,* if they are looking for just the right words to describe their subject. In revising, if their sketch is about a historical figure, they may decide to consult a biographical reference like *Merriam-Webster's Biographical Dictionary.* And in editing, they might turn to *Bartlett's Familiar Quotations* for a quotation to perk up the beginning or end of their sketches.

Resources ——

Peer Editing Forms and Rubrics

• *Portfolio Management System,* p. 123

Revision Strategy Transparencies

• *Workshop Resources,* p. 5

T161

As class members read the Student Model, encourage them to look for ideas that they can apply to revising their own work. You can extend the discussion by having students focus on questions like these:

❓ In the introduction, what specific words and phrases grab the reader?

❓ In the body, what specific details describe the dog's physical, behavioral, and personality traits that bring him vividly to life?

❓ Does the conclusion do its job? How might it have done its job even better?

❓ What strategies that this writer uses could be used for a human subject? What strategies would have to be changed for a human subject?

Proofreading

Have students proofread their own papers first and then exchange them with another student. Tell students to watch for mistakes in comparative and superlative adjectives and to look for general modifiers that they can change to precise words. Also have them check for run-on sentences; refer them to the Sentence Workshop on p. 163 for help in revising run-ons.

If time permits, the final copy should be put aside for at least a day before it is proofread for the final time by the author.

Remind students that they must spell accurately in final drafts. Suggest that they use a spelling checker if they are using a computer that has one. Make sure students understand that a spelling checker will not alert them to usage errors, such as the confusion of *they're, their* and *your, you're*.

Publishing

Consider making a bulletin-board display of the class's biographies, including, if possible, photographs of the subjects.

Reflecting

Have students respond to one of the following questions:

• What discoveries did I make about myself or about my relationship with the person I wrote about?

• What was the hardest part of writing this biography?

• What's my favorite part of this biography and why?

T162

■ *Evaluation Criteria*

A good biographical sketch

1. *makes the personality of the subject come alive*

2. *includes concrete details of the subject's appearance, behavior, and background*

3. *includes specific incidents to illustrate the subject's personality*

4. *shows why the subject is important to the writer*

Sentence Workshop
H E L P

Run-on sentences: page 163.

Communications Handbook
H E L P

See Proofreaders' Marks.

Publishing Tip

If possible, read or send your work to the person who inspired it. You might also submit your sketch to your school newspaper or literary magazine.

NO-TAIL SHERMAN

Every time people see him, they ask what he is. We always tell them that Sherman is his name, and that he is a schipperke. He is a black, small, compact dog that is half fur. He has a fox- or wolf-like face, short fox ears, and no tail. Sherman weighs seventeen pounds and is a sweet, affectionate dog, although he is hyper and jumps up on everyone he sees. He doesn't smell bad too often; but when he does smell, he smells like a rotten onion just found on the bottom of an old grocery sack. Unfortunately, his bark can often be heard with a *yip-brop-rorp* and a *bu-ru-ru-ru* that is sharper than a razor blade. He prances lightly and with a bouncing motion, like a cat with springs on his feet. When he wants to go out, he whines like a hungry seal. If he gets the chance, he will get into the refrigerator and eat the peanut butter if the jar is left open. Sherman has a different attitude from most dogs. Most dogs lick the garbage can and attack the postman. Sherman licks the postman and attacks the garbage can.

Sherman is the most unusual dog I have ever known. I guess that is why I love him so much.

—Matt Harris
University Laboratory School
Baton Rouge, Louisiana

The beginning catches the reader's attention.

The writer gives a detailed description of Sherman's appearance and personality.

These incidents also give the reader a sense of Sherman's personality.

The end makes clear Sherman's importance to the writer.

162 UNFORGETTABLE PERSONALITIES

Grading Timesaver

Rubrics for this Writer's Workshop assignment appear on p. 124 of the *Portfolio Management System*.

Sentence Workshop

OBJECTIVES
1. Identify run-on sentences
2. Correct run-on sentences by dividing them into shorter sentences or by adding a comma and a coordinating conjunction

RUN-ON SENTENCES

A run-on sentence is actually two or more sentences run together into one. In run-ons, what should be separate, clear thoughts becomes one confusing blur.

RUN-ON   Storm had scale eyes he watched as the sled was loaded.

It's often hard to tell where one idea in a run-on ends and the next one begins. One way to correct a run-on is to make it into separate sentences. Adding a period at the proper point brings the ideas in these sentences back into focus:

CORRECT   "Storm had scale eyes. **H**e watched as the sled was loaded."
                                    —Gary Paulsen, "Storm" (page 99)

Another way to correct run-ons is to add a comma and a coordinating conjunction (*and, but,* or *or*). Using a comma alone will not correct the run-on sentence. You must separate two complete ideas with a period (or a question mark or an exclamation point) or with a comma *and* a coordinating conjunction. Using a comma alone still results in a run-on sentence:

RUN-ON   Storm had scale eyes, he watched as the sled was loaded.

CORRECT   Storm had scale eyes, **and** he watched as the sled was loaded.

Writer's Workshop Follow-up: Revision

Exchange your biographical sketch for a classmate's. Proofread your partner's paper. Circle any run-on sentences you find, and suggest a correction for each. Exchange papers again, and decide for yourself how you will correct the run-ons your partner found.

Language Handbook HELP

See Run-on Sentences, page 738.

Technology HELP

See Language Workshop CD-ROM. Key word entry: run-on sentences.

Try It Out

Rewrite the following run-on sentences. Be sure to compare your revisions in class.

1. He would show it to me each time we stopped I would pet him on top of the head and take the stick from him.

2. I would very seriously erase even the touch of a smile from my face, later we'd laugh and laugh and howl.

3. Lincoln struggled hard to rise above his log-cabin origins by the time he ran for president he was a wealthy man.

4. Among the first people sold were two of Harriet Tubman's sisters, they went south with the chain gang on a Saturday.

SENTENCE WORKSHOP 163

Resources

Workshop Resources
• Worksheet, p. 39
Language Workshop CD-ROM
• Run-On Sentences

Mini-Lesson: Run-On Sentences
Write on the chalkboard this example of a run-on sentence: Storm had scale eyes he watched as the sled was loaded. Read the sentence aloud without pause, showing that it makes little sense. Point out that the sentence contains two complete thoughts that need to be separated. Explain these two ways to correct a run-on sentence: (1) with a period after the first sentence, and a capital letter at the beginning of the second; (2) with a comma and a coordinating conjunction between the two sentences. Correct the sentence on the chalkboard.

Try It Out
Possible Answers
1. He would show it to me each time we stopped. I would pet him on top of the head and take the stick from him.
2. I would very seriously erase even the touch of a smile from my face, and later we'd laugh and laugh and howl.
3. Lincoln struggled hard to rise above his log-cabin origins. By the time he ran for president, he was a wealthy man.
4. Among the first people sold were two of Harriet Tubman's sisters. They went south with the chain gang on a Saturday.

Assessing Learning

Quick Check: Run-On Sentences
Have students rewrite the following run-on sentences, using the revision techniques shown on p. 163. Possible corrections are provided.

1. Storm liked jokes I liked to watch him. [Storm liked jokes, and I liked to watch him.]

2. Storm took my hat he buried it in the snow. [Storm took my hat. He buried it in the snow.]

3. Storm dropped the stick when I held it out to him, he wouldn't take it. [Storm dropped the stick, and when I held it out to him, he wouldn't take it.]

4. Storm put the stick down in front of him before going to sleep it was there waiting when he woke up. [Storm put the stick down in front of him before going to sleep. It was there waiting when he woke up.]

5. Afterward, I watched for the stick it told me that I was doing the right thing. [Afterward, I watched for the stick. It told me that I was doing the right thing.]

T163

OBJECTIVES
1. Develop the practice of reading independently and regularly
2. Apply specific reading strategies to obtain meaning

Reading for Life

Independent Reading

Teaching the Lesson

Explain that the ability to read independently—to select a text and obtain meaning from it on one's own—is one of the most valuable skills a person can acquire. Ask volunteers to describe independent reading experiences—what they chose to read, how they approached the text, what they learned, and how they felt after reading the text. Guide students in recognizing various purposes for reading, the importance of using reading skills and strategies, and the benefits of sharing information.

Using the Strategies

Possible Responses

1. Students may choose any one of the cited books. Students' reasons should support their choice—for example, "*Woodsong* because I'd like to know more about Storm."
2. Any one of the four books could be read for enjoyment, depending on students' interests. A student who likes hunting and fishing, for example, would probably choose *Father Water, Mother Woods*.
3. The boxed commentary says that the excerpt about "Storm" was taken from *Woodsong*.

Situation

Your teacher asks you to pick a book to read on your own. You liked "Storm" by Gary Paulsen, and you find descriptions of other works by Paulsen in Meet the Writer on page 104. That's a good place to start.

When selecting a book for independent reading, use the following strategies.

Strategies

Find a book to read.

- Are you reading for your enjoyment? Do you have to write a book report? Make sure you pick a book that fits your purpose.

- In this textbook you'll find suggestions for books to read in Meet the Writer and Read On. Check both features when you're hunting for a book to read.

- Don't settle for a boring book. If the opening chapter seems dull, try other books.

Get the reading habit.

- You get this habit by reading regularly. Set a goal for

More Good Cooking by Gary Paulsen

Paulsen has cooked up a feast of adventure stories for young adults. If you're interested in wilderness-survival tales, try the novels *Dogsong* and *Hatchet* (both published by Bradbury). Both were named Newbery Award Honor Books by the American Library Association. If you prefer true stories, explore *Woodsong* (Bradbury), from which "Storm" is taken. You might also enjoy *Father Water, Mother Woods* (Delacorte), in which Paulsen reflects on his hunting and fishing experiences in the north woods.

—from Meet the Writer, page 104

---

yourself—a certain amount of reading time. Carry a book wherever you go.

Read quickly; read slowly.

- Adjust your reading rate to your purpose.

- Don't let a difficult word stop you. Try to **infer,** or guess, its meaning from the context, the words around it.

Use your reading skills.

- Make inferences and predictions.

- Notice how the writer creates characters and keeps you interested in them.

- Connect what you read with your own life.

Using the Strategies

1. Which book listed in the paragraph above would you pick for a book report? Why?

2. Which book would you read just for enjoyment? Why?

3. Which book tells more about a character you may have read about? How can you tell?

Extending the Strategies

Start a book club with a few friends. You can all read the same book and then discuss it.

Reaching All Students

Struggling Readers

One appropriate choice for these students, and one that makes an important cross-curricular connection, is the history textbook that they are currently studying. Have students work in pairs to use the techniques presented on this page to strengthen their methods of studying history and their grasp of grade-level content.

English Language Learners

Many of these students will welcome the chance to locate and read books about the history of their ancestral lands. Have students work with English-fluent partners if necessary, and with the school librarian, to locate appropriate books. Invite students to give written or oral reports to the class as a means of sharing their cultural heritage.

Advanced Learners

Depending on students' reading level, you and the school librarian might steer them toward works aimed a year or more above sixth grade level. Also guide students toward history-oriented magazines, such as *American Heritage* and *Smithsonian*. Encourage students with special interests, such as computers, dance, art, science, or math, to select and read books on their subjects.

Learning for Life

Researching Media Personalities

OBJECTIVES
1. Select a media celebrity, then collect, categorize, select, and discuss information about the person
2. Choose and complete a project (making a collage, creating an interview, writing and presenting copy for a newscast)

Problem

We rarely, if ever, get to meet the people we admire or are fascinated by. Everything we know about them comes to us indirectly, through TV, newspapers, or magazines. What do we learn about famous people from the media?

Project

Collect media stories about a well-known personality. Make a presentation about the kind of information you find and the way that information influences us.

Preparation

1. Working with a partner, select a media celebrity who interests you both.

2. Collect information about the person. Clip newspaper and magazine articles, and take notes on comments made about the person on radio and TV.

Procedure

1. Put the information you collected into categories, such as appearance, actions, quotes from the celebrity, and quotes about the celebrity.

2. Decide which information can be proved and which cannot. Also, note what categories contain the most information.

3. Discuss with your partner the following questions: Is the information you found trustworthy? How much of it is about the celebrity's appearance, style, or image? How much information is about the actions and attitudes of the celebrity? In what ways are you and others affected by media information about celebrities?

Presentation

Make your presentation in one of these ways:

1. Celebrity Collage

Make a collage showing media personalities in fields such as movies, TV, sports, and politics. Use magazine and newspaper articles, photographs, and quotes from radio and TV. Be sure your collage shows the kind of news that people receive about celebrities and the way they are influenced by it.

2. Interview

With your partner, create a skit about a celebrity being interviewed by a talk-show host. In preparing the interview, decide what kinds of questions the host will ask. What image of the celebrity will the audience get?

3. Newscast

Write copy for a newscast about your celebrity. What has your celebrity done that is newsworthy? How will you characterize the celebrity? Read your newscast to the class, or record it on videotape and play the tape.

Processing

Discuss this question with your classmates: How does media information about celebrities affect young adults?

LEARNING FOR LIFE **165**

Resources

Viewing and Representing
HRW Multimedia Presentation Maker
Students may wish to use the *Multimedia Presentation Maker* to create a collage.

Grading Timesaver

Rubrics for this Learning for Life project appear on p. 125 of the *Portfolio Management System*.

Developing Workplace Competencies

Preparation	Procedure	Presentation
• Working on teams • Making decisions • Acquiring data	• Classifying data • Evaluating data • Communicating ideas and information	• Using resources well • Thinking creatively • Exhibiting self-esteem

Collection Three

Machine Mania

Theme

The Future Is Now *The selections in this collection show how important machines are to us today and how they affect our imaginations. Some of these writers question the effects of machines and technology; others see "machines" at work even in the most delicate aspects of the natural world.*

Reading the Anthology

Reaching Struggling Readers

The Reading Skills and Strategies: Reaching Struggling Readers binder provides materials organized around eleven individual skill areas and coordinated with the Pupil's Edition to help students who have difficulty reading and comprehending text, or students who are reluctant readers. For Collection Three, the sixth-grade binder includes a Selection Skill Lesson that provides reading instruction and practice specific to a particular piece of literature (see the Collection Planner, p. T165C).

Reading Beyond the Anthology

Read On   Collection Three includes an annotated bibliography of books suitable for extended reading. The suggested books are related to works in this collection by theme, by author, or by subject. To preview the Read On for Collection Three, please turn to p. T227.

HRW Library   The *HRW Library* offers novels, plays, and short-story collections for extended reading. Each book in the Library includes one or more major works and thematically or topically related Connections. The Connections are magazine articles, poems, or other pieces of literature. Each book in the *HRW Library* is also accompanied by a Study Guide that provides teaching suggestions and worksheets. For Collection Three, the following titles are recommended.

THE CALL OF THE WILD
Jack London
This story of a heroic sled dog shows that human beings are ill-equipped to survive in a hostile environment. The call of the wild is the call of nature and of animal instinct.

THE TIME MACHINE and THE WAR OF THE WORLDS
H. G. Wells
These two classics of science fiction influenced the genre throughout the twentieth century. More than mere tales of scientific gadgetry, the stories show the effect of technology on people's lives.

Skills Focus

Selection or Feature	Reading Skills and Strategies	Elements of Literature	Language/ Grammar	Vocabulary/ Spelling	Writing	Listening/ Speaking	Viewing/ Representing
John Henry (p. 168) Anonymous African American	Dialogue with the Text, pp. 168, 176	Refrain, pp. 168, 176 Folk Heroes, p. 176			Write Lyrics, p. 177 Write the Next Chapter, p. 177		
Elements of Literature: Poetry: Sound Effects (p. 178)		Rhyme, pp. 178, 179 Alliteration, p. 178 Meter, pp. 178, 179 Free Verse, p. 179					
Ankylosaurus (p. 180) Jack Prelutsky	Use Prior Knowledge, p. 180	Onomatopoeia, pp. 181, 182 Rhythm, p. 182		Greek Roots, p. 182	Write a Poem Using Onomatopoeia, p. 182		Chart Data On Dioramas, p. 182 Do a Time Line, p. 182
Elements of Literature: Poetry: Seeing Likenesses (p. 183)		Figures of Speech, pp. 183–184 Personification, pp. 183–184					
The Toaster (p. 185) William Jay Smith **The Sidewalk Racer** (p. 187) Lillian Morrison **Things to Do If You Are a Subway** (p. 188) Bobbi Katz **Steam Shovel** (p. 190) Charles Malam		Metaphor, pp. 185, 192 Extended Metaphor, p. 185 Rhyme, p. 192 Alliteration, p. 192 Onomatopoeia, p. 192	Homophones, p. 193		Make Notes About How to Teach an Activity, p. 193 Write Riddles, p. 193 Write a Poem that Contains Homophones, p. 193		Create Art for a Poem, p. 193
Reading Skills and Strategies: Strategies for Reading Poetry (p. 194)	Read Poetry, p. 194 Use Prior Experience, p. 194	Rhythm, p. 194 Figurative Comparisons, p. 194	Punctuation in Poetry, p. 194	Use Context Clues, p. 194		Read Poetry Aloud, p. 194	
The Hill Mynah (p. 195) **The Hummingbird** (p. 197) Douglas Florian	Read Poetry, pp. 195, 198	Image, p. 198 Onomatopoeia, p. 198 Rhyme, p. 198			List Steps for Writing and Illustrating a Poem, p. 198 Write a Poem, p. 198		
Jimmy Jet and His TV Set (p. 199) Shel Silverstein	Scanning, pp. 199, 202	Rhyme Scheme, pp. 199, 202 Meter, pp. 199, 202			Write a Poem, p. 203 Write to a TV Network, p. 203		Make a Chart of Class's TV Habits, p. 203
The Fun They Had (p. 204) Isaac Asimov	Determine Cause and Effect, pp. 204, 212	Irony, pp. 204, 212 Main Idea, p. 212	End-Mark Errors, p. 214	Computer Words, p. 213 Word Roots, p. 214	Write a Journal Entry, p. 213 Make a Computer Dictionary, p. 213		Create a Time Capsule, p. 213 Illustrate a Dictionary, p. 213
No Questions Asked: The Nightingale (p. 215) Hans Christian Andersen	The **No Questions Asked** feature provides students with an unstructured opportunity to practice reading strategies using a selection that extends the theme of the collection.						
Speaking and Listening Workshop: Oral Interpretation (p. 228)	Identify Main Ideas and Key Phrases, p. 229				Prepare a Reading Script, p. 229	Oral Interpretation of a Poem, p. 228	
Writer's Workshop: How-To Essay (p. 230)		Chronological Order, p. 232	Use Transitions, p. 234		Write a How-To Essay, pp. 230–234		Use a Graphic Organizer to List Steps, p. 233
Sentence Workshop: Stringy Sentences (p. 235)			Stringy Sentences, p. 235		Revise Stringy Sentences, p. 235		
Reading for Life: Reading a Manual (p. 236)	Reading for Information, p. 236	Chronological Order, p. 236		Use Glossary to Define Unfamiliar Words, p. 236			Check Diagrams and Charts, p. 236
Learning for Life: Machines (p. 237)					Develop Instructions for Using a Machine, p. 237	Demonstrate a Machine, p. 237	Poster, p. 237 Design a Manual, p. 237

Skills Focus

Resources for this Collection

Note: All resources for this collection are available for preview on the *One-Stop Planner CD-ROM 1 with Test Generator.* All worksheets and blackline masters may be printed from the CD-ROM.

 **Internet Resources**
go.hrw.com LE0 6-3

Collection Planner

Selection or Feature	Reading and Literary Skills	Language and Grammar
John Henry (p. 168) Anonymous/African American **Connections: Working on the Railroad** (p. 174) Gloria A. Harris	• *Graphic Organizers for Active Reading,* Worksheet p. 13 • *Literary Elements:* Transparency 3; Worksheet p. 10	• *Daily Oral Grammar,* Transparency 11
Elements of Literature: Poetry: Sound Effects (p. 178)	• *Literary Elements,* Transparency 3	
Ankylosaurus (p. 180) Jack Prelutsky	• *Graphic Organizers for Active Reading,* Worksheet p. 14 • *Literary Elements:* Transparency 4; Worksheet p. 13	
Elements of Literature: Poetry: Seeing Likenesses (p. 183)	• *Literary Elements,* Transparency 4	
The Toaster (p. 185) William Jay Smith **The Sidewalk Racer or On the Skateboard** (p. 187) Lillian Morrison **Things to Do If You Are a Subway** (p. 188) Bobbi Katz **Steam Shovel** (p. 190) Charles Malam	• *Graphic Organizers for Active Reading,* Worksheet p. 15 • *Literary Elements:* Poetry Transparencies 1–5 Teaching Notes, p. 39	
The Hill Mynah (p. 195) **The Hummingbird** (p. 197) Douglas Florian	• *Graphic Organizers for Active Reading,* Worksheet p. 16	
Jimmy Jet and His TV Set (p. 199) Shel Silverstein	• *Graphic Organizers for Active Reading,* Worksheet p. 17	
The Fun They Had (p. 204) Isaac Asimov **Connections: Netiquette** Preston Gralla (p. 210)	• *Reading Skills and Strategies: Reaching Struggling Readers* • Selection Skill Lesson, p. 135 • *Graphic Organizers for Active Reading,* Worksheet p. 18	• *Grammar and Language Links:* End-Mark Errors, Worksheet p. 21 • *Language Workshop CD-ROM,* End Marks • *Daily Oral Grammar,* Transparency 12
No Questions Asked: **The Nightingale** (p. 215) Hans Christian Andersen *translated by* Anthea Bell	The **No Questions Asked** feature provides students with an unstructured opportunity to practice reading strategies using a selection that extends the theme of the collection.	
Speaking and Listening Workshop: Oral Interpretation (p. 228)		
Writer's Workshop: How-To Essay (p. 230)		
Sentence Workshop: Stringy Sentences (p. 235)		• *Workshop Resources,* p. 41 • *Language Workshop CD-ROM,* Stringy Sentences
Learning for Life: Machines: A User's Guide (p. 237)		

Collection Resources

- *Cross-Curricular Activities,* p. 18
- *Portfolio Management System:*
  Introduction to Portfolio Assessment, p. 1;
  Parent/Guardian Letters, p. 91
- *Formal Assessment,*
  Reading Application Test, p. 46
- *Test Generator,* Collection Test 💿

Vocabulary, Spelling, and Decoding	Writing	Listening and Speaking, Viewing and Representing	Assessment
	• *Portfolio Management System,* Rubrics for Choices, p. 126	• *Audio CD Library,* Disc 4, Track 2 🎧 • *Viewing and Representing:* Fine Art Transparency 7 📽 Worksheet p. 28 • *Portfolio Management System,* Rubrics for Choices, p. 126	• *Formal Assessment,* Selection Test, p. 35 • *Standardized Test Preparation,* p. 34 • *Test Generator* (One-Stop Planner CD-ROM) 💿
		• *Audio CD Library,* Disc 4, Track 3 🎧	• *Formal Assessment,* Literary Elements Test, p. 43
	• *Portfolio Management System,* Rubrics for Choices, p. 127	• *Audio CD Library,* Disc 4, Track 4 🎧 • *Portfolio Management System,* Rubrics for Choices, p. 127	• *Formal Assessment,* Selection Test, p. 36 • *Test Generator* (One-Stop Planner CD-ROM) 💿
			• *Formal Assessment,* Literary Elements Test, p. 44
	• *Portfolio Management System,* Rubrics for Choices, p. 128	• *Audio CD Library,* Disc 4, Tracks 5, 6, 7, 8 🎧 • *Viewing and Representing:* Fine Art Transparency 8 📽 Worksheet p. 32 • *Portfolio Management System,* Rubrics for Choices, p. 128	• *Formal Assessment,* Selection Test, p. 37 • *Standardized Test Preparation,* p. 36 • *Test Generator* (One-Stop Planner CD-ROM) 💿
	• *Portfolio Management System,* Rubrics for Choices, p. 129	• *Audio CD Library,* Disc 4, Tracks 9, 10 🎧 • *Portfolio Management System,* Rubrics for Choices, p. 129	• *Formal Assessment,* Selection Test, p. 39 • *Test Generator* (One-Stop Planner CD-ROM) 💿
	• *Portfolio Management System,* Rubrics for Choices, p. 130	• *Audio CD Library,* Disc 4, Track 11 🎧 • *Portfolio Management System,* Rubrics for Choices, p. 130	• *Formal Assessment,* Selection Test, p. 40 • *Test Generator* (One-Stop Planner CD-ROM) 💿
• *Words to Own,* Worksheet p. 10 • *Spelling and Decoding,* Worksheet p. 10	• *Portfolio Management System,* Rubrics for Choices, p. 131	• *Visual Connections,* Videocassette A, Segment 4 📼 • *Audio CD Library,* Disc 4, Track 12 🎧 • *Viewing and Representing:* Fine Art Transparency 9 📽 Worksheet p. 36 • *Portfolio Management System,* Rubrics for Choices, p. 131	• *Formal Assessment,* Selection Test, p. 41 • *Test Generator* (One-Stop Planner CD-ROM) 💿
		• *Audio CD Library,* Disc 4, Track 13 🎧	
			• *Portfolio Management System,* p. 132

	• *Workshop Resources,* p. 9
	• *Standardized Test Preparation:* Worksheet p. 130 📽 Transparencies 19–24 📽
			• *Portfolio Management System*
			  • Prewriting, p. 133
			  • Peer Editing, p. 134
			  • Assessment Rubric, p. 135

		• *Viewing and Representing,* HRW Multimedia Presentation Maker	• *Portfolio Management System,* Rubrics, p. 136

 Transparency   CD-ROM   Video   Audio CD

Machine Mania: People and Technology

Charlie Chaplin in the movie
Modern Times (1936).

Photofest/Kino International Corp.

166

OBJECTIVES

1. Read literature in different genres on the theme "Machine Mania: People and Technology"
2. Interpret literary elements used in the literature, with special emphasis on sound effects and figures of speech
3. Apply a variety of reading strategies, with special emphasis on learning to read poetry
4. Respond to the literature using a variety of modes
5. Learn and use word roots to create words
6. Plan, draft, revise, edit, proof, and publish a how-to essay
7. Prepare and present an oral interpretation of a poem
8. Learn how to recognize and fix stringy sentences
9. Demonstrate the ability to read a manual
10. Develop a set of instructions for using a machine to do one specific task

Introducing the Theme

Ask students to name as many machines as they can, and make a list on the chalkboard. What are these machines used for? How did these tasks get done before the machines were invented? Which machines are students glad to have and use? Which machines would they like to see eliminated? Why? After students have discussed the theme, explain that they will read a number of poems and stories that compare and contrast humans or animals with machines.

Responding to the Quotation

Carl Sandburg's poetry celebrates America and its working men and women. The quotation is taken from *The People, Yes* (1936), an epic poem celebrating the common people, who Sandburg believed will triumph in the end. What does this quotation suggest about machines? [Machines are easily controlled, but they have no pride, feelings, or individuality.]

Selection Readability

This Annotated Teacher's Edition provides a summary of each selection in the student book. Following each Summary heading, you will find one, two, or three small icons. These icons indicate, in an approximate sense, the reading level of the selection.

■ One icon indicates that the selection is easy.

■ ■ Two icons indicate that the selection is at an intermediate reading level.

■ ■ ■ Three icons indicate that the selection is challenging.

The machine yes the machine
never wastes anybody's time
never watches the foreman
never talks back.

—*Carl Sandburg*

RESPONDING TO THE ART

Charles Chaplin (1889–1977) was a genius of the silent-film era. Chaplin was born in England, where his mother, Hannah, was a star on the musical stage; Charlie made his stage debut at age five and was an instant success. A 1910 comedy tour of the United States led to a contract in 1913, and Chaplin embarked on his unique Hollywood film career.

Chaplin wrote, directed, and starred in numerous silent-screen comedies throughout the 1920s. He created a signature character known as the Little Tramp, a gentle little man in a bowler hat and shabby suit who triumphed over hard times.

Chaplin made only two films during the 1930s: *City Lights* and *Modern Times*. Although sound had come to motion pictures long since, Chaplin did not embrace it; these two films are largely silent, except for their musical scores. *Modern Times* is the story of a factory worker who suffers a mental breakdown from job stress (incessantly tightening bolts for the gigantic machinery shown here).

Writer's Notebook

Ask students to write a paragraph in their Writer's Notebook about the relationship between humans and machines. Encourage them to consider how machines facilitate the work of people in many industries. They should also consider the drawbacks of an increasingly technological world.

Resources

Portfolio Management System
- Introduction to Portfolio Assessment, p. 1
- Parent/Guardian Letters, p. 91

Formal Assessment
- Reading Application Test, p. 46

Test Generator
- Collection Test

Cross-Curricular Activities
- Teaching Notes, p. 18

Writing Focus: How-To Essay

The following **Work in Progress** assignments in this collection build to a culminating **Writer's Workshop** at the end of Collection 3.

- John Henry .... Explain how to use a tool (p. 177)
- Ankylosaurus .... Find out how to make a diorama (p. 182)
- The Toaster . . . . List steps for how-to instructions (p. 193)
- The Hill Mynah / The Hummingbird .. List steps for writing and illustrating a poem (p. 198)
- Jimmy Jet and His TV Set .... Describe steps for using a machine (p. 203)
- The Fun They Had .... List steps for operating a machine (p. 213)

Writer's Workshop: Expository Writing / How-To Essay (p. 230)

OBJECTIVES

OBJECTIVES

1. Read and interpret the ballad
2. Identify the ballad's refrain
3. Monitor comprehension
4. Express understanding through creative writing or music

SKILLS

Literary
• Identify a refrain

Reading
• Monitor comprehension

Writing
• Collect ideas for a how-to essay
• Continue a story

Music
• Write lyrics for a song

Planning

• **Block Schedule**
  Block Scheduling Lesson Plans with Pacing Guide

• **Traditional Schedule**
  Lesson Plans Including Strategies for English-Language Learners

• **One-Stop Planner**
  CD-ROM with Test Generator

Before You Read

JOHN HENRY

Make the Connection

Anything It Can Do, I Can Do Better

What can machines do better than people? Is there anything that people can do that machines can't do? In class, brainstorm to come up with a list of answers to these questions. Then, choose the best items from your list to fill in a chart like the one below. Think of at least three contests for each column.

Contests People Would Win	Contests Machines Would Win
songwriting	washing clothes

Reading Skills and Strategies

Dialogue with the Text

As you read "John Henry," keep a sheet of paper handy so that you can write down your reactions. One student's comments appear on pages 169 and 170 as an example. Remember that you create your own meanings from the poem. No one else will read it exactly the same way you do.

Elements of Literature

Refrain: Repeat After Me

The most obvious sound effect used in poetry and songs is the refrain. The refrain has been part of poems and songs for thousands of years. A **refrain** may consist of a few words, a line, or a whole stanza repeated at intervals. (The wording of some refrains varies from time to time.) Today almost every song you hear or sing has a refrain. Some refrains you might have heard are words and lines like "Kumbaya," "We shall overcome," and "Let my people go." The famous speech by Martin Luther King, Jr., is built on the refrain "I have a dream."

> A **refrain** is a repeated word, phrase, line, or group of lines in a poem or song or even in a speech.
>
> *For more on Refrain, see the Handbook of Literary Terms.*

Background

Literature and Social Studies

Nobody knows for sure if John Henry, the hero of this song, was a real person, but people began singing about him in the early 1870s. He was said to be an African American laborer in the construction crew working on the Big Bend Tunnel of the Chesapeake and Ohio Railroad. According to the legend, someone set up a contest between John Henry and a steam drill. If you can, listen to a recording of the song "John Henry."

go.hrw.com
LE0 6-3

Resources: Print and Media

Reading
• *Graphic Organizers for Active Reading*, p. 13
• *Audio CD Library*
  Disc 4, Track 2

Elements of Literature
• *Literary Elements*
  Transparency 3
  Worksheet, p. 10

Writing and Language
• *Daily Oral Grammar*
  Transparency 11

Viewing and Representing
• *Viewing and Representing*
  Fine Art Transparency 7
  Fine Art Worksheet, p. 28

Assessment
• *Formal Assessment*, p. 35
• *Portfolio Management System*, p. 126
• *Standardized Test Preparation*, p. 34
• *Test Generator (One-Stop Planner CD-ROM)*

Internet
• go.hrw.com (keyword: LE0 6-3)

When John Henry Was a Baby (1944–1947) by Palmer C. Hayden.

John Henry

anonymous African American

John Henry was about three days old
Sittin' on his papa's knee.
He picked up a hammer and a little piece of steel
Said, "Hammer's gonna be the death of me, Lord, Lord!
5   Hammer's gonna be the death of me."

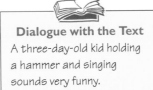

Dialogue with the Text
A three-day-old kid holding a hammer and singing sounds very funny.

Ⓐ

JOHN HENRY **169**

Summary ▪ ▪

As a baby, John Henry predicts that his death will be caused by a hammer. As an adult, he drives through rock with a hammer, digging tunnels for the railroad. When the captain plans to replace John Henry with a steam-powered drill, John Henry works even harder and cuts through fifteen feet of rock, compared with the steam drill's nine feet. But the exertion kills him. His wife, Polly Ann, takes his place. John Henry becomes a legend, and his ringing hammer strokes can still be heard for miles around.

Resources

Listening
Audio CD Library
A recording of this song is provided in the *Audio CD Library*:
• Disc 4, Track 2

Viewing and Representing
Fine Art Transparency
A fine art transparency of Palmer Hayden's *His Hammer in His Hand* can be used with this selection. See the *Viewing and Representing Transparencies and Worksheets*:
• Transparency 7
• Worksheet, p. 28

Ⓐ Reading Skills and Strategies
Dialogue with the Text
Point out the reader's questions and comments in the side-column feature Dialogue with the Text on pp. 169–170. Encourage students to write down questions of their own as they read the ballad. After they finish reading, students should be sure their questions have been answered.

Reaching All Students

Struggling Readers
Dialogue with the Text was introduced on p. 168 under Reading Skills and Strategies. For additional information on monitoring comprehension, see the *Reading Skills and Strategies* binder.

English Language Learners
Students may have difficulty with the dialect in the song. Explain to them that like all countries, the United States has spawned many regional dialects, which differ somewhat from standard English. Pair English language learners with native English speakers. The latter can help their partners with the song's unfamiliar spellings ("sittin'"), contractions ("gonna"), and expressions ("whop that steel on down").

Advanced Learners
Have students add more verses to the song, filling in some of the gaps in the story. For example, John Henry grows from babyhood to adulthood between the first two verses: What happens to him during that time? Make sure students maintain the rhyme scheme and meter of the song in their verses. Have students read their work aloud in class.

A Critical Thinking

Interpreting

? What do you think John Henry means by this? [He admits that a person is no match for a machine, but he is determined to prevail rather than be replaced.]

B Elements of Literature

Refrain

? Ask students to identify the repeated elements in each verse. [The fourth line of each verse is repeated as the fifth; "Lord, Lord!" ends the fourth line of every verse.] **What effect does this repetition have on the reader?** [Possible responses: The repetition of an idea or expression gives it greater impact; the repetition echoes the sound of hammer blows; "Lord, Lord!" shows the strength of John Henry's religious faith.]

C English Language Learners

Dialect

Make sure students understand this dialect. *Ain't* can mean "isn't," "don't," "haven't," or "hasn't." Dropping the final *g* from words that end in *-ing* is a common feature of some American dialects.

D Advanced Learners

Analyzing

? Why is John Henry able to win the race? [He has qualities the steam drill doesn't have: a will to win, courage, determination, and self-preservation.]

The captain said to John Henry,
"Gonna bring that steam drill 'round
Gonna bring that steam drill out on the job
Gonna whop that steel on down, Lord, Lord!
10　Whop that steel on down."

A
John Henry told his captain,
"A man ain't nothin' but a man
But before I let your steam drill beat me down
I'd die with a hammer in my hand, Lord, Lord!
15　I'd die with a hammer in my hand."

John Henry said to his shaker,°
"Shaker, why don't you sing?
I'm throwing thirty pounds from my hips on down
B Just listen to that cold steel ring, Lord, Lord!
20　Listen to that cold steel ring."

John Henry said to his shaker,
"Shaker, you'd better pray
'Cause if I miss that little piece of steel
Tomorrow be your buryin' day, Lord, Lord!
25　Tomorrow be your buryin' day."

The shaker said to John Henry,
"I think this mountain's cavin' in!"
John Henry said to his shaker, "Man,
C That ain't nothin' but my hammer suckin' wind,
　　　Lord, Lord!
30　Nothin' but my hammer suckin' wind."

The man that invented the steam drill
Thought he was mighty fine
D But John Henry made fifteen feet
The steam drill only made nine, Lord, Lord!
35　The steam drill only made nine.

16. shaker: worker who holds the drill.

Dialogue with the Text

I'm not sure what the captain is telling Henry. I think John Henry is supposed to make something.

Why does John Henry want to die with a hammer in his hand? Does it have to do with when he was a baby?

Why does John Henry want the shaker to sing while he is drilling?

That would be really scary if John Henry missed the piece of steel. The shaker would die. Would it be John Henry's fault?

Monique Hernandez

—Monique Hernandez
Ynez School
Monterey Park,
California

Listening to Music

"John Henry" (traditional), performed by Harry Belafonte and others

"I've Been Working on the Railroad" (traditional), performed by John Denver and others

"John Henry" is a work song—a song laborers sing to maintain the rhythm of their tasks and to make the time pass. "John Henry" is also the story of a larger-than-life hero, part of the same tradition that created Paul Bunyan and "Casey at the Bat."

Activities

1. After students have read "John Henry," have them listen to the musical version. Point out that the lyrics do not match the song as printed in the textbook; in the oral tradition, every tale, story, and song is a little different each time it is told. Have students identify and give their opinions of the differences.

2. After students read the essay "Working on the Railroad" and listen to the second song, have them compare and contrast the two songs in a class discussion.

John Henry hammered in the mountain
His hammer was striking fire
But he worked so hard, he broke his poor heart
He laid down his hammer and he died, Lord, Lord!

40   He laid down his hammer and he died.

John Henry had a little woman
Her name was Polly Ann
John Henry took sick and went to his bed
Polly Ann drove steel like a man, Lord, Lord!

45   Polly Ann drove steel like a man.

John Henry on the Right, Steam Drill on the Left (1944–1947) by Palmer C. Hayden.

The Museum of African American Art, Los Angeles.

JOHN HENRY **171**

E Reading Skills
and Strategies
**Dialogue with
the Text**

? What questions do you have at this
point in the story? [Possible questions:
What did John Henry die of? How did
the steam drill's inventor feel about it?
How did the baby John Henry know this
would happen?]

F **Appreciating Language**
Idioms

? What does the expression "like a
man" tell you about Polly Ann? Why is
it effective? [She is unusually strong. Her
ability to do the work of a man (who is
assumed to be stronger than she is)
echoes John Henry's ability to do the
work of a machine (which is assumed to
be stronger than he is).]

**Speaking and Listening:
Appreciating Spoken
Language**
Play the dramatic reading of this classic
poem for students (Disc 4, Track 2, in
the *Audio CD Library*). Ask students to
listen for the reader's variations in
tone, volume, and speed, especially in
the refrain. Then, ask them to discuss
how the sounds of the poem help
make it vivid and appealing.

Professional Notes

One day in 1879, young Laura Ingalls and her father watched the railroad men leveling the hilly Dakota prairie land to make a railroad grade. "Teams [of horses] and men were going slowly around in a circle, over the end of the grade and back to cross the plowed strip. The teams were pulling wide, deep shovels. These were the scrapers.... They kept on going steadily around the circle, over the plowed land and to the grade and over it and back to the plowed land again. Thirty teams and thirty scrapers, and all the four-horse teams and the plows, and all the drivers and the scraper holders, all were going round and round, all in their places and all moving in time, there on the open prairie, just like the works of a clock.... The whole afternoon had gone while Pa and Laura watched those circles moving, making the railroad grade.... Laura was still seeing the movement of men and horses in such perfect time that she could almost sing the tune to which they moved."

Read this excerpt aloud to students. Explain that John Henry worked in the East, while Pa and Laura watched the railroad men in the West, where the features of the land are very different.

Explain that the word *locomotive* comes from the Latin roots *locus,* meaning "place," and *motivus,* meaning "moving." A locomotive is an object that can move itself from place to place; it refers to a train driven by a steam engine or an electric motor.

B Elements of Literature
Refrain

? How is this verse different from all the others in the ballad? [It has a three-line refrain instead of a two-line refrain.] **Why do you think it is like this?** [Possible answers: It echoes the perpetual ring of John Henry's hammer; it marks the end of the ballad; it leaves readers with a feeling of triumph instead of tragedy, because John Henry's legend endures even after his death.]

LITERATURE AND SOCIAL STUDIES

Chinese and Irish immigrants also contributed greatly to the construction of the transcontinental railroad. Most of the Irish railroad workers had immigrated to the United States to escape the Potato Famine that began in 1845 and lasted until 1849. They worked the rails from the East Coast to Utah, and they were famous for being hard workers. Chinese immigrants labored almost every day of the month for about half the pay of the Irish workers. They volunteered for the most dangerous jobs, which involved working with explosives.

Students may want to read more about the railroad workers in the following books: *By the Shores of Silver Lake* by Laura Ingalls Wilder, *Tales from Gold Mountain: Stories of the Chinese in the New World* by Paul Yee, and *Ten Mile Day and the Building of the Transcontinental Railroad* by Mary Ann Fraser.

John Henry had a little baby
You could hold him in the palm of your hand
The last words I heard that poor boy say,
"My daddy was a steel-driving man, Lord, Lord!
50   My daddy was a steel-driving man."

They took John Henry to the graveyard
And they buried him in the sand
A And every locomotive comes a-roaring by
Says, "There lies a steel-driving man, Lord, Lord!
55   There lies a steel-driving man."

Well, every Monday morning
When the bluebirds begin to sing
You can hear John Henry a mile or more
B You can hear John Henry's hammer ring, Lord, Lord!
60   You can hear John Henry's hammer ring.

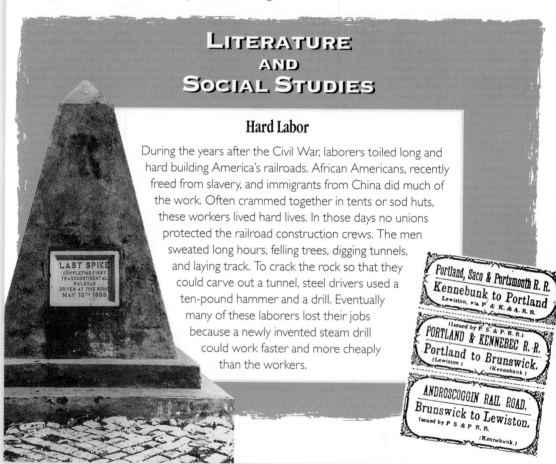

LITERATURE AND SOCIAL STUDIES

Hard Labor

During the years after the Civil War, laborers toiled long and hard building America's railroads. African Americans, recently freed from slavery, and immigrants from China did much of the work. Often crammed together in tents or sod huts, these workers lived hard lives. In those days no unions protected the railroad construction crews. The men sweated long hours, felling trees, digging tunnels, and laying track. To crack the rock so that they could carve out a tunnel, steel drivers used a ten-pound hammer and a drill. Eventually many of these laborers lost their jobs because a newly invented steam drill could work faster and more cheaply than the workers.

LAST SPIKE
COMPLETING FIRST
TRANSCONTINENTAL
RAILROAD
DRIVEN AT THIS POINT
MAY 10TH 1869

Portland, Saco & Portsmouth R. R.
Kennebunk to Portland
Lewiston, via P. & K. & A.R.R.

(Issued by P. S. & P. R. R.)
PORTLAND & KENNEBEC R. R.
Portland to Brunswick.
(Lewiston.)   (Kennebunk)

ANDROSCOGGIN RAIL ROAD.
Brunswick to Lewiston.
Issued by P. S. & P. R. R.
(Kennebunk.)

Using Students' Strengths

Visual Learners
As students read the song, they might benefit by filling in the graphic organizer located in *Graphic Organizers for Active Reading,* p. 13.

Kinesthetic Learners
Divide students into small groups to discuss how the language in the song helps readers feel the action and movements of the characters and machines. How do the song's rhyme scheme and rhythm suggest movement? Which vivid verbs and adjectives help "show" the characters and machines moving? How does the song's use of dialect help students "see" the story in motion? As students discuss these questions among themselves, move among the groups to hear their reactions and ideas.

He Laid Down His Hammer and Cried (1944–1947) by Palmer C. Hayden.

RESPONDING TO THE ART

Palmer C. Hayden (1893–1973) was born in Wide Water, Virginia. He studied art at New York City's Cooper Union. In 1927, he went to France to study at the École des Beaux Arts. Hayden painted African American subjects, and his work shows a strong influence from African motifs and designs. Some contemporary critics admired his portrayal of African American genre scenes. Others were disturbed by the exaggeration of African physical features, especially the eyes and lips; these exaggerations echoed a tradition of stereotypic white portrayals of black people. Hayden always denied that the exaggerations were intended to demean his subjects.

The paintings that illustrate this selection are part of a series of twelve canvases depicting John Henry's legend. (The fine art transparency that goes with this selection shows another painting from the series.) Hayden worked on this series for ten years, and it is considered his finest achievement.

Activities

1. In the first illustration, what is the baby John Henry pointing at? [the railroad tracks; the train] Compare and contrast this illustration with the song's first verse. [In the painting, John Henry looks much more than three days old; he is sitting on his mother's lap rather than his father's; the painting connects the railroad to the story right away.]

2. What is happening in the second illustration? [John Henry tries to drive spikes through the rock faster than the drill, on the left, can bore a hole.]

3. Why do you think John Henry is crying in the third illustration? Note that the song says he "laid down his hammer and he died." [He is saddened by the understanding that the machine will inevitably replace even the best workers.]

Making the Connections

Connecting to the Theme: "Machine Mania: People and Technology"

After students finish reading the song, discuss the collection's theme. What effect did the introduction of the steam drill have on the lives of railroad workers? What effect did it have on the building of the railroad? In the long run, were these effects positive or negative? Why? Have students keep these questions and answers in mind as they read the next selection. [Students should see that the drill means that the railroad will be completed sooner, but people will be deprived of jobs. Therefore, the lives of workers like John Henry and Polly Ann are made harder. Positive long-term effects: The faster the railroad is finished, the sooner people can travel conveniently across the country. Negative long-term effects: People are put out of work and can't feed their families; railroads create pollution.]

Connections

A MAGAZINE ARTICLE

Working on the Railroad   Gloria A. Harris

The song "I've Been Working on the Railroad" is about the African American railroad workers who laid ties, set rails, and did the jobs nobody else wanted. Even after the railroads were completed, many service positions were available to African Americans. The railroad industry was the biggest employer of black men in the post–Civil War era. The jobs were usually difficult and often dangerous, and many railroad workers created inventions to improve the efficiency and safety of their jobs.

One of the most dangerous jobs on early railroads was that of the brakeman. One of his jobs was to couple, or join, railroad cars together. To do this, he had to walk along the top of the train, then climb down the back of the last car like a spider. Bracing his back against the car, he waited for another train to back up close to his. If he was lucky, he dropped the coupling pin into a lock to connect the cars a split second before they came together. If he was not, he could be crushed between the two cars.

Andrew Beard, an Alabama railroad brakeman, lost his leg in just such an accident. While Beard was not the first to think of a better way to join railroad cars, he was the first to create an automatic coupler, called the Jenny Coupler, in the early 1890s. The genius of Beard's invention was that two railroad cars locked together just by being pushed against each other. A similar device is still used today.

Besides keeping the engine fueled, early railroad firemen were responsible for keeping the engine oiled to prevent overheating. To do this, the engineer had to stop the engine periodically, which usually meant bringing the locomotive to a halt. Oiling the engine was a hot, dirty, and dangerous job.

In 1872, Elijah McCoy invented a self-lubricating cup that dripped oil continuously onto the engine's moving parts even while it was going. He later received many patents[1] for improvements on his invention.

This "drip cup" was used throughout American industry to help extend the life of heavy machinery. The expression "Is it the real McCoy?" is said to have originated because many cheaper copies of McCoy's device were being sold. Industrial engineers wanted to be sure they were getting the best.

Most early trains rode on a single track, and the engineer had no way of knowing whether another train was coming the other way. Granville T. Woods found a way to send

Runaway locomotive at Hartford, Connecticut, roundhouse.
The Connecticut Historical Society, Hartford.

---

1. **patents:** government documents giving an inventor the exclusive right to make and sell a new invention.

Taking a Second Look

Review: Using Context Clues

The context of a word can help students understand what it means, even if the word is new to them. Context clues can also help students choose the correct definition of a word with multiple meanings. After looking at the surrounding words and grasping the sense of a whole sentence, students can determine which meaning of a word is correct. For example, *ain't* can mean "isn't," "aren't," "haven't," or "hasn't." The surrounding words will tell students which meaning is correct.

Activities

1. As students read this article, they will find both new words (*telegraphony, yardman*) and familiar words with new meanings (*ties, couple*). Have students list these words as they read the article.

2. Each time students write down a word that puzzles them, have them reread the sentence, looking for context clues. Sometimes words are directly defined within the text: "One of his jobs was to couple, or *join*, railroad cars together." Sometimes the writer gives only general hints: The word *ties* in the opening sentence clearly means "parts of a railroad track" because of the sense of the whole sentence.

3. After students have finished reading the article, have a class discussion in which they share definitions of words.

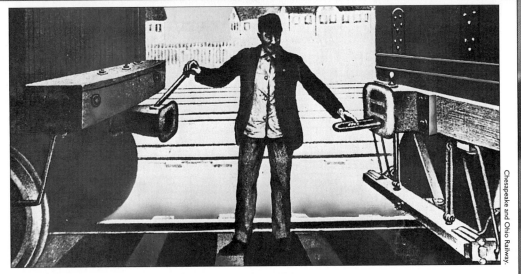

Old link-and-pin coupler.

Chesapeake and Ohio Railway.

C **Struggling Readers**
Using Context Clues
❓ What is a "telegraphony system"?
How do you know? [It is a system that
combines the telephone and telegraph;
the word contains both of those words,
and the writer explains its meaning.]

D **Critical Thinking**
Making Inferences
❓ Why would trains need alarms?
[Possible response: to warn passengers
and crew of danger; to warn other trains
that they are approaching; to scare cattle
or horses off the tracks.]

a message using the human voice. His
telegraphony system combined the telegraph
and telephone. Messages using Morse code[2]
or human speech could be sent over the
same wires using the same equipment. As a
result, engineers and conductors could be
warned of dangers that lay ahead.

In 1902, Woods obtained a patent for an
improvement to George Westinghouse's automatic air brake. Woods subsequently sold
the patent to the Westinghouse Company.
With the Westinghouse air brake, the cars
and the locomotive stopped at the same
time, avoiding many accidents.

Early railroads faced many other problems.
For example, early smokestacks often emitted sparks and soot that burned and soiled
passengers' clothing. One of the inventors
who received a patent for a better smoke-
stack was Landrow Bell, in 1871. Humphrey

H. Reynolds's window ventilator,[3] which received a patent in 1883, also helped solve
this problem.

In the 1890s, several inventors turned
their attention to improving the railway
switch, which moves a train from one track
to another. If a yardman threw a switch that
did not work properly, two trains might run
on the same track, with potentially disastrous
results. Patents for improvements of an elec-
trically controlled and operated railway
switch are listed for William H. Jackson and
William Purvis, 1897; William F. Burr, 1899;
Charles V. Richey, 1897; and Philip B.
Williams, 1900. Today trains switch from one
track to another, thanks in part to the work
of these inventors.

Another group of inventors worked on
safety devices such as railroad signals and train
alarms. Albert B. Blackburn received a patent
for a railroad signal in 1888, and Richard A.
Butler received one for a train alarm in 1897.

2. **Morse code:** system of dots and dashes, or short and
long sounds or flashes, used to represent letters or numbers in signaling, telegraphy, and so on.

3. **ventilator:** machine or object that brings in fresh air.

Connecting Across Texts

Connecting with "John Henry"
After students have read the article, ask them to
compare and contrast its attitude toward the
theme "Machine Mania: People and Technology"
with the attitude in the ballad of John Henry.
What is the most important difference between
the two? Which of the two attitudes do students believe is more true to life? Why? [Stu-
dents should see that in the song, a man and a
machine are in conflict; the steam drill threatens
to take away John Henry's job, and in the end it is

responsible for his death as he tries to outwork it.
In the article, machines don't replace workers but
help make their jobs easier and safer. Most students will probably think machines make people's
lives easier and help create new jobs. One good
example is that cash machines have not replaced
human bank tellers but have left them free to
cope with complex customer needs rather than
spending time on easy transactions.]

MAKING MEANINGS

First Thoughts

1. Possible answers: His performance is heroic, because it shows his sense of pride and self-worth; he is foolish, because it killed him.

Shaping Interpretations

2. Sample answer: Lines 33–35 show that John Henry outperforms the steam drill and wins the contest.

3. John Henry has great physical strength, and he faces near-impossible odds with courage and determination. As a baby, he lifts a hammer, speaks, and tells the future.

4. She does what is considered a man's job and does it well.

5. The passing locomotives and the sound of John Henry's hammer keep his name alive.

6. Refrains include "Lord, Lord!" and repeated lines in each stanza. The words "Lord, Lord" could be sung mournfully or triumphantly.

Extending the Text

7. Possible machines: Computers and microwave ovens have helped us become more efficient. Computers have caused a loss of privacy, and they keep people isolated from one another. Food heated in a microwave oven does not taste as good as food cooked in a convection oven.

8. Possible answers: People don't want to be replaced by machines; people are used to doing things a certain way and don't like change; people are concerned about the environment and don't like wasteful technology.

MAKING MEANINGS

First Thoughts

[respond]

1. What did you think of John Henry's trying to outperform a steam drill? Was this heroic or foolish? Why? Check your reading notes for ideas.

Shaping Interpretations

[interpret]
2. Who do you think eventually wins the contest between John Henry and the steam drill? Use lines from the song to support your answer.

[analyze]
3. **Folk heroes** are superheroes, people who have qualities admired by the people who give them lasting fame. How does John Henry show that he is a superhero, even a baby superhero?

[analyze]
4. How does Polly Ann show that she's a superhero, too?

[analyze]
5. Who or what keeps John Henry's name alive?

[identify]
6. What words do you think serve as **refrains** in this song? How could the refrains be sung differently each time they are used, to suggest different feelings?

Extending the Text

[generalize]
7. "Working on the Railroad" (see *Connections* on page 174) tells how the Jenny coupler, the drip cup, and the air brake improved life for railroad workers. What other machines have helped make our lives easier? How have they also caused trouble for some people?

[speculate]
8. Why do you think people sometimes oppose or fear new technology, even though in many cases machines can do the work better, faster, or more cheaply than people can?

Assessing Learning

Check Test: Short Answers

1. How old was John Henry when he predicted his own death? [three days]
2. What does John Henry have to race against? [a steam drill]
3. What is the shaker's job? [He holds the spike steady for John Henry to hit with the hammer.]
4. What does Polly Ann do after John Henry has to quit work? [She takes his place.]
5. What can people still hear on Monday morning? [They can hear the ring of John Henry's hammer.]

CHOICES: Building Your Portfolio

Writer's Notebook

1. Collecting Ideas for a How-To Essay

John Henry was an expert at driving in steel spikes with a hammer. Think of a tool or mechanical device that you use. Try to think of one with few if any moving parts. Here are some examples: a pencil sharpener, a screwdriver, a fork, and a window blind. Suppose you had to explain how to use the tool to an English-speaking alien from another galaxy. List the steps in the order in which you perform them.

> **Using a Flashlight**
> 1. Open flashlight to show batteries.
> 2. Take out batteries and check them.
> 3. Put back batteries; explain how + and - ("positive" and "negative") ends of the batteries line up.
> 4. Darken room.
> 5. Switch on flashlight.

Creative Writing/ Music

2. A Twenty-First-Century John Henry

Write the words to a song that might be sung in the future about a hero who challenges a new machine—maybe a computer or a talking car. Start with the hero's early life, and then tell the story of the big challenge. Try to find words you'll repeat for effect, like "Lord, Lord" in "John Henry." Your hero, of course, can be male or female. You can also switch the rules if you like: Have a machine challenge a person.

Creative Writing

3. John Henry: The Legend Lives On

Suppose John Henry had survived the contest. What would have happened to him next? Would he have continued working as a "steel-driving man," or would the steam drill have eventually replaced him? In one or two paragraphs, write the next chapter in the legend of John Henry.

Rubrics for each Choices assignment appear on p. 126 in the *Portfolio Management System.*

CHOICES: Building Your Portfolio

1. **Writer's Notebook** Suggest that each student see if a partner can identify the tool or device he or she has described.
2. **Creative Writing/Music** Students may want to set their lyrics to particular tunes. Encourage class performance of students' songs.
3. **Creative Writing** Remind students that a drill is as vulnerable as a person; it can break down, overheat, or lose parts.

Crossing the Curriculum

History

Have students research some aspect of the history of the railroad in the United States. Aspects that may interest students include
- the development of the New York City subway system (which opened in 1904 and was one of the first subways in the United States)
- the immigrant groups who built the railroads and subways (Chinese, Irish, and Italian)
- the scientific development of the early coal engines into modern high-speed trains
- the planning and completion of the transcontinental railroad. (Point out the photograph of the monument on p. 172, which commemorates the completion of the transcontinental railroad. Tell students that the completed railroad was called the Union Pacific.)

Have students work in small groups to select and research topics. They can use encyclopedias, history books, and the Internet. Encourage the use of visual and graphic aids.

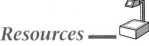

Resources

Elements of Literature
Sound Effects
For more instruction on sound effects, see *Literary Elements:*
• Transparency 3

Assessment
Formal Assessment
• Literary Elements Test, p. 43

Listening
Audio CD Library
• Disc 4, Track 3

Elements of Literature

This feature introduces students to a few of the various sound effects used in poetry—rhyme, alliteration, and meter. Students will learn what these terms mean and how to recognize them.

Mini-Lesson:
Sound Effects
Go through the examples on these pages with students. Make sure everyone understands the terms and their definitions. Then read aloud the first two stanzas of Edgar Allan Poe's "The Raven" or another poem that has emphatic rhyme and meter. Ask students to describe the rhymes, meter, and alliteration they hear.

POETRY: Sound Effects *by* John Malcolm Brinnin

Rhyme: Chiming Sounds

We all love **rhyme.** As soon as we hear or read words that sound alike and then notice that they occur in twos and threes, we know we are reading a poem in rhyme.

Rhyme can be as simple as the pairing of *moth* with *cloth* or a bit more complicated, like *antelope* matched with *cantaloupe.* Most rhymes are made by pairing the last word in one line with the last word in the next line. This is called **end rhyme.** Sometimes the last word in a line will be echoed by a word placed at the beginning or in the middle of the following line. This is called **internal rhyme.**

Rhyme makes the music in poetry, and it helps you to memorize lines, or stanzas, or even whole poems. Here is a stanza by a famous poet who uses rhymes to make even an invasion of rats seem funny.

And out of the houses the
  rats came tumbling;
Great rats, small rats, lean
  rats, brawny rats,
Brown rats, black rats,
  gray rats, tawny rats,
Grave old plodders, gay
  young friskers,
Fathers, mothers, uncles,
  cousins,
Cocking tails and pricking
  whiskers

—Robert Browning, from
  "The Pied Piper of
  Hamelin"

Repeating One Sound

Alliteration is the repetition of a single letter of the alphabet (as in "Peter Piper picked a peck of pickled peppers") or a combination of letters (as in "She sells seashells by the seashore"). It's just about the easiest form of repetition a poet can use. In "Cynthia in the Snow" the repeated faint hissing of *s* and *sh* sounds imitates the snow falling—"So beautiful it hurts."

Cynthia in the Snow

It SHUSHES.
It hushes
The loudness in the road.
It flitter-twitters,
And laughs away from me.
It laughs a lovely
  whiteness,
And whitely whirs away,
To be
Some otherwhere,
Still white as milk or shirts.
So beautiful it hurts.

—Gwendolyn Brooks

The Beat of a Poem

When poets are ready to put their ideas and feelings into words, they have to make a choice. They must ask themselves, Should this idea be expressed in lines regulated by a beat that sounds like ta-dum, ta-dum, ta-dum? Would it be expressed better in lines that sound like ordinary conversation, such as "Of course. You're right. I never thought of that. Give me a break. Let's drop the subject now."

Using Students' Strengths

Musical Learners
Have students find songs whose lyrics include examples of the sound effects discussed in this feature. Encourage them to look at familiar songs, such as Christmas carols, songs from musicals, or the national anthem. Have students play recordings of the songs in class. The class then can identify the literary elements and discuss their effect on the listener.

Applying the Element
Have each student choose a poem to read aloud in class. Students can choose any poem they like: a familiar nursery rhyme, a limerick, or a poem they have discovered in independent reading. If possible, bring in some poetry anthologies for students to look through.

Have each student read his or her poem aloud as the rest of the class listens. Have the class identify internal rhymes, end rhymes, alliteration, and meter. Encourage students to give their opinions on how well each poet used these elements to add meaning or feeling to his or her poem.

If they decide on a regular beat, all of the lines they write will be more or less the same length and have the same beat. This beat is called **meter**—a way of combining accented syllables with unaccented syllables to make a regular pattern. Robert Browning's lines on the rat invasion are written in meter. Read them aloud. You can't miss that beat.

If poets decide to ignore meter, they'll write in the loose groupings of words and phrases known as **free verse.** Just as there is no regular beat in conversation, there's no regular beat in free verse. Free verse is simply poetry written to sound like regular conversation.

How do you decide whether to write in meter or free verse? When you write a poem, you must trust yourself. Say what comes from your heart, in the form most natural to you.

Here is a poem in free verse about an unpoetic subject.

Good Hot Dogs

for Kiki

Fifty cents apiece
To eat our lunch
We'd run
Straight from school
Instead of home
Two blocks
Then the store
That smelled like steam
You ordered
Because you had the
   money
Two hot dogs and two
   pops for here
Everything on the hot dogs
Except pickle lily
Dash those hot dogs

Into buns and splash on
All that good stuff
Yellow mustard and onions
And french fries piled on
   top all
Rolled up in a piece of wax
Paper for us to hold hot
In our hands
Quarters on the counter
Sit down
Good hot dogs
We'd eat
Fast till there was nothing
   left
But salt and poppy seeds
   even
The little burnt tips
Of french fries
We'd eat
You humming
And me swinging my legs

—Sandra Cisneros

FROM THE EDITOR'S DESK
Because some states prohibit pictures of junk food in textbooks, we discussed whether we could illustrate this poem with a hot dog. We finally decided to go for it since this hot dog could actually be any kind of dog—even a tofu dog. Who knows?

Reaching All Students

Struggling Readers
Have students read aloud, in a group, the examples of rhymed and alliterative poetry and free verse shown on these pages. Let them *hear* the differences between the rhymed poems and Cisneros's free verse poem. If sound effects are not evident to students, encourage alternative readings of the same poem or offer to read the poem aloud yourself.

English Language Learners
Talk with students about sounds in English and how sounds are not always signaled by spellings. For example, sound out the words *though, throw, no,* and *toe,* all of which rhyme but are spelled differently. Then, sound out *through, bough,* and *cough,* which are spelled similarly but have different sounds. Have students list words that rhyme with *bead, word,* and *so.*

Advanced Learners
Ask students to choose a poem, either from their textbook or from independent reading, and have them identify the sound effects. How do the sound effects relate to the meaning of the poem? What effect do the sound effects have on the listener? Have students recite their poems to the class and follow with their responses.

OBJECTIVES
1. Read and interpret the poem
2. Identify onomatopoeia
3. Express understanding through creative writing or science

SKILLS
Literary
• Identify onomatopoeia
Writing
• Collect ideas for a how-to essay
• Write a poem
Science
• Research dinosaurs

Planning

• **Block Schedule**
  Block Scheduling Lesson Plans with Pacing Guide
• **Traditional Schedule**
  Lesson Plans Including Strategies for English-Language Learners
• **One-Stop Planner**
  CD-ROM with Test Generator

Before You Read

ANKYLOSAURUS

Make the Connection

Craze-osaurus

How about those dinosaurs? Sixty-five million years after they died out, they're still hot—the stars of blockbuster movies and best-selling books, the tops in toys and TV shows, and the list goes on.

Think-pair-share.

What do you think makes people so dinosaur crazy? Talk it over with a partner. Then, work together to draw a dinosaur outline like the one on this page. Label it with facts, phrases, questions,

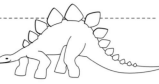

Why did they die out?

Ankylosaurus

Jack Prelutsky

A Clankity Clankity Clankity Clank!
Ankylosaurus° was built like a tank,
its hide was a fortress as sturdy as steel,
it tended to be an inedible meal.

5 B It was armored in front, it was armored behind,
there wasn't a thing on its minuscule mind,
C it waddled about on its four stubby legs,
nibbling on plants with a mouthful of pegs.

Ankylosaurus was best left alone,
10 D its tail was a cudgel of gristle and bone,
Clankity Clankity Clankity Clank!
Ankylosaurus was built like a tank.

2. **ankylosaurus** (aŋ'kə·lō·sôr'əs): heavily armored, short-legged dinosaur; also called ankylosaur.

180 MACHINE MANIA: PEOPLE AND TECHNOLOGY

 Resources: Print and Media

Reading
• *Graphic Organizers for Active Reading*, p. 14
• Audio CD Library
    Disc 4, Track 4

Elements of Literature
• *Literary Elements*
    Transparency 4
    Worksheet, p. 13

Assessment
• *Formal Assessment*, p. 36
• *Portfolio Management System*, p. 127
• *Test Generator (One-Stop Planner CD-ROM)*

Internet
• go.hrw.com (keyword: LE0 6-3)

and buzzwords that explain what makes dinosaurs fascinating favorites.

Quickwrite

What's your favorite dinosaur? Is it the meat-eating tyrannosaur? the gentle giant brontosaur? Briefly describe the dinosaur you like best.

Elements of Literature

Onomatopoeia: Crash! Bang! Clank!

Clank! The sound of that word—*clank*—tells you just what it means. That's because *clank* is a word, like *bark*, *buzz*, *roar*, and *hiss*, whose sound echoes its sense. In "Ankylosaurus," Jack Prelutsky uses *clankity clank*

as a sound effect that makes his monster sound like an army tank.

Onomatopoeia is the use of a word whose sound imitates or suggests its meaning.

For more on Onomatopoeia, see the Handbook of Literary Terms.

MEET THE WRITER

"There Are No Rules"

Jack Prelutsky (1940–   ) didn't like the poetry he read when he was growing up in New York City. "What about poems about the New York Yankees?" he'd ask himself. "Or my friend, the guy who would eat anything if you gave him enough money?"

Now, as one of today's most popular children's poets, he writes poems that come out of his own experience and imagination. He carries a notebook with him everywhere and constantly writes down ideas. About his note taking, he says:

66 I don't know ahead of time which of my notes are going to turn into a poem. A note can be anything. It can be a funny name, a joke, something I overheard, an idea that popped into my mind, a rhyme, an idea for a new game—there are no rules. 99

ANKYLOSAURUS 181

Summary

In an extended metaphor, the poet compares the ankylosaurus to an armored tank.

Resources

Listening

Audio CD Library

A recording of this poem is provided in the *Audio CD Library*:
• Disc 4, Track 4

Ⓐ Elements of Literature

Onomatopoeia

❓ Ask students to identify the internal rhyme in these lines. [*Clankity/Clank; Ankylosaurus/tank*] What does this sound effect contribute to the poem? [Possible answers: It makes the lines easier to remember; it echoes the sound the animal makes when it moves.]

Ⓑ Vocabulary Note

Latin Roots

❓ Ask students to define *minuscule*. What similar words does it look like? [It means "very small"; similar words include *minimal, miniature, minute, minus,* and *minor*.] Point out the Latin root *min-,* which always indicates "smaller" or "less." What does this word tell you about the dinosaur's intelligence? [It is scanty.]

Ⓒ Reading Skills and Strategies

Using Context Clues

❓ What are the dinosaur's "pegs"? [its teeth] What context clues tell you that? [The pegs are in his mouth, and he uses them to nibble.]

Ⓓ Vocabulary

Exact Meanings

❓ What is a *cudgel*? [It is a short, heavy club.]

Reaching All Students

Struggling Readers

Be sure students can pronounce the dinosaur's name. Have them practice saying it, using the pronunciation guide at the bottom of the page. It will help them to know that the first syllable of the name rhymes with "clank" and "tank."

English Language Learners

Although this poem is short, it includes some difficult vocabulary. Have students note any unfamiliar words as they read the poem. Encourage them to work with partners to

define the words and then to use a dictionary to define any words neither partner could identify. Partners can quiz one another on the new words until they both know all of them.

Advanced Learners

If possible, show "The Rites of Spring" segment from the film *Fantasia*. This segment shows the evolution of the dinosaurs and how they lived. Students will enjoy the music and animation. Challenge them to identify as many dinosaurs as they can.

BROWSING IN THE FILES

Writers on Writing. "I try to tell kids that poetry is not boring or a chore," says Jack Prelutsky. "It's not 'up there with the angels.' It is a natural continuation of everything else. It is one way a human being can tell another human being what's going on inside."

MAKING MEANINGS

First Thoughts

1. Students' pictures should suggest both dinosaurs and tanks.

Shaping Interpretations

2. An armored tank would make these noises because of its metal parts.
3. The poem is written in a ONE-two-three ONE-two-three rhythm. It suggests one heavy step followed by a little shaking of the earth, then another heavy step, and so on.
4. Possible words: *clumsy, heavy, slow, huge, thick, stupid, dangerous.*

Grading Timesaver

Rubrics for each Choices assignment appear on p. 127 in the *Portfolio Management System.*

CHOICES: Building Your Portfolio

1. **Writer's Notebook** Students should include research as part of the process. The diorama makers must know the kinds of terrains the dinosaurs lived in.
2. **Creative Writing** Encourage students to read their poems aloud in class. This will extend everyone's vocabulary of onomatopoeic words.
3. **Science/Making a Time Line** Ask the school librarian to suggest books on dinosaurs for information and for the origins of names.

Understanding Influences of Other Languages on the Spelling of English

Students should understand that knowledge of Greek roots can help them figure out the spelling of a word, as well as its meaning. For example, some students might be tempted to spell *hydrogen* as *hidrogen.* If they know that *hydro–* comes from the Greek word for "water," they will be able to see why it is not spelled with an *i.* Ask students to think of other words with *hydro–* (*hydrology, hydrophobia*). They might also think of words with *astro–, eco–, hypo–,* and *–vor–.*

MAKING MEANINGS

• First Thoughts

[visualize]   1. Draw a picture of what you see when you read this poem.

Shaping Interpretations

[analyze]   2. How do the *clankity clank's*—the **onomatopoeia** in lines 1 and 11—fit with the poem's other images of the ankylosaur?

[analyze]   3. Read the poem aloud to feel its beat. Pay special attention to the **rhythm** of the "Clankity Clankity Clankity Clank!" lines. How do they help you "see" the way the dinosaur moves?

[respond]   4. If you had to pick one word to describe the ankylosaur, what would it be?

CHOICES: Building Your Portfolio

Writer's Notebook

1. Collecting Ideas for a How-To Essay

If you have been to a museum of natural history, you might have seen the dioramas showing prehistoric animals in their natural habitats. How would you make a diorama that shows dinosaurs and where they lived? Collect your information in a chart:

How to Build a Dinosaur Diorama

Steps	Materials	Special Terms

Creative Writing

2. My Pick-osaurus

Look back at the Quickwrite you wrote about your favorite dinosaur (page 181). Develop these notes into a poem about this fascinating creature. Consider starting, as Prelutsky does, with a string of onomatopoeic words—that is, words whose sound imitates their meaning. For example, you might start a poem about a tyrannosaur this way:

Slash, crash, stomp, crunch
Tyrannosaur is eating lunch.

Chomp, munch, rip, tear—
What's he gnashing? *He* doesn't care.

Science/ Making a Time Line

3. Dino-Facts

Did all dinosaurs live on the earth at the same time? Research the facts and create a time line to share with your classmates.

For fun, include the meaning of each dinosaur name. *Dinosaur* comes from two **Greek roots,** *dino-,* meaning "monstrous," and *-saur,* meaning "lizard." What do you think *tyrannosaur* means?

Using Students' Strengths

Visual Learners

As visual learners read the poem, they might benefit by filling in the graphic organizer located in the *Graphic Organizers for Active Reading,* p. 14.

Naturalist Learners

Ask students how they feel about a living creature being compared to a machine. How does Prelutsky seem to feel about the natural world versus manufactured objects? Do students agree or disagree with him? Do students ever look at things in the natural world and mentally connect them to machines or humanly created objects? If so, what comparisons have they made? Have students choose partners to discuss their reactions with.

Elements of Literature

POETRY: Seeing Likenesses *by* John Malcolm Brinnin

Poetry lives and breathes because poets make especially imaginative comparisons— they have a special talent for seeing one thing in terms of something else, something very different. We call these comparisons between unlike things **figures of speech.** There are three main figures of speech: metaphors, similes, and personification.

Metaphors and Similes

"My baby sister's a doll," you might say, comparing your sister's size and sweetness to the perfection of a doll. At another time you might say, "My brother is a rat," comparing your poor brother to the nastiest little creature you can think of. In both cases you would be making a kind of comparison called **metaphor**—a form of comparison that directly compares two unlike things. A metaphor wastes no time in getting to the point.

On the other hand, if you had said, "My sister is *like* a doll," or, with a sudden change of heart, "My brother's as good *as* gold," you would in each case be making a **simile**—a form of comparison in which one thing is compared to another unlike thing by using specific words of comparison like *like*, *as*, and *resembles*.

Poets try to find unusual metaphors and similes. Christina Rossetti, when she was in love, used a simile and wrote, "My heart is like a singing bird." If she had made a metaphor, she would have written, "My heart *is* a singing bird." Emily Dickinson, thinking about the problems fame can bring, said "Fame is a bee." If she had made a simile, she would have said "Fame is *like* a bee."

Personification: Making the World Human

One of the most familiar kinds of comparison is **personification**—that is, speaking of something that is not human as if it had human abilities and human reactions. For instance, a

(continued on next page)

Peanuts reprinted by permission of United Feature Syndicate, Inc.

ELEMENTS OF LITERATURE: POETRY 183

Resources

Elements of Literature
Figures of Speech
For more instruction on figures of speech, see *Literary Elements:*
- Transparency 4

Assessment
Formal Assessment
- Literary Elements Test, p. 44

Elements of Literature

This feature introduces students to the three common figures of speech— metaphors, similes, and personification. Students will learn what these terms mean and how to distinguish them.
Mini-Lesson:
Figures of Speech
In this Peanuts cartoon, Lucy actually uses an ordinary comparison here, not a figure of speech. Comparing the batter's swing with her grandmother's swing is insulting, but it is not an imaginative simile. If Lucy had compared the batter's swing to the swing of a rusty gate (using the word *like*), she would have been using a simile. To qualify as a simile a comparison must be made between two things that are unlike— except in the way the poet points out to us. Challenge students to come up with a list of figures of speech Lucy might have used instead. Urge them to use their imaginations and make their comparisons as striking, original, and descriptive as possible. List students' figures of speech on the board, and have the class identify each as a metaphor, a personification, or a simile.

Using Students' Strengths

Visual Learners
Ask students to explain how figures of speech increase the visual impact of a text. How does a line like "Ankylosaurus was built like a tank" help them visualize the dinosaur? What does this line do that a line like "Ankylosaurus had very thick skin" does not? As they put their ideas and reactions into words, students will realize how much figures of speech enrich the impact of writing.

Applying the Element

Present students with the following figures of speech, and have them explain what is compared with what. Then, have them identify each figure as metaphor, personification, or simile. Have them explain their answers.

1. The budget went down the drain today. [metaphor]
2. The government is under fire from all sides. [metaphor]
3. The president put a lid on news leaks. [metaphor]
4. "The world will little note nor long remember what we say here, but it can never forget what they did here." (Abraham Lincoln) [personification]
5. "The fog comes on little cat feet." (Carl Sandburg) [metaphor]
6. "They that wait upon the Lord shall renew their strength; they shall mount up with wings as eagles...." (The Bible, Isaiah 40:31) [simile]

(continued from previous page)

newscaster might begin the six o'clock report by saying "Today the White House turned its back on the very last chance of relief the Hill was hoping for." Here, the White House personifies the presidency; and the Hill, or Capitol Hill, personifies Congress. What at first seems silly—a house being nasty to a hill—makes sense when we understand personification.

Here is another common example of personification: "The sky wept buckets all day long." In this example, a natural, nonhuman thing—the sky—is spoken of as though it had human abilities and human feelings. Isn't this description more interesting than a plain statement of fact, such as "Yesterday it rained for hours"?

Any of us can turn almost anything into imaginative language. After all, each of us has "a touch of the poet." This is partly what makes us human.

Your Poem, Man . . .

unless there's one thing seen
suddenly against another—a parsnip
sprouting for a President, or
hailstones melting in an ashtray—
nothing really happens. It takes
surprise and wild connections,
doesn't it? A walrus chewing
on a ballpoint pen. Two blue tail-
lights on Tyrannosaurus Rex. Green
cheese teeth. Maybe what we wanted
least. Or most. Some unexpected
pleats. Words that never knew
each other till right now. Plug us
into the wrong socket and see
what blows—or what lights up.
Try
      untried
            circuitry,
new
      fuses.
Tell it like it never really was,
man,
and maybe we can see it
like it is.

          —Edward Lueders

184 MACHINE MANIA: PEOPLE AND TECHNOLOGY

Reaching All Students

Struggling Readers

Have students look back at "Ankylosaurus" and identify the comparison Prelutsky makes in it. How do the poem's similes and metaphors help students understand what the animal looks like and how it moves? In the cartoon on p. 183, how does Lucy's comparison help students understand what kind of swing the batter has made? Encourage students to write their own sentences with metaphors and similes.

English Language Learners

Have each student choose a pet animal or an everyday object and write several figures of speech describing it—at least one of each of the three types they have studied in this lesson.

Then, have students share their results with classmates, who should comment on their effectiveness.

Advanced Learners

Have students discuss Lueders's poem. Their initial step should be to state what they think is the poem's main point. [Figures of speech have the power to help us see the world in new, fresh ways; they help us see how things in the world are connected.] What do Lueders's examples help them see or understand? Artistic students should illustrate this highly visual poem.

Before You Read

THE TOASTER / THE SIDEWALK RACER / THINGS TO DO IF YOU ARE A SUBWAY / STEAM SHOVEL

Make the Connection

Machine Biology

People have a way of talking about machines as if they were alive. Have you ever heard someone say that a car's engine "purrs" or "roars" or "hums" or "sings"?

Gearing up. Look over pages 186–190. What machines are described?

1. In a group, write a list of those machines and then brainstorm to add other machines to the list.

2. As a group, choose a machine.

3. Draw a gear diagram like the one below to explore your ideas about that machine.

4. Decide what living creature the machine would be if it came to life.

Quickwrite

Imagine that you're one of the machines on the brainstorming list. Write about yourself on a sheet of paper, but don't mention your name. See if a classmate can guess what you are from what you've written.

Elements of Literature

Metaphors: Anything Is Possible

In the imagination anything is possible. In two of the poems in this collection, machines become fierce, roaring, snorting animals.

Metaphor is what the writers of these poems use to identify the machinery with something alive. Such is the power of metaphor that you might never look at a steam shovel again without seeing a dinosaur. Notice how these poets hang on to their metaphors—they extend their comparisons all the way to the ends of their poems.

> **A** metaphor is a comparison between two unlike things in which one thing becomes another thing. An **extended metaphor** carries the comparison through an entire poem.
>
> *For more on Metaphor, see pages 183–184 and the Handbook of Literary Terms.*

For more on Metaphor, see pages 183–184 and the Handbook of Literary Terms.

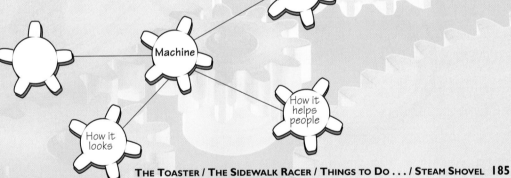

Summary ∎

In these four poems, a toaster and a subway train are compared to dragons, a skateboard rider to a sailor, and a steam shovel to a dinosaur.

Resources

Listening
Audio CD Library
A recording of these poems is provided in the *Audio CD Library:*
• Disc 4, Tracks 5, 6, 7, 8

Viewing and Representing
Fine Art Transparency
A fine art transparency of Arnold Jacobs's *Reflections: Tribute to Our Iron Skywalkers* can be used with this selection. See the *Viewing and Representing Transparencies and Worksheets:*
• Transparency 8
• Worksheet, p, 32

A **Elements of Literature**
Metaphors
❓ What is the "Dragon" in reality? How would you know this without looking at the picture? [It's a toaster. The poem says the dragon toasts bread, and it is "at my elbow," so it's an appliance on the counter or table rather than a stove or fireplace. The title tells us what the poem is about.]

B **Critical Thinking**
Challenging the Text
❓ Is a dragon a good metaphor for a toaster? Why or why not? [Possible answers: Yes, dragons breathe fire just as a toaster does; no, dragons are usually fierce and warlike, not tame or cooperative enough to make toast for someone.]

The Toaster
William Jay Smith

A silver-scaled Dragon with jaws flaming red
Sits at my elbow and toasts my bread.
I hand him fat slices, and then, one by one,
He hands them back when he sees they are done.

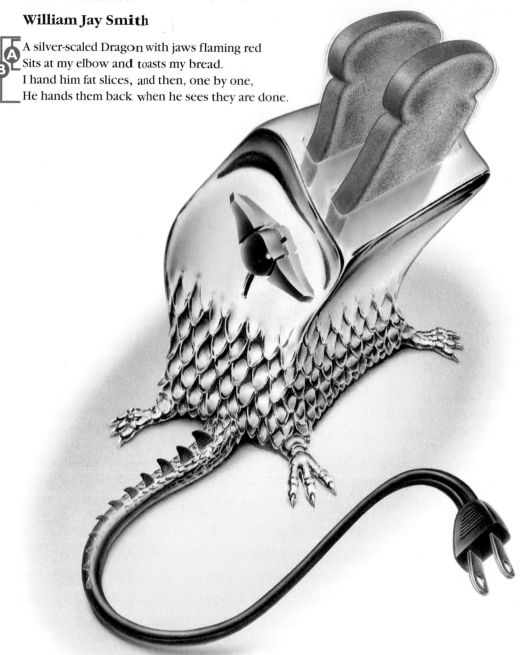

186 MACHINE MANIA: PEOPLE AND TECHNOLOGY

Reaching All Students

Struggling Readers
Have students make two-column charts, one for each poem. The columns for the first poem should be headed "Toaster" and "Dragon"; for the second, "Skateboard" and "Sailor"; for the third, "Subway" and "Dragon"; for the fourth, "Steam Shovel" and "Dinosaur." Before reading the poems, students can list words or phrases in each column that they associate with its heading. For example, words and phrases for "Dragon" might include "fierce," "breathes fire,"

and "imaginary animal." After reading the poems, students can decide whether the poets' comparisons are effective and explain why they do or do not think so.

English Language Learners
Have students choose partners to read the poems aloud with. Students should take turns reading and listening to all four poems. Partners should make sure they can both identify all four comparisons.

Advanced Learners
Have students locate and look at picture books with illustrations of dragons. What everyday objects besides toasters and steam shovels might dragons be compared to? Have students write their own short poems, each one containing an extended metaphor comparing a dragon to some inanimate object or machine. Students may want to illustrate their work and display it in class.

Ⓐ Elements of Literature
Alliteration
❓ Have students identify the repeated sound in ll. 1–7. Why did the poet repeat this particular sound? [The *s* sound is repeated. It echoes the sound of the wheels rushing over the sidewalk or street. It also suggests the sound of rushing water, which strengthens the comparison to a boat and sailor.]

Ⓑ Critical Thinking
Expressing an Opinion
❓ Whom or what does the pronoun "I" refer to? Explain. [It refers to the skater; he or she is a "human automobile."]

The Sidewalk Racer
or
On the Skateboard
Lillian Morrison

　　　Skimming
　　　an asphalt sea
　　　I swerve, I curve, I
　　　sway; I speed to whirring Ⓐ
5　　　sound an inch above the
　　　ground; I'm the sailor
　　　and the sail, I'm the
　　　driver and the wheel
　　　I'm the one and only
10　　　single engine Ⓑ
　　　human auto
　　　mobile.

THE SIDEWALK RACER **187**

Skill Link

Analyzing Illustrations
The contrasting styles of the illustrations for these poems provide a good opportunity for students to evaluate visual interpretations of texts.

Activities
1. Have students study each illustration before they read the poem that goes with it. Have

them write down their reactions to each illustration. What does it show? Do they like it? Why or why not?
2. Have students read each poem and compare and contrast it with the illustration. How well does the illustration capture the image in the text? How well does it present the metaphor in the poem?

3. Have students think about how they would have illustrated each poem. Ask them to choose one of the four poems and either draw a picture to illustrate it or describe their ideal illustration in words. Post students' illustrations in the classroom. Have students who wrote verbal descriptions read their descriptions aloud.

A Appreciating Language
Vivid Verbs
? Point out that every line of the poem starts with a verb. Why do you think the poet made this choice? [Possible responses: to help characterize the dragon as an active animal; to show the dragon's energy; to emphasize the speed and noise of the subway.]

B English Language Learners
Onomatopoeia
Have students say the word *zoom* aloud. Explain that its sound and meaning are closely related. *Zoom* is a word that was invented to imitate a sound. In this poem, *zoom* represents the sound of a speeding train.

C Cultural Connections
Express Trains
Explain to students that when used to describe a train, the word *express* means that the train "skips stops." The opposite of *express* in this sense is *local*, referring to a train that makes all stops on its route. Some subway systems, like the one in New York City, include both express and local tracks; the express trains stop only at major streets and transfer stations, while the locals make all the stops. Other subway systems, like the one in Washington, D.C., have only one set of tracks, and all the trains make all the stops.

Things to Do If You Are a Subway
Bobbi Katz

A Pretend you are a dragon.
Live in underground caves.
Roar about underneath the city.
Swallow piles of people.
Spit them out at the next station.
B Zoom through the darkness.
C Be an express.
Go fast.
Make as much noise as you please.

Using Students' Strengths

Visual Learners
As visual learners read the poems, they might benefit by filling in the graphic organizer located in the *Graphic Organizers for Active Reading,* p. 15.

Auditory Learners
Have volunteers read the four poems aloud. After each poem is read, have the class discuss how hearing the poem helps the listener appreciate the comparison the poet has made. Which images sound especially striking? Which words and phrases leap out at students because they like the sound of them? Do any of the poems look better on the page than they sound when read aloud? Which ones? Why?

LITERATURE AND REAL LIFE

Underground Poetry

The grim, noisy concrete-and-steel tunnels of the New York City subway are the last place you'd expect to find something as delicate and quiet as a poem. Imagine yourself, then, in a crowded subway train. As you scan the overhead ads about chewing gum and jeans, this phrase captures your attention: "Love is a word, another kind of open." You stop to think about these strange, beautiful words by the poet Audre Lorde, and the subway train becomes filled with magic and wonder.

Such moments of reading pleasure have become more and more common since the Metropolitan Transit Authority, in collaboration with the Poetry Society of America, began putting poems in New York City's subways and buses. The program, called Poetry in Motion, places two poems every month in all of New York's 5,900 subway cars and 3,700 buses.

Although the subways normally feature the work of professional poets, the MTA and the New York *Daily News* sought out amateur talent by cosponsoring a public poetry-writing contest. After heroically sifting through ten thousand entries, the *Daily News* selected winners in three categories—seventeen and under, adult, and sixty-five and over—all of which have appeared in the subways and buses. Here is the work of one of the winners, a fifteen-year-old student:

POETRY IN MOTION

Myself

So small, disheveled,
I never knew it was there.
Always, in New York
I must be like others,
Like the cool kids.
That is why I didn't know it existed –
That I could be...myself.

Abigail Friedman
Winner of DAILY NEWS Poetry Contest - Youth Division

MTA **New York City Transit**
In cooperation with the Poetry Society of America

THE TOASTER / THE SIDEWALK RACER / THINGS TO DO . . . / STEAM SHOVEL 189

Getting Students Involved

Cooperative Learning

Whose Turn Is It? Ask students to work in small groups to invent board games based on some of the comparisons in the poems. For example, students might design a subway system on the board, with each player's marker representing a dragon; advances may be made by answering questions about figures of speech, poetry, or other language arts–related topics.

Encourage students to use their imaginations and to make the boards as artistic and the games as much fun as possible. Set aside some class time for students to play the games.

Machine Skit. Organize students into groups of four to write, rehearse, and perform skits in which all four main characters of the poems—the toaster, the skateboard rider, the subway train, and the steam shovel—meet to work out a problem. Students may want to use the premise that each character can disguise itself as the animal or human being suggested in its poem. What problem will the machines face? How will they solve it? How will the disguises help? Have students perform their skits for the class.

Steam Shovel

Charles Malam

A The dinosaurs are not all dead.
I saw one raise its iron head
To watch me walking down the road
Beyond our house today.
5 Its jaws were dripping with a load
Of earth and grass that it had cropped.
It must have heard me where I stopped,
Snorted white steam my way,
B And stretched its long neck out to see,
10 And chewed, and grinned quite amiably!°

10. **amiably:** in a friendly way.

190 MACHINE MANIA: PEOPLE AND TECHNOLOGY

A Reading Skills and Strategies
  Visualizing
❓ Why might the poet think of a dinosaur when he sees a steam shovel? [Possible responses: It is big, slow, clumsy, and powerful; it has a long "neck" like a brontosaurus; it has huge "jaws" like a Tyrannosaurus rex.]

B Critical Thinking
  Drawing Conclusions
❓ How might the poet feel about dinosaurs? Why do you think so? [Possible responses: He likes them, because he describes this "dinosaur" as amiable, and it doesn't try to hurt him; he feels friendly toward them, because he characterizes this "dinosaur" as gentle and friendly.]

Making the Connections

Connecting to the Theme: "Machine Mania: People and Technology"
After students have read the poems, discuss the collection's theme. How do these poets view machines? Why might they think of machines as things to compare animals to? Why do students think the poets chose animals that are either extinct or imaginary? Do everyday animals lend themselves to comparison with machines? Students can share their ideas in a class discussion.

T190

MEET THE WRITERS

"Poetry Always Comes from Inside"

William Jay Smith

William Jay Smith (1918–) has Choctaw ancestors on his mother's side. His father was a corporal in the Sixth Infantry Band. Smith attended Washington University in St. Louis, Columbia University, Oxford University (where he was a Rhodes scholar), and the University of Florence. He has been a college teacher, a translator, and a member of the Vermont legislature.

Lillian Morrison

Lillian Morrison (1917–) was a librarian for almost fifty years. At the New York Public Library she was an expert in books and services for young adults. Besides writing poetry, she's always been interested in jazz, dancing, and sports—all kinds of sports. She has written so many poems about sports that she may hold the world record for it. In an introduction to *Sprints and Distances* (1965), one of her poetry collections, Morrison said:

❝ There is an affinity between sports and poetry. Each is a form of play. . . . Each has the power to take us out of ourselves and at times to lift us above ourselves. They go together naturally. . . . ❞

"I've been a fashion editor, social worker, and full time mom," says **Bobbi Katz** (1933–). Trained as an art historian, she's also taught and run a weekly radio program called *Arts in Action*. Now she works as a writer of fiction and poetry.

❝ My poetry always comes from inside—from my deep need to express a feeling. The child in me writes picture books. My fiction is almost not mine. The characters emerge and seem to tell their own stories. Even when writing within rigid boundaries that editors sometimes set, I find the characters become very real to me. I care what happens to them. ❞

Bobbi Katz

Charles Malam (1906–) was born in South Reygate, Vermont. He has written poems and one-act plays. His poems tend to look at everyday objects, such as steam shovels, in a light, playful way.

BROWSING IN THE FILES

Writers on Writing. "Children's poems must not only have a lilt to them; they must be graphic," writes William Jay Smith. "Children think in images, and their poet, to capture these images, must choose words that convey color and movement. Children's poems are never static but filled with action. Nouns and verbs predominate; adjectives are used sparingly. . . . Precision and concreteness are, of course, along with musicality, the chief demands on the children's poet."

About the Author. Lillian Morrison, the daughter of Russian immigrants, grew up in Jersey City, New Jersey. "Our playground was the street," she recalls. "We jumped rope, roller-skated, took turns racing around the block, timing each other, and played almost every kind of ball game. . . . Many of the poems in my book *The Sidewalk Racer* came out of the experiences in those years." Although she always liked reading and listening to poetry, Morrison did not begin writing until she was in her twenties.

Professional Notes

Carl Sandburg on Poetry

In 1928, the young poet Carl Sandburg published a list of "Tentative (First Model) Definitions of Poetry." Here are some excerpts:

"Poetry is the journal of a sea animal living on land, wanting to fly the air.

Poetry is a series of explanations of life, fading off into horizons too swift for explanations.

Poetry is a search for syllables to shoot at the barriers of the unknown and the unknowable.

Poetry is a dance music measuring buck-and-wing follies along with the gravest and stateliest dead-marches.

Poetry is a mock of a cry at finding a million dollars and a mock of a laugh at losing it.

Poetry is the opening and closing of a door, leaving those who look through to guess about what is seen during a moment.

Poetry is the capture of a picture, a song, or a flair, in a deliberate prism of words."

Share these excerpts with students. Have them add their own definitions of poetry to the list.

Student to Student

In this short student poem, a lawn mower is personified as an angry, menacing presence.

(A) Reading Skills and Strategies

Comparing and Contrasting

❓ How is this poem like and unlike the other four in this selection? [It also compares a machine to a living creature. However, it does not compare the machine to a specific animal.]

MAKING MEANINGS

First Thoughts

1. Encourage students to give their reading partners some thoughtful criticism and to accept helpful suggestions in return. After students have worked with their partners, encourage them to read aloud their favorite poems for the whole class.

Shaping Interpretations

2. Possible answers: toaster—efficient; subway—exuberant; steam shovel—friendly.

3. Possible answers: metaphor—"Steam Shovel" because its comparison is the most original; rhyme—"Steam Shovel" because its rhymes are not obvious; alliteration—"Sidewalk Racer" because the repeating *s* sounds echo the movement of a skateboard; onomatopoeia—"Subway" because sound is combined with action verbs, such as *roar, spit,* and *zoom*; mental images—"Subway" because of its vivid verbs.

Extending the Text

4. Possible answers: A refrigerator is the most helpful, because it keeps food from spoiling; a dentist's drill is the most fearful, because it can cause pain.

Student to Student

(A) The Lawn Mower

The lawn mower
roared with
sourness—
its dark
oil fuming
out with anger;
its jumpy
motion hardened
in stillness

—Taunya Woo
Washington Middle School
Olympia, Washington

MAKING MEANINGS
THE TOASTER / THE SIDEWALK RACER /
THINGS TO DO . . . / STEAM SHOVEL

First Thoughts

[interpret]
1. Choose your favorite poem and read it aloud to a partner. Show by your voice and movements how each machine moves and sounds.

Shaping Interpretations

[respond]
2. The machines in these poems have personalities. What words would you use to describe each of these creatures?

[analyze]
3. Suppose you're the judge of a poetry contest. Of the four poems on pages 186–190 and the one on this page, which would you give first prize for **metaphor**? for **rhyme**? for **alliteration**? for **onomatopoeia**? for **mental images**?

Extending the Text

[connect]
4. Of all the machines that have played a part in your life, which one has helped you the most? Which do you fear or resist the most strongly? Compare your thoughts with those of your classmates.

192 MACHINE MANIA: PEOPLE AND TECHNOLOGY

Assessing Learning

Check Test: Short Answers

1. What two machines are compared to a dragon? [a toaster and a subway train]
2. What does Charles Malam think of when he sees a steam shovel? [a dinosaur]
3. What does the "dragon" in the "The Toaster" poem do? [It toasts bread.]
4. What does the subway "dragon" do to its riders? [It swallows them up and then spits them out at the next station.]
5. How does the "dinosaur" react to the person passing by? [It "looks" at the person, stretches its "neck" out to see him, and "grins."]

Observation Assessment

Listen and observe as students read the poems aloud. Rate students from 1 to 4 (with 4 being the highest rating) in the following categories:

- pronunciation
- attention to punctuation
- dramatic interpretation
- clear understanding of the poem's meaning

CHOICES: Building Your Portfolio

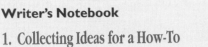

Writer's Notebook

1. Collecting Ideas for a How-To Essay

Picture yourself using a toaster to make breakfast. Think of something like skateboarding that you like to do outside. See yourself playing a team sport like soccer. Think about how you might teach another person to do something you do well. Jot down a list of steps. Beside each step, note the materials or equipment you need for it.

> **How to Make a Tortilla Pizza**
> 1. Spread cheese on one half of a tortilla. (tortilla, shredded cheese)
> 2. Fold tortilla in half.
> 3. Spread a little oil in frying pan and heat tortilla on both sides. (frying pan, cooking oil, spatula)

Creative Writing

2. Who Am I?

If you were to remove the titles from four of the five poems you just read, you'd have four riddles. Try writing riddles in which various machines describe themselves. In each riddle, for example, the machine might tell what it does, how it feels, and who its friends are. Your Quickwrite notes for page 185 may help you get started. Each riddle should be spoken by an "I." Try for a few rhymes. End each riddle with "Who am I?" Here's an easy one:

> I roar along the floor.
> I swallow balls of dust.

I'm never on a diet.
Click! I'm quiet.
Who am I?

Creative Writing

3. Sounds Like

Words that sound alike but have multiple meanings and spellings—such as *too*, *to*, and *two*—are called **homophones**. Several words in these poems—*red*, *sail*, *raise*, and *through*, for example—have homophones. (Think of *read*, *sale*, *rays*, and *threw*.) Brainstorm to come up with your own list of homophones, and then try writing a poem that contains at least three pairs of homophones. Here is an example:

> Once a dragon met eight knights. The dragon ate for seven nights.
>
> Now the knights are one or less. The dragon won the fight, I guess.

Art

4. It's a Subway! It's a Dragon! It's a Supermachine!

For one poem, create art to show the machine transformed so that it has taken on the personality of a living creature. You could draw a picture or make a collage or sculpture to illustrate the poem.

Rubrics for each Choices assignment appear on p. 128 in the *Portfolio Management System*.

CHOICES: Building Your Portfolio

1. **Writer's Notebook** Suggest that students choose something they do well that is relatively easy to explain.
2. **Creative Writing** Reassure students that their riddles need not rhyme; however, they should use vivid figures of speech and avoid clichés. Students can have fun trying to guess one another's riddles.
3. **Creative Writing** Suggest that students check their lists of homophones in a dictionary to make sure they are accurate.
4. **Art** Students can use the illustrations in their textbooks for inspiration. Post their finished work in the classroom.

Crossing the Curriculum

Art

Have students choose any machine they like and decide what kind of animal it resembles, either because of its appearance or because of the way it works. Have them draw or paint pictures showing the machine taking on the animal's personality and physical characteristics. For example, on p. 186, the toaster's plug becomes the dragon's tail, and the slots for bread become its mouth. Post students' work in the classroom.

OBJECTIVE
Learn strategies for reading poetry

Reading Skills and Strategies

This feature focuses on specific strategies, which can be immediately applied to the following selection, giving students the opportunity to practice each strategy using new material.

Mini-Lesson:
Reading Poetry

Go over the list of seven steps with students. Then have each student choose a poem, either from the textbook or from independent reading. Students may want to work on one of the poems they read on pp. 178–179. Students should apply each of the seven steps to their poems. After they finish this activity, have them write brief paragraphs evaluating these steps. Did the steps enrich their understanding of the poem?

Reading Skills and Strategies

STRATEGIES FOR READING POETRY

Don't let this happen to you:
There once was a man in our
  nation
Who suffered a bad situation.
  The poem he read
  Made no sense in his head
Because he ignored
  punctuation.

Seven Easy Steps to Reading Poetry

Punctuation is just one thing to look for when you're reading poems. Follow these guidelines, and poetry will come alive for you:

1. Read the poem aloud at least once. You'll find it easier to make sense of a poem if you hear how it sounds.

2. Pay attention to punctuation. Stop briefly at commas and semicolons, and stop longer after periods. If you see dashes, expect sudden shifts in thought. If you see no punctuation at the end of a line, don't pause.

3. Feel the poem's rhythm. Poetry has a special rhythmic sound, like music.

4. Poets choose their words very carefully. Use context clues to figure out the meanings of unfamiliar words. (Don't resist using a dictionary if you're stuck.) Do any words have more than one meaning?

5. Poets use comparisons. If you're reading a poem in which snowflakes are described as if they were insects, let the comparison create a picture in your mind. Think about *why* the poet chose *this* comparison. How does it make you feel?

6. Think about what the poem is saying to you. Does it relate to anything in your own life? Does it give you a new way of looking at something?

7. If you like the poem, memorize. Now it's yours.

CALVIN AND HOBBES. © Watterson. Reprinted with permission of UNIVERSAL PRESS SYNDICATE. All rights reserved.

Apply the strategy on the next page.

194 MACHINE MANIA: PEOPLE AND TECHNOLOGY

Reaching All Students

Struggling Readers
As students work on the Mini-Lesson, have them concentrate on Step 6. How does making connections to their own lives help them appreciate poetry? How does it affect their opinions about or interest in the poets? Do shared experiences make students wish they could talk with the poets? Encourage students to talk about why they like poems they can relate to their own lives.

English Language Learners
During their work on the Mini-Lesson, have students pay special attention to Steps 2, 4, and 5. Then, suggest that each student select a poem he or she likes and commit it to memory (Step 7) for a later recitation for the entire class.

Before You Read

THE HILL MYNAH / THE HUMMINGBIRD

Make the Connection

The Beauty of the Beasts

The poems you've just read are about some remarkable machines that make our life easier—or more fun. Poets looked at those machines and compared them to animals. Now, read two poems that look at birds and compare *them* to machines. It all goes to show you—in our imaginations, all things are possible.

Quickwrite

Think of an animal you have observed. Then, think of how that animal is like a machine. Maybe your cat purrs like an idling motor. Maybe your fish is like a submarine. If you let your imagination go, you can think of many more comparisons.

Reading Skills and Strategies

Reading Poetry: It's Different from Prose

You'll enjoy these two poems most if you read them aloud. For help in reading them, follow the steps for reading poetry outlined on page 194. Listen to the sounds in each poem. How does the poet make you hear the sounds each bird makes?

MEET THE WRITER*

A Mind That Lives in a New Territory Called Imagination

Douglas Florian (1950–   ) won his first art prize when he was ten years old. The son of an artist, Florian decided to become an artist himself when he was fifteen. Florian has created books of funny poems about animals and one devoted to insects—including termites, ticks, and locusts—called *Insectlopedia* (Harcourt). He illustrates his books with watercolors and pen-and-ink drawings.

*. . . AND ARTIST

OBJECTIVES
The Hill Mynah / The Hummingbird
1. Read and interpret the poems
2. Develop skills for reading poetry
3. Express understanding through creative writing

SKILLS
Reading
- Develop skills for reading poetry

Writing
- Collect ideas for a how-to essay
- Write a poem

Planning

- **Block Schedule**
  Block Scheduling Lesson Plans with Pacing Guide
- **Traditional Schedule**
  Lesson Plans Including Strategies for English-Language Learners
- **One-Stop Planner**
  CD-ROM with Test Generator

  Resources: Print and Media

Reading
- *Graphic Organizers for Active Reading*, p. 16
- *Audio CD Library*
  Disc 4, Tracks 9, 10

Assessment
- *Formal Assessment*, p. 39
- *Portfolio Management System*, p. 129
- *Test Generator (One-Stop Planner CD-ROM)*

Internet
- go.hrw.com (keyword: LE0 6-3)

Summary ■

In "The Hill Mynah," a mynah bird compares itself to a tape recorder that can speak any language and repeat any sound. In "The Hummingbird," the speaker compares a hovering hummingbird to a helicopter because their movements are similar.

Resources

Listening
Audio CD Library
A recording of these poems is provided in the *Audio CD Library:*
• Disc 4, Tracks 9, 10

Ⓐ Reading Skills and Strategies
Reading Poetry
❓ Should you pause or make a full stop at the end of each line when reading the first three lines aloud? Why or why not? [There is no end punctuation until "sing." Although each line is a complete sentence, the poet did not insert periods. This indicates that he wants the reader to pause only slightly.]

Ⓑ Appreciating Language
Word Choice
❓ After students have read the poem once, reread ll. 7–8. What do "gab" and "blab" mean? Why are they appropriate words here? [They mean to speak quickly and at length without thinking. The words are appropriate because tape recorders don't think; they just make noise.] What does "terse" mean? [concise, or the opposite of *gab* and *blab*]

RESPONDING TO THE ART

Douglas Florian (1950–)
first thought about being an artist when he was ten years old. He says, "I entered a national coloring contest. . . . Three months later the postman brought a brown parcel to our door. Inside was a pair of gold roller skates. I had placed second out of thousands of entries, and skated triumphantly around the neighborhood."
Activity. Ask students to draw their own interpretations of these poems.

T196

The Hill Mynah

Douglas Florian

Ⓐ
  I squawk
  I talk
    I even sing.
My voice can mimic anything.
5 In any tongue
  I can converse.
Ⓑ
  I gab
  I blab
    I'm never terse.
10 I echo every word that's said
  (A tape recorder's in my head.)

The Hummingbird

Douglas Florian

Barely bigger than your thumb,
See it hover, hear it hum,
With beating wings so fast they're blurred,
This *helicopter* of a bird.

THE HUMMINGBIRD 197

A Reading Skills and Strategies

Reading Poetry

❓ Have a volunteer read the poem aloud. How does listening to it help you appreciate the poem? [Possible responses: Its rhythm suggests the sound of a helicopter's propeller; alliteration makes it sound catchy and playful.]

B Elements of Literature

Metaphor

❓ Have students identify the metaphor. [A hummingbird is compared to a helicopter.] **Is the comparison surprising? Why or why not?** [Possible responses: It is not surprising because hummingbirds and helicopters move in similar ways; it is surprising because a hummingbird is tiny and delicate, and a helicopter is huge and loud.]

Speaking and Listening: Appreciating Spoken Language

Play the dramatic readings of these two contemporary poems about birds (Disc 4, Tracks 9 and 10, in the *Audio CD Library*). Ask students to notice where the reader pauses and changes volume in order to emphasize certain words and downplay others. Then, ask them to discuss how listening to the readings helps them imagine the subject of each poem.

Using Students' Strengths

Visual Learners

As visual learners read the poems, they might benefit by filling in the graphic organizer located in the *Graphic Organizers for Active Reading*, p. 16.

Auditory Learners

Divide students into small groups to discuss how Florian's use of language helps them hear the birds. Which words suggest particular sounds? Which phrases and rhymes echo the sounds of the tape recorder and helicopter? Encourage students to read the poems aloud as they discuss these questions.

MAKING MEANINGS

First Thoughts

1. Possible responses: "Hummingbird" provides a more vivid image because it describes how a helicopter moves; I preferred "Hill Mynah" because its comparison is so original and unexpected.

Shaping Interpretations

2. "Hill Mynah": *squawk, gab, blab.* "Hummingbird": *hum.*
3. The tone of both poems is humorous and affectionate. Florian loves birds and observes them closely. Like the poems, the paintings combine each bird with the object that best reflects the bird's behavior.
4. Rhymes: *thumb/hum; blurred/bird.* Alliteration: the repetition of *b* and *h* sounds throughout the poem.

Connecting with the Text

5. "Hill Mynah": *squawk/talk; sing/anything; converse/terse; gab/blab; said/head.* "Hummingbird": *thumb/hum; blurred/bird.* Other words that rhyme with these words: *stalk; sting/ring/king/everything; verse/worse/immerse/perverse; jab/crab/lab; bed/instead/lead/red; dumb/crumb/mum/strum; word/heard/stirred/purred.*

Grading Timesaver

Rubrics for each Choices assignment appear on p. 129 in the *Portfolio Management System*.

CHOICES: Building Your Portfolio

1. **Writer's Notebook** Encourage students to organize their five steps in chronological order.
2. **Creative Writing** Encourage students to read their poems aloud to see if their classmates can guess the identity of each poem's subject.

MAKING MEANINGS

First Thoughts

[visualize]
1. Which poem leaves you with a more vivid **image,** or picture? Tell which poem you like better and why.

Shaping Interpretations

[identify]
2. In each poem, find one example of **onomatopoeia** that echoes the sound that the bird makes.

[analyze]
3. **Tone** is the writer's attitude toward his audience or subject. What would you say is the tone of Florian's poems? What do you *see* in his watercolor paintings that has the same tone?

[identify]
4. Suppose that "The Hummingbird" were written as one long sentence in one long line. What rhymes and uses of alliteration would tell you that it should be written as a poem?

Connecting with the Text

[identify]
5. Many **rhyming words** in English do not look as if they rhyme. In "The Hill Mynah," for example, *squawk* and *talk* do not look like rhymes, but they are. (If *talk* were spelled *t-a-w-k*, the words would look like rhymes.) List the rhyming words in both poems. What other rhyming words in the poems do not look like rhymes? Think of other words that rhyme with the ones on your list, and add them. (For example, you could add *balk, caulk, gawk,* and *walk* to the list that includes *squawk* and *talk*.)

CHOICES: Building Your Portfolio

Writer's Notebook

1. Collecting Ideas for a How-To Essay

What's your favorite bird or insect? Imagine that you want to write a poem about it and illustrate the poem with a drawing or a painting. List five steps that you would take in the process of writing and illustrating a poem about a creature with wings.

Creative Writing

2. Extend-a-phor

Choose a bird, an insect, or any other animal, and write a brief poem about it. In your poem, compare one of the animal's features to a mechanical object (check your Quickwrite notes for ideas). Keep the animal unnamed in the body of your poem, as Florian does. Hint at the identity of your mystery animal by using sound effects that imitate the sound that the animal makes.

Making the Connections

Connecting to the Theme: "Machine Mania: People and Technology"

After students have read the two poems, discuss the collection's theme. How are these two poems similar to the four poems in the previous cluster? How are they different? Which poems did students like best, and why? Which comparisons did they think were funniest, most striking, or most thought-provoking? [Students should note that three of the four poems in the previous cluster compared machines to animals, while here the reverse is the case. Encourage them to give reasons for their preferences among the poems.]

Before You Read

JIMMY JET AND HIS TV SET

Make the Connection

Mad About Machines

This poem is about a boy who loves his TV. What machines are *you* crazy about? List three of them in order of importance in a chart like the one on this page. Record how much time you spend with each machine on a typical day. Write the best and worst effect the machine has on you. Then, compare charts with a partner. Based on what you each have written, would you say your involvement with machines is good or not so good?

Machine	Time	Best Effect	Worst Effect
1. TV	6 hrs.	I learn some things.	I get lazy.
2.			
3.			

Quickwrite

What if you were to decide to "break up" with one machine—your TV set?

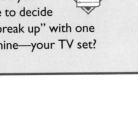

How would your life change? Think of how TV affects such things as your free time, your schoolwork, health, family life, and general knowledge. List the ways your life would be different if you lived without TV. If you don't watch TV, think of another machine you use a lot.

Elements of Literature

Mark That Rhyme; Scan That Rhythm

Poets will often use a pattern of rhymes in a poem, called a **rhyme scheme**. To find this pattern, mark the first line and all the lines that rhyme with it *a*; mark the second line and all the lines that rhyme with it *b*; and so on. For example, *abac* describes a four-line stanza in which only the first and third lines rhyme.

To chart **meter**, mark each stressed syllable with a (´) and each unstressed one with a (˘). This marking is called **scanning**. Here, for example, is how you might scan the first line of "Jimmy Jet":

I'll tell you the story
of Jimmy Jet

Rhyme scheme is the pattern of rhyming sounds at the ends of lines in a poem. **Meter** is the musical quality produced by the repeated pattern of stressed and unstressed syllables in a line. Finding this pattern is called **scanning**.

For more on Rhyme and Meter, see pages 178–179 and the Handbook of Literary Terms.

HRW go.hrw.com
LE0 6-3

JIMMY JET AND HIS TV SET **199**

Planning

• **Block Schedule**
  Block Scheduling Lesson Plans with Pacing Guide

• **Traditional Schedule**
  Lesson Plans Including Strategies for English-Language Learners

• **One-Stop Planner**
  CD-ROM with Test Generator

Summary ■

A boy named Jimmy Jet does nothing all day and night but watch television. Eventually, Jimmy's habit transforms him into a television set.

Resources

Listening
Audio CD Library
A recording of this poem is provided in the *Audio CD Library:*
• Disc 4, Track 11

Ⓐ Elements of Literature
Rhyme and Meter
❓ Have students identify the rhyme scheme and meter of this stanza. [Rhyme scheme: *abab.* Meter: l. 1 scans ˘ ´ ˘ ´ ˘ ˘ ´ ´; l. 2 scans ˘ ˘ ˘ ´ ˘ ´ ˘ ´; l. 3 scans ˘ ´ ˘ ´ ´ ˘ ´; and l. 4 scans ˘ ´ ˘ ´ ˘ ´.] What effect do these sound effects have on the reader? [Possible responses: The poem's rhythm makes it skip cheerfully along; the rhythm is fun.]

Ⓑ Appreciating Language
Repetition
❓ Have students identify repeated words and phrases in this verse. ["he watched all," "Show/shows"] What effect does this repetition have? [Possible responses: It gives the sound of the poem a catchy swing; it echoes the repetitiousness of Jimmy's TV habit.]

Jimmy Jet and His TV Set

Shel Silverstein

Ⓐ
I'll tell you the story of Jimmy Jet—
And you know what I tell you is true.
He loved to watch his TV set
Almost as much as you.

5 Ⓑ
He watched all day, he watched all night
Till he grew pale and lean,
From *The Early Show* to *The Late Late Show*
And all the shows between.

200 MACHINE MANIA: PEOPLE AND TECHNOLOGY

Listening to Music

"Jimmy Jet and His TV Set" by Shel Silverstein, performed by Shel Silverstein

The multitalented Shel Silverstein is best known for children's poetry, but he has also written several popular songs in a variety of different styles. These include the pop hit "Sylvia's Mother," performed by Dr. Hook & the Medicine Show; the humorous Johnny Cash hit "A Boy Named Sue"; the folk-style Civil War ballad "In the Hills of Shiloh," best known in a rendition by Judy Collins; and "Marie Laveau" and all the other songs on Bobby Bare's 1975 country album *Lullabys, Legends & Lies.* Silverstein's musical career dates back to his formation of the Red Onion Jazz Band in the late fifties. Like all the other songs in his collection *Where the Sidewalk Ends,* "Jimmy Jet and His TV Set" has been set to music and recorded by the author.
Activity
After students read the poem, have them listen to the musical version and evaluate its effectiveness. Then ask students to work in pairs to set another poem in the collection to a melody of their own.

He watched till his eyes were frozen wide,
10 And his bottom grew into his chair.
And his chin turned into a tuning dial,
And antennae grew out of his hair.

And his brains turned into TV tubes,
And his face to a TV screen.
15 And two knobs saying "VERT." and "HORIZ." 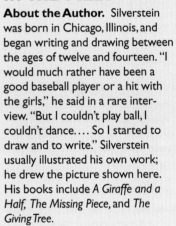 **C**
Grew where his ears had been.

And he grew a plug that looked like a tail
So we plugged in little Jim.
And now instead of him watching TV **D**
20 We all sit around and watch him.

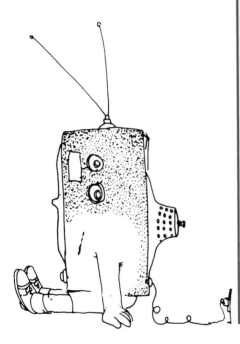

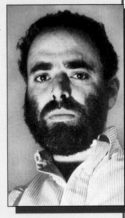
JIMMY JET AND HIS TV SET **201**

C Ⓒ **English Language Learners**
Abbreviations
See if students can guess the words these two abbreviations stand for and what the two knobs do. [The abbreviations stand for "vertical" and "horizontal"; the knobs can be turned to adjust a television picture in either direction.]

D Ⓓ **Reading Skills and Strategies**
Making Predictions
❓ What will happen to Jimmy's family? Why do you think so? [They will probably turn into TV sets because, like Jimmy, they watch TV all the time.]

BROWSING IN THE FILES

About the Author. Silverstein was born in Chicago, Illinois, and began writing and drawing between the ages of twelve and fourteen. "I would much rather have been a good baseball player or a hit with the girls," he said in a rare interview. "But I couldn't play ball, I couldn't dance. . . . So I started to draw and to write." Silverstein usually illustrated his own work; he drew the picture shown here. His books include *A Giraffe and a Half, The Missing Piece,* and *The Giving Tree.*

Using Students' Strengths

Visual Learners
As visual learners read the poem, they might benefit by filling in the graphic organizer located in the *Graphic Organizers for Active Reading,* p. 17.

Interpersonal Learners
Have students consider how television affects their relationships with other people. Do students usually watch TV alone or with friends? Do they talk with friends and family during the programs, or does everyone keep silent? Do they discuss the programs afterward? When students are bored or lonely, do they fall back on TV, or do they find a friend to talk to or a game to play? Have students gather in small groups to discuss their ideas and reactions.

First Thoughts

1. First choice: Students may point out that Jimmy's fate is literally impossible. Second choice: Students may be upset at Jimmy's family's indifference to his end. Third choice: Students may realize that television interferes with conversation and most other activities.

Shaping Interpretations

2. He freezes to his chair; he grows dials, tubes, and knobs; his face changes into a screen.

3. Stanza 1: *abab*. Stanzas 2–5: *abcb*. The difference sets the first stanza apart from the others. The first stanza is set off because it is an introduction.

4. The meter varies. Lines 6 and 8 scan ˇ ´ ˇ ´ ˇ. Lines like 10 and 12 scan ˇ ˇ ˇ ˇ ˇ ´ ˇ ´.

Connecting with the Text

5. Remind students that this question applies not only to habitual TV watchers but also to those who read incessantly or are slaves to any other habit.

Extending the Text

6. Students may say that they would limit the amount of television watched or forbid violent or adult entertainment. Ask them to explain their answers.

Challenging the Text

7. The speaker seems to think too much TV is a bad thing. Students may think Silverstein exaggerates (people do not watch TV constantly) or that he has a good point (TV prevents people from doing many other fun and interesting things).

First Thoughts

[respond]

1. Choose one of the following responses to the poem (or another response, if you don't agree with any of these), and explain your choice:
   • This poem is too silly to be serious.
   • This poem is too scary to be funny.
   • This poem made me think about TV in a new way.

Shaping Interpretations

[summarize]

2. In this poem a person becomes a machine instead of the other way around. How is Jimmy Jet transformed?

[analyze]

3. Use the letter code you learned earlier to mark the **rhyme scheme** (see page 199) in each stanza of "Jimmy Jet." Which stanza is different? Does the difference "make a difference"? Why or why not?

[analyze]

4. Read this poem aloud, and then copy several stanzas onto a separate sheet of paper. Scan them by marking the stressed and unstressed syllables in each line (see page 199). Is the **meter** identical in every line?

Connecting with the Text

[compare]

5. In line 4, the speaker suggests that you and Jimmy Jet are alike in some way. Is he right? Review your Quickwrite notes from page 199, and then answer the speaker.

Extending the Text

[extend]

6. If you were a parent, how much TV would you let your children watch? What would you worry about in regard to their TV viewing?

Challenging the Text

[evaluate]

7. How do you think the speaker feels about people who watch a lot of TV? Do you think Silverstein is too hard on them? Why or why not?

CALVIN AND HOBBES © Watterson. Reprinted with permission of UNIVERSAL PRESS SYNDICATE. All rights reserved.

202 MACHINE MANIA: PEOPLE AND TECHNOLOGY

Assessing Learning

Check Test: Short Answers

1. What does Jimmy Jet like best? [watching TV]
2. When does Jimmy Jet watch TV? [all the time; all day and all night]
3. What happens to Jimmy Jet's face? [It turns into a TV screen.]
4. What does Jimmy Jet become? [a TV set]
5. What does Jimmy's family do with him? [They plug him in and watch him.]

Interview Assessment

Have each student choose a poem from this collection. Talk with each student individually about his or her choice. What does the student like or dislike about the poem? Which sound effects and figures of speech can the student identify? What is the poem's rhyme scheme and meter? Assess each student in regard to his or her ability to identify and analyze the literary elements taught in the collection.

CHOICES: Building Your Portfolio

Writer's Notebook

1. Collecting Ideas for a How-To Essay

Jimmy Jet spent way too much time with his TV set. Think of a machine that takes up some of your time, but not *too* much of it. Maybe it's a video game, a refrigerator, a telephone, or a computer. Pick one machine that you'd hate not having. Tell how you make it do what you want it to do. List the steps in the process.

Answering Machine

1. When I get home, I check the machine.
2. I see the signal blinking.
3. I get paper and pencil.
4. I press the play button and listen.
5. I jot down messages.

Creative Writing

2. Download That Ode

Brainstorm to gather ideas for a poem that creates a comic picture of someone (possibly you) totally involved with a machine of some kind. List some ideas for images and some possible rhyming words (like *tape* and *escape* or *diskette* and *forget*). Then, team up with a classmate, and write the poem together.

Critical Writing/Math

3. Crunching the Tube

Survey your class's TV habits. Ask your classmates to keep a TV log for a week, recording when and what they watch. Have them also rate the programs they watch on a scale of 1 to 10, with 1 meaning "rotten" and 10 meaning "excellent." Put your findings in a chart like the one below. Use the results of your survey to write to the TV networks with suggestions for changes in their programming.

Our Class's TV Habits: One Typical Student	
Total hours/week of TV	
Average hours/day	
Heaviest viewing hours	
Most-watched program	
Highest-rated program	
Lowest-rated program	

JIMMY JET AND HIS TV SET 203

Grading Timesaver

Rubrics for each Choices assignment appear on p. 130 in the *Portfolio Management System*.

CHOICES: Building Your Portfolio

1. **Writer's Notebook** Suggest that students use a notebook like the one shown as a model for organizing their notes. Caution them not to forget steps they've grown accustomed to through routine.
2. **Creative Writing** Encourage students to illustrate their poems.
3. **Critical Writing/Math** Students may want to ask their math teachers for some help in organizing the data they collect, calculating averages, and so on. A quick review of business-letter format will help students garner more favorable attention from networks.

Making the Connections

Connecting to the Theme: "Machine Mania: People and Technology"

After students have read the poem, discuss the collection's theme. What point is Silverstein making about the effect of technology on people? How is Jimmy Jet's fate an instance of "machine mania"? Does technology have this kind of effect on the students or on anyone they know? Is there such a thing as too much technology? [Students should see that Silverstein suggests that if a person gets too attached to a machine, the person will lose his or her personality and ability to think. Students may think they spend too much time watching TV or playing computer games, or they may say this of friends or family members.]

OBJECTIVES

1. Read and interpret the story
2. Analyze irony
3. Identify causes and effects
4. Express understanding through creative writing, dictionary skills, or art
5. Use correct end marks
6. Create words from word roots

SKILLS

Literary
- Analyze irony

Reading
- Identify causes and effects

Writing
- Collect ideas for a how-to essay
- Write a journal entry
- Write a letter
- Make a dictionary of computer terms

Art
- Construct a time capsule
- Illustrate a dictionary

Grammar
- Use correct end marks

Vocabulary
- Create words from word roots

THE FUN THEY HAD

Make the Connection

Computer Craze

This fantasy was written in 1951. At that time, computers were huge, hulking machines humming day and night in refrigerated buildings. Those mainframe computers had wires, gears, dials, and circuit boards mounted on frames in cabinets. They were used only by specialists who stored information in them by creating patterns of holes on cards or tape. (That's why in this story a character writes for the computer in punch code.)

In the 1970s, twenty years after Asimov wrote this story, the silicon chip transformed computers. With the chip, computers became smaller, more powerful, and cheaper, as we know them today. They left their refrigerated buildings and entered our everyday lives.

Quickwrite

Write out your responses to these predictions about education by computer in 2155:

1. In 2155, we'll have no more printed books.

2. In 2155, computers will replace human teachers.

3. In 2155, we'll learn at home on computers.

HRW go.hrw.com
LE0 6-3

Elements of Literature

Irony: It Can Be a Surprise

When a situation turns out to be different from what you think it should be, you may feel a slight twinge of **irony.**

You might think it ironic, for example, that a botanist (a scientist who studies plants) is allergic to pollen. You might think it ironic, too, if someone wrote a hundred years ago, "People will never set foot on the moon because it would take too long to get there." People have gotten to the moon and may be on their way to Mars.

> **I**rony is the contrast between what is expected and what really happens.
>
> *For more on Irony, see the Handbook of Literary Terms.*

Reading Skills and Strategies

Cause and Effect: One Thing Leads to Another

A **cause** makes something happen. An **effect** is the result of something—of an event or a decision or a situation. To find a cause, ask "Why did this happen?" To find an effect, ask "What's the result of this?"

204 MACHINE MANIA: PEOPLE AND TECHNOLOGY

Resources: Print and Media

Reading
- *Reading Skills and Strategies*
  Selection Skill Lesson, p. 135
- *Graphic Organizers for Active Reading,* p. 18
- *Words to Own,* p. 10
- *Spelling and Decoding*
  Worksheet, p. 10
- *Audio CD Library*
  Disc 4, Track 12

Writing and Language
- *Daily Oral Grammar*
  Transparency 12
- *Grammar and Language Links*
  Worksheet, p. 21
- *Language Workshop CD-ROM*

Viewing and Representing
- *Viewing and Representing*
  Fine Art Transparency 9
  Fine Art Worksheet, p. 36

- *Visual Connections*
  Videocassette A, Segment 4

Assessment
- *Formal Assessment,* p. 41
- *Portfolio Management System,* p. 131
- *Test Generator (One-Stop Planner CD-ROM)*

Internet
- go.hrw.com (keyword: LE0 6-3)

The Fun They Had

Isaac Asimov

"Today Tommy found a real book!"

Margie even wrote about it that night in her diary. On the page headed May 17, 2155, she wrote, "Today Tommy found a real book!"

THE FUN THEY HAD **205**

Summary ▪▪

In May of 2155, people read everything on computer screens. One day, Tommy finds an antique—a book printed on paper. He and his friend Margie read about an old-fashioned school, where children of the same age learn the same things from a human teacher. They contrast this with their individual mechanical teachers. Margie, who hates this process of learning, thinks wistfully about the fun students must have had in those long-ago schools.

Planning

- **Block Schedule**
  Block Scheduling Lesson Plans with Pacing Guide
- **Traditional Schedule**
  Lesson Plans Including Strategies for English-Language Learners
- **One-Stop Planner**
  CD-ROM with Test Generator

Resources

Listening
Audio CD Library
A recording of this story is provided in the *Audio CD Library:*
- Disc 4, Track 12

Viewing and Representing
Fine Art Transparency
A fine art transparency of Frank R. Paul's *Amazing Stories* cover can be used with this selection. See the *Viewing and Representing Transparencies and Worksheets:*
- Transparency 9
- Worksheet, p. 36

Reaching All Students

Struggling Readers
Cause and Effect was introduced on p. 204 under Reading Skills and Strategies. For a lesson directly tied to this selection that teaches students to identify cause and effect by using a strategy called Text Reformulation, see the *Reading Skills and Strategies* binder:
- Selection Skill Lesson, p. 135

English Language Learners
Have students choose partners to read the selection aloud with. Encourage them to help one another pronounce and define new words. Every few paragraphs, partners should stop reading and discuss the story. What has happened so far? Who are the characters? What do students think will happen next?

Advanced Learners
Have students look carefully at a favorite book— at the words, the typeface, the illustrations, and the cover design. Ask them to feel the texture of the paper and the size and weight of the book. Tell them to pause as they look through the book to reread favorite passages. Then, have them describe this experience in a short essay. What value beyond the words printed in it does a book have? Why is a real book more precious than a computer printout of its text?

It was a very old book. Margie's grandfather once said that when he was a little boy, *his* grandfather told him that there was a time when all stories were printed on paper.

They turned the pages, which were yellow and crinkly, and it was awfully funny to read words that stood still instead of moving the way they were supposed to—on a screen, you know. And then, when they

"A man? How could a man be a teacher?"

turned back to the page before, it had the same words on it that it had had when they read it the first time.

Ⓐ "Gee," said Tommy, "what a waste. When you're through with the book, you just throw it away, I guess. Our television screen must have had a million books on it and it's good for plenty more. I wouldn't throw *it* away."

"Same with mine," said Margie. She was eleven and hadn't seen as many telebooks as Tommy had. He was thirteen.

She said, "Where did you find it?"

"In my house." He pointed without looking, because he was busy reading. "In the attic."

"What's it about?"

"School."

Ⓑ Margie was scornful. "School? What's there to write about school? I hate school." Margie always hated school, but now she hated it more than ever. The mechanical teacher had been giving her test after test in geography, and she had been doing worse and worse until her mother had shaken her head sorrowfully and sent for the county inspector.

He was a round little man with a red face

and a whole box of tools with dials and wires. He smiled at her and gave her an apple, then took the teacher apart. Margie had hoped he wouldn't know how to put it together again, but he knew how all right, and after an hour or so, there it was again, large and ugly, with a big screen on which all the lessons were shown and the questions were asked. That wasn't so bad. The part she hated most was the slot where she had to put homework and test papers. She always had to write them out in a punch code they made her learn when she was six years old, and the mechanical teacher calculated the mark in no time.

The inspector had smiled after he was finished and patted her head. He said to her mother, "It's not the little girl's fault, Mrs.

Ⓒ Jones. I think the geography sector was geared a little too quick. Those things happen sometimes. I've slowed it up to an average ten-year level. Actually, the overall pattern of her progress is quite satisfactory." And he patted Margie's head again.

Margie was disappointed. She had been hoping they would take the teacher away altogether. They had once taken Tommy's teacher away for nearly a month because the history sector had blanked out completely.

So she said to Tommy, "Why would anyone write about school?"

Tommy looked at her with very superior eyes. "Because it's not our kind of school,

Ⓓ stupid. This is the old kind of school that they had hundreds and hundreds of years ago." He added loftily, pronouncing the word carefully, "*Centuries* ago."

206 MACHINE MANIA: PEOPLE AND TECHNOLOGY

E Elements of Literature

Irony

⁉ What is ironic about the conversation? [Possible responses: The reader's expectations about teachers are reversed in this story; the reader's ordinary understanding of schools and teachers seems strange to Tommy and Margie.]

F Struggling Readers

Summarizing

Students may find the situation in this story confusing. At this point in the story, make sure they can summarize the features of the educational system used in 2155. [Teachers are computers. Students do all their schoolwork individually in their homes and submit it to the computers. The computers are individually programmed to match each student's abilities.]

"A man isn't smart enough."

"Sure he is. My father knows as much as my teacher."

"He can't. A man can't know as much as a teacher."

"He knows almost as much I betcha."

Margie wasn't prepared to dispute that. She said, "I wouldn't want a strange man in my house to teach me."

Tommy screamed with laughter. "You don't know much, Margie. The teachers didn't live in the house. They had a special building and all the kids went there." **F**

"And all the kids learned the same thing?"

Margie was hurt. "Well, I don't know what kind of school they had all that time ago." She read the book over his shoulder for a while, then said, "Anyway, they had a teacher."

"Sure they had a teacher, but it wasn't a *regular* teacher. It was a man."

"A man? How could a man be a teacher?" **E**

"Well, he just told the boys and girls things and gave them homework and asked them questions."

THE FUN THEY HAD 207

Getting Students Involved

Cooperative Learning

Play Ball! Have students play a video game that is based on a real game, such as chess or baseball. Then have them play the real, three-dimensional version of the game (or recall past experiences of playing it). Is playing this game with friends and in three dimensions more satisfying than playing it on a screen? Why? What are the differences between handling real game markers or chess pieces and clicking a mouse to move screen images of them? Would students abandon the real games in favor of the electronic versions? Why or why not? Have students discuss their experiences and ideas with their friends.

Hey, Teacher! Have students work in small groups to research old-fashioned one-room schoolhouses. What were they like? How did students learn? How did the teachers manage with students of so many different ages in one room? Interested students can read such young-adult novels as Dorothy Canfield Fisher's *Understood Betsy* and Laura Ingalls Wilder's *Farmer Boy, Little House on the Prairie,* and *These Happy Golden Years,* which give vivid portraits of old-fashioned schools in Vermont, New York, and North Dakota. Have students share what they learn with their classmates.

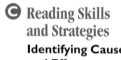
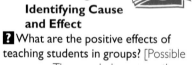
"Sure, if they were the same age."

Ⓐ "But my mother says a teacher has to be adjusted to fit the mind of each boy and girl it teaches and that each kid has to be taught differently."

"Just the same, they didn't do it that way then. If you don't like it, you don't have to read the book."

"I didn't say I didn't like it," Margie said quickly. She wanted to read about those funny schools.

They weren't even half finished when Margie's mother called, "Margie! School!"

Today's arithmetic lesson is on the addition of proper fractions. Please insert yesterday's homework in the proper slot.

208 MACHINE MANIA: PEOPLE AND TECHNOLOGY

Margie looked up. "Not yet, Mamma."

"Now," said Mrs. Jones. "And it's probably time for Tommy, too."

Margie said to Tommy, "Can I read the book some more with you after school?"

Ⓑ "Maybe," he said, nonchalantly. He walked away whistling, the dusty old book tucked beneath his arm.

Margie went into the schoolroom. It was right next to her bedroom, and the mechanical teacher was on and waiting for her. It was always on at the same time every day except Saturday and Sunday, because her mother said little girls learned better if they learned at regular hours.

The screen was lit up, and it said: "Today's arithmetic lesson is on the addition of proper fractions. Please insert yesterday's homework in the proper slot."

Margie did so with a sigh. She was thinking about the old schools they had when her grandfather's grandfather was a little boy. All the kids from the whole neighborhood came, laughing and shouting in the schoolyard, sitting together in the schoolroom, going home together at the end of the day. They learned the same things so they could help one another on the homework and talk about it.

And the teachers were people. . . .

The mechanical teacher was flashing on the screen: "When we add the fractions 1/2 and 1/4 . . ."

Margie was thinking about how the kids must have loved it in the old days. She was thinking about the fun they had.

MEET THE WRITER

A Writing Machine

Isaac Asimov (1920–1992) wrote or edited more than 470 books, as well as many short stories and scholarly articles. That's more books than any other American writer has turned out. Asimov also holds the unofficial record for writing about more different nonfiction subjects than any other writer in history. In fact, *The New York Times* called him a "writing machine."

Asimov was born in Russia and came to the United States with his parents when he was three years old. He submitted his first story to a science fiction magazine when he was only fourteen. The story was rejected, but the editor encouraged Asimov and helped him improve his writing.

Asimov talked about "The Fun They Had" in the first volume of his autobiography. A friend of his had asked him to write a short story for young readers. Asimov said:

66 I thought about it and decided to write a little story about school. What could interest children more? It would be about a school of the future, by way of teaching machines, with children longing for the good old days when there were old-fashioned schools that children loved. I thought the kids would get a bang out of the irony. 99

He wrote the story at one sitting and earned ten dollars for it—"a penny a word," Asimov says.

More by the Writing Machine

You'll find short stories about robots in Asimov's book *I, Robot* (Fawcett). His popular series of novels, called *The Foundation Trilogy* (Doubleday), covers thousands of years of "future history."

THE FUN THEY HAD **209**

Making the Connections

Connecting to the Theme: "Machine Mania: People and Technology"

After students have read the story, discuss the collection's theme. How has technology made Tommy and Margie's lives different from the students' lives? Are Tommy and Margie different from today's students in any way? How is education by a mechanical teacher different from working with a human teacher? [Students should see that everything about the learning process is different for Tommy and Margie; they work alone, and although their teachers are specially designed for them, a computer cannot have any kind of personal understanding of its students. Students should also note that Tommy and Margie don't seem much different from themselves and their friends.]

Connections

This essay lists a few basic rules of etiquette that everyone should follow when on-line.

Ⓐ English Language Learners
Technical Vocabulary
This essay is filled with computer-related jargon, or technical vocabulary. Pair students who have not worked much with computers with those who have. Computer-literate students can help their partners make sense of the unfamiliar terms. Encourage these students to share any knowledge they have about how the terms were invented.

You can use this essay to talk about word coinages and how we have always invented new words for new inventions. In this essay, for example, the word *cyber* is used to create new words (*cyberspace, cyberroad, Cyber-Shorthand*). Have students look up the prefix *cyber*. It comes from a Greek word for "helmsman" (*kybernātēs*) and was first used in 1948 to form the new word *cybernetics*. Cybernetics is the study of automatic control systems, such as the brain and computer electrical systems. The prefix *cyber-* has come to refer in general to computers. Perhaps students can use it to make up some words of their own. [*cyberfatigue, cyberburnout, cybernut*, etc.]

Ⓑ Appreciating Language
Coined Words
? Ask students to explain how the word *netiquette* was made. [by combining *net*, short for *Internet*, with *etiquette*] Why would the writer combine these words rather than saying "Internet etiquette"? [Possible responses: The words are easy to combine because the ending *-et* overlaps with the beginning *et-*; computer users often use abbreviations. Americans in general love to coin new words, and "netiquette" provides a clever short cut.]

Ⓒ Reading Skills and Strategies

Identifying Cause and Effect
Have students list the cause and effect in this paragraph. [Cause: You ignore the rules of netiquette. Effect: You lose your e-mail friends.]

Netiquette

Preston Gralla

Ⓐ Ⓑ **I**f you're going to go on-line, there are some rules of the cyberroad you should know about. It's etiquette on-line I'm talking about—what most people call **netiquette**—and it's all about being thoughtful of other people. You'll want to observe netiquette, because if you don't, you may find that no one will want to talk to you on-line. Ⓒ You won't have any e-mail buddies, and no one will bother to chat with you. So here are the main rules of netiquette:

- *Don't shout.* You know what Mom always told you about raising your voice? Well, the same holds true in cyberspace. Don't shout there, either. How can you shout in cyberspace? IF YOU USE CAPITAL LETTERS TO SEND MESSAGES, YOU'RE SHOUTING. So please, hold down your voice. Keep your hands off the *caps lock* key.

- *Don't use nasty language.* When you're on-line, there's a great temptation to use words that you might not use in person. Resist the temptation, though. Not only will people avoid you, but if you keep doing it, you could get banned from some areas and even a whole service.

- *Don't "flame."* When someone behaves obnoxiously by attacking people continu-

ously and for no reason, that's called a *flame.* Don't even think about doing it.

- *Don't harass.* Harassing means constantly bothering someone. This can be either in public or in private. Let me be clear about this. Don't do it. It's not nice. You'll lose friends. You can get kicked off an on-line service or even be charged with a crime.

- *Don't ruin cyberspace for others.* Maybe you've had a bad day. Your parents grounded you because you stayed out three hours too late last night. Or your teacher gave you a D on your history report. You may be tempted to go into a chat room and do something like hold down the 3 key this many times: 3333333333333333333333333333333. Don't do it. It's not fair to take out your bad mood on others.

User CyberShorthand for Chat, E-Mail, and Messages

Another way to show what you're thinking is to use a form of **shorthand**—let's call it *CyberShorthand*. For example, if you say something that you hope will be funny but could be taken the wrong way, you could use the CyberShorthand for "rolling on the floor, laughing"—ROFL. Generally, as in this case, the shorthand form uses the first letter of each word in a phrase. Here are some of the more popular CyberShorthands and what they mean:

ASAP	As soon as possible	IC	I see
<bg>	Big grin	IMO	In my opinion
BL	Belly laugh	IMHO	In my humble opinion
BRB	Be right back	L8R	Later
BTW	By the way	LD	Later, dude
B4N	Bye for now	LOL	Laughing out loud
CU	See you	SYSOP	System operator (person
CUL	See you later		who runs a bulletin board
DIKU?	Do I know you?		or chat room)
FAQ	Frequently asked question	TTUL	Talk to you later
FYI	For your information	Txs	Thanks
<g>	Grin	WU?	What's up?
GAL	Get a life	WYSIWYG	What you see is what
GMTA	Great minds think alike		you get

THE FUN THEY HAD 211

D Appreciating Language
Abbreviations

? Why do you think abbreviations are so popular? [Possible responses: They save time; they are like a secret code or language that people can share.] **Point out that** *ASAP* and *FYI* predate the computer age by many years. Have students list other abbreviations that are in common use. [OK, co-ed, e.g., bike, flu, net, gym, CD, PC, etc.]

Connecting Across Texts

Connecting with "The Fun They Had"
Have students look back at Margie's story in light of this essay. How has constant work with a computer affected Margie's life? What does this essay suggest about the effect computers have on language and communication? How is Margie's relationship to her teacher similar to relationships among e-mail buddies? If any students use the Internet for communication, have them share their thoughts about it. [Students should see that the Internet might physically isolate people from one another; people write notes to one another rather than talking face to face. The Internet also connects people together who live far apart. The Internet is also reshaping our language by creating a whole new vocabulary; some of the abbreviations on this page have become part of everyday speech.]

MAKING MEANINGS

First Thoughts

1. Possible responses: my school, because I can learn from other students; Margie's school, because she gets all of the teacher's attention.

Shaping Interpretations

2. Asimov might be troubled at the amount of computer use in present-day schools. He would probably like the idea of students working together on group projects, teaching and learning from one another.

3. Possible main idea: Things were better in the past. Agree: Life was less complicated without all the encroaching technology we now face. Disagree: Today, more and more people are educated, and we have greater freedom of choice.

4. Possible responses: Kids still hate homework; teachers are still needed; people still read. Most students will agree that these will be true of the future.

5. Possible responses: Yes, Margie looks back wistfully to an unfamiliar time, which the reader knows and probably dislikes; yes, technology is supposed to have improved things, but Margie thinks things were better in the past.

Connecting with the Text

6. Possible responses: I would be glad not to have to carry heavy books around; I would miss the feel of a book, its weight, its texture, and its smell; I would miss the difference in the illustrations in printed books.

7. Students' computer experiences will vary. Human teachers are less predictable, but each is unique. Human teachers can share many things, unlike a computer, which has only programmed knowledge. Human teachers can also understand students on an emotional level; computers can't.

Challenging the Text

8. Asimov's picture of computerized teaching is not unfair, but it is weighted by nostalgia and a strong belief in human relationships. Ways he is wrong: Computerized teachers have not yet replaced human teachers. Ways he is right: To some extent, computer programs can be tailored to the level of the student using them.

MAKING MEANINGS

• First Thoughts

[respond]
1. Which do you think is better—your school or the kind of "school" Tommy and Margie have? Why?

Shaping Interpretations

[infer]
2. Judging from this story, how do you think Asimov would feel about today's schools?

[interpret]
3. How would you state the message, or **main idea,** in this story? Do you agree with it? Why or why not?

[identify]
4. In Asimov's future world certain things have changed from the world we know. Other things have stayed the same. Name three things that, according to Asimov, time and science will *not* change. Do you agree with him?

[analyze]
5. Do you feel any **irony** when you read the last paragraph of "The Fun They Had"? Why?

Connecting with the Text

[respond]
6. Tell why you *would* or *wouldn't* like to live in a world without printed books.

[connect]
7. What good and bad experiences have you had with computers as "mechanical teachers"? Would you miss a human teacher? Why?

Challenging the Text

[evaluate]
8. Do you think Asimov gives a fair and correct picture of computerized teaching? In what ways would you say he got it right and wrong?

Reading Check

At the start of the story, Tommy has found a real book.

a. What is the **effect** of his discovery—in other words, what happens as a result of the discovery?

b. At the very end of the story, Margie thinks about the fun that kids must have had in the past. What has **caused** her to think this?

c. How does having a machine as a teacher **affect** Margie?

Reading Check

a. Margie learns about old-fashioned schools.

b. Kids in the past went to school together and were taught by a human being.

c. Margie hates school, especially handing in homework.

Assessing Learning

Check Test: Short Answers

1. What kind of books do Tommy and Margie read? [telebooks, which are read on a screen]

2. What is Margie's first reaction to the idea of a human teacher? [She thinks no person knows enough to teach.]

3. Where does Margie go to school? [at home, in a room next to her bedroom]

4. Why does Margie think the school in the book sounds like fun? [The kids learn together, and she would like to have a human teacher.]

CHOICES: Building Your Portfolio

Writer's Notebook

1. Collecting Ideas for a How-To Essay

Asimov could not imagine how important computers would become even before the twenty-first century. Tiny microprocessor chips work like computers in garage-door openers and in washing machines. They're used in video games, wristwatches, cameras, and calculators. You can find them even in toys. With a partner, choose one machine that uses a computer chip. Think of a process that you can carry out using that machine. Then, list the steps you take to complete the process. Add details that explain *how, when,* and *why,* if you need them.

> **Using the Remote**
> 1. Press power button to turn on TV.
> 2. Press button for channel you want.
> 3. Then, press the enter button.
> 4. Press the + button to make sound louder.
> 5. Press the - button to make sound softer.

Creative Writing

2. Earthdate: 2155

What do you think life will be like in the year 2155? Imagine that you're a young person living in that year. Write a journal entry that describes a normal day in your life—at your school, with your friends and your family, during your after-school activities. You might want to refer to the notes you made for the Quickwrite on page 204 for ideas.

Creative Writing/Art

3. The Fun We Have

What would you like students in the year 2155 to know about your life today? With your classmates, create a time capsule—a container that preserves things for the future. Use a large plastic or glass container that you can seal tightly. Decide what to put inside—your best artwork, photos, news articles, coins, letters to students of the future telling about today. Maybe you can even hide or bury your capsule so a class of the future might find it someday.

Dictionary Skills/Art

4. Compudiction

Computer users speak a new language. (See *Connections* on page 210.) They've invented new words, like *byte* and *floppy disk,* and they've given new meaning to some common words, like *mouse* and *chip.* With a partner, identify and define ten computer words. Combine your list with those of other students. Then, type all your word entries in alphabetical order. Illustrate any terms that can be shown in a drawing. Present your computer dictionary to your library.

Rubrics for each Choices assignment appear on p. 131 in the *Portfolio Management System.*

CHOICES: Building Your Portfolio

1. **Writer's Notebook** Suggest that students use a notebook like the one shown as a model for organizing their notes.
2. **Creative Writing** Challenge students to use their imaginations. Will schools in 2155 be anything like schools today? What will family life be like? What will children do for fun? What things won't change no matter how technologically advanced we become?
3. **Creative Writing/Art** Encourage students to include things that represent their everyday lives and their communities.
4. **Dictionary Skills/Art** Students may want to start their vocabulary search with the "Netiquette" article on pp. 210–211.

Crossing the Curriculum

Film

Have students get together in small groups to discuss a film about student-teacher relationships that they have seen. Possible films include *Mr. Holland's Opus; Stand and Deliver; Dangerous Minds; Lean on Me; The Power of One; Good-bye, Mr. Chips;* and *To Sir, with Love.* How does the teacher affect the lives of his or her students? What does he or she teach them that they could not have learned from a computer? How is the approach of other teachers in the film like the approach of a computer?

GRAMMAR LINK

Have students choose partners and read the dialogue between Margie and Tommy aloud. Have them pay attention to the end marks in the dialogue as a guide to how the sentences should sound—declarative (.), questioning (?), or emphatic (!). After students have had some time to practice, ask two volunteers to read the dialogue aloud for the class. Stop the readers frequently, and have the listeners identify the punctuation mark that ends the last sentence they heard.

Try It Out
Possible Responses

School would be fun that day! Margie was excited. She and Tommy were going to work together. They'd use just one mechanical teacher. Wouldn't they have fun? Of course they would!

VOCABULARY
Possible Responses

Telebat: a baseball bat that can hit any pitch out of Yankee Stadium.

Telebone: a trombone with an extra-long slide that can play an extra octave of notes.

Teledisc: a device that can transmit the sounds of outer space to your radio.

Telebook: a book that comes with a disk that can show you pictures of the story's setting.

Telepack: a backpack that includes a device for showing you views of any place on earth at any particular moment.

For information on *cyber* see p. T210. *Hyper* means "over, above," as in *hyperactive; mega* means "great, mighty, much," as in *megabyte; micro* means "small," as in *microchip* and *microscope.*

Resources ━━━━

Grammar
• *Grammar and Language Links,* p. 21

Vocabulary
• *Words to Own,* p. 10

Spelling
For related instruction, see
• *Spelling and Decoding,* p. 10

GRAMMAR LINK `MINI-LESSON`

• End All End-Mark Errors

Language Handbook HELP

See Sentences Classified by Purpose, pages 735–736; End Marks, pages 748–749.

Technology HELP

See Language Workshop CD-ROM. Key word entry: end marks.

The punctuation at the end of a sentence is called an **end mark.** Like stop signs, end marks prevent collisions. Read the following lines aloud. Can you tell where each sentence starts and ends?

> It was a very old book Margie's grandfather once said that there was a time when all stories were printed on paper

There are three end marks in English: a period (.), a question mark (?), and an exclamation point (!). Read the following examples aloud to see how changing the end mark can affect a sentence's meaning.

EXAMPLES "A man isn't smart enough**.**"

"A man isn't smart enough**?**"

A man isn't smart enough**!**

End marks differ in different languages. In Spanish, for example, a question mark or exclamation point appears both before and after a question or exclamation. (Punctuation marks at the beginning of a question or exclamation are *inverted*, or upside down.)

EXAMPLES ¿Qué pasa? [What's happening?] ¡Qué lastima! [What a shame!]

Try It Out

➤ Revise the paragraph below. Copy the paragraph, adding six missing end marks and capitalizing as needed.

School would be fun that day Margie was excited she and Tommy were going to work together they'd use just one mechanical teacher wouldn't they have fun of course they would

➤ As you proofread your own writing, highlight all your end marks. Then, check them. Ask yourself where each thought ends—really ends. Put an end mark there to show that the next word marks the beginning of a whole new thought. If you're in doubt, you might try reading your work aloud.

VOCABULARY `HOW TO OWN A WORD`

Rooting Out Meanings: "It's All Greek to Me"

Word roots are tools you can use to dig out the meaning of some words. For example, the Greek root *-tele-* means "far away." You'll find *-tele-* in *television, telescope,* and *telephone* because they all have meanings that involve distance.

Now, make up your own word, using the root *-tele-* to describe a machine of the future. Write a sentence describing your made-up machine, and add a picture.

Computer scientists often use the Greek language to form new terms. Use a dictionary to find the meanings of *-cyber-, -hyper-, -mega-,* and *-micro-.* What new words can you think of that use these old Greek roots?

Grammar Link Quick Check

Copy the following paragraph, adding end punctuation and capitalization as needed.

What a day Margie and Tommy's mechanical teachers broke down at exactly the same time the repairman could not come for at least five hours what did Margie and Tommy do they sat by the lake and read the wonderful book they had found

[What a day! Margie's and Tommy's mechanical teachers broke down at exactly the same time. The repairman could not come for at least five hours. What did Margie and Tommy do? They sat by the lake and read the wonderful book they had found.]

The Nightingale

Hans Christian Andersen
translated by Anthea Bell

In China, as of course you know, the Emperor is Chinese, and so are all his people. This story happened many years ago, but that makes it all the more worth hearing. Old tales should be told again before they are forgotten.

The Emperor had the most magnificent palace in the world, made all of fine porcelain,[1] so expensive and so fragile and delicate that you hardly dared touch it. Out in the garden grew wonderfully beautiful flowers, and the loveliest of all had little silver bells tied to them that rang as you went by so that you couldn't fail to notice them. Everything in the Emperor's garden was so ingeniously[2] laid out, and the garden itself stretched so far that even the gardener didn't know where it ended. If you went

"Travelers from every country in the world visited the Emperor's city and marveled at the city itself ..."

1. **porcelain** (pôr′sə·lin): fine, white china.
2. **ingeniously** (in·jēn′yəs·lē): skillfully or cleverly.

THE NIGHTINGALE 215

OBJECTIVES
1. Read and enjoy the story
2. Connect the story to the collection theme

No Questions Asked

The literature in No Questions Asked gives students the chance to read a selection for enjoyment and enrichment as they further explore the collection theme. Annotated questions in the margins of the Teacher's Edition should be considered optional. No follow-up questions appear after the selection.

The Emperor of China lives in a beautiful palace surrounded by exquisite and precious objects. Visitors to his city think the most beautiful thing in the city is the song of the nightingale. When the Emperor hears this, he sends his courtiers to find the bird and bring it to sing at the palace. The nightingale agrees, and its song enchants the Emperor and all his court. The nightingale is caged and made to stay at the palace. One day the Emperor of Japan sends the Emperor of China a mechanical nightingale, covered with sparkling jewels. As everyone exclaims at its beauty, the real nightingale flies away. Because the Emperor plays the mechanical bird all the time, it soon breaks down, and though it is repaired, it can only be played occasionally. Years pass, and the Emperor is about to die when the real nightingale reappears and sings, beguiling Death away. The Emperor asks the nightingale to stay forever, and it promises to return often and sing for him if he will keep the visits a secret.

Resources

Listening
Audio CD Library
A recording of this fairy tale is provided in the *Audio CD Library:*
• Disc 4, Track 13

Reaching All Students

Struggling Readers
Have students read this story with partners. At the end of each page, partners can pause to discuss what they have read so far. Each student should make sure his or her partner can summarize the story events up to this point and identify the characters and their relationships. Students should also predict what may happen next.

Advanced Learners
Have students form a small reading group. Students can select and read another of Andersen's tales, such as "The Little Mermaid," "The Wild Swans," or "The Steadfast Tin Soldier." (Students who have seen the animated film *The Little Mermaid* will be interested to learn how different the original story is!) Have students discuss the story together, comparing their impressions of it, what they like or dislike about it, and how it compares with "The Nightingale."

RESPONDING TO THE ART

Edmund Dulac (1882–1953) was born in Toulouse, France, to a middle-class family. He drew and painted all through childhood, but his father allowed him to study art only on the condition that he also study something more practical—law. When one of his paintings won a prize, Dulac was finally allowed to pursue full-time art study.

Dulac greatly admired such English designers and illustrators as Aubrey Beardsley and William Morris and decided to try his luck in London. His first work, illustrations for Charlotte Brontë's novel *Jane Eyre,* was well received and led to more commissions. Illustrated gift books were very popular in the early 1900s, and Dulac was hired to paint fifty pictures to illustrate *The Arabian Nights.* The book was a tremendous success, and the public bought all of the original paintings from the publishers. After this, Dulac produced one illustrated book every year, including *The Tempest, The Rubáiyát of Omar Khayyám, The Sleeping Beauty and Other Fairy Tales,* and *Stories from Hans Andersen.*

Activity. This rich illustration would be excellent to use as a test of students' observation skills. Have students write a paragraph telling exactly what they see in this painting. They should do two things: Describe the setting and the characters, and tell what they think is happening. Be sure to share paragraphs in class. Did anyone notice the man's long fingernails and the peacock feather coming out of his hat?

Ⓐ *Chinese Man with Two Women with Fans* (1911) by Edmund Dulac.

216 MACHINE MANIA: PEOPLE AND TECHNOLOGY

on beyond it you came to a very beautiful wood with tall trees and deep lakes. This wood went all the way down to the deep blue sea. Great ships could sail right in under its branches, and in the branches there lived a nightingale who sang so sweetly that even the poor fisherman, busy as he was when he came down to the sea at night to cast his nets, would stop and listen to its song. "Dear God, how beautiful it is!" he said. Then he had to get down to his work, and he forgot the bird, but when he came out next night and the nightingale sang again, he said the same: "Dear God, how beautiful it is!"

Travelers from every country in the world visited the Emperor's city and marveled at the city itself and the palace and the garden, but when they heard the nightingale, every one of them said, "Ah, that's the best thing of all!"

And when the travelers were home they said what they had seen, and learned men wrote books about the city and the palace and the garden, not forgetting the nightingale: They praised that most of all. And poets wrote wonderful verses about the nightingale who lived in the wood by the deep sea.

The books went all over the world, and at last they came to the Emperor too. He sat on his golden seat and read and read, nodding his head again and again with pleasure, for he was delighted with the wonderful descriptions of his city and his palace and his garden. And then he read: "But the nightingale is best of all."

"What's all this?" said the Emperor. "Nightingale? I never heard of it. So there is such a bird in my Imperial realm, in my own garden, and I haven't heard it? Well, to think what one may learn from books!"

And he summoned his Lord-in-Waiting, so very grand a gentleman that if anyone of lesser rank so much as spoke to him or asked him a question, he simply said, "P!" which means nothing at all.

"They say there is a remarkable bird called the nightingale here," said the Emperor, "and they say it's the finest thing in all my Empire. Why has nobody ever told me about this bird?"

"I never heard of it myself," said the Lord-in-Waiting. "It's never been presented at Court."

"I want it to come and sing for me this evening," said the Emperor. "It seems all the world knows what I have here, except me!"

"I never heard of it myself," repeated the Lord-in-Waiting. "But I'll look for it, and I'll find it."

Where was it to be found, though? The Lord-in-Waiting ran up and down all the flights of stairs, through great halls, down corridors, and no one he met had ever heard tell of the nightingale. So the Lord-in-Waiting went back to the Emperor and said it must be just a story made up by the people who wrote the books.

"Your Imperial Majesty mustn't believe everything he reads in books; they are full of invention and not to be trusted."

"But the book in which I read it," said the Emperor, "was sent to me by the high and mighty Emperor of Japan, so it must be true. I want to hear the nightingale! It is to come here this evening, and if it doesn't, I'll have the whole Court thumped in the stomach, right after they've had their supper."

"Tsing-pe!" said the Lord-in-Waiting, and he went off again and ran up and down the flights of stairs, through the halls, and down the corridors, and half the Court went with him, not wanting to be thumped in the stomach. They all asked about the remarkable nightingale, known to everyone else in the world but not to the Court. At last they found

THE NIGHTINGALE **217**

A Reading Skills and Strategies
Making Inferences

❓ What does this exchange imply about the courtiers? Explain your response. [Possible responses: They never leave the artificial world of the palace; they have no knowledge about natural things; their failure to recognize the sounds of cows and frogs suggests that they have a very limited view of life.]

B Elements of Literature
Theme

❓ What themes does the Lord's reaction suggest, given the beauty of the nightingale's song? [Possible response: Appearances can be deceptive; no one should prejudge; true beauty is sometimes not apparent to the eye.]

C Literature Connection

The nightingale's court adventure is echoed in a favorite George Selden story, "The Cricket in Times Square" (1960). Chester Cricket gets trapped in a picnic basket and is brought to New York by mistake. He escapes in the Times Square subway station, where he is rescued by a newsstand boy named Mario. Mario buys Chester a beautiful cage in Chinatown, and the cricket stays at the newsstand for a few weeks, bringing tears to commuters' eyes with his songs, sonatas, and operatic arias. Like the nightingale, Chester eventually returns to his wild home.

a poor little girl in the kitchen, who said "The nightingale? Oh, yes. I know the nightingale very well, and oh, how it can sing! I'm allowed to take some of the food left over from the table to my poor sick mother in the evenings, and she lives down by the shore, so when I'm on my way back, I stop for a rest in the wood and I hear the nightingale sing. It brings tears to my eyes, as if my mother were kissing me."

"Little kitchenmaid," said the Lord-in-Waiting, "I will get you a steady job here in the kitchen and permission to watch the Emperor eat his dinner if you can take us to the nightingale, for it is summoned to Court this evening."

So half the Court went out to the wood where the nightingale used to sing. And as they were going along, a cow began to moo.

"We've found the nightingale!" said the courtiers. "What a powerful voice for such a little creature! I've heard it somewhere before."

A "No, those are cows," said the little kitchenmaid. "We aren't nearly there yet."

Then they heard the frogs croaking in the pond.

"Exquisite!" said the Imperial Palace Chaplain. "Now that I hear it, its song is like little church bells."

"No, those are frogs," said the little kitchenmaid. "But I think we'll soon hear the nightingale now."

And then the nightingale began to sing.

"There it is!" said the little girl. "Listen, listen! It is sitting up there." And she pointed to a small gray bird up in the branches of the trees.

B "Can it be true?" said the Lord-in-Waiting. "I'd never have thought it! It looks like such an ordinary bird. All the color must have drained away from it at the sight of such grand people!"

"Little nightingale," called the kitchenmaid, "our gracious Emperor wants you to sing for him."

"He's very welcome," said the nightingale, and it sang so beautifully it was a joy to hear that song.

"Like glass bells!" said the Lord-in-Waiting. "And see the way its little throat quivers! And to think we never heard it before—what a success it will be at Court!"

"Shall I sing for the Emperor again?" asked the nightingale, who thought the Emperor himself was present.

"My dear, good little nightingale," said the Lord-in-Waiting. "I am pleased and proud to invite you to a party at Court this evening, where you will delight his Imperial Majesty with your lovely song."

"It sounds best out here in the green woods," said the nightingale, but it went along with them willingly enough on hearing it was the Emperor's wish.

What a cleaning and a polishing there was at the palace! The walls and floors, all made of porcelain, shone in the light of thousands of golden lamps. The loveliest of flowers, the chiming ones from the Emperor's garden, were placed along the corridor. With all the hurry and bustle there was such a draft that it made the bells ring out, and you couldn't hear yourself speak.

In the middle of the great hall where the Emperor sat, they placed a golden perch for the nightingale. The little girl, who now had the official title of Kitchenmaid, was allowed to stand behind the door. The entire Court was there, all dressed in their best, and they were all gazing at the little gray bird. The Emperor nodded to it.

And the nightingale sang so sweetly that tears rose to the Emperor's eyes and flowed

Listening to Music

Song of the Nightingale by Igor Stravinsky

Fairy tales have inspired many composers to write operas, ballets, and concert music. Examples include Peter Ilyich Tchaikovsky's ballet *Sleeping Beauty* (1890) and Jules Massenet's opera *Cendrillon* (Cinderella, 1891). Hans Christian Andersen's stories have inspired many composers, including Igor Stravinsky (1882–1971).

Stravinsky grew up in St. Petersburg, Russia,

but settled in France after the 1917 revolution. His "The Rites of Spring" caused audience riots in Paris in 1913. Stravinsky wrote a 45-minute opera/ballet of *The Nightingale* (1908–1914) and later arranged its music into a symphonic poem called "Song of the Nightingale" (*Chant du rossignol*, 1917). The real nightingale is played by the flute, and the mechanical one by the oboe.

Activity

Have students listen to the orchestral version of "Song of the Nightingale." Have them try to identify different parts of the story in the music. Then have a class discussion about how well students think the music captures different scenes and moods in "The Nightingale."

down his cheeks, and then the nightingale sang yet more beautifully, so that its song went right to the heart. The Emperor was so delighted that he said the nightingale was to have his own golden slipper to wear around its neck. But the nightingale thanked him and said it already had its reward.

"I have seen tears in the eyes of the Emperor, and what more could I wish for? An Emperor's tears have wonderful power; God knows that's reward enough for me." And it sang again in its sweet, lovely voice.

"That's the prettiest thing I ever heard," said the ladies standing by, and they poured water into their mouths and tried to trill when they were spoken to, thinking they would be nightingales too. Even the lackeys[3] and the chambermaids expressed satisfaction, which is saying a good deal, for such folk are the very hardest to please. In short, the nightingale was a great success.

And now it was to stay at Court, and have its own cage, and be allowed out twice by day and once by night. Twelve menservants

The Orange Tree Egg by Fabergé.
The Forbes Magazine Collection, New York.

3. **lackeys:** servants.

were to go with it, each holding tight to a silken ribbon tied to the bird's leg. Of course, going out like that was no pleasure at all.

The whole city was talking of the marvelous bird, and if two friends met, one would say, "Night," and the other would say, "Gale," and they sighed, and each knew exactly what the other meant. Eleven grocers' children were named after the bird, but not one of them could sing a note.

One day a big parcel came for the Emperor, with *Nightingale* written on it.

"Here's a new book about our famous bird," said the Emperor. But it wasn't a book; it was a little mechanical toy in a box, an artificial nightingale. It was meant to look like the real one, but it was covered all over with diamonds and rubies and sapphires. As soon as you wound the bird up, it sang one of the real nightingale's songs, and its tail went up and down, all shining with silver and gold. It had a little ribbon around its neck with the words: "The Emperor of Japan's nightingale is a poor thing beside the nightingale of the Emperor of China."

"How exquisite!" everyone said, and they

Professional Notes

The Creation of the Easter Eggs

"All the Easter eggs . . . are highly miniaturized, lavish productions, truly reflecting the wealth and splendour of the imperial court," wrote art historians Habsburg-Lothringen and Von Solodkoff in 1979. "Each one is a masterpiece in itself, representing hundreds of hours of workmanship. All the workshops—those of the goldsmiths, enamellers, miniature painters, lapidaries, and jewelers—collaborated to make them unique. . . . The coach in the Coronation Coach Egg of 1897, by Georg Stein, took fifteen months to complete. . . . Most of these elaborate works of art were several years in the making. From the first scale drawing embodying Fabergé's idea, right down to the specially constructed case, each step was controlled by the master and thoroughly discussed at the round table with all the workmen concerned."

RESPONDING TO THE ART

Edmund Dulac (see p. T216) loved Persian miniatures and studied them closely. Their influence over his work, both in color and style, is readily apparent. Rather than using conventional pastel colors, he adopted the richer, deeper shades seen in Eastern art: dark reds, brilliant yellows, and shades like magenta and violet. (See for example, the Chamberlain's robe in the watercolor on p. 224.) The night scenes in *The Arabian Nights* and "The Nightingale" gave him great freedom to explore these richer colors.

Activity. Who is the man in the painting? How do you know? [He is the fisherman mentioned on p. 217. He is on a little boat, he looks poor, and he is stopping to listen to the nightingale.] What time of day is it? How do you know? [Possible response: It is twilight, because the blues in the picture are grayed; it is nighttime on a moonlit night, because the crescent moon is visible above the fisherman's head.]

Chinese Man on Boat (1911) by Edmund Dulac.

220 MACHINE MANIA: PEOPLE AND TECHNOLOGY

Crossing the Curriculum

Film

Students may enjoy viewing the film *Hans Christian Andersen* (see p. 226). This charming musical tells a highly romanticized account of Andersen's life and includes a number of scenes showing how he was inspired to write some of his tales. Before students see the film, encourage them to locate and read more stories by Andersen.

Art

Andersen's stories have inspired many illustrators besides Edmund Dulac. Encourage students to look at other picture-book versions of Andersen's stories. Most public libraries have a wide variety of picture books. Students might want to look especially for other versions of "The Nightingale," such as the one illustrated by Nancy Ekholm Burkert. Have students bring the picture books to class and set aside some time for them to exchange books and study the illustrations. Whose work do students like best? Why? Students may want to create their own illustrations for "The Nightingale."

gave the man who had brought the artificial bird the title of Lord High Nightingale Bringer.

"Now they can sing together. We'll have a duet," said the Court.

So sing together they did, but it wasn't quite right, for the real nightingale sang in its own way, and the artificial bird's song worked by means of a cylinder inside it.

"It's not the new bird's fault," said the Master of the Emperor's Music. "It keeps perfect time and performs in my very own style." So the artificial bird was to sing alone. It was just as great a success as the real bird, and then it was so much prettier to look at! It glittered like jewelry.

It sang the same song thirty-three times, and still it wasn't tired. The Court would happily have heard the song again, but the Emperor thought it was time for the real nightingale to sing. But where had it gone? No one had noticed it flying out of the open window, out and away, back to its own green wood.

"What's all this?" said the Emperor, and all the courtiers said the nightingale was a most ungrateful creature. "But we still have the better bird," they said, and the mechanical nightingale had to sing the same song again, for the thirty-fourth time. It was a difficult song, and the Court didn't quite know it by heart yet. The Master of the Music praised the bird to the skies and actually stated that it was better than the real nightingale not just because of its plumage,[4] glittering with so many lovely diamonds, but inside too.

"For you see, my lords, and particularly your Imperial Majesty, you can never tell just what the real bird is going to sing, but with

4. **plumage** (plo͞om′ij): feathers of a bird.

the artificial bird it's all settled. It will sing like this and it won't sing any other way. You can understand it; you can open it up and see how human minds made it, where the wheels and cylinders lie, how they work, and how they all go around."

"My own opinion entirely," said everyone, and the Master of the Music got permission to show the bird to all the people next Sunday, for the Emperor said they should hear it too. And hear it they did, and they were as happy as if they had gotten tipsy on tea, for tea is what the Chinese drink; and they all said "Ooh!" and pointed their fingers in the air, and nodded. However, the poor fisherman who used to listen to the real nightingale said, "It sounds nice enough, and quite like the real bird, but there's something missing, I don't know what."

And the real nightingale was banished from the Emperor's domains.

The artificial bird had a place on a silk cushion next to the Emperor's bed. All the presents of gold and jewels it had been given lay around it, and it bore the title of Imperial Bedside-Singer-in-Chief, so it took first place on the left side: The Emperor thought the side upon which the heart lies was the better one, and even an Emperor's heart is on his left. And the Master of the Music wrote a book, in twenty-five volumes, about the mechanical bird. The book was very long and very learned and full of hard words in Chinese, so all the people at Court pretended to have read it for fear of looking stupid and being thumped in the stomach.

So it went on for a year. The Emperor, the Court, and all the other Chinese now knew every little trill of the mechanical bird's song by heart, but they liked it all the better for that. They could join in the song themselves,

A

A Reading Skills and Strategies
Connecting with the Text
❓ If you were the nightingale, would you want to leave the palace? Why or why not? [Possible responses: Yes, everyone seems to like the mechanical bird better, so there's no point in staying; no, the palace offers comfortable shelter, and the Emperor would soon grow tired of the mechanical bird.]

B Critical Thinking
Making Judgments
❓ Do you agree with the Master of the Music's reasoning? Why or why not? [Possible responses: No, the beauty and wonder of the nightingale are partly due to its mysteriousness and originality in nature; yes, things are more enjoyable and interesting when you can figure out exactly how they work.]

A Reading Skills and Strategies
Comparing and Contrasting
? What similarities and differences does this paragraph suggest exist between the two nightingales? [Differences: The real one sings when it wants to, but the mechanical one must sing on command; the real one could recover from an illness, but damage to the mechanical one is permanent. Similarities: The real one can get tired or sick, and the mechanical one can wear out.]

B Cultural Connections
Danse Macabre
Andersen's description of Death includes important similarities to the personification of death in medieval and Renaissance Europe. Andersen does not describe Death except to mention "great empty eye sockets" (p. 225). This implies that he is invoking the image of death as a skeleton, which was the image of death for centuries of European painting. Medieval paintings often show death as a skeleton, appearing to grin, as all skeletons do. Death appears at people's bedsides, beckoning them to follow him, and often wears a black hooded cloak. Charles Dickens gives a vivid description of this figure in his story *A Christmas Carol*, where it appears as the Ghost of Christmas Future.

and they did too. Even the street urchins[5] sang, "Tweet-tweet-tweet, cluck-cluck-cluck-cluck," and the Emperor sang too. How delightful it all was!

One evening, however, as the artificial bird was singing its very best and the Emperor lay in his bed listening, it went, "Twang!" and something broke inside it. The wheels whirred around and the music stopped.

The Emperor jumped straight out of bed and summoned his own doctor, but there was nothing the doctor could do. So they fetched the watchmaker, and after much talk and much tinkering about with it, he got the bird to work again after a fashion. However, he said it mustn't be made to sing very often, because the little pegs on the cylinders had worn out and there was no way of replacing them without spoiling the tune. This was very sad indeed. They let the mechanical bird sing just once a year, and even that was a strain on it, but the Master of the Music used to make a little speech crammed with difficult words, saying the bird was still as good as ever, and so then of course it was, just as he said.

Five years passed by, and then the whole country was in great distress, for the people all loved their Emperor, and now he was sick and likely to die. A new Emperor had already been chosen, and people stood in the street and asked the Lord-in-Waiting how the old one was.

He only said, "P!" and shook his head.

The Emperor lay in his great, magnificent bed, and he was cold and pale. The whole Court thought he was dead already, and the courtiers went off to pay their respects to the new Emperor. The lackeys of the bedchamber got together for a gossip, and the

maids-in-waiting were having a big coffee party. Cloth was laid down in all the halls and corridors so that you could hear no footfall, and all was quiet, very quiet. But the Emperor was not dead yet. Stiff and pale, he lay in his bed of state hung with velvet and with heavy golden tassels. There was a window open up above, and moonlight shone in on the Emperor and the mechanical nightingale.

The poor Emperor could hardly draw breath, and he felt as if something was sitting on his chest. He opened his eyes and saw that it was Death sitting there. Death was wearing his golden crown, and Death had his imperial golden saber[6] in one hand and his magnificent banner in the other. And strange faces peered out from among the folds of the great velvet hangings of the bed: Some were grim and hideous, others blessed and mild. They were the Emperor's good deeds and bad deeds all looking at him as Death sat there on his heart.

"Remember this?" they whispered, one by one. "Remember that?" And they reminded him of so many things that the sweat broke out on his forehead.

"No, no! I never knew!" said the Emperor. "Music!" he cried. "Music on the great Chinese drum to keep me from hearing what you say!"

But on they went, and Death kept nodding like a Chinese mandarin[7] at everything they said.

"Music, music!" cried the Emperor. "Sing, my little golden bird, oh, sing! I have given you gold and treasure; I myself hung my golden slipper around your neck, so sing for me now, sing!"

But the bird was silent, for there wasn't

---

5. **street urchins:** mischievous youngsters from the street.
6. **saber:** heavy sword with a curved blade.
7. **Chinese mandarin:** high official.

Connecting Across Texts

Connecting with "John Henry"
Have students turn back to the beginning of this unit and reread the story of the contest between John Henry and the steam drill. Have them compare and contrast it with the breakdown of the mechanical bird. John Henry dies because of his exertion; do students think the steam drill is as vulnerable as he is? What are machines vulnerable to that people (or nightingales) are not?

What can happen to an automobile that would not happen to a horse? What do you think John Henry's foreman might learn from reading "The Nightingale"? Students can share their ideas in a class discussion. [Students should realize that machines can break down, lose parts, overheat, and self-destruct in other ways. Machines are liable to be mistreated or otherwise overused by

careless people. Machines are not tireless; they have a certain life span, as do people and animals. People and animals know to rest when they are tired or to take care of themselves when they are sick or injured, but machines are at the mercy of the people who use them.]

Chinese Man in Bed with Goblin over Him (1911) by Edmund Dulac.

THE NIGHTINGALE 223

Dulac became a British subject in 1912. The success of his first five picture books (including the Andersen tales) led to a substantial book contract in 1914. Dulac agreed to produce twenty-five illustrations each for three books over three years. The outbreak of World War I canceled the contract, but Dulac did some important work during the war years. His *Fairy Tales of the Allied Nations* (1916) was highly praised. He did each illustration in the style of the country from which its story came.

Dulac applied his artistic abilities to many fields besides children's books—he designed theatrical sets and costumes, composed incidental music for plays, illustrated adult books (such as the poetry of his friend William Butler Yeats), designed postage stamps, and won renown for his humorous caricatures. Dulac died in 1953.

Activity. Ask students which image in this drawing attracts their attention first. [Most will say the little bird, encircled by the bright lantern. Some might be drawn to the chamberlain because he is the largest and most central figure.] Which of Dulac's illustrations do students like best? Why?

The Chamberlain Goes in Search of the Nightingale (1911) by Edmund Dulac.

224 MACHINE MANIA: PEOPLE AND TECHNOLOGY

anyone there to wind it up, and it could not sing without being wound. And Death gazed and gazed at the Emperor through his great empty eye sockets, and all was still, all was terribly still.

And at that moment the loveliest of songs was heard coming in through the window. It was the real nightingale sitting in the branches outside. It had heard of the Emperor's sickness, and so it had come to sing him a song of hope and comfort. And as it sang, the phantom shapes faded away, the blood flowed faster and faster through the Emperor's weak limbs, and Death himself listened and said, "Go on, go on, little nightingale!"

"Yes, if you give me that fine gold saber! Yes, if you give me that gorgeous banner! Yes, if you will give me the Emperor's crown!"

So Death gave all those treasures up, each for one of the nightingale's songs, and the nightingale sang on and on. It sang of the quiet churchyard where white roses grow, and the air is fragrant with elder flowers, and the fresh grass is wet with the tears of the bereaved.[8] Then Death longed for his own garden again, and he drifted away out of the window like cold white mist.

"Thank you, thank you," said the Emperor. "Most blessed of little birds, I know you now! I drove you away from my domains, yet you have sung away all those evil visions from my bed and driven Death from my heart. How can I reward you?"

"You have rewarded me already," said the nightingale. "I brought tears to your eyes the first time I sang to you, and I will never forget those tears. They are the jewels that rejoice a singer's heart. But you must sleep

8. **the bereaved** (bē·rēvd′): survivors of a person who recently died.

now and be fresh and strong when you wake. Now I will sing for you."

The nightingale sang, and the Emperor fell into a sweet, gentle, and refreshing slumber.

The sun was shining in on him through the window when he woke, feeling strong and healthy. None of his servants were back, for they all thought he was dead, but the nightingale still sat there singing.

"You must stay with me forever," said the Emperor. "You need never sing unless you want to, and I will break the artificial bird into a thousand pieces."

"Don't do that," said the nightingale. "It did the best it could, after all, so you should keep it. I cannot live or nest in a palace; but let me come to you when I feel like it, and I'll sit on the branch outside your window and sing in the evening to gladden your heart and fill it with thoughts. I will sing of those who are happy and those who are sad; I will sing to the bad and the good around you. A little singing bird flies far and wide, to the poor fisherman and the peasant's hut, to people very far from you and your Court. I love your heart more than I love your crown, yet that crown seems to have something sacred about it. I will come and sing for you, but you must promise me one thing."

"Anything," said the Emperor, and he stood there in the imperial robes he had put on again, holding his heavy golden saber to his breast.

"All I ask is that you will not let anyone know you have a little bird who tells you everything; that will be best."

Then the nightingale flew away.

The Emperor's servants came in to look at him lying dead, and they stood there amazed.

"Good morning," said the Emperor.

A Elements of Literature
Symbols
? Why does the nightingale ask for these things? [They are symbols that stand for the Emperor's life and his power. If Death lets them go, the Emperor will live.]

B Reading Skills and Strategies
Interpreting
? What does the nightingale sing of? [It sings of human joy and grief, of good and evil.] Whom does it sing for? [for the poor as well as for the Court] What does the bird mean when he says he loves the Emperor's heart more than his Crown? [He loves the person, not the person's wealth; he loves the person's capacity for love, not his power.]

Making the Connections

Connecting to the Theme: "Machine Mania: People and Technology"
After students have finished reading the story, discuss the collection theme. Why is it foolish to expect a machine to do exactly what a living creature can do? [Possible response: A machine can't take an active role; it can only be acted

upon.] If students could have only one thing and had to make a choice, which would they choose: a machine, such as a computer or a TV set? a garden? or a pet? Ask them to explain why.

MEET THE WRITER

A Fairy-Tale Life

Once upon a time, **Hans Christian Andersen** (1805–1875), the son of a poor shoemaker, lived in a small town in Denmark called Odense. As a boy, Hans loved the theater, but he couldn't pay for a ticket. So he made friends with an usher and got a copy of each program:

66 With this I seated myself in a corner and imagined an entire play, according to the name of the piece and the characters in it. That was my first unconscious poetizing. 99

A fortuneteller predicted a great future for Hans and said his hometown would someday be lit up in his honor. Hans was only fourteen when he went to Copenhagen to seek his fortune. By age twenty-eight, he had failed as a singer, actor, dancer, and writer. That year he began writing the fairy tales that soon made him known around the world. Ideas for these tales came from his life, he said.

66 [They] lay in my mind like seeds and only needed a gentle touch—the kiss of a sunbeam or drop of malice—to flower. 99

At the peak of his fame, Andersen fell in love with a great singer, Jenny Lind, who was nicknamed "the Swedish Nightingale." Andersen wrote "The Nightingale" in part to celebrate her beautiful voice and natural singing style, so different from the artificial Italian opera style fashionable at the time.

Every year around Christmas, until he was sixty-eight, Andersen published some new fairy tales. Late in his life his hometown of Odense hosted a festival for him, and the whole city was lit up in his honor. It's no wonder that Andersen called his autobiography *The Fairy Tale of My Life*!

More Fairy Tales

The collected works of Hans Christian Andersen include such beloved stories as "The Little Mermaid," "The Ugly Duckling," "The Steadfast Tin Soldier," "The Emperor's New Clothes," and "The Snow Queen." In 1952, a musical was made of Andersen's life, titled *Hans Christian Andersen,* starring Danny Kaye (Samuel Goldwyn). Your video store may have a copy of it for rent.

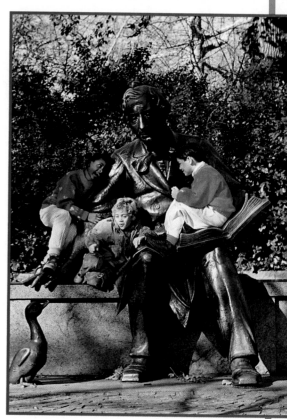

Statue of Hans Christian Andersen in Central Park, New York.

READ ON

• Low-Fat Diet

In Dean Marney's *The Computer That Ate My Brother* (Scholastic), Harry Smith gets a computer for his twelfth birthday. However, the games *this* computer plays are like no games Harry has ever seen. After the computer starts displaying thoughts of its own, Harry enlists the help of the eccentric Imogene S. Cuniformly, a retired math teacher, to solve the mystery in this lively tale of technology gone mad.

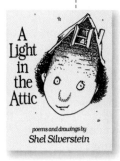

Poetic Tech

Discover the "Homework Machine" and "How to Make a Swing with No Rope or Board or Nails" in Shel Silverstein's *A Light in the Attic* (HarperCollins). In this imaginative collection of poems and drawings, you'll meet a boy who learns some funny things from TV commercials, find out what can happen when you push a button, and consider a guitar that can play and sing all by itself.

Flying Machines

They started out as bicycle salesmen with a dream. Against all odds they managed to do what no one had yet done: build a machine that could fly. *The Wright Brothers at Kitty Hawk* (Scholastic) by Donald J. Sobol is the story of the famous brothers, Orville and Wilbur Wright, who pioneered the aviation industry.

Other Picks

• Janet Asimov, *The Package in Hyperspace* (Walker). Spaceship passengers Ginnela and Pete Wade face the challenge of survival when their ship becomes disabled.
• Lee Bennett Hopkins, editor, *Click, Rumble, Roar* (Thomas Crowell). Twelve modern poets offer beautiful, unusual, and comic looks at machines and their effects on us.

READ ON
Portfolio Assessment Options
The following projects can help you evaluate and assess the reading your students do outside of class. Students can add videotapes, audiotapes, or slides of completed projects to their portfolios.

• **Role-Play a Dialogue**
Encourage pairs of students to respond to their selections by assuming the identities of two characters whom they have read about. Students should discuss topics of conversation and where they think the discussion may lead before they present their role-play for the class.

• **Design a Book Jacket**
Invite students to design book jackets for their chosen selections. A book jacket should depict some scene or theme that is central to the selection and include relevant jacket language, such as a plot summary and critic's blurb. Encourage students to use their imaginations, to be as creative as they like, and to use any medium they want. Display finished book jackets in class.

• **Write a Review** Have students write book reviews of their chosen selections. Remind them that a review is not a retelling of the contents or plot, but a critique of the work. Start students off with such questions as these: Why did you like or dislike this book? Would you recommend it? Why or why not?

• **Design a Time Line** Have students work together to create time lines for the major events in the selection they have chosen. Students can add annotations of great historical events that happened during the period their time lines cover. Encourage students to illustrate their time lines. Post their finished work in the classroom.

Speaking and Listening Workshop

Resources

Portfolio Management System
• *Performance Rubric, p. 132*

Introducing the Speaking and Listening Workshop

Point out to students that in everyday life, we communicate ideas both verbally and nonverbally. Review some basic nonverbal techniques, such as eye contact, posture, and common gestures (stop, come here, etc). Explain that ideas are also communicated by the rate, volume, pitch, and tone of a speaker's voice. In an oral reading, the speaker uses these techniques to convey his or her own interpretation of the poet's words. Choose a short poem, and model at least two different oral interpretations for students to illustrate the above points.

Try It Out
Encourage students to choose works to present that have a strong emotional appeal to them.

Determining Purpose
Before students listen to a speech, they should identify their purpose:
1. Will they listen critically because they think the speaker is not to be trusted?
2. Will they listen to gain information on a topic?
3. Will they listen to solve a particular problem?
4. Will they listen just to enjoy themselves?

Try It Out
Use the tips in this workshop to prepare and present an oral interpretation of one of the poems in this book (or another poem or group of poems approved by your teacher).

ORAL INTERPRETATION
BRINGING A POEM TO LIFE

When you read a work of literature aloud, you express its meaning with your voice and your body movements. This art is called **oral interpretation.** Poems, with their striking images and sounds, are especially well suited to oral interpretation.

Choosing a Poem

Find a poem that you like a great deal. You may like it for what it says to you, or you may like it for the way it sounds.

Getting to Know the Poem

Before you read your poem for an audience, you must know it inside out. Follow these steps to understand it better:

• Read the poem several times, both silently and aloud. As you read, think about the poem's meaning. What is the most important idea, or theme?

• Try to put this idea into your own words.

• Study the poem again. Does it express a strong emotion—anger, grief, or joy, for example?

Making Decisions

Poems can be presented in many ways. Here are some possibilities you'll want to consider:

• individual reading, in which a single reader presents a poem, either reading from a script or reciting from memory

• reading by two or more readers who read or recite different lines or parts of a poem

• choral reading, in which a group of readers presents a poem. Sometimes you can use two choruses: One possibility is a

---

Reaching All Students

Struggling Readers
Have students work in small groups to perform a Reader's Theater in which they share the responsibilities of oral reading. Instruct them to divide the lines in the poem equally among the members of the group, and encourage them to critique their own work. Ask them to perform the reading for the entire class once they have managed to settle on a delivery that suits them.

English Language Learners
Let students who are learning English work with more proficient English speakers on this activity. The proficient English speaker should read the poem aloud as many times as necessary and then mark the poem based on the decisions the two students make about key phrases, pauses, volume, pitch, and pace variation. Remind them to choose a short poem so that it may be easily memorized for performance.

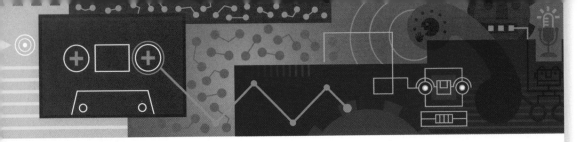

male chorus and a female chorus. Poems with refrains are often presented in choral readings.

- reading to musical accompaniment. Poets sometimes read to the strumming of guitars or other musical sounds. Sometimes readers use background sounds that relate to the poem. If you read "John Henry" aloud, for example, you might let the audience hear the sound of hammering, steady and strong, in the background.

Preparing a Reading Script

A reading script is a typed or neatly written copy of the poem that you have marked to show how you want to present the poem to your audience. Mark your script in this way:

- Underline or highlight key phrases or ideas.
- Draw a slash or vertical line wherever you will pause.
- Jot notes in the margin about changes in your volume, pitch, or pace as well as any gestures you plan to use.

Stepping Onstage

Poetry readings have become very popular all over the country—from cafés in New York City to bookstores in Austin and coffee shops in Seattle. Why not plan a poetry reading for your school or neighborhood? You might find that you enjoy sharing words that mean something to you.

CALVIN AND HOBBES © Watterson. Reprinted with permission of UNIVERSAL PRESS SYNDICATE. All rights reserved.

SPEAKING AND LISTENING WORKSHOP 229

Try It Out

Read this sentence: "I've seen that guy here before." Now, repeat the sentence to a friend. First, say the words as if you were afraid. Then, say them as if you were proud, annoyed, glad, or hiding something. Can your friend guess the emotions you are trying to show?

Teaching the Workshop

- Choose a short poem to copy onto a transparency, and model for students the steps in preparing a reading script described on p. 229.
- Read the poem aloud as you determine the key phrases, pauses, volume, pitch, and pace variations, and mark the poem accordingly.
- Using another poem, ask students to practice marking the stanzas as you have modeled, and ask volunteers to read them aloud.

Try It Out
Model for students how differences in volume, pitch, pace, and stress can change the emotional impact of a single sentence.

Grading Timesaver

Rubrics for this Speaking and Listening Workshop Assignment appear on p. 132 of *The Portfolio Management System*.

Reading Aloud in Selected Texts
When students read aloud, their reading should communicate their understanding of the text and should engage their listeners. To help students with their understanding of a text, suggest that they look up the meanings of unfamiliar words, pay attention to the words' connotations, and think about the writer's word choices. Then, ask them to paraphrase the work.

To help students engage their listeners, suggest that they choose their pitch, volume, and tone of voice to reflect meaning and mood, use stresses and pauses to emphasize important words and ideas, and vary their rate of speaking to punctuate and group ideas.

Students may enjoy applying these skills to some of these selected texts:
- "Foul Shot," p. 10
- "Cynthia in the Snow," p. 178
- "Ode to Mi Gato," p. 259
- "The Sneetches," p. 380
- "Macavity: The Mystery Cat," p. 429

Comparing Perceptions
After students listen to the poem, ask them to compare their perceptions of it. Did the speaker get the message across? Do they agree on the speaker's effectiveness?

Using Students' Strengths

Auditory Learners
Ask students to read their marked scripts aloud into a tape recorder. Have them play back the recording, listening for the appropriateness of their pauses, volume, pitch, and pace. Ask them to make any changes they think will improve their performance.

Interpersonal Learners
Provide the opportunity for students to perform their oral readings for other classes, for younger students, or for people in the community. Remind them to practice enough to feel comfortable performing in a public arena.

Writer's Workshop

MAIN OBJECTIVE
Write a how-to essay

PROCESS OBJECTIVES

1. Use appropriate prewriting techniques to identify and develop a topic
2. Create a first draft
3. Use evaluation criteria as a basis for determining revision strategies
4. Revise the first draft incorporating suggestions generated by self- or peer evaluation
5. Proofread and correct errors
6. Create a final draft
7. Choose an appropriate method of publication
8. Reflect on progress as a writer

Planning

- **Block Schedule**
  Block Scheduling Lesson Plans with Pacing Guide
- **One-Stop Planner**
  CD-ROM with Test Generator

Introducing the Writer's Workshop

- Point out that many activities in a person's daily routine involve some kind of process. List a few common activities on the chalkboard: for example, taking a shower, brushing your teeth, and tying your shoelaces. Explain that since we learned how to do these things a long time ago, the instructions or steps are no longer vivid in our minds. Have the class decide on a simple daily task and work together to list the steps involved in the process.
- If possible, bring in examples of how-to instructions from game boxes, computer programs, model kits, or crafts projects.

ASSIGNMENT
Write an explanation of how to do something.

AIM
To inform; to explain.

AUDIENCE
Your teacher and other adults or children a bit younger than you (you decide).

EXPOSITORY WRITING

HOW-TO ESSAY

One way to teach someone a process (giving a dog a bath, for instance) is to *show* how to do it. Another way is to *write* instructions that someone can follow. In this workshop you'll learn how to write instructions for a **process**. You'll explain **how to** do or make something.

Professional Model

How to Perform the Heimlich Maneuver

The Heimlich maneuver involves applying sudden sharp pressure (abdominal thrusts) to the front of the body. For a child over a year old, stand or kneel behind her and put both arms around her. Place your fists against the soft area above the child's navel and below her ribs. Put your other hand over your fist and push in and up four times, quickly and hard. This pressure forces the air out of her chest and along with it the object that is blocking her breathing. You may have to repeat these four thrusts several times.

The writers start with a definition of the technique.

The writers describe each step in the process.

The writers use an illustration to demonstrate the technique.

MAKE A FIST LIKE THIS, COVER IT WITH YOUR OTHER HAND.

PUSH IN AND UP FOUR TIMES

QUICKLY AND HARD.

The child or baby may eventually spit out the object or swallow it. In

  *Resources: Print and Media*

Writing and Language
- *Portfolio Management System*
  - Prewriting, p. 133
  - Peer Editing, p. 134
  - Assessment Rubric, p. 135
- *Workshop Resources*
  - Revision Strategy Teaching Notes, p. 9
  - Revision Strategy Transparencies 5, 6, 7

Assessment
- *Standardized Test Preparation*
  - Worksheet, p. 130
  - Transparencies 19–24

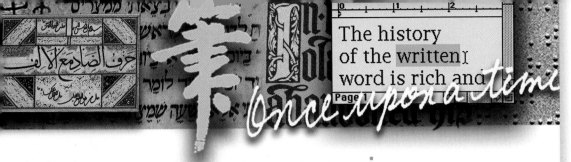

Teaching the Writer's Workshop

Prewriting

- Make sure students review their Writer's Notebook assignments. The notes they took throughout the collection will help them decide on an activity or process.
- If students get feedback from their classmates, urge the respondents to refrain from making value judgments or direct criticisms. When classmates rate each activity on a scale, remind them not to give higher ratings only to things they like to do, but to think of a wider audience.

(continued)

either case, as soon as he is breathing regularly, call the doctor.

It's important to remember that the Heimlich maneuver should not be performed on anyone who can talk, cry, or breathe, even with difficulty. An unnecessary Heimlich maneuver can do harm.

The writers end by adding an important piece of information.

—from *The New Complete Babysitters Handbook* by Carol Barkin and Elizabeth James

Prewriting

1. Writer's Notebook

Look back at your Writer's Notebook for this collection. You may want to explain how to do something you mentioned there. If you'd rather come up with a fresh idea to write about, try asking yourself these questions:

- Which activities am I good at?
- Which activities can be divided into steps?
- Which process will interest my audience most?
- Which process can I describe in a few paragraphs?

2. Getting Feedback

Another way to find ideas is to get feedback from people. On a sheet of paper, list three activities that you're considering. Below each, identify the audience you have in mind. Make several copies of your idea sheet, and give one to four or five classmates. Ask them to rate each activity on a scale from 1 to 5 to show how much they think

How to Keep Raccoons out of the Garbage Can
<u>Adults and classmates</u>
Rating: 5

How to Feed a Baby
<u>Classmates</u>   Rating: 2

How to Cure Hiccups
<u>Classmates</u>   Rating: 5

How to Remove Gum from Hair
<u>4th grade</u>   Rating: 4

How to Do Your Own Wash
<u>Classmates</u>   Rating: 2

WORK IN PROGRESS

How to Make Wrapping Paper

Steps	Equipment and Materials
1. Cover floor or table to protect it.	
2. Pour one paint color in each tray.	washable paints; 2 or 3 Styrofoam trays
3. Make designs and patterns.	big sheets of white paper
4. Dip printing tool into paint.	pieces of sponge, bottle caps, corncobs— whatever you want!
5. Let paper dry flat.	

WRITER'S WORKSHOP **231**

Reaching All Students

Struggling Writers

These students will benefit from a review of transitional words and phrases. Explain that *transitions* are words or phrases that connect one idea to another. Transitions can show cause and effect: *as a result, because, since, therefore.* They can show time: *after, before, finally, last, first, next.* They can show place: *above, below, across, nearby, next to.* Transitions can also show degrees of relevance or urgency: *mainly, first, last, more important.*

English Language Learners

Students learning English as a second language may prefer to brainstorm notes and even to generate a first draft in their native language. Encourage them to write in the language in which they are most fluent until they have recorded a satisfying introduction and sequence of events. Reassure students that their English versions do not need to be direct translations.

Drafting

- Work with the class to develop techniques for turning prewriting materials, such as notes, lists, and sketches, into complete sentences. Make sure that a logical sequence is maintained.
- Remind students to avoid personal comments in the bodies of their essays. They can save these observations for the opening and concluding sections of their essays.
- Remind students to double-space when they write their drafts. They should also leave extra space in the right margin. These blank spaces will be used for comments and editing marks.

Framework for a How-To Essay

You can organize your process paper in two ways. You can begin with a few sentences specifying all the ingredients and equipment needed for the process and then describe the steps (see the graphic organizer at the top of page 233). If you don't want to note all the equipment and materials at the beginning, list the ones needed with each step. The framework for your paper would then look like this:

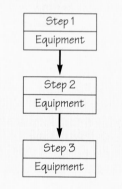

readers would like to learn about that process. (See the examples at the top of the right column on page 231.)

You might also ask your family and friends for ideas. They probably know your interests and skills better than anybody else. They may be able to come up with an idea no one else has thought of.

3. Listing Steps and Equipment

After you've found a topic for your how-to paper, (a) divide the process into steps and (b) list what's needed to do the activity. You might start by making a chart like the one in the right column on page 231. Notice that the steps are listed in **chronological,** or time, order. After you write down the steps, you may decide to move some around or cross out unnecessary ones. (If you're making your list on a computer, you can move steps around easily.) As you finalize your list of steps, keep your audience in mind. For an audience of third-graders, for instance, you may need to define some words or explain how or where to get ingredients or materials. Sixth-graders, on the other hand, may already know this information and may feel insulted if you include it.

Drafting

1. Organizing Your First Draft

Your Prewriting notes should contain most of the specific information you need. Keep looking at them as you write your first draft. Try to get your ideas down quickly.

You may want to **elaborate** on (describe in detail) some of the steps and equipment you listed. Be sure that any examples, descriptive details, or definitions you include with each step make it clearer. Don't add unnecessary information, even if it's interesting. Keep your readers focused on the process. Just describe each step fully, and move on to the next.

If you are explaining a process for readers younger than you, try to think of any questions they might have. Always keep safety issues in mind. For a how-to paper on making fry bread, for instance, you should explain to your readers how to tell when the oil is just hot enough. You should tell them how to place the dough into the cooking oil (*very carefully*).

Crossing the Curriculum

Science

A simple scientific process can serve as the subject of a how-to essay. Have students talk to their science teachers about possibilities. They might also present a demonstration of the process to the class after they read their how-to essays aloud. Make sure students clear their how-to science demonstration with you first.

Nature

Nature is a source of many possible subjects for a how-to essay. Students can describe how to grow a plant or how to take care of a garden. If students have pets at home, they might want to write about how they take care of their animals. Before they start their essays, they should make a list of steps involved in good animal care.

You may find the graphic organizer below helpful. Copy it, and add as many steps as you need. Write in complete sentences.

| Equipment, ingredients, and materials needed:_____ |
| _____ |
| Step 1_____ |
| _____ |
| Step 2_____ |
| _____ |
| Step 3_____ |
| _____ |

Sentence Workshop
H E L P

Stringy sentences:
page 235.

Communications Handbook
H E L P

See Proofreaders' Marks.

Using the Model

After students have completed their drafts, they may benefit from another look at the Student Model. Have students ask themselves the following questions.

❓ How does the writer interest the reader at the beginning?

❓ What details does the writer use to help the reader visualize the event?

❓ What techniques does this writer use that you might apply in your essay?

Student Model

How to Choose a Book You Will Enjoy

Do you ever feel that you will never find a book that you will like? Well, read on to find out what to do if you have trouble choosing a book you will like.

First, pick out five books that have interesting titles, or pick five that belong to your favorite book category. Then, just stare at each front cover. Examine the titles and pictures (if there are any). After this, read the back covers and the prefaces so you can get to know the main characters, the main idea, and the summary of the story. If what is written on the back interests you, keep the book. If it does not interest you, put it back on the shelf. You should only be left with two or three books. Now, read the title of each book carefully again and again until one of the titles seems more interesting to you than the others. Finally, read the first couple of chapters of the book you ended up with.

If the first couple of chapters are not interesting or are too hard for you to read, don't put the book back! Read on. Try to enjoy the book; try to understand it. But if you really can't go on, put the book back on the shelf.

If this process worked and you enjoyed the book you chose, write on a piece of paper the author's name and find more books by this author.

—Raisa Ali
Pacific Academy Preparatory School
Richmond, California

The intro-duction grabs the reader's attention by asking a question.

The writer breaks the process down into a series of steps.

The writer uses transitions (First, Then, After this, Now, Finally) to help the reader follow the steps in the process.

The writer concludes by referring to the process and adding a suggestion.

Evaluating and Revising

- Have students use the Evaluation Criteria to review their drafts and determine needed revisions.
- Point out that the revision phase is the time to add words, phrases, and sometimes sentences; to cross out things; to change things; to rearrange; and to get help in problem areas.
- Ask students to listen to the voice of their writing by reading it aloud. Then, have them, based on the reading, make adjustments so that the essay flows more smoothly.

Proofreading

Have students proofread their own papers first and then exchange them with other students. Suggest that students pay close attention to transitional words and phrases so that the chronological order of events in their how-to essays will be clear.

If time permits, the final copy should be put aside for at least a day before it is proofread one last time by the author.

Remind students that they must spell accurately in final drafts. Suggest that they use a spelling checker if they are using a computer that has one. Make sure students understand that a spelling checker will not alert them to errors involving homophones and homographs.

Publishing

Encourage students to present their essays to the audience they were written for. If they were written for an audience of younger children, students might want to compile a class collection of essays that can be shared with a younger class.

Reflecting

Suggest that students reflect on this assignment by answering the following questions:
1. What was the most difficult part of writing this essay?
2. What did I like best about writing this essay?
3. How can I use what I learned about informative writing in other forms of writing or in daily life?

Strategies for Elaboration

Using Transitions

Words like *first, next, later, before, after,* and *when* are called transitions. They act like traffic signals, telling readers when to take each step. Another kind of transition tells readers where things are or where they go. They are words and phrases that show location, such as *above, below, next to,* and *in the middle.* Use both types of transitions to make your how-to paper clear and easy to follow.

■ **Evaluation Criteria**

A good how-to paper

1. *describes the steps, equipment, and materials needed to complete the task*

2. *presents each step clearly so that anyone can perform it correctly*

3. *lists the steps in a logical (usually chronological) order*

4. *stays on track—sticks to the process being explained*

---

2. Beginning and Ending

The introduction of a process paper should be short and to the point. Try to hook your readers' attention and make them want to know more. In the first two or three sentences, identify the process you're going to describe. You may want to explain why you picked it and why it's fun or worth doing.

Here are some ideas for a strong conclusion:

- Refer to something you said in the introduction. For instance, tell how useful the process is. Don't repeat your exact words—add a new piece of information.
- Find a way to mention the audience. You might say, "I made my first fry bread when I was in the fourth grade. You're never too young to start having fun in the kitchen."
- Tell how sharing this process makes you feel. Include sensory details. If you've written a recipe, for instance, describe how the product smells and tastes.

Evaluating and Revising

Self-Evaluation

Ask yourself these questions:

- Have I made my instructions easy enough for my audience? Are they so easy that my paper will bore my readers? Is the vocabulary right for my audience?
- Does my introduction make readers want to keep reading? If not, what details can I add to give readers a reason for learning the process?
- Have I listed the steps in chronological order? What details can I add or take out to help readers understand and follow the steps? What transitions can I add to make it easy for readers to follow my explanation?
- Have I included all the equipment, materials, and ingredients that readers will need for each step?
- Have I stayed on track from beginning to end?
- Does my paper have a strong conclusion?

Grading Timesaver

Rubrics for this Writer's Workshop assignment appear on p. 135 of the *Portfolio Management System.*

Sentence Workshop

OBJECTIVES
1. Recognize stringy sentences
2. Learn techniques for revising stringy sentences

STRINGY SENTENCES

A secret of good writing is knowing how to vary the length of sentences. Too many short sentences in a row can make your writing seem choppy and your thoughts seem unconnected. However, ideas strung together with linking words like *and, but,* and *or* may create that enemy of all writers, the stringy sentence. Stringy sentences don't give readers a chance to pause between ideas. They don't show connections between ideas.

To revise a stringy sentence, you can do one of two things:

1. You can break the sentence into two or more sentences.
2. You can rewrite the sentence using phrases and subordinate clauses to show relationships more clearly.

Suppose you wrote this stringy sentence: "I went to the beach, and I hate sand, and it makes me itch." You could rewrite it like this: "I went to the beach, though I hate sand, which makes me itch." You could also write this: "Though I hate sand because it makes me itch, I went to the beach."

Here is another example of a stringy sentence, followed by Hans Christian Andersen's improvement:

STRINGY   Out in the garden grew wonderfully beautiful flowers, and the loveliest of all had little silver bells tied to them, and they rang as you went by, and you couldn't fail to notice them.

BETTER   "Out in the garden grew wonderfully beautiful flowers, and the loveliest of all had little silver bells tied to them that rang as you went by so that you couldn't fail to notice them."

—"The Nightingale," Hans Christian Andersen (page 215)

Writer's Workshop Follow-up: Revision

To catch stringy sentences, read your writing aloud. If you run out of breath before you get to the end of a sentence or if you hear too many *and*'s, you've probably written a stringy sentence.

Language Handbook HELP
See Revising Stringy Sentences, page 739.

Technology HELP
See Language Workshop CD-ROM. *Key word entry: stringy sentences.*

Try It Out

Rewrite the following passage to eliminate any stringiness. Be sure to compare your revised passages in class.

What a cleaning and a polishing there was at the palace, and the walls and the floors, all made of porcelain, shone in the light of thousands of golden lamps, and the loveliest of flowers, the chiming ones from the Emperor's garden, were placed along the corridor, and with all the hurry and bustle there was such a draft that it made the bells ring out, and you couldn't hear yourself speak.

Resources

Workshop Resources
• Worksheet, p. 41
Language Workshop CD-ROM
• Stringy Sentences

Teaching the Lesson

Choose a simple topic, such as birds, that everyone in the class will know something about. Have each student write a short statement about the topic on a piece of paper. Make copies of the statements, or write them on the chalkboard. Then have students work in pairs to write a paragraph about the topic, using the statements and avoiding stringy sentences. Have volunteers read their selections to the class to show sentence combinations that avoid stringy sentences.

Try It Out
Possible Answer
What a cleaning and a polishing there was at the palace. The walls and the floors, all made of porcelain, shone in the light of thousands of golden lamps. The loveliest of flowers, the chiming ones from the Emperor's garden, were placed along the corridor. With all the hurry and bustle, there was such a draft that it made the bells ring out. You couldn't hear yourself speak.

Assessing Learning

Quick Check: Stringy Sentences
Rewrite the following passage to correct any stringy sentences:
Margie did not like school, but she liked to read about schools from the past, and she did not like the mechanical teacher, and she hated the slot where she had to put in her homework, and she always had to write her homework in code so that the mechanical teacher could calculate her grade quickly.

[Possible answer: Margie did not like school, but she liked to read about schools from the past. She did not like the mechanical teacher, and she hated the slot where she had to put in her homework. She always had to write her homework in code so that the mechanical teacher could calculate her grade quickly.]

Teaching the Lesson

Point out to students that every computer game or program comes with a manual. So does every household appliance and every electronic device. Manuals help the owner to learn how to use the object he or she has just bought. If possible, bring in examples for students to look at.

Using the Strategies

1. To check a word's spelling, either click the Spelling button on the Standard toolbar or choose Spelling from the Tools menu.
2. *Menu* is a list of choices to select from; *select* means "to indicate one's choice."
3. To check the spelling of a single word, use a wildcard character, such as an asterisk (*) or a question mark (?).

Situation

You've heard that you can find misspellings in your writing with a computer, but you've never tried it. How can you find out what to do? You start by taking out the manual that came with your word processing software.

Strategies

Read to get information.
Reading a manual is a handy way to learn about a tool or program or to solve a problem.

- Think of a key word, like *Spelling,* that identifies the kind of information you're looking for. Then, check the **index,** the alphabetical list of subjects with page numbers, at the back.

- Read the directions slowly, word by word. Keep referring to the actual tool or program as you read.

Notice the order of steps.

- Directions are usually given in step-by-step, **chronological** order. Read about each step before moving on to the next.

To check spelling
1. Do one of the following:
   - On the Standard toolbar, click the Spelling button.
   - From the Tools menu, choose Spelling (ALT, O, S).
2. For each word that is displayed in the Not In Dictionary box, select the options you want.

Tip You can use a wildcard character, such as an asterisk (*) or question mark (?), to check the spelling of a single word. The asterisk can represent any number of characters, while the question mark represents only one character. For example, type **rec*ve** and select it. Click the Spelling button to learn how to spell "receive" correctly.

Look up unfamiliar words, abbreviations, and symbols.

- In the manual you may see words—like *menu, select,* and *tools*—used in new ways. You may also see abbreviations like ALT and CTRL and symbols like + and *. When you come across a new term, symbol, or abbreviation, look it up in the manual's glossary or index. If it isn't there, try using context to figure out its meaning.

Use graphic aids.

- Look for graphic aids like diagrams and charts. Try to match each feature you see in the graphic aid with a feature of the actual tool or software program.

Using the Strategies
1. Look at the information in the box above, which was taken from a manual. Describe two ways to check a word's spelling.

2. From the context, explain what *menu* and *select* mean in these directions.

3. How can you check the spelling of a single word?

Extending the Strategies
Help someone who is having a problem using a software program. Get the manual, and apply these strategies to help solve the problem.

Reaching All Students

Struggling Readers
Manuals for computers, electronic devices, and machines might intimidate some students. Provide them with simpler examples, such as manuals for a small tool or model kit. Emphasize that many manuals depend on pictures or schematic diagrams to explain certain processes. When reading instructions, it is helpful to visualize the process in our minds or to actually draw it on a piece of paper.

English Language Learners
Point out that many manuals are written in two or more languages. This is especially true these days because objects are manufactured to be sold around the world. These students may want to locate a manual that contains instructions written both in English and in their native language. They can cover the instructions written in English and write their own translations of the instructions from their native language.

Learning for Life

Machines: A User's Guide

Problem

Many people use machines to do their jobs. We all use machines every day to enrich or simplify our lives. To learn how to use a machine—whether it's a computer or a tractor—you usually need a set of instructions. What is involved in writing clear instructions for using a machine?

Project

Develop a set of instructions for using a machine to do one specific task.

Preparation

1. Find someone in your community who uses a machine on the job—a computer, a hydraulic jack, a pressure gauge. If you prefer, pick a machine you have at home that is somewhat difficult to use—such as a VCR, a food processor, or a thirty-five-millimeter camera.

2. If you've chosen a workplace machine, arrange to visit the person at work (with permission from your teacher and parents).

Explain your assignment, and ask for suggestions about a particular task for which you can write instructions, such as sending messages on a computer.

Procedure

1. If you're visiting a workplace, watch closely as the person uses the machine. Make notes on each action the person takes. Note all safety precautions. If possible, go over your notes with the person.

   After your visit, use your notes to write instructions for using the machine to do the task. You might include simple drawings if you think they help. Write a thank-you note to the person.

2. If you've chosen a machine in your home, think of a specific task to do. Carefully go through the process of using the machine to do the task. Take detailed notes on each step in the process. Afterward, use your notes to write a clear set of instructions.

Presentation

Present your machine instructions in one of the following ways:

1. Poster

Make an illustrated poster showing step by step how to use the machine for the task.

2. Instruction Manual

Design pages that could be part of an instruction manual for the machine.

3. Live Demonstration

For simple machines that can be brought into the classroom, arrange a live demonstration. Ask a classmate to do the task using your written instructions. (You will need to get your teacher's approval to bring equipment into the classroom.) See if your instructions are successful and easy to follow.

Processing

As a class, discuss the following question: What kinds of problems come up when you try to write clear instructions for using a machine?

LEARNING FOR LIFE **237**

Resources

Viewing and Representing
HRW Multimedia Presentation Maker
Students may wish to use the *HRW Multimedia Presentation Maker* when working on this activity.

Grading Timesaver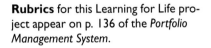

Rubrics for this Learning for Life project appear on p. 136 of the *Portfolio Management System*.

Developing Workplace Competencies

Preparation	Procedure	Presentation
• Making decisions • Acquiring data • Exhibiting sociability	• Evaluating actions • Processing information	• Thinking creatively • Teaching others

Collection Four

All Creatures Great and Small

Theme

Relationships Between People and Animals   *Some of the most enduring stories in the world are stories about humans and the animals who love and protect and help them. Here are stories that range from one about a patient goat who gives life to a little boy, to a true story about brave humans who rescue animals from a deadly flood.*

Reading the Anthology

Reaching Struggling Readers

The Reading Skills and Strategies: Reaching Struggling Readers binder provides materials coordinated with the Pupil's Edition (see the Collection Planner, p. T237C) to help students who have difficulty reading and comprehending text, or students who are reluctant readers. The binder for sixth grade is organized around eleven individual skill areas, and Selection Skill Lessons provide reading instruction and practice specific to particular pieces of literature in Collection Four.

Reading Beyond the Anthology

Read On   Collection Four includes an annotated bibliography of books suitable for extended reading. The suggested books are related to works in this collection by theme, by author, or by subject. To preview the Read On for Collection Four, please turn to p. T301.

HRW Library   The *HRW Library* offers novels, plays, and short-story collections for extended reading. Each book in the Library includes one or more major works and thematically or topically related Connections. The Connections are magazine articles, poems, or other pieces of literature. Each book in the *HRW Library* is also accompanied by a Study Guide that provides teaching suggestions and worksheets. For Collection Four, the following titles are recommended.

SOUNDER
William Armstrong
A loyal hunting dog becomes a boy's companion on the boy's long odyssey to find his father, who has been sentenced to a chain gang for stealing a ham to feed his hungry family.

WHERE THE RED FERN GROWS
Wilson Rawls
Two hounds provide companionship and triumph for a young boy in Oklahoma, but by the end of this touching novel, the boy must accept the deaths of both of his heroic friends.

Skills Focus

Selection or Feature	Reading Skills and Strategies	Elements of Literature	Language/ Grammar	Vocabulary/ Spelling	Writing	Listening/ Speaking	Viewing/ Representing
Zlateh the Goat (p. 240) Isaac Bashevis Singer	Dialogue with the Text pp. 240, 247	Suspense, pp. 240, 247 Character, p. 247 Main Events, p. 247	Pronouns and Antecedents, p. 249	Demonstrate Definitions, p. 249	List Jobs Animals Do with People, p. 248 Write a Dialogue Between an Animal and Yourself, p. 248	Perform the Story Using Pantomime, p. 248	
Stray (p. 250) Cynthia Rylant	Draw Inferences, p. 250 • Text Evidence • Prior Knowledge	Theme, pp. 250, 256 Plot, p. 250 Setting, p. 256	Pronouns and Contractions, p. 257 Possessive Pronouns, p. 257	Double Consonants, p. 257	Freewrite About a Pet, p. 256 Write from the Point of View of a Pet, p. 256 Write an Informative Article on the Cost of Dog Care, p. 256		
Ode to Mi Gato (p. 258) Gary Soto	Make Predictions, pp. 258, 261	Ode, pp. 258, 261 Images, p. 261			List Topics for a Report, p. 261 Write an Ode, p. 261	Read an Ode Aloud, p. 261	Illustrate the Poem, p. 261
Reading Skills and Strategies: Organizers (p. 262)	Use Text Organizers, p. 262 Sequence, p. 262 Understand Causes and Effects, p. 262	Narrative, p. 262 Main Events, p. 262					
The Flood (p. 263) Ralph Helfer	Use Chronology, p. 263 Map Sequence, pp. 263, 276	Narrative, p. 263 Main Events, pp. 263, 276	Pronoun References, p. 278 Antecedents, p. 278	Concrete and Abstract Words, p. 278	Write a List of Questions, p. 277 Research Wild Animals, p. 277	Debate a Topic, p. 277	Map Locations of Wild Animals, p. 277
Elements of Literature: The Main Idea (p. 279)	Identify the Main Idea, p. 279 Use a Graphic Organizer, p. 279	Topic, p. 279 Main Idea, p. 279					Use a Hand Organizer, p. 279
from **The Land I Lost** (p. 280) Huynh Quang Nhuong	Summarize, pp. 280, 289 Use a Graphic Organizer for Main Events and Supporting Details, p. 280	Main Events, pp. 280, 289 Supporting Details, p. 280 Autobiography, p. 280 Narrative, p. 288 Hero, p. 288 Conflict, p. 288 Resolution, p. 288	Pronouns as Objects of Prepositions, p. 290 • Prepositional Phrases • Objects	Synonyms, p. 290	Write Questions on Topics in the Story, p. 289 Write an Article About Crocodiles, p. 289 Write a Summary of the Story, p. 289 Write a Menu for a Vietnamese Meal, p. 289		Make Word Maps to Check the Meanings of Synonyms, p. 290
from **All I Really Need to Know I Learned in Kindergarten** (p. 291) Robert Fulghum	Find the Main Idea, pp. 291, 296 Identify Supporting Details, p. 291	Humorous Essay, p. 291 Essay, pp. 291, 296 Anecdote, p. 296	Exaggeration, p. 298	Compound Words, p. 298	Write a Humorous Essay or Poem, p. 297	Perform Songs or Poems, p. 297	Make a Word Web, p. 297 Draw a Cartoon, p. 297
No Questions Asked: A Nash Menagerie (p. 299) Ogden Nash				The **No Questions Asked** feature provides students with an unstructured opportunity to practice reading strategies using a selection that extends the theme of the collection.			
Writer's Workshop: Informative Report (p. 302)		Comparisons, p. 304 Main Idea, p. 304			Write an Informative Report, pp. 302–306		
Sentence Workshop: Wordy Sentences (p. 307)			Wordy Sentences, p. 307		Revise Wordy Sentences, p. 307		
Reading for Life: Searching the Internet (p. 308)	Use an Internet Directory, p. 308		Logical Key Words, p. 308				
Learning for Life: Teaching People About Animals (p. 309)					Write a Children's Story, p. 309 Write a Radio Announcement, p. 309	Interview an Animal Expert, p. 309	Create a Brochure, p. 309

Collection Four All Creatures Great and Small

Resources for this Collection

Note: All resources for this collection are available for preview on the *One-Stop Planner CD-ROM 1 with Test Generator.* All worksheets and blackline masters may be printed from the CD-ROM.

Internet Resources
go.hrw.com LE0 6-4

Collection Planner

Selection or Feature	Reading and Literary Skills	Language and Grammar

Zlateh the Goat (p. 240)
Isaac Bashevis Singer
	• *Reading Skills and Strategies: Reaching Struggling Readers*
	  • Selection Skill Lesson, p. 15
	• *Graphic Organizers for Active Reading,* Worksheet p. 19
		• *Grammar and Language Links:*
		  Pronoun-Antecedent Agreement,
		  Worksheet p. 23
		• *Language Workshop CD-ROM,*
		  Pronoun-Antecedent Agreement
		• *Daily Oral Grammar,*
		  Transparency 13

Stray (p. 250)
Cynthia Rylant
Connections: Mother Doesn't Want a Dog (p. 255)
Judith Viorst
	• *Reading Skills and Strategies: Reaching Struggling Readers*
	  • Selection Skill Lesson, p. 101
	• *Graphic Organizers for Active Reading,* Worksheet p. 20
		• *Grammar and Language Links:*
		  Pronoun and Contraction, Worksheet p. 25
		• *Language Workshop CD-ROM,*
		  Pronouns
		• *Daily Oral Grammar,*
		  Transparency 14

Ode to Mi Gato (p. 258) Gary Soto	• *Graphic Organizers for Active Reading,* Worksheet p. 21	

The Flood *from* **The Beauty of the Beasts** (p. 263)
Ralph Helfer
Connections: Trial by Fire (p. 275)
People Magazine
	• *Reading Skills and Strategies: Reaching Struggling Readers*
	  • Selection Skill Lesson, p. 140
	• *Graphic Organizers for Active Reading,* Worksheet p. 22
	• *Literary Elements:*
	  Transparency 5; Worksheet p. 16
		• *Grammar and Language Links:*
		  Pronoun References, Worksheet p. 27
		• *Language Workshop CD-ROM,*
		  Pronoun References
		• *Daily Oral Grammar,*
		  Transparency 15

Elements of Literature: The Main Idea (p. 279)	• *Literary Elements,* Transparency 5	

from **The Land I Lost** (p. 280)
Huynh Quang Nhuong
	• *Reading Skills and Strategies: Reaching Struggling Readers*
	  • Selection Skill Lesson, p. 86
	• *Graphic Organizers for Active Reading,* Worksheet p. 23
		• *Grammar and Language Links:*
		  Object Pronouns, Worksheet p. 29
		• *Language Workshop CD-ROM,*
		  Objects of Prepositions
		• *Daily Oral Grammar,*
		  Transparency 16

from **All I Really Need to Know I Learned in Kindergarten** (p. 291)
Robert Fulghum
	• *Reading Skills and Strategies: Reaching Struggling Readers*
	  • Selection Skill Lesson, p. 120
	• *Graphic Organizers for Active Reading,* Worksheet p. 24
		• *Grammar and Language Links:*
		  Style: Exaggeration, Worksheet p. 31
		• *Daily Oral Grammar,* Transparency 17

No Questions Asked: A Nash Menagerie (p. 299) Ogden Nash	The **No Questions Asked** feature provides students with an unstructured opportunity to practice reading strategies using a selection that extends the theme of the collection.	
Writer's Workshop: Informative Report (p. 302)		
Sentence Workshop: Wordy Sentences (p. 307)		• *Workshop Resources,* p. 43 • *Language Workshop CD-ROM,* Wordiness
Learning for Life: Teaching People About Animals (p. 309)		

Collection Resources

- *Cross-Curricular Activities*, p. 24
- *Portfolio Management System:*
  Introduction to Portfolio Assessment, p. 1;
  Parent/Guardian Letters, p. 93

- *Formal Assessment,*
  Reading Application Test, p. 62
- *Test Generator*, Collection Test 🔘

Vocabulary, Spelling, and Decoding	Writing	Listening and Speaking, Viewing and Representing	Assessment
• *Words to Own*, Worksheet p. 11 • *Spelling and Decoding*, Worksheet p. 11	• *Portfolio Management System*, Rubrics for Choices, p. 137	• *Audio CD Library*, Disc 5, Track 2 🎧 • *Viewing and Representing:* Fine Art Transparency 10 Worksheet p. 40 • *Portfolio Management System*, Rubrics for Choices, p. 137	• *Formal Assessment*, Selection Test, p. 50 • *Standardized Test Preparation*, p. 38 • *Test Generator* (One-Stop Planner CD-ROM) 🔘
• *Spelling and Decoding*, Worksheet p. 12	• *Portfolio Management System*, Rubrics for Choices, p. 138	• *Audio CD Library*, Disc 5, Track 3 🎧 • *Portfolio Management System*, Rubrics for Choices, p. 138	• *Formal Assessment*, Selection Test, p. 52 • *Standardized Test Preparation*, p. 40 • *Test Generator* (One-Stop Planner CD-ROM) 🔘
	• *Portfolio Management System*, Rubrics for Choices, p. 139	• *Visual Connections*, Videocassette A, Segment 5 📼 • *Audio CD Library*, Disc 5, Track 4 🎧 • *Portfolio Management System*, Rubrics for Choices, p. 139	• *Formal Assessment*, Selection Test, p. 54 • *Test Generator* (One-Stop Planner CD-ROM) 🔘
• *Spelling and Decoding*, Worksheet p. 13	• *Portfolio Management System*, Rubrics for Choices, p. 140	• *Audio CD Library*, Disc 6, Track 2 🎧 • *Portfolio Management System*, Rubrics for Choices, p. 140	• *Formal Assessment*, Selection Test, p. 55 • *Standardized Test Preparation*, pp. 42, 44 • *Test Generator* (One-Stop Planner CD-ROM) 🔘
			• *Formal Assessment*, Literary Elements Test, p. 61
• *Words to Own*, Worksheet p. 12 • *Spelling and Decoding*, Worksheet p. 14	• *Portfolio Management System*, Rubrics for Choices, p. 141	• *Audio CD Library*, Disc 6, Track 3 🎧 • *Portfolio Management System*, Rubrics for Choices, p. 141	• *Formal Assessment*, Selection Test, p. 57 • *Standardized Test Preparation*, p. 46 • *Test Generator* (One-Stop Planner CD-ROM) 🔘
• *Spelling and Decoding*, Worksheet p. 15	• *Portfolio Management System*, Rubrics for Choices, p. 142	• *Audio CD Library*, Disc 6, Track 4 🎧 • *Portfolio Management System*, Rubrics for Choices, p. 142	• *Formal Assessment*, Selection Test, p. 59 • *Standardized Test Preparation*, p. 48 • *Test Generator* (One-Stop Planner CD-ROM) 🔘
		• *Audio CD Library*, Disc 6, Track 5 🎧 • *Viewing and Representing:* Fine Art Transparency 11 Worksheet p. 44	

	• *Workshop Resources*, p. 15
	• *Standardized Test Preparation:* Worksheet p. 114 Transparencies 7–12
	• *Writer's Workshop 1 CD-ROM*, Report of Information 🔘
			• *Portfolio Management System*
			  • Prewriting, p. 143
			  • Peer Editing, p. 144
			  • Assessment Rubric, p. 145

		• *Viewing and Representing*, HRW Multimedia Presentation Maker	• *Portfolio Management System*, Rubrics, p. 146

 Transparency   CD-ROM   📼 Video   🎧 Audio CD

Collection Planner

OBJECTIVES

1. Read literature in different genres on the theme "All Creatures Great and Small"
2. Interpret literary elements with special emphasis on determining the main idea in a paragraph
3. Apply a variety of reading strategies, particularly using organizers to find the structure of a text
4. Respond to the literature in a variety of modes
5. Learn and use new words
6. Plan, draft, revise, edit, proof-read, and publish an informative report
7. Demonstrate the ability to understand and use strategies for searching the Internet
8. Explore through a variety of projects how to teach people about animals

Introducing the Theme

The selections in this collection explore animals, people, and the relationships between them—relationships that contain everything from love and interdependence to outright hostility. As students read, ask them to think about the kind of information about animals they would like to learn and share with others.

Responding to the Quotation

? George Eliot is the pseudonym of nineteenth-century English novelist Mary Ann Evans (1819–1880). **What quality in animals does she especially praise?** [Possible responses: their unquestioning acceptance; their lack of a judgmental attitude.] **Can all animals be our friends, or only certain animals?** [Many students will feel that only pets become our friends. Wild animals do not trust us, and we do not let ourselves become close to animals raised for food or clothing.]

Animals (1960) by Manuel Jiménez.

Writing Focus: Informative Report

The following **Work in Progress** assignments in this collection build to a culminating **Writer's Workshop** at the end of Collection 4.

• Zlateh the Goat	Think about animals and people teaming up (p. 248)
• Stray	Freewrite about an experience with a pet (p. 256)
• Ode to Mi Gato	List topics about cats that can be explored (p. 261)
• The Flood	Jot down questions and sources (p. 277)
• The Land I Lost	Write questions about topics on Vietnam (p. 289)
• All I Really Need to Know . . .	Make a word web of beliefs about an animal (p. 297)

Writer's Workshop: Expository Writing / Informative Report (p. 302)

Collection

Four

All Creatures Great and Small

*Animals are such
agreeable friends—
they ask no questions,
they pass no criticisms.*

—*George Eliot*

239

RESPONDING TO THE ART

Manuel Jiménez is a Mexican artist who works in Oaxaca. He pioneered the style of carving that Oaxacans use today through his discovery of the wood of the copalillo tree. These animals, reflecting a tradition of Mexican animal representation, were created around 1960.
Activity. The Oaxacan animals seem to embody human feelings and personalities. Ask each student to identify three of the animals, give each animal an appropriate name, and describe the animal's personality. (Perhaps the animal would want to speak as "I" and comment on the rest of the animals here.) Be sure to have them share their imaginings.

Writer's Notebook

WORK IN PROGRESS

Have students freewrite about how people and animals benefit each other and how they harm each other. You may want to have students consider ways human civilization and the animal kingdom can coexist in harmony as more and more territory is developed. Have them cite any species that they know to be endangered or perhaps an example of conservation that has allowed an animal population to flourish. Students' observation here may be developed in the Writer's Workshop on p. 302.

Resources ———

Portfolio Management System
• Introduction to Portfolio Assessment, p. 1
• Parent/Guardian Letters, p. 93
Formal Assessment
• Reading Application Test, p. 62
Test Generator
• Collection Test
Cross Curricular Activities
• Teaching Notes, p. 24

Selection Readability

This Annotated Teacher's Edition provides a summary of each selection in the student book. Following each Summary heading, you will find one, two or three small icons. These icons indicate, in an approximate sense, the reading level of the selection.

■ One icon indicates that the selection is easy.
■ ■ Two icons indicate that the selection is on an intermediate reading level.
■ ■ ■ Three icons indicate that the selection is challenging.

OBJECTIVES

1. Read and interpret the story
2. Identify suspense
3. Monitor comprehension
4. Express understanding through creative writing and performance
5. Identify pronouns and their antecedents and use them correctly in writing
6. Understand and use new words

SKILLS

Literary
- Identify suspense

Reading
- Monitor comprehension

Writing
- List ways people and animals work together
- Write a dialogue between oneself and an animal

Speaking/Listening
- Perform a pantomime of the story

Grammar/Language
- Identify pronouns and their antecedents and use them correctly in writing

Vocabulary
- Understand and use new words

Viewing/Representing
- Identify realistic elements in a painting (ATE)

Planning

- **Block Schedule**
  Block Scheduling Lesson Plans with Pacing Guide

- **Traditional Schedule**
  Lesson Plans Including Strategies for English-Language Learners

- **One-Stop Planner**
  CD-ROM with Test Generator

Before You Read

ZLATEH THE GOAT

Make the Connection

Animal Talk

Think-pair-share. What messages have animals sent you lately? Think of a time when you realized that an animal was telling you something or showing you how it felt. Share your story with a classmate. Then, fill in a class chart with the details of your story. What does your chart tell you about how animals "talk"? Take a few minutes to talk about your thoughts and feelings about animal-person communication.

Animal	What It Did	What It Was Saying
Julie's cat, Geege	stared out window all afternoon	wanted to go out and hunt birds

Elements of Literature

Suspense: What Happens Next?

As a reader, Singer liked stories that kept him wondering what would happen next. "From my childhood I have always loved tension in a story," wrote Singer. "To me a story is still a story where the reader listens and wants to know what happens."

At first, "Zlateh the Goat" seems to be just a story of a Jewish family in Poland and a boy who is sent to market with the family goat. Zlateh is an unusually appealing animal, though, and this account of her trip to the butcher could change your attitude toward goatdom. That's because an alarming change in the weather suddenly transforms this simple tale into a suspenseful page turner that makes you anxious to find out what happens next to the resourceful Aaron and his trusting Zlateh.

> **S**uspense is the anxious curiosity you feel about what will happen next in a story.
>
> *For more on Suspense, see the Handbook of Literary Terms.*

Reading Skills and Strategies

Dialogue with the Text

As you read this story, keep a sheet of paper next to the book so that you can record your thoughts. One student's comments appear on the first page as an example.

Background

Literature and Religion

"Zlateh the Goat" takes place at Hanukkah (khä′noo·kä′), a Jewish religious festival. Hanukkah, an eight-day holiday, is usually observed in December. Hanukkah celebrates the victory, in 165 B.C., of the Jewish fighters called the Maccabees over a huge Syrian army. After their victory, while the Maccabees were repairing damage to their Temple in Jerusalem, a miracle occurred. A tiny bit of oil for the holy lamp—barely enough for one day—lasted eight days. Do you see a miracle in Zlateh's story as well?

go.hrw.com
LEO 6-4

Preteaching Vocabulary

Words to Own

Have students work in small groups to copy the Words to Own and their definitions; to quiz each other on the meanings of the words; and then to work together to choose the two best answers to each of the following questions.

1. If a day were wet and drizzly, which things might *penetrate* a boy's clothing?
   dampness/cold/sunshine/heat
   [dampness/cold]

2. Besides an animal's hooves, what other *cleft* things might someone notice on a walk in the country?
   tree trunk/sun/blizzard/fence post
   [tree trunk/fence post]

3. What might create *chaos* in the outdoors?
   sunshine/blizzard/hurricane/drizzle
   [blizzard/hurricane]

4. After three days in a haystack with a goat, what smells might someone's clothing *exude*?
   goat/sun/hay/dirt [goat/hay]

Zlateh the Goat

Isaac Bashevis Singer

At Hanukkah time the road from the village to the town is usually covered with snow, but this year the winter had been a mild one. Hanukkah had almost come, yet little snow had fallen. The sun shone most of the time. The peasants complained that because of the dry weather there would be a poor harvest of winter grain. New grass sprouted, and the peasants sent their cattle out to pasture.

For Reuven the furrier[1] it was a bad year, and after long hesitation he decided to sell Zlateh the goat. She was old and gave little milk. Feyvel the town butcher had offered eight gulden[2] for her. Such a sum would buy Hanukkah candles, potatoes and oil for pancakes, gifts for the children, and other holiday necessaries for the house. Reuven told his oldest boy, Aaron, to take the goat to town.

Aaron understood what taking the goat to Feyvel meant, but he had to obey his father. Leah, his mother, wiped the tears from her eyes when she heard the news. Aaron's younger sisters, Anna and Miriam, cried loudly. Aaron put on his quilted jacket and a cap with earmuffs, bound a rope around Zlateh's neck, and took along two slices of bread with cheese to eat on the road. Aaron was supposed to deliver the goat by evening, spend the night at the butcher's, and return the next day with the money.

While the family said goodbye to the goat, and Aaron placed the rope around her neck, Zlateh stood as patiently and good-naturedly as ever. She licked Reuven's

> *In his twelve years Aaron had seen all kinds of weather, but he had never experienced a snow like this one.*

1. **furrier:** someone who makes and repairs articles made of fur.
2. **gulden:** gold or silver coins used in several European countries.

Dialogue with the Text

Is winter grain grown during the summer or winter?

I would feel bad if I had to sell one of my pets.

Candles, gifts . . . Hanukkah must be a holiday.

Everyone seems sad!

A It is definitely winter because Aaron put on a jacket, cap, and earmuffs.

No wonder everyone is upset— the goat will be butchered.

—Bea Sisaleumsok
Piedmont Lake Middle School
Apopka, Florida

ZLATEH THE GOAT 241

Summary

In a Polish village many years ago, twelve-year-old Aaron must sell the family's beloved goat, Zlateh, to the town butcher. Aaron sets out sadly with the goat, but their progress is halted by a blizzard. In order to survive, they burrow into a snow-covered haystack, and Aaron tells stories to Zlateh, who provides Aaron with milk. The suspense builds until the snow stops three days later. They return home, and no one again mentions selling Zlateh.

Resources

Listening
Audio CD Library
A recording of "Zlateh the Goat" is provided in the *Audio CD Library:*
• Disc 5, Track 2

Assessment
Formal Assessment
• Selection Test, p. 50
Test Generator
• Selection Test

Viewing and Representing
Fine Art Transparency
After students have read the story, ask them to compare and contrast Aaron and Zlateh with the figures in Henri Rousseau's *The Sleeping Gypsy.*
• Transparency 10
• Worksheet, p. 40

A Reading Skills and Strategies
Dialogue with the Text

? Why is everyone so sad? [The goat is a beloved pet, but she must be sold to the butcher to pay for the Hanukkah celebration.] Write down how you would feel if you were Aaron. [Answers will vary.]

Resources: Print and Media

Reading
• *Reading Skills and Strategies*
   Selection Skill Lesson, p. 15
• *Graphic Organizers for Active Reading,* p. 19
• *Words to Own,* p. 11
• *Spelling and Decoding,* p. 11
• *Audio CD Library*
   Disc 5, Track 2

Writing and Language
• *Daily Oral Grammar*
   Transparency 13
• *Grammar and Language Links*
   Worksheet, p. 23
• *Language Workshop CD-ROM*

Viewing and Representing
• *Viewing and Representing*
   Fine Art Transparency 10
   Fine Art Worksheet, p. 40

Assessment
• *Formal Assessment,* p. 50
• *Portfolio Management System,* p. 137
• *Standardized Test Preparation,* p. 38
• *Test Generator (One-Stop Planner CD-ROM)*

Internet
• go.hrw.com (keyword: LE0 6-4)

Ⓐ Elements of Literature

Dramatic Irony

❓ What do you know that Zlateh does not know? [This time she should not be so trusting; she is going to be slaughtered.]

Ⓑ Elements of Literature

Suspense

❓ The family expects the trip to take Aaron and Zlateh all day. What do you wonder when the weather changes? [Possible response: Students may wonder if they will get hurt or if they will even make it to the village.]

Ⓒ Reading Skills and Strategies

Dialogue with the Text

❓ What was your first thought on hearing that Aaron and Zlateh are both twelve years old? Jot down your response on a sheet of paper. [Possible response: It made me feel sad because Zlateh has been with Aaron all his life.]

Ⓓ Critical Thinking

Challenging the Text

❓ Do pets really communicate with their owners, or is the author simply giving human qualities to Zlateh? [Most students will feel that pets communicate with their owners.]

Ⓔ Elements of Literature

Suspense

❓ How does this passage increase the story's suspense? [Now Aaron cannot turn around and go home because he can no longer figure out directions. He and Zlateh could freeze to death.]

---

hand. She shook her small white beard. Ⓐ Zlateh trusted human beings. She knew that they always fed her and never did her any harm.

When Aaron brought her out on the road to town, she seemed somewhat astonished. She'd never been led in that direction before. She looked back at him questioningly, as if to say, "Where are you taking me?" But after a while she seemed to come to the conclusion that a goat shouldn't ask questions. Still, the road was different. They passed new fields, pastures, and huts with thatched roofs. Here and there a dog barked and came running after them, but Aaron chased it away with his stick.

Ⓑ The sun was shining when Aaron left the village. Suddenly the weather changed. A large black cloud with a bluish center appeared in the east and spread itself rapidly over the sky. A cold wind blew in with it. The crows flew low, croaking. At first it looked as if it would rain, but instead it began to hail as in summer. It was early in the day, but it became dark as dusk. After a while the hail turned to snow.

In his twelve years Aaron had seen all kinds of weather, but he had never experienced a snow like this one. It was so dense it shut out the light of the day. In a short time their path was completely covered. The

They passed new fields, pastures, and huts with thatched roofs.

wind became as cold as ice. The road to town was narrow and winding. Aaron no longer knew where he was. He could not see through the snow. The cold soon penetrated his quilted jacket.

Ⓒ At first Zlateh didn't seem to mind the change in weather. She too was twelve years old and knew what winter meant. But when her legs sank deeper and deeper into the snow, she began to turn her head and look at Ⓓ Aaron in wonderment. Her mild eyes seemed to ask, "Why are we out in such a storm?" Aaron hoped that a peasant would come along with his cart, but no one passed by.

The snow grew thicker, falling to the ground in large, whirling flakes. Beneath it Aaron's boots touched the softness of a plowed field. He realized that he was no longer on Ⓔ the road. He had gone astray. He could no longer figure out which was east or west, which way was the village, the town. The wind whistled, howled, whirled the snow about in eddies. It looked as if white imps were playing tag on the fields. A white dust rose above the ground. Zlateh stopped. She could walk no longer. Stubbornly she anchored her cleft

WORDS TO OWN

penetrated (pen′i·trāt′id) *v.*: made its way through.
cleft (kleft) *adj.*: formed with a partial split.

242 ALL CREATURES GREAT AND SMALL

Reaching All Students

Struggling Readers

Dialogue with the Text was introduced on p. 240. For a lesson directly tied to this selection that teaches students to monitor comprehension by using a strategy called Think-Aloud, see the *Reading Skills and Strategies* binder.
• Selection Skill Lesson, p.15

English Language Learners

The storm presents a variety of vocabulary words useful for describing cold weather. Words such as *snowflake, blizzard, hail,* and *frost* may be new to some English language learners. Ask students to jot down these and related words. Later have them discuss how the words are similar to and different from each other.

Advanced Learners

After students have read the story, invite advanced learners to compose three notes Aaron might have written to Zlateh or three that he might have written to his father, Reuven. Each one should reflect a different time in the story: before they leave home, their time in the haystack, and after they return home.

hooves in the earth and bleated as if pleading to be taken home. Icicles hung from her white beard, and her horns were glazed with frost.

Aaron did not want to admit the danger, but he knew just the same that if they did not find shelter, they would freeze to death. This was no ordinary storm. It was a mighty blizzard. The snowfall had reached his knees. His hands were numb, and he could no longer feel his toes. He choked when he breathed. His nose felt like wood, and he rubbed it with snow. Zlateh's bleating began to sound like crying. Those humans in whom she had so much confidence had dragged her into a trap. Aaron began to pray to God for himself and for the innocent animal.

Suddenly he made out the shape of a hill. He wondered what it could be. Who had piled snow into such a huge heap? He moved toward it, dragging Zlateh after him. When he came near it, he realized that it was a large haystack which the snow had blanketed.

Aaron realized immediately that they were saved. With great effort he dug his way through the snow. He was a village boy and knew what to do. When he reached the hay, he hollowed out a nest for himself and the goat. No matter how cold it may be outside, in the hay it is always warm. And hay was food for Zlateh. The moment she

Suddenly he made out the shape of a hill.

smelled it, she became contented and began to eat. Outside, the snow continued to fall. It quickly covered the passageway Aaron had dug. But a boy and an animal need to breathe, and there was hardly any air in their hide-out. Aaron bored a kind of a window through the hay and snow and carefully kept the passage clear.

Zlateh, having eaten her fill, sat down on her hind legs and seemed to have regained her confidence in man. Aaron ate his two slices of bread and cheese, but after the difficult journey he was still hungry. He looked at Zlateh and noticed her udders were full. He lay down next to her, placing himself so that when he milked her, he could squirt the milk into his mouth. It was rich and sweet. Zlateh was not accustomed to being milked that way, but she did not resist. On the contrary, she seemed eager to reward Aaron for bringing her to a shelter whose very walls, floor, and ceiling were made of food.

Through the window Aaron could catch a glimpse of the chaos outside. The wind carried before it whole drifts of snow. It was completely dark, and he did not know whether night had already come or

---

WORDS TO OWN
chaos (kā′äs′) n.: extreme confusion.

ZLATEH THE GOAT **243**

F **Reading Skills and Strategies**
Making Predictions
? How do you think the story will turn out? Write down your prediction, and come back to it later to compare it with the actual outcome of the story. [Possible responses: Some students might fear that Aaron and Zlateh will die, while others might have hope for their survival.]

G **Elements of Literature**
Dramatic Irony
Help students understand that Zlateh's distrust is ironic. Earlier, when she suspected nothing, Aaron was leading her to the butcher; now he is trying to help her.

H **Struggling Readers**
Summarizing
? What steps does Aaron take to make sure that he and Zlateh survive? [He finds a haystack and makes a nest for himself and Zlateh; he makes an air hole and keeps it open.]

RESPONDING TO THE ART
Maurice Sendak (1928–) is the author and illustrator of many popular children's stories, including *Where the Wild Things Are*. He began illustrating comic books while he was in high school and illustrated his first book when he was only nineteen.
Activity. Ask students how the illustrations accompanying this story help to tell the events of the story. How do they show the characters' emotions?

Using Students' Strengths

Verbal Learners
After students have read the story, ask pairs of students to list five common words to describe Reuven, five to describe Aaron, and five to describe Zlateh. Then have them use a dictionary or thesaurus to find synonyms they can use to extend or fine-tune their lists. Have them share their lists with the class.

Analyzing Details

? How do Aaron and Zlateh help each other? [Possible responses: They give each other warmth; Aaron keeps an air vent open for both of them, and Zlateh gives him milk. They give each other companionship and comfort.]

B Reading Skills and Strategies

Dialogue with the Text

? In this section, what are some of the things Zlateh might mean by "Maaaa, Maaaa"? Write on your sheet of paper what you think Zlateh means each time she responds to one of Aaron's questions. [Possible answers: concern, agreement, distress.]

whether it was the darkness of the storm. Thank God that in the hay it was not cold. The dried hay, grass, and field flowers ex-uded the warmth of the summer sun. Zlateh ate frequently; she nibbled from above, below, from the left and right. Her body gave forth an animal warmth, and Aaron cuddled up to her. He had always loved Zlateh, but now she was like a sister. He was alone, cut off from his family, and wanted to talk. He began to talk to Zlateh.

"Zlateh, what do you think about what has happened to us?" he asked.

"Maaaa," Zlateh answered.

"If we hadn't found this stack of hay, we would both be frozen stiff by now," Aaron said.

"Maaaa," was the goat's reply.

"If the snow keeps on falling like this, we may have to stay here for days," Aaron explained.

"Maaaa," Zlateh bleated.

"What does 'Maaaa' mean?" Aaron asked. "You'd better speak up clearly."

"Maaaa. Maaaa," Zlateh tried.

"Well, let it be 'Maaaa' then," Aaron said patiently. "You can't speak, but I know you understand. I need you and you need me. Isn't that right?"

"Maaaa."

Aaron became sleepy. He made a pillow out of some hay, leaned his head on it, and dozed off. Zlateh too fell asleep.

For three days Aaron and Zlateh stayed in the haystack.

When Aaron opened his eyes, he didn't know whether it was morning or night. The snow had blocked up his window. He tried to clear it, but when he had bored through to the length of his arm, he still hadn't reached the outside. Luckily he had his stick with him and was able to break through to the open air. It was still dark outside. The snow continued to fall and the wind wailed, first with one voice and then with many. Sometimes it had the sound of devilish laughter. Zlateh too awoke, and when Aaron greeted her, she answered, "Maaaa." Yes, Zlateh's language consisted of only one word, but it meant many things. Now she was saying, "We must accept all that God gives us—heat, cold, hunger, satisfaction, light, and darkness."

Aaron had awakened hungry. He had eaten up his food, but Zlateh had plenty of milk.

For three days Aaron and Zlateh stayed in the haystack. Aaron had always loved Zlateh, but in these three days he loved her more and more. She fed him with her milk and helped him keep warm. She comforted him with her patience. He told her many stories, and she always cocked her ears and listened.

WORDS TO OWN
exuded (eg·zyo͞od′id) v.: gave off.

Making the Connections

Connecting to the Theme: "All Creatures Great and Small"
Ask students to debate who are the "great" (large) and "small" creatures of this story.

Cultural Connections
Have students research midwinter holidays, including (but not limited to) Hanukkah, Christmas, and Kwanzaa. Ask each student to create a page of information about one holiday, such as its origin, date or dates, and how various cultures celebrate it.

Getting Students Involved

Cooperative Learning
The Village's Voice. Have students create a special edition of *The Village's Voice*, an imaginary newspaper for Aaron's village. It should feature the incident described in the story. Each student might contribute a separate element of the edition: layout, typing, printing, or word processing; a picture of Aaron and Zlateh at the haystack; an editorial; an advice column with letters from several readers; several news items about other events the class imagines having taken place around the same time; and other features suggested by the class. You may wish to begin the activity by brainstorming the list of contents for the edition. Allow volunteers to choose specific features to contribute, and assign other features according to students' interests and abilities.

When he patted her, she licked his hand and his face. Then she said, "Maaaa," and he knew it meant, I love you too.

The snow fell for three days, though after the first day it was not as thick and the wind quieted down. Sometimes Aaron felt that there could never have been a summer, that the snow had always fallen, ever since he could remember. He, Aaron, never had a father or mother or sisters. He was a snow child, born of the snow, and so was Zlateh. It was so quiet in the hay that his ears rang in the stillness. Aaron and Zlateh slept all night and a good part of the day. As for Aaron's dreams, they were all about warm weather. He dreamed of green fields, trees covered with blossoms, clear brooks, and singing birds. By the third night the snow had stopped, but Aaron did not dare to find his way home in the darkness. The sky became clear and the moon shone, casting silvery nets on the snow. Aaron dug his way out and looked at the world. It was all white, quiet, dreaming dreams of heavenly splendor. The stars were large and close. The moon swam in the sky as in a sea.

On the morning of the fourth day, Aaron heard the ringing of sleigh bells. The haystack was not far from the road. The peasant who drove the sleigh pointed out the way to him—not to the town and Feyvel the butcher, but home to the village. Aaron had decided in the haystack that he would never part with Zlateh.

Aaron's family and their neighbors had searched for the boy and the goat but had found no trace of them during the storm. They feared they were lost. Aaron's mother

and sisters cried for him; his father remained silent and gloomy. Suddenly one of the neighbors came running to their house with the news that Aaron and Zlateh were coming up the road.

There was great joy in the family. Aaron told them how he had found the stack of hay and how Zlateh had fed him with her milk. Aaron's sisters kissed and hugged Zlateh and gave her a special treat of chopped carrots and potato peels, which Zlateh gobbled up hungrily.

Nobody ever again thought of selling Zlateh, and now that the cold weather had finally set in, the villagers needed the services of Reuven the furrier once more. When Hanukkah came, Aaron's mother was able to fry pancakes every evening, and Zlateh got her portion too. Even though Zlateh had her own pen, she often came to the kitchen, knocking on the door with her horns to indicate that she was ready to visit, and she was always admitted. In the evening, Aaron, Miriam, and Anna played dreidel.[3] Zlateh sat near the stove, watching the children and the flickering of the Hanukkah candles.

Once in a while Aaron would ask her, "Zlateh, do you remember the three days we spent together?"

And Zlateh would scratch her neck with a horn, shake her white bearded head, and come out with the single sound which expressed all her thoughts, and all her love.

---

3. **dreidel** (drā′d′l): spinning top played with at Hanukkah. The top's four sides contain Hebrew letters that stand for "A great miracle happened there."

C Elements of Literature
Personification
? What human activity does Aaron imagine the world can do? [dream] What human activity does the moon seem to be performing? [swimming in the sky]

D Reading Skills and Strategies
Making Predictions
? Do you think Aaron will find it easy to convince his father that Zlateh should live? Why or why not? [Possible responses: Yes, because his father will be so glad to see Aaron and grateful to Zlateh for providing him with nourishment; no, because the family will still need money.]

E Reading Skills and Strategies
Identifying Cause and Effect
? Why does the weather create a need for the services of Aaron's father? [Reuven is a furrier, and people need warm fur coats, hats, and gloves in cold weather.]

F Cultural Connections
Hanukkah is celebrated for eight consecutive days. Each evening is marked by the lighting of one more candle than on the previous evening on an eight-branched candlestick called a *menorah*.

G Critical Thinking
Interpreting
? How has Zlateh's relationship with the family changed? [Possible response: now she is more like a friend than a pet. She is more than "just an animal."]

Resources
Assessment
Formal Assessment
• Selection Test, p. 50
Test Generator
• Selection Test

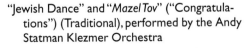

Listening to Music

"Jewish Dance" and "*Mazel Tov*" ("Congratulations") (Traditional), performed by the Andy Statman Klezmer Orchestra

Klezmer, from the Hebrew for "musical instrument," is the dance-oriented folk music of Eastern European Jews. It has similarities to early American jazz, especially in its tendency to rely on brass, woodwind, and percussion instruments rather than on strings. In Europe, klezmer bands often traveled from wedding to wedding to perform. Klezmer is also associated

with the Ukrainian (formerly Russian) city of Odessa, a thriving cultural center for late nineteenth-century Eastern European Jews, nicknamed "the New Orleans of the Russian Empire." In the early twentieth century, Jewish immigrants brought klezmer to the United States, where the jazz influence became more pronounced. Its popularity faded as Jews assimilated into the mainstream culture, but it revived with the blossoming of interest in folk and ethnic music in the 1960s and 1970s.

Activity
After students have read "Zlateh the Goat," briefly explain what klezmer music is, and play the representative musical selections for students. Then have a group of students reenact the story in pantomime to a background of klezmer music.

MEET THE WRITER

"Time Does Not Vanish"

Isaac Bashevis Singer (1904–1991) was born in a village like the one in this story and grew up in Warsaw, Poland, where his father was a rabbi. As a boy he read constantly and was curious about everything. Both of Singer's parents were skilled storytellers. Life teemed on Warsaw's Krochmalna Street. Singer recalled:

66 In our Warsaw apartment my father set up a rabbinical court. The people of Krochmalna Street came to our home to ask him for advice or to have him settle a dispute according to the law of the Torah. People also came to him to pour out their hearts. 99

Singer listened and watched carefully, storing scenes, people, and incidents he would write about for the rest of his life. His stories won him the Nobel Prize for Literature in 1978.

In "Zlateh the Goat" and many other stories, Singer keeps alive a way of life that no longer exists. He wrote:

66 Children are as puzzled by passing time as grown-ups. What happens to a day once it is gone? Where are all our yesterdays with their joys and sorrows? Literature helps us remember the past with its many moods. To the storyteller yesterday is still here as are the years and the decades gone by.

In stories time does not vanish. Neither do men and animals. For the writer and his readers all creatures go on living forever. What happened long ago is still present.

It is in this spirit that I wrote these tales. In real life many of the people that I describe no longer exist, but to me they remain alive and I hope they will amuse the reader with their wisdom, their strange beliefs, and sometimes with their foolishness.

I dedicate this book to the many children who had no chance to grow up because of stupid wars and cruel persecutions which devastated cities and destroyed innocent families. I hope that when the readers of these stories become men and women they will love not only their own children but all good children everywhere. 99

More Yesterdays That Are Still Here

If you liked "Zlateh the Goat," try reading *The Fools of Chelm and Their History* (Harper) or *A Day of Pleasure: Stories of a Boy Growing Up in Warsaw* (Farrar, Straus & Giroux).

246 ALL CREATURES GREAT AND SMALL

Assessing Learning

Check Test: True-False

1. When Aaron and Zlateh leave for town, the weather is already nasty. [False]
2. Aaron and Zlateh find shelter from the blizzard in a haystack. [True]
3. After Aaron sleeps for a while, he can no longer tell day from night. [True]
4. Food for Zlateh is a major problem while the storm continues to rage. [False]
5. After the storm, Aaron finishes his errand by taking Zlateh to the butcher. [False]

Standardized Test Preparation

For practice with standardized test format specific to this selection, see
• *Standardized Test Preparation,* p. 38
For practice in proofreading and editing, see
• *Daily Oral Grammar,* Transparency 13

MAKING MEANINGS

First Thoughts

[respond]

1. How did you react when the family decided to sell Zlateh to the butcher? How did you feel at the end of the story? Look back at your reading notes for ideas.

Shaping Interpretations

[consider]

2. Think of Aaron's behavior during the storm. What does it tell you about his **character**?

[respond]

3. Make a list of the moments in the story when you felt **suspense**.

[analyze]

4. What evidence in the story can you find to support this statement: "Zlateh the Goat" is a story about love?

[interpret]

5. Singer, who was a dedicated vegetarian, once said, "I love birds and all animals, and I believe that men can learn a lot from God's creatures." In this story, what does Aaron learn from Zlateh? What does Aaron's family learn?

[speculate]

6. Hanukkah is a celebration of a rebirth: The Temple at Jerusalem, which had been ruined, was rebuilt. Why do you suppose Singer set "Zlateh the Goat" during Hanukkah?

[respond]

7. Where in the story does Zlateh express her thoughts and ideas? Have your feelings about animal-person communication changed now that you've read the story?

Extending the Text

[compare/ contrast]

8. Think of another story or a movie about a close friendship between a person and an animal. What connections, if any, can you see between that story and Zlateh's?

[respond]

9. Aaron believes that Zlateh tells him "We must accept all that God gives us—heat, cold, hunger, satisfaction, light, and darkness." What do you think of this idea about acceptance?

> **Reading Check**
>
> Write four questions that deal with the **main events** in the story. Then, get together with a partner, and ask him or her these questions. Afterward, compare quizzes. Did you and your partner agree on what was important?

The Village (1973) by Marc Chagall.
©1999 Artists Rights Society (ARS), New York/ADAGP, Paris.

ZLATEH THE GOAT 247

> **Reading Check**
>
> Students should focus on important questions. Possible responses:
> 1. Why does Aaron set off with Zlateh?
> 2. How do Aaron and Zlateh survive the blizzard?
> 3. Why does the family decide not to sell Zlateh after all?
> 4. How does the family get the money it needs?

MAKING MEANINGS

First Thoughts

1. Many students may have been sad when Aaron had to take Zlateh to the butcher and glad when the family decided to keep her.

Shaping Interpretations

2. Aaron is religious (he prays for Zlateh and himself), knowledgeable (he knows that a haystack means safety and that he must make a vent for fresh air), loving (he does not abandon Zlateh), and patient.

3. Have students refer to the notes they made as they were reading the story. For example, they may recall the snowstorm as being a suspenseful moment.

4. Reuven wants to provide his family with a happy Hanukkah; Anna and Miriam cry when they learn that Zlateh is to be sold to the butcher; Aaron grows to love Zlateh like a sister; the family mourns when Aaron appears to be lost; and when Zlateh returns, no one considers selling her anymore.

5. Zlateh's patience and trust are examples to Aaron. Aaron and his family learn about the interdependence of humans and animals for survival and friendship.

6. Zlateh is supposed to die, but she is saved; Aaron and Zlateh come close to dying, but they survive; and Aaron's family believes he is dead, but he returns with Zlateh.

7. Zlateh expresses herself through her patient following of Aaron's lead, with her *Maaas* in the haystacks, and by asking admittance to the house on her own terms. Students may find that they are more convinced that animals can communicate with humans.

Extending the Text

8. Students may mention *Julie of the Wolves* by Jean Craighead George, in which a girl lost in an Arctic winter seeks help from wolves, or *Woodsong* by Gary Paulsen, about the author's competition in the Iditarod dogsled race.

9. Some students may agree with the idea of acceptance; some may not. Encourage them to explore their beliefs by listing the arguments for and against acceptance.

CHOICES: Building Your Portfolio

1. **Writer's Notebook**   Before students begin the activity, ask volunteers to share any examples of their having been helped by animals. Remind students to save their work. They may use it as prewriting for the Writer's Workshop on p. 302.

2. **Creative Writing**   Pairs of students might role-play their dialogues, acting as much like the animals they chose as possible. They may wish to tape-record the role-play and transcribe it later. Students who write dialogues with animals they know may wish to accompany their dialogues with photographs or illustrations of the animals.

3. **Performance**   Students can consult various plays or reader's theater pieces in this book and elsewhere for examples of stage directions. Allow students ample time to adjust their scripts and to rehearse.

CHOICES: Building Your Portfolio

Writer's Notebook

1. Collecting Ideas for an Informative Report

Animals and people often team up to get things done. Think about some of the jobs you've seen or heard about that animals do along with people.

- How do animals and people work to transport or carry things?

- How do animals help protect people or property?

- How do animals and people work together to find missing people or things?

I saw a blind person with a guide dog. Dogs can be "ears" for deaf people, too. Pets give love to old people. Do a report on animals who help people?

Creative Writing

2. Beastly Conversation

What would life be like if animals could express thoughts and feelings in human language? Think of an animal—a pet or other animal you know or a wild animal—with whom you'd like to have a conversation. Write a dialogue between the animal and you. See if you can capture the animal's personality through what it says.

Performance

3. Zlateh Live

Form a group to work on a performance of "Zlateh the Goat," using pantomime. In a pantomime, actors use body movements and facial expressions—but not their voices—to act out a story. Some pantomimes are totally silent; some have musical accompaniment; some use a narrator, who stands on the side or even offstage and reads the story aloud.

You'll have to make several decisions before you start working on your performance:

a. Who will write your script?

b. Who will be your director?

c. How many actors will you need?

d. How will you play Zlateh?

e. What props and scenery will you need?

The script is a typed version of the story as you will perform it. The script should show when actors enter and leave the stage. It should also describe some of their movements and feelings. Actors should mark up their copies of the script with notes on how to play their scenes.

GRAMMAR LINK   MINI-LESSON

Making Pronouns and Antecedents Agree

Language Handbook HELP

See Indefinite Pronouns, page 695.

Technology HELP

See Language Workshop CD-ROM. Key word entry: pronoun-antecedent agreement.

A pronoun usually refers to a noun or another pronoun, called its **antecedent**. Whenever you use a pronoun, make sure it agrees with its antecedent in number and gender. This is usually easy, except when you use certain pronouns as antecedents.

Use a singular pronoun to refer to *each, either, neither, one, everyone, everybody, no one, nobody, anyone, someone,* or *somebody.*

EXAMPLE

> Nobody wants to sell his or her pet to a butcher.

Nobody is singular, so you use the singular pronouns *his* and *her*. You need both *his* and *her* because the gender of *nobody* can be either masculine or feminine.

EXAMPLE

> Aaron's mother and sisters were very upset about Zlateh, and everyone had tears in her eyes.

Everyone is singular, so you use the singular pronoun *her*. You use *her* (rather than *his or her*) because *everyone* refers to Aaron's mother and sisters.

Try It Out

➤ In this paragraph about "Zlateh the Goat," make all the pronouns and their antecedents agree:

Anyone who loves animals will find their interest grabbed by "Zlateh the Goat." How can someone take their pet goat to be butchered, as Aaron does? Everybody knows what it's like to love their pets.

➤ When you proofread your own writing, circle each pronoun and draw an arrow from it to its antecedent. Check to see that each pronoun matches its antecedent in number and gender.

VOCABULARY   HOW TO OWN A WORD

WORD BANK
penetrated
cleft
chaos
exuded

Demonstrate It

1. The narrator says that the cold penetrated Aaron's quilted jacket. Act out how Aaron reacted.
2. Zlateh has cleft hooves. Sketch a picture of those hooves.
3. Aaron makes a window in the haystack that lets him see the chaos outside. Imitate the sounds Aaron probably heard.
4. Inside the shelter the "dried hay, grass, and field flowers exuded the warmth of the summer sun." Show how this probably affected Aaron.

ZLATEH THE GOAT **249**

GRAMMAR LINK

Ask students to select papers from their portfolios and to identify the pronouns and antecedents, correcting any that do not agree. Then have students exchange their papers with partners to check each other's work.

Try It Out
Answer
Anyone who loves animals will find *his or her* interest grabbed by "Zlateh the Goat." How can someone take *his or her* pet goat to be butchered, as Aaron does? Everybody knows what it's like to love *his or her* pet.

VOCABULARY

1. Students might hunch over, pull their jackets tight, and shiver.
2. Sketches should show the split hooves of a goat.
3. Students should imitate the various whining noises the wind made.
4. Students should act drowsy and contented.

Resources

Grammar
• *Grammar and Language Links,* p. 23

Vocabulary
• *Words to Own,* p. 11

Spelling
For related instruction, see
• *Spelling and Decoding,* p. 11

Grammar Link Quick Check

Revise the following sentences so that the pronouns agree with their antecedents.

1. Anyone who wants to sell their pet should think twice before they do it. [Anyone who wants to sell his or her pet should think twice before he or she does it *or* People who want to sell their pets should think twice before they do it.]

2. Everyone loves to see their pet. [Everyone loves to see his or her pet *or* All people love to see their pets.]

3. Each student has to do their own work. [Each student has to do his or her own work; all students have to do their own work.]

4. Nobody has ever lost their coat before. [Nobody has ever lost his or her coat before.]

OBJECTIVES

1. Read and interpret the story
2. Identify and analyze theme
3. Draw inferences
4. Express understanding through writing or math/problem solving
5. Identify pronouns and contractions and use them in writing
6. Spell words in which the final consonant is doubled or not before addition of a suffix

SKILLS

Literary
- Identify and analyze theme

Reading
- Draw inferences

Writing
- Freewrite about pets
- Write from a pet's point of view

Grammar
- Identify pronouns and contractions and use them in writing

Vocabulary
- Spell words in which the final consonant is doubled or not before addition of a suffix

Math/Problem Solving
- Research the cost of dog care

Viewing/Representing
- Express opinions about artistic choices (ATE)

Planning

- **Block Schedule**
  Block Scheduling Lesson Plans with Pacing Guide

- **Traditional Schedule**
  Lesson Plans Including Strategies for English-Language Learners

- **One-Stop Planner**
  CD-ROM with Test Generator

STRAY

Make the Connection

Puppy Love

Rate each of the following statements with a number from 0 to 4. (A rating of 0 means that you completely disagree; 4 means that you completely agree.) Record your ratings on a sheet of paper.

disagree 0 1 2 3 4 agree

1. Every family should have a dog.

2. Children can learn a lot from taking care of a dog.

3. Dogs are easy to train.

4. Having a dog for a pet costs almost nothing.

5. Stray dogs usually make good pets.

Save your responses. You'll refer to them after reading "Stray."

Quickwrite

Choose the statement above that you have the strongest opinion about. Jot down some real-life examples and details that support your opinion.

Elements of Literature

Theme: The Heart of a Story

Theme is the heart of a story. It is what the story reveals about our lives. Theme is different from plot. **Plot** is what happens in a story. **Theme** is what the story means. When you are asked to summarize a plot, you can start out by saying "The major events in this story are . . .". When you are asked to summarize a theme, you can start out by saying "This story showed me that . . .". Always think about how a story's theme relates to your own life. Also remember that no two readers will probably ever state a theme in exactly the same way.

> **T**heme is the idea about life revealed in a work of literature.
>
> *For more on Theme, see page 326 and the Handbook of Literary Terms.*

Reading Skills and Strategies

Drawing Inferences: Looking for Clues

An **inference** is a guess, but not just any kind of guess. It's a guess you can support with evidence from a text and from experience. To infer the theme of "Stray," follow these steps:

- Look for evidence, or clues, in the text. How do characters change? What do they learn about life?

- Think of evidence from your own experience. Try to make connections between the story and real life.

- Try to state what all of this evidence reveals about life and people in general.

There. You've inferred a theme.

go.hrw.com
LEO 6-4

250 **ALL CREATURES GREAT AND SMALL**

  Resources: Print and Media

Reading
- *Reading Skills and Strategies*
    Selection Skill Lesson, p. 101
- *Graphic Organizers for Active Reading,* p. 20
- *Spelling and Decoding,* p. 12
- *Audio CD Library*
    Disc 5, Track 3

Writing and Language
- *Daily Oral Grammar*
    Transparency 14

- *Grammar and Language Links*
    Worksheet, p. 25
- *Language Workshop CD-ROM*

Assessment
- *Formal Assessment,* p. 52
- *Portfolio Management System,* p. 138
- *Standardized Test Preparation,* p. 40
- *Test Generator (One-Stop Planner CD-ROM)*

Internet
- go.hrw.com (keyword: LEO 6-4)

stray

Cynthia Rylant

She cried herself to sleep.

In January, a puppy wandered onto the property of Mr. Amos Lacey and his wife, Mamie, and their daughter, Doris. Icicles hung three feet or more from the eaves of houses, snowdrifts swallowed up automobiles, and the birds were so fluffed up they looked comic.

The puppy had been abandoned, and it made its way down the road toward the Laceys' small house, its ears tucked, its tail between its legs, shivering.

Doris, whose school had been called off because of the snow, was out shoveling the cinder-block front steps when she spotted the pup on the road. She set down the shovel.

"Hey! Come on!" she called.

STRAY 251

Summary ■ ■

On a wintry January day, a puppy wanders into the lives of the Lacey family. Doris, the young daughter, wants to adopt the dog, but her parents say they cannot afford to feed it. However, the puppy stays on for several days, while icy roads prevent Mr. Lacey from taking it to the pound. Although Doris has avoided naming the dog so she won't become too attached to it, she cries all day when her father finally takes the dog to the pound. That evening she discovers that her father could not in good conscience leave the puppy in such a filthy place, so the dog is now hers. Doris understands the sacrifices her parents are making in allowing her to befriend a small, lost creature.

Resources

Listening
Audio CD Library
A recording of "Stray" is provided in the *Audio CD Library*:
• Disc 5, Track 3

Assessment
Formal Assessment
• Selection Test, p. 52
Test Generator
• Selection Test

Ⓐ Critical Thinking
Making Connections
? How would you feel if you were Doris? What would you want to do?
[Possible responses: Most students would feel sorry for the puppy and would want to rescue it.]

Reaching All Students

Struggling Readers
Drawing Inferences was introduced on p. 250. For a lesson directly tied to this selection that teaches students to draw inferences using a strategy called It Says . . . I Say, see the *Reading Skills and Strategies* binder.
• Selection Skill Lesson, p. 101

English Language Learners
After students have finished reading the story, evaluate their comprehension by asking them to work in pairs to write alternative titles for the story and to give the reasons for their choices. Collect their work, and then provide discussion practice by asking them to explain which specific parts of the selection influenced their choices of title.

Advanced Learners
Ask students to write a first-person narrative of the events in the story from the point of view of one of the characters: Doris, Mr. Lacey, Mrs. Lacey, or even the stray puppy. Remind students that a first-person narrative is one told by a character in a story, using the personal pronoun *I*. Suggest that students first discuss the different ways each character might look at the same events.

A **Reading Skills and Strategies**

Drawing Inferences

? Does Mrs. Lacey seem very sympathetic toward the puppy? How can you tell? [She doesn't; she stresses the word *that* when she asks, "Where did *that* come from?"—which implies the puppy is something she doesn't want in her house.]

Seated Girl with Dog (1944) by Milton Avery. Oil on canvas, 44″ x 32″.
Roy R. Neuberger Collection.

The puppy stopped in the road, wagging its tail timidly, trembling with shyness and cold.

Doris trudged through the yard, went up the shoveled drive and met the dog.

"Come on, pooch."

A "Where did *that* come from?" Mrs. Lacey asked as soon as Doris put the dog down in the kitchen.

Mr. Lacey was at the table, cleaning his fingernails with his pocketknife. The snow was keeping him home from his job at the warehouse.

252 ALL CREATURES GREAT AND SMALL

Getting Students Involved

Cooperative Learning

Family Role-Play. The story may arouse strong responses in students who have had an experience similar to Doris's—being in conflict with their parents about keeping a pet. Doris shows her unhappiness but takes very little action to resolve the conflict. Have three student volunteers role-play a conversation between Doris and her parents, in which Doris gives a full account of her reasons for keeping the puppy and in which her parents respond. After the first time through, have the rest of the class give suggestions to Doris and her parents about other arguments they could use. Then have the same volunteers or another group repeat the role-play, incorporating the suggestions that seem the most helpful.

"I don't know where it came from," he said mildly, "but I know for sure where it's going."

Doris hugged the puppy hard against her. She said nothing.

Because the roads would be too bad for travel for many days, Mr. Lacey couldn't get out to take the puppy to the pound in the city right away. He agreed to let it sleep in the basement, while Mrs. Lacey grudgingly let Doris feed it table scraps. The woman was sensitive about throwing out food.

By the looks of it, Doris figured the puppy was about six months old and on its way to being a big dog. She thought it might have some shepherd in it.

Four days passed and the puppy did not complain. It never cried in the night or howled at the wind. It didn't tear up everything in the basement. It wouldn't even follow Doris up the basement steps unless it was invited.

It was a good dog.

Several times Doris had opened the door in the kitchen that led to the basement, and the puppy had been there, all stretched out, on the top step. Doris knew it had wanted some company and that it had lain against the door, listening to the talk in the kitchen, smelling the food, being a part of things. It always wagged its tail, eyes all sleepy, when she found it there.

Even after a week had gone by, Doris didn't name the dog. She knew her parents wouldn't let her keep it, that her father made so little money any pets were out of the question, and that the pup would definitely go to the pound when the weather cleared.

Still, she tried talking to them about the dog at dinner one night.

"She's a good dog, isn't she?" Doris said, hoping one of them would agree with her.

Her parents glanced at each other and went on eating.

"She's not much trouble," Doris added. "I like her." She smiled at them, but they continued to ignore her.

"I figure she's real smart," Doris said to her mother. "I could teach her things."

Mrs. Lacey just shook her head and stuffed a forkful of sweet potato in her mouth. Doris fell silent, praying the weather would never clear.

But on Saturday, nine days after the dog had arrived, the sun was shining and the roads were plowed. Mr. Lacey opened up the trunk of his car and came into the house.

Doris was sitting alone in the living room, hugging a pillow and rocking back and forth on the edge of a chair. She was trying not to cry but she was not strong enough. Her face was wet and red, her eyes full of distress.

Mrs. Lacey looked into the room from the doorway.

"Mama," Doris said in a small voice. "Please."

Mrs. Lacey shook her head.

"You know we can't afford a dog, Doris. You try to act more grown-up about this."

Doris pressed her face into the pillow.

Outside, she heard the trunk of the car slam shut, one of the doors open and close, the old engine cough and choke and finally start up.

"Daddy," she whispered. "Please."

She heard the car travel down the road, and though it was early afternoon, she could do nothing but go to her bed. She cried herself to sleep, and her dreams were full of searching and searching for things lost.

It was nearly night when she finally woke up. Lying there, like stone, still exhausted, she wondered if she would ever in her life have anything. She stared at the wall for a while.

But she started feeling hungry, and she knew she'd have to make herself get out of

STRAY 253

B Reading Skills and Strategies

Drawing Inferences

❓ Where does Mr. Lacey mean the puppy is going? [Possible responses: back outside; to the pound.]

C Reading Skills and Strategies

Drawing Inferences

❓ Why do Doris's parents not say anything? Do they think the puppy is not good? [Possible responses: They don't want to argue with Doris; they don't want to build up Doris's hope that she might be able to keep the puppy. Though they can probably see that the puppy is good, they don't feel they can afford to feed an animal that is going to grow.]

D Critical Thinking

Interpreting the Text

❓ What does Mrs. Lacey mean by telling Doris to try to act "more grown-up"? [She means that Doris should accept—without crying—the fact that the family just can't afford a dog.]

Resources ⎯⎯⎯⎯

Assessment

Formal Assessment
• Selection Test, p. 52

Test Generator
• Selection Test

Making the Connections

Connecting to the Theme: "All Creatures Great and Small"

Both "Zlateh the Goat" and "Stray" are about the relationships between families and animals. The central human character in each story is a child; the father in each story changes his mind and allows the animal to live. Ask students to create Venn diagrams showing both similarities and differences in the stories. You can use the Venn diagram transparency from the transparency package.

Cultural Connections

Sometimes pets may also "work" for their living, by doing such things as herding livestock or helping people who have impaired vision or hearing. Pets can also be therapeutic for people who are sick or lonely. Have students comment on situations they know about in which animals help people.

Assessing Learning

Observation Assessment

As students discuss the story, use the following criteria to assess their understanding:
R = Rarely, S = Sometimes, O = Often

_____ 1. Addresses multiple perspectives

_____ 2. Uses the text to confirm and clarify ideas

_____ 3. Makes personal connections with the text

_____ 4. Makes connections with other texts

T253

Speculating

? What has happened to the dog? [Mr. Lacey brought it back home.] **Why do you think he didn't leave the puppy at the pound?** [Possible responses: He has become attached to the puppy too; he didn't like the pound; he didn't want to hurt Doris.]

B Elements of Literature

Theme

? What does the story say about life? [Sample responses: Love is more important than money; people decide what is important to them even if they have to make sacrifices; actions may say more than words.]

BROWSING IN THE FILES

About the Author. Cynthia Rylant sympathizes with people who must face hardships, perhaps because of her own difficult childhood. Her parents separated when she was four, and her father died when she was thirteen. She and her mother moved to West Virginia, and most of her stories are set amid that Appalachian landscape. After earning bachelor's and master's degrees in English and library science, Rylant worked as a college English professor and then in the children's department of a public library. It was at the library that she first became acquainted with children's literature. She claims that her own lack of early exposure to children's books made her a better author, since it allowed her to use her imagination more fully and to avoid "writing down" to children.

A Critic's Comment. According to *Children's Literature Review*, critics praise Rylant "for her straightforward approach, economic yet lyrical language, . . . and ability to express powerful emotions with restraint. . . . Thematically, she stresses the importance of family and all living things. . . . Her works ultimately convey understanding and hope."

---

bed and eat some dinner. She wanted not to go into the kitchen, past the basement door. She wanted not to face her parents.

But she rose up heavily.

Her parents were sitting at the table, dinner over, drinking coffee. They looked at her when she came in, but she kept her head down. No one spoke.

Doris made herself a glass of powdered milk and drank it all down. Then she picked up a cold biscuit and started out of the room.

A "You'd better feed that mutt before it dies of starvation," Mr. Lacey said.

Doris turned around.

"What?"

"I said, you'd better feed your dog. I figure it's looking for you."

Doris put her hand to her mouth.

"You didn't take her?" she asked.

"Oh, I took her all right," her father answered. "Worst-looking place I've ever seen. Ten dogs to a cage. Smell was enough to knock you down. And they give an animal six days to live. Then they kill it with some kind of a shot."

Doris stared at her father.

"I wouldn't leave an *ant* in that place," he said. "So I brought the dog back."

B Mrs. Lacey was smiling at him and shaking her head as if she would never, ever, understand him.

Mr. Lacey sipped his coffee.

"Well," he said, "are you going to feed it or not?"

MEET THE WRITER

"Our Lives Are Beautiful, Breathtaking"

Cynthia Rylant (1954–   ) spent part of her childhood with her grandparents in West Virginia. Remembering them fondly, she says:

❝ They lived life with strength, great calm, and a real sense of what it means to be devoted to and responsible for other people. The tone of my work reflects the way they spoke, the simplicity of their language, and, I hope, the depth of their own hearts. ❞

Why does Rylant—winner of the Newbery and other awards—like to write?

❝ I like to show the way our lives are beautiful, breathtak-ing, in the smallest things: shelling beans on a porch in the evening; sitting in a run-down shoe repair shop; wanting a pretty little lamp; giving saltines to the squirrels. I prefer writing about child characters because they have more possibilities. They can get away with more love, more anger, more fear than adult characters. They can be more moving. I like them more. I sympathize with them more. ❞

More from the Heart
Cynthia Rylant writes poetry, short stories, and novels. If you enjoyed "Stray," try the story collections *Every Living Thing* (Bradbury) and *A Couple of Kooks: And Other Stories About Love* (Orchard Books).

254

Assessing Learning

Check Test: True-False

1. The story is set in summer. [False]
2. Snow has given Doris a free day. [True]
3. Doris sees the puppy when she is staring out the window. [False]
4. Mr. Lacey lets the puppy stay in the basement. [True]
5. The puppy is left at the pound. [False]

Standardized Test Preparation

For practice with standardized test format specific to this selection, see
• *Standardized Test Preparation*, p. 40
For practice in proofreading and editing, see
• *Daily Oral Grammar*, Transparency 14

Mother Doesn't Want a Dog

Judith Viorst Ⓐ

Mother doesn't want a dog.
Mother says they smell,
And never sit when you say sit,
Or even when you yell.
5 And when you come home late at night
And there is ice and snow,
You have to go back out because
The dumb dog has to go.

Mother doesn't want a dog.
10 Mother says they shed,
And always let the strangers in
And bark at friends instead,
And do disgraceful things on rugs,
And track mud on the floor,
15 And flop upon your bed at night
And snore their doggy snore.

Mother doesn't want a dog.
She's making a mistake.
Because, more than a dog, I think
20 She will not want this snake.

STRAY 255

Connecting Across Texts

Connecting with "Stray"
Both "Stray" and "Mother Doesn't Want a Dog" reveal conflicts between children and parents about adopting a dog, and both have surprise endings. Ask pairs or triads of students to create dialogues between children and parents about the joys and responsibilities of owning pets. Encourage students to include humor or surprise endings in their dialogues, as Judith Viorst does in her poem.

Connections

The title of this amusing poem is repeated as a refrain in the first line of each stanza. The first two stanzas relate the disadvantages of dog ownership from Mother's point of view. In the final stanza, Mother's child—the speaker—reveals a quite different opinion of the relationship between people and animals, hinting that bringing Mother a snake may lead her to yield on the dog question.

Ⓐ Literary Connections

Critic Joanne Lewis Sears writes of Viorst, "Prolific, comical, practical and wise, Judith Viorst has given us kids' books, wry poems about getting older, a very funny novel—and some serious stuff." Viorst, a graduate of the Washington Psychoanalytic Institute, translates her scholarship into the stuff of daily life, as in her book *If I Were in Charge of the World and Other Worries: Poems for Children and Their Parents* (1987). With Viorst's trademark humor evident throughout, the book's more than forty poems deal with children's concerns, such as fear of the dark, pets, and relationships with other children and older people.

Ⓑ Elements of Literature
Speaker
❓ Who is the speaker of this poem? [a child who is reporting "Mother's" views about pets] Remind students that a reader shouldn't assume that a poem's speaker is the poet.

Ⓒ Appreciating Language
Repetition
Repetition of "And" suggests the endless disruptions associated with owning a dog—at least according to Mother.

Ⓓ Reading Skills and Strategies
Drawing Inferences
❓ What is surprising about the ending? [The speaker has brought home a snake.] Considering what the entire poem is about, why might the speaker have brought the snake home? [Sample response: to make Mother think that a dog might be preferable.]

MAKING MEANINGS

First Thoughts

1. Some students may feel the ending is unrealistic; others will be pleased that Doris can keep the puppy.

Shaping Interpretations

2. The puppy could not survive in winter without help. The weather delays the trip to the pound, and the family grows used to the dog.

3. Some students may agree that crying serves no useful purpose; others may argue that it is good to release feelings by crying.

4. Sample response: Sometimes people express their love more by what they do than by what they say.

Grading Timesaver

Rubrics for each Choices assignment appear on p. 138 in the *Portfolio Management System.*

CHOICES:
Building Your Portfolio

1. **Writer's Notebook**   Remind students to save and use their work as prewriting for the Writer's Workshop on p. 302.
2. **Creative Writing**   To prepare for the activity, ask students for examples of stories, folk tales, movies, or television programs that feature talking animals.
3. **Math/Problem Solving**   Encourage students who have dogs to also consult their parents on actual costs, including annual shots and other veterinarian bills.

MAKING MEANINGS

First Thoughts

[respond]

1. What were your feelings about Mr. Lacey's decision at the end of the story?

Shaping Interpretations

[generalize]

2. Why is the **setting**—a cold, snowy January—an important part of the story?

[respond]

3. After Doris cries, her mother tells her "to act more grown-up." Do you think this is good advice? Why or why not?

[synthesize]

4. What do you think the story's **theme** has to say about love and caring?

CHOICES: Building Your Portfolio

Writer's Notebook

1. Collecting Ideas for an Informative Report

To get ideas for an informative report on pets, freewrite about an experience with a pet or about one of the following topics:

- choosing the right pet
- training a pet
- finding homes for lost or abandoned pets

You might also find a good idea for a report in your notes for the Quickwrite on page 250.

Creative Writing

2. A First-Pet Point of View

Hardly any pets write stories about their owners. Pretend you are a pet you know. You might want to be Doris's stray or even the snake in "Mother Doesn't Want a Dog" (see *Connections* on page 255). Then, from the "first-pet point of view," write about your life.

Math/Problem Solving

3. How Much Is That Doggie . . . ?

Will having a dog break your budget? Find out the cost of caring for a dog. First, choose a breed of dog. Then, research how much food you would have to buy in a year and how much it would cost at your local supermarket. Next, call or visit a veterinarian's office to find out the cost of shots a dog would need. Also, find out the price of a dog license, a leash, and some toys.

   Present your information as an article for a consumer magazine.

GRAMMAR LINK   MINI-LESSON

Pronoun and Contraction Mix-ups

Language Handbook HELP

See Personal Pronouns, page 714; Contractions, page 759.

Technology HELP

See Language Workshop CD-ROM. Key word entry: pronouns.

Contractions	Possessive Pronouns
it's (it is/has)	its
they're (they are)	their
you're (you are)	your
who's (who is/has)	whose

1. Use an apostrophe to show where letters are missing in a **contraction** (a shortened form of a word or group of words):

   <u>Who's</u> [Who is] the girl with the puppy?

   Doris, <u>you're</u> [you are] a brave girl.

2. Don't use an apostrophe with a **possessive personal pronoun:**

   <u>They're</u> [they are] making <u>their</u> way up the walk.

   Doris, <u>you're</u> [you are] late, and <u>your</u> dog is waiting to be fed.

   "<u>Whose</u> dog is that? <u>Who's</u> [who is] asking?"

   The dog thinks <u>it's</u> [it is] never getting <u>its</u> dinner.

Try It Out

Write a dialogue between Doris and her parents in which Doris tries to persuade them to let her keep the puppy. Use *its, it's; your, you're; their, they're;* and *whose, who's* in your dialogue. Exchange dialogues, and check your partner's use of pronouns and contractions.

SPELLING   HOW TO OWN A WORD

Language Handbook HELP

See Adding Suffixes, page 763.

Consonants: Double or Nothing?

1. Double the final consonant before adding *-ing, -ed, -er,* or *-est* to a one-syllable word that ends in a vowel followed by a single consonant.

   EXAMPLE   stop + *-ed* = stopped

2. When a one-syllable word ends in two vowels followed by a single consonant, do *not* double the consonant before adding *-ing, -ed, -er,* or *-est.*

   EXAMPLE   feel + *-ing* = feeling

Start two lists in your Spelling Log, one for words ending with a single vowel and a consonant and the other for words ending with two vowels and a consonant. Refer to the lists when you proofread your work.

GRAMMAR LINK

After students have chosen passages from their portfolios to proofread, have them circle possessive pronouns with one color and contractions with another. Students may proofread their own work or exchange papers with partners and proofread each other's work.

Try It Out
Sample Response

"*It's* not going to be easy taking care of that puppy," Mrs. Lacey said. "*Who's* going to feed him when *you're* not around?"

"That's not going to be *your* responsibility," Doris said. "I'll take care of it."

"Well, if *you're* going to be so responsible, maybe you should find out *whose* dog it is." Mr. Lacey said. "*They're* probably out looking for it."

"I've checked *its* collar, but there wasn't an identification tag," Doris said, "And I haven't heard anything about it on the radio."

"*Their* own children are probably worried sick about that poor dog," Mrs. Lacey said.

SPELLING

Have students begin their lists by looking back through their own writing for words ending in *-ing, -ed, -er,* or *-est.* You might also suggest a few starter words (such as *wrap* or *shop*) that require a doubled consonant when a suffix is added and a few (such as *look* and *peal*) that do not.

Resources ———

Grammar
• *Grammar and Language Links,* p. 25

Spelling
For related instruction, see
• *Spelling and Decoding,* p. 12

Grammar Link Quick Check

Choose the correct possessive pronouns or contractions in the following sentences.

1. I can't believe <u>it's/its</u> been a month since Daddy came back with the puppy. [it's]

2. When he asked me <u>who's/whose</u> going to pay for the dog's upkeep, I said I would. [who's]

3. Diane said, "I can't believe <u>you're/your</u> going to be able to pay for that dog! Where will you get the money?" [you're]

4. But I've done really well, because the neighbors pay me to watch <u>they're/their</u> kids after school. [their]

OBJECTIVES
1. Read and interpret the poem
2. Identify an ode
3. Express understanding through writing and art

OBJECTIVES

1. Read and interpret the poem
2. Identify an ode
3. Express understanding through writing and art

SKILLS

Literary
- Identify an ode

Writing
- Gather ideas about topics relating to cats
- Write an ode about a person or pet

Art
- Illustrate images from the poems

Planning

- **Block Schedule**
  Block Scheduling Lesson Plans with Pacing Guide
- **Traditional Schedule**
  Lesson Plans Including Strategies for English-Language Learners
- **One-Stop Planner**
  CD-ROM with Test Generator

RESPONDING TO THE ART

This is an eighteenth-century copy of a painting done during the great Ming Dynasty in China (1368–1644). This charming painting was done on silk and is part of a handscroll. It is called *Spring Play in a T'ang Garden*. (T'ang was an earlier, very cultivated dynasty, 618–907.) Handscrolls show a series of connected scenes painted on a roll of thin material—in this case, silk.

Before You Read

ODE TO MI GATO

Make the Connection

I Know How You Felt

Think about all the love songs you hear on the radio. Love has also inspired poets to create tens of thousands of poems.

Quickwrite

Art is about feelings, too. Look at the artwork that illustrates this poem. What feelings do the colors and shapes suggest? Given these clues, try to **predict** the emotions you'll share in this poem. Jot down your ideas on a sheet of paper.

Elements of Literature

Ode: A Poem of Praise

When poetry lovers hear the word *ode,* they think of a poem written in a grand, dignified style, praising someone or something. Gary Soto brings the ode down to earth, using ordinary language and the rhythms of everyday speech as he celebrates his little cat, or *gato.*

> **A**n ode is a poem that pays tribute to someone or something of great importance to the poet.

 go.hrw.com
LE0 6-4

Spring Play in a T'ang Garden (detail) (18th century) by an unknown artist. Copy of a painting attributed to Hsuan Tsung (Ming dynasty). Handscroll; colors on silk.
The Metropolitan Museum of Art, New York. Fletcher Fund, 1947. (47.18.9). Photograph © 1979 The Metropolitan Museum of Art.

 — *Resources: Print and Media* —

Reading
- *Graphic Organizers for Active Reading,* p. 21
- *Audio CD Library*
  Disc 5, Track 4

Viewing and Representing
- *Visual Connections*
  Videocassette A, Segment 5

Assessment
- *Formal Assessment,* p. 54
- *Portfolio Management System,* p. 139
- *Test Generator (One-Stop Planner CD-ROM)*

Internet
- go.hrw.com (keyword: LE0 6-4)

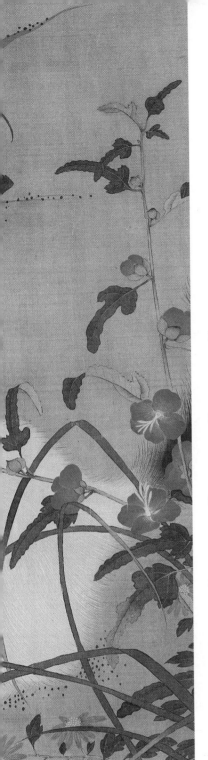

Ode to Mi Gato

Gary Soto

He's white
As spilled milk,
My cat who sleeps
With his belly
5   Turned toward
The summer sky.
He loves the sun,
Its warmth like a hand.
He loves tuna cans
10 And milk cartons
With their dribble
Of milk. He loves
Mom when she rattles
The bag of cat food,
15 The brown nuggets
Raining into his bowl.
And my cat loves
Me, because I saved
Him from a dog,
20 Because I dressed him
In a hat and a cape
For Halloween,
Because I dangled
A sock of chicken skin
25 As he stood on his
Hind legs. I love mi gato,
Porque I found
Him on the fender
Of an abandoned car.
30 He was a kitten,

With a meow
Like the rusty latch
On a gate. I carried
Him home in the loop
35 Of my arms.
I poured milk
Into him, let him
Lick chunks of
Cheese from my palms,
40 And cooked huevo
After huevo
Until his purring
Engine kicked in
And he cuddled
45 Up to my father's slippers.
That was last year.
This spring,
He's excellent at sleeping
And no good
50 At hunting. At night
All the other cats
In the neighborhood
Can see him slink
Around the corner,
55 Or jump from the tree
Like a splash of
Milk. We lap up
His love and
He laps up his welcome.

ODE TO MI GATO **259**

Reaching All Students

Struggling Readers
Have students stop after every few lines to write a summary of what they have read. For example, the first sixteen lines of "Ode to Mi Gato" might be summarized as follows: "My cat is white and sleeps on his back. He loves the sun, tuna cans, milk cartons, and Mom when she brings him food."

English Language Learners
Although the vocabulary in this poem is not difficult, English language learners may not comprehend some of Soto's figurative language. Ask them to sketch or explain in other words what is meant by each of the following:
• nuggets *raining* into a bowl (ll. 15–16)
• dangling a *sock* of chicken skin (ll. 23–24)
• a meow *like the rusty latch* (ll. 31–32)
• the *loop* of the speaker's arms (ll. 34–35)
• jump *like a splash of milk* (ll. 55–57)

Summary ■

This free-verse poem, an ode praising a cat, lists reasons why the cat and the speaker love each other. Using imagery that appeals to each of the senses, Soto gradually reveals the intensity of this relationship.

Resources

Viewing and Representing
Videocassette A, Segment 5
The *Visual Connections* segment "We're All in This Together" can be used to elicit post-reading discussion. See the *Visual Connections Teacher's Manual.*

Listening
Audio CD Library
A recording of this poem is provided in the *Audio CD Library:*
• Disc 5, Track 4

Assessment
Formal Assessment
• Selection Test, p. 54
Test Generator
• Selection Test

Ⓐ **Cultural Connections**
Spanish Words
Ask Spanish-speaking students to write the following words from the poem on the board and to pronounce and define them for the class: *mi gato* [mē gä′tō, "my cat"], *porque* [pôr · kā′, "because"], *huevo* [wā′vō, "egg"].

Ⓑ **Appreciating Language**
Word Choice
❓ Alert students to watch for words that create vivid sounds or pictures. Invite them to list three sensory words on a piece of paper or on the chalkboard. [Possible responses: *spilled, dribble, rattles, dangled, rusty latch, loop, lick, purring engine, cuddled, slink, splash of milk, lap up.*] **Which images do you especially enjoy?** [Sample response: dressing the cat up "In a hat and a cape / For Halloween."]

Ⓒ **Elements of Literature**
Ode
❓ In this ode, what does the speaker give to the cat? [Sample responses: welcome; love; food; a home.] **What does the cat give to the speaker?** [Sample responses: love; responsive purrs and meows; amusement.]

T259

MEET THE WRITER

"A Working Life"

Gary Soto (1952–   ) grew up in Fresno, California. His father worked at a raisin factory and his mother at a potato-processing plant. Today Soto writes poems and stories about the everyday joys and sorrows of people from backgrounds like his. In his time off he enjoys Aztec dance and karate.

66 I like to think of my poems as a working life, by which I mean that my poems are about commonplace, everyday things—baseball, an evening walk, a boyhood friendship, first love, fatherhood, a tree, rock 'n' roll, the homeless, dancing. The poems keep alive the small moments which add up to a large moment: life itself. 99

More Odes by Gary Soto

You can read more odes—about bathtubs, chicken wire, plumbing, and bricks—in Soto's book *Neighborhood Odes* (Harcourt Brace).

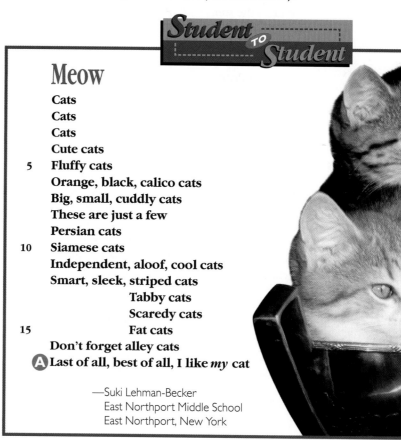

Student to Student

Meow

Cats
Cats
Cats
Cute cats
5   Fluffy cats
Orange, black, calico cats
Big, small, cuddly cats
These are just a few
Persian cats
10   Siamese cats
Independent, aloof, cool cats
Smart, sleek, striped cats
   Tabby cats
   Scaredy cats
15   Fat cats
Don't forget alley cats
Ⓐ Last of all, best of all, I like *my* cat

—Suki Lehman-Becker
East Northport Middle School
East Northport, New York

260   ALL CREATURES GREAT AND SMALL

Student to Student

The subject matter of this poem with the onomatopoeic title is cats—all kinds of cats, all sizes, all colors, all breeds, and all temperaments. The best cat of all, of course, is the speaker's.

Ⓐ **Critical Thinking**

Speculating

❓ Why is there so little in the poem about the speaker's cat and so much about other cats? [Sample response: Maybe the speaker is saying that there are many wonderful kinds of cats, but the best thing of all—the love of your own cat—can't really be described.]

Making the Connections

Connecting to the Theme: "All Creatures Great and Small"

In "Ode to Mi Gato," dozens of sensory details mark the special relationship between the speaker and his cat. The poet pays tribute to small, humble moments—as well as to more profound events from their history together (giving the cat a home and saving his life from a dog's attack). "Meow" concerns the way a single cat is part of a vast, varied world of felines.

Connecting Across Texts

Connecting with "Ode to Mi Gato"

Like Gary Soto's "Ode to Mi Gato," Suki Lehman-Becker's "Meow" is a poem in praise of cats. Ask students to brainstorm ideas for an original ode in response to Choice 2 on p. 261.

MAKING MEANINGS

MAKING MEANINGS

First Thoughts

[respond]
1. What picture did you get of the speaker of "Ode to Mi Gato"? Does the speaker seem to be a person you would like? Why?

Shaping Interpretations

[compare/contrast]
2. In the poem the speaker explains why he loves his cat and why it loves him. How are the reasons alike? How are they different?

[infer]
3. How does the speaker feel about the fact that the cat is "excellent at sleeping/And no good/At hunting"? How can you tell?

[predict]
4. What emotions does the poet share with you in "Ode to Mi Gato"? How did they match the **predictions** you made in your notes for the Quickwrite on page 258?

CHOICES: Building Your Portfolio

Writer's Notebook

1. Collecting Ideas for an Informative Report

"Ode to Mi Gato" and "Meow" (page 260) give you glimpses of the behavior of cats as well as impressions of their many breeds and types. If you were preparing a report on cats, what topics would you explore? Think about questions like these:

- How many breeds of cats are there?
- How are pet cats related to wild cats, such as cougars and lynxes?
- What was the special role of cats in ancient Egypt?

Creative Writing

2. Odes Aloud

Think of a special person or pet you'd like to praise in an **ode**. First, list some special details about your subject so that a reader will understand why you feel so strongly about it. Then, write your ode. You might get together with other ode writers to present an "Odes Aloud" reading.

Art

3. Artistic "Purrfection"

What images did you see as you read "Ode to Mi Gato" and "Meow"? Which of these pictures would be fun to illustrate? Choose a medium that you like, such as watercolors, colored pencils, markers, poster paints, photography, collage, or modeling clay. Then, create one or more of your favorite images.

ODE TO MI GATO **261**

Assessing Learning

Check Test: Short Answers
1. What color is the speaker's cat? [white]
2. Where did the speaker find the cat? [on an abandoned car]
3. What is one thing the cat is excellent at doing? [sleeping]
4. What does the cat not do very well? [hunt]
5. What do the speaker and the cat give each other? [love, affection]

First Thoughts
1. The speaker seems friendly, thoughtful, caring, and likable.

Shaping Interpretations
2. The cat loves the speaker because the speaker saved his life and plays with him. The speaker loves the cat because the cat is playful and grateful.
3. The speaker is amused by the cat's sleeping so much and not troubled by his lack of hunting ability. The speaker describes his cat with admiration and love.
4. Possible response: Soto shares feelings of love and amusement. Students should respond to the question before they check their Quickwrites.

Grading Timesaver

Rubrics for each Choices assignment appear on p. 139 in the *Portfolio Management System*.

CHOICES: Building Your Portfolio

1. **Writer's Notebook** Remind students to save their work. They may use it as prewriting for the Writer's Workshop on p. 302.
2. **Creative Writing** Suggest that students fill in a graphic organizer like the following for several possible ode subjects:

Possible subject	
Description	
Personality	
My feelings	

3. **Art** Students might bring in images from calendars or magazines in order to create collages. Those proficient in a computer drawing program might want to design their own hybrid cats.

OBJECTIVES

1. Appreciate the value of using organizers
2. Understand the uses of organizers, such as fish bones, hand organizers, and sequence charts

Reading Skills and Strategies

This feature focuses on a specific reading strategy that students can apply in the following selection.

Mini-Lesson:

Organizers

- After students have read the page, model the process of filling in the three organizers. Using student input, complete a sequence chart and a fish bone organizer on the board for the short story "Stray." Then show students another way of "seeing" the relationship of ideas by transferring the information in the fish bone chart to a hand organizer.

- Next, divide the class into three (or six) groups. Assign each group a different kind of organizer (fish bone, hand organizer, or sequence chart) to complete as they analyze the poem "Ode to Mi Gato." Ask the groups to draw their organizers on poster board and to present their finished products to the class. Encourage other class members to ask questions about how and why each group constructed its chart as it did.

- Finally, encourage students to use organizers as they read each remaining selection in the collection.

Reading Skills and Strategies

ORGANIZERS: FINDING THE STRUCTURE

Organizers are like road maps. They help you to find the **structure of a text** and to discover its meaning. Organizers come in many forms. You have already used some organizers in this text. You may also know about a kind of organizer called an **outline** (see page 685). Another useful organizer is a cluster diagram; you'll see one of these familiar maps on the opposite page.

Fish Bone and Handprint

A fish bone is another kind of organizer. Fish bones are especially useful when you're reading informative texts. They help you locate important ideas and their supporting details. You can use a fish bone to **infer** a text's main idea (see page 279). A fish bone appears at the right.

You can also find the structure of an informative text by making a "hand organizer." First, trace your hand. Then, list details in the fingers and write the main idea in the palm. (A hand organizer is shown on page 279.)

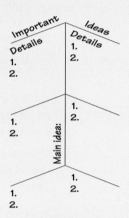

Sequence Chart

A **narrative** is an account of a series of related events. To review a narrative, use an organizer like the one at the right. When you read a narrative, you want to remember its **main events.** You also want to be sure you understand **causes and effects:** You want to be clear on how one event leads to another and then to another, and so on.

You can use a sequence chart as an aid for following the main events in stories and informative texts.

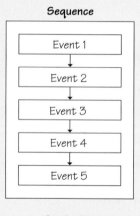

Sequence

Event 1 → Event 2 → Event 3 → Event 4 → Event 5

Apply the strategy on the next page.

Using Students' Strengths

Visual, Auditory, and Interpersonal Learners

If possible, include a mix of visual, auditory, and interpersonal learners in the groups working to create graphic organizers. Visual learners will naturally catch on to the concept of visual organizers, whereas auditory learners may need some assistance. Have visual learners explain the process orally as the students work together to complete the organizers. This oral instruction should help auditory learners grasp the concept more readily. The groups may choose to rely on visual learners as they work to complete the drawing portion of the assignment, and interpersonal learners may feel most comfortable presenting the graphic organizers to the class.

Before You Read

Make the Connection

The Beauty of the Beasts

The people in this story have some unusual ideas about how animals should be treated. Here's a chance to sort out your own thinking about animals before you start reading. (After you finish the story, you can see if it has changed your mind.) Copy the following list of ways people use animals. You can add other ways. Put a plus sign next to the uses you think are OK. Put a minus sign next to the uses you think are not OK.

People use animals for

- food
- clothing
- sport (hunting, fishing)
- entertainment (circuses, animal shows)
- display (zoos, animal reserves)
- medical research
- protection
- help (guide dogs)
- pets

go.hrw.com
LEO 6-4

Quickwrite

In the middle of a sheet of paper, write the word *Animals*. Review your pluses and minuses on ways animals are used. Then, create a map showing your ideas and feelings about animals.

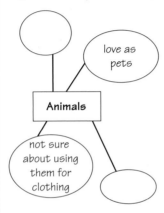

Reading Skills and Strategies

Using Chronology: Keeping Track of Events

This story is a kind of text called a **narrative.** Every narrative has the same basic structure, whether it's a fictional story or a true one, like "The Flood." All narra-tives are made up of a series of related events. Using **chronology,** keeping track of the order of events, will help you find and recall information in narratives. As you read, be aware of what happens, when it happens, and why it happens. Notice when the writer flashes back to an earlier time to explain events happening in the present. After you finish this story, you'll map its **main events** in a sequence organizer like the one on page 262. To start your sequence of events, read the opening paragraph now, and write down the story's first main event in the top box.

Drawing of a manatee by Olivia Borges Veras, 12 years old.

Summary ▪▪

In this nonfiction selection, Africa U.S.A., a ranch for 1,500 wild animals in southern California, is hit by a tremendous flood. The narrator and his co-workers work against enormous odds to free the animals from their cages and give them a chance to swim for their lives. (This would have been an impossible chore had most of the animals not had "affection training," which enables them to remain calm and cooperate with their rescuers. In contrast, some of the "fear-trained" animals must be tranquilized and so find it difficult to escape through the raging water.) Helping each other, animals and people struggle in the fast-moving water through two terrifying days and nights. The narrator is amazed to find that the majority of animals survive the ordeal. Damage to the ranch runs into millions of dollars, but most of the living things survive—thanks to the close relationships between the people and animals of the ranch.

Resources

Listening
Audio CD Library
A recording of this narrative is provided in the *Audio CD Library:*
• Disc 6, Track 2

 Reading Skills and Strategies
Using Chronology
Have students use the first paragraph to begin a sequence chart to track the narrative's main events. [Sample response: Day One, morning. It is raining, as it has been for weeks.]

Cages were starting to come loose from their foundations; the animals were swimming inside them, fighting for breath.

THE FLOOD

from The Beauty of the Beasts

Ralph Helfer

It was raining that morning, as usual. For weeks it had been coming down—sometimes heavily, with thunder and lightning, and sometimes with just a mist of light rain. But it was always there, and by now the blankets, the beds, and the whole house were constantly damp.

My career was at a peak. I'd spent twelve years struggling to get to the top, and I had finally made it. My life was pretty good. I had just completed the back-to-back shooting of *Daktari* and *Gentle Ben,* and I was living at our new ranch, Africa U.S.A., with 1,500 wild animals and a crew of dedicated keepers and trainers.

The ranch was beautiful. Nestled at the bottom of Soledad Canyon, about thirty miles north of Los Angeles, the property snaked for a mile down the canyon beside the banks of the Santa Clarita stream. The highway wound above it on one side, the railroad track on the other.

We'd had heavy rains before, and even a few floods, but nothing we couldn't handle. There was a flood-control dam above us, fifteen miles up the canyon, and we weren't too worried about the stream's overflowing. But just to make sure, we had asked the city's flood-control office to advise us. They checked their records for the biggest flood in the office's hundred-year history, and calculated that to handle one that size we would need a channel 100 feet wide, 12 feet deep, and 1 mile long. It cost us $100,000 and three months of hard work, but we built it. It was worth it to feel safe.

264 ALL CREATURES GREAT AND SMALL

  *Resources: Print and Media*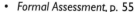

Reading
• *Reading Skills and Strategies*
  Selection Skill Lesson, p. 140
• *Graphic Organizers for Active Reading,* p. 22
• *Spelling and Decoding,* p. 13
• *Audio CD Library*
  Disc 6, Track 2

Elements of Literature
• *Literary Elements*
  Transparency 5
  Worksheet, p. 16

Writing and Language
• *Daily Oral Grammar*
  Transparency 15
• *Grammar and Language Links*
  Worksheet, p. 27
• *Language Workshop CD-ROM*

Assessment
• *Formal Assessment,* p. 55
• *Portfolio Management System,* p. 140
• *Standardized Test Preparation,* pp. 42, 44
• *Test Generator (One-Stop Planner CD-ROM)*

Internet
• go.hrw.com (keyword: LE0 6-4)

Toni and I had grabbed a few hours' sleep before leaving the house, which was located off the ranch up on a hill, and heading out into the rain again early this morning to make sure our animals were dry and safe.

On arriving at the compound, Toni went over to check on the "wild string," a group of lions, tigers, bears, and leopards that had been donated to us by people who never should have had them in the first place. Hopeless animal lovers that we were, we had taken them in, even though we know that very few spoiled mature animals could ever be indoctrinated[1] with affection training.

I checked at the office for messages, then headed for "Beverly Hills," our nickname for the area where our movie-star animals lived—Gentle Ben, Clarence the cross-eyed lion, Judy the chimp, Bullfrog the "talking" buffalo, Modoc the elephant, and many others. The rain had become a steady downpour by the time I arrived there. Everything seemed to be in order, so I went on to the rhinos. No problems there, either.

As I left the rhinos, I noticed that I could no longer jump over the stream that ran beside their barn. I was starting to get a little concerned. The sky was  now opening up with a vengeance.[2] I wrapped my poncho around me and continued my tour of inspection.

I was wondering how Toni was making out with the wild string when Miguel, a Mexican keeper who had been with us for

1. **indoctrinated** (in·däk′trə·nāt′id): taught.
2. **with a vengeance** (ven′jəns): with great force.

six years, arrived to care for the animals in the Beverly Hills section. He smiled his broad, gold-capped grin, then disappeared around a bend of the stream.

Then my head trainer, Frank Lamping, arrived. He told me that the earthen dam above us was about to go. To prevent the dam from bursting, the flood-control people were opening the floodgates to release the pressure. We were to watch out for some heavy water coming downstream.

The crew had all been working continuously from morning until night since the rains had begun, to make sure that the ranch was safe. Now we had to redouble our efforts.

I told Frank to check the stock area. A trainer yelled from the roadway above that he had the nursery section under control.

I found some pretty badly undermined cages in my area and set to work with a shovel to fill the erosion. I was looking down at my shovel, working hard, when I heard a noise. It was a low roar, and it was quickly becoming louder and closer. I remember just looking over my shoulder, and suddenly there it was—a wall of water carrying with it full-sized oak trees, sheds, branches. Down it came, crashing and exploding against the compound, uprooting cages, overturning buildings, trucks—anything in its way.

Instantly, everything was in chaos. Sheer panic broke out among the animals in the Beverly Hills section. Lions were roaring and hitting against the sides of their cages; bears were lunging against the bars; chimps were screaming. The water was starting to rock the cages. Some were already floating and were about to be swept downstream.

I didn't know what to do first! I raced for the cages, but was thrown down by the weight of the water. Miguel came running

THE FLOOD 265

B Reading Skills and Strategies
Drawing Conclusions
? Is Toni a man or a woman? Who is Toni? [The spelling suggests that Toni is a woman. She might be the narrator's partner.]

C Struggling Readers
Using Graphic Aids
Have students pause here to create two lists: one of people, including the narrator, and one of "special" animals. They should include brief identifying tags and add to their lists as they continue to read. [people—Frank Helfer (narrator), Toni (his partner), Miguel (Mexican keeper), Frank Lamping (head trainer); special animals—Gentle Ben (bear), Clarence (cross-eyed lion), Judy (chimpanzee), Bullfrog ("talking" buffalo), Modoc (elephant)]

D Appreciating Language
Sensory Words
? What words in these two paragraphs help you see, hear, and feel the chaos and terror of the sudden flood? [Sample responses: *louder, crashing, exploding, uprooting, overturning, chaos, panic, roaring, hitting, lunging, screaming.*]

E Reading Skills and Strategies
Responding to the Text
? What would you do first in such a situation? [Most students will say something about looking for ways to save the animals.]

Reaching All Students

Struggling Readers
Using Chronology to track events was introduced on p. 263. For a lesson directly tied to this selection that teaches students to use chronology by using a strategy called Retellings, see the *Reading Skills and Strategies* binder.
• Selection Skill Lesson, p. 140

English Language Learners
Students' vocabularies may not yet extend to the names of wild animals. Before they read the narrative, give them the following list, which includes all of the animals the narrative mentions, and have them look up the corresponding names in their native languages.

alligator	(Indian) buffalo	eagle	lion
aoudad	camel	eland	llama
bear	chimpanzee (chimp)	elephant	monkey
boa constrictor	deer	giraffe	python
		goat	rhinoceros (rhino)
		guanaco	tiger
		hippopotamus (hippo)	wolf
		jaguar	zebra
		leopard	

Ralph Helfer and his family with Zamba the lion.

over, yelling half in English and half in Spanish. I told him to grab a large coil of rope that was hanging in a tree nearby. I fastened it around me and, with Miguel holding the other end, I started out into the water. If I could just get to the cages, I could unlock them and set the animals free. At least then they could fend for themselves. It was their only chance. Otherwise, they would all drown in their cages.

A The water was rushing past me furiously. I struggled through it to Gentle Ben's cage, fumbling for the key. "Don't *drop* it!" I mumbled to myself. The key turned, I threw open the door, and the great old bear landed right on top of me in his panic for freedom.

I grabbed Ben's heavy coat and hung on as his massive body carried me to a group of cages holding more than twenty animals. The water was now five or six feet deep. Cages were starting to come loose from their foundations; the animals were swimming inside them, fighting for breath. I let go of Ben and grabbed onto the steel bars of one of the cages. My heart sank as I saw Ben dog-paddling, trying to reach the embankment. He never did. I could just barely make out his form as he was carried through some rough white water and around a bend before he was lost from view.

B One by one I released the animals—leopards, tigers, bears— talking as calmly as I could, even managing an oc- casional pat or kiss of farewell.

I watched as they were carried away, swept along with the torrent of water. Some would come together for a moment and would then be whisked away, as though a giant hand had come up and shoved them. Some went under. I strained to see whether any of these came up again, but I couldn't tell.

My wonderful, beloved animals were all fighting for their lives. I felt sick and helpless.

To my right, about thirty feet out in the water and half submerged, was a large, heavy steel cage on wheels with a row of four compartments in it. I managed to get to it just as the force of the current started to move it. I began to open the compartments, one by one, but now the cage was moving faster downstream, carrying me with it. I looked back to the shore, at Miguel. He saw the problem, and with his end of the rope he

Crossing the Curriculum

Geography

Have students use the locational references in the first four paragraphs of the selection to draw a map of Africa U.S.A., showing the flood-control channel and the habitats for various animals.

Zoology

Ask students interested in animal science to create a glossary of the animals mentioned in the narrative. Each entry should name the animal, briefly define or describe it, and explain where in the world it can be found. Students may wish to illustrate their work with pictures of animals that are hand-drawn, taken from magazines, downloaded from computer references, or drawn from print sources.

Mathematics

Paragraph four describes a flood control channel that was built for 100,000 dollars. That sounds like a lot of money, but ask students to compute the actual cost per cubic foot. They should diagram the channel, label its dimensions, compute the total cubic feet it contains, and then determine cost per cubic foot. [One mile = 5,280 feet; $5,280 \times 12 \times 100 = 6,336,000$ cubic feet; $\$100,000.00 \div 6,336,000 = \$0.016$, or just over $1\frac{1}{2}$¢ per cubic foot]

threw a dally around a large tree branch. We were running out of time. If the rope came to the end of its slack before I could get it off me and onto the cage, we would lose the cage. It was picking up speed, and the animals inside were roaring and barking in terror.

I decided to hold the cage myself, with the rope tied around my waist. There were two beautiful wolves in the last cage, Sheba and Rona. Toni and I had raised them since they were pups. I was at their door, fumbling with the lock, when the rope went taut. I thought it would cut me in half. I grabbed the steel bars with both hands, leaving the key in the lock, praying it wouldn't drop out. When I reached down once more to open the lock, the key fell into the water! I was stunned, frozen. I knew I had just signed those animals' death warrants. The water behind the cage was building up a wall of force. I held on as tightly as I could, but finally the cage was ripped out of my hands.

I fell backward into the churning water; when I surfaced, I could see the cage out in the mainstream, racing with the trees, bushes, and sides of buildings, heading on down the raging river. I looked for the last time at Sheba and Rona. They were looking at us quietly as if they knew, but their eyes begged for help. My tears joined the flood as my beloved friends were washed away.

By this time it had become clear to me what had happened. The floodgates on the dam had been opened, all right, but because the ground was already saturated with the thirty inches of rain that had fallen in the last few weeks, it wouldn't absorb any more. At the same time, the new storm had hit, pouring down another fourteen inches in just twenty-four hours. Together, these conditions had caused the flood.

It was a larger flood than any that had been recorded in the area in the last hundred years, and it was made worse because the water had been held up occasionally on its fifteen-mile journey down the canyon by debris in its path. When suddenly released, the water that had built up behind the naturally formed logjams doubled in force. By the time it reached us, huge waves had been built up: The water and debris came crashing down on us like a wall, then subsided, only to come crashing down again. We were to struggle through two days and nights of unbelievable havoc and terror, trying desperately to salvage[3] what we could of the ranch.

The storm grew worse. Heavy sheets of rain filled and overflowed our flood channel, undermining its sides until they caved in. By midmorning the Santa Clarita had become a raging, murderous torrent, 150 feet wide and 15 feet deep, moving through Africa U.S.A. with the speed and force of an express train. In its fury it wiped out a two-lane highway, full-grown oak trees, generator buildings—everything. Our sound stage was in a full-sized building, 100 feet long by 50 feet wide, but the water just picked it up like a matchbox and carried it away downstream, end over end, rolling it like a toy and depositing it on a sand embankment a mile away. Electric wires flared brightly as the water hit them. We rushed for the main switch to the sound stage, shutting everything down for fear of someone being electrocuted. Everywhere,

3. **salvage** (sal'vij): save from destruction.

THE FLOOD **267**

C Critical Thinking
Interpreting
❓ Why does the narrator feel so terrible when Sheba and Rona are swept away in their cages? [Possible responses: He and Toni raised them from pups; they are more like pets than wild animals.]

D Struggling Readers
Summarizing
The narrator breaks the narrative here to explain what caused the flood. Help students briefly summarize what he says. [The ground was saturated from earlier rains, and the new rainfall put so much pressure on the earthen dam that the floodgates needed to be opened. Backing up behind debris and then breaking free increased the force of the water flow by the time it reached the ranch.]

Getting Students Involved

Cooperative Learning
Animal Exploitation? Divide the class into mixed-ability groups of five to seven students to engage in problem-solving discussions about the use of animals for a variety of products. (This activity may also serve as preparation for Choice 2 on p. 277.) Ask each group first to brainstorm a list of products made from animals, such as fur coats, feather dusters, goose down pillows, wool sweaters, leather shoes and purses, and ivory chess pieces. Then, ask them to discuss the usefulness of the products and to offer alternative sources for producing them. Each group might organize its notes in a three-column chart like the one in the next column.

Use	Animal Product	Alternatives
Chess pieces	Elephant tusks	Wood, stone, plastic
Fur coats	Mink skins	Synthetic imitations
Wool sweaters	Sheep wool	Synthetics or cotton

T267

animals and people were in the water, swimming for safety.

We'd be half drowned, and then we'd make our way to the shore, cough and sputter, and go back into the water. You don't think at a time like that—you *do*. My people risked their lives over and over again for the animals.

A The waves next hit the elephant pens, hard. We moved the elephants out as the building collapsed and was carried downstream. Then the waves caught the camels' cage, pulling it into the water. One huge camel was

turning over and over as he was swept along. (I thought at the time that somewhere, someday, if that animal drowned, some archaeologist would dig up its bones and say, "There must have been camels in Los Angeles!")

We worked frenziedly. Bears, lions, and tigers were jumping out of their cages and immediately being swept downstream. Others were hanging onto our legs and pulling us under, or we were hanging onto them and swimming for shore. I unlocked the cheetah's cage and he sprang out over my head, right into the water, and was gone. Animals were everywhere.

I remember grabbing hold of a mature tiger as he came out of his cage. He carried me on his back to temporary security on the opposite bank as smoothly as if we'd rehearsed it.

Another time I found myself being carried downstream with Zamba, Jr., who was caught in the same whirlpool that I was. I grabbed his mane, and together we swam for the safety of the shore. After resting a bit, I managed to get back to the main area, leav-

Ranch hands with Raja the tiger on the set of the television series *Daktari*.

ing the lion in as good a spot as any. At least for the moment he was safe.

B As the storm rode on, the river was full of animals and people swimming together; there was no "kill" instinct in operation, only that of survival. Men were grabbing fistfuls of fur, clinging for life. A monkey grabbed a lion's tail, which allowed him to make it to safety.

Clarence the cross-eyed lion was in a state of panic. The river had surrounded him and was now flooding his cage. His trainer, Bob, waded across the water, put a chain on Clarence, took him out of his cage, and attempted to jump across the raging stream with him. But the lion wouldn't jump. The water was rising rapidly. Bob threw part of the chain to me. To gain some leverage,[4] I grabbed a pipe that was running alongside a building. As we both pulled, Clarence finally jumped, and just then the pipe I was holding onto came loose. It turned out to be a "hot" electric conduit, for when Clarence leaped and the pipe came loose, we all got a tremendous electric shock! Fortunately, the pipe also pulled the wires loose, so the shock only

4. **leverage** (lev′ər·ij): extra force; power to do something.

268 ALL CREATURES GREAT AND SMALL

Listening to Music

The Carnival of the Animals by Camille Saint-Saëns (san·säns′), performed by the Boston Pops

French composer Camille Saint-Saëns (1835–1921) was a child prodigy who began playing the piano before his third birthday. After graduating from the Paris Conservatory, where he won two awards, he became the organist at the Church of the Madeleine in Paris. His famous

works as a composer include the opera *Samson et Dalila*; the eerie tone poem *Danse macabre*; his Symphony No. 3; and *The Carnival of the Animals*, a suite for two pianos and orchestra. Subtitled "A Grand Zoological Fantasy," the *Carnival* presents over a dozen animals' portraits, including "Tortoises," "The Elephant," "Kangaroos," "Aquarium," and, most famous of all, "The Swan."

Activity

Point out that not only writers but also composers have created works about animals. To illustrate, play "The Elephant" or "The Swan" and some of the other musical portraits in Saint-Saëns's *Carnival*. Then have students work in pairs to create tunes or rhythms that portray different animals saved from the flood by Ralph Helfer and his colleagues.

lasted for an instant. Had it continued, it would certainly have killed us, as we were standing knee-deep in water.

We noticed a group of monkeys trapped in a small outcropping of dirt and debris in the middle of the river. Frank almost died trying to save them: He tied a rope around his waist and started across, but about halfway over he slipped and went under. We didn't know whether to pull on the rope or not. We finally saw him in midstream, trying to stay afloat. Whenever we pulled on the rope, he would go under. (We found out later that the rope had become tangled around his foot, and every time we yanked it, we were pulling him under!) But he made it, thank God, and he was able to swim the animals to safety.

We were racing against time. The river was still rising, piling up roots and buildings and pushing them along in front, forming a wall of destruction. The shouts of half-drowned men and the screams of drowning animals filled the air, along with thunder and lightning and the ever-increasing downpour of rain.

Throughout the turmoil and strife one thing was crystal clear to me, and that is that without affection training, all would have been lost. It was extraordinary. As dangerous and frightening as the emergency was, these animals remained calm enough to let themselves be led to safety when it was possible for us to do so.

Imagine yourself in a raging storm, with buildings crashing alongside of you. You make your way to a cage that houses a lion or a tiger, and the animal immediately understands why you're there and is happy to see you. You open the door, put a leash on the animal, and you both jump out into the freezing, swirling water. Together, you're swept down the stream, hitting logs, rolling over and over, as you try to keep your arms around the animal. Together, you get up onto the safety of dry land. You dry off, give your animal a big hug, and then go back in for another one.

There was one big cage left in the back section containing a lion. This lion was a killer who had been fear-trained rather than affection-trained. We went out to him. The other lions were being saved because we could swim with them, but this fellow was too rough. I got to the cage and opened the door. A couple of my men threw ropes on the lion and pulled, trying to get him out of his potential grave—but he wouldn't come out. He was petrified![5] We pulled and struggled and fought to get him out of the cage, but we couldn't do it, and we finally had to let him go.

Then the "wild string" panicked, and in their hysteria they attacked their rescuers as if they were enemies. In the end, we had to resort to tranquilizer guns. We fired darts into each fear-trained animal, and as they succumbed to[6] the medication, we held their bodies up above the water and carried them to safety. Tragically, there was not enough time to drag all of them to safety; several drowned in their drugged sleep before we could reach them.

The storm continued on into the night, and with the darkness came a nightmare of confusion. We worked on without sleep, sustained by coffee and desperation.

5. **petrified** (pe′tri·fīd′): frozen in fear.
6. **succumbed** (sə·kumd′) **to:** surrendered to; were overcome by.

Using Students' Strengths

Ranch hands at Africa U.S.A., with one of the 1,500 wild animals.

During that first night, it become clear that ancient Modoc, the elephant, the one-eyed wonder of the big top, had by no means outlived her capacity for calmness and courage in the face of disaster. Modoc took over, understanding fully what was at stake and what was required of her. Animal after animal was saved as she labored at the water's edge, hauling their cages to safety on higher ground. When the current tore a cage free and washed it downstream, Modoc got a firmer grip on the rope with her trunk and, with the power of several bulldozers, steadily dragged the cage back to safety. Then a trainer would attach the rope to an-other endangered pen, and Modoc would resume her labors.

We eventually became stranded with some of the animals on an island—this was all that was left of Africa U.S.A., plus the area alongside the railroad track. When the dam had burst upstream, the wall of water that hit the ranch divided into two fast-moving rivers. As time passed, the rivers widened and deepened until they were impossible to cross. As dusk fell on the second day, we realized that we were cut off from the mainland. Since it was the highest ground on the ranch, the island in the center had become the haven[7] for all the survivors. The office building, the vehicles, and about twenty cages were all well above the flooded zone and so were safe for the time being. The giraffes, some monkeys, and one lion were all housed in makeshift cages on the island. We all hoped the water would not rise any further.

Behind the office building ran a railroad track. By following the tracks for three miles, it would be possible to reach the highway. The problem would then be in crossing the torrent of water to get to the road.

I noticed that Bullfrog, our thousand-pound Indian buffalo, was gone. Buffaloes are known to be excellent swimmers. Surely *he* could survive! I asked around to see whether anyone had seen him. No one had. Bullfrog's cage had been at the entrance to the ranch, because he always greeted visitors with a most unusual bellow that sounded exactly like the word "Hi." Now he was gone, too. Would it ever end? I felt weak. The temperature had dropped, and the wind had come up. The windchill factor was now thirty degrees below zero.

7. **haven** (hā′vən): safe place; shelter.

270 ALL CREATURES GREAT AND SMALL

Professional Notes

Ancient Menageries and Spectacles

No one knows precisely when the first collections of animals were established, but ancient China, Iraq, Israel, Egypt, Greece, and Rome are among the cultures known to have collected rare and exotic beasts, usually for public exhibition. As a rule, the kings or other wealthy owners of these ancient menageries sought to collect a rich variety of creatures that would arouse wonder in the viewer. In contrast, the Greeks of Aristotle's time (the fourth century B.C.) were more interested in the scientific study of animals. One of the tasks of Aristotle's most famous pupil, Alexander the Great, was to send home samples of the new animals he encountered on his military expeditions. Romans of the first centuries B.C. and A.D. continued to maintain private menageries and aviaries for simple enjoyment, yet the Roman Empire is notorious for its second type of animal collection—animals (such as lions) destined for combat and death in the public spectacle of the arena. Exhibition and spectacle remained the purpose of many stationary and traveling collections of animals until well into modern times. Famous European menageries include those of Emperor Charlemagne in the eighth century and of King Philip VI (at the Louvre in Paris) in the fourteenth century.

There's something horrible about tragedy that occurs in the dark. I could hear the water running behind me, and every once in a while I'd hear a big timber go, or an animal cry, or a person shouting. It all seemed very unreal.

Throughout the night and all the next day the rain continued, and we worked on. **C** Luckily, help came from everywhere. The

highway, which we could no longer get to but which we could see, was lined with cars. Some people had successfully rigged up a bo's'n chair 50 feet in the air and were sending hot food and drink over to us, a distance of some 200 yards. Other people were walking three miles over the hills to bring supplies. Radio communication was set up by a citizens'-band club. Gardner McKay, the actor and a true friend, put his Mercedes on the track, deflated the tires, and slowly drove down to help us. One elderly woman prepared ham and coffee and brought it in at two o'clock in the morning, only to find on her return that her car had been broken into and robbed!

Then a train engine came down the track to help (just an engine—no cars). Three girls from the affection-training school volunteered to rescue the snakes. The girls climbed onto the cowcatcher[8] on the front of the engine. **D** We then wrapped about thirty feet of pythons and boa constrictors around their shoulders and told them where to take the snakes once they were on the other side. (There was, of course, no more electricity in the reptile and

8. **cowcatcher:** metal frame at the front of a train engine that clears objects from the track.

nursery area, and unless we could get the reptiles to some heat, they would surely die.) Goats, aoudads, and llamas all rode in the coal bin behind the engine. I'll never forget the look on one girl's face as the engine pulled out and a python crawled through her hair.

By four the next morning, some twenty people had, by one method or another, made it over to our island to help. Some chose a dangerous way, tying ropes around their middles and entering the water slowly, with those on the island holding the other ends of the ropes. Then, with the current carrying **E** them quickly downstream, they would look for a logjam or boulder to stop them so they could make their way to where we were.

I was having some coffee in the watchmen's trailer when the scream of an animal shattered the night. I dashed out to find a small group of people huddled together, trying to shine their flashlights on the animal who was out there in the dark, desperately struggling in the raging water. It had succeeded in swimming out of the turbulence in the middle of the stream, but the sides of the river were too slippery for it to get a foothold and climb to safety. In the dark, I couldn't make out which animal it was. Then I heard it: "Hi! Hi!" It was a call of desperation from Bullfrog, the buffalo, as he fought for his life. There was nothing we could do to help him, and his "Hi's" trailed down the dark, black abyss, fading as he was carried away around the bend.

Then Toni screamed at me in the dark, "Ralph, over here!" I fought my way through a maze of debris and water and burst into a clearing. There was Toni, holding a flashlight on—lo and behold—a big steel cage from Beverly Hills! It had been washed downstream and was lodged in the trunk of a toppled tree.

THE FLOOD **271**

C **Reading Skills and Strategies**

Using Chronology
Call students' attention to this sentence, in which the second day begins. After the chaos of the first day, it is another day of hard work, with many people coming to offer their help. Encourage students to watch for words and phrases such as *then* and *the next* to help them keep events in chronological order.

D **Critical Thinking**
Determining Author's Attitude
? Sometimes people assume that girls and women are afraid of snakes, mice, and certain other creatures. Does Helfer seem to think that? How do you know? [No, Helfer doesn't make that assumption. He matter-of-factly reports that three girls *volunteer* to deliver huge snakes to safety and that they allow the narrator and his helpers to drape the snakes all over them.]

E **Reading Skills and Strategies**

Using Chronology
Make sure that students notice the time clues in this passage. "By four the next morning" means during the second night, a clue confirmed by the phrase "shattered the night" in the first sentence of the following paragraph.

Professional Notes

Modern Zoos and Safari Parks
Modern zookeeping is usually dated to 1752, when the Imperial Menagerie was founded in Vienna. However, the concept behind most modern zoos dates to the nineteenth century, when zookeepers sought to give animals greater freedom of movement. In fact, the word *zoo* is short for *zoological garden*—a garden or park in which animals may roam. Zoos founded by zoological societies, such as the one established in London in 1828,

promote the scientific study of animals.

Since the mid-twentieth century a number of zoos have also been developed for breeding endangered species; moreover, many zoos now provide educational programs for students and the general public. Whereas urban zoos remain limited in space and must use animal "houses" with adjacent outdoor habitats, the modern safari park, such as the San Diego Zoo, imitates the African nature reserve. It offers acres of

fields through which visitors can drive, with the animals contained behind moats or ditches.

A Elements of Literature

Allusion

Sunlight on the "morning of the third day" carries symbolic overtones of resurrection and new life, as in the Bible stories of the resurrection of Jesus on the third day.

B Cultural Connections

The Peaceable Kingdom

The scene Helfer describes closely matches the biblical image of the coming of God's kingdom, when it is said that wolves and lambs, calves and lions shall lie down together (Isaiah 11:6–9). Helfer alludes directly to this biblical passage at the end of the paragraph. The image may be best known, however, through the works of American primitive artist Edward Hicks (1780–1849), who painted so many versions of *The Peaceable Kingdom* that nearly one hundred still survive.

Helfer, with an orangutan, talks with students at an Africa U.S.A. class.

It was still upright, but its back was facing us, and we couldn't see inside. We waded out to the cage. Toni kept calling, "Sheba, Rona, are you there? Please answer!" Our hearts were beating fast, and Toni was crying.

Hoping against hope that the wolves were still alive, we rounded the corner, half swimming, half falling. Then we eased up to the front of the cage and looked straight into two sets of the most beautiful eyes I'd ever seen. Rona and Sheba had survived! They practically jumped out of their skins when they saw us, as though to say, "Is it really *you*?" Toni had her key, and we unlocked the door. Both wolves fell all over us, knocking us into the water. They couldn't seem to stop licking our faces and whimpering. Thank God, at least *they* were safe!

A The rain finally let up on the morning of the third day. The sun came out, and at last we had time to stop, look around, and assess the damage. It was devastating,[9] and heartrending.

Most of the animals had been let out of their cages and had totally disappeared, including Judy, Clarence, Pajama Tops, the zebra, and Raunchy, our star jaguar. We knew a few others had definitely drowned. Both

9. **devastating** (dev′əs·tāt′iŋ): heartbreaking.

272 ALL CREATURES GREAT AND SMALL

rhinos were missing, and so were the hippos. Our beloved Gentle Ben had been washed away, along with hundreds of other animals.

I was sitting there looking at the wreckage when somebody put a cup of hot chocolate in my hand. It was Toni. She stood before me, as exhausted as I was, clothes torn and wet, hair astray, cold and shivering. What a woman! Earlier, she had managed to make her way to the Africa U.S.A. nursery, where all of the baby animals were quartered. Without exception, the babies had all followed her to safety. Not one baby animal had been lost.

The hot liquid felt good going down. I stood up and hugged and kissed Toni, and arm in arm we walked. The sun was just topping the cottonwoods. The river had subsided. All was quiet, except for an occasional animal noise: a yelp, a growl, a snort. All of the animals were happy to see the sun, to feel its warmth.

Toni and I felt only the heavy, leaden feeling of loss. Ten years were, literally, down the drain. We had just signed a contract with Universal Studios to open our beautiful ranch to their tours; this would now be impossible. A million dollars was gone, maybe more. But what was far worse was the loss of some of our beloved animals.

B We hiked to a ridge above the railroad track. Something caught my eye, and as we came near an outcrop of trees where we could have a better view, we looked over. There, on top of a nearby hill, we saw an incredible sight. Lying under the tree was Zamba, and at his feet, resting, were a multitude of animals. Deer, bears, tigers, llamas, all lying together peacefully. The animals must have fought their way clear of the treacherous waters and, together, climbed the hill, slept, and then dried off in the morning sun. They hadn't run away. In

---

Getting Students Involved

Cooperative Learning

Live at Five. Divide the class into three or four teams, each representing the staff of a television or radio news program. Each team's task is to make a plan and prepare a script for a news show that follows up events narrated in "The Flood." You may wish to help each group designate planners, writers, individuals to be portrayed, interviewers, recorders, and so on. Interested groups may wish to produce actual audio- or videotapes based on their scripts.

Newspaper. Alternatively, students might prepare a newspaper insert that covers the same or different events from "The Flood." In this case, each group should brainstorm a list of articles and illustrations for inclusion—everything from straight news and interviews with Ralph, Toni, Miguel, and Frank to diagrams of the flood's route and pictures of the animals. Again, interested groups may wish to lay out and reproduce copies of an actual newspaper insert.

fact, they seemed to be waiting for our next move. It was as though God had caused the flood to make me realize how powerful affection training is, how deep it had gone. The lamb could truly lie down with the lion, without fear, and could do it by choice!

We called Zam over to us and smothered him with hugs and kisses. As we climbed down to the ranch, the other animals joined us. Camels, giraffes, eland—all came along as we wound our way down.

So many people were there at the ranch! We were once again connected with the rest of the world. Exhausted, wet, wonderful people—true animal lovers. They had come from everywhere. Some were employees, some friends, some strangers. All greeted us as we came down the hill. Their faces expressed hope and love. They cared . . . and it showed.

We took the animals one by one and fed, cleaned, and housed them as best we could.

"Ralph, come quickly!" screamed a voice. "He made it, he made it! *He's alive!*"

"Who, who?" I screamed, and was met by a resounding "Hi, Hi!" From around the corner came Bullfrog—disheveled[10] and muddy, but alive!

"Hi, hi!"

Yes, *hi,* you big, lovable . . . hi! hi!

We began searching for the animals that were still lost. The ranch was a network of people and animals working together on the massive cleanup effort. Animals were straining to pull big trucks out of the water and muck. Bakery trucks were coming by with stale bread for the elephants. Farmers loaned us their skip loaders to round up the hippos and rhinos. (One hippo fell in love with the skip-loader bucket and coyly followed

10. **disheveled** (di·shev′əld): untidy; messy.

it home!) Charley and Madeline Franks, two loyal helpers, kept hot chili coming and must have dished out hundreds of meals. People from the Humane Society, Fish and Game, Animal Regulation, and the SPCA all helped to comfort and tend the animals.

Everyone was busy constructing makeshift cages. The medical-lab trailer was pulled out of the mud. The nursery building and all of its kitchen storage area had been completely submerged, and some of it had been washed away. However, what could be salvaged was taken up to the island for immediate use.

Outside the ranch, the animals began turning up everywhere. Elephants showed up in people's backyards. Eagles sat in the limbs of trees. Llamas and guanacos cruised the local restaurants and were seen in parking lots. There was no difficulty between animals and people.

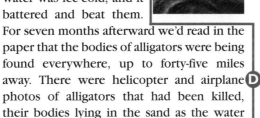

We had had dozens of alligators, some weighing two hundred to three hundred pounds. The whole pen had been hit by the water; we lost most of them because the water was ice-cold, and it battered and beat them. For seven months afterward we'd read in the paper that the bodies of alligators were being found everywhere, up to forty-five miles away. There were helicopter and airplane photos of alligators that had been killed, their bodies lying in the sand as the water subsided.

THE FLOOD **273**

C **Reading Skills and Strategies**
Connecting with the Text
? A *guanaco* (gwä · nä′kō) is a South American mammal related to the camel but without the hump. What would you do if one of these animals turned up in your yard? [Sample response: Call 911, the ASPCA, or a nearby zoo—and take a lot of pictures.]

D **Critical Thinking**
Analyzing Details
? Which group of animals suffered the most deaths? [alligators] Of the other animals, how many died? [only nine] How many of those had not been affection-trained to trust people? [five]

Resources ————

Assessment
Formal Assessment
• Selection Test, p. 55
Test Generator
• Selection Test

Assessing Learning

Check Test: Short Answers
1. What causes the flood that hits Africa U.S.A.? [weeks of rain; opening the floodgates]
2. How long does the flood last? [three days]
3. Which animals cooperate better with their human helpers—those trained by affection or those trained by fear? [affection-trained animals]
4. What is amazing about the number of survivors? [Aside from alligators, only nine animals die.]

Observation Assessment
As students work in groups to discuss the story or carry out other activities, use the following scale to rate their participation: A = Always, S = Sometimes, R = Rarely, N = Never
_____ 1. Stays on task
_____ 2. Listens to others with respect
_____ 3. Asks questions when understanding breaks down
_____ 4. Brings up new ideas
_____ 5. Helps the group achieve its goals

Standardized Test Preparation
For practice with standardized test format specific to this selection, see
• *Standardized Test Preparation,* pp. 42, 44
For practice in proofreading and editing, see
• *Daily Oral Grammar,* Transparency 15

A **Reading Skills and Strategies**
Responding to the Text
? How does the ending of the narra-
tive make you feel? [Most students will
share Helfer's joy at the return of Gentle
Ben.]

B **Elements of Literature**
Allusion
Helfer evokes another biblical image
with the rainbow. In Genesis, God
places the rainbow in the sky as a
pledge that the world will never again
be destroyed by a flood (Genesis
9:12–15).

Of 1,500 other animals, only nine had drowned. Five of these were animals that had not been affection-trained.

Only one animal remained lost and unaccounted for, and that was old Gentle Ben. I had last seen him being swept sideways down the river. We didn't have much hope for him.

I was starting to feel the full shock of everything that had happened. True, by some miracle most of the animals were safe, but other losses had been enormous. As the emergency lessened and mopping-up operations took over, I felt worse and worse. The shakes set in, and then I developed a high fever. The doctors said it was a walking pneumonia, and that rest, good food, and warmth were in order. But there were still too many things to do—now was not the time to stop. I did, however, need to find a place to sit down and relax for a while.

As I sat on a log, my body trembled with shock as well as illness. In looking over the debris, it seemed to me that everything I had worked for was gone. The emotional pain, the sheer physical exhaustion, and the pneumonia had overloaded me. I just couldn't handle any more. I had no more tears, no pain of any kind. I was numb. I sat in the middle of the chaos with an old blanket wrapped around me, unmoving, unable to give any more orders.

I had closed my eyes and was drifting off to sleep when something warm and wet on my face woke me up. I opened my eyes and saw Ben. *Gentle Ben had come home!!* I hugged him and cried like a big kid. I turned to get up to tell everyone, but I didn't have to. They were all there. Toni, joined by the rest, had brought him to me. He'd been found two miles down the canyon, mud-covered and a few pounds lighter, but safe! Tears were in everybody's eyes—and if you looked closely, it seemed that even old Ben had a few.

A beautiful rainbow arched its brilliant colors across the ravaged countryside, then was gone.

MEET THE WRITER

Finding a New Way

Ralph Helfer (1931–   ) always knew he wanted to spend his life working with animals. He began as a Hollywood stuntman, wrestling with bears, lions, tigers, and snakes in films. At that time, trainers thought that dangerous animals like bears and tigers could be controlled only through fear. People who trained animals to perform in circuses and films often used beating and electric shocks to show that they were in charge.

Helfer came to believe that animals would respond better to gentler methods. He developed a technique called "affection training," emphasizing love, patience, understanding, and respect. According to Helfer, affection-trained animals are easier to work with and more dependable than animals trained with traditional methods. Even young children can safely perform with affection-trained lions and bears.

Helfer's method proved highly successful. For many years he owned and operated the largest animal rental company in the world. His animals performed in many movies and TV commercials. They won twenty-six Patsy awards, the highest honor given to animals in show business. Helfer now spends most of his time in Africa, where he leads photographic safaris and works with organizations that protect wild animals.

"The Flood" is the final chapter in Helfer's book *The Beauty of the Beasts* (Tarcher).

Making the Connections

Connecting to the Theme:
"All Creatures Great and Small"
The collection theme comes from stanza one of a poem by Cecil Frances Alexander (1818–1895):

All things bright and beautiful,
All creatures great and small,
All things wise and wonderful,
The Lord God made them all.

Ask students to discuss how the attitude Helfer shows toward animals in "The Flood" echoes the attitude of the poet. [Both are respectful, admiring.]

Cultural Connections
People have different perceptions of animals. For example, in America, people generally regard cows as sources of beef and milk, whereas in India most people regard cows as sacred animals. Some Americans and Britons, raised on Winnie-the-Pooh stories, which include the character Kanga, view kangaroos fondly; however, Australian ranchers often see kangaroos as pests. People are divided in their feelings about animals. Deer are viewed as beautiful creatures, crop-eating nuisances, and game animals. List the following animals on the chalkboard, and ask students to give at least two completely different views of each: mice, cats, birds, rabbits, spiders, bats, snakes, and fish.

Trial by Fire

After battling a blaze in an abandoned auto shop on March 29 last year, New York City firefighters were startled to hear meowing. There, amid the smoke, sat three crying kittens; across the street were two more. Within moments, their mother, a badly injured calico,° was found nearby. "She had done her job and pulled them out one by one," says firefighter David Giannelli, who placed the animals in a box. "Her eyes were burnt shut, but she touched every one of those babies with the tip of her nose."

Taken to Long Island's North Shore Animal League, the kittens and their mother— named Scarlett at the shelter—were treated

Karen Wellen holds her newly adopted cat, Scarlett.

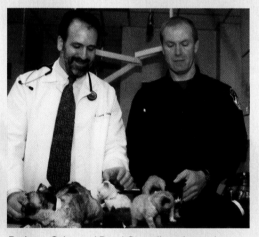

Dr. Larry Cohen and David Giannelli are happy that Scarlett and her kittens are on the road to recovery.

°**calico** (kal′i·kō′): cat with spots and markings of several colors.

for smoke inhalation and burns. "The instinct to save your young is very strong," says Dr. Bonnie Brown, North Shore's medical director. "This was just an extraordinary example." Sifting through some 2,000 adoption applications, administrators finally sent Scarlett home with Karen Wellen, a New York City writer, and her parents. (One kitten died from a viral infection; the others were placed in area homes.) Now three times a day, Scarlett—a plump 15 pounds—receives eye cream to counter damage to her lids but otherwise is healthy and loving. Karen can't believe her own luck: "This cat risked her life to save her kittens. To come out of it with such a sweet personality is amazing."

—from *People Magazine*, July 14, 1997

THE FLOOD **275**

Connections

This news feature focuses on a mother cat, a calico, who suffered serious burns in order to pull her five kittens from a fire in an abandoned auto shop in New York City. The mother cat— later named Scarlett—and her kittens were treated at Long Island's North Shore Animal League. One died; however, good homes were found for Scarlett and the other four. Scarlett still requires eye salve but is otherwise a happy, healthy, loving cat.

Ⓐ Reading Skills and Strategies
Finding the Main Idea
❓ What amazing feat does a mother cat perform? [She saves her five kittens from a fire, even though her own eyes are burned shut in the process.]

Ⓑ Critical Thinking
Making Connections
❓ How is Scarlett like the affection-trained animals you read about in "The Flood"? [She helps others to survive, not just herself, and has an affectionate attitude.]

Connecting Across Texts

Connecting with "The Flood"
Invite students to compare Scarlett in "Trial by Fire" with animals in "The Flood." Which animal in "The Flood" does Scarlett most remind them of? [Many students will mention Modoc, a female elephant who works tirelessly to haul other animals' cages out of the raging waters.] **What qualities does Scarlett have that we usually associate with human beings?** [Possible responses: motherly love; great courage.]

MAKING MEANINGS

First Thoughts

1. Encourage students to ask specific questions, such as "Where is Modoc now?" rather than questions with obvious answers, such as "How did you feel?"

Shaping Interpretations

2. Helfer has consulted the city's flood-control office and built the channel they recommended. The ranch is flooded because of an unusually heavy rainy season that threatens an earthen dam.

3. Helfer frees the animals so that they have a chance to swim to safety. He loves animals and feels that human beings are responsible for them.

4. One dramatic example is that of Modoc hauling cages to higher ground.

5. During the flood, affection-trained animals cooperate with human beings, whereas fear-trained animals must be tranquilized. More fear-trained animals are lost.

6. The flood could have lasted longer, more animals could have died, or some of his crew could have been lost. After the flood Helfer sees "a multitude of animals" lying together peacefully. This made Helfer realize the great power of his affection training—it saved his animals because they didn't panic and run away after the flood was over.

7. In "The Flood" animals help human beings swim to safety and later lie down peacefully together; in "Trial by Fire" a mother cat saves her kittens even though she must suffer severe burns to do so. These are qualities you expect human beings to show in times of crisis.

8. Lion, tiger, bear, leopard, chimpanzee, Indian buffalo, elephant, rhinoceros, wolf, camel, cheetah, monkey, giraffe, python, boa constrictor, goat, aoudad, llama, zebra, jaguar, hippopotamus, deer, eland, eagle, guanaco, alligator; students' responses will vary.

Connecting with the Text

9. Encourage students to include reasons—for example, "An elephant could move big objects out of my way."

MAKING MEANINGS

First Thoughts

[respond]

1. If you could meet Ralph Helfer, what would you ask him?

Shaping Interpretations

[analyze]

2. What has Helfer done to protect the ranch from a flood? Why, then, is the ranch flooded?

[interpret]

3. Why does Helfer free wild animals from their cages when the ranch is flooded? What does this action show about his feelings toward animals? What does it tell you about his feelings toward people?

[evaluate]

4. How do the animals help one another to survive?

[synthesize]

5. How do the events during and after the flood prove that affection training works?

[predict]

6. What could have happened that would have made the flood's impact on Helfer much worse? What does Helfer say he learns about life as a result of the flood?

[generalize]

7. What heroic qualities are shown by the animals in "The Flood" and by Scarlett in "Trial by Fire" (see *Connections* on page 275)? Are they qualities you usually think of as human? Explain.

[evaluate]

8. How good are you at noticing details? Helfer mentions twenty-six types of animals. See if you can list all of them. (Do not include the general categories *snake* and *reptile*—Helfer names specific types of each.) Then, pick three animals and tell what happens to them in the story.

Connecting with the Text

[connect]

9. If you could get a wild animal to follow you around like a pet, which animal would you choose? Tell why.

Challenging the Text

[respond]

10. Although Helfer loves animals, he keeps them in captivity, teaching them to perform in films and using the money to support the ranch. What are your thoughts and feelings about zoos and other displays of wildlife? How do you feel about animals' being taught to do tricks and perform for audiences? Review your cluster map for ideas.

276 **ALL CREATURES GREAT AND SMALL**

> **Reading Check**
>
> Working with a partner, finish your sequence organizer showing the **main events** in "The Flood." You can record your sequence in words or pictures or in a combination of both.

Challenging the Text

10. Some students may feel all captivity is wrong; others may feel that animals benefit from association with human beings when they are treated well.

> **Reading Check**
>
> Events should include the following:
> - Rain continues for weeks.
> - Floodgates are opened, and Africa U.S.A. is flooded.
> - Helfer unlocks cages.
> - Animals and human beings assist each other.
> - The flood continues for two more days.
> - Many people come to help.
> - Nearly all of the animals are saved.
> - Gentle Ben returns.

Writer's Notebook

1. Collecting Ideas for an Informative Report

You might want to write a report about one of the animals mentioned in "The Flood." Think about the questions you need to answer in a report. Try to come up with questions a scientist might ask. Jot down a list of questions that interest you and places where you might look to find answers.

Cheetah
- —Looks? Size? (Zoo)
- —What does it eat? (Zoo)
- —Where is it found? (Books from library)
- —Is it endangered? (Library)
- —Can it be trained? (Internet)

Debate/Science

2. Pro and Con

Look back at your ratings of ways animals are used, and pick one use. Find a classmate who feels the same way about this use and two classmates who strongly disagree. Ask the classmate who agrees with you to be your debate partner.

Next, do some research on the use you've chosen. See what you can find on the subject at the library and on the Internet. You might also try to get an opinion from an expert on the subject. Try to come up with at least three reasons to support your side of the argument. Then, with your partner, debate the two classmates who hold the opposite view.

Creative Writing

3. Make It Concrete

A concrete poem, like the one below, is shaped like its subject. Think of a subject for a concrete poem. You may want to choose just one word, like *rain*, *wave*, *dog*, or *pizza*. What shape does your subject suggest to you? What words does it suggest? Remember that the way you arrange the words should have something to do with their meaning.

Concrete Cat

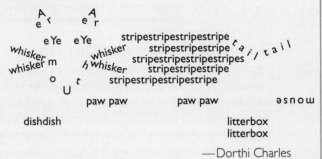

—Dorthi Charles

Rubrics for each Choices assignment appear on p. 140 in the *Portfolio Management System*.

CHOICES: Building Your Portfolio

1. **Writer's Notebook** Remind students to save their work. They may use it as prewriting for the Writer's Workshop on p. 302.
2. **Debate/Science** Explain that in a debate, each side argues for or against a specific proposition—for example, "Animals should/should not be used in police work because it is too dangerous." Each side presents the strongest arguments it can find. Usually a judge decides who has won the debate; you may wish to assign a panel of judges and give them criteria for evaluating the arguments.
3. **Creative Writing** Students may benefit from brainstorming a list of items that could be used as starting points for their concrete poems. Encourage them to choose objects whose shapes are varied. The poems then may be mounted on colorful poster board and displayed in the classroom.

GRAMMAR LINK

Ask students to exchange excerpts from their reading notes with partners. Have partners circle any pronouns whose antecedents they do not recognize. Then instruct them to take back their own notes and to revise the unclear sentences. Have partners exchange notes again to check each other's work.

Try It Out
Possible Answers
1. Would our animals be shot by frightened neighbors? We worried about the animals.
2. A buffalo tried to climb up the riverbank. The buffalo was covered with mud.
3. When the lion reached Ralph, Ralph hugged and kissed him.

VOCABULARY
Sample answers
1. Sight—big steel cage; cross-eyed lion
2. Smell—mud; ham and coffee
3. Taste—coffee; hot chocolate
4. Hearing—a yelp, a growl, a snort; crashing and exploding
5. Touch—python crawling through her hair; licking our faces

Resources ——————

Grammar
• *Grammar and Language Links,* p. 27

Spelling
For related instruction, see
• *Spelling and Decoding,* p. 13

GRAMMAR LINK   `MINI-LESSON`

Language Handbook HELP

See The Pronoun, page 694.

Technology HELP

See Language Workshop CD-ROM. Key word entry: pronoun reference.

Clear Pronoun References

You can use a pronoun to refer to a noun or to another pronoun, called an **antecedent.** To avoid confusion, make sure each pronoun you use clearly refers to its antecedent.

CONFUSING Ralph talked to Miguel and then waded out to Ben. <u>He</u> was terrified.

The pronoun *He* could refer to Ralph, Miguel, or Ben. Replace *He* with the right name or a phrase such as *The animal.*

CLEAR Ralph talked to Miguel and then waded out to Ben. <u>The animal</u> was terrified.

[Calvin and Hobbes comic strip]
Panel 1: I NEED HELP ON MY HOMEWORK. WHAT'S A PRONOUN?
Panel 2: A NOUN THAT LOST ITS AMATEUR STATUS.
Panel 4: MAYBE I CAN GET A POINT FOR ORIGINALITY.

CALVIN AND HOBBES © Watterson. Reprinted with permission of UNIVERSAL PRESS SYNDICATE. All rights reserved.

Try It Out
➤ Rewrite each item to make confusing pronoun references clear. (Each item can be corrected in more than one way.)

1. Would our animals be shot by frightened neighbors? We worried about them.

2. A buffalo tried to climb up the riverbank. It was covered with mud.

3. When the lion reached Ralph, he hugged and kissed him.

➤ Take out a piece of writing you are working on, and highlight all your pronouns. Then, find the antecedent for each pronoun and circle it. Are all your references clear?

VOCABULARY   `HOW TO OWN A WORD`

Concrete and Abstract Words: Picture This

Concrete is a word used to describe a poem that has the shape of an actual thing (see page 277). *Concrete* is also used to describe words that refer to actual things that can be seen, touched, tasted, smelled, or heard. Concrete words are words like *cat, ranch,* and *flood.* Each of these words names something that can be seen. The opposite of *concrete* is *abstract.* Abstract words name ideas or qualities. Some examples of abstract words are *beauty, truth,* and *peace.* Write down two concrete words or phrases from "The Flood" that appeal to each of these senses.

1. sight   2. smell   3. taste   4. hearing   5. touch

Grammar Link Quick Check

Rewrite the following sentences to clear up the confusing pronoun references.
1. Ralph was glad to see Gentle Ben. We were all glad that he survived the flood. [Ralph was glad to see Gentle Ben. We were all glad that Ben survived the flood.]
2. The monkey and the lion were swimming. The monkey was hanging on to his tail. [The monkey and the lion were swimming. The monkey was hanging on to the lion's tail.]

3. Ralph was nervous about releasing the tiger, but he did him no harm. [Ralph was nervous about releasing the tiger, but the tiger did Ralph no harm.]
4. Ralph and Toni found the wolves alive. They were excited to see them. [Ralph and Toni found the wolves alive. The wolves were excited to see them.]

Elements of Literature

OBJECTIVES
1. Distinguish and understand the meanings of "topic" and "main idea"
2. Use an organizer to infer the main idea from the details of a text

THE MAIN IDEA: What's It All About?

The **topic** is what a paragraph is all about. The **main idea** is the most important thing the paragraph says about the topic.

It's All in the Details

Most paragraphs do not state the main idea directly. It's up to you to figure out the main idea yourself. As you read the following paragraph, think about its topic. Then, decide which details about this topic are most important.

You might have heard the phrase "dead as a dodo." The story of the dodo is very sad—despite the humorous sound of its name.

Centuries ago the Portuguese were exploring the island of Mauritius, off the coast of Africa. On the island was a strange bird, one the Portuguese had never seen before. It was the size of a turkey and had short legs, a curved beak, and a fat body. Its wings were tiny, so it could not fly. The poor dodo had never seen people before, so it was not afraid of the Portuguese. This was a mistake. The Portuguese killed many of the birds just for sport (they didn't eat the dodos because the birds' flesh tasted funny). And the dodos faced another problem: The Portuguese had brought pigs, dogs, cats, and rats with them. The dodo laid its eggs in the open, making it easy for the newcomers' animals to eat the eggs and the hatching chicks. The last dodo died in 1681. If something is dead as a dodo, it will never come back.

Clearly, the topic of this paragraph is the dodo bird—all the sentences give details about its sad end. Which of these details are most important? Which should be part of a statement of the main idea?

Here is one way to organize the important details from the paragraph: Put the details listed in the fingers of a "hand organizer" together in a sentence or two that states the main idea.

When you read nonfiction, think about the topic and main ideas in each paragraph. It's a good way to make sure you are understanding what you're reading.

Hand organizer diagram:
- once found on Mauritius
- large, unable to fly
- no fear of humans—easily slaughtered
- eggs and young eaten by domestic animals
- died out in 1681

Main ideas: The last dodo died on Mauritius in 1681. Because it was friendly and could not fly, it was easily killed. Also, its eggs and chicks were eaten by the explorers' domesticated animals.

ELEMENTS OF LITERATURE: THE MAIN IDEA **279**

Resources

Elements of Literature
The Main Idea
For additional instruction on determining main ideas, see *Literary Elements:*
- Transparency 5

Assessment
Formal Assessment
- Literary Elements Test, p. 61

Elements of Literature

This feature explains the difference between topic and main idea and shows students how to use a hand organizer to infer the main idea from the details of a text.

Mini-Lesson:
The Main Idea
After students have read p. 279, make sure they understand the difference between topic and main idea. Help them to see how the main idea in the hand organizer is derived from the details drawn from the article about the dodo. Invite students to think of other useful and interesting ways to illustrate the relationship between a main idea and the details that support it. Examples include a tree trunk and branches and a chair's seat and legs.

Applying the Element
Break the class into small groups, and provide the groups with short paragraphs about animals and people. Have students work together to determine each paragraph's topic, important details, and main idea by using a hand organizer like the one in the text.

Reaching All Students

Struggling Readers
Have readers work together to determine the topic, important details, and main ideas of the feature. Ask them to use a graphic organizer, described on p. 262, to organize their thoughts.

Advanced Learners
Have students work together to determine the topic, important details, and main idea of a long piece of writing, such as an informative essay.

1. Read and interpret the nonfiction narrative
2. Summarize the nonfiction narrative
3. Express understanding through writing, writing/science, critical writing/summarizing, and research/social studies
4. Identify pronouns used as objects of prepositions and use them in writing
5. Understand and use new words
6. Understand and use synonyms

SKILLS

Reading/Writing
• Summarize the nonfiction narrative
• Generate a list of questions based on the nonfiction narrative
• Write a summary of the nonfiction narrative

Grammar/Vocabulary
• Identify pronouns used as objects of prepositions and use them in writing
• Understand and use new words
• Understand and use synonyms

Science/Social Studies
• Write an article about crocodiles
• Research Vietnamese cuisine and write a menu

Planning

• **Block Schedule**
  Block Scheduling Lesson Plans with Pacing Guide
• **Traditional Schedule**
  Lesson Plans Including Strategies for English-Language Learners
• **One-Stop Planner**
  CD-ROM with Test Generator

Before You Read

THE LAND I LOST

Make the Connection

Wild Kingdom

Think about crocodiles. They give most people the jitters. Maybe it's the needle-sharp teeth and steel-trap jaws or the scaly, prehistoric-looking skin. Maybe it's the way the deadly reptile lies like a log, half-hidden in the muck, waiting, just waiting. . . .

Quickwrite

Take a good look at the crocodile on page 288. Then, make a cluster diagram showing all the things you associate with crocodiles.

 go.hrw.com
LEO 6-4

Reading Skills and Strategies

Summarizing: Retelling the Story

When you **summarize** a story, you tell about its **main events** and **important details** in your own words. Summarizing is a useful skill to know because it helps you recall a story. As you read this excerpt from *The Land I Lost,* look for the main events and supporting details. Put them in an organizer like one of those described on page 262.

Background

Literature and Social Studies

One place you're likely to meet up with a crocodile is Vietnam, a tropical country in Southeast Asia with many warm, muddy rivers and open marshes and deltas. Vietnam is about the size of New Mexico, and as you can see on the map, it extends south from China in a long, narrow S-curve.

Most Americans probably still associate Vietnam with war. However, in this excerpt from his **autobiography,** Huynh Quang Nhuong (pronounced *whyng quong nuong*) recalls a more peaceful time in his beautiful country. He shows us a place where people visit with neighbors, fall in love, and work together to solve problems, just as people do all over the world.

Preteaching Vocabulary

Words to Own

Have students work with a partner to copy the Words to Own and their definitions, review the sentences in which the words occur, and write original sentences using each word. Then ask students to work together to choose the single best synonym for each Word to Own in the following exercise.

1. infested (overrun, visited, enjoyed) [overrun]
2. wily (intelligent, trustworthy, tricky) [tricky]
3. hallucination (memory, vision, thought) [vision]
4. placate (excite, befriend, calm) [calm]
5. avenge (apologize, get even, report) [get even]

from

THE LAND I LOST

Huynh Quang Nhuong

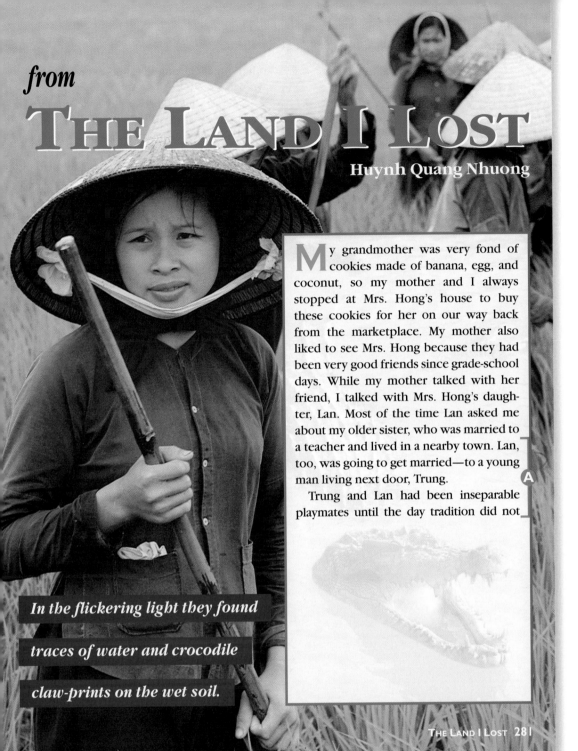

In the flickering light they found traces of water and crocodile claw-prints on the wet soil.

My grandmother was very fond of cookies made of banana, egg, and coconut, so my mother and I always stopped at Mrs. Hong's house to buy these cookies for her on our way back from the marketplace. My mother also liked to see Mrs. Hong because they had been very good friends since grade-school days. While my mother talked with her friend, I talked with Mrs. Hong's daughter, Lan. Most of the time Lan asked me about my older sister, who was married to a teacher and lived in a nearby town. Lan, too, was going to get married—to a young man living next door, Trung.

Trung and Lan had been inseparable playmates until the day tradition did not

THE LAND I LOST 281

Summary ■■

In this excerpt from an autobiography, the author relates events surrounding the marriage of Lan and Trung, young neighbors in Vietnam. After the ceremony, Lan goes to the river to bathe and is snatched out of the water by a crocodile. Trung's relatives conclude that nothing can be done for the unfortunate young woman. However, Trung thinks he hears Lan calling him—though friends and family think he is hallucinating—and finally he sees Lan waving at him from an island. (She escaped the old crocodile by playing dead.) Trung and his friends quickly rescue her, and because it seems as though she has returned from the dead, the couple's mothers hold a second wedding celebration.

Resources

Listening
Audio CD Library
A suspenseful reading of this narrative is provided in the *Audio CD Library:*
• Disc 6, Track 3

Assessment
Formal Assessment
• Selection Test, p. 57
Test Generator
• Selection Test

Ⓐ Elements of Literature
Flashback
❓ What change in time occurs between the first and second paragraphs? [The second paragraph is about events that happened before the events of the first paragraph. The second paragraph begins a memory, or flashback.]

Resources: Print and Media

Reading
• *Reading Skills and Strategies*
  Selection Skill Lesson, p. 86
• *Graphic Organizers for Active Reading*, p. 23
• *Words to Own*, p. 12
• *Spelling and Decoding*
  Worksheet, p. 14
• *Audio CD Library*
  Disc 6, Track 3

Writing and Language
• *Daily Oral Grammar*
  Transparency 16
• *Grammar and Language Links*
  Worksheet, p. 29
• *Language Workshop CD-ROM*

Assessment
• *Formal Assessment*, p. 57
• *Portfolio Management System*, p. 141
• *Standardized Test Preparation*, p. 46
• *Test Generator (One-Stop Planner CD-ROM)*

Internet
• go.hrw.com (keyword: LE0 6-4)

A Struggling Readers

Using Context Clues

Invite students to identify context clues that help them determine how the fish gets on the windowsill. [Clues such as "Trung was a skillful fisherman," "smile to herself," and "finally, she decided that Trung" can help students realize that Trung puts the fish there.]

B Critical Thinking

Analyzing Motivation

? Why is Lan so helpful? [Possible responses: She wants to please the mother of the young man she loves; she wants to please Trung by helping repair his net; she wants to make Trung happy; she wants to be with Trung.]

C Critical Thinking

Interpreting

? Why does Trung wish that nobody would move the chair? [Sample responses: He hopes Lan will come back, and he wants her place to be ready for her; he can more easily picture her sitting in the chair if no one moves it; in his mind, something of Lan remains in the chair as long as no one touches it.]

282 ALL CREATURES GREAT AND SMALL

allow them to be alone together anymore. Besides, I think they felt a little shy with each other after realizing that they were man and woman.

Lan was a lively, pretty girl, who attracted the attention of all the young men of our hamlet.[1] **A** Trung was a skillful fisherman who successfully plied[2] his trade on the river in front of their houses. Whenever Lan's mother found a big fish on the kitchen windowsill, she would smile to herself. Finally, she decided that Trung was a fine young man and would make a good husband for her daughter.

Trung's mother did not like the idea of her son giving good fish away, but she liked the cookies Lan brought her from time to time. **B** Besides, the girl was very helpful; whenever she was not busy at her house, Lan would come over in the evening and help Trung's mother repair her son's fishing net.

Trung was happiest when Lan was helping his mother. They did not talk to each other, but they could look at each other when his mother was busy with her work. **C** Each time Lan went home, Trung looked at the chair Lan had just left and secretly wished that nobody would move it.

One day when Trung's mother heard her son call Lan's name in his sleep, she decided it was time to speak to the girl's mother about marriage. Lan's mother agreed they should be married and even waived[3] the custom whereby the bridegroom had to give the bride's family a fat hog, six chickens, six ducks, three bottles of wine, and thirty kilos[4] of fine rice, for the two families had known each other for a long time and were good neighbors.

1. **hamlet:** village.
2. **plied:** worked at.
3. **waived:** gave up voluntarily.
4. **kilos:** kilograms, about 2.2 pounds each.

Reaching All Students

Struggling Readers

Summarizing was introduced on p. 280. For a lesson directly tied to this selection that teaches students to summarize using a strategy called Somebody Wanted But So, see the *Reading Skills and Strategies* binder.
- Selection Skill Lesson, p. 86

English Language Learners

Students may become confused about who is telling Trung and Lan's story. Point out that Huynh writes from the first-person point of view but plays no role in these events. Students may find it helpful to make a story map as they read, listing major events of the narrative in order of occurrence.

Advanced Learners

As students read, have them generate questions about Vietnamese society and customs. When they have finished, have them work in pairs to select the questions they find the most important or interesting. Students can then write them in the center of large sheets of paper, build webs around the questions by listing ways of finding answers, and share their webs with the class.

T282

The two widowed mothers quickly set the dates for the engagement announcement and for the wedding ceremony. Since their decision was immediately made known to relatives and friends, Trung and Lan could now see each other often. . . .

At last it was the day of their wedding. Friends and relatives arrived early in the morning to help them celebrate. They brought gifts of ducks, chickens, baskets filled with fruits, rice wine, and colorful fabrics. Even though the two houses were next to each other, the two mothers observed all the proper wedding day traditions.

First, Trung and his friends and relatives came to Lan's house. Lan and he prayed at her ancestors' altars and asked for their blessing. Then they joined everyone for a luncheon.

After lunch there was a farewell ceremony for the bride. Lan stepped out of her house and joined the greeting party that was to accompany her to Trung's home. Tradition called for her to cry and to express her sorrow at leaving her parents behind and forever becoming the daughter of her husband's family. In some villages the bride was even supposed to cling so tightly to her mother that it would take several friends to pull her away from her home. But instead of crying, Lan smiled. She asked herself, why should she cry? The two houses were separated by only a garden; she could run home and see her mother anytime she wanted to. So Lan willingly followed Trung and prayed at his ancestors' altars before joining everyone in the big welcome dinner at Trung's house that ended the day's celebrations.

Later in the evening of the wedding night, Lan went to the river to take a bath. Because

The two widowed mothers quickly set the dates for the engagement announcement and for the wedding ceremony.

THE LAND I LOST **283**

D Reading Skills and Strategies
Summarizing
Have students summarize the events and information described in the flashback. [Sample answer: Trung and Lan were inseparable playmates and are now attracted to each other. Lan is popular and pretty, and Trung is a skillful fisherman. When Trung's mother hears him call Lan's name in his sleep, she and Lan's mother agree that the couple should be married. The mothers agree to the terms of the marriage and announce the engagement.]

E Elements of Literature
Flashback
Help students recognize that this paragraph marks the end of the flashback and picks up the story that began with the excerpt's first paragraph.

F English Language Learners
Finding Sequence of Events
? What words in this paragraph help you understand the order of events? [*First, then*]

G Critical Thinking
Analyzing Character
? What does Lan's not crying suggest about her? [Sample responses: She is an independent thinker; she is less concerned about tradition than some other people are; she is too happy to be marrying Trung to worry about tradition.]

H Reading Skills and Strategies
Connecting with the Text
Invite students to compare the traditions the narrator describes with the wedding customs they know best.

Skill Link

Decoding: Two-Letter Vowel Spellings
Ask students if they know this rhyme:
   When two vowels go a-walking,
   The first one does the talking.
Explain that the rhyme is a mnemonic device that helps you remember how to decode a vowel *digraph*—two vowel letters that stand for one vowel sound. Review with students the vowel pairs that this rhyme applies to.
   ai for /ā/, as in *wait*
   ea and *ei* for /ē/, as in *eat* and *seize*

ie for /ī/, as in *lie*
oa for /ō/, as in *coat*
ui and *ue* for /o͞o/, as in *fruit* and *blue*
Point out that in these combinations the first vowel does the talking by, in effect, saying its own name, since the long sounds of the vowels sound the same as the letter names.
   Then explore with students some exceptions to the "two-vowel rule": *ai* stands for /e/ in *again*; *ea* stands for /e/ in *head* and /ēə/ in *idea*;

ei stands for /ā/ in *vein*; *ie* stands for /ī/ in *fierce*, /īə/ in *fiery*, /ē/ in *belief*, and /e/ in *friend*; and *ui* stands for /i/ in *build*.
Activity
Have students look for words in the selection with the following two-vowel spellings: *ai, ea, ei, ie, oa, ui*. List the words they find on the board. Read each word aloud and decide whether or not the rule about two vowels that "go a-walking" applies.

Ⓐ Appreciating Language
Word Choice

? How would the impact and meaning of the sentence change if the author had written "lived in" instead of "infested"? [*Lived in* carries no bad connotations; the sentence would become a simple statement of fact that arouses no alarm in the mind of the reader. *Infested* carries negative connotations: Rats *infest* houses; fleas *infest* dogs and cats; and lice *infest* people. The author's use of *infested* provides a hint that something bad will happen that involves crocodiles.]

Ⓑ Reading Skills and Strategies
Making Predictions

? Is the voice real? Is Trung imagining things? Or is there some other explanation for "the sound of Lan calling his name"? Ask students to write down a prediction of how they think the story will turn out. When they have finished reading the story, they can check the accuracy of their predictions.

Ⓒ Critical Thinking
Interpreting

? Why might Trung's relatives think that he is hallucinating? [Sample responses: They know how crocodiles behave, so they assume that Lan is dead; they might think that the old belief is merely a superstition and that Lan could not be calling; they might think that Trung is not in his right mind because of the grief involved in the sudden loss of his bride.]

Ⓐ crocodiles <u>infested</u> the river, people of our hamlet who lived along the riverbank chopped down trees and put them in the river to form barriers and protect places where they washed their clothes, did their dishes, or took a bath. This evening, a <u>wily</u> Ⓑ crocodile had avoided the barrier by crawling up the riverbank and sneaked up behind Lan. The crocodile grabbed her and went back to the river by the same route that it had come.

Trung became worried when Lan did not Ⓒ return. He went to the place where she was supposed to bathe, only to find that her clothes were there, but she had disappeared. Panic-stricken, he yelled for his relatives. They all rushed to the riverbank with lighted torches. In the flickering light they found traces of water and crocodile claw-prints on the wet soil. Now they knew that a crocodile had grabbed the young bride and dragged her into the river.

Since no one could do anything for the girl, all of Trung's relatives returned to the house, urging the bridegroom to do the same. But the young man refused to leave the place; he just stood there, crying and staring at the clothes of his bride.

Suddenly the wind brought him the sound of Lan calling his name. He was very frightened, for according to an old belief, a crocodile's victim must lure a new victim to his master; if not, the first victim's soul must stay with the beast forever.

Trung rushed back to the house and woke all his relatives. Nobody doubted he thought he had heard her call, but they all believed that he was the victim of a <u>hallucination</u>. Everyone pleaded with him and tried to convince him that nobody could survive when snapped up by a crocodile and dragged into the river to be drowned and eaten by the animal.

WORDS TO OWN

infested (in·fest′id) *v.:* inhabited in large numbers; swarmed.
wily (wīl′ē) *adj.:* sly.
hallucination (hə·lōō′si·nā′shən) *n.:* dreamlike vision of sights, sounds, and so on, that are not actually present.

Using Students' Strengths

Kinesthetic Learners

Have students research the size of crocodiles. Once they know how large crocodiles can grow, have students use old cardboard boxes to cut out a flat replica of a crocodile to better appreciate exactly how large a twelve- to fourteen-foot animal is. Students may draw the features of the crocodile on the cutout to make it more realistic.

D Reading Skills
and Strategies

Summarizing

Have students use an organizer, such as the sequence chart on p. 262, to list each event that happens during the night. Then have them give an oral or written summary of what Trung's night was like.

E Cultural Connections

Metric System

Vietnam, like most countries other than the United States, uses the metric system. Ask students to convert the metric number to an English unit of measurement, or simply tell them that six hundred meters is approximately four tenths of a mile.

F Elements of Literature

Plot

❓ What makes this event the **climax** of the story—the moment of greatest suspense, the turning point? [Sample responses: The reader wonders if Trung has gone mad or if Lan really has somehow survived being dragged off by a crocodile; the reader is anxious to find out what really happened to Lan and will look for the answer for the rest of the story.]

The young man brushed aside all their arguments and rushed back to the river. Once again, he heard the voice of his bride in the wind, calling his name. Again he rushed back and woke his relatives. Again they tried to persuade him that it was a hallucination, although some of the old folks suggested that maybe the ghost of the young girl was having to dance and sing to <u>placate</u> the angry crocodile because she failed to bring it a new victim.

No one could persuade Trung to stay inside. His friends wanted to go back to the river with him, but he said no. He resented them for not believing him that there were desperate cries in the wind.

Trung stood in front of the deep river alone in the darkness. He listened to the sound of the wind and clutched the clothes Lan had left behind. The wind became stronger and stronger and often changed direction as the night progressed, but he did not hear any more calls. Still he had no doubt that the voice he had heard earlier was absolutely real. Then at dawn, when the wind died down, he again heard, very clearly, Lan call him for help.

Her voice came from an island about six hundred meters away. Trung wept and prayed: "You were a good girl when you were still alive, now be a good soul. Please protect me so that I can find a way to kill the beast in order to free you from its spell and <u>avenge</u> your tragic death." Suddenly, while wiping away his tears, he saw a little tree moving on the island. The tree was jumping up and down. He squinted to see better. The tree had two hands that were waving at him. And it was calling his name.

Trung became hysterical and yelled for help. He woke all his relatives and they all rushed to his side again. At first they thought that Trung had become stark mad. They tried to lead him back to his house, but he fiercely

---

WORDS TO OWN

placate (plā′kāt′) v.: calm.
avenge (ə·venj′) v.: get revenge for some kind of injury; get even.

THE LAND I LOST **285**

Crossing the Curriculum

Social Studies

Have each student make a KWL chart like the one in the next column, and ask students to contribute to the first two columns. Then divide the class into groups to learn about Vietnam. They might use encyclopedias, books specifically devoted to Vietnam, and interviews with people from Vietnam or people who have been there. Students can then compare and contrast what they have learned with what is on the chart.

What Students **K**now	What Students **W**ant to Know	What Students **L**earned

LITERATURE AND LEGENDS

Examples of urban folklore that students may have heard include

- a drive to send hundreds of get-well cards to a boy in another country so that he can get into the *Guinness Book of World Records*
- someone biting into something disgusting in a hamburger or a taco at a fast-food restaurant

One key characteristic of urban legends is that they are always announced as having "really happened"—but always to someone you can't contact, such as a friend of a friend or the neighbor of a distant relative of someone you barely know. Ask students also to comment on details in the selection that suggest that it is at least partly a tall tale. [Possible responses: The woman escapes a crocodile because it becomes thirsty and doesn't eat her right away; the naked woman covers herself in leaves so that she looks like a tree jumping up and down.]

resisted their attempt. He talked to them incoherently[5] and pointed his finger at the strange tree on the island. Finally his relatives saw the waving tree. They quickly put a small boat into the river, and Trung got into the boat along with two other men. They paddled to the island and discovered that the moving tree was, in fact, Lan. She had covered herself with leaves because she had no clothes on.

5. **incoherently:** not clearly.

At first nobody knew what had really happened because Lan clung to Trung and cried and cried. Finally, when Lan could talk, they pieced together her story.

A Lan had fainted when the crocodile snapped her up. Had she not fainted, the crocodile surely would have drowned her before carrying her off to the island. Lan did not know how many times the crocodile had tossed her in the air and smashed her against the ground, but at one point, while being tossed in the air and falling back onto the

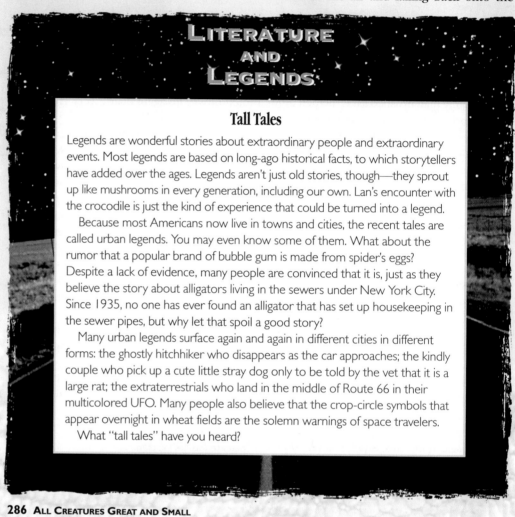

LITERATURE AND LEGENDS

Tall Tales

Legends are wonderful stories about extraordinary people and extraordinary events. Most legends are based on long-ago historical facts, to which storytellers have added over the ages. Legends aren't just old stories, though—they sprout up like mushrooms in every generation, including our own. Lan's encounter with the crocodile is just the kind of experience that could be turned into a legend.

Because most Americans now live in towns and cities, the recent tales are called urban legends. You may even know some of them. What about the rumor that a popular brand of bubble gum is made from spider's eggs? Despite a lack of evidence, many people are convinced that it is, just as they believe the story about alligators living in the sewers under New York City. Since 1935, no one has ever found an alligator that has set up housekeeping in the sewer pipes, but why let that spoil a good story?

Many urban legends surface again and again in different cities in different forms: the ghostly hitchhiker who disappears as the car approaches; the kindly couple who pick up a cute little stray dog only to be told by the vet that it is a large rat; the extraterrestrials who land in the middle of Route 66 in their multicolored UFO. Many people also believe that the crop-circle symbols that appear overnight in wheat fields are the solemn warnings of space travelers.

What "tall tales" have you heard?

Making the Connections

Connecting to the Theme: "All Creatures Great and Small"

Ask students to compare the crocodiles in *The Land I Lost* with the other animals in the collection. [Possible response: This story shows a scarier side of animal behavior.] Discuss whether they find this selection more realistic than the other selections they have read. [Sample responses: Yes, this selection reflects the fact that animals can be dangerous; no, all the selections are realistic.]

Getting Students Involved

Cooperative Learning

Listen to Me! Ask small groups of students to do some problem-solving. What can they do when they have something important to say, and people either do not believe them or refuse to listen? Encourage group members to brainstorm (and perhaps list) their ideas. Then have them compare their answers with the way Trung acts when he hears Lan calling him. What might Trung have done to get people to listen to him? Students might organize their ideas in a chart like the one below.

What I Do	What I Could Do	What Trung Does	What Trung Could Do
[Become angry]	[State my case calmly]	[Becomes hysterical]	[Ask for help to look for Lan]

crocodile's jaw, she regained consciousness. The crocodile smashed her against the ground a few more times, but Lan played dead. Luckily the crocodile became thirsty and returned to the river to drink. At that moment Lan got up and ran to a nearby tree and climbed up it. The tree was very small.

Lan stayed very still for fear that the snorting, angry crocodile, roaming around trying to catch her again, would find her and shake her out of the tree. Lan stayed in this frozen position for a long time until the crocodile gave up searching for her and went back to the river. Then she started calling Trung to come rescue her.

Lan's body was covered with bruises, for crocodiles soften up big prey before swallowing it. They will smash it against the

ground or against a tree, or keep tossing it into the air. But fortunately Lan had no broken bones or serious cuts. It was possible that this crocodile was very old and had lost most of its teeth. Nevertheless, the older the crocodile, the more intelligent it usually was. That was how it knew to avoid the log barrier in the river and to snap up the girl from behind.

Trung carried his exhausted bride into the boat and paddled home. Lan slept for hours and hours. At times she would sit up with a start and cry out for help, but within three days she was almost completely recovered.

Lan's mother and Trung's mother decided to celebrate their children's wedding a second time because Lan had come back from the dead.

Ⓑ Reading Skills and Strategies
Comparing/Contrasting
❓ How does Lan's behavior compare or contrast with Trung's? [Trung becomes hysterical, but Lan remains calm and in control.] How does Lan's behavior help her? [It enables her to stay alive.]

Ⓒ Critical Thinking
Interpreting
❓ What does the narrator mean by saying that Lan came "back from the dead"? [She was so close to death, it is as if she really had died; she was presumed dead.]

Resources
Assessment
Formal Assessment
• Selection Test, p. 57
Test Generator
• Selection Test

MEET THE WRITER
To Make People Happy
Huynh Quang Nhuong (1946–   ) was born in a small village in Vietnam between a deep jungle and a chain of high mountains. At the age of six, Huynh learned to tend his family's herd of water buffaloes. His favorite, named Tank, takes part in many of the adventures described in *The Land I Lost*. "Wild animals played a very large part in our lives," Huynh says. In addition to gentle animals, he remembers the fearsome ones that often threatened his village. "There were four creatures we feared the most: the tiger, the lone wild hog, the crocodile, and the horse snake."

Huynh left his village to study chemistry at the University of Saigon. When war broke out, "the land I love was lost to me forever," he recalls. Huynh was drafted into the army of South Vietnam. One day on the battlefield he was shot and paralyzed.

In 1969, Huynh left Vietnam to receive special medical treatment in the United States. He stayed, earned degrees in literature and French, and settled in Columbia, Missouri. His writing is a link between his two lands. He says:

66 I hope that my books will make people from different countries happy, regardless of their political adherences, creeds, and ages. 99

BROWSING IN THE FILES
About the Author. In his autobiographical book, *The Land I Lost: Adventures of a Boy in Vietnam,* Huynh describes events in the lives of the villagers in his native Mytho—a man teaching monkeys to pick tea leaves and hunt squirrels, a bridegroom killed by a snake on his wedding night, a bloody battle between the villagers and a wild hog. These events occurred before the beginning of the war that brought devastation to villages like Huynh's.

Assessing Learning

Check Test: Short Answers
1. What does Lan's mother find on the windowsill, and who left it there? [Lan's mother finds fish left by Trung.]
2. What does Lan do for Trung's mother? [Lan gives her cookies and helps her fix Trung's fishing net.]
3. Why does Lan's mother ignore the custom of the groom's giving gifts to the bride's family?

[The families have been friends and neighbors for years.]
4. What happens to Lan as she bathes on her wedding night? [She is taken away by a crocodile.]
5. How does Trung know that Lan is not dead? [He hears Lan crying for help, and he sees her waving to him from an island.]

Standardized Test Preparation
For practice with standardized test format specific to this selection, see
• *Standardized Test Preparation,* p. 46
For practice in proofreading and editing, see
• *Daily Oral Grammar,* Transparency 16

MAKING MEANINGS

First Thoughts

1. Feelings may include fear, relief, horror, or admiration.

Shaping Interpretations

2. Trung is the hero, and Lan is the heroine. Their biggest conflict is that the crocodile has carried Lan away. Additional conflicts include not being able to see each other very much before they are engaged, Trung being unable to convince people that he has heard Lan, and Lan needing to attract Trung's attention. The central conflict is resolved when Trung and his relatives rescue Lan.

3. The enemy is the crocodile. It is big, strong, experienced, and clever.

4. By escaping the crocodile, Lan shows that she is brave and resourceful. Some students may be surprised at her survival because she has never been in such danger before; others will recognize that she has always been an independent thinker.

Connecting with the Text

5. Some students may be even more afraid of crocodiles because this story shows how strong and sly they can be. Some may have more respect for them after finding out how smart they are.

6. Many students will say that they also value love, family, courage, and intelligence.

7. Some students may say they thought of urban dangers, such as traffic accidents and human predators, but others may say that the story was set in too remote a place to make them think about the dangers in their own environments.

Challenging the Text

8. Some students may believe that the narrative is factual since the events are presented so vividly. Some may wonder why the villagers do not look for Lan before they do. Asking the author whether or not the story is completely true is one way to verify the story's authenticity.

MAKING MEANINGS

First Thoughts

[respond]

1. How did you feel about what happens to Lan?

Shaping Interpretations

[comprehend]

2. Huynh tells a **narrative** about a girl's ordeal with a crocodile. In many ways a narrative is just like a short story, although it can be either fictional or true. Who are the **hero** and **heroine** of the story? What is their problem, or **conflict**? How do they **resolve** their problem?

[comprehend]

3. Who is the enemy in this narrative? What are the enemy's special powers that make him hard to conquer?

[respond]

4. Think of what you learn about Lan's **character** before she is attacked by the crocodile. Does it surprise you that she is able to escape? Why or why not?

Connecting with the Text

[respond]

5. What have you learned about crocodiles from the story of Lan and Trung? Look back at the cluster map you made for the Quickwrite on page 280. Have any of your ideas about crocodiles changed? Explain.

[connect]

6. This selection is about a faraway land where customs are very different from those in North America. What values and feelings do you share with Huynh's people?

[connect]

7. You may not have to worry about crocodiles, but every place has its dangers. Did this story make you think of any of the dangers where you live? Explain.

Challenging the Text

[challenge]

8. Does the story about the crocodile seem like a tall tale? Do you think this narrative is totally factual? How could this story be proved to be true?

288 ALL CREATURES GREAT AND SMALL

Reading Check

Imagine that you are Lan or Trung and you are telling your children about your engagement and wedding. Be sure to explain to them why you had two celebrations of your marriage.

Reading Check
Sample response:

Your father and I were very good friends as children, and since our parents were also friends and neighbors, we did not follow the usual wedding engagement rituals. On the day we were married, I went down to the river to bathe and was snatched up by an enormous old crocodile. I couldn't believe what was happening to me and surely thought that I would die. However, because I fainted and later played dead, the crocodile lost interest in me, and I quickly escaped by climbing a nearby tree. When it was safe to do so, I yelled to your father to help me. He was so overcome with grief that he did not entirely believe his ears. Yet he persisted in his belief that he heard me calling. A search was organized, and I was soon found and reunited with your father. We were then married a second time to celebrate my return.

CHOICES: Building Your Portfolio

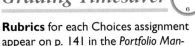

Writer's Notebook

1. Collecting Ideas for an Informative Report

This excerpt from Huynh's autobiography gives you a brief look at South Vietnamese village culture and life. There are references to Vietnamese wedding customs, religion, clothing, food, and fishing. Choose one or more topics from the story that interest you. Then, write some questions about each topic. Your questions should help you select information for your report.

> **Topic:** Vietnamese weddings
> **Questions:** Who performs the couple's ceremony? How is their wedding different from the weddings I know about?

Writing/Science

2. Croc On!

Imagine that you are publishing a travel guide for visitors to the Florida Everglades, where crocodiles and their relatives, alligators, are also found. Write an article about crocodiles for the guide. Include information about what American crocodiles look like, where they live, and how and what they hunt. To gather information, you might watch the video *Crocodiles: Here Be Dragons* by the National Geographic Society. Also, provide tips about what a person can do to avoid being attacked by a crocodile.

Critical Writing/ Summarizing

3. The Main Events

Writing a **summary** is a way of summing up the most important events in a story. Using your notes, write a summary of this excerpt from *The Land I Lost*. Tell about each major event in a complete sentence. If there are two **main events** in a part of the story, you may want to put both of them into one sentence. Use words and phrases like *then, after,* and *there* to show your readers when and where events happened. Use words and phrases like *because* and *as a result* to show connections between events.

Research/ Social Studies

4. On the Menu

This story and others in *The Land I Lost* mention foods—such as duck, coconut, and fish—that people in Vietnam often eat. Find out about other foods that are popular there. For instance, cooks prepare many dishes with a fermented fish sauce called *nuoc mam*. Then, write out a menu for a Vietnamese meal or a special banquet (like Trung and Lan's wedding luncheon).

Grading Timesaver

Rubrics for each Choices assignment appear on p. 141 in the *Portfolio Management System*.

CHOICES: Building Your Portfolio

1. **Writer's Notebook** After students have generated several questions, have them compare their questions with those of a partner or of several students in a small group. Remind students to save their work. They may use it as prewriting for the Writer's Workshop on p. 302.
2. **Writing/Science** Students might begin their reports by explaining the difference between crocodiles and alligators. Advanced learners could help students who are having difficulty by suggesting places to look for information and by modeling how to outline an article.
3. **Critical Writing/Summarizing** Have students use the notes they made after reading the story as the basis for their summaries.
4. **Research/Social Studies** If your community has Vietnamese restaurants, encourage students to contact the owners to ask for information.

Taking a Second Look

Review: Making Predictions

Remind students that as we read, we make inferences about what will happen next. We predict, or try to foretell, events based on what we have read already—using evidence from the text plus our own knowledge and experience. Making predictions requires us to think about information we have gathered and then to look ahead to consider what may happen next. This excerpt from *The Land I Lost* provides a good opportunity for students to practice this skill since it contains plenty of suspense.

Activities

1. Before they begin reading, invite students to think about the title and to scan the map and photographs that accompany the selection. What do they think this narrative will be about? Where do they predict it will take place? Do they think it will be fictional or real?

2. Encourage students to continue making predictions as they read. You might wish to start them off with the question "How will Trung and Lan be able to spend more time together?" After students finish reading, have them compare and contrast their predictions with the events that have actually unfolded in the narrative.

GRAMMAR LINK

Read p. 290 with students, picking out prepositions for a master list. Point out that some words, such as *before* and *after,* can be either prepositions or conjunctions, depending on how they are used. Then ask students to choose excerpts from their portfolios, circle prepositions that have pronouns as objects, and check to make sure that these pronouns are correct.

Try It Out
1. him
2. him
3. me
4. her

VOCABULARY

1. infested
   - Definition: inhabited in large numbers; swarmed over
   - Synonyms: filled; overrun
2. hallucination
   - Definition: dreamlike vision of sights, sounds, and so on, that are not actually present
   - Synonyms: vision; image; illusion
3. placate
   - Definition: to calm
   - Synonyms: soothe; pacify
4. avenge
   - Definition: get revenge for some kind of injury
   - Synonyms: retaliate; counterattack; get even

Resources

Grammar
- *Grammar and Language Link,* p. 29

Vocabulary
- *Words to Own,* p. 12

Spelling
For related instruction, see
- *Spelling and Decoding,* p. 14

GRAMMAR LINK MINI-LESSON

Pronouns as Objects of Prepositions

Language Handbook HELP

See *The Object Form,* page 715.

Technology HELP

See *Language Workshop CD-ROM. Key word entry: objects of prepositions.*

A **prepositional phrase** begins with a preposition and ends with a noun or pronoun, which is called the **object of the preposition.**

EXAMPLES

to Lan	about Trung
without her	for him
after her	to him

Always use the object form of a pronoun that is the object of a preposition. Choosing the current form of the pronoun isn't difficult when the object of a preposition is a single pronoun, but doing so can be troublesome when a preposition has two objects:

> Lan talked to Trung and I/me.

To figure out the correct choice, try out the sentence with just one pronoun at a time. (You wouldn't say "Lan talked to I.")

CORRECT   Lan talked to Trung and me.

Try It Out

For each sentence, decide which of the underlined pronouns is correct. Be prepared to explain your answers.

1. The neighbors talked excitedly about Lan and he/him.
2. For Lan and he/him the future looked bright.
3. Soon came an event that no one would wish on you or I/me.
4. To celebrate her survival, a second wedding was planned for she/her and Trung.

VOCABULARY HOW TO OWN A WORD

WORD BANK

infested
wily
hallucination
placate
avenge

Choose the Right Synonym

Even though **synonyms** are words with similar meanings, they're not always interchangeable. That's because synonyms often have distinct shades of meaning. The synonym map below for *wily* shows how to check the meanings of synonyms. Make a similar map for each of the other words in the Word Bank.

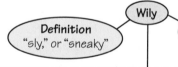

Wily

Definition "sly," or "sneaky"

Synonyms tricky, two-faced, crafty

"Tricky" and "crafty" could work since they show the crocodile was sly and sneaky. "Two-faced" doesn't really work since it suggests the human trait of saying one thing and meaning another.

290 ALL CREATURES GREAT AND SMALL

Grammar Link Quick Check

Choose the correct pronoun from each pair of pronouns.

1. Just between you and I/me, I like crocodiles. [me]
2. Liz says she hopes that no crocodile goes swimming with she/her. [her]
3. Bill's pet alligator Ralph goes swimming with he/him. [him]
4. Bill likes to swim under he/him and scratch his belly. [him]
5. Bill and Ralph? People are always talking about they/them. [them]

Before You Read

ALL I REALLY NEED TO KNOW I LEARNED IN KINDERGARTEN

Make the Connection

Spider Webbing

Do spiders give you the creeps, or do you see them as one of nature's wonders? How much do you actually know about spiders? You may remember songs, nursery rhymes, or stories about them.

Quickwrite

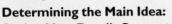

Put all your notions about spiders in a word web like this one:

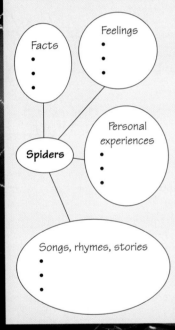

- Facts
- Feelings
- Spiders
- Personal experiences
- Songs, rhymes, stories

go.hrw.com
LE0 6-4

Elements of Literature

Humorous Essays: Tickling Your Funny Bone

Writers of **humorous essays** are something like stand-up comics: They entertain us by putting a funny spin or twist on odd or embarrassing moments from everyday life.

Yet writers of humorous essays aren't always just out for laughs. They often have other, more serious purposes in mind. As you read the following essay, see if you think the writer intends to do more than tickle your funny bone (but first read the essay just for fun).

> An **essay** is a short piece of nonfiction prose written from a personal point of view.
>
> *For more on the Essay, see the Handbook of Literary Terms.*

Reading Skills and Strategies

Determining the Main Idea: Seeing How Details Support the Main Idea

Almost every essay has a main idea. That's true even of humorous essays, like this one. The **main idea** is the point the writer is making.

The writer of this essay doesn't tell you the main idea directly. That might make his essay sound too heavy. To figure out the main idea, follow these steps:

- Look at the key details. See what ideas they support or develop.

- Look for details that build to a major idea stated several times in slightly different words.

- Pay special attention to details near the end of the selection. What major idea does the writer emphasize there?

Summary ■ ■

In this humorous first-person essay, the author relates (from both points of view) an anecdote about the accidental meeting of a woman and a spider. The woman walks into a spider web outside her door, emits a loud scream, and flees. The spider, experiencing a combination earthquake, tornado, and volcano, thinks she has inadvertently captured a human in her web and wonders what to do with something of this size. Admiring the spider's amazing abilities, the author uses figurative language to speculate on what humans could do with those abilities as he recalls the children's song, "The Eeensy-Weensy Spider."

Resources ——

Listening
Audio CD Library
An entertaining reading of this essay is provided in the *Audio CD Library:*
• Disc 6, Track 4

from

All I Really Need to Know I Learned in Kindergarten

Robert Fulghum

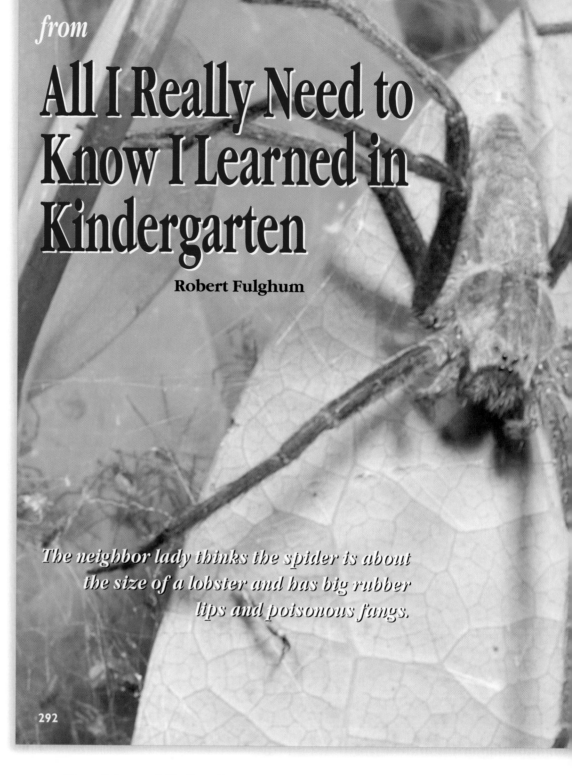

The neighbor lady thinks the spider is about the size of a lobster and has big rubber lips and poisonous fangs.

292

Reaching All Students

Struggling Readers
Determining Main Idea was introduced on p. 291. For a lesson directly tied to this selection that teaches students to determine main idea using a strategy called Most Important Word, see the *Reading Skills and Strategies* binder.
• Selection Skill Lesson, p. 120

English Language Learners
Working in pairs, one student should read the first paragraph aloud, and then the other student should summarize it. Students can switch roles for the second paragraph and continue to the end of the selection, switching roles at the end of each paragraph. For additional strategies to supplement instruction for English language learners, see
• *Lesson Plans Including Strategies for English-Language Learners*

Advanced Learners
The Doppler effect is footnoted on p. 293. When a sound is moving away from a hearer, the sound waves are stretched out, and the pitch is lowered. When a source approaches, the waves are compressed, raising the pitch. Ask students to present demonstrations of the Doppler effect by recording the sounds of a train, jet, or car approaching and moving away.

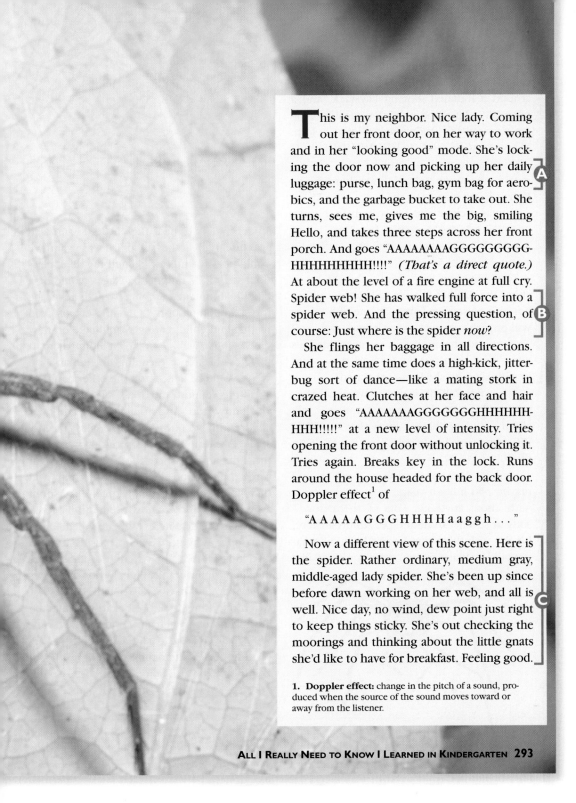

This is my neighbor. Nice lady. Coming out her front door, on her way to work and in her "looking good" mode. She's locking the door now and picking up her daily luggage: purse, lunch bag, gym bag for aerobics, and the garbage bucket to take out. She turns, sees me, gives me the big, smiling Hello, and takes three steps across her front porch. And goes "AAAAAAAAGGGGGGGGG-HHHHHHHHH!!!!" *(That's a direct quote.)* At about the level of a fire engine at full cry. Spider web! She has walked full force into a spider web. And the pressing question, of course: Just where is the spider *now?*

She flings her baggage in all directions. And at the same time does a high-kick, jitterbug sort of dance—like a mating stork in crazed heat. Clutches at her face and hair and goes "AAAAAAAGGGGGGGHHHHHH-HHH!!!!!" at a new level of intensity. Tries opening the front door without unlocking it. Tries again. Breaks key in the lock. Runs around the house headed for the back door. Doppler effect[1] of

"A A A A A G G G H H H H a a g g h . . ."

Now a different view of this scene. Here is the spider. Rather ordinary, medium gray, middle-aged lady spider. She's been up since before dawn working on her web, and all is well. Nice day, no wind, dew point just right to keep things sticky. She's out checking the moorings and thinking about the little gnats she'd like to have for breakfast. Feeling good.

---

1. **Doppler effect:** change in the pitch of a sound, produced when the source of the sound moves toward or away from the listener.

ALL I REALLY NEED TO KNOW I LEARNED IN KINDERGARTEN 293

A Elements of Literature

Humorous Essay

? How does the phrase "daily luggage" hint at a humorous tone in the essay? [It's an exaggerated way of referring to all the bags the speaker's neighbor carries with her when she leaves for work.]

B Critical Thinking

Making Connections

? How would you react if you walked into a spider web? You might wish to demonstrate your reactions with gestures and verbal sounds. [Most students will swipe at their hair or faces, duck, and twist their shoulders or bodies.]

C Reading Skills and Strategies

Determining the Main Idea

? How are the neighbor and the spider alike? [Both start out well-organized, efficient, cheerful, and feeling good.] **After** you have finished reading the essay, return to these opening paragraphs to see how Fulghum conveys details to support his main idea from the outset.

Getting Students Involved

Cooperative Learning

Read All About It. Place students in groups of five to create a newspaper. Each student can perform one task:

• write a front-page story about the incident
• draw a picture to accompany the story
• write an editorial about the event
• write letters to an advice columnist from the spider, the woman, and the narrator
• write the answers from the advice columnist

Spiderlogue. Ask a triad of students to create a dialogue the neighbor and the spider might have spoken after recovering from their traumatic experience. (The narrator could serve as moderator or advisor.) For instance, the neighbor might complain about the awful feel of a spider web in her face, and the spider might complain about the woman's destruction of a work of art. The narrator could then try to guide each to see the other's point of view and to come to some kind of understanding. [Perhaps the spider might agree not to spin webs across the front door, and the neighbor might agree not to remove webs from less critical locations.] Have the students perform their "Spiderlogue" for the class, and invite questions and comments relating to other possible outcomes or solutions.

Ready for action. All of a sudden everything breaks loose—earthquake, tornado, volcano. The web is torn loose and is wrapped around a frenzied moving haystack, and a huge piece of raw-but-painted meat is making a sound the spider never heard before: "AAAAAAAGGGGGGGGGGHHHHHHHHHH!!!!!!" It's too big to wrap up and eat later, and it's moving too much to hold down. Jump for it? Hang on and hope? Dig in?

Human being. She has caught a human being. And the pressing question is, of course: Where is it going, and what will it do when it gets there?

The neighbor lady thinks the spider is about the size of a lobster and has big rubber lips and poisonous fangs. The neighbor lady will probably strip to the skin and take a full shower and shampoo just to make sure it's gone—and then put on a whole new outfit to make certain she is not inhabited.

The spider? Well, if she survives all this, she will really have something to talk about—the one that got away that was THIS BIG. "And you should have seen the JAWS on the thing!"

Spiders. Amazing creatures. Been around maybe 350 million years, so they can cope with about anything. Lots of them, too—sixty or seventy thousand per suburban acre. It's the web thing that I envy. Imagine what it would be like if people were equipped like

spiders. If we had this little six-nozzled aperture[2] right at the base of our spine and we could make yards of something like glass fiber with it. Wrapping packages would be a cinch! Mountain climbing would never be the same. Think of the Olympic events. And mating and child rearing would take on new dimensions. Well, you take it from there. It boggles the mind. Cleaning up human-sized webs would be a mess, on the other hand.

All this reminds me of a song I know. And you know, too. And your parents and your children, they know. About the eensy-weensy spider. Went up the waterspout. Down came the rain and washed the spider out. Out came the sun and dried up all the rain. And the eensy-weensy spider went up the spout again. You probably know the motions, too.

What's the deal here? Why do we all know that song? Why do we keep passing it on to our kids? Especially when it puts spiders in such a favorable light? Nobody goes "AAAAAAAGGGGGGGGGGHHHHHHHHHH!!!!!" when they sing it. Maybe because it puts the life adventure in such clear and simple terms. The small creature is alive and looks for adventure. Here's the drainpipe—a long tunnel going up toward some light. The spider doesn't even think about it—just goes.

2. **aperture** (ap'ər·chər): opening or hole.

294 ALL CREATURES GREAT AND SMALL

Disaster befalls it—rain, flood, powerful forces. And the spider is knocked down and out beyond where it started. Does the spider say, "To heck with that"? No. Sun comes out—clears things up—dries off the spider. And the small creature goes over to the drainpipe and looks up and thinks it *really* wants to know what is up there. It's a little wiser now—checks the sky first, looks for better toeholds, says a spider prayer, and heads up through mystery toward the light and wherever.

Living things have been doing just that for a long, long time. Through every kind of disaster and setback and catastrophe. We are survivors. And we teach our kids about that.

And maybe spiders tell their kids about it, too, in their spider sort of way.

So the neighbor lady will survive and be a little wiser coming out the door on her way to work. And the spider, if it lives, will do likewise. And if not, well, there are lots more spiders, and the word gets around. Especially when the word is "AAAAAAAGGGGGGGGHHHHHHHHH!!!!"

MEET THE WRITER

The Winner of the "Refrigerator Door Prize"

Robert Fulghum (1937–) claims he learned all the important lessons about life in kindergarten. These include the following:

66 Share everything.

Play fair.

Don't hit people.

Put things back where you found them.

Clean up your own mess.

Say you're sorry when you hurt somebody. 99

A former minister, Fulghum began printing his funny but wise ideas about life in a church newsletter. People liked his columns and began cutting them out, copying them, and sending them to their friends. Soon radio commentators picked up his list of simple lessons, and so did "Dear Abby" and the *Reader's Digest.* Twenty years later his ideas finally became the book *All*

I Really Need to Know I Learned in Kindergarten.

Fulghum is proud to write essays that people put on their refrigerator doors. He told *People* magazine:

66 I'm pleased because you can really tell what's important to people by looking at their refrigerator doors. I won't ever win the Pulitzer Prize or the Nobel. But I've won the Refrigerator Door Prize. 99

More of Robert Fulghum's Funny Thoughts

If you liked this essay about spiders, you might enjoy reading other short, humorous essays in *All I Really Need to Know I Learned in Kindergarten* (Villard). You might also try Fulghum's next book, *Uh-Oh: Some Observations from Both Sides of the Refrigerator Door* (Villard).

295

D Reading Skills and Strategies

Determining the Main Idea
Invite students to restate the lesson Fulghum draws from the story about the neighbor and the spider. [Sample responses: All living things show a sense of resilience and courage when disaster strikes; animals are more like people than we usually think; all animals and people learn survival skills.]

E Elements of Literature

Humorous Essay
? Why do you think the narrator comes back to "AAAAAAAGGGGG-GGGHHHHHHHHHH!!!!" as the final "word" of the essay? [It ties everything together by taking readers back to the scene at the beginning of the essay.]

Resources

Assessment
Formal Assessment
• Selection Test, p. 59
Test Generator
• Selection Test

BROWSING IN THE FILES

About the Author. Robert Fulghum's *All I Really Need to Know I Learned in Kindergarten* is so popular that it has been published in ninety-three countries and twenty-seven languages. For a time another of his books, *It Was on Fire When I Lay Down on It,* joined it on *The New York Times* best-seller list. His later books include *True Love* (1997) and *Words I Wish I Wrote* (1997).

A Critic's Comment. Sarah Harvey says in the Toronto *Globe and Mail,* "Fulghum specializes in the celebration of the everyday event, the little domestic epiphany, the miracle of the meatloaf, the cosmic significance of jelly beans...."

Assessing Learning

Check Test: Short Answers

1. Where is the neighbor going at the beginning of the essay? [to work]
2. Where does the neighbor actually go? [back into her house]
3. What does the spider catch in her web? [the neighbor's head]
4. What song is the narrator reminded of? [the children's song about the "eensy-weensy spider"]
5. What lesson does the essay convey? [People and animals have learned to survive.]

Standardized Test Preparation

For practice with standardized test format specific to this selection, see
• *Standardized Test Preparation,* p. 48
For practice in proofreading and editing, see
• *Daily Oral Grammar,* Transparency 17

MAKING MEANINGS

First Thoughts

1. Sample responses: brush off the spider web; yell and scream; drop everything I was carrying.

Shaping Interpretations

2. Sample responses: There are two sides to every situation; people and animals are a lot alike; the best-made plans can be overturned in an instant.

3. The paragraphs illustrate the importance of not giving up in the face of adversity.

4. Sample responses: People should not fear a person or thing that is different; it is natural for living things to seek adventure and not to give up; setbacks can help all living things to learn and grow.

Connecting with the Text

5. Whether students agree with the main idea or not, they should give specific reasons for their opinions. For every example students give of people who have given up, others may counter with examples of perseverance, such as in setting sports records or reaching a goal despite a physical disability.

MAKING MEANINGS

First Thoughts

[respond]

1. Complete the following statement: If I were all dressed up and walked out my front door "full force into a spider web," I would . . . .

Shaping Interpretations

[evaluate]

2. Fulghum's **essay** begins with an **anecdote** (an′ik·dōt′), which is a very brief story told to make a point. What point do you think Fulghum is trying to make as the essay begins?

[analyze]

3. In the ninth and tenth paragraphs, why does Fulghum talk about the "eensy-weensy spider"?

[infer]

4. Is this essay about spiders, or is it really about something else? In one or two sentences, state what you think is Fulghum's **main idea.**

Connecting with the Text

[evaluate]

5. What do you think of the main idea of this essay? Do you agree with it? Why or why not?

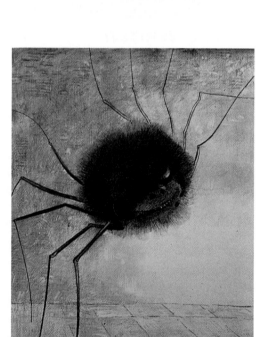

The Spider by Odilon Redon.

296 ALL CREATURES GREAT AND SMALL

CHOICES: Building Your Portfolio

Writer's Notebook

1. Collecting Ideas for an Informative Report

Fulghum's essay is about a creature that many people are afraid of or don't understand. Is there a "misunderstood" creature that you would like to help people understand better? Make a word web of people's beliefs and feelings about an animal such as a shark, bat, snake, toad, or worm. You may want to develop the spider web you made for the Quickwrite on page 291 instead.

How some people feel about snakes:

- Slimy
- Scaly
- Disgusting
- SNAKES
- Evil
- Dangerous

Creative Writing

2. Just Imagine

Human life would be different indeed if people could spin webs the way spiders do. Can you imagine other animal powers or skills you'd like to have? Write a humorous essay or poem describing how life would be different if people could walk on walls and ceilings like flies, tunnel like moles, run like cheetahs, or have some other animal power.

Art

3. Varmint Viewpoint

Can you imagine certain situations from an animal's point of view? For example,

how might the sport of fishing look to a fish? What might a bird think about birdwatching? How would a dog view a dog show? Jot down some funny thoughts and feelings these animals might have. Then, draw a cartoon or comic strip to illustrate your ideas. For inspiration, you might look at cartoons or comic strips like *Calvin and Hobbes, Garfield, Peanuts,* and *The Far Side.*

Research/Performance

4. "Along Came a Spider"

With two or three classmates, go to the library and find songs and poems about spiders or other "creepy" creatures. Perform the works for the rest of your class or for younger students. Use photos, drawings you've made, or videos to illustrate your performance.

Rubrics for each Choices assignment appear on p. 142 in the *Portfolio Management System.*

CHOICES: Building Your Portfolio

1. **Writer's Notebook** Call students' attention to the sample web next to the writing prompt. Remind students to save their work. They may use it as prewriting for the Writer's Workshop on p. 302.
2. **Creative Writing** As a prewriting exercise for this assignment, first have students list some of the things animals can do that people cannot. Then have students imagine the experience of possessing one of these animal skills.
3. **Art** If students cannot come up with a situation, ask them to discuss with a partner how Fulghum's neighbor might have reacted to a snake or a toad. How would the snake or toad have reacted in return? They can then draw the neighbor from the point of view of one of these animals.
4. **Research/Performance** Ask students to seek out recordings of the songs they find in the library. If they find sheet music but no recording, urge them to ask someone who reads music to teach them the tune. (If possible, include in every group a student who reads music.)

LANGUAGE LINK

Have students go through their notebooks, looking for entries that might be made humorous by exaggeration. Have them add the exaggeration and then share what they have written with the rest of the class. For an example of exaggeration, have the class reread "Jimmy Jet and His TV Set" by Shel Silverstein (p. 200). You could also read to the class "Sarah Cynthia Sylvia Stout Would Not Take the Garbage Out," another Silverstein poem, in which Sarah waits so long to take the garbage out that it reaches from New York to California and from the earth up to the sky.

Try It Out

Students may mention, for instance, the "high-kick, jitterbug sort of dance" the neighbor is said to do. The dance shows how upset the neighbor is to have walked into a spider web.

SPELLING

fire engine
haystack
gym bag
middle-aged
dew point
spider web
drainpipe
earthquake

Resources ——————

Language
• *Grammar and Language Links,* p. 31

Spelling
For related instruction, see
• *Spelling and Decoding,* p. 15

LANGUAGE LINK   MINI-LESSON

Style: Exaggeration Can Be Funny

Think about the last time you told a funny story about something that happened to you. Did you exaggerate some of the facts—just a little—to make people laugh? That's what Robert Fulghum does, for example, when he describes his neighbor screaming "at about the level of a fire engine at full cry."

Although a certain amount of exaggeration comes naturally to many of us when we tell a story out loud, we may "freeze up" when putting a funny experience on paper. Remember that good humorous writing should sound like one friend talking to another.

Try It Out

➤ Look through Fulghum's essay for another funny exaggeration. What comical picture does it put in your mind? How well does this exaggerated image get across the neighbor's view of spiders?

➤ Take out a humorous piece you have written. Tell the story or experience out loud to a friend, exaggerating some of the details in a funny way. Try to think of a comic comparison, like the one Fulghum used. Can you add a humorous exaggeration to your writing?

SPELLING   HOW TO OWN A WORD

Putting Words Together

A **compound word** is made up of two or more words. Together these words name one thing. Some compound words are written together as one word (*newspaper*). Some are joined by a hyphen (*all-star*). Others are written as two separate words (*air conditioner*).

Find the following compound words in the essay. Then, write each correctly—either as one word, as two words, or with a hyphen. Note: When you are not sure how to spell a compound word, look in a dictionary.

fire + engine	hay + stack	gym + bag
middle + aged	dew + point	spider + web
drain + pipe	earth + quake	

298 ALL CREATURES GREAT AND SMALL

Spelling Quick Check

Choose the correct way to combine the words in the parentheses: written as one word, joined by a hyphen, or written as two separate words. You may use a dictionary.
1. I know (some + body) who has a pet spider. [somebody]
2. I like the spider better than his (cocker + spaniel). [cocker spaniel]
3. We play with the spider in our (club + house). [clubhouse]
4. The rest of the time, the spider lives in a (fish + tank). [fish tank]
5. A spider can make a nice (eight + footed) friend. [eight-footed]

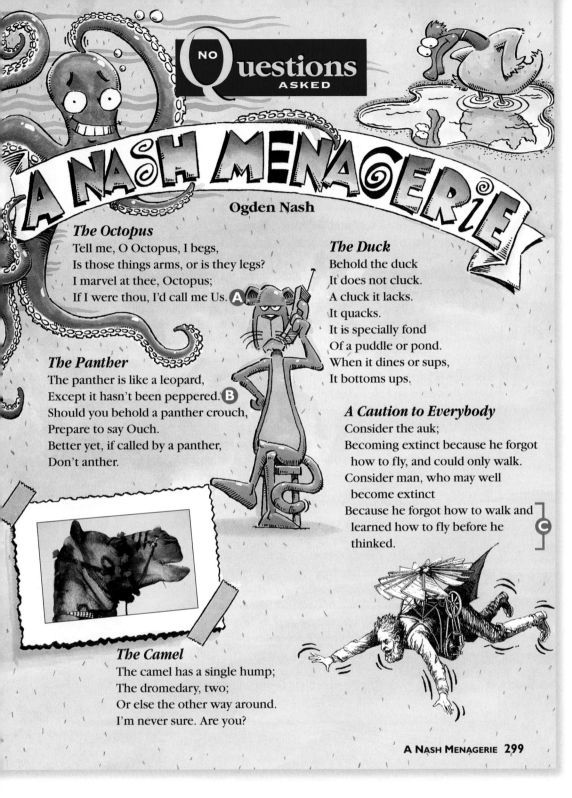

A NASH MENAGERIE

Ogden Nash

The Octopus
Tell me, O Octopus, I begs,
Is those things arms, or is they legs?
I marvel at thee, Octopus;
If I were thou, I'd call me Us. **A**

The Panther
The panther is like a leopard,
Except it hasn't been peppered. **B**
Should you behold a panther crouch,
Prepare to say Ouch.
Better yet, if called by a panther,
Don't anther.

The Camel
The camel has a single hump;
The dromedary, two;
Or else the other way around.
I'm never sure. Are you?

The Duck
Behold the duck
It does not cluck.
A cluck it lacks.
It quacks.
It is specially fond
Of a puddle or pond.
When it dines or sups,
It bottoms ups.

A Caution to Everybody
Consider the auk;
Becoming extinct because he forgot
   how to fly, and could only walk.
Consider man, who may well
   become extinct
Because he forgot how to walk and
   learned how to fly before he
   thinked. **C**

A NASH MENAGERIE **299**

Making the Connections

Connecting to the Theme:
"All Creatures Great and Small"
Have students determine what creatures Nash adds to the list of animals that appear in other selections. [The octopus, panther, duck, and auk are new; the camel was mentioned in "The Flood."] Then, have students think back over all the selections and complete a chart showing which animals especially caught their attention and what they learned about them.

Selection	Animal	Thing Learned
"A Nash Managerie"	[camel]	[can have one or two humps]
"All I Really Need to Know . . ."		
"The Land I Lost"		
"The Flood"		
"Ode to Mi Gato"		
"Stray"		
"Zlateh the Goat"		

OBJECTIVE
1. Read, enjoy, and understand the poems
2. Connect the poems to the Collection theme, "All Creatures Great and Small"

No Questions Asked

The literature in No Questions Asked gives students the chance to read a selection for enjoyment and enrichment as they further explore the collection theme. Annotated questions in the margins of the Teacher's Edition should be considered optional. No follow-up questions will appear after the selections.

These short, humorous poems use wordplay to describe five animals in unexpected ways.

Resources

Listening
Audio CD Library
A lively reading of these poems is provided in the *Audio CD Library*:
• Disc 6, Track 5

Viewing and Representing
Fine Art Transparency
Invite students to discuss Suzanne Duranceau's *The Paradise Vision* in relation to Nash's poems:
• Transparency 11
• Worksheet, p. 44

A Reading Skills and Strategies
Making Inferences
❓ What does Nash mean by saying, "I'd call me Us?" [An octopus should count as more than one because it has so many legs.]

B Reading Skills and Strategies
Visualizing
❓ What might something that has been "peppered" look like? [covered with black dots] Why is "peppered" a good way to describe a leopard? [Leopards have spots.]

C Struggling Readers
Paraphrasing
❓ How would you put these lines in your own words? [Sample response: People invent technology faster than they learn how to use it well.]

T299

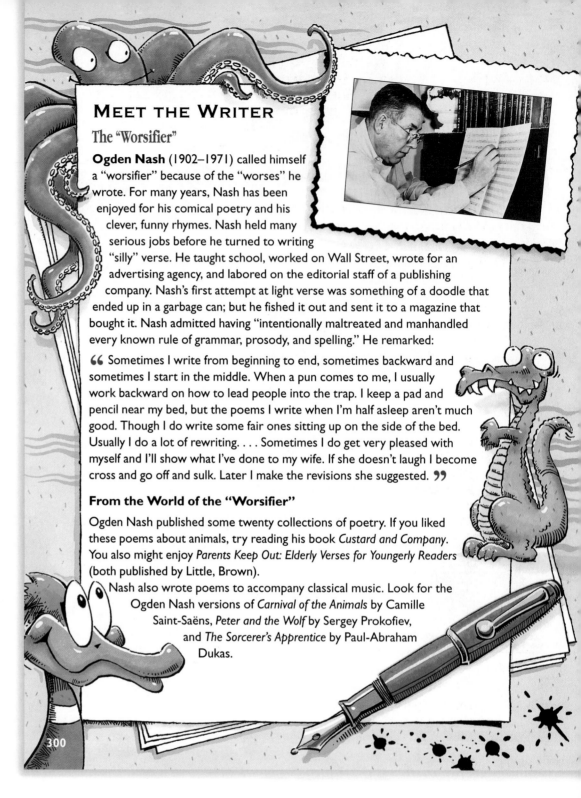

MEET THE WRITER

The "Worsifier"

Ogden Nash (1902–1971) called himself a "worsifier" because of the "worses" he wrote. For many years, Nash has been enjoyed for his comical poetry and his clever, funny rhymes. Nash held many serious jobs before he turned to writing "silly" verse. He taught school, worked on Wall Street, wrote for an advertising agency, and labored on the editorial staff of a publishing company. Nash's first attempt at light verse was something of a doodle that ended up in a garbage can; but he fished it out and sent it to a magazine that bought it. Nash admitted having "intentionally maltreated and manhandled every known rule of grammar, prosody, and spelling." He remarked:

" Sometimes I write from beginning to end, sometimes backward and sometimes I start in the middle. When a pun comes to me, I usually work backward on how to lead people into the trap. I keep a pad and pencil near my bed, but the poems I write when I'm half asleep aren't much good. Though I do write some fair ones sitting up on the side of the bed. Usually I do a lot of rewriting. . . . Sometimes I do get very pleased with myself and I'll show what I've done to my wife. If she doesn't laugh I become cross and go off and sulk. Later I make the revisions she suggested. "

From the World of the "Worsifier"

Ogden Nash published some twenty collections of poetry. If you liked these poems about animals, try reading his book *Custard and Company*. You also might enjoy *Parents Keep Out: Elderly Verses for Youngerly Readers* (both published by Little, Brown).

Nash also wrote poems to accompany classical music. Look for the Ogden Nash versions of *Carnival of the Animals* by Camille Saint-Saëns, *Peter and the Wolf* by Sergey Prokofiev, and *The Sorcerer's Apprentice* by Paul-Abraham Dukas.

300

Getting Students Involved

READ ON

In Good Hands

A thirteen-year-old Eskimo girl named Miyax runs away from home and gets lost on the tundra—a vast, treeless region of Alaskan wilderness—in Jean Craighead George's *Julie of the Wolves* (HarperCollins). Miyax is protected from a host of dangers by a pack of wolves, who gradually accept her as one of their own.

Family Ties

William H. Armstrong's *Sounder* (Harper & Row) tells the story of an African American sharecropper who is arrested for stealing food for his starving family. His son spends years searching for him. Then one day the young man and Sounder, the family's hunting dog, hear footsteps approaching the house. (This title is available in the HRW Library.)

Amusing Animals

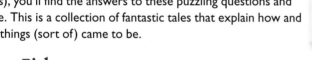

How did the rhinoceros get his wrinkly skin? How did the whale get the grating in his throat? And how *did* the camel ever get that hump? In Rudyard Kipling's *Just So Stories* (Watermill Press), you'll find the answers to these puzzling questions and more. This is a collection of fantastic tales that explain how and why things (sort of) came to be.

Other Picks

- Jane Langton, *The Fledgling* (HarperCollins). Meet Georgie, a girl who wants nothing more than to fly, and the mysterious Canada goose who shows her how.

- Walter Farley, *The Black Stallion* (Random House). A wonderful story about a friendship between a wild horse and a shipwrecked boy.

READ ON **301**

Writer's Workshop

MAIN OBJECTIVE
Write an informative report

PROCESS OBJECTIVES

1. Use appropriate prewriting techniques to identify and develop a topic
2. Create a first draft
3. Use evaluation criteria as a basis for determining revision strategies
4. Revise the first draft, incorporating suggestions generated by self- or peer evaluation
5. Proofread and correct errors
6. Create a final draft
7. Choose an appropriate method of publication
8. Reflect on progress as a writer

Planning

- **Block Schedule**
  Block Scheduling Lesson Plans with Pacing Guide
- **One-Stop Planner**
  CD-ROM with Test Generator

Technology HELP

See Writer's Workshop 1 CD-ROM. *Assignment: Report of Information.*

ASSIGNMENT

Write a report in which you present information on a topic.

AIM

To inform.

AUDIENCE

Your teacher and classmates.

EXPOSITORY WRITING

INFORMATIVE REPORT

Writing an **informative report** lets you expand and share your knowledge—about anything from dinosaurs to dynamite. In your report you'll be the expert, informing readers about a subject of your choice.

Professional Model

A century ago there were more than a hundred thousand elephants living in the forests of Asia. But as the needs and demands of our increasing human population have grown, most of the forests have been cut down or damaged, and elephant numbers have declined sharply. Now there are only thirty-five thousand Asian elephants left, and they are considered to be an endangered species.

Ten thousand Asian elephants live in the relatively small country of Myanmar, once known as Burma, in Southeast Asia. Though Myanmar is only about the size of Texas, five thousand wild elephants roam its forests in herds, as they have for thousands of years. Five thousand more, known as timber elephants, continue to live in the forests but work there with humans to extract valuable hardwoods, including teak, which are sold around the world.

The writers start by giving facts and reasons that lead to their main idea.

The writers present more facts and compare the size of Myanmar to that of Texas—a place readers can picture.

 *Resources: Print and Media*

Writing and Language
- *Portfolio Management System*
    - Prewriting, p. 143
    - Peer Editing, p. 144
    - Assessment Rubric, p. 145
- *Workshop Resources*
    - Revision Strategy Teaching Notes, p. 15
    - Revision Strategy Transparencies 8, 9
- *Writer's Workshop 1 CD-ROM*
    - Report of Information

Assessment
- *Standardized Test Preparation*, p. 114

(continued)

> The Asian elephant is the only endangered species that has a working partnership with humans. This partnership may be the key to saving these elephants from extinction.
>
> —from *In the Forest with the Elephants*
> by Roland Smith and Michel J. Schmidt

The last paragraph begins with an interesting statement and ends with a strong conclusion.

Prewriting

1. Writer's Notebook

If you have Writer's Notebook entries for this collection, review them for ideas for a report. If you prefer, try the suggestions that follow.

2. Brainstorming

a. Decide on a subject that interests you—perhaps sports or nature, animals or art. Then, join a few classmates who share your interest, and brainstorm for topics that relate to the subject. Pick one that appeals to you.

b. Write down two topics you know about and two you'd like to know about. Trade lists with a classmate, and ask questions about his or her topics. Then, answer your partner's questions about your topic.

3. Choosing and Narrowing Your Topic

Remember to think small. Choose and then narrow your topic so that you can cover it in several paragraphs.

Narrowing a Topic

Broad	Cats
Less broad	Wild cats
Narrow	Snow leopard

Framework for an Informative Report

Introduction (hook to catch readers' interest, with a clear statement of the main idea): _____
_____

Body (facts, anecdotes, and details, presented in a sensible order):

1. Topic:_____
   Details:_____
2. Topic:_____
   Details:_____
3. Topic: _____
   Details:_____

Conclusion (restatement of the main idea):_____
_____

Introducing the Writer's Workshop

- After giving students a few minutes to write down some questions they would like to answer in their research, list at least fifteen of their questions on the board. You might wish to stimulate student thinking with a few sample questions, such as: What were the first pets? How are bee colonies organized? How are elephants used as domestic animals?
- Lead a discussion in which students consider questions such as these: Why do you want or need to know the answer to a question? How might I find the answer? Who else might be interested in knowing this information? How could I present my findings?

Teaching the Writer's Workshop

- Read the Professional Model aloud while students follow in their textbooks. Pause to answer any questions and to point out the annotations to the right of the text.
- Remind students that they are already familiar with choosing a topic, writing a main idea, gathering and using details, and writing a composition with a beginning, a middle, and an end. Now they will be trying something new—researching and writing on an unfamiliar topic to inform others about what they have learned.

Prewriting
Have students use the techniques suggested on p. 303 (or any others that may be helpful to them) to come up with ideas for topics.

Reaching All Students

Struggling Writers
Have students work in pairs or small groups to help each other move from general to specific topics. Each student, in turn, should name a general topic that interests him or her (such as camels), and others should ask questions about the topic until a more specific topic emerges (such as "Why do camels have humps?").

English Language Learners
Meet with English language learners to discuss aspects of life in the United States that mystify members of their families, such as the meaning of certain customs or local ordinances. Help students choose a topic for which print resources exist. Students can write their papers with family members in mind as the intended audience.

Advanced Learners
Create small editing groups of students who can help peers proofread their papers. The good spellers may assist with spelling; students who understand good sentence structure may help correct awkward usage, and so on.

Organizing and Outlining Information from Multiple Sources

Students may have difficulty organizing information that they have collected from a variety of sources. Suggest that they sort through their notes and organize them into sets that cover the same idea. For example, for a report on the beginning of computers, a student might group together one set of notes that tells about the inventors of the computer and another set about the basic principles of computer technology.

Tell students that each set of notes should be about one main idea (for example, "the inventors of the computer"). In the next step of organizing information—the outline—the subject of each set of notes becomes a main heading. Have students take these steps before making an outline:

- Decide how to order the main ideas, and then write down the main ideas in the chosen order.
- Go through each set of notes, and put them in an order that makes sense. The main facts in each set are the outline's main subheadings. Write the subheadings under the appropriate main headings.

Drafting

- If you have not yet taught the Student Model, do so before students write their drafts.
- Remind students to use every other line as they write their drafts.
- Help students start strong by having them experiment with several strategies for their openers. Suggest that each student write one introduction that begins with a quotation, a second that begins with a description, a third that begins with a personal experience, and a fourth that begins with a question. After they have finished writing the body of their report, they can go back and choose the opener that is strongest and most appropriate.

Using Compiled Information to Raise Additional Questions

Sometimes when students write informative reports, their research will raise new questions. For example, if students are compiling information on Vietnamese culture, they may become interested in comparing and contrasting ancient and modern customs. Encourage students to use their completed research as a springboard for pursuing related topics.

Strategies for Elaboration

Comparisons make facts real to your readers. Imagine that you quote a fact like this: "The average giraffe drinks only 50 gallons of water per week." How can you help your readers understand how much water that is? With an almanac and a little math, you can add a comparison: "That's equal to about one bathtubful."

Many comparisons include the terms *like* and *as*:

- It attacks its prey *like* a race car passing the finish line.
- Newborn opossums are *as* small and pink *as* jellybeans.

As you draft your report, create comparisons to make your facts real to your readers.

Communications Handbook HELP

See Evaluating Sources; Taking Notes.

---

4. Considering Your Audience

You must make your information clear to your audience. To decide what to include, ask yourself these questions:

- What background information will my readers need?
- What information might interest them most?

5. Gathering Facts

a. **Finding information.** You might explore books, magazines, encyclopedias, newspapers, TV and video documentaries, and the Internet to find facts about your topic. You might also interview experts. Consult at least three sources before you begin writing.

b. **Taking notes.** Write your notes on 3- x 5-inch note cards. On each card, include the source of the information. Write in your own words, using phrases and incomplete sentences if you wish. If you do copy anything word for word, be sure to put quotation marks around it.

6. Planning and Outlining

An outline will help you plan. Arrange your facts in a sensible order. You could organize according to the subject's characteristics (as in the Student Model on page 305), by order of importance, or by time order. The framework on page 303 is a general guide for organizing a report.

Drafting

1. Starting Strong

Start with a bang. Open with a quotation, a vivid description, or a personal experience. If you wish, you can wait and draft your introduction after drafting the body.

2. Drafting the Body

The body of your report should be full of facts that support the controlling idea. Use your notes and outline as a guide. If you get new ideas as you write, add them if they improve the report. Illustrate facts with details and comparisons that create pictures in your readers' minds. Note, for example, the comparisons in the Student Model.

Using Students' Strengths

Auditory/Musical Learners

To provide practice in taking notes, have each student bring in one book or article on a topic. Working in groups, students can read aloud passages from their sources as others take notes. Group members should then compare notes to see whether they have heard the texts' most important points.

Visual Learners

Show the class a short, informative documentary video. Encourage students to identify features such as a strong start, a main idea, supporting facts, a clearly organized framework, and a memorable ending—as if they were reading an informative report. You can pause the video to discuss the elements as they occur or wait until the end of the video.

SNOW LEOPARD—THE PREDATOR!

The snow leopard seems calm from far away, but a run-in with one could lead to deadly consequences. The snow leopard's fur is not sleek, but it is thick and long which makes it easier for the snow leopard to adapt to the cold climate it lives in. The tropical leopard and many big cats have large ears in proportion to the size of their heads, but the snow leopard's ears are small. Its tail is also longer than other big cats' tails. The snow leopard's tail is three feet long and is used as a blanket in its cold habitat when it is sleeping.

The snow leopard is a predator. If it weren't for its cunning cleverness and its quick speed, the snow leopard's diet would be plants, bugs, and other small animals. It attacks its prey like a race car passing the finish line. It runs and runs until it gets there and attacks the prize. The snow leopard's movement is so quick that it makes its attack like stealing candy from a baby.

—Jenny Boscamp
Frost Elementary School
Chandler, Arizona

The title states the main idea.

The first sentence grabs our attention and reinforces the main idea.

The paper is clearly organized. This paragraph discusses the snow leopard's physical appearance. The last paragraph discusses its role as a predator.

Throughout, the writer provides specific facts and details.

Two colorful comparisons provide a strong conclusion.

3. Wrapping It Up

End your report by tying your ideas together. You might sum up your main idea or discuss your thoughts about the information. Consider closing with a vivid image.

4. Listing Your Sources

At the end of your paper, list your sources of information. Put them in alphabetical order by the authors' last names. Use the style guide in the Communications Handbook or one that your teacher selects.

Language/Grammar Link
H E L P

Problems with pronouns: pages 249, 257, 278, and 290. Exaggeration: page 298.

Communications Handbook
H E L P

See Listing Sources and Taking Notes.

As class members read the Student Model, be sure they understand each of the side notes. You can extend the discussion with the following questions:

❓ What main idea is expressed in the title?

❓ Where else does the report develop this idea?

❓ What interesting comparisons does the writer use to make facts real to readers?

Drawing Conclusions from Information Drawn from Multiple Sources

Weighing and assessing information from a variety of sources is a difficult process for some students. Caution them not to draw conclusions based on a single source. Before they draw a conclusion, advise them to be sure that each source

• is directly relevant to their topic
• is as up-to-date as possible
• is accurate and reliable
• presents representative points of view (if there are multiple opinions on the topic)

Choosing Reference Materials and Resources for Writing, Revising, and Editing

As students write, revise, and edit their reports, they should consult specific reference materials. For example, in writing their reports, they might want to look in a book of synonyms, such as *Roget's International Thesaurus* or *Webster's New Dictionary of Synonyms* if they are looking for just the right words to describe their topic. In revising, they may decide to consult an encyclopedia like *Collier's Encyclopedia* or *The World Book 1999 Multimedia Encyclopedia* if they need additional information on their topic. And in editing, they might want to check the *MLA Handbook for Writers of Research Papers* to be sure that they have cited their sources correctly.

Getting Students Involved

Cooperative Learning

You Took the Words Right Out of My Mouth. Before students begin taking notes for their reports, explain the importance of identifying and avoiding plagiarism (stealing another writer's exact words without giving credit). Give students practice in spotting and revising plagiarism by writing a paragraph yourself and including two or three plagiarized passages. Assign students to small groups and give them copies of your writing and the sources you used. Have students work together to check the paper against the sources to identify examples of plagiarism. Encourage them to suggest how you could have avoided plagiarism by using your *own* words to explain the ideas. Have each group create a suggested revision and read it aloud to the class.

Evaluating and Revising

Have students use the Evaluation Criteria provided here to review their drafts and determine needed revisions. You might ask students to work in small groups to read each other's papers, apply the criteria, and suggest visual aids each writer could attach to enhance the report.

Proofreading

Have students proofread their own papers first and then exchange papers with other students. For this assignment, remind students to be sure that pronouns agree with their antecedents.

If time permits, the final copy should be put aside for at least a day before it is proofread for the final time.

Publishing

To reach other audiences, students might bind their reports, arrange them by subject, and place them on a table or shelf in the school library. They might create posters or other visual aids (illustrations from magazines, computer programs, and other sources) to spark library users' interest. If English language learners have written for their families, suggest that they illustrate their report and read it aloud at home, translating if necessary as they proceed.

Reflecting

If students choose to include their informative reports in their portfolios, have them date their work and add a short reflection based on one of the starters below.

- The easiest thing about writing this report was . . .
- The next time I write a report, one thing I'll do differently is . . . because . . .
- The hardest thing about this assignment was . . .

Resources

Peer Editing Forms and Rubrics
- *Portfolio Management System,* p. 144

Revision Strategy Transparencies
- *Workshop Resources,* p. 15

■ *Evaluation Criteria*

A good informative report

1. *centers on one topic, supported by explanations and facts*
2. *presents information with authority*
3. *organizes information and observations in a way that makes sense*
4. *documents any outside sources used*

Publishing Tip

You and your classmates might bind your reports and put them in your library. Create visual aids to accompany them.

Sentence Workshop
HELP

Wordy sentences: page 307.

Communications Handbook
HELP

See Proofreaders' Marks.

Evaluating and Revising

1. Peer Review

Trade drafts with one or more classmates. Ask readers to highlight their favorite parts and answer these questions:

- What is the main idea?
- Is there anything that is unclear or confusing?
- Does the organization make sense? How might the writer improve it?

2. Self-Evaluation

Wait a day or two. Then, read over your draft and see if there are any parts you'd like to change. Ask yourself:

- What could I add to make my introduction stronger?
- Which parts could I write more about?
- How else might I tie my ideas together at the end?

3. Revising

Look at your readers' comments. Think about your self-evaluation. Decide what you'll add or change to make your report better. If your teacher wishes, list your sources at the end of your report.

Peanuts reprinted by permission of United Feature Syndicate, Inc.

Grading Timesaver

Rubrics for this Writer's Workshop assignment appear on p. 145 of the *Portfolio Management System.*

Assessing Learning

Standardized Test Preparation
For practice with standardized test prompts and formats, see
- *Standardized Test Preparation,* p. 114

BUILDING YOUR PORTFOLIO
Sentence Workshop

OBJECTIVES
1. Write with increasing accuracy
2. Revise to remove wordiness by deleting, combining, or re-arranging

WORDY SENTENCES

The best way to avoid wordiness in your writing is to write and rewrite. As you proofread and revise, delete unneeded words but keep or add exact ones. You can often say more by using fewer words. Here are three ways to eliminate wordiness from your sentences.

1. Replace a phrase with one word:

   WORDY On account of the fact that the roads were too bad for travel, Mr. Lacey couldn't take the car.

   REVISED Because the roads were too bad for travel, Mr. Lacey couldn't take the car.

2. Take out *who is* or *which is* or *that is*:

   WORDY We could see as far as the foot of the great mountain, which is Kilimanjaro.

   REVISED We could see as far as the foot of the great mountain, Kilimanjaro.

3. Delete a whole group of unnecessary words:

   WORDY In the month of January, a puppy wandered onto the property.

   REVISED In January a puppy wandered onto the property.

Writer's Workshop Follow-up: Revision

Take out your informative report, and exchange papers with a classmate. Circle any wordy sentences, and suggest a revision for each. Exchange papers again, and decide how you will revise the wordy sentences that your partner found in your paper.

Language Handbook HELP

See Revising Wordy Sentences, page 742.

Technology HELP

See Language Workshop CD-ROM. Key word entry: wordiness.

Try It Out

Revise each of these wordy sentences:

1. For Reuven, who was the furrier, it was a bad year.

2. In spite of the fact that it was early afternoon, she could do nothing but go to her bed.

3. During the time that my mother talked with her friend, I talked with Mrs. Hong's daughter.

4. At first they thought that Trung had gone crazy and had become stark mad.

Resources

Workshop Resources
• Worksheet, p. 43

Language Workshop CD-ROM
• Wordiness

Try It Out
Possible Answers
1. For Reuven the furrier, it was a bad year.
2. Although it was early afternoon, she could do nothing but go to bed.
3. While my mother talked with her friend, I talked with Mrs. Hong's daughter.
4. At first they thought Trung had gone crazy.

Assessing Learning

Quick Check: Wordy Sentences
Revise the following wordy sentences.

1. To Zlateh, who was the goat who was going to be sold, the whole adventure was quite disturbing. [To Zlateh, the goat who was going to be sold, the whole adventure was quite disturbing.]

2. In response to the fact that her parents would not let her keep the stray, Doris did not give the dog a name. [Because her parents would not let her keep the stray, Doris did not give the dog a name.]

3. During the rainy season, a flood that was sudden hit the ranch. [During the rainy season, a sudden flood hit the ranch.]

4. Due to the fact that Gary Soto loved his cat, he wrote an ode to him. [Because Gary Soto loved his cat, he wrote an ode to him.]

5. The Abominable Beast is the name that we have given to the crocodile that is the animal that attacked Lan. [The Abominable Beast is the name of the crocodile that attacked Lan.]

Using the Strategies

1. Facts/Current Events and Science and Math
2. Possible responses: Encyclopedias, Animals
3. A drawing could be found under the Fine Arts main subject area, in the Drawing, Coloring, or Art by Children subcategories.

Situation

You've been assigned to write a report about animals and ways they help people. Your teacher wants you to get information on your topic from three Web sites. You decide to write about spiders. Here are some strategies you can use to narrow your search.

http://sunsite.berkeley.edu/KidsClick/

Strategies

Find sites for kids.

Librarians across the country review and select sites to help students with their homework. To get a list of these sites, start with your public library's home page. A children's librarian can also give you a list of kids' sites, like the one above, and show you how to access them.

Use directories.

A **directory** is an index of sites grouped by subject.

- KidsClick! is a directory that librarians have put together for kids. It sorts sites into broad subject areas like Science and Math.

- There are three ways to find your topic on KidsClick! (1) You can type a key word—*spiders,* for instance—in the Search box. (2) You can click on the letter *s*, then go to *spiders*. (3) You can click on the subject area *animals,* then go to *spiders*.

Focus your search.

- Not all the sites listed will give you the information you're looking for. To save time, carefully read the brief description provided.
- Using a key word like *people* will produce too many "hits" (sites or links). Use a specific name instead.
- If you get a message like *Search Results: 0,* don't give

up. Try using synonyms for your key word, or use an additional key word. Check your spelling. Click on the help function.

Using the Strategies

1. Which of the two main subject areas shown above might have links to *spiders?*

2. Find two subcategories that seem likely to have information on spiders.

3. Where could you find a drawing or painting to illustrate your report?

Extending the Strategies

Show a friend how to find information on a favorite animal on the Web.

Learning for Life

Teaching People About Animals

OBJECTIVES
1. Generate ideas and questions for an interview
2. Interview someone who works with animals
3. Summarize and organize information gathered in the interview
4. Present information in various forms using available technology

Problem

As this collection shows, people have many different relationships with animals. How can we learn about animals and teach others about them?

Project

Find out more about animals by interviewing experts who work with them. Then, teach others what you've learned.

Preparation

1. With a group of two or three classmates, find someone to interview who works with animals. Some possibilities are
   - veterinarians • groomers
   - animal-shelter workers
   - trainers • zoo keepers
   - livestock farmers
2. Set up a time and place to interview the person. Be sure to get permission from your parents or teacher.
3. In your group, develop a list of questions to ask your animal expert. Here are some ideas:

- What do you like about the animals you work with?
- How are animals like people? How are they different?
- What are some common ways in which people misunderstand and mistreat animals?
- How can people learn to treat animals with kindness and respect?

Procedure

1. As a group, interview your expert. One student may ask questions while others take notes. Try to observe the person interacting with the animals he or she works with.
2. After the interview, review your notes as a group. Write a summary of the main points.
3. Write a note thanking the person for the interview.

Presentation

Choose one of these ways to teach others about animals:

1. Pet-Store Brochure

Create a pet-store brochure that includes photographs and descriptions of several pets. Write about the benefits of owning each pet and the way to care for it.

2. Children's Story

As a class, write a children's story about the importance of treating animals kindly. Include a character who loves animals and one who misunderstands and mistreats them. Illustrate the book and, if possible, share it with some young children.

3. Radio Spot

Write a brief radio announcement about an animal-related issue in your community. Examples are passing leash laws, supporting humane societies, and educating the public about pet diseases.

Processing

Discuss this question with your classmates: What responsibilities do people have toward animals?

LEARNING FOR LIFE 309

Resources

Viewing and Representing
HRW Multimedia Presentation Maker
Students may wish to use the *Multimedia Presentation Maker* to create vehicles that teach people about animals.

Grading Timesaver

Rubrics for this Learning for Life project appear on p. 146 of the *Portfolio Management System*.

Developing Workplace Competencies

Preparation	Procedure	Presentation
• Working on teams • Working well with people from diverse backgrounds • Stating the desired goal • Choosing the best alternative	• Acquiring data • Processing information • Interpreting information • Thinking creatively	• Teaching others • Communicating ideas and information • Synthesizing information • Applying technology

Justice for All

Theme

Justice for All   *The conflicts in these stories are driven by our sense of injustice—injustice toward a young outsider, toward a shy eleven-year-old, toward a young Japanese American about to be moved to an internment camp, toward a poor homeless man. Dr. Seuss's narrative poem that ends the collection presents a hilarious spoof of those who separate the world into "them" and "us."*

Reading the Anthology

Reaching Struggling Readers

The *Reading Skills and Strategies: Reaching Struggling Readers* binder provides materials coordinated with the Pupil's Edition (see the Collection Planner, p. T309C) to help students who have difficulty reading and comprehending text, or students who are reluctant readers. The binder for sixth grade is organized around eleven individual skill areas, and Selection Skill Lessons provide reading instruction and practice specific to particular pieces of literature in Collection Five.

Reading Beyond the Anthology

Read On   Collection Five includes an annotated bibliography of books suitable for extended reading. The books are related to works in this collection by theme, by author, or by subject. To preview the Read On for Collection Five, please turn to p. T393.

HRW Library   The *HRW Library* offers novels, plays, and short-story collections for extended reading. Each book in the Library includes one or more major works and thematically or topically related Connections. A Study Guide provides teaching suggestions and worksheets. For Collection Five, the following titles are recommended.

THE GLORY FIELD
Walter Dean Myers

Myers traces the experiences of an African American family that has been in this country for 241 years. The book also includes *Amistad Rising*, by Veronica Chambers, about the slave rebellion led by an African named Cinque.

FAREWELL TO MANZANAR
Jeanne Wakatsuki Houston and James D. Houston

This is the true story of how a Japanese American family copes with their removal to an internment camp during World War II. Jeanne was seven when she and her family lost their freedom.

Collection Planner

Skills Focus

Selection or Feature	Reading Skills and Strategies	Elements of Literature	Language/Grammar	Vocabulary/Spelling	Writing	Listening/Speaking	Viewing/Representing
All Summer in a Day (p. 312) Ray Bradbury	Dialogue with the Text, pp. 312, 323 Prior Knowledge, pp. 312, 323	Setting, p. 312 Title, p. 323	Figurative Language, p. 325	Semantic Mapping, p. 325	List Ways to Resolve a Conflict, p. 324 Write a New Ending for the Story, p. 324		Use a Chart to Compare a Planet with Earth, p. 324
Elements of Literature: The Short Story (p. 326)	Identify Plot Sequence, p. 326	Character, p. 326 Plot, p. 326 • Conflict • Climax Point of View, p. 326 Theme, p. 326					
Eleven/Once (p. 327) Sandra Cisneros *translated by* Liliana Valenzuela	Make Inferences, pp. 327, 334 Use Prior Knowledge, p. 327	Point of View, pp. 327, 335 Images, p. 334 Metaphors, p. 334	Punctuation of Dialogue, p. 336 • Direct Quote • Speaker Tag	Dropping of Silent e When Adding a Suffix, p. 336	List Support for a Position, p. 335 Write a Message to the Character, p. 335 Write the Story with a New Narrator, p. 335	Role-Play a Conversation Between Characters, p. 335	Design a Birthday Card for the Character, p. 335
Reading Skills and Strategies: Making and Adjusting Predictions (p. 337)	Make and Adjust Predictions, p. 337						Use a Graphic Organizer to Chart Predictions, p. 337
The Gold Cadillac (p. 338) Mildred D. Taylor	Use Symbols to Track Predictions, pp. 338, 353		Connotations, p. 355	Use Words in Context, p. 355	List and Support Positions, p. 354 Write a Letter to the Author, p. 354	Hold a Civil Rights Discussion, p. 354	Make a Road Map of the Characters' Car Trip, p. 354
The Bracelet (p. 356) Yoshiko Uchida	Make Generalizations, pp. 356, 363 State the Theme, pp. 356, 363	Theme, pp. 356, 363	Dialogue: Paragraph Breaks to Identify Speaker, p. 365	Use Words in a Research Context, p. 365	Jot Down Ideas on an Issue, p. 364 Write Dialogue, p. 364 Commemorate a Special Person, p. 364	Team-Teach on Japanese American Internment, p. 364	Use a Double-Entry Journal, p. 363
What Do Fish Have to Do with Anything? (p. 366) Avi	Chronological Order, p. 366 Use a Sequence Chart to Track Events, p. 366	Character, pp. 366, 376 • Character Change • Main Character Title, p. 376	Direct and Indirect Quotations, p. 378	Use Words in a Description Context, p. 378	Freewrite About Your Position on a Local Issue, p. 377 Create a Dialogue, p. 377 Write a Thank-You Note, p. 377	Conduct a Team Debate on Homelessness, p. 377	
The Sneetches (p. 379) Dr. Seuss	Apply Prior Knowledge, pp. 379, 385	Rhyme, pp. 379, 385, 386 Moral, p. 385 Rhythm, p. 386	Made-up Words, pp. 379, 385, 386		List Pros and Cons on Local Groups, p. 386 Write a Poem Like Dr. Seuss's, p. 386	Read "The Sneetches" to a Group of Young Children, p. 386	Make Up and Draw a Seusslike Creature, p. 386
No Questions Asked: The Southpaw (p. 387) Judith Viorst	The **No Questions Asked** feature provides students with an unstructured opportunity to practice reading strategies using a selection that extends the theme of the collection.						
Speaking and Listening Workshop: Social Interaction (p. 394)						Communicate Clearly, p. 394 Listen Actively, p. 395	
Writer's Workshop: Supporting a Position (p. 396)		Order of Importance, p. 400	Transitions, p. 400		Write an Essay Supporting a Position, pp. 396–400	Brainstorm Topics in a Group, p. 397	Use a Cluster Diagram for Positions, p. 397
Sentence Workshop: Combining Sentences by Inserting Words (p. 401)			Combining Sentences by Inserting Words, p. 401		Revise Sentences by Combining, p. 401		
Reading for Life: Evaluating Persuasion (p. 402)	Evaluate Persuasive Writing, p. 402	Perspective, p. 402	Loaded Words, p. 402				
Learning for Life: Persuading with Editorial Cartoons (p. 403)					Write a Letter to the Editor, p. 403	Plan a Cartoon Contest, p. 403	Create an Editorial Cartoon, p. 403

Resources for this Collection

Note: All resources for this collection are available for preview on the *One-Stop Planner CD-ROM 2 with Test Generator.* All worksheets and blackline masters may be printed from the CD-ROM.

Internet Resources
go.hrw.com LE0 6-5

Selection or Feature	Reading and Literary Skills	Language and Grammar
All Summer in a Day (p. 312) Ray Bradbury **Connections: Suit Helps Girl Enjoy Daylight** (p. 321) *The Gainesville Sun,* Lise Fisher	• *Graphic Organizers for Active Reading,* Worksheet p. 25 • *Literary Elements:* Transparency 6; Worksheet p. 19	• *Grammar and Language Links:* Style: Figurative Language, Worksheet p. 33 • *Daily Oral Grammar,* Transparency 18
Elements of Literature: The Short Story (p. 326)	• *Literary Elements,* Transparency 6	
Eleven/Once (p. 327) Sandra Cisneros *translated by* Liliana Valenzuela	• *Graphic Organizers for Active Reading,* Worksheet p. 26	• *Grammar and Language Links:* Punctuating Dialogue, Worksheet p. 35 • *Language Workshop CD-ROM,* Direct Quotations • *Daily Oral Grammar,* Transparency 19
The Gold Cadillac (p. 338) Mildred D. Taylor **Connections: I Was Not Alone** *from I Dream a World* (p. 350) Rosa Parks and Brian Lanker	• *Reading Skills and Strategies: Reaching Struggling Readers* • Selection Skill Lesson, p. 67 • *Graphic Organizers for Active Reading,* Worksheet p. 27	• *Grammar and Language Links:* Style: Connotations, Worksheet p. 37 • *Daily Oral Grammar,* Transparency 20
The Bracelet (p. 356) Yoshiko Uchida	• *Reading Skills and Strategies: Reaching Struggling Readers* • Selection Skill Lesson, p. 105 • *Graphic Organizers for Active Reading,* Worksheet p. 28	• *Grammar and Language Links:* Look Who's Talking, Worksheet p. 39 • *Language Workshop CD-ROM,* Dialogue • *Daily Oral Grammar,* Transparency 21
What Do Fish Have to Do With Anything? (p. 366) Avi	• *Graphic Organizers for Active Reading,* Worksheet p. 29 • *Literary Elements:* Transparency 7; Worksheet p. 22	• *Grammar and Language Links:* Direct and Indirect Quotations, Worksheet p. 41 • *Language Workshop CD-ROM,* Quotation Marks • *Daily Oral Grammar,* Transparency 22
The Sneetches (p. 379) Dr. Seuss (Theodor Geisel)	• *Graphic Organizers for Active Reading,* Worksheet p. 30	
No Questions Asked: The Southpaw (p. 387) Judith Viorst	The **No Questions Asked** feature provides students with an unstructured opportunity to practice reading strategies using a selection that extends the theme of the collection.	
Speaking and Listening Workshop: Social Interaction (p. 394)		
Writer's Workshop: Supporting a Position (p. 396)		
Sentence Workshop: Combining Sentences by Inserting Words (p. 401)		• *Workshop Resources,* p. 45
Learning for Life: Persuading with Editorial Cartoons (p. 403)		

Collection Resources

- *Cross-Curricular Activities*, p. 30
- *Portfolio Management System:*
  Introduction to Portfolio Assessment, p. 1;
  Parent/Guardian Letters, p. 95
- *Formal Assessment,*
  Reading Application Test, p. 78
- *Test Generator,* Collection Test

Vocabulary, Spelling, and Decoding	Writing	Listening and Speaking, Viewing and Representing	Assessment
• *Words to Own,* Worksheet p. 13 • *Spelling and Decoding,* Worksheet p. 16	• *Portfolio Management System,* Rubrics for Choices, p. 147	• *Audio CD Library,* Disc 7, Track 2 • *Portfolio Management System,* Rubrics for Choices, p. 147	• *Formal Assessment,* Selection Test, p. 66 • *Standardized Test Preparation,* p. 50 • *Test Generator* (One-Stop Planner CD-ROM)
			• *Formal Assessment,* Literary Elements Test, p. 77
• *Spelling and Decoding,* Worksheet p. 17	• *Portfolio Management System,* Rubrics for Choices, p. 148	• *Portfolio Management System,* Rubrics for Choices, p. 148	• *Formal Assessment,* Selection Test, p. 68 • *Standardized Test Preparation,* p. 52 • *Test Generator* (One-Stop Planner CD-ROM)
• *Words to Own,* Worksheet p. 14	• *Portfolio Management System,* Rubrics for Choices, p. 149	• *Audio CD Library,* Disc 7, Track 3 • *Portfolio Management System,* Rubrics for Choices, p. 149	• *Formal Assessment,* Selection Test, p. 70 • *Standardized Test Preparation,* pp. 54, 56 • *Test Generator* (One-Stop Planner CD-ROM)
• *Words to Own,* Worksheet p. 15 • *Spelling and Decoding,* Worksheet p. 18	• *Portfolio Management System,* Rubrics for Choices, p. 150	• *Visual Connections,* Videocassette B, Segment 6 • *Audio CD Library,* Disc 8, Track 2 • *Viewing and Representing:* Fine Art Transparency 12 Worksheet p. 48 • *Portfolio Management System,* Rubrics for Choices, p. 150	• *Formal Assessment,* Selection Test, p. 72 • *Standardized Test Preparation,* p. 58 • *Test Generator* (One-Stop Planner CD-ROM)
• *Words to Own,* Worksheet p. 16 • *Spelling and Decoding,* Worksheet p. 19	• *Portfolio Management System,* Rubrics for Choices, p. 151	• *Audio CD Library,* Disc 8, Track 3 • *Viewing and Representing:* Fine Art Transparency 13 Worksheet p. 52 • *Portfolio Management System,* Rubrics for Choices, p. 151	• *Formal Assessment,* Selection Test, p. 74 • *Standardized Test Preparation,* p. 60 • *Test Generator* (One-Stop Planner CD-ROM)
	• *Portfolio Management System,* Rubrics for Choices, p. 152	• *Audio CD Library,* Disc 8, Track 4 • *Portfolio Management System,* Rubrics for Choices, p. 152	• *Formal Assessment,* Selection Test, p. 76 • *Test Generator* (One-Stop Planner CD-ROM)
		• *Viewing and Representing:* Fine Art Transparency 14 Worksheet p. 56	
			• *Portfolio Management System,* p. 153
	• *Workshop Resources,* p. 19 • *Standardized Test Preparation:* Worksheet p. 106 Transparencies 1–6		• *Portfolio Management System* • Prewriting, p. 154 • Peer Editing, p. 155 • Assessment Rubric, p. 156
		• *Viewing and Representing,* HRW Multimedia Presentation Maker	• *Portfolio Management System,* Rubrics, p. 157

 Transparency CD-ROM Video Audio CD

Collection Planner

OBJECTIVES

1. Read literature in different genres centered on the theme "Justice for All"
2. Interpret literary elements used in the literature, with special emphasis on the short story
3. Apply a variety of reading strategies, with special emphasis on making and adjusting predictions
4. Respond to the literature using a variety of modes
5. Learn and use new words
6. Develop skill in social interaction
7. Plan draft, revise, edit, proof, and publish a persuasive essay
8. Combine sentences by inserting words
9. Demonstrate the ability to evaluate a persuasive argument
10. Explore, through a variety of projects, how editorial cartoons are used to express opinions

Introducing the Theme

The stories in this collection show characters dealing with various forms of injustice, including childhood cruelty, racial prejudice, and homelessness. As they read these selections, students will be reminded of ways that people in their own experience are—and are not—treated fairly.

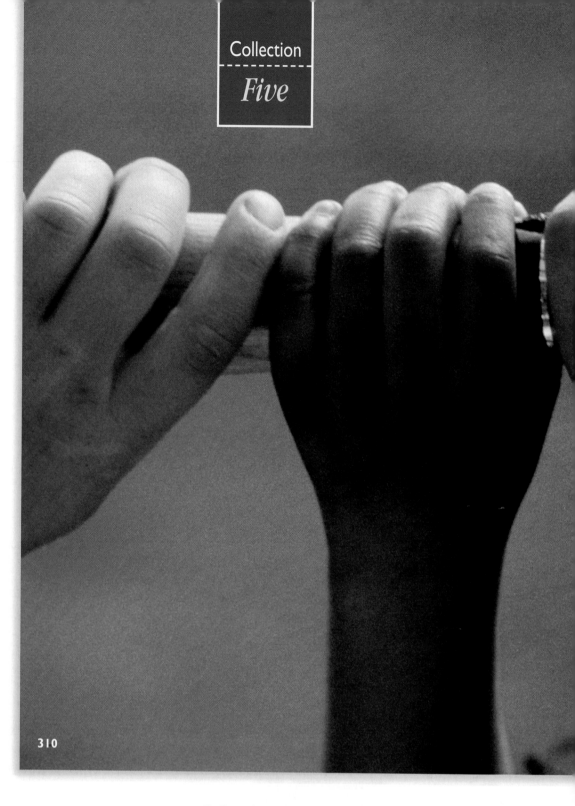

310

Selection Readability

This Annotated Teacher's Edition provides a summary of each selection in the student book. Following each Summary heading, you will find one, two, or three small icons. These icons indicate, in an approximate sense, the reading level of the selection.

■ One icon indicates that the selection is easy.

■ ■ Two icons indicate that the selection is on an intermediate reading level.

■ ■ ■ Three icons indicate that the selection is challenging.

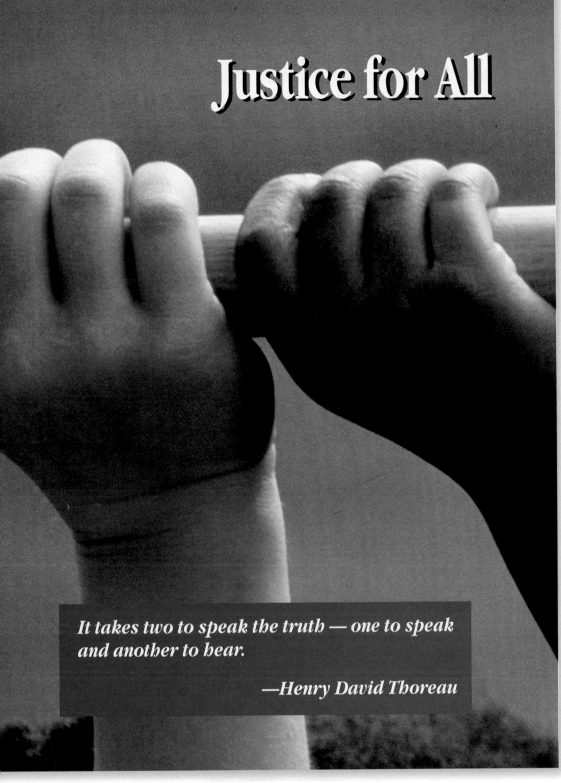

Justice for All

> *It takes two to speak the truth — one to speak and another to hear.*
>
> *—Henry David Thoreau*

Writing Focus: Supporting a Position

The following **Work in Progress** assignments in this collection build to a culminating **Writer's Workshop** at the end of Collection 5.

- All Summer in a Day   Brainstorm ideas for resolving a conflict (p. 324)
- Eleven / Once   List reasons supporting a position (p. 335)
- The Gold Cadillac   State opinions on issues (p. 354)
- The Bracelet   Jot down ideas you agree with (p. 364)
- What Do Fish Have to Do . . .   Freewrite about a community problem (p. 377)
- The Sneetches   Write about reasons for forming groups (p. 386)

Writer's Workshop: Persuasive Writing / Supporting a Position (p. 396)

Before You Read

ALL SUMMER IN A DAY

Make the Connection

The Outsider

In this story the children of Venus (that is, Venus as Ray Bradbury imagines it) lead very different lives from kids on Earth. One thing is still the same, though: Someone who differs from the rest of the crowd is seen as an outsider.

How does it feel to be an outsider? Do you understand why some people won't accept others into their group? Get together with a few classmates to fill in a diagram like the one below:

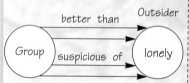

On the arrows leading from the Group circle, write words and phrases that describe how the group feels toward the outsider. In the Outsider circle, write how the outsider feels.

Elements of Literature

Setting: Margot's Never-Ending Rainy Day

Setting plays an important part in science fiction stories.

312 JUSTICE FOR ALL

Science fiction writers like to show us people living in a time and place very different from our own yet facing problems surprisingly similar to ours. This story takes place on an imaginary Venus sometime in the future. On this bleak planet, rain falls continuously for seven years. The unending rain is like torture for the main character, Margot, who longs for another setting—the bright, sunny Earth.

> **S**etting is the time and place of a story or play.
>
> *For more on Setting, see the Handbook of Literary Terms.*

Reading Skills and Strategies

Dialogue with the Text

As you read "All Summer in a Day," keep a sheet of paper next to the book so that you can record your questions, predictions, and responses to Bradbury's story. One student's responses appear on page 314 as an example.

go.hrw.com
LE0 6-5

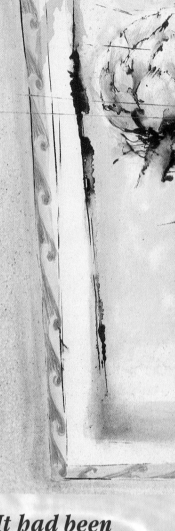

It had been raining for seven years . . .

Preteaching Vocabulary

Reflex (1988) by William Baggett.

ALL SUMMER in a DAY

Ray Bradbury

Summary ▪▪

On an imaginary version of the planet Venus, the sun shows its face for only two hours every seven years. Unremitting rain falls the rest of the time. Nine-year-old Margot anxiously waits with her classmates to witness the sun's brief appearance. She and her family moved to Venus from Earth five years ago, so she alone of her classmates remembers the sun. Margot has not adjusted to Venus, and there is talk that her family will take her back to Earth the following year.

The children resent Margot because she knows what the sun is like, and so they lock her in the closet while the teacher steps away. When the sun appears, the children romp in the gray jungle, marveling at the sun's warmth. Forced inside by the rain's return, the children remember Margot and release her from the closet—but it is too late, because the sun will not return for another seven years.

Resources

Listening
Audio CD Library
An exciting recording of this short story is included in the *Audio CD Library*:
• Disc 7, Track 2

RESPONDING TO THE ART
William Baggett (1946–   ) grew up in Tennessee and now makes his home in Mississippi.
Activity. Ask students what they think this person's feelings may be. Ask students what they think the story will be about.

   Resources: Print and Media

Reading
• *Graphic Organizers for Active Reading*, p. 25
• *Words to Own*, p. 13
• *Spelling and Decoding Worksheet*, p. 16
• *Audio CD Library* Disc 7, Track 2

Elements of Literature
• *Literary Elements Transparency 6 Worksheet*, p. 19

Writing and Language
• *Daily Oral Grammar Transparency 18*
• *Grammar and Language Links Worksheet*, p. 33

Assessment
• *Formal Assessment*, p. 66
• *Portfolio Management System*, p. 147
• *Test Generator (One-Stop Planner CD-ROM)*

Internet
• go.hrw.com (keyword: LE0 6-5)

A Elements of Literature
Figures of Speech
❓What does comparing the children to roses and weeds suggest about the children? [It suggests that there is a wide variety of children, some more attractive than others. "Weeds" also suggests that some of the children are wild and out of control.]

B Reading Skills and Strategies

Dialogue with the Text
❓What is your response to the story so far? What questions do you have? [Encourage students to respond to details such as the author's description of the rainy atmosphere and his use of very short and very long sentences. Students should form questions such as "Who are these children?" and "What are they doing here?"] How do your responses and questions compare with those of Paul Behee? [Students should have similar responses and questions and continue their dialogue with the text as they read the selection.]

C Reading Skills and Strategies
Identifying Setting and Characters
❓What do the descriptions here tell you about where the story is set and who the characters are? [It is set on the planet Venus, and the characters are children of the rocket men and women who came to Venus to set up civilization.]

D Elements of Literature
Setting
❓What effect does the setting seem to have on the children? [Possible response: The rain defines their lives, even invading their dreams. It is the single most important aspect of their existence.]

"Ready."

"Ready."

"Now?"

"Soon."

"Do the scientists really know? Will it happen today, will it?"

"Look, look; see for yourself!"

The children pressed to each other like so many roses, so many weeds, intermixed, peering out for a look at the hidden sun.

It rained.

It had been raining for seven years; thousands upon thousands of days compounded and filled from one end to the other with rain, with the drum and gush of water, with the sweet crystal fall of showers and the concussion[1] of storms so heavy they were tidal waves come over the islands. A thousand forests had been crushed under the rain and grown up a thousand times to be crushed again. And this was the way life was forever on the planet Venus, and this was the schoolroom of the children of the rocket men and women who had come to a raining world to set up civilization and live out their lives.

"It's stopping, it's stopping!"

"Yes, yes!"

Margot stood apart from them, from these children who could never remember a time when there wasn't rain and rain and rain. They were all nine years old, and if there had been a day, seven years ago, when the sun came out for an hour and showed its face to the stunned world, they could not recall. Sometimes, at night, she heard them stir, in remembrance, and she knew they were dreaming and remembering gold or a yellow crayon or a coin large enough to buy the world with. She knew they thought they remembered a warmness, like a blushing in the face, in the body, in the arms and legs and trembling hands. But then they always awoke to the tatting drum, the endless shaking down of clear bead necklaces upon the roof, the walk, the gardens, the forests, and their dreams were gone.

1. **concussion:** violent shaking or impact.

314 JUSTICE FOR ALL

Dialogue with the Text

Will what happen today?

What are they looking at? Sometimes my class rushes to the window to look at something interesting.

I can't even imagine rain for seven years nonstop!

I like how descriptively the author writes.

At my house it rains so hard it can break trees also.

Now I understand why the weather is different.

Do the students stay at school all day and night?

I wonder if I could remember what the sun was like if I hadn't seen it for seven years?

Is this a dream?

Paul Behee

—Paul Behee
Twain Harte School
Twain Harte, California

Reaching All Students

Struggling Readers
Use Paul Behee's comments on p. 314 to explain the types of comments one makes when using the Think-Aloud strategy. Think-Aloud comments include identifying problems (first two questions and a statement); making a comment (third statement); fixing the problems (sixth statement); making comparisons (eighth statement); picturing the text; and predicting. See the *Reading Strategies Handbook,* p. 115, in front of the *Reading Skills and Strategies* binder for information about Think-Aloud.

English Language Learners
Pair fluent and less fluent readers for an Echo Reading. Have fluent readers read the story aloud, paragraph by paragraph; then have the less fluent readers repeat the paragraphs. For additional strategies to supplement instruction for these students, see
• *Lesson Plans Including Strategies for English-Language Learners*

Advanced Learners
Have students prepare the work for an oral performance. They should decide first how many readers they will need. Then they can map out the story and assign parts. They might want to consider using a chorus to read some of the children's parts.

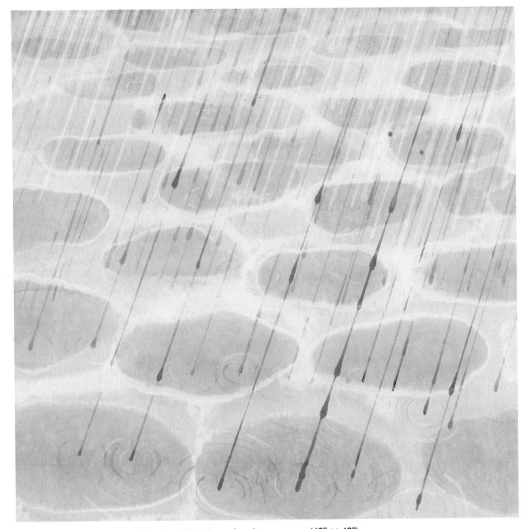

Japanese Rain on Canvas (1972) by David Hockney. Acrylic on canvas (48" × 48").
© David Hockney.

All day yesterday they had read in class about the sun. About how like a lemon it was, and how hot. And they had written small stories or essays or poems about it.

I think the sun is a flower
That blooms for just one hour.

That was Margot's poem, read in a quiet voice in the still classroom while the rain was falling outside.

"Aw, you didn't write that!" protested one of the boys.

"I did," said Margot. "I *did*."

"William!" said the teacher.

ALL SUMMER IN A DAY 315

Crossing the Curriculum

Health

Ask the class to investigate how the sun affects people's health, both physically and psychologically. To record their findings, students can create a chart listing the beneficial effects of the sun, the harmful effects of the sun, and the effects of no sun. Students can use a graphic organizer such as this one:

Sun's Benefits	Sun's Drawbacks	No Sun
[vitamin D]	[sunburn]	[death]

Science

How much rain falls in your region? Students can make a rain gauge to find out. They will need a large glass jar, a funnel, and a stiff plastic sheet. Have students bury the jar with its neck at ground level, cut a small hole in the plastic, place the plastic over the jar's neck, and jam the funnel through the hole in the plastic into the glass jar. At set intervals, students can lift out the jar and measure the amount of water that has collected. They can chart the results over a set period of time.

RESPONDING TO THE ART

The work of the American artist **John Marin** (1870–1953) was regularly exhibited, during the course of forty years, in the New York City gallery of the famous artist-photographer Alfred Stieglitz. Some of Marin's favorite subjects were New England landscapes and Manhattan skyscrapers. Casco Bay is in Maine.

Activity. Invite students to describe how the painting fits Margot's description of the sun as being "like a penny" and "like a fire in a stove." Ask them to use other similes to describe the painting ("The painting is like. . . .").

Ⓐ Elements of Literature

Setting

❓ How has life on Venus affected Margot? [It has affected her badly. She has become pale from the lack of sun, frail, and ill-looking.]

Ⓑ Reading Skills and Strategies

Dialogue with the Text

❓ Why do you think William picks on Margot? [Possible responses: He resents her having memories of the sun; he feels it is permissible to pick on her because she is an outsider; he is just cruel.] What do you predict might happen as a result of William's cruelty? [Possible responses: Nothing might happen; William might do something even more hurtful to Margot, such as prevent her from seeing the sun.]

Sunset, Casco Bay by John Marin.

The Roland P. Murdock Collection, Wichita Art Museum, Wichita, Kansas.

But that was yesterday. Now the rain was <u>slackening</u>, and the children were crushed in the great thick windows.

"Where's teacher?"

"She'll be back."

"She'd better hurry; we'll miss it!"

They turned on themselves like a feverish wheel, all tumbling spokes.

Ⓐ Margot stood alone. She was a very frail girl who looked as if she had been lost in the rain for years and the rain had washed out the blue from her eyes and the red from her mouth and the yellow from her hair. She was an old photograph dusted from an album, whitened away, and if she spoke at all her voice would be a ghost. Now she stood, separate, staring at the rain and the loud wet world beyond the huge glass.

Ⓑ "What're *you* looking at?" said William.

Margot said nothing.

"Speak when you're spoken to." He gave her a shove. But she did not move; rather she

---

WORDS TO OWN

slackening (slak′ən·iŋ) *v.* used as *adj.*: falling off; lessening.

---

316 JUSTICE FOR ALL

Professional Notes

Before the 1960s, our knowledge of Venus came from Earth-based telescopes. Since then, sophisticated space probes have provided new information.

We've discovered, for example, that Venus is the hottest planet in our solar system, about 860 degrees Fahrenheit. As a result of this tremendous heat, almost all the water on Venus has boiled away. Unlike Earth's atmosphere, which is mostly nitrogen and oxygen, the atmosphere of Venus is mostly carbon dioxide. It also contains sulfur dioxide, which combines with water vapor to produce poisonous sulfuric acid. We've also learned that there's no rain on Venus and little wind. One day is exactly like the next.

Ironically, even though Venus is very hot, the sun is always blocked by clouds. It does not shine even once every seven years. Clearly, the actual Venus is not the one Bradbury imagines in "All Summer in a Day."

let herself be moved only by him and nothing else.

They edged away from her; they would not look at her. She felt them go away. And this was because she would play no games with them in the echoing tunnels of the underground city. If they tagged her and ran, she stood blinking after them and did not follow. When the class sang songs about happiness and life and games, her lips barely moved. Only when they sang about the sun and the summer did her lips move as she watched the drenched windows.

And then, of course, the biggest crime of all was that she had come here only five years ago from Earth, and she remembered the sun and the way the sun was and the sky was when she was four in Ohio. And they, they had been on Venus all their lives, and they had been only two years old when last the sun came out and had long since forgotten the color and heat of it and the way it really was. But Margot remembered.

"It's like a penny," she said once, eyes closed.

"No, it's not!" the children cried.

"It's like a fire," she said, "in the stove."

"You're lying; you don't remember!" cried the children.

But she remembered and stood quietly apart from all of them and watched the patterning windows. And once, a month ago, she had refused to shower in the school shower rooms, had clutched her hands to her ears and over her head, screaming the water mustn't touch her head. So after that, dimly, dimly, she sensed it, she was different, and they knew her difference and kept away.

There was talk that her father and mother were taking her back to Earth next year; it seemed vital to her that they do so, though it would mean the loss of thousands of dollars to her family. And so, the children hated her for all these reasons of big and little consequence.[2] They hated her pale snow face, her waiting silence, her thinness, and her possible future.

"Get away!" The boy gave her another push. "What're you waiting for?"

Then, for the first time, she turned and looked at him. And what she was waiting for was in her eyes.

"Well, don't wait around here!" cried the boy savagely. "You won't see nothing!"

Her lips moved.

"Nothing!" he cried. "It was all a joke, wasn't it?" He turned to the other children. "Nothing's happening today. *Is* it?"

They all blinked at him and then, understanding, laughed and shook their heads. "Nothing, nothing!"

"Oh, but," Margot whispered, her eyes helpless. "But this is the day, the scientists predict, they say, they *know*, the sun . . ."

"All a joke!" said the boy, and seized her roughly. "Hey everyone, let's put her in a closet before teacher comes!"

"No," said Margot, falling back.

They <u>surged</u> about her, caught her up and bore her, protesting, and then pleading, and then crying, back into a tunnel, a room, a closet, where they slammed and locked the door. They stood looking at the door and saw it tremble from her beating and throwing herself against it. They heard her muffled cries. Then, smiling, they turned and went out and

---

2. **consequence:** importance; result.

- -
WORDS TO OWN
surged (sʉrjd) *v.*: swelled or pushed violently.
- -

ALL SUMMER IN A DAY 317

C Reading Skills and Strategies
Comparing and Contrasting
❓ How is Margot like the other children? How is she different from them? [Like the other children, Margot is nine years old and lives on Venus. Unlike them, she is frail, won't join the games, and remembers the sun. Also, she will sing only about the sun and the summer.]

D Critical Thinking
Analyzing
❓ What does Margot's reaction in the shower suggest about her emotional state? [Possible responses: All the rain on Venus has caused her to fear and hate water. She is very fragile emotionally, which has made her an outcast.]

E Struggling Readers
Questioning
❓ What is Margot waiting for that shows in her eyes? [She is waiting for the sun. The boy can see the desperate yearning in her eyes.]

F Reading Skills and Strategies

Dialogue with the Text
❓ Why do the other students lock Margot in the closet? [Possible responses: They resent her "pale snow face, her waiting silence, her thinness, and her possible future"; they hate her because she is different.]

Listening to Music

In a Summer Garden for Orchestra by Frederick Delius, performed by the London Symphony Orchestra

Frederick Delius (1862–1934), born in Bradford, England, created beautiful tone poems that reflected various aspects of nature, including orchestral "landscapes" named after places where he lived and worked. Some of the evocative titles of his compositions include *Florida, Over the Hills and Far Away, Paris,* and *Summer Night on the River.*

Activity
After students read "All Summer in a Day," play *In a Summer Garden for Orchestra,* and briefly discuss how some or all of its parts could be used as background music for a film version of Bradbury's story.

back down the tunnel, just as the teacher arrived.

"Ready, children?" She glanced at her watch.

"Yes!" said everyone.

"Are we all here?"

"Yes!"

The rain slackened still more.

They crowded to the huge door.

The rain stopped.

It was as if, in the midst of a film concerning an avalanche, a tornado, a hurricane, a volcanic eruption, something had, first, gone wrong with the sound apparatus, thus muffling and finally cutting off all noise, all of the blasts and repercussions and thunders, and then, second, ripped the film from the projector and inserted in its place a peaceful tropical slide which did not move or tremor. The world ground to a standstill. The silence was so immense and unbelievable that you felt your ears had been stuffed or you had lost your hearing altogether. The children put their hands to their ears. They stood apart. The door slid back and the smell of the silent, waiting world came in to them.

The sun came out.

It was the color of flaming bronze and it was very large. And the sky around it was a blazing blue tile color. And the jungle burned with sunlight as the children, released from their spell, rushed out, yelling, into the springtime.

"Now, don't go too far," called the teacher after them. "You've only two hours, you know. You wouldn't want to get caught out!"

But they were running and turning their faces up to the sky and feeling the sun on their cheeks like a warm iron; they were tak-

ing off their jackets and letting the sun burn their arms.

"Oh, it's better than the sun lamps, isn't it?"

"Much, much better!"

They stopped running and stood in the great jungle that covered Venus, that grew and never stopped growing, tumultuously,[3] even as you watched it. It was a nest of octopuses, clustering up great arms of fleshlike weed, wavering, flowering in this brief spring. It was the color of rubber and ash, this jungle, from the many years without sun. It was the color of stones and white cheeses and ink, and it was the color of the moon.

The children lay out, laughing, on the jungle mattress and heard it sigh and squeak under them, resilient and alive. They ran among the trees, they slipped and fell, they pushed each other, they played hide-and-seek and tag, but most of all they squinted at the sun until tears ran down their faces; they put their hands up to that yellowness and that amazing blueness and they breathed of the fresh, fresh air and listened and listened to the silence which suspended them in a blessed sea of no sound and no motion. They looked at everything and savored everything. Then, wildly, like animals escaped from their caves, they ran and ran in shouting circles. They ran for an hour and did not stop running.

And then——

In the midst of their running, one of the girls wailed.

3. **tumultuously:** wildly; violently.

WORDS TO OWN

tremor (trem′ər) *n.* used as *v.:* shake.
resilient (ri·zil′yənt) *adj.:* springy.
savored (sā′vərd) *v.:* delighted in; tasted or smelled.

Getting Students Involved

Cooperative Learning

Resolving Conflict. Ask groups of three students to form a "task force" to resolve the problem between Margot, the other children, and the teacher. As a group, students can brainstorm ideas; then each member should assume responsibility for writing down a proposal for one of the parties in the conflict. Students might use a graphic organizer, such as the one at the right. Suggest that students role-play a conversation among the three parties that helps resolve the conflict.

Teacher	Children	Margot
[have children apologize; take away their privileges]	[apologize; be nicer to Margot from then on]	[try to make friends with the others and understand their problems]

A Venus Vacation. Groups of students can practice persuasive writing by creating a travel campaign for tourism on Venus. The package can include brochures, posters, TV and radio ads, and flyers. Ask students to include sensory descriptions of the planet as they try to persuade others to visit Bradbury's Venus. Each group can present its advertising campaign to the class, who can then vote to decide which package is the most persuasive.

Everyone stopped.

The girl, standing in the open, held out her hand.

"Oh, look, look," she said trembling.

They came slowly to look at her opened palm.

In the center of it, cupped and huge, was a single raindrop.

She began to cry, looking at it.

They glanced quietly at the sky.

"Oh. Oh."

A few cold drops fell on their noses and their cheeks and their mouths. The sun faded behind a stir of mist. A wind blew cool around them. They turned and started to walk back toward the underground house, their hands at their sides, their smiles vanishing away.

A boom of thunder startled them, and like leaves before a new hurricane, they tumbled upon each other and ran. Lightning struck ten miles away, five miles away, a mile, a half-mile. The sky darkened into midnight in a flash.

They stood in the doorway of the underground for a moment until it was raining hard. Then they closed the door and heard the gigantic sound of the rain falling in tons and avalanches, everywhere and forever.

"Will it be seven more years?"

"Yes. Seven."

Then one of them gave a little cry.

"Margot!"

"What?"

"She's still in the closet where we locked her."

"Margot."

They stood as if someone had driven them, like so many stakes, into the floor. They looked at each other and then looked away. They glanced out at the world that was raining now and raining and raining steadily. They

Large Sun by David Finn.

could not meet each other's glances. Their faces were solemn and pale. They looked at their hands and feet, their faces down.

"Margot."

One of the girls said, "Well . . . ?"

No one moved.

"Go on," whispered the girl.

They walked slowly down the hall in the sound of cold rain. They turned through the doorway to the room in the sound of the storm and thunder, lightning on their faces, blue and terrible. They walked over to the closet door slowly and stood by it.

Behind the closet door was only silence.

They unlocked the door, even more slowly, and let Margot out.

ALL SUMMER IN A DAY **319**

Making the Connections

Connecting to the Theme:
"Justice for All"
After students have read the story, talk about the theme. Ask the class to define the word *justice*, using the dictionary. Then divide the class in half to debate whether or not Margot might ever be able to obtain justice for the terrible injustice that was done to her. As they frame their arguments, students can draw from the ideas they generated in the Cooperative Learning activity.

MEET THE WRITER

Space-Age Storyteller

Ray Bradbury (1920–   ) has been called the world's greatest science fiction writer. It's not a label Bradbury agrees with. He says simply: "I am a storyteller. That's all I've ever tried to be."

Although his stories are often set in space, the characters and emotions are pure Bradbury. In fact, Bradbury advises beginning writers to write from their own experiences:

66 Find out what excites and delights you, or what angers you most, then get it down on paper. After all, it is your individuality that you want to isolate. Work from the subconscious; store up images, impressions, data—then dip into this 'well of self' for your stories. 99

Bradbury also encourages young people to try to imagine what wonders the future might bring—just as he did when he was in school:

66 Everything confronting us in the next thirty years will be science fictional, that is, impossible a few years ago. The things you are doing right now, if you had told anyone you'd be doing them when you were children, they would have laughed you out of school. . . . I was the only person at Los Angeles High School who knew the Space Age was coming. Totally alone among four thousand students, I insisted we were going to get the rocket off the ground, and that made me the class kook, of course. I said, 'Well, we're going to do it anyway.' 99

More from Ray Bradbury's Universe

Bradbury's stories are collected in books such as *The Illustrated Man* (Bantam), *R Is for Rocket* (Bantam), *Twice-Twenty-Two* (Doubleday), and *The Stories of Ray Bradbury* (Knopf). Try starting with "Mars Is Heaven," "The Veldt," "The Sound of Summer Running," and "The Flying Machine." If reading a Bradbury novel interests you, try *Dandelion Wine* (Knopf).

Assessing Learning

Self-Assessment

To evaluate their participation in class discussions, have students answer the following questions in writing:

- Do I express my own opinions during the discussion?
- Do I support my opinions with specific details from the story?
- Am I willing to consider other points of view in addition to my own?
- Do I consider other people's feelings when I offer my opinions?

Check Test: True-False

1. In the story, the sun shines on Venus once every seven years. [True]
2. Margot will not play with the other children. [True]
3. Scientists on Venus predict the sun's reappearance. [True]
4. Margot was born on Venus. [False]
5. Margot is beating on the door when the children return to let her out. [False]

Standardized Test Preparation

For practice in proofreading and editing, see
- *Daily Oral Grammar*, Transparency 18

Suit Helps Girl Enjoy Daylight

LISE FISHER

Keystone Heights, Florida—Tinted goggles and grayish green fabric covered the three-year-old's face while blocking sunlight from Saturday morning's hazy sky. The suit, however, couldn't hide her enthusiasm.

While other families record events like their children's first steps and words, Steve and Michele Williams will be marking down this day for their daughter, Logan. It was her first play day in the sunlight protected in a "Cool Suit" that blocks the sun's rays, and the event went better than the Williamses could have imagined.

"It just opens up a whole lot of doors," said Logan's father. "The burden is off," a tearful Michele Williams said.

Doctors determined Logan had a rare genetic disease—xeroderma pigmentosum, or XP, as it is known—when she was eighteen months old. For the fewer than one thousand XP patients worldwide, exposure to ultraviolet radiation can lead to deadly skin cancers. The disease has no known cure.

Since the diagnosis, Logan has lived in a world of tinted windows and terror caused by the "bad light."

Light streaming in from a front door and bouncing off their refrigerator frightens the family. Getting Logan to a doctor's appointment has involved padding Logan with a helmet and clothes and covering the car's windows with plastic bags and blankets. She hasn't seen stores, and she marvels that they stock more than one box of cereal and a few toys. Barbara Pellechio, a teacher at Keystone Heights's McRae Elementary School, visits the girl two to three times a week at night because that's when Logan is awake. Like any young child, Logan is afraid of the dark even though it has been the only time she can go outside and play.

The clothing is based on technology from NASA and covers every inch of the little girl with tightly woven material to keep out the sun. Gloves outfitted with rough material for gripping hide her hands. An oversized shirt and pants that look and feel like a soft sweat suit cinch at her wrists and ankles. A hood secured with goggles conceals her freckled face.

Everything Logan did Saturday was a milestone for Logan's parents and for more than twenty of the family's friends and relatives. They kept pulling up in cars, in trucks, and even in the Keystone Heights fire engine.

Logan clutched purple and yellow flowers her parents bought and planted just for this day. She bounced on a trampoline with friends. Her hands found and clutched a lizard.

"This is probably the most special day of my life," said Alison Broadway, 33. The family friend was holding Logan when the girl spotted a butterfly. "I was holding her and she started squirming and screaming. . . . When they say miracles don't happen, they're wrong because one happened here today," said Broadway.

—from *The Gainesville Sun*

Logan Williams plays in her "Cool Suit."

Connections

This news article presents Logan, a young girl with a rare condition that makes her skin hypersensitive to ultraviolet light, forcing her to live her life indoors. Logan is excited about going outside for her first "play day" in the Florida sun with the help of a suit based on material technology from NASA.

A **Reading Skills and Strategies**
Comparing and Contrasting
? How is Logan like Margot in Bradbury's story "All Summer in a Day"? How is she different? [The sun plays a crucial role in both children's lives. Margot is prevented from seeing the sun by the cruelty of her peers; Logan is unable to go out in the sun because she suffers from a condition that makes the sun her enemy.]

B **Critical Thinking**
Speculating
? How might Logan's life change as a result of the suit? [Possible responses: She will be able to go outside during daylight hours and play with friends; she will be able to attend a regular school; she will be able to explore her environment with greater freedom.]

C **English Language Learners**
Questioning
? What does Alison Broadway mean when she says, "When they say miracles don't happen, they're wrong because one happened here today"? [She means that Logan's experiences with the outside world were at one time unimaginable, but not anymore.]

Connecting Across Texts

**Connecting with
"All Summer in a Day"**

In the story, Margot is treated unjustly by others because she is different. In "Suit Helps Girl Enjoy Daylight," Logan Williams is treated with compassion and generosity. Barbara Pellochio, Logan's teacher, makes special nighttime visits to help Logan with her studies. Her first daylight excursion in her protective suit is a celebration. Sharing in Logan's achievement, a family friend comments, "This is the most special day of my life." Despite the obvious setback of having such a rare disease, it seems that Logan has the kind of support needed to overcome the difficulty of avoiding exposure to daylight. Have students consider why the sun is so important to Margot and Logan.

The narrator of this student piece observes the barely noticeable activities in a garden's natural world at the end of the summer. She describes in great detail all of the plants, insects, and birds that surround her and concludes that they are better left undisturbed.

A Reading Skills and Strategies
Finding the Main Idea

❓ Why is the speaker sitting on a stone pathway between an herbal and a flower garden? [She is observing nature and finding some truths about her life from what she sees.]

B English Language Learners
Context Clues

Point out that the context clues "cricket," "grasshopper," and "have begun to sing" suggest that *katydids* are either other insects or birds. Explain that a *katydid* is an insect.

C Elements of Literature
Symbol

❓ What does the katydid represent to the writer? [Possible answer: It symbolizes many of the things that are out of the writer's reach and thus are best left undisturbed.]

Resources

Assessment
• *Standardized Test Preparation*, p. 50

Special Small World

It is late afternoon at the end of summer. At this time of year the trees are dressed in green. But the edges of leaves are starting to brown and curl. The leaves of the forest understory have dried up, so I can easily see the trunks of the oaks and hickories. I hear their nuts falling to the ground. I am sitting on a stone pathway between an herbal and a flower garden. Thyme, oregano, chives, and basil surround me on one side. The fragrance of the basil is overwhelming. A butterfly bush, burgundy snapdragons, orange marigolds, and the giant leaves of a zucchini plant that has vined its way seven feet from its original planting spot are on the other side. I am in a special small world where so much is happening, yet few would notice.

I am suddenly distracted by the sound of a nuthatch and the tufted titmice announcing their arrival at the bird feeder. A chickadee flies down from a maple, plucks a seed with its beak, and flies back to the tree, where it cracks open the shell and eats the contents. The bird repeats this procedure again and again, while a chipmunk scours the ground beneath the feeder searching for spilled sunflower seeds. Its cheeks are ballooning up with treasure. Five doves follow each other in a straight line across the southern sky. In the distance a family of crows is squawking too loudly. Their raucous calls are soon drowned out by the deafening drones of two—no, several male cicadas chanting to attract mates.

The crickets, unaware that I am here, chime in with their melodious chirps. I spy a spray of flowering oregano move. I notice that there is a large brown grasshopper on it. The hopper leaps into a forest of black-eyed Susans where the katydids have begun to sing. Now there is a chorus of chirpers filling the air with a symphony of sounds just as beautiful as any human composer could write.

A daddy longlegs is nestled between the branches of a basil bush, stalking its prey. A yellow jacket that has been darting around the flowers for quite some time finally lands on the drooping flower cluster of the butterfly bush beside me. In the light stream cast by the setting sun, a swarm of tiny white flies dance circles around each other like the ice crystals inside a growing cumulus cloud. I see a pale green katydid, but it is out of my reach. I feel frustrated. But then I realize that a lot of things in life are just out of reach.

Besides, what would I do with a katydid anyway? I would hold it, observe it for a while, and then I would let it go to live its own life.

—Casie Anne Smith
Pierre Van Cortlandt Middle School
Croton-on-Hudson, New York

Connecting Across Texts

Connecting with "All Summer in a Day"

In "All Summer in a Day," Margot is locked in a closet and denied an afternoon in the sun because she is an outsider. In "Special Small World," the narrator observes nature in a tiny part of her world. Have students contrast the depressing environment of Venus with the nurturing environment of "Special Small World."

MAKING MEANINGS

First Thoughts

[respond]   1. How do you feel about what the other children do to Margot in Bradbury's story? What do you think she does when they let her out? Refer to your reading notes for ideas.

Shaping Interpretations

[interpret]   2. Why do you think the children lock Margot in a closet when they know how much the sun means to her?

[interpret]   3. When the children remembered that Margot was still in the closet (page 319), they "looked at each other and then looked away.... Their faces were solemn and pale. They looked at their hands and feet, their faces down." What do these details tell you about how they feel?

[interpret]   4. How is Logan like Margot (see *Connections* on page 321)?

[speculate]   5. How do you think the writer of "Special Small World" (page 322) would react to the **setting** on Venus?

[interpret]   6. What do you think the **title** of Bradbury's story means? Do you think it's a good title? Why or why not?

Connecting with the Text

[apply]   7. What do you think now about outsiders and the groups who pick on them? Refer to the diagram you completed before you read the story.

Extending the Text

[evaluate]   8. Do you think the hardships faced by pioneers are worth it? Would you volunteer to be a colonist on a distant planet? Explain why or why not.

Challenging the Text

[evaluate]   9. Bradbury's ending leaves some questions unanswered. Do you think he should have shown what happens when Margot gets out of the closet, or do you like the story as it is? Explain.

ALL SUMMER IN A DAY 323

Reading Check

a. At the beginning of Bradbury's story, why are the children so excited?

b. The children in this story live on Venus. What is the weather like there?

c. How is Margot different from the other children?

d. What happens while Margot is in the closet? What happens at the end?

Reading Check

a. They expect the sun to come out for the first time in seven years.

b. It is rainy, stormy, and cold.

c. She is pale, thin, quiet, and unhappy. She moved to Venus from Ohio when she was four and remembers the sun, unlike her peers.

d. The sun comes out for two hours, and the children play outside. At the end, the children let Margot out of the closet. We don't know what happens next.

Challenging the Text

9. Students might like the ending because it seems real or dislike it because it does not come to a conclusion and explain Margot's fate.

MAKING MEANINGS

First Thoughts

1. Students are likely to feel angry at the children's cruelty. They may predict that Margot cries, screams, or goes into a withdrawn state when she is released.

Shaping Interpretations

2. The children may envy her memory of the sun, hate her for having the chance to return to Earth, or resent her for being different.

3. They are too ashamed to look each other in the eye.

4. Both Logan and Margot wish to see the sun but cannot. Margot is prevented from seeing the sun by her classmates; Logan cannot go outside because she suffers from a rare condition.

5. Possible responses: She would be excited and would find the gardens and the jungle fascinating because she is a keen observer; she would be bored because the rain makes everything seem dull.

6. The title means that the sun comes out only once every seven years, so all of summer is compressed into one day. Students may like the title because it is unusual and catches their interest. Encourage them to think of alternate titles, if they dislike this one.

Connecting with the Text

7. Some students will have more sympathy for outsiders, but others may still lack sympathy for those who do not fit in. The problem of "outsiders," of course, is a very real one in middle schools.

Extending the Text

8. Some students may say that the excitement, adventure, and challenge of exploration balance the hardships, and so they would welcome the chance to be colonists. Others might argue that nothing would persuade them to trade the pleasures of life on Earth for this inhuman climate. If some brave explorers, such as astronauts, were not willing to endure deprivation, and even pain, what would happen to the human race and its quest for knowledge?

CHOICES: Building Your Portfolio

1. **Writer's Notebook** With each selection, a Writer's Notebook appears as the first option in the Choices section. These brief work-in-progress assignments build toward the writing assignment in the Writer's Workshop at the end of the collection. If students save their work for their Writer's Notebook activities as they move through the collection, they should be able to use some of them as starting points for the workshop.

2. **Creative Writing** Students can create a flow chart to help them make sure that their proposed ending works with the rest of the story. As they write, students can discuss their endings with the class to receive feedback about continuity.

3. **Science/Research** To gather information, students can access space-related Web pages, such as the National Space Science Data Center's Planetary Sciences Web page. The site includes photo galleries and information on all the planets. *You may want to preview any Internet activity you suggest to students. Because these resources are sometimes public forums, their content can be unpredictable.*

CHOICES: Building Your Portfolio

Writer's Notebook

1. Collecting Ideas for Supporting a Position

You can find some good ideas for an essay supporting a position by thinking of issues that concern people everywhere. That doesn't mean you have to write about global issues, like war or the greenhouse effect. You can find good ideas by thinking about problems that you've read about or experienced. For example, what problems between in-groups and outsiders have you noticed at your school? List a few examples; then, brainstorm with a group of classmates to gather ideas for resolving one of the conflicts.

> **Issue:**
> Some kids are made fun of because of the way they dress.
> **Solutions:**
> —have a dress code
> —make everyone wear a uniform

Creative Writing

2. End to End

Write a new ending for the story, beginning with this sentence: "They unlocked the door and let Margot out." Your ending should answer these questions:

a. What do Margot, the children, and the teacher say and do?

b. Have any of the children's feelings or attitudes changed? If so, how?

c. What does Margot's future hold?

Discuss your story endings with your classmates. Did any of you end the story the same way?

Science/Research

3. Armchair Astronauts

To find out more planetary facts, form a research team with seven classmates. **Your mission.** Explore the eight other planets in our solar system—Mercury, Venus, Mars, Jupiter, Saturn, Uranus, Neptune, and Pluto. **Your method.** Research one planet per team member and fill out a data sheet. **Your goal.** Compare the data and then decide which planet to explore on a space mission. Use the data sheet shown here (information has been filled in for Earth).

Data Sheet	
Planet	**Earth**
Diameter	25,000 miles
Distance from Sun	93 million miles
Time it takes to go around Sun	365 Earth days
Climate	Varies from torrid to frozen, with large temperate areas.
Number of moons	1
Fascinating facts	Intelligent life exists there.

Using Students' Strengths

Kinesthetic Learners

As a prewriting exercise for Choice 2, have students work in small groups to act out possible revised endings to the story. Have them evaluate each ending to see if it fits with the established plot, characters, and theme.

Intrapersonal Learners

After they complete Choice 3, students can post their results on the school or class Web page. They can also create their own Web page to share their findings and receive feedback from others. This interaction can also help students correct any errors or misconceptions in their conclusions. *You may want to work with students as they post their findings on the Internet. Because these resources are sometimes public forums, feedback can be unpredictable.*

LANGUAGE LINK MINI-LESSON

See Figure of Speech.

Handbook of Literary Terms HELP

Style: Figurative Language

Figurative language is language based on unusual comparisons that are not literally true.

1. A **simile** is a comparison between two unlike things, using a word such as *like, as,* or *resembles.*

   EXAMPLE "The children pressed to each other <u>like</u> so many roses, so many weeds. . . ."

2. A **metaphor** compares two unlike things without using a word such as *like, as,* or *resembles.*

   EXAMPLE "She was an old photograph dusted from an album, whitened away. . . ."

3. **Personification** is a special kind of metaphor in which a nonhuman thing is talked about as if it were human.

   EXAMPLE ". . . if there had been a day, seven years ago, when the sun came out for an hour and showed its face to the stunned world, they could not recall."

Try It Out

1. Draw a picture to illustrate each of Bradbury's figures of speech.

2. Use at least three figures of speech to describe your favorite place or a place you just hate.

VOCABULARY HOW TO OWN A WORD

WORD BANK

slackening
surged
tremor
resilient
savored

Semantic Mapping

A strategy called **semantic mapping** can help you understand the hard words you come across in your reading.

Using the map on the right as a model, try mapping three of the words listed in the Word Bank. Before you begin, find each word in the story and note how it's used. You can find synonyms for your maps in reference books called **synonym finders.** You can also check **reference software** and on-line libraries. Before you list a synonym on a map, see if you can use it in the story to replace the word from the Word Bank.

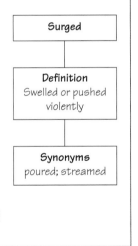

Surged

Definition
Swelled or pushed violently

Synonyms
poured; streamed

ALL SUMMER IN A DAY **325**

Language Link Quick Check

Have students identify each of the following figures of speech as a simile, metaphor, or personification.

1. Margot is as shy as a rabbit. [simile]
2. The sun smiled on the children. [personification]
3. The children acted like monsters, putting Margot in a closet. [simile]
4. Margot is a flower, and without the sun she will not grow. [metaphor]
5. The closet held Margot in its clutches. [personification]

LANGUAGE LINK

Have students select a piece of writing from their portfolios and identify any figures of speech they used.

Try It Out

1. Pictures will vary, but each one should represent the two things being compared.
2. Sample answers: *Simile*—My neighborhood garden is like an oasis in a desert of concrete and asphalt. *Metaphor*—My neighborhood garden is a harbor for tired city souls. *Personification*—My neighborhood garden breathes its flowery breath into my window.

VOCABULARY

Sample Answers

slackening
Definition
lessening
Synonyms
lessening; loosening up

surged
Definition
swelled or pushed violently
Synonyms
increased; rushed; rose

tremor
Definition
shake
Synonyms
quake; vibrate; quiver; tremble; shiver

resilient
Definition
springy (in this context)
Synonyms
elastic; flexible

savored
Definition
delighted in; tasted or smelled
Synonyms
relished

Resources ———

Language
• *Grammar and Language Links,* p. 33
Vocabulary
• *Words to Own,* p. 13

OBJECTIVES

1. Identify elements of literature in the short story
2. Define *characters, plot, conflict, climax, theme,* and *point of view*
3. Recognize these elements in a short story

Resources

Elements of Literature
The Short Story
For more instruction on the short story, see *Literary Elements:*
• Transparency 6

Assessment
Formal Assessment
Literary Elements Test, p. 77

Elements of Literature

This lesson discusses how writers combine *characters, plot, conflict, climax, theme,* and *point of view* to create a short story.

Mini-Lesson:
The Short Story
As students read the essay, chart the basic elements of the short story on the chalkboard: *characters, plot, conflict, climax, theme,* and *point of view.* Ask students to select a story or movie they have all read or seen and to identify each of the elements as you fill in the columns on the chart. Remind students to reread the essay if they have trouble with the basic elements. See the following chart for an example:

Story	["The Three Little Pigs"]
Characters	[First Pig, Second Pig, Third Pig, Big Bad Wolf]
Plot	[The Big Bad Wolf eats the First and Second Pigs. He climbs down the chimney of the Third Pig's house and falls into a pot of boiling water.]
Conflict	[The Big Bad Wolf wants to eat the pigs, but they do not want to be eaten.]
Climax	[The Big Bad Wolf climbs down the chimney.]
Theme	[Be prepared; listen to advice.]
Point of View	[third-person omniscient]

THE SHORT STORY: The Main Ingredients *by* John Leggett

You've probably heard of the main parts of a story—**characters**, **plot**, **point of view**, and **theme**. Let's look at how they work in a story you probably know—"The Three Little Pigs."

Who's Who?

Characters are the people or animals in a story who are involved in some kind of **conflict**, or struggle.

The main characters in "The Three Little Pigs" are the wolf and three pigs. All of the pigs are house builders. The wolf is sly and crafty, with an appetite for pork. The first two pigs are carefree and careless. They throw together houses of straw and sticks and think that these will keep them safe from slobbering wolves. The third pig, on the other hand, is an intelligent little porker. He builds a sturdy house of bricks.

What Happens?

The sequence of events in a story is called the **plot**. All the events in a plot must logically lead from one to the other. As you know, in this plot the wolf and the three little pigs are on a collision course. The wolf wants his pork dinner. The pigs want to live safely in their new houses. This is the **conflict**, or struggle, that drives the plot.

As the story develops, the wolf seems to be getting what he wants. First, the first little pig's straw house caves in; second, the second little pig's stick house does the same. By now, the villain has wolfed down two pigs.

By the time the wicked wolf is squeezing himself down the chimney of the third pig's house, the events of the plot are at a **climax**. That's the point where tension in the story is greatest. What will the third little pig do to avoid becoming wolf chow? You learn the answer when the wolf falls into a pot of boiling water.

Who Tells It?

In this story we know exactly how scared the pigs are and how hungry and sure of himself the wolf is. That's because the story is told by a narrator who knows everything that's going on. This means that the story has an **omniscient** (äm·nish′ənt) point of view. What if the wolf (or a pig) were telling the story in the **first person**, using the word *I* and revealing only his own thoughts and feelings? How would the story be different? (You might want to try to write it and see what happens.)

What's It All About?

The **theme** of a story is its message about life. One theme of "The Three Little Pigs" might be "Always prepare for the worst." The story could have other themes, too. Can you think of one?

Using Students' Strengths

Verbal Learners
Have students work in groups of four or five. Invite each student to tell a brief story while the rest of the group listens and takes notes on the short story elements. Then the group should work together to identify the *characters, plot, conflict, climax, theme,* and *point of view* in each student's story.

Logical/Mathematical Learners
Students can create story charts, diagrams, or other visuals to show the six elements that make up a short story and how they work together to create meaning. Invite each student to display his or her visual and explain its meaning to the class.

Before You Read

ELEVEN/ONCE

Make the Connection

I Can't Believe That Happened

We all have different opinions about what is embarrassing. With a group, make a list of embarrassing situations you've faced, seen on television, or read about in a story. Then, rank each situation on a scale from 1 to 4, 1 being slightly embarrassing and 4 being "crawl-under-a-rock" embarrassing.

Quickwrite

Jot down answers to the following questions:

- What do you do when you're embarrassed?
- How do you try to avoid being embarrassed?

go.hrw.com
LE0 6-5

Elements of Literature

Point of View: The First-Person Narrator

This story lets us get into the mind of a girl on her eleventh birthday. The story is told from the **first-person point of view:** The narrator is a character in the story who speaks as "I." In a story told in the first person, we learn a great deal about the narrator's thoughts and feelings. We don't learn what other people are thinking and feeling, however. We know only what the narrator tells us.

Reading Skills and Strategies

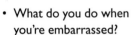

Making Inferences: Guessing Games

An **inference** is a kind of guess. When you **make inferences** as you read, you look for clues; then you guess what will happen next and what it all means. Base your inferences on your own experiences, and combine that information with clues you find in the story. (This is one guessing game you can't lose, because you're an expert at being eleven.)

A story told from the **first-person point of view** is told by a character who refers to himself or herself as "I."

For more on Point of View, see the Handbook of Literary Terms.

Background

"Eleven" appears here both in English, the language in which Sandra Cisneros writes, and in Spanish, the language she learned from her parents.

If you know Spanish, compare the translation with the original as you read. If you don't, look for words in the Spanish version that remind you of English words you know (such as *necesites*, *mamá*, and *plástico*). As a Spanish speaker could tell you, the word *once* is pronounced "ôn'sā" and means "eleven."

ELEVEN / ONCE 327

OBJECTIVES

1. Read and interpret the short story
2. Identify first-person point of view
3. Make inferences
4. Express understanding through writing, art, or performance
5. Identify and use punctuation in dialogue
6. Understand the rule for adding suffixes to words ending in silent e

SKILLS

Literary
- Identify first-person point of view

Reading
- Make inferences

Writing
- Collect ideas for a persuasive essay
- Make a birthday card
- Rewrite the story using another first-person narrator

Speaking/Listening
- Create a role-play

Grammar
- Identify and use punctuation in dialogue

Spelling
- Add suffixes to words ending in silent e

Viewing/Representing
- Discuss how a painting relates to a short story (ATE)

Planning

- **Block Schedule**
  Block Scheduling Lesson Plans with Pacing Guide
- **Traditional Schedule**
  Lesson Plans Including Strategies for English-Language Learners
- **One-Stop Planner**
  CD-ROM with Test Generator

  Resources: Print and Media

Reading
- *Graphic Organizers for Active Reading,* p. 26
- *Spelling and Decoding*
  Worksheet, p. 17

Writing and Language
- *Daily Oral Grammar*
  Transparency 19
- *Grammar and Language Links*
  Worksheet, p. 35
- *Language Workshop CD-ROM*

Assessment
- *Formal Assessment,* p. 68
- *Portfolio Management System,* p. 148
- *Standardized Test Preparation,* p. 52
- *Test Generator (One-Stop Planner CD-ROM)*

Internet
- go.hrw.com (keyword: LE0 6-5)

Summary ▪ ▪

This realistic first-person story is told by Rachel on her eleventh birthday. It's a confusing time for Rachel, and the day grows even worse when her teacher, Mrs. Price, insists that an ugly red sweater she has found must belong to Rachel. Although Rachel protests, Mrs. Price insists that Rachel wear the sweater. In agony, Rachel dons the hated sweater and begins weeping, but soon after, another girl remembers that the sweater is hers. Although Mrs. Price tries to gloss over the situation, Rachel's birthday has been spoiled by the injustice. (The story also appears in Spanish.)

Ⓐ Reading Skills and Strategies

Making Inferences

❓ Based on the speaker's description of getting older, how do you think she feels about turning eleven? [Possible responses: She is worried about her approaching birthday and maturing. She is also concerned that she won't feel any older.]

Ⓑ Elements of Literature

First-Person Point of View

❓ Why do you think the narrator uses the pronoun "you" at the beginning of the story? [The first-person narrator is speaking directly to us, the readers. The use of "you" draws us into the story.]

Eleven

Sandra Cisneros

When you wake up on your eleventh birthday you expect to feel eleven, but you don't.

Ⓐ What they don't understand about birthdays and what they never tell you is that when you're eleven, you're also ten, and nine, and eight, and seven, and six, and five, and four, and three, and two, and one. And when you wake up on your eleventh birthday you expect to feel eleven, but you don't. You open your eyes and everything's just like yesterday, only it's today. And you don't feel eleven at all. You feel like you're still ten. And you are—underneath the year that makes you eleven.

Like some days you might say something stupid, and that's the part of you that's still ten. Or maybe some days you might need to sit on your mama's lap because you're scared, and that's the part of you that's five. And maybe one day when you're all grown up maybe you will need to cry like if you're three, and that's okay. That's what I tell Mama when she's sad and needs to cry. Maybe she's feeling three.

Because the way you grow old is kind of like an onion or like the rings inside a tree trunk or like my little wooden dolls that fit one inside the other, each year inside the next one. That's how being eleven years old is.

Ⓑ You don't feel eleven. Not right away. It takes a few days, weeks even, sometimes even months before you say Eleven when they ask you. And you don't feel smart eleven, not until you're almost twelve. That's the way it is.

Only today I wish I didn't have only eleven years rattling inside me like pennies in a tin Band-Aid box. Today I wish I was one hundred and two instead of eleven because if I was one hundred and two I'd have known

328 JUSTICE FOR ALL

Reaching All Students

Struggling Readers

Students may have trouble realizing that most of the story takes place inside a young girl's mind. Use the strategy Story Impressions to help students. Before reading the story, give students the following list of words: *eleven, birthday, embarrassed, teacher, sweater*. Have them get into groups and write down what they think this story will be about, based on those words.

For more information on the Story Impressions strategy, see p. 101 in the *Reading Strategies Handbook*.

English Language Learners

Have students create a word map that describes the narrator. Students should write "Rachel" in the middle of a piece of paper. Read the first page aloud, and have students jot down words

that describe Rachel, such as "eleven" and "scared." As students read, have them add more words that describe Rachel's character, feelings, and appearance. For additional strategies to supplement instruction for these students, see
- *Lesson Plans Including Strategies for English-Language Learners*

Girl Seated at Table by Rosa Ibarra.

what to say when Mrs. Price put the red sweater on my desk. I would've known how to tell her it wasn't mine instead of just sitting there with that look on my face and nothing coming out of my mouth.

"Whose is this?" Mrs. Price says, and she holds the red sweater up in the air for all the class to see. "Whose? It's been sitting in the coatroom for a month."

"Not mine," says everybody. "Not me."

"It has to belong to somebody," Mrs. Price keeps saying, but nobody can remember. It's an ugly sweater with red plastic buttons and a collar and sleeves all stretched out like you could use it for a jump-rope. It's maybe a thousand years old and even if it belonged to me I wouldn't say so.

Maybe because I'm skinny, maybe because

she doesn't like me, that stupid Sylvia Saldívar says, "I think it belongs to Rachel." An ugly sweater like that, all raggedy and old, but Mrs. Price believes her. Mrs. Price takes the sweater and puts it right on my desk, but when I open my mouth nothing comes out.

"That's not, I don't, you're not . . . Not mine," I finally say in a little voice that was maybe me when I was four.

"Of course it's yours," Mrs. Price says. "I remember you wearing it once." Because she's older and the teacher, she's right and I'm not.

Not mine, not mine, not mine, but Mrs. Price is already turning to page thirty-two, and math problem number four. I don't know why but all of a sudden I'm feeling sick inside, like the part of me that's three wants to come out of my eyes, only I squeeze them

ELEVEN 329

RESPONDING TO THE ART

About the Artist. The Puerto Rican artist **Rosa Ibarra** often uses her children as models. Her paintings concentrate on the human figure and employ strong colors. Ibarra uses a style called *impasto,* in which the paint is applied to the canvas in thick layers, producing an almost sculptural effect.

Activity. Ask students to point out how color is used to reflect the image of the narrator as she is portrayed in the story. Urge them to find examples in the story to support their opinions about the use of color.

C English Language Learners
Compound Words
Point out that a *coatroom* is a closet in which coats are kept. Students can figure this out by dividing the word into its two parts, *coat* and *room.*

D Reading Skills and Strategies

Making Inferences
❓ Why doesn't Rachel assert herself and refuse to accept the sweater? [Possible responses: She is frightened of Mrs. Price; she doesn't want to make a fool of herself in front of the class.]

Using Students' Strengths

Kinesthetic Learners
Invite students to pantomime Rachel's response to putting on the red sweater. Have students use the description of the event as a guide to the emotion they should be expressing. After each pantomime, have the class explain what emotion they saw and which aspects of nonverbal communication and body language they used to make their inferences.

Logical/Mathematical Learners
Have students make graphic organizers based on the narrator's image of wooden dolls nested inside one another. Students can start by drawing an outline of Rachel at eleven and then, on the inside, drawing smaller and smaller outlines of her at the ages she mentions in the story. Students should label the large outline "11" and the smaller outlines "10," "5," "4," and "3," respectively. Then have students write quotations from the story inside the appropriate outlines.

A Struggling Readers
Using Context Clues
❓ What does Mrs. Price mean when she tells Rachel that "that's enough"? [She means that Rachel should stop being upset about the sweater and pushing it off her desk.]

B Reading Skills and Strategies
Making Inferences
❓ Why does Rachel wish that she were invisible? [She wants to escape from Mrs. Price's insensitive treatment; she is embarrassed to be seen crying.]

C Critical Thinking
Speculating
❓ Why does Mrs. Price pretend that nothing is wrong? [Possible responses: She might feel embarrassed or guilty; she might still think that the sweater belongs to Rachel; she might want to continue with the lesson.]

D Elements of Literature
First-Person Point of View
Ask: "What details about her experience does the narrator not describe?" [She doesn't say why the teacher was cruel or why her classmate said the sweater was hers. She does not explain why she does not speak out or refuse to put on the sweater.] Note how the first-person narrative focuses us completely on Rachel's thoughts and feelings. A Choices activity asks students to imagine how this story would change if the teacher were the narrator. They should also imagine how the story would change if it were told by an omniscient narrator, someone who is not in the story but who can tell us all about every character in the story.

shut tight and bite down on my teeth real hard and try to remember today I am eleven, eleven. Mama is making a cake for me for tonight, and when Papa comes home everybody will sing Happy birthday, happy birthday to you.

But when the sick feeling goes away and I open my eyes, the red sweater's still sitting there like a big red mountain. I move the red sweater to the corner of my desk with my ruler. I move my pencil and books and eraser as far from it as possible. I even move my chair a little to the right. Not mine, not mine, not mine.

In my head I'm thinking how long till lunchtime, how long till I can take the red sweater and throw it over the schoolyard fence, or leave it hanging on a parking meter, or bunch it up into a little ball and toss it in the alley. Except when math period ends Mrs. Price says loud and in front of everybody, "Now, Rachel, that's enough," because she sees I've shoved the red sweater to the tippy-tip corner of my desk and it's hanging all over the edge like a waterfall, but I don't care.

"Rachel," Mrs. Price says. She says it like she's getting mad. "You put that sweater on right now and no more nonsense."

"But it's not——"

"Now!" Mrs. Price says.

This is when I wish I wasn't eleven, because all the years inside of me—ten, nine, eight, seven, six, five, four, three, two, and one—are pushing at the back of my eyes when I put one arm through one sleeve of the sweater that smells like cottage cheese, and then the other arm through the other and stand there with my arms apart like if the

sweater hurts me and it does, all itchy and full of germs that aren't even mine.

That's when everything I've been holding in since this morning, since when Mrs. Price put the sweater on my desk, finally lets go, and all of a sudden I'm crying in front of everybody. I wish I was invisible but I'm not. I'm eleven and it's my birthday today and I'm crying like I'm three in front of everybody. I put my head down on the desk and bury my face in my stupid clown-sweater arms. My face all hot and spit coming out of my mouth because I can't stop the little animal noises from coming out of me, until there aren't any more tears left in my eyes, and it's just my body shaking like when you have the hiccups and my whole head hurts like when you drink milk too fast.

But the worst part is right before the bell rings for lunch. That stupid Phyllis Lopez, who is even dumber than Sylvia Saldívar, says she remembers the red sweater is hers! I take it off right away and give it to her, only Mrs. Price pretends like everything's okay.

Today I'm eleven. There's a cake Mama's making for tonight, and when Papa comes home from work we'll eat it. There'll be candles and presents and everybody will sing Happy birthday, happy birthday to you, Rachel, only it's too late.

I'm eleven today. I'm eleven, ten, nine, eight, seven, six, five, four, three, two, and one, but I wish I was one hundred and two. I wish I was anything but eleven, because I want today to be far away already, far away like a runaway balloon, like a tiny *o* in the sky, so tiny-tiny you have to close your eyes to see it.

Skill Link

Decoding: Compound Words
Remind students that a compound word is a word formed by combining two words. Most compounds are written as one word, but a compound can also be written with a hyphen or as two words.

Compounds that are adjectives or verbs, such as *top-heavy*, usually use hyphens. Hyphens are also used in compounds that might be confusing if written as one word, such as *get-together*. Explain that there are two ways to distinguish a compound word from two words that are used together. One is stress. In a compound, one of the component words usually has reduced stress. Compare *may be* and *maybe* in this sentence: *I may be there tomorrow, but maybe I'll just stay home.* The other way is meaning. A compound word takes on a new meaning that is somewhat different from the meaning of the two parts, as shown by *brainstorm, ghostwriter,* and *couch potato.*

Activities
Have students work with partners on the following activities:
1. Find examples in the selection of compound words that are written as one word, as a hyphenated word, and as two words.
2. List compound words that are recent additions to English, such as *mousepad*.

Once

Sandra Cisneros
translated by Liliana Valenzuela

Lo que no entienden acerca de los cumpleaños y lo que nunca te dicen es que cuando tienes once, también tienes diez, y nueve, y ocho, y siete, y seis, y cinco, y cuatro, y tres, y dos, y uno. Y cuando te despiertas el día que cumples once años esperas sentirte once, pero no te sientes. Abres tus ojos y todo es tal como ayer, sólo que es hoy. Y no te sientes como si tuvieras once para nada. Todavía te sientes como si tuvieras diez. Y sí los tienes—debajo del año que te vuelve once.

Como algunos días puede que digas algo estúpido, y ésa es la parte de tí que todavía tiene diez. O tal vez algunos días necesites sentarte en el regazo de tu mamá porque tienes miedo, y ésa es la parte de tí que tiene cinco. Y tal vez un día cuando ya eres grande tal vez necesitas llorar como si tuvieras tres, y está bien. Eso es lo que le digo a Mamá cuando está triste y necesita llorar. Tal vez se siente como si tuviera tres.

Porque el modo como uno se hace viejo es un poco como una cebolla o los anillos adentro de un tronco de árbol o como mis muñequitas de madera que embonan una adentro de la otra, cada año adentro del siguiente. Así es como es tener once años.

No te sientes once. No luego luego. Tarda varios días, hasta semanas, a veces hasta meses antes de que dices Once cuando te preguntan. Y no te sientes inteligente once, no hasta que casi ya tienes doce. Así es.

Sólo que hoy quisiera no tener tan sólo once años repiqueteando adentro de mí como centavitos en una caja de Curitas. Hoy quisiera tener ciento dos años en lugar de once porque si tuviera ciento dos hubiera sabido qué decir cuando la Srita. Price puso el suéter rojo sobre mi escritorio. Hubiera sabido cómo decirle que no era mío en lugar de quedarme sentada ahí con esa cara y con nada saliendo de mi boca.

"¿De quién es esto?" dice la Srita. Price, y levanta el suéter arriba en el aire para que toda la clase lo vea. "¿De quién? Ha estado metido en el ropero durante un mes."

"Mío no," dice todo el mundo. "Mío no."

"Tiene que ser de alguien," la Srita. Price sigue diciendo, pero nadie se puede acordar. Es un suéter feo con botones de plástico rojos y un cuello y unas mangas todas estiradas como si lo pudieras usar para una cuerda de saltar. Tal vez tiene mil años y aún si fuera mío no lo diría.

Tal vez porque soy flaquita, tal vez porque

Teaching the Translation

Sandra Cisneros writes in English. As you see, the story has been translated into Spanish by Liliana Valenzuela. Your approach to this story in Spanish will depend, of course, on the makeup of your classroom.

If you have students who are Spanish speakers, you can use the story for oral reading. You might assign several students to share the narrator's part and assign other students to take the speaking roles of Mrs. Price and the students.

Spanish-speaking students might also try their hands at translating Cisneros's text into Spanish. Or they could evaluate Liliana Valenzuela's translation.

The story can provide a rich opportunity for all students to examine a single text told in two languages. The two versions will also give them an opportunity to find similarities and differences in the texts. Here are some questions you might ask the class:
1. How is the title pronounced in Spanish? [(ōn'sā)] Ask Spanish speakers: What word in English is also spelled o-n-c-e, and how is it pronounced?
2. Where can they find the numbers eleven to one in Spanish? [in the first paragraph] Do any of the Spanish numbers resemble English words? [Look at *siete, seis, tres,* and *uno.*]
3. How do Spanish speakers say "birthday"? What does the Spanish word literally mean? [*Cumpleaños* literally means "He or she completes years."]
4. What is the Spanish word for "cake"? [*pastel*]
5. How do Spanish speakers say "Happy birthday"? [*Feliz cumpleaños.*]
6. What is the Spanish word for "sweater"? [*suéter*] Does it sound like the English word?

Taking a Second Look

Review: Summarizing
Remind students that when they summarize a text, they create a short restatement of a story's main events or of an essay's essential ideas. Discuss with the class how a summary provides a complete picture of a text using only a few words. Point out that the best summaries are complete but concise. A summary of a narrative, such as "Eleven," includes the main events and shows cause and effect. Be sure students understand that a summary is shorter than the original text and written in their own words.

Activities
1. Have students summarize the key events in "Eleven." Be sure they indicate the effects of the teacher's insistence that Rachel wear the sweater.
2. Have students summarize the author's biography on p. 333.
3. Ask students to list three ways that summarizing is important in the reading process. Help them see how stopping to summarize main ideas or key events can help them understand and remember the text. It can also help them pinpoint portions of the text that might be unclear.

7. How did the translator deal with phrases like "tippy-tip corner of my desk" [*"la orillita de mi escritorio"*] and "tiny-tiny" [*"chiquitita chiquitita"*] in the last line?

8. Have students skim the story to find Spanish words that resemble English words. Using a good dictionary, they can figure out which words come from a common source.

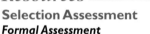

FROM THE EDITOR'S DESK

We were the first to publish several of Cisneros's short stories in school literature anthologies—in fact, we published some of her stories before they appeared anywhere else. The wonderful stories that came to us in manuscript were "Eleven," "Three Wise Guys," and "Salvador Late or Early."

Resources

Selection Assessment
Formal Assessment
• Selection Test, p. 68
Test Generator
• Selection Test

no le caigo bien, esa estúpida de Sylvia Saldívar dice, "Creo que es de Raquel." Un suéter feo como ése, todo raído y viejo, pero la Srita. Price le cree. La Srita. Price agarra el suéter y lo pone justo en mi escritorio, pero cuando abro la boca no sale nada.

"Ese no es, yo no, tú no estás . . . No es mío," digo por fin con una vocecita que tal vez era yo cuando tenía cuatro.

"Claro que es tuyo," dice la Srita. Price. "Me acuerdo que lo usaste una vez." Porque ella es más grande y la maestra, tiene la razón y yo no.

No es mío, no es mío, no es mío, pero la Srita. Price ya está pasando a la página treinta y dos, y al problema de matemáticas número cuatro. No sé por qué pero de repente me siento enferma adentro, como si la parte de mí que tiene tres quisiera salir por mis ojos, sólo que los aprieto duro y muerdo con mis dientes bien duro y me trato de acordar que hoy tengo once, once. Mamá me está haciendo un pastel para hoy en la noche, y cuando Papá venga a casa todos van a cantar Feliz Cumpleaños, feliz cumpleaños a tí.

Pero cuando el mareo se me pasa y abro los ojos, el suéter rojo todavía está ahí parado como una montañota roja. Muevo el suéter rojo para la esquina de mi escritorio con mi regla. Muevo mi lápiz y libros y goma tan lejos de él como sea posible. Hasta muevo mi silla un poquito a la derecha. No es mío, no es mío, no es mío.

En mi cabeza estoy pensado cuándo falta para el recreo, cuánto falta hasta que pueda agarrar el suéter rojo y tirarlo por encima de la barda de la escuela, o dejarlo ahí colgado sobre un parquímetro, o hacerlo bolita y aventarlo en el callejón. Excepto que cuando acaba la clase de mate la Srita. Price dice fuerte y enfrente de todos, "Vamos, Raquel,

ya basta," porque ve que empujé el suéter rojo hasta la orillita de mi escritorio y está colgado sobre la orilla como una cascada, pero no me importa.

"Raquel," dice la Srita. Price. Lo dice como si se estuviera enojando. "Ponte ese suéter inmediatamente y déjate de tonterías."

"Pero no es——"

"¡Ahora mismo!" dice la Srita. Price.

Es cuando quisiera no tener once, porque todos los años dentro de mí—diez, nueve, ocho, siete, seis, cinco, cuatro, tres, dos, y uno—están empujando por detrás de mis ojos cuando pongo un brazo por una manga del suéter que huele a requesón, y luego el otro brazo a través de la otra y me paro con mis brazos separados como si el suéter me hiciera daño y sí, todo sarnoso y lleno de gérmenes que ni siquiera son míos.

Ahí es cuando todo lo que he estado guardando dentro desde esta mañana, desde cuando la Srita. Price puso el suéter en mi escritorio, por fin sale, y de repente estoy llorando enfrente de todo mundo. Quisiera ser invisible pero no lo soy. Tengo once y hoy es mi cumpleaños y estoy llorando como si tuviera tres enfrente de todos. Pongo mi cabeza sobre el escritorio y entierro mi cara en mis brazos estúpidos de suéter de payaso. Mi cara toda caliente y la baba saliéndose de mi boca porque no puedo parar los ruiditos de animal que salen de mí, hasta que ya no quedan lágrimas en mis ojos, y sólo está mi cuerpo temblando como cuando tienes hipo, y toda la cabeza me duele como cuando bebes leche demasiado aprisa.

Pero lo peor sucede justo antes de que suene la campana para el recreo. Esa estúpida Phyllis López, que es todavía más tonta que Sylvia Saldívar, ¡dice que se acuerda que el suéter rojo es de ella! Me lo quito inme-

Making the Connections

Connecting to the Theme: "Justice for All"
After students have read the story, talk about the collection theme. Divide the class into groups to decide how the story is connected to the theme "Justice for All." Do they think Rachel is treated unjustly? Is Mrs. Price being deliberately unjust, or is she merely insensitive to Rachel's feelings? Be sure to compare Rachel with Margot in "All Summer in a Day." [Both girls are very sensitive and suffer for it.]

diatamente y se lo doy a ella, sólo que la Srita. Price hace de cuenta como si no pasara nada.

Hoy tengo once años. Hay un pastel que Mamá está haciendo para hoy, y cuando Papá llegue a casa del trabajo nos lo comeremos. Va a haber velitas y regalos y todos van a cantar Feliz Cumpleaños, feliz cumpleaños a tí, Raquel, sólo que ya es demasiado tarde.

Hoy tengo once años. Tengo once, diez, nueve, ocho, siete, seis, cinco, cuatro, tres, dos, y uno, pero quisiera tener ciento dos. Quisiera tener cualquier cosa menos once, porque hoy quiero estar ya lejos, lejos como un globo que se escapó, como una pequeña *o* en el cielo, tan chiquitita chiquitita que tienes que cerrar los ojos para verla.

MEET THE WRITER

"Inside I'm Eleven"

Sandra Cisneros (1954–) was born in Chicago and grew up speaking Spanish and English. Although she sometimes had a hard time in school, she eventually became a teacher and a highly acclaimed writer. Her childhood experiences, her family, and her Mexican American heritage all find a place in her writing.

In much of her writing, Cisneros explores the feeling of being shy and out of place.

66 What would my teachers say if they knew I was a writer? Who would've guessed it? I wasn't a very bright student. I didn't much like school because we moved so much and I was always new and funny-looking. . . . At home I was fine, but at school I never opened my mouth except when the teacher called on me, the first

time I'd speak all day.

When I think how I see myself, I would have to be at age eleven. I know I'm older on the outside, but inside I'm eleven. I'm the girl in the picture with skinny arms and a crumpled shirt and crooked hair. I didn't like school because all they saw was the outside of me. 99

Sandra Cisneros Inside Out

Another memorable Cisneros character narrates the novel *The House on Mango Street* (Random House). Esperanza is a young girl who wishes for a lot of things in her life, including a new name. She would like to be called Zeze the X.

ELEVEN / ONCE 333

Assessing Learning

MAKING MEANINGS

First Thoughts

1. Some students might have insisted that the sweater wasn't theirs and refused to put it on; others might have asked friends for help in revealing the truth. Be sure students understand what Rachel reveals about herself when she puts on the despised sweater. (She feels four years old; she sees the teacher as older and therefore right. She is shy and has little self-esteem.)

Shaping Interpretations

2. Rachel means that we often still feel the way we did when we were very young. She means we are the sum of our experiences.

3. Mrs. Price assumes that Rachel would own an ugly red sweater and not admit it.

4. Students can infer that Rachel is sensitive and cannot overcome this unpleasant incident. The humiliation over the sweater has ruined her birthday.

Connecting with the Text

5. Some students would feel bad for Rachel; others might think she is overreacting. Some might not understand why she is upset. Answers about helping Rachel will vary. Some students might say they would have explained to the teacher that she had hurt Rachel's feelings because the sweater did not belong to Rachel; others would have done nothing because they would not have felt it was their place to intercede.

6. Some students would feel ashamed that the teacher thought they owned such an old, smelly sweater, but everyone would feel embarrassed about crying in class.

7. Since birthdays are emotional days for most people, many students might find their day ruined by an incident like this. Most people want to feel special and loved on their birthday.

Challenging the Text

8. The image of the nesting dolls is very effective because a doll is an image of a person; the metaphors of tree rings and an onion are also highly compelling because they suggest layers of experience hidden from the outside world.

MAKING MEANINGS

First Thoughts

[respond]

1. If you were Rachel, what would you have done when Mrs. Price said "You put that sweater on right now"? Be sure to look back at the notes you made for the Quickwrite on page 327.

Shaping Interpretations

[interpret]
2. What does Rachel mean when she says "when you're eleven, you're also ten, and nine" and so on (page 328)?

[interpret]
3. What assumptions does Mrs. Price seem to make about Rachel?

[infer]
4. What **inference** can you make about the kind of person Rachel is when she says "everybody will sing Happy birthday . . . , only it's too late" (page 330)?

Connecting with the Text

[connect]
5. How did you react to the scene where Rachel begins to cry in class (page 330)? If you had been in her class, would you have done anything? Why or why not?

[apply]
6. Would you be embarrassed if you were in Rachel's situation? Look back at the list you made before you read the story. Which situations do you find the most embarrassing?

[evaluate]
7. Do you think an incident like the one described in this story would ruin your birthday celebration? Explain why or why not.

Challenging the Text

[evaluate]
8. Think about the different **images** and **metaphors** that Cisneros uses to describe getting older—rings on a tree, layers of an onion, pennies in a Band-Aid box, wooden dolls fitting inside one another. Which do you think are the most interesting or accurate descriptions of growing up? Do you think any of these images are not effective?

Reading Check

With a small group of your classmates, do these activities to review the story together:

a. At the beginning of the story, Rachel says that you're acting younger than eleven when you do certain things. Make a list of the things she mentions.

b. Rachel compares growing older to three objects. Make sketches of the ones you remember.

c. Briefly describe what happens to Rachel after Mrs. Price asks "Whose is this?"

Reading Check

a. Rachel includes saying stupid things, sitting on your mother's lap, and crying.

b. Student sketches should show nesting dolls, layers in an onion, and rings in a tree.

c. Mrs. Price says the sweater is Rachel's and makes her put it on, even though Rachel does not claim the sweater and clearly does not want to wear it. Rachel's embarrassment is made worse when Phyllis Lopez remembers that the sweater is hers and claims it. Rachel takes off the sweater, but her day—her birthday, at that—has been ruined.

CHOICES: Building Your Portfolio

Writer's Notebook

1. Collecting Ideas for Supporting a Position

Rachel puts up with the injustice of having to wear the ugly red sweater because she can't convince Mrs. Price that it isn't hers. She takes a position but is unable to support it with reasons. Think about a difficult situation that you might face. Then, take a position and list some reasons supporting it.

> **Situation:**
> Big brother started smoking when he got to college.
> **Position:**
> Quit now!
> **Reasons:**
> —cancer
> —it smells
> —expensive

Creative Writing/Art

2. Happy Birthday to You!

Make a birthday card for Rachel with a special message in it. In your message, try to cheer her up. Then, share with Rachel what becoming or being eleven means to you. Illustrate the card with a picture that expresses your message.

Performance

3. Speak Your Piece

Imagine this: It's Rachel's twenty-first birthday. She is visiting her old school when she sees Mrs. Price. Ten years have passed since the sweater incident. Yet Rachel recalls every detail as she walks over to her old teacher. . . .

You take it from there.

With a partner, role-play for the class a conversation between Rachel and Mrs. Price. Is Rachel still upset about the incident? What does she say? Does her old teacher remember what happened? What explanation might Mrs. Price give for her actions?

Creative Writing

4. It All Depends on Your Point of View

"Eleven" is told from the **first-person point of view,** with Rachel as the narrator. She uses the words *I, me,* and *mine* as she tells about her humiliating experience with the red sweater. What would Mrs. Price say about the incident if she were the first-person narrator? How would another student in the class tell it? Rewrite the story, using another first-person narrator of your choice.

Rubrics for each Choices assignment appear on p. 148 in the *Portfolio Management System*.

CHOICES: Building Your Portfolio

1. Writer's Notebook Remind students to save their work. They may be able to use it later as a prewriting for the Writer's Workshop.

2. Creative Writing/Art Encourage students to compose their messages in rhymes. While the messages can be humorous or serious, they should all serve to cheer Rachel up on her eleventh birthday.

3. Performance Students should start by discussing how both Rachel and Mrs. Price might feel about the situation a decade later. Students can then use these ideas as a basis for their role-play.

4. Creative Writing Students can work in pairs to probe the other narrator's views on the incident. Students might also want to ask their parents or other adults for input to help them probe Mrs. Price's point of view.

Using Students' Strengths

Auditory/Musical Learners

In connection with Choice 2, have students work in groups of three or four to prepare singing telegrams to express their good wishes to Rachel. Students can write their own songs or fit their words to existing tunes. Invite each group to perform its song for the class.

Intrapersonal Learners

Have students write answers to the questions in Choice 3 before they develop and practice their role-playing. This will give students more time to consider the characters' possible feelings and reactions as they meet ten years later.

GRAMMAR LINK

Have students select a piece of writing from their portfolios that contains dialogue. Then direct them to use highlighters to color the punctuation marks in the dialogue. Have students exchange papers with a partner and check the punctuation for mistakes. To summarize the lesson, students can make posters with the rules for punctuating dialogue. Display the posters prominently to encourage students to use dialogue correctly in their writing.

Try It Out

Point out that many words other than *says* can be speaker tags, such as *shouts, asks, answers, thinks, interrupts, adds, observes,* and *reminds.* Urge students to look for these words as they proofread their writing.

SPELLING

Answers

1. making
2. moved
3. strangely
4. coming
5. grateful

Resources ———————

Grammar
• *Grammar and Language Links,* p. 35

Spelling
• *Spelling and Decoding,* p. 17

GRAMMAR LINK `MINI-LESSON`

Punctuating Dialogue

Follow these tips when you include dialogue in your own writing:

1. Put beginning and ending quotation marks around a **direct quotation**—a person's exact words.

   EXAMPLE **"Whose is this?"** says Mrs. Price.

2. A **speaker tag** is a phrase such as *he said* that identifies the speaker. When the speaker tag comes before a quotation, put a comma after the tag. If the speaker tag interrupts the quotation, put a comma before the tag and a comma or period after it.

   EXAMPLES Mrs. Price says**,** "Put it on now."

   "Rachel**,**" she says**,** "put it on now."

3. If a quotation comes before the speaker tag, insert a comma, question mark, or exclamation point before the ending quotation mark. Never use a period before the speaker tag.

   EXAMPLES "Whose sweater is this**?**" she asks.
   "Not mine**,**" says everybody.

4. Always begin a *new* quotation with a capital letter.

   EXAMPLE Mrs. Price says, "**P**ut it on now."

Language Handbook HELP

See Quotation Marks, pages 755-757.

Technology HELP

See Language Workshop CD-ROM. Key word entry: direct quotations.

Try It Out

➤ Find a piece of your own writing that contains dialogue. Proofread it for correct punctuation. If you make many mistakes punctuating dialogue, copy the example sentences on the left in your Writer's Notebook. Use them for quick reference when you're proofreading.

SPELLING `HOW TO OWN A WORD`

Language Handbook HELP

See Adding Suffixes, page 763.

How to Make Silent *E* Go Quietly

". . . I wish I didn't have only eleven years <u>rattling</u> inside me. . . ."

Before the word *rattle* was changed to *rattling,* it had a silent e on the end. In general, when you add a **suffix**, or ending, that begins with a vowel, knock off the silent e. Leave the silent e on when the suffix begins with a consonant, as in this example: "I felt <u>hopeless</u> about reaching an <u>agreement</u>." Try adding suffixes yourself:

1. "Mama is <u>make</u> + <u>ing</u> a cake for me for tonight. . . ."
2. I <u>move</u> + <u>ed</u> the sweater to the corner of my desk.
3. Mrs. Price asked me why I was acting so <u>strange</u> + <u>ly</u>.
4. ". . . I can't stop the little animal noises from <u>come</u> + <u>ing</u> out of me. . . ."
5. I'm so <u>grate</u> + <u>ful</u> to Mama for the birthday cake.

Grammar Link Quick Check

Have students revise the following dialogue by adding commas, end marks, and quotation marks where necessary.

1. I think the sweater belongs to Rachel said Sylvia ["I think the sweater belongs to Rachel," said Sylvia.]
2. That sweater Rachel said is too big for me ["That sweater," Rachel said, "is too big for me."]
3. Mrs. Price said Rachel stop crying [Mrs. Price said, "Rachel, stop crying."]
4. I can't Rachel answered I wish I could ["I can't," Rachel answered. "I wish I could."]
5. Rachel moaned My birthday is ruined [Rachel moaned, "My birthday is ruined."]

Reading Skills and Strategies

OBJECTIVES
1. Make and adjust predictions
2. Use a Prediction Trail to track predictions

MAKING AND ADJUSTING PREDICTIONS

What do you predict these two canine friends are about to do? Hard to tell? You don't have much information. What if you knew this:

- They have just spotted a rabbit. Now what do you predict?
- Someone is standing in front of them holding a tasty dog biscuit. Do you have a different prediction?

In life we are constantly making predictions and then adjusting them as we gain new information. We do the same thing when we read. We make **predictions** from the information we've been given and from our prior knowledge. When we get new information, we often make adjustments to these predictions.

The Prediction Trail

One way to chart your own process of making and adjusting predictions is to use a graphic like the trail below.

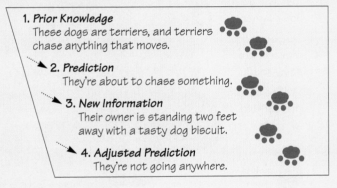

1. *Prior Knowledge*
   These dogs are terriers, and terriers chase anything that moves.

2. *Prediction*
   They're about to chase something.

3. *New Information*
   Their owner is standing two feet away with a tasty dog biscuit.

4. *Adjusted Prediction*
   They're not going anywhere.

Follow That Gold Cadillac

As you read "The Gold Cadillac," you'll find yourself making predictions and changing them. After you've finished, try making a prediction trail.

Apply the strategy on the next page.

Reading Skills and Strategies

This feature helps students learn to make predictions and then adjust their predictions as they receive new information. Students practice the skill by using a graphic organizer, the Prediction Trail, that allows them to track information as it unfolds.

Mini-Lesson:

Making and Adjusting Predictions
Have volunteers read aloud the text on p. 337. Be sure students understand the difference between the two bulleted questions. Then discuss the steps in the Prediction Trail. Ask volunteers to define and give examples of *prior knowledge* and *adjusted prediction*.

To help students apply the skill to reading, ask them to think of a story they have recently read. Did they make guesses about what would happen? If they did, what events in the story led them to make these predictions? Did the story turn out as they had thought it would? Then, with the students' participation, you might make a Prediction Trail based on a story the class has read, such as "All Summer in a Day," using the example below:

Passage in Text	"Margot stood alone."
First Prediction	[Her classmates will ignore her.]
First Outcome	They put her in a closet.
Second Prediction	[They will stand outside the closet and laugh at her.]
Second Outcome	They play in the sun and forget her.

Reaching All Students

Struggling Readers

Be sure students understand that all readers, at some time or other, make predictions that turn out to be "wrong." Students shouldn't be afraid to make predictions based on their own knowledge and experience and on evidence from the story—even if their guesses differ from the story's actual events. Many writers like to surprise their readers with endings that are impossible to predict, and many readers enjoy being surprised. Sometimes, too, the story clues are hard to find or confusing. Students might try making predictions with a partner or in small groups.

English Language Learners

Students may have difficulty with some of the vocabulary on p. 337. You may want to preteach the words *adjusting, predicting, canine, inference,* and *graphic*. Then have students find these words in their text and use context clues and visual clues to reinforce their meaning.

OBJECTIVES

1. Read and interpret the short story
2. Track predictions
3. Express understanding through writing, panel discussion, art, or research
4. Identify and use words with connotative power
5. Understand and use new words

SKILLS

Reading
- Track predictions

Writing
- Collect ideas for a persuasive essay
- Write a letter

Speaking/Listening
- Research information about the civil rights movement and hold a panel discussion

Art/Research
- Make a road map

Language
- Identify and use words with connotative power

Viewing/Representing
- Respond to a painting (ATE)
- Discuss how a painting relates to a short story (ATE)

Planning

- **Block Schedule**
  Block Scheduling Lesson Plans with Pacing Guide

- **Traditional Schedule**
  Lesson Plans Including Strategies for English-Language Learners

- **One-Stop Planner**
  CD-ROM with Test Generator

T338

Before You Read

THE GOLD CADILLAC

Make the Connection

Injustice for Some

Do the following scenarios seem to describe another world?

- separate drinking fountains for whites and African Americans
- restaurants in which African Americans are not allowed to eat
- restroom doors in gas stations with signs barring African Americans

They used to be a reality, right here in the United States. The civil rights movement of the 1950s and 1960s ended some forms of segregation, but the story you are about to read takes place before segregation was ended.

Quickwrite

Write down your thoughts on the scenes listed above. How do you feel about them? What would you do if segregation were a reality today?

Reading Skills and Strategies

Tracking Your Predictions

As you read this story, you'll notice little symbols in the text. When you see a symbol, turn back to this page and make a prediction based on the questions next to that symbol.

★ Do you predict the mother will be happy about the new car?

■ From what the uncle said, what do you predict will happen on the trip?

▲ What do you predict the policemen will do to 'lois's father?

◆ Do you predict they will keep going south?

● Will he keep the Cadillac?

 go.hrw.com
LEO 6-5

338 JUSTICE FOR ALL

Resources: Print and Media

Reading
- *Reading Skills and Strategies*
  Selection Skill Lesson, p. 67
- *Graphic Organizers for Active Reading*, p. 27
- *Words to Own*, p. 14
- *Audio CD Library*
  Disc 7, Track 3

Writing and Language
- *Daily Oral Grammar*
  Transparency 20

- *Grammar and Language Links*
  Worksheet, p. 37

Assessment
- *Formal Assessment*, p. 70
- *Portfolio Management System*, p. 149
- *Standardized Test Preparation*, pp. 54, 56
- *Test Generator (One-Stop Planner CD-ROM)*

Internet
- go.hrw.com (keyword: LE0 6-5)

The GOLD CADILLAC

Mildred D. Taylor

*"We got us
a Cadillac!"
Wilma and I
proclaimed in unison.*

My sister and I were playing out on the front lawn when the gold Cadillac rolled up and my father stepped from behind the wheel. We ran to him, our eyes filled with wonder. "Daddy, whose Cadillac?" I asked.

And Wilma demanded, "Where's our Mercury?"

My father grinned. "Go get your mother and I'll tell you all about it."

"Is it ours?" I cried. "Daddy, is it ours?"

THE GOLD CADILLAC 339

Summary ▪▪

The story takes place in the 1950s and is narrated by a young African American girl named 'lois. 'Lois's father loves the new gold Cadillac he has just bought, but her mother refuses to ride in it, since it was bought without her consent and with money intended for a house. The father decides to drive the car to Mississippi to visit his parents. 'Lois's mother agrees to go. The family gets as far as Memphis before a white police officer, believing that the grand car has been stolen, throws 'lois's father in jail. When he is released, the family, terrified of another encounter with the police, returns to Memphis and borrows a cousin's Chevy. The family spends a week in Mississippi, and 'lois questions her father about segregation laws that keep black people out of some restaurants and hotels. After returning home, the father sells the Cadillac and buys an old Ford. 'Lois never forgets the gold car and the fear and injustice her family faced in the South.

Resources

Listening
Audio CD Library
A recording of this short story is included in the *Audio CD Library:*
• Disc 7, Track 3

A Reading Skills and Strategies
Making Inferences
❓Why are the girls' eyes filled with wonder? [A Cadillac is an expensive luxury car. They can't believe the car belongs to them.]

B Struggling Readers
Using Context Clues
Explain that a *Mercury* is a make (or brand) of car. Students can infer this because the father is driving a Cadillac, not a Mercury.

Preteaching Vocabulary

Words to Own
Have students read the Words to Own and their definitions listed at the bottom of the selection pages. Ask students to identify something that is *evident* in the classroom. Ask them to name something they'd find in a *rural* setting. Ask what a *heedful* person might do at an intersection. Ask how *ignorance* might get someone in trouble.

Reaching All Students

Struggling Readers
Making Predictions was introduced on p. 338. For a lesson directly tied to this selection that teaches students to make predictions by using a strategy called Story Impressions, see the *Reading Skills and Strategies* binder:
• Selection Skill Lesson, p. 67

English Language Learners
You may have to explain that Cadillacs are costly luxury cars and that many people consider them symbols of wealth and status. Have students list some of today's status symbols, such as certain types of clothing and jewelry. These students also might be unaware of the discrimination that African Americans faced before the civil rights movement. Explain that racial segregation was a standard practice and a legal requirement in many southern states. For additional strategies to supplement instruction for these students, see
• *Lesson Plans Including Strategies for English-Language Learners*

A Reading Skills and Strategies

Tracking Your Predictions

❓ What clues might make you predict the mother will be happy about the new car? unhappy? [Her surprise indicates that she could be either pleased or displeased. Students might predict that she will be unhappy because her husband did not consult her about such an expensive purchase.]

B Critical Thinking

Analyzing

❓ Why do you think the mother reacts this way about the car? [Possible responses: She thinks the new car is far too expensive; she resents not being consulted before the purchase; she does not like ostentatious items like this.]

"Get your mother!" he laughed. "And tell her to hurry!"

Wilma and I ran off to obey, as Mr. Pondexter next door came from his house to see what this new Cadillac was all about. We threw open the front door, ran through the downstairs front parlor and straight through the house to the kitchen, where my mother was cooking and one of my aunts was helping her. "Come on, Mother-Dear!" we cried together. "Daddy say come on out and see this new car!"

A "What?" said my mother, her face showing her surprise. "What're you talking about?" ★

"A Cadillac!" I cried.

"He said hurry up!" relayed Wilma.

And then we took off again, up the back stairs to the second floor of the duplex. Running down the hall, we banged on all the apartment doors. My uncles and their wives stepped to the doors. It was good it was a Saturday morning. Everybody was home.

"We got us a Cadillac! We got us a Cadillac!" Wilma and I proclaimed in unison.[1] We had decided that the Cadillac had to be ours if our father was driving it and holding on to the keys. "Come on see!" Then we raced on, through the upstairs sunroom, down the front steps, through the downstairs sunroom, and out to the Cadillac. Mr. Pondexter was still there. Mr. LeRoy and Mr. Courtland from down the street were there too, and all were admiring the Cadillac as my father stood proudly by, pointing out the various features.

"Brand-new 1950 Coupe deVille!" I heard one of the men saying.

"Just off the showroom floor!" my father said. "I just couldn't resist it."

My sister and I eased up to the car and

1. **in unison:** speaking the same words at the same time.

peeked in. It was all gold inside. Gold leather seats. Gold carpeting. Gold dashboard. It was like no car we had owned before. It looked like a car for rich folks.

"Daddy, are we rich?" I asked. My father laughed.

"Daddy, it's ours, isn't it?" asked Wilma, who was older and more practical than I. She didn't intend to give her heart too quickly to something that wasn't hers.

"You like it?"

"Oh, Daddy, yes!"

He looked at me. "What 'bout you, 'lois?"

"Yes, sir!"

My father laughed again. "Then I expect I can't much disappoint my girls, can I? It's ours, all right!"

Wilma and I hugged our father with our joy. My uncles came from the house, and my aunts, carrying their babies, came out too. Everybody surrounded the car and owwed and ahhed. Nobody could believe it.

Then my mother came out.

B Everybody stood back grinning as she approached the car. There was no smile on her face. We all waited for her to speak. She stared at the car, then looked at my father, standing there as proud as he could be. Finally she said, "You didn't buy this car, did you, Wilbert?"

"Gotta admit I did. Couldn't resist it."

"But . . . but what about our Mercury? It was perfectly good!"

"Don't you like the Cadillac, Dee?"

"That Mercury wasn't even a year old!"

My father nodded. "And I'm sure whoever buys it is going to get themselves a good car. But we've got ourselves a better one. Now stop frowning, honey, and let's take ourselves a ride in our brand-new Cadillac!"

My mother shook her head. "I've got food

Professional Notes

In 1950, when the story takes place, the Cadillac was the undisputed luxury car. A Coupe de Ville cost a staggering $3,995, and a convertible $4,144. As the decade progressed, Cadillac continued to be the automotive trendsetter. The 1957 and 1958 Eldorados, for example, had special, unmistakable tail treatment, called *shark fins*. The cone-shaped tail lights mimicked the exhaust flame of a rocket.

By the 1970s, however, public taste shifted. The Arab oil embargo of 1973 made the Cadillac's huge engine unpopular. In addition, imports started to dent the domestic market as buyers began to realize they could get luxury cars from abroad. Cadillac came nose-to-nose with Germany's Mercedes-Benz.

on the stove," she said and, turning away, walked back to the house.

There was an awkward silence, and then my father said, "You know Dee never did much like surprises. Guess this here Cadillac was a bit too much for her. I best go smooth things out with her."

Everybody watched as he went after my mother. But when he came back, he was alone.

"Well, what she say?" asked one of my uncles.

My father shrugged and smiled. "Told me I bought this Cadillac alone, I could just ride in it alone."

Family No. 9 (1968) by Charles Alston.
Courtesy of Harry Henderson.

Another uncle laughed. "Uh-oh! Guess she told you!"

"Oh, she'll come around," said one of my aunts. "Any woman would be proud to ride in this car."

"That's what I'm banking on," said my father as he went around to the street side of the car and opened the door. "All right! Who's for a ride?"

"We are!" Wilma and I cried.

All three of my uncles and one of my aunts, still holding her baby, and Mr. Pondexter climbed in with us, and we took off for the first ride in the gold Cadillac. It was a glorious ride, and we drove all through the city of Toledo. We rode past the church and past the school. We rode through Ottawa Hills, where the rich folks lived, and on into Walbridge Park and past the zoo, then along the

Maumee River. But none of us had had enough of the car, so my father put the car on the road and we drove all the way to Detroit. We had plenty of family there, and everybody was just as pleased as could be about the Cadillac. My father told our Detroit relatives that he was in the doghouse with my mother about buying the Cadillac. My uncles told them she wouldn't ride in the car. All the Detroit family thought that was funny, and everybody, including my father, laughed about it and said my mother would come around.

It was early evening by the time we got back home, and I could see from my mother's face she had not come around. She was angry now not only about the car, but that we had been gone so long. I didn't understand that, since my father had called her as soon as we reached Detroit to let her know where we were. I had heard him myself. I didn't understand either why she did not like that fine Cadillac and thought she was being terribly disagreeable with my father. That night, as she tucked Wilma and me in bed, I told her that too.

"Is this your business?" she asked.

"Well, I just think you ought to be nice to Daddy. I think you ought to ride in that car with him! It'd sure make him happy."

"I think you ought to go to sleep," she said and turned out the light.

THE GOLD CADILLAC 341

C Critical Thinking

Analyzing

❓ Why does the narrator's father smile? [Possible response: He is embarrassed at having to admit that he angered his wife; he thinks what his wife said was funny.]

D English Language Learners

Idioms

Explain that someone is *in the doghouse* when he or she has done something wrong. Ask students to speculate on the origin of the idiom. [A dog might be confined to a doghouse as punishment.]

Using Students' Strengths

Verbal Learners

Have students work in small groups to create titles for the major sections of the story. For instance, the section of the story in which the narrator's mother refuses to ride in the Cadillac might be called "Mother-Dear Won't Ride." Students should divide the story into at least six parts. Have each group write its titles and then compare them with the titles written by other groups. Students should cite details to justify their choice of title.

Mathematical Learners

Have students research the costs of cars today and compare those figures with the prices of cars in 1950. This family is saving for a house; students might also research the prices of homes in Toledo, Ohio, today and compare them with 1950 prices. Suggest that they present their research in graphic form.

A Elements of Literature
Motivation
❓ Why is the mother angry that her husband bought the Cadillac? [They were saving money for a house.]

B Critical Thinking
Speculating
❓ Why would the father buy a Cadillac when he and his wife are saving for a house? [Possible responses: He thinks he can have both; he wants to appear wealthy for his family and friends; he has always wanted a luxury car and believes he deserves one.]

C Reading Skills and Strategies
Drawing Conclusions
❓ How would you describe the narrator's life, based on the details in this paragraph? [Possible responses: happy, interesting, fun, contented, prosperous, full of togetherness.]

Later I heard her arguing with my father. "We're supposed to be saving for a house!" she said.

"We've already got a house!" said my father.

"But you said you wanted a house in a better neighborhood. I thought that's what we both said!"

"I haven't changed my mind."

"Well, you have a mighty funny way of saving for it, then. Your brothers are saving for houses of their own, and you don't see them out buying new cars every year!"

"We'll still get the house, Dee. That's a promise!"

"Not with new Cadillacs we won't!" said my mother, and then she said a very loud good night, and all was quiet.

The next day was Sunday, and everybody figured that my mother would be sure to give in and ride in the Cadillac. After all, the family always went to church together on Sunday. But she didn't give in. What was worse, she wouldn't let Wilma and me ride in the Cadillac either. She took us each by the hand, walked past the Cadillac where my father stood waiting, and headed on toward the church three blocks away. I was really mad at her now. I had been looking forward to driving up to the church in that gold Cadillac and having everybody see.

On most Sunday afternoons during the summertime, my mother, my father, Wilma, and I would go for a ride. Sometimes we just rode around the city and visited friends and family. Sometimes we made short trips over to Chicago or Peoria or Detroit to see relatives there or to Cleveland, where we had relatives too, but we could also see the Cleveland Indians play. Sometimes we joined our aunts and uncles and drove in a

caravan[2] out to the park or to the beach. At the park or the beach, Wilma and I would run and play. My mother and my aunts would spread a picnic, and my father and my uncles would shine their cars.

But on this Sunday afternoon, my mother refused to ride anywhere. She told Wilma and me that we could go. So we left her alone in the big, empty house, and the family cars, led by the gold Cadillac, headed for the park. For a while I played and had a good time, but then I stopped playing and went to sit with my father. Despite his laughter he seemed sad to me. I think he was missing my mother as much as I was.

That evening, my father took my mother to dinner down at the corner cafe. They walked. Wilma and I stayed at the house, chasing fireflies in the back yard. My aunts and uncles sat in the yard and on the porch, talking and laughing about the day and watching us. It was a soft summer's evening, the kind that came every day and was expected. The smell of charcoal and of barbecue drifting from up the block, the sound of laughter and music and talk drifting from yard to yard were all a part of it. Soon one of my uncles joined Wilma and me in our chase of fireflies, and when my mother and father came home, we were at it still. My mother and father watched us for a while, while everybody else watched them to see if my father would take out the Cadillac and if my mother would slide in beside him to take a ride. But it soon became evident that the din-

2. **caravan:** group of cars traveling together.

WORDS TO OWN
evident (ev′ə·dənt) *adj.:* easily seen or understood; obvious.

Taking a Second Look

Review: Making Inferences

Remind students that an inference is an educated guess based on information in the text and on the reader's prior knowledge and experience. Explain to students that as they read, they are constantly having to make inferences about ideas and details that writers do not reveal directly. Be sure students understand that when they make inferences, they come to conclusions by reasoning from evidence that

may be only hinted at or implied. Remind them also that as they continue to read, they may revise their inferences.

Activities

1. Point out that when we make inferences about characters, we make intelligent guesses about what characters are like, what their feelings are, what their motivations are—all

based on evidence from the text. Ask students to make two inferences about the character of the narrator's father and mother.

2. Ask students to make inferences about the story's setting: What was life like for African Americans in the North and the South in the 1950s?

I was proud to say that car belonged to my family.

ner had not changed my mother's mind. She still refused to ride in the Cadillac. I just couldn't understand her objection to it.

Though my mother didn't like the Cadillac, everybody else in the neighborhood certainly did. That meant quite a few folks too, since we lived on a very busy block. On one corner was a grocery store, a cleaner's, and a gas station. Across the street was a beauty shop and a fish market, and down the street was a bar, another grocery store, the Dixie Theater, the cafe, and a drugstore. There were always people strolling to or from one of these places, and because our house was right in the middle of the block, just about everybody had to pass our house and the gold Cadillac. Sometimes people took in the Cadillac as they walked, their heads turning for a longer look as they passed. Then there were people who just outright stopped and took a good look before continuing on their way. I was proud to say that car belonged to my family. I felt mighty important as people called to me as I ran down the street. "'Ey, 'lois! How's that Cadillac, girl? Riding fine?" I told my mother how much everybody liked that car. She was not impressed and made no comment.

Since just about everybody on the block knew everybody else, most folks knew that my mother wouldn't ride in the Cadillac. Because of that, my father took a lot of good-natured kidding from the men. My mother got kidded too, as the women said if she didn't ride in that car, maybe some other woman would. And everybody laughed about it and began to bet on who would give in first, my mother or my father. But then my father said he was going to drive the car south into Mississippi to visit my grandparents, and everybody stopped laughing.

My uncles stopped.
So did my aunts.
Everybody. **D**

"Look here, Wilbert," said one of my uncles, "it's too dangerous. It's like putting a loaded gun to your head."

"I paid good money for that car," said my father. "That gives me a right to drive it where I please. Even down to Mississippi."

My uncles argued with him and tried to talk him out of driving the car south. So did my aunts, and so did the neighbors, Mr. LeRoy, Mr. Courtland, and Mr. Pondexter. They said it was a dangerous thing, a mighty dangerous thing, for a black man to drive an expensive car into the <u>rural</u> South.

"Not much those folks hate more'n to see a northern Negro coming down there in a fine car," said Mr. Pondexter. "They see those Ohio license plates, they'll figure you coming down uppity, trying to lord your fine car over them!"

I listened, but I didn't understand. I didn't understand why they didn't want my father **E** to drive that car south. It was his.

"Listen to Pondexter, Wilbert!" cried another uncle. "We might've fought a war to **F** free people overseas, but we're not free here!"

WORDS TO OWN
rural (roor'əl) *adj.*: having to do with country life.

D **Advanced Learners**
Style
? How would you read this passage aloud? What effect does the writer achieve with the two short, choppy sentences and the fragment "Everybody"? [Sample answer: I would read it slowly, haltingly. The short, choppy sentences and the fragment give the impression of stopping, just as the laughing stops. The style creates suspense.]

E **Elements of Literature**
Theme
? Why is the narrator confused about the reaction to her father's decision to drive south? [Possible response: She has not experienced racism or segregation, so she doesn't understand her family's concern.]

F **Historical Connections**
This comment refers to the fact that African Americans fought and died in World War II to free Europe and Asia from tyranny, but, ironically, they were still not free at home: Segregation laws were still in effect in many southern states. Most of these laws were abolished in Supreme Court rulings and federal legislation that included *Brown v. the Board of Education of Topeka* (1954), the Civil Rights Act of 1964, and the Voting Rights Act of 1965.

Skill Link

Style: Connotation
Use this activity before you teach the Language Link activity on page 355. It will help you assess students' understanding of the connotative power of words.

For each word on the following chart, have students circle + if the word has a positive connotation, circle – if the word has a negative connotation, or circle 0 if the word does not have any connotation.

Word	Connotation			
1. slender	+	–	0	[+]
2. scrawny	+	–	0	[–]
3. cheap	+	–	0	[–]
4. thrifty	+	–	0	[+]
5. house	+	–	0	[0]
6. home	+	–	0	[+]
7. abundant	+	–	0	[+]
8. meager	+	–	0	[–]
9. drudge	+	–	0	[–]
10. worker	+	–	0	[+]

(A) Man, those white folks down south'll lynch[3] you soon's look at you. You know that!" ■

Wilma and I looked at each other. Neither one of us knew what *lynch* meant, but the word sent a shiver through us. We held each other's hand.

(B) My father was silent, then he said: "All my life I've had to be <u>heedful</u> of what white folks thought. Well, I'm tired of that. I worked hard for everything I got. Got it honest, too. Now I got that Cadillac because I liked it and because it meant something to me that somebody like me from Mississippi could go and buy it. It's my car, I paid for it, and I'm driving it south."

(C) My mother, who had said nothing through all this, now stood. "Then the girls and I'll be going too," she said.

"No!" said my father.

My mother only looked at him and went off to the kitchen.

My father shook his head. It seemed he didn't want us to go. My uncles looked at each other, then at my father. "You set on doing this, we'll all go," they said. "That way we can watch out for each other." My father took a moment and nodded. Then my aunts got up and went off to their kitchens too.

All the next day, my aunts and my mother

3. **lynch:** kill a person without legal authority, usually by hanging. Lynchings are committed by mobs that have taken the law into their own hands.

cooked and the house was filled with delicious smells. They fried chicken and baked hams and cakes and sweet potato pies and mixed potato salad. They filled jugs with water and punch and coffee. Then they packed everything in huge picnic baskets, along with bread and boiled eggs, oranges and apples, plates and napkins, spoons and forks and cups. They placed all that food

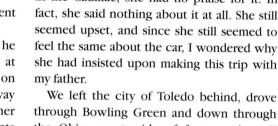

Open Road, from the series *Landscape of the Apocalypse* (1972) by Martin Hoffman. Acrylic on canvas (60" X 80").
Virginia Museum of Fine Arts, Richmond, Virginia. The Sydney and Frances Lewis Contemporary Art Fund. Photo: Ron Jennings. © 2000 Virginia Museum of Fine Arts.

on the back seats of the cars. It was like a grand, grand picnic we were going on, and Wilma and I were mighty excited. We could hardly wait to start.

My father, my mother, Wilma, and I got into the Cadillac. My uncles, my aunts, my cousins got into the Ford, the Buick, and the Chevrolet, and we rolled off in our caravan headed south. Though my mother was finally riding in the Cadillac, she had no praise for it. In fact, she said nothing about it at all. She still seemed upset, and since she still seemed to feel the same about the car, I wondered why she had insisted upon making this trip with my father.

We left the city of Toledo behind, drove through Bowling Green and down through the Ohio countryside of farms and small towns, through Dayton and Cincinnati, and across the Ohio River into Kentucky. On the

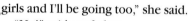

WORDS TO OWN

heedful (hēd′fəl) *adj.:* paying close attention to.

Crossing the Curriculum

Geography/Mathematics

Have students make two different maps tracking the route the narrator's family could take from Toledo through Dayton, Cincinnati, and Bowling Green, Kentucky. The first map should trace a scenic course; the second map, a more direct route. Then have students calculate the mileage for both routes and decide which one they would take if they were making this trip today. Have them explain their choice.

other side of the river, my father stopped the car and looked back at Wilma and me and said, "Now from here on, whenever we stop and there're white people around, I don't want either one of you to say a word. *Not one word!* Your mother and I'll do the talking. That understood?"

"Yes, sir," Wilma and I both said, though we didn't truly understand why.

My father nodded, looked at my mother, and started the car again. We rolled on, down Highway 25 and through the bluegrass hills of Kentucky. Soon we began to see signs. Signs that read: WHITE ONLY, COLORED NOT ALLOWED. Hours later, we left the Bluegrass State and crossed into Tennessee. Now we saw even more of the signs saying: WHITE ONLY, COLORED NOT ALLOWED. We saw the signs above water fountains and in restaurant windows. We saw them in ice cream parlors and at hamburger stands. We saw them in front of hotels and motels, and on the restroom doors of filling stations. I didn't like the signs. I felt as if I were in a foreign land.

I couldn't understand why the signs were there, and I asked my father what the signs meant. He said they meant we couldn't drink from the water fountains. He said they meant we couldn't stop to sleep in the motels. He said they meant we couldn't stop to eat in the restaurants. I looked at the grand picnic basket I had been enjoying so much. Now I understood why my mother had packed it. Suddenly the picnic did not seem so grand.

Finally we reached Memphis. We got there at a bad time. Traffic was heavy and we got separated from the rest of the family. We tried to find them but it was no use. We had to go on alone. We reached the Mississippi state line, and soon after, we heard a police siren. A police car came up behind us. My father slowed the Cadillac, then stopped. Two white policemen got out of their car. They eyeballed the Cadillac and told my father to get out. ▲

"Whose car is this, boy?" they asked.

I saw anger in my father's eyes. "It's mine," he said.

"You're a liar," said one of the policemen. "You stole this car."

"Turn around, put your hands on top of that car, and spread-eagle," said the other policeman.

My father did as he was told. They searched him and I didn't understand why. I didn't understand either why they had called my father a liar and didn't believe that the Cadillac was his. I wanted to ask, but I remembered my father's warning not to say a word, and I obeyed that warning.

The policemen told my father to get in the back of the police car. My father did. One policeman got back into the police car. The other policeman slid behind the wheel of our Cadillac. The police car started off. The Cadillac followed. Wilma and I looked at each other and at our mother. We didn't know what to think. We were scared.

The Cadillac followed the police car into a small town and stopped in front of the police station. The policeman stepped out of our Cadillac and took the keys. The other policeman took my father into the police station.

"Mother-Dear!" Wilma and I cried. "What're they going to do to our daddy? They going to hurt him?"

"He'll be all right," said my mother. "He'll be all right." But she didn't sound so sure of that. She seemed worried.

We waited. More than three hours we waited. Finally my father came out of the

D Historical Connections

During the first half of the twentieth century, racial segregation, either overt or covert, was common in most aspects of American life. In the South, "separate but equal" facilities for blacks and whites became the norm. It was not until the 1954 Supreme Court ruling in *Brown v. Board of Education* that the doctrine of "separate but equal" regarding segregated schools was overturned. Nonetheless, change was slow. Three years after the Brown decision, then-President Eisenhower had to use federal troops to escort African American students into a "white" school in Little Rock, Arkansas. Some segregation laws (called Jim Crow laws) continued in effect into the 1960s.

E Elements of Literature
Irony

❓ Why does the narrator's mother pack the picnic? [Ironically, the mother packs the picnic basket not because the family is going on a pleasant outing, but because they will not be allowed in restaurants in the South because of their color.]

F Reading Skills and Strategies

Tracking Your Predictions

❓ How do you predict the policemen will react to 'lois's father? [Possible responses: They will be angry that he is driving such a grand car; they will think he stole the car; they will want to arrest him.]

G Vocabulary Note
Connotations

It is an insult for the policeman to call the father "boy."

H Critical Thinking
Analysis

❓ Why does the mother say that the father will be all right, even though she is clearly worried? [She wants to reassure the children.]

Getting Students Involved

Cooperative Learning

Students can create a "found poem" with words and phrases from "The Gold Cadillac." After students have read the story, divide the class into groups of four students each. Have each group skim the story to find eight vivid words and phrases. Next, have each group select its top four phrases. Then have one reader from each group read one phrase aloud at a time. Continue around the room without stopping until all the phrases have been read.

B ⬤ **Reading Skills and Strategies**
Identifying Cause and Effect

❓ Why doesn't the family go to a hotel instead of pulling over into a grove of trees? [Hotels are restricted to "whites only."]

LITERATURE AND SOCIAL STUDIES

Point out to students that in 1910, only one in ten African Americans lived outside the South. During both World War I and World War II, however, tens of thousands of African Americans left the South for other regions. For example, in just ten years, from 1940 to 1950, the number of African Americans in the western states more than tripled. Today, more than half of all African Americans live in the North. However, many African Americans living in the North maintain strong ties with the South through relatives who still live there.

Resources

Assessment
• Standardized Test Preparation, p. 54

---

police station. We had lots of questions to ask him. He said the police had given him a ticket for speeding and locked him up. But then the judge had come. My father had paid the ticket and they had let him go.

He started the Cadillac and drove slowly out of the town, below the speed limit. The police car followed us. People standing on steps and sitting on porches and in front of stores stared at us as we passed. Finally we were out of the town. The police car still followed. Dusk was falling. The night grew black, and finally the police car turned around and left us.

We drove and drove. But my father was tired now and my grandparents' farm was still far away. My father said he had to get some sleep, and since my mother didn't drive, he pulled into a grove of trees at the side of the road and stopped.

"I'll keep watch," said my mother.

"Wake me if you see anybody," said my father.

"Just rest," said my mother.

So my father slept. But that bothered me. I needed him awake. I was afraid of the dark and of the woods and of whatever lurked there. My father was the one who kept us

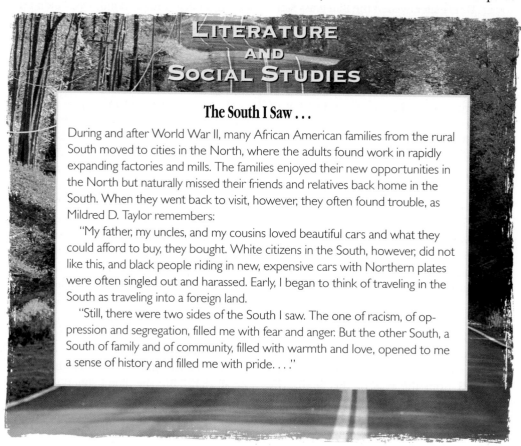

LITERATURE AND SOCIAL STUDIES

The South I Saw . . .

During and after World War II, many African American families from the rural South moved to cities in the North, where the adults found work in rapidly expanding factories and mills. The families enjoyed their new opportunities in the North but naturally missed their friends and relatives back home in the South. When they went back to visit, however, they often found trouble, as Mildred D. Taylor remembers:

"My father, my uncles, and my cousins loved beautiful cars and what they could afford to buy, they bought. White citizens in the South, however, did not like this, and black people riding in new, expensive cars with Northern plates were often singled out and harassed. Early, I began to think of traveling in the South as traveling into a foreign land.

"Still, there were two sides of the South I saw. The one of racism, of oppression and segregation, filled me with fear and anger. But the other South, a South of family and of community, filled with warmth and love, opened to me a sense of history and filled me with pride. . . ."

Professional Notes

After the Civil War, the Thirteenth, Fourteenth, and Fifteenth Amendments to the Constitution abolished slavery and made the recently freed slaves citizens. However, after a period of change in the South known as Reconstruction came to an end in 1877, the states of the old Confederacy passed laws to deny African Americans their freedom. These came to be known as "Jim Crow" laws from the name of a character in minstrel shows insulting to African Americans. Jim Crow laws enforced racial segregation in schools, restaurants, parks, and transportation, among many other places. Most Jim Crow laws were abolished in 1964 with the passage of the Civil Rights Act, which prohibited discrimination based on race, color, religion, or national origin. Change came slowly, however, especially with regard to segregated schools, which were outlawed in 1954. In the early 1970s, fewer than half the South's schools had been desegregated.

In the North and West, many black students also attended segregated schools. These schools were considered unconstitutional only where they could be proved to have originated in unlawful state action. To achieve integration, children were often transported on school buses to various schools. The explosive issue of "busing" was resolved in 1974 by the Supreme Court.

safe, he and my uncles. But already the police had taken my father away from us once today, and my uncles were lost.

"Go to sleep, baby," said my mother. "Go to sleep."

But I was afraid to sleep until my father woke. I had to help my mother keep watch. I figured I had to help protect us too, in case the police came back and tried to take my father away again. There was a long, sharp knife in the picnic basket, and I took hold of it, clutching it tightly in my hand. Ready to strike, I sat there in the back of the car, eyes wide, searching the blackness outside the Cadillac. Wilma, for a while, searched the night too, then she fell asleep. I didn't want to sleep, but soon I found I couldn't help myself as an unwelcome drowsiness came over me. I had an uneasy sleep, and when I woke, it was dawn and my father was gently shaking me. I woke with a start and my hand went up, but the knife wasn't there. My mother had it.

My father took my hand. "Why were you holding the knife, 'lois?" he asked.

I looked at him and at my mother. "I—I was scared," I said.

My father was thoughtful. "No need to be scared now, sugar," he said. "Daddy's here and so is Mother-Dear." ◆

Then after a glance at my mother, he got out of the car, walked to the road, looked down it one way, then the other. When he came back and started the motor, he turned the Cadillac north, not south.

"What're you doing?" asked my mother.

"Heading back to Memphis," said my father. "Cousin Halton's there. We'll leave the Cadillac and get his car. Driving this car any farther south with you and the girls in the car, it's just not worth the risk."

And so that's what we did. Instead of driving through Mississippi in golden splendor, we traveled its streets and roads and highways in Cousin Halton's solid, yet not so splendid, four-year-old Chevy. When we reached my grandparents' farm, my uncles and aunts were already there. Everybody was glad to see us. They had been worried. They asked about the Cadillac. My father told them what had happened, and they nodded and said he had done the best thing.

We stayed one week in Mississippi. During that week I often saw my father, looking deep in thought, walk off alone across the family land. I saw my mother watching him. One day I ran after my father, took his hand, and walked the land with him. I asked him all the questions that were on my mind. I asked him why the policemen had treated him the way they had and why people didn't want us to eat in the restaurants or drink from the water fountains or sleep in the hotels. I told him I just didn't understand all that.

My father looked at me and said that it all was a difficult thing to understand and he didn't really understand it himself. He said it all had to do with the fact that black people had once been forced to be slaves. He said it had to do with our skins being colored. He said it had to do with stupidity and ignorance. He said it had to do with the law, the law that said we could be treated like this here in the South. And for that matter, he added, any other place in these United States where folks thought the same as so many folks did here in the South. But he also said, "I'm hoping one day though we can drive that

---

WORDS TO OWN
ignorance (igʹnər·əns) n.: lack of knowledge.

THE GOLD CADILLAC 347

C **Reading Skills and Strategies**

Tracking Your Predictions

❓ Do you predict that the family will keep going south? What are your clues? [The father's determination suggests they will continue south, but his recognition of his child's terror suggests he will place his family's safety first and turn around.]

D **Elements of Literature**
Character

❓ What does the father's decision to turn back and switch cars reveal about his character? [He places his family and their safety first. His love for them and his desire to keep them safe is more important to him than his pride in driving a beautiful car.]

E **Struggling Readers**
Figures of Speech

Explain that the phrase "golden splendor" means driving in the gold Cadillac. It might suggest driving in a golden carriage or even the sun itself.

Using Students' Strengths

Interpersonal Learners
After the family's experience in Mississippi, 'lois is so terrified of further trouble that she sleeps with a knife. Have students role-play scenes in which they explain the situation to 'lois and reassure her that she will be safe. Students can draw information from the text and supplement it by using their own experiences with fear and injustice. After each group presents its scene, have the class decide which approaches were most effective in calming the child's fear and why.

Verbal Learners
On August 28, 1963, the Rev. Dr. Martin Luther King, Jr., delivered his famous "I Have a Dream" speech as the keynote address at the March on Washington for Jobs and Freedom. Speaking from the steps of the Lincoln Memorial, Dr. King called for justice for all Americans. Ask students to obtain a copy of the speech and deliver an excerpt from it to the class. The speech can be found on the Internet and in books about the March on Washington.

long road down here and there won't be any signs. I'm hoping one day the police won't stop us just because of the color of our skins and we're riding in a gold Cadillac with northern plates."

When the week ended, we said a sad goodbye to my grandparents and all the Mississippi family and headed in a caravan back toward Memphis. In Memphis, we returned Cousin Halton's car and got our Cadillac. Once we were home, my father put the Cadillac in the garage and didn't drive it. I didn't hear my mother say any more about the Cadillac. I didn't hear my father speak of it either. ●

Some days passed, and then on a bright Saturday afternoon while Wilma and I were playing in the back yard, I saw my father go into the garage. He opened the garage doors

wide so the sunshine streamed in and began to shine the Cadillac. I saw my mother at the kitchen window staring out across the yard at my father. For a long time, she stood there watching my father shine his car. Then she came out and crossed the yard to the garage, and I heard her say, "Wilbert, you keep the car."

He looked at her as if he had not heard.

"You keep it," she repeated and turned and walked back to the house.

My father watched her until the back door had shut behind her. Then he went on shining the car and soon began to sing. About an hour later he got into the car and drove away. That evening when he came back, he was walking. The Cadillac was nowhere in sight.

"Daddy, where's our new Cadillac?" I demanded to know. So did Wilma.

Meet the Writer
Weaving Memories into Fiction

Mildred D. Taylor (1943–   ) tells about the memories behind "The Gold Cadillac":

66 For a few years when I was a child, I lived in a big house on a busy street with my mother, my father, my sister, and many aunts and uncles and cousins. We were originally a Mississippi family who had migrated to the industrial North during and after World War II. My father was the first of the family to go to the North and that was when I was only three weeks old. When I was three months old, my mother, my older sister, and I followed. A year after our arrival, my parents bought the big house on the busy street. During the next nine years, aunts and uncles and cousins from both sides of the family arrived yearly from Mississippi and stayed in that big house with us

Making the Connections

Connecting to the Theme: "Justice for All"
After students have read the story, talk about the collection theme. Ask the class what motivates the police to treat the narrator's father so unjustly. Then have students work in small groups to decide if they agree with the father's decision to sell the Cadillac.

He smiled and put his hand on my head. "Sold it," he said as my mother came into the room.

"But how come?" I asked. "We poor now?"

"No, sugar. We've got more money towards our new house now, and we're all together. I figure that makes us about the richest folks in the world." He smiled at my mother, and she smiled too and came into his arms.

After that, we drove around in an old 1930s Model A Ford my father had. He said he'd factory-ordered us another Mercury, this time with my mother's approval. Despite that, most folks on the block figured we had fallen on hard times after such a splashy showing of good times, and some folks even laughed at us as the Ford rattled around the city. I must admit that at first I

was pretty much embarrassed to be riding around in that old Ford after the splendor of the Cadillac. But my father said to hold my head high. We and the family knew the truth. As fine as the Cadillac had been, he said, it had pulled us apart for a while. Now, as ragged and noisy as that old Ford was, we all rode in it together, and we were a family again. So I held my head high.

Still, though, I thought often of that Cadillac. We had had the Cadillac only a little more than a month, but I wouldn't soon forget its splendor or how I'd felt riding around inside it. I wouldn't soon forget either the ride we had taken south in it. I wouldn't soon forget the signs, the policemen, or my fear. I would remember that ride and the gold Cadillac all my life.

until they had earned enough to rent another place or buy houses of their own.

I loved those years. There were always cousins to play with. There was always an aunt or uncle to talk to when my parents were busy, and there seemed always to be fun things to do and plenty of people to do them with. On the weekends the whole houseful of family often did things together. Because my father, my uncles, and my older male cousins all loved cars, we often rode in caravan out to the park where the men would park their cars in a long, impressive row and shine them in the shade of the trees while the women spread a picnic and chatted, and my sister, younger cousins, and I ran and played. Sometimes we traveled to

nearby cities to watch a baseball game. And sometimes we took even longer trips, down country highways into the land called the South.

I have many good memories of those years, including the year my father brought home a brand-new Cadillac. I also have memories of those years that long troubled me. I have woven some of those memories into this story of fiction called 'The Gold Cadillac.' **99**

More Memories Woven into Fiction

To explore Taylor's writing, read *Song of the Trees* (Dial) and *Roll of Thunder, Hear My Cry* (Puffin), winner of the Newbery Medal for distinguished American literature for children.

THE GOLD CADILLAC **349**

D **Reading Skills and Strategies**
Making Inferences
? What other reasons might the narrator's father have for selling the Cadillac? [Possible responses: He wants to please his wife; he has decided there are better ways to express his pride.]

E **Elements of Literature**
Theme
? What has the narrator learned from the experience she relates? [Possible responses: She has learned that family unity is more important than the judgment of outsiders; that racism can threaten her family; and that the world can be an unfair place.]

Resources
Formal Assessment
• Selection Test, p. 70
Test Generator
• Selection Test

BROWSING IN THE FILES

About the Author. Mildred Taylor comes from a long line of storytellers, and her work is influenced by their oral tradition. "I wanted to include the teachings of my own childhood," she says of her work, "the values and principles upon which I and so many other black children were reared. I wanted to show a family united by love and self-respect, as parents strong and sensitive attempted to guide their children successfully, without harming their spirits, through the hazardous maze of living in a discriminatory society. I wanted to show happy, loved children, about whom other children of all colors, or of all cultures, could say, 'I really like them, I feel what they feel.'"

Assessing Learning

Check Test: Short Answers
1. How does the narrator's mother feel about the new car? [She disapproves of it.]
2. What state is the family from, and what state are they traveling to? [They live in Ohio and are traveling to Mississippi.]
3. Where do the police think the father got the car? [They think he stole it.]
4. What does the father do with the Cadillac at the end of the story? [He sells it.]
5. Whom does the father call "the richest folks in the world"? [his family]

Observation Assessment: Reading
As you watch students read silently, use the following criteria for informal assessment:
1. Students look back at the work.
2. Students pause to think while reading.
3. Students consult a source, such as a dictionary or glossary, for clarification.

Standardized Test Preparation
For practice with standardized test format specific to this selection, see
• *Standardized Test Preparation*, p. 56
For practice in proofreading and editing, see
• *Daily Oral Grammar*, Transparency 20

Connections

In this interview, Rosa Parks tells the story behind her refusal to give up her seat on a bus in Montgomery, Alabama, in 1955. Her decision to confront the injustices of American society had major ramifications, both for herself and her country.

Ⓐ Critical Thinking

Making Connections

❓ Which of the narrator's experiences in "The Cadillac" might explain why Rosa Parks would not feel free? [Possible responses: seeing the hateful "Whites Only, Colored Not Allowed" signs; seeing her father taken away by the police on a trumped-up charge.]

Ⓑ English Language Learners

Using Context Clues

Men's alterations means "altering men's suits to make them fit." Rosa Parks was a tailor in a department store.

Ⓒ Struggling Readers

Idioms

When the driver tells Rosa Parks and the black man sitting with her, "Y'all make it light on yourselves," he means that he thinks it would be easier for them to just give up their seats.

Speaking and Listening: Distinguishing Fact and Opinion

Rosa Parks states facts and opinions in her interview. Remind students that a fact can be proved true and that an opinion cannot be supported with evidence. Ask students to explain what facts Rosa Parks cites to demonstrate social injustice in the 1950s. Then, ask them to suggest places where they can **verify** these facts (for example, an encyclopedia or a history book). Finally, ask students to find one or two opinions that Parks expresses in the interview.

Connections — AN INTERVIEW

I Was Not Alone

An interview with Rosa Parks by Brian Lanker from *I Dream a World*

When Rosa Parks refused to give up her seat on a Montgomery, Alabama, bus in 1955, her silent defiance spoke for a whole people. Her arrest sparked a 381-day bus boycott,[1] which ignited the civil rights movement and changed America. Fired from her tailoring job, she moved to Detroit, Michigan, where she was a special assistant to Congressman John Conyers for twenty-five years. She is the founder and president of the Rosa and Raymond Parks Institute for Self-Development, inaugurated[2] in 1988.

As far back as I can remember, being black in Montgomery we were well aware of the inequality of our way of life. I hated it all the time. I didn't feel that, in order to have some freedom, I should have to leave one part of the United States and go to another part of the same country just because one was South and one was North.

My mother believed in freedom and equality even though we didn't know it for reality during our life in Alabama.

In some stores, if a woman wanted to go in to try a hat, they wouldn't be permitted to try it on unless they knew they were going to buy it, or they put a bag on the inside of it. In the shoe stores they had this long row of seats, and all of those in the front could be vacant, but if one of us would go in to buy, they'd always take you to the last one, to the back of the store. There were no black salespersons.

At the Montgomery Fair [a department store] I did men's alterations. Beginning in December coming up to the Christmas holiday, the work was a bit heavy. When I left the store that evening, I was tired, but I was tired every day. I had planned to get an electric heating pad so I could put some heat to my shoulder and my back and neck. After I stepped up on the bus, I noticed this driver as the same one who had evicted me from another bus way back in 1943.

Just back of the whites there was a black man next to one vacant seat. So I sat down with him. A few white people boarded the bus and they found seats except this one man. That is when the bus driver looked at us and asked us to let him have those seats. After he saw we weren't moving immediately, he said, "Y'all make it light on yourselves and let me have those seats."

When he saw that I was still remaining in the seat, the driver said, "If you don't stand up, I'm going to call the police and have you arrested." I said, "You may do that."

1. **boycott:** act of joining together and refusing to deal with a company for political reasons.
2. **inaugurated:** formally begun.

Listening to Music

"We Shall Overcome" and "This Little Light" (Traditional), performed by Joan Baez

Just as African American slaves often sang the religious songs known as spirituals to make coded protests against slavery, so, too, did the champions of civil rights in the 1950s and 1960s make use of religious songs to express a social message. Among the two most famous examples are "We Shall Overcome," a turn-of-the-century Baptist hymn that became something of an anthem for the civil rights movement, and "This Little Light," another traditional hymn turned freedom song. Both songs were recorded by gospel and other choral groups associated with the civil rights movement and by folk-rock singers of the 1960s; both were widely sung at the era's civil rights marches.

Activity

After students have read the selections in this cluster, play the two songs, and explain that both were popular in the civil rights movement of the mid-twentieth century. Then have students work in small groups to write and perform a dramatic scene, based on the selections, in which one of the songs figures in the events or background.

D **Reading Skills and Strategies**
Responding to the Text
? How would you feel if you were in the police officer's position? Why?
[Possible responses: Students might feel angry that they had to enforce an unjust law and upset that Rosa Parks was not being treated fairly. Some students might say that the policeman was just doing his job, enforcing the law, and had no sense of injustice.]

E **Cultural Connections**
A *test case* is one intended to test a law and set a legal precedent. Rosa Parks hoped that if she could win the right to sit where she wanted on the bus, then all African Americans would have the same right.

Mrs. Rosa Parks, forty-three, sits in the front of a city bus as a Supreme Court ruling that banned segregation on the city's public transit system takes effect.

Two policemen came and wanted to know what was the trouble. One said, "Why don't you stand up?" I said, "I don't think I should have to." At that point I asked the policemen, "Why do you push us around?" He said, "I don't know, but the law is the law and you're under arrest." **D**

The decision was made by the three of us, my husband, my mother, and me, that I would go on and use my case as a test case, challenging segregation on the buses. **E**

When I woke up the next morning and realized I had to go to work and it was pouring down rain, the first thing I thought about was the fact that I never would ride a segregated bus again. That was my decision for me and not necessarily for anybody else.

People just stayed off the buses because I

(continued on next page)

Connecting Across Texts

Connecting with "The Gold Cadillac"
In "The Gold Cadillac," the narrator and her family are treated unjustly when they travel to Mississippi in their beautiful gold Cadillac. Police officers insult and harass the narrator's father, jail him on a false charge, and follow the family to the city limits to make sure they really leave. In "I Was Not Alone," Rosa Parks defies the injustice of the Jim Crow laws when she refuses to give up her seat on a Montgomery bus. Have students work in small groups to brainstorm ways that people can fight injustice. When the groups are finished working, list all their ideas on the board. Then discuss the advantages and disadvantages of each method. You might want to extend the discussion to people like Mahatma Gandhi, Nelson Mandela, and Aung San Suu Kyi, the Burmese freedom fighter and winner of the Nobel Peace Prize in 1991.

A Struggling Readers

Summarizing

❓ How did other African Americans in Montgomery aid the boycott? [They stayed off the buses, gave people rides, and held mass meetings. Black cab companies charged bus fare instead of the higher cab fare.]

B Critical Thinking

Speculating

❓ Why would some whites say that what Rosa Parks did freed them, too? [Possible answers: They did not think that segregation was right either; they no longer had to feel guilty about the way people were treated under segregation; they felt no one is free if everyone isn't free.]

C Elements of Literature

Character

❓ Why does Rosa Parks say she must continue the struggle? [Despite the success of the bus boycott and the subsequent passage of the Civil Rights Act of 1964, discrimination still exists. Rosa Parks realizes that the battle isn't over until all discrimination has been abolished.]

D Reading Skills and Strategies

Comparing and Contrasting

❓ How does Rosa Parks view segregation? [She sees it as an extension of slavery.]

---

was arrested, not because I asked them. If everybody else had been happy and doing well, my arrest wouldn't have made any difference at all.

The one thing I appreciated was the fact that when so many others, by the hundreds and by the thousands, joined in, there was a kind of lifting of a burden from me individually. I could feel that whatever my individual desires were to be free, I was not alone. There were many others who felt the same way.

A The first thing that happened after the people stayed off was the black cab companies were willing to just charge bus fare instead of charging cab fare. Others who had any kind of car at all would give people rides. They had quite a transportation system set up. Mass meetings were keeping the morale up. They were singing and praying and raising money in the collection to buy gasoline or tires.

There was a lot of humor in it, too. Somebody told a story about a [white] husband who had fired the family cook because she refused to ride the bus to work. When his wife came home, she said, "If you don't go get her, you better be on your way." Some white people who were not wanting to be deprived of their domestic help[3] would just go themselves and pick up the people who were working for them.

The officials really became furious when they saw that the rain and bad weather or distance or any other problem didn't matter.

B Many whites, even white Southerners, told me that even though it may have seemed like the blacks were being freed, they felt more free and at ease themselves. They thought

3. **domestic help:** household servants: cooks, maids, or drivers.

that my action didn't just free blacks but them also.

Some have suffered much more than I did. Some have even lost their lives. I just escaped some of the physical—maybe not all—but some of the physical pain. And the pain still remains. From back as far as I can remember.

When people made up their minds that they wanted to be free and took action, then there was a change. But they couldn't rest on just that change. It was to continue.

C It just doesn't seem that an older person like I am should still have to be in the struggle, but if I have to be in it then I have no choice but to keep on.

I've been dreaming, looking, for as far back as I had any thought, of what it should be like to be a human being. My desires were to be free as soon as I had learned that there had been slavery of human beings and that I was a descendant from them. If there was a D proclamation[4] setting those who were slaves free, I thought they should be indeed free and not have any type of slavery put upon us.

4. **proclamation:** official announcement.

Rosa Parks at the annual NAACP Image Awards, Pasadena, California, 1997.

Assessing Learning

Check Test: Short Answers

1. What kind of work did Rosa Parks do in Montgomery? [men's alterations; tailoring]
2. What was Rosa Parks arrested for? [refusing to give up a seat on a bus to a white rider]
3. What was the purpose of the bus boycott Rosa Parks started? [to integrate the buses]
4. How did African American cab companies help the boycott? [They charged bus fare, not cab fare.]
5. Why did Rosa Parks say she was not alone? [Many people agreed with her and helped her.]

Self-Assessment: Reading

Have students use the following criteria to assess their reading. They might rate themselves on each item: 1 = rarely; 2 = sometimes; 3 = very often.

1. I can isolate key details in a passage.
2. I can vary my reading rate as needed.
3. I can use context clues to define unfamiliar words and expressions.
4. I can summarize the selection.
5. I can identify the main idea or theme.

MAKING MEANINGS

First Thoughts

[respond]
1. Do you think selling the Cadillac is the right thing to do? Why or why not?

Shaping Interpretations

[interpret]
2. What do you think the gold Cadillac stands for in the eyes of Wilbert and his neighbors?

[interpret]
3. How can you tell that 'lois's parents love each other even though they disagree about the car?

[interpret]
4. How do you think the journey south changes 'lois? How does her father change?

[interpret]
5. Near the end of the story, 'lois thinks her family might be poor. What does her father mean when he says they may be "the richest folks in the world"?

Connecting with the Text

[apply]

6. Have you ever met with an injustice that changed your view of the world? Describe your experience and how you felt about it. How do those feelings compare with the feelings you described in your notes for the Quickwrite on page 338?

[evaluate]

7. Go back to the **predictions** you made as you read. Draw a trail showing your predictions and the adjustments you made to those predictions (see page 337).

Extending the Text

[synthesize]
8. What have this story and "I Was Not Alone" (see *Connections* on page 350) shown you about deciding when to stand up for your rights and when to compromise?

[evaluate]
9. Do you think that what happens to 'lois's father in the 1950s could happen in the United States today? Why or why not?

Reading Check
a. She thinks it is a waste of money that could be better spent on a new house.
b. They admire it very much.
c. They are afraid of violence against them.
d. They accuse him of stealing the Cadillac.
e. He sells the Cadillac to please his wife and to put aside the money toward a new house.

MAKING MEANINGS

First Thoughts

1. Some students may say it is better to save money for a house; others may argue that the Cadillac represents pride and self-respect and so should be kept.

Shaping Interpretations

2. The car represents success, pride, self-respect, status, and overcoming discrimination.
3. 'lois's parents try to overcome their disagreements. They treat each other with respect and are not afraid to change their opinions to adjust to each other's vision and values. In the end, they hold each other in their arms.
4. She understands the obstacles her parents have overcome and the battles she will have to fight. Her father now is more interested in having his family safe and together than in showing off his prosperity.
5. He means that the family is rich because they have each other.

Connecting with the Text

6. Students may have been treated unfairly by a classmate, friend, relative, or teacher. *Students should not say anything that would make them uncomfortable. As an alternative, allow them to describe injustice experienced by someone else.*
7. Students can track their predictions on a chart like this:

Clue	Prediction	Outcome

Extending the Text

8. "The Gold Cadillac" shows that you should compromise when your family might be harmed by defiance. "I Was Not Alone" shows that justice can be achieved through protest and unity.
9. While the racist signs have been taken down and there are now laws against discrimination, what happened to 'lois's father in the 1950s can and does happen today because some people are motivated by ignorance and hate.

CHOICES: Building Your Portfolio

1. **Writer's Notebook** Remind students to save their work. They may use it as prewriting for the Writer's Workshop on pp. 396–400.
2. **Writing a Letter** Help students use the correct style for a business letter by referring them to the model in the Communications Handbook (p. 691). Point out the heading, inside address, salutation, body, closing, and signature. Students can answer the prewriting questions alone or with partners. Be sure students are courteous in their remarks to the writer.
3. **Research/Panel Discussion** As students begin their research, encourage them to consult a print or on-line encyclopedia for an overview of their topic. For more in-depth information, students can consult *The Civil Rights Movement in America* by Patricia and Frederick McKissack.
4. **Art/Research** Be sure students start by establishing a scale and a compass rose so that their maps are accurate. Students may wish to check their work by using a computerized map-maker, such as TripMaker.

CHOICES: Building Your Portfolio

Writer's Notebook

1. Collecting Ideas for Supporting a Position

Some people spend a lifetime fighting for a cause, such as racial equality. Think of one or two issues that *you* really care about. Try to come up with issues that other people care about as well. Write a sentence identifying each issue and stating your opinion on it. Then, give one or two reasons supporting your position.

> —Kids should not be banned from the mall on Saturday nights.
>
> —Boys and girls should be taught in separate classrooms.

Writing a Letter

2. Dear Author

Write a letter to Mildred Taylor expressing your opinions and feelings about her story. To help organize your thoughts, you might want to answer these questions:

- Was the story believable?
- Did what happened to the family make you feel uncomfortable, or did it make you feel something completely different?
- Do you have any questions you would like the author to answer?

Research/ Panel Discussion

3. Journey Toward Equality

The civil rights movement ended much of the discrimination of the kind that 'lois and her family faced on their car trip. With a group of classmates, research one of these topics: the Jim Crow laws; *Brown v. Board of Education of Topeka, Kansas;* Dr. Martin Luther King, Jr., and the 1955 Montgomery bus boycott; the Civil Rights Act of 1964. Write down some facts about your topic. Then, present a panel discussion for the rest of the class.

Art/Research

4. Road Map

Make a road map showing the route the family took on their trip south. Check the text to find where the trip started and ended. Also, be sure you know the places the family passed through and stopped at. Illustrate your map, showing some details of the trip. Look at the illustrated map on page 137 for ideas. If you are not sure of any parts of the route, make the best decisions you can using the information in the text.

Systematic Word Study Across Content Areas and in Current Events

After students have completed the vocabulary activity on using glossaries and dictionaries (see p. 647), encourage them to create their own vocabulary logs of words they discover in newspapers, in magazines, and on-line. Students may want to compile specialized logs for specific content areas, such as science and social studies, with words they encounter while reading about current events.

Entries should include a pronunciation and a definition of each word and a sentence that uses the word correctly. Recommend that students add fifteen words a week to their logs, and encourage them to share their entries with the class. Consider keeping your own log as a model for the class.

LANGUAGE LINK

Style: Connotations

Handbook of Literary Terms
HELP

See Connotation.

Connotations are the feelings and associations that have come to be attached to certain words. For example, the narrator's father might have called the gold Cadillac *dazzling*, but her mother might have said it was *showy*. Both words suggest that the car looked great, but one word has a positive connotation (*dazzling*) while the other has a negative connotation (*showy*); their effects are therefore very different.

Think about why Mildred D. Taylor used *proclaimed* in this sentence: "'We got us a Cadillac!' Wilma and I <u>proclaimed</u> in unison."

The writer could have used *declared* or *announced*. Both of those words also mean "made known publicly." *Proclaimed* emphasizes the greatness of the new car, however. It makes us think of an orator proclaiming ideas in a speech or a president proclaiming the end of a war.

Think of the different feelings and associations attached to the following words, all of which mean more or less the same thing:

fragrance   scent   smell   odor   stink

Try It Out

Discuss the connotations of the underlined word in each of these sentences from the story. List other words that have roughly similar meanings but more positive or more negative connotations.

1. "There were always people <u>strolling</u> to or from one of these places. . . ."

2. "I was afraid of the dark and of the woods and of whatever <u>lurked</u> there."

A tip for writers: A **thesaurus** can help you replace a dull word with a **synonym** (a word with the same meaning) that has the connotations you want. Use the thesaurus sparingly, though—don't hide your natural style behind a wall of "thesaurus words."

VOCABULARY   HOW TO OWN A WORD

WORD BANK
evident
rural
heedful
ignorance

Talk About It

Be sure you can support your answers to these questions.

1. Is it <u>evident</u> to you that some Americans still discriminate against others on the basis of race?
2. What are some of the pros and cons of living in a <u>rural</u> area?
3. Should the narrator's father have been <u>heedful</u> when his relatives begged him not to drive south?
4. Is <u>ignorance</u> the chief cause of prejudice?

LANGUAGE LINK

Have students select a piece of writing from their portfolios and choose key words in it. Then have them list synonyms for each important word they identified and decide if any of the synonyms improve their papers.

Try It Out

1. *strolling* (positive); *walking* (neutral); *wandering* (somewhat negative); *patrolling* (negative)
2. *lurked* (negative); *hid* (less negative); *lay* (neutral); *was* (neutral)

VOCABULARY

Possible Answers

1. Yes; for example, Mexican immigrants are looked down on in many places.
2. Pro: The country offers peace and quiet, away from the frantic pace of the city. Con: In the country, you are isolated and don't have things like museums and lots of movies.
3. Yes, the narrator's father should have paid attention to his family's pleas.
4. Yes, lack of knowledge and experience can lead to prejudice; no, ignorance is only one cause of prejudice, not the chief cause, which is learned hatred.

Resources

Language
• *Grammar and Language Links,* p. 37

Vocabulary
• *Words to Own,* p. 14

Using Reference Aids to Clarify Usage

Students who enjoy thinking about word choice and shades of meaning may want to use a dictionary, thesaurus, or synonym finder to discover a precise word to use in place of a vague word or phrase in their writing. Students can turn to p. 685 to see an example of the way synonyms are listed in a thesaurus.

Language Link Quick Check

Have students identify the connotations of the underlined words as positive or negative. (Does everyone agree?)

1. He is a <u>fussy</u> person. [negative]
2. Gloria is <u>particular</u> about her friends. [positive]
3. Kay <u>enjoys talking</u>. [positive]
4. Gar is <u>gabby</u>. [negative]
5. Michael is <u>gossipy</u>. [negative]

OBJECTIVES

1. Read and interpret the short story
2. Analyze theme
3. Make generalizations
4. Express understanding through writing, art, or social studies/research
5. Identify and use techniques for presenting dialogue
6. Understand and use new words

SKILLS

Literary
• Analyze theme

Reading
• Make generalizations

Writing
• Collect ideas for a persuasive essay
• Write a dialogue
• Research questions generated by the story

Art
• Draw a picture or make a collage

Grammar
• Identify and use techniques for presenting dialogue

Vocabulary
• Define and use new words

Viewing/Representing
• Use a photograph to help visualize the story's setting (ATE)

Planning

• **Block Schedule**
  Block Scheduling Lesson Plans with Pacing Guide

• **Traditional Schedule**
  Lesson Plans Including Strategies for English-Language Learners

• **One-Stop Planner**
  CD-ROM with Test Generator

Before You Read

THE BRACELET

Make the Connection

Never Again

The author of the story that follows had a purpose: She wanted to tell a true story to teach us a lesson about the need for trust and compassion.

During World War II, the U.S. government imprisoned thousands of Japanese Americans in internment camps. In this story the author describes what it was like to be one of those imprisoned.

Quickwrite

What stories or movies can you think of in which painful events are used to teach us *never* to repeat mistakes? Give at least two examples and describe the lessons you learned.

Elements of Literature

Theme: It's All About Life

Theme is the special message that a reader takes away from a story. **Plot** tells us what happens in a story, while **theme** tells us what the point is. Theme is what the writer is saying about life.

A story's theme is usually not stated directly by the writer. A story may have several themes, and different readers often find different themes in the same story.

> **T**heme is the idea about life revealed in a work of literature.
>
> *For more on Theme, see page 326 and the Handbook of Literary Terms.*

Reading Skills and Strategies

Making Generalizations: Sifting the Evidence

When you make a **generalization,** you look at evidence and make a broad statement about what it tells you. A statement about a story's theme is a kind of generalization. To make a statement about the theme of "The Bracelet," follow these steps:

• Look for an important idea about life that the characters discover because of what happens in the story.

• State the idea in a general way. Make it apply not just to the story but to real life. One of the themes of "The Gold Cadillac" can be stated this way: "Envy can make people cruel."

HRW go.hrw.com
LE0 6-5

No one knew exactly what was going to happen to us.

Preteaching Vocabulary

Words to Own

After students read the Words to Own and their definitions listed at the bottom of the selection pages, have partners play "Guess My Word!" To play, the first player gives synonyms until the second player guesses the word. When all four words have been used, players switch roles and play again. Then have students select the best synonym for each word that follows.

1. **evacuated** [possible synonyms: abandoned, cleared, removed]

2. **interned** [possible synonyms: imprisoned, confined, detained]

3. **aliens** [possible synonyms: outsiders, strangers, foreigners]

4. **forsaken** [possible synonyms: abandoned, outcast, deserted]

The Bracelet

Yoshiko Uchida

"Mama, is it time to go?"

I hadn't planned to cry, but the tears came suddenly, and I wiped them away with the back of my hand. I didn't want my older sister to see me crying.

"It's almost time, Ruri," my mother said gently. Her face was filled with a kind of sadness I had never seen before.

I looked around at my empty room. The clothes that Mama always told me to hang up in the closet, the junk piled on my dresser, the old rag doll I could never bear to part with— they were all gone. There was nothing left in my room, and there was nothing left in the rest of the house. The rugs and furniture were gone, the pictures and drapes were down, and the closets and cupboards were empty. The house was like a gift box after the nice thing inside was gone; just a lot of nothingness.

It was almost time to leave our home, but we weren't moving to a nicer house or to a new town. It was April 21, 1942. The United States and Japan were at war, and every Japanese person on the West Coast was being <u>evacuated</u> by the government to a concentration camp. Mama, my sister Keiko,

---

WORDS TO OWN

evacuated (ē·vak′yōō·āt′id) v.: removed from the area.

THE BRACELET 357

Summary ▪ ▪

This story is set in 1942, when America is at war with Japan. Suddenly, all Japanese Americans are viewed with suspicion. As a result, Ruri's Japanese American family is uprooted from its home in Berkeley, California, and sent to an internment camp. Before the family leaves, Ruri's best friend, Laurie, comes to say goodbye. Laurie gives Ruri a bracelet with a heart. Touched, Ruri vows to wear the bracelet forever, but it disappears when the family arrives at the camp. Ruri is distraught, but her mother reassures her by explaining that the people we love are always with us, in our hearts.

Resources

Viewing and Representing
Videocassette B, Segment 6
The segment "War, Internment, and Atonement" explores the Japanese American experience during World War II. For full lesson plans and worksheets, see the *Visual Connections Teacher's Manual*.

Listening
Audio CD Library
A dramatic recording of this short story is included in the *Audio CD Library*:
• Disc 8, Track 2

Viewing and Representing
Fine Arts Transparency
A transparency of Norman Rockwell's *The Right to Know* can be used to spark discussion before students read "The Bracelet." See The *Viewing and Representing Transparencies and Worksheets*:
• Transparency 12
• Worksheet, p. 48

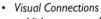

Resources: Print and Media

Reading
• *Reading Skills and Strategies*
  Selection Skill Lesson, p. 105
• *Graphic Organizers for Active Reading*, p. 28
• *Words to Own*, p. 15
• *Spelling and Decoding*
  Worksheet, p. 18
• *Audio CD Library*
  Disc 8, Track 2

Writing and Language
• *Daily Oral Grammar*
  Transparency 21
• *Grammar and Language Links*
  Worksheet, p. 39
• *Language Workshop CD-ROM*

Viewing and Representing
• *Viewing and Representing*
  Fine Art Transparency 12
  Fine Art Worksheet, p. 48

• *Visual Connections*
  Videocassette B, Segment 6

Assessment
• *Formal Assessment*, p. 72
• *Portfolio Management System*, p. 150
• *Standardized Test Preparation*, p. 58
• *Test Generator (One-Stop Planner CD-ROM)*

Internet
• go.hrw.com (keyword: LE0 6-5)

Theme

? The internment of Japanese Americans during World War II shocks many people even today. How people confront injustice is an important aspect of the story's theme. Why does Ruri think that the relocation might all be a terrible mistake? [Possible response: What has happened to her family is so sudden, cruel, and unfair that she cannot quite believe that it is true.]

B Historical Connections

Very early in the morning of December 7, 1941, the Japanese launched a surprise air attack on Pearl Harbor in Hawaii in an attempt to destroy America's Pacific fleet. The attack was brutally successful: 8 American battleships, 10 other naval vessels, and about 150 aircraft were destroyed. About 2,335 military personnel were killed. The attack was part of the strategy of Japan, which was fighting World War II on the side of the Axis powers (Germany and Italy), and motivated America to join on the side of the Allies, the nations (Great Britain, China, France, and Russia) associated against the Axis.

C Reading Skills and Strategies

Making Generalizations

? The story is set in 1942. How long has Ruri's father lived in America? [He has lived here for twenty-five years.] What generalization can you make about his feelings for America based on the length of time he has lived in the country? [He must be happy in America and loyal to our country if he has lived here so long and raised his children here.]

D Elements of Literature

Simile

? Find the simile in this sentence. What does this comparison suggest about Laurie? [Simile: "her face drooped like a wilted tulip." This comparison suggests that she is beautiful but very sad.]

and I were being sent from our home, and out of Berkeley, and eventually out of California.

A The doorbell rang, and I ran to answer it before my sister could. I thought maybe by some miracle a messenger from the government might be standing there, tall and proper and buttoned into a uniform, come to tell us it was all a terrible mistake, that we wouldn't have to leave after all. Or maybe the messenger would have a telegram from Papa, who was <u>interned</u> in a prisoner-of-war camp in Montana because he had worked for a Japanese business firm.

B The FBI had come to pick up Papa and hundreds of other Japanese community leaders on the very day that Japanese planes had bombed Pearl Harbor. The government thought they were dangerous enemy <u>aliens</u>. If it weren't so sad, it would have been funny. Papa could no more be dangerous than the mayor of our city, and he was every bit as **C** loyal to the United States. He had lived here since 1917.

When I opened the door, it wasn't a messenger from anywhere. It was my best friend, **D** Laurie Madison, from next door. She was holding a package wrapped up like a birthday present, but she wasn't wearing her party dress, and her face drooped like a wilted tulip.

"Hi," she said. "I came to say goodbye."

She thrust the present at me and told me it was something to take to camp. "It's a bracelet," she said before I could open the package. "Put it on so you won't have to pack

---

WORDS TO OWN

interned (in·tʉrnd') v.: detained or confined.
aliens (āl'yənz) n.: foreigners.

---

358 JUSTICE FOR ALL

Reaching All Students

Struggling Readers
Making Generalizations was introduced on p. 356. For a lesson directly tied to this story that teaches students to use prior knowledge by using a strategy called Most Important Word, see the *Reading Skills and Strategies* binder:
• Selection Skill Lesson, p. 105

English Language Learners
To introduce the story, work with students to examine the title, the quotations from the story on pp. 356 and 361, and the illustrations. Then have students predict what the story will be about. For additional strategies to supplement instruction for English language learners, see
• *Lesson Plans Including Strategies for English-Language Learners*

it." She knew I didn't have one inch of space left in my suitcase. We had been instructed to take only what we could carry into camp, and Mama had told us that we could each take only two suitcases.

"Then how are we ever going to pack the dishes and blankets and sheets they've told us to bring with us?" Keiko worried.

"I don't really know," Mama said, and she simply began packing those big impossible things into an enormous duffel bag—along with umbrellas, boots, a kettle, hot plate, and flashlight.

"Who's going to carry that huge sack?" I asked.

But Mama didn't worry about things like that. "Someone will help us," she said. "Don't worry." So I didn't.

Laurie wanted me to open her package and put on the bracelet before she left. It was a thin gold chain with a heart dangling on it. She helped me put it on, and I told her I'd never take it off, ever.

"Well, goodbye then," Laurie said awkwardly. "Come home soon."

"I will," I said, although I didn't know if I would ever get back to Berkeley again.

I watched Laurie go down the block, her long blond pigtails bouncing as she walked. I wondered who would be sitting in my desk at Lincoln Junior High now that I was gone. Laurie kept turning and waving, even walking backward for a while, until she got to the corner. I didn't want to watch anymore, and I slammed the door shut.

The next time the doorbell rang, it was Mrs. Simpson, our other neighbor. She was going to drive us to the Congregational Church, which was the Civil Control Station where all the Japanese of Berkeley were supposed to report.

THE BRACELET 359

E Elements of Literature
Theme
? The writer provides these details of the evacuation to show how the family members face their ordeal with dignity and courage. These details also help readers understand the story's theme: that maintaining values and standards can help people withstand injustice. What does the mother say that reveals her faith in human nature? ["Someone will help us."]

F Elements of Literature
Symbols
? A symbol is a thing that stands for something beyond itself. What does the bracelet symbolize? [The bracelet is a symbol of the girls' friendship. The heart symbolizes Laurie's love, which comforts Ruri in a difficult time.]

G Reading Skills and Strategies
Making Generalizations
? From Laurie's actions, what generalizations can you make about the reactions of non-Japanese people to the situation? [Possible responses: Some of them felt sorry for the people being uprooted; some of them believed that relocating Japanese Americans to internment camps was unjust; some of them had close personal bonds with their Japanese American friends and neighbors.]

Taking a Second Look

Review: Chronological Order

Remind students that when stories are related in chronological order, the events are arranged in the order in which they happened, from start to finish. To help readers follow the chronological order of events, writers often include cue words, such as *first, then, next, finally,* and *last.* "The Bracelet" is related in chronological order. Although the narrator is relating a story that happened to her many years before, she is presenting the events in the same order in which they originally occurred.

Activities

1. As students read the story, have them construct a time line to track the chronological order of events narrated.

2. After students have read the story, challenge them to explain why the author recounts events in chronological order. Why is the specific order of events especially important in this narrative? How might the story's effect on the reader change if Laurie's visit were presented as a flashback, an event remembered by Ruri while she is in the camp?

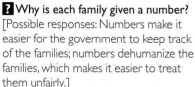

A Reading Skills and Strategies

Making Generalizations

❓Why is each family given a number? [Possible responses: Numbers make it easier for the government to keep track of the families; numbers dehumanize the families, which makes it easier to treat them unfairly.]

B Critical Thinking

Interpreting

❓What do you learn about Ruri's parents from Ruri's memories of the irises? [Possible responses: that they love each other very much; that they treat each other with kindness and respect.]

C Critical Thinking

Speculating

❓A *bayonet* is a daggerlike steel weapon attached to the muzzle end of a gun and used for stabbing in hand-to-hand combat. The weapon was named after the French town of Bayonne, where it was first made and used. Why do you think the writer specifically mentions the bayonets? [Sample answer: Bayonets are terrifying weapons, so they convey the panic and fear everyone felt.]

D Elements of Literature

Theme

❓Some of the information in this paragraph confirms a generalization you made on p. 358 (annotation C). What additional information is revealed in this passage? [The wartime internment of Japanese Americans was unnecessary and unjust. Most Japanese Americans were citizens because they were born in the United States, although their parents, born in Japan, could not become U.S. citizens.]

It was time to go. "Come on, Ruri. Get your things," my sister called to me.

It was a warm day, but I put on a sweater and my coat so I wouldn't have to carry them, and I picked up my two suitcases. **(A)** Each one had a tag with my name and our family number on it. Every Japanese family had to register and get a number. We were Family Number 13453.

Mama was taking one last look around our house. She was going from room to room, as though she were trying to take a mental picture of the house she had lived in for fifteen years, so she would never forget it.

(B) I saw her take a long last look at the garden that Papa loved. The irises beside the fish pond were just beginning to bloom. If Papa had been home, he would have cut the first iris blossom and brought it inside to Mama. "This one is for you," he would have said. And Mama would have smiled and said, "Thank you, Papa San"° and put it in her favorite cut-glass vase.

But the garden looked shabby and <u>forsaken</u> now that Papa was gone and Mama was too busy to take care of it. It looked the way I felt, sort of empty and lonely and abandoned.

When Mrs. Simpson took us to the Civil Control Station, I felt even worse. I was scared, and for a minute I thought I was going to lose my breakfast right in front of everybody. There must have been over a thousand Japanese people gathered at the church. Some were old and some were young. Some were talking and laughing, and some were crying. I guess everybody else was scared too. No one knew exactly what was going to happen to us. We just knew we were being taken to the Tanforan Racetracks,

which the army had turned into a camp for the Japanese. There were fourteen other camps like ours along the West Coast.

(C) What scared me most were the soldiers standing at the doorway of the church hall. They were carrying guns with mounted bayonets. I wondered if they thought we would try to run away and whether they'd shoot us or come after us with their bayonets if we did.

A long line of buses waited to take us to camp. There were trucks, too, for our baggage. And Mama was right; some men were there to help us load our duffel bag. When it was time to board the buses, I sat with Keiko, and Mama sat behind us. The bus went down Grove Street and passed the small Japanese food store where Mama used to order her bean-curd cakes and pickled radish. The windows were all boarded up, but there was a sign still hanging on the door that read, "We are loyal Americans."

(D) The crazy thing about the whole evacuation was that we were all loyal Americans. Most of us were citizens because we had been born here. But our parents, who had come from Japan, couldn't become citizens because there was a law that prevented any Asian from becoming a citizen. Now everybody with a Japanese face was being shipped off to concentration camps.

"It's stupid," Keiko muttered as we saw the racetrack looming up beside the highway. "If there were any Japanese spies around, they'd have gone back to Japan long ago."

"I'll say," I agreed. My sister was in high school and she ought to know, I thought.

°**San:** Japanese term added to names to indicate respect.

WORDS TO OWN
forsaken (fər·sā′kən) *adj.*: abandoned; deserted.

Skill Link

Grammar: Look Who's Talking
Use this activity before you teach the Grammar Link activity on p. 365 to help you assess students' understanding of punctuating dialogue. Review how to punctuate dialogue. Be sure students can identify speaker's tags, words such as *said, cried,* and *explained.* Then have students punctuate each of the following direct quotations from the story. They will have to add commas and quotation marks.

1. Hi she said. I came to say goodbye. ["Hi," she said. "I came to say goodbye."]

2. It's a bracelet she said before I could open the package. Put it on so you won't have to pack it. ["It's a bracelet," she said before I could open the package. "Put it on so you won't have to pack it."]

3. Who's going to carry that huge sack? I asked. ["Who's going to carry that huge sack?" I asked.]

4. Well, goodbye then Laurie said awkwardly. Come home soon. ["Well, goodbye then," Laurie said awkwardly. "Come home soon."]

5. It's so stupid Keiko muttered. ["It's so stupid," Keiko muttered.]

When the bus turned into Tanforan, there were more armed guards at the gate, and I saw barbed wire strung around the entire grounds. I felt as though I were going into a prison, but I hadn't done anything wrong.

We streamed off the buses and poured into a huge room, where doctors looked down our throats and peeled back our eyelids to see if we had any diseases. Then we were given our housing assignments. The man in charge gave Mama a slip of paper. We were in Barrack 16, Apartment 40.

"Mama!" I said. "We're going to live in an apartment!" The only apartment I had ever seen was the one my piano teacher lived in. It was in an enormous building in San Francisco, with an elevator and thick-carpeted hallways. I thought how wonderful it would be to have our own elevator. A house was all right, but an apartment seemed elegant and special.

We walked down the racetrack, looking for Barrack 16. Mr. Noma, a friend of Papa's, helped us carry our bags. I was so busy looking around I slipped and almost fell on the muddy track. Army barracks had been built everywhere, all around the racetrack and even in the center oval.

Mr. Noma pointed beyond the track toward the horse stables. "I think your barrack is out there."

He was right. We came to a long stable that had once housed the horses of Tanforan, and we climbed up the wide ramp. Each stall had a number painted on it, and when we got to 40, Mr. Noma pushed open the door.

"Well, here it is," he said, "Apartment 40."

The stall was narrow and empty and dark. There were two small windows on each side of the door. Three folded army cots were on the dust-covered floor, and one light bulb

"Those are things we can carry in our hearts . . ."

dangled from the ceiling. That was all. This was our apartment, and it still smelled of horses.

Mama looked at my sister and then at me. "It won't be so bad when we fix it up," she began. "I'll ask Mrs. Simpson to send me some material for curtains. I could make some cushions too, and . . . well . . ." She stopped. She couldn't think of anything more to say.

Mr. Noma said he'd go get some mattresses for us. "I'd better hurry before they're all gone." He rushed off. I think he wanted to leave so that he wouldn't have to see Mama cry. But he needn't have run off, because Mama didn't cry. She just went out to borrow a broom and began sweeping out the dust and dirt. "Will you girls set up the cots?" she asked.

It was only after we'd put up the last cot that I noticed my bracelet was gone. "I've lost Laurie's bracelet!" I screamed. "My bracelet's gone!"

We looked all over the stall and even down the ramp. I wanted to run back down the track and go over every inch of ground we'd walked on, but it was getting dark and Mama wouldn't let me.

I thought of what I'd promised Laurie. I wasn't ever going to take the bracelet off, not even when I went to take a shower. And now I had lost it on my very first day in camp. I wanted to cry.

I kept looking for it all the time we were in Tanforan. I didn't stop looking until the day

THE BRACELET 361

E **Appreciating Language**
Connotations
? What connotations does the word *apartment* have for Ruri? [She associates the word with elegance and exclusiveness.]

F **Reading Skills and Strategies**
Making Predictions
? What do you predict Ruri's apartment will be like? Why? [Students should predict that the family's apartment is going to be small, crude, and rough because the government is unlikely to inter prisoners in fine homes.]

G **Elements of Literature**
Theme
? The mother's dignified response to the family's situation helps you understand the story's theme: that maintaining values and standards can help people withstand injustice. Why does Ruri's mother plan to fix up the apartment? [Possible responses: She wants to cheer up her daughters and make the best of a terrible situation; she refuses to lower her values and standards even in a dreadful situation such as this.]

H **Reading Skills and Strategies**
Making Generalizations

? What effect will losing the bracelet have on Ruri's friendship with Laurie? [Possible response: Losing the bracelet will not harm the friendship because Laurie will understand.] In general, what role do objects play in friendships? [Objects are physical reminders of friendships.]

Making the Connections

Connecting to the Theme:
"Justice for All"
When students have completed the story, talk about the collection's theme. Explain that in 1944, the Supreme Court ruled that forcing Japanese Americans into internment camps was unconstitutional. But not until 1965 did the U.S. Congress end discrimination against Asians in immigration laws, such as the discrimination that prevented Ruri's parents from becoming American citizens. Divide the class into small groups to discuss other ways that the government could have dealt with its fear and suspicion toward Japanese Americans during World War II.

A Reading Skills
and Strategies
**Making
Generalizations**

? Why are friends important? [Possible responses: They offer support when other people are being unjust; they help us achieve our goals; they are fun to be with.]

**BROWSING
IN THE FILES**

About the Author. Yoshiko Uchida also wrote versions of traditional Japanese folk tales. For example, "Momotaro: Boy-of-the-Peach" tells the story of a boy who jumps out of an enormous peach that a Japanese woman finds floating down the river where she is washing clothes. She and her husband take care of the boy until he is fifteen and goes off to perform a good deed. Uchida first heard this story from her mother.

Writers on Writing. Uchida started keeping a journal the day she graduated from elementary school. "I was trying to hold on to and somehow preserve the magic as well as the joy and sadness of certain moments in my life," she explains. "I guess that's really what books and writing are all about."

Resources ——————

Formal Assessment
• Selection Test, p. 72

Test Generator
• Selection Test

we were sent to another camp, called Topaz, in the middle of a desert in Utah. And then I gave up.

But Mama told me never mind. She said I didn't need a bracelet to remember Laurie, just as I didn't need anything to remember Papa or our home in Berkeley or all the people and things we loved and had left behind.

"Those are things we can carry in our hearts and take with us no matter where we **A** are sent," she said.

And I guess she was right. I've never forgotten Laurie, even now.

MEET THE WRITER

So It Won't Happen Again

Yoshiko Uchida (1921–1992) was a senior in college when the United States entered World War II. Like most other people of Japanese descent on the West Coast, Uchida and her family were uprooted by the government and forced to go to an internment camp. There, she and her family lived at Tanforan Racetrack in horse stall 40, answering to Family Number 13453 instead of their own name. Later Uchida gave the same horse stall and family number to the fictional family she created in her short story "The Bracelet."

Uchida said that in writing about the internment camps, she tried to give readers a sense of the courage and strength that enabled most Japanese Americans to endure this tragedy.

There was another reason that she wrote about the camps:

❝ I always ask the children why they think I wrote *Journey to Topaz* and *Journey Home*, in which I tell of the wartime experiences of the Japanese Americans. . . . 'To tell how you felt? To tell what happened to the Japanese people?'

'Yes,' I answer, but I continue the discussion until finally one of them will say, 'You wrote those books so it won't ever happen again.'

And that is why I wrote this book. I wrote it for the young Japanese Americans who seek a sense of continuity with their past. But I wrote it as well for all Americans, with the hope that through knowledge of the past, they will never allow another group of people in America to be sent into desert exile ever again. **❞**

More Light on the Past

In addition to *Journey to Topaz: A Story of the Japanese-American Evacuation* (Creative Arts) and its sequel, *Journey Home* (Macmillan), Uchida wrote a trilogy about a young Japanese American girl called Rinko who lives in California during the 1930s. The trilogy includes *The Jar of Dreams, The Best Bad Thing,* and *The Happiest Ending* (all McElderry Books).

362 JUSTICE FOR ALL

Assessing Learning

Check Test: True-False

1. Ruri's father has been put in an internment camp in New York. [False]
2. Laurie gives Ruri a bracelet to remember her by. [True]
3. The family is housed in an old stable. [True]
4. The family's room is large and clean. [False]
5. Laurie comes to visit Ruri at the camp. [False]

Peer Assessment

After students have finished their group activities, have them write one positive comment about the contribution of each of the other group members. They should also write one suggestion for improvement for each group member, framed in a useful and positive way.

Standardized Test Preparation

For practice with standardized test format specific to this selection, see
• *Standardized Test Preparation,* p. 58
For practice in proofreading and editing, see
• *Daily Oral Grammar,* Transparency 21

MAKING MEANINGS

First Thoughts

[respond]

1. As you were reading the story, what particular passages or scenes said the most to you? In a double-entry journal like the one below, copy the passages from the text, and note your thoughts.

Passage	My Response
"I was scared, and . . . thought I was going to lose my breakfast. . . ."	She helps me see how terrified she must have been.

Reading Check

Imagine you're Ruri writing a letter from Tanforan Race-track to your friend Laurie. Tell her three things: Let her know what happened to your family after you left Berkeley; describe what the camp is like; and tell her what happened to the bracelet she gave you.

Shaping Interpretations

[interpret]

2. Ruri says the garden "looked the way I felt, sort of empty and lonely and abandoned" (page 360). What does she remember about the first iris? How does that memory make Ruri feel as she looks at the now shabby garden?

[analyze]

3. Uchida says she wanted to show how Japanese Americans survived their uprooting with strength and courage. Describe scenes in the story where Ruri or her mother shows these qualities.

[interpret]

4. What is the story's **theme**? State this theme in the form of a **generalization** about life.

Connecting with the Text

[connect]

5. How do you think you and your family would behave if you were in the same situation as Ruri? When you first started this story, how did you predict it was going to end? How accurate was your prediction?

Extending the Text

[evaluate]

6. Uchida said she wrote about the internment of Japanese Americans so that nothing like it would ever occur in the United States again. Do you think it's possible that such an injustice could happen again? Explain.

Challenging the Text

[evaluate]

7. Does the author successfully teach a lesson in this story? Does she do this as well as the authors of the stories and the directors of the movies you listed in your notes for the Quickwrite on page 356? Explain.

THE BRACELET 363

Reading Check
Sample response:
Dear Laurie,
    We have arrived safely at Tanforan Racetrack. I imagined that our apartment would be a beautiful and elegant place. Imagine my shock when we were placed in a small, smelly stall! It is narrow and dark, with two small windows on each side of the door. There are three army cots and a light bulb dangling from the ceiling. The camp is very muddy, too. But that's not the worst of it.

    The most terrible thing happened when we set up the last cot—I noticed my bracelet was gone! We looked all over the stall and even down the ramp. I wanted to check every inch of ground outside, but it was getting dark and Mama wouldn't let me. I was so sad that I wanted to cry, but Mama comforted me when she said that I didn't need the bracelet to remember you— I will carry your kindness in my heart forever.
Your friend,
Ruri

MAKING MEANINGS

First Thoughts

1. Students might include the scene in which Laurie gives Ruri the bracelet, the scene where Ruri loses the bracelet, and the scene with the soldiers and bayonets.

Shaping Interpretations

2. Ruri remembers her father giving her mother the first iris blossom, which makes her feel even sadder as she surveys the ruined garden.
3. Scenes include the family members' great dignity as they pack, assemble for the relocation, and arrive at the horse stall. Ruri's mother's optimism in the face of adversity shows her strength and bravery.
4. Possible responses: No one can take away something you carry in your heart; friendship means a great deal during adversity; it is important to maintain one's values and standards during times of injustice and hardship.

Connecting with the Text

5. Students may say that their family would also stick together and face adversity as a unit. They might have predicted that Ruri and her family would be exempt from the relocation because they have been in America for so long or that someone would hide them so that they would not have to live in an internment camp.

Extending the Text

6. Some students will say that it can indeed happen again if we forget the events of the past. Others might claim that we could never again be so unjust since we learn from our mistakes.

Challenging the Text

7. Some students might argue that the lesson is clear since it is stated near the bottom of p. 360 ("The crazy thing . . . camps."). Others might not grasp the author's lesson easily since the events she describes happened over fifty years ago and are difficult to relate to.

Rubrics for each Choices assignment appear on p. 150 in *the Portfolio Management System.*

CHOICES:
Building Your Portfolio

1. **Writer's Notebook** Remind students to save their work, which they may use as prewriting for the Writer's Workshop on pp. 396–400.
2. **Creative Writing** First have students skim the story for clues to Laurie's character. Then students can reread the parts of the story where Ruri argues against relocating Japanese Americans to internment camps.
3. **Art/Writing** Remind students to choose a subject they would not mind sharing with the class.
4. **Social Studies/Research** Students can ask their social studies or history teachers for help in locating World War II resources.

RESPONDING TO THE ART

Ansel Adams (1902–1984) was fourteen years old when he vacationed with his family at Yosemite National Park, took photographs with his first camera, and fell in love with the park and photography. Adams decided to become a photographer. He was enormously successful, and his images of nature continue to be extremely popular.
Activity. Ask students how the photograph helps them to visualize the story's setting.

CHOICES: Building Your Portfolio

Writer's Notebook
1. Collecting Ideas for Supporting a Position

Look through school and local newspapers to find an issue you feel strongly about. Check the editorials and letters to the editor—that's where people write about situations and events that mean a lot to them. Jot down ideas that might work for you.

—All kids should have good health care.

—Kids should be forced to do volunteer work.

Creative Writing
2. Loyal Laurie

Laurie was a loyal friend to Ruri at a time when many Americans were turning against Americans of Japanese descent. Imagine a situation at Laurie's school in which a classmate says that the internment camps are a good idea. What would Laurie say to that person? Write the dialogue you think the two classmates might have.

Art/Writing
3. Gone but Not Forgotten

Is there someone in your life whom you'll always carry in your heart? Draw a picture of the person or make a collage that shows how you feel about him or her. Under the illustration, write a few lines explaining why you will always remember the person.

Social Studies/Research
4. Revisiting the Camps

Reading "The Bracelet" may have raised questions in your mind about the treatment of Japanese Americans during World War II. You might wonder about issues like these:

- What reasons did the U.S. government give for forcing these Americans to leave their homes?
- Why do you think most Japanese Americans went along with the evacuation order?
- Why did the rounding up of Japanese Americans take place mainly on the West Coast?

With a partner, research these and any other questions you have. Then, share the information you find by team-teaching a history lesson to your class.

Courtesy of the Library of Congress.

Manzanar War Relocation Center in California (1943) by Ansel Adams.

Reaching All Students

Struggling Readers
As a prewriting exercise for Choice 2, have students use a tape recorder to brainstorm ideas for their dialogue. Pairs of students can also play the roles of Laurie and Ruri and discuss their feelings about the World War II relocation of Japanese Americans to internment camps.

Advanced Learners
For Choice 3, students may write their explanations in poetry rather than prose. Challenge students to experiment with different verse forms, such as sonnets, free verse, or ballads.

GRAMMAR LINK

Look Who's Talking

**Language
Handbook
H E L P**

*See
Quotation
Marks,
pages 756-
757.*

**Technology
H E L P**

*See
Language
Workshop
CD-ROM.
Key word
entry:
dialogue.*

What's wrong with the way the following dialogue is presented?

> "Well, goodbye then," Laurie said awkwardly. "Come home soon." "I will," I said, although I didn't know if I would ever get back to Berkeley again.

Is it hard to tell when Laurie stops talking and Ruri starts? To avoid this kind of confusion, writers usually start a new paragraph whenever the speaker changes in a conversation. Here's how the dialogue above looks in the story. Notice how much easier it is to tell when Laurie stops speaking and Ruri starts:

> "Well, goodbye then," Laurie said awkwardly. "Come home soon."
>
> "I will," I said, although I didn't know if I would ever get back to Berkeley again.

Try It Out

Here is a dialogue between two students discussing the story. Copy the dialogue, inserting the appropriate paragraph breaks.

"I admired the way Ruri and her family handled the camp," said Tamika. "I don't know," said José. "I think I would have put up more resistance. After all, they lost their homes and should have been angry." "I disagree," retorted Tamika. "They wanted to prove they were loyal citizens, and they did."

Go back to the story, and find examples of dialogue in which a new paragraph is used to show a change in speaker.

VOCABULARY HOW TO OWN A WORD

WORD BANK	Research It
evacuated *interned* *aliens* *forsaken*	1. How are people <u>evacuated</u> during floods and other disasters? 2. Consult an encyclopedia to find out which states Japanese Americans were <u>interned</u> in during World War II. 3. Imagine that you're a filmmaker making a documentary on the treatment of <u>aliens</u> in the United States. Write a one-sentence summary of your film, identifying the people you want to focus on. 4. How would a <u>forsaken</u> pet feel?

THE BRACELET 365

GRAMMAR LINK

Have students select a piece of writing from their portfolio that contains dialogue. Then have them exchange papers with a partner to check that they have punctuated and indented each line correctly. As they work, students can read the dialogue aloud, each partner taking a part. Point out to students that if changes of speaker are confusing, poor formatting may be the cause.

Try It Out

"I admired the way Ruri and her family handled the camp," said Tamika.

"I don't know," said José. "I think I would have put up more resistance. After all, they lost their homes and should have been angry."

"I disagree," retorted Tamika. "They wanted to prove they were loyal citizens, and they did."

VOCABULARY
Possible Answers
1. They are taken by bus, car, and air transportation to shelters, often in schools and other public buildings.
2. The Japanese Americans were interned in Colorado, Utah, Texas, California, Arizona, and New Mexico.
3. My film will focus on Mexican immigrants in the United States.
4. The pet might feel sad and lonely.

Resources ————

Grammar
• *Grammar and Language Links*, p. 39
Vocabulary
• *Words to Own*, p. 15

Grammar Link Quick Check

Have students copy the following dialogue, inserting the appropriate paragraph breaks:
"When will Ruri come home?" Laurie asked her mother. "I don't have any idea, but I'm afraid it may be a long time," her mother answered. "I miss her," Laurie said sadly.

["When will Ruri come home?" Laurie asked her mother.

"I don't have any idea, but I'm afraid it may be a long time," her mother answered.

"I miss her," Laurie said sadly.]

WHAT DO FISH HAVE TO DO WITH ANYTHING?

Planning

- **Block Schedule**
  Block Scheduling Lesson Plans with Pacing Guide
- **Traditional Schedule**
  Lesson Plans Including Strategies for English-Language Learners
- **One-Stop Planner**
  CD-ROM with Test Generator

Make the Connection

What's Your Opinion?

Rate the following opinions about life, which are expressed in the following story. Use this scale to rank the statements: 1 = disagree, 2 = no opinion, 3 = agree.

a. "Parents need to protect their children."

b. "Questions that have no answers shouldn't be asked."

c. "Money will cure a lot of unhappiness."

d. "People are ashamed of being unhappy."

Quickwrite

From the list, choose a statement that you agree or disagree with. Explain why you feel the way you do.

go.hrw.com
LE0 6-5

Elements of Literature

Character Change: When People Grow, It Shows

When people learn from things that happen to them, they change. This is true in fiction, just as it is in real life. As you read this story, you'll watch a character grow because of his experiences.

The writer doesn't tell you directly that this character changes. Instead, he lets the character's actions show you what's going on. He also makes you think about why some people learn new things from life while others remain "blind."

> In stories the main **character** often changes as a result of the story's events.
>
> *For more on Character, see page 326 and the Handbook of Literary Terms.*

Reading Skills and Strategies

Chronological Order: Moments in Time

When a story is told in **chronological order,** the events are arranged in the order in which they happen. As you read "What Do Fish Have to Do with Anything?" keep track of the events by filling in a sequence chart like the one here.

| event | → | event | → | event |

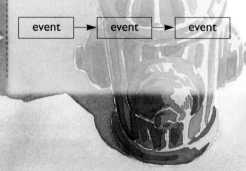

366 JUSTICE FOR ALL

Preteaching Vocabulary

Words to Own

Have students read the Words to Own and their definitions at the bottom of the selection pages. Then have them create a four-panel cartoon that presents a story about fish, using all four vocabulary words correctly. Have students trade papers with a partner to make sure they have used the words correctly. Then display the cartoons in the classroom.

What Do Fish Have to Do with Anything?

"Maybe you can't buy happiness, but you can rent a lot of it."

Avi

Every day Mrs. Markham waited for her son, Willie, to come out of school when it was over. They walked home together. If asked why, Mrs. Markham would say, "Parents need to protect their children."

One Monday afternoon as they approached their apartment building, she suddenly tugged at Willie. "Don't look that way," she said.

"Where?"

"At that man over there."

As they walked, Willie stole a look back over his shoulder. A man Willie had never seen before was sitting on a red plastic milk crate near the curb. His matted, streaky gray hair hung like a ragged curtain over a dirty face. His shoes were torn. Rough hands lay upon his knees. One hand was palm up.

WHAT DO FISH HAVE TO DO WITH ANYTHING? 367

Summary ■

As the story opens, fifth-grader Willie Markham is walking home from school with his mother. Willie asks his mother about a beggar they pass, but she is unsympathetic to his plight. At home, Willie has a snack and does his homework, all the time wondering about the beggar. The next day, Willie asks the beggar about unhappiness, hoping to help his mother, who has been sad since his father left. The beggar shares his cure for unhappiness: "What a person needs is always more than they say." When the beggar is gone the next day, Willie asks his mother about him. She explains she had the police remove him. Willie tells his mother she is like the fish who live in dark, underwater caves and cannot see.

Resources ───

Listening
Audio CD Library
A dramatic recording of this short story is included in the *Audio CD Library*:
• Disc 8, Track 3

Viewing and Representing
Fine Arts Transparency
A transparency of Carmen Lomas Garza's *Cumpleaños (Birthday Party)* can be used to spark discussion before students read the story. See the *Viewing and Representing Transparencies and Worksheets*:
• Transparency 13
• Worksheet, p. 52

Ⓐ Elements of Literature
Character
❓ What does Willie's action tell you about his character? [Possible responses: He is curious; he is sometimes disobedient.]

Resources: Print and Media ───

Reading
• *Graphic Organizers for Active Reading,* p. 29
• *Words to Own,* p. 16
• *Spelling and Decoding*
    Worksheet, p. 19
• *Audio CD Library*
    Disc 8, Track 3

Elements of Literature
• *Literary Elements*
    Transparency 7
    Worksheet, p. 22

Writing and Language
• *Daily Oral Grammar*
    Transparency 22
• *Grammar and Language Links*
    Worksheet, p. 41
• *Language Workshop CD-ROM*

Viewing and Representing
• *Viewing and Representing*
    Fine Art Transparency 13
    Fine Art Worksheet, p. 52

Assessment
• *Formal Assessment,* p. 74
• *Portfolio Management System,* p. 151
• *Standardized Test Preparation,* p. 60
• *Test Generator (One-Stop Planner CD-ROM)*

Internet
• go.hrw.com (keyword: LE0 6-5)

A Critical Thinking

Evaluating

❓ Do you think Mrs. Markham is telling Willie the truth when she says that they can't afford to give the beggar anything? Why or why not? [Possible responses: Yes, it seems they live in a poor neighborhood, and so it is unlikely that they can afford to be generous; no, she is just stingy or uncaring or doesn't want to encourage begging.]

B Reading Skills and Strategies

Making Inferences

❓ What can you infer about Mrs. Markham from her comment? [Possible responses: She accepts things at face value; she doesn't like to look below the surface or question too deeply.]

C Elements of Literature

Character

❓ How did the encounter with the homeless man affect Willie? [Possible responses: He is curious about the man and others like him; he is no longer satisfied with evasive answers.]

D Critical Thinking

Interpreting

❓ What does the salesperson's statement mean? [It implies that people are wrong when they say that money and happiness are not related.]

"What's the matter with him?" Willie asked.

Keeping her eyes straight ahead, Mrs. Markham said, "He's sick." She pulled Willie around. "Don't stare. It's rude."

"What kind of sick?"

Mrs. Markham searched for an answer. "He's unhappy," she said.

"What's he doing?"

"Come on, Willie; you know. He's begging."

"Did anyone give him anything?"

"I don't know. Now come on, don't look."

"Why don't you give him anything?"

A "We have nothing to spare."

When they got home, Mrs. Markham removed a white cardboard box from the refrigerator. It contained poundcake. Using her thumb as a measure, she carefully cut a half-inch-thick piece of cake and gave it to Willie on a clean plate. The plate lay on a plastic mat decorated by images of roses with diamondlike dewdrops. She also gave him a glass of milk and a folded napkin.

Willie said, "Can I have a bigger piece of cake?"

Mrs. Markham picked up the cake box and ran a manicured pink fingernail along the nutrition information panel. "A half-inch piece is a portion, and a portion contains the following nutrients. Do you want to hear them?"

"No."

B "It's on the box, so you can accept what it says. Scientists study people and then write these things. If you're smart enough, you could become a scientist. Like this." Mrs. Markham tapped the box. "It pays well."

Willie ate his cake and drank the milk. When he was done, he took care to wipe the crumbs off his face as well as to blot the milk moustache with the napkin.

His mother said, "Now go on and do your homework. You're in fifth grade. It's important."

Willie gathered up his books that lay on the empty third chair. At the kitchen entrance he paused. "What *kind* of unhappiness does he have?"

C "Who's that?"

"That man."

Mrs. Markham looked puzzled.

"The begging man. The one on the street."

"Could be anything," his mother said, vaguely. "A person can be unhappy for many reasons."

"Like what?"

"Willie . . ."

"Is it a doctor-kind of sickness? A sickness you can cure?"

"I wish you wouldn't ask such questions."

"Why?"

"Questions that have no answers shouldn't be asked."

"Can I go out?"

"Homework first."

Willie turned to go.

D "Money," Mrs. Markham suddenly said. "Money will cure a lot of unhappiness. That's why that man was begging. A salesperson once said to me, 'Maybe you can't buy happiness, but you can rent a lot of it.' You should remember that."

The apartment had three rooms. The walls were painted mint green. Willie walked down the hallway to his room, which was at the front of the building. By climbing up on the windowsill and pressing against the glass, he could see the sidewalk five stories below. The man was still there.

It was almost five when he went to tell his mother he had finished his school assign-

---

WORDS TO OWN

vaguely (vāg'lē) *adv.:* not clearly; uncertainly.

Reaching All Students

Struggling Readers

To help students analyze each character's decision-making process, have them complete a chart like the following one. Students should list each character's choices and their consequences, as well as alternative choices and their possible results.

Character	Choice	Result	Other Choice	Other Result
Willie				
Mrs. Markham				
homeless man				

English Language Learners

Students may wonder why homeless people exist in America, one of the richest countries in the world. Explain that even though the United States has a welfare system, many people do not qualify for assistance; others have no access to the system or have mental or physical problems that prevent them from seeking aid. For additional strategies to supplement instruction for English language learners, see

• *Lesson Plans Including Strategies for English-Language Learners*

ments. She was not there. He found her in her bedroom, sleeping. Since she had begun working the night shift at a convenience store—two weeks now—she took naps in the late afternoon.

For a while Willie stood on the threshold,[1] hoping his mother would wake up. When she didn't, he went to the front room and looked down on the street again. The begging man had not moved.

Willie returned to his mother's room.

"I'm going out," he announced softly.

Willie waited a decent interval[2] for his mother to waken. When she did not, Willie made sure his keys were in his pocket. Then he left the apartment.

Standing just outside his door, he could keep his eyes on the man. It appeared as if he had still not moved. Willie wondered how anyone could go on without moving for so long in the chilly October air. Was staying in one place part of the man's sickness?

During the twenty minutes that Willie watched, no one who passed looked in the beggar's direction. Willie wondered if they even saw the man. Certainly no one put any money into his open hand.

A lady leading a dog by a leash went by. The dog strained in the direction of the man sitting on the crate. The dog's tail wagged. The lady pulled the dog away. "Heel!" she commanded.

The dog—tail between its legs—scampered to the lady's side. Even so, the dog twisted around to look back at the beggar.

1. **threshold:** entrance or entryway.
2. **interval:** period of time between two events.

Willie grinned. The dog had done exactly what he had done when his mother told him not to stare.

Pressing deep into his pocket, Willie found a nickel. It was warm and slippery. He wondered how much happiness you could rent for a nickel.

Squeezing the nickel between his fingers, Willie walked slowly toward the man. When he came before him, he stopped, suddenly nervous. The man, who appeared to be looking at the ground, did not move his eyes. He smelled bad.

"Here." Willie stretched forward and dropped the coin into the man's open right hand.

"Bless you," the man said hoarsely, as he folded his fingers over the coin. His eyes, like high beams on a car, flashed up at Willie, then dropped.

Willie waited for a moment, then went back up to his room. From his front room he looked down on the street. He thought he saw the coin in the man's hand but was not sure.

After supper Mrs. Markham got ready to go to work. She kissed Willie good night. Then, as she did every night, she said, "If you have regular problems, call Mrs. Murphy downstairs. What's her number?"

"274-8676," Willie said.

"Extra bad problems, call Grandma."

"369-6754."

"Super-special problems, you can call me."

"962-6743."

"Emergency, the police."

"911."

E Reading Skills and Strategies
Chronological Order

❓ How does Willie spend his weekdays? Trace the sequence of events of a typical day in Willie's life. [Willie goes to school; his mother picks him up after school; she gives him a snack; he does his homework while she naps; and he stays home alone while she works the night shift at the convenience store.]

F Elements of Literature
Character

❓ What does Willie learn from the dog? Why does he grin? [Willie learns that dogs, like people, sometimes do the opposite of what they are told to do. Willie grins because he recognizes his own behavior in the dog's actions.]

G Critical Thinking
Speculating

❓ Why does Willie give money to the homeless man, especially when his mother told him to stay away? [Possible responses: He feels compassion for the man; he is curious to see what his mother feared; he wants something from the homeless man in exchange for the money.]

H Reading Skills and Strategies
Making Inferences

❓ Why does Mrs. Markham give Willie all these phone numbers? [Possible responses: She is a responsible parent and wants her son to be prepared in case of an emergency. She is afraid that something will happen to Willie while she is gone.]

Crossing the Curriculum

Nutrition/Mathematics
Have students bring in the nutritional labels from a variety of processed foods, such as a jar of peanut butter, a packaged cake, a canned vegetable or fruit, a box of cereal, or a package of cheese. Have students calculate the nutrients in an average serving of each food. Which food has the most salt? the most protein? the most calories?

Health
Staying home alone after school is a reality for many children in America. Have students work in teams to design a "Home Alone Poster" that children could use to help ensure their safety when their parents aren't home. The poster could include emergency numbers, advice about fire safety, and first aid measures. Combine everyone's ideas to create a class poster that you may wish to make available to other children in the school and community.

Cultural Connections

Homeless Children

Children are the fastest-growing segment of homeless people. Although statistics on the homeless vary, at least 100,000 children are without shelter every day in the United States. That's enough children to fill all the seats in three football stadiums. Most of these children are under five years old.

Some children are homeless because their parents are, but others end up on the streets because they leave home. There are also "throwaway" children who are evicted from their homes because of conflicts with their parents. Homeless teenagers live anywhere they can—in alleys, parks, and abandoned buildings.

Professional Notes

How many people in America are actually homeless? Since homeless people have no permanent residence, it is a daunting task to locate people who need help—or even figure out how many people are actually homeless.

Before 1987, advocates for the homeless believed that more than two million Americans were without permanent shelter. That year, the Urban Institute, located in Washington, D.C.,

conducted a survey and concluded that there were between 355,000 and 445,000 homeless Americans. In 1989, writer Peter H. Rossi placed the figure as high as half a million in his book *Down and Out in America*.

In 1990, the government tried to take an accurate count of the number of homeless people in America. The census workers focused on one night: March 20, 1990. They found 228,621

people in shelters and 49,793 people on the street.

But whether the number of homeless people is 300,000 or 3,000,000 (as some estimates claim), we can conclude that there are too many people in America who struggle daily to find shelter.

"Don't let anyone in the door."

"I won't."

"No television past nine."

"I know."

"But you can read late."

"You're the one who's going to be late," Willie said.

"I'm leaving," Mrs. Markham said.

After she went, Willie stood for a long while in the hallway. The empty apartment felt like a cave that lay deep below the earth. That day in school Willie's teacher had told them about a kind of fish that lived in caves. These fish could not see. They had no eyes. The teacher had said it was living in the dark cave that made them like that.

Before he went to bed, Willie took another look out the window. In the pool of light cast by the street lamp, Willie saw the man.

On Tuesday morning when Willie went to school, the man was gone. But when he came home from school with his mother, he was there again.

"*Please* don't look at him," his mother whispered with some urgency.

During his snack Willie said, "Why shouldn't I look?"

"What are you talking about?"

"That man. On the street. Begging."

"I told you. He's sick. It's better to act as if you never saw them. When people are that way, they don't wish to be looked at."

"Why not?"

Mrs. Markham thought for a while. "People are ashamed of being unhappy."

"Are you sure he's unhappy?"

"You don't have to ask if people are unhappy. They tell you all the time."

"Is that part of the sickness?"

"Oh, Willie, I don't know. It's just the way they are."

Willie contemplated the half-inch slice of cake his mother had just given him. He said, "Ever since Dad left, you've been unhappy. Are you ashamed?"

Mrs. Markham closed her eyes. "I wish you wouldn't ask that."

Willie said, "Are you?"

"Willie . . ."

"Think he might come back?"

"It's more than likely," Mrs. Markham said, but Willie wondered if that was what she really thought. He did not think so. "Do you think Dad is unhappy?"

"Where do you get such questions?"

"They're in my mind."

"There's much in the mind that need not be paid attention to."

"Fish that live in caves have no eyes."

"What are you talking about?"

"My teacher said it's all that darkness. The fish forget to see. So they lose their eyes."

"I doubt she said that."

"She did."

"Willie, you have too much imagination."

After his mother went to work, Willie gazed down onto the street. The man was there. Willie thought of going down, but he knew he was not supposed to leave the building when his mother worked at night. He decided to speak to the man tomorrow.

Next afternoon—Wednesday—Willie said to the man, "I don't have any money. Can I still talk to you?"

The man's eyes focused on Willie. They were gray eyes with folds of dirty skin beneath them. He needed a shave.

WORDS TO OWN

urgency (ur′jən·sē) *n.*: insistence; need for fast action.
contemplated (kän′təm·plāt′id) *v.*: studied carefully.

WHAT DO FISH HAVE TO DO WITH ANYTHING? **371**

A **Reading Skills and Strategies**
Chronological Order
? When did Willie learn about the sightless fish? Why do you think he remembers them now? [Willie learned about the fish earlier that day in school. He remembers them now because the apartment seems empty, like a cave, without his mother.]

B **Critical Thinking**
Speculating
? Why is it so important to Mrs. Markham that her son not look at the homeless man? [Possible responses: She is afraid of the homeless man; she wants to protect her son from negative experiences and thoughts.] **How do you think her attitude will affect Willie?** [Possible responses: It will make him more curious about the man; it will make him afraid of the man.]

C **Critical Thinking**
Speculating
? Why doesn't Mrs. Markham want Willie to ask her about her unhappiness? [Possible responses: The question is painful to her; she wants to shield Willie from the truth about her feelings.]

D **Elements of Literature**
Character
? Why does Willie bring up the sightless fish at this point in their conversation? [Possible responses: Willie sees that his mother is blinding herself to reality by refusing to answer his questions; he now understands that you can't make a situation—or person—go away by ignoring it.]

Using Students' Strengths

Auditory Learners
Have students work in groups of seven to create a news broadcast of the police arriving on the scene and forcing the homeless man to leave. One student in each group can be the news director in charge of the broadcast; another student can be the news anchor, who summarizes what is happening. A third student can be a reporter interviewing students who play the roles of the homeless man, a police officer, Willie, and Mrs. Markham.

Naturalist Learners
There are more than twenty kinds of fish that cannot see. They live in caves deep in the ocean. In the oceans off the coast of the eastern United States, for example, the sightless *cavefish* or *blind-fish* compensate for their lack of sight with a sharp sense of touch. They have small sense organs all over their bodies that enable them to feel what they cannot see. Have students research more about sightless fish, report their findings in a couple of paragraphs, and add illustrations.

An *Adam's apple* is the lump of thyroid cartilage in the front of the neck. Much larger in men than in women, it got its name from the belief that a piece of the forbidden fruit in the Garden of Eden, popularly regarded as an apple, got stuck in Adam's throat.

B Reading Skills and Strategies

Making Inferences

? What does the homeless man's answer suggest about his feelings? [It suggests that he really is unhappy and is ashamed or embarrassed to admit this to others.]

C Reading Skills and Strategies

Chronological Order

? How much time has passed since Willie last spoke with the man? [It is the following day; today is Friday, and they last spoke on Thursday.]

D Critical Thinking

Interpreting

? Why does the homeless man say that Willie can see? [Possible responses: because Willie pays attention to him; because Willie is aware that others are unhappy and he wants to help them; because Willie asks important questions.]

"My mother said you were unhappy. Is that true?"

"Could be," the man said.

"What are you unhappy about?"

The man's eyes narrowed as he studied Willie intently. He said, "How come you want to know?"

Willie shrugged.

"I think you should go home, kid."

"I am home." Willie gestured toward the apartment. "I live right here. Fifth floor. Where do you live?"

"Around."

"*Are* you unhappy?" Willie persisted.

A The man ran a tongue over his lips. His Adam's apple bobbed.

Willie said, "I'm trying to learn about unhappiness."

"Why?"

"I don't think I want to say."

"A man has the right to remain silent," the man said and closed his eyes.

Willie remained standing on the pavement for a while before walking back to his apartment. Once inside his own room, he looked down from the window. The man was still there. At one moment Willie was certain he was looking at the apartment building and the floor on which Willie lived.

The next day—Thursday—after dropping a nickel in the man's palm, Willie said, "I've decided to tell you why I want to learn about unhappiness."

The man gave a grunt.

B "See, I've never seen anyone look so unhappy as you do. So I figure you must know a lot about it."

The man took a deep breath. "Well, yeah, maybe."

Willie said, "And I need to find a cure for it."

"A *what*?"

"A cure for unhappiness."

The man pursed his lips and blew a silent whistle. Then he said, "Why?"

"My mother is unhappy."

"Why's that?"

"My dad left."

"How come?"

"I don't know. But she's unhappy all the time. So if I found a cure for unhappiness, it would be a good thing, wouldn't it?"

"I suppose."

Willie said, "Would you like some cake?"

"What kind?"

"I don't know. Cake."

"Depends on the cake."

C On Friday Willie said to the man, "I found out what kind of cake it is."

"Yeah?"

"Poundcake. But I don't know why it's called that."

"Probably doesn't matter."

For a moment neither said anything. Then Willie said, "In school my teacher said there are fish that live in caves and the caves are dark, so the fish don't have eyes. What do you think? Do you believe that?"

"Sure."

"You do? How come?"

"Because you said so."

"You mean, just because someone *said* it you believe it?"

"Not someone. You."

Willie said, "But, well, maybe it *isn't* true."

The man grunted. "Hey, do you believe it?"

Willie nodded.

D "Well, you're not just anyone. You got eyes. You see. You ain't no fish."

"Oh."

WORDS TO OWN

intently (in·tent′lē) *adv.*: with attention firmly directed.

Taking a Second Look

Review: Monitoring Comprehension
Remind students that when they monitor their comprehension, they use reading strategies to help them think about the mental processes involved in reading, recognize when they are having trouble, and choose appropriate strategies to comprehend a text better. Review the following reading strategies:

• **Rereading**—Go back to the last point at which you understood the text and reread the passage more slowly. You may have missed some important information.

• **Using Resources**—Use resources such as a dictionary, glossary, thesaurus, encyclopedia, almanac, or atlas to gather information and clarify aspects of the text.

• **Questioning**—Ask questions about aspects of the text that you don't understand, such as the vocabulary, topic, or organization.

Activities

1. Have students work in small groups to demonstrate how they approach a confusing portion of the text.

2. Students can work in pairs to find any unfamiliar references in "What Do Fish Have to Do with Anything?" and then locate their meanings in a resource text.

3. Ask students to write five questions about parts of the story that are confusing to them. Then have students exchange papers with a classmate and try to answer each other's questions.

"What a person needs is always more than they say."

"What's your name?"

"Willie."

"That's a boy's name. What's your grown-up name?"

Willie thought for a moment. "William, I guess." **[E]**

"And that means another thing."

"What?"

"I'll take some of that cake."

Willie smiled. "You will?"

"Just said it, didn't I?"

"I'll get it."

Willie ran to the apartment. He took the box from the refrigerator as well as a knife, then hurried back down to the street. "I'll cut you a piece," he said.

As the man looked on, Willie opened the box, then held his thumb against the cake to make sure the portion was the right size. **[F]** With a poke of the knife he made a small mark for the proper width.

Just as he was about to cut, the man said, "Hold it!"

Willie looked up. "What?"

"What were you doing with your thumb there?"

"I was measuring the right size. The right portion. One portion is what a person is supposed to get."

"Where'd you learn that?"

"It says so on the box. You can see for yourself." He held out the box.

The man studied the box, then handed it back to Willie. "That's just lies," he said.

"How do you know?"

"William, how can a box say how much a person needs?"

"But it does. The scientists say so. They measured, so they know. Then they put it there."

"Lies," the man repeated.

Willie studied the man. His eyes seemed bleary.[3] "Then how much should I cut?" he asked.

The man said, "You have to look at me, then at the cake, and then you're going to have to decide for yourself."

"Oh." Willie looked at the cake. The piece was about three inches wide. Willie looked up at the man. After a moment he cut the cake into two pieces, each an inch and a half wide. He gave one piece to the man and kept the other. **[G]**

"Bless you," the man said, as he took the piece and laid it in his left hand. He began to break off pieces with his right hand and one by one put them into his mouth. Each piece was chewed thoughtfully. Willie watched him piece by piece.

When the man was done, he dusted his hands of crumbs.

"Now I'll give you something," the man said.

"What?" Willie said, surprised.

"The cure for unhappiness."

"You know it?" Willie asked, eyes wide. The man nodded.

"What is it?"

"It's this: What a person needs is always more than they say." **[H]**

Willie thought for a while. "Who's *they*?" he asked.

---

3. **bleary:** dim or blurred, as from lack of rest.

WHAT DO FISH HAVE TO DO WITH ANYTHING? **373**

E Critical Thinking

Analyzing

? Why does the homeless man want to know Willie's "grown-up name"? Why does Willie have to think for a minute? [Sample responses: The homeless man is treating Willie like an adult. Willie is so used to being treated like a child that he doesn't know how to respond for a moment. He is rarely called by his full name.]

F Struggling Readers

Finding Details

? Why does Willie measure the cake the way he does? [He is imitating his mother.]

G Elements of Literature

Character

? What does Willie learn from the homeless man? How does it change him? [Possible responses: He learns to think for himself; he learns to be generous; he learns that each person is an individual and has his or her own needs—no one is "average."]

H Elements of Literature

Theme

? What does the homeless man mean? What is his special message or idea about life? [Possible responses: People need more than they realize; our needs can be psychological as well as physical; a person is not always aware of what he or she needs or cannot always admit it.]

Skill Link

Grammar: Direct and Indirect Quotations

Use this activity before you teach the Grammar Link activity on p. 378 to help you assess students' ability to distinguish between direct and indirect quotations.

Review the difference between direct and indirect quotations. Remind students that a speaker's exact words are set off with quotation marks, while indirect quotations are not. For each of the following statements, have students write D if the sentence is a direct quotation and I if it is an indirect quotation.

1. "Don't look that way," she said. [D]
2. As they walked, Willie told his mother all about his day in school. [I]

3. "Money will cure a lot of unhappiness," Mrs. Markham said suddenly. [D]
4. "I wish you wouldn't ask so many questions," she snapped. [D]
5. Mrs. Markham explained all about beggars to Willie. [I]

A Elements of Literature
Character
❓ Why does Willie give the man the other piece of cake? How has Willie grown as a person? [Sample responses: Willie understands what the man has said, that a person needs more than he or she can say. Willie has matured; he has gained knowledge that helps him appreciate the complexities of life and deal with its difficulties.]

B Critical Thinking
Speculating
❓ Why do you think Mrs. Markham is so upset with Willie? [Possible responses: She is afraid that the homeless man will hurt Willie; she is angry that Willie has disobeyed her; she does not like the ideas the homeless man has put into Willie's head.]

C Reading Skills and Strategies
Drawing Conclusions
❓ What do you think happened to the man? [Possible responses: He moved on because he found food or shelter in another part of town; the police forced him to move on; Willie's mother had him removed from the area so Willie couldn't talk to him anymore.]

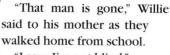

FROM THE EDITOR'S DESK

We wanted a short story by Avi for this theme because he so often writes about justice and doing the right thing, and his work is very popular with middle schoolers. We contacted Avi, told him our theme, asked if he would write a story for us—and held our breath. This sensitive story is what arrived.

The man pointed to the cake box. "The people on the box," he said.

A ⎡ Willie thought for a moment; then he gave the man the other piece of cake.
⎣ The man took it, saying, "Good man," and then ate it.

The next day was Saturday. Willie did not go to school. All morning he kept looking down from his window for the man, but it was raining and he did not appear. Willie wondered where he was but could not imagine it.

Willie's mother woke about noon. Willie sat with her while she ate the breakfast he had made. "I found the cure for unhappiness," he announced.

"Did you?" his mother said. She was reading a memo from the convenience store's owner.

"It's, 'What a person needs is always more than they say.'"

His mother put her papers down. "That's nonsense. Where did you hear that?"

"That man."

"What man?"

"On the street. The one who was begging. You said he was unhappy. So I asked him."

"Willie, I told you I didn't want you to even look at that man."

"He's a nice man . . . "

"How do you know?"

"I've talked to him."

"When? How much?"

Willie shrank down. "I did, that's all."

B ⎡ "Willie, I forbid you to talk to him. Do you understand me? Do you? Answer me!"

"Yes," Willie said, but in his mind he decided he would talk to the man one more time. He needed to explain why he could not talk to him anymore.

On Sunday, however, the man was not there. Nor was he there on Monday.

C ⎡ "That man is gone," Willie said to his mother as they walked home from school.
"I saw. I'm not blind."
"Where do you think he went?"
⎣ "I couldn't care less. And you might as well

Making the Connections

Connecting to the Theme: "Justice for All"

After students have read the story, talk about the collection theme. Ask students which character or characters in the story have been denied justice: Willie, Mrs. Markham, the homeless man—or all of them? Divide the class into three equal groups, and assign one character to each group. Have each group decide how its character has been treated unjustly and how the situation could be corrected. Have each group select a spokesperson to present its conclusion. As a class, draw parallels between this and other stories students have read in this collection.

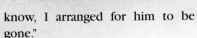

know, I arranged for him to be gone."

Willie stopped short. "What do you mean?"

"I called the police. We don't need a nuisance like that around here. Pestering kids."

"He wasn't pestering me."

"Of course he was."

"How do you know?"

"Willie, I have eyes. I can see."

Willie stared at his mother. "No, you can't. You're a fish. You live in a cave."

"Willie, don't talk nonsense."

"My name isn't Willie. It's William." Turning, he walked back to the school playground.

Mrs. Markham watched him go. "Fish," she wondered to herself; "what do fish have to do with anything?"

MEET THE WRITER

"Don't Be Satisfied with Answers Others Give You"

Avi (1937–) says he became a writer out of sheer stubbornness. In elementary school and high school, he failed many subjects, not knowing at the time that he had a serious learning disability. Still, he was determined to prove to everyone that he could write if he just set his mind to it. First he tried to write plays, then novels for adults, but he had little success. He didn't discover his true audience until he became a father and took an interest in writing for children and young adults.

66 Only when my own kids came into my life did I start to write for young people. I was to find what I did best. Writing for kids has been at the center of my life ever since. 99

Avi offers the following advice to young people thinking of becoming writers:

66 Listen and watch the world around you. Try to understand why things happen. Don't be satisfied with answers others give you. Don't assume that because everyone believes a thing, it is right *or* wrong. Reason things out for yourself. Work to get answers on your own. 99

More About Why Things Happen

Avi has written many novels about strong-willed young people making tough decisions in challenging or dangerous situations. These include *Wolf Rider: A Tale of Terror* (Macmillan); *Windcatcher* (Macmillan); *The True Confessions of Charlotte Doyle* (Orchard), a Newbery Honor Book and the winner of the Boston Globe–Horn Book Award for fiction in 1991; and *The Barn* (Orchard).

WHAT DO FISH HAVE TO DO WITH ANYTHING? **375**

D **Elements of Literature**
Character
❓ What does Willie learn about his mother? How does it change him? [Sample response: Willie learns that his mother refuses to see the truth. As a result, Willie now tries to face important but unpleasant issues, such as the homeless, on his own.]

E **Critical Thinking**
Speculating
❓ Why does Willie insist on being called "William"? [Possible response: Willie has matured because of his experiences with his mother and the homeless man; he wants to be treated in a more adult manner.]

F **Elements of Literature**
Symbols
❓ What do the sightless fish represent or symbolize? [The fish symbolize blindness. They represent Mrs. Markham's unwillingness to respect all people or listen to what they say.]

BROWSING IN THE FILES

About the Author. Avi (pronounced "Ah-vee") Wortis keeps in contact with his readers by making regular visits to schools. "I always ask to speak to the learning-disabled kids," he says. "They come in slowly, waiting for yet another pep talk, more instructions. Eyes cast down, they won't even look at me. Their anger glows. I don't say a thing. I lay out pages of my own copy-edited manuscripts, which are covered with red marks. 'Look here,' I say, 'see that spelling mistake. There, another spelling mistake. Looks like I forgot to put a capital letter there. Oops! Letter reversal.' Their eyes lift. They are listening. And I am among friends."

Resources

Selection Assessment
Formal Assessment
• Selection Test, p. 74
Test Generator
• Selection Test

Assessing Learning

Check Test: Fill-in-the-Blank

1. In the afternoon, Willie eats a snack of _____. [pound cake]
2. Mrs. Markham doesn't want Willie to talk to the _____. [homeless man]
3. Mrs. Markham works the night shift at a(n) _____. [convenience store]
4. To Mrs. Markham, unhappiness can be cured with _____. [money]
5. The homeless man is taken away by the _____. [police]

Standardized Test Preparation

For practice with standardized test format specific to this selection, see
• *Standardized Test Preparation*, p. 60
For practice in proofreading and editing, see
• *Daily Oral Grammar,* Transparency 22

MAKING MEANINGS

First Thoughts

1. Some students may have felt angry, while others might have felt relieved that Willie will be safe from the "bleary-eyed man."

Shaping Interpretations

2. Mrs. Markham is afraid the homeless man will harm Willie; also, she does not want him exposed to life's unpleasantness.

3. She has been unhappy since Willie's father left. Willie gives the homeless man food and attention; he tries to find a cure for his mother's unhappiness.

4. Mrs. Markham says the story isn't true and that Willie has too much imagination; the homeless man believes the information, because he realizes Willie is an honest person and would not lie.

5. Willie says the portion size is noted on the box, but the homeless man says Willie should look at him and then decide the proper amount. The homeless man then tells Willie the cure for unhappiness: A person always needs more than he or she says. The homeless man is telling Willie to think for himself and to treat each person as an individual.

6. Willie insists on being called William because he wants to assert his independence. The name change shows that Willie is maturing; he is becoming less of a child and more of an adult.

Connecting with the Text

7. Statement a. can be found on p. 367, b. and c. on p. 368, and d. on p. 371. Mrs. Markham makes all the statements, applying a. and b. to Willie, c. to herself, and d. to the homeless man. Students are likely to have changed their opinion about some of the statements.

Extending the Text

8. Students should see that Avi's advice has to be applied judiciously or it is unwise. For example, if someone tells you to avoid a hot stove, there is no reason to doubt the advice.

Challenging the Text

9. Willie's mother says this at the end of the story. It is a good title because it sums up the story's theme: Refusing to face reality leads to unhappiness.

T376

MAKING MEANINGS

First Thoughts

[respond]

1. How did you feel when you learned that Mrs. Markham has called the police?

Shaping Interpretations

[interpret]

2. Why doesn't Mrs. Markham want Willie to look at or talk to the homeless man?

[identify]

3. According to Willie, why is his mother unhappy? How does Willie try to help both his mother and the homeless man?

[identify]

4. Willie's mother and the homeless man react differently to the information about the fish with no eyes. What does each one say?

[synthesize]

5. Summarize the conversation Willie and the homeless man have about the right amount of poundcake to serve a person. What do you think the homeless man is trying to say to Willie?

[analyze]

6. Why do you think Willie wants to be called William at the end? What does this show about the way his **character** has grown and changed during the story?

Connecting with the Text

[connect]

7. Look back at the statements you responded to before you read the story. Where are they expressed in the story? Has reading the story changed the way you look at these opinions?

Extending the Text

[evaluate]

8. On page 375, Avi says, "Don't be satisfied with answers others give you. Don't assume that because everyone believes a thing, it is right *or* wrong. Reason things out for yourself. Work to get answers on your own." Is this good advice, or could it lead to trouble? Explain your opinion.

Challenging the Text

[evaluate]

9. Who says, "What do fish have to do with anything?" When? Does the quotation make a good **title** for the story? Why or why not?

376 JUSTICE FOR ALL

Reading Check

Imagine that you're Willie and you're going to the police to try to explain what happened with the homeless man. Describe your meetings with him, and explain why your mother called the police. Tell the police why you want to help him. Use your sequence chart to make sure that you cover all the important events.

Reading Check

Sample response:

Monday afternoon, I saw a homeless man on the street. While my mother napped that afternoon, I went outside and watched the homeless man for twenty minutes. Then I gave the man a nickel. On Wednesday, I asked the man why he was unhappy, but he did not answer. On Thursday, I gave the man a nickel and some pound cake and told him about the blind fish. He told me the cure for unhappiness.

On Saturday, I told my mother all about our meeting, but she forbade me to talk to the homeless man. The man was gone on Sunday and did not return on Monday, either. My mother told me she had the police take him away. That's why I'm here at the station house. Please help the homeless man because he is unhappy and hungry.

CHOICES: Building Your Portfolio

Writer's Notebook

1. Collecting Ideas for Supporting a Position

The problem of homelessness hits home for Willie when he befriends a man begging on the street. What problems or issues in your community have you been noticing and thinking about lately? Try to recall articles that you've read or stories that you've seen on the news. Then, freewrite about an issue that makes you want to take a stand. State your position in a sentence, and list a few supporting reasons.

> TV news story about lonely people in hospitals made me sad. Could try to get kids to start volunteer visitor club at school.

Creative Writing

2. Meeting of Minds

Imagine that Willie meets the homeless man again and they have another conversation. What would they say to each other? Write a short conversation between them. Looking at some of their talks in the story might give you ideas and help you use dialogue.

A Letter

3. Thanks from the Heart

In the story Willie meets someone who changes the way he thinks about life. Have you ever had an experience with someone who taught you something valuable about life? Write a thank-you note you wish you could send to that person. You may want to send your note to this special person.

Debate

4. Pros and Cons

Hold a debate on the following question: In some cities, people can be arrested for begging or sleeping on the streets. Do you think this is fair? Why or why not?

First, come up with a statement that answers the question. Then, choose two teams: one to argue *for* the statement and one to argue *against* it. Have each team do research to find facts and statistics to back up its point of view. Before and after the debate, take a class vote on the issue to see if people change their minds.

WHAT DO FISH HAVE TO DO WITH ANYTHING? **377**

Grading Timesaver

Rubrics for each Choices assignment appear on p. 151 in the *Portfolio Management System*.

CHOICES: Building Your Portfolio

1. **Writer's Notebook** Remind students to save their work, which they may use as prewriting for the Writer's Workshop on pp. 396–400.
2. **Creative Writing** Before students write their dialogues, have them work in pairs to role-play possible conversations. They should take turns playing the two roles.
3. **A Letter** Have students create a prewriting web to generate specific examples to include in their letters.
4. **Debate** Students may wish to consult the *Reader's Guide* or the *New York Times Index* for accounts of recent controversies concerning the homeless. Rabbi Charles A. Kroloff has written a hypertext book called *54 Ways You Can Help the Homeless,* available on the Internet. *You may want to preview any Internet activity that you suggest to students. Because these resources are sometimes public forums, their content can be unpredictable.*

Using Compiled Information to Raise Additional Questions

Sometimes when students prepare for debates, such as the debate on people's rights in Choice 4 above, their research will raise new questions to pursue. For example, in compiling information on begging in the streets, students may become interested in a question related to freedom of speech. Encourage students to use their research as a springboard for exploring related topics.

Using Students' Strengths

Interpersonal Learners

As a prewriting exercise for Choice 1, have students explain to the class the problem they have chosen and ask for suggestions. Students can also interview community leaders to gather information about key social issues in their region.

Kinesthetic Learners

As students prepare their arguments for the debate, encourage them to consider the effect of their nonverbal communication. Point out that posture and effective hand movements can help persuade an audience as much as words. For example, as they speak, students should stand straight, shoulders back, and make eye contact with members of the audience. Students can practice their body language in front of a mirror to isolate and reinforce effective gestures.

GRAMMAR LINK

Have students select from their portfolios writing that contains dialogue. Then have them rewrite the direct quotations as indirect quotations. Students should work in pairs to check each other's work; they should make sure that the indirect quotations correctly summarize the direct quotations.

Try It Out
Possible Answers

1. a. "What's the matter with him?" Willie asked. [Willie asked what was wrong with him.]
   b. Willie said, "Can I have a bigger piece of cake?" [Willie asked for a bigger piece of cake.]
   c. "Are you unhappy?" Willie persisted. [Willie kept asking the man if he was unhappy.]
2. That day in school, Willie's teacher had said, "There is a kind of fish that lives in caves. These fish cannot see. They have no eyes." The teacher also said, "It is because they live in the dark cave that they are like that."

VOCABULARY
Possible Responses

1. Students should give unspecific descriptions, lacking details.
2. Students should convey pressure and intensity.
3. Students should show anticipation.
4. Students should lean forward, make eye contact, and show great attention to their partner's words.

Resources ———

Grammar
• *Grammar and Language Links*, p. 41
Vocabulary
• *Words to Own*, p. 16

GRAMMAR LINK   MINI-LESSON

Direct and Indirect Quotations

Language Handbook HELP

See Quotation Marks, page 755.

Technology HELP

See Language Workshop CD-ROM. Key word entry: quotation marks.

In the story Willie has several conversations with his mother and with the homeless man. The exact words of those talks are put in quotation marks and are called **direct quotations**.

EXAMPLE Willie said, "Would you like some cake?"

Sometimes, though, instead of quoting someone's exact words, Avi summarizes what the person said. These summaries, called **indirect quotations,** are not placed in quotation marks.

EXAMPLE That day in school Willie's teacher had told them about a kind of fish that lived in caves. These fish could not see. They had no eyes. The teacher had said it was living in the dark cave that made them like that.

Try It Out

1. Find three direct quotations in the story, and rewrite them as indirect quotations.

2. Look at the example of an indirect quotation at the left. Rewrite it as a direct quotation, using the exact words Willie's teacher might have used. Remember to put her words in quotation marks.

VOCABULARY   HOW TO OWN A WORD

WORD BANK

vaguely
urgency
contemplated
intently

Act It Out

With a partner, follow these instructions to show what the Word Bank words mean.

1. Describe <u>vaguely</u> to your partner an event you attended recently—a movie, concert, or game.
2. Using words or gestures or both, ask your partner with <u>urgency</u> to do something.
3. On your birthday you <u>contemplated</u> eating a delicious piece of cake. Show how you were feeling.
4. Have a conversation with your partner. Show that you are listening to each other <u>intently</u>.

378 JUSTICE FOR ALL

Grammar Link Quick Check

Have students identify each item as a direct or indirect quotation. Then have them rewrite direct quotations as indirect quotations and rewrite indirect quotations as direct quotations.

1. "Could be anything," his mother said. [Direct. Indirect: His mother said it could be anything.]
2. "He's unhappy," she said. [Direct. Indirect: She said that he was unhappy.]
3. Mrs. Markham said that she was leaving. [Indirect. Direct: "I'm leaving," Mrs. Markham said.]
4. Willie said that he was trying to learn about unhappiness. [Indirect. Direct: Willie said, "I'm trying to learn about unhappiness."]
5. Willie said, "I need to find a cure for it." [Direct. Indirect: Willie said that he needed to find a cure for it.]

Before You Read

THE SNEETCHES

Make the Connection

Justice for All

This collection of stories is called Justice for All. Dr. Seuss uses some unusual characters to give us another lesson in justice.

Think tank. In a small group, make a list of injustices you are aware of. Discuss events you've read about in newspapers or magazines. List some of the reasons people are rejected or are treated unjustly. (Reasons may be as simple as the clothes people wear or as complex as their personal beliefs.)

Quickwrite

Decide which item on your group's list is the greatest injustice. Explain why you feel the way you do and how you think the injustice could be remedied.

Elements of Literature

Rhymes: *Sneetches* and *Eaches*

Everyone knows what a rhyme is: two words that have the same chiming sounds. When asked the question "What is rhyme?" Dr. Seuss replied, "A rhyme is something without which I would probably be in the dry-cleaning business." To make sure his poems galloped along with catchy rhymes, Dr. Seuss often invented words to rhyme with real words. For instance, throughout "The Sneetches" he rhymes the real word *stars* with the made-up word *thars*. For that matter, who ever heard of Sneetches before Dr. Seuss invented them?

Rhyme is the repetition of accented vowel sounds, and all sounds following them, in words that are close together in a poem.

For more on Rhyme, see pages 178–179 and the Handbook of Literary Terms.

go.hrw.com
LE0 6-5

Summary ■

In this humorous poem, the Star-Belly Sneetches consider themselves superior to the Plain-Belly Sneetches. A traveling con artist, Sylvester McMonkey McBean, takes advantage of the Plain-Belly Sneetches' envy and sells them belly stars. As a result, stars are no longer valued, so the Sneetches with the original stars have them removed. The newly starred Sneetches then want their stars taken off. The cycle continues—"Off again! On again!"—until the Sneetches are confused about who should and shouldn't have a star. When all their money is spent, McBean leaves town, and the Sneetches finally realize that both groups of Sneetches are equal.

Resources

Listening
Audio CD Library
A humorous recording of this poem is included in the *Audio CD Library:*
• Disc 8, Track 4

Ⓐ Elements of Literature
Rhyme
❓ What real word does the invented word *thars* replace? [*theirs*] Why doesn't the author use *theirs*? [It wouldn't rhyme, and it isn't funny.]

Ⓑ Elements of Literature
Alliteration
❓ Alliteration is the repetition of initial consonant sounds. Identify the alliteration in this line. [*snoots, sniff, snort*] Why do you think Seuss uses alliteration? [Possible answers: It makes the line flow smoothly; it reinforces the Sneetches' "snootiness."]

Ⓒ English Language Learners
Explain to students that frankfurters (also called *hot dogs*) and marshmallows are often put on sticks and roasted over a grill at outdoor parties or picnics.

Ⓓ Reading Skills and Strategies
Main Idea
❓ What real-life differences divide people into opposing groups? [Possible responses: religion, race, clothing, money.]

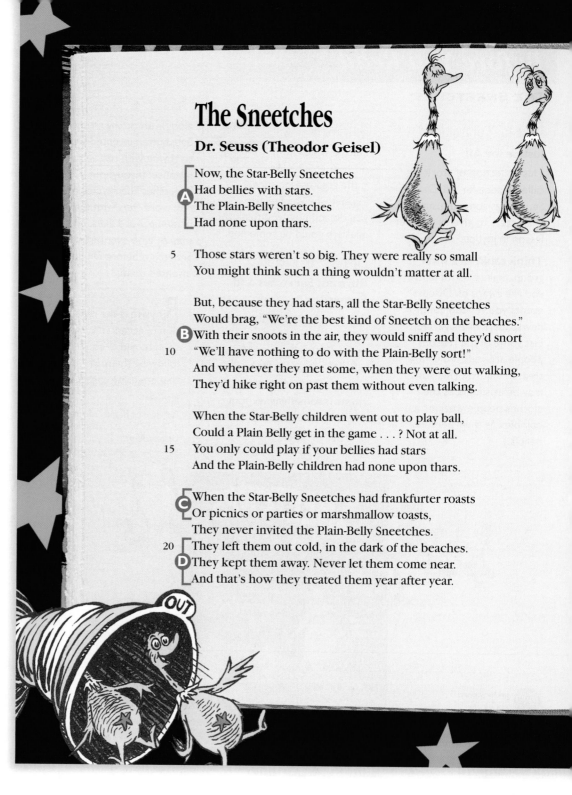

The Sneetches
Dr. Seuss (Theodor Geisel)

Ⓐ Now, the Star-Belly Sneetches
Had bellies with stars.
The Plain-Belly Sneetches
Had none upon thars.

5 Those stars weren't so big. They were really so small
You might think such a thing wouldn't matter at all.

But, because they had stars, all the Star-Belly Sneetches
Would brag, "We're the best kind of Sneetch on the beaches."
Ⓑ With their snoots in the air, they would sniff and they'd snort
10 "We'll have nothing to do with the Plain-Belly sort!"
And whenever they met some, when they were out walking,
They'd hike right on past them without even talking.

When the Star-Belly children went out to play ball,
Could a Plain Belly get in the game . . . ? Not at all.
15 You only could play if your bellies had stars
And the Plain-Belly children had none upon thars.

Ⓒ When the Star-Belly Sneetches had frankfurter roasts
Or picnics or parties or marshmallow toasts,
They never invited the Plain-Belly Sneetches.
20 They left them out cold, in the dark of the beaches.
Ⓓ They kept them away. Never let them come near.
And that's how they treated them year after year.

Reaching All Students

Struggling Readers
To help struggling readers understand the poem's challenging language and theme, have them read with a partner. Have one student read a stanza of the poem aloud while the second student listens. Then the second student should ask the first one a question about the stanza. Students should continue alternating roles until they have finished the poem.

English Language Learners
Pair English language learners with advanced learners. Have partners read the poem together and list all the unfamiliar words. Students can look up each word in the dictionary to see if it is real or invented and to find its definition. Then have them create definitions for the invented words based on context. For additional strategies to supplement instruction for English language learners, see
• *Lesson Plans Including Strategies for English-Language Learners*

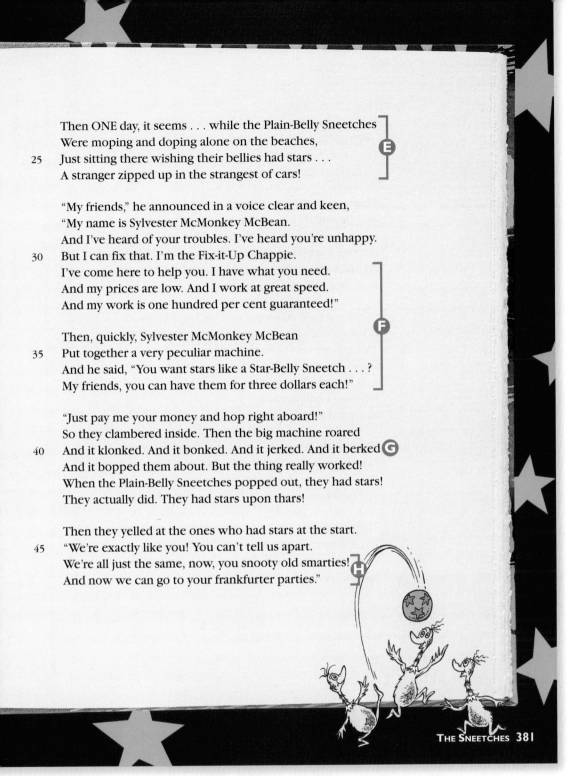

Then ONE day, it seems . . . while the Plain-Belly Sneetches
Were moping and doping alone on the beaches,
25 Just sitting there wishing their bellies had stars . . .
A stranger zipped up in the strangest of cars!

"My friends," he announced in a voice clear and keen,
"My name is Sylvester McMonkey McBean.
And I've heard of your troubles. I've heard you're unhappy.
30 But I can fix that. I'm the Fix-it-Up Chappie.
I've come here to help you. I have what you need.
And my prices are low. And I work at great speed.
And my work is one hundred per cent guaranteed!"

Then, quickly, Sylvester McMonkey McBean
35 Put together a very peculiar machine.
And he said, "You want stars like a Star-Belly Sneetch . . . ?
My friends, you can have them for three dollars each!"

"Just pay me your money and hop right aboard!"
So they clambered inside. Then the big machine roared
40 And it klonked. And it bonked. And it jerked. And it berked
And it bopped them about. But the thing really worked!
When the Plain-Belly Sneetches popped out, they had stars!
They actually did. They had stars upon thars!

Then they yelled at the ones who had stars at the start.
45 "We're exactly like you! You can't tell us apart.
We're all just the same, now, you snooty old smarties!
And now we can go to your frankfurter parties."

THE SNEETCHES 381

Elements of Literature
Rhyme
❓ What words rhyme in this stanza? [*sneetches/beaches; stars/cars*] What is the stanza's rhyme scheme? [*aabb*] Why do you think Dr. Seuss uses this rhyme scheme? [Sample response: The pairs of rhymed couplets are humorous, bouncy, and rhythmic.]

Critical Thinking
Analyzing
❓ Why does McBean come to the Sneetches' town? [He comes to make money off their prejudice, not to help them resolve their differences.]

Elements of Literature
Onomatopoeia
❓ Onomatopoeia is the use of a word whose sound imitates or suggests its meaning. Onomatopoeic words sound like the thing they refer to. *Boom, growled,* and *plunked* are examples of onomatopoeia. What onomatopoeic words does Dr. Seuss use in this line? [*klonked, bonked, jerked,* and *berked*]

Reading Skills and Strategies
Making Predictions
❓ What do you predict will happen next? What clues in the text helped you make your prediction? [Sample response: The Sneetches are motivated by feelings of superiority. Since the Sneetches who once had no stars now have stars, the Sneetches with the original belly stars will probably want to have their stars removed. The newly starred Sneetches will then want their stars off.]

Using Students' Strengths

Kinesthetic Learners
Sylvester McMonkey McBean roars into town with his odd star machine. Have small groups of students create models of McBean's machine. Students should use found objects, such as boxes, foil, empty tubes, cans, and coat hangers, to create their machines. Have each group demonstrate its machine for the class.

Auditory/Musical Learners
Invite students to set "The Sneetches" to music or create rap versions of the poem. For their musical versions, students should maintain the "Sneetches" story, rhyme scheme, and moral. However, they can shorten the poem or substitute verses or lines of their own. Ask students to perform their songs for the class. You may wish to tape record or videotape the performances.

A **Elements of Literature**
Irony
? Irony is a contrast between what is expected and what really happens. What is ironic about the Star-Belly Sneetches at this point? [The original Star-Belly Sneetches still believe they are superior, even though the other Sneetches now have stars on their bellies.]

B **Reading Skills and Strategies**
Connecting with the Text
? Name some examples of fashion styles that are popular one day and outdated the next. [Possible responses: platform shoes, fleece pullovers, baggy pants.] Why do you think people flock to these fads? [Possible responses: They want to look fashionable and feel popular; they want to feel as if they are part of a special group.]

C **Elements of Literature**
Rhyme
List other words that rhyme with *mad* and *bad*. [Possible responses: *lad, add, dad, had, fad, sad, tad, pad, cad.*]

"Good grief!" groaned the ones who had stars at the first.
A "We're *still* the best Sneetches and they are the worst.
50   But, now, how in the world will we know," they all frowned,
"If which kind is what, or the other way round?"

Then up came McBean with a very sly wink
And he said, "Things are not quite as bad as you think.
So you don't know who's who. That is perfectly true.
55   But come with me, friends. Do you know what I'll do?
I'll make you, again, the best Sneetches on beaches
And all it will cost you is ten dollars eaches."

B "Belly stars are no longer in style," said McBean.
What you need is a trip through my Star-*Off* Machine.
60   This wondrous contraption will take *off* your stars
So you won't look like Sneetches who have them on thars."
And that handy machine
Working very precisely
Removed all the stars from their tummies quite nicely.

65   Then, with snoots in the air, they paraded about
And they opened their beaks and they let out a shout,
"We know who is who! Now there isn't a doubt.
The best kind of Sneetches are Sneetches without!"

C Then, of course, those with stars all got frightfully mad.
70   To be wearing a star now was frightfully bad.
Then, of course, old Sylvester McMonkey McBean
Invited *them* into his Star-Off Machine.

Crossing the Curriculum

Mathematics

It's plain that Sylvester McMonkey McBean roars into town with a plan: to get as much of the Sneetches' money as he can. But how much does he get? Have students create charts or graphs showing how much money McBean makes, assuming that there are 75 Star-Belly Sneetches, 125 Plain-Belly Sneetches, and 8 star changes for each Sneetch (4 on and 4 off). Remind students that McBean charges different prices for putting stars on and for taking them off.

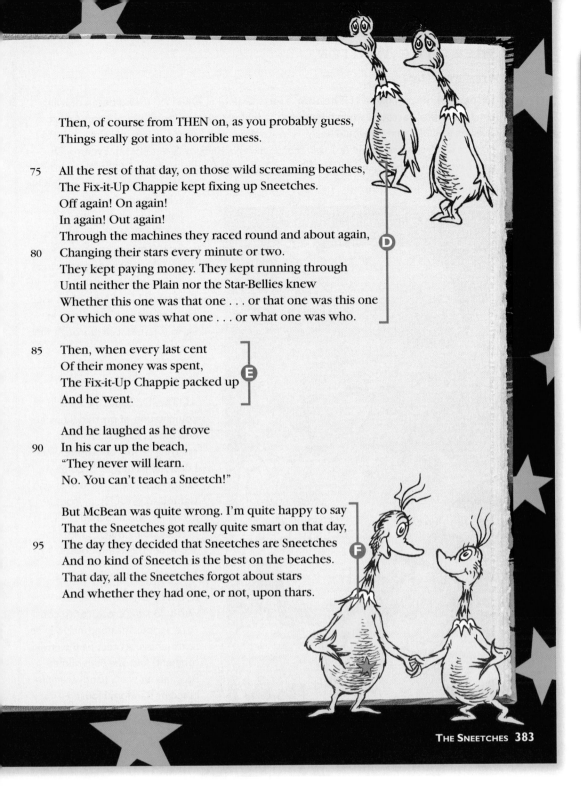

Then, of course from THEN on, as you probably guess,
Things really got into a horrible mess.

75　All the rest of that day, on those wild screaming beaches,
The Fix-it-Up Chappie kept fixing up Sneetches.
Off again! On again!
In again! Out again!
Through the machines they raced round and about again,
80　Changing their stars every minute or two.
They kept paying money. They kept running through
Until neither the Plain nor the Star-Bellies knew
Whether this one was that one . . . or that one was this one
Or which one was what one . . . or what one was who.

85　Then, when every last cent
Of their money was spent,
The Fix-it-Up Chappie packed up
And he went.

And he laughed as he drove
90　In his car up the beach,
"They never will learn.
No. You can't teach a Sneetch!"

But McBean was quite wrong. I'm quite happy to say
That the Sneetches got really quite smart on that day,
95　The day they decided that Sneetches are Sneetches
And no kind of Sneetch is the best on the beaches.
That day, all the Sneetches forgot about stars
And whether they had one, or not, upon thars.

D

E

F

THE SNEETCHES **383**

RESPONDING TO THE ART
Theodore Seuss Geisel
(1904–1991) wrote and illustrated forty-seven books, which have been translated into eighteen languages. In 1984, he won a special Pulitzer Prize for his lifetime contribution to education and entertainment.
Activity. Ask students to point out the details Seuss uses to show the Sneetches' emotions of joy and despair. [Possible responses: joy—upturned beaks, wide-open eyes, upturned faces, clasped hands; despair—droopy postures, down-turned mouths, sad eyes.]

D **Elements of Literature**
　Rhyme
? What words rhyme in this stanza? [*beaches/Sneetches; two/through/knew/who*] What is the stanza's rhyme scheme? [*aabbbcccdc*] Why does Dr. Seuss vary from his usual *aabb* rhyme scheme? [Possible responses: He wants to show the Sneetches' hysteria and their frantic racing around; he wants to add variety to the poem's sound.]

E **Reading Skills and Strategies**
　Drawing Conclusions
? Why does the Fix-it-Up Chappie leave? [He has taken all the Sneetches' money, so he has no reason to stay.]

F **Critical Thinking**
　Evaluating
? Why are the Sneetches smart now? [They know that they are all equal and that it is not important whether or not they have stars.]

Resources

Selection Assessment
Formal Assessment
• Selection Test, p. 76
Test Generator
• Selection Test

Making the Connections

Connecting to the Theme:
"Justice for All"
After students finish the poem, have them discuss how the Sneetches achieve justice for all. Ask students how the resolution of this poem is different from the endings of all the other selections in this collection. Lead students to see that this is the only selection in which the characters finally set aside their differences and realize that everyone is equal and should be treated the same. In the other selections, the injustices are not resolved. Discuss with the class ways that people can work together to make sure everyone is treated fairly.

About the Author. The May 1954 issue of *Life* magazine claimed that children were having difficulty learning to read because their books were boring. This sparked Geisel's publisher, Bennett Cerf, to present Geisel with a list of 400 words that first-graders should know, to be used as the basis for an elementary reader. Nine months later, Geisel had used 220 of the words to create *The Cat in the Hat,* an instant success. Six years later, Cerf bet Geisel fifty dollars that he couldn't write an entire book using only fifty words. Geisel won the bet with *Green Eggs and Ham.*

Writers on Writing. Where did Dr. Seuss get all his wild ideas? Tongue firmly in cheek, he once claimed, "I get all my ideas in Switzerland near the Forka Pass. There is a little town called Gletch, and two thousand feet up above Gletch there is a small hamlet called Uber Gletch. I go there on the fourth of August every summer to get my cuckoo clock repaired. While the cuckoo is in the hospital, I wander around and talk to the people in the streets. They are very strange people, and I get my ideas from them."

MEET THE WRITER

Creature Feature

Dr. Seuss is the pen name of **Theodor Seuss Geisel** (1904–1991), who began drawing fantastic animal cartoons while he was still a child. (His father ran the local zoo.) An art teacher told him that he would never learn to draw, and twenty-seven publishers rejected his first children's book, *And to Think That I Saw It on Mulberry Street* (1937). Even so, Dr. Seuss went on to write and illustrate more than forty children's classics, full of nonsense rhymes, wacky creatures, and his special brand of wisdom.

Judging by the number of books Dr. Seuss has sold—at least 200 million copies—he is one of the most popular writers in history. As he did in "The Sneetches," Dr. Seuss often used his zany characters to look at serious issues as if "through the wrong end of a telescope."

Dr. Seuss explained how he decided on his pen name:

Courtesy of Bill Nelson.

66 The 'Dr. Seuss' name is a combination of my middle name and the fact that I had been studying for my doctorate when I decided to quit to become a cartoonist. My father had always wanted to see a Dr. in front of my name, so I attached it. I figured by doing that, I saved him about ten thousand dollars. 99

More Creature Features

Books by Dr. Seuss that use wacky-looking creatures to convey a serious message include *The Lorax* (about protecting the environment) and *The Butter Battle Book* (about war). (Both are published by Random House.)

384 JUSTICE FOR ALL

Assessing Learning

Check Test: Short Answers

1. Where do the Sneetches live? [on beaches]
2. Which Sneetches think they are best? [Star-Belly Sneetches]
3. How much does McBean charge for putting stars on? [three dollars]
4. How much does he charge for removing stars? [ten dollars]
5. What kind of Sneetches do the Sneetches finally decide are the best? [Neither—they finally decide that all Sneetches are equal.]

Ongoing Assessment

Use the following chart to assess students' written responses to literature.
A=Always S=Sometimes R=Rarely N=Never

Criteria	Rating
States reasoned viewpoints	
Entertains contrary interpretations	
Cites textual evidence to support views	
Understands literary elements	
Makes connections to the reading	

MAKING MEANINGS

MAKING MEANINGS

First Thoughts

[respond]

1. Complete the following sentences:
   - My favorite lines in this poem are . . .
   - I was surprised when . . .
   - I think this poem is about . . .

Shaping Interpretations

[respond]

2. What one word would you use to describe the Star-Bellies? the Plain-Bellies?

[interpret]

3. What opinion does McBean have of the Sneetches in general? Why do you think he is right (or wrong)?

[interpret]

4. Why do the Sneetches finally change their behavior?

[analyze]

5. What words has Dr. Seuss made up to keep his lines **rhymed**?

[interpret]

6. What do you think is the **moral**, or lesson, of this poem? Do you think it is an important one?

Connecting with the Text

[connect]

7. What real-life people behave like the Sneetches or like Sylvester McMonkey McBean? For ideas, look back at your think-tank list or your notes for the Quickwrite on page 379.

Extending the Text

[evaluate]

8. Do you think people can change their attitudes, the way the Sneetches finally did? Give reasons for your answer.

> ### Reading Check
> a. Why do one group of Sneetches think they are better than another group? How do they treat the other group?
>
> b. What offer does McBean make to the Plain-Bellies? What offer does he then make to the Star-Bellies?
>
> c. When does McBean finally leave? What happens afterward?

THE SNEETCHES **385**

First Thoughts

1. Possible responses:
   - My favorite lines in this poem are ll. 75–84 because they are fast and funny.
   - I was surprised when the Sneetches set aside their star problems and decided to accept each other.
   - I think this poem is about intolerance and justice.

Shaping Interpretations

2. The Star-Bellies: snooty, arrogant, proud. The Plain-Bellies: envious, jealous, insecure.
3. McBean thinks the Sneetches are stupid creatures who cannot learn, but in the end he is wrong because they learn to get along.
4. Possible response: They can't tell which Sneetches originally did or did not have a star, and so they just give up the argument.
5. *Sneetches, thars, Chappie, berked, eaches*
6. Sample response: People should not judge others on the basis of their appearance or look down on others because they are different. It is an important lesson because it pertains to important life experiences.

Connecting with the Text

7. Students may cite snobs or bigots or certain politicians. Remind students not to cite classmates.

Extending the Text

8. Students who think people can change long-held prejudices might cite our "mosaic," multicultural society and the advances we've made in civil rights; those who feel we cannot change our attitudes might cite racial or class tensions that continue to exist despite great efforts to uproot them.

Reading Check
Sample responses:

a. The Sneetches with stars on their bellies look down on the Sneetches who do not have stars on their bellies. The Star-Belly Sneetches won't have anything to do with the Plain-Belly Sneetches.

b. McBean offers to put stars on the Plain-Bellies for three dollars each. He offers to take the stars off the Star-Bellies for ten dollars each.

c. McBean leaves when he gets all the money the Sneetches have. Afterward, the Sneetches decide that no kind of Sneetch is best, and they all become friends.

Rubrics for each Choices assignment appear on p. 152 in the *Portfolio Management System*.

CHOICES:
Building Your Portfolio

1. **Writer's Notebook** Remind students to save their work, which they may use as prewriting for the Writer's Workshop on pp. 396–400.
2. **Creative Writing** Encourage students to base their wacky creature on some real-life creature, such as a chicken, mouse, or frog. Lead students to link their creature's name to its appearance, for logic as well as humor.
3. **Critical Thinking** Suggest that students start by focusing on ads that use celebrity endorsements.
4. **Reading Aloud** Students may wish to create some removable stars that they can put on and take off as props at appropriate points in their performance. Students can adhere the stars with double-sided tape.

CHOICES: Building Your Portfolio

Writer's Notebook

1. Collecting Ideas for Supporting a Position

It seems to be human nature for people to band together and form groups, as the Sneetches did. Think of groups that have formed in either your community or your school. Then, write down positive and negative reasons for forming groups like these.

> Group: *social club*
> Positive reasons:
> *to do things*
> *together*
> Negative reasons:
> *snobbishness*

Creative Writing

2. Seuss on the Loose

Sketch a wacky creature who thinks he, she, or it is superior to other creatures. Think of some absurd reason for the creature's snobbism. In Dr. Seuss's story it's stars on the belly. Then, make up a name and turn your character into the inspiration for a short poem in the style of Dr. Seuss. Be sure to use a singsong rhythm, lots of rhyme, and a few invented words. Finally, collect your poems and doodles in an anthology entitled "Loosely Seuss."

Critical Thinking

3. Sneetch Snobs

McBean uses snob appeal to make money on his Star-On and Star-Off Machines. Snob appeal works on those who want to seem superior to others. What ads and commercials today seem to promise to make you just like people who are rich and famous? Collect magazine ads that you think use snob appeal to sell something. Then, in a group, pass around the pictures and discuss whether the ads are successful in turning people into Sneetch snobs.

Reading Aloud

4. Teach the Sneetch

With a partner, read "The Sneetches" aloud to a group of young children. Decide in advance how you want to divide the reading. For example, one of you may want to read all the Star-Belly parts and the other all the Plain-Belly parts. Before your performance, practice reading the poem out loud, playing up all the silly sound effects and exaggerating the characters. After you read, ask the children what they thought of the poem. Do any of their responses surprise you?

Using Students' Strengths

Auditory/Musical Learners

As students create their wacky creatures for Choice 2, encourage them to experiment with funny voices. Partners can also tape-record their performance, inviting several classmates to contribute their voices to the soundtrack as well. Students might want to add sound effects and background music to make their readings more humorous.

Kinesthetic Learners

As they research advertisements and commercials for Choice 3, invite students to extend the activity by creating their own ad campaign for Star-On and Star-Off Machines. The ads should be aimed at Sneetches who wish to remove their stars (or acquire them).

The Southpaw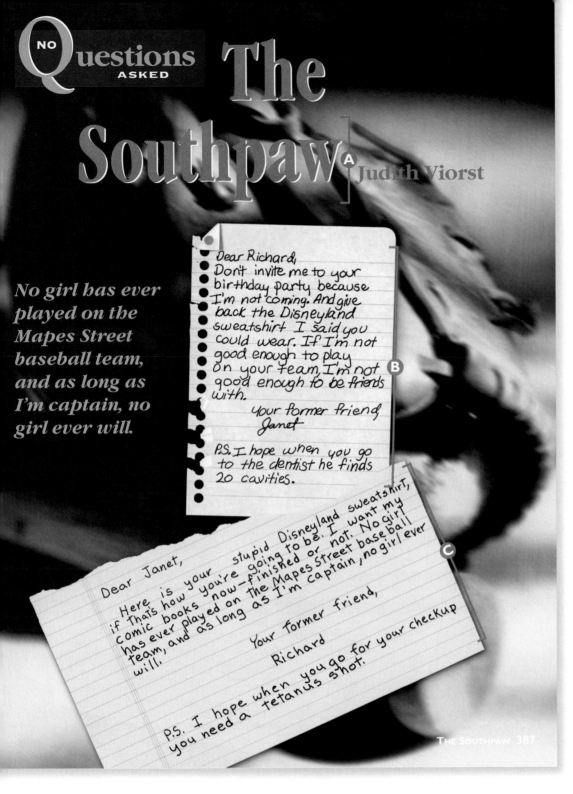
Judith Viorst

No girl has ever played on the Mapes Street baseball team, and as long as I'm captain, no girl ever will.

> Dear Richard,
> Don't invite me to your birthday party because I'm not coming. And give back the Disneyland sweatshirt I said you could wear. If I'm not good enough to play on your team, I'm not good enough to be friends with.
>
> Your former friend,
> Janet
>
> P.S. I hope when you go to the dentist he finds 20 cavities.

> Dear Janet,
> Here is your stupid Disneyland sweatshirt, if that's how you're going to be. I want my comic books now—finished or not. No girl has ever played on the Mapes Street baseball team, and as long as I'm captain, no girl ever will.
>
> Your former friend,
> Richard
>
> P.S. I hope when you go for your checkup you need a tetanus shot.

THE SOUTHPAW 387

Reaching All Students

Struggling Readers
Make sure that students are not having trouble deciphering the handwritten notes or their order on the page. You might have students duplicate the story's format and exchange a similar series of letters with a friend.

English Language Learners
You might want to give students a quick explanation of the game of baseball—its importance in American culture and its rules. If you are unfamiliar with the rules of the game, ask students who are baseball fans to explain it.

OBJECTIVE
1. Read and enjoy a short story
2. Connect the story to the collection theme

No Questions Asked

The literature in No Questions Asked gives students the chance to read a selection for enjoyment and enrichment as they further explore the collection theme. Annotated questions in the margins of the Teacher's Edition should be considered optional. No follow-up questions will appear after the selection.

This short story is told in the form of notes exchanged by former friends Janet and Richard. Janet insists that girls should be allowed to play on the Mapes Street baseball team. As captain of the team, Richard adamantly refuses and doesn't understand the unfairness of the situation. The two continue to trade notes laden with insults and threats, as well as with references to their past friendship. Janet campaigns hard, reminding Richard of her batting average and making not-so-subtle references to the team's losing streak. Because of illness and injury to his male teammates, Richard is forced to change his attitude. Janet strikes a tough bargain: a package deal with her as pitcher and three other girls as well. Justice finally prevails on the Mapes Street baseball team.

A Cultural Connections
Southpaw is a baseball term for a left-handed pitcher. In the ballpark in Chicago where the term originated around 1885, the pitcher's left arm was to the south.

B Reading Skills and Strategies
Responding to the Text
❓ What is your first impression of Janet? [Possible responses: She is very upset; she is not someone who lets other people push her around.]

C Reading Skills and Strategies
Making Inferences
❓ What was the relationship between Richard and Janet before he said she could not play on his team? [They were friends and shared some possessions.]

A **Literary Connections**

? A novel written in the form of an exchange of letters is called an *epistolary novel*. The term is derived from *epistle,* which is another word for *letter.* "The Southpaw" is an epistolary story. What do you think of telling a story through letters? [Possible responses: I like it because it makes the story seem real; I don't like it because there is no narrator.]

B **Reading Skills and Strategies**
Responding to the Text
? What do you think of Richard's suggestion that Janet take up knitting? [Possible responses: Richard is mean—he is saying that Janet can do only what he thinks of as girls' things; Richard is funny—he is trying to make Janet mad.]

C **Reading Skills and Strategies**
Drawing Conclusions
? What does Richard mean when he says, "Wait until Friday"? [He is implying that his team will finally win.]

Resources

Viewing and Representing
Fine Arts Transparency
The transparency of a painting by Greg Ragland can be used to stimulate discussion as students read the selection.
• Transparency 14
• Worksheet, p. 56

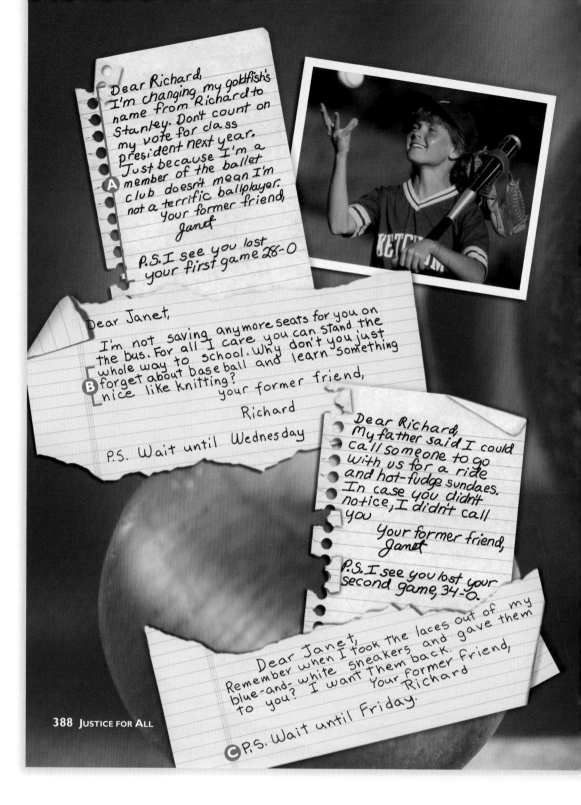

388 JUSTICE FOR ALL

T388

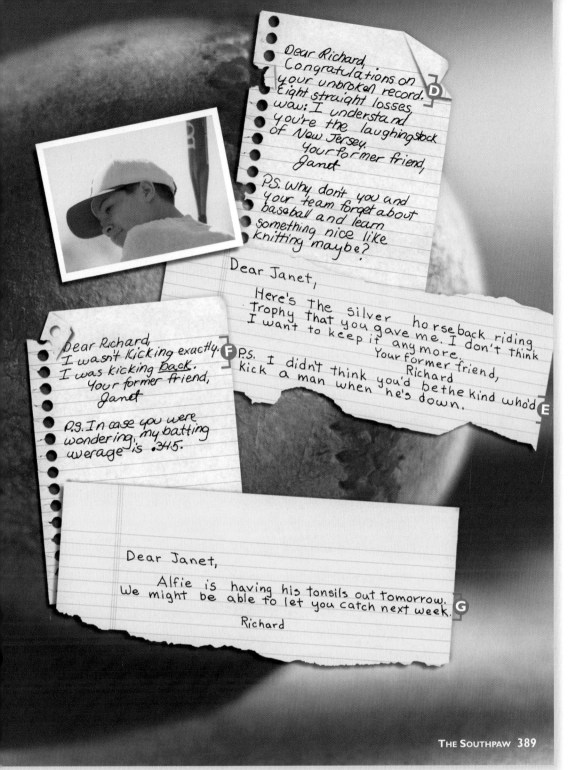

Dear Richard,
Congratulations on your unbroken record. Eight straight losses, wow: I understand you're the laughingstock of New Jersey.
Your former friend,
Janet

P.S. Why don't you and your team forget about baseball and learn something nice like knitting maybe?

Dear Janet,
Here's the silver horseback riding trophy that you gave me. I don't think I want to keep it any more.
Your former friend,
Richard

P.S. I didn't think you'd be the kind who'd kick a man when he's down.

Dear Richard,
I wasn't kicking exactly. I was kicking _back_.
Your former friend,
Janet

P.S. In case you were wondering, my batting average is .345.

Dear Janet,
Alfie is having his tonsils out tomorrow. We might be able to let you catch next week.
Richard

THE SOUTHPAW 389

D **Elements of Literature**
Irony
? What does the phrase an "unbroken record" usually mean? [It usually refers to a team winning all its games.] **How does Janet use it here?** [She is referring to the fact that Richard's team has lost all its games.]

E **Reading Skills and Strategies**
Making Inferences
? How do you think Richard feels? [Possible responses: He feels sorry for himself because his team keeps losing; he tries to make her feel guilty.]

F **Critical Thinking**
Expressing an Opinion
? Do you agree with Janet? Is "kicking back" a justified response? [Possible responses: Yes, Richard started it when he wouldn't let her play on his team; no, even if he wouldn't let her play on the team, she shouldn't make fun of his defeats.]

G **Reading Skills and Strategies**
Identifying Cause and Effect
? What causes Richard to offer Janet the possibility of playing on his team? [One of the players is sick.] **What does this gesture suggest about Richard?** [Possible responses: He is desperate; he has changed his mind about having a girl on the team; he misses Janet's friendship.]

Making the Connections

Connecting to the Theme: "Justice for All"

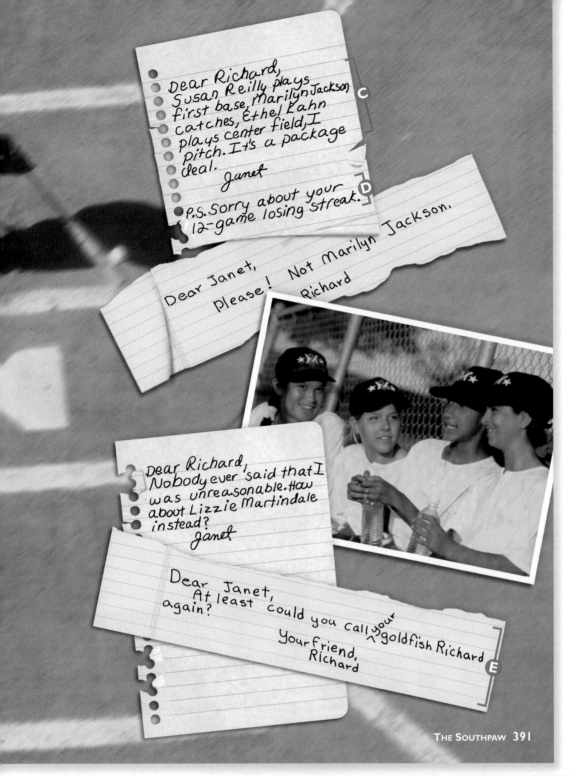

Dear Richard,
Susan Reilly plays first base, Marilyn Jackson catches, Ethel Kahn plays center field, I pitch. It's a package deal.
Janet
P.S. Sorry about your 12-game losing streak.

Dear Janet,
Please! Not Marilyn Jackson.
Richard

Dear Richard,
Nobody ever said that I was unreasonable. How about Lizzie Martindale instead?
Janet

Dear Janet,
At least could you call your goldfish Richard again?
Your friend,
Richard

C **Critical Thinking**
Interpreting
? What does it say about Janet that she wants her girlfriends to play, too? [Possible responses: She cares about the rights of others, not just her own rights; she drives a hard bargain.]

D **Critical Thinking**
Speculating
? Why do you think Janet says that she is sorry? [Possible responses: She is reminding Richard of his losses to get him to give in and let her and the other girls play; despite their argument, she really does care about Richard.]

E **Elements of Literature**
Theme
? What lesson does this story teach? What is the writer saying about life? [Possible responses: The writer's message is that you should not be mean to people because someday you may need their help; the writer's point is that girls should be allowed the same opportunities as boys; the writer is implying that boys should not look down on girls.]

THE SOUTHPAW 391

Selection	Injustice	Outcome
"All Summer in a Day"	[hurting someone because she is different]	[The other children let Margot out.]
"Eleven"	[not believing that someone is telling the truth]	[Rachel is unhappy and embarrassed.]
"The Gold Cadillac"	[segregation/stopping someone because he is African American and driving a new Cadillac]	[The narrator's family unites to overcome discrimination.]
"The Bracelet"	[putting loyal Japanese Americans in internment camps]	[Ruri and her family maintain their dignity.]
"What Do Fish Have to Do with Anything?"	[homelessness/lack of compassion]	[Willie learns a lesson, but the homeless man is taken away by the police.]
"The Sneetches"	[snobbery]	[The Sneetches wise up.]
"The Southpaw"	[sexism/underestimating someone's ability because she is a girl]	[Janet gets to play after all, and so do her girlfriends.]

MEET THE WRITER

Laughing at Everyday Life

Judith Viorst (1931–   ) decided when she was only seven years old that she wanted to be a writer. She sent out "terrible poems about dead dogs, mostly," to magazines in hopes of getting them published. In those days she liked to write about "deadly-serious things," but she later found success in writing books that help people of all ages laugh at the ups and downs of everyday life.

Viorst has based many of her books on the experiences of her own family. When her oldest son, Anthony, started giving his younger brothers a hard time, for example, she wrote a children's book called *I'll Fix Anthony* (1969) to cheer up the younger ones. When her son Alexander was having lots of bad days, she wrote *Alexander and the Terrible, Horrible, No Good, Very Bad Day* (1972) to help him cope.

More Very Bad (and Some Very Good) Days

In addition to the books mentioned above, you might also enjoy *The Tenth Good Thing About Barney* and *Rosie and Michael* (both published by Aladdin).

READ ON

To Be or Not to Be

Pocahontas had every reason in the world to be happy in the spring of her eleventh year. She was the special favorite of her father, the chief of her tribe. She was accepted by the white settlers. Disaster struck when Pocahontas was kidnapped and forced to give up her people's ways. In *The Double Life of Pocahontas* (Puffin) by Jean Fritz, peace between two very different worlds depends on the decision of one young girl.

Dog Days

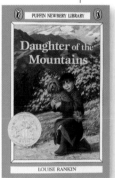

Would you travel alone across a dangerous mountain range to track down thieves? Momo's valuable Lhasa Apso dog is stolen by robbers in *Daughter of the Mountains* (Puffin) by Louise Rankin. She risks her life to find her beloved Pempa in this lively adventure set high in the Himalayas during the last years of British rule.

Children of the Caribbean

Nenna and her brother Man-Man track down a thief in their Jamaican village. Tukku-Tukku loses more than just fights with his friend and rival, Samson, until one day the tables are turned. These stories of justice and more are told with great spirit in *A Thief in the Village and Other Stories of Jamaica* (Puffin) by James Berry.

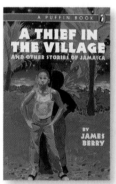

Other Picks

- Willo Davis Roberts, *Jo and the Bandit* (Atheneum). After the stagecoach she is riding in gets held up, Josephine "Jo" Whitman helps catch the bandits and faces some surprises.

- Harriette Gillem Robinet, *Mississippi Chariot* (Atheneum). Shortning Bread Jackson hatches a plan to save his innocent father from a Mississippi jail in the 1930s.

Speaking and Listening Workshop

OBJECTIVES
1. Practice social skills
2. Learn how to make introductions
3. Learn strategies for carrying on a conversation and being an active listener

Resources

Portfolio Management System
- *Performance Rubric,* p. 153

Introducing the Speaking and Listening Workshop

Tell students that the skills taught in the Speaking and Listening Workshop will help them feel more comfortable in social situations and help them make others feel more at ease. Ask them to make lists of social situations in which they have participated. Give students a couple of examples to get them started, such as a birthday party or eating out at a restaurant with their family. Then have students share with the class the social situations they have listed. After students have read the workshop, have them return to these situations and discuss how what they have learned applies.

Try It Out
Possible Answers
_____, this is my brother _____.
Mr. Jordan, this is _____ _____.
Hello, my name is _____ _____.
Uncle Rupert, this is my music teacher, Mr. [Ms.] _____. Uncle Rupert is a professional violinist, Mr. [Ms.] _____.

Try It Out
Form a group with two or three classmates. Then, practice these encounters:

- Introduce your brother to a new friend of yours.
- Introduce your school's basketball star to Michael Jordan.
- Introduce yourself to two aliens from Venus.
- Introduce your music teacher to your uncle Rupert, a professional violinist.

SOCIAL INTERACTION

In this workshop you'll practice social skills that can help you get to know, and feel more confident with, the people you meet.

How to Make Introductions
When you're with people you know but who don't know one another, you need to introduce them. When you meet people for the first time, you need an introduction. Follow these suggestions for making smooth, polite introductions:

- When you introduce friends your own age, first names are usually enough. ("Alex, this is Marta.")
- When you introduce a younger person to an older person, say the older person's name first. ("Uncle Rupert, this is my friend Nick. Nick, this is my uncle, Rupert Brooke.")
- If no one else is there to introduce you, introduce yourself. Begin by asking a question or telling something about yourself. ("Hi, I'm Toshiko. Have you been playing chess long?")
- If you know that the people you're introducing have something in common, bring it up. ("Kim, I want you to meet Chris and Samantha. They like camping, too. Chris and Sam, this is Kim. She just got back from the Grand Canyon.")

Conversation: Communicating Clearly
Have you ever played catch with a friend? A good conversation has the same slow, easy back-and-forth. Try some of these skills when you start your next conversation:

- Express yourself. Don't be afraid to voice an opinion. ("Junk food is terrible" or "I think junk food is great" is a stronger remark than "Junk food? Uh, I don't know. I guess it's OK.")
- Be confident. Speak clearly and forcefully, and look at the

Reaching All Students

Struggling Speakers
It is important when involved in a conversation to ask questions that cannot be answered with a simple yes or no. Have students practice asking open-ended questions. Ask students to think of two questions that they might ask each of the following people: their mother's best friend, a foreign exchange student, a friend's grandfather, and a new member of the basketball team.

English Language Learners
Different cultures or countries often have different social standards and practices. For example, making direct eye contact is considered to be rude behavior in some countries. Ask students to share conversational practices from their native countries. How do people make introductions? Is it acceptable behavior to introduce yourself to a stranger? Do body language and gestures play an important role in conversation?

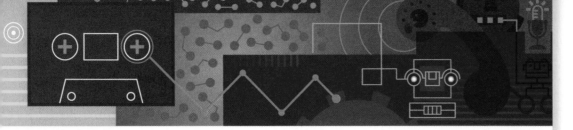

person you're talking to. If you mumble or turn away from your listener while you speak, nobody will follow what you're saying.

- Ask good questions. A conversation isn't a speech—it's a give-and-take. To show that you're interested in hearing what the other person has to say, try to ask questions that can't be answered with a simple yes or no.

- Be polite. Don't attack the opinions of the person you're talking to—even if you disagree with him or her. Instead, look for common ground.

Listening Actively

You haven't mastered the art of conversation until you've learned to listen well. Here are some ways to sharpen your listening skills:

- Concentrate. When someone is talking, pay attention. Don't just wait for the person to stop talking so that you can speak.

- Respond. Active listeners show how they feel about what's being said. Look at the speaker. Nod, smile—react!

- Reflect. To show the speaker that you understand, summarize what he or she has said. ("So you prefer soccer to lacrosse?")

- Ask questions. If you're not sure what someone means, ask. The speaker will be flattered that you're paying such close attention.

- Share your experiences. By comparing stories, you show that you understand how someone feels.

Try It Out

To hone your listening skills, ask a classmate to tell you a story as vividly as possible. As you're listening, try to form a mental picture of the places and people involved. When your classmate has finished, retell the story in your own words. How much can you remember? Did you forget any important details?

Teaching the Speaking and Listening Workshop

- Focus on examples of social interaction drawn from the stories in this collection. For example, you might want to discuss with students why Margot has trouble interacting with her classmates. Have students draw up a list of questions that she might ask them or that they might ask her to start a conversation.

- If possible, videotape segments from television talk shows. Have the class analyze the interaction between the host and each guest. How do the guests introduce themselves? How does the host introduce a guest? What questions does the talk-show host ask to initiate conversation? Do gestures and eye contact play an important role?

Try It Out

Record both versions of the story. Then have the students listen to the recordings for details left out of the second version. Students should discuss why details were left out, how the first speaker could have made them more memorable, and how the listener could have noted them. Finally, students should switch roles and practice speaking and listening with a new story.

Grading Timesaver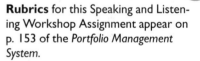

Rubrics for this Speaking and Listening Workshop Assignment appear on p. 153 of the *Portfolio Management System*.

Using Students' Strengths

Intrapersonal Learners
Have students write in their journals about their feelings in social situations, especially those in which they must interact with people they do not know. Then have them describe the skills they would like to learn in order to feel more confident. *Remind students that they need not write or share anything that makes them uncomfortable.*

Kinesthetic Learners
Divide the class into pairs or small groups to act out scenarios that require the skills explained in this workshop. Then have each pair or group choose one scenario to perform for the class. Allow students enough time to plan and rehearse their scenarios.

Interpersonal Learners
Have a small group of students create and perform for the class a brief skit dramatizing the importance of speaking up clearly and confidently. A character might not be assertive in warning the other characters of a problem—with bad results. On the other hand, a character might successfully solve a problem for the group with a well-stated good suggestion.

T395

Planning

- **Block Schedule**
  Block Scheduling Lesson Plans with Pacing Guide
- **One-Stop Planner**
  CD-ROM with Test Generator

Introducing the Writer's Workshop

- Bring in local newspapers and news magazines for students to look at. Reading articles on community, national, and international issues will inspire students to formulate their own opinions on these or similar issues. In addition, the editorial section of the newspaper can provide students with examples of how professional writers support their opinions.

BUILDING YOUR PORTFOLIO

Writer's Workshop

ASSIGNMENT
Write an essay in which you state your position on an issue that is important to you and provide reasons supporting your position.

AIM
To persuade.

AUDIENCE
Your classmates or anyone affected by the issue. (You choose.)

Looking at the Good and the Bad on Community Issues	
Dog park	• Good: Dogs need space to run. • Bad: Dogs ruin the grass, and people need more parks.
Streetlights	• Good: Needed for safety. • Bad: Too many now; they waste valuable energy.
Bike lanes	• Good: Bicyclists need lanes to travel safely. • Bad: Bikes are hazards for cars.

396 JUSTICE FOR ALL

PERSUASIVE WRITING

SUPPORTING A POSITION

In this collection you've read about people dealing with different kinds of injustice. You've seen some fight for what they believed was right. In this Writer's Workshop you'll have a chance to take and defend a stand on an issue that you feel strongly about. You'll write a paper in which you

- discuss an issue that people disagree about
- talk about the **pros** and **cons**—the reasons for and against different positions on the issue
- tell where you stand on the issue
- give at least three reasons for supporting your position

Professional Model

Exercise is important for kids these days because they spend a lot of time sitting in front of TV and computer screens. Some people say young people don't need to worry about exercise. Kids have always been more active than adults. However, studies show that kids today are less fit than they were twenty years ago.

    Experts in children's health say that young people should be getting at least thirty minutes of physical activity every day. Kids who exercise are more confident, get fewer injuries, and are less likely to feel stressed out.

    Look for an activity that will increase your overall physical fitness. It doesn't

The writer introduces the issue.

The writer includes a counter-argument.

The writer states facts as support.

  Resources: Print and Media

Writing and Language
- *Portfolio Management System*
  Prewriting, p. 154
  Peer Editing, p. 155
  Assessment Rubric, p. 156
- *Workshop Resources*
  Revision Strategy Teaching Notes, p. 19
  Revision Strategy Transparencies 10, 11, and 12

Assessment
- *Standardized Test Preparation, p. 106*

(continued)

> have to be a team sport. Run, swim, bike, dance, walk quickly. Check with your doctor to find out what some reasonable goals are for you. Then, try to meet them.
>
> It's important for kids to do their bit to keep our planet from being taken over by couch-potato people. Get the fitness habit, so you can stay healthy for all of your life.
>
> —"Get Off the Couch" by Lynn Hovland

The writer suggests ways to take action.

The writer ends by re-stating the issue.

Prewriting

1. Writer's Notebook

Look through your Writer's Notebook entries for this collection. Search for ideas that you want to expand into a paper supporting a position. To get more ideas, try the brainstorming suggestion below.

WORK IN PROGRESS

2. Brainstorming

To find issues that people disagree about, get together with a group of classmates. Brainstorm topics that concern people in your school, your community, the nation, and the world. Spend just two or three minutes brainstorming issues affecting each of these groups of people. Then, each group member should

- pick one issue in each area
- jot down different opinions on that issue
- share all the issues and opinions with the group

It's up to parents to decide.

NO—in the summer it's light until 9:00 P.M.

Should there be an 8:00 P.M. curfew for kids twelve years old and younger (unless with an adult)?

YES—kids should be home, not out on the streets.

Kids get into gangs.

Tell what happened to Angie.

Language/Grammar Link
H E L P

Figurative language: page 325. Punctuating dialogue: page 336. Connotations: page 355. Paragraphing dialogue: page 365. Direct and indirect quotations: page 378.

Prewriting

- If students work together in groups to brainstorm topics, remind them to listen carefully to each other's opinions. Even if they do not agree with a classmate's opinion, they should respect it.
- Make sure that the issues students choose to write about are not too broad. If the issue they choose is too general, suggest that they focus on a specific aspect of it. For example, if they choose to write about pollution, they may want to limit their thoughts on the issue to noise pollution or the damage done by automobile emissions to the environment.

Drafting

- Ask students to think about why they feel strongly about the problems they have chosen. Suggest that they try to communicate in writing the same sense of urgency they feel. Students' own experiences may be especially compelling.
- Remind students to present the views of their opponents fairly and to explain calmly why they are not convinced by them. A fair presentation of opposing views gives a writer credibility and thus makes an argument more convincing, not less.
- It is important for students to support their opinions with facts and statistics. Newspapers and news magazines are a good source of supporting evidence. The Internet is also a source of information. However, make sure students realize that the information provided on web sites can be inaccurate and biased. Point out that information on web sites sponsored by academic and nonprofit institutions is likely to be more reliable than that on commercial sites.
- Remind students to double-space when they write their drafts. They should also leave extra space in the right margin. These blank spaces will be used for comments and editing marks.

Reaching All Students

Struggling Writers

These students will benefit from a quick review of the difference between fact and opinion. Remind them that a statement of fact contains information that can be proved true, whereas a statement of opinion expresses a personal belief or attitude. Inform students that an opinion must be supported by facts in order to make it valid, effective, and convincing.

English Language Learners

Students learning English as a second language may prefer to brainstorm notes and even to generate a first draft in their native language. Encourage them to write in the language in which they are most fluent until they have recorded a satisfying introduction and presented reasons to support their opinion. Reassure students that their English versions do not need to be direct translations.

After students have completed their drafts, they may benefit from another look at the Student Model on p. 399. Have students ask themselves the following questions:

- ❓ How does the writer interest the reader at the beginning?
- ❓ What is the writer's opinion? Do I agree with it? Why or why not?
- ❓ What evidence does the writer supply to support her opinion?
- ❓ What techniques does this writer use that I might apply in my essay?

Framework for an Essay Supporting a Position

Introduction (statement of the issue, the pros and cons of different positions on the issue, and your position): _____

_____

Reason 1 with two supporting details (facts, examples, and personal experiences):

_____

Reason 2 with two supporting details: _____

_____

Conclusion (restatement of your opinion and a call to action): ___

_____

Communications Handbook
H E L P

See Proofreaders' Marks.

Sentence Workshop
H E L P

Combining sentences by inserting words: page 401.

3. Choosing an Issue and Finding Reasons

Now that you have a lot of issues to choose from, you're ready to make the big decision. First, look for an issue that matters to you (try to pick one that others will consider important, too). Second, make sure you see reasons to support different sides. Remember that you have to come up with **counter-arguments,** arguments *against* the position you'll take.

Clustering may help you find different positions on an issue. First, state the issue in the form of a question. Write the question in the middle of a sheet of paper, and draw a big circle around it. Then, write down the position you want to take. Circle that, too. On the other side of the big circle, write and circle another position people might take on the issue. As you come up with reasons for each position, write them down. Connect them to the position they support. Write down evidence—facts, examples, and personal experiences—supporting each reason. The model on the left is an example of clustering.

4. Targeting Your Audience

In persuasive writing, you want to persuade your readers to agree with your position. You might even want to move them to take the action you recommend. Before you start writing, think about whom you're trying to persuade. Then, imagine yourself in your readers' shoes. What does the audience already know about this issue? What do you need to explain? What counterarguments could your audience make, and how might you answer them?

Drafting

1. Starting Strong

One way to grab your readers' attention is to make your first sentence short. You could start with a surprising fact or a question like "Why should we care about the Amazon rain forest?"

Let your first paragraph set the stage. Tell what the issue is and why it's important to you—and to your audience. Then, briefly present the pros and cons of the issue. You can state your position at this point or save that information for a later paragraph. Whether you state it early in your paper or later, be sure to make your position clear!

Using Students' Strengths

Auditory Learners
After students have written their drafts, have partners read their drafts aloud to each other. When the writer says something that is confusing or unclear to the listener, the listener should tell the writer to stop so that they can discuss the source of the problem. Then have students exchange drafts and read them again so that they hear their own words spoken by another.

Intrapersonal Learners
As students work through the Writer's Workshop, have them track their progress in their journals or notebooks by using a two-column chart. In the first column, students should record what work they do; in the second column, they should record how that work contributes to the goal of writing a persuasive essay.

Visual Learners
Have students color-code their drafts to help them see the structure of their papers and to fix any organizational problems. They should highlight the introduction with one color, the statement of the opinion with a second color, the supporting evidence and reasons with a third, possible objections and responses to them with a fourth, and the conclusion with a fifth.

Makx a Diffxrxncx!

As I start this lxttxr, thosx who rxad it might think somxthing is wrong and stop rxading at this point. But plxasx kxxp on rxading.

As you can sxx, for onx lxttxr of thx alphabxt I havx substitutxd an "x." Somx of you might find this strangx. Lxt mx xxplain.

A lot of pxoplx don't think that onx pxrson in this world can makx any diffxrxncx. But lxt mx txll you this. In history wx havx all sxxn and hxard pxoplx who havx stood up for what thxy bxlixvx in. Thxy havx indxxd madx a diffxrxncx in our livxs. It only takxs onx pxrson to changx somxthing and makx xvxryonx's lifx a lot bxttxr. Considxr rxcycling: It only takxs onx pxrson to rxcyclx; thxn xvxryonx xlsx will follow. If wx all thought only of oursxlvxs, thx world would bx a disastrous placx right now. Thx ozonx layxr would bx gonx and wx would all bx harmxd by thx sun.

It only takxs onx pxrson to comx right out and say hx or shx carxs. What I'm saying is to lxt go of our pridx and do what you bxlixvx is right. If you arx confidxnt, thxn you will succxxd. You should know that you can makx a diffxrxncx.

Now, what doxs all this havx to do with mx writing "x's" instxad of "e's"? Did it xvxr occur to you that if onx lxttxr can makx a diffxrxncx, thxn so can onx pxrson? Xvxn though this is a small xxamplx, it shows that if onx tiny lxttxr in thx alphabxt can makx such a diffxrxncx in a pixcx of writing, thxn, of coursx, onx pxrson can makx a diffxrxncx in thx world today.

—Elena Chen
Ridgely Middle School
Lutherville, Maryland

First appeared in *Merlyn's Pen: The National Magazines of Student Writing.*

The use of the letter x grabs the reader's attention right away.

The writer mentions a counterargument and then refutes it.

Examples support the writer's point.

The writer urges readers to take action.

In a strong conclusion the writer restates her main point. The x's persuade us that one person can make a difference.

2. Making Your Case

In the next three paragraphs, you'll try to persuade your audience to agree with you. In each paragraph, give one convincing reason to support your position. Then, elaborate on that reason with two items of support—facts, examples, or personal experiences.

Evaluating and Revising

- Have students use the Evaluation Criteria on p. 400 to review their drafts and determine needed revisions.
- Point out that the revision phase is the time to add words, phrases, and sometimes sentences; to cross out things; to change things; to rearrange things; and to get help with problem areas.
- Ask students to listen to the voice of their writing by reading it aloud. Then, based on the reading, they should make adjustments so that the essay flows more smoothly. Remind them to listen for awkward sentence constructions and to look for nouns and verbs they can make more specific and vivid.
- If they traded drafts with a partner, have them read their partner's comments carefully. They should think about each strength and weakness their partner pointed out. Do they need to add more supporting details? Did their partner question the introduction or conclusion? If so, they should think about ways to make it more effective.
- Allow students ample time for peer reviews. Schedule peer-review sessions in advance of the final draft of the assignment to allow students time to think about each other's comments.
- Remind students that their comments are for the purpose of helping one another write better papers, even if they disagree with the papers they are reviewing. Comments are not for criticizing people.
- Remind students to accept the comments of others with good grace because the comments are meant to help them, not hurt their feelings.

Crossing the Curriculum

Computer Science and Technology

Encourage students to use word-processing programs for prewriting, as well as for drafting and revising. Students may be able to input ideas faster than they can write them by hand. The computer also offers greater freedom to experiment with various orders of presentation and to save alternative expressions of the same ideas.

Proofreading

Have students proofread their own papers first and then exchange them. If students used direct quotations in their essays, they should make sure that they punctuated them correctly.

If time permits, the final copy should be put aside for at least a day before it is proofread for the final time by the author.

Publishing

Have each student write a brief statement indicating the intended audience of his or her essay. Encourage students to get their essays to the audience they were written for. If their essays deal with school or community issues, suggest that they publish them in the school paper or post them on the school's Web site.

Reflecting

Suggest that students reflect on their papers by answering the following questions:

1. What was the most difficult part of writing this essay?
2. What did I like best about writing this essay?
3. Do I think my essay will convince people that my opinion is right?
4. How can I use what I learned about persuasive writing in other forms of writing or in daily life?

Resources

Peer Editing Forms and Rubrics
• *Portfolio Management System*, p. 155

Revision Strategy Transparencies
• *Workshop Resources*, p. 19

Grading Timesaver

Rubrics for this Writer's Workshop assignment appear on p. 156 of the *Portfolio Management System*.

Strategies for Elaboration

To support your position, you can use

• facts (including statistics)
• examples
• definitions
• expert opinions, especially direct quotations
• anecdotes (very short stories, such as personal experiences)
• appeals to emotion
• cause-and-effect predictions (for example, the results of a particular course of action)

■ *Evaluation Criteria*

A good position paper

1. *clearly states the issue*
2. *gives two or more positions on the issue or courses of action*
3. *clearly states the writer's position on the issue*
4. *gives sound, convincing reasons to support a position*
5. *stays on track from first sentence to last*
6. *is organized logically, with transitions connecting ideas*

Try to use different kinds of support. Personal experiences are interesting, but if you depend totally on them, you may give your audience the impression that you can't find other kinds of support. The list at the left may help you find ways to elaborate on your reasons.

3. Organizing the Evidence

Arrange your reasons and support so that they make sense. Many writers use **order of importance** for this kind of paper: They save their strongest reason for last. Use transitions between sentences and paragraphs to lead readers from one idea to the next. For instance, to emphasize ideas, you might use transitions such as *mainly, last,* and *most important.* To contrast two courses of action, you might use transitions like *on the other hand, another,* and *however.*

4. Ending with a Knockout

In your conclusion, strongly restate your position. Drive your point home by telling what's wrong with opposing positions. End by urging readers to agree with you or to follow the course of action you support. To organize your ideas, use the Framework for an Essay Supporting a Position (page 398).

Evaluating and Revising

Trade your draft for a classmate's. After you've read your partner's draft, answer the following questions:

• How does the writer get me interested in the issue?

• Does the writer clearly state the issue? Does the writer support this position with interesting, convincing reasons?

• Which reasons and supporting details are strongest? Which ones need more elaboration?

• Does the writer state and answer any counterarguments?

• How can the introduction and conclusion be strengthened?

• What do I like most about this essay?

Make all the changes that you think will improve your paper.

T400

Sentence Workshop

OBJECTIVE
Learn how to combine sentences by inserting key words or phrases

COMBINING SENTENCES BY INSERTING WORDS

A simple way to combine short sentences is to pull a key word or phrase from one sentence and insert it into the other sentence. Sometimes you can just add the key word or phrase to the first sentence and drop the rest of the second sentence.

TWO SENTENCES   I wish I'd known what to say when Mrs. Price put the ugly sweater on my desk. The sweater was <u>red</u>.

COMBINED   I wish I'd known what to say when Mrs. Price put the ugly <u>red</u> sweater on my desk.

Other times you'll need to change the form of the key word or a word in the key phrase. When you do so, you often add an ending such as *-ed, -ing, -ful,* or *-ly* to make an adjective or adverb. In its new form the word can be used to describe another word in the sentence.

EXAMPLES   fear → feared   use → useful
            hang → hanging   final → finally

TWO SENTENCES   Willie <u>pressed deep into his pocket</u>. He found a nickel.

COMBINED   "<u>Pressing deep into his pocket</u>, Willie found a nickel."

—Avi, "What Do Fish Have to Do with Anything?" (page 369)

Writer's Workshop Follow-up: Revision

Exchange your paper supporting a position for a classmate's. If you find passages with too many short sentences, suggest ways to combine some of them. Look over your essay, and see if any short sentences can be combined to eliminate repeated words or ideas.

Language Handbook HELP

See Inserting Words, page 740; Inserting Groups of Words, pages 740–741.

Technology HELP

See Language Workshop CD-ROM. Key word entry: sentence combining.

Try It Out

Combine the two sentences in each item by inserting the underlined key word into the first sentence. See the directions in parentheses for changing the key word.

1. There was a silence after Willie's mother said she'd called the police. The silence was <u>awkward</u>.

2. The crazy thing was that we were all loyal citizens. We were <u>U.S.</u> citizens.

3. Margot thought of the way the sun and the sky looked in Ohio. She was in a <u>daydream</u>. (Add *-ing.*)

4. Rachel sat at her desk, trying not to cry. She was <u>silent</u>. (Add *-ly.*)

Teaching the Lesson

Resources
Workshop Resources
• Worksheet, p. 45
Language Workshop CD-ROM
• Sentence Combining

Demonstrate to the class the need for combining short, choppy sentences by reading the following paragraph to them:

"The Sneetches" is a poem. It is hilarious. I read it. I had fun. Dr. Seuss wrote it.

Then combine the sentences into one sentence, such as the following: I had fun reading "The Sneetches," a hilarious poem by Dr. Seuss.

Ask students which version they prefer. Then have them create short, choppy paragraphs for a partner to combine.

Try It Out
Possible Answers
1. There was an awkward silence after Willie's mother said she'd called the police.
2. The crazy thing was that we were all loyal U. S. citizens.
3. Daydreaming, Margot thought of the way the sun and the sky looked in Ohio.
4. Rachel sat silently at her desk, trying not to cry.

Assessing Learning

Quick Check: Combining Sentences by Inserting Words

Combine the following pairs of sentences by inserting the underlined word or words from one sentence into the other. Answers will vary.

1. I was afraid of losing my wallet. My wallet was a <u>new leather</u> wallet. [I was afraid of losing my new leather wallet.]

2. The workers <u>pulled together on the old door</u>. The workers were able to enter the house that had stood empty for a decade or more. (Change *-ed* to *-ing.*) [Pulling together on the old door, the workers were able to enter the house that had stood empty for a decade or more.]

3. The teacher provided information about mammals. The information was <u>interesting</u>. [The teacher provided interesting information about mammals.]

4. Juanita had the highest score on the exam. It was the <u>last</u> exam. [Juanita had the highest score on the last exam.]

OBJECTIVES
1. Learn how to evaluate a persuasive argument
2. Learn how to analyze the writer's perspective and how to evaluate the writer's choice of details and words

Teaching the Lesson

Have students apply the strategies that they learned in the Writer's Workshop to evaluate the persuasive argument in this feature. Have them consider the following questions: How strong are the writer's introduction and conclusion? Is the writer's use of facts, statistics, and examples effective? Does the lack of personal experiences or examples detract from the argument? Is the evidence organized in a logical fashion?

Using the Strategies

Answers

1. The writer believes that people should respect and protect rain forests. The writer's position is not stated directly.
2. Possible reasons: Rain forests contain 50 to 70 percent of the planet's life forms; many species become extinct each day; rain forests are being destroyed at an alarming rate.
3. Loaded words include *paradise, lush, moth-eaten, forced, driven, insist, demolishing,* and *productive.* Most students will agree that the writing would be less effective without these words.
4. The statistics included by the writer are especially convincing. Students might like the writer's use of a simile, or they might like the fact that the writer's opinion is implied rather than directly stated.

Reading for Life
Evaluating a Persuasive Message

Situation

In the essay excerpted at the right, a student explains why she thinks the rain forests must be saved. How convincing is her argument? Use the following strategies when you evaluate persuasive writing.

Strategies

Find the main idea.

- Identify the topic and the writer's opinion on the topic. How clearly is the opinion stated?

Evaluate the writer's choice of details and words.

- Which details are especially striking?
- Does the vocabulary fit the audience and the purpose?
- Does the writer use loaded words—words that stir up strong feelings, like *stupid* and *heartbroken*?

Analyze the writer's perspective, or point of view.

- Does the writer present just one point of view? Does he or she discuss several sides of the argument?
- How much does the writer

> **Rain Forest Rights**
> Once a paradise of lush vegetation, the Amazon rain forest can now be likened to a moth-eaten carpet, a proud wild animal forced to be a caged zoo exhibit. Every second, 2.47 acres are destroyed, the equivalent of two football fields. One hundred thirty-seven species of life are driven into extinction every day! Rain forests cover only two percent of the earth, yet they contain fifty to seventy percent of life forms on this planet. However, we still insist on burning, cutting, and otherwise completely demolishing the most productive and complex ecosystem on the planet.
>
> —Aviv Gazit, writing in *The Vocal Point,*
> Boulder's first electronic student newspaper
> Centennial Middle School, Boulder, Colorado

http://bvsd.k12.co.us/cent/Newspaper/Newspaper.html

know about the subject? Can you believe what he or she says?

- What reasons does the writer give to support his or her position? Are the reasons backed up with evidence?

Using the Strategies

1. What is the writer's position on the rain forests? Does she state it directly, or do you have to *infer* it?
2. Find three reasons given by the writer to support saving the rain forests.

3. Find two or three words that you consider loaded. Would the writing be more effective or less effective without them?
4. Do you find the writer's argument convincing? What do you like best about her essay?

Extending the Strategies

- Find an editorial in a newspaper or in your school paper. Use the strategies you've learned to evaluate the writer's message.

402 JUSTICE FOR ALL

Reaching All Students

Struggling Readers
These student might have trouble grasping the statistics presented by the writer. Explain that an *acre* is a unit of land that measures 43,560 square feet. Explain that *percent* means "per hundred" and that the symbol for *percent* is %. Although 2 percent is a relatively small amount, 50 to 70 percent is an overwhelming figure—one that is hard to ignore. Point out that statistics are a form of evidence that carry a lot of weight in our number-crunching society.

English Language Learners
Point out that protecting the environment is a relatively recent concern in America's cultural history. The "green movement" started in earnest in the 1960s. There are now a number of organizations, such as Green Peace, that focus on the environment. The term *ecosystem* refers to a system made up of a community of animals, plants, and bacteria and its interrelated physical and chemical environment—in short, all the components that come together to create a natural setting.

Learning for Life

Persuading with Editorial Cartoons

OBJECTIVES
1. Analyze editorial cartoons
2. Create an editorial cartoon to express an opinion about a topic

Problem

Something's bothering you. You see an issue that's dividing your friends, your family, or your community, and you want to shake people up and get them thinking about it. How do you get your point across?

Project

Study editorial cartoons and decide what qualities make them effective. Create an editorial cartoon that expresses your opinion about a topic.

Preparation

1. Clip from newspapers or magazines five or more editorial cartoons about unjust situations.

2. Form a small group and vote on the two best cartoons from those that the group members have found. Then, make a list of the strengths of a good cartoon—for example, exaggeration and humor.

3. In your group, think of an issue that affects your school or community or the nation. Choose something you feel strongly about. Then, think of a visual image that will get your opinion across.

Procedure

1. As a group, write a brief statement about what you want your cartoon to communicate.

2. Make some sketches of your visual image, working either individually or together. Vote for the one that works best.

3. Decide if you want to add words to your cartoon. The words could be

   • a caption—a brief statement or quotation under the illustration

   • dialogue—words spoken by one or more characters and enclosed in speech balloons

   • a title

4. Make the final drawing.

Presentation

Use your cartoons in one of the following ways:

1. Letter to the Editor

Submit your cartoon to your school newspaper, along with a letter to the editor saying why you think the cartoon should be published.

2. Cartoon Contest

Plan a cartoon contest to be judged by a committee of students and teachers. Work with the group to decide what qualities the judges should look for in the cartoons.

3. Cartoon Anthology

As a class, put together a collection of cartoons. Group them by topic. For each cartoon, include a paragraph or two explaining the importance of the issue the cartoon comments on.

Processing

Discuss this question with your classmates: Would you rather express your opinion by drawing a cartoon or by giving a speech? Explain.

Resources

Viewing and Representing
HRW Multimedia Presentation Maker
Students may wish to use the *Multimedia Presentation Maker* when working on this activity.

Grading Timesaver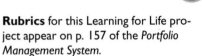

Rubrics for this Learning for Life project appear on p. 157 of the *Portfolio Management System.*

Developing Workplace Competencies

Preparation	Procedure	Presentation
• Using resources well	• Communicating ideas	• Leading others
• Working on teams	• Monitoring performance	• Solving problems
• Acquiring data	• Making decisions	• Predicting consequences
• Interpreting information	• Exhibiting sociability	• Applying the solution
• Thinking creatively	• Choosing the best alternative	• Monitoring acceptance of the solution
• Identifying central issues and problems	• Clarifying the problem	• Evaluating actions

Onstage!

Theme

Onstage! *This collection provides three short, lively plays for students to perform right in the classroom—along with Connections and special features that show students how to move from page to stage.*

Reading the Anthology

Reaching Struggling Readers

The Reading Skills and Strategies: Reaching Struggling Readers binder provides materials coordinated with the Pupil's Edition (see the Collection Planner, p. T403C) to help students who have difficulty reading and comprehending text, or students who are reluctant readers. The binder for sixth grade is organized around eleven individual skill areas and offers the following options:

-  **MiniReads** are short, easy texts that give students a chance to practice a particular skill and strategy before reading selections in the Pupil's Edition. Each MiniRead Skill Lesson can be taught independently or used in conjunction with a Selection Skill Lesson.

- **Selection Skill Lessons** Selection Skill Lessons allow students to apply skills introduced in the MiniReads. Each Selection Skill Lesson provides reading instruction and practice specific to a particular piece of literature in the Pupil's Edition.

Reading Beyond the Anthology

Read On

Collection Six includes an annotated bibliography of books suitable for extended reading. The suggested books are related to works in this collection by theme, by author, or by subject. To preview the Read On for Collection Six, please turn to p. T479.

HRW Library

The *HRW Library* offers novels, plays, and short story collections for extended reading. Each major work in the Library includes thematically or topically related Connections. A Study Guide provides teaching suggestions and worksheets. For Collection Six, the following titles are recommended.

FAMOUS STORIES FOR PERFORMANCE

This collection offers dramatizations of famous stories, like "The Man Without a Country" and "The Devil and Daniel Webster"—plus "Pyramus and Thisby," the play-within-a-play in *A Midsummer Night's Dream.*

A MIDSUMMER NIGHT'S DREAM
William Shakespeare

It can be done! You can help middle-school students stage this comedy, which is full of the tricks students love: mistaken identity, farce, magic potions, and silly lovers.

Selection or Feature	Reading Skills and Strategies	Elements of Literature	Language/ Grammar	Vocabulary/ Spelling	Writing	Listening/ Speaking	Viewing/ Representing
Elements of Literature: Drama (p. 406)	Experience Self-Recognition Through Drama, p. 406	Drama, p. 406 • Basic Situation • Complications • Climax • Resolution • Acts					
Reading Skills and Strategies: Forming Opinions (p. 407)	Fact vs. Opinion, p. 407						
The Adventure of the Speckled Band (p. 408) Sir Arthur Conan Doyle *dramatized by* Mara Rockliff	Form Opinions, pp. 408, 418 Make Predictions, pp. 408, 431	Foreshadow, p. 408 Suspense, p. 408 Chronological Order, p. 418 Motive, p. 431 Mood, p. 431		Word Analogies, p. 433 British Terms, p. 433	Develop and Apply Criteria to Evaluate the Play, p. 432 Dramatize a Scene from the Story "Duffy's Jacket," p. 432	Stage and Perform a Scene from "Duffy's Jacket," p. 432 Perform a Scene from the Play, p. 432	Design a Set Diorama or a Full-Scale Stage Set for a Production of the Play, p. 432
From Page to Stage (p. 434) Joann Leonard	Interpret a Script, p. 435	Theater, pp. 434–438 • Story/Dialogue • Staging • Action and Acting • Scenic Design and Costumes				Practice Voice Exercises, p. 436 Perform Acting Exercises, p. 437	
Blanca Flor (p. 439) Angel Vigil	Recognize Cause and Effect, pp. 439, 448, 460 Support an Opinion with Text Evidence, p. 460	Folk-Tale Motifs, pp. 439, 448, 460 Character, p. 460 Ending, p. 460 Setting, p. 460		Foreign Words as Food Names, p. 448	Practice Persuasive Writing by Listing Pro or Con Arguments on Staging This Play, p. 460 Retell *Blanca Flor* in a New Setting, p. 460		Draw or Paint the Duende in His Home, p. 460
Rumpelstiltskin (p. 462) Jakob and Wilhelm Grimm *dramatized by* Mara Rockliff	Form and Support Opinions, pp. 462, 473, 474	Folk Tales, pp. 462, 473, 474 Character Types, pp. 462, 473 Motifs, p. 473 Ending, p. 473		Denotations and Connotations, p. 475	Evaluate the Potential of the Tale for Screen Adaptation, p. 474 Compare Grimm Fairy Tales, p. 474 Write a Fairy Tale of Your Own, p. 474	Rehearse and Perform a Group Reading of One Act of the Play, p. 474	
No Questions Asked: Stars of Stage, Screen . . . and Social Studies Class *a photo essay by* Jack Manning (p. 476)	The **No Questions Asked** feature provides students with an unstructured opportunity to practice reading strategies using a selection that extends the theme of the collection.						
Writer's Workshop: Evaluation (p. 480)	Recognize Evaluation, p. 480	Plot, p. 480 Character, p. 480	Quotation Marks, p. 484 Styling of Titles, p. 484		Persuasive Writing: Write an Evaluation, pp. 480–484	Discuss and Support Your Opinion with a Partner, p. 481	
Sentence Workshop: Combining Sentences by Using Groups of Words (p. 485)			Use Groups of Words to Combine Sentences, p. 485		Revise Sentences, p. 485		
Reading for Life: Understanding Induction and Deduction (p. 486)	Understand How a Writer Makes an Argument, p. 486 • Induction • Deduction						
Learning for Life: Settling Conflicts with Friends (p. 487)					Write an Advice Manual on Settling Conflicts, p. 487	Discuss Conflicts in a Group, p. 487 Create an Ad for "Friendship Week," p. 487	Design a Board Game That Rewards Teamwork, p. 487 Design an Advice Manual, p. 487

Collection Six Onstage!

Resources for this Collection

Note: All resources for this collection are available for preview on the *One-Stop Planner CD-ROM 2 with Test Generator.* All worksheets and blackline masters may be printed from the CD-ROM.

 **Internet Resources**
go.hrw.com LE0 6-6

Selection or Feature	Reading and Literary Skills	Language and Grammar
Elements of Literature: Drama (p. 406)	• *Literary Elements,* Transparency 8	
The Adventure of the Speckled Band (p. 408) Sir Arthur Conan Doyle *dramatized by* Mara Rockliff **Connections: Duffy's Jacket** (p. 425) Bruce Coville **Connections: Macavity: The Mystery Cat** (p. 429) T. S. Eliot	• *Reading Skills and Strategies: Reaching Struggling Readers* • MiniRead Skill Lesson, p. 149 • Selection Skill Lesson, p. 157	• *Daily Oral Grammar,* Transparencies 27, 28
From Page to Stage (p. 434) Joann Leonard		
Blanca Flor (p. 439) Angel Vigil **Connections: Star Struck** (p. 457) Chris Krewson	• *Literary Elements:* Transparency 8; Worksheet p. 25	• *Daily Oral Grammar,* Transparencies 25, 26
Rumpelstiltskin (p. 462) Jakob and Wilhelm Grimm *dramatized by* Mara Rockliff **Rumpelstiltskin** (p. 471) Rosemarie Künzler *translated by* Jack Zipes	• *Literary Elements:* Transparency 8; Worksheet p. 25	• *Daily Oral Grammar,* Transparencies 23, 24
No Questions Asked: Stars of Stage, Screen . . . and Social Studies Class (p. 476) Jack Manning	The **No Questions Asked** feature provides students with an unstructured opportunity to practice reading strategies using a selection that extends the theme of the collection.	
Writer's Workshop: Evaluation (p. 480)		
Sentence Workshop: Combining Sentences by Using Groups of Words (p. 485)		• *Workshop Resources,* p. 47 • *Language Workshop CD-ROM,* Sentence Combining
Learning for Life: Settling Conflicts with Friends (p. 487)		

Collection Planner

Collection Resources

- *Cross-Curricular Activities*, p. 43
- *Portfolio Management System:*
  Introduction to Portfolio Assessment, p. 1;
  Parent/Guardian Letters, p. 97

- *Formal Assessment,*
  Reading Application Test, p. 89
- *Test Generator,* Collection Test

Vocabulary, Spelling, and Decoding	Writing	Listening and Speaking, Viewing and Representing	Assessment
			• *Formal Assessment,* Literary Elements Test, p. 88
• *Words to Own,* Worksheet p. 17	• *Portfolio Management System,* Rubrics for Choices, p. 158	• *Audio CD Library,* Disc 9, Track 2 • *Portfolio Management System,* Rubrics for Choices, p. 158	• *Formal Assessment,* Selection Test, p. 82 • *Standardized Test Preparation,* pp. 62, 64 • *Test Generator* (One-Stop Planner CD-ROM)
	• *Portfolio Management System,* Rubrics for Choices, p. 159	• *Audio CD Library,* Disc 10, Track 2 • *Viewing and Representing:* Fine Art Transparency 15; Worksheet p. 60 • *Portfolio Management System,* Rubrics for Choices, p. 159	• *Formal Assessment,* Selection Test, p. 84 • *Test Generator* (One-Stop Planner CD-ROM)
	• *Portfolio Management System,* Rubrics for Choices, p. 160	• *Visual Connections,* Videocassette B, Segment 7 • *Audio CD Library,* Disc 11, Track 2 • *Portfolio Management System,* Rubrics for Choices, p. 160	• *Formal Assessment,* Selection Test, p. 86 • *Standardized Test Preparation,* pp. 66, 68 • *Test Generator* (One-Stop Planner CD-ROM)

	• *Workshop Resources,* p. 25
	• *Standardized Test Preparation:* Worksheet p. 122 Transparencies 13–18
	• *Writer's Workshop 1 CD-ROM,* Evaluation
			• *Portfolio Management System*
			  • Prewriting, p. 161
			  • Peer Editing, p. 162
			  • Assessment Rubric, p. 163

		• *Viewing and Representing,* HRW Multimedia Presentation Maker	• *Portfolio Management System,* Rubrics, p. 164

 Transparency   **CD-ROM**   **Video**   **Audio CD**

T403D

Collection Planner

Collection

Six

OBJECTIVES

1. Read examples of dramatic literature
2. Identify the basic elements used in drama
3. Apply a variety of reading strategies to the plays
4. Respond to the plays in a variety of modes
5. Learn and use new words
6. Plan, draft, revise, proof, and publish an essay of evaluation
7. Demonstrate skill in combining sentences using groups of words
8. Demonstrate an understanding of inductive and deductive reasoning
9. Explore through a variety of projects ways of settling conflicts

Introducing the Theme

Ask for a show of hands to find out how many students have seen live plays and how many have read plays. Also ask for a show of hands about how many students have seen movies and how many have seen dramas on television. Most or all students will have seen the screen media; fewer will have seen live plays. Compare and contrast the experiences of viewing these media. How is seeing a live play like seeing a movie or television show, and how is it different? Contribute your own ideas, especially if students have few experiences of live theater. Wrap up the discussion by telling students that in this collection they will have a chance to participate in live theater themselves.

Resources

Portfolio Management System
- Introduction to Portfolio Assessment, p. 1
- Parent/Guardian Letters, p. 97

Formal Assessment
- Reading Application Test, p. 89

Test Generator
- Collection Test

Cross-Curricular Activities
- Teaching Notes, p. 43

A play isn't a text. It's an event.
—Tom Stoppard

Selection Readability

This Annotated Teacher's Edition provides a summary of each selection in the student book. Following each Summary heading, you will find one, two, or three small icons. These icons indicate, in an approximate sense, the reading level of the selection.

- ■ One icon indicates that the selection is easy.
- ■ ■ Two icons indicate that the selection is on an intermediate reading level.
- ■ ■ ■ Three icons indicate that the selection is challenging.

ONSTAGE!

405

Writing Focus: Evaluation

The following **Work in Progress** assignments in this collection build to a culminating **Writer's Workshop** at the end of Collection 6.

- The Adventure of the Speckled Band   List criteria for evaluating a play (p. 432)
- Blanca Flor   List arguments for or against a play (p. 460)
- Rumpelstiltskin   Note good and bad points of a play (p. 474)

Writer's Workshop: Persuasive Writing / Evaluation (p. 480)

Responding to the Quotation

Read the quotation aloud and ask: "How is a play different from a short story or novel?" "What is an *event?*" [Stoppard means that the written dialogue and stage directions are only part of a play; the play comes completely to life only when it is performed onstage—when it becomes a live event, a *happening,* a *spectacle.*] Tom Stoppard is a famous present-day British playwright and screenwriter.

RESPONDING TO THE ART

This photograph shows some of Joann Leonard's young drama students in their costumes. On p. 434 you'll find a lively article written by Leonard in which she gives students tips on how to bring a play to life onstage. The photographs in this collection for *The Adventure of the Speckled Band* and for *Rumpelstiltskin* show more of Leonard's students in costumes especially produced for the plays in this book.

Activity. Ask students to imagine the kinds of characters these students are portraying. What kind of play could include all these characters? Students might improvise the dialogue that these characters are having.

Writer's Notebook

Ask students to write notes on a movie or TV show they really like, or one they really hate. Have them jot down reasons for their strong feelings. In their opinions, what makes a play (in the movies or on TV) interesting? They might discuss the categories used for the Academy Awards and comments they've heard or read by professional reviewers or critics.

Resources

Elements of Literature
Drama
For more instruction on drama, see
Literary Elements:
• Transparency 8
Assessment
Formal Assessment
• Literary Elements Test, p. 88

Elements of Literature

This feature, written by dramatist Robert Anderson, sets forth some of the most important elements found in dramatic literature, including character, conflict, and the stages of plot development. It then connects the audience's understanding of conflict onstage with their recognition and resolution of conflict in life.

Mini-Lesson:
Drama

Ask students to work in groups and choose a favorite television show, movie, or play. They should then determine their drama's **basic situation, complications, climax,** and **resolution.** Guide them by reminding them of the definitions of these "bare bones" of drama and by asking questions that lead students to recall important details of the dramas they have chosen.

Applying the Element

Have students prepare a simple chart or list of the four "bare bones" of drama for *The Adventure of the Speckled Band,* the play they are about to read. Then, as students read the play, have them fill in specific details for each element.

Elements of Literature

DRAMA: Before Our Eyes *by* Robert Anderson

Why do we love plays so much? Probably for the same reasons that we enjoy any form of storytelling: Plays show us people in action, facing conflicts. Plays help us share feelings of suspense, horror, satisfaction, fear, love, sadness, joy, wonder. Even more, plays allow us to share an experience with actors and with the people who sit with us in the theater, at the movies, or even in our living rooms.

The Four Big "Bones"

All plays are made up of four "bare bones." The **basic situation** in a play usually involves a person (or several people) who wants something badly. In many musical comedies a boy wants a girl, or a girl wants a boy. In murder mysteries a detective wants to solve a crime.

As the person tries to get what he or she wants so badly, **complications** make things difficult: The parents of the boy don't like the girl,

or all the clues at the crime scene have been washed away by the rain. This is what people mean when they say "the plot thickens."

Toward the end of the play is the **climax.** This is the most emotional and intense part of the play: The character we're rooting for either gets what he or she wants or loses it. In action movies the climax is the big shootout or car chase.

In the **resolution** all the problems are resolved, or worked out—happily or unhappily. The play is over.

Give Me a Break

Long plays are broken up into smaller parts, called **acts.** Each act may contain many different scenes or camera shots. Usually each act ends at an especially dramatic moment—TV plays, for example, often end each act with a crisis. We wait through all those commercial breaks because we want to find out what happens next.

Characters We Care About

The characters in dramas change, or their relationships change, as they try to get what they want. Most dramas have at least two characters, because characters need to interact with other characters. Think about it—a person rarely changes without the influence of others. Also, some of the characters must be people we care about. It would be hard to sit through a play full of characters we disliked.

The Shock of Recognition

Drama offers us the gift of self-recognition. As we watch the characters try to overcome their conflicts, we may see ourselves or people we know. As we recall our own hopes, failures, and triumphs, we realize that other people in the audience feel this "shock of recognition" as well. In these ways, drama connects us with one another.

406 ONSTAGE!

Using Students' Strengths

Visual and Kinesthetic Learners
Ask students to suppose that they must explain to someone from another planet what plays are. The catch is that humans can communicate with the creatures only by using the sense of sight and the gestures and illustrations that appeal to the sense of sight—the two species have no other senses in common. Have students demonstrate how they would explain to this creature from another world what a play is.

Musical/Auditory Learners
Adapt the Visual Learners activity so that the only sense the humans and the creatures share is hearing. Then wrap up the activities by emphasizing that in reality, the wonderful thing about plays is that they involve all these senses.

Reading Skills and Strategies

FORMING OPINIONS

What are the facts and what are the opinions expressed by the speaker in the poem at the right? It's easy to tell facts from opinions if you remember these points:

- A statement of **fact** contains information that can be proved true.

  FACT   Judith Viorst wrote the poem on this page.

- A statement of **opinion** expresses a personal belief or attitude.

  OPINION   Judith Viorst is a good poet.

Valid Opinions

A **valid opinion** is a judgment or belief supported by facts. These two opinions are valid—they're supported by facts:

- I think Judith Viorst is a clever poet: By printing her poem upside down, she makes us realize that *she* might be the weird one.

- I think Judith Viorst's poem is just OK; Ogden Nash's poems are much cleverer and have funnier rhymes.

These two opinions are not valid—they're not supported by facts:

- I think Judith Viorst is a silly poet.
- I think "Weird!" is a good poem.

Opinions Can Change

Strategic readers constantly form opinions and change them as they get to know the characters in a story. As the characters change, the readers' opinions of them change, too. Readers draw new inferences and form new opinions from what the characters say or do.

As you read *The Adventure of the Speckled Band,* the characters and events will probably begin to seem real to you even though the play is set in a world very different from your own. You'll make inferences and form opinions from the characters' words and actions. Read on and see what *you* think. You're sure to enjoy the play. (In case you didn't notice, *that* was an opinion.)   **Apply the strategy on the next page.**

> ### WEIRD!
>
> My sister Stephanie's in love.
> (I thought she hated boys.)
> My brother had a yard sale and
> Got rid of all his toys.
> My mother started jogging, and
> My dad shaved off his beard.
> It's spring—and everyone but me
> Is acting really weird.
>
> —Judith Viorst

Reaching All Students

Struggling Readers

To teach valid opinions, give the following example: Sharon comes home to find her favorite cookie jar empty with the dog sitting next to it, holding the lid between its paws and with cookie crumbs in its whiskers. Explain that the opinion that the dog ate the cookies is supported by evidence. There might be some other explanation for the dog's appearance: someone may have smeared the dog's whiskers with crumbs and placed the jar nearby as a prank. But at present there is no evidence for this opinion, so it is not valid.

Recommend that students make a graphic organizer like the following to differentiate fact and opinion in other situations.

Situation	Fact, Opinion, or Valid Opinion	Why?
[Joe thinks Mike stole his baseball glove because Mike said he liked the glove]	[Opinion]	[No evidence to support Joe's idea]

OBJECTIVES

1. Distinguish between fact and opinion
2. Distinguish between valid, factually supported opinions and invalid, unsupported opinions

Reading Skills and Strategies

This feature focuses on a specific reading strategy, which students apply in the following selection.

Mini-Lesson: Forming Opinions

- Have students determine the facts in the poem "Weird." [brother selling toys, mother jogging, dad shaving beard, spring arriving] Ask how these facts can be confirmed. [through observation] Ask what other ways students know of to check facts. [Possible responses: Consult an encyclopedia, a dictionary, an atlas, or other reference book, or ask an expert.] Then have students determine the opinion in this poem. [that the speaker is the only one not acting strangely] Ask if this opinion is supported by the facts. [Possible response: No; the upside-down printing shows the speaker to be acting strangely, and the actions she reports do not seem strange.]

- Have students work in pairs to make lists of five facts and five opinions about your school. Topics might include the school building, a school team, the library, and the cafeteria.

As students read *The Adventure of the Speckled Band,* have them practice forming valid opinions by filling out a graphic organizer like the one below.

Valid Opinion	Text Support
[British in 1883 had customs that were different from American customs today]	[Helen wears a black veil; landlady wakes up her tenants to announce a visitor]

T407

OBJECTIVES

1. Read and interpret the play
2. Identify foreshadowing and analyze suspense
3. Form and analyze opinions
4. Express understanding through writing, performance, drama, or art
5. Understand and use new words
6. Complete analogies

SKILLS

Literary
- Identify foreshadowing
- Analyze suspense

Reading
- Form and analyze opinions

Writing
- Collect ideas for an evaluation

Vocabulary
- Define and use new words

Performance
- Dramatize a scene

Drama
- Rehearse and perform a scene or a whole play

Art
- Design a stage set

Viewing and Representing
- Match images to text (ATE)

Planning

- **Block Schedule**
  Block Scheduling Lesson Plans with Pacing Guide

- **Traditional Schedule**
  Lesson Plans Including Strategies for English-Language Learners

- **One-Stop Planner**
  CD-ROM with Test Generator

THE ADVENTURE OF THE SPECKLED BAND

Make the Connection

Elementary, My Dear Watson

Have you heard of Sherlock Holmes? He's fiction's most brilliant detective, famous for his ability to figure out a lot from the least bit of evidence. Sherlock Holmes can look at a footprint and tell his friend Dr. Watson almost everything about the person who made it. Sometimes he solves mysteries without even leaving his chair.

Quickwrite

How much can *you* figure out from a few words and a picture? Look at the title and the photograph on the opposite page. Read the quotation in large type. What do you predict will happen in this play? What *is* the speckled band, and what is the mystery about it? Write down your guesses.

Reading Skills and Strategies

Forming Opinions

As you read this play, work along with the legendary Sherlock Holmes to solve the case. Notice when your opinion about the solution changes. Do you find it changing whenever Holmes discovers something new?

Elements of Literature

Foreshadowing and Suspense: Hinting at an Uncertain Future

Writers use **foreshadowing** to give us clues to things that will happen later in a story. Foreshadowing builds **suspense;** it makes us anxious about what will happen next. This short scene shows how foreshadowing works:

Holmes (*to a young woman who has just entered his sitting room*). Please sit down, and I'll get you a cup of tea. I see that you are shivering.

Helen. It is not cold which makes me shiver.

Holmes. What is it, then?

Helen. It is fear, Mr. Holmes. It is terror.

> **F**oreshadowing is the use of details that hint at events that will occur later in a story. **Suspense** is the anxious curiosity we feel about what will happen next. Foreshadowing intensifies our suspense.
>
> *For more on Foreshadowing and Suspense, see the Handbook of Literary Terms.*

 go.hrw.com
LE0 6-6

Background

Detective Fiction

When you read detective fiction, you become a detective, too. The writer gives you all the facts you need to solve the mystery. It is up to you to put the puzzle together and answer the big question. In most detective stories the question is "Who did it?" What is the question in this play?

The play takes place in England more than one hundred years ago. The main character is Sherlock Holmes, a freelance detective. Holmes and his good friend Dr. Watson, both bachelors, share rooms, or what we would call an apartment today. Their rooms include a sitting room, bedrooms, and rooms for their housekeeper.

Preteaching Vocabulary

Words to Own

Have students locate the Words to Own and their definitions on the bottom of the text pages. Then ask students to answer the following questions.

1. Is an **associate** a person, a place, or a thing?
2. If a fact is **trivial**, is it important or unimportant?
3. If the light coming into a room is **feeble**, is the room dark or bright?
4. Name at least three things that are not usually **visible**.
5. If you **deduced** an answer to a question, what did you do?

THE ADVENTURE OF THE SPECKLED BAND

Sir Arthur Conan Doyle, *dramatized by* **Mara Rockliff**

"It's a wicked world, and when a clever man turns his brain to crime, it is the worst of all."

The students in this production are part of Joann Leonard's MetaStages, a drama program for youth at Pennsylvania State University. A list of the cast is on page vii.

Characters

Sherlock Holmes, the great detective

Dr. Watson, his loyal friend

Helen Stoner, their client, about thirty years old

Julia Stoner, her sister

Dr. Roylott, Helen and Julia's violent stepfather

Setting: England, early April 1883.

Summary ▪▪

Act One: Scene 1. One morning Sherlock Holmes and Dr. Watson find a young woman, Helen Stoner, dressed in mourning, sitting on their sofa and shivering from fear. Helen relates that she has been raised by her stepfather on an estate that is heavily mortgaged and that her sister Julia died mysteriously two years earlier, just before Julia was about to get married. Helen is now frightened for her own life.
Scene 2. In a flashback, Helen and Julia act out the story of Julia's death. Julia mentions a whistle she has heard in the middle of the night (she decides it must be the Gypsies who camp on the estate). The scene reverts to the present, and Holmes questions Helen further, discovering that she keeps her door locked because of her stepfather's collection of Indian animals. We return to the flashback, hear a whistle and a clanging sound, and see Julia stagger out of her room and drop dead, crying out about a "speckled band." The scene shifts back to the present. Helen says no evidence pointed to a cause for Julia's death; she believes the "speckled band" refers to the spotted kerchiefs the Gypsies wear. Helen says she has come to see Holmes because now she, too, is engaged to marry and she, too, has heard the low whistle. After Holmes notes that the stepfather has caused the bruises on her arm, Helen exits. Her stepfather, Dr. Roylott, then roars in and threatens Holmes.

FROM THE EDITOR'S DESK

We went to the drama department of Pennsylvania State University, where Joann Leonard runs a children's theater group called MetaStages, to shoot the photographs for *The Adventure of the Speckled Band* and *Rumpelstiltskin.* We thought it was important to use real sixth graders to portay scenes from the plays. The photographer took a roll of film for each shot, and the actors were conscientious about staying in character throughout the long day of shooting.

Resources: Print and Media

Reading
- *Reading Skills and Strategies*
  MiniRead Skill Lesson, p. 149
  Selection Skill Lesson, p. 157
- *Words to Own,* p. 17
- *Audio CD Library*
  Disc 9, Track 2

Writing and Language
- *Daily Oral Grammar*
  Transparencies 27, 28

Assessment
- *Formal Assessment,* p. 82
- *Portfolio Management System,* p. 158
- *Standardized Test Preparation,* pp. 62, 64
- *Test Generator (One-Stop Planner CD-ROM)*

Internet
- go.hrw.com (keyword: LE0 6-6)

Ⓐ Reading Skills and Strategies

Forming Opinions

? What is Dr. Watson's theory of the crime? [Dr. Roylott hired the Gypsies to kill Julia.] Do you agree or disagree with it? Why? [Possible responses: agree, because Julia claimed her death was due to a "band," and the metallic sound may have been caused by Gypsies removing the metal bar that locked the shutters; disagree, because the evidence against the Gypsies is not strong enough; whereas the circumstantial evidence strongly implies that Dr. Roylott himself committed the murder.]

Ⓑ Critical Thinking

Interpreting

? Why does Holmes answer Roylott with irrelevant, trivial remarks about the weather and flowers? [Possible response: He is trying to arouse Roylott's anger in order to verify Helen's description of her stepfather.]

may have been caused by the bar securing the shutters falling back in place.

Ⓐ **Watson.** You think the doctor hired the Gypsies to kill her? But how did they do it?

Holmes. I cannot imagine. But——

[*The door flies open and* DR. ROYLOTT *storms in. He is huge and evil looking, with a top hat and a long coat.*]

Roylott (*angrily*). Which one of you is Holmes?

Holmes (*calmly*). I am, sir. But who are you?

Roylott. I am Dr. Grimesby Roylott.

Holmes. Indeed, doctor. Please have a seat.

416 ONSTAGE!

Roylott. I will do nothing of the kind. My stepdaughter has been here. I traced her here. What has she been saying to you?

Holmes. It is a little cold for this time of year.

Ⓑ **Roylott** (*shouting*). What has she been saying to you?

Holmes. But I have heard that the tulips promise to do well.

[ROYLOTT *shakes his fist.*]

Roylott. You think you can put me off, do you? I know you, you scoundrel. I've heard of you before. Holmes the meddler. Holmes the busybody!

Skill Link

Speaking and Listening: Determining Purposes for Listening

Remind students that different people may listen to the same words for different purposes. Indeed, the same person may listen for different purposes at different times. Ask students to imagine a stage production of *The Adventure of the Speckled Band* with an audience of four people. One listener is attending the play for pure enjoyment. A second listener is a teacher attending the play in order to learn about life in England in the late 1800s. A third person, an aspiring writer, is attending the play in order to learn how to write mysteries. The fourth audience member, a professional theater director, is attending the play in order to gain ideas about what makes a performance good or bad. Invite small groups of students to discuss what these different audience members might learn from seeing the play.

Holmes (*laughing*). Your conversation is most entertaining. When you go out, please close the door behind you.

Roylott. I will go when I've had my say. Don't you dare meddle with my affairs. I am a dangerous man to make angry! See here.

[*He grabs a metal poker*[4] *from the fireplace and bends it in half.*]

Roylott. See that you keep yourself out of my grip.

[*He hurls the poker back into the fireplace and storms out.*]

Holmes (*laughing*). What a friendly person. I'm not so bulky, but if he had stayed I might have shown him that my grip is not much more <u>feeble</u> than his own. **C**

[*He picks up the poker and straightens it out.*]

Holmes. And now, let's have some breakfast, Watson!

4. **poker:** metal rod used to stir fires.

WORDS TO OWN
feeble (fē′bəl) *adj.*: weak; without force.

THE ADVENTURE OF THE SPECKLED BAND, ACT ONE 417

Assessing Learning

MAKING MEANINGS

First Thoughts

1. Accept a wide variety of possible opinions; for example, it is a snake, a necktie, a headband, a band of musicians.

Shaping Interpretations

2. She goes to Holmes because she fears something terrible is about to happen. Most students will agree that she is right to feel afraid, from the evidence of her sister's death, her stepfather's violence, and the mysterious repetition of the low, whistling sound.

3. Julia died shortly before she was about to be married, a marriage that would have diverted an inheritance from her stepfather to herself. Her death occurred in her locked bedroom, where she was apparently alone at the time. No evidence as to a cause of death was found. A strange sound was heard before her death. Her last words had to do with a speckled band.

4. Possible response: His actions show that he is dangerously violent, perhaps mentally ill. Most students will say that they worry that Roylott is about to commit further violence against Helen, Holmes, or both. They probably also felt suspense (anxiety) when Helen told of her sister's strange death.

5. Answers will vary. Suspenseful scenes include Helen's visit to Holmes, when we worry about her safety; the flashback scene of Julia's death, when we wonder what could have caused her death and worry that the same thing will happen to Helen; the entrance of Roylott, when we worry about what he will do to Helen and to Holmes.

6. During the flashback, we see the events of Julia's death and learn of the whistle, the locked doors, the clanging sound.

7. Possible responses: Roylott killed Julia, on the evidence of his violent nature and his potential financial gain. Or, someone else killed Julia, because Roylott is too obvious a suspect.

Connecting with the Text

8. Possible responses: I would have seen the danger coming far in advance and would have left. Or, I might have wished to leave, but a proper Victorian middle-class young

T418

MAKING MEANINGS (ACT ONE)

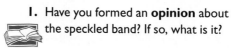

First Thoughts

[respond]
1. Have you formed an **opinion** about the speckled band? If so, what is it?

Shaping Interpretations

[infer]
2. Why does Helen Stoner come to see Sherlock Holmes? From what she tells him, do you think she's right to feel afraid? Why or why not?

[summarize]
3. Summarize what you know at this point about the circumstances of Julia's strange death.

[infer]
4. The beastly Grimesby Roylott also visits Holmes. What do his actions and appearance tell you about him?

[infer]
5. List the points in this act where you felt **suspense**. (What were you worried about?)

[connect]
6. In Scene 2 a technique called **flashback** takes you back to events that happened earlier. What events take place during the flashback?

[infer]
7. Who or what do you think killed Julia? Give evidence to support your opinion.

Connecting with the Text

[connect]
8. If you were Helen, would you have stayed in the house for two years after your sister's death? Why or why not?

Extending the Text

[extend]
9. Think of other detectives in novels, movies, and TV shows. In what ways are they like Sherlock Holmes? In what ways are they different? Which are professional detectives, and which are freelancers who regularly outsmart the police?

418 ONSTAGE!

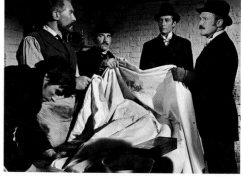

Scene from *A Study in Terror* (1965), starring John Neville as Sherlock Holmes.

lady would have felt that marriage was her only possible escape route. After all, where could she go?

Extending the Text

9. Responses will vary according to students' experiences. (Remind them of childhood stories, such as those about the intrepid Nancy Drew.) Today we have a much wider range of detective types than in Doyle's day, from hardened law enforcement officers to innumerable individual amateur sleuths.

Act Two

Dr. Roylott's estate

Scene 1

The scene takes place in two bedrooms: ROYLOTT's *and* JULIA's. ROYLOTT's *room includes a chair set against the wall, a metal safe with a small bowl on top, and a small loop of rope hung on the corner of the bed.* JULIA's *room includes a thick rope bell pull*  *hanging from the wall next to* ROYLOTT's *room, the tasseled end resting on the bed.* WATSON *and* HELEN *are standing in* JULIA's *room.* HOLMES *is crawling around on the floor, looking through a magnifying glass.*

Watson. So this is the room in which Julia used to sleep, and in which you've been sleeping for the last two nights because of the repairs on your own room.

Helen. Truthfully, Dr. Watson, the repairs hardly seemed necessary. I believe they were just an excuse to move me from my room.

[HOLMES *leaps to his feet.*]

Holmes. Ah! That is very interesting.

[*He walks over to the window, opens it, and tries unsuccessfully to force the shutters open.*]

Holmes. Hmm! This certainly presents some difficulties. No one could get into this room through the window if the shutters were closed.

[*He sits down and thinks, frowning. Suddenly he points to the bell pull.*]

Holmes. What does that bell communicate with?

Helen. It rings in the housekeeper's room.

Holmes. It looks newer than the other things.

Summary ▪▪

Act Two: Scene 1. Holmes, with Helen, examines Julia's bedroom, in which he discovers a dummy bell rope and a ventilator, installed shortly before Julia's death, which connects to Roylott's room. Holmes also examines Roylott's room and discovers a safe and a saucer of milk. Announcing that he has solved the mystery, Holmes says that he and Watson will witness the evening's activities in Julia's room.
Scene 2. Night. Holmes and Watson, in Julia's room, notice that her bed is clamped to the floor. Suddenly, they hear a hissing sound, and Holmes lashes at a snake coming down the bell pull, driving it back through the ventilator into Roylott's adjoining room. There it bites Roylott fatally.
Epilogue. Holmes explains the process by which Roylott, in the past, sent the snake into the room to kill Julia.

Ⓐ Cultural Connections

A bell pull is a rope connected to a bell in another room. In affluent Victorian homes, the residents would call their servants by pulling the rope, which rang a bell in the servants' quarters.

Using Students' Strengths

Logical Learners

Invite students, either individually or in a small group, to try to identify flaws in the plot of *The Adventure of the Speckled Band.* These may consist of reasons why facts or clues in the play aren't convincing; for example, why there seem to be only three bedrooms in a house belonging to very rich people; why Helen would agree to sleep in the same bedroom where her sister died, especially when she suspected there was little reason to. Still other logical flaws might consist of broader questions of believability; for example, why wouldn't Roylott notice that the snake had been prevented from entering Julia's room and protect himself? Couldn't someone as clever and vicious as Roylott have killed both women in some other way that would seem like an accident? Ask your student detectives to write up a report explaining their opinion of the solidity or flimsiness of the case.

A English Language Learners
Multiple Meaning Words
Make sure students understand that in this context, a *dummy* is something that doesn't work. The bell pull doesn't ring; it has been placed in the room to fool people.

B English Language Learners
Vocabulary Development
A *ventilator* is an air passageway leading from one room to another or from a room to the outside. If your classroom has a ventilator grille or heating register, ask a volunteer to point it out.

C Elements of Literature
Foreshadowing and Suspense
? What might the dummy bell rope and ventilator have to do with what happens next? [Accept reasonable responses. The actual answer, which should not be revealed at this point, is that the two devices serve as a passageway for a poisonous snake in the adjoining room.]

D Reading Skills and Strategies
Making Predictions
? What do you think the saucer of milk might be for? [Most will think it's for a cat; some might think it is poisoned.]

E Critical Thinking
Interpreting
? Why is it worst when a clever person turns to crime? [A clever person's crimes may be the hardest to detect; a clever person's potential contribution to society is wasted that way.]

Helen. Yes, it was put there only a couple of years ago.

Watson. Your sister asked for it, I suppose?

Helen. No, I never heard of her using it. We had no servants. We always used to get what we wanted for ourselves.

[HOLMES *jumps out of his seat and gives the bell pull a tug.*]

A **Holmes.** Why, it's a dummy.

Watson. Won't it ring?

Holmes. No, it's not even attached to a wire. You can see it is just hanging from a hook, just

B above the ventilator opening on the wall.

Helen. How strange! I never noticed that before.

Holmes. That's not the only strange thing about this room. For example, what a fool a builder must be to put in a ventilator to the next room, when with the same trouble he could have it open to the outside air!

Helen. That is also a recent addition, done about the same time as the bell rope. There were several little changes carried out about that time.

Holmes. They seem to have been changes of
C a most interesting nature—dummy bell ropes and ventilators which do not ventilate. Now, with your permission, Miss Stoner, I'd like to see the doctor's room.

[*They move into the next room.* HOLMES *walks around slowly, examining everything with great interest. He taps the safe.*]

Holmes. What's in here?

Helen. My stepfather's business papers. I saw him open it once, but it was some years ago.

Holmes. There isn't a cat in it, by any chance?

Helen. No, of course not. What a strange idea!
D **Holmes** (*picking up the bowl*). Then what is this saucer of milk for?

420 ONSTAGE!

Helen. I don't know. We don't have a cat. But there is the cheetah and the baboon.

Watson. Well, a cheetah is just a big cat.

Holmes. But a saucer of milk doesn't go very far in satisfying its wants, I daresay.

[*He squats down in front of the chair and examines it carefully with his magnifying glass.*]

Holmes. I've seen enough. (*Sighs*) It's a
E wicked world, and when a clever man turns his brain to crime, it is the worst of all. Tonight, Miss Stoner, after your stepfather goes to bed, you must go quietly back to your own room on the end. Dr. Watson and I will sneak in and keep watch in the middle room.

[HELEN *lays her hand on his arm.*]

Helen. I believe you have made up your

Getting Students Involved

Enrichment Activity
Speaking and Listening. Have students work in groups to improvise a scene of life at the Roylott estate—a scene not including Holmes or Watson, but focusing on the daily lives of Helen, Dr. Roylott, and (if the scene takes place in the past) Julia. Encourage students to act out what the characters were like as people and how they felt about one another, based on what students learned about them in *The Adventure of the Speckled Band.*

mind about this mystery, Mr. Holmes. Can't you tell me what caused my sister's death?

Holmes. We will all discover the truth tonight.

Scene 2

Only JULIA's *room is now visible onstage;* ROYLOTT's *room is hidden with a curtain or screen.* JULIA's *room is dimly lit.* HOLMES *and* WATSON *are crouched beside the bed. A walking stick lies next to* HOLMES.

Holmes. You know, Watson, I should have warned you before bringing you with me tonight. There is a distinct element of danger.

Watson. Danger! You must have seen more in this room than I did.

Holmes. No, I think we saw all the same things. But I may have deduced a little more.

Watson. I saw nothing remarkable except the bell rope, and what purpose that could have, I must confess, is more than I can imagine.

Holmes. You saw the ventilator, too?

Watson. Yes, but I don't think it's such an unusual thing to have a small opening between two rooms. It's so small a rat could hardly pass through it.

Holmes. I knew that we would find a ventilator before we ever came here.

Watson (*surprised*). My dear Holmes!

Holmes. Don't you remember when Miss Stoner said that her sister could smell the cigar smoke coming from her stepfather's room?

WORDS TO OWN

visible (viz′ə·bəl) *adj.*: capable of being seen; observable.
deduced (dē·dōōst′) *v.*: reasoned out; concluded from known facts or evidence.

F ● **Elements of Literature**
Foreshadowing and Suspense
? How do these last two speeches in Scene 1 build suspense for the next scene? [They make the audience feel that a solution to the mystery is going to be revealed in the next scene. This "hooks" the audience, maintaining interest while the scene shifts.]

G ● **Elements of Literature**
Drama
? In a well-constructed play, every detail matters. If a playwright shows a character putting a gun in a drawer in Act One, we expect the gun to reappear at some point later in the play. What might be the importance of Holmes's walking stick? [Perhaps Holmes is going to use the stick as a weapon.]

H ● **Elements of Literature**
Foreshadowing and Suspense
? How does this little speech of Holmes's contribute to suspense? [It tells the audience that danger looms.]

I ● **Reading Skills and Strategies**
Forming Opinions
? Do you share Watson's opinion that there is nothing remarkable on the premises? [Possible response: No, the ventilator, dummy bell pull, and saucer of milk together create a set of unusual clues.]

Getting Students Involved

T421

Ⓐ Advanced Students
Drawing Conclusions
❓ What connection can you imagine between the ventilator, the rope, and Julia's death? [Accept a variety of theories without revealing the actual solution.]

Ⓑ Struggling Readers
Questioning
❓ What do you think is Holmes's purpose in hitting the bell pull with his stick? [Accept a variety of theories without revealing the answer: that he is hitting the snake.] Continue reading in order to learn the explanation, which is coming soon.

Ⓒ Struggling Readers
Questioning
❓ What do you think the scream means? [Accept a variety of answers. The answer, that Roylott has died, is about to be revealed.]

Ⓓ Reading Skills and Strategies
Making Predictions
Encourage students to review any predictions they made previously and any opinions they formed about the manner of Julia's death. Ask if students guessed that a snake was the "weapon," and if so, on what evidence they based their theory.

Ⓔ Vocabulary Note
Tell students that an *epilogue* is a section at the end of a novel or play that sums up or comments on the action or gives more information. In a mystery, the epilogue usually contains the detective's explanation of the crime.

Ⓕ Critical Thinking
Challenging the Text
❓ Has it really been proven that no one could have entered through the window or door? [Possible responses: Yes, the window was barred and the door was locked; no, locks can be picked and bars can be removed and replaced.]

Ⓖ Critical Thinking
Interpreting
❓ How could Holmes tell by looking at the chair that someone had been standing on it? [He undoubtedly saw shoe or foot imprints, perhaps dirt from shoes.] Remember that Holmes probably inspected the chair with his magnifying glass.

T422

Watson. But what harm could there be in a ventilator?

Ⓐ **Holmes.** Well, it's a curious coincidence of timing, don't you think? A ventilator is made, a rope is hung, and a lady who sleeps in the bed dies. Doesn't that strike you as interesting?

Watson. I can't see the connection.

Holmes. Do you notice anything peculiar about this bed?

Watson. No.

Holmes. It is clamped to the floor. The lady could not move her bed. It must always be in the same position relative to the ventilator and the rope.

Watson. Holmes! I think I begin to see what you are——

Ⓑ [*A hissing sound is heard.* HOLMES *grabs the walking stick, springs to his feet, and begins lashing wildly at the bell pull.* WATSON *watches, bewildered.*]

Holmes. You see it, Watson? You see it?

Ⓒ [*There is a long, low whistle.* HOLMES *stops hitting the bell pull and stares up at the ventilator. A horrible scream is heard from the direction of* ROYLOTT's *room. It is a man's voice.* HOLMES *and* WATSON *stare at each other.*]

Watson. What can it mean, Holmes?

Holmes. It means that it is all over. And perhaps it is for the best. Let's go.

[*The curtain is drawn back and* ROYLOTT's *room is revealed. The safe is open.* ROYLOTT *is sitting on the chair in a long dressing gown, eyes fixed on the ceiling, an expression of horror frozen on his face. He is dead. Around his head is wrapped a yellow snake with brown speckles.*]

Ⓓ **Holmes.** It is a swamp adder! The deadliest

422 ONSTAGE!

---

snake in India. He has died within ten seconds of being bitten!

Watson (*whispers*). The band! The speckled band!

Ⓔ Epilogue
The house on Baker Street

WATSON, HOLMES, *and* HELEN *sit drinking tea in the sitting room.*

Helen. How on earth did you figure it out, Mr. Holmes?

Holmes. At first, Miss Stoner, the presence of the Gypsies, and your sister's use of the word "band" to describe what she saw, brought me to an entirely mistaken conclusion.

Watson. Ah, yes, yes.

Ⓕ **Holmes.** But when I saw that no one could have gotten in the window or the door, I reconsidered. My attention was quickly drawn to the ventilator, and then to the bell rope which hung down to the bed. The discovery that this was a dummy, and that the bed was clamped to the floor, made me suspect that the rope was there as a bridge for something passing through the hole and coming to the bed. The idea of a snake instantly occurred to me, and when I remembered that the doctor had other animals from India, I was sure I was on the right track.

Helen. Of course! The cheetah and the baboon!

Ⓖ **Holmes.** Then I inspected his chair and saw that he was in the habit of standing on it, which he would need to do to open the ventilator and put the snake in.

Watson. Oh, that's why you were looking so closely at the chair.

Holmes. The snake provided a type of poison

Crossing the Curriculum

Art
Have students make posters to advertise *The Adventure of the Speckled Band*. The poster should depict an important scene, character, or event in the play. Ask students to write one or two sentences of advertising copy to go on the poster. Remind students that the purpose of the poster is to make people want to see the play: the poster should emphasize drama, suspense, and other exciting elements.

Making the Connections

Connecting to the Theme: "Onstage!"
Remind students that *The Adventure of the Speckled Band* was originally a short story rather than a play. Invite students to discuss the following questions:

• What is there about this story that made it a good choice to turn into a play?
• What scenes or events in the play did you find most suspenseful or exciting?
• Would you rather read the play or see it performed? Explain.

which would not appear on a chemical test, and it would take a very sharp-eyed coroner to notice the two tiny holes on the victim's body where the snake had done its work.

Helen. And what of the whistle and the metallic clang?

Holmes. Dr. Roylott had trained the snake, using the milk we saw, to return to him when he whistled so your sister wouldn't see it there in the morning. The clang was obviously caused by him closing the door of the safe on the snake when it returned home. He must have sent the snake through night after night, waiting for the night when it finally would bite your sister and kill her.

Helen. But why?

Holmes. The good doctor did not want to give up your mother's money when you and your sister got married. Having successfully stopped one marriage, when you became engaged he decided to try the same strategy again.

Watson. So when you heard the hissing sound, you attacked the snake with your cane, driving it back through the ventilator.

Holmes. And my blows made it angry enough to turn on its master at the other end. No doubt I am indirectly responsible for Dr. Roylott's death. I cannot say it will weigh very heavily on my conscience.

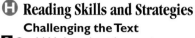 **Reading Skills and Strategies**
Challenging the Text

❓ Could Holmes have known in advance that by hitting the snake, he would drive it back to Roylott's room? [Possible responses: No, the snake could have fallen to the floor of Julia's room and killed Holmes or Watson; yes, the ventilator hole was small—big enough for only a rat (or a snake) to go through—so as soon as Holmes heard it, he could drive it back.]

Resources

Selection Assessment
Formal Assessment
• Selection Test, p. 82
Test Generator
• Selection Test

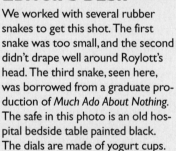
FROM THE EDITOR'S DESK
We worked with several rubber snakes to get this shot. The first snake was too small, and the second didn't drape well around Roylott's head. The third snake, seen here, was borrowed from a graduate production of *Much Ado About Nothing*. The safe in this photo is an old hospital bedside table painted black. The dials are made of yogurt cups.

Assessing Learning

Check Test: True-False

1. Dr. Watson brilliantly solves the case of *The Adventure of the Speckled Band*. [False]
2. Roylott, after being caught, confesses his crime. [False]
3. Because of the bravery of Holmes and Watson, Helen escapes with her life. [True]
4. The snake entered Julia's room a few nights before it attacked her. [True]
5. The Gypsies warned Helen of what was about to happen. [False]

Standardized Test Preparation

For practice with standardized test formats specific to this selection, see
• *Standardized Test Preparation*, pp. 62, 64
For practice in proofreading and editing, see
• *Daily Oral Grammar*, Transparencies 27, 28

LITERATURE AND SCIENCE

Interested students could research the biology of poisonous snakes and present a brief report to the class. They could focus on these questions: What is snake venom, and what does it do to its victims? How do snakes inject their poison? What are the major poisonous snakes? Under what circumstances are poisonous snakes likely to attack a person?

BROWSING IN THE FILES

About the Author. Sir Arthur Conan Doyle wrote novels as well as short stories about Sherlock Holmes. The first novel, *A Study in Scarlet,* was rejected by a number of publishers before finally being published—without great acclaim—in 1887. Two years later, an American editor who had liked *A Study in Scarlet* commissioned a second Holmes novel, *The Sign of Four,* which became a success. Perhaps the most well-known Holmes novel is *The Hound of the Baskervilles.*

Writers on Writing. Sir Arthur Conan Doyle found writing novels about Holmes more congenial than writing short stories about him:"[E]very story really needed as clear-cut and original a plot as a longish book would do. One cannot without effort spin plots at such a rate. They are apt to become thin and break."

LITERATURE AND SCIENCE

Cobra Copy

Questions: What exactly *is* the "speckled band" in this play? Holmes identifies it as a swamp adder, a type of snake that does not actually exist. Readers have raised other questions: Since snakes have no ears, how could the snake have responded to Dr. Roylott's whistle? Can a snake be trained to crawl up and down a bell pull? Do snakes drink milk?

Answers: Even though snakes do not have outside ear openings, they are very sensitive to low vibrations. Cobras—deadly snakes found in India—will drink milk when water is not available.

Is this "loathsome serpent" a cobra? Although we'll never know for sure, Doyle's "speckled band" has become one of literature's famous snakes.

MEET THE WRITER

"I Think of Slaying Holmes"

Arthur Conan Doyle (1859–1930) often complained that he wrote more about Sherlock Holmes than he ever wanted to. Doyle created the most famous detective of all time, but he grew to dislike him. In 1891, Doyle wrote to his mother, "I think of slaying Holmes . . . and winding him up for good and all. He takes my mind from better things."

In fact, Doyle considered Sherlock Holmes such a distraction from his serious writing that he killed him off in a story called "The Final Problem." The public outcry that followed forced Doyle to bring his hero back to life. More Sherlock Holmes adventures followed: Doyle wrote a total of fifty-six stories and four novels about the supersleuth.

The son of an Irish artist, Doyle was born in Edinburgh, Scotland, and was trained to be a doctor. His medical practice brought in little income, so he began writing stories to earn money.

Although detective stories had always fascinated Doyle, the ones he read annoyed him. In most of the stories, the case seemed to be solved through luck, or the solution was never explained. In his first Sherlock Holmes book, *A Study in Scarlet,* Doyle created a different kind of detective story. Unlike the detectives in earlier stories, Holmes solves cases with his amazing powers of deductive reasoning. All but four of the Sherlock Holmes stories are told by the detective's pleasant but dull friend Dr. Watson. Compared with Dr. Watson, Holmes seems even more brilliant!

Sherlock Holmes lives on today not only in Doyle's stories, which have been translated into sixty-three languages, but in hundreds of films. Holmes still serves as a model for detectives, both real and fictional. One California-based detective who tracks down lost pets is called Sherlock Bones.

Duffy's Jacket

Bruce Coville

If my cousin Duffy had the brains of a turnip it never would have happened. But as far as I'm concerned, Duffy makes a turnip look bright. My mother disagrees. According to her, Duffy is actually very bright. She claims the reason he's so scatterbrained is that he's too busy being brilliant inside his own head to remember everyday things. Maybe. But hanging around with Duffy means you spend a lot of time saying, "Your glasses, Duffy," or "Your coat, Duffy," or— well, you get the idea: a lot of three-word sentences that start with "Your," end with "Duffy," and have words like *book, radio, wallet,* or whatever it is he's just put down and left behind, stuck in the middle.

Me, I think turnips are brighter.

But since Duffy's my cousin, and since my mother and her sister are both single parents, we tend to do a lot of things together—like camping, which is how we got into the mess I want to tell you about.

Personally, I thought camping was a big mistake. But since Mom and Aunt Elise are raising the three of us—me, Duffy, and my little sister, Marie—on their own, they're convinced they have to do man-stuff with us every once in a while. I think they read some book that said

me and Duffy would come out weird if they don't. You can take him camping all you want. It ain't gonna make Duffy normal.

Anyway, the fact that our mothers were getting wound up to do something fatherly, combined with the fact that Aunt Elise's boss had a friend who had a friend who said we could use his cabin, added up to the five of us bouncing along this horrible dirt road late one Friday in October. **(A)**

It was late because we had lost an hour going back to get Duffy's suitcase. I suppose it wasn't actually Duffy's fault. No one remembered to say, "Your suitcase, Duffy," so he couldn't really have been expected to remember it.

"Oh, Elise," cried my mother, as we got deeper into the woods. "Aren't the leaves beautiful?" **(B)**

That's why it doesn't make sense for them to try to do man-stuff with us. If it had been our fathers, they would have been drinking beer and burping and maybe telling dirty stories instead of talking about the leaves. So why try to fake it?

Anyway, we get to this cabin, which is about eighteen million miles from nowhere, and to my surprise, it's not a cabin at all. It's a house. A big house.

Connections

In this utterly simple, comic short story (which is little more than a joke, but the kind of joke middle schoolers like), the fifteen-year-old narrator travels to a house in the woods with his mother, his Aunt Elise, his absent-minded cousin, Duffy, and his younger sister, Marie. In the house, the characters find a sign warning of a mysterious "sentinel." When they take a walk in the woods, the narrator senses they are being followed. Unfortunately, Duffy, as usual, has left his jacket behind. That evening, the two mothers leave their teenagers alone in the house. The nervous teens hear a scratching noise at the door and grow frightened. The narrator sees a large shape entering the barn; later, it approaches the house. The teens theorize that the Sentinel of the Woods has tracked them, using the scent of Duffy's jacket. At last the door opens, the Sentinel steps into the house, says, "You forgot your jacket, stupid," throws the garment down, and returns to the woods.

(A) **Struggling Readers**
Summarizing
This is a good place to ask students to pause and summarize what they have learned so far in the story.

(B) **Critical Thinking**
Challenging the Text
? Do you agree with the narrator's view of how men and women act? [Some students will agree while others may find the narrator's view stereotypical.]

Reaching All Students

Struggling Readers
Struggling readers should have no trouble with a Coville text. This story presents a good opportunity for oral reading. Students should pay special attention to the dialogue and try to read it in ways that make these comic characters come alive. A relaxed oral reading session might encourage students to ham it up and enjoy their performance.

English Language Learners
Point out colloquialisms and nonstandard usages, such as, "Me, I think turnips are brighter," and "It ain't gonna make Duffy normal." Invite English-fluent students to comment on whether they themselves would speak that way.

Advanced Learners
Encourage advanced students to read the story in a critical spirit, by asking questions such as, "Did you think the story was really funny?" and "Do you think the story was scary?" Accept negative answers that are supported by reasons, as well as positive answers that are similarly supported.

"Oh, my," said my mother as we pulled into the driveway.

"Isn't it great?" chirped Aunt Elise. "It's almost a hundred years old, back from the time when they used to build big hunting lodges up here. It's the only one in the area still standing. Horace said he hasn't been able to get up here in some time. That's why he was glad to let us use it. He said it would be good to have someone go in and air the place out."

Leave it to Aunt Elise. This place didn't need airing out—it needed fumigating. I never saw so many spiderwebs in my life. From the sounds we heard coming from the walls, the mice seemed to have made it a population center. We found a total of two working lightbulbs: one in the kitchen, and one in the dining room, which was paneled with dark wood and had a big stone fireplace at one end.

"Oh, my," said my mother again.

Duffy, who's allergic to about fifteen different things, started to sneeze.

"Isn't it charming?" asked Aunt Elise hopefully.

No one answered her.

Four hours later we had managed to get three bedrooms clean enough to sleep in without getting the heebie-jeebies—one for Mom and Aunt Elise, one for Marie, and one for me and Duffy. After a supper of beans and franks we hit the hay, which I think is what our mattresses were stuffed with. As I was drifting off, which took about thirty seconds, it occurred to me that four hours of housework wasn't all that much of a man-thing, something it might be useful to remember the next time Mom got one of these plans into her head.

Things looked better in the morning when we went outside and found a stream where we could go wading. ("Your sneakers, Duffy.")

Later we went back and started poking around the house, which really was enormous.

That was when things started getting a little spooky. In the room next to ours I found a message scrawled on the wall. BEWARE THE SENTINEL,° it said in big black letters.

When I showed Mom and Aunt Elise they said it was just a joke and got mad at me for frightening Marie.

Marie wasn't the only one who was frightened.

We decided to go out for another walk. ("Your lunch, Duffy.") We went deep into the woods, following a faint trail that kept threatening to disappear but nerve actually faded away altogether. It was a hot day, even in the deep woods, and after a while we decided to take off our coats.

When we got back and Duffy didn't have his jacket, did they get mad at him? My mother actually had the nerve to say, "Why didn't you remind him? You know he forgets things like that."

What do I look like, a walking memo pad?

Anyway, I had other things on my mind—like the fact that I was convinced someone had been following us while we were in the woods.

I tried to tell my mother about it, but first she said I was being ridiculous, and then she accused me of trying to sabotage the trip.

So I shut up. But I was pretty nervous, especially when Mom and Aunt Elise announced that they were going into town—which was twenty miles away—to pick up some supplies (like lightbulbs).

"You kids will be fine on your own," said Mom cheerfully. "You can make popcorn and

°**sentinel:** guard.

Using Students' Strengths

Visual Learners

This story is prime material for students' illustrations, since it portrays contemporary American youngsters in a recognizable domestic setting that is made comically eerie. Invite students to imagine that they are children's book illustrators who have been asked to submit possible pictures for an illustrated edition of "Duffy's Jacket." Have them provide a sample of at least three illustrations.

Linguistic Learners

Challenge students to rewrite the first paragraph of the story in the voice of someone very different from a middle-class teenager speaking colloquially. It might be, for example, the first-person voice of the narrator's mother, or the third-person voice of an omniscient adult narrator (one who knows everything about the story and is not identified with a specific character). Enthusiastic students may wish to try more than one new voice. Ask students to read their paragraphs aloud. You might ask listening classmates to guess what kind of person is narrating the revision; otherwise, have the author of the revision identify the narrator beforehand.

play Monopoly. And there's enough soda here for you to make yourselves sick on."

And with that they were gone.

It got dark.

We played Monopoly.

They didn't come back. That didn't surprise me. Since Duffy and I were both fifteen they felt it was okay to leave us on our own, and Mom had warned us they might decide to have dinner at the little inn we had seen on the way up.

But I would have been happier if they had been there.

Especially when something started scratching on the door.

"What was that?" asked Marie.

"What was what?" asked Duffy.

"That!" she said, and this time I heard it, too. My stomach rolled over, and the skin at the back of my neck started to prickle.

"Maybe it's the Sentinel!" I hissed.

"Andrew!" yelled Marie. "Mom told you not to say that."

"She said not to try to scare you," I said. "I'm not. *I'm* scared! I told you I heard something following us in the woods today."

Scratch, scratch.

"But you said it stopped," said Duffy. "So how would it know where we are now?"

"I don't know. I don't know what it is. Maybe it tracked us, like a bloodhound."

Scratch, scratch.

"Don't bloodhounds have to have something to give them a scent?" asked Marie. "Like a piece of clothing, or—"

We both looked at Duffy.

"Your jacket, Duffy!"

Duffy turned white.

"That's silly," he said after a moment.

"There's something at the door," I said frantically. "Maybe it's been lurking around all day, waiting for our mothers to leave. Maybe it's been waiting for years for someone to come back here."

Scratch, scratch.

"I don't believe it," said Duffy. "It's just the wind moving a branch. I'll prove it."

He got up and headed for the door. But he didn't open it. Instead he peeked through the window next to it. When he turned back, his eyes looked as big as the hard-boiled eggs we had eaten for supper.

"There's something out there!" he hissed. *"Something big!"*

"I told you," I cried. "Oh, I knew there was something there."

"Andrew, are you doing this just to scare me?" said Marie. "Because if you are—"

Scratch, scratch.

"Come on," I said, grabbing her by the hand. "Let's get out of here."

I started to lead her up the stairs.

"Not there!" said Duffy. "If we go up there, we'll be trapped."

"You're right," I said. "Let's go out the back way!"

The thought of going outside scared the daylights out of me. But at least out there we would have somewhere to run. Inside—well, who knew what might happen if the thing found us inside.

We went into the kitchen.

I heard the front door open.

"Let's get out of here!" I hissed.

We scooted out the back door. "What now?" I wondered, looking around frantically.

"The barn," whispered Duffy. "We can hide in the barn."

"Good idea," I said. Holding Marie by the hand, I led the way to the barn. But the door was held shut by a huge padlock.

427

T427

C **Elements of Literature**

Foreshadowing and Suspense

❓ What aspects of this passage made you feel suspense? [the fact that the kids are being left alone; the cheerfulness of the mothers; the very short paragraphs that heighten suspense; the darkness; the sentence, "I would have been happier if they had been there."]

D **Struggling Readers**

Breaking Down Difficult Text

Work with students to make sure they understand the gist of the conversation about the bloodhound. Ask volunteers to explain, if necessary, that a bloodhound tracks people by their scent. Remind students that Duffy left his jacket in the woods. Then ask them what conclusion they draw. Direct attention to the line, "Your jacket, Duffy!" and ask them what it means. [The narrator and Marie have drawn the conclusion that the Sentinel tracked them using the scent on Duffy's jacket.]

E **Critical Thinking**

Making Judgments

❓ Do you think Duffy really saw a monster out there? Why or why not? [Possible responses: No, because Duffy is foolish and because the story seems to be comical and fictional; yes, because it's important to the plot that Duffy confirms the narrator's assertion that there's something there.]

Foreshadowing and Suspense

? How does the writer use the sounds and the look of words to increase suspense? [The repeated thumping and knocking sounds and the use of italic type invite readers to hear something scary. The very short, one-line paragraphs that announce the approach of the creature create suspense.]

B Reading Skills and Strategies

Responding to the Text

? Does the story turn out to be scary, funny, both, or neither? [It is intended to be both, but student responses may differ.] Do you like this ending, and if not, what kind of ending would you have preferred?

BROWSING IN THE FILES

Bruce Coville (1950–), a very popular YA writer, grew up in central New York State and has worked as a teacher, a salesman, an assembly line worker, a toy maker, and a gravedigger. He is best known for his fantasy novels for young people, such as *Jeremy Thatcher, Dragon Hatcher*.

Writers on Writing. Very conscious of the writer's role as teacher, Coville comments, "I do not expect a child to read my picture books and suddenly discover the secret of the universe. I do hope that something from my works will tuck itself away in the child's mind, ready to present itself as a piece of the puzzle on some future day when he or she is busy constructing a view of the world that will provide at least a modicum of hope and dignity."

The wind was blowing harder, but not hard enough to hide the sound of the back door of the house opening, and then slamming shut.

"Quick!" I whispered. "It knows we're out here. Let's sneak around front. It will never expect us to go back into the house."

Duffy and Marie followed me as I led them behind a hedge. I caught a glimpse of something heading toward the barn and swallowed nervously. It was big. Very big.

"I'm scared," whispered Marie.

"*Shhhh!*" I hissed. "We can't let it know where we are."

We slipped through the front door. We locked it, just like people always do in the movies, though what good that would do I couldn't figure, since if something really wanted to get at us, it would just break the window and come in.

"Upstairs," I whispered.

We tiptoed up the stairs. Once we were in our bedroom, I thought we were safe. Crawling over the floor, I raised my head just enough to peek out the window. My heart almost stopped. Standing in the moonlight was an enormous, manlike creature. It had a scrap of cloth in its hands. It was looking around—looking for us. I saw it lift its head and sniff the wind. To my horror, it started back toward the house.

"It's coming back!" I yelped, more frightened than ever.

"How does it know where we are?" asked Marie.

I knew how. It had Duffy's jacket. It was tracking us down, like some giant bloodhound.

We huddled together in the middle of the room, trying to think of what to do.

A minute later we heard it.

Scratch, scratch.

None of us moved.

Scratch, scratch.

428 ONSTAGE!

We stopped breathing, then jumped up in alarm at a terrible crashing sound.

The door was down.

We hunched back against the wall as heavy footsteps came clomping up the stairs.

I wondered what our mothers would think when they got back. Would they find our bodies? Or would there be nothing left of us at all?

Thump. Thump. Thump.

It was getting closer.

A *Thump. Thump. Thump.*

It was outside the door.

Knock, knock.

"Don't answer!" hissed Duffy.

Like I said, he doesn't have the brains of a turnip.

It didn't matter. The door wasn't locked. It came swinging open. In the shaft of light I saw a huge figure. The Sentinel of the Woods! It had to be. I thought I was going to die.

The figure stepped into the room. Its head nearly touched the ceiling.

Marie squeezed against my side, tighter than a tick in a dog's ear.

The huge creature sniffed the air. It turned in our direction. Its eyes seemed to glow. Moonlight glittered on its fangs.

Slowly the Sentinel raised its arm. I could see Duffy's jacket dangling from its fingertips.

And then it spoke.

B "You forgot your jacket, stupid."

It threw the jacket at Duffy, turned around, and stomped down the stairs.

Which is why, I suppose, no one has had to remind Duffy to remember his jacket, or his glasses, or his math book, for at least a year now.

After all, when you leave stuff lying around, you never can be sure just who might bring it back.

BEWARE THE SENTINEL

Connecting Across Texts

Connecting with *The Adventure of the Speckled Band*

Ask students to provide ideas to fill in a chart on the chalkboard identifying ways in which "Duffy's Jacket" and *The Adventure of the Speckled Band* are alike and different. A sample chart is shown.

Alike	Different
They're scary.	One is a play; one is a short story.
They are suspenseful.	Settings: England 1883 vs. U.S. today.
A mystery is solved at the end.	*The Adventure of the Speckled Band* is a real mystery. "Duffy's Jacket" is sort of a joke.

Macavity: The Mystery Cat

T. S. Eliot

T. S. Eliot is best known for his serious poetry, but he also wrote funny poems about cats. He collected these poems in a book called Old Possum's Book of Practical Cats. *Eliot was a cat lover who gave his own pets names like Pettipaws, Wiscus, and George Pushdragon.*

Since Macavity is a British cat, you'll see British names like Scotland Yard, the Flying Squad, and the Foreign Office. You'll also find that Eliot calls Macavity "the Napoleon of crime." Eliot borrowed the phrase from one of the Sherlock Holmes stories, in which the detective refers to his archrival, the master criminal Professor Moriarty, as "the Napoleon of crime."

Macavity's a Mystery Cat: he's called the Hidden Paw—
For he's the master criminal who can defy the Law.
He's the bafflement of Scotland Yard, the Flying Squad's despair:
For when they reach the scene of crime—*Macavity's not there!*

5   Macavity, Macavity, there's no one like Macavity,
He's broken every human law, he breaks the law of gravity.
His powers of levitation would make a fakir° stare,
And when you reach the scene of crime—*Macavity's not there!*
You may seek him in the basement, you may look up in the air—
10   But I tell you once and once again, *Macavity's not there!*

Macavity's a ginger cat, he's very tall and thin;
You would know him if you saw him, for his eyes are sunken in.
His brow is deeply lined with thought, his head is highly domed;
His coat is dusty from neglect, his whiskers are uncombed.
15   He sways his head from side to side, with movements like a snake;
And when you think he's half asleep, he's always wide awake.

7. **fakir** (fə·kir′): Hindu or Moslem holy man, thought by some to perform wonders.

THE ADVENTURE OF THE SPECKLED BAND **429**

Edward Gorey (1925–   ) is
an American illustrator and writer
famous for his satiric black-and-
white illustrations, often published
in small books of comic verse
with mock-Edwardian themes.
Gorey's drawings poke fun at such
subjects as the literary life, upper-
class tastes, Gothic mystery stories, and high society.
Activity. Ask students to evaluate the drawing of Macavity, referring to details in the poem. What
is Macavity doing here? [perhaps
levitating]

**BROWSING
IN THE FILES**

T. S. Eliot (1888–1965), who was
born in St. Louis but later became
a British subject, is one of the
most influential poets of the twentieth century. His most famous
serious poem is *The Waste Land.*
Eliot also wrote a series of
humorous poems about cats, *Old
Possum's Book of Practical Cats,*
which was made into the long-
running Broadway hit musical
Cats! Eliot himself loved cats. "Old
Possum" is the nickname given to
the very distinguished poet by his
friend, poet Ezra Pound.

**Speaking and Listening:
Analyzing the Use of Aesthetic
Language**
Read this poem aloud at least twice.
Then, have students list words and
phrases that dramatize Macavity's
movements and reveal his character.
Ask them also to discuss how they
respond to the poem's rhythm and
refrain.

Macavity, Macavity, there's no one like Macavity,
For he's a fiend in feline shape, a monster of depravity.
You may meet him in a by-street, you may see him in the square—
20   But when a crime's discovered, then *Macavity's not there!*

He's outwardly respectable. (They say he cheats at cards.)
And his footprints are not found in any file of Scotland Yard's.
And when the larder's looted, or the jewel-case is rifled,°
Or when the milk is missing, or another Peke's° been stifled,
25   Or the greenhouse glass is broken, and the trellis past repair—
Ay, there's the wonder of the thing! *Macavity's not there!*

And when the Foreign Office find a Treaty's gone astray,
Or the Admiralty lose some plans and drawings by the way,
There may be a scrap of paper in the hall or on the stair—
30   But it's useless to investigate—*Macavity's not there!*
And when the loss has been disclosed, the Secret Service say:
"It *must* have been Macavity!"—but he's a mile away.
You'll be sure to find him resting, or a-licking of his thumbs,
Or engaged in doing complicated long division sums.

35   Macavity, Macavity, there's no one like Macavity,
There never was a Cat of such deceitfulness and suavity.°
He always has an alibi, and one or two to spare:
At whatever time the deed took place—MACAVITY WASN'T THERE!
And they say that all the Cats whose wicked deeds are widely known
40   (I might mention Mungojerrie, I might mention Griddlebone)
Are nothing more than agents for the Cat who all the time
Just controls their operations: the Napoleon of Crime!

23. rifled (rī'fəld): searched through; looted.
24. Peke's: *Peke* is short for *Pekingese,* a kind of small dog with long hair and short legs.
36. suavity (swäv'ə·tē): here, smoothness to the point of insincerity.

Connecting Across Texts

**Connecting with *The Adventure of the
Speckled Band***
Have students work in groups to create a
poem about Sherlock Holmes that imitates
the rhythm and perhaps some of the lines of
Eliot's poem. Tell students they must think of a
refrain that describes Holmes.

You might also have a group of students write
a shrinklet (a plot reduced to its barest bones)
about some encounter Holmes has with The
Hidden Paw.

MAKING MEANINGS (ACT TWO)

First Thoughts

[respond]

1. Look back at the guesses you made about the mystery in *The Adventure of the Speckled Band*. How close did you come to the real explanation?

Shaping Interpretations

[interpret]

2. In mysteries a **red herring** is a false clue thrown in to distract or confuse the reader. What is the red herring in this play? How does it mislead the characters? How did it confuse or distract you?

[interpret]

3. The murderer in a murder mystery must have a **motive** for committing the crime. What is the murderer's motive in this play?

[predict]

4. What happens to Dr. Roylott in the end? What did you expect Holmes and Watson to find when they entered his room?

[synthesize]

5. Look at the clues in the box above. Which clues in Act One **foreshadow**, or hint at, events in Act Two?

[connect]

6. Who does Holmes say is "indirectly responsible" for Dr. Roylott's death? If Holmes were tried for killing him and you were on the jury hearing the case, what would your verdict be?

Extending the Text

[identify]

7. Mystery writers use certain elements to create an eerie **mood,** or atmosphere, in their stories. Here are some of the elements they use to make us anxious:

- stormy weather
- mysterious letters
- strange noises
- nighttime settings
- houses in lonely, isolated places
- monstrous or deadly creatures

   Which ones are used by Bruce Coville (see *Connections* on page 425)? by Arthur Conan Doyle?

Challenging the Text

[compare]

8. Part of the fun of reading detective stories is challenging the plot. Do you see any flaws in this plot? Do any details still puzzle you or fail to make sense?

> ### Reading Check
>
> Choose four clues from the following list, and explain how each one helps Sherlock Holmes solve the mystery.
>
> **a.** the fake bell pull
>
> **b.** the smell of cigar smoke
>
> **c.** the low whistle
>
> **d.** the saucer of milk
>
> **e.** the marks on Dr. Roylott's chair
>
> **f.** the ventilator
>
> **g.** the bed secured to the floor

MAKING MEANINGS

First Thoughts

1. Guesses will vary. Be sure students compare their guesses.

Shaping Interpretations

2. The red herring in this case is the Gypsy camp. It misleads the characters and readers into thinking Gypsies killed Julia. Invite students to discuss whether or not they were fooled by the red herring.

3. Roylott's motive is to retain all the money his deceased wife left to him and his stepdaughters.

4. He is killed by the snake. Some students might have expected to find him dead; most will be surprised.

5. Clues b and c, which appear in Act One, foreshadow events in Act Two.

6. He says that he is responsible. Possible verdict: Not guilty on grounds of self-defense (Holmes might have been attacked by the snake) and because there is no evidence that Holmes actively sought Roylott's death.

Extending the Text

7. Both writers use all the elements except for mysterious letters. However, both works include mysterious messages or statements: in "Duffy's Jacket," the sign, "Beware the Sentinel," and in *The Adventure of the Speckled Band*, Julia's warning, "It was the band! The speckled band!"

Challenging the Text

8. Students' responses should include specific details.

Reading Check

a. The bell pull served as a bridge for something traveling through the ventilator to the bed.

b. The smell of cigar smoke told Holmes that there must be an air passageway connecting Roylott's room to Julia's.

c. The low whistle told Holmes that Roylott had trained the snake to return to his room.

d. The saucer of milk was used by Roylott to train the snake.

e. The marks on Roylott's chair showed that it had been stood upon, something Roylott would need to do in order to open the ventilator to let out the snake.

f. The ventilator provided the passageway along which the snake traveled from Roylott's room to the bell pull in Julia's room.

g. The bolted bed ensured that the occupant would be in the right position to be bitten when the snake descended the bell pull.

Grading Timesaver

Rubrics for each Choices assignment are provided on p. 158 in the *Portfolio Management System*.

CHOICES: Building Your Portfolio

1. **Writer's Notebook**   Have students work in groups of three or four to brainstorm criteria (which may include some or all of those shown on this page, as well as other criteria). Groups should continue free discussion to rate the play and state reasons.
2. **Dramatic Performance**   After students select roles, the next step will be to divide the story into scenes and choose one scene to dramatize. Suggest that students write down a list of the story's scenes and circle the one they agree upon.
3. **Oral Performance**   For help, see pp. 228–229, the Speaking and Listening Workshop.
4. **Art**   This activity can be combined with Choice 3, but does not need to be. Students designing sets may simply draw pictures of sets in pencil on paper, or may choose a more ambitious medium, including building an actual set for the performance in Choice 3. For dioramas, a cardboard box or even a shoebox can be used.

CHOICES: Building Your Portfolio

Writer's Notebook

1. Collecting Ideas for an Evaluation

When you evaluate a play, you decide how good or bad it is and then support your opinion with reasons and evidence. The first step in evaluating a play is deciding on your **criteria:** What qualities do you think a good mystery play has? Write down the criteria that are important to you. Then, judge *The Adventure of the Speckled Band* against these criteria. (You might try rating it on a scale of one to ten.) Jot down some reasons and evidence to support your judgment. Evidence might include details from the play, comparisons with another mystery (maybe a book or a movie), or explanations of your personal preferences.

> - Criteria for a good mystery
> - Originality
> - Believability
> - Suspense
> - Lots of surprises
> - Scary details

Performance

2. Duffy Scene

Form a group, and choose a scene from "Duffy's Jacket" to dramatize. Then, prepare a performance of the scene. Here are some decisions you'll have to make before the curtain goes up:

a. Who will write the script?

b. Who will be the director?

c. What props and scenery will you need?

d. How will you portray the Sentinel (if it appears in your scene)?

Oral Performance

3. Macavity Alive!

With a group, prepare an oral reading of "Macavity: The Mystery Cat" (see *Connections* on page 429). Read the poem carefully to decide how to present it: Will you use a chorus to read the refrain, *Macavity's not there!,* for example? How many readers will you need? Will you wear costumes? Will you use background noise or music? Before your performance, present your reading to a test group. Use their responses to perfect your presentation.

Art

4. Set the Scene

Make a diorama of the stage set of *The Adventure of the Speckled Band*. A **diorama** is a miniature re-creation of a scene, made by placing figures and objects in a box. The box stands on its side, so that the diorama looks like a real stage set. Construct a diorama illustrating a setting in the play, perhaps one in the Roylott mansion. Before you begin, list all the details in the play that describe this setting. Which of these details add to the play's eerie mood?

432 ONSTAGE!

T432

WORD BANK

associate
trivial
feeble
visible
deduced

Analogies

An **analogy** shows how one pair of words is related to another pair. Completing analogies is a fun mental exercise. First you figure out the relationship between a pair of words. Then you complete another pair with a similar relationship.

EXAMPLE   *Teacher* is to *instructor* as *partner* is to

_____.

Teacher and *instructor* have similar meanings. To complete the analogy, find a word that is similar in meaning to *partner*. If you were limited to Word Bank words, you'd choose *associate*. Use a Word Bank word to complete each analogy below.

1. *Happy* is to *joyful* as *weak* is to _____.
2. _____ is to *important* as *sweet* is to *sour*.
3. *Addition* is to *added* as *deduction* is to _____.
4. *Ear* is to *audible* as *eye* is to _____.

British Terms

Sir Arthur Conan Doyle wrote "The Adventure of the Speckled Band" more than one hundred years ago (the adaptation you just read was written recently). Some of the words in Doyle's story are still commonly used in Britain but have fallen out of use in the United States. For example, we would probably call Holmes's "sitting room" a living room. Below are some phrases and sentences from Doyle's story. Each contains a word, shown in italics, that is used differently from the way it is used by Americans today. Using a dictionary, define each italicized word as Doyle uses it here. Do Americans use the word today? If so, what does it usually mean?

LOOK
IN THE
BOOT.

1. "'*Pray* draw up to it, and I shall order you a cup of hot coffee. . . .'"
2. "'There is no vehicle *save* a dogcart which throws up mud in that way. . . .'"
3. "'And the lady, I *fancy,* is Miss Stoner. . . .'"
4. "'. . . within a *fortnight* of the day which had been fixed for the wedding . . .'"
5. "It was a *homely* little room. . . ."

VOCABULARY

Answers to Analogies
1. feeble
2. trivial
3. deduced
4. visible

Answers to British Terms
1. **Pray:** Doyle uses it to mean "implore, beseech." Today we use *pray* to mean "address God or ask God for something or praise God."
2. **Save:** Doyle uses it as a preposition to mean "except" or "unless." Today we use *save* to mean "preserve from harm, put away money or goods for the future, deliver from sin, avoid."
3. **Fancy:** Doyle uses it as a verb to mean "imagine." Today we use *fancy* as an adjective to mean "extravagant, ornamental, elaborate."
4. **Fortnight:** Doyle uses it to mean "two weeks" (from Old English, meaning "fourteen nights"). Americans do not use the word.
5. **Homely:** Doyle uses the word to mean "homey, comfortable, homelike." Today we use *homely* to mean "not good looking, plain." It is not a complimentary word.

Note the illustration that shows how Americans can be confused by British English. This tourist thinks *boot* means "high shoes or overshoes," but the Englishwoman is referring to the trunk of her car.

Resources ——————

Vocabulary
• *Words to Own,* p. 17

T433

OBJECTIVES
1. Identify a variety of jobs in the theater
2. Prepare to take part in a theatrical production

From Page to Stage

This features should stir students' enthusiasm for the theater. It gives them a brief glimpse of the many, varied tasks theater professionals carry out, such as directing, acting, or designing stage sets, costumes, lighting, and sound. The chart that opens the feature links students' aptitudes, personal tastes, and, implicitly, learning styles to specific forms of participation in theater.

Mini-Lesson:
From Page to Stage

Make a cluster diagram on the chalkboard, with the word *Plays* in the central circle. Begin discussion of this broad topic by asking students to think about and offer theories on the question, "When did people first put on plays, and why?" Many scholars believe that prehistoric drama began in religious ceremonies, in which participants acted out the roles of gods or spirits. Some of these ceremonies may have been intended to produce successful hunts or fruitful crops; masks and costumes may have been used to represent gods and animal spirits, as is still done in some cultures and traditions. The sheer enjoyment of acting out roles, dancing, and singing must have added emotional power to such ceremonies.

Discussion of drama's origins can lead into a discussion of why people throughout the world love plays. Encourage students to describe their own experiences seeing or participating in plays, and feel free to include your own experiences. Add new circles to the cluster to note significant elements of theater that are mentioned. These may range from specific functions, such as acting or set design, to more abstract and personal rewards of participation in the theater, such as "thrill of performing" or "fame" or "magical feeling."

From Page to Stage
by Joann Leonard

Where Do You Fit In?

If you like . . .	you could be . . .
writing stories	a playwright
planning strategy and coaching the team	a director
pretending you're someone else	an actor
creating environments and moods	a scenic, lighting, or sound designer
designing and making clothes	a costume designer, cutter, or draper
designing and overseeing construction projects	a technical director or master electrician
building things and creating interesting objects	a stage carpenter or prop master
making music	a composer, singer, or musician
creating or performing dances	a choreographer or dancer
organizing and supervising people and overseeing details	a stage manager
advertising and selling products	a publicist or box office manager
participating in events that make you laugh, cry, think, and dream	a member of the audience

If you can see yourself in any of these roles, the theater has a place for you. These are just a few of the jobs involved in transforming a script into a live performance.

434 ONSTAGE!

Using Students' Strengths

Kinesthetic Learners
The physical and vocal exercises on pp. 436–437 give these students a chance to let go and utilize their physical abilities. Use the chart on p. 434 to show students that there are many possible functions in the theater that may appeal to them, including acting, dancing, choreography, and stage carpentry.

Interpersonal Learners
You might suggest that these students create an organizational flow chart of people they would like to work with or people they would like to supervise in their chosen role.

Ideas into Words

"Once upon a time . . ." Since ancient times, people everywhere have told stories—in tents lined with yak-wool blankets, in castles hung with tapestries, in grass huts on sun-drenched shores, in adobe dwellings, in your own home at mealtime or bedtime. People tell stories to explain the mysteries of the universe, to share hopes and fears, or just to have fun.

Plays are stories that are acted out. The people who created the first dramas may have used animal skins as costumes and mud or berry pulp as makeup. The flickering flames of a communal fire may have been their lighting effects. For sound effects they may have thumped a hollow tree trunk with a stick or shaken a seed pod.

Modern dramatic performances probably bear little resemblance to those early dramas. Even so, every play still begins with a story. This story is written in the form of **dialogue** by a **playwright.** In the theater the story is brought to life for an audience.

Words into Images

If you were staging the story of Little Red Riding Hood, would you set it as a traditional fairy tale? Would you look at it from the wolf's point of view, as a story about human intrusion into his territory? In what other ways might you present the story? Interpreting the script and developing an overall concept that communicates the story most powerfully is the job of the **director.**

The director works with the designers on the look and sound of the play. If you were directing *Rumpelstiltskin* (page 463), you'd have to decide whether Rosa should appear in a miniskirt or a medieval surcoat. You'd have to decide whether she'd bake her gingersnaps in a microwave or on an open hearth.

The director tells the actors when and where to enter and exit. The director also coaches them on their movements and interpretations of character. The director must stage the play so that the audience can see, hear, and believe the story.

At the start of a new production, actors learn their lines and stage movements, or *blocking.* The director shows them where to move and how to perform each scene. The photographs in this essay are from the Inter-Active Theater Company in Houston, Texas.

Reaching All Students

Historical Connections

How Did Drama Begin?

A definitive answer to this question is not known, but it is generally considered that theater as the Western world knows it began in ancient Greece. The great philosopher Aristotle says that drama began in a religious ceremony, in a choral hymn sung to honor the Greek god Dionysus. As the hymn was sung, the leader of the chorus exchanged dialogue with the group as a whole. In 534 B.C., a great innovation was made: the leader of the chorus, a man named Thespis, selected one of the members of the chorus to exchange solo speeches with him. This was the very beginning of dramatic action, and to this day, in honor of this innovator, actors are called *thespians*. The first of the great Greek tragic playwrights, Aeschylus, added a second actor, and his successor, Sophocles, added a third. Thus, Western drama was born. You might ask students if they know the story of how and why drama developed in other cultures.

Exercise your voice:
First, let loose a big, noisy yawn to relax all the muscles in your throat and jaw. Next, take a deep breath, letting the air fill your belly. Then, recite this phrase: "The tip of the tongue, the lips and the teeth and the jaw." Pronounce all the sounds clearly, as if you were trying to communicate with someone in another room. This exercise uses all the parts of the mouth that shape words in English.

Now, imagine that your voice is a ball. Throw (project) it to the other side of the room. Did you use enough energy and volume to allow someone on the other side to catch it?

Images into Action

Have you ever acted? Yes! As a child you probably pretended to be a prince or princess, an airplane or a dog, a rock singer or a superhero.

Have you ever done mime? Yes! Mime was your first language. Before you could say "bye-bye" or recite the alphabet, you understood much of what people said through their body language. You knew when they were happy or angry or upset. You communicated with them by pointing, frowning, smiling, and opening your eyes wide with wonder. Our bodies tell stories all the time, and people read those stories. In a play an actor reveals character through movement as well as dialogue.

Actors use their bodies, imaginations, and emotions, combined with clues in the script, to make their characters believable. Actors ask themselves, "What does my character *want*? How does my character *feel*?" Actors also try to observe real people who are like their characters. They study people's behavior: how they walk, talk, sit, eat. Actors study a carpenter's hands to learn how they differ from a magician's hands. They train their voices and bodies to be strong, flexible, and expressive in order to transform themselves effectively.

Descriptions into Pictures

A bare stage becomes a forest, with birds chirping in the distance. Paint and plywood become the marble floor of a mansion. Dyes on a piece of canvas become the ancient mossy stones of a castle. A few strands of Christmas lights behind a translucent backdrop become a star-studded night. These are illusions created by **scenic, lighting,** and **sound designers.** These designers study the play's setting and transform the theater (or classroom) into another

Costume construction is an important part of putting on a play. This production calls for a four-headed giant.

The scenic designer decides how the stage will look. This is a finished set.

place, another time. The designers work closely with the technical director, master electrician, carpenters, scene painters, prop persons, and other technicians to create a set.

Characters into Costumes

For the Broadway production of *The Lion King,* the designers had a huge budget and more than a year to create the fabulous masks and costumes. For your production of *Rumpelstiltskin,* on the other hand, you have a shoestring budget and just one week until performance. As the costume designer, you have to be creative. For the king's royal robe, you buy a red skirt (the biggest you can find) at a thrift shop, cut it up the middle, and decorate it with gold fabric paint or secondhand costume jewelry. For the strange little man's costume, you glue burlap strips onto an old sweat shirt.

The **costume designer** researches the fashions of the period in which a play is set and sketches the actors' costumes. After the costumes are approved, the designer buys fabric, draws patterns, cuts and stitches garments, schedules fittings, selects accessories (items like belts, gloves, and jewelry), styles hair and wigs, and designs makeup. The costume designer helps create the magical world of the play.

Production to the Public

The **production and administrative staffs** may include a stage manager, a publicist, box office personnel, a house manager, ushers, and bookkeepers. Although they work behind the scenes, their contribution is vital to the success of a production. Even if you are performing a play in the classroom, without sets and lights and with just a few costumes, everyone must collaborate (work together) to bring the play to life.

Exercise your body and your imagination: First, form a group with a few classmates, and pick a leader. Then, walk around the room. When the leader claps and tells you what to become, stop and follow the command. Here are a few sample commands:

- "You are a balloon being blown up."

- "You are a circus performer—let us see who you are."

- "You are a statue in a museum."

- "You are walking through a jungle on a path choked with vines. It is hot, and mosquitoes are buzzing all around you. Show us how you feel."

- "You are a sea creature. Show us how you move around and how you eat."

Background

Point out to students that acting is to a great extent a physical job. Ask, "What aspects of acting require physical skills and training?" [fighting without getting hurt, running, dancing, moving gracefully in front of an audience, and performing tasks determined by specific roles, such as boxing, lifting heavy objects, or riding horses] Many successful actors find it useful to learn dance, gymnastics, or martial arts to acquire strength and coordination.

Additional Background

Ask students if they have heard the expression, "Break a leg." Tell them that it is an expression, a sort of secret signal, that actors say to wish each other good luck before a performance. (They believe that wishing *good* luck will bring bad luck.)

In this scene from the play, all the elements have come together.

An Important Lesson for Stage and Life: Expect the Unexpected

Minor emergencies—forgotten lines, ripped costumes, missed light cues—constantly arise in the theater. Dealing with the unexpected onstage is an important part of working in the theater—and is also excellent practice for the dramas of real life.

A young actor named Robby fractured his leg just one day before a performance. He returned the following day wearing a cast that went from his toes to his thigh. His stiff peg leg would have been great if he were playing Long John Silver in *Treasure Island,* but it posed a real challenge for him in the role he was playing: He was part of a group of kids racing around as they time-warped through cyberspace back to pioneer days.

Theater is about using your imagination, so we quickly found a solution to Robby's problem: a wheelchair. After silencing an annoying squeak in the wheels with lubricating oil provided by a helpful janitor, we were set. The other cast members adjusted their positions onstage, and each time the characters "reeled through time," one of the actors would zoom the wheelchair around the stage. The show went on looking as if it were just the way it had been planned.

We all kidded Robby, telling him that he shouldn't take it literally when people said "break a leg" to wish him good luck. (After the show, he had a real "cast" party.)

Sometimes a production kit comes to the rescue. Moments before going onstage, an actress named Sara discovered a rip in her pants. No problem. An inside patch was quickly made from a roll of duct tape in the production kit, and the curtain went up only a few seconds late. Simple items like safety pins, a needle and thread, scissors, a hot-glue gun, a hammer and nails, pliers, and bandages—along with quick thinking—can be backstage lifesavers.

Where Do You Come In?

Now you have an idea of how your interests and talents might be used in taking a play from page to stage. When the curtain comes down and the audience applauds the effort of so many imaginations, hands, and hearts, what part will you have played?

438 ONSTAGE!

Before You Read

BLANCA FLOR

Make the Connection

The Great Escape

You and your friend are running as fast as you can from a pair of bad guys, but they're getting closer and closer.

Luckily, your friend has magic powers. She pulls out a comb and throws it behind her. It turns into a fence, and the bad guys have to stop and climb it.

Soon they're gaining on you again. This time your friend pulls out a hairbrush. She throws it on the ground, and it turns into a forest. Eventually, though, the bad guys make their way through it and you hear their footsteps behind you again.

Now what? Your friend takes out a mirror and throws it down behind her. It turns into a lake, too wide for the bad guys to swim across. At last you're safe.

The play you're about to read, *Blanca Flor,* is based on a traditional European story, part of which is retold above. Tales usually change as they travel. Look for changes that make the play version different from the tale.

Quickwrite

Pick three items in your classroom, and imagine that they are magical objects, like the ones in the folk tale. What would they turn into if you threw them behind you? How would they help you escape from danger?

Reading Skills and Strategies

Cause and Effect: Why Things Happen

A **cause** makes something happen. An **effect** is what happens as the result of a cause.

Without cause and effect, a story would make no sense. Things would just happen one after another, with no reason or connection.

As you read *Blanca Flor,* notice how the play is held together by cause and effect. What **causes** the characters to act the way they do? What are the **effects** of their actions?

Elements of Literature

Motifs in Folk Tales: Again and Again

In the folk tale retold above, the heroine throws three items behind her in her flight to safety. In "Cinderella," three sisters take turns trying on a glass slipper. In folk tales we come across certain elements, like the number three, again and again. The number three is a motif (mō·tēf'), an element that appears frequently in literature. Here are other familiar motifs:

- the use of magic
- metamorphoses, or transformations
- impossible tasks
- villains
- maidens in danger and heroes who rescue them

> A **motif** is an element that appears again and again in literature.

BLANCA FLOR **439**

Summary ■

Scenes 1–5: Juanito, a young man, leaves his home with his parents' blessing to seek his fortune. Walking through a forest, he encounters a *Duende,* a mischievous, magical creature, who eats Juanito's tortillas and points him along a path with a warning to be careful. Juanito comes to a house in a clearing, where a beautiful young woman, Blanca Flor, urges him to flee before the evil magician who has imprisoned her, Don Ricardo, returns. Don Ricardo has a history of enslaving young men who have been tempted to try to help Blanca Flor escape; he tests them with impossible tasks and, after they fail the test, forces them to work until they die. Don Ricardo returns and confronts Juanito, who agrees to do three tasks in order to win Blanca Flor's freedom. Two tasks—draining a lake in one day and doing a year's agricultural work in one day—prove impossible for a human being. Blanca Flor intercedes. She puts Juanito to sleep by combing his hair and then performs the tasks through her own magic. The third task will be too difficult even for Blanca Flor's magic, and the two young people flee.

FROM THE EDITOR'S DESK

We spent a lot of time searching for a good play to use with sixth graders, and we discovered this one almost too late. It was found in the Austin Public Library in a little book of plays that was snuggled in the "new" section. When we began talking about the humor in the play and the fun we would have acting out the farcical parts, we knew the play would be a hit with sixth graders.

BLANCA FLOR

Angel Vigil

— Resources: Print and Media —

Reading
- *Audio CD Library,*
  Disc 10, Track 2

Elements of Literature
- *Literary Elements*
  Transparency 8
  Worksheet, p. 25

Writing and Language
- *Daily Oral Grammar*
  Transparencies 25, 26

Viewing and Representing
- *Viewing and Representing*
  Fine Art Transparency 15
  Fine Art Worksheet, p. 60

Assessment
- *Formal Assessment,* p. 84
- *Portfolio Management System,* p. 159
- *Test Generator (One-Stop Planner CD-ROM)*

Internet
- go.hrw.com (keyword: LE0 6-6)

Characters

The Narrator
Juanito, a young man
The Duende (dwen′dā), a gnomelike, mischievous creature who lives in the forest
Blanca Flor, a young woman
Don[1] **Ricardo,** an evil man
Don Ramon, the father of Juanito
Doña[2] **Arlette,** the mother of Juanito
Two Doves, actors in costume

Scene 1: In the forest

The Narrator. *Blanca Flor,* "White Flower." There never was a story with such a beautiful name as this story of Blanca Flor. At the beginning of our story, a young man named Juanito has left home to seek his fortune in the world. With the blessing of his parents to aid and protect him, he has begun what will be a fantastic adventure. At the beginning of his journey, he wanders into a forest and stops by a stream to rest and eat some of the tortillas his mother had packed for his journey.

[JUANITO *enters and walks around the stage as if looking for a comfortable place to rest. He finally decides upon a spot and sits down. He takes out a tortilla from his traveling bag and he begins to talk to himself.*]

Juanito. Whew! I'm hot. This river looks like a good spot to rest for a while. I'm so tired. Maybe this journey wasn't such a good idea. Right now I could be home with *la familia* eating a good supper that *mamacita* cooked for us. But no, I'm out in the world seeking my fortune. So far I haven't found very much,

1. **Don** (dän): Spanish for "Sir" or "Mr."
2. **Doña** (dô′nyä): Spanish for "Lady" or "Madam."

and all I have to show for my efforts are two worn-out feet and a tired body . . . oh, and don't forget (*holding up a dried tortilla*) a dried-out tortilla . . . (*He quickly looks around as if startled.*) What was that? (*He listens intently and hears a sound again.*) There it is again. I know I heard something . . .

[As JUANITO *is talking,* THE DUENDE *enters, sneaking up behind him.*]

Juanito. Must be my imagination. I've been out in the woods too long. You know, if you're alone too long, your mind starts to play tricks on you. Just look at me. I'm talking to my tortilla and hearing things . . .

The Duende (*in a crackly voice*). Hello.
Juanito. Yikes! Who said that! (*He turns around quickly and is startled to see* THE DUENDE *behind him.*) Who are you?
The Duende (*with a mischievous twinkle in his eye*). Hello.
Juanito. Hello . . . who, who are you? And where did you come from?

[THE DUENDE *grabs the tortilla out of* JUANITO's *hand and begins to eat it. During the rest of the scene* THE DUENDE *continues to eat tortillas.*]

Juanito. Hey, that's my tortilla.
The Duende (*in a playful manner*). Thank you very much. Thank you very much.
Juanito (*to the audience*). He must be a forest Duende. I've heard of them. They're spirits who live in the wood and play tricks on humans. I better go along with him or he might hurt me. (*He offers* THE DUENDE *another tortilla.* THE DUENDE *takes the tortilla and begins to eat it, too.*) I hope he's not too hungry. If he eats all my tortillas, I won't have

Background

According to Angel Vigil, in his preface to the anthology *¡Teatro! Hispanic Plays for Young People, Blanca Flor* is based on the folk drama tradition of the Hispanic Southwest, which dates back to the Spanish colonial culture in America. The period of Spanish colonization in America coincided with the Golden Age of literature in Spain, the period from the late 1500s through the 1600s. Among the many Spanish playwrights of the time whose works are still read and performed are Lope de Vega (1562–1635) and Calderón de la Barca (1600–1681).

Ⓐ Reading Skills and Strategies
Reading Aloud
If you have Spanish-speaking students in your class, ask one to pronounce the names of the characters aloud.

Ⓑ Vocabulary Note
Using Context Clues
Have a non–Spanish-speaking student use context clues to figure out the meaning of the Spanish words *la familia* ("the family") and *mamacita* (an affectionate term for "mother," like "Mama" or "Mommy").

Ⓒ Elements of Literature
Tone/Humor
❓ Say, "oh, and don't forget . . . a dried-out tortilla" in the tone of voice Juanito might use. What tone of voice is it? [disgusted, ironic] What does his remark suggest that the mood of this play is going to be? [It will contain some humor.]

Ⓓ Elements of Literature
Motifs in Folk Tales
❓ What folk tale motifs can you find in the character of the Duende? [The use of magic; tricksters.]

Reaching All Students

Struggling Readers
Cause and Effect was introduced on p. 439. A strategy that will help students identify cause and effect is Text Reformulation. For information on using this strategy see the *Reading Strategies Handbook,* p. 107 in the *Reading Skills and Strategies* binder.

English Language Learners
Students whose first language is Spanish can enrich the class's experience of *Blanca Flor* by clarifying elements of Latin American culture in the play. For English language learners from other cultures, explain that the play comes from the Hispanic culture of the Southwest. Then concentrate on the English in the text. For additional strategies, see
• *Lesson Plans Including Strategies for English-Language Learners*

Advanced Learners
Have students read folk tales from around the world in search of motifs that they encounter in *Blanca Flor.* Ask each student to choose two cultures other than the Hispanic culture of the Americas, and to read at least two tales from each culture. Encourage students to look for the motifs listed on p. 439 and to discover additional ones that recur in tales.

A Elements of Literature

Motifs in Folk Tales

This interchange between Juanito and the Duende contains two motifs found in many tales (but not included on the list on p. 439): the divergent path and the warning. Motifs can often be found not only in folk tales but in modern literature as well; for example, the divergent path is in Robert Frost's poem "The Road Not Taken" and the warning is in Herman Melville's novel *Moby-Dick.* In *Blanca Flor*, interestingly, the warning goes along with encouragement.

B Reading Skills and Strategies

Cause and Effect

❓ Juanito goes down a certain path because the Duende points that way. What might be the effect of Juanito's taking the path? [Accept a wide range of responses; the actual effect is the meeting with Blanca Flor and thus the rest of the play.]

C Elements of Literature

Motifs in Folk Tales

❓ What two motifs on the list on p. 439 are introduced in Blanca Flor's situation? [villains; maidens in danger]

---

any left, and it'll be days before I get food again. I'll have to eat wild berries like an animal. (*He reaches for the tortilla and* THE DUENDE *hits his hand.*) Ouch, that hurt!

The Duende. Looking for work, eh?

Juanito. Now I know he's a Duende. He can read minds.

The Duende. No work here. Lost in the forest. No work here.

Juanito. I know that. We're in the middle of the forest. But I know there'll be work in the next town.

The Duende. Maybe work right here. Maybe.
Juanito. Really. Where?

[THE DUENDE *points to a path in the forest.* JUANITO *stands up and looks down the path.*]

Juanito. There's nothing down that path. I've been down that path and there is nothing there.

The Duende. Look again. Look again. Be careful. Be careful. (*He begins to walk off, carrying the bag of tortillas with him.*)

Juanito. Hey, don't leave yet. What type of work? And where? Who do I see? Hey, don't leave yet!

The Duende (THE DUENDE *stops and turns*). Be careful. Danger. Danger. (*He exits.*)

Juanito. Hey! That's my bag of tortillas. Oh, this is great. This is really going to sound good when I get back home. My tortillas? . . . Oh, they were stolen by a forest Duende. Not to worry . . . (*He yells in the direction of the departed* DUENDE.) And I'm not lost! . . . This is great. Lost and hungry and no work. I guess I'm never going to find my fortune in the world. But what did he mean about work . . . and be careful . . . and danger. I've been down that path and there was nothing there . . . I don't think there was anything there. Oh well, there is only one way to find out. It

442 ONSTAGE!

---

certainly can't get much worse than things are now, and maybe there is work there.

[JUANITO *exits, in the direction of the path* THE DUENDE *indicated.*]

Scene 2: Farther in the forest

The Narrator. In spite of the Duende's warning, Juanito continued on the path of danger. As he came into a clearing, he came to a house and saw a young woman coming out of it.

[JUANITO *enters,* BLANCA FLOR *enters from the opposite side of the stage and stops, remaining at the opposite side of the stage.*]

Juanito. Where did this house come from? I was here just yesterday and there was no house here. I must really be lost and turned around. (*He sees the young woman and waves to her.*) Hey! Come here. Over here!

[BLANCA FLOR *runs to* JUANITO.]

Blanca Flor (*with fear in her voice*). How did you find this place? You must leave right away. The owner of this place is gone, but he will return soon. He leaves to do his work in the world, but he will return unexpectedly. If he finds you here, you'll never be able to leave. You must leave right away.

Juanito. Why? I haven't done anything.

Blanca Flor. Please, just leave. And hurry!

Juanito. Who are you? And why are you here?

Blanca Flor. I am Blanca Flor. My parents died long ago, and I am kept by this man to pay off their debts to him. I have to work day and night on his farm until I can be free. But he is mean, and he has kept prisoner others who have tried to free me. He makes them work until they die from exhaustion.

Juanito. Who would be so mean?

Blanca Flor. His name is Don Ricardo.

Using Students' Strengths

Logical Learners

Like mystery stories, folk tales can be fun to poke holes in (see *The Adventure of the Speckled Band*, pp. 409–423). Get a small group of these learners together, or have one student work independently, to write out a list of all the logical flaws and problems of believability that can be found in *Blanca Flor*. Make sure students

understand that the existence of magic in the tale is not in itself a logical flaw; it is one of the rules by which the story, like a game, works. Logical flaws would be inconsistencies within the rules of the story. For example, if Don Ricardo's powers end at the border of his lands, how can his curse extend farther? And if Blanca

Flor has such impressive powers, why couldn't she have escaped on her own? Have students report their analysis to the class. Then invite discussion of the question: "Do these flaws spoil a story for you, or can you enjoy it anyway?"

D Elements of Literature

Motifs in Folk Tales

? What motif discussed on p. 439 do you find in Don Ricardo's statement? [The importance of the number three.]

E Reading Skills and Strategies

Making Predictions

? What do you predict will happen when Juanito tries to do the tasks? [Possible responses: He's the hero and in fairy tales anything is possible; he'll succeed at one of the tasks and free Blanca Flor; he'll fail and be rescued by Blanca Flor or the Duende.]

F Reading Skills and Strategies

Cause and Effect

? What is the cause of Juanito's staying? [He wants to save Blanca Flor.] What will its effects be? [Possibly that he and Blanca Flor will fall in love and escape Don Ricardo]

[DON RICARDO *enters, suddenly and with great force.*]

Don Ricardo (*addressing* JUANITO). Why are you here! Didn't she tell you to leave!

Blanca Flor (*scared*). Don't hurt him. He is lost in the forest and got here by mistake. He was just leaving.

Don Ricardo. Let him answer for himself. Then I will decide what to do with him.

Juanito (*gathering all his courage*). Yes, she did tell me to leave. But . . . but I am in the world seeking my fortune and I am looking for work. Is there any work for me to do here?

Don Ricardo. Seeking your fortune! They always say that, don't they, Blanca Flor. Well, I will give you the same chance I have given others. For each of three days, I will give you a job. If in three days you have completed the jobs, then you may leave. If not, then you will work here with me until you are dead. What do you say, fortune-seeker?

Blanca Flor (*pulling* JUANITO *aside*). Do not say yes. You will never leave here alive. Run and try to escape.

Juanito. But what about you? You are more trapped than anybody.

Blanca Flor. That is not your worry. Just run and try to escape.

Juanito (*suddenly turning back to* DON RICARDO). I will do the work you ask.

Don Ricardo (*laughing*). Blanca Flor, it is always your fault they stay. They all think they will be able to set you free. Well, let's give this one his "fair" chance. (*To* JUANITO) Here is your first job. See that lake over there? Take this thimble (*he gives a thimble to* JUANITO)

BLANCA FLOR, SCENES 1–5 **443**

FROM THE EDITOR'S DESK

We often work with editors in our juvenile trade division to find selections and illustrators for *Elements of Literature*. We discovered the magical illustrations of Carlos Vazquez in a book on the shelf in the trade department and thought his use of animal motifs and brilliant colors were a perfect match for *Blanca Flor*.

Crossing the Curriculum

Mathematics/Social Studies

The "powers of three" have often been noted both in mathematics and in cultural lore. Have pairs of students investigate the special qualities this number possesses in those two realms. The cultural importance of the number three can be found in folklore (three blind mice, three little pigs, three billy goats gruff). Among the mathematical properties of three is that any number, however large, is divisible by three if the sum of its digits is divisible by three. Encourage students to find more examples and to create a poster or display illustrating their findings.

Music

Ask one or more students to create a tune for the song the doves sing on p. 455. Possible modes of performance include solo singing, singing with an *a cappella* (unaccompanied) group, and singing with instrumental accompaniment.

LITERATURE AND DRAMATIC ARTS

To get students to use these terms, tell them to suppose that they are going to plan a stage performance of *Blanca Flor*. This will involve finding actors for the roles, finding jobs for everyone else, and conducting rehearsals and other preparations. Tell the class that you are going to give them an "impossible task" to complete. The task is: In the discussion, they must use correctly all the terms on the list within a given time limit, such as ten minutes.

Onstage and Backstage: Theater Talk

audition (n.): short performance to show or test the ability of an actor (also called a **tryout**)

backstage: the part of the stage that is hidden from the audience, including the areas on either side and in back

block (v.): map out the movements of actors on the stage

"Break a leg!": theater expression for "Good luck!" Theater people, who are often superstitious, consider the expression "Good luck" to be bad luck.

cast (n.): the actors in a play

cast (v.): choose actors for the parts in a play

character: person in a play who is portrayed by an actor

choreographer (kôr′ē·äg′rə·fər): one who plans movements, such as dances or sword fights, and teaches them to actors

crew: team that does one type of work, such as building or moving scenery

cue: signal that tells an actor when to speak or move

curtain call: appearance onstage after a play to respond to the applause of the audience

director: one who interprets a play and works closely with actors and designers to create it

dress rehearsal: full rehearsal, with actors in costume and sets in place, that occurs shortly before opening night

A Critical Thinking

Extending

❓ What other tasks can you describe that would be as impossible as moving a lake with a thimble? [Possible responses: Counting the grains of sand on a beach; moving a mountain with a shovel; filling the Grand Canyon with pebbles.] What other impossible tasks do you know of from fairy tales? [Possible responses: Spinning straw into gold; finding a girl whose foot fits a glass slipper.]

B Elements of Literature

Motifs in Folk Tales

You might point out, as an aside, that Juanito himself seems to have heard many folk tales and to be familiar with their motifs.

C Struggling Readers

Identifying Pronoun Antecedents

If students seem puzzled by the reference to "ours," direct them to the last sentence in Blanca Flor's previous speech: ". . . his magic is stronger than any of ours." What makes this word puzzling, for Juanito as well as the reader, is that it has no antecedent: Blanca Flor does not say whom it refers to in addition to herself. It seems to imply that she belongs to a family or community of magical people.

---

and use it to carry all the water in the lake to that field over there.

A **Juanito.** You want me to move a lake with a thimble?!

Don Ricardo. You wanted work, fortune-seeker. Well, this is your job. Have it finished by morning or your fate will be the same as all the others who tried to save poor Blanca Flor. (*He exits.*)

B **Juanito.** What type of man is he? I have heard legends of evil men who keep people captive, and in my travels I heard many stories of young men seeking their fortunes who were never seen again, but I always thought they were just stories.

Blanca Flor. You have had the misfortune to get lost in a terrible part of the forest. Didn't anyone warn you to stay away from here?

Juanito. Yes . . . one person did. But I

444 ONSTAGE!

thought he was a forest Duende, and I didn't really believe him.

C **Blanca Flor.** It was a forest Duende. In this part of the forest there are many creatures with magic. But my keeper, his magic is stronger than any of ours.

Juanito. Ours? . . . What do you mean, ours? Are you part of the magic of this forest?

Blanca Flor. Do not ask so many questions. The day is passing by, and soon it will be morning.

Juanito. Morning. I'm supposed to have moved the lake by then. I know this job is impossible, but while God is in his heaven there is a way. I will do this job. And when I am done, I will help you escape from here.

[JUANITO *and* BLANCA FLOR *exit.*]

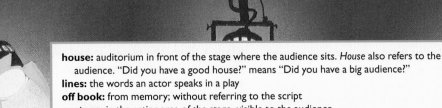

house: auditorium in front of the stage where the audience sits. *House* also refers to the audience. "Did you have a good house?" means "Did you have a big audience?"

lines: the words an actor speaks in a play

off book: from memory; without referring to the script

onstage: in the acting area of the stage, visible to the audience

opening night: first performance of a play

prompt (v.): remind an actor of his or her lines

prop: movable object that is placed or used in a set, not including costumes or scenery

read-through: gathering of the cast to read an entire script out loud

rehearsal: practice performance of a play or part of a play. A rehearsal of a whole play is a **run-through.**

scene: section of a play

script (n.): written text of a play

set (n.): acting area, complete with scenery and props

set designer: one who researches and designs sets and scenery

stage directions: instructions that tell actors where and how to move on the stage and how to say their lines

stage manager: assistant to the director who oversees all aspects of a production, including rehearsals, props, and technical elements

technical rehearsal: rehearsal during which sound cues, light cues, and set changes are practiced

wings: areas on the sides of the stage where actors wait to make their entrances, out of the audience's sight

D Reading Skills and Strategies

Cause and Effect

? What causes Juanito to cry, and what effects does his crying have? [He cries because he seems to be doomed; his crying moves Blanca Flor to pity, which in effect motivates her to use her powers to help him.] Draw a simple chart, using arrows to lead from a cause to its effect and to the next cause.

E Elements of Literature

Motifs in Folk Tales

? What motifs do you find in this event? [the use of magic; transformations; impossible tasks]

Scene 3: The next morning

JUANITO *and* BLANCA FLOR *enter. As* THE NARRATOR *speaks,* JUANITO *and* BLANCA FLOR *act out the scene as it is described.*

The Narrator. Juanito took the thimble and started to carry the water from the lake. He worked as hard as he could, but soon he began to realize that the job really was an impossible one, and he knew he was doomed. He sat down and began to cry because his luck had abandoned him and because his parents' blessings offered no protection in that evil place. Blanca Flor watched Juanito's valiant effort to move the water. As she watched him crying, her heart was touched, and she decided to use her powers to help him. She knew that it was very dangerous to use her powers to help Juanito and to cross Don Ricardo, but she felt it was finally time to end her own torment. As Juanito cried, Blanca Flor took out her brush and began to brush his hair. She cradled Juanito in her arms and her soothing comfort soon put him to sleep . . .

[*As soon as* JUANITO *is asleep,* BLANCA FLOR *gently puts his head down and leaves, taking the thimble with her.*]

The Narrator. When Juanito awoke, he frantically looked for the thimble and, not finding it, ran to the lake. When he reached the lake, he stood at its banks in amazement. All the water was gone. He looked over to the other part of the field, and there stood a lake where before there was nothing. He turned to look for Blanca Flor, but instead there was Don Ricardo.

BLANCA FLOR, SCENES 1–5 445

Taking a Second Look

Review: Forming Opinions

Remind students that a **fact** contains information that can be proven true, while an **opinion** expresses a belief or attitude. A **valid opinion** is one that is supported by facts.

Activities

1. Have students write down one fact about the play. [Example: The Duende eats Juanito's tortillas.]

2. Have students write an opinion which the fact might support. [Example: The Duende is mischievous.]

3. Ask volunteers to take turns reading their facts and their opinions aloud. Ask the class to assess (a) whether the fact is really a fact, (b) whether the opinion is really an opinion, (c) whether the opinion is valid. Whenever the answer is "No," have the student revise the fact or opinion.

Ⓐ Struggling Readers

Finding Sequence of Events

The sentence, "You are to clear that ground. . ." lists, in chronological order, the steps a farmer would take in order to turn forest land into a farm, raise a crop of wheat, and turn the wheat into bread. Ask students to speculate about how long this multiple task would take the typical farmer to complete. [Possible response: At least a year.] If you live in a farming community, students may be experts at answering this question.

Ⓑ Reading Skills and Strategies

Making Predictions

❓ What is going to happen while Juanito is asleep, based on what happened the last time he fell asleep under the spell of Blanca Flor's hairbrush? [Possible response: The rocks will be moved, seeds planted, wheat grown and harvested, wheat ground and baked into a loaf of bread.]

Ⓒ Elements of Literature

Suspense

❓ What question do you want the answer to? [What could this third task be?]

Ⓓ Reading Skills and Strategies

Cause and Effect

❓ What is causing Juanito and Blanca Flor to run? [The third task will be impossible even for Blanca Flor to perform, so this is their only chance to escape.] If Don Ricardo kills Juanito, what will be the cause? [Blanca Flor has helped Juanito.]

Ⓔ Elements of Literature

Motifs in Folk Tales

❓ What motif is the Narrator using here? [the importance of the number three] What question is put in your mind here? [Why is she spitting?]

[DON RICARDO *enters.*]

Don Ricardo (*in full force and very angry*). This must be the work of Blanca Flor, or else you have more power than I thought. I know Blanca Flor is too scared to ever use her powers against me, so as a test of your powers, tomorrow your next job will not be so easy. See that barren³ ground over on the side of the mountain? You are to clear that ground, plant seeds, grow wheat, harvest it, grind it, cook it, and have bread for me to eat before I return. You still have your life now, but I better have bread tomorrow. (*He exits, with a flourish.*)⁴

[JUANITO *exits.*]

Scene 4: The next morning

As THE NARRATOR *speaks,* JUANITO *and* BLANCA FLOR *enter and act out the scene as it is described.*

The Narrator. Immediately upon waking the next morning, Juanito tried to move the rocks in the field, but they were impossible to move because of their great size. Once again, Juanito knew that his efforts were useless. He went over to the new lake and fell down in exhaustion. As he lay in the grass by the lake, Blanca Flor came to him once more and began to brush his hair. Soon, Juanito was asleep.

[BLANCA FLOR *exits.*]

The Narrator. As before, when he awoke, Juanito dashed to the field to make one last attempt to do his work. When he got there, he again stopped in amazement. The field was clear of rocks, and the land had been planted and harvested. As he turned around, there stood Blanca Flor.

---

3. **barren:** not producing crops or fruit.
4. **flourish:** sweeping movement.

446 ONSTAGE!

[BLANCA FLOR *enters.*]

Blanca Flor (*she hands a loaf of bread to* JUANITO). Give this to Don Ricardo.
Juanito. How did you do this?

[DON RICARDO *enters, quickly.*]

Don Ricardo. What do you have?
Juanito (*shaking with fear*). Just . . . just this loaf of bread. (*Giving the bread to* DON RICARDO) Here is the bread you asked for.
Don Ricardo (*very angry*). This is the work of Blanca Flor. This will not happen again. Tomorrow, your third job will be your final job, and even the powers of Blanca Flor will not help you this time! (*He exits.*)
Blanca Flor. Believe me, the third job will be impossible to do. It will be too difficult even for my powers. We must run from here if there is to be any chance of escaping his anger. He will kill you because I have helped you. Tonight I will come for you. Be ready to leave quickly as soon as I call for you.

[JUANITO *and* BLANCA FLOR *exit.*]

Scene 5: Later that night

On one side of the stage, JUANITO *sits waiting. On the other side,* BLANCA FLOR *is in her room grabbing her traveling bag. As she leaves her room, she turns and mimes spitting three times as* THE NARRATOR *describes the action.*

The Narrator. Late that night, as Juanito waited for her, Blanca Flor packed her belongings into a bag. Before she left the house, she went to the fireplace and spat three times into it.

[BLANCA FLOR *joins* JUANITO.]

Blanca Flor (*quietly calling*). Juanito . . . Juanito.
Juanito. Blanca Flor, is it time?

Professional Notes

Critical Comment

Folk tales have come under extensive scrutiny by literary critics and social scientists who find meanings in them that extend to the contemporary world. Psychoanalysts, including Sigmund Freud, Carl Jung, and Otto Rank, have analyzed the characters in folk tales and myths as if they were patients, and the themes of the tales as if they contained keys for healing the neurosis of our time. Psychoanalyst Bruno Bettelheim examined the effects of fairy tales on child development in his book *The Uses of Enchantment.* More recently, feminist literary critics have analyzed such tales as "Cinderella" and "Sleeping Beauty" for the origins of gender roles. One theory of the meaning of *Blanca Flor*—for you rather than your students—is that Don Ricardo symbolically fills the role of a traditional father. He keeps Blanca Flor at home, where he exercises a veto power over his potential sons-in-law by testing their mettle. When a suitor comes along whom his "daughter" falls in love with, Don Ricardo's opposition proves weak; the lovers are able to sidestep his powers, and he becomes oddly feeble in his attempts to stop them, almost as if he were acceding to their escape. Yet even after they leave his domain, Don Ricardo retains, through his curse, an inhibiting hold over their psyches.

ⒻStruggling Readers
Breaking Down Difficult Text/Visualizing
Make sure students understand the following important facts about this scene: (1) only the Narrator is onstage, (2) the actors playing Don Ricardo and Blanca Flor speak from offstage, (3) Don Ricardo, from another room, is checking to find out if Blanca Flor is in her room, (4) Blanca Flor's spit, in the fireplace, has magically acquired the power to speak in her voice and thus fool Don Ricardo into thinking she is still in the room. To help students visualize this setup, you might suggest that they draw a quick cartoon of what the stage looks like, including speech balloons showing where the voices are coming from.

Blanca Flor. Yes. We must leave quickly, before he finds out I am gone, or it will be too late.

Juanito. Won't he know you are gone as soon as he calls for you?

Blanca Flor. Not right away. I've used my powers to fool him. But it won't last long. Let's go!

[JUANITO *and* BLANCA FLOR *exit.*]

The Narrator. When Don Ricardo heard the noise of Juanito and Blanca Flor leaving, he called out . . .

Don Ricardo (*from offstage*). Blanca Flor, are you there?

The Narrator. The spit she had left in the fireplace answered.

Blanca Flor (*from offstage*). Yes, I am here.

The Narrator. Later, Don Ricardo called out again.

Don Ricardo (*from offstage*). Blanca Flor, are you there?

The Narrator. For a second time, the spit she had left in the fireplace answered.

Blanca Flor (*from offstage*). Yes, I am here.

The Narrator. Still later, Don Ricardo called out again, a third time.

Don Ricardo (*from offstage*). Blanca Flor, are you there?

The Narrator. By this time, the fire had evaporated Blanca Flor's spit, and there was no answer. Don Ricardo knew that Blanca Flor was gone, and that she had run away with Juanito. He saddled his horse and galloped up the path to catch them before they escaped from his land.

BLANCA FLOR, SCENES 1–5 **447**

Skill Link

Word Origins
Use this activity before you teach the vocabulary exercise on p. 448, which has students find the meanings of words for foods. Many such words have colorful etymologies, or origins. The activity is also applicable to the vocabulary exercise on p. 461, which has students study English words that come from Spanish. You might either repeat the activity at that point, or remind students about it.

Remind students that in many dictionaries, the origin of a word is given after its pronunciation and syllabification and before its meanings. Have students browse through a dictionary, preferably unabridged, to find one example of each of the following:

- a word that comes from Latin
- a word that comes from German
- a word that comes from a non–European language

Have students write the definition and origin of each word and report them to the class. You might have students work in groups of three.

MAKING MEANINGS

First Thoughts

1. Possible responses: yes, because in folk tales the good guys live happily ever after; no, I think this play will have an ending with a twist.

Shaping Interpretations

2. Possible response: It is both an encouragement and a warning: the Duende wants Juanito to go down the path but knows it will be difficult and wants to help him. I would have gone down the path because I like adventure.

3. Possible responses: She pities Juanito for his sorrow; she has fallen in love with him; she has spent so much time as Don Ricardo's captive that she is finally determined to leave. The text gives two reasons: "her heart was touched" by Juanito's efforts and despair; "she felt it was finally time to end her own torment."

4. All of the motifs are present. Locations of some of them are given in the following side-margin annotations in this Teacher's Edition: pp. T441D, T442C, T443D, T445E, T446E. Encourage students to find them elsewhere in the play as well. Advanced students may find additional, unlisted motifs (see p. 442, annotation A).

VOCABULARY

Possible Answers

Specific foods chosen will depend upon students' tastes and their skill at using dictionaries. For students who have trouble thinking of examples, you might suggest the following: hamburger, frankfurter (and other German foods), pasta (and other Italian foods), chow mein (and other Chinese foods), sushi (and other Japanese foods), enchilada, taco (and other Mexican foods).

MAKING MEANINGS (SCENES 1–5)

First Thoughts

[predict]

1. Do you think Blanca Flor and Juanito will escape from Don Ricardo? Why or why not?

Shaping Interpretations

[interpret]

2. The narrator says that Juanito goes down the path "in spite of the Duende's warning." Did you hear the Duende's words as a warning, as encouragement, or as something else? Would you have gone down the path? Explain.

[infer]

3. Why do you think Blanca Flor decides to help Juanito even though she hasn't helped any of the young men before? (Does the text hint at more than one reason?)

[identify]

4. How many of the **motifs** listed on page 439 can you find in Scenes 1–5? Try to find at least four.

Reading Check

Match each **cause** in the left-hand column with its **effect** in the right-hand column.

a. The Duende points to a path in the forest.

b. Juanito hears Blanca Flor's story.

c. Juanito ignores Blanca Flor's warning and refuses to leave.

d. Blanca Flor moves the lake for Juanito.

1. Juanito decides to try to rescue Blanca Flor.

2. Don Ricardo catches Juanito on his land.

3. Juanito meets Blanca Flor.

4. Don Ricardo gives Juanito a harder task.

VOCABULARY `HOW TO OWN A WORD`

Eating Your Words

Have you ever eaten a *tortilla,* as the Duende does in the play? a *croissant?* a *bagel?*

The names of these foods come from Spanish, French, and Yiddish. When English speakers began eating these foods, they brought the names into the English language. After all, *bread* is a good word, but it certainly fails to capture the specific—and delicious—qualities of tortillas, croissants, and bagels.

What is your favorite food? Use an unabridged dictionary to find out where its name comes from and when the name came into the English language.

Reading Check
Answers
a. 3
b. 1
c. 2
d. 4

Scene 6: In the forest

JUANITO *and* BLANCA FLOR *enter, running and out of breath.*

Juanito. Blanca Flor, we can rest now. We are free.

Blanca Flor. No, Juanito, we will not be free until we are beyond the borders of Don Ricardo's land. As long as we are on his land, his powers will work on us.

Juanito. How much farther?

Blanca Flor. Remember the river where you met the Duende? That river is the border. Across it we are free.

Juanito. That river is still really far. Let's rest here for a while.

Blanca Flor. No, he is already after us. We must keep going. I can hear the hooves of his horse.

Juanito (*he looks around desperately*). Where? How can that be?

Blanca Flor. He is really close. Juanito, come stand by me. Quickly!

Juanito (*still looking around*). I don't hear anything.

Blanca Flor (*grabbing him and pulling him to her*). Juanito! Now!

[*As* THE NARRATOR *describes the action,* JUANITO *and* BLANCA FLOR *act out the scene.* BLANCA FLOR *does not actually throw a brush. She mimes throwing the brush and the action.*]

The Narrator. Blanca Flor looked behind them and saw that Don Ricardo was getting closer. She reached into her bag, took her brush, and threw it behind her. The brush turned into a church by the side of the road. She then cast a spell on Juanito and turned him into a little old bell ringer. She turned herself into a statue outside the church.

[DON RICARDO *enters, as if riding a horse.*]

Don Ricardo (*addressing the bell ringer* [*Juanito*]). Bell ringer, have you seen two young people come this way recently? They would have been in a great hurry and out of breath.

Juanito (*in an old man's voice*). No . . . I don't think so. But maybe last week, two young boys came by. They stopped to pray in the church . . . Or was it two girls. I don't know. I am just an old bell ringer. Not many people actually come by this way at all. You're the first in a long time.

Don Ricardo. Bell ringer, if you are lying to me you will be sorry. (*He goes over to* BLANCA FLOR [*the statue*], *who is standing very still, as a statue. He examines the statue very closely and then addresses the bell ringer* [*Juanito*].) Bell ringer, what saint is this a statue of? The face looks very familiar.

Juanito. I am an old bell ringer. I don't remember the names of all the saints. But I do know that the statue is very old and has been here a long time. Maybe Saint Theresa or Saint Bernadette.

Don Ricardo. Bell ringer, if you are lying, I will be back! (*He exits.*)

Juanito. Adiós, Señor!

[BLANCA FLOR *breaks her pose as a statue and goes to* JUANITO.]

Blanca Flor. Juanito, Juanito. The spell is over.

Juanito. What happened? I did hear the angry hooves of a horse being ridden hard.

Blanca Flor. We are safe for a while. But he will not give up, and we are not free yet.

[JUANITO *and* BLANCA FLOR *exit.*]

Summary ■

Scenes 6–10: Blanca Flor's magic gives the couple a head start on Don Ricardo. When the villain gives chase, Blanca Flor's magic enables the couple to be metamorphosed into different people or objects and to evade his notice. As the couple reach freedom past the boundary of Don Ricardo's magic, he brings a curse upon them, saying that the first embrace Juanito receives will make him forget Blanca Flor. This comes true: When Juanito's parents embrace him, he loses all memory of Blanca Flor and allows his parents to arrange his marriage with another girl. Blanca Flor, broken-hearted, goes to live in a nearby village, where she becomes known for her virtue. When Juanito's village holds a celebration for him, Blanca Flor magically turns a strand of her hair and a strand of his hair into two singing doves and presents them to Juanito as a wedding gift. Hearing the doves sing of the couple's adventures, Juanito remembers all and embraces Blanca Flor; they will live happily ever after.

Ⓐ Elements of Literature

Motifs in Folk Tales

? What motif or motifs can you find in this scene? [the use of magic; metamorphoses, or transformations]

Professional Notes

Gender Roles

Historically, in Western civilization and many other cultures, it has been believed that men are stronger, more physically capable, and more adventurous than women—that men are the rescuers and women the rescued. The motif of "maidens in danger and heroes who rescue them" can be viewed as an outgrowth of this social assumption. In the present-day world this assumption is being examined and to some extent altered. Challenge students to think about the following statement and to find evidence either supporting or opposing it: "In *Blanca Flor,* it is not so much the hero who rescues the maiden, it is the maiden who rescues the hero." [Possible responses: support—Blanca Flor performs the tasks set by Don Ricardo when Juanito is unable to, magically conceals her escape with Juanito from Don Ricardo, and finally rescues Juanito from marriage to someone he doesn't love by helping him overcome the curse; opposition—Blanca Flor herself acts as if she needs rescuing, she has never escaped on her own, and Juanito's recovery of his memory rescues her from loneliness.]

Scene 7: Farther into the forest

The Narrator. Blanca Flor and Juanito desperately continued their escape. As they finally stopped for a rest, they had their closest call yet.

[BLANCA FLOR *and* JUANITO *enter.*]

Juanito. Blanca Flor, please, let's rest just for a minute.

Blanca Flor. OK. We can rest here. I have not heard the hooves of his horse for a while now.

Juanito. What will he do if he catches us?

Blanca Flor. He will take us back. I will be watched more closely than ever, and you will——

Juanito (*sadly*). I know. Was there ever a time when you were free? Do you even remember your parents?

Blanca Flor. Yes. I have the most beautiful memories of my mother, our house, and our animals. Every day, my father would saddle the horses and together we would——

Juanito. Blanca Flor . . . I hear something.

Blanca Flor (*alarmed*). He's close. Very close.

[*As* THE NARRATOR *describes the action,* JUANITO *and* BLANCA FLOR *act out the scene.* BLANCA FLOR *does not actually throw a comb. She mimes throwing the comb and the action.*]

The Narrator. Blanca Flor quickly opened her bag and threw her comb behind her. Immediately the comb turned into a field of corn. This time she turned Juanito into a scarecrow, and she turned herself into a stalk of corn beside him.

[DON RICARDO *enters, as if riding a horse.*]

Don Ricardo. Where did they go? I still think that the bell ringer knew more than he was saying. They were just here. I could hear their scared little voices. Juanito will pay for this, and Blanca Flor will never have the chance to escape again. . . . Now where did they go? Perhaps they are in this field of corn. It is strange to see a stalk of corn grow so close to a scarecrow. But this is a day for strange things. (*He exits.*)

Blanca Flor. Juanito, it is over again. Let's go. The river is not far. We are almost free.

[JUANITO *breaks his pose as a scarecrow and stretches and rubs his legs as* BLANCA FLOR *looks around apprehensively.*][5]

Juanito. Blanca Flor, that was close. We have to hurry now. The river is just through these trees. We can make it now for sure if we hurry.

The Narrator. But they spoke too soon. Don Ricardo had gotten suspicious about the field of corn and returned to it. When he saw Juanito and Blanca Flor he raced to catch them.

[DON RICARDO *enters suddenly and sees them.*]

Don Ricardo. There you are. I knew something was wrong with that field of corn. Now you are mine.

[*As* THE NARRATOR *describes the action,* JUANITO *and* BLANCA FLOR *act out the scene.* BLANCA FLOR *does not actually throw a mirror. She mimes throwing the mirror and the action.*]

The Narrator. When Blanca Flor saw Don Ricardo, she reached into her bag and took out a mirror, the final object in the bag. She threw the mirror into the middle of the road. Instantly, the mirror became a large lake, its waters so smooth and still that it looked like a mirror as it reflected the sky and clouds.

5. **apprehensively:** fearfully; uneasily.

451

FROM THE EDITOR'S DESK

Artist Carlos Vazquez was born in Mexico where he studied physics and art. He now teaches bilingual adult education in New York City. You might see if students note that Juanito is always shown with a small lizard on or near his shoulder. Vazquez does this as a trademark. In his children's book about a young heroine named América, the heroine is always shown with a bird on her shoulder or flying near her.

Professional Notes

Both as professionals and as readers, we keep returning to folk tales. They operate on so many levels: The same tale can be listened to in preschool, read in a modern retelling in elementary school, reread in its original form at the university and again in maturity, and loved equally well at each stage, only gaining in rich-

ness with each new encounter. For contemporary Americans, this may be especially true because we find ourselves in a time of changing values, and folk tales are, above all, expressions of community values. Those of us who have lived through such changes may be startled and delighted (or for that matter, distressed and

enlightened) by what we find on rereading a folk tale we have not looked at for decades. When the tale involves the meaning of being a man or a woman, as in *Blanca Flor,* a reaction is almost inevitable.

A Elements of Literature

Motifs in Folk Tales

? The motif of a curse is familiar from such tales as "Sleeping Beauty" and "Snow White." What motifs from the list on p. 439 are also found here? [use of magic; villains] Note that in "Sleeping Beauty" and "Snow White" the curse also involves a maiden who must be rescued.

B Reading Skills and Strategies

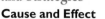

Cause and Effect

? What effect do you think the curse will have when Juanito goes to meet his family? [Encourage reasonable guesses; the actual answer is that his parents' embrace activates the curse.]

C Reading Skills and Strategies

Making Predictions

? What do you think the "next chapter" in Juanito's "great adventure" will be about? [Accept reasonable predictions; the actual answer is that it will be about how he returns to his community and forgets Blanca Flor, and how love then conquers the curse.]

D Advanced Learners

Analyzing/Making Generalizations

The conversation between Doña Arlette and Don Ramon includes several statements about basic issues in family life: (1) "the best thing to do was return home and make my fortune right here"; (2) "It is easier for a father to know those things. A mother will never stop worrying about her children"; (3) "there is no stopping children who want to grow up"; (4) "He has our blessing and permission to go, and that will be what brings him back safe to us." Ask students to rephrase each of those as a generalization about parents and their children. Then have students discuss whether they agree or disagree with these generalizations, and why.

When Don Ricardo got to the lake, all he saw was two ducks, a male and a female, swimming peacefully in the middle of the lake. Suddenly, the ducks lifted off the lake and flew away. As they flew away, Don Ricardo knew that the ducks were Juanito and Blanca Flor, and that they were beyond his grasp. As they disappeared, he shouted one last curse.

[JUANITO *and* BLANCA FLOR *exit.*]

A **Don Ricardo.** You may have escaped, Blanca Flor, but you will never have his love. I place a curse on both of you. The first person to embrace him will cause him to forget you forever! (*He exits.*)

Scene 8: Near Juanito's home

BLANCA FLOR *and* JUANITO *enter.*

The Narrator. Disguised as ducks, Blanca Flor and Juanito flew safely away from that evil land and escaped from Don Ricardo. They finally arrived at Juanito's home, and using Blanca Flor's magical powers, they returned to their human selves.

Juanito. Blanca Flor, we are close to my home. Soon we will be finally safe forever. I will introduce you to my family, and we will begin our new life together . . . Blanca Flor, why do you look so sad? We have escaped the evil Don Ricardo, and soon we will be happy forever.

Blanca Flor. We have not escaped. His final curse will forever be over us.

Juanito. Remember, that curse will work only in his own land. You yourself told me that once we were beyond the borders of his land, his powers would have no hold on us.

Blanca Flor. His powers are very great, Juanito.

Juanito. Blanca Flor, you have never ex-

452 ONSTAGE!

plained to me the source of your own powers. Are your powers also gone?

Blanca Flor. The powers have always been in the women of my family. That is why Don Ricardo would not let me leave. He was afraid that I would use my powers against him. I have never been away from that land, so I do not know about my powers in this new land.

B **Juanito.** You will have no need for your powers here. Soon we will be with my family. Wait outside while I go and tell my family that I have returned from seeking my fortune, safe at last. Then I will tell them that the fortune I found was you.

Blanca Flor. Juanito, remember the curse.

Juanito. I am not afraid of any curse. Not with you here with me. All my dreams have come true. Come, let's go meet my family.

[JUANITO *and* BLANCA FLOR *exit.*]

Scene 9: At Juanito's home

DON RAMON *and* DOÑA ARLETTE *are sitting at home passing the time with idle talk.*

C **The Narrator.** Juanito's parents had waited patiently for their son to return from seeking his fortune in the world. They did not know that his return home was only the beginning of another chapter of his great adventure.

Doña Arlette. Do you ever think we will hear from Juanito? It has been months since he left to seek his fortune in the world.

D **Don Ramon.** We will hear word soon. I remember when I left home to seek my fortune in the world. Eventually, I found that the best thing to do was return home and make my fortune right here, with my *familia* at my side. Soon he will discover the same thing and you will have your son back.

Doña Arlette. It is easier for a father to

Getting Students Involved

Enrichment Activity

Writing: I Used to Be…But Now I Am…
Invite groups of three to work together on a poem entitled "I Used to Be . . . But Now I Am…," about the character Blanca Flor. Each line of the poem should follow the pattern of the title, but with words or phrases inserted where the ellipses (three dots) were. Thus, each line relates information, or in some cases

opinions, about who the character is and how she has changed. The poem should be at least six lines long, with each group member contributing at least two lines. There is no upper limit—the more such statements students make about the character, the better they will understand her! Ask groups to read their poems aloud.

know those things. A mother will never stop worrying about her children.

Don Ramon. I worry about the children just as much as you do. But there is no stopping children who want to grow up. He has our blessing and permission to go, and that will be what brings him back safe to us. Soon. You just wait.

[JUANITO *enters. His parents are overjoyed to see him.*]

Juanito. Mama! Papa! I am home.
Doña Arlette. *¡Mi 'jito!*[6]
Don Ramon. Juanito!

[*Overjoyed with seeing* JUANITO, *his parents rush and embrace him.*]

Doña Arlette. God has answered my prayers. *Mi 'jito* has returned home safe.

6. ***mi 'jito*** (mē hē′tō): contraction of *mi hijito,* Spanish for "my little son."

Don Ramon. Juanito, come sit close to us and tell us all about your adventures in the world. What great adventures did you have?

Juanito. I had the greatest adventures. For the longest time I was unlucky and unable to find work but finally I . . . I . . .

Doña Arlette. What is it? Are you OK? Do you need some food?

Juanito. No, I'm OK. It's just that I was going to say something and I forgot what I was going to say.

Don Ramon. Don't worry. If it is truly important, it'll come back.

Juanito. No, I've definitely forgotten what I was going to say. Oh well, it probably wasn't important anyway.

Doña Arlette. Did you meet someone special? Did you bring a young woman back for us to meet?

Juanito. No, I didn't have those kind of adventures. Pretty much nothing happened,

E Elements of Literature
Motifs in Folk Tales
You might point out to students that reunions, especially reunions of parents and children, are common motifs in folk tales. So are reunions of lovers, as will occur later in the play.

F Struggling Readers
Noting Details
❓ What important event may occur when Juanito embraces someone? [He may forget Blanca Flor.] **How do you know this?** [It was stated earlier, when Don Ricardo put his curse on the couple.]

G Reading Skills and Strategies
Cause and Effect
❓ What is the cause of Juanito's forgetfulness? [Don Ricardo's curse] **What do you think its effects will be?** [Accept reasonable answers, such as, Blanca Flor and Juanito will be separated and unhappy; Juanito will fall in love with someone else.]

Getting Students Involved

Cooperative Learning
Writing Summaries. Divide the class into groups of four. Assign each student a character from *Blanca Flor.* Juanito, Blanca Flor, and Don Ricardo should be represented in every group; the fourth student should be assigned the role of the Duende. Have students discuss the events of the play from the points of view of their assigned characters. Then have each member independently write a summary of the play from his or her character's point of view. (Although the Duende only appears at the beginning of the play, he has magic powers and apparently knows much about what is going on; he may even be steering events toward a conclusion he desires. So his point of view is perhaps the most interesting of all.) Have each student read his or her summary aloud within the group. Peers may comment or ask questions about any points raised in their group's summaries.

Elements of Literature
Suspense
? What questions do you have at this point in the plot? [Possible responses: Will Juanito fall in love with Don Emilio's daughter? Will Juanito remember his adventures in time?]

B Struggling Readers
Finding Details/Making Predictions
? Several months pass between Scene 9 and Scene 10. What kinds of things might have happened in that time? [Possible responses: Juanito could be married; Blanca Flor could have been recaptured.]

C Reading Skills and Strategies
Responding to the Text
? What do you hope will happen at the celebration? [Possible responses: Juanito will remember Blanca Flor; Blanca Flor will fight Emilio's daughter over Juanito.]

D English Language Learners
Vocabulary Development/ Pronunciation
Show students a picture of a *dove*, and say the word aloud. What English words rhyme with it? [love, glove] What English words that have *ove* at the end do *not* rhyme with it? [move, stove] You might ask students how to say *dove* in their first language. In Spanish, it is the beautiful word *paloma*.

---

and then I finally decided that it was just best to come home.

Don Ramon (*to* DOÑA ARLETTE). See what I told you? That is exactly what I said would happen.

Doña Arlette. Now that you are home, it is time to settle down and start your own family. You know our neighbor Don Emilio has a younger daughter who would make a very good wife. Perhaps we should go visit her family this Sunday.

Juanito. You know, that would probably be a good idea. I must admit that I was hoping I would find love on my adventures, but I have come home with no memories of love at all. Perhaps it is best to make my fortune right here, close to home.

Don Ramon (*to* DOÑA ARLETTE). See? That is exactly what I said would happen.

[*All exit.*]

Scene 10: Months later at Juanito's home

The Narrator. Blanca Flor had seen the embrace and knew that the evil curse had been fulfilled. Brokenhearted, she traveled to a nearby village and lived there in hopes that one day the curse could be broken. The people of the village soon got to know Blanca Flor and came to respect her for the good person she was. One day, Blanca Flor heard news that a celebration was being held in honor of Juanito's return home. She immediately knew that this might be her one chance to break the curse. From the times when she had brushed Juanito's hair, she had kept a lock of his hair. She took one strand of his hair and made it into a dove. She then took one strand of her own hair and turned it into another dove. She took these two doves to Juanito's celebration as a present.

[JUANITO *and* DON RAMON *are sitting talking.*]

Don Ramon. Juanito, what was the most fantastic thing that happened on your adventures?

Juanito. Really, Father, nothing much at all happened. Sometimes I begin to have a memory of something, but it never becomes really clear. At night I have these dreams, but when I awake in the morning I cannot remember them. It must be some dream I keep trying to remember . . . or forget.

Don Ramon. I remember when I went into the world to seek my fortune. I was a young man like you . . .

[DOÑA ARLETTE *enters.*]

Doña Arlette. Juanito, there's a young woman here with a present for you.

Juanito. Who is it?

Doña Arlette. I don't really know her. She is the new young woman who just recently came to the village. The women of the church say she is constantly doing good works for the church and that she is a very good person. She has brought you a present to help celebrate your coming home safe.

Juanito. Sure. Let her come in.

[BLANCA FLOR *enters with the two* DOVES. *The* DOVES *are actors in costume.*]

Blanca Flor (*speaking to* JUANITO). Thank you for giving me the honor of presenting these doves as gifts to you.

Juanito. No. No. The honor is mine. Thank you. They are very beautiful.

Blanca Flor. They are special doves. They are singing doves.

Doña Arlette. I have never heard of singing doves before. Where did you get them?

Blanca Flor. They came from a special

Making the Connections

Connecting to the Theme: "Onstage!"
After students finish reading the play, remind them of the collection focus—Onstage!—and that the play *Blanca Flor* was adapted from a spoken and written folk tale. Discuss the question, "If you had your choice of either reading *Blanca Flor* as a tale, listening to a storyteller tell the tale, or seeing the play performed, which would you choose, and why?" (Note that reading the tale would not be the same as reading the play script.)

Then remind students about Scene 5, in which, after Blanca Flor spits into the fireplace, the stage is left empty as the characters talk from the wings. Ask students how the scene would be described in a narrative tale. Then ask them to imagine how it would be shot in a movie, where the camera could show many different shots, such as a close-up of the fireplace, close-ups of Blanca Flor's and Don Ricardo's

faces, shots of each character in his or her surroundings, and split-screen shots of both characters side by side. (You might want to make quick sketches of these types of shots at the chalkboard.) Which of the three modes of presenting this scene do students think is most effective, most "magical"—stage, film, or print—and why?

E Critical Thinking

Analyzing

? What kind of music would you compose for the doves' song? (Note that songs are used for similar effect in some of Shakespeare's comedies.)

F Reading Skills and Strategies

Cause and Effect

? What effect does the doves' singing have on Juanito? [It makes him remember his adventures with Blanca Flor.] In view of that fact, what effect does their singing have on the play? [Possible response: It makes the happy ending possible.]

Resources ⎯⎯⎯⎯⎯

Selection Assessment

Formal Assessment
• Selection Test, p. 84

Test Generator
• Selection Test

---

place. A place where all things have a magic power. There are no other doves like these in the world.

Don Ramon. Juanito, what a gift! Let's hear them sing!

Doña Arlette. Yes, let's hear them sing.

Blanca Flor (*to* JUANITO). May they sing to you?

Juanito. Yes, of course. Let's hear their song.

[*Everyone sits to listen to the* DOVES' *song. As the* DOVES *begin to chant, their words begin to have a powerful effect on* JUANITO. *His memory of* BLANCA FLOR *returns to him.*]

Doves. Once there was a faraway land
A land of both good and evil powers.
A river flowed at the edge like a steady hand
And it was guarded by a Duende for all the
   hours.

Of all the beautiful things the land did hold
The most beautiful with the purest power
Was a young maiden, true and bold
Named Blanca Flor, the White Flower.

Juanito. I remember! The doves' song has made me remember. (*Going to* BLANCA FLOR) Blanca Flor, your love has broken the curse. Now I remember all that was struggling to come out. Mama, Papa, here is Blanca Flor, the love I found when I was seeking my fortune.

[JUANITO *and* BLANCA FLOR *embrace.*]

Don Ramon. This is going to be a really good story!

[*All exit, with* JUANITO *stopping to give* BLANCA FLOR *a big hug.*]

BLANCA FLOR, SCENES 6–10 455

Assessing Learning

Check Test: Short Answers

Identify each of the following characters by stating briefly his or her role in the play.

1. Juanito [hero]
2. Blanca Flor [heroine]
3. the Duende [trickster, magician]
4. Don Ricardo [villain]
5. Don Emilio's daughter [would-be wife of Juanito]

Standardized Test Preparation

For practice in proofreading and editing, see
• *Daily Oral Grammar*, Transparencies 25, 26

MEET THE WRITER

"My Living Relatives Were Sources of Folklore"

Angel Vigil (1947–   ) was born in New Mexico and was raised "in a large, traditional Hispanic extended family, with loving grandparents and plenty of aunts and cousins." Storytelling was an important part of family life. Vigil says in *The Corn Woman:*

66 I was amazed to discover that my living relatives were sources of folklore. . . . I felt it was my calling to do what I could to make sure that the rich oral tradition of my childhood would continue through my generation. 99

Although *Blanca Flor* is based on a traditional European tale, the play also draws on Hispanic folklore. The mischievous little tricksters called *duendes* make trouble for people in stories told throughout the Hispanic Southwest.

Vigil is an award-winning collector and teller of stories. Most of the legends and folk tales he retells—sometimes in the form of plays—come from the Hispanic oral tradition. Vigil is also a performer and stage director and serves as chairman of the Fine and Performing Arts Department and director of drama at Colorado Academy in Denver.

Hispanic Artistry

You can find other plays based on Hispanic stories in Vigil's *¡Teatro! Hispanic Plays for Young People* (Teacher Ideas Press). You might also enjoy reading *The Corn Woman: Stories and Legends of the Hispanic Southwest* (Libraries Unlimited). Vigil's most recent collection, *Una Linda Raza* (Fulcrum Publishing), includes stories and plays, along with recipes, crafts, art, songs, dances, and historical information.

456 ONSTAGE!

Star Struck

Drama camp teaches youngsters basics of theater

CHRIS KREWSON

UNIVERSITY PARK, Pennsylvania—Thirty-two children face each other on the floor. They're divided into four circles, and this first day of camp they're all tied up.

"All right, I want you to grab someone's hand—not the person next to you," instructs Joann Leonard, the camp's director and organizer of the chaotic scene. "Now grab someone else's hand—but you shouldn't be holding the same person's two hands. Ready? Now I want you to get untangled."

Getting untangled was just the beginning of the week for MetaStages director Leonard and her thirty-two campers, ranging from nine to sixteen years old. This mixer, held at 10:00 A.M. Thursday, with these groups of knotted children, is the first lesson in the weeklong drama camp.

"Teamwork—that's what theater is," Leonard said. "Getting in all kinds of knots, and the bigger the knot, the better."

Leonard has been running MetaStages for the past seven years, holding the weeklong camps in the spring, summer, and fall seasons. She organizes her campers into two groups, grades four to seven and eight to twelve, and each rehearses scripts she wrote.

In the summers, MetaStages is held in the Pavilion Theatre, the livestock-building-turned-theater-space, with the audience surrounding the stage on three sides.

Right now, the Stages crew have all gotten loose on the stage floor, and Leonard is busy organizing them into their age groups. The Reds—the younger children—are to head downstairs to learn some elementary mime. The older children—the Blues—are going to stay upstairs and work on performance.

But they don't break until Leonard offers another tidbit of advice.

"When your families and friends come, they won't just see Christopher, Jillian, or Maggie. They're going to see your charac-

ters," Leonard assured her brood. "And you'll blow them away."

Heidi Vogel, the Blue group's instructor, begins with "group humiliation." She waves the Blues into a circle, then tells them, one at a time, to step inside the circle.

Then, Vogel explains, they are to "make a random sound and motion. One person makes it," she says, "then everyone repeats. Then we all clap and say 'Yes!'"

While the Blues are being humiliated—and giggling with the results, ranging from raspberries to dramatic falls to the floor—the younger Reds are working on a silent art.

The mirrored walls of the Pavilion Studio are echoing with their none-too-quiet efforts. Mark Olsen, a former professional

MetaStages drama camp director Joann Leonard works with campers on how to weave while maintaining the audience's interest in their play, *Song of the Sea,* during rehearsal. Molly Ryan, 10, center, and Ben Olson, 10, right, both of State College, are playing storytellers.

Centre Daily Times/Michelle Klein

BLANCA FLOR 457

Connections

This newspaper article describes events at Joann Leonard's MetaStages camp, as campers prepare a theatrical production.

Ⓐ Critical Thinking
Expressing Opinions
Ask a group of five or six students to try the exercise in front of the class; or, alternatively, have students imagine the exercise. Ask, "What does the exercise teach?" [Possible responses: cooperation, inventive problem solving.]

Ⓑ Vocabulary Note
Understanding Word Parts
Tell students that the prefix *meta-* is a difficult Greek prefix with many meanings, including "after," "later," "behind," "beyond," and "occurring with"; it often indicates a change in something, or indicates a focus on the topic designated by the root word that follows the "meta" prefix. The name *MetaStages* indicates that the program focuses on the stage. Students are already familiar with a "meta" word from this collection: *metamorphosis.* Ask them to describe the meaning of *meta-* in *metamorphosis.* ["Change": a metamorphosis is a change in form.]

Ⓒ English Language Learners
Understanding Idioms
Make sure students understand that the verb *break* in this instance doesn't mean to break in two! It means to take a break—to take a short rest.

Ⓓ English Language Learners
Understanding Idioms
Ask volunteers to suggest other expressions whose meaning is similar to *you'll blow them away.* [Possible responses: You'll impress them; you'll amaze them; you'll knock them out; you'll knock them for a loop.]

Ⓔ Vocabulary Note
Tell students that *random* means "chosen by chance, without plan or prearrangement."

A Critical Thinking
Making Connections
By this point, students have encountered enough basic exercises to begin practicing acting if they wish. Have students look back at the physical and vocal exercises in From Page to Stage (pp. 434–438). Encourage interested students to get together as a group and to invent and try out new acting exercises of their own, inspired by the ones they have read.

B Appreciating Language
Theater Talk
Have students look up *block* in the Literature and Dramatic Arts glossary on p. 444. Ask a volunteer to explain the statement, "the plays have all been 'blocked.'" [The actors' movements in all the plays have been planned.]

C Vocabulary Note
Synonyms
? What term on p. 445 must be a synonym for *off-lines*? ["off book"]

D Critical Thinking
Interpreting
? According to Joann Leonard, what benefits will children gain from participating in MetaStages? [Possible responses: self-confidence, the ability to speak in public, conquest of fear.]

Leonard fixes Jessica Hovick's costume. The 11-year-old resident of Port Matilda is also playing a storyteller.

Centre Daily Times/Michelle Klein

mime and Penn State performance movement teacher, works on their warm-up exercises.

"OK, I want everyone to pretend you're balloon people," Olsen says, guiding the children around the room. "And if you hit somebody, you gently float away."

Day Three at MetaStages is a bit more like, well, work. The kids have been working with their scripts—the Reds with *Song of the Sea,* a translated folk tale from Finland, and the Blues with *Johnny Appleseed in Cyberspace.*

By the third day of camp, the plays have all been "blocked." Each camper knows where they're supposed to be onstage, and they've started working on characters.

There's another challenge that starts on Day Three, Leonard said. It's the first time the campers go "off-lines," or stop using their scripts.

"It's always a little rocky when you first go off-lines," Leonard said. "And they have a lot of lines to learn for kids."

While the first two days of camp were mostly fun, Leonard said, Day Three ups the ante.

"Monday and Tuesday, they probably left thinking, 'Wow, that was fun,'" Leonard said with a grin. "We started to ride them a little harder today. And tomorrow, well, that'll be a little harder. But on Friday, with the performance, they'll be so amazed at what they've done."

Day Five of camp is the crowning moment. After a morning of technical rehearsals, working to coordinate the lights and sounds, the campers have enough time for only one dress rehearsal apiece before showtime.

The dress rehearsals run almost smoothly—only a few campers forget lines and one or two of the younger children have a tendency to rush, to blur the words together, or to not project. But Olsen and Leonard are supportive, gently trying to pull it all together.

The rest of the rehearsals end without any major mistakes, and the children gather for one last pep talk before their performance, but Leonard is already sure they'll succeed.

"We want to encourage them to have a voice. So when they need to use that voice, they can do it with confidence," Leonard said. "Sure, when they come here, some of them are afraid to say their names out loud. But by the end, they're so proud of how they've grown."

—from the *Centre Daily Times*

458 ONSTAGE!

Connecting Across Texts

Connecting with *Blanca Flor*
Ask groups of three or four students to imagine that they are participants in MetaStages and are going to perform a scene from *Blanca Flor.* They will have a five-day week in which to prepare, with their performance occurring at the end of the fifth day. Ask your groups to discuss what they would want to do and achieve on each day, what problems they might face, and how they would solve those problems. Each group should choose a specific scene from *Blanca Flor,* and the discussion, at least with regard to later days in MetaStages, should refer to specific aspects of that scene. Point out that since the article by Chris Krewson does not clearly distinguish between days one and two, or between days four and five, students are free to develop their own ideas on how to prepare a play. Have one member in each group take notes on the discussion; finally, have groups report to the class on their process and its outcome.

When I Was in *Oklahoma!*

It was my first year in our neighborhood theater program, called Main Street Theater. The play was *Oklahoma!*, and my friend Hanna and I tried out for parts. Neither of us knew what to expect—this was our first year in the program, and neither of us knew much about *Oklahoma!* I remember being very shy and embarrassed when I had to sing a song in front of the director.

After our tryout, we had to wait a few days (which seemed like forever) before we would know if we got a part. And then finally one day I remember running across the street with my friend, both of us hoping that the chart that lists the parts would *finally* be up. And it was.

I got the part of Fay (who in the world is that?) and my friend got Kate (she was a mystery as well). So we both went home, eager to get the script on the first day of rehearsal and see how many lines we had. The day arrived, the first day of rehearsal! We got the scripts. Hanna and I glanced at each other excitedly. Now we would finally get to see what the roles of Kate and Fay were like! We sat down, and I remember eagerly and excitedly leafing through the script. But as we went, page by page, neither of us spotted one line, not one! Eventually we came to the end of the script, and neither of us had a single line! I think we were more surprised than upset.

For about three months we rehearsed. I was onstage for some of the play, but I would kind of just stand there and react to whatever the other people onstage were saying. There were a lot of songs, though, so I got to sing a lot, and even dance. Then we got our costumes—that was fun. Both Hanna and I got two dresses to wear, a daytime dress and an evening dress. I remember that Hanna's daytime dress was really nice, but my evening dress was great.

Eventually, the day of the play arrived. I remember being a bit nervous, but not too much. My aunt came and so did my grandpa and, of course, my parents. My aunt did my hair in two braids. I think I messed up only once (since there wasn't much to mess up on): I came on a little late for a scene.

So that was it. Even though my part was small, everyone told me what a good job I did, and I got flowers. I think I was pretty much relieved it was over, maybe a little bit sad, too. Now I've been in the theater for four years and my parts have gotten bigger and bigger. I don't regret doing that small part in *Oklahoma!* It actually taught me that when you do something for the first time, you can't expect too much. But that doesn't mean it won't get better, and in the theater, you'll always have fun.

—Emily Goodridge
The Marymount School
New York, New York

Student to Student

Oklahoma! is a musical comedy, with the book and lyrics written by Oscar Hammerstein II and the music by Richard Rodgers. *Oklahoma!* opened on Broadway at the St. James Theatre on March 31, 1943. The New York run lasted five years with 2,212 performances. *Oklahoma!* was a groundbreaker musical in that for the first time music was used to advance the plot—the lyrics and melodies were integral to the unfolding of the musical's story, rather than being mere unrelated interludes. As you can see from Emily's essay, *Oklahoma!* is a favorite among middle and high schoolers, with its large cast of male and female characters, its American western setting, and its gorgeous music (songs include "Oh What a Beautiful Morning," "People Will Say We're in Love," and the rousing chorus "Oklahoma!").

Connecting Across Texts

Connecting with *Blanca Flor* and "Star Struck"

Open whole-class discussion of the following question: "Now that you've read *Blanca Flor* and two articles about young people's experiences in the theater, are you more interested in having a theater experience yourself?" Have students explain their responses. As an alternative or supplement to the discussion, ask students to write their individual answers in their journals. Then ask a few volunteers to read their answers aloud.

MAKING MEANINGS

First Thoughts

1. Sample responses: I liked it because it was romantic; I disliked it because it wasn't a surprise.

Shaping Interpretations

2. The major "threes" are: Don Ricardo prepares to give Juanito three tasks (Scene 2); Blanca Flor spits three times into the fireplace (Scene 5); Don Ricardo calls out to Blanca Flor three times (Scene 5); Blanca Flor throws three magic objects from her bag (Scenes 6–7). Less obvious "threes" are: Juanito, Blanca Flor, and Don Ricardo make a three-person household, as do Juanito and his parents.

3. Possible responses: The parents, because they show concern and care and disagree like real parents; or, Juanito, because, unlike Blanca Flor and Don Ricardo and the Duende, he doesn't have magic powers, and because he is forgetful, like a real person.

Challenging the Text

4. Sample responses: I would have revealed the truth at that point; I would have stopped his parents from embracing Juanito; I would have done exactly what Blanca Flor did, because it resulted in the best possible ending.

Extending the Text

5. Putting on a play fosters teamwork because a play is always a team activity (even a one-person show involves a technical crew and often a director as well as the solo performer); even if members of the team have personal conflicts, they must resolve them or put them aside long enough for a successful production to be put on. Students who agree with Leonard will probably make statements similar to the foregoing; students who disagree may say that stars, playwrights, and directors are so much more important than other members of a theatrical team that their positions may go to their heads and make them uncooperative.

T460

MAKING MEANINGS (SCENES 6–10)

First Thoughts

[respond]
1. Did you like the way the play ended? Why or why not?

Shaping Interpretations

[identify]
2. The number three is a common **motif**. How many times can you find things happening in threes in *Blanca Flor*?

[analyze]
3. Who do you think is the most lifelike character in this play? Give evidence from the text to support your opinion.

Challenging the Text

[connect]
4. If you were Blanca Flor, would you have just walked away when Juanito's mother came to embrace him? What else could you have done?

Extending the Text

[connect/ speculate]
5. Joann Leonard has said that teamwork is what theater is all about (see **Connections** on page 457). Do you agree or disagree with Leonard's statement? How might putting on a play foster cooperation and teamwork?

Reading Check

Using the events in Scenes 6–10, make a cause-and-effect matching game like the one on page 448. Trade papers with a partner, and play the game he or she has made.

CHOICES: Building Your Portfolio

Writer's Notebook

1. Collecting Ideas for an Evaluation

Your class is going to put on a play, and one of the plays being considered is *Blanca Flor*. Before the class decides, you have a chance to make your case for or against *Blanca Flor*. Decide which side you're on, and list your arguments. Put check marks next to the three arguments you think are the most convincing.

Creative Writing

2. A Change of Scenery

Retell the story of *Blanca Flor*, setting it in another time and place (perhaps your neighborhood today). Here are some questions to consider:

- What will the names of the characters be?
- What impossible tasks will the hero be given?
- What items will be thrown down during the chase, and what will they become? (Look for ideas in your Quickwrite.)

Art

3. Portrait of a Duende

What does the Duende look like? What does he do when he's not stealing tortillas and confusing young men? Where does he sleep at night? Does he have a family? Draw or paint the Duende in his home, deep in the forest.

Reading Check

Remind student to make sure their partners' cause-and-effect matches are faithful to the play. A sample matching game follows. Answers are in brackets.

Cause	Effect
a. Blanca Flor throws magic objects from her bag. [2]	**1.** Don Ricardo puts his curse on Juanito.
b. Blanca Flor and Juanito escape from Don Ricardo's lands. [1]	**2.** Blanca Flor and Juanito undergo metamorphosis.
c. Juanito's parents embrace him. [4]	**3.** Juanito remembers Blanca Flor.
d. Doves sing at the celebration for Juanito. [3]	**4.** Juanito forgets Blanca Flor.

Word Origins: Words from Spanish

The English language has borrowed many words from Spanish, and more come into English all the time. We eat *tortillas, enchiladas,* and *chili.* Sometimes we say goodbye to our friends by calling "*Adios.*"

You can sometimes figure out the meaning of an unfamiliar Spanish word by thinking of English words that resemble it. (If Spanish is your first language, you can figure out the meanings of some English words the same way.)

Find an English dictionary that tells you the origins of words—the languages they come from. Then, look up each of the words in the first column of the chart below. In the second column, write down the word's Spanish meaning or the original Spanish word or root. In the third column, write down the English meaning (either look in the dictionary or draw on your own knowledge).

Word	Spanish Meaning or Original Spanish	English Meaning
tornado	*tornar,* "to turn"	rapidly rotating column of air; whirlwind
pueblo		
patio		
canyon		
mustang		
mosquito		

BLANCA FLOR **461**

Rubrics for each Choices assignment appear on p. 159 in the *Portfolio Management System.*

CHOICES: Building Your Portfolio

1. **Writer's Notebook** Students may enjoy working on their lists with partners. One partner might propose reasons for choosing *Blanca Flor* and the other partner, reasons against it; or, both partners may brainstorm for both categories. Remind students to save their work. They may use it as prewriting for the Writer's Workshop on pp. 480–484.

2. **Creative Writing** In addition to students' own neighborhoods, you might suggest some settings that are historically or culturally interesting, such as the United States at the time of the American Revolution, or Sherlock Holmes's London. Bear in mind that the names, tasks, and objects may in some instances remain the same across settings.

3. **Art** Students might brainstorm answers to the questions about the Duende's lifestyle before beginning their individual drawings.

VOCABULARY
Answers

pueblo: Spanish meaning, "people, village"; English meaning, "an Indian village of the American Southwest."

patio: Spanish meaning, "courtyard enclosed by columns"; English meaning, "the courtyard of a house; an area outside a house where people sit or eat."

canyon: Spanish meaning, "a deep, narrow valley or gorge"; English meaning, same.

mustang: Spanish meaning, "stray animal"; English meaning, "a wild horse of the American West descended from the domestic horses brought by Spanish settlers."

mosquito: Spanish meaning, "little fly"; English meaning, "a member of the fly family *Culicidae,* in which the females suck the blood of animals."

T461

OBJECTIVES

1. Read and interpret the play
2. Identify character types in a dramatization of a folk tale
3. Express understanding through writing and performance
4. Identify connotations and denotations of words

SKILLS

Literary
- Identify character types in a dramatization of a folk tale

Writing
- Take notes to evaluate appealing and unappealing aspects of a play
- Compare and evaluate folk tales

Speaking and Listening
- Perform a reading of a one-act play

Vocabulary
- Identify connotations and denotations of words

Planning

- **Block Schedule**
  Block Scheduling Lesson Plans with Pacing Guide
- **Traditional Schedule**
  Lesson Plans Including Strategies for English-Language Learners
- **One-Stop Planner**
  CD-ROM with Test Generator

Resources

Listening
Audio CD Library
An entertaining performance of the play is provided in the *Audio CD Library*.
- Disc 11, Track 2

RUMPELSTILTSKIN

Make the Connection

Older Than the Hills

The story of Rumpelstiltskin is much, much older than anybody alive today. Like "Cinderella" and "Sleeping Beauty," it's a European folk tale recorded by Jakob and Wilhelm Grimm in the 1800s—long before the days of tape recorders and CD-ROMs.

For hundreds of years, people have listened to and loved these stories. Why have they remained so popular? Some think it's because these stories express deep, universal wishes and fears—feelings shared by people the world over.

What's Your Opinion?

Read the statements in the chart above. Decide whether you think each statement is true of people in real life and of characters in folk tales. Then, record your opinion by writing *agree* or *disagree* in the second and third columns. Discuss your opinions with your classmates.

Quickwrite

Pick a statement that you strongly agree or disagree with. Freewrite for a few minutes about why you feel as you do.

Statement	Real Life	Folk Tales
It's easy to tell who's good and who's bad.		
Good always wins out over bad in the end.		
People are sometimes greedy.		
People sometimes value wealth above love.		

Elements of Literature

Character Types

Think of some familiar folk-tale characters: the handsome prince, the wicked stepmother, the cruel stepsisters, the strange little man with magic powers. Such characters are either all good or all bad. Unlike people in real life, these **character types** do not

use their unusual experiences to grow or change. They are always the same.

> The characters in folk tales are **character types**—familiar, unchanging figures whom we meet in one story after another.

 go.hrw.com
LE0 6-6

462 ONSTAGE!

  Resources: Print and Media

Reading
- *Audio CD Library*
  Disc 11, Track 2

Elements of Literature
- *Literary Elements*
  Transparency 8
  Worksheet, p. 25

Writing and Language
- *Daily Oral Grammar*
  Transparencies 23, 24

Viewing and Representing
- *Visual Connections*
  Videocassette B, Segment 7

Assessment
- *Formal Assessment*, p. 86
- *Portfolio Management System*, p. 160
- *Standardized Test Preparation*, pp. 66, 68
- *Test Generator (One-Stop Planner CD-ROM)*

Internet
- go.hrw.com (keyword: LE0 6-6)

Rumpelstiltskin

a German folk tale, retold by
Jakob and **Wilhelm Grimm**

dramatized by **Mara Rockliff**

The students in this production are part of Joann
Leonard's MetaStages, a drama program for youth
at Pennsylvania State University. A list of the cast
is on page vii.

Characters

The narrator
A boastful miller
Rosa, his teenage daughter
A young king
A very strange little man

Setting: A small village, once upon a time.

RUMPELSTILTSKIN 463

Summary ∎

This play is a modernized dramatization of the well-known folk tale collected by the Brothers Grimm. In this version, a poor miller boasts to the king that his clever and beautiful daughter, Rosa, can spin straw into gold. As a joke and to teach the miller a lesson, the king takes the girl to his palace and demands that she spin straw into gold. If she succeeds, the king says he will marry her. If she fails, he claims she will be put to death. While Rosa sits hopelessly, lamenting her father's boast, a mysterious little man appears and offers to spin the straw into gold in exchange for Rosa's necklace. When the king walks in, he is amazed to see gold up to his ankles. Not really wanting to marry a girl he hardly knows, the king stalls for time by giving Rosa twice as much straw to spin into gold. Again, the little man appears, and Rosa gives him her ring in exchange for his spinning. The king then gives Rosa three times as much straw to spin. When the little man appears again, Rosa has nothing left to trade, so he asks her to promise him her first-born son. Thinking that it will be a long time before she has a baby and that the little man will have forgotten their deal by then, Rosa agrees. Eventually, Rosa and the king are married, and their first child is born. Soon afterward, the little man reappears and demands the baby. Horrified, Rosa refuses him. The little man then gives her three nights to guess his name, or he will take the baby. As the third night approaches, Rosa's father stops by the palace and tells his daughter about a strange little man he saw in the woods, who was singing a song in which he revealed his name as Rumpelstiltskin. When the little man returns for the last time, Rosa finally guesses his name correctly. Enraged, Rumpelstiltskin stamps his feet and disappears forever.

Reaching All Students

Struggling Readers

Help students understand the nuances of meaning of the body language described in the stage directions. Have students demonstrate the following actions from the play:

- sighs, shakes her head, and goes back to her book
- She buries her face in her hands in complete mortification.
- He draws his finger across his throat dramatically.
- sits alone, her chin on her fists, looking glum
- look around in amazement
- shrinks back horrified
- does a strange little victory dance
- startled

English Language Learners

For students unfamiliar with the traditional version of this European folk tale, you may want to read aloud from the original *Grimm's Fairy Tales* before students read the play and the Connections feature. In addition, since the characters in the play speak in contemporary language that is highly idiomatic and colloquial, students will need help "translating" many of the idioms.

Act One

At the mill

Narrator. Once upon a time there was a miller who lived with his teenage daughter, Rosa, in a little house by the village mill. He made a pretty good living as a miller, but he dreamed of something better for his daughter.

Miller. You don't have to stay in this hick town, Rosa. With your brains, you can do anything. You could be the first astronaut on Mars. You could go to Hollywood and be a movie director. You could learn seventeen African languages and study the social habits of tigers and zebras and——

Rosa (*looking up from a book*). What*ever*, Dad. I'm trying to read, OK?

Miller. That's my girl! Always reading. A mind like a steel trap. You make your old dad proud.

[ROSA *sighs, shakes her head, and goes back to her book.*]

Narrator. One day they were sitting on the porch of their little house and the young king came by. The miller just couldn't stop himself . . .

Miller (*rushing up*). Hey, King, King! Hang on! Wait up!

King. Yes?

Miller. Listen, I know you don't want to stop and talk to me. Why should you talk to me? I'm just a boring old miller, nothing special, nobody important. But you have *got* to meet my daughter, Rosa. She is really something— smart, pretty, talented, too.

Rosa. This is *so* embarrassing.

King (*to the* MILLER, *politely*). How nice.

[*He starts to move on, but the* MILLER *grabs his arm.*]

Miller. Hey, I'm not just saying it because I'm

her father. This girl is the cream of the crop, the top of the heap, the bee's knees, the cat's pajamas. She is all that and a bag of chips, as you kids say.

Rosa. Oh, *Dad.*

[*She buries her face in her hands in complete mortification.*]

King (*to the* MILLER, *amused*). Well, that's wonderful. You must be very proud.

Miller. You know, a nice young king like you, rattling around that great big palace all alone, it isn't right. You need a queen to keep you company, help you make all those tough decisions. Someone with a head for politics, someone with a good public image, someone handy around the house.

King. I'll keep that in mind.

[*He tries to move on again.*]

Miller. Why rush off so fast? Stay, stay, have a cup of tea, a gingersnap, baked fresh by my daughter this morning. She makes incredible gingersnaps, the best in the village. And look, see those solar panels on the roof? My Rosa built and installed them all by herself. She's a whiz. She can do anything. She . . . she . . . hey, if she wanted to she could put straw on a spinning wheel and spin it into gold!

Rosa. *Dad!*

King (*to himself*). This guy is unbelievable. Doesn't he ever give it a rest? I think it's time somebody taught him a lesson. I'll call his bluff, throw a scare into him. (*To the* MILLER) Spins straw into gold, eh? That's something I'd like to see.

Miller (*nervously*). Oh, well you know . . . a figure of speech, of course. Just a manner of speaking, you understand——

King. I understand perfectly! You said your daughter could spin straw into gold. What a

---

Professional Notes

Heroes and Magical Helpers
Writer and editor Joanna Cole has explained the significance of folk tales featuring magical helpers in the following way: "The heroes' relationship with the magical helpers can be understood as their willingness to partake of what their surroundings have to offer, their acceptance of good fortune when it comes their way. . . .

Thus, whether or not they are the cleverest or most highly favored of youths, the heroes and heroines of the tales sow the seeds for their own success by engaging with the world in a receptive, creative manner. And the happy ending of the tales, far from being an unrealistic 'fairy tale' fantasy, as some would have it, shows that maturity and independence will surely come to those who have such an attitude toward themselves and life."

talent! There's plenty of straw around here, so she must have made you very rich already. I guess you won't mind if I take her back to the palace so she can spin some gold for me, too.

Miller. But—I didn't mean——

King. Of course you did! (*With mock severity*) Now, I *know* you wouldn't lie to the king, would you?

Miller. No, no, certainly not, no, not at all, never, but I——

King. I should hope not! I'm going to take your daughter home with me tonight and give her all the straw she wants. If she spins it into gold, I'll marry her and make her the queen and you can come and live in the palace with us. But if she can't, well . . . (*He draws his finger across his throat dramatically.*)

[*The* KING *takes* ROSA's *hand and pulls her away, leaving the unhappy* MILLER *behind.*]

Miller. Me and my big mouth!

Act Two

In the palace

ROSA *sits alone, her chin on her fists, looking glum.*

Narrator. The young king took Rosa back to his palace and locked her with a spinning wheel in a room full of straw. "Like father, like daughter," the king thought to himself. "The way her dad goes on about her, that girl must be totally stuck up. I bet she could use a good lesson too." So the king let Rosa go on thinking he was seriously expecting her to spin straw into gold, or else . . . (*draws finger across throat dramatically*).

Rosa. I don't believe this. This time my dad has *really* done it. No way can I spin straw into gold. I can't even spin, for crying out loud. We always get our clothes at the mall. Now what am I supposed to do?

E **Reading Skills and Strategies**
Making Inferences

❓ What does the king mean when he draws his finger across his throat dramatically? [He means that Rosa will die if she cannot spin straw into gold.] Is he serious? How do you know? [No, he is not serious. He revealed earlier that he was just trying to teach the miller a lesson. And, according to the stage directions, he speaks with "mock severity" or phony harshness.]

F **Critical Thinking**
Expressing an Opinion

❓ Do you think it is cruel of the king to let Rosa think she is going to die if she can't spin straw into gold? Give reasons for your answer. [Possible responses: Yes, it is cruel because Rosa is an innocent victim, not responsible for her father's boastfulness; no, it is not cruel because the king believes that the miller's boastfulness has made Rosa "stuck up," or conceited, and that she needs to be taught a lesson, too.]

G **English Language Learners**
Interpreting Idioms

English language learners may need help interpreting this passage. Explain that the idiom "has *really* done it" means "has really done something bad or stupid." The word *really* is italicized to indicate that Rosa emphasizes it when she speaks. The idiom "No way" means "There is no way I can do this" or "It's impossible for me." The idiom "for crying out loud" simply indicates strong feelings similar to another dated oath, "for goodness' sakes!"

Getting Students Involved

Cooperative Learning

The Trial of Rumpelstiltskin. After students finish reading the play, suggest that they imagine that, instead of disappearing at the end of the play, Rumpelstiltskin is caught and put on trial for attempting to take the queen's baby. Assign the roles of Rumpelstiltskin, the prosecuting attorney, the defense attorney, the judge, and Rosa. Then have these students prepare and role-play a trial, after which the class will play jury and decide on a verdict.

Writing Activity

Fairy-Tale Updates. Ask students to write their own updated versions of their favorite fairy tales. Encourage them to imagine contemporary variations on the classic character types, use contemporary dialogue, and/or change the endings to reflect contemporary values. Have students read their updated fairy tales to the class.

[*Suddenly a very strange* LITTLE MAN *appears.*]

Little Man. Hey hey hey, here I am, now the party can begin! (*Sees* ROSA) Well, hello there, little lady. Why the long face? Let's see if we can turn that frown upside down. (*Winks*)

Rosa. Oh, great. Just when I thought things couldn't possibly get any worse. Who are *you*?

Little Man. I am the man, little lady, the man with the plan, and that is all you need to know. So what seems to be the problem?

Rosa. The king locked me in with all this straw, and he says I have to spin it into gold by morning, and if I don't . . . (*She draws her finger across her throat.*)

Little Man. Well, well, well, this is your lucky day, my young friend. A little trick like that is nothing for old— (*he catches himself*) —yours truly. But, you know, we've all got to look out for number one . . .

Rosa. Excuse me?

Little Man. What's the payoff? The bottom line? What's in it for me?

Rosa. Oh! (*Thinks*) You can have my genuine imitation pearl necklace if you want.

[*She takes it off and hands it to him.*]

Little Man. What a fashion statement! You've got yourself a deal, little lady.

[*He snaps his fingers and disappears. Just then the* KING *walks in, and he and* ROSA *look around in amazement.*]

Rosa (*to herself*). Wow, he actually did it! Gold up to my ankles. I can't believe it.

King (*to himself*). I can't believe it. Gold up to my ankles. This was just supposed to be a joke. I never thought she'd actually pull it off. Now what am I going to do? I don't want to marry this girl. I hardly even know her. I've got to stall for time until I think of something. (*To* ROSA) Not bad, not bad for practice. But

that wasn't enough straw for a real test. I'm giving you twice as much tonight, and I want you to spin it into gold or else . . . (*He draws his finger across his throat dramatically and walks out.*)

Rosa. What a creep.

[*The* LITTLE MAN *reappears.*]

Little Man. Hey hey hey, I'm back and I am better than ever. Did you miss me?

Rosa. Now I'm in even bigger trouble than before. The king gave me twice as much straw, and I'm supposed to spin that into gold, too.

Little Man. You have come to the right place, little lady. But you can't play if you don't pay. How about a little sweetener?

Rosa. Want my cubic zirconium diamond ring?

[*She takes off the ring and hands it to him.*]

Little Man. Flashy, baby, flashy!

[*He snaps his fingers and disappears. Just then the* KING *walks in, and he and* ROSA *look around in amazement.*]

Rosa. He did it again! Gold up to my knees. I can't believe it.

King (*to himself*). I can't believe it. Gold up to my knees. I have to admit, if she is conceited, she's got a good reason to be. Maybe everything her dad said was true. Now what do I do? Some joke. Looks like I'm the one who's being taught a lesson. I need more time. (*To* ROSA) Not bad, not bad. Still, it looks like beginner's luck to me. I'm giving you three times as much straw tonight, and I want you to spin it into gold or else . . . (*He draws his finger across his throat dramatically and walks out.*)

Rosa. What a loser. How did *he* get to be a king, anyway?

RUMPELSTILTSKIN, ACT TWO 467

Taking a Second Look

Review: Making Generalizations

Remind students that when they make generalizations they make a statement that applies to life in general or to a whole group of people. For example, point out that the statements in the chart on the Before You Read page (p. 462) are all generalizations. Generalizations are used to describe the theme, or message about life, that a story conveys.

Activities

1. After students finish reading the play, have them read aloud the generalizations in the chart on p. 462 and tell which one best expresses the theme of the play.

2. Now ask students if they can make up a better generalization to express the story's theme.

3. Tell students that the theme of the Connections story on p. 471 is different from the theme of the play. Have them read the story and suggest a generalization that conveys its theme.

A. Critical Thinking

Making Judgments

❓ What is your opinion of the Little Man? Do you find him likable in some ways? Why or why not? [Possible responses: Some students may find the Little Man's sense of humor and his helpfulness appealing. Others may say that these qualities do not make up for his greed and his willingness to take advantage of someone who appears to be in a desperate situation.]

B. Critical Thinking

Extending the Text

❓ What popular actor might you cast in the part of the Little Man if the play were being made into a movie? [Possible responses: Danny DeVito, Robin Williams, Adam Sandler, Billy Crystal, Woody Allen, or other comic actors.]

C. Reading Skills and Strategies

Connecting with the Text

❓ What other choices might Rosa have considered in this situation? What might you have done in her place? [Possible responses: Some students may say that Rosa could have kept bargaining with the Little Man, promising him a share of her riches after she became queen; others may say she could have tried to escape from the palace or thrown herself on the king's mercy when he returned, explaining about the Little Man and his deals. Some students may argue that, from Rosa's point of view, accepting the Little Man's deal seemed the only realistic option.]

[*The* LITTLE MAN *reappears.*]

A **Little Man.** What's a nice girl like you still doing in a place like this? Don't tell me the king *still* wasn't satisfied. (*Sighs*) Everybody's a critic in this town, you know?

Rosa. Look, this time he's given me three times as much straw as before. Can you turn it all into gold?

Little Man. Sure thing, snookums, if you make it worth my while.

Rosa. I haven't got anything left to give you. But if you'll just help me this one last time, I'll give you anything you want after I get out of here.

Little Man (*slyly*). How about . . . your first-born child?

Rosa. What? Are you crazy?

B **Little Man.** Hey, take it or leave it. I guess you'd rather . . . (*He draws his finger across his throat dramatically.*)

C **Rosa** (*to herself*). I'm only a teenager, anyway. By the time I have a baby, he'll probably be too old to remember what I promised. (*To the* LITTLE MAN) Okay, whatever. Just turn this straw into gold before the king gets back.

Narrator. So the very strange little man turned all the straw into gold for the third time. When the king came back and saw the gold, he broke down and apologized to Rosa, explaining how it had all started as a joke. She didn't think it was very funny, but she appreciated his honesty, so she admitted in turn that she hadn't really spun the straw into gold herself. They both felt better then and even started to like each other a little bit.

D Rosa went back home to her father, who was very relieved to see her again, though he couldn't help going on about how clever she was to have gotten herself out of that jam.

The young king came by to visit the next day, and again the day after, and the day after

that. Pretty soon they were inseparable, and eventually, once Rosa finished law school, they got married and lived happily ever after. For a while, anyway.

Act Three

In the palace

ROSA *walks back and forth, holding a small bundle in her arms and humming.*

Narrator. Ten years after the incident with the straw and the gold, the king and the queen had their first baby. Rosa couldn't have been happier. But then, one night, as she was putting the baby to sleep, the strange little man returned.

E **Little Man.** What a lovely little nipper, and it's mine, mine, mine! I just couldn't be happier.

[*He reaches for the baby and* ROSA *shrinks back, horrified.*]

F **Rosa.** No! You can't take my baby. It was a nonbinding verbal agreement without witnesses and—and—I was a minor at the time and my legal guardian didn't cosign and—and—I promised under duress and——

Little Man. OK, OK, stop! I can stand anything but lawyer talk. How about a little guessing game instead? If you can guess my name, you can keep the baby. I'll even give you three nights to guess it. Is that fair or what? More than fair, if you ask me. I'm just too nice, that's my problem. Everybody takes advantage of me. Story of my life.

G **Narrator.** The first night, Rosa tried all the ordinary names from her baby-naming book.

Rosa. Is it James?

Little Man. No.

Rosa. Is it Ken? Is it Louis?

Little Man. No and no.

Listening to Music

Rumpelstiltskin by David Sanborn and Ricky Peterson, performed by David Sanborn

Musician and composer David Sanborn (1945–) began playing wind instruments as physical therapy following a childhood bout with polio. A native of Tampa, Florida, he was performing at age fourteen with famous blues artists like Albert King and Little Milton. During the 1960s, Sanborn joined the Paul Butterfield Blues Band, whose brand of rhythm and blues

was popular with the hard-rock crowd. He then worked with Stevie Wonder, David Bowie, and other pop-music stars before branching off on his own. Today Sanborn generally plays alto sax and sometimes flute in a distinctive jazz-blues-rock fusion style, recording mainly original compositions that he writes with Ricky Peterson, the keyboard artist in his band.

Activity

After students have read *Rumpelstiltskin*, have them listen to the Sanborn-Peterson composition of the same name. Ask students to describe ways in which the music reflects the story.

Rosa. Is it Scott? Is it Ted? Is it Tom? Is it Doug?

Little Man (*laughing meanly*). No, no, no, NO!

Narrator. The second night, she tried the strangest, silliest, most peculiar names she'd ever heard of. After all, he was a very strange little man.

Rosa. Is it Gofannon?

Little Man. No.

Rosa. Is it Nexus? Is it Paxus?

Little Man. No and no.

Rosa. Is it Keenan? Is it Rollie? Is it Ayden Rain? Is it . . . Free Radical?

Little Man. No, no, no, NO!

[*He does a strange little victory dance and disappears.*]

Narrator. Rosa was beside herself with worry. The final night was approaching and she'd tried every name she could imagine. Then her father stopped by on his way to his wing of the palace.

Miller. What's wrong, honey? Anything I can do to help?

Rosa. Don't I wish. I think I'm going to have to figure this one out by myself, though.

Miller. Well, here's a funny story that might take your mind off your problem. I was walking through the woods this morning when I

RUMPELSTILTSKIN, ACT THREE **469**

Making the Connections

Cultural Connections

Among the many folk tales from around the world that feature the motif of a magical helper are the following: "The Baba Yaga" (Russia), "How the Rajah's Son Won the Princess Labam" (India), "The Magic Kettle" (Japan), "The Magic Orange Tree" (Haiti), and "The Search for the Magic Lake" (Ecuador). You can find all of these stories in Joanna Cole's *Best-Loved Folktales of the World*. Another good collection is Jane Yolen's *Favorite Folktales from Around the World*. Cole's collection is arranged by country of origin, while Yolen's is arranged by theme.

D **Reading Skills and Strategies**

Comparing/Contrasting

? In what way does the end of Act Two remind you of other fairy tales you have read? In what ways is it different? [Possible similarity: The king and the beautiful young girl who performed an impossible task get married. Possible differences: The king and the girl do not fall in love immediately and do not marry until several years later; the beautiful young girl goes to law school first.]

E **Elements of Literature**

Character Types

? Does the Little Man seem to have changed in any way in the ten years that have passed since Act Two? [No, he is still greedy, insists on keeping the deal they made ten years ago, and still has a tendency to repeat things three times.]

F **Vocabulary Note**

Jargon

In her argument, Rosa uses legal jargon and arguments appropriate to someone who has just finished law school. Make sure students understand the following legal terms and concepts: A *verbal agreement* is one that is spoken and not written down. Because no third person witnessed their conversation, Rosa argues that the agreement is *nonbinding*, meaning that, legally, she is not required to honor it. A *minor* is a young person who is not yet an adult and thus not empowered to make legal agreements without the consent of a parent or legal guardian, who must *cosign* the agreement, along with the minor.

G **Elements of Literature**

Folk Tale Motifs

? What common motifs used in folk tales are repeated in this part of the play? [The motifs of the difficult task and the number three are repeated, as the Little Man gives Rosa three nights to guess his name.]

H **English Language Learners**

Interpreting Idioms

Make sure these students understand that the phrase *beside herself* is an idiom meaning "very upset."

T469

suddenly came to a clearing, where I saw a very strange little man with his back to me. He was so busy dancing and singing—not very well, I might add—that he didn't even notice me. His song went something like this: (*Sings*)

> "Beebopaloolah, I'm taking that baby.
> Rub-a-dub-dub, I don't mean maybe.
> Ding dong bell, I'll never tell.
> And she'll *never* guess my name is RUMPELSTILTSKIN!"

[ROSA *runs to her father and hugs him.*]

Rosa. Dad, this makes up for everything. Thanks!

Miller (*startled*). Are you feeling OK?

[*He walks out shaking his head. As soon as he's gone, the* LITTLE MAN *appears.*]

Little Man. Well, little lady, ready for one last shot before I skedaddle with the moppet?

Rosa. Is it . . . Navy Gravy?
Little Man. No way, José!
Rosa. Is it . . . is it . . . Felix Bizaoui?
Little Man. Ho, ho, ho, and no, no, no!

[*He reaches for the baby, and* ROSA *steps back.*]

Rosa. Is it . . . could it be . . . could it possibly be . . . RUMPELSTILTSKIN?

[*The* LITTLE MAN *shrieks, horribly enraged. He jumps up and down and stamps his foot, which goes right through the floor. Then he stamps his other foot, which also goes through the floor. Then he falls completely through the floor and disappears.*]

Rosa. All right!

Narrator. The strange little man never came back, and this time the king and Rosa and her father really did live happily ever after. For a good long while, anyway.

The End

Rumpelstiltskin

Rosemarie Künzler, *translated by Jack Zipes*

After the miller had boasted that his daughter could spin straw into gold, the king led the girl into a room filled with straw and said, "If you don't spin this straw into gold by tomorrow morning, you must die."

Then he locked the door behind him. The poor miller's daughter was scared and began to cry. Suddenly a little man appeared and asked, "What will you give me if I spin the straw into gold for you?"

After the girl gave him her necklace, the little man sat down at the spinning wheel, and *whiz, whiz, whiz,* three times the wheel went round, and soon the spool was full and had to be replaced. And so it went until morning. By then all the straw had been spun into gold.

When the king saw this, he was pleased. He immediately brought the miller's daughter to a larger room, also filled with straw, and ordered her again to spin the straw into gold by morning if she valued her life. And again the miller's daughter cried until the little man appeared. This time she gave him the ring from her finger. The little man began to make the wheel whiz, and by morning all the straw was spun into gold.

RUMPELSTILTSKIN **471**

Connections

In this version of the classic folk tale, the miller boasts to the king that his daughter could spin straw into gold, and so the king imprisons the girl and demands that she perform this task. Twice a little man called Rumpelstiltskin appears to her and magically spins the straw into gold in return for the young girl's necklace and her gold ring. When the king demands for a third time that the young girl spin straw into gold, the little man demands her first child as payment for his help. The young girl refuses. The little man then becomes enraged and stamps his foot. His action jars open the prison door, enabling the young girl to escape.

Ⓐ Reading Skills and Strategies
Comparing Texts
❓ How does the first paragraph of this story compare to Act One of the play? [Possible responses: The paragraph quickly summarizes the events that lead up to the girl's impossible task, while the play dramatizes the events with clever dialogue. In the play the miller, the king, and Rosa are given distinct personalities, while in the opening paragraph of the story, they are not.] In this version, does the king's threat of death seem serious? [yes]

Ⓑ Critical Thinking
Analyzing Folk Tale Motifs
❓ Why do you think the author describes the sound of the spinning wheel? [Possible responses: The vivid description helps bring the story to life; the words "whiz, whiz, whiz" emphasize the folk tale motif of things happening in sets of three.]

Professional Notes

Critical Comment: Feminist Tales

Jack Zipes, the translator of this story, is a scholar who has edited several volumes of feminist fairy tale anthologies, including *Don't Bet on the Prince* and *The Outspoken Princess and The Gentle Knight.* In his Introduction to *Don't Bet on the Prince,* he explains his interest in these tales: "In reviewing the contemporary feminist experiments, I want to focus on those tales that reveal the manifold ways in which present-day writers have rearranged familiar motifs and characters and reversed plot lines to provoke readers to rethink conservative views of gender and power.... In the fairy tales for younger readers the most noticeable change in the narratives concerns the heroine who actively seeks to define herself, and her self-definition determines the plot. As she moves to complete this task, traditional fairy-tale topics and motifs are transformed to indicate the necessity for gender rearrangement and the use of power for achieving equality."

Ask students how this retelling reflects these concerns.

A Reading Skills and Strategies
Comparing Texts
❓ In this version of the story, what seems to be the king's motivation for asking the miller's daughter to spin straw into gold? [He seems to be very greedy, wanting more and more gold.] How does his motivation compare with that of the king in the play? [In the play, the king simply wants to teach the boastful miller a lesson; he doesn't seem to care much about the gold; he keeps asking the girl to spin more because he thinks she can't do it and he isn't sure he wants to marry her.]

B Reading Skills and Strategies
Comparing Texts
❓ So far, how does this version of *Rumpelstiltskin* compare with the version you heard as a child? [So far, the story follows the plot of the traditional Grimm's fairy tale.]

C Elements of Literature
Character Types
❓ In this version, how does the miller's daughter suddenly break out of the traditional character type of the beautiful young girl? [Instead of desperately agreeing to Rumpelstiltskin's deal, she calls him crazy, says she doesn't want to marry the king and would never give her child away.] How did you feel about this surprising change of character? [Possible responses: Students may find this variation funny and may cheer the girl on for being so brave and showing common sense instead of passively accepting her fate; they may have a new respect for this character and feel her response is more realistic than the one in the traditional fairy tale.]

D Critical Thinking
Determining Author's Purpose or Slant
❓ Why do you think the author changed the ending of the story? [Possible responses: She wanted to create a more modern, "liberated" version; she wanted to create a more sensible heroine who took charge of her fate, instead of passively accepting it.]

T472

When the king saw the gold, he was overjoyed. But he was still not satisfied. He led **A** the miller's daughter into an even larger room and said, "If you spin this straw into gold by tomorrow, you shall become my wife."

When the girl was alone, the little man appeared for the third time and asked, "What will you give me if I help you?" **B** But the miller's daughter had nothing to give away.

"Then promise to give me your first child when you become queen."

These words jolted her and finally made her open her eyes.

C "You're crazy!" the miller's daughter yelled. "I'll never marry this horrible king. I'd never give my child away."

"I'm not going to spin. I'll never spin again!" the little man screamed in rage. "I've spun in vain!"

The little man stamped with his right foot so ferociously that it went deep into the **D** ground and jarred the door to the room open. Then the miller's daughter ran out into the great wide world and was saved.

472 ONSTAGE!

Connecting Across Texts

Connecting with the Play
Rumpelstiltskin

Both the play by Mara Rockliff and this story by Rosemarie Künzler are attempts to modernize the traditional Grimm's fairy tale "Rumpelstiltskin." In the play, Rockliff modernizes the language and the motivations of the characters, but the plot is resolved in the traditional way: The miller's daughter promises Rumpelstiltskin her first-born child, marries the king, wins back the child by guessing the magical little man's name, and lives happily ever after. Künzler's story, on the other hand, begins in the traditional way and then takes a surprising turn at the climax, which changes the message of the tale: The miller's daughter refuses to promise Rumpelstiltskin her first-born child and refuses to marry the "horrible king." She then "ran out into the great wide world and was saved."

MAKING MEANINGS

First Thoughts

[respond]

 1. Which of our deepest wishes do you think *Rumpelstiltskin* expresses? Do you think it also expresses some of our fears? Explain. (Check your Quickwrite notes for ideas.)

Shaping Interpretations

[interpret]

2. Which people in the play represent the **character types** listed below? Do you see any variations?

   • the handsome young prince

   • the beautiful young girl

   • the magician

[apply]

3. Look back at the list of **motifs** on page 439. Which motifs can you find in *Rumpelstiltskin*? List two or three.

[evaluate]

4. What details in the play make it modern? What do you think of modernized fairy tales like this one?

Challenging the Text

[evaluate]

5. Some people say that fairy tales are too violent and frightening for children. How do you feel about this issue? Refer to the story "Rumpelstiltskin" (see *Connections* on page 471) in your answer.

[synthesize]

6. The play ends happily for the miller, his daughter, and the king—but what about Rumpelstiltskin? He makes a bargain in good faith with the miller's daughter. He works hard. What do you think about the way he is treated? How would you change the ending to make it a happy one for the "strange little man"? (Make your ending a happy one for Rosa, too—don't take away the baby!)

Extending the Text

[evaluate]

7. Would you rather read this play in story form or see it performed? What are the advantages and disadvantages of reading a book? of seeing a play (or a movie)?

> **Reading Check**
>
> Recap the main events of the play by making three cartoon panels, one for each act. In each panel, draw a picture of one important event in that act. Use dialogue bubbles to show what the characters say at that point in the drama.

RUMPELSTILTSKIN, ACT THREE **473**

Reading Check
Possible cartoon panels:
Act One: A picture of the king, the miller, and Rosa at the miller's house: The miller is saying: "She can do anything. If she wanted to she could spin straw into gold!" The king is saying: "I'm taking her to the palace! If you're telling the truth, I'll marry her. If not, she dies!" Rosa is thinking: "Oh, no, Dad! You and your big mouth!"
Act Two: A picture of Rosa and the Little Man in the locked room at the palace. The Little Man is saying: "I'll help you one last time if you promise me your first-born son." Rosa is saying: "What! Are you crazy? Oh, all right, just do it—quickly!"
Act Three: A picture of Rosa clutching her baby and saying: "Is it . . . Rumpelstiltskin?" The angry Little Man is stomping his foot and disappearing through the floor, screaming, "No fair! You cheated! Aiieeee!"

MAKING MEANINGS

First Thoughts

1. The story of Rumpelstiltskin reflects our desires to be able to turn ordinary materials into precious gold; to have a magic helper save us from disaster; to have fantastic luck; to live happily ever after. It also reflects our fears of undeserved tragedy (in this case, betrayal by the father) and of losing things most precious to us.

Shaping Interpretations

2. The handsome young prince is represented by the king; the beautiful young girl is Rosa; and the magician is Rumpelstiltskin. The king varies from the traditional type because he does not want to marry Rosa and does not rescue her.

3. Students might mention the motif of the impossible task (spinning straw into gold, guessing Rumpelstiltskin's name), the use of magic, and the use of the number three. (The king asks Rosa to spin straw into gold three times, and Rumpelstiltskin gives Rosa three nights to guess his name.)

4. Modern details include the diction, or word choice, and references to astronauts, Hollywood, movie directors, solar panels, the mall, an imitation pearl necklace, a cubic zirconium diamond ring, and Rosa's going to law school. Most students will feel these changes make the story funny and more enjoyable.

Challenging the Text

5. Some students may say that the real threat of death is too frightening for children. Others may say that fairy tales are not too frightening because good always wins over evil or because the stories help children to deal with real fears that they experience anyway.

6. Some may say the Little Man got what he deserved because he was greedy. To give him a happy ending, Rosa could offer him treasure or a position at court.

Extending the Text

7. Encourage discussion and concrete reasons for student preferences.

T473

Rubrics for each Choices assignment appear on p. 160 in the *Portfolio Management System*.

CHOICES: Building Your Portfolio

1. **Writer's Notebook** Point out the sample notes in the notebook graphic. Suggest that students add a third head, *Suggested Changes*, to their notes. Remind them to give reasons why they like the good points and dislike the bad points. Also remind them to save their work as possible prewriting for the Writer's Workshop on pp. 480–484.

2. **Critical Writing** To make this activity more manageable, you might choose four Grimm's fairy tales, such as "Rapunzel," "The Elves and the Shoemaker," "The Golden Goose," "Snow White and Rose Red," and "Hansel and Gretel." Divide the class into four groups, and assign each group to read one of the four stories and compare it to "Rumpelstiltskin." Then have the whole class meet to compare and contrast all the stories.

3. **Performance** To help students prepare for their performance, ask four volunteers to do a "cold" reading of the first column of dialogue in Act I. After they read, ask other students to make suggestions for improving the performances. On the chalkboard, write suggestions for performing each of the characters. Use the same process to help students develop the character of the Little Man in Act II.

4. **Creative Writing** Some students who are artistically talented might want to tell their own fairy tale in the form of cartoon panels. See pp. 582–585 for inspiration.

CHOICES: Building Your Portfolio

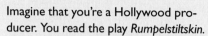

Writer's Notebook

1. Collecting Ideas for an Evaluation

Imagine that you're a Hollywood producer. You read the play *Rumpelstiltskin*. Would you say that it's a hit waiting to happen—or a flop? Take notes on what you like and what you don't like about the script, and explain why. What changes can you suggest to make the play more appealing to today's movie audiences? (On the right are one reader's notes for an evaluation of "All Summer in a Day" by Ray Bradbury.)

Good points
—surprise ending
—strange setting
—Kids like it.

Bad points
—a lot of cruelty

Comparing and Contrasting Stories

2. Grimm Reading

Borrow a copy of *Grimm's Fairy Tales* from the library. Read at least two tales in the collection. Write two paragraphs comparing and contrasting the stories and naming three similarities and three differences between them. Write a third paragraph telling which story you like best, and why. (Be sure to put quotation marks around the titles of the stories.)

Performance

3. Rumpel-radio

With a small group, rehearse and perform a reading of one act of the play. Do either a live dramatic reading in front of the class or a taped reading for an imaginary radio broadcast.

Look closely at stage directions that tell you how lines should be spoken. Sometimes the dialogue itself gives you clues to the way the characters feel. Work on using your voice to convey emotions like pride, amusement, and nervousness. Your group may want to pick a director to help actors rehearse their lines.

Creative Writing

4. A New Fairy Tale

Refer to the list of folk-tale **motifs** (page 439) and the discussion of **character types** often found in folk tales (page 462). Write a fairy tale of your own, using at least three of these character types or motifs. You can write a takeoff on an old fairy tale or an entirely new story, and set it in the past, the present, or the future. You might want to start out in the usual way: "Once upon a time."

Denotations and Connotations: Finding the Right Word

Do you think Rosa would rather be called a *girl*, a *woman*, or a *lady*? These three words have similar **denotations**, or dictionary meanings, but different connotations. **Connotations** are the feelings and ideas that have become attached to certain words. Connotations can be positive or negative. A word with positive connotations calls up good feelings; a word with negative connotations calls up bad feelings.

Rosa probably wouldn't mind if friends called her a *girl*. For many people, *girl* suggests a fun-loving, unmarried young female. In some situations, though, calling someone a *girl* is a put-down: It can suggest someone who doesn't act her age. *Woman* suggests someone who is older and more responsible; you'd expect a woman to know more than a girl. *Lady* suggests someone in a high position, as in *first lady*. It also connotes a woman with good manners.

Why do you think Rumpelstiltskin calls Rosa "little lady"? Is he showing her respect or making fun of her? Notice that Rosa chooses to call herself a *teenager*. What connotations does *teenager* have for you?

As an old saying goes, "I am careful; you are thrifty; he is stingy." Sometimes a word has such unfavorable connotations that you may decide never to use it. Here are five words that usually have negative connotations. For each word, think of another word that has the same general meaning but more positive connotations. You may want to use a dictionary.

scrawny   fat   old   smelly   cheap

RUMPELSTILTSKIN **475**

Possible Answers

You could suggest that students make a chart like the following. This is a good exercise to assign to groups.

Negative	Positive
scrawny	slender, thin, slim, lean
fat, chubby, huge, obese, overweight	healthy, rounded
old, aged, decrepit, elderly	senior
smelly, stinky	fragrant
cheap	inexpensive, reasonable

Students who enjoy drawing might draw other cartoons showing the differences in connotations. Other words that you might extend the lesson with are *firm, stubborn, obstinate; stingy, frugal, thrifty; young, immature; odd, unusual, weird, eccentric; carefree, careless; solitude, loneliness.*

Using Reference Aids to Clarify Usage

Students who need help in distinguishing the shades of meaning among the vocabulary words may find clues to their usage in a dictionary, thesaurus, or synonym finder. Students can turn to p. 686 to see an example of the way synonyms are presented in the dictionary.

The literature in No Questions Asked gives students the chance to read a selection for enjoyment and enrichment as they further explore the collection theme. Annotated questions in the margins of the Teacher's Edition should be considered optional. No follow-up questions will appear after the selection.

This photo essay documents the daily life of young students/actors who attend the Professional Performing Arts School in New York City.

Background

Broadway Theater

For decades the Times Square neighborhood, clustered around the broad avenue called Broadway in midtown Manhattan, has been the center of commercial theater in New York City and a tourist attraction for visitors from all over the world. Recently this once gritty neighborhood has been renovated and revitalized by major corporations such as Disney. Broadway theaters are especially known for their lavish productions of new musicals such as *The Lion King, Ragtime, The Phantom of the Opera, Miss Saigon, CATS, Titanic,* and *Les Miserables,* and for their revivals of classic musicals such as *The Sound of Music, Annie Get Your Gun,* and *Guys and Dolls.*

Cultural Connections

Alvin Ailey American Dance Theater

The Alvin Ailey American Dance Theater was founded in 1958 by Alvin Ailey, Jr., a dancer and choreographer. The company eventually became an international showcase for African American dancers and choreographers, making triumphant tours throughout the world. After Ailey's death in 1989, famed dancer Judith Jamison became artistic director of the company. Today the Alvin Ailey American Dance Theater is a vibrant part of the dance theater scene in New York City.

Stars of Stage, Screen... and Social Studies Class

a photo essay by **Jack Manning**

D on't be fooled by their size. These young people are all seasoned veterans of Broadway. They are currently appearing in shows like *The Lion King, The Sound of Music, Les Misérables,* and the forthcoming revival of *Annie Get Your Gun.*

They are also students at the Professional Performing Arts School. Since 1990 the public school, on West Forty-eighth Street in the theater district, has been offering students in grades six to twelve a college-preparatory program along with professional classes that include acting, singing, and dancing.

The theater (as well as television and films) is more than child's play to these hard-working students. First they must pass a tough audition just to enroll in the school.

Then they get the opportunity to spend their mornings in academic classes like Spanish, physics, or calculus and their afternoons honing their stage skills at the school and at places like the Alvin Ailey American Dance Center. Some of the older students somehow find the time to take college courses, too. All in a day's work.

Students include, from left at table, Imani Parks, Cassidy Ladden, and Alicia Morton. Behind them, holding paper, from left, David Sanchez, Ashley Perry, and Marshall Pailet.

Getting Students Involved

Cooperative Learning

Students may enjoy working together on their own photo essay saluting local young people active in the performing arts. Assign some students to photograph the subjects at school, in rehearsal, and backstage before a performance. Other students will be responsible for taping interviews about the rewards and stresses of being a student performer, while a third group can lay out the photo essay.

Dreams, indeed: Among students in Broadway shows, from left, are Barry Cavanagh, David (Dakota) Sanchez, Cassidy Ladden, Alicia Morton, Imani Parks, and Marshall Pailet.

Sara Zelle, who is in the cast of *The Sound of Music*, has a singing lesson at the Professional Performing Arts School with Chuck Vassallo.

It can be a long day for a scholar-dancer: Graham Bowen, one of five siblings in his family in the arts school, prepares for a performance at the Neil Simon Theater.

Background

Performing Arts Schools

Other middle schools and high schools in the United States that offer special programs in the performing arts include the Las Vegas Academy of International Studies, Performing and Visual Arts; the Chicago Academy for the Arts; the High School for the Performing and Visual Arts in Houston, Texas; the Vine Middle Performing Arts and Sciences School in Knoxville, Tennessee; the School of the Arts in Charlotte, North Carolina; the School for Creative and Performing Arts in Cincinnati, Ohio; and the Whitfield School in St. Louis, Missouri.

Critical Thinking

Expressing an Opinion

Discuss with students the subject of attendance at a special performing arts high school like this one. [Some students may say that attending such a school is a good idea because it gives students a head start on their careers, while also preparing them for college. Others may say that such a program sounds too stressful and allows little time for just being a teenager. They may feel that students would be better off attending a regular high school and then pursuing their career ambitions after high school.]

Crossing the Curriculum

Art

Have students research other careers related to the performing arts such as costume design, makeup, set design, and lighting. Have them report on what kind of specialized training is required for these careers and where such training is available in your area. If possible, have students interview experts from a local theater company or college drama department to obtain firsthand information.

T477

Additional Background

The Lion King

The Broadway production of *The Lion King* won six Tony Awards in 1998—Best Choreography, Best Costume Design, Best Director, Best Lighting Design, Best Scenic Design, and Best New Musical. The guiding force behind the musical was director and costume designer Julie Taymor, whose bold, experimental combination of live performers, puppets, and masks transformed the animated movie into an unforgettable stage experience.

A dance teacher, Donna Morse, takes time with Christopher Trowsdale, one of the children in the current revival of The Sound of Music.

Backstage at The Lion King, three of the school's students: David (Dakota) Sanchez plays young Simba, and Ashley Perry, left, and Imani Parks alternate as young Nala.

478 ONSTAGE!

Professional Notes

Julie Taymor, the director of *The Lion King,* commented in an interview about the importance of her own early experiences in the theater: "Because I am from Boston, I didn't go to Broadway regularly as a child. But I do remember loving musicals, really loving them. At 11 or 12, I started doing children's theater in Boston, doing *Cinderella* and *Snow White* and all of that. When I was 13, I joined the Theatre Workshop of Boston with Julie Portman and became involved in theater where actors create their own material. When I went to Oberlin, I worked with Herbert Blau (founder of the Actor's Workshop). Bill Irwin, myself, and a number of other actors worked with Blau creating material from scratch, from concepts. So that was a big part of my training and why I am capable of creating original material that is not based on a play, but a concept or a novel or a story."

READ ON

A Powerful Imagination

An angel, a vampire, a troop of elves—these are among the characters that appear in *Oddly Enough* (Harcourt Brace) by Bruce Coville. Each of the nine short stories in this collection will startle and surprise you. You can see Coville's imagination at work again in *Jennifer Murdley's Toad* (Harcourt Brace). In this adventure story you'll meet Jennifer, who would give anything to be beautiful. One day she stumbles into a magic shop, where she finds a warty old toad that can talk. He can imitate Humphrey Bogart, a tiger, traffic sounds, and Niagara Falls.

Twisty Tales

If you're hooked on Sherlock Holmes, you can find all fifty-six stories and four novels starring the famous detective in *Sherlock Holmes: The Complete Novels and Stories,* Volumes I and II (Bantam) by Sir Arthur Conan Doyle. Try starting with "The Adventure of the Dying Detective," "The Red-Headed League," and *The Hound of the Baskervilles.*

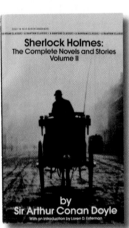

Other Picks

- Ronn Smith, *Nothing but the Truth* (Avon). A boy is forced to fight for his rights when he finds himself at the center of a conflict that rocks his school and community. This play is based on an award-winning novel by Avi.

- Lev Ustinov, *Seven Fairy Tales for Theater* (The Dramatic Publishing Company). These plays, based on traditional stories given a modern twist, are filled with snappy dialogue and ordinary situations—and all the enchantment you'd expect to find in a fairy tale.

Writer's Workshop

MAIN OBJECTIVE

Write an evaluation of a work

PROCESS OBJECTIVES

- Use appropriate prewriting techniques to identify and develop a topic
- Create a first draft
- Use evaluation criteria as a basis for determining revision strategies
- Revise the first draft, incorporating suggestions generated by self- or peer evaluation
- Proofread and correct errors
- Create a final draft
- Choose an appropriate method of publication
- Reflect on progress as a writer

Planning

- **Block Schedule**
  Block Scheduling Lesson Plans with Pacing Guide
- **One-Stop Planner**
  CD-ROM with Test Generator

Technology HELP

See Writer's Workshop 1 CD-ROM. Assignment: Evaluation.

ASSIGNMENT

Write an evaluation of a work such as a book, movie, TV show, story, poem, or play.

AIM

To persuade; to inform.

AUDIENCE

Your teacher, classmates, or friends or the readers of your school or local newspaper.

Items You Might Evaluate	
movie	tape or CD
book	story
TV show	play

PERSUASIVE WRITING

EVALUATION

When you tell a friend about a good book you've read or a television program you didn't like, you're making an **evaluation,** or judgment. You're giving your opinion on whether something is good or bad. If your friend questions your opinion, you'll probably give reasons to back up your judgment.

Professional Model

Here is an evaluation of a book.

The Well by Mildred D. Taylor
With this book, Mildred D. Taylor brings us a prequel to the saga of the Logan family. Ten-year-old David and his brother Hammer take us through a dry, hot summer when all the wells run dry except the one on their family's land. In contending with the mean-spirited Simmses, the boys struggle with the undercurrents and overt suspicions that define race relations in the old South, as well as the heartrending injustice of the times. The adult characters are finely etched, especially the mother and feisty old grandmother. The persistence of familial history and memories is beautifully delineated. Above all, this is a book about pride. It's hard to put down, as are Taylor's other books, *Roll of Thunder, Hear My Cry* and *Let the Circle Be Unbroken*.

—Uma Krishnaswami,
www.childrenslit.com

In the second and third sentences the writer briefly describes the plot.

The writer gives examples of things she liked about the book: the characters and the focus on family history.

The writer ends with a judgment: "It's hard to put down."

  Resources: Print and Media

Writing and Language
- *Portfolio Management System*
  - Prewriting, p. 161
  - Peer Editing, p. 162
  - Assessment Rubric, p. 163

- *Workshop Resources*
  - Revision Strategy Teaching Notes, p. 25
  - Revision Strategy Transparencies 13, 14
- *Writer's Workshop 1 CD-ROM*
  - Evaluation

Assessment
- *Standardized Test Preparation*
  - Worksheet, p. 122
  - Transparencies 13-18

Prewriting

1. Writer's Notebook

Review your Writer's Notebook to find ideas for an evaluation. If your notes are not satisfactory and you're still looking for something to evaluate, try the brainstorming activity below.

2. Brainstorming

What do you love? What do you hate? Which is the best TV show? Which is the worst? With classmates, brainstorm to come up with lists of books, movies, concerts, or other forms of entertainment. Consider categories like the following:

- all-time favorites
- the funniest
- the absolute worst
- the most heartwarming
- the most unusual
- the most powerful

3. Choosing a Topic and Rating It

Skim your lists of ideas for a work that you feel strongly about and want others to know about. Then, write a sentence or phrase stating your opinion of it.

4. Defining Your Standards

Your judgments are based on **criteria**, or standards—your own personal rating system. Just what are those standards? To identify them, try this with a partner:

a. Begin by stating your opinion: "I think this story is exciting but silly."

b. Your partner should then ask you a simple question, like "Why?"

Topic: _A Whole New Ball Game_, a book by Sue Macy
Judgment: very good
Standards:
1. is interesting and holds my attention
2. presents facts accurately
3. includes specific examples and details
4. contains some funny or exciting parts

Framework for an Evaluation

Introduction (name and description or summary of subject): _____

Your judgment: ____

_____

Standards, in order of importance:

1. _____
   Example: _____
2. _____
   Example: _____
3. _____
   Example: _____

Conclusion (restatement or recommendations): _____

Before you begin the workshop, give students your own oral review of a recent episode of a popular TV series. First, briefly summarize the plot of the episode. Then give your opinion of the show, along with two or three specific reasons why you did or did not like it. Ask students who also saw the show to give their opinions and to support them with reasons. Emphasize that we all evaluate books, movies, TV shows, and music every day. To be persuasive, though, an evaluation must include relevant reasons why the evaluator liked or disliked the work.

Teaching the Writer's Workshop

Read aloud the Professional Model, define any unfamiliar words for students, and point out the sentences referred to in the annotations on the model. Help students analyze the structure of the evaluation: (1) The writer first briefly summarizes the plot of the book; (2) Then she gives several reasons why she likes the book; (3) She concludes with a final judgment.

Reaching All Students

Struggling Writers

Encourage these students to choose a short story or TV show to evaluate rather than a long book or movie. You might also give them a more specific Framework for an Evaluation, such as the following, to guide them:

Name of my book/show:

_____

What the book/show is about: _____

_____

_____

I liked/did not like the book/show because:
it has realistic/dull etc. characters
EXAMPLE: _____
it has funny/exciting/scary etc. events
EXAMPLE: _____
it has good/bad dialogue
EXAMPLE: _____

English Language Learners

To help these students make a good start on the assignment, meet with them individually to discuss their topics and to help them fill out the Framework for an Evaluation form shown on p. 481 of the Student's Edition, or the more specific framework shown under Struggling Writers at the left.

Prewriting

Recommend that students list their criteria in order of importance on a sheet of paper they can keep in front of them as they work.

Drafting

Remind students to double space when they write their drafts. They should also leave extra space in the right margin for comments and editing marks.

- To model good beginnings, give students examples of openings you might use in a review of a popular TV show such as *The X-Files*:

  QUOTATION: "The truth is out there," according to the creators of *The X-Files,* "but week after week it seems to mysteriously escape from agents Mulder and Scully."

  QUESTION: Does the FBI really have a team of agents to investigate mysterious, unexplainable events and conspiracies like the ones in *The X-Files?* I hope so.

  TELL A STORY: The first time I watched *The X-Files,* I couldn't believe my eyes—and I didn't have a clue what was going on. So the next time it was on, I taped the show and watched it again and again.

- Also model other ways of reaching out to readers:
  "If you like fast and funny shows with lots of snappy dialogue...."
  "If you like books that make you feel like the main character is your best friend...."
  "If you're a Stephen King fan, you'll love...."

<table>
<tr><td>

Strategies for Elaboration

To spot details and quotations that make good examples, look for

- words, phrases, or scenes that stay in your mind. They'll stay in your readers' minds, too.

- comparisons or surprises: "They were like pioneers exploring the new world."

Remember: Quotations are like spices—they add flavor, but a few go a long way. Don't quote a whole passage when one sentence or phrase makes a powerful statement.

</td></tr>
</table>

---

c. Try to answer the question by stating what you value in a story (or movie, or book, or whatever your topic is), giving reasons, offering evidence, or doing whatever seems appropriate.

d. Your partner should continue to question you (maybe just asking "Why?" again). Try to keep clarifying your answers so that your standards become more obvious.

5. Judging Your Criteria

Before you start your draft, make a list of the criteria you've identified. Which are most important to you? Which don't count quite as much? You might discuss your standards by order of importance—either from most important to least important or from least important to most important.

Drafting

1. Drafting a Beginning

Beginnings are tough, so play around a bit. Rather than using a boring "This paper is about . . ." opening, start with a catchy quotation or a question that will grab your reader's attention. Tell a brief story or set the scene.

2. Reaching Out to Readers

As you begin drafting, keep your readers in mind. Ask yourself, "Which of my readers would probably enjoy the work I'm evaluating? Which probably wouldn't enjoy it?" Notice that the Student Model on page 483 specifies the kind of reader who would enjoy the book.

3. Supporting Your Opinion with Evidence

In the body of your evaluation, make a convincing case for your opinion. "I thought it was silly" doesn't say much. "I thought it was silly because a kid wouldn't worry so much about a job," followed by some details, is more persuasive.

Use specific details and examples from the work or from your own experience to support your points. You may also want to make comparisons with other works or cite the opinions of authorities.

Getting Students Involved

Cooperative Learning

Fans' Notes. Before they begin their drafts, invite students interested in the same book, movie, or TV show to hold a fan club meeting to discuss or debate important aspects of the work, such as important characters and key scenes. Appoint a secretary to tape record or take notes of important points made by each member. As they draft, students can share the "minutes" of their meeting and use them for ideas to include in their evaluation.

4. Wrap It Up

End by stating your opinion once again. Restate your case briefly, or give one more convincing reason in support of your evaluation.

Sentence Workshop
H E L P

Combining sentences by using groups of words: page 485.

Using the Model

- As class members read the Student Model, be sure they understand the side notes. Then have the class discuss how well the model satisfies each of the four Evaluation Criteria listed on p. 484.
- Ask students, for example, what specific criteria the student author used to judge the book. [She evaluated it on the basis of how interesting and exciting it was, how much personal detail it included, how fun it was to read, how appealing the women in the book were, and how important their accomplishments were to other women.]
- Suggest that students refer to the model frequently as they draft their own reviews.

Student Model

from a review of A WHOLE NEW BALL GAME

A Whole New Ball Game by Sue Macy is an exciting description of the All American Girls Professional Baseball League (AAGPBL). It explains, in an interesting way, how women got involved with baseball, how they played, and in what ways it was different from men's baseball. It also tells personal details about the players. What made the book fun to read was details such as the time a fan yelled out to Pepper Paire, "I see you haven't gotten any smaller since last year." Without skipping a beat she yelled back, "I see your mouth hasn't lost any weight either."

Every woman in the league was brave. I love this about them. They were like pioneers exploring the new world. They were brave in so many ways. First of all they were doing something women had never done before. They were up against a very strong thing—society. Second, they were leaving home for the first time and some were as young as fourteen. . . .

The writer names the book and its author.

Here, the writer briefly describes the book.

The writer uses a funny example and quotations to support her view.

The writer responds personally to the book.

(continued)

Using Students' Strengths

Interpersonal Learners

Pairs of students who hold different opinions about the same work might draft their evaluations as a debate rather than as a written review. Suggest that they first fill out their Frameworks for an Evaluation individually, then meet to informally debate each item on their list of Standards. Have each student take notes on the informal debate, prepare responses to the other's criticism, and present his or her final position to the class.

Evaluating and Revising

Direct students to use the Evaluation Criteria provided here to review their drafts and to determine needed revisions. When students trade evaluations for peer review, remind them to phrase their comments in a positive way, pointing out the parts they like and making suggestions for improvement, rather then simply criticizing the weaker parts.

Proofreading

Before students proofread, they should read the Proofreading Tips on this page and, if necessary, review the rules of using quotation marks and italics on p. 754 of the Language Handbook.

Publishing

Ask students to show their work to an interested friend or to submit their reviews to the school or local newspaper. For more publishing suggestions, see the Getting Students Involved note below.

Reflecting

Ask students to name the step of the writing process that was the biggest challenge for them. Invite them to suggest how they can make that step easier on their next assignment.

Resources

Peer Editing Forms and Rubrics
- *Portfolio Management System*, p. 162

Revision Strategy Transparencies
- *Workshop Resources*, p. 25

Grading Timesaver

Rubrics for this Writer's Workshop assignment appear on page 163 of the *Portfolio Management System*.

■ *Evaluation Criteria*

A good evaluation

1. *identifies and describes the work*

2. *makes a clear judgment based on specific criteria*

3. *supports the judgment with reasons and examples*

4. *restates or reinforces the judgment in a strong conclusion*

Communications Handbook HELP

See Listing Sources and Taking Notes; Proofreaders' Marks.

Proofreading Tips

- When you write a review, pay special attention to the use of quotation marks.

- Put titles of full-length works in italic type; put titles of shorter works in quotation marks.

Student Model (continued)

I recommend this book to everybody, but especially to those who are interested in women's rights and those who love the game of baseball. I wish the league had never stopped. This way my friends and I could have women role models that played baseball and we wouldn't have to feel as if we were being too "tomboyish."

—Merenda Garnett-Kranz
Home School
Louisa, Virginia

In the conclusion the writer recommends the book to everyone. She also identifies readers who might find it especially appealing.

Evaluating and Revising

Peer Review

Trade evaluations with a classmate. As you read your partner's paper, ask yourself questions like these:

- Which parts show most clearly how the writer feels about the work?

- Was I convinced by the writer's judgments? How might the writer strengthen his or her opinion?

- What do I like best about the evaluation?

Think about your reader's comments. Then, use them to revise your evaluation.

Getting Students Involved

Enrichment Activity
Talking Back to the Reviewer. To add interest to this assignment, you might have students research reviews of their favorite movie or TV show and find a review that they strongly disagree with. They can then write their review as a response to the professional critic. If the review appears in a newspaper or magazine that accepts letters to the editor, students might submit their review for publication.

Cooperative Learning
On-line Fan Club. If a group of students are fans of a particular movie, TV show, or writer, encourage them to set up their own Web site about their choice. Students can publish their reviews on their Web site, and invite visitors to respond to their opinions.

OBJECTIVES
Revise choppy sentences by combining them, using groups of words

COMBINING SENTENCES BY USING GROUPS OF WORDS

I saw my friend Cito. He was at the corner. He told me about a basketball game. The game was at the playground. It was two blocks away.

You don't need to be an English teacher to see what's wrong with the paragraph above. It's like an old car moving by fits and starts down a street: It moves forward a couple of feet, stalls, then jerks forward another few feet, stalls, and dies. What it doesn't do is flow smoothly. The problem is too many short sentences in a row. The solution is **combining sentences** by taking a group of words from one sentence and adding it to another sentence.

EXAMPLE

I saw my friend Cito at the corner. He told me about a basketball game at the playground two blocks away.

A choppy, start-and-stop five-sentence jalopy of a passage has become a smooth, lean machine of only two sentences. Here are some other examples:

CHOPPY   I went to the playground and looked. I looked through the playground fence.

COMBINED   I went to the playground and looked through the playground fence.

Writer's Workshop Follow-up: Revision

Take out your evaluation. Read it aloud to yourself, listening for sentence groups that sound short and choppy. Then, trade papers with a classmate, and listen as he or she reads your paper aloud. Revise your paper to get rid of any choppiness that you notice.

Language Handbook HELP

See Inserting Groups of Words, pages 740–741.

Technology HELP

See Language Workshop CD-ROM. *Key word entry: sentence combining.*

Try It Out

Rewrite each of these choppy passages to make a single smooth sentence. Can you think of different ways to revise each passage?

1. Grimesby Roylott bends the poker. He bends it in half.

2. Holmes and Watson go to Stoke Moran. They go that afternoon.

3. Julia died a week before the wedding. She died in a mysterious and terrible way.

4. We don't have a cat. There is a cheetah and a baboon.

Resources —————

Workshop Resources
• Worksheet, p. 47
Language Workshop CD-ROM
• Sentence Combining
Try It Out
Possible Responses
1. Grimesby Roylott bends the poker in half.
2. Holmes and Watson go to Stoke Moran that afternoon. Or: That afternoon, Holmes and Watson go to Stoke Moran.
3. Julie died in a mysterious and terrible way a week before the wedding.
4. We don't have a cat, but there is a cheetah and a baboon.

Assessing Learning

Quick Check: Combining Sentences by Using Groups of Words

Revise the following passages by combining sentences using groups of words.

1. The miller says that Rosa can spin straw. She can spin it into gold. [The miller says that Rosa can spin straw into gold.]

2. The king pretends to believe the miller. He does it as a joke. [As a joke, the king pretends to believe the miller.]

3. The king takes Rosa. He takes her to the palace. [The king takes Rosa to the palace.]

4. Rosa promises Rumpelstiltskin something. She promises him her first-born child. [Rosa promises Rumpelstiltskin her first-born child.]

5. Rosa marries the king. She marries him after she finishes law school. [Rosa marries the king after she finishes law school.]

6. Eventually Rosa outsmarts Rumpelstiltskin. She does it by guessing his name. [Eventually Rosa outsmarts Rumpelstiltskin by guessing his name.]

Reading for Life

Understanding Induction and Deduction

OBJECTIVES

1. Demonstrate an understanding of inductive and deductive reasoning
2. Learn to analyze and evaluate inductive and deductive reasoning in arguments

Teaching the Lesson

Ask students if they've ever felt that something wasn't right about another person's argument but couldn't quite put their finger on it. Explain to them that inductive and deductive reasoning are two essential ways people use to defend their opinions, and that understanding these techniques will help them evaluate the arguments of others. (Students will also learn that induction and deduction are two ways they can organize their own arguments—whether oral presentations or written ones.)

To introduce the lesson, demonstrate with another teacher an argument with which students can easily identify, such as whether school should run throughout the year with more interim vacations. Model the two approaches (without being confined by them), so that students can see that both can be used to argue effectively. Afterward, have students decide whose argument they found to be more compelling and why.

Using the Strategies

1. Tim Wong uses inductive reasoning. Jenny Suarez uses deductive reasoning.
2. Sample responses: Jenny's argument is more logical because she clearly shows why she prefers *The Adventure of the Speckled Band.* Tim's argument is well supported and well organized. He sticks to the point.
3. Sample response: Jenny's argument that only little kids like books about magic is simply not true and can be considered insulting. My father reads fantasy all the time. Her comment about real life doesn't stick to the point.

Situation

Two students in the class are discussing the plays in this collection. What strategies can you use to evaluate their arguments?

Strategies

Learn what it means to argue logically.
A logical argument is based on correct reasoning. When you argue logically, you back up opinions with facts. You stick to the point. You attack ideas, but not the person who has the ideas. You avoid insults, exaggerations, and other language that might make your audience angry.

Look for the way the writer presents and supports arguments.

- In *Rumpelstiltskin,* the miller (who is also Rosa's father) says that Rosa makes great gingersnaps. She's also installed solar panels on the roof. From this evidence he concludes that Rosa can do anything—she can even spin straw into gold. The miller is using **inductive**

Jenny Suarez argues: "I like plays about people and events that could be real. *The Adventure of the Speckled Band* is like that. Only little kids would like books about people with magic powers. Maybe they're afraid of real life. Sherlock Holmes is someone who could have lived. That's why I liked reading a play about him."

Tim Wong argues: "Straw turns into gold. Spit talks. People have magic powers. You never know what's going to happen next. Reading *Rumpelstiltskin* or *Blanca Flor* is like taking a trip to another world. It's a lot easier than taking a plane or driving someplace. That's the kind of play I like to read."

---

reasoning when he builds an argument in this way. He moves from specific facts or observations to a general conclusion based on those facts.

- **Deductive reasoning** goes in the opposite direction. It starts with a general idea or opinion. Then it presents specific reasons to support that idea or opinion. Here's an example of deductive reasoning.

    General idea: Jackie Marshall should be president of the Drama Club.

    Supporting reasons: She loves acting, she helps build sets, and she's good at publicity.

Using the Strategies

Read the students' arguments above. Then, answer these questions:

1. Which student uses mostly inductive reasoning? Which uses mostly deductive reasoning?
2. Which student's argument seems more logical to you? (Ignore your own opinion of the plays, and focus on the arguments themselves.)
3. Analyze each argument, using the information on this page. What flaws, if any, can you find in each student's reasoning?

Extending the Strategies

Look for an editorial or a letter to the editor. See if you can find places where the writer uses inductive or deductive reasoning.

486 ONSTAGE!

Reaching All Students

Struggling Readers

Be sensitive to students who are able to recall the definitions for *induction* and *deduction,* but seem unable to apply them consistently or get the two definitions mixed up. There is a level of abstraction in understanding and evaluating arguments that students may need some time to master.

Advanced Learners

Ask students to watch and record a portion of a Sunday morning political program. Have them analyze the arguments made and determine whether the reasoning employed was mainly inductive or deductive. Then have students bring their recordings to class for a demonstration of their observations and judgments.

Learning for Life

Settling Conflicts with Friends

OBJECTIVES
1. Learn ways to resolve interpersonal conflicts
2. Develop conflict resolution awareness through a variety of projects

Problem

No matter who you are, there will be times when you come into conflict with a friend. How can we settle conflicts with others and still be friends?

Project

Find out how people solve conflicts and remain friends.

Preparation

1. In a group of four or five, think about times when you've had disagreements with friends. Why did the disagreements happen? How did you settle them? Did you remain friends?

2. Think about characters in literature, TV, or movies who had conflicts with friends. How did they handle their conflicts? Did their friendships last?

3. In your group, discuss the following questions: Which ways of settling conflicts seem to work best? Which don't work at all?

Procedure

1. With the class, discuss the thoughts you've come up with in your group. Put together a set of guidelines for settling conflicts. Try to come up with at least ten, such as the following:

   - Put yourself in the other person's shoes. How do you feel?
   - Offer to take turns getting your way. Say, "I'll do it your way this time if you do it my way next time."
   - Get a third person to listen and suggest a solution.

2. Next, make a list of methods that wouldn't work and would probably make the conflict worse. For example, insisting on getting your way is selfish and doesn't solve anything.

3. Take a class vote on the most important dos and don'ts of settling conflicts.

Presentation

Present what you've learned in one of these formats:

1. Advice Manual

With a small group, put together an advice manual explaining the dos and don'ts of settling conflicts with friends. Include examples to illustrate your points.

2. Teach the Children

Design a game in which there are no losers and the players are rewarded for working together. It can be a board game or an outdoor game.

3. Ad for Friendship Week

As a class, prepare an ad for Friendship Week that could be aired on radio or TV. Produce an audiotape or a videotape explaining the dos and don'ts of resolving conflicts. Use skits, songs, slogans, or any combination of these to get your points across.

Processing

Write a reflection using this starter: The world would be a better place if conflicts were settled by . . . .

Resources

Viewing and Representing
HRW Multimedia Presentation Maker
Students may wish to use the *Multimedia Presentation Maker* to create vehicles that teach people about conflict resolution.

Grading Timesaver

Rubrics for this Learning for Life project appear on p. 164 of the *Portfolio Management System*.

Developing Workplace Competencies

Preparation	Procedure	Presentation
• Comparing similarities and differences • Examining alternatives • Choosing best solution	• Evaluating data • Synthesizing information	• Working on teams • Teaching others • Thinking creatively

Explaining Our World: Fact and Fiction

Collection Planner *(sidebar)*

Theme

Explaining Our World: Fact and Fiction *All people are curious about the world and why it works the way it does. Some people imagine the answers to the "How?" and "Why?" questions we all ask; others provide factual research.*

Reading the Anthology

Reaching Struggling Readers

The Reading Skills and Strategies: Reaching Struggling Readers binder provides materials coordinated with the Pupil's Edition (see the Collection Planner, p. T487C) to help students who have difficulty reading and comprehending text, or students who are reluctant readers. The binder for sixth grade is organized around eleven individual skill areas and offers the following options:

- Mini Read   MiniReads are short, easy texts that give students a chance to practice a particular skill and strategy before reading selections in the Pupil's Edition. Each MiniRead Skill Lesson can be taught independently or used in conjunction with a Selection Skill Lesson.

- **Selection Skill Lessons**   Selection Skill Lessons allow students to apply skills introduced in the MiniReads. Each Selection Skill Lesson provides reading instruction and practice specific to a particular piece of literature in the Pupil's Edition.

Reading Beyond the Anthology

Read On   Collection Seven includes an annotated bibliography of books suitable for extended reading. The suggested books are related to works in this collection by theme, by author, or by subject. To preview the Read On for Collection Seven, please turn to p. T559.

HRW Library   The *HRW Library* offers novels, plays, and short-story collections for extended reading. Each book in the Library includes one or more major works and thematically or topically related Connections. The Connections are magazine articles, poems, or other pieces of literature. Each book in the *HRW Library* is also accompanied by a Study Guide that provides teaching suggestions and worksheets. For Collection Seven, the following title is recommended.

TUCK EVERLASTING
Natalie Babbitt
One of the questions people ask is, can we find a way to live forever? It is a question that has yielded myths and folk tales for centuries. This fantasy imagines a magical stream that confers immortality on the people who drink from it —with unexpected results.

Skills Focus

Selection or Feature	Reading Skills and Strategies	Elements of Literature	Language/ Grammar	Vocabulary/ Spelling	Writing	Listening/ Speaking	Viewing/ Representing
Loo-Witt, The Fire-Keeper (p. 490) Nisqually Myth *retold by* Joseph Bruchac	Dialogue with the Text, pp. 490, 495 Identify Insights, pp. 490, 495	Origin Myth, pp. 490, 495, 496 Metamorphosis, pp. 495, 496 Folk Tale, p. 496	Formation of Noun Plurals, p. 497	Correct Spelling of Noun Plurals, p. 497 American Indian Names, p. 497	Record Observations, p. 496 Write a Myth, p. 496 Write a Metamorphosis Myth, p. 496	Do a Reader's Theater Performance of a Myth, p. 496	Design a Cover for a Collection of Class Origin Myths, p. 496
from **Volcano** (p. 498) Patricia Lauber	List Questions on a *5W-How?* Chart, pp. 498, 509 Read Informative Writing, pp. 498, 509	Figures of Speech, pp. 498, 511 Suspense, p. 509 Myth, p. 509 Personification, p. 511	Scientific Language, pp. 498, 509 Imaginative Language, p. 498	Use Context to Define Scientific Terms, p. 498 Use Words in the Context of a Scientific Report, p. 511	Compare Observations, p. 510 Captions for a Map of Volcano Eruptions, p. 510 Label a Diagram of Mount St. Helens, p. 510		Make a World Map Comparing Eruptions, p. 510 Diagram the Effects of the Eruption, p. 510
Elements of Literature: Subjective and Objective Writing (p. 512)	Critical Reading, p. 512 Fact and Opinion, p. 512	Objective and Subjective Writing, p. 512					
The Dog of Pompeii (p. 513) Louis Untermeyer	Compare and Contrast Texts: Fiction vs. Nonfiction, pp. 513, 526, 527	Historical Fiction, pp. 513, 526, 527 Ending, p. 526 Setting, pp. 526, 527		Use Words in Context, p. 527	Compare Characters, p. 527 Write an Ending, p. 527 Write a Historical Fiction Piece, p. 527		
The Seventh Sister (p. 528) Cindy Chang	Establish a Purpose for Reading: Match Purpose to Text, pp. 528, 535	How-and-Why Tale, pp. 528, 535	Commas to Separate Adjectives in a Series, p. 536	Words with Silent Consonants, p. 536	List Observed Traits of a Real Person, p. 535 Create a How-and-Why Story, p. 535 Write a Report on Our Galaxy, p. 535	Think-Pair-Share on How-and-Why Story Ideas, p. 535	
Reading Skills and Strategies: Reading for Varied Purposes (p. 537)	Narrative and Informative Text, p. 537	Main Idea, p. 537 Details, p. 537 Subject, p. 537					
Scanning the Heavens *from* **Science in Ancient China** (p. 538) George Beshore	Reading for Varied Purposes, pp. 538, 543	Main Idea, pp. 538, 543	Items in a Series, p. 544 Serial Commas, p. 544	Use a Cluster Diagram for Word Meanings, p. 544	Describe What You Observe in Your Kitchen, p. 543 Report on an Astronomy Article, p. 543		Make a Time Line of Technological Discoveries in China, p. 543
How the Snake Got Poison (p. 545) Zora Neale Hurston	Compare and Contrast Texts, pp. 545, 551	Oral Tradition, pp. 545, 551 Folk Tale, pp. 545, 551, 552 Nonfiction, p. 545	Dialect, p. 553	Homonyms, p. 553	Describe an Animal's Defenses, p. 552 Create an Animal How-and-Why Tale, p. 552	Present an Oral Reading of the Story, p. 552	Draw a Comic-Strip Version of the Story, p. 552
No Questions Asked: Why Dogs Chase Cats (p. 554) *retold by* Julius Lester	The **No Questions Asked** feature provides students with an unstructured opportunity to practice reading strategies using a selection that extends the theme of the collection.						
Speaking and Listening Workshop: Speaking to Inform (p. 560)		Point of View, p. 560				Prepare and Give an Informative Speech, pp. 560–561	
Writer's Workshop: Observational Writing (p. 562)		Sensory Details, p. 565	Use Vivid Words, p. 565		Write an Observational Essay, pp. 562–566		Use a Chart to Record Details, p. 565
Sentence Workshop: Combining Sentences Using Connecting Words (p. 567)			Combine Sentences Using Conjunctions p. 567		Revise Sentences, p. 567		
Reading for Life: Reading a Science Book (p. 568)	Read a Science Book, p. 568				Formulate and List Research Questions, p. 568		Use Maps, Charts, and Tables, p. 568
Learning for Life: Explaining Our World: Scientific Research (p. 569)					Research a Science Topic, p. 569	Hold a Science Fair, p. 569 Videotape a Science Show, p. 569	Create a Class Science Mural, p. 569

Collection Seven Explaining Our World: Fact and Fiction

Resources for this Collection

Note: All resources for this collection are available for preview on the *One-Stop Planner CD-ROM 2 with Test Generator.* All worksheets and blackline masters may be printed from the CD-ROM.

Internet Resources
go.hrw.com LE0 6-7

Collection Planner

Selection or Feature	Reading and Literary Skills	Language and Grammar
Loo-Wit, the Fire-Keeper (p. 490) Joseph Bruchac	• *Graphic Organizers for Active Reading,* Worksheet p. 31	• *Grammar and Language Links:* Forming the Plural of Nouns, Worksheet p. 43 • *Language Workshop CD-ROM,* Plurals of Nouns • *Daily Oral Grammar,* Transparency 29

from **Volcano** (p. 498)
Patricia Lauber
	• *Reading Skills and Strategies: Reaching Struggling Readers*
	  • Selection Skill Lesson, p. 29
	  • Selection Skill Lesson, p. 144
	• *Graphic Organizers for Active Reading,* Worksheet p. 32
	• *Literary Elements:*
	Transparency 9; Worksheet p. 28
		• *Grammar and Language Links:*
		Style: Comparisons in Science Writing,
		Worksheet p. 45
		• *Daily Oral Grammar,*
		Transparency 30

Elements of Literature: Subjective and Objective Writing (p. 512)	• *Literary Elements,* Transparency 9	
The Dog of Pompeii Louis Untermeyer (p. 513) **Connections: Pompeii** (p. 524) Robert Silverberg	• *Reading Skills and Strategies: Reaching Struggling Readers* • Selection Skill Lesson, p. 29 • *Graphic Organizers for Active Reading,* Worksheet p. 33	• *Daily Oral Grammar,* Transparency 31

The Seventh Sister (p. 528)
Cindy Chang
	• *Reading Skills and Strategies: Reaching Struggling Readers*
	  • MiniRead Skill Lesson, p. 161
	  • Selection Skill Lesson, p. 170
	• *Graphic Organizers for Active Reading,* Worksheet p. 34
		• *Grammar and Language Links:*
		Using Commas, Worksheet p. 47
		• *Language Workshop CD-ROM,*
		Commas
		• *Daily Oral Grammar,*
		Transparency 32

Scanning the Heavens *from* **Science in Ancient China** (p. 538) George Beshore	• *Reading Skills and Strategies: Reaching Struggling Readers* • Selection Skill Lesson, p. 175 • *Graphic Organizers for Active Reading,* Worksheet p. 35	• *Grammar and Language Links:* Using Commas, Worksheet p. 49 • *Language Workshop CD-ROM,* Commas • *Daily Oral Grammar,* Transparency 33
How the Snake Got Poison (p. 545) Zora Neale Hurston **Connections: Snakes: The Facts and the Folklore** (p. 550) Hilda Simon	• *Graphic Organizers for Active Reading,* Worksheet p. 36	• *Grammar and Language Links:* Style: Dialect, Worksheet p. 51 • *Daily Oral Grammar,* Transparency 34
No Questions Asked: Why Dogs Chase Cats (p. 554) Julius Lester	The **No Questions Asked** feature provides students with an unstructured opportunity to practice reading strategies using a selection that extends the theme of the collection.	
Speaking and Listening Workshop: Speaking to Inform (p. 560)		
Writer's Workshop: Observational Writing (p. 562)		
Sentence Workshop: Combining Sentences Using Connecting Words (p. 567)		• *Workshop Resources,* p. 49 • *Language Workshop CD-ROM,* Combining Sentences
Learning for Life: Explaining Our World: Scientific Research (p. 569)		

Collection Resources

- *Cross-Curricular Activities,* p. 49
- *Portfolio Management System:*
  Introduction to Portfolio Assessment, p. 1;
  Parent/Guardian Letters, p. 99
- *Formal Assessment,*
  Reading Application Test, p. 107
- *Test Generator,* Collection Test 💿

Vocabulary, Spelling, and Decoding	Writing	Listening and Speaking, Viewing and Representing	Assessment
• *Spelling and Decoding,* Worksheet p. 20	• *Portfolio Management System,* Rubrics for Choices, p. 165	• *Audio CD Library,* Disc 12, Track 2 🎧 • *Portfolio Management System,* Rubrics for Choices, p. 165	• *Formal Assessment,* Selection Test, p. 94 • *Standardized Test Preparation,* p. 70 • *Test Generator* (One-Stop Planner CD-ROM) 💿
• *Words to Own,* Worksheet p. 18 • *Spelling and Decoding,* Worksheet p. 21	• *Portfolio Management System,* Rubrics for Choices, p. 166	• *Visual Connections,* Videocassette B, Segment 8 📼 • *Audio CD Library,* Disc 12, Track 3 🎧 • *Viewing and Representing:* Fine Art Transparency 16 🎨 Worksheet p. 64 • *Portfolio Management System,* Rubrics for Choices, p. 166	• *Formal Assessment,* Selection Test, p. 96 • *Test Generator* (One-Stop Planner CD-ROM) 💿
			• *Formal Assessment,* Literary Elements Test, p. 106
• *Words to Own,* Worksheet p. 19	• *Portfolio Management System,* Rubrics for Choices, p. 167	• *Audio CD Library,* Disc 12, Track 4 🎧 • *Portfolio Management System,* Rubrics for Choices, p. 167	• *Formal Assessment,* Selection Test, p. 98 • *Standardized Test Preparation,* pp. 72, 74 • *Test Generator* (One-Stop Planner CD-ROM) 💿
• *Spelling and Decoding,* Worksheet p. 22	• *Portfolio Management System,* Rubrics for Choices, p. 169	• *Audio CD Library,* Disc 13, Track 2 🎧 • *Portfolio Management System,* Rubrics for Choices, p. 169	• *Formal Assessment,* Selection Test, p. 100 • *Standardized Test Preparation,* p. 76 • *Test Generator* (One-Stop Planner CD-ROM) 💿
• *Words to Own,* Worksheet p. 20 • *Spelling and Decoding,* Worksheet p. 23	• *Portfolio Management System,* Rubrics for Choices, p. 170	• *Audio CD Library,* Disc 13, Track 3 🎧 • *Viewing and Representing:* Fine Art Transparency 17 🎨 Worksheet p. 68 • *Portfolio Management System,* Rubrics for Choices, p. 170	• *Formal Assessment,* Selection Test, p. 102 • *Standardized Test Preparation,* p. 78 • *Test Generator* (One-Stop Planner CD-ROM) 💿
	• *Portfolio Management System,* Rubrics for Choices, p. 171	• *Audio CD Library,* Disc 13, Tracks 4, 5 🎧 • *Portfolio Management System,* Rubrics for Choices, p. 171	• *Formal Assessment,* Selection Test, p. 104 • *Standardized Test Preparation,* p. 80 • *Test Generator* (One-Stop Planner CD-ROM) 💿
		• *Audio CD Library,* Disc 13, Track 6 🎧	
			• *Portfolio Management System,* p. 172
	• *Workshop Resources,* p. 29 • *Writer's Workshop 1 CD-ROM,* 💿 Observational Writing		• *Portfolio Management System* • Prewriting, p. 173 • Peer Editing, p. 174 • Assessment Rubric, p. 175
		• *Viewing and Representing,* HRW Multimedia Presentation Maker	• *Portfolio Management System,* Rubrics, p. 176

 Transparency   **CD-ROM**   **Video**   🎧 **Audio CD**

Collection Planner

T487D

OBJECTIVES

1. Read literature in different genres on the theme "Explaining Our World: Fact and Fiction"
2. Interpret literary elements used in the literature with special emphasis on subjective and objective writing
3. Apply a variety of reading strategies, particularly reading for varied purposes
4. Respond to the literature in a variety of modes
5. Learn and use new words
6. Develop skill in speaking to inform
7. Plan, draft, revise, proof, and publish observational writing
8. Combine sentences using connecting words
9. Demonstrate the ability to read a science book
10. Explore through a variety of projects how scientific research helps to explain our world

Introducing the Theme

Fiction and factual writing provide alternative viewpoints of the world. When the fiction is in the form of folklore, it often presents imaginative explanations for phenomena of the natural world. Factual writing, on the other hand, relies upon scientific data. This collection pairs selections from these two genres, and the writers consider subjects such as the origins of volcanoes, stars, and snakes. Before students read, explain that both folklore and factual writing can be based on observation, yet only factual writing is based on observations than can be verified by scientific experiment.

Explaining Our World: Fact and Fiction

'Tis strange—but true; for truth is always strange;
Stranger than fiction.

—George Gordon, Lord Byron

488

Writing Focus: Observational Writing

The following **Work in Progress** assignments in this collection build to a culminating **Writer's Workshop** at the end of Collection 7.

- Loo-Wit, the Fire-Keeper — Record details of something in nature (p. 496)
- Volcano — Jot down details about a photograph (p. 510)
- The Dog of Pompeii — Describe a place using revealing details (p. 527)
- The Seventh Sister — List traits of an admirable person (p. 535)
- Scanning the Heavens — Record sensory details noticed in a kitchen (p. 543)
- How the Snake Got Poison — Describe defenses of an animal or a plant (p. 552)

Writer's Workshop: Descriptive Writing / Observational Writing (p. 562)

Responding to the Quotation

Explain that Lord Byron was a great English poet of the early nineteenth century. Ask what two things Byron is comparing. [truth and fiction] Then have students brainstorm a list of the strangest true things they have heard of. Write the suggestions in one column on the board. Next ask students to brainstorm a list of the strangest things they have read about in fiction or seen in fictional movies or television shows. Write those in another column on the board. Have the class discuss the two lists in light of Byron's quotation. Then ask for suggestions on why truth can be stranger than fiction.

Writer's Notebook

To give students prewriting experience in preparation for the Writer's Workshop on pp. 562–566 (on Observational Writing), have them describe exactly what they see in the art on pp. 488–489. They should look for colors, shapes, natural phenomena, people, animals, actions. Have them open their notes with "I see . . ."

Resources

Portfolio Management System
• Introduction to Portfolio Assessment, p. 1
• Parent/Guardian Letters, p. 99
Formal Assessment
• Reading Application Test, p. 107
Test Generator
• Collection Test
Cross-Curricular Activities
• Teaching Notes, p. 49

Selection Readability

This Annotated Teacher's Edition provides a summary of each selection in the student book. Following each Summary heading, you will find one, two, or three small icons. These icons indicate, in an approximate sense, the reading level of the selection.

■ One icon indicates that the selection is easy.
■ ■ Two icons indicate that the selection is on an intermediate reading level.
■ ■ ■ Three icons indicate that the selection is challenging.

Before You Read

LOO-WIT, THE FIRE-KEEPER

Make the Connection

Greener Pastures

Have you ever heard the expression "The grass is always greener on the other side of the fence"? The expression doesn't have much to do with how much water a field of grass gets. It has more to do with how we feel about what we have. Write down your ideas about the expression. Describe times in your life when you felt that the grass was greener on the other side.

Elements of Literature

Origin Myths

Asking "Why?" is part of being human. Usually we can figure out the causes of events, but occasionally things stump us. Faced with a puzzling situation, people of ancient times often made up an explanation in the form of a story or tale, known as an **origin myth.** Such myths were passed down by word of mouth from generation to generation.

> **A**n **origin myth** is a story that explains how something in the world began or was created.
>
> *For more on Myth, see page 598 and the Handbook of Literary Terms.*

Reading Skills and Strategies

Dialogue with the Text

"Loo-Wit, the Fire-Keeper" is an origin myth. As you read, jot down your thoughts on what the myth reveals about human behavior. One student's comments appear on the first page.

Background

Literature and Social Studies

"Loo-Wit, the Fire-Keeper" explains the origin of some of the natural features of Washington and Oregon. (See the map of this area on page 500.) The river gorges, mountains, and American Indian peoples mentioned in this myth are all real. The Klickitat, one of the rival peoples in the myth, are now part of the Yakima Nation, a confederation of peoples in south-central Washington. Many of the Multnomah peoples mentioned in the myth were wiped out by an epidemic of measles in 1832.

Loo-Wit, the Fire-Keeper

The Creator gave everyone all that was needed to be happy.

a Nisqually myth, retold by

Joseph Bruchac

When the world was young, the Creator gave everyone all that was needed to be happy.

The weather was always pleasant. There was food for everyone and room for all the people. Despite this, though, two brothers began to quarrel over the land. Each wanted to control it. It reached the point where each brother gathered together a group of men to support his claim. Soon it appeared there would be war.

The Creator saw this and was not pleased. He waited until the two brothers were asleep one night and then carried them to a new country. There a beautiful river flowed and tall mountains rose into the clouds. He woke them just as the sun rose, and they looked out from the mountaintop to the land below. They saw what a good place it was. It made their hearts good.

"Now," the Creator said, "this will be your land." Then he gave each of the brothers a bow and a single arrow. "Shoot your arrow into the air," the Creator said. "Where your arrow falls will be the land of your people, and you shall be a great chief there."

The brothers did as they were told. The older brother shot his arrow. It arched over the river and landed to the south in the valley of the Willamette River. There is where he and his people went, and they became the Multnomahs. The younger brother shot his arrow. It flew to the north of the great river. He and his people went there and became the Klickitats.

Dialogue with the Text

This paragraph sparks a picture in my mind of when the world was first created and everything was peaceful.
How perfect! I wish the world was still like that today.

It's surprising what great lengths people will go to get their way or to gain control.

To me, the Creator reminds me of my family. No matter what I do, they forgive me.

I wonder when the brothers will fight over their new land?

I hope the two brothers appreciate the Creator and use their second chance wisely by not arguing over the land.

Meagan Gilner

—Meagan Gilner
Western Middle School
Russiaville, Indiana

LOO-WIT, THE FIRE-KEEPER 491

Summary ▪▪

Though the Creator has made a happy world, two brothers quarrel over who will control the land. To resolve the dispute, the Creator takes both men to a fine new land and has each shoot an arrow to determine which stretch of land each man and his followers will control. The older brother and his people get the land south of the Columbia River, in the valley of the Willamette River, and become the Multnomahs. The other brother and his people settle to the north and become the Klickitats. The Creator builds a bridge over the river, so that the two peoples may visit one another as long as they live in peace. After the people begin to covet each other's land, the Creator punishes them by taking away fire. When the people beg for its return, the Creator gets fire from Loo-Wit, an old woman who lived apart and was not greedy. In return, the Creator makes her young and beautiful. However, another conflict arises: both chiefs want to marry Loo-Wit. To end the squabble, the Creator turns the Klickitat chief into Mt. Adams and the Multnomah chief into Mt. Hood. Loo-Wit, now in the form of Mt. St. Helens, is placed between the two.

Resources

Listening
Audio CD Library
A recording of this myth is provided in the *Audio CD Library:*
• Disc 12, Track 2

Selection Assessment
Formal Assessment
• Selection Test, p. 94

Test Generator
• Selection Test

Ⓐ Elements of Literature
Origin Myths
❓ What details tell you that this is an origin myth? [Possible responses: The expression "When the world was young"; mention of a Creator; description of a happy original state.]

Reaching All Students

Struggling Readers
Encourage students to make lists of questions as they progress through the myth. Remind them that questions can address anything from confusing details of plot or setting to why characters behave as they do. After they have finished reading, have students work in pairs or small groups to answer one another's questions.

English Language Learners
This myth features English versions of Native American names, such as *Multnomah, Klickitat,* and *Willamette.* Explain that languages often borrow words from each other. For example, various Native American languages are the sources for the English words *chipmunk, hickory, moccasin, moose, pecan, skunk, squash,* and *toboggan.* Invite students to translate into their native languages a handful of especially challenging words used in the myth.

A English Language Learners

Multiple Meaning Words

? The word *heart* can refer either to a physical organ or to human feelings. In this case, which meaning does *hearts* have? [human feelings]

B Critical Thinking

Analyzing Dialogue

? According to this dialogue, what causes the two groups of people to quarrel? [Each group thinks that the other group has better land.]

C Struggling Readers

Identifying Cause and Effect

? How does the Creator punish humans for being greedy and for quarreling? [He darkens the sky and takes away fire.]

D Reading Skills and Strategies

Dialogue with the Text

Ask students to keep a sheet of paper at hand as they read. Encourage them to jot down any questions that occur to them. For example, if the Creator gave humans fire in the first place, why does he need to borrow fire from a human being to give it back to them?

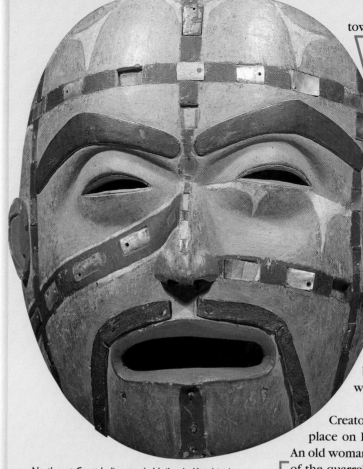

Northwest Coast Indian mask, Heiltsuk, Kwakiutl.

Neg./trans. no. 1576, Courtesy Department of Library Services.
American Museum of Natural History.

Then the Creator made a Great Stone Bridge across the river. "This bridge," the Creator said, "is a sign of peace. You and your peoples can visit each other by crossing over this bridge. As long as you remain at peace, as long as your hearts are good, this bridge will stand."

For many seasons the two peoples remained at peace. They passed freely back and forth across the Great Stone Bridge. One day, though, the people to the north looked south toward the Willamette and said, "Their lands are better than ours." One day, though, the people to the south looked north toward the Klickitat and said, "Their lands are more beautiful than ours." Then, once again, the people began to quarrel.

The Creator saw this and was not pleased. The people were becoming greedy again. Their hearts were becoming bad. The Creator darkened the skies and took fire away. Now the people grew cold. The rains of autumn began and the people suffered greatly.

"Give us back fire," they begged. "We wish to live again with each other in peace."

Their prayers reached the Creator's heart. There was only one place on Earth where fire still remained. An old woman named Loo-Wit had stayed out of the quarreling and was not greedy. It was in her lodge only that fire still burned. So the Creator went to Loo-Wit.

"If you will share your fire with all the people," the Creator said, "I will give you whatever you wish. Tell me what you want."

"I want to be young and beautiful," Loo-Wit said.

"That is the way it will be," said the Creator. "Now take your fire to the Great Stone Bridge above the river. Let all the people come to you and get fire. You must keep the fire burning there to remind people that their hearts must stay good."

492 EXPLAINING OUR WORLD: FACT AND FICTION

Listening to Music 🎵

Symphony No. 50 ("Mt. St. Helens")
by Alan Hovhaness, performed by Seattle Symphony Orchestra

American composer Alan Hovhaness (1911–   ) grew up in Massachusetts, where he is said to have begun writing music at age four. He has composed over four hundred works; he has also been known to destroy in periodic bonfires, compositions that no longer please

him. This has not been the fate of his popular Symphony No. 50. Hovhaness once explained that he didn't see the first eruption of Mt. St. Helens, but he heard it; for that reason, the symphony opens with the pounding of a bass drum followed by loud trombones, then percussion, and even cannon shots to create the effect of the mountain ripping apart.

Activity

Before students read "Loo-Wit, the Fire-Keeper," ask them to listen to the opening of Hovhaness's symphony and to create (in words or pictures) images that the music brings to mind. Then explain that the music is about the volcanic eruption of Mt. St. Helens and that students will read a myth about that volcanic mountain.

The next morning, the skies grew clear and the people saw the sun rise for the first time in many days. The sun shone on the Great Stone Bridge, and there the people saw a young woman as beautiful as the sunshine itself. Before her, there on the bridge, burned a fire. The people came to the fire and ended their quarrels. Loo-Wit gave each of them fire. Now their homes again became warm and peace was everywhere.

One day, though, the chief of the people to the north came to Loo-Wit's fire. He saw how beautiful she was and wanted her to be his wife. At the same time, the chief of the people to the south also saw Loo-Wit's beauty. He, too, wanted to marry her. Loo-Wit could not decide which of the two she liked better. Then the chiefs began to quarrel. Their peoples took up the quarrel, and fighting began.

When the Creator saw the fighting, he became angry. He broke down the Great Stone Bridge. He took each of the two chiefs and changed them into mountains. The chief of the Klickitats became the mountain we now know as Mount Adams. The chief of the Multnomahs became the mountain we now know as Mount Hood. Even as mountains, they continued to quarrel, throwing flames and stones at each other. In some places, the stones they threw almost blocked the river between them. That is why the Columbia

River is so narrow in the place called The Dalles° today.

Loo-Wit was heartbroken over the pain caused by her beauty. She no longer wanted to be a beautiful young woman. She could no longer find peace as a human being.

The Creator took pity on her and changed her into a mountain also, the most beautiful of the mountains. She was placed so that she stood between Mount Adams and Mount

°**The Dalles** (dalz): town in Oregon on the steep, rocky banks of the Columbia River.

Northwest Coast Indian mask.

Neg./trans. no. 1574, Courtesy Department of Library Services. American Museum of Natural History.

E **Struggling Readers**
Summarizing
Have students pause to summarize the three chances the Creator has given the people to live in peace. [He gives them everything they need; he takes the brothers to a new country; he clears the skies and tells Loo-Wit to return fire to everyone.]

F **Background**
Have students consult an atlas to find Mt. Adams (elevation 12,276 feet), north of the Columbia River in Washington. They can also find Mt. Hood (elevation 11,235 ft.), south of that river in Oregon. To the southwest of Mt. Hood is the Willamette River.

G **Critical Thinking**
Interpreting Details
? What causes the Creator to change Loo-Wit into a mountain? [The creator wishes to be kind.] How do you imagine she feels about the change? [Possible response: Loo-Wit is pleased and grateful.]

RESPONDING TO THE ART
These portrait masks were probably carved from wood in the mid-19th century. The Kwakiutl, like other peoples of the Pacific Northwest, wore the masks at potlatches—ceremonies at which people demonstrate their importance and generosity by giving away their possessions. At these ceremonies, Kwakiutl ancestors were spoken to, and their returning spirits were represented by the mask wearers.
Activity. Have students identify and describe various features of the masks, such as their colors, shapes, and texture. Discuss why a mask might be a good way to represent something mysterious.

Using Students' Strengths

Visual Learners
Since the narrative contains a complex series of events and spans a long period of time, you might have visual learners plot the events on time lines beginning with "The world was young" and ending with the eruption of Mt. St. Helens. Students could decorate their time lines with illustrations of important events from the myth.

Kinesthetic Learners
Invite students to act out the metamorphoses in the myth. For example, a student might pretend to be one of the brothers as he is turned into a volcano and then erupts. Another might pretend to be Loo-Wit as she is changed from an old woman into a young and beautiful one.

A Background

Have students find Mt. St. Helens (elevation 8,364 ft.) on a map or globe. It stands to the west of Mt. Adams in the state of Washington.

B Elements of Literature

Origin Myths

? According to the myth, what causes Mt. St. Helens to erupt? [The Creator and Loo-Wit have been made unhappy by the people's mistreatment of the land.]

C Reading Skills and Strategies

Dialogue with the Text

Invite students to share some observations and questions they recorded while reading.

Resources

Selection Assessment
Formal Assessment
• Selection Test, p. 94
Test Generator
• Selection Test

BROWSING IN THE FILES

About the Author. Poet and folklorist Joseph Bruchac has also had a long career as a teacher in American colleges, in a high school in Ghana, and in a prison.

Hood, and she was allowed to keep the fire within herself which she had once shared on the Great Stone Bridge. Eventually, she became known as Mount St. Helens and she slept peacefully.

Though she was asleep, Loo-Wit was still aware, the people said. The Creator had placed her between the two quarreling mountains to keep the peace, and it was intended that humans, too, should look at her beauty and remember to keep their hearts good, to share the land and treat it well. If we human beings do not treat the land with respect, the people said, Loo-Wit will wake up and let us know how unhappy she and the Creator have become again. So they said, long before the day in the 1980s when Mount St. Helens woke again.

MEET THE WRITER

"The Earth Lasts Longer Than Our Footsteps"

Joseph Bruchac (1942–   ) was born and raised near Saratoga Springs, New York, in a house that he still lives in today. As a child, Bruchac was especially close to his grandfather, a member of the Abenaki people.

Today Bruchac often retells the tales and myths of Native American peoples. His poems also draw on this rich heritage, as well as on his deep love of nature.

66 If you have ever walked in the mountains and seen, as I have, names carved on trees, and cans and bottles by the trails, you may have felt a kind of sorrow. I believe that if we do things to nature, we will suffer for it in the long run. . . . The earth lasts longer than our footsteps. . . . To me that is a comforting thought, perhaps because I have been reminded by my American Indian teachers that this earth is our mother. If we treat it well, it will treat us well in return. 99

The Storytelling Connection

Bruchac believes that "storytelling keeps us humane and connects us with past generations." To connect with other retellings of Native American tales by Joseph Bruchac, read *Turkey Brother and Other Tales: Iroquois Folk Stories* (Crossing Press), *Thirteen Moons on Turtle's Back: A Native American Year of Moons* (Philomel), and *The First Strawberries: A Cherokee Story* (Dial).

494 EXPLAINING OUR WORLD: FACT AND FICTION

Making the Connections

Connecting to the Theme: "Explaining Our World: Fact and Fiction"

Remind students of the collection theme, and ask them to list at least three things the myth tries to explain. [Possible responses: war and peace; fire; Mt. Adams and Mt. Hood, and the eruptions of Mt. St. Helens.]

Assessing Learning

Check Test: Short Answers

1. What was the weather like when the world was young? [pleasant]
2. How does each brother get land for his people? [by shooting an arrow at the Creator's request and taking the land where the arrow falls]
3. What does the Creator do when people become unhappy with the land they have? [He takes away fire.]
4. How does the Creator change Loo-Wit? [She first becomes young and beautiful; later she is changed into a mountain.]
5. How do Mt. Adams and Mt. Hood quarrel? [They throw flames and stones at each other.]

Standardized Test Preparation

For practice with standardized test format specific to this selection, see
• *Standardized Test Preparation*, p. 70
For practice in proofreading and editing, see
• *Daily Oral Grammar*, Transparency 29

MAKING MEANINGS

First Thoughts

[respond]

1. Complete two of the following statements. Look back at your Dialogue with the Text notes for ideas.
   - If I were one of the two brothers, I would/would not . . .
   - If I were Loo-Wit, I would/would not . . .
   - I was surprised when . . .

Shaping Interpretations

[interpret]

2. What natural features or events does this **origin myth** explain?

[identify]

3. A **metamorphosis** in literature is a magical change of someone or something from one shape or form to another. How many metamorphoses can you find in this myth? Describe them.

[infer]

4. What behavior and attitudes does the Creator reward? What does he punish? What beliefs do you think the myth encourages?

Extending the Text

[connect]

5. What **conflicts** in the story are caused by greed or envy—the feeling that "the grass is greener on the other side of the fence"? What similar conflicts do greed and envy cause in the world today?

[evaluate]

6. The Creator hoped that the sight of beautiful Mount St. Helens would make people remember to treat the land well and to share it. Has the Creator's plan worked? What do you think is needed to persuade people to share the land and treat it well?

Challenging the Text

[respond]

7. What **title** would you have given this myth?

Reading Check

a. Why do the two brothers begin to quarrel?

b. What is the meaning and purpose of the Great Stone Bridge that the Creator gives to the two peoples?

c. What does Loo-Wit give to the people, and what does she get in return?

d. What does the Creator do to the two chiefs when they begin to quarrel over Loo-Wit?

e. According to the myth, what will happen to humans if they are greedy and do not treat the land with respect?

Reading Check

a. Each wants to control the land.

b. The bridge means peace and sharing. The peoples of the two brothers can cross it to visit each other.

c. Loo-Wit gives the people fire, and she receives youth and beauty from the Creator.

d. He changes them into mountains.

e. Loo-Wit, now Mt. St. Helens, will erupt to show people that she and the Creator are unhappy with them.

MAKING MEANINGS

First Thoughts

1. Sample answers:
   - I would try to make peace.
   - I would do exactly what Loo-Wit did.
   - the brothers were turned into mountains.

Shaping Interpretations

2. The creation of Mt. Adams, Mt. Hood, The Dalles, and Mt. St. Helens, and the eruption of the volcanoes.

3. Loo-Wit becomes young and beautiful. The chief of the Klickitat becomes Mt. Adams. The chief of the Multnomah becomes Mt. Hood. Loo-Wit becomes Mt. St. Helens.

4. The Creator rewards people for being content with what they have and punishes greed. The myth suggests that peaceful behavior will be rewarded and that aggressive behavior will be punished.

Extending the Text

5. In the story, greed and envy cause conflicts over control of the land and a conflict over Loo-Wit. Students may mention present-day conflicts for political or personal control of land and people.

6. Possible responses: The plan has worked because people who see the beauty of the land are inspired to preserve it; the eruption of Mt. St. Helens shows that the plan has not worked and that the land is being destroyed. Students may mention techniques ranging from better education to tougher penalties for those who harm the environment.

Challenging the Text

7. Sample answers: "When the World Was Young"; "Three Mountains and a River"; "Loo-Wit, The Volcano."

Rubrics for each Choices assignment are provided on p. 165 in the *Portfolio Management System.*

CHOICES: Building Your Portfolio

1. **Writer's Notebook** Encourage students to observe their subjects for several minutes, if possible, before they begin to record their impressions. Remind them to use as many of their five senses as possible. If students save their work, they may use it as prewriting for the Writer's Workshop on pp. 562–566.

2. **Creative Writing** Students might wish to write their myths about the features of nature they observed for Choice 1.

3. **Creative Writing** Have students consider choosing problems in today's world—such as poverty, injustice, war, or personal unhappiness—that they would most want to solve.

4. **Research/Reader's Theater** Productions could be relatively simple, with groups no larger than the number of parts, or relatively elaborate, with writers, stagehands, and other production assistants.

CHOICES: Building Your Portfolio

Writer's Notebook

1. Collecting Ideas for Observational Writing

Observe something in nature. Pick an animal, a plant, a body of water, the weather, or some other natural element you can watch for a while. With notes, sketches, or photos, record how long you observe your subject and exactly what happens at different times.

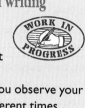

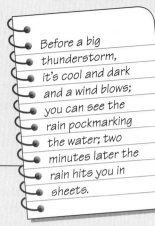

Before a big thunderstorm, it's cool and dark and a wind blows; you can see the rain pockmarking the water; two minutes later the rain hits you in sheets.

Creative Writing

2. "When the World Was Young..."

Write your own myth explaining the origin of a natural feature, such as a mountain, river, desert, cave, or marsh. Usually origin myths (like the one about Loo-Wit) describe something people did to anger the gods. Often these myths deal with punishments for bad behavior or rewards for good acts. Collect your class origin myths in a book. Design a cover and give your collection a title.

Creative Writing

3. That Changes Everything!

In myths and folk tales a **metamorphosis**, or magical change in form, often helps solve a seemingly unsolvable problem. Think of a difficult problem in the world today, and then imagine a magical metamorphosis that resolves the problem. Remember that in a metamorphosis anything is possible. Some stories of metamorphosis are wish-fulfillment stories. What wish will come true in your myth?

Research/Reader's Theater

4. Tell Me Why

With a group of students, find another origin myth to share with your class (perhaps one that explains the change of seasons, the origin of fire, the reason death came to the world, or the origin of the moon or stars). Review the myth to decide the best way to divide up parts for a reader's theater. For example, you may want to choose a narrator and assign characters' speaking parts to everyone else. Think of a title for your performance and present your reading to an audience.

GRAMMAR LINK | MINI-LESSON

Forming the Plurals of Nouns

Language Handbook HELP

See Forming the Plurals of Nouns, pages 764-765.

Technology HELP

See Language Workshop CD-ROM. Key word entry: plurals of nouns.

1. Add *-s* to form the plural of most nouns.

   EXAMPLES brother**s**, cloud**s**, mountain**s**, flame**s**, stone**s**

2. Add *-es* to form the plural of nouns ending in s, x, z, *ch*, or *sh*.

   EXAMPLES lens**es**, tax**es**, waltz**es**, patch**es**, dish**es**

3. Add *-es* to words ending in a *consonant* plus *o*. Add *-s* to words ending in a *vowel* plus *o*.

   SINGULAR tomato, stereo

   PLURAL tomato**es**, stereo**s**

4. When a noun ends in a *consonant* plus *y*, change the *y* to *i* and add *-es*. When a noun ends in a vowel plus *y*, just add *-s*.

   SINGULAR puppy, holiday

   PLURAL pupp**ies**, holiday**s**

5. There are some exceptions to the rules above for forming plurals.

   EXAMPLES men, women, children, geese, mice, data

Try It Out

Proofread the following paragraph, correcting errors in the spelling of plural nouns.

Heros play an important part in many origin myths. For example, the discovery of fire is often credited to a hero who must endure clashs with the gods and much suffering. After several trys the hero steals fire and shares it with all the mans, womans, and childs of his world. In the Greek myths the godes punish this hero by letting a vulture eat his liver forever. Mythes show the fears, hopes, and wishs that people around the world share.

VOCABULARY | HOW TO OWN A WORD

American Indian Names: From Sea to Shining Sea

Many rivers, mountains, and other landmarks in the United States were given English versions of Indian names, from the Appalachian Mountains in the East to the Willamette River in the West. Use a dictionary or an encyclopedia to answer these questions.

1. Which states' names come from American Indian languages? List five names.
2. What does the place name *Mohave* mean?
3. Sometimes pioneers did not know the meanings of the names the Indians used. What is the real meaning of the name *Chicago*? What American Indian language is it from?
4. What American Indian names survive in your part of the world?

LOO-WIT, THE FIRE-KEEPER **497**

GRAMMAR LINK

Ask students to select passages from their portfolios and to underline each plural noun. Students should then make a chart that enables them to organize all the plural nouns they have used into five labeled boxes, each label indicating one way to form a plural noun. Have students enter each noun in the appropriate box.

Try It Out

Heroes; myths; clashes; tries; men; women; children; gods; myths; wishes

VOCABULARY

Answers

1. Alabama, Alaska, Arizona, Arkansas, Connecticut, Hawaii, Illinois, Iowa, Kansas, Massachusetts, Michigan, Minnesota, Mississippi, Missouri, Nebraska, North Dakota, Ohio, Oklahoma, South Dakota, Tennessee, Texas, Utah, Wisconsin, Wyoming, and perhaps Idaho, Kentucky, and Oregon
2. *Mohave* (or *Mojave*) refers to an American Indian people living along the Colorado River in Arizona.
3. *Chicago* is from the Algonquian language family and means "place of the wild onion."
4. Answers will vary according to your location. Have students look up the origins of local place names in a dictionary or local history, if possible.

Resources ———

Grammar
- *Grammar and Language Links,* p. 43

Spelling
For related instruction, see
- *Spelling and Decoding,* p. 20

Grammar Link Quick Check

Form the plurals of the following words:
1. table [tables]
2. church [churches]
3. potato [potatoes]
4. monkey [monkeys]
5. foot [feet]

T497

1. Read and understand the non-fiction excerpt
2. Recognize and understand features of informative writing
3. Express understanding through writing, reading a map, research/writing/art, and art/writing
4. Identify imaginative comparisons in science writing, and use such comparisons in writing
5. Understand and use new words

SKILLS

Reading
- Recognize and understand features of informative writing
- Answer questions about a map

Writing
- Collect ideas for observational writing
- Write captions for a diagram
- Write map labels

Grammar/Language
- Understand and use imaginative comparisons in science writing

Vocabulary
- Understand and use new words

Art
- Compare volcanic eruptions by drawing a map
- Draw diagrams of stages of volcanic activity

Planning

- **Block Schedule**
  Block Scheduling Lesson Plans with Pacing Guide
- **Traditional Schedule**
  Lesson Plans Including Strategies for English-Language Learners
- **One-Stop Planner**
  CD-ROM with Test Generator

Before You Read

VOLCANO

Make the Connection

Explosive Questions

When you hear the word *volcano*, what questions erupt in your mind? With your classmates, begin brainstorming *5W-How?* questions on volcanoes. To come up with questions, try previewing the photos and other illustrations in this selection.

Quickwrite

Jot down all the questions you have about volcanoes. Record your questions on a chart like the one below.

5W-How?	Examples
Who?	
What?	What is lava made of?
Why?	Why *do* volcanoes erupt?
When? Where?	
How?	How do scientists study volcanoes?

go.hrw.com
LEO 6-7

Reading Skills and Strategies

Informative Writing: Making It Clear

Informative writing provides facts about a real-life event or phenomenon. When you read informative writing, you have to know how to read these features:

Graphic aids. Tables, charts, graphs, photographs, diagrams, maps, and their explanatory captions help you visualize what the author is talking about. Before you

read an informative text, preview the graphic aids by skimming the pages to look at the illustrations and to read a few lines here and there. The visual materials will give you a good idea of what the text is about.

Cause-and-effect explanations. Science writers usually show how one event is connected to another.

Scientific terms. New scientific words are often defined in context or through clues in the passage.

Imaginative language. Science writers, just like fiction writers, often use imaginative comparisons, or figures of speech, to clarify difficult ideas or to help you visualize something.

As you read "Volcano," make use of all the informative-writing features that Patricia Lauber has included to help you understand what happens when the earth erupts.

498 EXPLAINING OUR WORLD: FACT AND FICTION

Preteaching Vocabulary

Words to Own

Have students work in pairs to study the Words to Own and their definitions and to quiz each other on the meanings of the words. Draw their attention to the fact that each of the four words describes some kind of action. Then have pairs work together to choose the word that is the best response to each statement below.

1. You would use the word *lumbered* to describe this creature's movements.
   a bee / a bird / a bear / a snake [a bear]

2. You would probably *never* use the word *billowing* to describe the way this moves.
   smoke / a snake / fog / a sail [a snake]

3. It would be impossible to clear off or clean this by *scouring* it.
   water / a frying pan / a tile floor / a rock [water]

4. This would be a good word to describe the movement of something that is *churned*.
   calm / smooth / impatient / violent [violent]

With the earthquake of March 20, 1980, Mount St. Helens woke from a sleep of 123 years.

from Volcano

Patricia Lauber

The Volcano Wakes

For many years the volcano slept. It was silent and still, big and beautiful. Then the volcano, which was named Mount St. Helens, began to stir. On March 20, 1980, it was shaken by a strong earthquake. The quake was a sign of movement inside St. Helens. It was a sign of a waking volcano that might soon erupt again.

Mount St. Helens was built by many eruptions over thousands of years. In each eruption hot rock from inside the earth forced its way to the surface. The rock was so hot that it was molten, or melted, and it had gases

VOLCANO **499**

Summary ■■■

Mount St. Helens, a volcano in Washington, erupted suddenly on May 18, 1980. After explaining the scientific causes for an eruption, the author describes the geological history of Mount St. Helens from the mid-nineteenth century to 1980. The eruption that spring killed 57 people and countless plants and animals. It spread destruction over 230 square miles, and left the mountain 1,200 feet lower than it had been. Entire forests were flattened by a "stone wind" that resulted when superheated water inside the mountain was released. After six more eruptions, Mount St. Helens was studied by scientists hoping to learn better ways to predict eruptions and to understand how life returns after volcanic eruptions.

Resources

Viewing and Representing
Videocassette B, Segment 8
Molten Mountains gives students an opportunity to watch real volcanoes erupting.

Listening
Audio CD Library
A recording of this excerpt is provided in the *Audio CD Library*:
• Disc 12, Track 3

Selection Assessment
Formal Assessment
• Selection Test, p. 96
Test Generator
• Selection Test

Viewing and Representing
Fine Art Transparency
Mt. Vesuvius, by J. M. W. Turner, is a dramatic image that can be used to spark students' interest in this selection.
• Transparency 16
• Worksheet, p. 64

Resources: Print and Media

Reading
• *Reading Skills and Strategies*
  Selection Skill Lesson, p. 29
  Selection Skill Lesson, p. 144
• *Graphic Organizers for Active Reading*, p. 32
• *Words to Own*, p. 18
• *Spelling and Decoding* Worksheet, p. 21
• *Audio CD Library*
  Disc 12, Track 3

Elements of Literature
• *Literary Elements*
  Transparency 9
  Worksheet, p. 28

Writing and Language
• *Daily Oral Grammar*, Transparency 30
• *Grammar and Language Links*,
  Worksheet p. 45

Viewing and Representing
• *Viewing and Representing*
  Fine Art Transparency 16

Fine Art Worksheet, p. 64
• *Visual Connections*
  Videocassette B, Segment 8

Assessment
• *Formal Assessment*, p. 96
• *Portfolio Management System*, p. 166
• *Test Generator (One-Stop Planner CD-ROM)*

Internet
• go.hrw.com (keyword: LE0 6-7)

A Reading Skills and Strategies

Informative Writing

Have students read and reread this passage in order to clarify the meanings of the scientific terms, *magma* and *lava*. [*Magma* denotes "melted rock inside a volcano"; *lava* is "melted rock that flows outside a volcano".]

B Background

Pumice is such a light rock that it floats. When the mountain Krakatau erupted on an Indonesian island in 1883, so much pumice was thrown into the air that it covered the surface of the sea for miles.

C Reading Skills and Strategies

Informative Writing

? What three kinds of graphic aids appear on this page, and what kind of information does each one provide? [The diagram shows a cutaway view of a volcano; the map shows the locations of volcanoes in Oregon and Washington; the photograph shows a volcano erupting.]

D English Language Learners

Questioning

Encourage students to pause after reading each page in order to review and update their *5W-How* charts.

A trapped in it. The name for such rock is magma. Once the molten rock reaches the surface it is called lava. In some eruptions the magma was fairly liquid. Its gases escaped gently. Lava flowed out of the volcano, cooled, and hardened. In other eruptions the magma was thick and sticky. Its gases burst out violently, carrying along sprays of molten rock. As it blasted into the sky, the rock cooled and hardened. Some of it rained down B as ash—tiny bits of rock. Some rained down as pumice—frothy rock puffed up by gases.

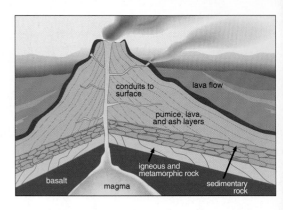

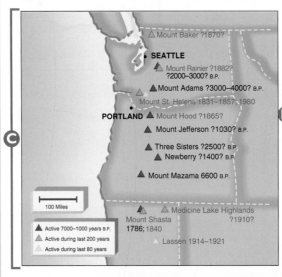

Together the lava-flows, ash, and pumice built a mountain with a bowl-shaped crater at its top. St. Helens grew to a height of 9,677 feet, so high that its peak was often hidden by clouds. Its big neighbors were D built in the same way. Mount St. Helens is part of the Cascade Range, a chain of volcanoes that runs from northern California into British Columbia.

In the middle 1800s, a number of small

(Above) A volcano is a place where hot, molten rock from inside the earth comes to the surface. Mount St. Helens was built by many eruptions over thousands of years.

(Left) Map shows the Cascade Range in the United States and the periods in which each volcano last erupted. Question marks mean that dates are not certain; B.P. means "before the present time."

500 EXPLAINING OUR WORLD: FACT AND FICTION

Reaching All Students

Struggling Readers

The use of Cause and Effect in Informative Writing was introduced on p. 498. For a lesson directly tied to this selection that teaches students to use cause and effect using a strategy called Text Reformulation, see the *Reading Skills and Strategies* binder
• Selection Skill Lesson, p. 144

English Language Learners

Because this excerpt contains many scientific terms and concepts, you may wish to read sections of the text aloud to the class. You might also use graphic aids, including chalkboard drawings, to help students visualize the meanings of words such as *lava, molten, earthquake, eruption,* and *avalanche.* For additional strategies to supplement instruction for these students, see
• *Lesson Plans Including Strategies for English-Language Learners*

Advanced Learners

Students interested in geology might enjoy doing independent research on the causes and consequences of volcanic eruptions. Others might look up news reports from 1980 on the Mount St. Helens eruptions in order to create their own news reports for the class. Still other students might create drawings, paintings, or dioramas of Mount St. Helens.

Mount St. Helens spouting volcanic steam, April 1980.

eruptions took place. Between 1832 and 1857, St. Helens puffed out clouds of steam and ash from time to time. It also gave off small flows of lava. Then the mountain fell still. /

For well over a hundred years the volcano slept. Each spring, as winter snows melted, its slopes seemed to come alive. Wildflowers bloomed in meadows. Bees gathered pollen and nectar. Birds fed, found mates, and built nests. Bears <u>lumbered</u> out of their dens. Herds of elk and deer feasted on fresh green shoots. Thousands of people came to hike, picnic, camp, fish, paint, bird-watch, or just enjoy the scenery. Logging crews felled tall trees and planted seedlings.

These people knew that Mount St. Helens was a volcano, but they did not fear it. To them it was simply a green and pleasant mountain, where forests of firs stretched up the slopes and streams ran clear and cold. /

The mountain did not seem so trustworthy to geologists (scientists who study the earth). They knew that Mount St. Helens was dangerous. It was a young volcano and one of the most active in the Cascade Range. In 1975, two geologists finished a study of the volcano's past eruptions. They predicted that Mount St. Helens would erupt again within 100 years, perhaps before the year 2000.

The geologists were right. With the earthquake of March 20, 1980, Mount St. Helens woke from a sleep of 123 years. Magma had forced its way into the mountain, tearing apart solid rock. The snapping of that rock set off the shock waves that shook St. Helens. That quake was followed by many others. Most of them were smaller, but they came so fast and so often that it was hard to tell when one quake ended and another began.

On March 27, people near Mount St. Helens heard a tremendous explosion. The volcano began to blow out steam and ash that stained its snow-white peak. Small explosions went on into late April, stopped, started again on May 7, and stopped on May 14.

The explosions of late March opened up two new craters at the top of the mountain. One formed inside the old crater. The other formed nearby. The two new craters grew bigger. Soon they joined, forming one large crater that continued to grow during the next few weeks. Meanwhile, the north face of the mountaintop was swelling and cracking. The swelling formed a bulge that grew outward at a rate of five to six feet a day.

Geologists were hard at work on the

WORDS TO OWN

lumbered (lum'bərd) v.: moved heavily, clumsily, and often noisily.

VOLCANO **501**

E **Critical Thinking**
Speculating
? Why do you think the author spends so much time describing the volcano's peaceful, beautiful qualities? [Possible responses: She wants to create a dramatic contrast with the violence that is soon to come; she wants to help students appreciate the natural beauty of a volcano.]

F **Reading Skills and Strategies**
Making Inferences
? How do geologists predict volcanic eruptions? [They study a volcano's past eruptions.]

G **Reading Skills and Strategies**

Informative Writing
? What causes the earthquake? [The force of the magma pushing upward snaps the rock holding it back.] **What is the effect of the earthquake?** [A series of explosions follows the quake, creating new craters.]

Using Students' Strengths

Naturalist Learners
Ask students to do research to determine what species of plants, animals, insects, and birds were present on Mount St. Helens before its eruption and what species, new or old, have lived there since.

Verbal Learners
Have students make a glossary of scientific terms used in this excerpt. Entries for each word should include a definition, a key to pronunciation, and any interesting information about the word's origin. For example, the word *volcano* comes from the Latin word *Volcanus*, the name of the ancient Roman god of fire. Students might draw or find illustrations for some of the words and then publish their glossaries as handouts or posters.

waking volcano. They took samples of ash and gases, hoping to find clues to what was happening inside. They placed instruments on the mountain to record earthquakes and the tilting of ground. They kept measuring the bulge. A sudden change in its rate of growth might be a sign that the volcano was about to erupt. But the bulge grew steadily, and the ash and gases yielded no clues.

By mid-May, the bulge was huge. Half a mile wide and more than a mile long, it had swelled out 300 feet.

On Sunday morning, May 18, the sun inched up behind the Cascades, turning the sky pink. By 8:00 A.M. the sun was above the mountains, the sky blue, the air cool. There was not one hint of what was to come.

At 8:32, Mount St. Helens erupted. Billowing clouds of smoke, steam, and ash hid the mountain from view and darkened the sky for miles.

The eruption went on until evening. By its end a fan-shaped area of destruction stretched out to the north, covering some 230 square miles. Within that area 57 people and countless plants and animals had died.

Geologists now faced two big jobs. One was to keep watch on the mountain to find out if more eruptions were building up. If so, they hoped to learn how to predict the eruptions.

The other job was to find out exactly what had happened on May 18. Most volcanic eruptions start slowly. Why had Mount St.

WORDS TO OWN
billowing (bil′ō·iŋ) v. used as adj.: swelling and rising.

Mount St. Helens partially covered with volcanic ash, April 1980.

Crossing the Curriculum

Violent eruption of Mount St. Helens and ash cloud.

E Reading Skills and Strategies

Informative Writing

? Writers of informative nonfiction need to keep the reader interested in the topic at hand. What stylistic strategy does the author use here to help keep readers interested? [She asks questions and implies that the answers are forthcoming.]

F Struggling Readers

Using Graphic Aids

Encourage students to refer to this map when they read descriptions of the eruption and its effects. You might point out that the map shows three different types of destruction, indicated by three colors. It also shows how the initial avalanche, colored red, moved toward Spirit Lake as well as along the valley of the North Fork Toutle River.

Helens erupted suddenly? What events had caused the big fan-shaped area of destruction? What had become of the mountaintop, which was now 1,200 feet lower?

The answers to these questions came slowly as geologists studied instrument records and photographs, interviewed witnesses, and studied the clues left by the eruption itself. But in time they pieced together a story that surprised them. This eruption turned out to be very different from the ones that built Mount St. Helens.

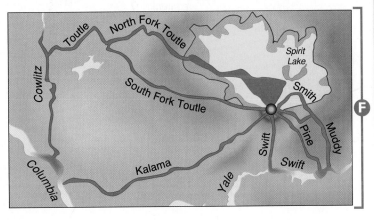

Yellow marks the area of destruction caused by the blast. Orange marks the area where trees were left standing but were killed by the heat. Red shows the avalanche path.

VOLCANO 503

Getting Students Involved

Cooperative Learning

In Our Own Backyard. Have small groups of students work together to learn about geological features in your area and to present their findings to the class. Different groups might be assigned different features, such as fault lines or mountain ranges. Have groups begin by discussing how best to utilize the strengths of each group member. For example, a student who is good at writing could record the group's activities, and an artistic student might design visual aids.

Enrichment Activity

Reciprocal Teaching. Have pairs of students study this selection by means of Reciprocal Teaching. Each student reads a portion of the text aloud to his or her partner. Challenge students to pay close attention to the text and to formulate and answer questions based on both listening and reading.

(A) Reading Skills and Strategies

Identifying Cause and Effect

Challenge students to trace the chain of causes and effects presented in this important passage. Many students may benefit from making simple cause-and-effect charts of the process, using arrows to connect related events. [Under pressure, the water inside the mountain becomes superheated. The avalanche tears open the mountain, causing the hot water to quickly change to steam. This in turn causes an explosion, shattering and spewing rock.]

(B) Reading Skills and Strategies

Informative Writing

❓ The author uses imaginative language in the form of figures of speech. What does she compare the tree trunks to? [straws] What does this comparison tell you about the force of the blast? [It was immense.] Ask students to look at the photograph of downed trees on this page and to suggest other possible comparisons. [Possible responses: pick-up or match sticks; a field of shattered skeletons; popsicle sticks; whiskers.]

The Big Blast

The May 18 eruption began with an earthquake that triggered an avalanche. At 8:32 A.M., instruments that were miles away registered a strong earthquake. The pilot and passengers of a small plane saw the north side of the mountain rippling and churning. Shaken by the quake, the bulge was tearing loose. It began to slide, in a huge avalanche that carried along rock ripped from deep inside Mount St. Helens.

The avalanche tore open the mountain. A scalding blast shot sideways out of the opening. It was a blast of steam, from water heated by rising magma.

Normally water cannot be heated beyond its boiling point, which is 212 degrees Fahrenheit at sea level. At boiling point, water turns to a gas, which we call steam. But if water is kept under pressure, it can be heated far beyond its boiling point and still stay liquid. (That is how a pressure cooker works.) If the pressure is removed, this superheated water suddenly turns, or flashes, to steam. As steam it takes up much more room—it expands. The sudden change to steam can cause an explosion.

Before the eruption Mount St. Helens was like a giant pressure cooker. The rock inside it held superheated water. The water stayed liquid because it was under great pressure, sealed in the mountain. When the mountain was torn open, the pressure was suddenly relieved. The superheated water flashed to steam. Expanding violently, it shattered rock inside the mountain and exploded out the opening, traveling at speeds of up to 200 miles an hour.

The blast flattened whole forests of 180-foot-high firs. It snapped off or uprooted the trees, scattering the trunks as if they were straws. At first, this damage was puzzling. A wind of 200 miles an hour is not strong enough to level forests of giant trees. The explanation, geologists later discovered, was

The blast leveled forests of huge firs. The tiny figures of two scientists (lower right) give an idea of the scale.

Taking a Second Look

Review: Summarizing

Remind students that a summary is a short restatement of the main events or essential ideas of a text. It is shorter than the original text and is written in the reader's own words. A good summary includes important factual information and is arranged in a logical order. Since it contains a great deal of factual information, this selection provides a good opportunity for students to practice this skill.

Activities

1. Work with the class to summarize the second and third paragraphs of the selection (pp. 499–500). Have one or more volunteers read the text aloud. Then invite students' comments about which ideas, facts, and descriptions are essential and which should be omitted. On the chalkboard, write a summary of two to four sentences based on students' responses.

2. Have groups of four or five students work together to create a summary of the entire selection. Divide the text into equal portions and have each group member summarize one portion. Then each group should read its summaries aloud in sequence. They can then revise and combine them into a single summary. Remind students to use statements of cause and effect when possible.

that the wind carried rocks ranging in size from grains of sand to blocks as big as cars. As the blast roared out of the volcano, it swept up and carried along the rock it had shattered.

The result was what one geologist described as "a stone wind." It was a wind of steam and rocks, traveling at high speed. The rocks gave the blast its great force. Before it, trees snapped and fell. Their stumps looked as if they had been sandblasted. The wind of stone rushed on. It stripped bark and branches from trees and uprooted them, leveling 150 square miles of countryside. At the edge of this area other trees were left standing, but the heat of the blast scorched and killed them.

The stone wind was traveling so fast that it overtook and passed the avalanche. On its path was Spirit Lake, one of the most beautiful lakes in the Cascades. The blast stripped the trees from the slopes surrounding the lake and moved on.

Meanwhile the avalanche had hit a ridge and split. One part of it poured into Spirit Lake, adding a 180-foot layer of rock and dirt to the bottom of the lake. The slide of avalanche into the lake forced the water out. The water sloshed up the slopes, then fell back into the lake. With it came thousands of trees felled by the blast.

The main part of the avalanche swept down the valley of the North Fork of the Toutle River. There, in the valley, most of the avalanche slowed and stopped. It covered 24 square miles and averaged 150 feet thick.

The blast itself continued for 10 to 15 minutes, then stopped. Minutes later, Mount St. Helens began to erupt upward. A dark column of ash and ground-up rock rose miles into the sky. Winds blew the ash eastward.

Ash blanketed the trees like snow.

Lightning flashed in the ash cloud and started forest fires. In Yakima, Washington, some 80 miles away, the sky turned so dark that street lights went on at noon. Ash fell like snow that would not melt. This eruption continued for nine hours.

Shortly after noon the color of the ash column changed. It became lighter, a sign that the volcano was now throwing out mostly new magma. Until then much of the ash had been made of old rock.

At the same time, the volcano began giving off huge flows of pumice and ash. The material was very hot, with temperatures of about 1,000 degrees Fahrenheit, and it traveled down the mountain at speeds of 100 miles an hour. The flows went on until 5:30 in the afternoon. They formed a wedge-

VOLCANO **505**

C **Struggling Readers**
Rereading
? Encourage students to reread this passage to be sure they understand that the term *stone wind* was coined by a scientist. Then ask what a stone wind is. [a strong wind that carries steam and rocks through the air] **What causes the stone wind on Mount St. Helens?** [the force of steam exploding through the opening created by the avalanche]

D **Reading Skills and Strategies**
Informative Writing
Call students' attention to the imaginative language the author uses to describe the visual effects of the eruption. Point out that though the author's main purpose is to inform readers, she is also careful to engage their senses and imagination.

E **Critical Thinking**
Extending the Text
Invite students to compare the speed of the lava flow to the speed of other fast-moving objects they are familiar with. [Possible responses: It's faster than a car on a superhighway; it's as fast as a major-league fastball.]

Skill Link

Reading: Recognize and Interpret Literary Devices
Remind students that good science writers look for opportunities to use imaginative language in their descriptions and explanations of the natural world. One way they do this is by using figurative language to compare two seemingly unlike things.
Activity
Have students read the following examples of figurative language from pp. 504–505. Ask students to identify the two things being compared and to explain how each comparison deepens their understanding of a fact or process.

1. Before the eruption Mount St. Helens was like a giant pressure cooker. [Mount St. Helens, pressure cooker; can better visualize build-up of pressure inside volcano]

2. It snapped off or uprooted the trees, scattering the trunks as if they were straws. [tree trunks, straws; emphasizes explosion's power by comparing trunks to small, light objects]

3. The wind carried rocks ranging in size from grains of sand to blocks as big as cars. [blocks of rock, cars; stresses rocks' hugeness by comparing them to objects that are larger than most rocks]

**Informative
Writing**
Encourage students to compare this
photograph of the volcano's mudflow
with the map on p. 503. Both graphic
aids illustrate the flow of volcanic
material toward Spirit Lake and along
the Toutle River. North is the direction
at the top of the map on p. 503 (Spirit
Lake is on the northeastern slope of
Mount St. Helens). In order to align
the two pictures, students can give the
photo a 180 degree turn or give the
map a 180 degree turn. Point out that
the photograph shows the northern
face of the volcano.

B **Appreciating Language**

**Comparisons in Science
Writing**
? What two things does the author
compare by simile in this paragraph?
[The author compares the mudflow to
wet concrete.]

A

An eruption on March 19, 1982, melted snow and caused this mudflow. The smaller part of the flow went into Spirit Lake (lower left), while the larger part traveled down the Toutle River.

shaped plain of pumice on the side of the mountain. Two weeks later temperatures in the pumice were still about 780 degrees.

Finally, there were the mudflows, which started when heat from the blast melted ice and snow on the mountaintop. The water mixed with ash, pumice, ground-up rock, and dirt and rocks of the avalanche. The result was a thick mixture that was like wet concrete, a mudflow. The mudflows traveled fast, scouring the landscape and sweeping down the slopes into river valleys. Together their speed and thickness did great damage.

The largest mudflow was made of avalanche material from the valley of the North Fork of the Toutle River. It churned

(Above) A geologist records information about the blast.

WORDS TO OWN

scouring (skour'iŋ) v. used as adj.: removing as if by
  cleaning and scraping; sweeping away.
churned (churnd) v.: moved violently.

506 EXPLAINING OUR WORLD: FACT AND FICTION

Using Students' Strengths

Interpersonal Learners
Have students work together to create and present a radio or television news broadcast of the
eruption. They might focus on the main eruption of May 18 or on the events of a series of
days before or after. Encourage students to use
additional research and information from the
text to write scripts for their broadcasts. Alternatively, groups of students could role-play a discussion with people who witnessed the

eruption. The witnesses might include people
who saw Mount St. Helens at different times
and from different places: above the mountain in
a small plane during the eruption; on a ridge
above Spirit Lake; in Yakima; on the Columbia
River, and so on. Witnesses might also include
people who visited the mountain shortly before
the eruption.

Verbal Learners
The meanings of many key terms in this article
can be inferred from their contexts. Have students study sentences from the text to write
definitions for *avalanche, crater, ash,* and *eruption.*
Then have them use a dictionary to verify their
inferences. Remind students that they may use
the same process with other unfamiliar words
they encounter.

down the river valley, tearing out steel bridges, ripping houses apart, picking up boulders and trucks and carrying them along. Miles away it choked the Cowlitz River and blocked shipping channels in the Columbia River.

When the sun rose on May 19, it showed a greatly changed St. Helens. The mountain was 1,200 feet shorter than it had been the morning before. Most of the old top had slid down the mountain in the avalanche. The rest had erupted out as shattered rock. Geologists later figured that the volcano had lost three quarters of a cubic mile of old rock.

The north side of the mountain had changed from a green and lovely slope to a fan-shaped wasteland.

At the top of Mount St. Helens was a big, new crater with the shape of a horseshoe. Inside the crater was the vent, the opening through which rock and gases erupted from time to time over the next few years.

In 1980, St. Helens erupted six more times. Most of these eruptions were explosive—ash soared into the air, pumice swept down the north side of the mountain. In the eruptions of June and August, thick, pasty lava oozed out of the vent and built a dome. But both domes were destroyed by the next eruptions. In October the pattern changed. The explosions stopped, and thick lava built a dome that was not destroyed. Later eruptions added to the dome, making it bigger and bigger.

During this time, geologists were learning to read the clues found before eruptions. They learned to predict what St. Helens was going to do. The predictions helped to protect people who were on and near the mountain.

Among these people were many natural scientists. They had come to look for survivors, for plants and animals that had lived through the eruption. They had come to look for colonizers, for plants and animals that would move in. Mount St. Helens had erupted many times before. Each time life had returned. Now scientists would have a chance to see how it did. They would see how nature healed itself.

Arnica flowers blooming on the Lang Ridge in 1984, four years after the eruption of Mount St. Helens.

Making the Connections

BROWSING IN THE FILES

About the Author. About becoming a writer, Patricia Lauber says, "I had been a small child who adored stories and was fortunate enough to have a mother who liked to read to me. But there never seemed to be enough time. As a result, first grade was probably the most exciting year of my entire education. I discovered that I knew how to read. Now I no longer had to depend on my mother's being free when I wanted a story. Next year I learned to print and also to spell a few words. An undreamed-of world appeared: I could make up my own stories and poems and write them down. I knew at once what I was going to be...."

A Critic's Comment. When *Volcano: The Eruption and Healing of Mount St. Helens* became a 1987 Newbery Honor Book, reviewer Jo Carr commented in *Horn Book* magazine that the judges "showed great wisdom in choosing this perfect book."

FROM THE EDITOR'S DESK

We like the fact that our fictional accounts of volcanoes—"Loo-Wit, the Fire-Keeper" and "The Dog of Pompeii"—are linked to specific, real volcanoes, and that our nonfiction excerpt, *Volcano*, is as dramatic as a short story.

MEET THE WRITER

Science Is Her Specialty

Patricia Lauber (1924–   ) is best known for her informational books on a wide variety of topics, including alligators, rivers, planets, robots, and cattle ranching. Here, she explains why she decided to write "Volcano":

66 Volcanoes have always interested me, and so when Mount St. Helens erupted I followed the story closely in newspapers and magazines and I built a file of clippings. But I wasn't thinking of writing a book about the eruption. Rather, I was planning to add the story to an already published book that I had written about volcanoes, by way of bringing it up-to-date.

One day, though, I was reading a magazine article about the volcano and came across a small photograph. It showed a young fireweed plant pushing its way up through a crack in the volcanic ash—ash that was thick enough and strong enough to support the weight of a grown man. Suddenly I knew the book that I wanted very much to write. It would tell about the eruption, how and why it took place. It would also tell how, in time, life came back, as it always does, to a place that looked as barren as the moon.

Before I could write the book, I had, of course, to wait for life to start coming back, wait for natural scientists to make their studies of what was happening. All the time I was scared that some other author would have the same idea and write the story before I did. Finally, the time was right for me to make a trip to Mount St. Helens (I live in Connecticut), to see for myself what had happened and to talk to the scientists who were studying the mountain and its life. Then I was at last able to tell the story of fearsome destruction but also of healing, of the return of life. 99

Assessing Learning

Check Test: Short Answers

1. How was Mount St. Helens built up? [by many eruptions of molten rock over thousands of years]
2. During what year did the most recent eruptions take place? [1980]
3. When can water be heated past its normal boiling point? [when it is under pressure]
4. After the eruptions of 1980, was Mount St. Helens shorter or taller than it had been before? [shorter]

Observation Assessment

As students respond to oral readings of this selection or other selections, use the following checklist to assess their listening.

1=Never   2=Sometimes   3=Always

_____ Pays attention to oral presentation

_____ Listens without interrupting

_____ Participates in discussion

_____ Seems to understand what is read

Standardized Test Preparation

For practice in proofreading and editing, see
• *Daily Oral Grammar,* Transparency 30

MAKING MEANINGS

First Thoughts

[respond]

1. What is the most interesting fact that you learned about volcanoes in general from this selection? about Mount St. Helens in particular?

Shaping Interpretations

[respond]

2. Like fiction writers, science writers try to create **suspense.** They want to make us eager to read on to find out what happens next. Where in this selection do you think the writer builds suspense? At these moments, what questions did she plant in your mind?

[identify]

3. Look back at the list of **informative-writing** features described on page 498. Which features does Lauber use in "Volcano"? Which feature did you find most helpful as you read? Why?

Connecting with the Text

[compare/ contrast]

4. "Loo-Wit, the Fire-Keeper" (page 491) is a myth that describes Mount St. Helens as a woman who erupts in anger at humankind. Compare and contrast that mythical account with this article. What strengths do you see in each? Which do you prefer—the story or the science?

Extending the Text

[generalize]

5. Why do you think people like to read about natural disasters?

Challenging the Text

[evaluate]

6. Science writers, like all nonfiction writers, have to know their audience. Lauber's book about volcanoes was written for young adults. Do you think the writer succeeded in making difficult scientific concepts clear? Is anything unclear? Did you find the answers to the *5W-How?* questions you listed in the chart you prepared for the Quickwrite on page 498?

> **Reading Check**
>
> With a small group of your classmates, create a **time line** that shows all the major events surrounding the eruption of Mount St. Helens—before, during, and after. For your time line, focus on what the volcano was doing, what geologists were doing, and how the eruption affected the surrounding countryside.

> **Reading Check**
>
> Be sure students include the following events in their time lines: Small eruptions build up volcano; geologists predict an eruption before the year 2000; earthquakes cause explosions, creating new craters; geologists look for clues in ash; Mount St. Helens erupts suddenly; fan-shaped area of destruction is created; geologists study destructive effects.

MAKING MEANINGS

First Thoughts

1. Possible responses: the fact that rock becomes hot enough to melt; the fact that Mount St. Helens erupted so suddenly and violently on a peaceful morning.

Shaping Interpretations

2. Possible response: A moment of suspense occurs in the description of the beautiful spring setting of the sleeping Mount St. Helens immediately before the eruption. Lauber excites the reader's curiosity about what will happen to the plants, animals, and people she has described.

3. Lauber uses all the features on the list. Many students will say they found the explanations of scientific terms such as *magma* and *lava* most helpful because these words are defined in the middle of a description of a volcanic eruption—when interest is at a peak.

Connecting with the Text

4. Possible responses: The myth's strength is in teaching people through its storytelling to take care of the land and each other; the article's strength is in teaching respect for the power of nature by conveying information vividly.

Extending the Text

5. Possible responses: People are awestruck by the power of nature; people are excited by dangers that don't threaten them personally; people like to learn about worlds outside their own.

Challenging the Text

6. Possible response: The writer generally succeeds in making scientific concepts clear, but some questions remain, such as exactly how the bulge on the north face was formed. Students will probably have found the answers to many, but not all, of their *5W-How?* questions.

Grading Timesaver

Rubrics for each Choices assignment appear on p. 166 of the *Portfolio Management System*.

CHOICES:
Building Your Portfolio

1. **Writer's Notebook** Encourage students to take at least ten or fifteen seconds to study the image before beginning to jot down notes. Remind students to save their work. They may use it as prewriting for the Writer's Workshop on pp. 562–566.

2. **Reading a Map**
   Answers:
   a. the Cascade Range
   b. Mount Shasta
   c. before the present time
   d. Three Sisters
   e. Mount Jefferson

3. **Research/Writing/Art** Students might also include the 1991 eruption of Mount Pinatubo in the Philippines, which threw so much ash and so many chemicals into the air that the temperature of the entire world dropped about one degree Fahrenheit.

4. **Art/Writing** Students can show what is happening inside the mountain as well as what is happening outside it.

CHOICES: Building Your Portfolio

Writer's Notebook

1. Collecting Ideas for Observational Writing

To practice observing details, find a partner and choose one of the photos in this selection to study carefully. Working alone, jot down every detail you observe in the picture. Afterward, compare your notes with your partner's. Did you and your partner observe different details? Did you and your partner describe some details differently?

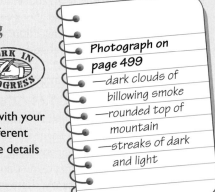

Photograph on page 499
—dark clouds of billowing smoke
—rounded top of mountain
—streaks of dark and light

Reading a Map

2. Map It

To help readers understand a science article, an author will often include **graphic aids**, such as charts, graphs, diagrams, maps, and photographs. These graphic aids are often accompanied by captions, which explain what the aids are about.

Use the map and caption on page 500 to answer the following questions:

a. What does the map show?

b. Which is farther away from Mount Jefferson—Mount Shasta or Mount Rainier?

c. What do the letters B.P. stand for?

d. Which is closer to Mount Mazama—Lassen Peak or Three Sisters?

e. Which volcano is between Mount Hood and Three Sisters?

Research/Writing/Art

3. A Lava Lineup

Compare the eruption of Mount St. Helens with other volcanic eruptions in history, such as that of Vesuvius (A.D. 79) in Pompeii, Italy (see page 524), and that of Krakatau (1883) in Indonesia. Were some eruptions even bigger, longer lasting, or more destructive? Find out for yourself—and make your findings easy for others to see—by creating a lava lineup. Draw a large world map, mark the location of each eruption, and give the date and other information next to the mark.

Art/Writing

4. Three Views of the Mountain

Imagine you're a geologist studying Mount St. Helens. Draw three diagrams to show the mountain before, during, and after the giant eruption. Use details in "Volcano" as your guide. Be sure to write a caption that explains each diagram.

LANGUAGE LINK | MINI-LESSON

Handbook of Literary Terms
H E L P

See Personification.

Style: Comparisons in Science Writing

Science writers, like all writers, sometimes describe one thing in terms of something else, even though it is not actually the same thing. These imaginative comparisons between two seemingly unlike things are called **figures of speech**. **Personification** is a figure of speech. It describes an object as if it had human qualities. In "Volcano," Patricia Lauber adds power to her description of St. Helens by making the mountain seem in many ways like a person.

1. Actions of the volcano are sometimes described as if they were human actions.

    EXAMPLES "For many years the volcano slept. . . . Then the volcano . . . began to stir."

2. The volcano, like a person, seems to have personality traits.

    EXAMPLE "The mountain did not seem so trustworthy to geologists. . . ."

Try It Out

1. Suppose you're a science writer. Use personification or another figure of speech to rewrite each description below.

    • After being inactive for more than a hundred years, the volcano became active.

    • At the base of the mountain was a wasteland.

    • Geologists began to see ways to predict the volcano's eruptions.

2. Think of three natural or mechanical things to write about. Write a sentence describing each thing, using personification to help readers form vivid images.

VOCABULARY | HOW TO OWN A WORD

WORD BANK	Vocabulary for the Workplace: A Scientific Report
lumbered billowing scouring churned	Imagine you are a scientist sent to investigate an erupting volcano and file a report. Use the words in the Word Bank to describe what you observed at the scene.

LANGUAGE LINK

Ask students to bring in papers they have written for science classes. Have them work in pairs to look for opportunities to add personification to some of their scientific explanations. Encourage them to focus on verbs that tell how an object reacts or changes. They might use a chart like the one below.

Object	Verb	Personification
Volcano	Erupts	Awakens
Tree	Vibrates	Shudders

Try It Out
Possible answers

1. • After sleeping for more than a hundred years, the volcano awakened.
   • At the base of the mountain, a wasteland reached out like a hand.
   • Geologists began to see ways to predict the volcano's tantrums.
2. Sample responses: His car is sick. The wind moaned in the treetops. The blue jays are always scolding my cat.

VOCABULARY

Before students answer, have them review pp. 501–506 to study the vocabulary words in context. You might wish to combine this activity with students' work on Choices 1, 3, or 4 (p. 510).

Resources ———

Language
• *Grammar and Language Links,* p. 45
Vocabulary
• *Words to Own,* p. 18
Spelling
For related instruction, see
• *Spelling and Decoding,* p. 21

Language Link Quick Check

Rewrite the following descriptions, using personification to make them livelier.
1. A thick mudflow covered the mountainside. [Possible response: A thick mudflow smothered the mountainside.]
2. Suddenly, the mountain erupted. [Possible response: Suddenly, the mountain coughed up lava, ash, and steam.]

3. Heavy stones flew in the wind. [Possible response: The wind picked up heavy stones and threw them as if they were snowballs.]
4. Later, new plants appeared on the volcano slope. [Possible answer: Later, new plants populated the volcano slope.]

Resources

Elements of Literature
Subjective and Objective Writing
For additional instruction on subjective and objective writing, see *Literary Elements:*
• Transparency 9
Assessment
Formal Assessment
• Literary Elements Test, p. 106

Elements of Literature

This feature describes the difference between objective and subjective approaches to nonfiction writing. The essay also encourages students to consider issues underlying objectivity and subjectivity as they read nonfiction.
Mini-Lesson:
Subjective and Objective Writing
Have students read the pupil page. Then give an example of an opinion, such as, "The seashore is beautiful," as well as a fact about the same subject, such as, "The seashore is rocky." Ask students to brainstorm other pairs of fact-opinion statements about nature or other everyday topics.

Applying the Element
Ask students to choose a topic they are familiar with and to write an objective paragraph about it. Then have students write a subjective paragraph about the same topic.

SUBJECTIVE AND OBJECTIVE WRITING: Facts vs. Feelings

You're a newspaper reporter with a big story: A disaster—a hurricane, an earthquake, or a flood—has hit your community. How do you write your story?

You have some choices. You could approach the topic **objectively**. That means you'd state the facts and statistics and keep your personal feelings out of it. You'd gather data. You'd get experts to tell you about the causes of the disaster. You'd conduct interviews to show your readers how the disaster affected people's lives.

On the other hand, you might want to approach the same topic **subjectively**. Then you'd share your own feelings, thoughts, and opinions about the disaster. You might describe what went through your mind as the earthquake shook you out of bed. You might say it's a shame that people never work together until a disaster strikes. You might ex-

press your anger that there was no warning.

Objective Writing: Just the Facts

"Volcano" by Patricia Lauber is a good example of objective writing. Lauber's purpose is to inform us—to help us see a volcanic eruption from different angles. She describes what the volcano was doing, how it affected the surrounding countryside, and how geologists were responding.

This is the kind of objectivity we expect from a science article or a news story. Lauber doesn't share her feelings about Mount St. Helens. We don't learn anything about Patricia Lauber; we learn about volcanoes.

Subjective Writing: Your Angle

In some types of nonfiction, we expect subjective writing.

Personal essays, for example, are subjective. When you're writing about losing every soccer game in a season or celebrating the Fourth of July, your thoughts and feelings matter. Your readers will know you better after they read your essay.

Be a Critical Reader

When you're reading a history book or a newspaper editorial or when you're watching the television broadcast of a speech, think about the differences between subjective and objective writing. When you read nonfiction, always ask yourself: "Am I reading something subjective? Are these the writer's opinions? Or are these facts—statements that can be proved?"

Be a critical reader. Be alert to the difference between what's personal (subjectivity) and what's provable (objectivity).

Reaching All Students

Struggling Readers/English Language Learners
Have students work in pairs to identify the opinions and facts in a piece of nonfiction writing from a local newspaper. Have students use a chart like the one at the right to evaluate each statement in the piece. Then have students determine whether the piece is subjective or objective.

Question	Fact	Opinion
Does the statement reveal the writer's emotions?		
Does the statement say whether something is good or bad?		
Does the statement tell only what happened?		

Advanced Learners
Emphasize that objectivity and subjectivity can often be found in the same piece of writing, even when the writer uses one mode primarily. For example, supposedly factual news stories often imply the views of the writers or the newspaper. Ask students to study a newspaper in order to discover subjective statements in front-page news stories. Have students report their findings to the class in an oral report.

Before You Read

THE DOG OF POMPEII

Make the Connection

Run or Hide?

It's noon on a hot, steamy day near the end of summer. You're on your way home. Suddenly the sky turns as dark as night. People begin shouting at each other, "What's going on? Is it a fire? a hurricane? a tornado? Is an asteroid falling?"

All anybody knows is that a disaster is about to happen. Will you run home? Will you try to get as far away as you can? Will you look for a place to hide?

Quickwrite

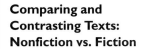

Imagine that you have thirty minutes before disaster strikes. Jot down a few sentences telling what you will do. If you'll hide, tell where. If you'll run, who or what will you take with you?

Elements of Literature

Historical Fiction: Bread and Bones

This story takes place in Pompeii, a real Roman city that was buried by a volcanic eruption in A.D. 79.

Archaeologists uncovered most of what we know about Pompeii. They dug up houses, artwork, tools, and household objects that tell us much about life in ancient Rome. They found the bones of humans and animals who had not been able to escape. They even found rock-hard loaves of bread baked almost two thousand years ago. Notice how the author of this story weaves some of these facts with fiction to bring a piece of history to life.

> **H**istorical fiction combines an imaginative story with facts about events that happened in the past. Some historical fiction uses actual historical figures along with fictional characters.

Reading Skills and Strategies

Comparing and Contrasting Texts: Nonfiction vs. Fiction

When you **compare** texts, you tell how they're alike. When you **contrast** texts, you tell how they're different.

"Volcano" (page 499) and "The Dog of Pompeii" are similar in that they are both about volcanoes. The big difference is that "Volcano" is nonfiction, while "The Dog of Pompeii" is fiction. After you read this disaster story, you'll have a chance to compare it with a nonfiction account of the same event.

Cave Canem (Beware the Dog). Ancient Roman floor mosaic from Pompeii.

go.hrw.com
LE0 6-7

THE DOG OF POMPEII **513**

Summary ...

Tito, a blind orphan, lives in the streets of ancient Pompeii with his dog, Bimbo, who retrieves food for the youth three times daily. One day Tito hears a conversation among men who disagree about whether Mt. Vesuvius is giving warnings of an eruption. He is awakened that night by Bimbo: the eruption has begun. Bimbo helps Tito to escape by leading him to the sea. Tito is taken into a boat, but Bimbo disappears. Eighteen hundred years later, archaeologists discover the preserved skeleton of a dog with a flat raisin cake in its mouth.

Background

The ruins of Pompeii are about a dozen miles south of the city of Naples. Mt. Vesuvius, the only active volcano on the mainland of Europe, has erupted many times since the destruction of Pompeii, notably in 472, 512, 1631, 1872, 1906, and 1944.

Resources

Listening
Audio CD Library
A recording of "The Dog of Pompeii" is provided in the *Audio CD Library:*
• Disc 12, Track 4

Selection Assessment
Formal Assessment
• Selection Test, p. 98
Test Generator
• Selection Test

THE DOG OF POMPEII

Louis Untermeyer

"When the smoke tree above Vesuvius grows to the shape of an umbrella pine, look to your lives."

514

RESPONDING TO THE ART

Explain to students that in the illustrations for this selection, the artist has superimposed figures in period Roman costume against the present-day ruins of Pompeii. This juxtaposition is neither accurate nor realistic.

Activity. Ask students to discuss the emotional effect of mixing Pompeii's past and present in one image. Does it intensify or diminish the story's impact?

 Resources: Print and Media

Reading
• *Reading Skills and Strategies*
  Selection Skill Lesson, p. 29
• *Graphic Organizers for Active Reading*, p. 33
• *Words to Own*, p. 19
• *Audio CD Library*
  Disc 12, Track 4

Writing and Language
• *Daily Oral Grammar*
  Transparency 31

Assessment
• *Formal Assessment*, p. 98
• *Portfolio Management System*, p. 167
• *Standardized Test Preparation*, pp. 72, 74
• *Test Generator (One-Stop Planner CD-ROM)*

Internet
• go.hrw.com (keyword: LE0 6-7)

Tito and his dog Bimbo lived (if you could call it living) under the wall where it joined the inner gate. They really didn't live there; they just slept there. They lived anywhere. Pompeii was one of the gayest of the old Latin towns, but although Tito was never an unhappy boy, he was not exactly a merry one. The streets were always lively with shining chariots and bright red trappings; the open-air theaters rocked with laughing crowds; sham battles and athletic sports were free for the asking in the great stadium. Once a year the Caesar[1] visited the pleasure city and the fireworks lasted for days; the sacrifices[2] in the forum were better than a show.

But Tito saw none of these things. He was blind—had been blind from birth. He was known to everyone in the poorer quarters. But no one could say how old he was, no one remembered his parents, no one could tell where he came from. Bimbo was another mystery. As long as people could remember seeing Tito—about twelve or thirteen years—they had seen Bimbo. Bimbo had never left his side. He was not only dog but nurse, pillow, playmate, mother, and father to Tito.

Did I say Bimbo never left his master? (Perhaps I had better say comrade, for if anyone was the master, it was Bimbo.) I was wrong. Bimbo did trust Tito alone exactly three times a day. It was a fixed routine, a custom understood between boy and dog since the beginning of their friendship, and the way it worked was this: Early in the morning, shortly after dawn, while Tito was still dreaming, Bimbo would disappear.

When Tito awoke, Bimbo would be sitting quietly at his side, his ears cocked, his stump of a tail tapping the ground, and a fresh-baked bread—more like a large round roll—at his feet. Tito would stretch himself; Bimbo would yawn; then they would breakfast. At noon, no matter where they happened to be, Bimbo would put his paw on Tito's knee and the two of them would return to the inner gate. Tito would curl up in the corner (almost like a dog) and go to sleep, while Bimbo, looking quite important (almost like a boy), would disappear again. In half an hour he'd be back with their lunch. Sometimes it would be a piece of fruit or a scrap of meat, often it was nothing but a dry crust. But sometimes there would be one of those flat rich cakes, sprinkled with raisins and sugar, that Tito liked so much. At suppertime the same thing happened, although there was a little less of everything, for things were hard to snatch in the evening, with the streets full of people. Besides, Bimbo didn't approve of too much food before going to sleep. A heavy supper made boys too restless and dogs too stodgy[3]—and it was the business of a dog to sleep lightly with one ear open and muscles ready for action.

But, whether there was much or little, hot or cold, fresh or dry, food was always there. Tito never asked where it came from and Bimbo never told him. There was plenty of rainwater in the hollows of soft stones; the old egg woman at the corner sometimes gave him a cupful of strong goat's milk; in the grape season the fat winemaker let him have drippings of the mild juice. So there was no danger of going hungry or thirsty. There was plenty of everything in Pompeii—if you knew where to find it—and if you had a dog like Bimbo.

1. **Caesar** (sē′zər): Roman emperor. The word *Caesar* comes from the family name of Julius Caesar, a great general who ruled Rome as dictator from 49 to 44 B.C.
2. **sacrifices:** offerings (especially of slaughtered animals) to a god or gods.

3. **stodgy** (stä′jē): heavy and slow in movement.

THE DOG OF POMPEII 515

Ⓐ Elements of Literature
Historical Fiction
❓ What parts of the description are historical, and what parts are fictional? [Possible response: The descriptions of life in Pompeii are historical; the descriptions of Tito and Bimbo are fictional.]

Ⓑ Determining Author's Purpose
Encourage students to read this passage with and without the sections in parentheses. Ask why they think the author included these additional phrases. [Possible responses: He wanted to show how similar the boy and dog are—they are "in tune" with each other; he wanted to include humor and to make ancient times seem more accessible.]

Ⓒ Elements of Literature
Historical Fiction
You might suggest that the description of the raisin cake is both historical and fictional. Encourage students to tell how it connects to something historical and how it connects to something fictional. [It is historical because it refers to a kind of ancient Roman cake. It is fictional in that it is an aspect of a fictional character's daily life.] You might also point out that copies of some ancient Roman cookbooks and literary descriptions of ancient Roman meals have survived.

Ⓓ Reading Skills and Strategies

Comparing and Contrasting Texts
Both "The Dog of Pompeii" and the excerpt from *Volcano* describe scenes of calm and contentment before a volcanic eruption. Ask students to compare and contrast these treatments.

Reaching All Students

Struggling Readers
Comparing and Contrasting Texts was introduced on p. 513. For a lesson in which students compare and contrast this selection with the excerpt from *Volcano* by using a strategy called Likert Scales, see the *Reading Skills and Strategies* binder
• Selection Skill Lesson, p. 29

English Language Learners
You might wish to divide the story into short sections and use Echo Reading. An English-fluent partner can read a section aloud first, followed by an English language learner. For additional strategies to supplement instruction for these students, see
• *Lesson Plans Including Strategies for English-Language Learners*

Advanced Learners
Have students take notes while reading in order to write reviews of the story. Their notes and reviews should include positive and negative responses to the author's fictional treatment of the historical subject matter. Remind them to cite specific details from the story to support their points.

A Critical Thinking
Challenging the Text

? How does the author know what games ancient Roman children played—or does he *not* really know? [Possible responses: He might have found information about Roman children's games in reference books or in ancient literature; the author might be guessing, and this guess could be based on games modern Western children have played for generations.] You might research the history of one or more of these games.

B Elements of Literature
Historical Fiction

? List all the details you learn about Roman life from this passage. Through what senses does Tito experience these details? [the food served at a feast, how clothes were kept moth-free, the use of fumes to cure a fever, and the different foods found in a market; Tito experiences the details through his senses of smell and hearing.]

As I said before, Tito was not the merriest boy in Pompeii. He could not romp with the other youngsters and play "hare and hounds" **A** and "I spy" and "follow your master" and "ball against the building" and "jackstones" and "kings and robbers" with them. But that did not make him sorry for himself. If he could not see the sights that delighted the lads of Pompeii, he could hear and smell **B** things they never noticed. He could really see more with his ears and nose than they could with their eyes. When he and Bimbo went out walking, he knew just where they were going and exactly what was happening.

"Ah," he'd sniff and say, as they passed a handsome villa,[4] "Glaucus Pansa is giving a grand dinner tonight. They're going to have three kinds of bread, and roast pigling, and stuffed goose, and a great stew—I think bear stew—and a fig pie." And Bimbo would note that this would be a good place to visit tomorrow.

Or, "H'm," Tito would murmur, half through his lips, half through his nostrils. "The wife of Marcus Lucretius is expecting her mother. She's shaking out every piece of goods in the house; she's going to use the best clothes—the ones she's been keeping in pine needles and camphor[5]—and there's an extra girl in the kitchen. Come, Bimbo, let's get out of the dust!"

Or, as they passed a small but elegant dwelling opposite the public baths, "Too bad! The tragic poet is ill again. It must be a bad fever this time, for they're trying smoke

4. **villa:** large house.

5. **camphor** (kam′fər): strong-smelling substance used to keep moths away from clothing. Camphor is still used for this purpose.

Using Students' Strengths

Visual Learners
The descriptions in the story are often not visual, since Tito is blind. Encourage students to pause and imagine visual details that might have been included if Tito were sighted. Ask students to draw or sketch what they imagine aspects of Tito's world looked like.

Kinesthetic Learners
Like many people without sight, Tito is skilled at making his way in the world using his other senses. Have sighted students imagine how they would make their way to—and through a day at—school without sight. Invite them to take a mental trip through an "ordinary" day and to write a list of aural and tactile cues that would help them make their way. Any visually impaired students would be excellent tutors for this activity.

Interpersonal Learners
After they have read the story, have pairs of students imagine that they are Pompeiians in A.D. 79. Invite them to discuss and write down a plan for escaping a volcanic eruption. The first order of business will be to make a list of problems or obstacles to overcome. Remind students that their only escape route is the sea.

fumes instead of medicine. Whew! I'm glad I'm not a tragic poet!"

Or, as they neared the forum, "Mm-m! What good things they have in the macellum[6] today!" (It really was a sort of butcher-grocer-marketplace, but Tito didn't know any better. He called it the macellum.) "Dates from Africa, and salt oysters from sea caves, and cuttlefish, and new honey, and sweet onions, and—ugh!—water-buffalo steaks. Come, let's see what's what in the forum." And Bimbo, just as curious as his comrade, hurried on. Being a dog, he trusted his ears and nose (like Tito) more than his eyes. And so the two of them entered the center of Pompeii.

The forum was the part of the town to which everybody came at least once during the day. It was the central square, and everything happened here. There were no private houses; all was public—the chief temples, the gold and red bazaars, the silk shops, the town hall, the booths belonging to the weavers and jewel merchants, the wealthy woolen market, the shrine of the household gods. Everything glittered here. The buildings looked as if they were new—which, in a sense, they were. The earthquake of twelve years ago had brought down all the old structures and, since the citizens of Pompeii were ambitious to rival Naples and even Rome, they had seized the opportunity to rebuild the whole town. And they had done it all within a dozen years. There was scarcely a building that was older than Tito.

Tito had heard a great deal about the earthquake, though being about a year old at the time, he could scarcely remember it. This particular quake had been a light one—as earthquakes go. The weaker houses had been shaken down, parts of the outworn wall had been wrecked; but there was little loss of life, and the brilliant new Pompeii had taken the place of the old. No one knew what caused these earthquakes. Records showed they had happened in the neighborhood since the beginning of time. Sailors said that it was to teach the lazy city folk a lesson and make them appreciate those who risked the dangers of the sea to bring them luxuries and protect their town from invaders. The priests said that the gods took this way of showing their anger to those who refused to worship properly and who failed to bring enough sacrifices to the altars and (though they didn't say it in so many words) presents to the priests. The tradesmen said that the foreign merchants had corrupted the ground and it was no longer safe to traffic in imported goods that came from strange places and carried a curse with them. Everyone had a different explanation and everyone's explanation was louder and sillier than his neighbor's.

They were talking about it this afternoon as Tito and Bimbo came out of the side street into the public square. The forum was the favorite promenade[7] for rich and poor. What with the priests arguing with the politicians, servants doing the day's shopping, tradesmen crying their wares, women displaying the latest fashions from Greece and Egypt, children playing hide-and-seek among the marble columns, knots of soldiers, sailors, peasants from the provinces[8]—to say noth-

---

7. **promenade** (präm′ə·nād′): public place where people stroll.
8. **provinces:** places far from the capital, under Roman control.

- -

WORDS TO OWN
ambitious (am·bish′əs) *adj.*: eager to succeed or to achieve something.

- -

THE DOG OF POMPEII 517

---

6. **macellum** (mə·sel′əm): market, especially a meat market.

C Reading Skills and Strategies
Connecting with the Text
? What kinds of modern places resemble the ancient Roman forum? [Possible responses: a mall; a town square; a shopping center; a marketplace.]

D Critical Thinking
Making Judgments
? Do the ancient Romans sound superstitious, scientific, or both? [Possible responses: superstitious, in that they thought disasters were caused by the will of the gods; scientific, because they kept records of the volcano's activity.]

E Struggling Readers
Breaking Down Difficult Text
Help students break down this long, difficult sentence. Draw their attention to the series of phrases—beginning with the words "the priests";"servants";"women";"children";"knots"; and "those"—that precede the sentence's main clause:"the square was crowded to its last inch."

Crossing the Curriculum

Social Studies
As described on this page, the forum was the most important public space in the city in ancient Roman times. Have students research information about the evolution and structure of the forum. Students might create a historical fictional account of a day in the forum, using their imagination as well as information from their research.

Architecture
The ruins of Pompeii have helped archaeologists and architects learn about the transition from Greek to Roman architecture that was occurring in the first century A.D. Suggest that students interested in architecture conduct research into the kinds of structural design and materials that were prominent at this period of time. Some students may create drawings or scale models of temples, civic buildings, baths, or private homes.

Food
Students interested in food might want to research information about the kinds of food that were common in Pompeii and ancient Rome. In the selection, Tito describes some foods that were part of a feast. Encourage students to pursue more information in an encyclopedia or books on ancient Rome.

Ⓐ Elements of Literature

Historical Fiction

❓One tried-and-true technique of historical fiction is to present dialogue about historical issues in the mouths of fictional characters. Is Rufus right or wrong in his judgment about the volcano? [wrong]

Ⓑ Background

Sicily is a large island to the southwest of the "toe" of Italy. One of the "two towns" is probably Catania; the other may refer to any of the other municipalities that ring Mount Etna—Paternò, Biancavilla, Adrano, Bronte, Randazzo, Taormina, Riposto, Giarre, or Acireale. Situated on the eastern coast of the island, Mount Etna is (at over 10,000 feet) the highest active volcano in Europe. Scientists estimate that Etna has been active for more than two-and-a-half million years.

Ⓒ Reading Skills and Strategies

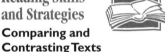

Comparing and Contrasting Texts

Have students compare the warnings of eruption from Mount St. Helens in the excerpt from *Volcano* and the warning from Vesuvius described on this page. How are the signals similar? How are they different? [Sample answer: Both eruptions were preceded by smoke and ash rising from the craters; an explosion and several earthquakes preceded the Mount St. Helens explosion; the smoke from Vesuvius became thicker.]

Ⓓ Historical Connections

Naples is the third-largest city in modern Italy (after Rome and Milan) and is the southernmost of the three. Founded as a Greek colony, it was captured by the Romans in the fourth century B.C.

Ⓔ Elements of Literature

Historical Fiction

Point out that writers of historical fiction often like to highlight similarities between their historical settings and the present. The tension between the big city of Naples and the smaller town of Pompeii reflects the sometimes troubled relations today between cities like New York, London, Rome, Tokyo, Bangkok, Bombay, Nairobi, and Buenos Aires and their suburbs.

ing of those who merely came to lounge and look on—the square was crowded to its last inch. His ears even more than his nose guided Tito to the place where the talk was loudest. It was in front of the shrine of the household gods that, naturally enough, the householders were arguing.

Ⓐ "I tell you," rumbled a voice which Tito recognized as bath master Rufus's, "there won't be another earthquake in my lifetime or yours. There may be a tremble or two, but earthquakes, like lightnings, never strike twice in the same place."

"Do they not?" asked a thin voice Tito had never heard. It had a high, sharp ring to it and Tito knew it as the accent of a stranger.

Ⓑ "How about the two towns of Sicily that have been ruined three times within fifteen years by the eruptions of Mount Etna? And were they not warned? And does that column of smoke above Vesuvius mean nothing?"

Ⓒ "That?" Tito could hear the grunt with which one question answered another.

"That's always there. We use it for our weather guide. When the smoke stands up straight, we know we'll have fair weather; when it flattens out, it's sure to be foggy; when it drifts to the east——"

"Yes, yes," cut in the edged voice. "I've heard about your mountain barometer.[9] But the column of smoke seems hundreds of feet higher than usual and it's thickening and spreading **Ⓓ** like a shadowy tree. They say in Naples——"

"Oh, Naples!" Tito knew this voice by the little squeak that went with it. It was Attilio the cameo cutter.[10] "They talk while we suffer. Little help we got from them last time. **Ⓔ** Naples commits the crimes and Pompeii pays the price. It's become a proverb with us. Let them mind their own business."

"Yes," grumbled Rufus, "and others', too."

9. **barometer** (bə·räm′ət·ər): instrument for measuring atmospheric pressure. Barometers are used in forecasting changes in the weather.

10. **cameo cutter:** artist who carves delicate pictures on gems or shells.

Taking a Second Look

Review: Describing Mental Images

Remind students that as they read they visualize details by combining descriptions in a text with prior knowledge and experience to make mental pictures of situations, characters, events, and actions in the text. In most texts, images are primarily visual; yet images can also appeal to the senses of hearing, touch, taste, and smell.

Activities

1. Have students select passages in which details are presented from Tito's vantage point. Ask students to take note of the images formed in their own mind from these descriptions. Have them think of visual details that would correspond to the author's images. Then have students expand the story passages by adding descriptions of the visual details they see in their mind.

2. Invite students to draw the scenes they have just written. Have students list the details they have added on the backs of the pictures.

"Very well, my confident friends," responded the thin voice, which now sounded curiously flat. "We also have a proverb—and it is this: *Those who will not listen to men must be taught by the gods.* I say no more. But I leave a last warning. Remember the holy ones. Look to your temples. And when the smoke tree above Vesuvius grows to the shape of an umbrella pine, look to your lives."

Tito could hear the air whistle as the speaker drew his toga about him, and the quick shuffle of feet told him the stranger had gone.

"Now what," said the cameo cutter, "did he mean by that?"

"I wonder," grunted Rufus. "I wonder."

Tito wondered, too. And Bimbo, his head at a thoughtful angle, looked as if he had been doing a heavy piece of pondering. By nightfall the argument had been forgotten. If the smoke had increased, no one saw it in the dark. Besides, it was Caesar's birthday and the town was in a holiday mood. Tito and Bimbo were among the merrymakers, dodging the charioteers who shouted at them. A dozen times they almost upset baskets of sweets and jars of Vesuvian wine, said to be as fiery as the streams inside the volcano, and a dozen times they were cursed and cuffed. But Tito never missed his footing. He was thankful for his keen ears and quick instinct—most thankful of all for Bimbo.

They visited the uncovered theater, and though Tito could not see the faces of the actors, he could follow the play better than most of the audience, for their attention wandered—they were distracted by the scenery, the costumes, the byplay, even by themselves—while Tito's whole attention was centered in what he heard. Then to the city walls, where the people of Pompeii watched a mock naval battle in which the city was at-tacked by the sea and saved after thousands of flaming arrows had been exchanged and countless colored torches had been burned. Though the thrill of flaring ships and lighted skies was lost to Tito, the shouts and cheers excited him as much as any, and he cried out with the loudest of them.

The next morning there were two of the beloved raisin-and-sugar cakes for his breakfast. Bimbo was unusually active and thumped his bit of a tail until Tito was afraid he would wear it out. The boy could not imagine whether Bimbo was urging him to some sort of game or was trying to tell him something. After a while, he ceased to notice Bimbo. He felt drowsy. Last night's late hours had tired him. Besides, there was a heavy mist in the air—no, a thick fog rather than a mist—a fog that got into his throat and scraped it and made him cough. He walked as far as the marine gate[11] to get a breath of the sea. But the blanket of haze had spread all over the bay and even the salt air seemed smoky.

He went to bed before dusk and slept. But he did not sleep well. He had too many dreams—dreams of ships lurching in the forum, of losing his way in a screaming crowd, of armies marching across his chest, of being pulled over every rough pavement of Pompeii.

He woke early. Or, rather, he was pulled awake. Bimbo was doing the pulling. The dog had dragged Tito to his feet and was urging the boy along. Somewhere. Where, Tito did not know. His feet stumbled uncertainly; he was still half asleep. For a while he noticed nothing

---

11. **marine gate:** gate in a city wall leading to the sea.

WORDS TO OWN

proverb (präv′ərb′) *n.:* well-known traditional saying that expresses a truth.

THE DOG OF POMPEII **519**

Skill Link

Identifying How Sayings Reflect Cultures

Every culture has wise sayings, or proverbs. In "The Dog of Pompeii," the author cites the Roman saying "Those who will not listen to men must be taught by the gods."

Activity

Have students discuss this saying in light of what it reveals about cultural and religious values in ancient Rome. [Students might mention such ideas as the Romans' belief in more than one divine power, in the importance of responsibility and prudence in human affairs, and in the possibility that the gods can inflict hardship.] In addition, have students brainstorm more recent sayings (from American culture or other cultures) that convey a similar central idea. [Possible responses include "Those who live by the sword die by the sword," "An ounce of prevention is worth a pound of cure," and "Forewarned is forearmed."]

Introduce the term *archaeology* to students and ask if anyone knows what it means. Explain that archaeologists study the civilizations and cultures of the past by examining the things the people of those cultures left behind. Archaeologists dig up the remains of ancient towns, villages, or campsites. Pottery, sculpture, writing on clay tablets, jewelry, clothing, building materials, human bones, and food remains are among the items that give archaeologists clues to the way the people of the past lived. Usually, these items are found broken rather than whole, and when there are enough fragments of a single item, they must be pieced together skillfully. More often, archaeologists make inferences from assorted fragments of various objects. Encourage students to think of archaeology as a kind of detective work that discovers clues to the ancient cultures of such peoples as the Aztecs, Mayans, Romans, Greeks, Egyptians, and Hebrews.

Ⓐ Reading Skills and Strategies

Comparing and Contrasting Texts

❓ Compare and contrast Louis Untermeyer's and Patricia Lauber's descriptions of volcanic eruptions. How would you explain some of the similarities and differences? [Both authors use imaginative language effectively. Lauber's account is more scientific than Untermeyer's. His descriptions, on the other hand, contain a sense of mystery and dread—perhaps because his account of the eruption is filtered through the experiences of individual characters.]

Ⓑ Struggling Readers

Visualizing

Encourage students to visualize this scene to clarify what is happening. Help students to understand that the people of Pompeii are panicking and running past Tito and Bimbo.

LITERATURE AND SOCIAL STUDIES

A City Frozen in Time

The volcano that destroyed the city of Pompeii also preserved it. Excavations there began in the eighteenth century. Archaeologists brought the past to life as they uncovered buildings, furniture, food, paintings, and tools. They also found about two thousand hollow forms of humans and animals that had been frozen in place by the ash that buried them.

An Italian archaeologist named Giuseppe Fiorelli found a way to make molds of the bodies, by pumping a kind of liquid plaster into the forms they had left in the ashes. When the plaster hardened, the ash around it was chipped off. The remaining plaster casts are perfect images of the buried bodies.

Today three quarters of old Pompeii has been unearthed. You can visit Pompeii as a tourist; no time machine is necessary. You can walk the same streets, look at the same buildings, and stare at the same volcano, sleeping for now, that the unsuspecting residents of Pompeii saw for the last time on that day nearly two thousand years ago.

Ⓐ except the fact that it was hard to breathe. The air was hot. And heavy. So heavy that he could taste it. The air, it seemed, had turned to powder—a warm powder that stung his nostrils and burned his sightless eyes.

Then he began to hear sounds. Peculiar sounds. Like animals under the earth. Hissings and groanings and muffled cries that a dying creature might make dislodging the stones of his underground cave. There was no doubt of it now. The noises came from underneath. He not only heard them—he could feel them. The earth twitched; the twitching changed to an uneven shrugging of the soil. Then, as Bimbo half pulled, half coaxed him across, the ground jerked away from his feet and he was thrown against a stone fountain.

The water—hot water—splashing in his face revived him. He got to his feet, Bimbo steadying him, helping him on again. The noises grew louder; they came closer. The cries were even more animal-like than before, but now they came from human Ⓑ throats. A few people, quicker of foot and more hurried by fear, began to rush by. A family or two—then a section—then, it seemed, an army broken out of bounds. Tito, bewildered though he was, could recognize Rufus as he bellowed past him, like a water buffalo gone mad. Time was lost in a nightmare.

It was then the crashing began. First a sharp crackling, like a monstrous snapping of twigs; then a roar like the fall of a whole forest of trees; then an explosion that tore earth and sky. The heavens, though Tito could not

---

WORDS TO OWN

coaxed (kōkst) *v.*: gently urged or tried to persuade.
revived (ri·vīvd′) *v.*: brought back to life or to a waking state.

Crossing the Curriculum

Social Studies

The eruption of Mt. Vesuvius may have become the best-known event of A.D. 79, but most people in the world at the time were unaware of it because of the absence of news media. Moreover, throughout and beyond the Roman Empire and in the non-Roman world too, other fascinating things were happening. Have groups of students do library research to find out what other important events occurred in A.D. 79. What was happening in the city of Rome as well as in China, India, Africa, and North and South America?

Have groups design the front page of a newspaper that includes at least one story from each continent. The newspaper should have an appropriate name and illustrations. Encourage each student to contribute at least one story. Allow students to broaden the time span (to a decade or a generation, if they wish) and to report on broad developments as well as specific events.

see them, were shot through with continual flickerings of fire. Lightnings above were answered by thunders beneath. A house fell. Then another. By a miracle the two companions had escaped the dangerous side streets and were in a more open space. It was the forum. They rested here awhile—how long, he did not know.

Tito had no idea of the time of day. He could feel it was black—an unnatural blackness. Something inside—perhaps the lack of breakfast and lunch—told him it was past noon. But it didn't matter. Nothing seemed to matter. He was getting drowsy, too drowsy to walk. But walk he must. He knew it. And Bimbo knew it; the sharp tugs told him so. Nor was it a moment too soon. The sacred ground of the forum was safe no longer. It was beginning to rock, then to pitch, then to split. As they stumbled out of the square, the earth wriggled like a caught snake and all the columns of the temple of Jupiter[12] came down. It was the end of the world—or so it seemed. To walk was not enough now. They must run. Tito was too frightened to know what to do or where to go. He had lost all sense of direction. He started to go back to the inner gate; but Bimbo, straining his back to the last inch, almost pulled his clothes from him. What did the creature want? Had the dog gone mad?

Then suddenly he understood. Bimbo was telling him the way out—urging him there. The sea gate, of course. The sea gate—and then the sea. Far from falling buildings, heaving ground. He turned, Bimbo guiding him across open pits and dangerous pools of bubbling mud, away from buildings that had caught fire and were dropping their burning beams. Tito could no longer tell whether the

12. **Jupiter:** the supreme god in the religion of the Romans.

noises were made by the shrieking sky or the agonized people. He and Bimbo ran on—the only silent beings in a howling world.

New dangers threatened. All Pompeii seemed to be thronging toward the marine gate and, squeezing among the crowds, there was the chance of being trampled to death. But the chance had to be taken. It was growing harder and harder to breathe. What air there was choked him. It was all dust now—dust and pebbles, pebbles as large as beans. They fell on his head, his hands—pumice stones from the black heart of Vesuvius. The mountain was turning itself inside out. Tito remembered a phrase that the stranger had said in the forum two days ago: "Those who will not listen to men must be taught by the gods." The people of Pompeii had refused to heed the warnings; they were being taught now—if it was not too late.

Suddenly it seemed too late for Tito. The red-hot ashes blistered his skin, the stinging vapors tore his throat. He could not go on. He staggered toward a small tree at the side of the road and fell. In a moment Bimbo was beside him. He coaxed. But there was no answer. He licked Tito's hands, his feet, his face. The boy did not stir. Then Bimbo did the last thing he could—the last thing he wanted to do. He bit his comrade, bit him deep in the arm. With a cry of pain, Tito jumped to his feet, Bimbo after him. Tito was in despair, but Bimbo was determined. He drove the boy on, snapping at his heels, worrying his way through the crowd, barking, baring his teeth, heedless of kicks or falling stones. Sick with hunger, half dead with fear and sulfur fumes, Tito pounded on, pursued by Bimbo. How long, he never knew. At last he staggered through the marine gate and felt soft sand under him. Then Tito fainted. . . .

C Elements of Literature

Historical Fiction

Of course, one aspect of the "miracle" of Tito's survival is the fact that he is a fictional character. You might wish to point out that the protagonist in historical fiction is often the reader's "person on the scene." The author faces the challenge of how to keep this key character alive for as long as possible without straining the reader's sense of belief.

D Critical Thinking

Making Connections

After students have read Robert Silverberg's article, "Pompeii" (p. 524), they will understand that Tito's drowsiness is caused by carbon monoxide poisoning from the gas released by the eruption. You might wish to have them return to this passage briefly after reading "Pompeii."

E English Language Learners

Finding Sequence of Events

Guide students through this potentially challenging sentence containing three infinitives. You might ask a student volunteer to read the sentence aloud as other students listen for words that indicate that more than one event is being described. If necessary, draw students' attention to the way the author uses the word *then* twice to indicate a particular order of events.

F Critical Thinking

Making Judgments

? What lesson do you think the people are being taught? [Possible responses: to take precautions; to heed the warnings of the wise; to respect nature.]

G Reading Skills and Strategies

Responding to the Text

? What did you think or feel when Bimbo bit Tito? [Possible answers: shocked; upset.] **Do you think Bimbo did the right thing?** [Possible responses: Yes, the act saved Tito's life; no, because a dog should never bite its master.]

Making the Connections

Connecting to the Theme:
"Explaining Our World:
  Fact and Fiction"

Historical fiction is, for many readers, one of the most enjoyable ways to learn facts about the past. For writers of this genre, factual research is a necessary part of the writing process; yet readers should not necessarily accept all the details in a work of historical fiction as factually accurate. Point out to students that fiction writers have license to alter, and sometimes even distort, the historical record for the sake of

entertainment. After guiding students through a discussion of these issues, invite them (as a class) to search "The Dog of Pompeii" for information about the Roman Empire in A.D. 79. Then have them conduct research in the library or on the Internet to verify the accuracy of the facts in the selection.

Activity. Ask students to work in small groups to prepare a first-person account of the events depicted in the illustration. Have students develop the narrative with Tito as the narrator and remind them to have Tito retell not only what happened to him but how he felt about his experiences. They might imagine Tito retelling his experiences years later to a younger listener. Have one student from each group read the group's narrative to the class.

522

Someone was dashing seawater over him. Someone was carrying him toward a boat.

"Bimbo," he called. And then louder, "Bimbo!" But Bimbo had disappeared.

Voices jarred against each other. "Hurry— hurry!" "To the boats!" "Can't you see the child's frightened and starving!" "He keeps  calling for someone!" "Poor boy, he's out of his mind." "Here, child—take this!"

They tucked him in among them. The oarlocks creaked; the oars splashed; the boat rode over toppling waves. Tito was safe. But he wept continually.

"Bimbo!" he wailed. "Bimbo! Bimbo!"

He could not be comforted.

Eighteen hundred years passed. Scientists were restoring the ancient city; excavators were working their way through the stones and trash that had buried the entire town. Much had already been brought to light—statues, bronze instruments, bright mosaics,[13] household articles; even delicate paintings had been preserved by the fall of ashes that had taken over two thousand lives. Columns were dug up, and the forum was beginning to emerge.

It was at a place where the ruins lay deepest that the director paused.

"Come here," he called to his assistant. "I think we've discovered the remains of a building in good shape. Here are four huge millstones that were most likely turned by slaves or mules—and here is a whole wall standing with shelves inside it. Why! It must have been a bakery. And here's a curious thing. What do you think I found under this heap where the ashes were thickest? The skeleton of a dog!"

13. **mosaics** (mō-zā′iks): pictures or designs made by inlaying small bits of stone, glass, tile, or other materials in mortar.

"Amazing!" gasped his assistant. "You'd think a dog would have had sense enough to run away at the time. And what is that flat thing he's holding between his teeth? It can't be a stone."

"No. It must have come from this bakery. You know it looks to me like some sort of cake hardened with the years. And, bless me, if those little black pebbles aren't raisins. A raisin cake almost two thousand years old! I wonder what made him want it at such a moment."

"I wonder," murmured the assistant.

MEET THE WRITER

Reviving an Old World

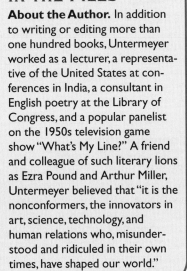

Louis Untermeyer (1885–1977) may have been thinking of this story when he described the writer's job as the "struggle somehow to revive an old world, or create a new one."

As a child, Untermeyer loved to read, but he disliked school, especially math. His parents expected him to go to college, but he dropped out of high school when he was sixteen. For the next twenty-two years he worked in his family's jewelry business. He says he did not become serious about working or writing until he met the poet Robert Frost in 1915. Frost became Untermeyer's lifelong friend. It was Frost who encouraged Untermeyer to quit his day job and become a full-time writer.

Today Untermeyer is best known not for his own writing but for the very popular collections of poetry he put together, some for children and some for adults. In his autobiography *From Another World* he describes himself as a friend to three generations of poets.

THE DOG OF POMPEII **523**

 A **Struggling Readers**
Reading Aloud
Encourage students to read this paragraph aloud and to use a different voice for each separate speech. Draw their attention to the opening and closing quotation marks that indicate six separate exclamations from as many as six speakers.

B **Reading Skills and Strategies**
Comparing and Contrasting Texts
Untermeyer's narrative advances almost two thousand years in one bold sentence. Patricia Lauber moves forward just a short distance in time to discuss the aftermath of the eruption of Mount St. Helens. Ask how each writer's strategy is appropriate for his or her subject. [Possible response: Eighteen hundred years really did pass before the destruction of Pompeii became "news" again. However, the eruption of Mount St. Helens was immediate news around the world.]

Resources
Selection Assessment
Formal Assessment
• Selection Test, p. 98
Test Generator
• Selection Test

BROWSING IN THE FILES
About the Author. In addition to writing or editing more than one hundred books, Untermeyer worked as a lecturer, a representative of the United States at conferences in India, a consultant in English poetry at the Library of Congress, and a popular panelist on the 1950s television game show "What's My Line?" A friend and colleague of such literary lions as Ezra Pound and Arthur Miller, Untermeyer believed that "it is the nonconformers, the innovators in art, science, technology, and human relations who, misunderstood and ridiculed in their own times, have shaped our world."

Assessing Learning

Check Test: True-False
1. Pompeii was a city in the ancient Roman Empire. [True]
2. Pompeii was destroyed by a flood in A.D. 79. [False]
3. Tito walks on crutches with the aid of Bimbo. [False]
4. Tito and Bimbo are killed when Pompeii is destroyed. [False]
5. The reader last sees Bimbo with a raisin cake in his mouth. [True]

Standardized Test Preparation
For practice with standardized test format specific to this selection, see
• *Standardized Test Preparation*, pp. 72, 74
For practice in proofreading and editing, see
• *Daily Oral Grammar*, Transparency 31

Connections

This is a piece of historical writing based on research, specifically on the human and animal remains unearthed by archaeologists in the ruins of Pompeii. To enliven the history, the author has created plausible anecdotes about the attempts of some citizens to escape the disastrous volcanic eruptions of A.D. 79.

Ⓐ Reading Skills and Strategies

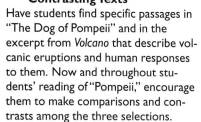

Comparing and Contrasting Texts

Have students find specific passages in "The Dog of Pompeii" and in the excerpt from *Volcano* that describe volcanic eruptions and human responses to them. Now and throughout students' reading of "Pompeii," encourage them to make comparisons and contrasts among the three selections.

Ⓑ Critical Thinking

Determining Author's Purpose

❓ On what might Robert Silverberg have based his account of the behavior of a specific dog in ancient Pompeii? [Possible response: A dog's skeleton may have been found by archaeologists. Of course, those archaeologists would not have seen the dog struggling or heard it barking. These details are deduced by the author from his knowledge of dogs and how they would be likely to behave in these circumstances.] What is the purpose of made-up details in a non-fiction article or book? [Possible responses: They make history seem real for the reader; they are entertaining.]

Ⓒ Background

An earthquake following a volcanic eruption is no coincidence: volcanic eruptions can cause local earthquakes.

Connections | **A HISTORY**

POMPEII

Robert Silverberg

Ⓐ The people of Pompeii knew that doom was on hand, now. Their fears were doubled when an enormous rain of hot ashes began to fall on them, along with more lapilli.[1] Pelted with stones, half smothered by ashes, the Pompeiians cried to the gods for mercy. The wooden roofs of some of the houses began to catch fire as the heat of the ashes reached them. Other buildings were collapsing under the weight of the pumice stones that had fallen on them.

In those first few hours, only the quick-witted managed to escape. Vesonius Primus, the wealthy wool merchant, called his family together and piled jewelry and money into a sack. Lighting a torch, Vesonius led his little band out into the nightmare of the streets. Ⓑ Overlooked in the confusion was Vesonius' black watchdog, chained in the courtyard. The terrified dog barked wildly as lapilli struck and drifting white ash settled around him. The animal struggled with his chain, battling fiercely to get free, but the chain held, and no one heard the dog's cries. The humans were too busy saving themselves.

Many hundreds of Pompeiians fled in those first few dark hours. Stumbling in the darkness, they made their way to the city gates, then out, down to the harbor. They boarded boats and got away, living to tell the tale of their city's destruction. Others preferred to remain within the city, huddling inside the temples, or in the public baths, or in the cellars of their homes. They still hoped that the nightmare would end—that the tranquility of a few hours ago would return. . . .

It was evening, now. And new woe was in store for Pompeii. The earth trembled and quaked! Roofs that had somehow withstood the rain of lapilli went crashing in ruin, bury-Ⓒing hundreds who had hoped to survive the eruption. In the forum, tall columns toppled as they had in 63.[2] Those who remembered that great earthquake screamed in new terror as the entire city seemed to shake in the grip of a giant fist.

Three feet of lapilli now covered the ground. Ash floated in the air. Gusts of poisonous gas came drifting from the belching crater, though people could still breathe. Roofs were collapsing everywhere. Rushing throngs, blinded by the darkness and the smoke, hurtled madly up one street and down the next, trampling the fallen in a crazy, fruitless dash toward safety. Dozens of people plunged into dead-end streets and found themselves trapped by crashing buildings. They waited there, too frightened to run farther, expecting the end.

The rich man Diomedes was another of those who decided not to flee at the first sign of alarm. Rather than risk being crushed by the screaming mobs, Diomedes calmly led the members of his household into the solidly built basement of his villa. Sixteen people

1. **lapilli** (lə·pil'ī'): small pieces of hardened lava.

2. There had been an earthquake in Pompeii sixteen years before Vesuvius erupted.

524 EXPLAINING OUR WORLD: FACT AND FICTION

Connecting Across Texts

Connecting with "The Dog of Pompeii"

"Pompeii" and "The Dog of Pompeii" describe the same historical event from two different standpoints: the former is nonfiction, and the latter is historical fiction. In "Pompeii," the author's primary purpose is informing the reader about the eruption, whereas Untermeyer's primary purpose is entertaining the reader. To achieve his purpose, each author combines techniques of narrative and informa-tive writing; each incorporates careful research on the facts of the eruption gleaned from archaeological evidence, and each uses characters—human and animal—whose individual dramas give special life to the story of the eruption. In "The Dog of Pompeii," however, the characters are central to the work and are involved in a plot; in "Pompeii," they merely illustrate historical events.

"Pompeii" can also be compared and contrasted with the excerpt from *Volcano*. In each of these nonfiction articles about volcanic eruptions, the author uses imaginative language to describe scenes; both Silverberg and Lauber also explain scientific terms and make cause-effect connections.

T524

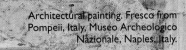

Architectural painting. Fresco from Pompeii, Italy, Museo Archeologico Nazionale, Naples, Italy.

altogether, as well as his daughter's dog and her beloved little goat. They took enough food and water to last for several days.

But for all his shrewdness and foresight, Diomedes was undone anyway. Poison gas was creeping slowly into the underground shelter! He watched his daughter begin to cough and struggle for breath. Vesuvius was giving off vast quantities of deadly carbon monoxide that was now settling like a blanket over the dying city.

"We can't stay here!" Diomedes gasped. Better to risk the uncertainties outside than to remain here and suffocate. "I'll open the door," he told them. "Wait for me here."

Accompanied only by an old and faithful servant, who carried a lantern to light Diomedes' way in the inky blackness, the nobleman stumbled toward the door. He held the silver key in his hand. Another few steps and he would have been at the door, he could have opened it, they could have fled into the air—but a shroud of gas swooped down on him. He fell, still clutching the key, dying within minutes. Beneath the porch, fourteen people waited hopefully for him, their lives ticking away with each second. Diomedes did not return. At the last moment, all fourteen embraced each other, servants and masters alike, as death took them.

The poison gas thickened as the terrible night continued. It was possible to hide from the lapilli, but not from the gas, and Pompeiians died by the hundreds. Carbon monoxide gas keeps the body from absorbing oxygen. Victims of carbon monoxide poisoning get sleepier and sleepier, until they lose consciousness, never to regain it. All over Pompeii, people lay down in the beds of lapilli, overwhelmed by the gas, and death came quietly to them. Even those who had made their way outside the city now fell victim to the spreading clouds of gas. It covered the entire countryside.

In a lane near the forum, a hundred people were trapped by a blind-alley wall. Others hid in the stoutly built public bathhouses, protected against collapsing roofs but not against the deadly gas. Near the house of Diomedes, a beggar and his little goat sought shelter. The man fell dead a few feet from Diomedes' door; the faithful goat remained by his side, its silver bell tinkling, until its turn came.

All through the endless night, Pompeiians wandered about the streets or crouched in their ruined homes or clustered in the temples to pray. By morning, few remained alive. Not once had Vesuvius stopped hurling lapilli and ash into the air, and the streets of Pompeii were filling quickly. At midday on August 25, exactly twenty-four hours after the beginning of the holocaust,[3] a second eruption racked the volcano. A second cloud of ashes rose above Vesuvius' summit. The wind blew ash as far as Rome and Egypt. But most of the new ashes descended on Pompeii.

The deadly shower of stone and ashes went unslackening into its second day. But it no longer mattered to Pompeii whether the eruption continued another day or another year. For by midday on August 25, Pompeii was a city of the dead.

3. **holocaust:** great destruction of life.

THE DOG OF POMPEII **525**

Getting Students Involved

MAKING MEANINGS

First Thoughts

1. Possible responses: Bimbo behaves like real dogs in the news who save their masters.

Shaping Interpretations

2. Untermeyer shifts the setting to a twentieth-century archaeological dig on the site of Pompeii; the change creates dramatic surprise and brings readers closer to the story. The mystery of Bimbo's disappearance is answered.

3. Possible responses: carbon monoxide poisoning, panicking crowds, falling volcanic material, and preserved remains are found in both selections.

4. The story provides human emotion and shows the effects of historical events on specific characters whom we have come to know well.

Connecting with the Text

5. Possible response: The dog loved his master so much (or was so bound by habit) that it risked death in order to get his master's daily food.

6. Possible responses: glad he's alive; grateful for Bimbo's heroic action; grief-stricken over Bimbo's death; confused.

7. Possible responses: I would have run to the first available boat; I would have panicked.

Challenging the Text

8. Possible response: The story is still exciting because of its interesting characters and dramatic events.

Extending the Text

9. Possible response: People are thrilled by danger and fear injury or death. Stories about danger provide thrills without the possibility of physical harm. Students should provide appropriate supporting reasons for liking or disliking a specific disaster film.

T526

MAKING MEANINGS

First Thoughts

[connect] 1. Does Bimbo behave like any real dogs you've known or read about? Give an example.

Shaping Interpretations

[synthesize] 2. Where are we at the end of the story? Why do you think Untermeyer changes the setting near the story's end? What big question is answered at the end of the story?

[compare]   3. Compare details in the story with details in "Pompeii" (see *Connections* on page 524). Find three details that are similar in the two texts.

[respond] 4. "The Dog of Pompeii" is an example of **historical fiction**. How does the story add to your understanding of the eruption of Vesuvius? What does it give you that you don't get from Silverberg's historical account?

Connecting with the Text

[infer] 5. How would you answer the question the director asks at the end about the raisin cake?

[connect] 6. How do you think Tito feels several days after the eruption of Vesuvius? Describe how he might feel about what Bimbo did for him.

[connect]   7. What would you have done if you had been in Pompeii the day Vesuvius erupted? Look back at your Quickwrite notes for ideas.

Challenging the Text

[generalize] 8. "The Dog of Pompeii" was first published in 1932. Do you think the story is still interesting to readers today? Why or why not?

Extending the Text

[generalize] 9. Why do you think stories and movies about disaster are so popular? Think of a disaster movie you've seen recently, and tell what you liked and what you didn't like about it.

Reading Check

a. Why does Tito depend on Bimbo to bring food?

b. What sign does the volcano give before it erupts?

c. In what two ways does Bimbo help Tito escape?

d. What finally happens to Bimbo?

e. Why are scientists surprised to find a dog buried in the ruins?

Reading Check

a. Tito is a poor, blind orphan.

b. Its smoke thickens and spreads.

c. Bimbo guides Tito through the crowd and wakes him with a bite.

d. Bimbo dies trying to get a raisin cake for Tito.

e. They feel that an unchained dog could have escaped.

CHOICES: Building Your Portfolio

Writer's Notebook

1. Collecting Ideas for Observational Writing

Untermeyer paints a detailed picture of ancient Pompeii. We feel as if he had been there and seen its markets and shops, smelled its odors, and observed its people and their activities. Take notes on a place you know well, perhaps one where you can sit and observe for a while. Describe what you see, smell, and hear. Try to find details that reveal how you feel about the place.

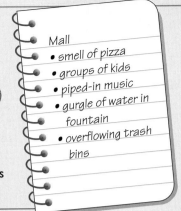

Mall
- smell of pizza
- groups of kids
- piped-in music
- gurgle of water in fountain
- overflowing trash bins

Comparing Texts

2. It's a Dog's Life

Writers know that people are interested in animals, and they often use animal characters in stories to reveal something to us about our own lives. Compare the dog in "Storm" (see page 97) with Bimbo, the dog of Pompeii. Is the writer of each story trying to say something about how *people* should live and act?

Creative Writing/Art

3. Bring Bimbo Back

Do you think the ending of "The Dog of Pompeii" is too sad? Rewrite the story from the point where Tito staggers toward the marine gate. You may want to leave out the shift in setting or to change what the scientists found. Create an illustration for your "happy ending."

Research/ Narrative Writing

4. Historical Fiction

Think of another historical event or period, and write a story about an imaginary person who was there. Possibilities include the building of the Pyramids, life in the ancient Greek city of Sparta or Athens, and the first Thanksgiving at Plymouth. To make your story authentic, do some research.

VOCABULARY HOW TO OWN A WORD

WORD BANK	Creature Questions
ambitious	1. Do you think that an <u>ambitious</u> owner could make any dog a star?
proverb	2. Write a <u>proverb</u> that expresses a truth about animals.
coaxed	3. If you <u>coaxed</u> a cat and a dog, which one might be persuaded first?
revived	4. How would you create a <u>revived</u> interest in saving an endangered species?

THE DOG OF POMPEII 527

Grading Timesaver

Rubrics for each Choices assignment appear on p. 167 in the *Portfolio Management System*.

CHOICES: Building Your Portfolio

1. **Writer's Notebook** Remind students to save their work. They may use it as prewriting for the Writer's Workshop on pp. 562–566.
2. **Comparing Texts** Have groups of two to four students discuss the comparison, using charts to keep track of the points they make.
3 and 4. **Creative Writing/Art/ Research/Narrative Writing** Encourage students to "publish" a class magazine containing their new story endings, illustrations, and historical narratives. Some students may act as fact checkers to be sure that the historical information in the narratives is accurate.

VOCABULARY
Possible Answers
1. An owner who sets high goals for his pet could certainly get a lot of recognition.
2. Dogs are man's best friend.
3. Dogs are more easily persuaded to come, sit, or stay, but especially when they are rewarded with food.
4. I would choose an endangered species that received a lot of media attention some time ago, the spotted owl, say, and then I would create a new advertising campaign that includes a Web site.

OBJECTIVES

1. Read and interpret the folk tale.
2. Identify and analyze a how-and-why tale
3. Establish purposes for reading
4. Express understanding through writing, creative writing, and critical writing/science
5. Punctuate adjectives in a series correctly
6. Understand and use strategies for spelling words with silent consonants

SKILLS

Literary
- Identify and analyze a how-and-why tale

Reading
- Establish purposes for reading

Writing
- Collect ideas for observational writing
- Write a how-and-why story
- Write a scientific report about the galaxy

Grammar/Language
- Use commas to separate adjectives in a series

Planning

- **Block Schedule**
  Block Scheduling Lesson Plans with Pacing Guide
- **Traditional Schedule**
  Lesson Plans Including Strategies for English-Language Learners
- **One-Stop Planner**
  CD-ROM with Test Generator

Before You Read

THE SEVENTH SISTER

Make the Connection

I Wonder

Life is full of *why* questions: Why do two stars shine more brightly than the rest? Why do dogs bury bones? Why do crickets chirp?

Think-pair-share.

Make up three questions about things in nature you're curious about. Share your list with a partner. Together, choose one question that appeals to both of you. Think of some ideas for a fun story to explain the answer to your question.

Quickwrite

Write down the story ideas that you liked best. Save your notes to use after you've read the selection.

Elements of Literature

How-and-Why Tales: Q-and-A Stories

Before scientists discovered some of the answers to puzzling *why* questions, people around the world used their imaginations to explain what they saw in nature. They made up stories like "The Seventh Sister" to explain how something in the world came to be.

> **A how-and-why tale** is a story that explains *how* something came to be and *why* it is the way it is.

Reading Skills and Strategies

Establishing Purposes for Reading: Matching Purpose to Text

We read for many purposes. We read for enjoyment, to solve a problem or get information, or to gain a better understanding of people, including ourselves. Often we have several purposes when we read. Here is a how-and-why story told long ago that explains how two special stars came to be. What purpose would you establish for reading this story?

HRW go.hrw.com
LE0 6-7

The Seventh Sister

a Chinese folk tale, retold by
Cindy Chang

528 EXPLAINING OUR WORLD: FACT AND FICTION

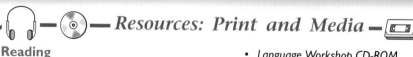

Resources: Print and Media

Reading
- *Reading Skills and Strategies*
  MiniRead Skill Lesson, p. 161
  Selection Skill Lesson, p. 170
- *Graphic Organizers for Active Reading*, p. 34
- *Spelling and Decoding*, Worksheet, p. 22
- *Audio CD Library*, Disc 13, Track 2

Writing and Language
- *Daily Oral Grammar*, Transparency 32
- *Grammar and Language Links*, Worksheet, p. 47

- *Language Workshop CD-ROM*

Assessment
- *Formal Assessment*, p. 100
- *Portfolio Management System*, p. 169
- *Standardized Test Preparation*, p. 76
- *Test Generator (One-Stop Planner CD-ROM)*

Internet
- go.hrw.com (keyword: LE0 6-7)

Long ago, in the heavens above, seven beautiful maidens wove the glorious tapestry° of the night sky. Each night, celestial magpies spread the tapestry over the earth. But the sun's early rays melted the night, so that day after day, the maidens' nimble fingers had to fly across their looms to complete their task before sunset. They sang as they worked, and their music drifted through the clickety-clack, clickety-clack of their looms.

°**tapestry:** heavy woven cloth with decorative designs and pictures.

"Happiness shall be yours, gentle man."

THE SEVENTH SISTER **529**

Summary ■ ■

This ancient Chinese folk tale tells of seven beautiful maidens who have the daily task of weaving the tapestry of the night sky. Each new day arrives when the sun's rays melt the tapestry. One day, as the sisters fill their jars at a silver pond at the end of the rainbow, Chang, a cowherd, sees them and falls in love with the youngest, Mei. As instructed by a magpie in a dream, Chang hides Mei's magic robe, so she is unable to return to the sky. Instead, she stays and falls in love with Chang. The next day, the sun refuses to move across the sky. Mei realizes that the sun is angry at her; she must return to her weaving so that night can fall. Separated from Chang, Mei weeps, and her tears form the stars of the Milky Way. In another dream, Chang learns how to reach Mei. Once a year, a flock of magpies forms a bridge across the Milky Way so that the two lovers can be together for a single night. Chang and Mei can be seen as stars in the night sky. Thus, the how-and-why tale explains how and why the Milky Way and the bright stars on either side of it came to be.

Resources ────

Listening

Audio CD Library

A recording of this folk tale is provided in the *Audio CD Library:*
• Disc 13, Track 2

Selection Assessment

Formal Assessment
• Selection Test, p. 100

Test Generator
• Selection Test

Crossing the Curriculum

Music

If possible, invite students to listen to recordings of Chinese folk songs from a local library's audio collection. Ask students to think about—and to describe—how the Chinese songs compare and contrast with folk or popular music from another culture.

Art

After students have finished reading the folk tale, encourage them to design and create their own illustrations for the story. Remind them to choose from a variety of media, including collage, different types of paint, pencils, charcoal, markers, and clay.

**Establishing
Purposes for Reading**

? Reflect on the purposes you established for reading this folk tale. Do you think the tale will give you a better understanding of people? Will it contain useful information? Will it be enjoyable to read? [Students may already sense that any or all of these purposes are appropriate for reading "The Seventh Sister."]

B Reading Skills and Strategies

Comparing/Contrasting

? How are Mei and Chang different and alike? [Sample responses: Mei lives in the sky and Chang on earth. She makes fine silks, and he works the soil. They both work; both are sad and lonely; both make music.]

C Critical Thinking

Making Judgments

? What do you think of Chang's taking Mei's robe as a way of gaining her love? [Possible responses: It seems unfair, cruel, selfish, and self-defeating; in a folk tale, it makes sense to follow instructions given in a dream; taking it is necessary to their meeting.]

D Appreciating Language

**Using Commas to Separate
Adjectives in a Series**

Point out the commas between *cool* and *babbling* and between *warm* and *rising*. Tell students that an important rule of grammar is that a comma separates two or more adjectives that precede the noun they modify. Mention that students will practice the rules for such comma usage in the Grammar Link on p. 536.

Though all the sisters were known for their beauty and talent, the youngest, Mei, was the most clever. She made silks finer than the fluffiest clouds, and cloth more colorful than the brightest birds. Yet, even surrounded by the beauty of heaven, Mei was sad and lonely, and her sad song echoed through the sky.

Below, in the grassy lowlands of China, there lived a cowherd named Chang. Every morning, he would rise before the sun and eat a meal of rice porridge and tea. Chang would then begin his long day in the fields, plowing and tilling the soil with his only companion, an ox.

One evening, after a long hot day, Chang rested upon the bank of a small gentle stream. "Even though you are only an ox, you are my closest friend," Chang sighed. "I am not happy, but I do not know what I am missing. Perhaps the answers are in the stars." Then he looked into the sky and filled the air with the sweet, sad songs of his flute.

As night fell, the sky turned from blue to lavender and Chang drifted off to sleep. He dreamed that a magpie flew to him and spoke. "Happiness shall be yours, gentle man. Follow the willow trees to the silver pond where the rainbow ends. There, seven maidens gather water to brighten the stars in the sky. The youngest and fairest is Mei. She will remain with you, if you remember one thing. You must hide her magical outer robe, for without it she cannot return to the heavens." With that, the magpie flew away.

Chang awoke with a start. He looked at his ox, resting in the still waters. "I know of no magical ponds," Chang said softly. "Perhaps it is only a silly dream." He patted his ox fondly. "We need to be on the lookout for magical ponds!" laughed Chang as he stared into the night.

The next morning brought a soft, misty rain. Chang set off through the wetness toward a distant field. He passed a small pond shaded from the rain by graceful willow trees. As he stopped to look, the morning's mist began to turn into a rainbow. And beneath the rainbow were seven maidens, chatting and singing.

Each maiden was filling a jar made of moonbeams with water from the pond. And, though each was more lovely than the other, Chang thought the youngest was the fairest of all. "My life would be complete if this fair maiden were part of it," Chang thought.

As he watched, Chang noticed seven robes upon the trees in the distance and remembered his dream. "It is just as the magpie said!" Chang whispered to his ox. Quietly, he grabbed the most delicate robe and hid it.

As the afternoon shadows grew longer, a magpie's song rang through the willows. One by one, the maidens took their outer robes and flew back to their celestial homes. All except for Mei, who looked frantically for hers. Her sisters called for her to hurry. Mei started to cry as she watched her sisters leaving her behind.

Mei's tears were more than Chang's heart could bear. He stepped forward from his hiding place and played a soft song of welcome. Mei smiled at his song, which told of cool, babbling streams and the warm, rising sun. She sang to him about the white sky and her own unhappiness. Soon love songs fluttered about them like butterflies.

The two were so happy, they never noticed that the sun rose earlier than usual the next morning. Mei sent Chang off to work with a kiss, a noon meal of pork and rice wrapped in tea leaves, and a loving scratch for Ox.

Reaching All Students

Struggling Readers

Establishing Purposes for Reading is introduced on p. 528. For a lesson in which students establish purpose using a strategy called Probable Passage, see the *Reading Skills and Strategies* binder

- MiniRead Skill Lesson, p. 161
- Selection Skill Lesson, p. 170

English Language Learners

Work with students to list the words they do not know. Then have them form groups to make a master list of unfamiliar words and to share the task of studying the context and looking up the words in a dictionary. Each group can then prepare its own glossary of difficult words from the selection. For additional strategies to supplement instruction, see

- *Lesson Plans Including Strategies for English-Language Learners*

Advanced Learners

Tell students that folk tales have *motifs*, that is, simple story elements that appear in somewhat different forms in many folk tales. Ask students to find ideas, images, or situations in "The Seventh Sister" that remind them of similar elements in other folk tales. Then invite students to find other tales containing motifs such as celestial siblings, weaving as fate, love between humans and other-worldly beings, and trickery.

LITERATURE AND ASTRONOMY

Diamonds in the Sky

The Milky Way is a giant galaxy of stars, dust, and gas held in place by gravity (the tendency of objects in space to move toward one another). For many years, scientists depicted the galaxy as a pinwheel-shaped spiral with star-studded arms. New evidence, however, suggests that the Milky Way may actually be made up of a thick bar of stars with two or more curved arms at each end of the bar. Whatever its exact shape, the Milky Way galaxy is our home. Our star—the Sun—is just one of billions of stars in the Milky Way, and the Milky Way is just one of billions of galaxies in the universe.

Over the centuries, people from many cultures around the world have been fascinated by the great "river of light" that the Milky Way forms in the night sky, and they have made up stories about it. The Sumerians saw the Milky Way as a great serpent. The Vikings thought the pale light of the galaxy was the road their dead warriors followed on the way to their final rest in Valhalla. The Pawnee Indians saw the light as a cloud of dust formed by a buffalo and a horse chasing each other across the sky.

No matter how sophisticated our scientific advances, the vast universe in which we live will probably always remain largely a mystery that will continue to touch the human imagination. As we wonder about our night sky, we can feel a special sense of connection with our ancestors around the world who made up wonderful stories that helped them feel at home in a strange, often overpowering universe.

The sun was hot. Often, Chang stopped to rest from the scorching heat. His ox moved slowly and finally stopped. Chang looked up at the sun. He knew they had been working all day, yet the sun was no lower than when they had started. "This is very strange," Chang said to the owner of the land.

"The sun is angry," the landowner said. "It is past eight o'clock in the evening, yet the sun does not move. We must have displeased her. But what have we done? What can we do?" Both men scratched their heads in confusion.

Chang arrived home to find Mei sipping a cool cup of tea. "Mei, the sun has made it too hot to work. What has made her so angry?"

THE SEVENTH SISTER **531**

A Advanced Learners
Making Inferences
❓ What can you infer about the values of traditional Chinese culture from the way Mei and Chang respond to the sun's anger? [Possible response: Both Mei and Chang react dutifully, sacrificing their personal happiness for the good of the world as a whole. This could imply that in traditional China, people valued the welfare of the community above that of the individual, or dutifulness above romantic fulfillment.]

B Background
Relatives of crows, magpies live in Europe, Asia, and North America. Most magpies have black wings and tails and white underparts, though the black may be colored with bronze or green. Known for their noisy chatter, magpies sometimes imitate the calls of other birds or even human speech.

C Elements of Literature
Personification
Help students identify all the words and phrases on this page that personify the sun. [angry, tired, rest, grateful sigh]

D Elements of Literature
How-and-Why Tale
❓ What actual heavenly bodies are explained by Mei's tossing "stars across the sky"? [meteors, or shooting stars]

Mei burst into tears. "It is my fault," she said. "The sun is angry with me."

"What do you mean?" asked Chang.

A "Without my help, my sisters have not been able to finish the tapestry of the night sky. The sun has not been able to rest, so she is tired and angry," Mei said with tears streaming down her beautiful face. "I must return."

Chang was quiet as he realized they could not be together. At last, he said in a low voice, "Yes, you must return. Without your work, we will all suffer. You must finish the tapestry of the night sky."

B Gently, Chang took Mei's robe from its hiding place and wrapped it around her shoulders. She flew higher and higher into the sky. A flock of magpies accompanied Mei on her journey.

C That night, the sun seemed to sink with a grateful sigh as once again the night sky spread across the earth. People slept contentedly, since the sun was no longer angry. But Chang could only sit by the door of his simple hut, filling the night sky with his sweet, sad songs.

D Mei returned to her work on the tapestry of the night. Often, she tossed stars across the sky to remind Chang of her love. As she worked, Mei's tears fell onto her loom and became the stars that fill the night sky. So many stars were formed that they became the mighty Milky Way, dividing the sky in two.

At night, Chang watched the shooting stars and thought of Mei. One night, a magpie came to Chang in a dream. "Happiness shall be yours, gentle man," the magpie said. "The way to Mei is within your reach. Return

532 Explaining Our World: Fact and Fiction

Skill Link

Decoding: Letters That Are Seen and Not Heard

Discuss silent letters. There are familiar ones such as the *k* in *knee* and the *g* in *gnaw*. Explain that *t* may be the letter that is most often seen but not heard. It is silent when it follows *s* in words like *listen* and *nestle*. *T* is also silent in words like *scratch*, *watch*, and *itch*, where it is part of the spelling for /ch/.

Explain that when *t* is not silent, it often stands for a sound other than /t/. When *t* comes before *i* or *u*, the consonant sound is not /t/ but /ch/ or /sh/: as in *actual*, *motion*, *mixture*. Point out that dictionary pronunciations show /t/ in words like *clickety-clack*, *ninety*, and *matter*, but if you listen to people saying these words, *t* often sounds more like /d/.

D is another silent letter in words like *bridge*, *edge*, and *porridge*, where it is part of the spelling for /j/. When the inflectional ending *-ed* is added to some words, the sound you hear is not /d/ but /t/: as in *worked*, *looked*.

Activity
Have students work with partners to think of and list five examples of the following:
• words in which *t* is silent
• words in which *d* is silent
• words in which *t* is pronounced /d/
• words in which *t* is pronounced /ch/ or /sh/
See the helpful suggestion regarding regional pronunciations on p. T536 under "Spelling."

T532

to the silver pond. There you will find a magpie feather that will take you to Mei. Go quickly, my friend."

Chang awoke and hurried to the pond. There, nestled among the roots of the willows, he saw one lone feather shimmering in the moonlight. Grasping it, he raised his arm and said, "Take me to Mei!" He flew higher and higher into the sky, where Mei was waiting for him.

But, alas, the vast Milky Way separated Chang from his beloved Mei. "What are we to do now?" cried Chang in despair.

Suddenly a flock of magpies appeared from every corner of the world. As their wings touched, their bodies formed a bridge.

Mei and Chang ran lightly across it into each other's waiting arms and their voices rang out in joyous song.

"When you are together, Mei cannot work and all the earth suffers," said the magpie from Chang's dream. "But your love is good and strong, so once a year, we will form a bridge to unite you."

You can still see Chang and Mei in the nighttime sky. On one side of the Milky Way, Mei is a bright star completing the tapestry of the night sky. On the other side, another bright star, the ever-faithful Chang, awaits the seventh day of the seventh month, when he can be with his beloved for one special night.

ⓔ Critical Thinking
Making Connections
Have students compare and contrast the bridge in this story with the Great Stone Bridge in "Loo-Wit, the Fire-Keeper." [In this tale, a bridge of birds across the sky allows separated lovers to reunite; in "Loo-Wit, the Fire-Keeper," a stone bridge made by the Creator permits two related peoples to visit one another in peace. In both narratives, bridges are symbols of harmony and union.]

ⓕ Reading Skills and Strategies
Drawing Conclusions
❓ What do you think this story is saying about love? [Possible response: People in love sometimes have to make sacrifices and overcome obstacles in order for their love to survive.]

ⓖ Critical Thinking
Making Connections
❓ How would you compare and contrast this story with "Loo-Wit, the Fire-Keeper"? [Possible responses: Both explain the origins of natural phenomena—the features of the night sky in the Chinese tale and the features of the earth in "Loo-Wit, the Fire-Keeper." "Loo-Wit" has an explicit moral message, while "The Seventh Sister" merely implies a moral. Though love appears in both tales, "The Seventh Sister" is more of an outright love story.]

Resources

Selection Assessment
Formal Assessment
• Selection Test, p. 100
Test Generator
• Selection Test

Assessing Learning

Check Test: Short Answers
1. Before Chang meets Mei, what is his only companion? [his ox]
2. What do the seven sisters weave each day? [the tapestry of the night sky]
3. What lifts Chang into the sky? [a magpie feather]
4. What are the seven maidens' water jars made of? [moonbeams]

Standardized Test Preparation
For practice with standardized test format specific to this selection, see
• *Standardized Test Preparation*, p. 76
For practice in proofreading and editing, see
• *Daily Oral Grammar*, Transparency 32

Making the Connections

Connecting to the Theme:
"Explaining Our World:
Fact and Fiction"
Ask students whether they prefer to read myths and legends like "Loo-Wit, the Fire-Keeper" and "The Seventh Sister," modern historical fiction like "The Dog of Pompeii," or factual articles such as the excerpt from *Volcano*. Have them consider how each form has its way of helping us understand our world. Encourage students to explain the reasons for their choices.

Student to Student

This is an original how-and-why tale written by a contemporary student, giving her own imaginative explanation for the stars.

A ### Reading Skills and Strategies
Making Predictions
? Based on the first paragraph, do you think this explanation of why there are stars in the sky will be fact or fiction? [Most students will correctly predict that Morgan's piece will be fictional.]

B ### Critical Thinking
Analyzing Humor
? How would you explain the humor in the name "H & H"? [Possible responses: It makes fun of the kinds of names that businesses and other bureaucracies often have today; it's funny to think of God running into a headquarters to get approval for his plans.]

C ### Vocabulary Note
Word Origins
In fact, the word *star* traces its lineage to the Latin word *stella,* and the Greek word *aster.* Point out that—since there are thousands of human languages—God would need to think of thousands of words for *star.*

Why There Are Stars in the Sky

A Once upon a time, long, long ago, God was sitting up in Heaven all alone thinking hard—and when I say thinking hard, he was thinking hard!

God would sit up all day and all night staring into the sky without moving or saying a word. Do you know why he was thinking? Well, God had a problem. You see, he was just starting to create all humankind and animals and plants. He had a place for the humans when they died, which was Heaven, but since there were so many humans, there wasn't enough room for any of the animals. If he didn't find a place soon, his plans would be ruined!

So God continued to sit and think and sit and think until it became really dark. He was staring into the velvet-black sky, and suddenly an idea burst into his head out of nowhere! He knew where to put the animals! God ran into the H&H (which stands **B** for "Headquarters and Heaven") and spilled his plans out as fast as spilling milk! Here is what he said:

"Hello, all fellow angels. You know how I have been having difficulty trying to figure out where to put the animals when they pass away. Well, I have figured it out! You know at night it gets really dark and you can't see a

thing! Well, I was thinking while I was staring into the sky that we need some kind of lights to brighten up the night sky. Then I thought, well, the animals' spirits can go up into the sky and they can form bright, large lights of gas to brighten it up! When an animal dies, its spirit will be the brightest light for the night or nights until another animal dies! Isn't that a brilliant idea?"

"But what do we call them?" asked one of the angels.

C "Ah, but you see, I have thought of that also. Since I got the idea from staring into the sky, I decided to use the first four letters of the word *staring,* which form the word *star.* That's what we'll call them!"

Well, you see, the H&H angels had a vote on what to do with the animals' spirits, and the votes came out to be one no and nine yeses. (What happened to the one difficult angel? He lost his wings and down he went. But that's a different story.) So God and the angels were happy with the new "star" idea. And that is why there are stars in the sky (and so many of them, must I mention).

—Morgan Faris Novak
Loggers Run Community Middle School
Boca Raton, Florida

Connecting Across Texts

Connecting with "The Seventh Sister"
Both "The Seventh Sister" and "Why There Are Stars in the Sky" are how-and-why tales explaining the origin of the stars. Invite students to brainstorm lists of similarities and differences between the two pieces. [There are many specific differences in details, of course, but both tales pose imaginative supernatural origins for the stars. "The Seventh Sister" is an old folk tale, the product of a long tradition of anonymous retellings, whereas "Why There Are Stars in the Sky" is the creative effort of a present-day writer whose name we know. Both tales spring from the same human impulse to use the imagination to explain our world.]

MAKING MEANINGS

First Thoughts

[respond]
1. If you could send a skywriting message to Chang and Mei, what would you say?

Shaping Interpretations

[generalize]
2. What makes "The Seventh Sister" a **how-and-why tale**?

[analyze]
3. How is this a story about the power of love? How is it also a story about compassion—that feeling for others that makes us merciful and kind?

Connecting with the Text

[connect]
4. Would you have made the same decision as Mei? Why or why not?

[analyze]
5. What **purpose** did you establish for reading "The Seventh Sister," and why did you choose it? Did your purpose change while you were reading?

Reading Check

a. What do the seven beautiful maidens do in the heavens?

b. Why is Chang unhappy at the start of the tale?

c. How does Chang get Mei to stay with him on earth?

d. Why is the sun unhappy, and what does Mei decide to do about it?

e. How is Chang finally able to rejoin Mei?

CHOICES: Building Your Portfolio

Writer's Notebook

1. Collecting Ideas for Observational Writing

Mei is a responsible character. She is willing to give up her own happiness for the happiness of others. Think of a real person who has a trait that you admire (such as friendliness or honesty). Then, list the things you've observed about that person. Concentrate on what the person says and does.

Creative Writing

2. Why, Oh Why?

In "Why There Are Stars in the Sky" (page 534), the writer invents a tale to explain how the stars came to brighten the night sky. Look back at the story ideas you recorded for the Quickwrite on page 528, or think of a question you still wonder about today. Write a how-and-why story that explains the mystery.

Critical Writing/ Science

3. Star Facts

If you were to travel back in time to meet the original tellers of this tale, what scientific explanation of the Milky Way could you give them? Prepare a short report that describes the size, shape, and composition of our galaxy. Include any facts you find interesting. (See Literature and Astronomy on page 531.)

Reading Check
a. They weave the tapestry of the night sky.
b. He misses something, but he doesn't know what.
c. He hides her magic robe.
d. The sun cannot rest because the sisters cannot finish the tapestry of the night without Mei. Mei returns to help her sisters.
e. Once a year, magpies form a bridge across the Milky Way to bring Chang and Mei together.

MAKING MEANINGS

First Thoughts

1. Sample messages: Chang and Mei—Your Love Is Good and Strong!; Chang and Mei—Thank You for Giving Us the Stars!

Shaping Interpretations

2. It explains how and why the stars, the Milky Way, meteors, and two bright stars on opposite sides of the Milky Way came to be.

3. It is about the love of Chang and Mei, which overcomes obstacles in order to endure. It is also about Chang and Mei's compassion for others in the world, as well as the magpies' concern for Chang and Mei. Less importantly, the tale shows the bond between Chang and his ox.

Connecting with the Text

4. Possible responses: Yes, because depriving the world of night would be harmful to many; no, I would have stayed with Chang because love is the most important thing in life. If students say "no," be sure they justify their decision in terms of its devastating effects on the world.

5. Possible response: My purpose was enjoyment. As I read, I added the purpose of learning about Chinese traditions and values.

Grading Timesaver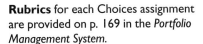

Rubrics for each Choices assignment are provided on p. 169 in the *Portfolio Management System*.

CHOICES: Building Your Portfolio

1. **Writer's Notebook** Students may use their notes as prewriting for the Writer's Workshop on pp. 562–566.

2. **Creative Writing** Invite students to read their stories aloud to the class.

3. **Critical Writing/Science** Before students start their research, have them list possible sources of scientific information, such as encyclopedia articles and science textbooks. Suggestions for use of the Internet are found on p. 308.

GRAMMAR LINK

Ask students to choose paragraphs from their portfolios and to identify any series of two or more adjectives preceding nouns. Students should check the punctuation of each series, using the rules on the pupil's page. Students who only rarely use two or more adjectives to modify a single noun might be encouraged to write new examples of such sentences for their portfolios. Be sure they read the helpful hint on p. 536, example 3, beginning "To decide . . ."

Try It Out
Answers

Chang was a lonely Chinese cowherd. He played sweet, sad songs on his flute. One night he had a dream about seven magical sisters. He finally met the youngest, cleverest sister. The two young people fell in love.

SPELLING

Because of regional differences in pronunciation, some students may pronounce consonants that others do not. Remind students to look up the pronunciations of words in a dictionary. To think of words, just run through the alphabet. Here are some examples: *batch, catch, hatch, latch, match, patch, watch, badge, dodge, edge, hedge, sedge, wedge.*

Resources ——————

Grammar
• *Grammar and Language Links*, p. 47
Spelling
For related instruction, see
• *Spelling and Decoding*, p. 22.

GRAMMAR LINK   `MINI-LESSON`

Language Handbook H E L P

See Items in a Series, page 750.

Technology H E L P

See Language Workshop CD-ROM. Key word entry: commas.

Using Commas to Separate Adjectives in a Series

1. Use commas to separate two or more adjectives before the noun they modify.

   EXAMPLE Chang "filled the air with the sweet, sad songs of his flute."

2. Do not place a comma between an adjective and a noun that immediately follows it.

   INCORRECT The next morning brought a soft, misty, rain.

   CORRECT "The next morning brought a soft, misty rain."

3. If the second or last adjective in a series is closely connected in meaning to the noun, do not use a comma before that adjective.

   INCORRECT "The Seventh Sister" is a beautiful, Chinese myth.

   CORRECT "The Seventh Sister" is a beautiful Chinese myth.

   To decide if a comma is needed, add the word *and* between the adjectives (beautiful *and* Chinese, for example). If the *and* sounds strange, don't use a comma.

> **Try It Out**
>
> Proofread the following paragraph, adding commas where necessary and taking out unnecessary commas.
>
> Chang was a lonely, Chinese cowherd. He played sweet sad songs on his flute. One night he had a dream about seven magical sisters. He finally met the youngest, cleverest sister. The two, young people fell in love.

SPELLING   `HOW TO OWN A WORD`

> ### The Consonants You Can't Hear
>
> Two words in "The Seventh Sister"—*porridge* and *bridge*—have a silent *d;* one word—*scratched*—has a silent *t.* Many words that end in *ge* or *ch* also have silent consonants. To get used to these spellings, play this game with a partner: Say a word with a silent consonant, such as *scratch* or *clutch, budge* or *ledge.* Your partner must think of a rhyming word. For example, if you say *scratch,* your partner may say *match* or *catch,* which have silent letters. Use a dictionary if you need help spelling the rhyming words. Then, make a list of the words with silent consonants that you and your partner have found.

536 EXPLAINING OUR WORLD: FACT AND FICTION

Grammar Link Quick Check

Add commas to the following sentences where necessary. Not all sentences are incorrect.

1. Mei is a beautiful[,] caring[,] intelligent maiden.
2. Chang is a poor Chinese cowherd. [No change.]
3. They both sing beautiful[,] sad songs.
4. Chang rides a shimmering magpie feather up to the sky. [No change]
5. Mei and Chang share a strong[,] faithful love.

Reading Skills and Strategies

OBJECTIVES
1. Distinguish between narrative and informative texts
2. Match reading purpose and method to text subject
3. Learn to use question sheets to remember information

READING FOR VARIED PURPOSES: NARRATIVE AND INFORMATIVE TEXTS

Narrative and Informative: What's the Difference?

A book about science is different from a novel, so you read them differently. A science book explains how and why things happen. It is an informative text that provides facts or theories about real-life events. A novel or short story is a narrative text; it tells a story. When you read a story, you expect to meet characters, follow a plot, and experience a setting. You expect to be entertained, to appreciate the writer's craft, and to discover something about your own life and about people.

If you try to read a science text about astronomy (the study of stars) the way you would read a short story, you may end up having to read about stars all over again. That's because narrative and informative texts are written for different purposes and should be approached in different ways.

Matching Purpose to Subject

It's important to match your purpose for reading to your method of reading and the material you're reading—your subject matter. If you're reading a mystery story for pleasure, you can read in a relaxed way. You may even race to the end to find out "who done it." If you're reading a scientific text for information, however, you'll want to proceed slowly and carefully. You may even reread certain parts to make sure you understand them.

You can make informative texts easier to remember by using question sheets to examine what you've read. (See the box at the left.)

Question Sheet for Informative Texts

1. What is the topic? _____

2. Do I understand what I'm reading? _____

3. What parts should I reread? _____
   _____

4. What are the main ideas and details?

   Main idea: _____   Main idea: _____

   Details: _____   Details: _____

   Main idea: _____   Main idea: _____

   Details: _____   Details: _____

5. Summary of what I learned:
   _____
   _____

Apply the strategy on the next page.

READING SKILLS AND STRATEGIES **537**

Reading Skills and Strategies

This feature focuses on a specific reading strategy that students can apply immediately in the following selection.
Mini-Lesson:
Reading for Varied Purposes

- Before students read the feature, ask them what kinds of movies they like. They will probably cite popular films with strong narratives. Then have students imagine that they are watching an informative (documentary) movie or video at school which they will be tested on. Would they watch this film the same way they watch a movie? Students will realize that their viewing differs according to their purpose—getting information or being entertained. Their approach to print material also depends on the subject and on their purpose for reading.

- Next, work through the lesson with the class. You might wish to have two or more students read aloud selected passages from a sixth grade science text and from a short story or novel. Encourage students to *hear* differences in tone and style.

- You might wish to have students brainstorm a list of examples of informative texts on the chalkboard. Possible responses could include history books and science books and also directions on product labels, encyclopedia articles, newspaper stories, and data in an almanac.

- After students have finished reading the feature, ask them to prepare a question sheet like the one on the pupil's page and to use it as they read "Scanning the Heavens" on pp. 539–542. They may revise their answers as they read and after they discuss the nonfiction excerpt.

Reaching All Students

Struggling Readers

One good strategy to use with Reading for Varied Purposes is called Probable Passage. For information on using this strategy, see p. 43 of the *Reading Strategies Handbook* in the front of the *Reading Skills and Strategies* binder.

English Language Learners

Encourage these students to preview reading assignments by skimming for clues that will help them determine a purpose for reading. Point out that many informative texts contain graphic aids, section headings, and numbered items, steps, or questions. Narrative texts are more likely to contain dialogue and descriptive details.

Advanced Learners

Ask students to describe the kinds of texts they usually read and their purpose for reading each text. Then have them describe how their reading strategies differ from one text to another.

OBJECTIVES

1. Read and interpret the nonfiction excerpt
2. Adjust reading strategies based on purposes for reading
3. Express understanding through writing, critical writing/research, and science/social studies
4. Use commas to separate items in a series
5. Understand and use new words

SKILLS

Reading
- Read for varied purposes

Writing
- Collect ideas for observational writing
- Write a report about an article

Grammar/Language
- Use commas to separate items in a series

Vocabulary
- Learn and use new words
- Make a cluster diagram for a vocabulary word

Science/Social Studies
- Make a time line

Viewing/Representing
- Analyze details of a painting and draw inferences from them (ATE)
- Identify details in art (ATE)

Planning

- **Block Schedule**
  Block Scheduling Lesson Plans with Pacing Guide
- **Traditional Schedule**
  Lesson Plans Including Strategies for English-Language Learners
- **One-Stop Planner**
  CD-ROM with Test Generator

Before You Read

SCANNING THE HEAVENS

Make the Connection

Sky Signs

Ever since ancient times, astronomers in all cultures have closely observed the movements of the Moon, Sun, and stars. What do the heavenly bodies tell us? Get together with a group, and brainstorm to come up with reasons why studying the sky might have been important to early people. What might they have learned from scanning the heavens?

Quickwrite

Think about what you learned from your brainstorming. Then, write down what *you* think is the most important benefit that ancient people gained from studying the heavens.

 go.hrw.com
LE0 6-7

Reading Skills and Strategies

Reading for Varied Purposes: Narrative and Informative Texts

Before you read "Scanning the Heavens," skim the text and consider these questions:

- What will this selection be about?
- What do the subheads tell me?

- Will the vocabulary be difficult or easy for me?
- How fast or slowly will I read this selection?

While you read "Scanning the Heavens," think about the main ideas and details the writer presents. Keep asking yourself if you're understanding what you're reading.

The first Chinese writing, which was scratched onto bones over 3,500 years ago, shows that people already knew that the year was 365¼ days long.

Eclipse of the Moon seen through clouds.

Total eclipse of the Moon.

538 EXPLAINING OUR WORLD: FACT AND FICTION

Preteaching Vocabulary

Words to Own

Have students find the two Words to Own for this selection, *celestial* and *revolution*, at the bottom of the text pages. Have students read the definitions and pronunciations, and then ask them to answer the following questions.

1. Name at least two different kinds of celestial objects. [Possible responses: stars, planets, asteroids, moons, comets, satellites, meteors.]
2. How long does it take the earth to make one revolution around the sun? [one year]

T538

Scanning the Heavens

from Science in Ancient China

George Beshore

Technological progress was important to the Chinese, but from ancient times they also applied themselves to pure science. Astronomy, the study of the stars, was one pure-science field.

Marco Polo[1] described thirteenth-century Beijing as a city of about five thousand stargazers, all interested in the movements of heavenly bodies for one reason or another. Some of them were astrologers, who fancied they could discover what to expect in the future by plotting the movements of the stars and planets. Others were astronomers, who carefully measured the orbits of distant celestial bodies and predicted tides, seasonal changes, and other natural events on earth by the things they learned from their study of the stars. These thirteenth-century astronomers came from a long line of scientists that stretches back to prehistoric times. Some of the earliest accurate stellar[2] observations recorded anywhere in the world were made by these ancient stargazers.

---

1. **Marco Polo** (1254–1324): Italian trader and traveler who became famous for his travels in central Asia and China.
2. **stellar:** of the stars or of a star.

WORDS TO OWN

celestial (sə·les′chəl) *adj.:* of or in the sky or universe, as planets, stars, and so on.

Halley's comet.

SCANNING THE HEAVENS **539**

Summary ▪▪▪

The ancient Chinese studied the stars as both astrologers and astronomers. They developed a calendar based on the stars, made accurate predictions of eclipses, accurately calculated the duration of the year and the lunar month, and observed novas, sunspots, and comets.

Resources

Listening
Audio CD Library
A recording of this nonfiction excerpt is provided in the *Audio CD Library:*
• Disc 13, Track 3

Selection Assessment
Formal Assessment
• Selection Test, p. 102
Test Generator
• Selection Test

Viewing and Representing
Fine Art Transparency
The fine art transparency *Women Reaching for the Moon* by Rufino Tamayo can be used to heighten students' interest in the selection.
• Transparency 17
• Worksheet, p. 68

A Vocabulary Note
Using Context Clues
? What is the difference between astrologers and astronomers?
[Astrologers try to predict future events in the human world by studying the stars; astronomers are scientists who study celestial bodies to predict the natural events and changes on Earth.]

Resources: Print and Media

Reading
• *Reading Skills and Strategies*
   Selection Skill Lesson, p. 175
• *Graphic Organizers for Active Reading*, p. 35
• *Words to Own*, p. 20
• *Spelling and Decoding*,
   Worksheet, p. 23
• *Audio CD Library*, Disc 13, Track 3

Writing and Language
• *Daily Oral Grammar*, Transparency 33

• *Grammar and Language Links*,
   Worksheet, p. 49
• *Language Workshop CD-ROM*

Viewing and Representing
• *Viewing and Representing*
   Fine Art Transparency 17
   Fine Art Worksheet, p. 68

Assessment
• *Formal Assessment*, p. 102
• *Portfolio Management System*, p. 170
• *Standardized Test Preparation*, p. 78
• *Test Generator (One-Stop Planner CD-ROM)*

Internet
• go.hrw.com (keyword: LE0 6-7)

Ⓐ Reading Skills and Strategies

Reading for Varied Purposes

Suggest that students use the headings of the three parts of this selection to determine what their purpose or purposes for reading will be, and to prepare themselves to adjust reading rates accordingly. Also, remind students to fill out their question sheets as they read.

Ⓑ Background

A year is the time it takes the earth to circle the sun. (A day is the time it takes the earth to rotate on its own axis.) The year is not an exact number of days: one day is added to our calendar every four years, on February 29, to make up for the extra quarter-day in each solar year.

A lunar month is the time it takes for the moon to revolve once around the earth, or to go through one cycle of its phases. This is not exactly the same as our calendar month, which is approximately one-twelfth of a year.

Ⓒ Cultural Connections

Antares is the brightest star in the constellation Scorpius, and, for us, one of the twenty brightest stars in the sky.

Ⓐ Practical Needs

The accurate observation of heavenly bodies is necessary for many reasons. Farmers need a calendar to tell them when it is safe to plant their crops in the spring without danger of frost or freezing weather. Spring floods are caused by melting snow in far-off mountains. Floods can be predicted with reasonable accuracy if people keep track of the months that pass to know when such events generally occur. China has always depended on its farmers to produce food for the many people who live there, so an astronomer who could devise an accurate calendar received high honors in ancient times.

Other, more subtle knowledge can be gained by observing the skies. A priest or king who can predict eclipses of the sun or moon will seem to possess divine knowledge. Those who can forecast these events are often credited with being able to foretell other happenings. The common people often worship such leaders and are more likely to listen to their warnings and to obey their commands.

Ⓑ Tradition says that the first astronomical observatories in China were built over four thousand years ago by Huang-Ti, an emperor who, according to legend, also taught the people how to write, play music, and raise silkworms. There is no way to know if this is true; but the first Chinese writing, which was scratched onto bones over 3,500 years ago, shows that people already knew that the year was 365¼ days long. This is amazingly close to the length of the year as it is measured today (365.24219 days). It is also more accurate than calculations made by other people who lived that far back in time.

By the thirteenth century B.C. the Chinese had recorded the length of the lunar month as 29.53 days—extremely close to the

29.530879 days measured by modern scientists. (A lunar month is one <u>revolution</u> of the moon around the earth.) Chinese astronomers developed an accurate calendar with twelve lunar months in each year that started on the winter solstice. The winter solstice is the time around December 22 when the sun is at its southernmost point in the winter skies. Twelve lunar months gave them a year of approximately 360 days. In order to adjust this to the true year, the emperor added an extra month from time to time (approximately once every seven years). He had to rely upon his astronomers to tell him when to insert this month, and that added to their prestige in royal circles.

Strange Stellar Events

Chinese astronomers began recording eclipses of the moon as far back as 1361 B.C. They noted an eclipse of the sun a century and a half later in 1217 B.C. and began keeping regular records of eclipses after that. As early as 1000 B.C. the Chinese could accurately predict when an eclipse of the sun or moon would occur from such observations. It would be another five hundred years before astronomers in the West learned how to do this.

Ⓒ Chinese astronomers also noticed that strange stars sometimes appear suddenly, burn brightly for a short time, then disappear. Called guest stars, the first of these to be recorded appeared in the vicinity of a star now called Antares around 1300 B.C. The newcomer lasted for only two days.

WORDS TO OWN

revolution (rev′ə·lōō′ shən) *n.*: the time taken for an object in space, such as a star or planet, to go around another object and return to its original position.

---

540 EXPLAINING OUR WORLD: FACT AND FICTION

Reaching All Students

Struggling Readers

Reading for Varied Purposes was introduced on p. 538. For a lesson directly tied to this selection that teaches students to vary reading purpose using a strategy called Say Something, see the *Reading Skills and Strategies* binder
• Selection Skill Lesson, p. 175

English Language Learners

Supplement the data in this excerpt with illustrations of the celestial phenomena discussed. For example, display diagrams or charts showing the orbit of Earth around the sun, the orbit of the moon around Earth, a solar eclipse, and sun spots. For additional strategies to supplement instruction for these students, see
• *Lesson Plans Including Strategies for English-Language Learners*

Advanced Students

Invite students to read about the development of astronomical research in Western cultures and then compare and contrast it with the information in this excerpt. The end of the selection provides students with a natural transition to study *current* theories of the cosmos.

T540

Today we would call a guest star a nova. Dozens of times every year, distant stars exhaust the nuclear fuel that makes them burn. Just before collapsing, such stars explode. They appear to burn more brightly (to the naked eye) for a brief time before disappearing from view.

The Chinese also observed and recorded sunspots, which are caused by flares on the surface of the sun. They saw comets, which pass near the solar system from distant space. Halley's comet, which last swung around the sun in the winter of 1985–86, has returned to the solar system at intervals of approximately seventy-five years throughout the ages. The Chinese observed a comet that may have been Halley's in the year 467 B.C. Another sighting in 240 B.C. was definitely this comet; the Chinese kept records of many visits by Halley's and other comets during the centuries that followed. By the sixth century A.D. they had realized that these celestial wanderers reflect the sun's light rather than shining on their own. A thousand years earlier, in the fourth century B.C., they had figured out that the moon reflects the light of the sun instead of producing its own energy.

Cosmic Views

As the Chinese accumulated more and more knowledge about the heavenly bodies, some of their philosophers formulated ideas about the nature of the universe. Throughout their long history the Chinese people have basi-

Chinese painting of an astronomer (1675).

The Granger Collection, New York.

SCANNING THE HEAVENS 541

Ⓓ Background

Stars such as the sun are mostly made up of hydrogen gas. Atoms of hydrogen collide to form atoms of helium in thermonuclear explosions similar to those detonated in a hydrogen bomb. These collisions release huge amounts of energy in the form of heat and light that make life on earth possible. There is so much fuel in our sun that this process can continue for billions of years.

Sunspots are magnetic storms on the gaseous surface of the sun. They are dark because their temperature is lower than that of the surrounding surface. Sunspot activity peaks about every eleven years and may cause magnetic storms and electrical interference on earth.

Comets are composed mainly of dust and gas. The gases at their cores are frozen into ice, making comets like huge, dirty, outer-space snowballs. Since their orbits around the sun are very long, comets pass near earth infrequently. Halley's comet last appeared in March and April of 1986; it is due back in approximately 2061.

RESPONDING TO THE ART

This anonymous painting shows a Chinese astronomer with a globe that represents the heavens. The circles on the globe represent stars and planets; those connected by lines indicate constellations. The device on top of the globe is an astrolabe, an old instrument once used to find the altitude of the stars.

Activity. Ask students to speculate on what the astronomer is doing with his hands. [calculating] Ask students to infer the social status of early Chinese astronomers from this figure's appearance and clothing. [He is richly dressed and therefore probably has high social status.]

Using Students' Strengths

Visual Learners

Show pictures of the solar system, eclipses of the sun and moon, and sunspots. Before students read the selection, ask them to speculate on what humans could have learned about the heavenly bodies before the invention of the telescope. Have students check their speculations after they have read the selection.

Naturalist Learners

Provide students with star guides, which can be found in books, star maps, and star globes; or have students use star guides they already possess. Have them report on what the night sky currently looks like in your part of the world. How does the configuration of stars, planets, constellations, and other visible bodies change through the year? Students could prepare an illustrated report for presentation to the class.

Astronomers now believe that the universe is very large but may not go on forever. It may turn back on itself, so that if one could somehow go far enough in one direction, he or she would end up back at the starting point! Contemporary scientists speculate that the universe is between twelve and fourteen billion years old.

RESPONDING TO THE ART

The Tang Dynasty (A.D. 618–906) has been called China's Golden Age. A stable government and a prosperous populace encouraged all kinds of art to flourish. Traders and artisans from the Middle East also influenced artistic styles at this time.
Activity. Ask students to identify some or all of the animals in the engraving. Tell students that each year of the Chinese calendar is named for an animal—rat, ox, tiger, hare, dragon, snake, horse, sheep, monkey, fowl, dog, and pig.

Resources

Selection Assessment
Formal Assessment
• Selection Test, p. 102
Test Generator
• Selection Test

---

cally had three different theories about the cosmos.[3]

The oldest of these was that the earth, which they thought of as being flat or slightly curved, floated on water. Overhead, the sky was a curved dome; the stars were fixed to its surface. The sun and moon had movements of their own, crossing this domed sky at regular intervals.

By the second century B.C. the Chinese had altered their view of the universe. They began to think of it as a giant egg. The earth was the yolk at the center of this curved universe. Around the earth stretched the curved sky like the inside of an eggshell. The Chinese calculated the size of this universe, giving the diameter of the egg as 2,032,300 li, or approximately 700,000 miles (over one million kilometers). (A li is a unit of Chinese measurement equal to approximately one

3. **cosmos:** the universe considered as a harmonious and orderly system.

---

third of a mile, or about half a kilometer.) Philosophically, the Chinese admitted that they had no idea what lay beyond the celestial "egg."

In the third century A.D. the Chinese came up with their third and final version of what the cosmos is like. Called the Hsüan Yeh, or "infinite, empty space" teaching, this theory held that the blue sky that seems to arch overhead is an optical illusion. Instead, they said, space goes on and on. By the eighth century they added that this universe had existed for a hundred million years.

These theories gave the Chinese a framework to go along with their observations of the phenomena that they saw in the skies. However, most of China's astronomers concentrated on cataloging celestial events and figuring out calendars for the farmers to use on earth, preferring to leave philosophical questions about the universe to those who wanted to investigate such matters.

A celestial sphere from the Tang dynasty (A.D. 618–906). Color engraving.
The Granger Collection, New York.

MEET THE WRITER

A Modern Observer of an Ancient World

George Beshore is a world traveler and photographer and an expert on science and the environment. For more than thirty years, he has explained science and technology through his writing. He is the author of several hundred newspaper and magazine articles, movie scripts, speeches, books, and educational publications. "Scanning the Heavens" is an excerpt from his book *Science in Ancient China* (1988).

More Travels in Time and Space

Continue your journey through the ancient world with Beshore's *Science in Early Islamic Culture* (Franklin Watts).

Making the Connections

Connecting to the Theme: "Explaining Our World: Fact and Fiction"
In seeking to explain the origins of the world, the people of ancient China created myths, in addition to making objective observations. Ask students to summarize and discuss the explanations of the cosmos, presented in this selection and in "The Seventh Sister." Have students discuss what is gained—and lost—by solving some of the mysteries of nature.

Assessing Learning

Check Test: Short Answers
1. What is the scientific study of the stars called? [astronomy]
2. What famous comet was sighted by the people of ancient China? [Halley's comet]
3. Where does the light of comets come from? [the sun]
4. What did the "infinite, empty space" theory say? [Space has no limit, and the universe is a hundred million years old.]

Standardized Test Preparation
For practice with standardized test format specific to this selection, see
• *Standardized Test Preparation*, p. 78
For practice in proofreading and editing, see
• *Daily Oral Grammar*, Transparency 33

MAKING MEANINGS

First Thoughts

[respond]

1. Complete these statements:
   - I was surprised to learn that . . .
   - I'd like to ask the author . . .

Shaping Interpretations

[generalize]

2. State the **main idea** of this selection in your own words.

[compare]

3. What did the ancient Chinese gain by studying the sky? Do the facts in the selection match your guesses for the Quickwrite on page 538?

Connecting with the Text

[connect]

4. Which of the three ancient views of the universe did you find most interesting? Why?

[compare/contrast]

5. What connections can you see between "Scanning the Heavens" and "The Seventh Sister" (page 528)? Which selection did you enjoy more? Why?

Reading Check

Copy the Question Sheet for Informative Texts on page 537, and fill it out for this selection. Do the part titles within the selection help you figure out the **main ideas**?

CHOICES: Building Your Portfolio

Writer's Notebook

1. Collecting Ideas for Observational Writing

Astronomers, like other scientists, are keen observers. Most writers are also. Writers use vivid sensory details to record exactly what they saw, heard, smelled, tasted, and touched. Spend some time in your kitchen. Describe exactly what you observe.

Record as many sensory details as you can.

Critical Writing/Research

2. Still Scanning

What are astronomers doing now? Use the *Readers' Guide to Periodical Literature* or a database to find current articles on astronomy. For instance, you might read about the Hubble telescope. Choose an article to write a report on.

Science/Social Studies

3. Ancient Chinese Know-How

The Chinese built suspension bridges, made cast iron, used natural gas for fuel, made paper, used wheelbarrows, and powered machines with falling water long before Westerners did. Find out about these and other examples of Chinese technology. Make a **time line** that shows when each first came into use in China.

Using Compiled Information to Raise Additional Questions

Sometimes when students do reports, such as the one on astronomers in Choice 2 above, their research will raise new questions. For example, in compiling information on contemporary astronomy, students may become interested in comparing and contrasting the training of ancient and modern astronomers. Encourage students to use their research as a springboard for pursuing related topics.

Reading Check

Have students share their question sheets through discussion. Most students will find that the part titles reflect main ideas, such as ancient Chinese astronomers' discoveries and theories.

MAKING MEANINGS

First Thoughts

1. Possible answers:
   - . . . Chinese astronomers knew so much so long ago.
   - . . . how ancient Chinese astronomers knew the moon shines with reflected light.

Shaping Interpretations

2. Possible answer: Before the telescope was invented, ancient Chinese astronomers made many accurate observations of the celestial bodies.
3. They learned when it was safe to plant their crops, when floods were likely, and when eclipses would arrive. This knowledge brought security, power, and prestige.

Connecting with the Text

4. Possible answers: The flat-earth theory, because it seems like a reasonable guess; the egg theory, because it's so strange; the "infinite, empty space" theory, because it seems almost true.
5. Each selection tells what some people in China believed about the stars. Some students will prefer the more factual, objective account, while others will prefer the imaginative, narrative account, which includes human motives and feelings.

Grading Timesaver

Rubrics for each Choices assignment are provided on p. 170 of the *Portfolio Management System*.

CHOICES: Building Your Portfolio

1. **Writer's Notebook**   You might have a pair of students model a Think Aloud activity. One partner should describe sensory details in the classroom while the other takes notes.
2. **Critical Writing/Research**   Encourage students to choose topics that they can comfortably understand.
3. **Science/Social Studies**   Before students draw their time lines, create a sample time line of local or other familiar events on the chalkboard during class discussion.

GRAMMAR LINK

Ask students to compose sentences that contain three or more items in a series and not to separate those items with commas. They can use the sentence marked "Incorrect" on the pupil page as a model. Then have them ask a partner to read their sentences and discuss why they are difficult to follow. For example, in the given incorrect sentence, a reader might think the sentence is saying that the emperor taught the people "to write play music" rather than "to write and to play music." After the discussion, ask partners to work together to punctuate the sentences correctly.

Try It Out

Some teachers and writers omit the final comma in a series, before the conjunction. Thus, in each example below, the second comma is optional.

- The astronomers predicted tides, seasonal changes, and other natural events on Earth.
- Strange stars appear suddenly, burn brightly for a short time, and then disappear.
- The Chinese theories about the universe were sometimes surprisingly accurate, sophisticated, and useful.

VOCABULARY

Possible Answers

For the word *celestial*, students might ask:

- What are some celestial bodies?
- How do scientists study celestial bodies?
- Which celestial bodies can we see without a telescope?

Resources

Grammar
- *Grammar and Language Links*, p. 49

Vocabulary
- *Words to Own*, p. 20

Spelling
For related instruction, see
- *Spelling and Decoding*, p. 23

T544

GRAMMAR LINK [MINI-LESSON]

Language Handbook HELP

See Items in a Series, page 750.

Technology HELP

See Language Workshop CD-ROM. Key word entry: commas.

Using Commas to Separate Items in a Series

What's wrong with this sentence?

INCORRECT The emperor taught the people how to write play music and raise silkworms.

Did you have to reread the sentence to figure out exactly what three things the emperor taught? If so, it's because three items are written one after the other without any commas to separate them.

CORRECT The emperor "taught the people how to write, play music, and raise silkworms."

Three or more items written one after the other are called a **series**. Always use commas to separate items in a series. Use a comma before *and* but not after it. Note: Do not use commas to separate items in a series if you join all items with *and*.

Try It Out

Copy the sentences below, adding commas to separate the items in a series.

1. The astronomers predicted tides seasonal changes and other natural events on Earth.

2. Strange stars appear suddenly burn brightly for a short time and then disappear.

3. The Chinese theories about the universe were sometimes surprisingly accurate sophisticated and useful.

VOCABULARY [HOW TO OWN A WORD]

WORD BANK

celestial
revolution

Cluster It

Filling out a cluster diagram can help you discover what you know about a word. On a separate sheet of paper, fill out a diagram like the one here, about the meanings of *revolution*. Then, create your own cluster diagram based on the word *celestial*.

What revolutions in history do I know about?
•
•

What changes in today's world can be called revolutions?

Revolution

What revolutions occur in the movements of a car?
•
•

How many revolutions around the Sun does Earth make in a year?
•

544 EXPLAINING OUR WORLD: FACT AND FICTION

Grammar Link Quick Check

Insert commas to separate items in a series in the sentences that follow.

1. Light from car headlights[,] neon signs[,] streetlights[,] houses[,] and businesses interferes with telescopes.
2. Astronomers like to place their observatories away from cities[,] towns[,] and even highways.
3. Observatories have been placed in deserts[,] on mountains[,] and on islands.
4. Light pollution is as much a problem for astronomers as water pollution is for fish. [no change]
5. Astronomers do not want light pollution to keep them from seeing planets[,] stars[,] comets[,] and galaxies.

Before You Read

HOW THE SNAKE GOT POISON

Make the Connection

Fight, Flight, or Bite

Jaws or claws, elephant trunks or the scent of skunks, wings or stings, quills or bills: Every animal on earth has at least one adaptation, or natural feature that helps it survive. Scientists may tell you how and why these adaptations came about. Storytellers aren't interested in such explanations. Storytellers see an animal's interesting features and think of a story to explain them.

Quickwrite

Let your imagination go free, and jot down *your* answer to this question: Why does the snake have poison?

Elements of Literature

Oral Tradition: "Tell Me That Story"

All of our literature begins with the oral tradition. Before writing was invented, and even long since, stories have been sung or recited. They were told to children at bedtime, to friends huddled around a warm fire at night, and to people gathered in a dusty market square. Today we gather around television to hear and see a story. Long ago the "television set" was a person, an oral storyteller. The teller's tales—some funny, some sad, some puzzling—linked many generations and formed the culture's **oral tradition.**

> A group's **oral tradition** is its folk tales, songs, and poems that have been passed on orally over generations.
>
> *For more on Oral Tradition, see the Handbook of Literary Terms.*

Background

Literature and Real Life

Zora Neale Hurston traveled to the South in the 1930s to gather stories that had been passed on for many years by storytellers of African descent. She recorded these folk tales in the kind of language used by these storytellers. Her snake story *must* be read aloud.

Rooster.
Shelburne Museum, Shelburne, Vermont. Photography by Ken Burris.

Reading Skills and Strategies

Comparing and Contrasting Texts: Looking for Similarities and Differences

Both of the selections you're about to read are about snakes. One is a folk tale; the other is nonfiction. Do they have any details in common?

 go.hrw.com
LE0 6-7

Summary ▪▪

This humorous African American folk tale explains the origins of rattlesnakes' venom and rattling tails. Complaining of being trampled, a snake visits God and begs for protection. After God gives him poison for his mouth, other animals complain that the snake now kills everything that moves near him. Thus, God gives the snake a warning bell, or rattle, for his tail. The tale closes with a traditional storyteller's rhyme.

Background

Only one-fifth of the world's approximately 2,700 species of snakes are poisonous. Poisonous snakes include various coral snakes, as well as the rattlesnake, copperhead, water moccasin, bushmaster, and fer-de-lance. Though coral snakes rarely attack unless threatened, others may attack without provocation. The fangs of poisonous snakes are hollow, like hypodermic needles, and inject venom that attacks the victim's nervous system.

Resources ——

Listening
Audio CD Library
A recording of this folk tale is provided in the *Audio CD Library:*
• Disc 13, Track 4

Selection Assessment
Formal Assessment
• Selection Test, p. 104
Test Generator
• Selection Test

HOW THE SNAKE GOT POISON

an African American folk tale, retold by
Zora Neale Hurston

"When they tromps on you, protect yourself."

Reaching All Students

Struggling Readers
Have pairs or small groups read the selection aloud sentence by sentence, or paragraph by paragraph. Encourage students to pause occasionally and summarize or paraphrase what they have read and to ask questions about words or phrases that are confusing. Also encourage rereading for fluency.

English Language Learners
Students may struggle to understand the dialect in this tale. After listening to the audiocassette, students might read the story on their own or in pairs, writing down words and phrases that pose special difficulty. You might also wish to read the tale aloud to students. For additional strategies to supplement instruction for these students, see
• *Lesson Plans Including Strategies for English-Language Learners*

Advanced Learners
Recommend that students read "Looking for Zora," Alice Walker's afterword to Zora Neale Hurston's book *I Love Myself When I Am Laughing . . . And Then Again When I Am Looking Mean and Impressive.* Walker's essay is a moving account of her search for Hurston's unmarked grave. It should give students an idea of how significant the recovery of folk tales such as this one has been for many African Americans.

Crawling Snake (1988) by Sultan Rogers.
Courtesy of the University Museum, University of Mississippi Cultural Center.

Well, when God made the snake, he put him in the bushes to ornament the ground. But things didn't suit the snake, so one day he got on the ladder and went up to see God.

"Good mawnin', God."

"How do you do, Snake?"

"I ain't so many, God, you put me down there on my belly in the dust and everything trods upon me and kills off my generations. I ain't got no kind of protection at all."

God looked off toward immensity and thought about the subject for a while. Then he said, "I didn't mean for nothin' to be stompin' you snakes like that. You got to have some kind of a protection. Here, take this poison and put it in your mouth, and when they tromps on you, protect yourself."

So the snake took the poison in his mouth and went on back.

So after a while, all the other varmints went up to God.

"Good evenin', God."

"How you makin' it, varmints?"

"God, please do somethin' 'bout that snake. He's layin' in the

HOW THE SNAKE GOT POISON 547

RESPONDING TO THE ART

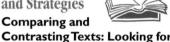

Sultan Rogers (1922–   ), an African American artist from Mississippi, learned from his father how to carve small likenesses of animals. He continued carving to relieve the tedium of his job monitoring the workings of machinery in a chemical plant. Rogers's carvings are humorous and sometimes satirical, and he claims that images of what he will carve appear in his dreams; then he "just carves them out."

Activity. Have students discuss how closely Rogers's carving *Crawling Snake* captures the character of the snake in Hurston's tale. [Possible response: Both seem to have a humorous quality and other humanlike traits.]

A **Reading Skills and Strategies**

Comparing and Contrasting Texts: Looking for Similarities and Differences
Have students preview the folk tale and the essay "Snakes: The Facts and the Folklore" (p. 550) by skimming the titles, texts, and illustrations. Have students make preliminary comparisons and contrasts and then read on to validate or modify them.

B **Elements of Literature**

Oral Tradition
❓ What word in the first sentence most clearly suggests that this tale was originally told orally? ["Well"]

Using Students' Strengths

Visual Learners
You might wish to invite visual learners to draw pictures of the snake before (and after) it receives the poison and the bell.

Interpersonal Learners
Have pairs of students improvise a confrontation between the snake and another animal after the snake has poison but before it has the bell. Ask them to make up dialogue as they go, but remind them to keep the conflict in mind and to work toward a resolution of the conflict.

Auditory/Musical Learners
Invite a skilled storyteller to tell the story aloud to the class, or play the audiocassette recording. Engage listeners actively by having them write a sentence or two describing what they enjoyed most about the tale immediately after the reading.

bushes there with poison in his mouth and he's strikin' everything that shakes the bush. He's killin' up our generations. We're scared to walk the earth."

So God sent for the snake and told him:

"Snake, when I give you that poison, I didn't mean for you to be hittin' and killin' everything that shakes the bush. I give you that poison and told you to protect yourself when they tromples on you. But you killin' everything that moves. I didn't mean for you to do that."

The snake say, "Lord, you know I'm down here in the dust. I ain't got no claws to fight with, and I ain't got no feet to get me out the way. All I can see is feet comin' to tromple me. I can't tell who my enemy is and who is my friend. You give me this protection in my mouth and I use it."

God thought it over for a while then he says:

"Well, Snake, I don't want your generations all stomped out and I don't want you killin' everything else that moves. Here, take this bell and tie it to your tail. When you hear feet comin', you ring your bell, and if it's your friend, he'll be careful. If it's your enemy, it's you and him."

So that's how the snake got his poison and that's how come he got rattles.

Biddy, biddy, bend, my story is end.
Turn loose the rooster and hold the hen!

Pair of parrots.
Shelburne Museum, Shelburne, Vermont.
Photograph by Ken Burris.

548 EXPLAINING OUR WORLD: FACT AND FICTION

Making the Connections

MEET THE WRITER

Pitching Head Foremost into the World

Zora Neale Hurston (c. 1903–1960) was born in Eatonville, Florida, the first incorporated African American town in the United States. She described it as "a city of five lakes, three croquet courts, three hundred brown skins, three hundred good swimmers, plenty guava, two schools, and no jailhouse." From her birth she heard stories:

66 When I pitched head foremost into the world, I landed in the crib of Negroism. From the earliest rocking of my cradle, I had known about the capers Brer Rabbit is apt to cut and what the Squinch Owl says from the housetop. 99

Hurston was more or less on her own after age nine, when her mother died. She supported herself with odd jobs around Florida; to get a college education, she moved to Washington, D.C., and New York City. There, she studied folklore and anthropology at Barnard College and became part of the Harlem Renaissance of the 1920s, a time of great achievement for African American artists and writers. Her research led to her book *Mules and Men* (1935), the first book of black folklore ever collected by an African American.

The end of Hurston's life wasn't what this joyous writer would have expected. Eventually the literary world forgot about her, and she died in poverty in Florida. Critics have a way of changing their minds, however, and so does the public. Now Hurston is seen again as one of the great, original voices in American literature.

Humdingers from Hurston

Hurston retells other African American folk tales in *Mules and Men* (HarperCollins), the collection that includes "How the Snake Got Poison."

The Granger Collection, New York.

BROWSING IN THE FILES

About the Author. Zora Neale Hurston landed in the middle of the Harlem Renaissance when she came to New York to attend Barnard College. During her years in New York City, she studied with Franz Boas, the famous anthropologist, at Columbia University. She traveled to Haiti to do fieldwork on voodoo and then returned to the United States to collect African American folk tales in the South. Since her rediscovery in the 1970s, Hurston has gained recognition as an important American writer for her novel *Their Eyes Were Watching God* (1937). Her autobiography is titled *Dust Tracks on a Road.*

Assessing Learning

Check Test: True-False

1. God puts the snake in the bushes to hide it from the world. [False]
2. God gives the snake poison to protect it. [True]
3. The other animals are glad that the snake got poison. [False]
4. God takes the poison away from the snake after the other animals complain. [False]
5. The snake is given a bell to ring as a warning. [True]

Standardized Test Preparation

For practice with standardized test format specific to this selection, see
- *Standardized Test Preparation*, p. 80

For practice in proofreading and editing, see
- *Daily Oral Grammar*, Transparency 34

This factual article gives the scientific explanation for the rattlesnake's venom and the rattling noise made by its tail. It also dispels misinformation on the function of these two features of the rattlesnake's anatomy.

Ⓐ English Language Learners
Breaking Down Difficult Text

To familiarize students with unfamiliar vocabulary and encourage them to read the rest of the article, take some time before reading to discuss the meanings of words such as *appendages*, *unique*, *segments*, and *molt*. You might begin by reviewing some of the best methods of finding the meanings of new words: using context clues, using prior knowledge, and consulting a dictionary or thesaurus.

Ⓑ Struggling Readers
Summarizing

Encourage struggling readers to pause and then to summarize the opposing arguments about the rattles. [Some people think it's naive or silly to believe that rattlesnakes want to warn enemies away. The warning does in fact protect the snake by keeping large animals from crushing it.]

Ⓒ Critical Thinking
Analyzing Details

❓ Why would the snake rather use its rattle to warn off intruders than use its venom? [It needs to save its venom to use against prey, in order to get food.]

Developing Vocabulary by Listening to Literature Read Aloud

Students can acquire vocabulary by listening to selections read aloud. The vocabulary in this science essay may challenge some students. Read the essay aloud to the students. Ask them to jot down unfamiliar words as they listen. (Students might list *appendages*, *segments*, and *attributing*.) Write some of the words on the board, and ask students to figure out their meanings. Students can draw on their own experience and use context to guess a word's meaning. Or have students complete a chart like the one on p. 325 to help uncover the meaning of unfamiliar words.

Connections | **A**
SCIENCE ESSAY

Snakes: The Facts and the Folklore

Hilda Simon

Ⓐ The series of tail appendages that is found only in the rattlesnakes and has given them their name is a unique organ not found in any other kind of snake. These hard, horny pieces are segments of unshed skin, an additional one being added at every molt. The newborn rattler cannot rattle, because it has only one rounded scale, or button, at the tip of its tail. Only when several loose segments have been added can the snake produce its characteristic sound, which is more a buzz than a rattle. The popular idea that one segment is added every year and that therefore the snake's age corresponds to the number of rattle segments is erroneous,° for snakes may shed their skin four times a year when they are young, and segments of the rattles of older snakes tend to break off, so that very old snakes usually have no more than eight or ten.

°**erroneous:** containing or based on error; mistaken; wrong.

Ⓑ There has been much discussion about whether the rattlesnakes really want to give warning when they sound their rattles. Some people have pooh-poohed this idea as attributing charitable intentions to the snake. However, the rattling sound definitely *is* meant as a warning, although its purpose is to protect the snake rather than the offending party. By sounding the rattle, the snake can often prevent a large animal, such as a buffalo, from stepping on it accidentally and crushing it. Ⓒ Furthermore, the venom is primarily the snake's means of securing food, and it therefore would rather scare off a potential enemy than waste the venom in self-defense. Even as the pit represents an evolutionary advance in pit vipers over the ordinary vipers, so the rattle is an advance over the rattleless pit vipers, which is the reason why scientists consider rattlesnakes to be the most highly evolved of the entire order.

Connecting Across Texts

Connecting with "How the Snake Got Poison"

Ask students to make lists of characteristics of snakes as described in "How the Snake Got Poison" and in "Snakes: The Facts and the Folklore." Then have students work in pairs or small groups to compare their lists, labeling each item as either fact or fiction. The whole class might then discuss what they learned about snakes from the two selections.

MAKING MEANINGS

First Thoughts

[respond]

1. What do you think of God's solution to the conflict between the snake and the other varmints?

Shaping Interpretations

[respond]

2. Hurston wrote her story using the kind of language in which it was told, in order to preserve the African American **oral tradition.** How do you like the rhyme she included at the end of the story? What other words and phrases in the story help you imagine how the African American storyteller spoke?

[compare/contrast]

3. Compare the imaginative story "How the Snake Got Poison" with the factual "Snakes: The Facts and the Folklore" (see *Connections* on page 550). Collect your details in a chart like the one below. (How well did Hurston's storyteller know snakes?)

	Folk Tale	Fact
Purpose of venom		
Purpose of rattle		

Connecting with the Text

[generalize]

4. Does this story have something to say about how to deal with people who threaten you? about how to deal with those in authority in order to get what you want?

[connect]

5. What lines in the story made you laugh? Read them aloud again.

Reading Check

Retell the events of the story by writing sentences to follow these words:

First _____
So _____
But _____
Then _____
Finally _____

HOW THE SNAKE GOT POISON **551**

MAKING MEANINGS

First Thoughts

1. Possible answers: I like the solution because it helps both the snake and the other animals. I dislike the solution because the snake can still use its poison harmfully.

Shaping Interpretations

2. Some students will see that the rhyme is funny and clever. Phrases that suggest how the storyteller spoke include "Good mawnin'," "I ain't so many, God," "How you makin' it, varmints?" and "He's killin' up our generations."

3. Possible responses:
   Purpose of Venom: Folk Tale—to protect itself;
   Fact—primarily to secure food.
   Purpose of Rattle: Folk Tale—to warn intruders;
   Fact—to warn intruders.
Students may conclude that the storyteller in the folk tale had a fair but not thorough knowledge of venomous snakes.

Connecting with the Text

4. The story implies that people should protect themselves in a fair and nonviolent way, if possible. It shows that presenting a problem or complaint to an authority should be done in a respectful and rational manner.

5. Students may select lines from the text, such as "How you makin' it, varmints?" and "I didn't mean for you to be hittin' and killin' everything that shakes the bush."

Reading Check
Possible responses:
- First the snake complains to God that he is in danger on the ground.
- So God gives him poison as a protection.
- But the snake begins killing all the other animals.
- Then the other animals complain to God.
- Finally God gives the snake a bell that he can ring to warn the other animals.

Rubrics for each Choices assignment appear on p. 171 in the *Portfolio Management System*.

CHOICES: Building Your Portfolio

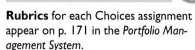

1. **Writer's Notebook** Let students work in small groups to share ideas about animals and plants they have seen (or read about) defending themselves. Remind students to save their notes. They may use them as prewriting for the Writer's Workshop on pp. 562–566.

2. **Creative Writing** For students who have trouble thinking up story ideas, provide the option of using a chart like the following so they can organize their thoughts before they write.

Creature	[Bee]
Annoying/dangerous qualities	[Sting]
How the animal got this quality	[Borrowed a needle from a tailor to use in protecting its honey]

3. **Art/Creative Writing** Let students work either singly or in pairs. Bring in some newspaper comics for them to use as models—or have volunteers do so.

4. **Oral Reading** Model the activity for students by reading part of the story aloud to them, changing your voice for the various roles. Encourage students to regard the dialect with respect, not ridicule, reminding them that all ethnic and regional groups have a dialect but not everyone in the group necessarily speaks that way.

CHOICES: Building Your Portfolio

Writer's Notebook

1. Collecting Ideas for Observational Writing

God tells the snake in the folk tale: "You got to have some kind of a protection." Choose an animal or plant that you've observed defending itself, either in real life or in photographs or on film. Describe the animal's or plant's natural defenses.

The snake's long, narrow shape lets it slither into cracks and holes where its enemies can't follow.

Creative Writing

2. Another Varmint Speaks Up

"How the Snake Got Poison" shows how the world might look from the point of view of a snake, an animal that frightens many people. Think of another creature that many people don't like (for example, a bat, mosquito, bee, or spider), and write a how-and-why tale about how the animal got its annoying or dangerous qualities. If you want to write about snakes, add to the story you started for the Quickwrite on page 545.

Art/Creative Writing

3. Folk-Tale Comics

Draw and write a comic-strip version of this story. First, choose the most important events, and decide on one or two illustrations for each. Then, figure out how much dialogue you can pick up from the story and how much you need to rewrite to fit the small space for each panel. Compare your strip with strips done by your classmates. Did you all choose the same scenes?

Oral Reading

4. Snake Charmer

Get together with three classmates and prepare to charm your class with a read-aloud of "How the Snake Got Poison." Pick one of the roles: the narrator, the snake, God, or the varmints. Speak the part in a conversational voice, making the dialect sound natural. Decide which words to emphasize and which to say softly or loudly. Then, practice, practice, practice before you perform. You may want to take on this challenge instead: Read the entire story aloud by yourself, changing your voice to suit the various roles.

• Style: Dialect—The Voice of the People

Handbook of Literary Terms
HELP

See Dialect.

Do you *make* the bed or *make up* the bed? Would you order a *sub* with "the woiks" (a long sandwich with all the extras) or a *hero* with "the works" or just a *grinder*? It depends on which **dialect** of English you speak. People from different regions of the United States and from different ethnic and social groups speak different varieties of English, with different vocabularies, pronunciations, and sentence structures. These different forms of English are called dialects. Everyone uses some form of dialect, and no dialect is better or worse than any other.

Test your classmates. How do they pronounce these words: *water, car, morning?*

Try It Out

A tip for writers: To make story characters come to life for your readers, make sure they speak in a dialect that suits their age, region, and social group. To develop your skill at writing dialect, take notes on or tape-record the conversations you hear around you. Try to reproduce exactly the way people talk. Listen to the way they pronounce words, the special words they use, and the way they put their sentences together.

Have students choose a piece of writing from their portfolios that has at least two characters and dialogue. Ask students to rewrite the dialogue of one of the characters, using a dialect that the character might realistically speak. Suggest that students read the dialogue aloud with a partner. Then invite students to discuss how the use of dialect changes their responses to the character who speaks it.

Try It Out
Avoid giving students the impression that speech in stories should always or usually be rendered as dialect. Dialect is used in relatively few contemporary works of fiction, usually for social realism or humor or both. In fact, dialect can be offensive if not used with utmost sensitivity. Dialect also "dates" quickly, especially when it is rendered through the use of misspellings. Note that—except for apostrophes in place of dropped g's—Zora Neale Hurston uses few misspellings in rendering dialect. Instead she relies on vocabulary and idiom to reproduce a distinctive way of speaking.

SPELLING   HOW TO OWN A WORD

Homonyms: *Past* and *Passed*

Read the following sentences, and notice how *past* and *passed* are used. *Past* and *passed* are **homonyms** (häm′ə·nimz′), words that are pronounced the same but have different meanings and spellings.

In the far *past*, snakes had no protection, so God *passed* out some poison to them. Then every time another animal went *past* them, the snakes would bite. When the other animals complained, God *passed* out rattles to the snakes so they could warn other creatures as they *passed* by.

Passed is used only as a verb. It is the past tense of the verb *pass.*
Past can be a noun, an adjective, or a preposition but *never* a verb.

INCORRECT	We *past* a red car on the highway.	
CORRECT	We *passed* a red car on the highway.	
CORRECT	We went *past* a red car on the highway.	

Write a description of some things you saw on your way to school today. Use the words *past* and *passed* correctly. Let a classmate check your work. Has it *passed* (or *past*) the spelling check?

SPELLING
Descriptions will vary. Students should use *past* at least once as a noun (the distant past), once as an adjective (the past few days), and once as a preposition (drove past the mall).

Resources

Language
• *Grammar and Language Links,* p. 51

Spelling Quick Check

Use the words *past* and *passed* correctly in the following sentences.

1. A snake slithered *past/passed* me yesterday. [past]

2. He *past/passed* me before I could react. [passed]

3. The snake was on the road a mile *past/passed* the intersection. [past]

4. My troubles with the snake have now *past/passed.* [passed]

5. I wrote about the snake in the *past/passed* tense. [past]

No Questions Asked

The literature in No Questions Asked gives students the chance to read a selection for enjoyment and enrichment as they further explore the collection theme. Annotated questions in the Teacher's Edition should be considered optional. No follow-up questions appear after the selection.

Cat and Dog are great friends until they are forced to go their separate ways in search of food. Dog promises not to follow Cat to Adam and Eve's house, where Cat earns his keep by catching mice. After many hard struggles, Dog eventually goes to Adam's house for food. Adam appreciates Dog's ability to warn the family when a dangerous animal approaches. Though Adam wants to keep both Cat and Dog, Cat insists that Dog keep his promise never to seek food in the same place as Cat. So Adam sends Dog to the home of his son, Seth. The tale illustrates why dogs still chase cats: They want to be friends as they once were.

Resources

Listening
Audio CD Library
A lively reading of this tale is provided in the *Audio CD Library*:
• Disc 13, Track 6

Ⓐ **Reading Skills and Strategies**
Responding to the Text
❓ What is surprising about this statement? [Sample response: dogs and cats rarely get along well together.]

Why Dogs Chase Cats

an African American folk tale, retold by **Julius Lester**

Ⓐ **There weren't two creatures in creation who were better friends than Dog and Cat.**

554

Reaching All Students

Struggling Readers
Encourage students to read the tale aloud with partners. Then invite them to take turns retelling successive passages of the tale to one another. Pairs of students might also benefit from acting out the roles of Dog, Cat, and the other characters.

English Language Learners
Students may have more success understanding the folk tale's straight narrative passages than its playful, lyrical passages, which make extensive use of figurative language and idioms. Help them work through sentences in which Lester uses repetition and imagery ("Long before . . . "; "From sunup to sundown, from moonup to moondown"). For additional strategies to supplement instruction for these students, see
• *Lesson Plans Including Strategies for English-Language Learners*

Advanced Learners
Have students imagine that they are writers assigned to produce a factual essay called "How Dogs and Cats Became Pets." Tell them that this essay will accompany "Why Dogs Chase Cats," just as "Snakes: The Facts and Folklore" accompanies "How the Snake Got Poison." Have them use an encyclopedia to research the history of animal domestication. After the whole class has read this folk tale, have essay writers read their work aloud to classmates.

Long before this time we call today, and before that time called yesterday, and even before "What time is it?" the world wasn't like it is now.

Long before time wound its watch and started ticking and chasing after tomorrow, which it can never catch up to, well, that was the time when Dog and Cat were friends. There weren't two creatures in creation who were better friends than Dog and Cat. From sunup to sundown, from moonup to moondown, Dog and Cat did everything together and never a cross word passed between them.

That's how matters stood until hard times came to visit and decided to stay awhile. Hard times are what you have when you look in your dinner plate and all you see is your face looking back at you.

After a few days of not finding anything to eat, Dog and Cat knew they had to do something. But what?

They scratched their fleas and thought. They thought and scratched each other's fleas. They stopped thinking and stopped scratching. That was when Dog got an idea.

"There's only one thing we can do."

"What's that?" Cat wanted to know.

"We must go our separate ways. It's easier for one to find food than it is for two."

Cat agreed.

"I know where you can find food," Dog continued.

"Where?" Cat asked eagerly.

"Go to Adam's house."

"What will you do?"

"Don't worry about me," Dog said. "I'll find something somewhere."

"But what if you don't?" Cat wondered.

"Well, maybe I'll have to come to Adam's house."

That was what Cat was afraid of. "You eat more than I do. If you come where I am, you'll eat everything and there won't be enough for me. We have to promise that we will never look for food in the place where the other one is."

Dog promised and Cat promised and the two friends went their separate ways.

Cat went to Adam's house. When Eve saw Cat sitting on the back porch, she thought he was the cutest thing she'd ever seen. She picked him up, put him on her lap, and started stroking him. When night came, Eve brought Cat to bed with her. Adam didn't like the idea of sleeping in the same bed with an animal, but he didn't want to get into an argument with Eve about it.

In the middle of the night, Adam was awakened suddenly by a noise. He sat up. By the light of the moon, he saw Cat catching a mouse. Seeing how useful Cat was going to be, Adam treated him very kindly from that day on, and Cat was never hungry because there were many mice to catch.

WHY DOGS CHASE CATS 555

B Elements of Literature
Figurative Language
To help students better understand the role of figurative language in making writing interesting, have them paraphrase this passage in plain language. [Possible response: Long ago, cats and dogs were friends.] Ask what the main metaphor in the passage is. [The metaphor is a ticking watch.]

C English Language Learners
Interpreting Idioms
Encourage students to use context to figure out the meaning of the idiom *how matters stood.* If necessary, help them to see that this expression means "how things were."

D Reading Skills and Strategies
Connecting with the Text
? What is your definition of hard times? [Possible responses: When a person has too little money to pay bills; when a person cannot get enough to eat.]

E Critical Thinking
Analyzing Details
? What physical detail does the tale give to show that Dog and Cat were friends? [They scratched each other's fleas.]

F Cultural Connections
Make sure students know that Adam and Eve were the first man and woman in the Book of Genesis in the Bible.

Getting Students Involved

Cooperative Learning
Animal Social Relationships. Dog and Cat help each other by scratching each other's fleas. Are there other species that aid each other in their grooming or survival? Have cooperative groups research ways in which certain animal species interact socially. Members of each group should assume responsibility for tasks such as locating information, taking notes, writing a report, illustrating the report, and presenting the report to the class.

Enrichment Activity
Oral Report. When, where, how, and why did humans first domesticate animals? Encourage students to learn about how species, such as horses, donkeys, sheep, goats, cattle, camels, yaks, water buffalo, and chickens were tamed. Suggest that students work in groups, with one or two members specializing in each animal. Have each group present an oral report. Each group might illustrate a world map by marking the locations of early domestication of each animal.

A Elements of Literature
Imagery
? Call students' attention to the striking image, "Dog could hear a raindrop fall on cotton." What is the literal meaning of this image? [Dog could hear the softest sounds.]

B Elements of Literature
Personification
? In what way is the moon compared to a human being? [It is female and has fears that a person might have.]

C Struggling Readers
Rereading
Ask students to reread this passage containing the brief conversation between Dog and Wolf. Urge them to visualize the animals' positions and movements to help them determine what is happening. Ask what is Wolf's motive—what is he secretly trying to do—in telling Dog to chase the noise. [Some students may say Wolf is trying to get rid of Dog; others may say Wolf genuinely wants Dog to scare off whatever is approaching the cave.]

D Reading Skills and Strategies
Drawing Conclusions
? What does Dog's willingness to face down a gorilla for some food tell you about Dog? [Possible responses: He is so hungry he'll risk his life for food; he is not very bright; he is brave.]

Dog was not as lucky. The first night after he and Cat separated, Dog went to the cave of Wolf and asked for shelter.

Wolf said he was welcome to stay but not to ask for any food. Wolf scarcely had enough for himself.

Dog found a spot near the front of the cave, settled down and went to sleep. Everybody knows that Dog has the best hearing of almost any animal in the world. Dog could hear a raindrop fall on cotton.

In the darkest part of the night, the time of night that's so scary even Moon wishes she had someplace to hide, Dog woke up suddenly.

He listened. He heard trees and bushes being torn out of the ground, and footsteps in the distance. He ran to the back of the cave, where Wolf was sleeping.

"Something is coming!"

"If you run it away, I'll give you some of my food."

Dog ran back to the front of the cave and waited. The footsteps got louder and louder until out of the forest, holding a tree in each hand, came Gorilla.

Dog growled his growliest growl. He rushed at Gorilla and barked his barkiest bark. Gorilla looked down, picked Dog up, and threw him over his shoulder. It was three days and five nights before Dog came down to earth.

Poor Dog didn't know what to do. He wandered and he wandered, but no one had

Using Students' Strengths

Visual Learners
Invite students to retell the folk tale in comic-strip form. Remind them to include speech balloons and other standard comic-strip techniques, such as thought balloons, captions, and graphic lines indicating action or movement. Encourage students to illustrate the events of the tale and to invent new dialogue, characters' thoughts, and additional episodes, if they wish.

Verbal Learners
Invite students to compose their own folk tales about animal species that appeal to them. The goal should be to create an entertaining story that gives a fictional explanation for an animal's characteristics or behavior—such as for a snake's shape or for a sheep's submissiveness. As prewriting, students might jot down a list of animals and their interesting features or habits. Students might then choose the detail they find most appealing, and invent fictional reasons for its existence.

more than a few scraps of food to share with him. He was so hungry there was nothing to do but go to Adam's house.

When Adam saw Dog in the backyard, he immediately liked him. He gave Dog something to eat. After he'd filled his stomach, Dog crawled underneath the porch and went to sleep.

In the middle of the night, Dog woke up suddenly. He heard something! He started barking. Adam awoke, grabbed his bow and arrow, and hurried outside. There, in the darkness, he saw a rhinocehorse. Adam shot arrows at it and drove the rhinocehorse away.

Adam patted Dog on the head and told him he could stay forever. His barking had saved Adam's and Eve's lives.

The next morning when Eve put Cat outside, the first thing Cat saw was Dog lying beneath a shade tree.

"What're you doing here?" Cat asked angrily.

Dog started explaining about what a hard time he'd had and how there was more than enough food at Adam's for the two of them.

Cat didn't want to hear a word. "We made a promise and you broke it."

"Let's go to Adam and maybe he can solve our problem," Dog suggested.

Adam listened while Cat said his say. Then he listened to Dog say his say. When each had finished saying their say, it was Adam's turn to say.

"Dog, let there be no mistake. You and Cat made a

promise and you broke it. However, Cat, you must understand that I am the one who told Dog he could stay here. There is more than enough food for both of you. I need both of you. Cat, you are useful for catching mice. Dog, you warn me when danger is around. I want you both to stay."

"No!" said Cat. "No, no, no!"

"Why?" Adam asked.

"Because," said Cat, "a promise is a promise."

Dog pleaded with Cat. He reminded Cat that they had been best friends since water was wet. Nothing Dog said could change Cat's mind.

Finally Adam said to Dog, "I'm sorry, but you're going to have to go."

"Where can I go?" Dog wanted to know.

"My son, Seth, lives down the road and around the curve."

So Dog went to live with Seth and he was very happy there.

But from that time to this, whenever a dog sees a cat, he chases after it because he still wants the cat to be his friend.

WHY DOGS CHASE CATS 557

E Reading Skills and Strategies
Making Generalizations
? What generalization does the story suggest about men and women's preferences for dogs or cats? [Sample answer: Men prefer dogs, and women prefer cats.] Why do you agree or disagree with this generalization? [Students should provide anecdotes, logical reasons, and any factual evidence to support their opinions.]

F Critical Thinking
Expressing an Opinion
? Do you agree with Cat that "a promise is a promise" or with Dog that there are sometimes good reasons to break a promise? Explain your view. [Possible responses: Keeping promises is essential because it is the basis for trusting others; promises should be kept whenever possible, but for Dog, breaking the promise was a matter of life or death.]

G Critical Thinking
Extending the Text
? For what other reasons are dogs and cats nice to have around? [Possible responses: Dogs are loyal and fun to play with; cats are cuddly; both offer companionship.]

H Reading Skills and Strategies
Responding to the Text
? Is this a fictional or a factual explanation of why dogs chase cats? [fictional] Why do you think dogs chase cats? [Possible responses: To shoo them away; to practice hunting; to play.]

Making the Connections

**Connecting to the Theme:
"Explaining Our World:
Fact and Fiction"**
Have students fill out a chart like the following, listing the facts and fiction from the selections in this collection, including "Why Dogs Chase Cats."

Facts	Fiction
[A rattlesnake's rattle is made of unshed skin.]	[The rattle is a bell given to the snake by God to ward off intruders.]
[Dogs chase cats.]	[A cat hunts mice in Adam and Eve's house.]

About the Author. In addition to African American folk tales and narratives from African American history, Julius Lester, the son of a Methodist minister, also has retold Jewish folk tales. In *How Many Spots Does a Leopard Have? and Other Stories,* he combines folk tales from both African and Jewish traditions. He writes in his introduction to the collection, "Although I am of African and Jewish ancestry, I am also an American. . . . I have fitted the story to my mouth and tongue." Lester wrote about his conversion to Judaism in his 1988 autobiography, *Lovesong: Becoming a Jew.* Lester told an interviewer, "Children's literature is the one place where you can tell a story. Just straight, tell a story, and have it received as narrative without any literary garbage. I've done a fair amount of historically based fiction that would be derided as adult literature because it's not 'sophisticated.' I'm just telling a story about people's lives. In children's literature I can do that."

MEET THE WRITER

Folk Tales: "More Fun Than Television"

Julius Lester (1939–   ) grew up in Missouri, Tennessee, and Arkansas. During his childhood he absorbed the rich traditions, stories, and music of African Americans in the rural South.

After college, Lester did many things. He was active in the civil rights movement in the 1960s. He played the banjo and performed with popular folk singers like Judy Collins. For a while he had his own radio and TV shows in New York City. However, writing became his lifework.

Lester explains why he retells folk tales:

❝ They're more fun than television. There is also the sense that there are people behind these tales as opposed to an author behind the stories. For me folk tales are . . . creations, and we'll never know who the creators are. That's wonderful and mysterious to me. They're a distillation of an entire people's learning and knowledge and wisdom into a very brief tale. Implied are values of the worth of ordinary people, and that's a value that I consider very important. I want to communicate to children that you don't have to *be* somebody to have worth. And here are all these tales that you love, and the same things are inside you. ❞

More Tales Handed Down by the Writer

You'll find more of Lester's entertaining folk tales in *The Tales of Uncle Remus: The Adventures of Brer Rabbit* (Dial), *How Many Spots Does a Leopard Have? and Other Tales* (Scholastic), and *The Knee-High Man and Other Tales* (Dial).

The Granger Collection, New York.

558 EXPLAINING OUR WORLD: FACT AND FICTION

Assessing Learning

Check Test: Short Answers

1. What do the two friends promise? [They will never look for food in the same place.]
2. Which animal goes to Adam and Eve's house first? [Cat]
3. What does Gorilla do to Dog? [He throws Dog into the air.]
4. Who breaks the promise? How? [Dog, by going to Adam and Eve's house to look for food.]
5. According to the tale, why do dogs chase cats? [Dogs want cats to be their friends.]

READ ON

Clever Fools

In eight stories passed down from his great-great-grand-mother, Isaac Bashevis Singer tells of fools, imps, and a lazy man saved by love. *When Shlemiel Went to Warsaw* (Farrar, Straus & Giroux) is a book full of enchanting and comic tales.

Peek into the East

Dive into the magical Chinese tales of *The Rainbow People* (HarperCollins) by Laurence Yep. You'll find a land of dragons, money that pours from heaven, and a man who uses his nose to sniff out riches.

The Voice of a People

Meet Bruh Rabbit, Aunt Fish-Horse, and the Hairy Man. Virginia Hamilton tells African American folk tales filled with riddles, trickery, and fantasy. *The People Could Fly: American Black Folktales* (Knopf) brings to life stories first told by Africans held as slaves as a way to voice their fears, hopes, and dreams of freedom.

A Better Planet

Travel to cultures around the world in the pages of *Peace Tales: World Folktales to Talk About* (Linnet) by Margaret Read MacDonald. See how these clever tales get people thinking and talking about the power of peace.

Sustained Silent Reading

Virginia Hamilton's collection of African American folk tales would be a good book to assign for sustained silent reading.

To help students monitor their reading, have them try the strategy called "Say something . . . silently" or "Think silently." Give them these directions: (1) Preview what you are about to read. What predictions about the content of the tales can you offer based on the titles and illustrations? (2) As you read, pause from time to time to think about your responses, your questions, and any connections you make to real-life experiences or to other stories. Reread any confusing passages to clarify them. (3) After you have finished reading, make a list of the most important ideas in the collection.

Speaking and Listening Workshop

OBJECTIVES

1. Choose a topic for a speech
2. Plan and deliver a speech

Resources

Performance Rubric
- *Portfolio Management System*, p. 172

Introducing the Speaking and Listening Workshop

- Before students read the workshop, play a short "how-to" video segment (perhaps one or two minutes long) on a familiar subject such as cooking, home repair, or gardening. Ask students to note the speaker's manner and tone. Then play the segment a second time so that students can focus on the information being conveyed by the speaker.
- Ask students to recall times when they learned information effectively from teachers, parents, coaches, siblings, or peers. Invite students to describe the situations and to explain exactly what made the instructors effective.
- Based on the above discussion, ask the class to brainstorm a list of qualities that make teaching effective.

Try It Out

Students pretending to learn to tie their shoes may need to be reminded to do exactly what their instructors say—neither more nor less.

Determining Purpose

Before students listen to an informative speech, be sure that they have clarified their purpose in listening: Do they wish to learn something, solve a problem, or find the answer to some question? Should they bring a notebook to the presentation?

Try It Out

Do you think teaching is easy? Try this: Using only verbal instructions, teach a classmate to tie his or her shoelaces. Remember: No pointing or demonstrating is allowed.

SPEAKING TO INFORM

People teach through speech every day. A chef tells her assistant how to stuff a chicken. A coach tells his quarterback how to execute a new play. A park ranger tells a group of scouts how to track a mountain lion. In this workshop, you'll give a three- to five-minute "speech to teach." Your speech will inform classmates *about* a topic or teach them *how to do* something.

Choosing a Topic

Choosing a topic is often the hardest part of speaking to inform. Ask yourself:

- What can I do well? (Think about hobbies, sports, school subjects, or family activities that show your talents.)

- What can I teach my audience? (If you speak a language besides English, for instance, you could teach your classmates a few phrases or a song.)

- What topic seems interesting and exciting to me?

If you're still having trouble coming up with a topic, ask your family and friends what they'd like to learn about from you.

Setting Your Purpose

The purpose of your speech is to teach. Just exactly what do you want your audience to learn, though? To set your purpose, complete the following sentence: I want my audience to understand that . . . .

Say you would like to talk about dog training. "I want my audience to understand that dog training" is not a complete sentence, so it can't be your purpose. "Dog training" is just a topic. "I want my audience to understand that *discipline and fairness are the keys to dog training*" is a purpose.

Considering Your Audience

If you consider your audience's **point of view** as you prepare

---

Using Students' Strengths

Intrapersonal Learners
Encourage these students to practice in privacy until they know their material well. In small groups, intrapersonal learners can listen to one another's speeches. You might allow very shy students to tape speeches.

Interpersonal Learners
Allow a group of students to work together on planning and delivering a longer speech, in which each member speaks for three to five minutes.

Invite other group members to ask questions or make polite comments to aid any speaker who becomes hesitant or nervous.

Logical/Mathematical Learners
Students might practice their speeches by solving mathematical problems on the board in front of classmates. They can explain each step they take to find the solution to the problem.

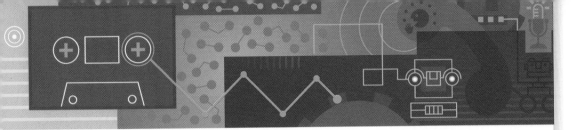

your speech, you'll be able to keep your listeners interested and involved. Ask yourself these questions:

- What do my listeners already know about my topic? (Do they know what a tamale is, or should I explain that before I teach them my uncle's recipe?)

- How can I get my audience to care about what I have to say? (Can I tell them that if they learn how to grow organic tomatoes, they can make their own ketchup and help the environment, too?)

- How can I organize my speech so that it will be easy for my listeners to follow?

Giving Your Speech

As you practice giving your speech, think about these tips:

- Don't write out your speech word for word. Instead, make a note card for each main point or step; this will allow you to speak naturally and look at your audience.

- Speak slowly and clearly, making sure you can be heard even at the back of the room.

- Pause after each point or step to make sure that your listeners understand. If there are any questions, answer them before you go on.

- Relax. Smile. Tell a joke—even if it is just to say how nervous you are. The more at ease you seem, the more comfortable your audience will be.

Try It Out

Choose a partner to help you rehearse your speech. Ask your partner to think about these questions as you speak:

- Can I picture clearly what is being said? If not, what do I need to know to fill in the gaps?

- Does the information seem accurate and complete?

- Does anything I'm hearing seem to contradict my own experience?

- How can I use this information?

PEANUTS, reprinted by permission of United Feature Syndicate, Inc.

SPEAKING AND LISTENING WORKSHOP **561**

Teaching the Speaking and Listening Workshop

- Tell students that the best way to learn how to give a speech is to go ahead and give one. As with playing a musical instrument or kicking a soccer ball, practice is the key to success.

- You may wish to spend some time discussing the fact that public speaking is an activity that makes many people feel nervous. (In fact, studies have shown that speaking in public makes many people more nervous than anything else in life!) Reassure nervous students that they have lots of company. Since nervousness is natural in performance situations, encourage students to accept these feelings and move on—rather than to try to eradicate the feelings.

- Some people allow their nervousness about public speaking to prevent them from practicing speaking, but practice is exactly what will help them become more comfortable with speaking to a group of people. You might wish to stress that this workshop is a chance to practice and that students aren't expected to give a flawless speech.

Try It Out
Suggest that students make audio or video recordings of their rehearsal speeches. Have them replay the speeches with their partners, pausing every sentence or two to answer the questions and make other observations.

Comparing Perceptions
After the speech is delivered, be sure that students compare perceptions of the speech. Do they agree on the speaker's message? Do they agree on the speaker's effectiveness?

Reaching All Students

Struggling Learners
Some students who struggle with reading and writing may be surprisingly fluent speakers. Allow students' personal preferences to guide them in deciding how extensively to take notes and write drafts for their speeches. Also, you might allow considerable latitude for students to choose their own topics. (You might be surprised at what they know.)

English Language Learners
Encourage students to use graphic aids, such as charts and drawings, to help them explain the topic or process they wish to convey. Invite students to teach their audience something about their native languages or cultures. Students teaching songs or phrases in their native languages may want to write the words, with English translations, on chart paper.

Advanced Learners
You may need to remind students to choose topics that will be interesting to the rest of the class. Also bear in mind that students' level of academic proficiency may or may not correlate with their level of comfort about public speaking. Invite students of mixed abilities and personality types to rehearse together, exchange strategies, and share encouragement.

Writer's Workshop

MAIN OBJECTIVE
Write an observational essay

PROCESS OBJECTIVES

1. Use appropriate prewriting techniques to identify and develop a topic
2. Create a first draft
3. Use evaluation criteria as a basis for determining revision strategies
4. Revise the first draft, incorporating suggestions generated by self- or peer evaluation
5. Proofread and correct errors
6. Create a final draft
7. Choose an appropriate method of publication
8. Reflect on progress as a writer

Planning

- **Block Schedule**
  Block Scheduling Lesson Plans with Pacing Guide
- **One-Stop Planner**
  CD-ROM with Test Generator

Technology HELP

See Writer's Workshop 1 CD-ROM. *Assignment: Observational Writing.*

ASSIGNMENT

Write an essay describing something you have observed.

AIM

To inform; to express yourself.

AUDIENCE

Your teacher, classmates, family, or friends.

DESCRIPTIVE WRITING

OBSERVATIONAL WRITING

No one else experiences the world exactly as you do. In **observational writing** you present your view of something you have observed closely over a period of time. You describe all its details, especially those related to your five senses.

Professional Model

Margaret E. Murie made detailed observations of life in the Alaskan back country during the early 1920s. Here she describes the way the tundra, the arctic plain, looks after nightfall.

The sky is midnight blue and fully spangled with stars, and the moon is rising brighter and brighter behind the pointed trees. In the north a flicker of green and yellow; then an unfurled bolt of rainbow ribbon shivering and shimmering across the stars—the Aurora. The dogs begin to speed up; we must be nearing a cabin; yes, there it is, a little black blotch on the creek bank. The air is cold and tingling, fingers are numb. A great dark form flops slowly across the trail—a great horned owl, the speaking spirit of the wilderness.

— from *Two in the Far North* by Margaret E. Murie

The writer tells what time of day it is.

She uses colors to paint a picture of the scene.

She uses details that appeal to the senses of sight and touch.

The details she chooses help us feel as if we were there.

   Resources: Print and Media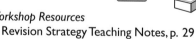

Writing and Language
- *Portfolio Management System*
  Prewriting, p. 173
  Peer Editing, p. 174
  Assessment Rubric, p. 175

- *Workshop Resources*
  Revision Strategy Teaching Notes, p. 29
  Revision Strategy Transparencies 15, 16
- *Writer's Workshop 1 CD-ROM*
  Observational Writing

Prewriting

1. Writer's Notebook

If you have Writer's Notebook entries for this collection, review them. Decide if you want to expand an entry. If you prefer, try the following activities.

2. Quickwriting

- **Looking.** Closely observe a person or an object that you already know well. Look until you see something you hadn't noticed before, until the person or object seems somewhat unfamiliar. What's new? Can you describe it?

- **From your memory.** Remember a place where you have been happy. Describe it in detail. Focus on sounds, smells, tastes, sights, and physical sensations.

- **Animal antics.** Recall an animal that you've spent time watching. It may be a pet, a zoo animal, or even an insect. Describe how the animal looks, sounds, and behaves.

- **Focus on firsts.** Do you remember the first time you rode a bike, visited a city, did a science experiment, or tasted a new food? Gather your observations of some favorite "firsts."

3. Choosing Your Topic and Audience

Pick any topic that interests you and that you can observe (or recall) in detail. Try thinking of your essay as a magazine

"All I see is more trees."

WRITER'S WORKSHOP 563

Introducing the Writer's Workshop

- Read the Professional Model on p. 562 as students follow along.
- Be sure students understand the side margin comments. Ask them to identify specific details this previous reader noticed.
- Discuss with students the characteristics of good observational writing:
  1. a clearly defined subject and setting
  2. details that bring the subject and setting to life
  3. an observer's interesting point of view
- Be sure students understand their own purpose in creating observational writing: to describe something they have observed closely over a period of time.

Remind students to choose a situation that they will not mind sharing with others.

Teaching the Writer's Workshop

Prewriting

Have students use the techniques suggested on pp. 563–564 (or any others that may be helpful to them) to come up with ideas.

Remind students that observing comes *before* writing, and that they should observe with as many of their senses as possible. Remind them to remain quiet and still so as not to disrupt their own (or others') observations. Then have students write nonstop for three minutes, writing whatever comes to mind without editing themselves.

Reaching All Students

Struggling Learners

Assure students that the topic they choose need not be exotic, such as the wildlife of the Alaskan tundra. You might point out, in fact, that students will be able to write more knowledgeably and vividly about things close to home that they have come to know well over a long time. Encourage students to quickwrite to remember as many details as possible, and then to mark the details that they consider the strongest.

English Language Learners

Some of these students may have access to fascinating material that many other students don't have. They may be able to observe American culture in fresh new ways if they were not born into it. In addition, they may be able to offer unique observations about the process of getting used to a new environment. Students might prefer to freewrite in their first language before switching over to English to draft and revise.

Advanced Learners

Have students transform their observational writing into narrative or lyric poetry. Some students may discover that much of an observational essay can take the form of a "found poem" if they put it into verse instead of prose.

T563

Prewriting (continued)

As each student thinks of at least three possible topics, make a list on the chalkboard of all students' topics. Remind students to postpone deciding on topics for their essays until they have considered the entire list. After students have chosen topics, urge them to answer the following questions:

- Who is going to read this?
- Why will they read it?
- After they have read my essay, what do I want my readers to think, feel, know, and do?

To help students stay on track, have them state their topic and intended audience in the margins of their first draft.

Drafting

You may want students to examine the Student Model on p. 565 before they begin their drafts.

Organizing

Remind students that many writers do not rely on only one organizational pattern. For example, in the excerpt from *Volcano,* Patricia Lauber describes the eruption of Mount St. Helens in chronological order on pp. 501–502. Elsewhere, she explains the causes and effects of volcanic eruptions. And in one such explanation, on pp. 504–507, Lauber uses spatial order to describe the effects of the eruption from the top to the bottom of the volcano. These organizational methods are effective because each segment comes at an appropriate moment to give the reader relevant information in the most interesting way.

Framework for Observational Writing

Introduction (states subject plus time, place, and background information):

_____
_____

Your observations:

1. _____
   Specifics: _____
2. _____
   Specifics: _____
3. _____
   Specifics: _____
4. _____
   Specifics: _____

Conclusion (may include your main impression, your feelings, or your questions about what you observed):

_____
_____
_____

---

article. Would your audience be readers of a magazine about animals and nature, like *National Geographic World*? a magazine about sports, like *Sports Illustrated for Kids*? When you write, keep your readers in mind.

Drafting

1. Starting with a Context

You'll want to identify your subject at the beginning of your essay. In the first few sentences you should also present the context (the time and place of your observations) along with any background information your readers may need.

2. Organizing

Here are several ways to organize your observation:

a. **Spatial order.** When you organize details spatially, you tell where they are located—moving, for example, from left to right or from near to far. Writers often use spatial order when they describe a scene.

b. **Chronological order.** When you organize chronologically, you put details in time order. This organization is best suited to describing an activity or an event. Note that the Student Model on page 565 is organized chronologically.

c. **Order of importance.** When you organize by order of importance, you present details from most to least important or from least to most important. This type of organization helps convey your feelings about a subject.

3. Elaboration: Painting with Specifics

As you present your observations, go into detail. Facts, sensory details, and actions are three types of specifics you can include. Use a chart like the one at the top of the next page to record all the details and actions you observe.

Using Students' Strengths

Visual Learners

As a supplement or alternative to freewriting, encourage students to draw in sketchbooks in order to recall and select topics and details.

Auditory/Musical Learners

As part of students' recollection process, suggest that they close their eyes and *hear* what was happening in the settings and during the events.

Naturalist Learners

This Writer's Workshop is well suited to this learning style. Encourage students to use specific natural phenomena, such as seasonal plant growth, weather, stars, and moonlight, as topics. Remind students to use images from as many senses as possible.

POPCORN NIGHTS

We entered, greeted by the warm, lingering smell of freshly popped corn. The bright blue bowl of popcorn, with ribbons of steam floating delicately off each kernel, lured us to it. I tasted a piece and let it remain there for a moment before swallowing. I picked up the bowl, and out we went into the dark and muggy night. Walking as quickly as we could without spilling the popcorn into the long grass, we hurried on our way. Barefoot, with our jeans rolled to our knees, the damp grass poked and danced on our toes as the wind became powerful hands that caressed our hair. Finally we reached our destination, a tent set up with a faint light glowing in the corner of my back yard.

— Sharon Orthey
Warren Township High School
Gurnee, Illinois

The title identifies the subject and the time of day.

The writer uses lots of details that appeal to the senses of touch, smell, sight, and taste.

She uses figurative language to describe the grass and the wind.

She uses chronological order to describe the action.

Topic: Carrying a bowl of popcorn

facts
• night
• bowl of popcorn
• tent in back yard

sensory details
• popcorn—warm, lingering smell
• night—dark, muggy, windy
• tent light—faint, glowing

actions
• tasting the popcorn
• picking up the bowl
• carrying the popcorn outside

Strategies for Elaboration

When you write an observational essay, use exact verbs, nouns, adjectives, and adverbs to express just what you mean.

Notice that in the Professional Model on page 562, the sky is described not just as blue and starry but as "midnight blue" and "spangled with stars."

In your writing, don't describe a car simply as "yellow" when it's actually "lemon yellow" or "mustard colored." Don't write that a boy is "on a sofa" when you might say that he "sprawls," "curls," or "snoozes" there.

Challenge yourself to add at least five exact words when you revise your draft.

As students read the Student Model, be sure they read and understand the side notes. Extend the discussion with questions like the following:
? How does the writer use facts, sensory details, and actions to describe the "popcorn nights"?
? Can you find facts, sensory details, and actions in your prewriting?
If students can find these items, suggest that they use them in their drafts. If their prewriting does not contain such elements, suggest that students add some when they draft and revise.

Evaluating and Revising

1. Reworking Your Draft

Reread your first draft, looking for the main impression of your subject. Try to sum up that main impression in a phrase or a sentence. For example, the writer of the Professional Model

Getting Students Involved

Cooperative Learning
Two Pairs of Eyes, Ears, and Hands. Take the class on a writer's field trip to a location that is rich in sensory stimuli. It may be someplace very near, such as the school kitchen or gymnasium or an art room. Students should work in pairs to record the things they see, hear, smell, taste, and touch. After returning to class, have each pair share their list of details with another pair and compile a group list. One member of each group can then read the list to the class.

Enrichment Activity
Usage. Help students become sensitive to an overabundance of description in their writing. Suggest that students select a handful of important details when describing an object, rather than describe everything about it. Urge them to find a few exact, vivid words—especially nouns and verbs—instead of many approximate or vague words. Have students watch out for long, stringy descriptive phrases in their writing. In such phrases, students should look at each word, evaluate its importance, and cross out any that seem unimportant.

Evaluating and Revising

Have students use the Evaluation Criteria provided here to review their drafts and determine needed revisions.

Proofreading

Have students proofread their own papers first and then exchange them with another student. For this assignment, remind students to be particularly careful of punctuation of adjectives or other items in a series.

If time permits, the final copy should be put aside for at least a day before it is proofread for a final time by the author.

Publishing

Here are some ideas for publishing students' observations:

- Invite groups of classmates to create and illustrate magazines.
- Suggest that students submit their essays to magazines that publish student writing, such as *Stone Soup*. (Help students find out how to submit their essays, or ask the school librarian for such help.)
- Have students read their essays aloud to the class or to a small group. Students might wish to play audio tapes of their own choosing as background music for oral readings.

Reflecting

If students would like to include their observational writing in their portfolio, have them date it and add a short reflection based on questions such as these:

- Why did I choose this topic?
- Which details do I like best?
- Which parts of my observational essay are especially well written? Why?
- How might I use the skills of observational writing in other assignments, in other classes, or in life outside school?

Resources

Peer Editing Forms and Rubrics
- *Portfolio Management System,* p. 174

Revision Strategy Transparencies
- *Workshop Resources,* p. 29

■ *Evaluation Criteria*

Good observational writing

1. *clearly identifies the subject*

2. *makes the time and place clear*

3. *uses detailed description to help the reader hear, see, feel, smell, or taste the subject*

4. *organizes details in a clear way*

5. *reveals the writer's feelings about the subject*

Language/Grammar Link
H E L P

Forming plural nouns: page 497. Personification: page 511. Using commas in a series: pages 536 and 544.

Sentence Workshop
H E L P

Combining sentences by using connecting words: page 567.

Communications Handbook
H E L P

See Proofreaders' Marks.

---

on page 562 might have stated her main impression as "Words can never describe the mystery and beauty of this land."

For your second draft, look for ways to sharpen that impression. You might go through the draft and circle a few points you've made that seem important. Then, try to say something more about each one. Think, too, about your reactions to what you're seeing. If you have a certain feeling about the person or object you're observing, search for details that might convey that feeling.

2. Peer Review

Trade papers with a classmate. Ask your reader to do the following:

- Circle the parts of the essay that are the easiest to picture.
- Write the main impression at the bottom of the essay.
- Note any questions about the setting, background, or subject.

Afterward, discuss responses to the essays with your partner.

3. Self-Evaluation

Reread your essay, and answer the following questions:

- Where could I add more facts or other details?
- Which nouns, verbs, adjectives, and adverbs could I replace with more exact ones?
- Would my observations be clearer if I put them in spatial order or chronological order or order of importance?

4. Revising

Think about your reader's responses and your own ideas for changing your essay. If your reader had questions about the time and place of your observations or about your subject, you need to add more information at the beginning of the essay. If your reader's statement of your main impression was very different from your statement of it, consider adding specifics to make your focus clearer.

Grading Timesaver

Rubrics for this Writer's Workshop assignment appear on p. 175 of the *Portfolio Management System.*

BUILDING YOUR PORTFOLIO

Sentence Workshop

OBJECTIVES
1. Identify compound subjects, compound verbs, and conjunctions
2. Combine two sentences by using conjunctions

COMBINING SENTENCES BY USING CONNECTING WORDS

By using connecting words, called **conjunctions**, you can join sentences and sentence parts that are closely related in meaning.

Sometimes two closely related sentences have the same subject or verb. If two sentences have the same subject, you can combine them by making a **compound verb.** If the sentences have the same verb, you can combine them by making a **compound subject.**

The conjunction you use is important. It tells your readers how the two subjects or the two verbs are related to each other. Use *and* to join similar ideas.

TWO SENTENCES	The older brother saw what a good place it was. The younger brother also saw what a good place it was.
COMBINED	The older brother and the younger brother saw what a good place it was. [compound subject]

Use *but* to join contrasting ideas.

TWO SENTENCES	The volcano was quiet on March 19. It erupted on March 20.
COMBINED	The volcano was quiet on March 19 but erupted on March 20. [compound verb]

Use *or* to show a choice between ideas.

TWO SENTENCES	An owl may have made that noise. The wind may have made that noise.
COMBINED	An owl or the wind may have made that noise. [compound subject]

Writer's Workshop Follow-up: Revision

Exchange your observational essay for a classmate's. Mark any passages that contain too many short sentences in a row, and suggest ways of combining them by joining subjects or verbs. Exchange papers again, and revise any choppy sentences your partner found.

Language Handbook HELP

See Using Connecting Words, page 741.

Technology HELP

See Language Workshop CD-ROM. Key word entry: combining sentences.

Try It Out

Use *and, but,* or *or* to combine each of the following pairs of sentences. The hints in parentheses will help you.

1. You can cross over this bridge. Your peoples can cross over this bridge. (Use *and.*)
2. He saw how beautiful she was. He kept his distance. (Use *but.*)
3. The blast stripped the trees from the slopes surrounding the lake. The blast moved on. (Use *and.*)
4. Mei could return to her sisters in the sky. Mei could stay with Chang. (Use *or.*)

Resources ———

Workshop Resources
- Worksheet, p. 49

Language Workshop CD-ROM
- Combining Sentences

Try It Out
Possible Answers
1. You and your peoples can cross over this bridge.
2. He saw how beautiful she was but kept his distance.
3. The blast stripped the trees from the slopes surrounding the lake and moved on.
4. Mei could return to her sisters in the sky or stay with Chang.

Assessing Learning

Quick Check: Combining Sentences by Using Connecting Words
Combine the following sentences. Use the hints in parentheses.

1. Mario saw the rabbit. Theresa saw the rabbit Anwar saw the rabbit. Hilda saw the rabbit. (Use *and.*) [Maria, Theresa, Anwar, and Hilda saw the rabbit.]
2. The rabbit saw the children. The rabbit stopped. (Use *and.*) [The rabbit saw the children and stopped.]

3. The rabbit was frightened. The rabbit did not run away. (Use *but.*) [The rabbit was frightened but did not run away.]
4. The children want to see the rabbit again. The children will go for another walk to look for it. (Use *and.*) [The children want to see the rabbit again and will go for another walk to look for it.]

5. If the children walk quietly, they may spot another rabbit. If the children walk quietly, they may even see a fox. (Use *or.*) [If the children walk quietly, they may spot another rabbit or may even see a fox.]

OBJECTIVES
1. Learn to use a science text-book to find information
2. Discover how a science text-book is organized
3. Use the parts of a textbook to locate information

Teaching the Lesson

Ask students to describe something interesting that they recently learned from their science textbook. Confirm that a science textbook is a rich resource of useful, fascinating information. Explain that this lesson will help students improve their skills in using a science textbook.

Using the Strategies

Answers
1. Chapter 26, Lesson 6, p. 512
2. Sample answers: Glaciers are thick sheets of ice; ice from glaciers forms icebergs; glaciers are found in cold geographic regions; glaciers can be 3,000 meters thick.
3. All of Canada and much of the northern United States and a small portion of South America in the area of modern Chile and Peru were covered by glaciers.

Extending the Strategies

Remind students to choose aspects of nature that they know something about but would like to know more about. Skimming and scanning their science textbook as described in the lesson will give them ideas on the range of topics scientists have explored.

Reading for Life

Reading a Science Book

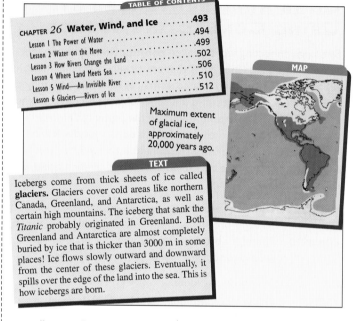

Situation

You've just read about how volcanoes change the earth. You've heard that glaciers also made huge changes in the earth, and you want to learn more. You decide to start with your science book.

Strategies

Focus your research.

• List questions you want your research to answer.

Use the text's structure to find information.

• Skim the **table of contents** to see how information in your textbook is organized. Scan unit headings and chapter titles. Do you see your research topic mentioned there?

• Think of some key words related to your topic. Search the **index** for those words. Check *glaciers,* of course, but don't stop there. Look for entries like *Ice Age* and *erosion.*

Use graphic features.

Look for **maps, charts, tables,** and photographs, which present a lot of information in

TABLE OF CONTENTS

CHAPTER 26 **Water, Wind, and Ice** **493**
Lesson 1 The Power of Water 494
Lesson 2 Water on the Move 499
Lesson 3 How Rivers Change the Land 502
Lesson 4 Where Land Meets Sea 506
Lesson 5 Wind—An Invisible River 510
Lesson 6 Glaciers—Rivers of Ice 512

MAP

Maximum extent of glacial ice, approximately 20,000 years ago.

TEXT

Icebergs come from thick sheets of ice called **glaciers.** Glaciers cover cold areas like northern Canada, Greenland, and Antarctica, as well as certain high mountains. The iceberg that sank the *Titanic* probably originated in Greenland. Both Greenland and Antarctica are almost completely buried by ice that is thicker than 3000 m in some places! Ice flows slowly outward and downward from the center of these glaciers. Eventually, it spills over the edge of the land into the sea. This is how icebergs are born.

a small space. Be sure to read the labels on graphic features and the captions carefully. A **caption** is the text beside or under each graphic feature. It tells you what you're looking at.

Using the Strategies

Answer the following questions about the material above, which is from a science textbook.

1. Look at the table of contents, and tell where you would find a lesson on glaciers.

2. List three things that you learned about glaciers.

3. How much of North and South America was once covered by glaciers?

Extending the Strategies

What in the natural world do you wonder about? Using the strategies you've learned here, look in your science textbook for information on a subject that interests you.

Reaching All Students

Struggling Learners

These students should work with others and with you to "walk through" the parts of a textbook. They may find it helpful to flag the various parts of a textbook with adhesive notes. Point out that the table of contents is always in the front of a book and lists the book's formal parts or sections in order. The index, on the other hand, is a comprehensive list, in alphabetical order, of the subjects covered in the book. An index entry will list every page in the book that gives information on the subject of the entry.

Learning for Life

Explaining Our World: Scientific Research

OBJECTIVES
1. Select and research a scientific topic alone or with a partner
2. Organize scientific research information, and choose and develop a method of presenting the research

Problem

Throughout history, people have tried to explain the world around them. Early on, myths provided explanations, but science has long since taken over that role. We now understand much that was unknown in ancient times. What natural phenomenon or other scientific topic do you want to learn about? How can you research it?

Project

Research a natural phenomenon or another scientific topic, and explain it to others.

Preparation

1. Pick a partner, and select a scientific topic that interests both of you. Make sure the topic is narrow enough to be studied in some detail. For example, choose lightning rather than weather, or choose life in the ocean's depths rather than the ocean.

2. Decide where you can find information on your topic.

For example, you might look at

- encyclopedias
- science textbooks
- science magazines, such as *Discover*
- science sections of news magazines and newspapers

Procedure

1. Working alone or with your partner, research your topic. Get together with your partner to organize your notes in clear categories.

2. Figure out how to present some of your material in a visual format—in a chart, graph, diagram, or map, for example.

Presentation

Choose one of these ways to present what you've learned:

1. Science Fair

Hold a science fair in your class. Partners should present their topics to the class in oral reports accompanied by visual aids, which might include photographs, diagrams, charts, and live demonstrations. After the fair, class members should write brief reports on what they learned at the fair.

2. Children's Science Show

Working with a group, plan and make a videotape that explains your topic to young children. Be sure to use clear and simple explanations and to include charts or diagrams. You might also include a demonstration. If possible, arrange to have the video shown to a second- or third-grade class.

3. Science Mural

As a class, create a large mural that explains several science topics. Include photographs, diagrams, charts, and maps.

Processing

Write a reflection, using this starter:

- One thing I learned about researching is . . .

LEARNING FOR LIFE **569**

Resources

Viewing and Representing
HRW Multimedia Presentation Maker
Students may wish to use the *Multimedia Presentation Maker* to display visual aids for their science fairs, charts or diagrams for their videotapes, or collage items for their murals.

Grading Timesaver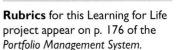

Rubrics for this Learning for Life project appear on p. 176 of the *Portfolio Management System*.

Using Tables of Contents to Organize Information
Tell students to be sure to study the table of contents of a book when they are conducting research using a variety of sources. Studying the table of contents offers a quick method of evaluating the usefulness of a text. Tell students that a table of contents is an outline of a book's organization. It shows how a book is divided (for example, into sections) and how the sections are arranged (for example, chronologically or by geographical region). Some books have overviews or summaries for each chapter that can help students decide whether or not the book's information is relevant to their research.

Developing Workplace Competencies

Preparation	Procedure	Presentation
• Identifying central issues and problems • Exhibiting sociability • Choosing the best alternative • Clarifying the problem • Making decisions	• Acquiring data • Evaluating data • Interpreting information • Solving problems • Thinking creatively	• Communicating ideas and information • Selecting equipment • Applying technology to specific tasks • Teaching others • Working in teams

Collection Eight

Tell Me a Tale

Theme

Tell Me a Tale   It's a tradition as old as the human race—to tell stories to explain the world, to create heroic role models, to teach children the values of generosity and courage, to express our hopes of one day finding a world of perfect happiness and peace.

Reading the Anthology

Reaching Struggling Readers

The *Reading Skills and Strategies: Reaching Struggling Readers* binder provides materials coordinated with the Pupil's Edition (see the Collection Planner, p. T569C) to help students who have difficulty reading and comprehending text, or students who are reluctant readers. The binder for sixth grade is organized around eleven individual skill areas and offers the following options:

- **MiniRead**   MiniReads are short, easy texts that give students a chance to practice a particular skill and strategy before reading selections in the Pupil's Edition. Each MiniRead Skill Lesson can be taught independently or used in conjunction with a Selection Skill Lesson.

- **Selection Skill Lessons**   Selection Skill Lessons allow students to apply skills introduced in the MiniReads. Each Selection Skill Lesson provides reading instruction and practice specific to a particular piece of literature in the Pupil's Edition.

Reading Beyond the Anthology

Read On   Collection Eight includes an annotated bibliography of books suitable for extended reading. The suggested books are related to works in this collection by theme, by author, or by subject. To preview the Read On for Collection Eight, please turn to p. T657.

HRW Library   The *HRW Library* offers novels, plays, and short-story collections for extended reading. Each book in the Library includes one or more major works and thematically or topically related Connections. The Connections are magazine articles, poems, or other pieces of literature. Each book in the *HRW Library* is also accompanied by a Study Guide that provides teaching suggestions and worksheets. For Collection Eight, the following titles are recommended.

A CHRISTMAS CAROL
Charles Dickens
This famous story tells of Scrooge, the miser who is transformed after he undertakes a perilous journey through his own past, present, and future.

TREASURE ISLAND
Robert Louis Stevenson
This story has classic adventure: a boy who sets off to find a buried treasure, an evil villain, a desert island, and pirates that send shivers down the reader's back.

Skills Focus

Selection or Feature	Reading Skills and Strategies	Elements of Literature	Language/ Grammar	Vocabulary/ Spelling	Writing	Listening/ Speaking	Viewing/ Representing
Medusa's Head (p. 572) Greek Myth *retold by* Olivia Coolidge	Dialogue with the Text, pp. 572, 586 Summarize the Text, p. 586	Myths and Mythic Heroes, pp. 572, 586 Quest, p. 586	Words from Myths, p. 588	Use Words in the Context of Myths, p. 588	Make Up a Story About a Character Who Can Become Invisible, p. 587 Update the Myth, p. 587		Create a Star Map of Constellations Named for Greek Mythical Figures, p. 587
Baucis and Philemon (p. 589) Greek Myth *retold by* Olivia Coolidge	Cross-Cultural Connections, pp. 589, 595, 596 Use a Chart to Organize Ideas, p. 595	Metamorphosis, pp. 589, 595, 596 Theme, p. 596 Story, p. 596 Plot, p. 596	Homophones: *Their, There,* and *They're,* p. 597	Spelling Words with Silent Letters, p. 597	Jot Down Ideas for a Metamorphosis, p. 596 Write an Essay on How the Myth Evokes a Theme, p. 596	Invent a Myth with a Moral, and Present It to the Class, p. 596	Draw the Transformation of Baucis and Philemon, p. 596
Elements of Literature: Mythology (p. 598)	Connect with Mythical Themes, p. 598	Myth, p. 598 • Origin Myth • Greek Myth • Roman Myth		Origin of the Word *Myth,* p. 598			
Quetzalcoatl (p. 599) Mexican Myth *retold by* Amy Cruse	Make Predictions, pp. 599, 605 Use Prior Knowledge, p. 599	Golden-Age Myth, pp. 599, 605, 606 Myth, pp. 605, 606	*Effect* vs. *Affect,* p. 607	Use Words in the Context of Myths, p. 607	Prewrite a Sequel to "Quetzalcoatl," p. 606 Make a Nahuatl-English Dictionary, p. 606 Write Display Panels for an Art Exhibit, p. 606		Make Replicas or Draw Pictures of Toltec Art, p. 606
Elements of Literature: Folk Tales (p. 608)		Folk Tale, p. 608 Character, p. 608 Tricksters, p. 608					
Reading Skills and Strategies: Using Word Parts to Build Meanings (p. 609)			Prefixes, p. 609 Suffixes, p. 609	Use Prefixes and Suffixes to Determine Word Meanings, p. 609			
Ali Baba and the Forty Thieves (p. 610) Persian Folk Tale *retold by* Walter McVitty	Use Word Parts to Determine Meaning, pp. 610, 622 Use a Time Line, p. 620	Suspense, p. 620 Fantasy, p. 620 Title, p. 620 Point of View, p. 621	Words from Arabic, p. 622	Prefixes, Suffixes, pp. 610, 622 Word Roots, p. 622	Write a Plot That Uses the Number Three, p. 621 Rewrite the Tale from Morgiana's Point of View, p. 621	Present a Group Reading of the Opening Pages of the Tale, p. 621	Design and Sketch the Three Costumes Worn by the Robber Chief, p. 621
The Emperor's New Clothes (p. 623) Hans Christian Andersen		Theme, pp. 623, 636, 637 Setting, p. 637 Character, p. 637 Plot Events, p. 637	Formal English, p. 638 Informal English, p. 638	Idioms, p. 638	Note Ideas for Story Themes, p. 637 Write About Your Favorite Clothes, p. 637 Extend the Story, p. 637	Present a Reader's Theater Reading of the Story, p. 637	
He Lion, Bruh Bear, and Bruh Rabbit (p. 639) African American Folk Tale *retold by* Virginia Hamilton	Use a Graphic to Track Sequence of Main Events and Cause and Effect, p. 646	Tricksters, pp. 639, 646 Folk Tale, pp. 639, 646 Main Events, p. 646	*To, Too,* and *Two,* p. 647	Use of a Glossary, p. 647	Create a Trickster and Freewrite for a Story, p. 646	Present a Reading or Performance of the Folk Tale or of One of Aesop's Fables, p. 646	
No Questions Asked: Dragon, Dragon (p. 648) John Gardner	The **No Questions Asked** feature provides students with an unstructured opportunity to practice reading strategies using a selection that extends the theme of the collection.						
Writer's Workshop: Story (p. 658)		Character, pp. 659–660 Plot, p. 660	Style: Realistic Dialogue, p. 660		Write a Story, pp. 658–662		
Sentence Workshop: Joining Sentences (p. 663)			Compound and Complex Sentences, p. 663		Revise Choppy Sentences, p. 663		
Reading for Life: Reading a Map and a Time Line (p. 664)	Read a Map and a Time Line, p. 664						Use a Map's Legend, Key, and Scale, p. 664
Learning for Life: Making Oral Presentations (p. 665)					Write a Folk Song Based on a Story, p. 665	Plan a Storytelling Festival, p. 665 Reader's Theater, p. 665	

Skills Focus

T569B

Resources for this Collection

Note: All resources for this collection are available for preview on the *One-Stop Planner CD-ROM 2 with Test Generator.* All worksheets and blackline masters may be printed from the CD-ROM.

Internet Resources
go.hrw.com LE0 6-8

Selection or Feature	Reading and Literary Skills	Language and Grammar
Medusa's Head (p. 572) Olivia Coolidge **Connections: Perseus and the Gorgon's Head** (p. 582) Marcia Williams	• *Reading Skills and Strategies: Reaching Struggling Readers* • Selection Skill Lesson, p. 33 • *Graphic Organizers for Active Reading,* Worksheet p. 37	• *Grammar and Language Links:* Words from Myths, Worksheet p. 53 • *Daily Oral Grammar,* Transparency 35
Baucis and Philemon (p. 589) Olivia Coolidge	• *Reading Skills and Strategies: Reaching Struggling Readers* • MiniRead Skill Lesson, p. 179 • Selection Skill Lesson, p. 186 • *Graphic Organizers for Active Reading,* Worksheet p. 38 • *Literary Elements:* Transparency 10; Worksheet p. 31	• *Grammar and Language Links:* Homophones, Worksheet p. 55 • *Language Workshop CD-ROM,* Words Often Confused • *Daily Oral Grammar,* Transparency 36
Elements of Literature: Mythology (p. 598)	• *Literary Elements,* Transparency 10	
Quetzalcoatl (p. 599) Amy Cruse	• *Reading Skills and Strategies: Reaching Struggling Readers* • Selection Skill Lesson, p. 71 • *Graphic Organizers for Active Reading,* Worksheet p. 39	• *Grammar and Language Links:* Words Often Confused, Worksheet p. 57 • *Language Workshop CD-ROM,* Words Often Confused • *Daily Oral Grammar,* Transparency 37
Elements of Literature: Folk Tales (p. 608)	• *Literary Elements,* Transparency 11	
Ali Baba and the Forty Thieves (p. 610) Walter McVitty	• *Reading Skills and Strategies: Reaching Struggling Readers* • Selection Skill Lesson, p. 49 • *Graphic Organizers for Active Reading,* Worksheet p. 40 • *Literary Elements:* Transparency 11; Worksheet p. 34	• *Grammar and Language Links:* Words from Other Languages, Worksheet p. 59 • *Daily Oral Grammar,* Transparency 38
The Emperor's New Clothes (p. 623) Hans Christian Andersen **Connections: King Long Shanks** (p. 630) Jane Yolen	• *Graphic Organizers for Active Reading,* Worksheet p. 41	• *Grammar and Language Links:* Style: Formal and Informal English, Worksheet p. 61 • *Daily Oral Grammar,* Transparency 39
He Lion, Bruh Bear, and Bruh Rabbit (p. 639) Virginia Hamilton **Connections: The Fox and the Crow** (p. 644) Aesop *dramatized by* Mara Rockliff	• *Graphic Organizers for Active Reading,* Worksheet p. 42	• *Grammar and Language Links:* Proofreading *To, Too* and *Two,* Worksheet p. 63 • *Language Workshop CD-ROM,* Homonyms • *Daily Oral Grammar,* Transparency 40
No Questions Asked: Dragon, Dragon (p. 648) John Gardner	The **No Questions Asked** feature provides students with an unstructured opportunity to practice reading strategies using a selection that extends the theme of the collection.	
Writer's Workshop: Story (p. 658)		
Sentence Workshop: Joining Sentences (p. 663)		• *Workshop Resources,* p. 51
Learning for Life: Making Oral Presentations (p. 665)		

Collection Resources

- *Cross-Curricular Activities,* p. 55
- *Portfolio Management System:*
  Introduction to Portfolio Assessment, p. 1;
  Parent/Guardian Letters, p. 101
- *Formal Assessment,*
  Reading Application Test, p. 127
- *Test Generator,* Collection Test

Vocabulary, Spelling, and Decoding	Writing	Listening and Speaking, Viewing and Representing	Assessment
• *Words to Own,* Worksheet p. 21 • *Spelling and Decoding,* Worksheet p. 24	• *Portfolio Management System,* Rubrics for Choices, p. 177	• *Audio CD Library,* Disc 14, Track 2 • *Portfolio Management System,* Rubrics for Choices, p. 177	• *Formal Assessment,* Selection Test, p. 113 • *Standardized Test Preparation,* p. 82 • *Test Generator* (One-Stop Planner CD-ROM)
• *Spelling and Decoding,* Worksheet p. 25	• *Portfolio Management System,* Rubrics for Choices, p. 178	• *Audio CD Library,* Disc 14, Track 3 • *Portfolio Management System,* Rubrics for Choices, p. 178	• *Formal Assessment,* Selection Test, p. 115 • *Test Generator* (One-Stop Planner CD-ROM)
			• *Formal Assessment,* Literary Elements Test, p. 125 • *Standardized Test Preparation,* p. 84
• *Words to Own,* Worksheet p. 22 • *Spelling and Decoding,* Worksheet p. 26	• *Portfolio Management System,* Rubrics for Choices, p. 179	• *Audio CD Library,* Disc 14, Track 4 • *Viewing and Representing:* Fine Art Transparency 18 Worksheet p. 72 • *Portfolio Management System,* Rubrics for Choices, p. 179	• *Formal Assessment,* Selection Test, p. 117 • *Standardized Test Preparation,* p. 86 • *Test Generator* (One-Stop Planner CD-ROM)
		• *Visual Connections,* Videocassette B, Segment 9	• *Formal Assessment,* Literary Elements Test, p. 126
• *Spelling and Decoding,* Worksheet p. 27	• *Portfolio Management System,* Rubrics for Choices, p. 180	• *Audio CD Library,* Disc 14, Track 5 • *Viewing and Representing:* Fine Art Transparency 19 Worksheet p. 76 • *Portfolio Management System,* Rubrics for Choices, p. 180	• *Formal Assessment,* Selection Test, p. 119 • *Standardized Test Preparation,* p. 88 • *Test Generator* (One-Stop Planner CD-ROM)
• *Spelling and Decoding,* Worksheet p. 28	• *Portfolio Management System,* Rubrics for Choices, p. 181	• *Audio CD Library,* Disc 15, Track 2 • *Portfolio Management System,* Rubrics for Choices, p. 181	• *Formal Assessment,* Selection Test, p. 121 • *Test Generator* (One-Stop Planner CD-ROM)
	• *Portfolio Management System,* Rubrics for Choices, p. 182	• *Audio CD Library,* Disc 15, Track 3 • *Portfolio Management System,* Rubrics for Choices, p. 182	• *Formal Assessment,* Selection Test, p. 123 • *Standardized Test Preparation,* p. 90 • *Test Generator* (One-Stop Planner CD-ROM)
		• *Audio CD Library,* Disc 15, Track 4 • *Viewing and Representing:* Fine Art Transparency 20 Worksheet p. 80	
	• *Workshop Resources,* p. 33 • *Writer's Workshop 1 CD-ROM,* Story		• *Portfolio Management System* • Prewriting, p. 183 • Peer Editing, p. 184 • Assessment Rubric, p. 185
		• *Viewing and Representing,* HRW Multimedia Presentation Maker	• *Portfolio Management System,* Rubrics, p.186

Transparency   CD-ROM   Video   Audio CD

OBJECTIVES

1. Read a collection of myths and folk tales
2. Interpret literary elements used in the literature, with special emphasis on the elements of myths and folk tales
3. Apply a variety of reading strategies, particularly using word parts to build meaning
4. Respond to the literature in a variety of modes
5. Learn and use new words
6. Develop skills in reading a map and time line
7. Plan, draft, revise, edit, proof, and publish a story
8. Combine short sentences into a compound or complex sentence
9. Explore oral storytelling through a variety of projects

Introducing the Theme

The selections in this collection are myths and folk tales. The main characters include a daring hero, a generous old couple, a vulnerable god, a clever servant, a foolish emperor, an obedient son, and some intelligent animals. The stories describe superhuman quests, miraculous transformations, tragic conflicts, and comic exploits. As with all myths and folk tales, these selections provide valuable lessons about human nature.

As students read the selections, remind them to look for elements that they have seen or heard in other stories and to identify elements that they can incorporate into stories of their own.

Resources

Portfolio Management System
• Introduction to Portfolio Assessment, p. 1
• Parent/Guardian Letters, p. 101
Formal Assessment
• Reading Application Test, p. 127
Test Generator
• Collection Test
Cross-Curricular Activities
• Teaching Notes, p. 55

Tell Me a Tale

*In the joy of story,
in the power of story,
to create a world of
power and joy
for all living beings.*

— *Floating Eagle Feather*

Selection Readability

This Annotated Teacher's Edition provides a summary of each selection in the student book. Following each Summary heading, you will find one, two or three small icons. These icons indicate, in an approximate sense, the reading level of the selection.

■ One icon indicates that the selection is easy.
■ ■ Two icons indicate that the selection is on an intermediate reading level.
■ ■ ■ Three icons indicate that the selection is challenging.

Tales (1988) by Jonathan Green, Naples, Florida.
Oil on masonite (24″ × 36″). Photograph by Tim Stamm.

571

Responding to the Quotation

? What stories have you read or heard that gave you a sense of power or joy? [Students may identify any stories they have enjoyed reading or hearing.] Encourage visual learners to mention movies or television shows that have given them joy or a sense of their own self-worth or power. Ask students to cite specific events and other details. Students may mention such things as happy endings and main characters with whom they identified or wanted to emulate.

RESPONDING TO THE ART

This painting by **Jonathan Green** (1955–   ) is modeled after Green's great-uncle Ebenezer Stewart, who was a master storyteller of tales from the African American folk tradition. (Other work by Green appears on pp. 111 and 112.)

Activity. Ask students what is happening in this picture, how they think this picture relates to the title of the collection, and what feelings they think the people in the picture are experiencing.

Writer's Notebook

Have students freewrite about an experience of hearing, reading, or telling a great story. The experience may be linked to family members, acquaintances, or visits to a library or museum. Tell students to focus on recalling details from the story and what was most exciting about the experience. Remind students to keep their notes for possible use in the Writer's Workshop on narrative writing on p. 658.

Writing Focus: Story

The following **Work in Progress** assignments in this collection build to a culminating **Writer's Workshop** at the end of Collection 8.

• Medusa's Head	Make up a story about an invisible character (p. 587)
• Baucis and Philemon	Jot down ideas for a story about a change (p. 596)
• Quetzalcoatl	Make up a character (p. 606)
• Ali Baba and the Forty Thieves	Plan a story that uses the number three (p. 621)
• The Emperor's New Clothes	Gather ideas for a story about people (p. 637)
• He Lion, Bruh Bear, and Bruh Rabbit	Freewrite about a trickster character (p. 646)

Writer's Workshop: Narrative Writing / Story (p. 658)

OBJECTIVES

1. Read and interpret the myth
2. Identify characteristics of mythic heroes
3. Monitor comprehension
4. Express understanding through creative writing or science/art
5. Identify words from myths; use a dictionary or other reference source to understand modern words derived from mythological names
6. Understand and use new words

SKILLS

Literary
• Identify characteristics of mythic heroes

Reading
• Monitor comprehension

Writing
• Collect ideas for a story
• Update a myth

Grammar/Language
• Identify and use words from myths

Vocabulary
• Define and use new words

Science/Art
• Make a star map

Viewing/Representing
• Discuss how a piece of sculpture relates to a myth (ATE)

Planning

• **Block Schedule**
  Block Scheduling Lesson Plans with Pacing Guide

• **Traditional Schedule**
  Lesson Plans Including Strategies for English-Language Learners

• **One-Stop Planner**
  CD-ROM with Test Generator

Before You Read

MEDUSA'S HEAD

Make the Connection

Fickle Finger of Fate

The idea of fate is important in this Greek myth. *Fate* refers to a power that is believed to decide the future no matter what we do. You learn right away in this story that a king has received bad news from an oracle (ôr′ə·kəl)—a priest or priestess who can foretell the future. He has learned that one day he will be killed by his own grandson.

Think about this for a few minutes. Then, discuss with several classmates what it would be like to know what is going to happen in the future.

Reading Skills and Strategies

Dialogue with the Text

As you read this story, jot down your responses to it. You may want to ask questions about unfamiliar words and predict what will happen next. On page 575, you'll see what one student thought as she began reading.

go.hrw.com
LE0 6-8

572 TELL ME A TALE

Elements of Literature

Mythic Heroes: More Than Human

What characters can fly, become invisible, and call on other supernatural powers in the fight against evil? You'll probably think of comic-book characters such as Batman or Superman. In "Medusa's Head" you'll meet a mythic hero, Perseus, who can do all these things—and more.

In the world of myth, heroes do the things we wish we could do and the things we are glad we don't have to do. Heroes in myths represent the hopes and fears of the people who create them.

Heroes in myths are often helped by gods. Sometimes they are even gods themselves. These superheroes usually have supernatural powers, and they always face great difficulties and challenges (like slaying a monster). Often the mythic hero saves a whole society from ruin.

Gorgon (sixth century B.C.).
Museo Archeologico, Syracuse, Sicily, Italy.
Scala/Art Resource, New York.

> A **mythic hero** is a powerful person with unusual gifts who undertakes superhuman tasks, sometimes with help from the gods.
>
> *For more on Myth, see page 598 and the Handbook of Literary Terms.*

Preteaching Vocabulary

Words to Own

Have students read the five Words to Own and the definitions at the bottom of the selection pages. If necessary, provide help in pronouncing the words. Then ask students to use context clues to identify the correct word for each sentence that follows.

1. Never stopping, the nine planets move in [perpetual] orbit around the sun.
2. As the day ended, the sun [descended] behind the western horizon.
3. Looking up, we saw bats hanging from the dark [recesses] of the cave.
4. Suddenly, the rabbit disappeared from the magician's hands, leaving the audience in a state of [perplexity].
5. The hummingbird [hovered] over the flower in order to drink the nectar.

MEDUSA'S HEAD

a Greek myth,
retold by **Olivia Coolidge**

Horror stiffened his arm as he hovered over her with his sword uplifted.

MEDUSA'S HEAD **573**

Summary ■ ■ ■

King Acrisios wants a son to succeed him, but the oracle tells him that he will have no son and that he will be killed by a grandson born to his only daughter, Danae. In an attempt to alter fate, the king imprisons Danae, but Zeus takes pity on her and gives her a son named Perseus. Angry and afraid, Acrisios puts Danae and Perseus into a wooden chest and casts them into the sea. Mother and son are rescued when the chest lands on an island ruled by Polydectes, who falls in love with Danae but is rejected by her. In order to get Perseus out of the way so he can coerce Danae, Polydectes pretends to marry someone else, and when Perseus asks what he can give the king as a wedding gift, the king sets up his demise by asking for the head of the Gorgon Medusa. Undaunted, Perseus sets to the task, aided by Athena, who tells him first to go to the sisters Phorcides who will in turn tell him how to get the hat of darkness, the winged sandals, and the knapsack for Medusa's head. When the hero gets this magic equipment, Athena gives him a shield and Hermes gives him a sword of adamant, for nothing else will kill Medusa. Athena warns Perseus not to look directly at the Gorgons, or he will be turned to stone; he must look only at their reflection in his shield. After reaching the Gorgons and taking Medusa's head, Perseus flies across the Libyan desert, lets Atlas see Medusa's head, which turns him into a mountain, and rescues Andromeda, who was about to be sacrificed to appease Poseidon. Perseus returns to his mother with Andromeda as his bride and uses the Gorgon's head to turn the wicked Polydectes to stone. Afterward, Perseus goes to seek Acrisios, his grandfather. He engages in an athletic contest in the kingdom of Argos and throws a discus, which is caught by the wind and goes straight for Acrisios. The discus hits Acrisios in the foot and causes the king to die of shock.

Resources: Print and Media

Reading
- *Reading Skills and Strategies*
  Selection Skill Lesson, p. 33
- *Graphic Organizers for Active Reading*, p. 37
- *Words to Own*, p. 21
- *Spelling and Decoding*, Worksheet, p. 24
- *Audio CD Library*, Disc 14, Track 2

Writing and Language
- *Daily Oral Grammar*
  Transparency 35

- *Grammar and Language Links*
  Worksheet, p. 53

Assessment
- *Formal Assessment*, p. 113
- *Portfolio Management System*, p. 177
- *Standardized Test Preparation*, p. 82
- *Test Generator (One-Stop Planner CD-ROM)*

Internet
- go.hrw.com (keyword: LE0 6-8)

Resources

Listening

Audio CD Library

An exciting recording of this myth is included in the *Audio CD Library:*
- Disc 14, Track 2

Ⓐ Critical Thinking

Classifying

❓ As a way of helping students become familiar with the names of the characters in the selection, organize the names into different categories using the list and the following questions: Which characters are gods? [Apollo, Zeus, Hermes, Nereus, Poseidon] Which character is a goddess? [Athena] Which characters are kings? [Acrisios, Polydectes, Cepheus] Who is a queen? [Cassiopeia] Which characters are princesses? [Danae, Andromeda] Which characters are brothers of kings? [Proitos and Dictys] Which character is the son of a human and a god? [Perseus] Which characters are groups of sisters? [Gorgons and Phorcides] Create a chart to show the different categories of characters.

Characters and Places

King Acrisios (ə·crē′sē·ōs′) **of Argos** (är′gäs′): Argos was an ancient city and kingdom in southern Greece.

Proitos (prō·ē′tōs): brother of King Acrisios.

Danae (dan′ā·ē′): daughter of King Acrisios. She bears Zeus's son Perseus.

Apollo: Greek god of light, medicine, poetry, and prophecy. The oracle of Apollo was a priest or priestess through whom the god was believed to speak.

Zeus (zyo͞os): king of the Greek gods.

Dictys (dic′tis): fisherman, brother of Polydectes. They lived on the island of Seriphos.

Polydectes (päl′ē·dek′tēz): king of Seriphos.

Perseus (pʉr′sē·əs): son of Danae and Zeus.

Gorgons: three fearful sisters who had brass hands, gold wings, and serpentlike scales. Medusa, the youngest Gorgon, had snakes for hair and could turn people to stone merely by looking at them.

Athene (ə·thē′nē): Greek goddess of crafts, war, and wisdom. Also spelled *Athena*.

Phorcides (fôr′sə·dēz): three sisters who live in a cave and have only one eye and one tooth between them.

Hermes (hʉr′mēz′): messenger of the gods.

Cepheus (sē′fē·əs): king of Ethiopia.

Cassiopeia (kas′ē·ō·pē′ə): queen of Ethiopia.

Andromeda (an·dräm′ə·də): daughter of King Cepheus and Queen Cassiopeia. She was chained to a rock to calm the anger of the sea god Poseidon.

Nereus (nir′ē·əs): a minor sea god.

Poseidon (pō·sī′dən): god of the sea.

574 TELL ME A TALE

Reaching All Students

Struggling Readers

Have students read the Connections cartoon on p. 582 before reading this selection. This will help them become familiar with the numerous characters and the complicated plot of the story. After they have read "Medusa's Head" and the cartoon Connections feature, have students compare the two versions of the story. Use the lesson, Comparing Story Variants, in the *Reading Skills and Strategies* binder.
- Selection Skill Lesson, p. 33

English Language Learners

Pronouncing some of the names of the characters and places may pose difficulties for some students. You may want to guide students in pronouncing the words, using a choral reading or call-and-response strategy, modeling each pronunciation and having students repeat it.

Advanced Learners

Have students consult a modern-day map of the Mediterranean region and attempt to locate the countries that might correspond to Larissa, Argos, and Seriphos in the selection. Some students may also want to research myths or folk tales originating from other areas on the map, such as Spain, Italy, Sicily, Asia Minor, Egypt, and Ethiopia.

T574

King Acrisios of Argos was a hard, selfish man. He hated his brother, Proitos, who later drove him from his kingdom, and he cared nothing for his daughter, Danae. His whole heart was set on having a son who should succeed him, but since many years went by and still he had only the one daughter, he sent a message to the oracle of Apollo to ask whether he should have more children of his own. The answer of the oracle was terrible. Acrisios should have no son, but his daughter, Danae, would bear him a grandchild who should grow up to kill him. At these words Acrisios was beside himself with fear and rage. Swearing that Danae should never have a child to murder him, he had a room built underground and lined all through with brass. Thither he conducted Danae and shut her up, bidding her spend the rest of her life alone.

It is possible to thwart the plans of mortal men, but never those of the gods. Zeus himself looked with pity on the unfortunate girl, and it is said he <u>descended</u> to her through the tiny hole that gave light and air to her chamber, pouring himself down into her lap in the form of a shower of gold.

When word came to the king from those who brought food and drink to his daughter that the girl was with child, Acrisios was angry and afraid. He would have liked best to murder both Danae and her infant son, Perseus, but he did not dare for fear of the gods' anger at so hideous a crime. He made, therefore, a great chest of wood with bands of brass about it. Shutting up the girl and her baby inside, he cast them into the sea, thinking that they would either drown or starve.

Again the gods came to the help of Danae, for they caused the planks of the chest to swell until they fitted tightly and let no water in.

The chest floated for some days and was cast up at last

WORDS TO OWN
descended (dē·send'id) *v.:* moved from a high place to a lower one; came down.

Dialogue with the Text

Why is there hatred between Acrisios and Proitos?

What is an oracle?
Where is the wife?
Could they adopt children?
Had Danae already had the opportunity to have a child?

Could people talk or communicate through the hole?

Does wood or brass dissolve in salt water?
What will happen to Danae and the child?

Katie Gaddis

— Katharine ("Katie") Gaddis
Westview Middle School
Longmont, Colorado

MEDUSA'S HEAD **575**

B Cultural Connections
In feudal European monarchies, the eldest male child of a ruler almost always succeeded the ruler. This line of succession was part of a system known as *primogeniture*, in which the eldest son was the sole legal heir of the estate of one or both parents. This system has largely vanished today, but is still adhered to in most remaining monarchies, such as the British royal family, in which the eldest son, or daughter if there is no son, inherits the throne.

C Elements of Literature
Mythic Heroes
❓ From this description, what powers does Zeus have? [He can peer into the lives of mortals and change into different shapes and materials, such as a "shower of gold."]

D Reading Skills and Strategies

Dialogue with the Text
❓ Look at Katherine Gaddis's questions in the column at the right of the page. What questions did you have as you read this page? [Students may have had some of the same questions as "Katie." Other possible questions are: How did King Acrisios become so hard and selfish and why did he deserve to be killed? What kind of person is Danae?]

Skill Link

Decoding: Unusual Spellings for Long and Short Vowels
Ask students to pronounce the following pairs of words from p. 575: *kill, build; he, sea.* Point out that both words in each pair have the same vowel sound (short *i*; long *e*) but the sound is spelled differently in each word. Explain that for many short vowel sounds, one vowel letter stands for one vowel sound as in *hen, pig, hop,* and *bug;* long vowel sounds may be spelled with one or two vowels, as in *go* and *mean.* Ask students to pronounce the words *myth* and *nymph.* What conclusions can they draw about the short *i* spelling? [It is sometimes spelled with a *y*]. Explain that the vowel sound with the most variant spellings in "Medusa's Head" is short *e.* For example, it is spelled *ai* in *said* and *again,* *ea* in *head* and *heavy,* and *ie* in *friends.*

Activity
Have students read the following words from the myth and sort them by the sound represented by *ea*: short *e* as in *head,* long *e* as in *sea,* etc.

already	great	overspread
appease	beneath	ceased
dreadful	heard	idea
instead	ocean	sheath
threatened	weakened	weary

A Elements of Literature

Mythic Heroes

? What qualities does Perseus have that indicate he might be a hero? [He is handsome, stronger than most young men, and a leader.]

B Reading Skills and Strategies

Dialogue with the Text

? What type of present do you think Polydectes will ask Perseus to get? Why? [Possible response: Polydectes will ask Perseus to bring something dangerous or impossible to get, because he wants Perseus to perish.]

C Appreciating Language

Recognizing Simile

? To what two animals does the author compare the Gorgons? [a serpent and a wild boar] What images come to mind from these comparisons? [The comparisons create images of ugliness, meanness, and danger.]

D Struggling Readers

Finding Sequence of Events

? What steps must Perseus take in order to slay the Gorgon? [He must first go to the sisters Phorcides, then to the nymphs where he'll get the hat of darkness, winged sandals, and knapsack. Next, he must take the shield Athena gives him and the sword from her brother Hermes. When he is near the Gorgon, he must turn his eyes away and kill her by using the reflection in the shield to guide the blow of his sword.]

on an island. There Dictys, a fisherman, found it and took Danae to his brother, Polydectes, who was king of the island. Danae was made a servant in the palace, yet before many years had passed, both Dictys and Polydectes had fallen in love with the silent, golden-haired girl. She in her heart preferred Dictys, yet since his brother was king, she did not dare to make her choice. Therefore she hung always over Perseus, pretending that mother love left her no room for any other, and year after year a silent frown would cross Polydectes' face as he saw her caress the child.

At last, Perseus became a young man, handsome and strong beyond the common and a leader among the youths of the island, though he was but the son of a poor servant. Then it seemed to Polydectes that if he could once get rid of Perseus, he could force Danae to become his wife, whether she would or not. Meanwhile, in order to lull the young man's suspicions, he pretended that he intended to marry a certain noble maiden and would collect a wedding gift for her. Now the custom was that this gift of the bridegroom to the bride was in part his own and in part put together from the marriage presents of his friends and relatives. All the young men, therefore, brought Polydectes a present, excepting Perseus, who was his servant's son and possessed nothing to bring. Then Polydectes said to the others, "This young man owes me more than any of you, since I took him in and brought him up in my own house, and yet he gives me nothing."

Perseus answered in anger at the injustice of the charge, "I have nothing of my own, Polydectes, yet ask me what you will, and I will fetch it, for I owe you my life."

At this Polydectes smiled, for it was what he had intended, and he answered, "Fetch me, if this is your boast, the Gorgon's head."

Now the Gorgons, who lived far off on the shores of the ocean, were three fearful sisters with hands of brass, wings of gold, and scales like a serpent. Two of them had scaly heads and tusks like the wild boar, but the third, Medusa, had the face of a beautiful woman with hair of writhing serpents, and so terrible was her expression that all who looked on it were immediately turned to stone. This much Perseus knew of the Gorgons, but of how to find or kill them, he had no idea. Nevertheless, he had given his promise, and though he saw now the satisfaction of King Polydectes, he was bound to keep his word. In his perplexity, he prayed to the wise goddess Athene, who came to him in a vision and promised him her aid.

"First, you must go," she said, "to the sisters Phorcides, who will tell you the way to the nymphs who guard the hat of darkness, the winged sandals, and the knapsack which can hold the Gorgon's head. Then I will give you a shield, and my brother Hermes will give you a sword, which shall be made of adamant, the hardest rock. For nothing else can kill the Gorgon, since so venomous is her blood that a mortal sword, when plunged in it, is eaten away. But when you come to the Gorgons, invisible in your hat of darkness, turn your eyes away from them and look only on their reflection in your gleaming shield. Thus you may kill the monster without yourself being turned to stone. Pass her sisters by, for they are immortal, but smite off the head of Medusa with the hair of writhing snakes.

WORDS TO OWN

perplexity (pər·pleks′ə·tē) *n.*: bewilderment; confusion.

Taking a Second Look

Review: Summarizing

Point out that when readers summarize, they present the main events and essential ideas of a text in a few words. Discuss how summarizing helps readers remember and understand a text and share it with others. Summarizing is also a useful way to record the most important points of a text, and can help readers analyze and evaluate the material.

Activities

1. Ask students to write a summary of what they have read in "Medusa's Head" so far. Then have them exchange papers and edit each other's summaries. Students can add to their summaries as they read the myth.

2. At the end of the reading, create a class summary by compiling individual summaries.

Then put it in your knapsack and return, and I will be with you."

The vision ended, and with the aid of Athene, Perseus set out on the long journey to seek the Phorcides. These live in a dim cavern in the far north, where nights and days are one and where the whole earth is overspread with perpetual twilight. There sat the three old women mumbling to one another, crouched in a dim heap together, for they had but one eye and one tooth between them, which they passed from hand to hand. Perseus came quietly behind them, and as they fumbled for the eye, he put his strong, brown hand next to one of the long, yellow ones, so that the old crone thought that it was her sister's and put the eye into it. There was a high scream of anger when they discovered the theft, and much clawing and groping in the dim recesses of the cavern. But they were helpless in their blindness and Perseus could laugh at them. At length, for the price of their eye, they told him how to reach the nymphs, and Perseus, laying the eye quickly in the hand of the nearest sister, fled as fast as he could before she could use it.

Again it was a far journey to the garden of the nymphs, where it is always sunshine and the trees bear golden apples. But the nymphs are friends of the wise gods and hate the monsters of darkness and the spirits of anger and despair. Therefore, they received Perseus with rejoicing and put the hat of darkness on his head, while on his feet they bound the golden, winged sandals, which are those Hermes wears when he runs down the slanting sunbeams or races along the pathways of the wind. Next, Perseus put on his back the silver sack with the gleaming tassels of gold, and flung across his shoulder the black-sheathed sword that was the gift of Hermes. On his left arm he fitted the shield that Athene gave, a gleaming silver shield like a mirror, plain without any marking. Then he sprang into the air and ran, invisible like the rushing wind, far out over the white-capped sea, across the yellow sands of the eastern desert, over strange streams and towering mountains, until at last he came to the shores of the distant ocean which flowed round all the world.

There was a gray gorge of stone by the ocean's edge, where lay Medusa and her sisters sleeping in the dim depths of the rock. All up and down the cleft, the stones took fantastic shapes of trees, beasts, birds, or serpents. Here and there, a man who had looked on the terrible Medusa stood forever with horror on his face. Far over the twilit gorge Perseus hovered invisible, while he loosened the pale, strange sword from its black sheath. Then, with his face turned away and eyes on the silver shield, he dropped, slow and silent as a falling leaf, down through the rocky cleft, twisting and turning past countless strange gray shapes,

Medusa by Michelangelo Caravaggio (1573–1610).
Uffizi, Florence, Italy. Scala/Art Resource, New York.

- -

WORDS TO OWN
perpetual (pər·pech′ o͞o·əl) *adj.*: continual; constant.
recesses (rē′ses·əz) *n.*: hollow places.
hovered (huv′ərd) *v.*: stayed suspended in the air.

- -

MEDUSA'S HEAD 577

RESPONDING TO THE ART
Michelangelo Caravaggio (1573–1610) was a master of realism and naturalism in painting. He used ordinary people as models and employed extreme contrasts of light and darkness known as *chiaroscuro* to give his paintings an intense, dramatic quality. See also his painting entitled *Fruit basket* on pp. 590–591.
Activity. Ask students to describe the features of the painting that seem faithful to the description of Medusa. Ask them how *they* picture Medusa.

E **Reading Skills and Strategies**
Identifying Cause and Effect
❓ Why does Perseus take the sisters' eye? [to bribe them into telling him how to get to the nymphs]

F **Elements of Literature**
Mythic Heroes
❓ Heroes do things we wish we could do, but they also do things we're glad we don't have to do. What can Perseus do that you wish you could do? [Possible response: run in the air, be invisible like the wind.] What does he do that you're glad you don't have to do? [Possible response: track down and kill a horrible monster that could turn him to stone.]

G **Elements of Literature**
Suspense
❓ What details in this scene create a sense of fear and concern about what will happen next? [Possible responses: the strange gray shapes, the deep cave where the sisters sleep, the men turned to stone, the echo of the waves, Perseus's fear.]

Using Students' Strengths

Interpersonal Learners
Pair students and have each partner portray one of a pair of characters such as Danae and Acrisios, Danae and Dictys, Perseus and Polydectes. Have each pair role-play an encounter in which the two characters try to resolve a key issue in the myth, such as Acrisios's imprisonment of Danae, Dictys's rescue of Danae and her child, or Polydectes's sending Perseus on a dangerous quest. You may want to have student partners perform their role-play for the class.

Logical/Mathematical Learners
Have students create a graphic organizer that depicts the relationships among the various characters in the myth. Each part of the organizer should be labeled with the name of the character and contain details that explain the character's role in the myth. Lines connecting two or more characters can show their relationship. A portion of a sample graphic organizer appears at right.

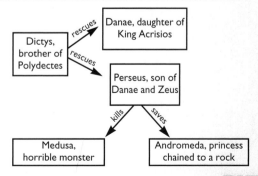

T577

Dialogue with the Text

❓ This is the second time the author has used the word *writhed*. What do you think the word means? [*Writhed* means "squirmed or twisted."] What clues helped you define the word? [The clues are "snakes," "round," and "troubled by an evil dream."] What do you already know that helped you define the word? [Possible response: I know how snakes move.]

B Elements of Literature

Plot

❓ This is the **climax** or most exciting part of the story—when the conflict is about to be resolved. What possibly could happen to Perseus now? [Possible responses: He could be turned to stone; he could be killed; he could escape without Medusa's head; he could triumph.]

C Elements of Literature

Origin Myths

❓ Remember that myths often explain the origin of things. What is being explained here? [This part of the myth explains how snakes came to be in Africa.]

D Critical Thinking

Speculating

❓ Why do you think Atlas wants to look at Medusa's head? [He wants to be turned to stone so holding up the world will be easier.]

---

down from the bright sunlight into a chill, dim shadow echoing and reechoing with the dashing of waves on the tumbled rocks beneath. There on the heaped stones lay the Gorgons sleeping together in the dimness, and even as he looked on them in the shield, Perseus felt stiff with horror at the sight.

Two of the Gorgons lay sprawled together, shaped like women, yet scaled from head to foot as serpents are. Instead of hands they had gleaming claws like eagles, and their feet were dragons' feet. Skinny metallic wings like bats' wings hung from their shoulders. Their faces were neither snake nor woman, but part both, like faces in a nightmare. These two lay arm in arm and never stirred. Only the blue snakes still hissed and writhed round the pale, set face of Medusa, as though even in sleep she were troubled by an evil dream. She lay by herself, arms outstretched, face upwards, more beautiful and terrible than living man may bear. All the crimes and madnesses of the world rushed into Perseus' mind as he gazed at her image in the shield. Horror stiffened his arm as he hovered over her with his sword uplifted. Then he shut his eyes to the vision and in the darkness struck.

There was a great cry and a hissing. Perseus groped for the head and seized it by the limp and snaky hair. Somehow he put it in his knapsack and was up and off, for at the dreadful scream the sister Gorgons had awakened. Now they were after him, their sharp claws grating against his silver shield. Perseus strained forward on the pathway of the wind like a runner, and behind him the two sisters came, smelling out the prey they could not see. Snakes darted from their girdles,° foam flew from their tusks, and the

° **girdles:** belts or sashes.

great wings beat the air. Yet the winged sandals were even swifter than they, and Perseus fled like the hunted deer with the speed of desperation. Presently the horrible noise grew faint behind him, the hissing of snakes and the sound of the bat wings died away. At last the Gorgons could smell him no longer and returned home unavenged.

By now, Perseus was over the Libyan desert, and as the blood from the horrible head touched the sand, it changed to serpents, from which the snakes of Africa are descended.

The storms of the Libyan desert blew against Perseus in clouds of eddying sand, until not even the divine sandals could hold him on his course. Far out to sea he was blown, and then north. Finally, whirled around the heavens like a cloud of mist, he alighted in the distant west, where the giant Atlas held up on his shoulders the heavens from the earth. There the weary giant, crushed under the load of centuries, begged Perseus to show him Medusa's head. Perseus uncovered for him the dreadful thing, and Atlas was changed to the mighty mountain whose rocks rear up to reach the sky near the gateway to the Atlantic. Perseus himself, returning eastwards and still battling with the wind, was driven south to the land of Ethiopia, where King Cepheus reigned with his wife, Cassiopeia.

As Perseus came wheeling in like a gull from the ocean, he saw a strange sight. Far out to sea the water was troubled, seething and boiling as though stirred by a great force moving in its depths. Huge, sullen waves were starting far out and washing inland over sunken trees and flooded houses. Many miles of land were under water, and as he sped over them, he saw the muddy sea lapping around the foot of a black, upstanding rock. Here on

---

Crossing the Curriculum

Geography

Perseus travels to many places before, during, and after his quest. Have groups of students create maps that depict the places Perseus visits. The maps should identify the geographic locations mentioned in the myth and the path that Perseus follows. Point out that not all the locations can be found on a contemporary map. Suggest that students refer to the map on p. 574 for approximate locations of Polydectes's island, for example.

a ledge above the water's edge stood a young girl chained by the arms, lips parted, eyes open and staring, face white as her linen garment. She might have been a statue, so still she stood, while the light breeze fluttered Ⓔ her dress and stirred her loosened hair. As Perseus looked at her and looked at the sea, the water began to boil again, and miles out a long gray scaly back of vast length lifted itself above the flood. At that, there was a shriek

Ⓔ **Reading Skills and Strategies**
Dialogue with the Text
❓ What do you think will happen to the girl chained to the rock? Why?
[Possible response: Perseus will rescue her because he is a hero.]

Perseus beheading the Medusa. From a temple in Selinunte, an ancient Greek colony in Sicily.

Galleria Nazionale, Palermo, Italy. Scala/Art Resource, New York.

RESPONDING TO THE ART

This Greek sculpture appears on a building in Selinunte, an early Greek settlement on the southern coast of Sicily. This is a *relief sculpture*, which means that it has figures that project from surrounding plane surfaces. This type of sculpture developed later than the freestanding variety. Many of the figures in ancient Greek sculpture wear what is called an "archaic smile," a mysterious small smile that does not always fit either the figure or the situation. **Activity.** First, have students identify the three figures in this sculpture. [left to right: man turned to stone, Perseus, Medusa] Then have students explain why the figure of Medusa doesn't quite fit her description in the myth. [In the myth, Medusa is described as having the face of a beautiful woman; the face in this figure is anything but beautiful.] Finally, have students compare the figure of Medusa in this sculpture with the figure on pp. 572–573.

MEDUSA'S HEAD **579**

Getting Students Involved

Cooperative Learning

Frozen in Time. Divide the class into groups of four to perform a tableau from the myth, based on a scene of their choice. Two students should each portray a character, voicing the character's concerns and plans in that particular scene. For example, in the scene in which Perseus fails to give Polydectes a wedding gift, Polydectes might say, "I will humiliate Perseus for not getting me a gift and then send him on a dangerous quest. Then I'll be rid of that annoying young man." The remaining two students serve as recorder and director. The recorder writes down the character's lines, the director taps each "frozen" character in turn, signaling the character to come to life and perform his or her role.

A Reading Skills and Strategies

Dialogue with the Text

❓ What is your reaction to Andromeda and her situation? Why? [Possible responses: She has been treated horribly and is lucky to be saved by Perseus; she may be a danger to Perseus if he tries to rescue her.]

B Elements of Literature

Mythic Heroes

❓ How do Perseus's actions fit the definition of what a mythic hero does? [He saves Andromeda and possibly her parents' kingdom from ruin; he uses the supernatural powers of flight and Medusa's head to conquer the beast sent by Poseidon.]

C Reading Skills and Strategies

Making Inferences

❓ Why was the temple a good place for Danae and Dictys to take refuge? [Possible responses: They would be protected there by the gods; Polydectes was afraid of the gods and would not harm Danae and Dictys in a place of worship.]

D Elements of Literature

Plot

❓ Here is another exciting moment in the story. How do you think it compares with the moment at which Perseus slays Medusa and escapes the Gorgons? [Possible responses: Some students may say Perseus's escape from the Gorgons was more dramatic because his life was in danger; others may say returning to Polydectes with Medusa's head and turning him into stone is more dramatic because it ends the conflict between Polydectes and Danae and Perseus.]

from a distant knoll where he could dimly see the forms of people, but the girl shrank a little and said nothing. Then Perseus, taking off the hat of darkness, alighted near the maiden to talk to her, and she, though nearly mad with terror, found words at last to tell him her tale.

Her name was Andromeda, and she was the only child of the king and of his wife, Cassiopeia. Queen Cassiopeia was exceedingly beautiful, so that all people marveled at her. She herself was proud of her dark eyes, her white, slender fingers, and her long black hair, so proud that she had been heard to boast that she was fairer even than the sea nymphs, who are daughters of Nereus. At this, Nereus in wrath stirred up Poseidon, who came flooding in over the land, covering it far and wide. Not content with this, he sent a vast monster from the dark depths of the bottomless sea to ravage the whole coast of Ethiopia. When the unfortunate king and queen had sought the advice of the oracle on how to appease the god, they had been ordered to sacrifice their only daughter to the sea monster Poseidon had sent. Not daring for their people's sake to disobey, they had chained her to this rock, where she now awaited the beast who should devour her.

Perseus comforted Andromeda as he stood by her on the rock, and she shrank closer against him while the great gray back writhed its half-mile length slowly towards the land. Then, bidding Andromeda hide her face, Perseus sprang once more into the air, unveiling the dreadful head of dead Medusa to the monster, which reared its dripping jaws yards high into the air. The mighty tail stiffened all of a sudden, the boiling of the water ceased, and only the gentle waves of the receding ocean lapped around a long, gray ridge of stone. Then Perseus freed

Andromeda and restored her to her father and beautiful mother. Thereafter, with their consent, he married her amid scenes of tremendous rejoicing, and with his bride set sail at last for the kingdom of Polydectes.

Polydectes had lost no time on the departure of Perseus. First he had begged Danae to become his wife, and then he had threatened her. Undoubtedly, he would have got his way by force if Danae had not fled in terror to Dictys. The two took refuge at the altar of a temple whence Polydectes did not dare drag them away. So matters stood when Perseus returned. Polydectes was enraged to see him, for he had hoped at least that Danae's most powerful protector would never return. But now, seeing him famous and with a king's daughter to wife, he could not contain himself. Openly he laughed at the tale of Perseus, saying that the hero had never killed the Gorgon, only pretended to, and that now he was claiming an honor he did not deserve. At this, Perseus, enraged by the insult and by reports of his mother's persecution, said to him, "You asked me for the Gorgon's head. Behold it!" And with that he lifted it high, and Polydectes became stone.

Then Perseus left Dictys to be king of that island, but he himself went back to the Grecian mainland to seek out his grandfather, Acrisios, who was once again king of Argos. First, however, he gave back to the gods the gifts they had given him. Hermes took back the golden sandals and the hat of darkness, for both are his. But Athene took Medusa's head, and she hung it on a fleece around her neck as part of her battle equipment, where it may be seen in statues and portraits of the warlike goddess.

Perseus took ship for Greece, but his fame had gone before him, and King Acrisios fled

Making the Connections

**Connecting to the Theme:
"Tell Me a Tale"**

After students have finished reading the myth, discuss aspects of the characters and events that make this a good story and one that has endured for thousands of years. Explore aspects such as the evil King Acrisios, the role of fate, the help of the gods, the mysterious birth of the hero, the hero's quest and deeds, and the happy ending. Ask students how the myth relates to present-day situations, relationships, wishes, and fears.

secretly from Argos in terror, since he remembered the prophecy and feared that Perseus had come to avenge the wrongs of Danae. The trembling old Acrisios took refuge in Larissa, where it happened the king was holding a great athletic contest in honor of his dead father.

Heroes from all over Greece, among whom was Perseus, came to the games. As Perseus was competing at the discus throwing, he threw high into the air and far beyond the rest. A strong wind caught the discus as it spun, so that it left the course marked out for it and was carried into the stands. People scrambled away to right and left. Only Acrisios was not nimble enough. The heavy weight fell full on his foot and crushed his toes, and at that, the feeble old man, already weakened by his terrors, died from the shock. Thus the prophecy of Apollo was fulfilled at last; Acrisios was killed by his grandson. Then Perseus came into his kingdom, where he reigned with Andromeda long and happily.

E Elements of Literature
Mythic Heroes
❓ How is Acrisios's death ironic?
[His death is ironic because he tried to escape his fate but happened to be exactly where death awaited him; it is also ironic because readers expect Perseus to kill Acrisios by a heroic deed, not by accident.]

MEET THE WRITER
A Twist of Fate

Olivia Coolidge (1908–   ) was enjoying a perfectly normal childhood in London with a perfectly normal dislike for Greek literature (which her father was urging her to read) when she twisted her ankle. For three months a cruel sprain kept her from going outside to play, and so she read—and read. Pretty soon she was even reading Greek poetry, and she made a shocking discovery. She loved it!

As happens sometimes in Greek myths, the young woman gladly accepted her fate: a lifelong love of the classics. (The word *classics* is used to describe Greek myths and other timeless works.) Her interest led her to Oxford University, where she continued her studies in the classics. Later, reflecting on why her own stories often spring from the classics, Olivia Coolidge noted:

66 I write about history, biography, and

ancient legends for teens because I am more interested in values that always have been of concern to people than I am in the form we express them in at this moment. Distant places and past ages show that these values are not expressed better in the United States in the twentieth century, but merely differently. My general purpose therefore is to give a picture of life. 99

More Pictures of Life

"Medusa's Head" comes from Coolidge's *Greek Myths* (Houghton Mifflin), a collection of stories about Greek gods and heroes.

MEDUSA'S HEAD 581

Assessing Learning

Check Test: Questions and Answers
1. What prophecy does the oracle give Acrisios? [Acrisios won't have a son, and his grandson will kill him.]
2. Why does Perseus seek Medusa's head? [Polydectes wants it as a wedding gift.]
3. Where does Perseus get the hat of darkness, sandals, and knapsack? [from the nymphs]
4. How does Perseus save Andromeda? [by turning the monster to stone with Medusa's head]
5. How does Acrisios die? [He is killed by a discus thrown by Perseus.]

Self-Assessment
Help students evaluate their approaches to reading with the following assessment.

1=Rarely   2=Sometimes   3=Frequently
_____ I try to predict upcoming events.
_____ I reread earlier parts of the story to help me understand confusing passages.
_____ I make sure I understand what I read by asking myself questions as I read.
_____ I try to figure out unfamiliar words by using context clues.

Standardized Test Preparation
For practice with standardized test format specific to this selection, see
• *Standardized Test Preparation*, p. 82
For practice in proofreading and editing, see
• *Daily Oral Grammar*, Transparency 35

Connections

This cartoon provides a different view of the events in the myth of Perseus and the Gorgon's head.

Ⓐ Reading Skills and Strategies

Dialogue with the Text

Be sure to have students write down their responses to this witty cartoon.

Ⓑ Critical Thinking

Analyzing

❓ **What makes this kind of story-telling interesting?** [Possible response: The pictures tell the story, and the words provide additional details and humor. Together, the pictures and the words make the story lively and amusing, like most cartoons.]

Ⓒ Elements of Literature

Tone

❓ **How is the tone of the cartoon different from the tone of the story? What details help you infer the tone in each work?** [Possible response: The tone of the story is solemn and serious, while the cartoon's tone is light and humorous. The myth uses formal English, including words such as *perplexity* and phrases such as "horror stiffened his arm." The cartoon uses informal English, including words such as "zillionth," "drip," "gimme," and phrases such as "...that'll make you stone dead."]

Using Students' Strengths

Kinesthetic Learners

Ask students to perform "Perseus and the Gorgon's Head" as a brief play, using the cartoon as their script. Each performance should run about five minutes and contain sound effects, background music, and simple props and costumes as well as appropriate actions, gestures, and body language. Guide students to include all the myth's relevant details but also to capture the cartoon's playful spirit.

Interpersonal Learners

Students can set up a mediation team in which they attempt to resolve the differences between King Acrisios, Perseus, and Danae. Students should explore the use of logic, emotion, compromise, and role-playing, or other methods to try to resolve the differences among the characters. Then have students write an alternative ending to the myth based on the results of their mediation.

(Pages 582–585) *Perseus and the Gorgon's Head* from the book *Greek Myths for Young Children* copyright ©1991 by Marcia Williams.

Reprinted by permission of Walker Books, Ltd, London. Published in the U.S. by Candlewick Press, Cambridge, Massachusetts.

(continued on next page)

D English Language Learners

Interpreting Idioms

? The "it" that Perseus is to sleep on is his decision. "To sleep on it" means to wait until morning to take action. What happens in the pictures that makes this meaning clear? [The pictures show Perseus pausing to sleep and think about his next action.]

E Elements of Literature

Mythic Heroes

? Does Perseus seem heroic in this retelling of the story? Why or why not? [Possible responses: Yes, because he still performs superhuman deeds and shows great bravery; no, because he seems comical.]

A English Language Learners
Synonyms

❓ In "Medusa's Head" the nymphs give Perseus a knapsack in which to put Medusa's head. What word in the cartoon version is a synonym for *knapsack*? [*bag*] Point out that other synonyms for *knapsack* include *satchel*, *backpack*, and *bookbag*.

B Elements of Literature
Mythic Heroes

❓ What great dangers does Perseus face in this scene? [He might be killed or turned to stone.] What might happen if he fails? [His mother might be forced to marry a man she detests.]

Skill Link

Using a Dictionary or Other Reference Source

Use this review before you teach the Language Link activity and before students begin the Language Link Mini-Lesson, both on p. 588. It will help you assess students' understanding of basic reference sources.

1. A *dictionary* is a book or software program that lists words in alphabetical order and gives their meaning, pronunciation, syllabification, and origin. A dictionary can also provide a word's synonyms and antonyms.
2. An *encyclopedia* is a book, set of books, or software program that contains information about specific subjects. Subjects are arranged in alphabetical order.
3. An *atlas* is a book of maps.
4. An *almanac* is a book of facts, including information on governments, countries, awards, population, and sports records.

Activities

Have students explain which reference source they would consult for each task:
1. How to pronounce *prophecy* [dictionary]
2. Find background on the myth of Perseus [encyclopedia]
3. Find a map of modern Greece [atlas]
4. Find synonyms for *mercurial* [dictionary]
5. Find the population of modern Greece [almanac]

As he leapt into the air, Medusa's sisters woke.

Quickly, Perseus donned the helmet and instantly vanished from their sight.

His journey home was not an easy one.

But, after a year, he arrived at Seriphus.

Perseus found his mother hiding from King Polydectes in the temple.

So he went on to the palace.

Polydectes was convinced that Perseus had long since been turned to stone.

The king was horrified to see him alive.

But before he could speak, Perseus pulled out Medusa's head.

Its gaze immediately turned the king to stone.

Perseus then rescued his mother and, before leaving the island, crowned Dictys the new King of Seriphus.

They sailed for Argos where, later, Perseus accidentally killed King Acrisius, as the oracle had predicted.

Connecting Across Texts

Connecting with "Medusa's Head"

Have students compare and contrast the myth "Medusa's Head" with the cartoon "Perseus and the Gorgon's Head." Ask them to arrange their ideas on a Venn diagram. They can use the following Venn diagram as a model:

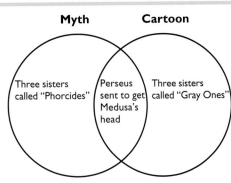

Myth — Three sisters called "Phorcides"

Perseus sent to get Medusa's head

Cartoon — Three sisters called "Gray Ones"

MAKING MEANINGS

First Thoughts

1. Most students are apt to find Perseus brave, strong, determined, loyal, and superhuman. Students who agree that there are modern heroes such as Perseus should give names and describe the person's qualities and deeds. Students who disagree should explain why, possibly citing the absence of truly superhuman capabilities such as flying through the air.

Shaping Interpretations

2. Perseus is at least part god because his father was a god. He is bold, courageous, and a natural leader. With the help of the gods, he can fly and become invisible. In addition, Perseus helps a number of people, including Danae, Dictys, and Andromeda.

3. In the story, what the oracle said would happen happened—even to a king—so fate must apply to everyone. Some students may feel that fate plays a strong role in life; others might argue that we control our own destiny.

Extending the Text

4. Students should cite specific movies or television shows that remind them of the story of Perseus and should describe the similar elements.

Challenging the Text

5. The Greeks believed in fate and valued physical strength, bravery, justice, and the wisdom of the gods. They thought there were "magical" explanations for things in the natural world.

MAKING MEANINGS

First Thoughts

[respond]

1. What do you think of Perseus? Do we have such heroes today? Refer to your reading notes for your responses to the story.

Shaping Interpretations

[interpret]

2. Why is Perseus a good example of a **mythic hero**? (Think about how he handles the challenges on his **quest** and how the gods help him.)

[interpret]

3. How does this myth show that no one can escape fate? What do you think of the ancient Greek idea that everything is decided in advance by fate?

Extending the Text

[extend]

4. Modern stories of action heroes often resemble ancient myths. What movies or TV shows remind you of the story of Perseus? Think about

   a. the hero threatened at birth
   b. the beautiful woman in danger
   c. the awful monster
   d. the role played by magic
   e. the perils faced by the hero
   f. the people who help the hero
   g. the final triumph of good over evil

Challenging the Text

[synthesize]

5. If this tale were all you knew of the ancient Greeks, what could you tell about them from analyzing it? What characteristics did they value in people? How did they look at the world around them?

586 TELL ME A TALE

Reading Check

Test yourself by filling in the missing events in this **summary** of Perseus' story.

a. Acrisios is told he will be killed by his grandson.

b. _____

c. Zeus visits Danae as a shower of gold.

d. Perseus and his mother are cast out to sea.

e. _____

f. King Polydectes orders Perseus to bring back Medusa's head.

g. _____

h. Perseus finds the sisters Phorcides.

i. _____

j. Perseus visits the nymphs.

k. _____

l. Perseus finds Medusa.

m. _____

n. Perseus sees Andromeda chained to a rock.

o. _____

p. Perseus changes Polydectes to stone.

q. _____

r. Perseus kills Acrisios with a discus.

Reading Check

b. Acrisios locks Danae in an underground room.

e. Danae and Perseus are found by Dictys and made servants to King Polydectes. Both men fall in love with Danae.

g. Athena tells Perseus how to get Medusa's head.

i. Perseus forces the Phorcides to tell him how to reach the nymphs.

k. The nymphs give Perseus tools that will help him conquer Medusa.

m. Perseus cuts off Medusa's head and shows it to Atlas, who turns to stone.

o. Perseus rescues Andromeda by turning the sea monster to stone.

q. Perseus then goes to find Acrisios.

T586

CHOICES: Building Your Portfolio

Grading Timesaver

Rubrics for each Choices assignment appear on p. 177 in the *Portfolio Management System*.

Writer's Notebook

1. Collecting Ideas for a Story

Make up a story about a character who can become invisible. Jot down some ideas about the following:

- the way the character becomes invisible
- things an invisible character could do that someone else couldn't do
- the dangers an invisible person would face

If you wish, tell your story in the form of a cartoon (see *Connections* on page 582).

Other drivers did double takes as I passed, invisible in the driver's seat. Then—a shrill police siren. Quick! Off with my magic glasses!

Creative Writing

2. Updating the Myth

Suppose you wanted to set the myth of Perseus in the year 2000 and make it into a movie. In a paragraph, tell how you would update the main details of the story. Here are some questions you should answer before you write your proposal:

a. Who would the hero be?

b. Who would Perseus' father be?

c. A character who's a wicked king would probably be unrealistic in 2000. What kind of job would a modern Polydectes have?

d. What task would Perseus perform for Polydectes?

e. Who or what would take the place of Medusa?

f. How would the hero be rewarded?

g. Who would Andromeda be, and what would she be threatened by?

h. What modern names would you give to Perseus, Danae, Polydectes, and the others?

Science/Art

3. Mythic Stars

If you look up, you might see Andromeda and her mother, Queen Cassiopeia, tonight. That's because according to myth, they both turned into constellations. The constellation Cassiopeia is located opposite the Big Dipper across the North Pole. The constellation Andromeda is south of Cassiopeia and northeast of Pegasus. (Pegasus, by the way, was a winged horse who sprang full-grown from Medusa's neck!) Do some research and make a star map that shows these and other constellations named for characters in Greek myths. Try to find and read the myths about these famous figures.

CHOICES: Building Your Portfolio

1. **Writer's Notebook** Remind students to save their work. They may use it as prewriting for the Writer's Workshop on pp. 658–662. If students wish to tell their story as a cartoon, suggest they make a storyboard, showing the different events they would include.

2. **Creative Writing** Have students look through newspapers and news magazines to find ideas for characters' challenges, deeds, and qualities. This will also help them find contemporary names for their characters.

3. **Science/Art** Divide the class into two groups. The first group should create the star map, while the second group researches the characters for whom the constellations are named. Provide students with books and other information about stars and constellations, or take them to the library to find material on their own. Visit a local planetarium, if there is one.

Using Students' Strengths

Verbal Learners

For Choice 2, have students start by working in pairs to summarize the story. As they work, ask students to discuss how they would update the story, considering changes in events, characters, and settings. When students have gathered some materials, one partner can present ideas while the other takes notes. Then students can switch roles and continue the brainstorming.

Visual/Spacial Learners

For Choice 3 have students make large reproductions of one or two specific constellations. Students can use poster board or butcher paper. Mount the constellations on the ceiling. If possible, let students use glow-in-the-dark paint on their constellations for a more dramatic effect.

LANGUAGE LINK

Try It Out

1. Mars—planet; candy bar.
   Venus—planet; *Venus' flytrap* is a plant.
   Saturn—planet; automobile.
   Apollo—space program; a famous theater in Harlem.
   Mercury—planet; space program; automobile; element.
   Jupiter—planet.
   Vulcan—species from *Star Trek;* *vulcanized* means a way of treating rubber with heat.
   Poseidon—underwater missile.
2. Possible answers
   - Hermes was the messenger of the gods, famous for his speed.
   - Today, the word *atlas* refers to a collection of maps. It came to be used this way because collections of maps sometimes have an image of Atlas (holding up the world) on the title page.

VOCABULARY

Sample responses

1. Perseus <u>hovered</u> in the air above the Gorgons and then <u>descended</u> to the ground.
2. When Perseus is told to get the Gorgon's head, he is full of <u>perplexity</u> because he doesn't know how to do it.
3. Atlas had the <u>perpetual</u> task of holding up the heavens; his job never ended.
4. In the <u>recesses</u> of the cave lived the hideous Gorgons.

Resources ———

Language
- *Grammar and Language Links,* p. 53

Vocabulary
- *Words to Own,* p. 21

Spelling
- *Spelling and Decoding,* p. 24

LANGUAGE LINK   MINI-LESSON

Style: Words from Myths

The Greek and Roman names for the gods and other mythological figures have become the names of many things in modern life. For instance, Pluto, the name of the god of the underworld, is now the name of a planet and a cartoon character. Medusa, the name of the monster in this myth, is also the name of an adult jellyfish, which has tentacles that sting. (Why is this name a good one?)

STING

Try It Out

1. How have these mythological names been used in the modern world? Are some names used for more than one thing?

Mars	Mercury
Venus	Jupiter
Saturn	Vulcan
Apollo	Poseidon

2. Use a dictionary or other reference source to answer the following questions:
   - Why is Hermes a good emblem for a messenger service?
   - The sight of Medusa's face changed the giant Atlas into a mountain. How is the word *atlas* used today? Why did it come to be used this way?

VOCABULARY   HOW TO OWN A WORD

WORD BANK
descended
perplexity
perpetual
recesses
hovered

Own It

1. Use the words *descended* and *hovered* to explain how Perseus captures Medusa's head.
2. Write a sentence using the word *perplexity* to explain how Perseus feels when he's told to fetch the Gorgon's head.
3. Write a sentence using the word *perpetual* to explain what Atlas's job is.
4. Write a sentence using the word *recesses* to describe the den of the Gorgons.

588 TELL ME A TALE

Language Link Quick Check

Have students answer each of the following questions.

1. Which space programs are named after Greek and Roman heroes or gods? [Apollo and Mercury]
2. How has the military used the name of the Greek god Poseidon? [Poseidon missiles]
3. Who is Hermes? [the Greek messenger of the gods]
4. What is an atlas? [a book of maps]

Before You Read

BAUCIS AND PHILEMON

Make the Connection

Here's to Hospitality

Suppose you were traveling centuries ago, long before the existence of freeways, fast-food restaurants, and motels. Hungry and footsore, you would have to find shelter as night approached. You'd probably stop at a house along the way and ask for a meal and a bed. Chances are you'd get what you asked for. Hospitality, or generosity to guests, was a sacred duty in the ancient world. In Greece, people were expected to share what they had—even with strangers.

Quickwrite

Freewrite about what you think makes a guest feel welcome.

Elements of Literature

Metamorphosis: Shifting Shapes

A **metamorphosis** is a total change in shape or form. The change from a larva to a butterfly is a metamorphosis. The wormlike larva goes through an incredible change in form to become a beautiful butterfly. A tadpole goes through a metamorphosis to become a frog. Metamorphosis is important in mythology. "Baucis and Philemon" begins with a metamorphosis in which the gods Zeus and Hermes change into humans. In myths, gods can transform anyone or anything into any form they choose. As you read this myth, look for another amazing metamorphosis.

> **etamorphosis** is a magical change from one shape or form to another one.

Reading Skills and Strategies

Recognizing Connections That Cross Cultures: Ties That Bind

Recognizing **connections** is part of the fun of reading. As you read "Baucis and Philemon," look for connections between this story from long ago and real life today. In particular, think about the message of the myth. How is that message important today? Do any characters in "Baucis and Philemon" remind you of people you know?

go.hrw.com
LEO 6-8

BAUCIS AND PHILEMON **589**

Summary ■■

The gods Zeus and Hermes come to Earth in human form. As they travel, they are refused food and shelter by everyone except a poor old couple, Baucis and Philemon. Wife and husband serve the strangers the best they have, and when the wine bowl fills itself, the couple realizes that their visitors are gods. To reward the elderly couple for their generosity, the gods ask them to choose whatever they wish. Philemon asks only that their humble cottage become a temple for the gods and that he and his wife be allowed to serve there. When pressed for a further reward, Philemon requests that he and Baucis die at the same time, since they have been together so long. Years later, when the generous, humble couple die, they change into two trees with intertwined branches.

Resources

Listening
Audio CD Library
An exciting recording of this myth is included in the *Audio CD Library*:
• Disc 14, Track 3

BAUCIS AND PHILEMON

a Greek myth, retold by
Olivia Coolidge

They were prompt to ask the strangers in and to set their best before them.

Fruit Basket by Michelangelo
Caravaggio (1573–1610).
Pinacoteca Ambrosiana, Milan, Italy.
Scala/Art Resource, New York.

590 TELL ME A TALE

Resources: Print and Media

Reading
• *Reading Skills and Strategies*
  MiniRead Skill Lesson, p. 179
  Selection Skill Lesson, p. 186
• *Graphic Organizers for Active Reading*, p. 38
• *Spelling and Decoding*
  Worksheet, p. 25
• *Audio CD Library*
  Disc 14, Track 3

Elements of Literature
• *Literary Elements*
  Transparency 10
  Worksheet, p. 31
Writing and Language
• *Daily Oral Grammar*
  Transparency 36
• *Grammar and Language Links*
  Worksheet, p. 55
• *Language Workshop CD-ROM*

Assessment
• *Formal Assessment*, p. 115
• *Portfolio Management System*, p. 178
• *Test Generator (One-Stop Planner CD-ROM)*
Internet
• go.hrw.com (keyword: LE0 6-8)

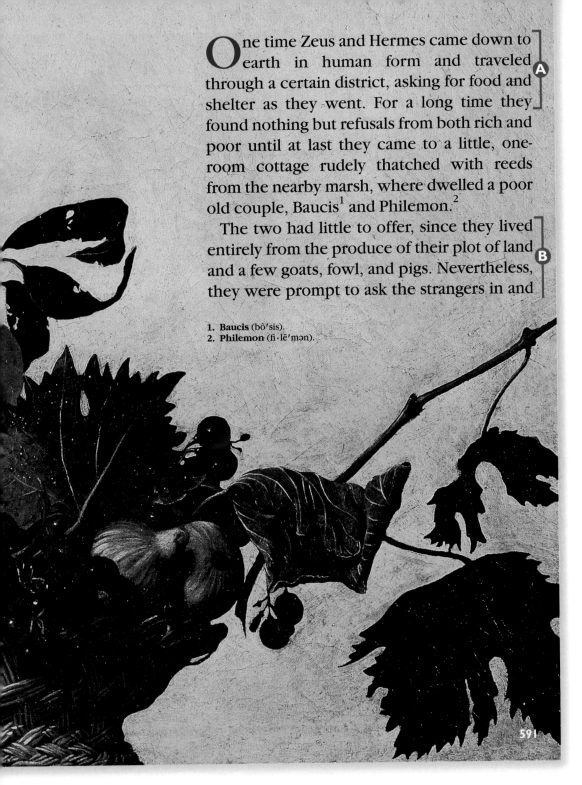

One time Zeus and Hermes came down to earth in human form and traveled through a certain district, asking for food and shelter as they went. For a long time they found nothing but refusals from both rich and poor until at last they came to a little, one-room cottage rudely thatched with reeds from the nearby marsh, where dwelled a poor old couple, Baucis[1] and Philemon.[2]

The two had little to offer, since they lived entirely from the produce of their plot of land and a few goats, fowl, and pigs. Nevertheless, they were prompt to ask the strangers in and

1. **Baucis** (bô′sis).
2. **Philemon** (fi·lē′mən).

A **Elements of Literature**

Metamorphosis

? What metamorphosis occurs at the start of the story? [Zeus and Hermes disguise themselves as humans.]

B **Reading Skills and Strategies**

Recognizing Connections that Cross Cultures

? How is the behavior of Baucis and Philemon similar to that of people you may know today? [Possible response: They live modestly, but they are respectful, kind, and generous toward others.]

RESPONDING TO THE ART

Michelangelo Caravaggio created paintings of extraordinary naturalism, evident in the realistic details of this still life. Although Caravaggio closely studied the work of the great Renaissance master, Michelangelo, he insisted that nature was his only teacher. **Activity.** Have students identify the realistic elements in this painting, such as the worm holes in the apple.

591

Reaching All Students

Struggling Readers

Recognizing Connections that Cross Cultures was introduced on p. 589. For a lesson in which students recognize themes across cultures using a strategy called Semantic Differential, see the *Reading Skills and Strategies* binder:

• MiniRead Skill Lesson, p. 179
• Selection Skill Lesson, p. 186

English Language Learners

Some students may be unfamiliar with the English names of some of the foods mentioned in this myth. Review the words and, if necessary, provide pictures or verbal descriptions of the food items. Invite students to describe special foods they would serve to honored guests. For additional strategies to supplement instruction for English language learners, see

• *Lesson Plans Including Strategies for English-Language Learners*

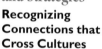

Ⓐ Struggling Readers

Using Context Clues

❓ How do you know that Baucis is the wife and Philemon the husband? [Baucis is referred to as "her."]

Ⓑ Reading Skills and Strategies

Recognizing Connections that Cross Cultures

❓ So far, what message do you think the myth has for people today? [Possible responses: Be kind to strangers; generosity is more important than money or material goods; giving to others has its own kind of reward.]

Ⓒ Critical Thinking

Hypothesizing

❓ How does the wine bowl fill up again? [The gods use their powers to refill it.]

---

to set their best before them. The couch that they pulled forward for their guests was roughly put together from willow boughs, and the cushions on it were stuffed with straw. One table leg had to be propped up with a piece of broken pot, but Baucis scrubbed the top with fragrant mint and set some water on the fire. Meanwhile Philemon ran out into the garden to fetch a cabbage and then lifted down a piece of home-cured bacon from the blackened beam where it Ⓐ hung. While these were cooking, Baucis set out her best delicacies on the table. There were ripe olives, sour cherries pickled in wine, fresh onions and radishes, cream cheese, and eggs baked in the ashes of the fire. There was a big earthenware bowl in the midst of the table to mix their crude, home-made wine with water.

The second course had to be fruit, but there were nuts, figs, dried dates, plums, grapes, and apples, for this was their best season of the year. Philemon had even had it in mind to kill their only goose for dinner, and there was a great squawking and cackling that went on for a long time. Poor old Philemon wore himself out trying to catch that goose, but somehow the animal always got away from him until the guests bade him let it be, for they were well served as it was. It was a good meal, and the old couple kept pressing Ⓑ their guests to eat and drink, caring nothing that they were now consuming in one day what would ordinarily last them a week.

At last the wine sank low in the mixing bowl, and Philemon rose to fetch some more. But to his astonishment as he lifted the wine-Ⓒ skin to pour, he found the bowl was full again as though it had not been touched at all. Then he knew the two strangers must be gods, and he and Baucis were awed and afraid. But the

592 TELL ME A TALE

Jupiter and Mercury at the Home of Baucis and Philemon by Adam Elsheimer.
Staatliche Kunstsammlungen, Dresden Gemäldegalerie Alte Meister, Germany. Kavaler/Art Resource, New York.

gods smiled kindly at them, and the younger, who seemed to do most of the talking, said, "Philemon, you have welcomed us beneath your roof this day when richer men refused us shelter. Be sure those shall be punished who would not help the wandering stranger, but you shall have whatever reward you choose. Tell us what you will have."

The old man thought for a little with his

Using Students' Strengths

Naturalist Learners

Have students work in pairs to find out more about the cultivation of various fruits and vegetables mentioned in the myth. Each pair should research three different plants. After students finish their research, have pairs present their findings to the class. Encourage students to include sketches or photographs to help the audience visualize each type of plant.

can boast of. In this small cottage, humble though it is, the gods have sat at meat. It is as unworthy of the honor as we are. If, therefore, you will do something for us, turn this cottage into a temple where the gods may always be served and where we may live out the remainder of our days in worship of them."

"You have spoken well," said Hermes, "and you shall have your wish. Yet is there not anything that you would desire for yourselves?"

Philemon thought again at this, stroking his straggly beard, and he glanced over at old Baucis with her thin, gray hair and her rough hands as she served at the table, her feet bare on the floor of trodden earth. "We have lived together for many years," he said again, "and in all that time there has never been a word of anger between us. Now, at last, we are growing old and our long companionship is coming to an end. It is the only thing that has helped us in the bad times and the source of our joy in the good. Grant us this one request, that when we come to die, we may perish in the same hour and neither of us be left without the other."

He looked at Baucis and she nodded in approval, so the old couple turned their eyes on the gods.

"It shall be as you desire," said Hermes. "Few men would have made such a good and moderate request."

Thereafter the house became a temple, and the neighbors, amazed at the change, came often to worship and left offerings for the support of the aged priest and priestess there. For many years Baucis and Philemon lived in peace, passing from old to extreme old age. At last, they were so old and bowed that it seemed they could only walk at all if they clutched one another. But still every

eyes bent on the ground, and then he said: "We have lived together here for many years, happy even though the times have been hard. But never yet did we see fit to turn a stranger from our gate or to seek a reward for entertaining him. To have spoken with the immortals[3] face to face is a thing few men

3. **immortals:** ancient Greek gods.

BAUCIS AND PHILEMON **593**

D ## Reading Skills and Strategies
Responding to the Text
? If you were in the same position as Baucis and Philemon, what reward would you ask from the gods? Why? [Possible responses: Students might ask for good health, great wealth, fame, or some outstanding skills.]

E ## Reading Skills and Strategies
Recognizing Connections that Cross Cultures
? What does Philemon's request suggest about what he and his wife value? Whom do you know with these same values? [Philemon's request suggests that he and his wife value each other and their marriage. Students may mention family members, neighbors, acquaintances, or characters from current events, history, movies, television, or fiction.]

F ## Appreciating Language
Homophones
? Which meaning does *there* have— "belonging to two or more people," "in that place," or "a short form of *they are*"? How do you know? [It means "in that place." The context indicates that people left objects in that location.]

Making the Connections

Connecting to the Theme: "Tell Me a Tale"
After students have read the myth, have them create a word web to show their reactions to the story. Start by having a volunteer write the phrase "power and joy" in the center of the board or on chart paper. Then have other students describe incidents and details from the story that show these qualities. Guide the class in recognizing how the qualities of power and pleasure help make this myth universal and enduring.

Drawing Conclusions

? Based on this description, what do you think was an important value to the ancient Greeks? [Possible responses: religion, service to the gods, modesty, loyalty.]

B Elements of Literature

Metamorphosis

? What metamorphosis occurs at the end of the myth? [Baucis and Philemon are transformed into trees.]

A evening they would shuffle a little way down the path that they might turn and look together at the beautiful little temple and praise the gods for the honor bestowed on them. One evening it took them longer than ever to reach the usual spot, and there they turned arm in arm to look back, thinking perhaps that it was the last time their limbs **B** would support them so far. There as they stood, each one felt the other stiffen and change and only had time to turn and say once, "Farewell," before they disappeared. In their place stood two tall trees growing closely side by side with branches interlaced. They seemed to nod and whisper to each other in the passing breeze.

594 TELL ME A TALE

Assessing Learning

Check Test: True-False

1. Baucis and Philemon are gods who come to earth as humans. [False]
2. Zeus and Hermes enjoy the older couple's hospitality. [True]
3. Baucis and Philemon wish to die together when their time comes. [True]
4. Baucis and Philemon's cottage is transformed into a mansion. [False]
5. Baucis and Philemon change into birds. [False]

Peer Assessment

Have students complete the following assessment after a cooperative learning activity.
A = Always S = Sometimes N = Never
1. I listened to my partners' ideas.
2. My partners listened to my ideas.
3. My partners and I shared the work fairly.
4. My partners and I were positive about the project.
5. I enjoyed working with my partners.

Standardized Test Preparation

For practice in proofreading and editing, see
- *Daily Oral Grammar*, Transparency 36

MAKING MEANINGS

MAKING MEANINGS

First Thoughts

[respond]

1. Finish one or more of these sentences:
   - If I were Philemon, I would have wished for . . .
   - This myth made me realize that . . .
   - I found the ending . . . because . . .

Shaping Interpretations

[interpret]

2. How does the **metamorphosis** of Baucis and Philemon suit their characters? If you could ask them how they felt about it, what do you think they'd say?

[interpret]

3. In a myth a **metamorphosis** can be a reward, a punishment, or just a disguise. Which types of metamorphoses occur in this myth? What purpose does each transformation serve? You might organize your ideas in a chart like this:

Metamorphosis	Type and Purpose
Zeus and Hermes become humans.	The gods disguise themselves. Their purpose is . . .

[interpret]

4. The ancient myths teach lessons about how we ought to behave. What lessons do you think the Greeks learned from this story?

Connecting with the Text

[generalize]

5. Look at your notes for the Quickwrite on page 589. Do Baucis and Philemon show the kind of hospitality you describe? How do you think Zeus and Hermes would be treated today?

Extending the Text

[synthesize]

6. "Baucis and Philemon" shows the value of caring for those in need. Can you think of ways in which people in your community show that they have taken this message to heart?

Reading Check

a. Why did the two gods come down to earth?

b. When did Baucis and Philemon realize the strangers were gods?

c. How did the old couple please the gods?

d. What were Philemon's two wishes? In what ways did they come true?

First Thoughts

1. Possible responses:
   - If I were Philemon, I would have wished for fame and fortune.
   - This myth made me realize that goodness, generosity, and kindness to strangers will be rewarded.
   - I found the ending happy because Baucis and Philemon got their wish and were united after they died.

Shaping Interpretations

2. The ending is suitable because Baucis and Philemon lived a simple, modest life close to each other and nature. They might say, "Now we will have that life for eternity."

3. Zeus and Hermes become humans as a disguise to test people's hospitality. The cottage is turned into a temple, and the elderly couple, at the ends of their lives, are turned into trees as a reward for their hospitality.

4. The Greeks learned that it is important to share what they have and to be generous to everyone, even to strangers.

Connecting with the Text

5. Students may say that the gods would not be invited into someone's home because today we are not as trusting toward strangers or because it can be dangerous to do so.

Extending the Text

6. Answers may include holding clothing and food drives for the poor, serving as a foster parent, or doing volunteer work at hospitals and retirement homes.

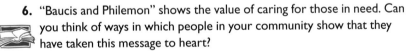

Reading Check

a. The gods came down to earth to see if people showed hospitality to others, especially toward strangers.

b. They realized the strangers were gods when the bowl of wine refilled itself.

c. They were generous, even though they were poor and had little to share.

d. Philemon asked the gods to turn their home into a temple and to let him and Baucis die together. The gods do turn their home into a temple, and, when it comes time for the couple to die, the gods transform them into trees with interlacing branches.

Rubrics for each Choices assignment appear on p. 178 in the *Portfolio Management System*.

CHOICES: Building Your Portfolio

1. **Writer's Notebook** Remind students to save their work. They may use it as prewriting for the Writer's Workshop on pp. 658–662. Point out to students that the story ideas they select may have more than one metamorphosis, as was the case in this myth.

2. **Writing About Theme** Before students begin to write, have them review the story and jot down at least three examples from it that support the theme they have chosen. Remind students to consider including these examples in their paragraph.

3. **Oral Storytelling** Have students brainstorm a list of lessons they feel are important. If necessary, prompt students with suggestions, such as "Respect others" and "Be responsible for yourself." You might also suggest that students brainstorm consequences of bad behavior.

4. **Art** Divide the class into an appropriate number of groups, and assign each group one picture in the series. Display the completed series of pictures in the classroom.

CHOICES: Building Your Portfolio

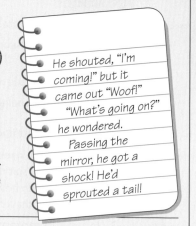

Writer's Notebook

1. Collecting Ideas for a Story

The gods Zeus and Hermes magically changed into ordinary humans, and Baucis and Philemon turned into trees. Metamorphosis occurs in other myths and tales too. Maybe you know about the prince who turned into a frog, or King Midas, whose touch turned everything into gold. Write down ideas for a story about a metamorphosis. Be sure to describe a magical change in shape or form that one of the characters undergoes.

> He shouted, "I'm coming!" but it came out "Woof!"
> "What's going on?" he wondered.
> Passing the mirror, he got a shock! He'd sprouted a tail!

Writing About Theme

2. All Is Revealed

A **theme** is an idea about life that is revealed in a work of literature. Here are some themes from "Baucis and Philemon":

- People who are generous to others will be rewarded.
- You do not need to be wealthy to be generous.
- Always be kind to strangers, for there is no telling who they might be.

Choose one of these themes to write about in a paragraph or two. Use details from the myth to show how the story expresses this message or idea.

Oral Storytelling

3. A Myth for Today

"Baucis and Philemon" taught a lesson to people of long ago. What lesson would you teach people today? With a partner, think of something you both believe is important. What story could you tell to teach the lesson? Invent a plot in which characters who behave well are rewarded and people who behave badly are punished. Make a story map of your ideas. Practice telling the story to your partner. Then, together present your modern myth to the class.

Art

4. Taking Root

Can you picture Baucis and Philemon as they stiffen, change, and become rooted to the spot? Draw a series of pictures showing the transformation. In the first drawing, show the couple close together, arm in arm. In the last drawing, show two tall trees nodding to each other, with branches intertwined like arms. In the in-between sketches, show the stages of this marvelous metamorphosis.

Using Students' Strengths

Kinesthetic Learners
As students brainstorm ideas for metamorphoses for Choice 1, invite volunteers to act out the changes in front of the class. Begin with the example on the pupil page, of the prince who turned into a frog.

Naturalist Learners
Suggest to these students that they consider themes that relate to nature and biology as they complete Choice 3. Invite students to skim survival handbooks or nature magazines and list ideas related to outdoor activities.

GRAMMAR LINK

MINI-LESSON

Language Handbook HELP

See Personal Pronouns, page 714; Contractions, page 759; Glossary of Usage: their, there, they're, page 770.

Technology HELP

See Language Workshop CD-ROM. Key word entry: words often confused.

• The Homophones *Their, There,* and *They're*

Are you confused about when to use *their, there,* and *they're*? There are good reasons for mixing these words up. They're **homophones**—words that are pronounced the same although their meanings are different.

their	A pronoun—the possessive form of *they*: "... The old couple kept pressing their guests to eat and drink."
there	An adverb that means "in that place": "There as they stood, each one felt the other stiffen. . . ."
	A word used with forms of the verb *to be,* usually at the beginning of a sentence: "There were ripe olives, sour cherries pickled in wine. . . ."
they're	A contraction of *they are:* They're happy to be together.

Try It Out

In these sentences the words *their, there,* and *they're* have been omitted. Copy the sentences, and write the correct word in the blank.

1. "_____ was a big earthenware bowl in the midst of the table to mix ____ crude, homemade wine with water."

2. "The second course had to be fruit, but ____ were nuts, figs, dried dates, plums, grapes, and apples, for this was ____ best season of the year."

3. Philemon and Baucis tell ____ guests that ____ happy to die together.

SPELLING   **HOW TO OWN A WORD**

Silent Letters

If English spellings always followed logic, you might write, "Ghilemon oghered the gods ghigs and other ghruit," instead of "Philemon offered the gods figs and other fruit." You might, that is, if *gh* always sounded like *f,* as in *rough*. In some words, *gh* is unvoiced—*boughs, though, neighbors,* and *thought,* for example. Do unvoiced letters spell trouble for you? If so, try this:

- Keep a list of such words (start your list by finding three words with silent letters in the story).

- Highlight *silent* letters in *loud* colors.

- Use different colors for different unvoiced letters or combinations of letters.

BAUCIS AND PHILEMON 597

GRAMMAR LINK

Have students select a piece of writing from their portfolios and highlight the words *their, there,* and *they're*. Ask students to check whether they used each word correctly and to make any necessary changes. Have students exchange papers with a partner to check each other's work.

Try It Out
1. There, their
2. there, their
3. their, they're

SPELLING

To provide an example, give students a short list of words such as *taught* and *fought* with the silent letters highlighted.

Resources ———

Grammar
- *Grammar and Language Links,* p. 55

Spelling
- *Spelling and Decoding,* p. 25

Grammar Link Quick Check

The words *their, there,* and *they're* are used incorrectly in the following sentences. Have students fix each sentence by using the correct homophone.

1. Zeus and Hermes change there shape from gods to humans. [their]
2. They go to earth, and their they meet Baucis and Philemon. [there]
3. Baucis and Philemon are poor, but they're kindness impresses the gods. [their]
4. Though the gods are strangers, there treated like royalty by Baucis and Philemon. [they're]
5. As a reward, Baucis and Philemon ask to die together when there time comes. [their]

Resources

Elements of Literature
Mythology
For more instruction on the elements of mythology, see *Literary Elements:*
• Transparency 10

Assessment
Formal Assessment
• Literary Elements Test, p. 125
Standardized Test Preparation
• Mini-Test, p. 84

Elements of Literature

This lesson explains how myths are central to human experience, including their universality and common characteristics.

Mini-Lesson:
Mythology
After students read and discuss p. 598, ask the following questions:
1. What are some things that myths explain? [how things in the world came to be, why the seasons change, why certain religious rituals are practiced, and what happens after death]
2. Why are we so familiar with Greek and Roman myths? [because they contain truths about human life; because much of Western civilization is based on ancient Greek culture; because these myths have been written down for more than two thousand years]
3. What do myths help us understand about our lives? [Myths help us understand the joys we experience and the challenges we face.]

Applying the Element
Read aloud a myth that explains the origin of a natural phenomenon, such as thunder, the cycle of day and night, or the seasons. Then read a scientific explanation of the same phenomenon. Ask students to respond to each explanation. Which one do they find more interesting? Which one do they think is true?

Elements of Literature

MYTHOLOGY: Echoes of Our Lives *by* Joseph Bruchac

Myths Make Us Human

Probably the first stories people ever told were **myths**—stories that explain their relationships with the gods and with the powers of creation. Myths are central to human experience. All over the world—in Europe or Asia, in Australia or Africa, in North America or South America, on the many Pacific Islands—we find great bodies of myths.

Although the myths may differ greatly in their details, all of them explain how, long ago, things came to be. Polynesian people tell how the god Maui goes fishing and catches the Hawaiian Islands on his magical hook, pulling them up out of the deep. Lakota Indian people tell how life on earth began with Tunka-shila, "Grandfather Rock," rising up out of fire to create dry land and clouds. The Greeks tell how, out of Chaos, Earth and Sky were born.

Myths may also explain such big questions as why we suffer, why seasons change, why a religious ritual is practiced, or what happens after death. These are serious matters, so it is wise to treat all myths with respect.

Myths of Greece and Rome

In the Western world the best-known myths are from ancient Greece and Rome. There are a number of reasons for that. First, these myths are great stories that contain essential truths about life. Second, Western civilization is based largely on the social and cultural foundations of ancient Greece. Most European languages, including English, contain words from Greek and Latin. (*Myth*, for example, comes from the Greek *mythos*, "story.") Third, tales of the Greek and Roman gods and goddesses have been written down for more than two thousand years. We have had a long time to become familiar with them.

It's important to remember that the myths of ancient Greece and Rome are only one small part of the body of myths. There are thousands of different cultures, and myths are part of every one.

The Myths of Our Lives

In many ways our own lives echo the great mythic tales about journeys of heroes. Like those heroes, we are born, we must grow and learn how to overcome problems, we are given advice by those who are older and wiser, and we must all, finally, face the challenge of death. Whether it is the story of Perseus guided by a wise goddess as he seeks to defeat the monster Medusa or it is the Native American Ojibway tale of Manabozho taking the advice of his wise grandmother as he fights the Fever Monster, a great myth helps us to understand the joys and challenges of our own lives.

598 TELL ME A TALE

Using Students' Strengths

Kinesthetic Learners
Have pairs or small groups present a simple myth in pantomime. Students should select a myth, brainstorm appropriate movements to convey the plot, allocate roles, rehearse, and finally present the myth to the class. Presenters may either give the name of the myth and a brief verbal description or present the myth with no introduction and ask the class to identify the subject and plot.

Visual Learners
Students can create a time line or cartoon tracing their own personal myth. Students should start with the earliest years they can remember and note the problems they overcame, the advice they were given, and how they used this advice to grow wiser. Urge students to be as specific as possible in evaluating their own experiences and creating their personal myths.

Before You Read

QUETZALCOATL

Make the Connection

The Good Old Golden Age

This myth tells of ancient Mexico's Golden Age, when the Toltec people were ruled by Quetzalcoatl (ket·säl'kō·ät''l)—their god and hero. During this time the people had all the good things in life—"no one was in want and no one was unhappy."

Round robin. If you ruled a country, what would you do to make life happy and peaceful and productive for the people? With a group of three or four classmates, brainstorm to discover the things a country needs to be happy and prosperous. Then, choose a group member to tell the rest of the class what you discussed.

Quickwrite

Keeping your discussions in mind, write down two or three major changes that you think would create a Golden Age of peace and prosperity in your country. Jot down your reasons for proposing each change.

go.hrw.com
LEO 6-8

Reading Skills and Strategies

Making Predictions: Guessing What Comes Next

"Long ago, there was a land where everyone was happy." A story that starts that way is almost begging you to **make predictions** about what will come next. To make good predictions, think about

- what's already happened in a story
- clues and hints that the author gives you
- your own knowledge and experience of life and storytelling

Elements of Literature

Golden-Age Myths

How did unhappiness come into the world? Ever since language was created, people have told stories to answer puzzling and fascinating questions such as this. Many cultures have myths about a long-ago **Golden Age** when the world was filled with peace, happiness, and prosperity. Do you think any Golden Age can last forever? The mythmakers seem to agree on the answer to that question—so they tell their stories about the glories of the Golden Age and why it didn't last.

QUETZALCOATL **599**

Planning

- **Block Schedule**
  Block Scheduling Lesson Plans with Pacing Guide
- **Traditional Schedule**
  Lesson Plans, Including Strategies for English-Language Learners
- **One-Stop Planner**
  CD-ROM with Test Generator

Preteaching Vocabulary

Words to Own

Have students read the Words to Own and their definitions listed at the bottom of the selection pages. Then have students select the correct antonym for each of the words from the following chart.

1. abundance [a]	a. lack	b. plenty	c. overflow
2. prosperity [b]	a. wealth	b. poverty	c. a lot
3. induce [c]	a. urge	b. persuade	c. prevent
4. devise [a]	a. destroy	b. plan	c. invent
5. resolve [b]	a. decide	b. give up	c. turn

QUETZALCOATL

a Mexican myth, retold by Amy Cruse

Summary ■

Quetzalcoatl, a god from the land of Sunrise, rules the Toltecs of Mexico (see the sites on the map, p. 599) and has created for them a peaceful and prosperous existence.

Tezcatlipoca, a god of the Toltecs' neighbors, is jealous of Quetzalcoatl and gives him wine, which he is unaccustomed to and which makes him drunk. While Quetzalcoatl is intoxicated, Tezcatlipoca brings misery and ruin to the Toltecs. After recovering, Quetzalcoatl is grieved to see what has happened and decides to leave the Toltecs. He destroys some of the gifts he gave to the Toltecs and buries others, because he refuses to reveal his secrets of prosperity to the other jealous gods. The god then begins a perilous journey back to his homeland. Centuries later, the native people, believing that Quetzalcoatl would return to rule over a new golden age, mistake the Spanish conqueror Cortés for Quetzalcoatl.

Resources ——

Listening
Audio CD Library
An exciting recording of this myth is included in the *Audio CD Library:*
• Disc 14, Track 4

 Elements of Literature

Golden-Age Myths
❓ What clues tell you this story is a Golden-Age myth? [It says that Quetzalcoatl came to the Toltecs in order to help them become happy and prosperous.]

The Mexicans believed that one day he would come back again . . .

Characters

Quetzalcoatl (ket·säl′kō·ät′′l): chief god of the Toltecs.

Tezcatlipoca (tez·kät′lē·pō′kə): god of the people who were neighbors of the Toltecs. Tezcatlipoca was jealous of Quetzalcoatl.

Hernando Cortés (kôr·tez′) (1485–1547): Spanish soldier and explorer who conquered Mexico.

Long, long ago, hundreds of years before the people of Europe knew anything about the great land of America, a people called the Toltecs lived in the southern part of what is today Mexico. They were ruled by Quetzalcoatl, the great god of the sun and the wind, who had left his home in the Land of the Sunrise so that he might teach the Toltecs and help them to become a happy and prosperous nation. He was an old man with a flowing white beard, and he wore a long, black robe fringed with white crosses. He

Resources: Print and Media ——

Reading
• *Reading Skills and Strategies*
Selection Skill Lesson, p. 71
• *Graphic Organizers for Active Reading*, p. 39
• *Words to Own*, p. 22
• *Spelling and Decoding*
Worksheet, p. 26
• *Audio CD Library*
Disc 14, Track 4

Writing and Language
• *Daily Oral Grammar*
Transparency 37
• *Grammar and Language Links*
Worksheet, p. 57
• *Language Workshop CD-ROM*

Viewing and Representing
• *Viewing and Representing*
Fine Art Transparency 18
Fine Art Worksheet, p. 72

Assessment
• *Formal Assessment*, p. 117
• *Portfolio Management System*, p. 179
• *Standardized Test Preparation*, p. 86
• *Test Generator* (One-Stop Planner CD-ROM)

Internet
• go.hrw.com (keyword: LE0 6-8)

was kind and wise, and while he reigned over them, the Toltecs were very happy. Everything in the country prospered. The maize crops were more abundant than they had ever been before; the fruits were larger and more plentiful. It is even said that the cotton grew in all sorts of colors, richer and rarer than could be produced by any dyes. The hills and valleys were gay with flowers, and bright-colored birds flitted through the air, filling the land with joyous song.

But the king-god Quetzalcoatl thought that

if his people were to be really happy, they must not spend their days in the idle enjoyment of all this loveliness and plenty. They must work and learn to take a pride in working as well as they possibly could. So he taught them many useful arts—painting and weaving and carving and working in metals. He taught them how to fashion the gold and silver and precious stones which were found in great abundance throughout the country into beautiful vessels and ornaments, and how to make marvelous many-tinted garments and hangings from the feathers of birds. Everyone was eager to work, and because each man did his share, there was plenty of leisure for all. No one was in want and no one was unhappy. It seemed as if, for these fortunate Toltecs, the Golden Age had really come.

The people of the neighboring states were very jealous when they saw the prosperity of the Toltecs. The gods of these people were fierce and warlike, and they hated Quetzalcoatl because he was so unlike themselves. They plotted together to destroy the peace and good government which he had established.

Tezcatlipoca, the chief of these gods, disguised himself as a very old man and went to the palace of Quetzalcoatl.

"I desire to speak with your master, the king," he said to the page who admitted him.

"That you cannot do," replied the page, "for the king is at present ill and can see no one."

"Nevertheless, go and take my message," said Tezcatlipoca, "and come back and tell me what he says."

WORDS TO OWN
abundance (ə·bun′dəns) *n.*: great plenty.
prosperity (prä·sper′ə·tē) *n.*: wealth.

QUETZALCOATL **601**

Ⓑ Reading Skills and Strategies
Making Predictions
❓ The world of the Toltecs is filled with peace and prosperity—it is truly a "Golden Age." Do you predict such happiness will last? Why or why not? [Possible responses: Yes, it will last because Quetzalcoatl is a wise leader; no, it cannot last because no Golden Age can endure.]

Ⓒ Struggling Readers
Summarizing
❓ What types of work does Quetzalcoatl teach his people? [He teaches them how to paint, weave, carve, work in metal, and make ornaments, vessels, clothes, and ornamental hangings.]

Ⓓ Reading Skills and Strategies
Making Predictions
❓ How do you think Quetzalcoatl's warlike neighbors will bring about his downfall? [Possible responses: They might spread vicious rumors about Quetzalcoatl; they might try to kill him; they might destroy the crops or cause illness.]

Ⓔ Elements of Literature
Golden-Age Myths
❓ What does Quetzalcoatl's illness suggest about the Golden Age? Why? [Possible response: The fact that Quetzalcoatl is ill suggests that the end of the Golden Age is on its way. This is strange because gods usually don't get sick.]

RESPONDING TO THE ART
Artist **David Stevenson** has illustrated the Quetzalcoatl myth for us in the style of the Mayan frescoes found in the crumbling rooms of the site called Bonampak in the Mexican state of Chiapas. The beautiful but grisly murals date from the eighth century. For more information on this site, refer interested students to *National Geographic*, February 1995. **Activity.** Have students identify details of Quetzalcoatl's appearance that reflect descriptions in the myth. Ask: What other parts of the myth are shown in the art?

Reaching All Students

Struggling Readers
Making Predictions was introduced on p. 599. For a lesson directly tied to this selection that teaches students to make predictions using a strategy called Probable Passage, see the *Reading Skills and Strategies* binder:
• Selection Skill Lesson, p. 71

English Language Learners
For additional strategies to supplement instruction for English language learners, see
• *Lesson Plans Including Strategies for English-Language Learners*

Advanced Learners
Suggest that interested students do research on the Greek myth of the Golden Age. How does that Golden Age compare with the one in this Mexican myth?

? How does this part of the myth warn people of the dangers of alcohol? [Possible responses: It shows that Quetzalcoatl loses his reason because of alcohol; it shows that other people may take advantage of you if you drink too much. The results of excessive drinking can be disastrous, as they are here.]

B Historical Connections

Some historians believe that the myth of Tezcatlipoca's victory over Quetzalcoatl is probably based on fact. From about the ninth through the twelfth centuries, the Toltec dominated central Mexico. A priestly class ruled their civilization during the ninth century, and peace prevailed, as described in this myth. Around the tenth century, though, the military took control from the priests, ending the "Golden Age" of peace and prosperity.

C Cultural Connections

Myths often have multiple versions, and this origin story is no different. According to this version of the myth, Quetzalcoatl vanishes on a raft of snakes. In another version, he is exiled from Tula, capital of the Toltecs, by Tezcatlipoca. Quetzalcoatl then travels down the Atlantic coast (the so-called "divine water"), burns in a blaze of glory, and is metamorphosed into the planet Venus.

D Elements of Literature

Golden-Age Myths
? Quetzalcoatl refuses to share his secrets of prosperity. What does this suggest about the Toltecs' Golden Age? [Possible responses: It will not last; it will not be re-created.]

The page soon returned, saying that the king would see his visitor, and Tezcatlipoca went in. He bowed low and respectfully before the god and said that he had come to bring him a drug that would at once cure him of his illness.

"I have been expecting you for some days," answered Quetzalcoatl, "and I will take your medicine, for my illness troubles me greatly."

Then Tezcatlipoca poured out a cupful of his medicine, which was really nothing but the strong wine of the country. Quetzalcoatl tasted it and liked it very much; he did not know what it was, for he never drank wine. After drinking the cupful, he declared that he already felt better, so that it was easy to induce him to drink cupful after cupful of this new, pleasant-tasting medicine. Very soon the wine had its effect, and he could no longer think clearly or act wisely or take his usual place as the ruler of the country. Tezcatlipoca took care to keep him supplied with plenty of the tempting drink, so that he remained for some time in this state of intoxication.

This was Tezcatlipoca's opportunity, and he used it to the full. He set to work to bring upon the happy Toltecs every kind of misery that he could devise. He stirred up strife between them and their neighbors, and in many cunning ways he used his magic arts to lure large numbers of them to destruction. He brought plagues upon them and disasters in which many lost their lives until, at last, by his wicked devices, the once happy land was brought to a state much worse than that of its barbarous neighbors.

When Quetzalcoatl shook off the evil influence of the wine given to him by his enemy and came to his true self once more, the grief which he felt at seeing all his work undone

made him resolve to leave the Toltecs and go back whence he had come. But first he determined to destroy what he could of the gifts he had given to the people. He burned the houses he had built and changed the cacao trees from which the Toltecs had obtained so much valuable food into useless mesquites. He buried his treasures of gold and silver in one of the deep valleys. All the bright-plumaged birds he commanded to follow him back to his own country; and, full of anger and grief, he set out on his long journey, taking with him a train of pages, and musicians to lighten the way with their flute-playing. On the road, as he passed through the neighboring states, he was met by some of the gods of these lands. These gods were his enemies and were glad to see him depart, but before he went, they hoped to gain from him some of his secrets.

"Why are you going away?" asked one, "and whither are you bound?"

"I am going back to my own country," Quetzalcoatl answered.

"But why?" the other asked again.

"Because my father, the Sun, has called for me."

"Go then," replied the gods. "But first tell us some of the secrets which are known to you alone concerning the arts you practice, for we know there is no one who can paint and weave and work in metals as you can."

"I will tell you nothing," replied Quetzalcoatl. He took all the treasures he had brought with him and cast them into a foun-

---

WORDS TO OWN

induce (in·do͞os′) v.: persuade.
devise (di·vīz′) v.: create; invent.
resolve (ri·zälv′) v.: decide.

Skill Link

Usage: *Effect* vs. *Affect*
Use this activity before teaching the Language Link on p. 607. Ask students to describe what happens when Quetzalcoatl drinks the wine. [He becomes intoxicated.] Ask students how they could use the word *effect* to express the same idea. [Possible answers: The wine has a bad *effect* on Quetzalcoatl; the *effect* of the wine on Quetzalcoatl is harmful.] Point out that the word *effect* is a noun in these sentences

and means "a result." Ask students why Tezcatlipoca acts as he does. [He is jealous.] Ask how students would use the word *affect* to express this idea. [Possible answer: Jealousy can *affect* someone's behavior.] Point out that *affect* is a verb and means "have an influence on." Ask students to supply *effect* or *affect* appropriately in these sentences:

1. The King's illness has a bad [*effect*] on the people.
2. The wine [*affects*] how Quetzalcoatl feels.
3. The [*effects*] of disease cause people to die.
4. Tezcatlipoca's evil deeds [*affect*] the Toltecs.

E Critical Thinking

Interpreting

? What is surprising about Quetzal-coatl's behavior in this scene? [Possible response: After his bad experience with wine, he drinks some more.]

F Reading Skills and Strategies

Making Predictions

? What do you think will happen to Quetzalcoatl? [Possible responses: He will perish in the terrible cold; he will survive because he is a god.]

RESPONDING TO THE ART

Activity. Dave Stevenson believes that the better the research is, the better the final piece of art is. Ask students to examine this illustration closely and to identify all the details in it, based on a close reading of the text. Ask them to make comparisons between what they've read and what they see in the illustration. Be sure they identify the plumed serpent at the top right.

tain nearby, which was called the Water of Precious Stones; and he went on his way, paying no heed to the entreaties of the disappointed gods.

As they journeyed on, the road grew increasingly harder and more dangerous, but Quetzalcoatl, his staff in his hand, pressed steadily forward; and his train, though they were weary and nearly exhausted, followed him. Only once did they stop to rest, and that was when an enchanter met Quetzalcoatl and gave him a cup of wine. The wine sent the god into a deep sleep, but in the morning he had recovered from its effects and was ready to set out once more.

That day was a terrible one for the travelers. At each step it grew colder and colder, and the poor pages, used to the sunny skies of their native land, felt their limbs gradually becoming numb and useless. At length Quetzalcoatl led the way through a narrow valley between a volcano and the Sierra Nevada, or Mountain of Snow. Here the cold was so intense that the pages one by one sank down and died. Quetzalcoatl mourned over them with many tears and sang wild songs of grief; then, sadly, he went on his way, still weeping bitterly.

He had now to cross a great mountain. He climbed up one side; then, when he had

QUETZALCOATL **603**

Making the Connections

Connecting to the Theme: "Tell Me a Tale"

When students have finished reading the myth, have them make a two-column chart showing what the Toltec culture is like during Quetzal-coatl's reign and after his departure. In the left column, students should describe the "Golden Age" of the Toltecs; in the right column, they should describe the Toltec downfall.

Quetzalcoatl's Reign	
During	After
abundant fruit and crops	Cacao trees turned into useless mesquites

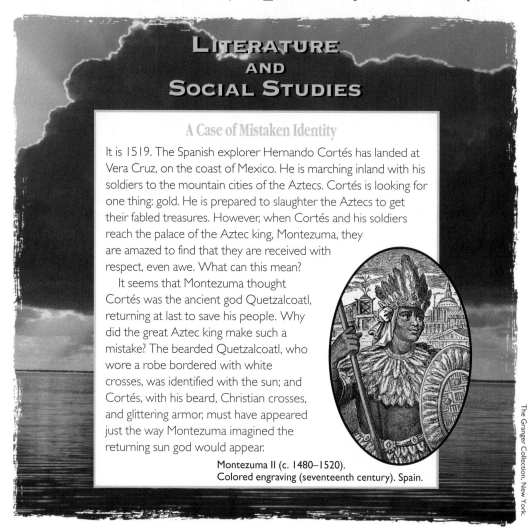

MAKING MEANINGS

MAKING MEANINGS

First Thoughts

[respond]

1. How did you respond when Quetzal-coatl left, destroying all the gifts he had given to the Toltecs?

Shaping Interpretations

[predict]

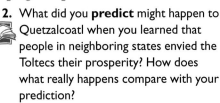

2. What did you **predict** might happen to Quetzalcoatl when you learned that people in neighboring states envied the Toltecs their prosperity? How does what really happens compare with your prediction?

[interpret]

3. This **myth** explains how unhappiness came to exist on earth. What troubles are explained by Tezcatlipoca's cunning and Quetzalcoatl's anger?

[interpret]

4. How does the myth explain the origin of deposits of gold, silver, and precious stones?

[interpret]

5. One of the tragic events in history was the Aztecs' allowing Cortés into their mountain city and then being brutally overcome by this man they thought was their god. Explain how the Aztecs' hope for their god's return led to their down-fall.

[analyze]

6. According to this myth, what qualities should the people have looked for in Cortés to find out if he was really their god?

Extending the Text

[synthesize]

7. Look back at your notes for the Quickwrite on page 599. How are your ideas about a **Golden Age** like Quetzalcoatl's? How are they different?

Reading Check

a. Describe some of the ways in which the Toltecs prosper under Quetzal-coatl's rule.

b. How are the gods of the Toltecs' neighbors differ-ent from Quetzalcoatl?

c. How does Tezcatlipoca trick Quetzalcoatl? What happens to the Toltecs as a result?

d. Describe the hardship of Quetzalcoatl's perilous journey back to his own land.

e. Why did the people want Quetzalcoatl to return? What happened when the Spanish conquerors came?

Drawing of Quetzalcoatl, the Plumed Serpent, from a fifteenth-century sculpture.

First Thoughts

1. Students might have felt sad or angry that Quetzalcoatl punished the Toltecs for actions that were beyond their control.

Shaping Interpretations

2. Students might have predicted that people in neighboring states would envy the Toltecs' happiness and prosperity and try to destroy it.

3. Tezcatlipoca's cunning explains how envious, unscrupulous people can take advantage of others to shatter peace and prosperity. Quetzalcoatl's anger explains how guilt can lead to anger because of having given in to temptation.

4. The myth explains that Quetzalcoatl buried the treasure he had given to the Toltecs. Deposits of gold, silver, and precious stones are found buried in the earth.

5. Cortés landed at the place from which Quetzalcoatl was supposed to have departed. His appearance—the beard, cross, armor—and the timing of his arrival led to the impression that he was Quetzal-coatl. Because of their firm belief in the god's return, they did not care-fully scrutinize the invader.

6. The people should have looked for an older man with a long white beard and a long black robe fringed with crosses. He should have been wise, kind, and generous.

Extending the Text

7. Students are apt to envision a Golden Age very similar to Quetzal-coatl's version, filled with peace and prosperity.

Reading Check

a. The crops are bountiful and the country is full of flowers and birds. The people have creative work and ample leisure time. Everyone is happy and there is no strife.

b. The neighbors' gods are jealous, mean, and warlike, while Quetzalcoatl is kind and wise.

c. He gives Quetzalcoatl wine that he says is medicine. The Toltecs are left unprotected and Tezcatlipoca uses his power to shatter their peace and bring strife and death.

d. The roads are dangerous and hard to travel. It gets colder and colder. There are steep moun-tains to climb, and many people die.

e. The people wanted Quetzalcoatl to bring back the Golden Age of happiness and pros-perity. The Aztecs thought the Spanish con-queror Cortés was Quetzalcoatl returning.

Rubrics for each Choices assignment appear on p. 179 in the *Portfolio Management System*.

CHOICES:
Building Your Portfolio

1. **Writer's Notebook** Remind students to save their work. They may use it as prewriting for the Writer's Workshop on pp. 658–662. Encourage students to use a graphic organizer such as a semantic web to help them generate specific details to describe the ruler or troublemaker.

2. **Creative Writing** Bring pictures of modern Mexico to class. Have students use the pictures to help them describe what Quetzalcoatl finds when he returns to Mexico.

3. **Research/Critical Thinking** Help students use the pronunciation key in the dictionary to say each word correctly. Tell students to write each definition as it would appear in a dictionary.

4. **Research/Art/Writing** Work with students to list the kinds of art the Toltecs created as described in the story. Have students write the list on the chalkboard for use in choosing which types of art they will research and write about.

CHOICES: Building Your Portfolio

Writer's Notebook

1. Collecting Ideas for a Story

Try creating a storybook character who is a leader (like Quetzalcoatl) or a trouble-maker (like Tezcatlipoca). List details about your character's appearance, powers, and special interests. Who are the people your character helps or harms? Think of a problem for your character to solve or a conflict your character gets mixed up in.

> A wise ruler gave his warring people special glasses that made them hate war. People wore the glasses all the time. Brought peace to the kingdom.

Creative Writing

2. Sun God Sequel

Suppose Quetzalcoatl comes back years later to re-create the Golden Age for his people. Write a description of what he looks like when he returns to Mexico, what he finds there, and what he does. Brainstorm with classmates, and before you write, fill out the chart that follows. Be sure to review the description of the god at the beginning of this myth.

The Return of Quetzalcoatl		
What he looks like	What he finds on his return	What he decides to do

Research/Critical Thinking

3. Words from Nahuatl

In the 1600s, as settlers in America pushed westward, they picked up many words from Mexico. Several came from Nahuatl, the principal Aztec tongue. Make a Nahuatl-English dictionary by looking up the Nahuatl origin of the following English words in a good dictionary. Tell what each word means in Nahuatl and what it means in English.

chili   tamale
chocolate   tomato
coyote

Research/Art/Writing

4. On Display

Suppose you want to display three major examples of Toltec art. First, reread "Quetzalcoatl," noting the kind of art the Toltecs created. You can continue your research at a library. Then, choose three items from your notes, and become an expert on them. Make replicas or draw pictures of the objects. Then, write a paragraph for each object on a display card, telling museum goers something that will add to their appreciation of this piece of art. Remember that clothing can be art; so can weaving, baskets, and jewelry.

Using Students' Strengths

Kinesthetic/Verbal Learners
For Choice 2, invite small groups of students to role-play Quetzalcoatl's return based on the information in their charts. Guide them to incorporate interesting dialogue and actions in their creative writing.

Visual Learners
Encourage these students to brainstorm effective ways to display the artwork and written descriptions for Choice 4. Some students may use ideas based on museum or department store displays they have seen.

GRAMMAR LINK | MINI-LESSON

Language Handbook HELP

See Glossary of Usage: affect, effect, page 766.

Technology HELP

See Language Workshop CD-ROM. Key word entry: words often confused.

Effect vs. *Affect*

Did Quetzalcoatl effect or affect positive changes among the Toltecs? Did Tezcatlipoca's troublemaking have a negative affect or effect? If you're confused about using *effect* and *affect*, you're not alone. This confusion affects many writers, and its effects can be seen in their work.

- **Effect** as a verb means "accomplish" or "bring about."

  To effect a major change in people's lives, Quetzalcoatl had to be wise and powerful.

- **Effect** as a noun means "the result of some action."

  Very soon the wine had its effect, and Quetzalcoatl could not think clearly or act wisely.

- **Affect** is usually a verb. It means "impress" or "influence."

  Did learning to weave, carve, and paint affect the people's everyday lives?

Try It Out

Which word completes each sentence correctly?

1. The changes that Tezcatlipoca affected/effected brought misfortune to the once-happy land.

2. Quetzalcoatl was deeply affected/effected when he saw all his work undone.

3. How did Quetzalcoatl's leaving affect/effect his people?

4. Cacao trees' turning into useless mesquites was one affect/effect of the god's anger.

5. If Quetzalcoatl ever does return, he will affect/effect great changes.

GRAMMAR LINK

Have students select three pieces of writing from their portfolios. Ask them to highlight the words *effect* and *affect* in each piece and look for these words in other contexts, such as textbooks or newspapers, to see if they have been used correctly. Students should make any necessary changes and exchange papers with a partner to check each other's work.

Try It Out
1. effected
2. affected
3. affect
4. effect
5. effect

VOCABULARY

Sample responses
1. In a Golden Age, the prosperity of people results from an abundance of crops, resources, skills, and art.
2. Tezcatlipoca will devise a plan to give you wine to induce a drunken state.
3. My decision is made; I resolve to leave this land and go back to my own country.

Resources ————

Grammar
- *Grammar and Language Links,* p. 57

Vocabulary
- *Words to Own,* p. 22

Spelling
- *Spelling and Decoding,* p. 26

VOCABULARY | HOW TO OWN A WORD

WORD BANK	Own It
abundance *prosperity* *induce* *devise* *resolve*	1. Use the words *abundance* and *prosperity* to describe a Golden Age. 2. Use *devise* and *induce* in a message to warn Quetzalcoatl about Tezcatlipoca. 3. Use *resolve* in a sentence from a brief farewell speech Quetzalcoatl might make to the Toltecs.

QUETZALCOATL 607

Grammar Link Quick Check

Have students choose the correct word in the following sentences.

1. The students' ability to concentrate on their lesson was effected/affected by the sounds outside the window. [affected]
2. The affect/effect of the sounds was disturbing to the students. [effect]
3. The teacher affected/effected the situation by closing the window. [affected]
4. The lesson on the Golden Age myths had a deep affect/effect on the students. [effect]
5. To effect/affect a Golden Age in their lifetime would take hard work. [effect]

OBJECTIVES

1. Recognize how folk tales are stories by and about people
2. Trace the history of folk tales
3. Recognize differences between folk tales and myths

Resources

Elements of Literature
Folk Tales
For more instruction on the elements of folk tales, see *Literary Elements:*
• Transparency 11

Assessment
Formal Assessment
• Literary Elements Test, p. 126

Viewing and Representing
Visual Connections
• Videocassette B, Segment 9

Elements of Literature

This lesson defines folk tales and describes their origins. It also describes some of the differences between folk tales and myths.
Mini-Lesson:
Folk Tales
After students read and discuss the essay, have them paraphrase differences and similarities between myths and folk tales. For example:

• Similar folk tales are found in many different cultures, while myths tend to stay in the area where they were developed because they are tied to religious beliefs.
• Both myths and folk tales have been passed down through the oral tradition.
• Both teach lessons about life. Although many myths explain how things came to be, folk tales provide lessons about morality.
• Characters in myths are gods and superhuman, while characters in folk tales are usually ordinary people.

Applying the Element
Ask students to compare and contrast one specific folk tale or fairy tale they've read or heard with one of the myths they've read so far in this collection. Students may make a chart or diagram showing differences and similarities in characters, settings, lessons, or themes.

FOLK TALES: The People's Stories *by* Joseph Bruchac

What is a folk tale? Until folk tales are written down, they are a major part of the oral, or spoken, traditions of the common people. A **folk tale** is the kind of story that is entertaining and meaningful enough to be remembered and shared for generation after generation. Folk tales are the kinds of stories told to children at bedtime and around the fire late at night after the family's work is done.

Traveling Tales

Folk tales travel from one culture to another with great ease. The basic story line of one folk tale will often turn up in another culture thousands of miles away. Myths, on the other hand, because of their connection with religion and belief, do not move around so easily.

In West Africa, for example, we find the stories of Anansi the Spider. Anansi is both a spider and a human being. He originated among the Akan people of Ghana, where children still love tales of his greed and trickery. Anansi always outwits those who are bigger and stronger, such as the python and the lion.

When West Africans were brought as slaves to the Western Hemisphere, they brought their folklore with them. In Jamaica, where many Akans were taken, stories of Anansi, the trickster spider, are popular to this day. In the United States, where African languages were forbidden by the slave owners, Anansi became Aunt Nancy. In the stories of Joel Chandler Harris, a white writer who wrote down tales he collected from Africans held in slavery, Anansi became Uncle Remus. In some southern tales, Anansi the Spider was replaced by the trickster Brer Rabbit, who also uses cleverness to defeat those who are bigger and stronger than he is. Brer Rabbit might be the ancestor of Bugs Bunny, a more recent rabbit trickster.

The People of Folk Tales

The central characters in myths are often gods and superhuman beings. The characters in folk tales, although they may have fantastic adventures and may even have magic powers, are ordinary by comparison.

If the characters in folk tales are less than godlike, it may be because they reflect the people who told the tales. The heroes of the African folk tales told in America were often **tricksters,** such as Brer Rabbit or High John the Conqueror, characters who used their wits to overcome those who were stronger than they but not nearly as clever. This is also true in the folk tales of Europe, in which clever peasants outsmart powerful kings and queens. In folk tales, what we wish for usually comes true.

Using Students' Strengths

Interpersonal Learners
Have students work in small groups to recall folk tales, fairy tales, or tall tales with which they are familiar. Students should attempt to recall or find out the specific cultural origin of the stories they recall and indicate the country or continent of origin on a map. Encourage students to identify common features among the folk tales they recall by sharing their recollections and research with the entire class.

Auditory/Musical Learners
Folk songs are an important part of many students' cultural heritage. Have students recall folk songs (including chants and spirituals) that they've heard. Some students may bring in a recording of a folk song to share with the class. Ask them to determine what characteristics folk songs share with folk tales.

Reading Skills and Strategies

OBJECTIVES
1. Use word parts to build meaning
2. Learn common prefixes and suffixes

USING WORD PARTS TO BUILD MEANINGS

Sometimes you can figure out the meaning of an unfamiliar word if you analyze the meaning of its parts. The more prefixes and suffixes you know, the more words you'll be able to figure out.

A **prefix** is a word part added to the beginning of a word or root. A **suffix** is a word part added to the end of a word or root. The charts at the right show common prefixes and suffixes.

In the next story, you'll encounter forty thieves, piles of treasure—and prefixes and suffixes. See if you can uncover the hidden word parts.

Common Prefixes		
Prefix	**Meaning**	**Examples**
bi-	two; doubly	bicycle, bicultural
dis-	opposing; away	dislike, discomfort
in-	not	incomplete, incapable
mis-	wrong; badly	misspell, misunderstand
non-	not	nonhuman, nonstop
over-	too much; above	overdone, overcoat
pre-	before	prepay, prejudge
re-	again; returning to	replace, research
semi-	half; partly	semicircle, semisweet
sub-	under	subtitle, submarine
un-	not	unhappy, unwise

Common Suffixes		
Suffix	**Meaning**	**Examples**
-able	capable of being	respectable, laughable
-en	make	deepen, lengthen
-ful	full of	stressful, doubtful
-ion	act or condition of	inspection, reaction
-less	without	penniless, hopeless
-ly	in a certain way	quickly, smoothly
-ness	quality of being	togetherness, happiness
-ous	characterized by	luxurious, dangerous

Apply the strategy on the next page. ▶

READING SKILLS AND STRATEGIES **609**

Reading Skills and Strategies

This feature identifies some of the most commonly used prefixes and suffixes and gives examples of words that include these affixes.

Mini-Lesson:
Using Word Parts to Build Meanings

- Review the prefixes and suffixes with students. Encourage them to suggest additional examples for each prefix and suffix.
- Write additional prefixes and suffixes on the chalkboard and ask students to think of words that include them. Make two charts on the board like those below to record students' answers. Ask volunteers to use the words in sentences.

Prefix	Meaning	Example
anti-	against, opposite	antisocial
co-	jointly, together	coordinate
inter-	between, among	interview
post-	after, following	postscript

Suffix	Meaning	Example
-ate	become, cause	activate
-dom	state, condition	freedom
-hood	condition, quality	childhood
-ize	make, cause to be	dramatize

Using Students' Strengths

Verbal Learners
Have students work in small groups to create mnemonic devices to help them remember the meaning of the various prefixes and suffixes. Possibilities include rhymes, songs, associations, and similar letter sounds. For example, to remember the suffix -able, students can link it to the word "capable"; if you're able, you're capable. Have each group share their best mnemonics with the class.

Visual Learners
Have students create symbols or drawings to represent some of the prefixes and suffixes. For example, to indicate the prefix semi-, students might use a fraction (1/2) or half-circle; for the suffix -en, students might draw a hand or two hands joined together. Encourage students to be creative in their development of symbols and drawings.

T609

Before You Read

ALI BABA AND THE FORTY THIEVES

Make the Connection

Finders Keepers?

Suppose you saw a gang of thieves hide a bag containing hundreds of thousands of dollars? What would you do?

Quickwrite

What problems might keeping the money create? What problems might it solve? What problems might arise if you turned the money in? Freewrite for a few minutes about all the possible consequences.

Reading Skills and Strategies

Using Word Parts

In this incredible tale you'll encounter a subterranean treasure, an unwise thief, and a clever sleuth. Be a detective yourself, and hunt out the **prefixes** and **suffixes** in this paragraph. (Review the charts on page 609.) If you come across unfamiliar words in your reading, take them apart. A prefix or a suffix might help you unravel the meaning.

610 TELL ME A TALE

go.hrw.com
LE0 6-8

Ali Baba
and the
Forty Thieves

a Persian folk tale, retold by **Walter McVitty**

Long ago, in the land of Persia, there lived two brothers, Cassim and Ali Baba. Cassim married a rich but unpleasant woman and became a wealthy merchant, while Ali Baba married a poor but kindly woman and lived a humble life by cutting wood and selling it in the marketplace.

One day, while working in the forest, he saw a band of evil-looking men riding toward him. Fearing they might be robbers and cutthroats, he hid himself among the branches of a tree, which was growing beside a very large rock.

Forty men, all armed with long swords, brought their horses to a halt, right underneath this tree. Their leader sprang from his horse and called to the rock, *"Open, Sesame!"*

At once the rock opened, revealing a cave, into which the robbers bundled their bulging saddlebags. The rock then closed

Piled before him was a great treasure—expensive silks, costly rugs, and heaps of gold and silver.

behind them, and all was silent.

Ali Baba looked on in amazement. He dared not leave his tree in case the bandits suddenly came out and caught him spying on them, for he knew that would surely mean death.

After some time, the rock opened up once more and the forty thieves came out, their saddlebags now empty. As they mounted their horses, their leader raised his hand and called out, *"Close, Sesame!"* The rock closed up once again and the robbers rode off.

Fascinated by what he had seen, Ali Baba climbed down from his tree and stood before the rock. He was curious to see if the magic words would work for him too. *"Open, Sesame!"* he cried, and behold, the great rock opened at his command.

Trembling with excitement, he entered the cave. The door closed behind him. Instead of being dark and gloomy as he

ALI BABA AND THE FORTY THIEVES **611**

Summary ▪ ■

Ali Baba, a humble woodcutter, sees robbers hiding treasure in a cave sealed with a rock. The rock moves when the robbers command, "Open, Sesame!" Later, Ali Baba uses the command to move the rock and take some of the treasure. Ali Baba's rich brother, Cassim, learns about the treasure, but he gets trapped when he forgets the password. When the robbers return and discover Cassim in their cave, they kill him. Morgiana, Ali Baba's clever servant, arranges for the cobbler to sew Cassim's body together, but the robbers learn of the ruse and plot to kill Ali Baba. Morgiana repeatedly foils their plans. Finally, she stabs the disguised robber chief during a dance, saving Ali Baba's life.

Resources 🎧

Listening
Audio CD Library
A suspenseful recording of this folk tale is included in the *Audio CD Library*:
• Disc 14, Track 5

Ⓐ Reading Skills and Strategies
Comparing/Contrasting
❓ How are Ali Baba and Cassim different? [Possible responses: Cassim is a wealthy merchant, married to a rich but unpleasant woman. Ali Baba is a poor woodcutter, married to a poor but kind woman.]

Ⓑ English Language Learners
Questioning
❓ An expression like "Open, Sesame" is called a magical saying or a password. What other magical sayings do you know that are used in folk tales and stories? [Possible responses: "Abracadabra," "Presto," "Alakazam."]

Resources: Print and Media

Reading
• *Reading Skills and Strategies*
  Selection Skill Lesson, p. 49
• *Graphic Organizers for Active Reading,* p. 40
• *Spelling and Decoding*
  Worksheet, p. 27
• *Audio CD Library*
  Disc 14, Track 5

Elements of Literature
• *Literary Elements*
  Transparency 11
  Worksheet, p. 34

Writing and Language
• *Daily Oral Grammar*
  Transparency 38
• *Grammar and Language Links*
  Worksheet, p. 59

Viewing and Representing
• *Viewing and Representing*
  Fine Art Transparency 19
  Fine Art Worksheet, p. 76

Assessment
• *Formal Assessment,* p. 119
• *Portfolio Management System,* p. 180
• *Standardized Test Preparation,* p. 88
• *Test Generator (One-Stop Planner CD-ROM)*

Internet
• go.hrw.com (keyword: LE0 6-8)

B Vocabulary Note

Words in Context

? What does the word *measure* mean here? ["to weigh"] What context clue helped you figure out the meaning? ["weighing pan"]

C Reading Skills and Strategies

Using Word Parts

? How can you use the suffix *-ful* to define the word *careful*? [*-ful* means "full of," so *careful* must mean "cautious," "watchful"]

D Critical Thinking

Classifying

? The words *barley* and *rye* name kinds of grain. Based on what you know about the word *sesame*, what makes Cassim's cries funny? [He cries out the names of grains, but they are the wrong ones.]

---

expected, the cave was well lit, for there was a hole in its roof.

Ali Baba was astonished by what he saw. Piled before him was a great treasure—expensive silks, costly rugs, and heaps of gold and silver.

Although poor, Ali Baba was not a greedy man. He quickly filled a few sacks with gold coins, just enough for his two donkeys to carry.

"Open, Sesame!" he commanded again, and hurried out. Remembering to say *"Close, Sesame!"* he then led his donkeys home.

When Ali Baba's wife saw the gold, she was speechless. He told her what he had seen and done and said to her, "You must promise to tell no one about this. We will bury the treasure and use it but a little at a time. Then no one will be suspicious. But first we must measure it. While I dig the hole, run to my brother Cassim's house and borrow his weighing pan—but remember, say nothing more."

Cassim's wife was very curious to know what Ali Baba could possibly have that was worth measuring, so she placed some suet° on the bottom of the pan. When it was returned to her, she was astonished to find a piece of gold stuck to the suet. She became jealous and angry and said to her husband, "Your brother Ali Baba is so wealthy he does not just *count* his gold. He has to *measure* it, like grain! He pretends to be poor, but he must be richer than all of us."

When he saw the scales and the gold coin, Cassim, too, grew jealous and angry. He ran to his brother's house and was just in time to see him putting the last of the gold into the

°**suet:** animal fat used in cooking.

hole. And so Ali Baba had to tell his brother the whole story.

Trembling with excitement, the greedy Cassim cried, "In the morning I will go to the cave myself—with *ten* donkeys. I will be richer than you!"

"Be careful, brother," warned Ali Baba. "If the forty thieves catch you, they will surely kill you."

Cassim soon found the rock and, saying

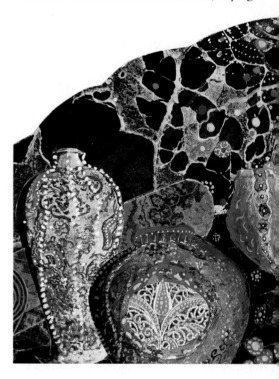

the magic words, opened up the cave and fell upon its treasure. He piled the gold into sack after sack. But when the time came for him to leave, he could not remember the magic words. *"Open, Barley!"* he cried in panic, but of course nothing happened. He tried again and again. *"Open, Rye! Open, Caraway!"* But it was no use. He was now a prisoner.

Reaching All Students

Struggling Readers
Using Word Parts was introduced on p. 610. For a lesson directly tied to this selection that teaches students to use word parts using a strategy called Vocabulary Trees, see the *Reading Skills and Strategies* binder:
• Selection Skill Lesson, p. 49

English Language Learners
Have students practice making predictions to help them follow the story's plot. Students should stop reading after every two or three paragraphs to make a prediction. At the same time, have them check previously made predictions and identify clues or evidence in the selection that help them revise their predictions. For additional strategies, see
• *Lesson Plans Including Strategies for English-Language Learners*

Advanced Learners
Have students prepare a plot outline for this folk tale. They should summarize key events so far and add to the outline as they continue reading. For additional support, review the main features of summarizing with students in Taking a Second Look on p. T613.

Later that day the forty thieves returned. When they saw the ten donkeys tied up outside the cave, they knew that someone had discovered their secret. With swords drawn, they rushed inside and killed Cassim without mercy and cut him into six parts.

"We will leave his body inside the cave," said the robber chief, "as a warning to anyone else who might be foolish enough to try to steal our treasure."

As the day wore on, Cassim's wife, waiting at home, grew more and more worried. When her husband did not return that night, she ran weeping to Ali Baba to ask for his help.

In the morning he went to the cave, where he found the remains of Cassim's body, which he brought back in a sack. When he arrived at his own house, he called for his servant Morgiana, an orphan who had been raised as a daughter by Ali Baba and his wife. She had grown into a brave and wise woman and knew how to solve problems of all kinds.

Ali Baba told her of the terrible fate which had overtaken his brother and said to her, "While I go to break the sad news to his widow, you must think of some way in which we can bury these six pieces so that people will think that Cassim died a natural death. Otherwise, everyone will learn our secret and then the robbers will come and murder us all."

"I will try," she promised.

The next day Morgiana went to the workplace of an old cobbler and said, "Look, Mustapha, here is a gold coin. For this, I want you to bring your needle and thread and come with me. But first, I must bandage your eyes, for you must not know where you are going."

This she did and led him through the streets and down into the cellar of Ali Baba's house, where she removed the blindfold. Giving him another gold coin, she said, "I wish you to sew the pieces of this body together. If you work quickly and well, you shall have another gold coin."

When he had finished, Morgiana led Mustapha back to his shop and paid him as arranged. "Remember, you must tell nobody what you have done or where you have been," she warned him.

Cassim was then buried properly, all in one piece, and nobody suspected how he had really met his death.

When the forty thieves returned to their cave and discovered that Cassim's body had been taken away, they knew that someone else had also found their cave. "We must find that person and kill him," said their leader.

He sent the bravest and smartest of the thieves into the city to find out if anybody

ALI BABA AND THE FORTY THIEVES 613

E Elements of Literature
Folk Tale
❓ What lesson does this folk tale teach about greediness? Do you think the lesson applies today? Why or why not? [Possible response: The folk tale teaches that people who are greedy are punished. Some students may say the lesson applies today because some greedy people who steal or cheat are caught and punished; others may say the lesson doesn't apply today because people can be greedy for good things, like developing skills and taking advantage of opportunities.]

F Reading Skills and Strategies
Using Word Parts
❓ What other words do you know that have the prefix over-, meaning "too much, above"? [Possible responses: overalls, overcast, overcoat, overcome, overdress, overdue, overeaten, overflow, overhang, overhead, overland, overlap, overlook, overpower, overrun, overshoes, oversleep, overtime.]

G Reading Skills and Strategies
Making Predictions
❓ What do you think Morgiana will do to make people believe that Cassim has died a natural death? [Possible response: She will have the cobbler sew Cassim's body together so no one will know that he was dismembered.]

H Critical Thinking
Hypothesizing
❓ Why do the thieves want to kill the person who found their cave? What does this reveal about the thieves? [Possible response: They think this person might return to the cave to take more of their treasure. This shows that the thieves are cruel, merciless, and motivated entirely by self-interest.]

Taking a Second Look

Review: Summarizing
Remind students that when they summarize a text they should do the following:
- look for the main idea
- reread closely, identifying the supporting details of the main idea
- rewrite the main idea and important supporting details in their own words
- make sure they've expressed the main idea and details in fewer words than the original text.

Activities
1. Have students write a summary of the events so far in "Ali Baba and the Forty Thieves."
2. Have students summarize a scene or major event from one of the myths they've read in this collection.
3. Have students summarize an article from a newspaper, magazine, or textbook.

A Cultural Note

Allah is "the Supreme Being" in the Islamic religion.

B Elements of Literature
Characterization

? What does this scene reveal about the cobbler's character? [Possible response: The cobbler is greedy, like Cassim, and dishonest, like the robbers, because he is willing to accept money from the thief to betray Morgiana.]

C Reading Skills and Strategies
Drawing Conclusions

? Why does Morgiana mark all the doors with the same mark? [Possible responses: So that the thieves will not know which door is her master's; so one house cannot be distinguished from the other.]

knew of a man whose body had been cut into six parts and buried. When this messenger arrived in the city, only one shop, the cobbler's, was open.

"Goodness me, old man," said the thief to Mustapha, "how do you manage to sew so neatly, in such dim light?"

A "I may be old," replied Mustapha, "but Allah has blessed me with good eyesight. And just as well, too, because a short while ago I had to sew up a body which had been cut into six parts. When I had finished, nobody would have guessed that poor man had not died in one piece."

The robber could hardly believe his luck. "I will give you five gold coins if you will show me where you performed such a marvel," he pleaded.

B "I cannot be sure of the direction, for I was led there blindfolded," Mustapha replied. "Perhaps if I were blindfolded once more, I might be able to lead you there by the sense of touch alone."

And so, bandaged afresh, he was able to find the way to Ali Baba's house with little trouble—and was well pleased with his reward. The delighted robber placed a mark on the door with a piece of white chalk and, sending Mustapha back to his shop, hurried away to the forest to tell his leader of his success.

C Shortly afterwards, when the servant Morgiana returned from the market, she saw the white mark on her master's door. Suspecting this to have been placed there by some unknown enemy, she fetched some chalk and marked all the other doors in the street in exactly the same way.

When the robber returned to the city with his comrades, he was dismayed to find how easily he had been tricked. "I must be dreaming," he cried. "I marked only one door and now I cannot tell which one it was."

The robber chief was so angry that, as soon as his men returned to the forest, he cut off the unfortunate messenger's head. He

614 TELL ME A TALE

Skill Link

Word Origins

To help you assess students' ability to use dictionary etymologies use this activity before you teach the Language Link activity on p. 622. Remind students that part of the dictionary entry for a word includes the history of the word, or the language from which the word originated. The origin of the word appears in square brackets. Point out that since space is limited, the different languages are abbreviated—

for example, E stands for English, F stands for French, L for Latin, Ar for Arabic, OE for Old English, ME for Middle English, and OHG for Old High German. Finally, explain that the symbol <, meaning "from," shows that a word is descended from one language to another. Advise students that when checking the origin of a word, they should find the earliest usage, which will be the last abbreviation cited in a list.

Activity

Have students use a dictionary to identify the origin of these words:

1. cobbler [Middle English]
2. jealous [Latin]
3. measure [Greek]
4. murder [Greek]
5. robber [German]
6. sack [Greek or Hebrew]
7. servant [Old French]
8. silk [Greek]
9. thief [Old High German]
10. touch [Latin]

now sent another thief into the city to find Mustapha, who was able to find the door of Ali Baba's house once again. The robber marked this door with red chalk, but later, when the thieves came two by two into the city, they found that the clever Morgiana had made identical marks on the doors of all the houses in the street. Therefore, they returned to the forest and cut off the head of the second messenger.

The robber chief now decided to do the job himself. With Mustapha's help, he soon found the house, but instead of marking it, he memorized its every detail so that he could find it again, even in the dark. Then he returned to the forest and told his comrades of his plan to murder all who lived in that house.

A few nights later, disguised as an oil merchant, he arrived at Ali Baba's house with nineteen donkeys, each of which carried two large jars. Only one of these jars had oil in it. All the rest concealed the thieves, one to

each. The robber chief asked Ali Baba if he would be kind enough to allow him to rest his animals for the night in his courtyard, as he was a stranger in the city and had nowhere to sleep.

Ali Baba did not recognize the robber chief, and being a generous man, he offered the oil merchant the hospitality of his house. The donkeys were unloaded and fed, and Morgiana was asked to prepare a meal for the guest.

Later that night the robber chief returned to the courtyard and whispered to each of his men in turn, "Stay hidden until I throw some pebbles from my window into the yard. This will be the signal to climb out of your jar and kill everybody in the house."

Still later that night, Morgiana was working in the kitchen when the oil lamp began to go out. As there was no more oil in the house, she decided to borrow a cupful from one of the merchant's jars. Just as she was about to remove the lid of the first jar, she was

ALI BABA AND THE FORTY THIEVES **615**

D Elements of Literature
Folk Tale
❓ How are the characters in this folk tale different from the characters you read about in myths, such as "Baucis and Philemon"? [Possible responses: The myths described gods, such as Hermes and Zeus. This folk tale describes characters such as Ali Baba and the robber chief, who are ordinary humans.]

E Critical Thinking
Determining Author's Purpose
❓ Why does the author include this detail about Ali Baba's generosity and hospitality? [Possible responses: It increases the story's suspense, describes Ali Baba's character, and suggests that generosity will be rewarded.]

F Reading Skills and Strategies
Using Word Parts
❓ What prefix can you find in the word *remove*? [re-] What does the prefix mean? [again, returning to]

Using Students' Strengths

Verbal/Kinesthetic Learners
Suggest that small groups of students present sections of this story as a Reader's Theater. Help students organize their presentation by asking them to select a director to oversee the production. Be sure that students understand that a Reader's Theater involves sitting or standing in the front of the room and reading from the book. Encourage the use of appropriate gestures, and allow students time to rehearse.

Logical/Mathematical Learners
When Ali Baba first encounters the thieves and learns the secret of the cave, he has a few options. In real life, most situations can also be approached in a variety of ways. Ask students to develop a Consequence Tree chart to help them sort Ali Baba's choices and evaluate his decision. Students should write Ali Baba's situation in the center of the tree and list his choices as branches.

A Elements of Literature

Folk Tale

? How is Morgiana heroic in the tradition of folk tales? [Possible response: She uses her wits to overcome those who are stronger than she is but not nearly as clever.]

B Critical Thinking

Making Connections

? What other story in this collection includes hospitality as an important issue? ["Baucis and Philemon"]

C English Language Learners

Using Context Clues

? What is a "dagger"? What clues helped you figure out the word's meaning? [A dagger is a kind of weapon. Clues include the fact that a robber who comes to Ali Baba's house to kill everyone is carrying one; it is hidden in his robe.]

D Reading Skills and Strategies

Using Word Parts

? What does the prefix *dis-* mean? How can you use this prefix to define "disbelief"? [The prefix *dis-* means "not." To disbelieve is to not believe.]

surprised to hear a voice come from inside it, asking, "Is it time to come out yet?"

Understanding the situation at once, the clever Morgiana whispered, "No, not yet."

As she went from jar to jar, she heard the same question and gave the same answer, until she came to the one jar which contained the oil.

A Morgiana took enough oil from this jar to fill all the kettles in the house. She placed these on the kitchen fire and brought them to the boil. Then she carried the kettles into the courtyard and poured their contents into each of the pots in turn. The oil was so hot that the robbers were killed instantly, before they could cry out.

At midnight, when the robber chief threw his pebbles from the upstairs window, he could not understand why his men did not spring from their jars, waving their swords. Thinking they must have fallen asleep, he crept into the courtyard to awaken them. When he discovered that his companions were all dead, he fled at once to the forest to work out a new plan of revenge.

In the morning, Morgiana told her master what she had done. Ali Baba was so grateful to her that he made her his chief housekeeper. Then, with the help of another servant, he dug a great pit in his garden and buried the thirty-seven bodies, and life returned to normal once more.

One day Ali Baba's son, who now looked after Cassim's old shop, said to his father, "I have recently become acquainted with a merchant who is new to the market. I have shared a midday meal with him B five times without returning his hospitality. Perhaps we could hold a fine feast in his honor."

Thus it was that the robber chief, disguised in a long beard, came to be invited to eat in the house of the man he planned to kill. The moment she saw him, however, the wise Morgiana C guessed who he really was and why he had come—especially when she noticed a dagger partly hidden in the folds of his robe.

After all had eaten, Morgiana appeared before the company, dressed as a dancer, and offered to entertain them. Everyone was captivated by the beautiful girl and her curious dance, which involved the use of a small dagger. However, delight soon turned to horror when, advancing toward the robber-guest, Morgiana suddenly plunged the dagger into his heart.

D Ali Baba cried out in disbelief, "Morgiana! What have you done? This man was an honored guest in my house. We shall be ruined forever."

Making the Connections

Connecting to the Theme: "Tell Me a Tale"

After students have finished reading the folk tale, have them form two groups to decide which characters were brave and clever— and which ones were too trusting and naive. Students should cite specific evidence in the folk tale to support their conclusions. Then ask the class if they think the reward Morgiana received was equal to the deeds she did for Ali Baba and his family. You may want to set up this discussion as a debate.

"Master, I have saved your life," replied Morgiana. "Your guest was none other than the robber chief, who came here to kill you." So saying, she removed the false beard from the dead man's face and pointed to the dagger hidden in his robe.

When Ali Baba saw that his guest was indeed the oil seller and captain of thieves, he realized that Morgiana had saved his life yet again. Overcome by joy, he cried, "Morgiana, my child, my daughter, will you be my daugh- 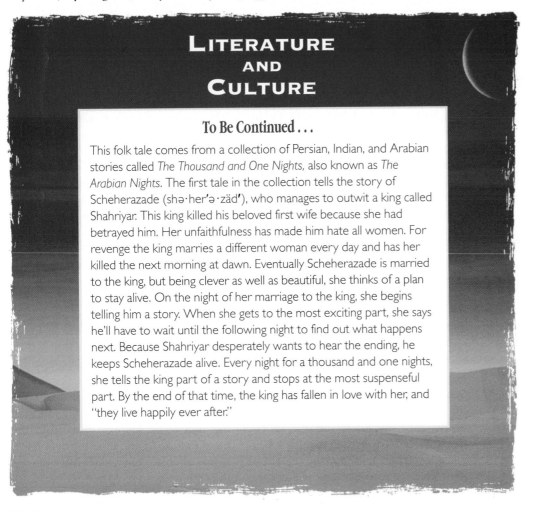ter in very truth and marry this handsome young man, my son?"

The wedding took place that very day and there was much feasting and rejoicing in the house.

In time, Ali Baba revealed the secret of the cave to his son, and his son to his son, and they shared their riches wisely and generously, so that Allah blessed them, every one, and the whole city loved and honored them dearly for the rest of their days.

LITERATURE AND CULTURE

To Be Continued . . .

This folk tale comes from a collection of Persian, Indian, and Arabian stories called *The Thousand and One Nights,* also known as *The Arabian Nights.* The first tale in the collection tells the story of Scheherazade (shə·her'ə·zäd'), who manages to outwit a king called Shahriyar. This king killed his beloved first wife because she had betrayed him. Her unfaithfulness has made him hate all women. For revenge the king marries a different woman every day and has her killed the next morning at dawn. Eventually Scheherazade is married to the king, but being clever as well as beautiful, she thinks of a plan to stay alive. On the night of her marriage to the king, she begins telling him a story. When she gets to the most exciting part, she says he'll have to wait until the following night to find out what happens next. Because Shahriyar desperately wants to hear the ending, he keeps Scheherazade alive. Every night for a thousand and one nights, she tells the king part of a story and stops at the most suspenseful part. By the end of that time, the king has fallen in love with her, and "they live happily ever after."

ALI BABA AND THE FORTY THIEVES 617

E Struggling Readers
Interpreting Idioms
When Ali Baba calls Morgiana his "daughter," he does not mean that she is his real daughter. Rather, he means that he will now accept her into the family as if she were his real daughter.

F Elements of Literature
Folk Tales
❓ Based on this folk tale, which qualities are rewarded and which qualities are punished? [Possible responses: Loyalty, daring, caution, intelligence, moderation, generosity, and honesty are rewarded; dishonesty and greed are punished.] Do we have the same values today? Give examples to support your conclusion. [Possible responses: Our values are the same today, as shown by the people we respect and admire and the people we distrust and avoid.]

LITERATURE AND CULTURE
Today, scholars believe that *The Thousand and One Nights* is a series of stories collected over many years. Evidence links the stories to many different countries: India, Iran, Iraq, Egypt, Turkey, and possibly even Greece. For example, the names of the main characters are Iranian, not Arabic. The material was once part of the oral tradition, and different writers transcribed it. At least six different layers of stories have been identified, dating from the eighth century to the sixteenth century.

Assessing Learning

Check Test: Short Answers
1. Ali Baba finds a fortune in a [cave].
2. The password to move the rock is ["Open, Sesame!"]
3. Cassim's body is cut into [six] pieces.
4. Morgiana kills the thieves hiding in the jars with boiling [oil].
5. Morgiana kills the chief robber with a [dagger].

Self-Assessment
Have students evaluate their critical reading by using the following criteria.
1=Rarely   2=Sometimes   3=Frequently
_____ I read the pictures, captions, and titles before I read the folk tale.
_____ I try to predict upcoming events.
_____ I reread confusing parts of the story for clarification.
_____ I try to figure out unfamiliar words by using context clues.

Standardized Test Preparation
For practice with test format specific to this selection, see
• *Standardized Test Preparation,* p. 88
For practice in proofreading and editing, see
• *Daily Oral Grammar,* Transparency 38

Student to Student

In their grandfather's garden, John and Sue discover a talking snake who promises them a reward if they undertake three tasks: retrieve a dead eagle from under the watchful eye of a lion, bring the eagle and a knife to an old woman who will remove its bones, and secure from a man two cupfuls of soil. When John and Sue return to the snake with the bones and the soil he is miraculously transformed into a king and grants them three wishes that make them and their grandfather prosperous and happy.

A Reading Skills and Strategies
Making Predictions

❓ What do you predict the story will be about, based on its title? [Possible response: The story will be about two children, John and Sue, and a talking snake who befriends them.]

B English Language Learners
Using Context Clues

❓ Based on this part of the story, what is a "garden snake"? [Possible response: It is a harmless snake that lives in a garden.]

C Struggling Readers
Summarizing

❓ What three things does the snake want the children to do? [First, go to the forest and get the eagle guarded by the lion. Second, go deeper into the forest and give the eagle and a knife to the old lady who lives in a shack but keep the eagle's bones. Third, go to another shack and ask the old man there for two cups of soil.]

D Critical Thinking
Speculating

❓ Why do the children withhold their plans from their grandfather? [Possible response: Their grandfather would not believe a snake talked to them; he would not let them follow the snake's instructions because they could lead to danger.]

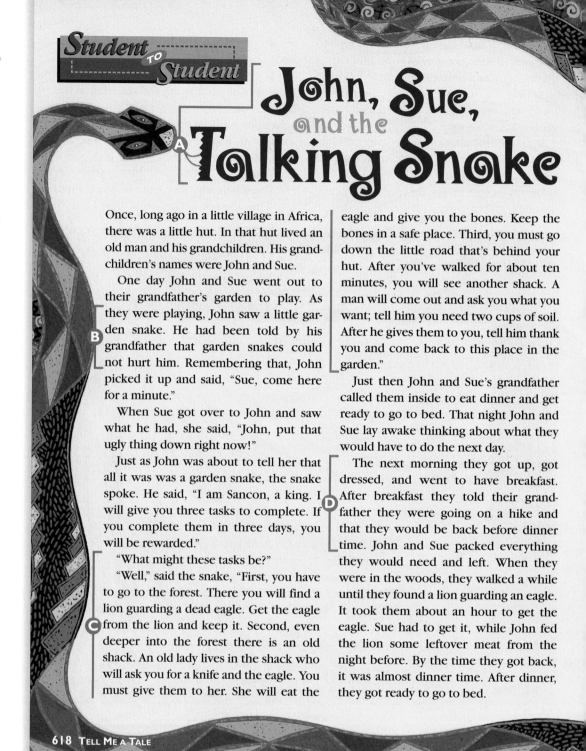

John, Sue, and the Talking Snake

Once, long ago in a little village in Africa, there was a little hut. In that hut lived an old man and his grandchildren. His grandchildren's names were John and Sue.

One day John and Sue went out to their grandfather's garden to play. As they were playing, John saw a little garden snake. He had been told by his grandfather that garden snakes could not hurt him. Remembering that, John picked it up and said, "Sue, come here for a minute."

When Sue got over to John and saw what he had, she said, "John, put that ugly thing down right now!"

Just as John was about to tell her that all it was was a garden snake, the snake spoke. He said, "I am Sancon, a king. I will give you three tasks to complete. If you complete them in three days, you will be rewarded."

"What might these tasks be?"

"Well," said the snake, "First, you have to go to the forest. There you will find a lion guarding a dead eagle. Get the eagle from the lion and keep it. Second, even deeper into the forest there is an old shack. An old lady lives in the shack who will ask you for a knife and the eagle. You must give them to her. She will eat the eagle and give you the bones. Keep the bones in a safe place. Third, you must go down the little road that's behind your hut. After you've walked for about ten minutes, you will see another shack. A man will come out and ask you what you want; tell him you need two cups of soil. After he gives them to you, tell him thank you and come back to this place in the garden."

Just then John and Sue's grandfather called them inside to eat dinner and get ready to go to bed. That night John and Sue lay awake thinking about what they would have to do the next day.

The next morning they got up, got dressed, and went to have breakfast. After breakfast they told their grandfather they were going on a hike and that they would be back before dinner time. John and Sue packed everything they would need and left. When they were in the woods, they walked a while until they found a lion guarding an eagle. It took them about an hour to get the eagle. Sue had to get it, while John fed the lion some leftover meat from the night before. By the time they got back, it was almost dinner time. After dinner, they got ready to go to bed.

Using Students' Strengths

Intrapersonal Learners

In part, "John, Sue, and the Talking Snake" portrays the children's relationship to their grandfather. Invite students to make an "Extended Family Tree" showing the people who are important to them. The tree can include, but is not limited to, people who are blood relatives. For example, students can include family friends, neighbors, playmates, and teachers as well as parents, siblings, and grandparents. Then have students notate and explain some of the things they have learned from the people they included in their "family tree."

Naturalist Learners

Snakes can't talk, but other animals *have* learned to communicate with humans. For example, some apes have been taught to communicate with people by using sign language. Have students find out more about the work being done on ape-human communication at the Yerkes Primate Research Center (Atlanta, Georgia) and other research centers. Ask students to share their findings with the class.

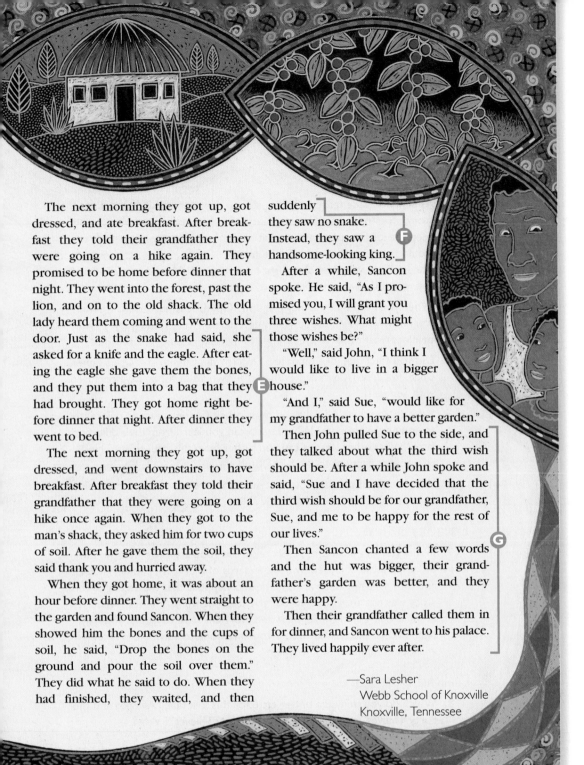

The next morning they got up, got dressed, and ate breakfast. After breakfast they told their grandfather they were going on a hike again. They promised to be home before dinner that night. They went into the forest, past the lion, and on to the old shack. The old lady heard them coming and went to the door. Just as the snake had said, she asked for a knife and the eagle. After eating the eagle she gave them the bones, and they put them into a bag that they had brought. They got home right before dinner that night. After dinner they went to bed.

The next morning they got up, got dressed, and went downstairs to have breakfast. After breakfast they told their grandfather that they were going on a hike once again. When they got to the man's shack, they asked him for two cups of soil. After he gave them the soil, they said thank you and hurried away.

When they got home, it was about an hour before dinner. They went straight to the garden and found Sancon. When they showed him the bones and the cups of soil, he said, "Drop the bones on the ground and pour the soil over them." They did what he said to do. When they had finished, they waited, and then

suddenly they saw no snake. Instead, they saw a handsome-looking king.

After a while, Sancon spoke. He said, "As I promised you, I will grant you three wishes. What might those wishes be?"

"Well," said John, "I think I would like to live in a bigger house."

"And I," said Sue, "would like for my grandfather to have a better garden."

Then John pulled Sue to the side, and they talked about what the third wish should be. After a while John spoke and said, "Sue and I have decided that the third wish should be for our grandfather, Sue, and me to be happy for the rest of our lives."

Then Sancon chanted a few words and the hut was bigger, their grandfather's garden was better, and they were happy.

Then their grandfather called them in for dinner, and Sancon went to his palace. They lived happily ever after.

—Sara Lesher
Webb School of Knoxville
Knoxville, Tennessee

E Reading Skills and Strategies
Making Predictions

❓ So far, the story is following a standard pattern for a folk tale: talking animals, three requests, and a quest. Based on this pattern, what do you think will happen next? Why? [Possible responses: The snake will use the bones for some kind of metamorphosis; the grandfather will find out about the snake; the children will be rewarded for their efforts.]

F Elements of Literature
Metamorphosis

❓ What metamorphosis occurs in the story? [The snake changes into a king.]

G Critical Thinking
Determining the Author's Purpose

❓ What point do you think the writer is making in this story? [Possible response: You can find wonderful things even in your own backyard; unusual circumstances and challenges may result in rich rewards.]

Connecting Across Texts

Connecting with "Ali Baba and the Forty Thieves"

Have students describe ways in which "John, Sue, and the Talking Snake" and "Ali Baba" are alike and different. Points of discussion may include the fact that one is a real folk tale, the other is a made-up folk tale; both have examples of fantasy; both have characters who are like real people—but one has a talking animal, the other does not; one has a series of quests for the main characters, the other has a series of dangerous situations that are eliminated through clever thinking; both have a happy ending. Students can display the similarities and differences between the two folk tales on a chart or a Venn diagram.

MAKING MEANINGS

First Thoughts

1. Some students may have taken more gold, arguing that the money did not belong to the thieves. Others would not have taken any gold since it would be considered stolen property.

Shaping Interpretations

2. Possible stopping points include after Ali Baba warns Cassim about entering the thieves' cave, after the thief marks Ali Baba's house, after Ali Baba welcomes the thief disguised as an oil merchant, and after the robber chief is invited into Ali Baba's house.

3. Some students may cite the cobbler's sewing Cassim together, although others might say a team of surgeons could do this. Some may say the cobbler's finding his way blindfolded to Ali Baba's house; others may say a blind person might be able to find his or her way back. Most students will agree that some robbers would have recognized a voice other than the robber chief's and would have cried out before dying from the shock of the hot oil.

4. It is funny that Cassim confuses other grains with sesame. Corn, rice, wheat.

5. Cassim is greedy and easily made jealous while Ali Baba is moderate about his self-interests and much more cautious. The story teaches that greed is punished and moderation, loyalty, honesty, and courage are rewarded.

6. Both Ali Baba and his son are hospitable to the robber chief. The robber chief has been hospitable to Ali Baba's son.

Extending the Text

7. Ali Baba might have to face charges of breaking and entering and robbery; Morgiana would be charged with murder. Calling the police and reporting the robbers would solve the problems.

Challenging the Text

8. The first title fits because the story involves the consequences of something Ali Baba did; the second title also fits because Morgiana's cleverness protects Ali Baba.

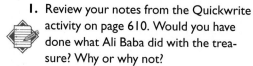

MAKING MEANINGS

First Thoughts

[respond]

1. Review your notes from the Quickwrite activity on page 610. Would you have done what Ali Baba did with the treasure? Why or why not?

Shaping Interpretations

[interpret]

2. As Scheherazade (page 617) told this story, she stopped at exciting points to keep the king in **suspense** so that he wouldn't kill her *that* night. Find four places where you think she might have stopped. (Would you have been able to predict what would happen next?)

[interpret]

3. When you read that the magic charm "Open, Sesame!" opens a cave, you know you've entered the strange, unreal world of **fantasy.** In your opinion, what other events in the story couldn't happen in real life?

[interpret]

4. Did you catch the joke on page 612? Why did Cassim say *"Open, Barley! Open, Rye! Open, Caraway!"* (What other words might he have confused with *Sesame?*)

[interpret]

5. Why do you think Ali Baba and his brother, Cassim, react so differently to finding the treasure? What lesson can you learn from their different fates? What other lessons can you gather from this tale? (Hint: Think about what happens to the faithful and clever Morgiana.)

[analyze]

6. What details show that hospitality to strangers was an important value to the people who told this story?

Extending the Text

[connect]

7. In this story, as in almost all folk tales, the good are rewarded and the evil are punished. Judged by the standards of their own people, Ali Baba and Morgiana are admirable and heroic. Suppose that the setting of this story was not ancient Persia but twentieth-century America. What criminal charges might Ali Baba and Morgiana have to face? If you had been in their place, what would you have done to solve the problems without committing any "crimes"?

Challenging the Text

[synthesize]

8. Which do you think is a better **title** for this folk tale, "Ali Baba and the Forty Thieves" or "Morgiana and the Forty Thieves"? Why?

Reading Check

Make a story **time line** for "Ali Baba and the Forty Thieves." List all the story's events in the order in which they occur. You can use the time line to help you retell the story to a friend.

Reading Check

- Ali Baba discovers where forty thieves hide their riches, and he takes some.
- Cassim goes to the cave to take some of the treasure, but the robbers catch him and cut him into six pieces.
- Morgiana has the cobbler sew Cassim's body back together.
- The cobbler leads a thief to Ali Baba's house.
- The thief marks the house with white chalk, but Morgiana marks all the houses with white chalk so the robbers cannot find Ali Baba.
- The same thing happens with red chalk.
- The robber chief, posing as an oil merchant, comes to Ali Baba's house.
- Morgiana kills the thieves with boiling oil and later stabs the robber chief to death.
- Morgiana marries Ali Baba's son.

CHOICES: Building Your Portfolio

Writer's Notebook

1. Collecting Ideas for a Story

Three has always been the most popular number in myths and tales. In "John, Sue, and the Talking Snake" (page 618), for example, the main characters perform three tasks and get three wishes. Try using the number three to plan the plot of an original story. You might have three brothers who go three different ways, or you might give a character three tasks or riddles to solve.

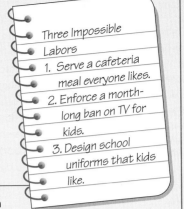

> Three Impossible Labors
> 1. Serve a cafeteria meal everyone likes.
> 2. Enforce a month-long ban on TV for kids.
> 3. Design school uniforms that kids like.

Creative Writing

2. To Catch a Thief

Rewrite this tale from Morgiana's point of view. After all, she's the one who keeps outwitting the thieves. Show her to be the gutsy, strong-willed woman she is. For example, Morgiana might demand a share of Ali Baba's

gold to keep rescuing him from the thieves. You might call your tale "To Catch a Thief" or "Mobsters Meet Morgiana."

Art

3. Fake It!

The robber chief is a master of disguise. Twice he hides his true identity from Ali Baba (although the clever Morgiana recognizes him in his second disguise). Suppose that you're a costume designer planning the robber's outfits for a dramatization of this story. Create three sketches of the robber chief's costumes: one as himself, the other as a fake oil merchant, and a third as a fake shop merchant.

Drama

4. "Open, Sesame!"

Do a group reading of the opening pages of the story, in which Ali Baba and later his brother, Cassim, enter the cave of the thieves. You'll need a narrator as well as readers for the parts of Ali Baba, Cassim, Cassim's wife, and the robber chief. First, practice reading the parts silently. Then, present the scenes to the whole class. Be sure to read with expression, especially when you come to the scene where Cassim can't remember the charm "Open, Sesame!"

Rubrics for each Choices assignment appear on p. 180 in the *Portfolio Management System*.

CHOICES: Building Your Portfolio

1. **Writer's Notebook** Remind students to save their work. They may use it as prewriting for the Writer's Workshop on pp. 658–662.
2. **Creative Writing** Have students use the time line of the major events in the story they created in the Reading Check on p. 620. Ask students to jot down a sentence in the first person, from Morgiana's point of view, that explains how Morgiana would react to each event. Students can use this rough outline as they write their stories.
3. **Art** Read aloud sections of the story that describe the robber chief. Then discuss with students what the robber chief might have been wearing.
4. **Drama** Divide the class into groups of five. Write the characters' names, including the narrator, on individual strips of paper. Have students pick one strip from a jar to determine which character he or she will play.

Using Students' Strengths

Verbal Learners

For Choice 2, invite pairs of students to interview Morgiana for a newspaper article or television news segment. One student can role-play the reporter and the other can role-play Morgiana. Suggest that students reread the folk tale in order to find information they can use to form interview questions and give substance to Morgiana's character.

Intrapersonal Learners

To help students identify with their character in Choice 4, have them reread the story silently. Ask them to jot down notes to describe what their character is feeling and thinking. Students can also construct a "history" to fill in gaps in the character's past.

LANGUAGE LINK

Have students select three pieces of writing from their portfolios. Ask them to select any five words and look up their origins and original meanings in the dictionary.

Try It Out

Here are two sample word graphs:

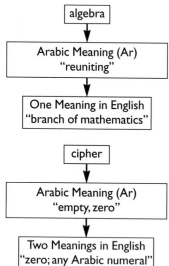

algebra
↓
Arabic Meaning (Ar)
"reuniting"
↓
One Meaning in English
"branch of mathematics"

cipher
↓
Arabic Meaning (Ar)
"empty, zero"
↓
Two Meanings in English
"zero; any Arabic numeral"

VOCABULARY

Sample Responses

1. **dismounted:** *dis-* = prefix; *mounted* = root. Meaning: got down from a horse, got off
   darkness: *dark* = root, *-ness* = suffix. Meaning: night time, without light
   unloaded: *un-* = prefix, *load* = root, *-ed* = suffix. Meaning: discharged
   disappeared: *dis-* = prefix, *appear* = root, *-ed* = suffix. Meaning: vanished

2. **faithful:** *faith* = root, *-ful* = suffix. Meaning: loyal
   returned: *re-* = prefix, *turn* = root, *-ed* = suffix. Meaning: gave back
   unknown: *un-* = prefix, *known* = root. Meaning: not familiar

3. **careless:** *care* = root, *-less* = suffix. Meaning: reckless
   respectable: *respect* = root, *-able* = suffix. Meaning: worthy of respect, socially acceptable
   unfortunately: *un-* = prefix, *fortune* = root, *-ate* = suffix, *-ly* = suffix. Meaning: unluckily

Resources

Language
• *Grammar and Language Links* p. 59

Spelling
• *Spelling and Decoding*, p. 27

LANGUAGE LINK MINI-LESSON

Style: Words from Arabic

WORDS FROM ARABIC

algebra
candy
cipher
elixir
ghoul
jasmine
mohair
saffron
satin
sequin
sheik
sherbet
tariff
zenith
zero

Many English words were born in foreign countries. The words at the left come from Arabic, a language spoken in a number of countries today. Some Arabic words came directly into our language. Others passed through other languages—Spanish, French, Italian—before becoming English words. How many of these words borrowed from Arabic do you know?

Try It Out

1. Using a dictionary, make a word graph for eight of the words borrowed from Arabic. Here's an example.

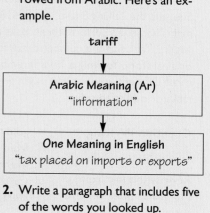

tariff
↓
Arabic Meaning (Ar)
"information"
↓
One Meaning in English
"tax placed on imports or exports"

2. Write a paragraph that includes five of the words you looked up.

VOCABULARY HOW TO OWN A WORD

Using Language Structure: Prefixes and Suffixes

Many words are built from word roots and affixes.

• A **word root** is the main part of a word. In the word *unpleasant* the root is *-pleas-*.
• An **affix** is a word part added to the beginning or end of a root. In the word *unpleasant*, *un-* and *-ant* are affixes.
• A **prefix** is an affix, like *un-*, added to the beginning of a root.
• A **suffix** is an affix, like *-ant*, added to the end of a root. Sometimes the spelling of a root changes when you add a suffix to it.

Identify the parts of each underlined word in the following sentences. Find the meaning of prefixes and suffixes in the lists on page 609. Tell what the whole word means.

1. The thieves <u>dismounted</u> in the <u>darkness</u>, <u>unloaded</u> their bags, and <u>disappeared</u> through the magic door.
2. <u>Faithful</u> Morgiana <u>returned</u> to Ali Baba and told him he had an <u>unknown</u> enemy.
3. <u>Careless</u> of her own safety, Morgiana proved that the guest, who seemed <u>respectable</u>, was <u>unfortunately</u> the robber chief.

622 TELL ME A TALE

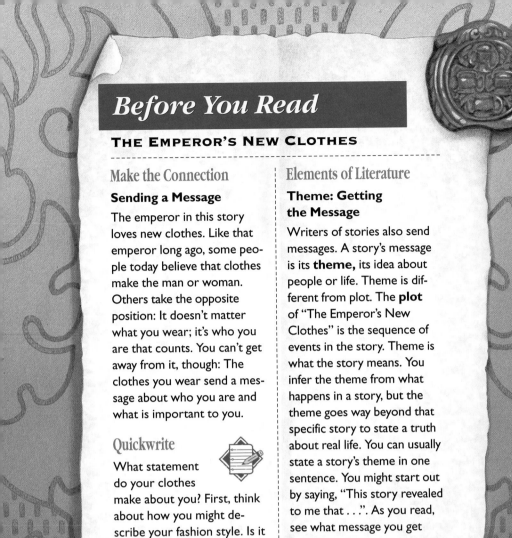

Before You Read

THE EMPEROR'S NEW CLOTHES

Make the Connection

Sending a Message

The emperor in this story loves new clothes. Like that emperor long ago, some people today believe that clothes make the man or woman. Others take the opposite position: It doesn't matter what you wear; it's who you are that counts. You can't get away from it, though: The clothes you wear send a message about who you are and what is important to you.

Quickwrite

What statement do your clothes make about you? First, think about how you might describe your fashion style. Is it classic? wild? preppy? grunge? hip-hop? natural? If none of those adjectives fit, think of words that describe the clothes you like to wear. Then, think about the message they send about who you are and what you like. Jot down notes on your answers to these questions.

Elements of Literature

Theme: Getting the Message

Writers of stories also send messages. A story's message is its **theme,** its idea about people or life. Theme is different from plot. The **plot** of "The Emperor's New Clothes" is the sequence of events in the story. Theme is what the story means. You infer the theme from what happens in a story, but the theme goes way beyond that specific story to state a truth about real life. You can usually state a story's theme in one sentence. You might start out by saying, "This story revealed to me that . . .". As you read, see what message you get from this story.

> **T**heme is the idea about life revealed in a work of literature.
>
> *For more on Theme, see page 326 and the Handbook of Literary Terms.*

go.hrw.com
LE0 6-8

623

Summary ▪ ▪

The Emperor spends all his money on clothes because he is so fond of them. One day two swindlers come to town, claiming they can make clothes that are invisible to anyone who is stupid or unfit for his or her job. The Emperor wants the extraordinary clothes and pays the swindlers, who pretend to weave and sew a magnificent outfit for him. Fearing they will be judged incompetent or foolish, the wise minister, honest official, and chamberlains claim to see the clothes. The fraud continues as the Emperor walks through town in his new "clothes" until a child cries, "But he has nothing on at all." Afraid of appearing foolish, the Emperor and his procession continue walking down the street.

Resources

Listening
Audio CD Library
A dramatic recording of this folk tale is included in the *Audio CD Library:*
• Disc 15, Track 2

624 TELL ME A TALE

  Resources: Print and Media

Reading
• *Graphic Organizers for Active Reading,* p. 41
• *Spelling and Decoding*
    Worksheet, p. 28
• *Audio CD Library*
    Disc 15, Track 2

Writing and Language
• *Daily Oral Grammar*
    Transparency 39
• *Grammar and Language Links*
    Worksheet, p. 61

Assessment
• *Formal Assessment,* p. 121
• *Portfolio Management System,* p. 181
• *Test Generator (One-Stop Planner CD-ROM)*
Internet
• go.hrw.com (keyword: LE0 6-8)

THE EMPEROR'S NEW CLOTHES

Hans Christian Andersen

Many years ago there lived an Emperor who was so fond of new clothes that he spent all his money on them. He did not care for his soldiers, or for the theater, or for driving in the woods, except to show off his new clothes. He had an outfit for every hour of the day, and just as they say of a king, "He is in the council chamber," so they always said of him, "The Emperor is in his dressing room."

The great city where he lived was very lively, and every day many strangers came there. One day two swindlers came. They claimed that they were weavers and said they could weave the finest cloth imaginable. Their colors and patterns, they said, were not only exceptionally beautiful, but the clothes made of this material possessed the wonderful quality of being invisible to

A **Reading Skills and Strategies**
Making Inferences
? What can you infer about the Emperor's character from this opening description? [Possible responses: He is not a good emperor; he is foolish; he is very shallow and vain.]

B **English Language Learners**
Word Origin
? The word "swindler" means someone who gets money or property by cheating or tricking someone else. What trick are these swindlers playing? [Possible response: They pretend to make clothes that can't be seen by anyone who is unfit for office or very stupid.]

Reaching All Students

Struggling Readers

Give students a KWL chart like the one at the right and have them complete the first two columns before they read. Ask them to read the story carefully to find the information they need to complete the third column on their charts.

K	W	L
What I Know	**What I Want to Know**	**What I Learned**
[Kings are sometimes characters in fairy tales.]	[What role the king plays in this story]	[The king is fooled because he is vain.]

English Language Learners

Ask students to describe traditional stories from their native culture and to identify common elements, such as trickster figures, royal characters, and moral lessons. Then have students predict which of these elements they might encounter in "The Emperor's New Clothes" and why. For additional strategies for English language learners, see

• *Lesson Plans Including Strategies for English-Language Learners*

any man who was unfit for his office, or who was hopelessly stupid.

"Those must be wonderful clothes," thought the Emperor. "If I wore them, I should be able to find out which men in my empire were unfit for their posts, and I could tell the clever from the stupid. Yes, I must have this cloth woven for me without delay." So he gave a lot of money to the two swindlers in advance, so that they could set to work at once.

They set up two looms[1] and pretended to be very hard at work, but they had nothing on the looms. They asked for the finest silk and the most precious gold, all of which they put into their own bags, and worked at the empty looms till late into the night.

"I should very much like to know how they are getting on with the cloth," thought the Emperor. But he felt rather uneasy when he remembered that whoever was not fit for his office could not see it. He believed, of course, that he had nothing to fear for himself, yet he thought he would send somebody else first to see how things were progressing.

Everybody in the town knew what a wonderful property the cloth possessed, and all were anxious to see how bad or stupid their neighbors were.

"I will send my honest old minister to the weavers," thought the Emperor. "He can judge best how the cloth looks, for he is intelligent, and nobody is better fitted for his office than he."

So the good old minister went into the room where the two swindlers sat working at the empty looms. "Heaven help us!" he thought, and opened his eyes wide. "Why, I cannot see anything at all," but he was careful not to say so.

1. **looms:** machines used for weaving thread into cloth.

626 TELL ME A TALE

Both swindlers bade him be so good as to step closer and asked him if he did not admire the exquisite pattern and the beautiful colors. They pointed to the empty looms, and the poor old minister opened his eyes even wider, but he could see nothing, for there was nothing to be seen. "Good Lord!" he thought, "can I be so stupid? I should never have thought so, and nobody must know it! Is it possible that I am not fit for my office? No, no, I must not tell anyone that I couldn't see the cloth."

"Well, have you got nothing to say?" said one, as he wove.

"Oh, it is very pretty—quite enchanting!" said the old minister, peering through his glasses. "What a pattern, and what colors! I shall tell the Emperor that I am very much pleased with it."

"Well, we are glad of that," said both the weavers, and they described the colors to him and explained the curious pattern. The old minister listened carefully, so that he might tell the Emperor what they said.

Now the swindlers asked for more money, more silk, and more gold, which they required for weaving. They kept it all for themselves, and not a thread came near the loom, but they continued, as before, working at the empty looms.

Soon afterward the Emperor sent another honest official to the weavers to see how they were getting on and if the cloth was nearly finished. Like the old minister, he looked and looked but could see nothing, as there was nothing to be seen.

"Is it not a beautiful piece of cloth?" said the two swindlers, showing and explaining the magnificent pattern, which, however, was not there at all.

"I am not stupid," thought the man, "so it

Taking a Second Look

Review: Making Inferences
Remind students that an *inference* is a guess based on information in the text and on the reader's prior knowledge and experience. Explain to students that as they read, they are constantly inferring information that writers do not state directly. As an example, remind students that they used information in the first paragraph of "The Emperor's New Clothes," plus their prior knowledge and experience, to infer that the Emperor is vain, foolish, and not a good leader. Be sure

students understand that when they make inferences, they come to decisions by reasoning from evidence that is only hinted at or implied.

Activity
Point out that when readers make inferences about a character, they make intelligent guesses about what the character is like, and what the character's feelings are; readers also make judgments about the character's actions and behavior based on evidence from the text.

As students read, have them make inferences about the Emperor and the swindlers by answering the following questions:
- Are the swindlers smart or just ordinary people?
- What motivates the minister to go along with the deception?
- What point is the writer making by referring to the minister as "honest"?
- What keeps the Emperor and minister from speaking the truth?

G Advanced Learners
Using Word Parts
❓ What smaller word appears in *courtiers*? [court] Using this information and other clues in the sentence, what does *courtiers* mean? [Courtiers are attendants at a *court*, such as councilors and nobles.]

G Elements of Literature
Theme
❓ What condition do the Emperor's thoughts and actions show? [Possible responses: Though he is a powerful leader, he is afraid to look foolish or unfit to lead; some people "buy into" a lie and then are too embarrassed to let it go and tell the truth; everyone has self-doubts from time to time.]

H Reading Skills and Strategies
Making Predictions
❓ What do you think will happen when the Emperor wears his new "clothes" outside? [Possible responses: Everyone will keep quiet to avoid being embarrassed or embarrassing the Emperor; some brave person will tell the truth; some people will laugh.]

must be that I am unfit for my high post. It is ludicrous,[2] but I must not let anyone know it." So he praised the cloth, which he did not see, and expressed his pleasure at the beautiful colors and the fine pattern. "Yes, it is quite enchanting," he said to the Emperor.

Everybody in the whole town was talking about the beautiful cloth. At last the Emperor wished to see it himself while it was still on the loom. With a whole company of chosen courtiers, including the two honest councilors who had already been there, he went to the two clever swindlers, who were now weaving away as hard as they could but without using any thread.

"Is it not magnificent?" said both the honest statesmen. "Look, Your Majesty, what a pattern! What colors!" And they pointed

2. **ludicrous** (lōō′di·krəs): ridiculous; laughable.

to the empty looms, for they imagined the others could see the cloth.

"What is this?" thought the Emperor. "I do not see anything at all. This is terrible! Am I stupid? Am I unfit to be Emperor? That would indeed be the most dreadful thing that could happen to me!"

"Yes, it is very beautiful," said the Emperor. "It has our highest approval," and nodding contentedly, he gazed at the empty loom, for he did not want to say that he could see nothing. All the attendants who were with him looked and looked, and, although they could not see anything more than the others, they said, just like the Emperor, "Yes, it is very fine." They all advised him to wear the new magnificent clothes at a great procession that was soon to take place. "It is magnificent! beautiful, excellent!" went from mouth to mouth, and everybody seemed delighted.

THE EMPEROR'S NEW CLOTHES **627**

Crossing the Curriculum

History/Social Studies

The main character in this story is an emperor, the ruler of an empire. Have students research information about world empires of the past and their leaders. Possible empires include Egypt (under Thutmose III), China (various dynasties), Japan (various emperors, including Hirohito), France (Napoleon), The Holy Roman Empire (Otto I and others), Rome (various Caesars), and Great Britain (Queen Victoria and later rulers). Which nation today has an emperor? Suggest that students prepare reports on the lands or countries included in an empire, the length of rule of a specific emperor, and two or three important events related to the empire. Ask students to present their reports to the class.

A Elements of Literature

Description

? This paragraph contains descriptions that appeal to some of the five senses. Which descriptions appeal to which senses? [Possible responses: sight—"sixteen candles;" touch—"pretended to take the cloth from the loom;" sound—"snipped the air with big scissors."]

B Appreciating Language

Formal and Informal English

? Notice the words the swindlers use here. Are they using formal or informal English? [Formal English] Why are they using it? [Possible responses: They are using an appropriate level of language to address an Emperor; they are still trying to flatter and deceive the Emperor, so they are using especially polite language.]

The Emperor awarded each of the swindlers the cross of the order of knighthood to be worn in their buttonholes, and the title of Imperial Court Weavers.

A Throughout the night preceding the procession, the swindlers were up working, and **B** they had more than sixteen candles burning. People could see how busy they were, getting the Emperor's new clothes ready. They pretended to take the cloth from the loom, they snipped the air with big scissors, they sewed with needles without any thread, and at last said: "Now the Emperor's new clothes are ready!"

The Emperor, followed by all his noblest courtiers, then came in. Both the swindlers held up one arm as if they held something, and said: "See, here are the trousers! Here is the coat! Here is the cloak!" and so on. "They are all as light as a cobweb! They make one feel as if one had nothing on at all, but that is just the beauty of it."

"Yes!" said all the courtiers, but they could not see anything, for there was nothing to see.

"Will it please Your Majesty graciously to take off your clothes?" said the swindlers. "Then we may help Your Majesty into the new clothes before the large mirror!"

The Emperor took off all his clothes, and the swindlers pretended to put on the new clothes, one piece after another. Then the Emperor looked at himself in the glass from every angle.

"Oh, how well they look! How well they fit!" said all. "What a pattern! What colors! Magnificent indeed!"

"They are waiting outside with the canopy which is to be borne over Your Majesty in the procession," announced the master of ceremonies.

628 TELL ME A TALE

Skill Link

Vocabulary: Interpreting Idioms

Use this activity to assess students' understanding before you teach the Vocabulary activity on p. 638. Explain that *idioms* are expressions that mean something beyond their simple definition or literal translation. For example, the idiom "in hot water" does not mean just "immersed in water between 98 and 212 degrees Fahrenheit." It means "in deep trouble." Explain that idioms give a language richness by expressing meaning in a nonliteral way.

Activities

1. Discuss each of the following idioms: "see red"; "walking on eggshells"; "I'm all ears"; "put his foot in his mouth."
2. Have students collect several idioms by listening to friends, relatives, radio, or television. Have students write down the idioms, give the literal and figurative meanings, and share them with the class.

"Well, I am quite ready," said the Emperor. "Doesn't my suit fit me beautifully?" And he turned once more to the mirror so that people would think he was admiring his garments.

The chamberlains, who were to carry the train, fumbled with their hands on the ground as if they were lifting up a train. Then they pretended to hold something up in their hands. They didn't dare let people know that they could not see anything.

And so the Emperor marched in the procession under the beautiful canopy, and all who saw him in the street and out of the windows exclaimed: "How marvelous the Emperor's new suit is! What a long train he has! How well it fits him!" Nobody would let the others know that he saw nothing, for then he would have been shown to be unfit for his office or too stupid. None of the Emperor's clothes had ever been such a success.

"But he has nothing on at all," said a little child.

"Good heavens! Hear what the innocent child says!" said the father, and then each whispered to the other what the child said: "He has nothing on—a little child says he has nothing on at all!" "He has nothing on at all," cried all the people at last. And the Emperor too was feeling very worried, for it seemed to him that they were right, but he thought to himself, "All the same, I must go through with the procession." And he held himself stiffer than ever, and the chamberlains walked on, holding up the train which was not there at all.

To read about Hans Christian Andersen, see Meet the Writer on page 226.

THE EMPEROR'S NEW CLOTHES **629**

C Elements of Literature
Theme
❓ What truth about real life do you see in the Emperor's comments and actions? [Possible responses: Some people are so conceited that they do not realize when they are being foolish; a person may say or do anything to maintain the appearance of competence and control.]

D Struggling Readers
Multiple-Meaning Words
❓ What does the word *train* mean in this passage? What clues help you to figure out the meaning? [Possible response: It means "a part of a costume that hangs down and drags behind." Clues are "suit" in the preceding paragraph; "carry," "lifting up," and "hold something up in their hands."]

E Elements of Literature
Plot
❓ This is a suspenseful moment in the plot. What details help to create an anxious feeling about what will happen? [Possible response: The chamberlains' fumbling with the "train," and the words "They didn't dare let people know that they could not see anything."]

F Elements of Literature
Theme
❓ Why does the Emperor decide to continue with the procession, even though he and everyone else knows that he is not wearing any clothing? [Possible responses: The Emperor is too proud and vain to admit the truth; the Emperor feels that he must maintain his dignity at all costs; a reversal would imply weakness.]

Making the Connections

Connecting to the Theme: "Tell Me a Tale"

After students have finished reading the fairy tale, have them discuss the collection theme, focusing on this question: How are people today like or unlike the characters in "The Emperor's New Clothes"? Half the class can argue that people aren't as vain or gullible as the Emperor, his courtiers, and subjects, nor as boldly deceptive as the swindlers. The other half can argue the opposite. Encourage students to draw examples from their observations and from stories in the news to make their point.

Connections

"King Long Shanks" is a zany adaptation of the folk tale, "The Emperor's New Clothes." In this version, the emperor is a frog.

RESPONDING TO THE ART

Activity. Ask students to predict what this story might be about, based on the illustration. Have them compare the illustration on this page with those for "The Emperor's New Clothes." What similar elements do they find? What differences?

Connections A **SHORT STORY**

KING Long Shanks

Jane Yolen

630 TELL ME A TALE

Sustained Silent Reading

To assess how your students are mastering sustained silent reading, try this project.

Tell students to suppose that they are putting together a collection of humorous stories for sixth-graders. Their task is to evaluate stories and decide which ones kids their age would enjoy reading—which ones would give them something to laugh about. Then, ask students to read Yolen's story silently in class. Tell them to write a few sentences in their logs when they have finished reading, noting whether they had any trouble with the story (if so, what gave them trouble?) and what aspects of the story they liked best and least. When students have finished reading, have them meet in groups to discuss their notes. See if the class can come to an agreement on whether or not the story should be included in a collection of humorous stories for sixth-graders.

While students are reading silently, you should circulate and give help when it is requested.

King Long Shanks had very good legs and was a nice shade of green. Everyone said so. So it had to be true.

The cook said it.

The gardener said it.

The butler, maid, and doorman said it.

The lords-in-waiting said it.

And the two visiting tailors said it, too. Not once but many times.

"Fine legs," said the small tailor.

"Fine long legs," said the tall tailor.

"Fine long strong legs," they said together. "And a very nice shade of green."

So when the two tailors added, "We have just the thing to show off those fine long strong legs, Your Majesty," King Long Shanks ordered: "Tell me."

So they did. The small tailor stretched very high (to make himself taller). And the tall tailor squatted very low (to make himself smaller). Then they whispered simultaneously and at the same time in King Long Shanks' ears.

The cloth is green,
The cloth is blue,
The very shade
That's right for you.

The cloth is blue,
The cloth is red,
To match the jewel
Inside your head.

The cloth is red,
The cloth is gold,
And only the true
and good
and honest
and smart
and loyal
Can it behold.

"What do you mean?" roared King Long Shanks. He was not fond of poetry, especially poetry that bumped in the wrong places and pretended to mean much more than it did. It made him go all cranky. "How can there be a cloth that is green and blue and red and gold? How can it match my head and the jewel inside it? How did you know about that jewel, anyway? It's a family secret."

He had many questions.

The tailors had many answers.

"It's a plaid cloth, sire," they said.

"It's a magic plaid cloth, sire," they said.

"It's a mysterious magic plaid cloth, sire," they said.

"And besides," they said, "it's very expensive."

Now, King Long Shanks did not know a lot about fashion, but he *did* know that expense was a good part of it.

"Show me," he ordered.

So the two tailors held their hands out, first wide apart, then close together. "What do you think?" they asked.

A Elements of Literature

Repetition

❓Repetition links this story to the oral tradition of fairy tales and fables. What words does the writer repeat? [The phrase "said it" is repeated.] What effect does the writer create by using repetition? [Possible responses: Repetition makes the story easier to remember; it makes the story more enjoyable; it helps to establish the tone.]

B Critical Thinking

Making Connections

❓How is the cloth in this story similar to the cloth the swindlers weave in "The Emperor's New Clothes"? [Possible responses: In both cases, the cloth is said to be visible only to people who are smart, honest, and loyal.]

C English Language Learners

Finding Details

❓Plaid cloth is fabric that has a pattern of checks or squares of various sizes, formed by colored bands and lines that cross each other. What details in the story help you understand the meaning of "plaid"? [Possible response: The different colors mentioned suggest a pattern of some sort.]

D Elements of Literature

Theme

❓What lesson about life do you think the author is suggesting here? [Possible responses: The author suggests that just because something is expensive does not mean that it is valuable; Long Shanks's vanity leads him to think that something expensive must be good.]

Using Students' Strengths

Verbal Learners

In both "The Emperor's New Clothes" and "King Long Shanks," the swindlers convince a monarch to buy something that doesn't exist. Have verbal learners create an ad campaign to sell a nonexistent item of their own creation. In their sales pitch, students should appeal to their audience's vanity. After students present their ad campaigns, have the class decide how willing people would be to purchase each item.

Kinesthetic Learners

Students can role-play the scene described on this page—the tailors trying to convince King Long Shanks that he must have this very special cloth. Arrange students in groups of three, two students playing the tailors, one performing as the King. Encourage students to stretch and squat as directed in the story and to use other appropriate facial and bodily gestures.

Musical/Auditory Learners

Have students create a melody for the repeated phrases in the story. Students might sing and record their versions. If some students are skilled on an instrument, have them play the melody while others sing it.

Since there appeared to be nothing between their hands but air, King Long Shanks did not know *what* to think. So he did what he always did when he wanted to pretend he understood something and didn't. He looked at the ceiling, hummed his favorite pond tune, and waited for a passing fly.

KA–ZAAAACK! He caught the fly with his tongue, then looked back at the tailors with a seriously informed expression.

"It's an *invisible* plaid cloth," said the tall tailor.

"Only someone who is true, good, honest, and smart can see the cloth," added the small tailor.

"And loyal," reminded the tall tailor.

"No one can question *my* loyalty," said King Long Shanks, "since it is loyalty to me."

"No one does," the tailors said quickly. "But the cloth is a sure way to check on the rest of the kingdom."

King Long Shanks swallowed the fly. "Then I will want a complete outfit," he said. He touched the air between the tailors, as if feeling a piece of cloth. "Lovely color." Then he turned on his fine long strong legs and leaped away.

The tailors spent many hours sewing their invisible cloth. The small tailor sewed large stitches. The tall tailor sewed tiny stitches. They cut and shaped and measured and cut again.

"Mother," said the princess one day as she watched them work, "there is nothing there. No cloth, no coat, no . . ."

"Hush," said the queen, "or your father will think you disloyal. Eat your flies."

"Mother," said the prince, "there really *is* nothing there. No pants, no socks, no . . ."

"Double hush," said the queen. "Loyalty begins at home. Your bugs are getting cold."

And because the queen and the princess

632 TELL ME A TALE

Crossing the Curriculum

and the prince said nothing, no one else said anything at all. Not the cook. Not the gardener. Not the butler, maid, or doorman. Not the lords-in-waiting.

And certainly not the tailors, who were, after all, being paid for their work.

Since no one said anything, King Long Shanks believed what he wanted to believe. Or needed to believe. Or thought he believed. Except for once, when he asked, "Are you *sure* that cloth is . . . well . . . right for me?" **E**

The small tailor stretched himself very high (to make himself taller). And the tall tailor squatted very low (to make himself smaller). Then they whispered simultaneously and at the same time in King Long Shanks' ears.

> The cloth is short,
> The cloth is long,
> For you it's right,
> Another—wrong.
>
> The cloth is narrow,
> The cloth is wide,
> So you can wear
> Your clothes with pride.
>
> The cloth is thick,
> The cloth is thin,
> And only the true
>   and good
>   and honest
>   and smart
>   and loyal— **F**

"I know, I know," interrupted King Long Shanks because he hated their poetry, and besides he didn't want them to suspect he couldn't see anything. KA–ZAAAACK! He ate another fly hastily and felt exceedingly cranky.

"You know everything, sire," said the small tailor.

"That's why you get the big bucks, Your Majesty," said the tall tailor. **G**

And then they smiled simultaneously and at the same time. It was not a pretty sight.

And so the tailors continued to sew on an invisible cloth that no one dared say was not there for fear of being thought a ninny, a nonny, a numbskull, or a nincompoop. And disloyal besides. **H**

Days went by. Weeks even. And at last it was time for the Summer Parade, when lily pads opened their big broad petals and the air fair hummed with insects.

King Long Shanks called the tailors to his throne room. "Will my new outfit be ready for the big parade?" he asked.

"That is exactly what we have been aiming for, sire," said the small tailor.

"We will sew you into it ourselves," the tall tailor added.

"For all your loyal subjects to see," they said together.

And on the morning of the parade, the two tailors, their hands full of the invisible cloth, dressed the king themselves.

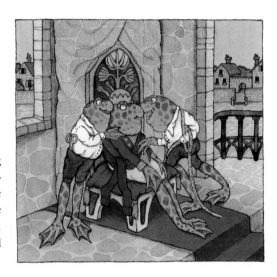

THE EMPEROR'S NEW CLOTHES **633**

E Elements of Literature
Theme
❓ What lesson can people learn from King Long Shanks's inability to believe the truth about the cloth? [Possible responses: People should not be afraid to speak up and tell the truth; it is important to set aside our pride and accept the truth; despite the opinions of others, we should trust ourselves.]

F Elements of Literature
Repetition
❓ Where did you last read this poem? [p. 631] Why do you think the writer repeats it here? [Possible responses: The tailors want to convince the king that the cloth is real at a moment when the king has expressed a doubt; the repetition makes this story sound like an old-fashioned fairy tale or fable.]

G Appreciating Language
Formal and Informal English
❓ What does it mean to "get the big bucks"? [It means to be paid a high salary.] How is the language in this story different from the language in "The Emperor's New Clothes"? [Possible response: The language in this story is not as formal and includes slang and colloquial expressions.]

H Appreciating Language
Interpreting Idioms
❓ What do *ninny, nonny, numskull,* and *nincompoop* all mean? [They all mean the same thing: "a dumb or silly person."] What clues helped you infer the meaning? ["that no one dared say was not there for fear of being thought a..."]

Taking a Second Look

Review: Monitoring Comprehension
Remind students that *reading strategies* are study techniques or aids that help to increase a reader's comprehension of a text. Readers monitor their comprehension when they think about what they are doing while they are reading, recognize when they are having trouble, and choose appropriate strategies to better comprehend a text. Point out that being a successful reader means recognizing when you're stuck and selecting the appropriate strategies for getting unstuck.

Activities
1. Have students read a paragraph or two of text and paraphrase it. Then have the students reread the text and note details and inferences that they recognize because they have reread the text.
2. Have students read a paragraph or two of text and form questions as they read. Then have students look for answers and describe how their questions helped improve their understanding of the text.
3. Finally, have groups of students identify the various resources they can use to help monitor their comprehension. These include text organizers, side notes, footnotes, dictionaries, glossaries, encyclopedias, and almanacs.

First they put on his invisible shirt.

Then his invisible shorts.

Then his invisible jacket and cloak and socks and shoes.

"We have a hat as well, Your Majesty," they said.

"I will wear my crown," King Long Shanks said. "So my loyal subjects will know me."

They brought him the royal mirror.

King Long Shanks stared and stared.

A "Toadally majestic," said the tall tailor.

"Ribeting," said the small tailor.

And they laughed secretly behind their hands simultaneously and at the same time.

King Long Shanks did not notice them laugh. He was too busy staring.

"The mirror cannot, of course, show you

634 TELL ME A TALE

how wonderful the outfit is," said the small tailor.

"After all," added the tall tailor, "a mirror is **B** not true or good or honest or smart."

"Or loyal," they said together.

"Well, at least you are right about one thing," said King Long Shanks, glancing at his reflection one last time.

"We are?" they asked.

"This outfit certainly shows off my fine long strong legs." He turned, went down the hall and out into the courtyard, where the Summer Parade was about to begin.

The queen and prince and princess were waiting there, dressed in their finery. The cook and the gardener were there as well. And so were the butler, maid, and doorman, and all the lords-in-waiting. And round them were the guards from the guardhouse, the soldiers from the armory, the townsfolk and farmfolk and the folk who tended the woods. In fact, everyone from the entire kingdom was there, waiting to walk in the parade that wound down from the palace to the pond, where the king would declare the opening of Summer.

C Only the two tailors were missing. They

Connecting Across Texts

Connecting with "The Emperor's New Clothes"
Explore with the class how "King Long Shanks" is clearly a humorous retelling of "The Emperor's New Clothes." Point out that while the stories share many similarities, they also have several important differences, especially in tone, character, and outcome. Divide the class into small groups to compare and contrast the two stories. Students can show their results in a chart such as the one at the right.

Story	Similarities	Differences
"The Emperor's New Clothes"	[monarch tricked into buying invisible clothing]	[characters are people]
"King Long Shanks"		[characters are frogs]

T634

brothers and sisters and cousins. "Hush! We are loyal to our king."

They were all the way down to the pond when the tad spoke again, in a voice the waters carried. "Mama, Papa, brothers and sisters and cousins—King Long Shanks is bare! His fine long strong legs and—*everything*!"

Just then a breeze rippled the pond and it looked like all the lily pads were laughing. That set the child and her brothers and sisters and cousins and mama and papa—and finally the woodfolk and farmfolk and townsfolk—to grinning. And *that* set the soldiers from the armory, the guards from the guardhouse, the butler and maid and doorman to giggling. And *that* set the cook and gardener to guffawing. And *that* made the prince and princess collapse in the green grass in hysterics.

Only the queen was somber. Silently she tore off a piece of her own beautiful gown and covered King Long Shanks with it, for she was the most loyal one of them all.

As to the tailors, they never entered *that* particular kingdom again with their magic cloth. But they played their same trick on one hundred and one other kings and emperors around the world. You may have heard of them.

However, none of those one hundred and one other kings and emperors had legs nearly as good or fine or long or strong—or green— as King Long Shanks. Of that I am sure.

had already collected their pay and were well on their way to the next kingdom.

There was a murmur when King Long Shanks appeared, dressed in his invisible clothes. But the queen had warned them all. And since they were all really terribly loyal to their king, the parade started with not one comment.

The parade was halfway to the pond when a little tad spoke up. "Mama," she said. "Papa—look at the king. He has no . . ."

"Hush!" her mama and papa said.

They were three-fourths of the way to the pond when the tad spoke up again. "But Mama, but Papa, really, King Long Shanks has no . . ."

"Hush!" said her mama and papa and her

MORAL

True loyalty cannot be measured as simply as cloth. But it covers a lot more than legs.

THE EMPEROR'S NEW CLOTHES 635

D Critical Thinking

Making Connections

❓ How is the tad similar to the child in "The Emperor's New Clothes"? How is she different? [Possible response: Like the child, the tadpole sees the truth. However, unlike the child, the tad is, at first, prevented from speaking.]

E Reading Skills and Strategies

Drawing Conclusions

❓ Why does the queen help the king in his moment of great embarrassment? [Possible responses: She loves him and does not want to see him humiliated; she feels responsible since she could have intervened before the parade.]

F Elements of Literature

Theme

❓ What is the theme or main idea of this story? [Possible responses: Loyalty is a very important quality to find in a person; it is very hard to tell who will be loyal and who will not be.]

Assessing Learning

Check Test: True-False

1. King Long Shanks is a frog. [True]
2. Two swindlers promise to make the king a beautiful outfit of plaid fabric. [True]
3. The king refuses to march in the Summer Parade because he feels cranky. [False]
4. A tad tries to tell everyone that the king has no clothes on, but she is not allowed to speak. [True]
5. The queen is not loyal to King Long Shanks. [False]

Self-Assessment: Reading

This assessment helps students evaluate their approaches to reading.

1=Rarely　　2=Sometimes　　3=Frequently

____ I try to predict upcoming events.

____ I reread earlier parts of the story in order to understand confusing passages.

____ I make sure I understand what I read by asking myself questions as I read.

____ I try to figure out unfamiliar words by using context clues.

Standardized Test Preparation

For practice in proofreading and editing, see
• *Daily Oral Grammar*, Transparency 39

First Thoughts

1. Some students would have stayed silent for fear of appearing foolish or to protect the Emperor from embarrassment; others might have spoken out and ended the charade.

Shaping Interpretations

2. The swindlers claim their cloth is invisible to anyone who is unfit for office or who is stupid. The Emperor wants to use the cloth to find out which of his subjects are unfit for their posts and who is clever and who is stupid.

3. The Emperor asks his honest old minister and another honest official to check the cloth. Both are too afraid of looking stupid or unfit to reveal the truth.

4. The adults do not want to look foolish, but a child is not hindered by arrogance or excess pride. Andersen sees children as more honest than adults.

5. The Emperor emerges as arrogant and unyielding.

6. Most students will select choice b, since it is shown most clearly by the two honest advisors and the adults watching the parade.

7. "King Long Shanks" describes frogs, not people; has a queen who helps the king; and uses informal language. Students are apt to prefer the second story because it is funny.

Connecting with the Text

8. Students can cite con men and women who sell various dubious, useless products. They might also cite rulers or elected officials who suffer from excessive pride and delusion.

MAKING MEANINGS

First Thoughts

[respond]

1. If you had been watching the emperor's procession, how would you have reacted?

Shaping Interpretations

[explain]

2. What special quality do the swindlers claim their cloth has? Why is the emperor interested in the swindlers' cloth?

[identify]

3. What people are asked by the emperor to check the cloth? Why won't any of them admit that they see nothing?

[interpret]

4. Why won't any adults admit that the emperor is wearing no clothes? Why do you suppose a child is not afraid to speak the truth? What seems to be the storyteller's opinion of children as opposed to his opinion of adults?

[interpret]

5. The emperor continues to march even though everyone knows he's wearing no clothes. What message about himself does he send by this action?

[interpret]

6. Readers often find different **themes** in the same story. Choose one of the following statements and tell why you think it's the best theme for "The Emperor's New Clothes." Come up with a better one if you can.

   a. People should not trust strangers.

   b. People are often afraid to speak the truth because they fear that others will think them stupid.

   c. An honest person can always be trusted to tell the truth.

   d. Children always tell the truth.

[contrast]

7. The author of "King Long Shanks" (see *Connections* on page 630) based her story on "The Emperor's New Clothes." List three important **differences** between the stories. Which story did you enjoy more?

Connecting with the Text

[connect]

8. What kinds of people today remind you of characters in "The Emperor's New Clothes" or "King Long Shanks"?

Reading Check

Imagine that you are the emperor. The procession is over and night has fallen. You take out your diary to write about your day. Tell what events led up to the procession, what happened during the procession, and how you feel about its outcome.

Reading Check
Sample response:

I have never been so embarrassed in all my life—me, the Emperor! When the two "tailors" came to town, I was excited that they could make a fabric that could help me tell who was fit for office and who was not. Like everyone else, I was tricked. How was I to know that they were con men? It was an honest mistake! I was so embarrassed to march through town without any clothes, but I had to go through with the procession. I could not let my subjects see that I had been fooled by some swindlers. I think I acted with the dignity of my position as Emperor.

CHOICES: Building Your Portfolio

Writer's Notebook

1. Collecting Ideas for a Story

Gather ideas for a story that would reveal an idea about life or people. You can either update "The Emperor's New Clothes" or make up your own. Start with the message you want to teach. Take notes on the settings, characters, and events you might want to use.

Message:
Children tell the truth.

Settings
• police station
• apartment

Characters
• brother and sister
• detective

Events
• robbery
• chase on skateboards

Reader's Theater

2. No Costumes Needed

Find some friends who are willing to prepare a reading of "The Emperor's New Clothes" for the class. A narrator could read the descriptive and explanatory material. Each reader could read the lines of a different character. Rehearse your reading at least twice before presenting it. Try to speak the way you think your character would speak. Vary the tone and volume of your voice to show different feelings.

Expository Writing

3. A Fashion Statement

In your Quickwrite, you took some notes on the clothes you like to wear and what your clothes say about you. Refer to your notes now, and write a paragraph about you and your favorite clothes. You might even illustrate your paragraph. Be sure to include a topic statement in your paragraph, either as the first or last sentence. Your topic statement should sum up the main point you are making about your clothes.

Creative Writing

4. The Final Scene

Extend the story by telling what happens after the procession. If the swindlers are still around, what does the emperor say to them? Has this experience changed the way the emperor feels about himself, his money, his clothes, and the people he trusted? Will the bold little child be part of your final scene?

Grading Timesaver
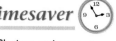

Rubrics for each Choices assignment appear on p. 181 in the *Portfolio Management System*.

CHOICES: Building Your Portfolio

1. **Writer's Notebook**   Remind students to save their work. They may use it as prewriting for the Writer's Workshop on pp. 658–662. Suggest that students look through a book of aphorisms for possible lessons their story could teach.
2. **Reader's Theater**   Also guide students to suit their body language, posture, and gestures to the characters they are playing. As students practice, suggest they look in a mirror or seek comments from others.
3. **Expository Writing**   Have students make a word web to help them generate adjectives and adverbs they can use to describe their favorite outfits in greater detail.
4. **Creative Writing**   Before students begin writing, have them consider several different ways the story could be extended. Students should jot down their ideas and related plot details in a graphic organizer. They can then share their ideas with classmates and receive some peer feedback before deciding on the story's final outcome.

Using Students' Strengths

Interpersonal Learners
For Choice 2, have students select someone to serve as director. This director should help students organize and practice their roles. The director can also take a role in the production, but his or her primary job should be as the facilitator.

Kinesthetic Learners
To help students describe their clothing more specifically in Choice 3, suggest they try on their outfits at home and analyze the appeal. Students can study their reflection in a mirror, handle the fabric, or examine how the clothes are constructed, for example. Students should incorporate these sensory details into their writing.

LANGUAGE LINK

Have students select three pieces of writing from their portfolios and analyze the level of diction they used in each. Students should identify specific sentences or paragraphs in which they've used formal or informal English. Have partners exchange papers and check each other's assessments.

Try It Out
Sample responses
1. No one is going to reveal that the weavers are disreputable scoundrels who are planning to swindle the Emperor.
2. All the guys were chicken because they thought they'd be dissed as too dopey to do their jobs.
3. The child's remark was astounding, but he would never invent such a comment.
4. The Emperor thought the jig was up, but he just kept walking, even though he was naked.

VOCABULARY

Sample responses
1. pulling the wool over everybody's eyes: fooling everybody
2. mouth to mouth: passed a message on
3. anything fishy going on: anything suspicious happening
4. stick out their necks: take a risk
5. came to a head: reached a climax
6. felt like a million dollars: felt very good
7. dressed to kill: dressed very well
8. spilled the beans: revealed the secret
9. made a monkey out of the emperor: made a fool out of him

Resources ━━━━━

Language
• *Grammar and Language Links*, p. 61
Spelling
• *Spelling and Decoding*, p. 28

LANGUAGE LINK `MINI-LESSON`

Style: Formal and Informal English

Which sentence sounds as if it came from "The Emperor's New Clothes"?

FORMAL Many years ago, there lived an Emperor who was fond of new clothes.

INFORMAL There used to be an Emperor who was wild about looking cool.

You're right, of course, if you guessed the first sentence. That one has a formal tone, and "The Emperor's New Clothes" is written in formal English. **Formal English** is what you use on serious occasions, like speaking at your graduation. Formal English doesn't include colloquial (conversational) expressions, like *wild about*, or slang words, like *cool*. Some people think that formal written English should not even include contractions, like *he'd*. **Informal English** is the English you use every day, especially when speaking to your friends. It almost always includes contractions and colloquial expressions.

> **Try It Out**
>
> Rewrite each sentence. Make the informal sentences formal and the formal sentences informal.
>
> 1. No one's going to let anybody in on the secret that the weavers are bad guys up to no good.
> 2. Everyone was afraid to be shown unfit for his office or stupid.
> 3. It's crazy what that little kid said, but there's no way he'd make up something like that.
> 4. It seemed to the emperor that the child was right, but he continued to walk on, wearing no clothes.

VOCABULARY `HOW TO OWN A WORD`

Interpreting Idioms

An **idiom** is an expression like "clothes make the man" or "head over heels in love." An idiom is a group of words that together mean something beyond the definitions of the individual words. People often use idioms when they speak informally.

Find ten idioms in the following paragraph. Working with a partner, tell what each idiom means. Then, tell what each idiom would mean if you translated it literally.

> The weavers pretended to be hard at work, but they were really pulling the wool over everybody's eyes. "It's beautiful, excellent!" went from mouth to mouth. No one thought there was anything fishy going on. The emperor's servants certainly were not willing to stick out their necks. Things came to a head during the procession. The emperor felt like a million dollars. He thought he was dressed to kill. Then a child spilled the beans: The weavers had made a monkey out of the emperor.

Language Link Quick Check
━━━━━━━━━━━━━━━━

Have students explain what each idiom means.
1. It's raining cats and dogs. [It's raining very heavily.]
2. He hit the ceiling. [He got very angry.]
3. She lost her head. [She lost control of herself.]
4. The Emperor flipped out. [The Emperor got angry.]
5. Don't bust a gasket! [Don't lose your temper.]

Before You Read

HE LION, BRUH BEAR, AND BRUH RABBIT

Make the Connection

Teaching Tales

Folk tales like this one originally came from Africa. On the surface the stories seem to be entertaining tales about big, mean animals and crafty little ones. If you read between the lines, however, you might discover that the teller of this tale is really talking about something else.

Quickwrite

Would you choose to be the strongest person in the world or the smartest person in the world? Make your decision. Then, write two or three sentences describing the first thing you'd do with all that power.

go.hrw.com
LE0 6-8

Elements of Literature

The Trickster

Remember Bugs Bunny, Tweety the Canary, Mighty Mouse, and Roadrunner? They always play the underdog in cartoons, but it doesn't matter how big their enemies are; these underdogs win every time. That's because they're **tricksters,** a type of underdog character that shows up in stories time and again all over the world. Although they often act silly, tricksters are usually quite clever. What's more, their tricks often teach important lessons. Don Coyote, Anansi the Spider, Raven—these are just a few of the famous tricksters in folk tales. Brer Rabbit, who is called Bruh (Brother) Rabbit in this story, is one of the trickiest.

> A **trickster** is a character in literature who relies on cleverness to outwit or trick more powerful opponents.

Planning

- **Traditional Schedule**
  Lesson Plans Including Strategies for English-Language Learners
- **One-Stop Planner**
  CD-ROM with Test Generator

639

Summary ▪ ▪

He Lion disturbs the other animals with his roar, "ME AND MYSELF, ME AND MYSELF." Seeking help, the other animals ask Bruh Bear and Bruh Rabbit to speak to he Lion. Bruh Bear and Bruh Rabbit ask he Lion to stop roaring, but he refuses, claiming that he alone is king of the forest. Bruh Bear and Bruh Rabbit point out that Man is in fact the king of the forest and take he Lion to see him. The first Man they encounter, however, is only nine years old and no challenge to he Lion; the second Man is ninety and also harmless. But the third Man is a 21-year-old hunter with a rifle who fires twice at he Lion and nearly kills him. As a result, he Lion learns his lesson and settles down.

Resources 🎧

Listening
Audio CD Library
A humorous recording of this folk tale is included in the *Audio CD Library:*
• Disc 15, Track 3

Ⓐ Elements of Literature

Dialect
❓ This folk tale is written in *dialect,* a way of speaking characteristic of a particular region or group of people. In a dialect, certain words are spelled and pronounced differently. What are some characteristics of this dialect? [The final "g" is left off nouns (*mornin*) and verbs (*huntin, fishin*); there are sentence fragments; extra pronouns are added (*he* Lion).]

Ⓑ Cultural Connections

In some segments of African American culture, adults may be addressed as "sister" or "brother," followed by their first names. Thus, a woman named Sue might be called "Sister Sue"; a man named Henry might be "Brother Henry." The term "Bruh" in this story is a dialect version of "Brother."

He Lion, Bruh Bear, and Bruh Rabbit

an African American folk tale,
retold by **Virginia Hamilton**

Ⓐ
Say that he Lion would get up each and every mornin. Stretch and walk around. He'd roar, "ME AND MYSELF. ME AND MYSELF," like that. Scare all the little animals so they were afraid to come outside in the sunshine. Afraid to go huntin or fishin or whatever the little animals wanted to do.

"What we gone do about it?" they asked one another. Squirrel leapin from branch to branch, just scared. Possum[1] playin dead, couldn't hardly move him.

He Lion just went on, stickin out his chest and roarin, "ME AND MYSELF. ME AND MYSELF."

The little animals held a sit-down talk, and one by one and two by two and all by all, Ⓑ they decide to go see Bruh Bear and Bruh Rabbit. For they know that Bruh Bear been around. And Bruh Rabbit say he has, too.

So they went to Bruh Bear and Bruh Rabbit. Said, "We have some trouble. Old he Lion, him scarin everybody, roarin every mornin and all day, 'ME AND MYSELF. ME AND MYSELF,' like that."

1. **possum:** short for *opossum,* a tree-dwelling mammal with a long tail that plays dead when in danger.

640 TELL ME A TALE

🎧 💿 — *Resources: Print and Media* — 📼 📽

Reading
• *Graphic Organizers for Active Reading,* p. 42
• *Audio CD Library*
  Disc 15, Track 3

Writing and Language
• *Daily Oral Grammar*
  Transparency 40
• *Grammar and Language Links*
  Worksheet, p. 63
• *Language Workshop CD-ROM*

Assessment
• *Formal Assessment,* p. 123
• *Portfolio Management System,* p. 182
• *Standardized Test Preparation,* p. 90
• *Test Generator (One-Stop Planner* CD-ROM)

Internet
• go.hrw.com (keyword: LE0 6-8)

"Why he Lion want to do that?" Bruh Bear said.

"Is that all he Lion have to say?" Bruh Rabbit asked.

"We don't know why, but that's all he Lion can tell us and we didn't ask him to tell us that," said the little animals. "And him scarin the children with it. And we wish him to stop it."

"Well, I'll go see him, talk to him. I've known he Lion a long kind of time," Bruh Bear said.

"I'll go with you," said Bruh Rabbit. "I've known he Lion most long as you."

That bear and that rabbit went off through the forest. They kept hearin somethin. Mumble, mumble. Couldn't make it out. They got farther in the forest. They heard it plain now. "ME AND MYSELF. ME AND MYSELF."

"Well, well, well," said Bruh Bear. He wasn't scared. He'd been around the whole forest, seen a lot.

"My, my, my," said Bruh Rabbit. He'd seen enough to know not to be afraid of an old he lion. Now old he lions could be dangerous, but you had to know how to handle them.

The bear and the rabbit climbed up and up the cliff where he Lion had his lair.[2] They found him. Kept their distance. He watchin them and they watchin him. Everybody actin cordial.[3]

"Hear tell you are scarin everybody, all the little animals, with your roarin all the time," Bruh Rabbit said.

"I roars when I pleases," he Lion said.

"Well, might could you leave off the noise first thing in the mornin, so the little animals can get what they want to eat and drink?" asked Bruh Bear.

"Listen," said he Lion, and then he roared:

2. **lair:** resting place of a wild animal; den.
3. **cordial** (kôr′jəl): warm and friendly.

"ME AND MYSELF. ME AND MYSELF. Nobody tell me what not to do," he said. "I'm the king of the forest, *me and myself.*"

"Better had let me tell you somethin," Bruh Rabbit said, "for I've seen Man, and I know him the real king of the forest."

He Lion was quiet awhile. He looked straight through that scrawny lil Rabbit like he was nothin atall. He looked at Bruh Bear and figured he'd talk to him.

"You, Bear, you been around," he Lion said.

"That's true," said old Bruh Bear. "I been about everywhere. I've been around the whole forest."

"Then you must know somethin," he Lion said.

"I know lots," said Bruh Bear, slow and quiet-like.

"Tell me what you know about Man," he Lion said. "He think him the king of the forest?"

"Well, now, I'll tell you," said Bruh Bear, "I been around, but I haven't ever come across Man that I know of. Couldn't tell you nothin about him."

So he Lion had to turn back to Bruh Rabbit. He didn't want to but he had to. "So what?" he said to that lil scrawny hare.

"Well, you got to come down from there if you want to see Man," Bruh Rabbit said. "Come down from there and I'll show you him."

He Lion thought a minute, an hour, and a whole day. Then, the next day, he came on down.

He roared just once, "ME AND MYSELF. ME AND MYSELF. Now," he said, "come show me Man."

So they set out. He Lion, Bruh Bear, and Bruh Rabbit. They go along and they go along, rangin the forest. Pretty soon, they come to a clearin. And playin in it is a little fellow about nine years old.

"Is that there Man?" asked he Lion.

HE LION, BRUH BEAR, AND BRUH RABBIT 641

"Why no, that one is called Will Be, but it sure is not Man," said Bruh Rabbit.

So they went along and they went along. Pretty soon, they come upon a shade tree. And sleepin under it is an old, olden fellow, about ninety years olden.

"There must lie Man," spoke he Lion. "I knew him wasn't gone be much."

"That's not Man," said Bruh Rabbit. "That fellow is Was Once. You'll know it when you see Man."

So they went on along. He Lion is gettin tired of strollin. So he roars, "ME AND MYSELF. ME AND MYSELF." Upsets Bear so that Bear doubles over and runs and climbs a tree.

"Come down from there," Bruh Rabbit tellin him. So after a while Bear comes down. He keepin his distance from he Lion, any-

how. And they set out some more. Goin along quiet and slow.

In a little while they come to a road. And comin on way down the road, Bruh Rabbit sees Man comin. Man about twenty-one years old. Big and strong, with a big gun over his shoulder.

"There!" Bruh Rabbit says. "See there, he Lion? There's Man. You better go meet him."

"I will," says he Lion. And he sticks out his chest and he roars, "ME AND MYSELF. ME AND MYSELF." All the way to Man he's roarin proud, "ME AND MYSELF, ME AND MYSELF!"

"Come on, Bruh Bear, let's go!" Bruh Rabbit says.

"What for?" Bruh Bear wants to know.

"You better come on!" And Bruh Rabbit takes ahold of Bruh Bear and half drags him

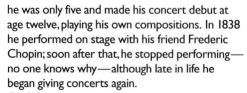

Listening to Music

to a thicket. And there he makin the Bear hide with him.

For here comes Man. He sees old he Lion real good now. He drops to one knee and he takes aim with his big gun.

Old he Lion is roarin his head off: "ME AND MYSELF! ME AND MYSELF!"

The big gun goes off: PA-LOOOM!

He Lion falls back hard on his tail.

The gun goes off again. PA-LOOOM!

He Lion is flyin through the air. He lands in the thicket.

"Well, did you see Man?" asked Bruh Bear.

"I seen him," said he Lion. "Man spoken to me unkind, and got a great long stick him keepin on his shoulder. Then Man taken that stick down and him speakin real mean. Thunderin at me and lightnin comin from that stick, awful bad. Made me sick. I had to turn around. And Man pointin that stick again and thunderin at me some more. So I come in here, cause it seem like him throwed some stickers at me each time it thunder, too."

"So you've met Man, and you know zactly what that kind of him is," says Bruh Rabbit.

"I surely do know that," he Lion said back.

Awhile after he Lion met Man, things were some better in the forest. Bruh Bear knew what Man looked like so he could keep out of his way. That rabbit always did know to keep out of Man's way. The little animals could go out in the mornin because he Lion was more peaceable. He didn't walk around roarin at the top of his voice all the time. And when he Lion did lift that voice of his, it was like, "Me and Myself and Man. Me and Myself and Man." Like that.

Wasn't too loud atall.

MEET THE WRITER

Telling Tales

Virginia Hamilton (1936–   ) has lived for most of her life, in the place where she was born and raised, Yellow Springs, Ohio. It's where her grandfather settled after he escaped from slavery in pre–Civil War days. Virginia was named for the state where her grandfather had lived before he escaped.

About her family and Yellow Springs, the place she calls home, Hamilton says:

66 My mother's 'people' were warm-hearted, tight with money, generous to the sick and landless, close-mouthed, and fond of telling tales and gossip about one another and even their ancestors. They were a part of me from the time I understood that I belonged to all of them. My uncle King told the best tall tales; my aunt Leanna sang the finest sorrowful songs. My own mother could take a slice of fiction floating around the family and polish it into a saga. So could my father. He, having come from a Creole family that wandered the face of this country and Canada, was always a traveling man, if only in his mind.

After a leave of fifteen years, when I lived in New York City, I returned to that village [Yellow Springs]. Knowing who and what I am, I can go home. With a bit of city style and humor, I can claim what is left of the land. I am only reclaiming what was given to me without comment so long ago—that freedom and dependence which was partly happiness. 99

Making the Connections

Connecting to the Theme: "Tell Me a Tale"

Of all the stories in the collection so far, this one reflects most clearly the origins of myths and folk tales in an oral tradition, owing to its use of informal English and dialect in the narration and dialogue. Have students discuss the other stories preceding this one, with an emphasis on evaluating whether the stories, as presented, seem closer to an oral or a written tradition. Encourage students to cite specific examples of narration and dialogue to support their conclusions.

Connections

Two of Aesop's fables have been dramatized for a reader's theater.

Ⓐ Critical Thinking
Speculating

❓What do you think of when you think of foxes? [Possible responses: clever, smart, sneaky, quick, sly.] What do you think of when you think of crows? [Possible responses: noisy, smart, bullying.] What do you think might happen in a story involving these two animals? [Possible response: One animal will try to outsmart or trick the other.]

Ⓑ Reading Skills and Strategies
Making Predictions

❓How do you think the fox could get the cheese from the crow? [Possible responses: The fox could trick the crow by making her think the cheese is spoiled; the fox could scare the crow so she drops the cheese and flies away.]

Ⓒ Elements of Literature
The Trickster

❓How does the fox trick the crow? [The fox flatters the crow so she opens her mouth and drops the cheese.]

Ⓓ Elements of Literature
Theme

❓What is the main idea of this folk tale? State it in your own words. [Possible responses: Don't let a need for flattery get the best of you; beware of people who are too flattering because they may take advantage of you.]

THE FOX AND THE CROW

Aesop, *dramatized by Mara Rockliff*

Narrator. One fine morning a Fox was wandering through the woods, enjoying the lovely spring weather.

Fox. Lovely spring weather is all very well, but a fox can't live on sunshine and fresh air. I could use some breakfast right about now.

Narrator. Suddenly he noticed a Crow sitting on the branch of a tree above him. The Fox didn't think much of crows as a rule, but this particular Crow had something very interesting in her beak.

Fox. Cheese. Mmm. A nice big yellow chunk of cheese. I would love that cheese. I deserve that cheese. But how can I get that cheese?

Narrator. The Fox thought awhile, and then he called up to the Crow.

Fox. Good morning, you fabulous bird.

Narrator. The Crow looked at him suspiciously. But she kept her beak closed tightly on the cheese and said nothing.

Fox. What beautiful beady eyes you have! And you certainly look great in black feathers. I've seen a lot of birds in my time, but you outbird them all. A bird with your good looks must have a voice to match. Oh, if only I could hear you sing just one song. Then I would know you were truly the Greatest Bird on Earth.

Narrator. Listening to all this flattery, the Crow forgot her suspicion of the Fox. She forgot her cheese, too. All she could think

644 TELL ME A TALE

of was impressing the Fox with a song. So she opened her beak wide and let out a loud "Caw!" Down fell the cheese, right into the Fox's open mouth.

Fox. Thanks! That tasted every bit as good as it looked. Well, now I know you have a voice—and I hope I never have to hear it again. But where are your brains?

All Together. If you let flattery go to your head, you'll pay the price.

Assessing Learning

Check Test: Matching Items
Have students match the characters to the actions.

Bruh Bear	1. so terrified he played dead
Bruh Rabbit	2. scared everyone with his roaring
Man	3. the trickster
He Lion	4. had been around the whole forest
Possum	5. tried to kill he Lion

[Bruh Bear=4, Bruh Rabbit=3, Man=5, He Lion=2, Possum=1]

Observation Assessment: Reading
Use the following criteria to assess students' comprehension of the folk tales.

1= Always   2=Sometimes   3=Never

Criteria	Rating
Understands the genre	
Probes characters' behavior	
Summarizes the plot	
Makes reasonable predictions	
Understands the moral	

Standardized Test Preparation
For practice with standardized test format specific to this selection, see
• *Standardized Test Preparation*, p. 90
For practice in proofreading and editing, see
• *Daily Oral Grammar*, Transparency 40

THE WOLF AND THE HOUSE DOG

Aesop, *dramatized by Mara Rockliff*

Narrator. Once there was a Wolf who never got enough to eat. Her mouth watered when she looked at the fat geese and chickens kept by the people of the village. But every time she tried to steal one, the watchful village dogs would bark and warn their owners.

Wolf. Really, I'm nothing but skin and bones. It makes me sad just thinking about it.

Narrator. One night the Wolf met up with a House Dog who had wandered a little too far from home. The Wolf would gladly have eaten him right then and there.

Wolf. Dog stew . . . cold dog pie . . . or maybe just dog on a bun, with plenty of mustard and ketchup . . .

Narrator. But the House Dog looked too big and strong for the Wolf, who was weak from hunger. So the Wolf spoke to him very humbly and politely.

Wolf. How handsome you are! You look so healthy and well fed and delicious—I mean, uh, terrific. You look terrific. Really.

House Dog. Well, you look terrible. I don't know why you live out here in these miserable woods, where you have to fight so hard for every crummy little scrap of food. You should come live in the village like me. You could eat like a king there.

Wolf. What do I have to do?

House Dog. Hardly anything. Chase kids on bicycles. Bark at the mailman every now and then. Lie around the house letting people pet you. Just for that they'll feed you till you burst—enormous steak bones with fat hanging off them, pizza crusts, bits of chicken, leftovers like you wouldn't believe.

Narrator. The Wolf nearly cried with happiness as she imagined how wonderful her new life was going to be. But then she noticed a strange ring around the Dog's neck where the hair had been rubbed off.

Wolf. What happened to your neck?

House Dog. Oh . . . ah . . . nothing. It's nothing, really.

Wolf. I've never seen anything like it. Is it a disease?

House Dog. Don't be silly. It's just the mark of the collar that they fasten my chain to.

Wolf. A chain! You mean you can't go wherever you like?

House Dog. Well, not always. But what's the difference?

Wolf. What's the difference? Are you kidding? I wouldn't give up my freedom for the biggest, juiciest steak in the world. Never mind a few lousy bones.

Narrator. The Wolf ran away, back to the woods. She never went near the village again, no matter how hungry she got.

All Together. Nothing is worth more than freedom.

HE LION, BRUH BEAR, AND BRUH RABBIT **645**

A Reading Skills and Strategies
Identifying Cause and Effect
❓ What causes the wolf to be so hungry? [People in town fear her and scare her away every time she tries to steal some food.]

B English Language Learners
Interpreting Idioms
In America a "dog on a bun" is usually called a *hot dog* or a *frankfurter*. The writer uses the phrase "dog on a bun" to create humor.

C Reading Skills and Strategies
Drawing Conclusions
❓ What responsibilities does the house dog have? [He must chase kids on bicycles, bark at the postal carrier, and let the humans pet him.] Why do you think the dog makes his life seem so easy? [Possible responses: It really is easy; the dog is trying to persuade the wolf that living a dog's life is desirable.]

D Critical Thinking
Speculating
❓ Why is the dog embarrassed by the ring around its neck? [Possible responses: He knows it is a sign that he is not really free; he thinks it's unattractive.]

E Elements of Literature
Theme
❓ How would you state the author's theme in your own words? [Possible responses: Freedom is the most valuable thing we have; we should not trade all the treasure in the world for our freedom.]

Connecting Across Texts

Connecting with "He Lion, Bruh Bear . . ."

Have students compare and contrast "He Lion, Bruh Bear, and Bruh Rabbit" with Aesop's two fables, "The Wolf and the House Dog" and "The Fox and the Crow." Have them identify and describe the *trickster* in each story and decide which one fits each category below, and why:

Most interesting _____

Most successful _____

Least successful _____

MAKING MEANINGS

First Thoughts

1. Some students may argue that he Lion deserved to be nearly killed because he was bothering everyone with his vanity; others may believe that humiliation would have been sufficient discipline.

Shaping Interpretations

2. A rabbit is small, quick, and agile.
3. He Lion means that only he matters; he puts his needs above all others'.
4. He Lion realizes that Man, not he, is the king of the jungle. He has been humbled.
5. This tale teaches that it is better to be smart than strong, for the smart rabbit triumphs over the strong lion.

Connecting with the Text

6. Bullies in school and aggressive captains of industry could be compared to he Lion, while activists might be compared to Bruh Rabbit.

Grading Timesaver

Rubrics for each Choices assignment appear on p. 182 in the *Portfolio Management System*.

CHOICES: Building Your Portfolio

1. **Writer's Notebook** Remind students to save their work. They may use it as prewriting for the Writer's Workshop on pp. 658–662.
2. **Performance** Students should select the tone of their performance—humorous or serious—and then consider including the story's dialect or revising the language.

MAKING MEANINGS

First Thoughts

[respond]

1. Does he Lion get what he deserves, or is Bruh Rabbit too mean to him? Explain.

Shaping Interpretations

[interpret]

2. What is it about rabbits that might make people think they would be good **tricksters**?

[interpret]

3. What does he Lion mean when he roars "ME AND MYSELF, ME AND MYSELF"?

[infer]

4. At the end of the story, he Lion roars less loudly and less often. Why?

[interpret]

5. According to this tale, is it better to be smart or to be strong? Why do you think so? (Think back to the decision you made for your Quickwrite.)

Connecting with the Text

[interpret]

6. Animals in folk tales often talk and act like people. In the real world today, what kind of people are like Bruh Rabbit or he Lion?

Reading Check

Use a graphic like the one below to trace the **sequence of main events** in this tale. Be sure to show **cause and effect**—the way each event leads to the next.

Event 1 → Event 2 → and so on

CHOICES: Building Your Portfolio

Writer's Notebook

1. Collecting Ideas for a Story

Make up a trickster (trickster characters are often animals), and freewrite for a story. You might tell how the trickster outwits a character who is much stronger, uses a trick to teach someone a lesson, or plays a trick that backfires.

Performance

2. You're On!

Get together with a group of classmates interested in preparing "He Lion . . ." or one of the fables by Aesop (see *Connections* on page 644) for classroom presentation. You can either do a live performance with props and costumes or tape your reading. If you decide on "He Lion . . . ,"

break the story into scenes. Decide if you need a narrator to provide details not supplied in the dialogue. Write out each character's lines. You may want to get together with groups who prepared the other two stories and present them in sequence.

Reading Check

Sample response:
[Event 1] He Lion disturbs all the other animals with his roaring.
[Event 2] Bruh Rabbit and Bruh Bear ask he Lion to stop roaring in the morning; he refuses, claiming to be king of the jungle. They claim Man is king.
[Event 3] Bruh Rabbit, he Lion, and Bruh Bear see a nine-year-old boy.
[Event 4] They see a ninety-year-old man.
[Event 5] They see the hunter, who shoots at he Lion twice.
[Event 6] He Lion learns his lesson and stops roaring so loud.

GRAMMAR LINK MINI-LESSON

To, Too, and Two

Technology HELP

See Language Workshop CD-ROM. *Key word entry: homonyms.*

Sometimes the sound-alike words *to*, *too*, and *two* can seem like tricksters. Don't let them fool you. Notice how they're used in this paragraph:

The little animals went to Bruh Bear and Bruh Rabbit. Those two animals had been around more than the others. Everyone agreed that he Lion was making too much noise. He had to stop scaring the children.

Remembering what each word means will help you use it correctly.

- **to:** toward; in the direction of; part of the infinitive form of a verb
- **too:** also; more than enough
- **two:** a number: one plus one

Try It Out

Choose the correct word from the underlined pair in each sentence.

1. He Lion didn't like talking <u>too/to</u> Bruh Rabbit.

2. He Lion's roar was <u>too/to</u> loud for Bruh Bear, so Bruh Bear climbed a tree.

3. He Lion thought he wanted <u>two/to</u> see Man.

4. The animals saw <u>too/two</u> fellows, a little one and an old one, before they saw Man.

5. After he had seen Man, he Lion was more peaceable; he was quieter, <u>to/too</u>.

VOCABULARY HOW TO OWN A WORD

Using a Glossary

A **glossary** defines words that the reader of a book might find difficult. A glossary usually appears at the back of a book. It looks a little like a dictionary, but it's much shorter. Notice these points about the glossary of this book (page 773):

- It tells you how to pronounce each word.
- It identifies the part of speech.
- It gives you the meaning of the word as it used in the book.

Look back at "He Lion, Bruh Bear, and Bruh Rabbit," and find four words that you think readers might not know. (Don't pick dialect words like *Bruh* and *atall*.) Write a glossary entry for each word, following the style used in this book's glossary. Check a dictionary for pronunciation. Be sure to use a definition that fits the context of the word in the story.

EXAMPLE **lair** (ler) *n.*: resting place of a wild animal; den.

HE LION, BRUH BEAR, AND BRUH RABBIT 647

GRAMMAR LINK

Have students select three pieces of writing from their portfolios and underline every *to*, *too*, and *two*. Students should check to see if they used the words correctly. Then have students exchange papers with a partner and check each other's assessments.

Try It Out
1. to
2. too
3. to
4. two
5. too

VOCABULARY

As they work, direct students to pay close attention to the word's part of speech. This will help them define the word correctly in context.

Resources

Language
- *Grammar and Language Links*, p. 63

Using the Glossary to Find Pronunciations

If students have trouble pronouncing a particular word, they should turn to the guide to pronunciation symbols that appears at the bottom of p. 773, the first page of the Glossary. The guide contains words and symbols that will help students decode unfamiliar words.

Grammar Link Quick Check

Have students underline the correct homonym in each sentence.

1. He Lion liked <u>to/too</u> scare all the animals. [to]
2. They were all afraid of him, <u>two/too</u>. [too]
3. One day, <u>two/too</u> of the animals visited he Lion. [two]
4. "We have <u>to/too</u> talk," Bruh Rabbit said. [to]
5. "<u>Too/To</u> many animals have complained about you," Bruh Bear added. [Too]

OBJECTIVES
1. Read and enjoy the story
2. Connect the selection to the collection theme

No Questions Asked

The literature in No Questions Asked gives students the chance to read a selection for enjoyment and enrichment as they further explore the collection theme. Annotated questions in the margins of the Teacher's Edition should be considered optional. No follow-up questions will appear after the selection.

   A king offers to give half his kingdom plus the princess' hand in marriage to whoever can slay the dragon that is menacing his kingdom. One by one, the wise cobbler's three sons accept the challenge. The first two sons disregard their father's advice to recite a poem to the dragon, and both end up in the dragon's belly. The youngest son recites the poem, the dragon falls down in hysterical laughter, and the boy manages to lop off his head. The boy then frees his brothers, and the three sons find the wizard's missing book of spells, enabling the wizard to restore the queen from a rosebush to her human form. The successful son marries the princess and gains half the kingdom.

Resources

Listening
Audio CD Library
A humorous recording of this story is included in the *Audio CD Library:*
• Disc 15, Track 4

Viewing and Representing
• Fine Art Transparency 20
• Fine Art Worksheet, p. 80

Reaching All Students

English Language Learners
Students may not understand the meaning of *spell* as "a magical chant or formula intended to bring about a dramatic change in a person or thing." They may also have trouble with idioms such as "slipped his mind," "at his wits end," "racked his brain," and "leave well enough alone." Provide explanations as necessary. For additional strategies to supplement instruction for English language learners, see
• *Lesson Plans Including Strategies for English-Language Learners*

Advanced Learners
Remind students that some fairy tales and folk tales have a *moral,* a lesson that teaches readers how they should behave or what they should believe. Point out that the moral can be directly stated or indirectly implied. Explain that the moral is not directly stated in this story. Suggest that as students read the tale they take notes on characters' actions and on events, so that they can decide what the moral is after they've read the entire selection.

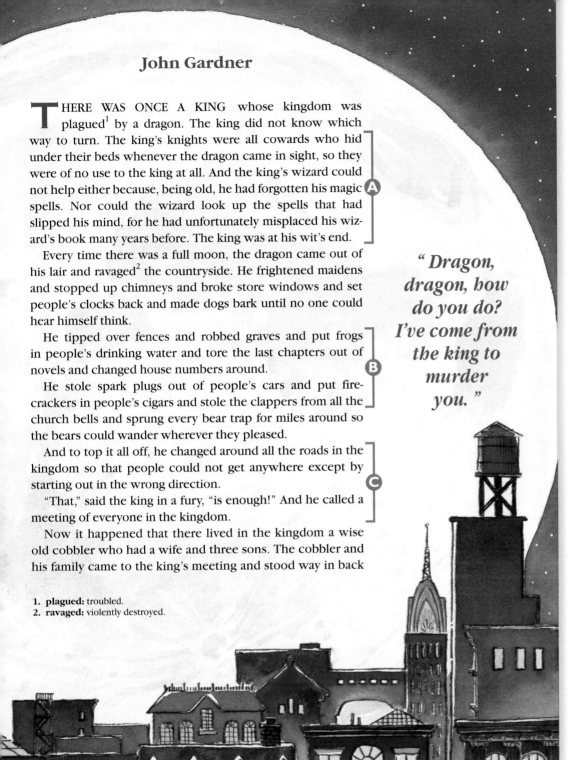

John Gardner

THERE WAS ONCE A KING whose kingdom was plagued[1] by a dragon. The king did not know which way to turn. The king's knights were all cowards who hid under their beds whenever the dragon came in sight, so they were of no use to the king at all. And the king's wizard could not help either because, being old, he had forgotten his magic spells. Nor could the wizard look up the spells that had slipped his mind, for he had unfortunately misplaced his wizard's book many years before. The king was at his wit's end.

Every time there was a full moon, the dragon came out of his lair and ravaged[2] the countryside. He frightened maidens and stopped up chimneys and broke store windows and set people's clocks back and made dogs bark until no one could hear himself think.

He tipped over fences and robbed graves and put frogs in people's drinking water and tore the last chapters out of novels and changed house numbers around.

He stole spark plugs out of people's cars and put firecrackers in people's cigars and stole the clappers from all the church bells and sprung every bear trap for miles around so the bears could wander wherever they pleased.

And to top it all off, he changed around all the roads in the kingdom so that people could not get anywhere except by starting out in the wrong direction.

"That," said the king in a fury, "is enough!" And he called a meeting of everyone in the kingdom.

Now it happened that there lived in the kingdom a wise old cobbler who had a wife and three sons. The cobbler and his family came to the king's meeting and stood way in back

1. **plagued:** troubled.
2. **ravaged:** violently destroyed.

" Dragon, dragon, how do you do? I've come from the king to murder you. "

Ⓐ Critical Thinking
Making Connections
❓ How are the knights and the wizard in this fairy tale different from those in other fairy tales you've read or heard? [Possible responses: The knights in this story are cowardly instead of brave; the wizard is forgetful instead of clever.]

Ⓑ Elements of Literature
Characterization
❓ How would you describe this dragon? What are his character traits? [Possible response: This dragon is clever, mischievous, funny, and a nuisance.]

Ⓒ Reading Skills and Strategies
Identifying Cause and Effect
❓ Which one of the dragon's tricks causes the king to be so angry that he calls a meeting to do something about the dragon? [The dragon has changed all the roads in the kingdom around so that people cannot find their way.]

Making the Connections

**Connecting to the Theme:
"Tell Me a Tale"**
Have students work in small groups to determine the similarities among the myths, folk tales, and fairy tales in this collection. Students can record their responses in a chart such as this one:

Similarities	Examples
[The number three]	[Perseus had three parts to his quest; Morgiana saves Ali Baba three times; the cobbler has three sons and each tries to slay the dragon; he Lion encounters three forms of Man.]

A **Elements of Literature**

Plot

❓ Why do you think the king asked the cobbler to attend the meeting? [Possible responses: The cobbler is described as "wise"; the king may want everyone present so he can explore all possibilities; the cobbler has three sons who are likely to play a role in the story.]

B **English Language Learners**

Briticisms

One meaning of the word *deuce* is "bad luck" or "the devil." "What the deuce" is a mild curse, indicating that the speaker is annoyed.

C **Elements of Literature**

Irony

❓ How is the king's comment about his wife ironic? [Possible responses: It's not what you'd expect a husband to say in this situation—you'd expect him to be alarmed or shocked, but he isn't; he seems not to care.]

D **Reading Skills and Strategies**

Making Predictions

❓ Do you think the eldest son will slay the dragon? Why or why not? [Possible responses: Yes, because he's the eldest and he may be the strongest and smartest; no, because he seems too confident; no, because things come in threes in fairy tales, so it is more likely that the third son will succeed.]

A by the door, for the cobbler had a feeling that since he was nobody important, there had probably been some mistake, and no doubt the king had intended the meeting for everyone in the kingdom except his family and him.

"Ladies and gentlemen," said the king when everyone was present, "I've put up with that dragon as long as I can. He has got to be stopped."

All the people whispered amongst themselves, and the king smiled, pleased with the impression he had made.

But the wise cobbler said gloomily, "It's all very well to talk about it—but how are you going to do it?"

And now all the people smiled and winked as if to say, "Well, King, he's got you there!"

The king frowned.

"It's not that His Majesty hasn't tried," the queen spoke up loyally.

"Yes," said the king, "I've told my knights again and again that they ought to slay that dragon. But I can't *force* them to go. I'm not a tyrant."

"Why doesn't the wizard say a magic spell?" asked the cobbler.

"He's done the best he can," said the king.

The wizard blushed and everyone looked embarrassed. "I used to do all sorts of spells and chants when I was younger," the wizard explained. "But I've lost my spell book, and I begin to fear I'm losing my memory too. For instance, I've been trying for days to recall **B** one spell I used to do. I forget, just now, what the deuce it was for. It went something like—

> Bimble,
> Wimble,
> Cha, Cha
> CHOOMPF!"

Suddenly, to everyone's surprise, the queen turned into a rosebush.

"Oh dear," said the wizard.

"Now you've done it," groaned the king.

"Poor Mother," said the princess.

"I don't know what can have happened," the wizard said nervously, "but don't worry, I'll have her changed back in a jiffy." He shut his eyes and racked his brain for a spell that would change her back.

C But the king said quickly, "You'd better leave well enough alone. If you change her into a rattlesnake, we'll have to chop off her head."

Meanwhile the cobbler stood with his hands in his pockets, sighing at the waste of time. "About the dragon . . ." he began.

"Oh yes," said the king. "I'll tell you what I'll do. I'll give the princess' hand in marriage to anyone who can make the dragon stop."

"It's not enough," said the cobbler. "She's a nice enough girl, you understand. But how would an ordinary person support her? Also, what about those of us that are already married?"

"In that case," said the king, "I'll offer the princess' hand or half the kingdom or both—whichever is most convenient."

The cobbler scratched his chin and considered it. "It's not enough," he said at last. "It's a good enough kingdom, you understand, but it's too much responsibility."

"Take it or leave it," the king said.

"I'll leave it," said the cobbler. And he shrugged and went home.

D But the cobbler's eldest son thought the bargain was a good one, for the princess was very beautiful, and he liked the idea of having half the kingdom to run as he pleased. So he said to the king, "I'll accept those terms, Your Majesty. By tomorrow morning the dragon will be slain."

650 TELL ME A TALE

Taking a Second Look

Review: Setting Purpose for Reading

Remind students that setting a purpose for reading a selection helps them focus their attention and helps them improve their comprehension of the selection. Different purposes include the following: to understand the plot, theme, or main ideas; to find specific information, such as facts or details; to appreciate the author's craft; and to enjoy the selection. Suggest that students follow these steps when they set a purpose for reading:

- Skim the selection to get a general idea of what it is about.
- Write down several questions that you want to find answers to as you read.
- Use the 5W-How words (Who? What? Where? When? Why? and How?) to form your questions.

Activities

1. Ask students what questions they have in mind as they are reading "Dragon, Dragon."

Suggest that they form some questions if they have not already done so.

2. Ask students to apply the steps at left to set a purpose for reading the Writer's Workshop on pp. 658–662.

3. Ask students to describe a purpose they set in the past for reading a selection. What was the selection? What did they learn or what did they experience while reading the selection?

"Bless you!" cried the king.

"Hooray, hooray, hooray!" cried all the people, throwing their hats in the air.

The cobbler's eldest son beamed with pride, and the second eldest looked at him enviously. The youngest son said timidly, "Excuse me, Your Majesty, but don't you think the queen looks a little unwell? If I were you, I think I'd water her."

"Good heavens," cried the king, glancing at the queen, who had been changed into a rosebush, "I'm glad you mentioned it!"

Now the cobbler's eldest son was very clever and was known far and wide for how quickly he could multiply fractions in his head. He was perfectly sure he could slay the dragon by somehow or other playing a trick on him, and he didn't feel that he needed his wise old father's advice. But he thought it was only polite to ask, and so he went to his father, who was working as usual at his cobbler's bench, and said, "Well, Father, I'm off to slay the dragon. Have you any advice to give me?"

The cobbler thought a moment and replied, "When and if you come to the dragon's lair, recite the following poem.

Dragon, dragon, how do you do?
I've come from the king to murder you.

Say it very loudly and firmly, and the dragon will fall, God willing, at your feet."

"How curious!" said the eldest son. And he thought to himself, "The old man is not as wise as I thought. If I say something like that to the dragon, he will eat me up in an instant. The way to kill a dragon is to outfox him." And keeping his opinion to himself, the eldest son set forth on his quest.

When he came at last to the dragon's lair, which was a cave, the eldest son slyly disguised himself as a peddler and knocked on the door and called out, "Hello there!"

"There's nobody home!" roared a voice.

The voice was as loud as an earthquake, and the eldest son's knees knocked together in terror.

"I don't come to trouble you," the eldest son said meekly. "I merely thought you might be interested in looking at some of our brushes. Or if you'd prefer," he added quickly, "I could leave our catalog with you and I could drop by again, say, early next week."

"I don't want any brushes," the voice roared, "and I especially don't want any brushes next week."

"Oh," said the eldest son. By now his knees were knocking together so badly that he had to sit down.

Suddenly a great shadow fell over him, and the eldest son looked up. It was the dragon. The eldest son drew his sword, but the dragon lunged[3] and swallowed him in a single

3. **lunged** (lunjd): plunged forward suddenly.

DRAGON, DRAGON **651**

A Reading Skills and Strategies
Making Predictions
? What prediction can you make about the second son's ability to slay the dragon? What clues help you predict? [Possible responses: The second son will fail. Although he is strong, fairy tales and folk tales group events in threes, so it is more likely that the third son will succeed; the author describes the second son similarly to the way he described the first son, who also failed.]

B Reading Skills and Strategies
Comparing/Contrasting
? How does the second son's reaction to his father's advice compare to the eldest son's reaction? What conclusion can you draw? [Possible responses: Both sons think the cobbler's advice is odd and useless. The second son will fail, just as the eldest son did.]

C Cultural Connections
There are a great many superstitions associated with the moon in general and with a full moon in particular. For example, some people believe that a full moon drives all the clouds from the sky. The full moon is also believed to affect people's moods negatively. The term *lunatic*, an insane person, originally meant someone who was "moon-struck."

gulp, sword and all, and the eldest son found himself in the dark of the dragon's belly. "What a fool I was not to listen to my wise old father!" thought the eldest son. And he began to weep bitterly.

"Well," sighed the king the next morning, "I see the dragon has not been slain yet."

"I'm just as glad, personally," said the princess, sprinkling the queen. "I would have had to marry that eldest son, and he had warts."

Now the cobbler's middle son decided it was his turn to try. The middle son was very strong and was known far and wide for being able to lift up the corner of a church. He felt perfectly sure he could slay the dragon by simply laying into him, but he thought it would be only polite to ask his father's advice. So he went to his father and said to him, "Well, Father, I'm off to slay the dragon. Have you any advice for me?"

The cobbler told the middle son exactly what he'd told the eldest.

"When and if you come to the dragon's lair, recite the following poem.

652 TELL ME A TALE

Dragon, dragon, how do you do?
I've come from the king to murder you.

Say it very loudly and firmly, and the dragon will fall, God willing, at your feet."

"What an odd thing to say," thought the middle son. "The old man is not as wise as I thought. You have to take these dragons by surprise." But he kept his opinion to himself and set forth.

When he came in sight of the dragon's lair, the middle son spurred his horse to a gallop and thundered into the entrance, swinging his sword with all his might.

But the dragon had seen him while he was still a long way off, and being very clever, the dragon had crawled up on top of the door so that when the son came charging in, he went under the dragon and on to the back of the cave and slammed into the wall. Then the dragon chuckled and got down off the door, taking his time, and strolled back to where the man and the horse lay unconscious from the terrific blow. Opening his mouth as if for a yawn, the dragon swallowed the middle son in a single gulp and put the horse in the freezer to eat another day.

"What a fool I was not to listen to my wise old father," thought the middle son when he came to in the dragon's belly. And he too began to weep bitterly.

That night there was a full moon, and the dragon ravaged the countryside so terribly that several families moved to another kingdom.

"Well," sighed the king in the morning, "still no luck in this dragon business, I see."

"I'm just as glad, myself," said the princess, moving her mother, pot and all, to the window, where the sun could get at her. "The cobbler's middle son was a kind of humpback."

Professional Notes

Dragons are legendary monsters found in nearly all cultures, although they have widely different meanings.

To the ancient Hebrews and Christians, the dragon is most often a symbol of evil, death, and destruction. In the Christian tradition, the dragon represents sin, which is why these fantastical creatures are usually shown crushed under the heels of saints. But to other cultures, the dragon stands for good rather than evil. Ancient Greeks and Romans, for instance,

believed that dragons could translate the world's secrets to humans. As a result, Roman legions and ancient Norsemen used the dragon as a military symbol. Britain's Celtic conquerors used the dragon as a symbol of the king. Even today, the dragon is inscribed on the shield of the prince of Wales.

In Asian culture, the dragon is a symbol of good luck. For this reason, it is China's national emblem. The dragon is considered god-like to those who follow the Taoist tradition.

Now the cobbler's youngest son saw that his turn had come. He was very upset and nervous, and he wished he had never been born. He was not clever, like his eldest brother, and he was not strong, like his second-eldest brother. He was a decent, honest boy who always minded his elders.

He borrowed a suit of armor from a friend of his who was a knight, and when the youngest son put the armor on, it was so heavy he could hardly walk. From another knight he borrowed a sword, and that was so heavy that the only way the youngest son could get it to the dragon's lair was to drag it along behind his horse like a plow.

When everything was in readiness, the youngest son went for a last conversation with his father.

"Father, have you any advice to give me?" he asked.

"Only this," said the cobbler. "When and if you come to the dragon's lair, recite the following poem.

Dragon, dragon, how do you do?
I've come from the king to murder you.

Say it very loudly and firmly, and the dragon will fall, God willing, at your feet."

"Are you certain?" asked the youngest son uneasily.

"As certain as one can ever be in these matters," said the wise old cobbler.

And so the youngest son set forth on his quest. He traveled over hill and dale and at last came to the dragon's cave.

The dragon, who had seen the cobbler's youngest son while he was still a long way off, was seated up above the door, inside the cave, waiting and smiling to himself. But minutes passed and no one came thundering in. The dragon frowned, puzzled, and was tempted to peek out. However, reflecting that patience seldom goes unrewarded, the dragon kept his head up out of sight and went on waiting. At last, when he could stand it no longer, the dragon craned[4] his neck and looked. There at the entrance of the cave stood a trembling young man in a suit of armor twice his size, struggling with a sword so heavy he could lift only one end of it at a time.

At sight of the dragon, the cobbler's youngest son began to tremble so violently that his armor rattled like a house caving in. He heaved with all his might at the sword and got the handle up level with his chest, but even now the point was down in the dirt. As loudly and firmly as he could manage, the youngest son cried—

Dragon, dragon, how do you do?
I've come from the king to murder you!

"What?" cried the dragon, flabbergasted. "You? *You?* Murder *Me???*" All at once he began to laugh, pointing at the little cobbler's son. *"He he he ho ha!"* he roared, shaking all over, and tears filled his eyes. *"He he*

4. **craned:** stretched (the neck) as a crane does.

DRAGON, DRAGON **653**

D **Elements of Literature**
Theme
? What traits does the author suggest are most effective against evil? [Possible response: He suggests that decency, honesty, and respect for elders are more effective than cleverness and strength.]

E **Critical Thinking**
Speculating
? Do you think the youngest son will follow his father's advice? Why or why not? [Possible response: Yes, because he listens to his elders and respects their wisdom.]

F **Historical Connections**
Armor was supposed to give the most protection with the least weight, but a full suit of medieval armor weighed from forty to sixty pounds. Armor worn in tournaments weighed at least twice as much. It's no wonder the third son is trembling under the weight of all that metal.

G **Reading Skills and Strategies**
Identifying Cause and Effect
? What causes the dragon to laugh at the third son? [Possible responses: He does not think that such a small, weak opponent poses any threat to him; he finds the poem ridiculous.]

Using Students' Strengths

Verbal Learners
The cobbler directs his sons to disarm the dragon with a silly poem. Have students write other brief silly rhymes the cobbler's sons could use that would have the same effect on the dragon. The poems should be in the form of rhyming couplets. Then have students read their poems to the class to see which ones elicit the most laughter and would thus be most effective against the dragon.

RESPONDING TO THE ART

Activity. Ask students to identify the humorous elements of the illustration. Have students consider what they might add to make the illustration even funnier.

654 TELL ME A TALE

Taking a Second Look

Review: Identifying Main Idea/ Supporting Details

Remind students that the *main idea* of a work of literature is the message, opinion, insight, or lesson that is the focus of the work. Explain that the main idea is the most important idea that a writer wants a reader to remember. A writer may state the main idea directly or let readers infer it from the details.

Point out that *supporting details* are the information the writer includes to support or explain the main idea. Be sure students understand that supporting details are small bits of information, such as facts, examples, or descriptions that the writer includes to further develop, explain, or illustrate the main idea.

Activities

1. Have students identify the theme, or main idea, in "Dragon, Dragon."
2. Ask students to list at least five details that support the main idea.
3. Students can also write a summary that states the main idea and the important supporting details.

he ho ho ho ha ha!" laughed the dragon. He was laughing so hard he had to hang onto his sides, and he fell off the door and landed on his back, still laughing, kicking his legs helplessly, rolling from side to side, laughing and laughing and laughing.

The cobbler's son was annoyed. "I *do* come from the king to murder you," he said. "A person doesn't like to be laughed at for a thing like that."

"*He he he!*" wailed the dragon, almost sobbing, gasping for breath. "Of course not, poor dear boy! But really, *he he*, the *idea* of it, *ha ha ha!* And that simply ri*dic*ulous *poem!*" Tears streamed from the dragon's eyes, and he lay on his back perfectly helpless with laughter.

"It's a good poem," said the cobbler's youngest son loyally. "My father made it up." And growing angrier he shouted, "I want you to stop that laughing, or I'll—I'll—" But the dragon could not stop for the life of him. And suddenly, in a terrific rage, the cobbler's son began flopping the sword end over end in the direction of the dragon. Sweat ran off the youngest son's forehead, but he labored on, blistering mad, and at last, with one supreme heave, he had the sword standing on its handle a foot from the dragon's throat. Of its own weight the sword fell, slicing the dragon's head off.

"*He he ho huk,*" went the dragon—and then he lay dead.

The two older brothers crawled out and thanked their younger brother for saving their lives. "We have learned our lesson," they said.

Then the three brothers gathered all the treasures from the dragon's cave and tied them to the back end of the youngest brother's horse and tied the dragon's head on behind the treasures and started home. "I'm glad I listened to my father," the youngest son thought. "Now I'll be the richest man in the kingdom."

There were hand-carved picture frames and silver spoons and boxes of jewels and chests of money and silver compasses and maps telling where there were more treasures buried when these ran out. There was also a curious old book with a picture of an owl on the cover, and inside, poems and odd sentences and recipes that seemed to make no sense.

When they reached the king's castle, the people all leaped for joy to see that the dragon was dead, and the princess ran out and kissed the youngest brother on the forehead, for secretly she had hoped it would be him.

"Well," said the king, "which half of the kingdom do you want?"

"My wizard's book!" exclaimed the wizard. "He's found my wizard's book!" He opened the book and ran his finger along under the words and then said in a loud voice, "Glmuzk, shkzmlp, blam!"

Instantly the queen stood before them in her natural shape, except she was soaking wet from being sprinkled too often. She glared at the king.

"Oh dear," said the king, hurrying toward the door.

A Critical Thinking
Interpreting
? Do you think this is what the cobbler thought would happen when he advised his sons to recite the poem? Why or why not? [Possible response: Yes, because the poem could not affect the dragon any other way. Further, the cobbler has been described as wise, and his actions reinforce that description.]

B Elements of Literature
Main Idea/Theme
? What lesson did the brothers learn? [Possible responses: The brothers learned that they should listen to their father; they learned that they should respect the opinions of their parents or people who are wiser than they are.]

C Reading Skills and Strategies
Making Inferences
? What might this book be? [It is probably the wizard's book of spells.] What clues help you infer this? [Possible responses: The book is described as containing "poems and odd sentences and recipes that seemed to make no sense." These are the wizard's magic spells and chants. The book was said to have been misplaced earlier in the story.]

Getting Students Involved

Cooperative Learning
Arrange students in a Think-Pair-Share to rework "Dragon, Dragon" as a children's picture book. Students should first select the key scenes and then rewrite them to suit a second-to third-grade audience. Then have group members divide up the tasks of planning the layout of the book (number of pages, placement of illustrations and text, and so on), writing the text, illustrating the pages and combining the pages and binding them into a book. When they are finished with their picture books, each group can read them to younger students.

MEET THE WRITER

A Twister of Tales

With characters like the hero who is so weak and puny he can't lift the sword and the wizard who can't remember his magic, **John Gardner** (1933–1982) poked fun at old-fashioned fairy tales. The story you've just read is from *Dragon, Dragon, and Other Tales* (1975), his first collection for young readers. Gardner became famous with *Grendel* (1971), a novel for adults that offers a twist on the well-known English epic *Beowulf*. The epic is about the hero Beowulf, who battles and finally defeats the monster Grendel. Gardner twists this tale by telling his story from the monster's point of view.

When Gardner was young, his favorite storytellers were Charles Dickens and Walt Disney, the producer of animated films. Gardner believed that both created wonderful cartoon images, told stories that were as direct as fairy tales, and knew the value of broad comedy spiced up with a little weeping. Gardner kept a bust of Dickens in his study "to keep me honest."

Gardner was only forty-nine years old when he died in a motorcycle accident.

John Gardner's Garden of Tales

For more twisted fairy tales, read the other stories in *Dragon, Dragon, and Other Tales*. For twisted verses, look for Gardner's *A Child's Bestiary* (both published by Random House), a popular collection of humorous poems about animals.

READ ON

Fight to the Finish

After he conquers Troy, Ulysses angers the gods, who determine that his voyage home will last ten years. On the journey he meets the one-eyed Cyclops; the sorceress Circe, who turns men into pigs; and the nightmarish monsters Scylla and Charybdis. *The Adventures of Ulysses* (Scholastic), retold by Bernard Evslin, recounts the story of a great man's tortured path and his fight to reclaim his home.

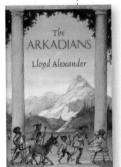

Three's Company

Join the charming bean counter Lucian as he crashes his way through an epic adventure in *The Arkadians* (Dutton) by Lloyd Alexander. Lucian's companions are a hotheaded girl and a donkey-poet. You'll find romance, magic, and wisdom in this unforgettable story.

Signs of Light

On his eleventh birthday, Will Stanton discovers two strange doors standing alone on a snowy hill. After he enters one of them, he learns that he is the last of the immortal Old Ones, and his whole life changes. In *The Dark Is Rising* (Aladdin) by Susan Cooper, Will searches for the six magical signs that will save the world.

Icy Enchantments

Find out what happened to the powerful gods and goddesses of the Aesir in *Norse Gods and Giants* (Doubleday) by Ingri and Edgar Darin d'Aulaire. Explore fantastic worlds of trolls, elves, gnomes, and more in this exciting collection of tales.

Writer's Workshop

Planning

- **Block Schedule**
  Block Scheduling Lesson Plans with Pacing Guide
- **One-Stop Planner**
  CD-ROM with Test Generator

Technology HELP

See Writer's Workshop 1 CD-ROM. *Assignment: Story.*

ASSIGNMENT
Write an original story.

AIM
To be creative.

AUDIENCE
Children, teenagers, or adults (you decide).

NARRATIVE WRITING

STORY

When you write a **story,** you draw on your experience and your original ideas to create a new, imaginary world.

Professional Model

This excerpt from a Japanese folk tale illustrates many of the elements of fiction.

Long, long ago, in a small village nestled beside the Sea of Japan, there lived two brothers. The older brother was very wealthy and owned many things, but the younger brother was poor and had nothing.

One day, toward the end of December, when the people of the land were preparing to welcome the New Year, the younger brother went to his brother's home to borrow some rice.

"We have no rice for New Year's breakfast," he said. "Will you lend me just a little? I shall return it as soon as I can."

But the older brother was greedy, and he did not want to lend even a small amount of rice. "I haven't any to spare," he said, and he turned his brother away.

The young brother was sad and disappointed. He walked slowly down the narrow dirt road that led back to

The setting is revealed in the first sentence.

The second sentence introduces the two main characters.

The events of the plot begin.

Dialogue is used to develop the younger brother's personality.

The main problem, or conflict, is introduced.

658 TELL ME A TALE

Resources: Print and Media

Writing and Language
- *Portfolio Management System*
    Prewriting, p. 183
    Peer Editing, p. 184
    Assessment Rubric, p. 185
- *Workshop Resources*
    Revision Strategy Teaching Notes, p. 33
    Revision Strategy Transparencies 17, 18

- *Writer's Workshop 1 CD-ROM*
    Story

The history
of the written
word is rich and
Page 1

Once upon a time

(continued)

> his house. What would he say to his wife, coming home empty-handed? What would they eat on New Year's Day? He looked out at the cold blue sea, beating against the shore. He looked up at the murky skies full of the promise of snow, but he found no comfort anywhere.
>
> —from "The Magic Mortar," retold by Yoshiko Uchida

The setting adds to the problem.

Prewriting

1. Writer's Notebook

Are there any entries in your Writer's Notebook you'd like to develop into a story? If not, try the activities below.

2. Freewriting and Brainstorming

a. Start with yourself. Often we write best about what we know best. Think of experiences you've had that you feel comfortable sharing with others. Freewrite about one or more of them. Use your experience as the basis of your story, but feel free to make changes that might improve your story.

b. Character watch. Begin with characters. Think of adults, children, and animals who have caught your attention. Then, use your imagination to freewrite about them. To flesh out each character, write a profile of him or her. Use the Character Profile on the right as a guide.

Character Profile
Name:
Age:
Family:
Friends:
Home:
Wishes:
Physical appearance:
Favorite clothes:
Personality traits:
Typical behavior:
Favorite places:
Special qualities or talents:

WRITER'S WORKSHOP **659**

Introducing the Writer's Workshop

Read the Professional Model as the students follow along, and encourage them to discuss their reactions to the story. How is the opening like openings in other stories they've read? What is the conflict that the writer introduces? What details provide insight into the characters' traits and goals?

- Be sure students understand the side-margin comments. Ask them to identify the setting, characters, plot, conflict, and dialogue.
- Discuss with students what makes an effective short story:
  1. vivid characters—realistic or fantastic
  2. a dramatic conflict
  3. interesting dialogue
  4. engaging details
  5. a compelling plot
- Be sure students understand the purpose of their writing: to write a short story.
- Remind students to choose a topic or character they find personally interesting; this will help them convey their enthusiasm to the reader.

Teaching the Writer's Workshop

Prewriting

Have students use the techniques suggested on this and the next page (or any other methods that may be helpful to them) to come up with ideas. For example, students may want to write a sequel to a story they have read, using the same characters and introducing new conflicts, additional characters, and perhaps a new setting.

- To help students identify the details they can include in their character profiles, have them first make a character profile of themselves or of a familiar character in a story they've read. Students should list distinguishing characteristics. Then suggest that students invent similar details for their characters to make them realistic and compelling.
- In addition, have students review the stories in this collection before determining their main character's goals and problems.

Reaching All Students

Struggling Writers

If some students are having difficulty starting their writing, suggest they make storyboards or story maps that outline their ideas. Encourage students to use as much visual detail as they can when they make their storyboards or maps, so they can later re-create those visual details with words.

Advanced Learners

Invite these students to consider using more advanced storytelling techniques. For example, they might incorporate flashbacks and flash forwards. They might also consider telling their story from an intriguing point of view. Students can also explore the effects they can create with symbolism and figures of speech.

T659

Prewriting (continued)

- Ask students to identify the primary obstacles their characters face. Remind them to create plausible goals for their characters so their plots will make sense. Point out that unusual characters, such as mythical beings or fairy tale characters, can have unusual goals. However, the problems must be solved logically— that is, in relation to the character's skills, traits, and to any help he or she may have.

As they create their plot, students should . . .

- Consider the *theme* or main idea they wish to convey.
- Be sure to include a beginning, middle, and end.
- Decide where to place the *climax,* or point of greatest interest. Remind students that the climax usually comes very close to the end of the story.
- Resolve all loose ends, so the reader isn't left wondering about a character or event mentioned in the story.

Strategies for Elaboration

Listening can help you write realistic **dialogue**—words spoken by characters in a story. Take time to listen closely to people talking. Notice the following:

- use of contractions and slang
- use of half-finished sentences and phrases
- interruptions—how, when, and why speakers interrupt one another

Read your dialogue aloud, or ask a classmate to do so. Keep changing it until it sounds real.

Language Link
H E L P

Formal and informal English: page 638.

Sentence Workshop
H E L P

Joining sentences: page 663.

660 TELL ME A TALE

---

3. Looking for Trouble

To make a story, you have to give your main character a problem to resolve. For example, your character may have to deal with a natural disaster or a challenging contest or the loss of a friend. Brainstorm to come up with problems and ways your character would deal with them.

4. Hatching a Plot

For your **plot,** the core of your story, plan four elements:

- a problem (also called a **conflict**)
- a **series of events** that the problem sets in motion
- a **high point,** or **climax,** when the problem is settled
- an **outcome,** which shows how things work out afterward

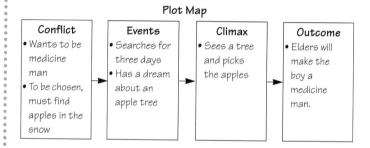

Plot Map

Conflict	Events	Climax	Outcome
• Wants to be medicine man • To be chosen, must find apples in the snow	• Searches for three days • Has a dream about an apple tree	• Sees a tree and picks the apples	• Elders will make the boy a medicine man.

5. Sketching the Setting

The following questions will help you plan your setting:

- Is your story set in the past, the present, or the future?
- At what time of day and in what season does your story begin? Is the setting part of the conflict?
- What time period does your story cover—hours? days? years?
- What objects and scenery are important to the setting?

Using Students' Strengths

Kinesthetic Learners

Encourage students to improvise the action in their stories. Explain that acting out some of the scenes will help them be sure they have added enough details to make the events logical or convincing. Students may need to work in small groups to complete this activity.

Interpersonal Learners

Provide opportunities for students to talk about their plots with other students. Sharing their information offers students an opportunity to get informal feedback on the characters, settings, and themes they have chosen. It also helps them organize and clarify their writing and use supporting details effectively.

APPLES IN THE SNOW

Snow Child used to be called Little Bear. He was as free as the wind with his Cherokee family and was very happy. The only thing he longed for was to become the sacred medicine man of the tribe.

The elders, though, thought it unwise for him to become the medicine man. They said that he was too wild and too young. But Little Bear persisted. Finally, the elders said, "Go out into the hills. If you can find apples in the snow, it will be a sign that the Great Spirit wills you to become our medicine man."

Little Bear fasted all day. Then he set out into the hills. He climbed and searched to no avail for that day and the next. He stopped often to pray to Mon-o-La, the earth, and to the Great Spirit.

Then, on the third night, Little Bear had a dream. He dreamed that he was standing by a golden apple tree. Around it the snow was melted. Then from inside the tree came a musical voice. "Come pick my apples. I grow them for you, for you, for you. . . ." Little Bear awoke. He tried to think what the dream meant. While he thought, he walked up the hill.

Thinking and walking, he soon reached the top. There he began to pray. When he opened his eyes, there was the golden apple tree of his dream. He waited for the voice to come, but when it did not, he decided that it had spoken in his dream and that was enough. So he picked the apples and started down the mountain, thanking the goodness of the spirits. When he turned to look at the tree, it was gone.

When he reached his village, there was great feasting. The elders told him that the golden tree was the tree of Mon-o-La. So Little Bear became Snow Child and would soon become the tribe's sacred medicine man.

—Jane Caflisch
Kensington, Maryland

The first paragraph introduces the main character and tells us what he wants.

This dialogue establishes Little Bear's main conflict: The elders think he is too young.

A series of events is narrated.

Sensory details paint a picture of the dream's setting.

This is the high point, or climax. Little Bear has met his challenge.

The conflict is resolved.

As class members read the Student Model, be sure they understand the side notes. You can extend the discussion by having students respond to the following questions:

? Why does the writer introduce the main character and his goal in the first sentence?

? What purpose does the dialogue serve?

? What is the story's plot? How would you arrange the main events on a time line?

? Which sensory details did you find most effective? Why?

? What happens in the climax, the point of greatest interest?

? How is the conflict resolved?

? What other techniques does the writer use that you might use in your story?

Getting Students Involved

Cooperative Learning

Arrange students in a Think-Pair-Share to evaluate the opening paragraphs of their stories. Remind students that the reader's attention is often won or lost with a story's opening lines. Have one member of the group read his or her opening paragraph aloud. The other members should listen carefully, think about their responses, then share their responses with a partner. The partners should then agree on a response to share with the entire group. Have students continue the activity until every member has had a chance to share his or her opening paragraph. Then have students work together to revise opening paragraphs, as needed. Encourage them to consider opening their stories with dialogue or description to generate reader interest and suggest their theme.

Enrichment Activity

After students have written their second drafts, have them consider their tone and style of writing. For example, did they select the appropriate level of word choice for their subject, audience, and purpose? Where could they add dialogue and sensory details to enliven their writing? Students should also read their stories aloud to hear the rhythm of their sentences.

Drafting

- If you have not yet taught the Student Model, do so before students begin their drafts.
- Remind students to use every other line when they write their drafts. They should also leave extra space in the right margin for comments and editing marks.

Evaluating and Revising

Allow students time for their stories to sit and "cool off" between drafts. Explain that problems often become much clearer if you let some time elapse between writing and revision.

- Remind students not to be afraid to make significant changes as they revise. Explain that they will most likely change the order of paragraphs, delete sections, and add new passages.
- If students are using a computer, have them save successive drafts in different computer files. Point out that they might find a use for deleted material later.

Publishing

Students who wouldn't mind sharing their story with a larger audience should look to the school literary magazine, newspaper, or Web site for publication.

Reflecting

Students might prepare a brief reflection on what they learned from the process of writing a short story by answering these questions:

- What did you learn about your ability to imagine and create a story?
- What did you learn about the process of writing?

To focus students' thinking, have them review the evaluation criteria for "a good story."

Resources ━━━

Peer Editing Forms and Rubrics
- *Portfolio Management System*, p. 184

Revision Strategy Transparencies
- *Workshop Resources*, p. 33

Grading Timesaver

Rubrics for the Writer's Workshop assignment appear on p. 185 of the *Portfolio Management System*.

■ *Evaluation Criteria*

A good story

1. *centers on a major conflict that a character has to solve*
2. *includes a series of related events that reach a climax*
3. *provides a vivid description of the setting*
4. *uses dialogue and actions to develop the characters*
5. *ends with a resolution of the conflict*

Language/Grammar Link
H E L P

Homophones: pages 597 and 647. Effect *vs.* affect: page 607.

Communications Handbook
H E L P

See Proofreaders' Marks.

Publishing Tip
Working with classmates, gather your stories into a class literary magazine.

Drafting

1. Write the Middle First

Start right in with the events of your story. Write quickly, using action details and putting the events in time order. If your writing takes you in a direction you didn't expect, see where it leads.

2. Craft a Strong Beginning

Your first few sentences should pull your readers into the story. Make your readers curious by creating suspense or by showing your characters in action.

3. Round Out the Ending

Show how your characters have been affected by the problem and by the way it was settled. Have they changed or learned a lesson? How will their future be different now?

Evaluating and Revising

1. Details, Details!

Details make the difference between a flat story and a story with zing. Think about how you could improve your story.

- Where could you add action details to bring events to life?
- Where could you replace explanations with dialogue (words that characters say)?
- Where could you add sensory details to create more vivid pictures of your characters or setting?

2. Self-Evaluation

Reread your story, keeping the evaluation guidelines in mind. Look for parts of your story that don't seem to work. Would it help to move them? Could you replace them with details or dialogue? Plan changes that you think are necessary.

3. Revising

Make any changes you think would improve your story. As a last touch, add a snappy title that relates to your characters, setting, or plot.

Reaching All Students

English Language Learners

English language learners may have difficulty with idiomatic expressions, especially when they have to select the correct preposition to follow a particular word. To the right are some especially troublesome combinations you may wish to help students learn:

Incorrect	Revised
apologize about	apologize for
bored of	bored with
capable to	capable of
in search for	in search of
interested about	interested in
outlook of life	outlook on life
puzzled on	puzzled at, puzzled by
similar with	similar to

Other tricky prepositions include *among/between, could of/could have,* and *off of/off.*

Sentence Workshop

OBJECTIVES
1. Identify ways to join sentences
2. Create compound and complex sentences

JOINING SENTENCES

Suppose you're writing a summary of "Medusa's Head" and you notice the short, choppy sentences beginning to pile up:

ORIGINAL   King Acrisios is an evil, selfish man. His brother, Proitos, drives him from his kingdom. Acrisios cares nothing for his daughter, Danae. He wants to have a son to succeed him. His wife bore him no son. He asks the oracle of Apollo for advice.

By using a comma plus *or, but,* or *and,* you can connect two related sentences that express equally important ideas. The result is a **compound sentence.**

REVISION   King Acrisios is an evil, selfish man**, and** his brother, Proitos, drives him from his kingdom.

You can also combine short sentences when one sentence helps explain the other sentence by telling *how, where, why,* or *when.* You can show this connection by adding words such as *after, although, as, because, before, if, since, so that, until, when, whether,* and *while.* The result is a **complex sentence.** Your choice of a word to combine your sentences will depend on what you want your new sentence to say.

REVISION   Acrisios cares nothing for his daughter, Danae, **because** he wants to have a son to succeed him. **Since** his wife bore him no son, he asks the oracle of Apollo for advice.

Writer's Workshop Follow-up: Revision

Take out your story, and exchange papers with a classmate. Mark any passages that seem dull and choppy because of too many short sentences. Then, suggest ways of combining the sentences. Exchange papers again, and revise yours to eliminate any choppiness your partner found.

Language Handbook
H E L P

See Combining Sentences, page 739.

Try It Out

Rewrite this paragraph by combining sentences, using the techniques discussed. Compare your revisions in class.

Zeus and Hermes come to earth in disguise. They ask for food and shelter. Baucis and Philemon have little to offer. Still, they are generous to the strangers. The gods offer Baucis and Philemon a reward. They have been hospitable.

Resources

Workshop Resources
• Worksheet p. 51

Try It Out
Sample Answers
Zeus and Hermes come to earth in disguise, **and** they ask for food and shelter. Baucis and Philemon have little to offer, **but** they are generous to the strangers. The gods offer Baucis and Philemon a reward **because** they have been hospitable.

Assessing Learning

Quick Check: Varying Sentence Structure
Have students identify the following sentences as compound or complex.
1. Acrisios tries to avoid his fate, but it catches up to him in the end. [compound]
2. Ali Baba makes Morgiana his chief housekeeper because she is clever, brave, and strong. [complex]
3. The Emperor is embarrassed when a child says he has no clothes on. [complex]
4. The lion roars boastfully, and the other animals are afraid to walk in the forest. [compound]
5. The dragon brings mayhem to the town until the cobbler's youngest son slays the monster. [complex]

OBJECTIVES
1. Use a map to identify geographic locations
2. Use a compass rose to identify directions on a map
3. Recognize and analyze events on a time line
4. Use a time line to indicate the chronology of important events

Teaching the Lesson

Ask students to describe kinds of maps they have seen or used. [Possible responses: road maps, globe, street maps, atlases.] Ask students to describe time lines they have seen. [Possible responses: important dates in history (in a textbook or museum exhibit), important periods in Earth's development (in a science book).] Explain that a map can help students find specific places, distances between places, and the compass direction of one place in relation to another. Point out that a time line can help students recognize and explain how events occurred in time.

Using the Strategies

Answers
1. north
2. The United States of America
3. She was married and became a U. S. citizen.
4. Mexico, Spain, the United States

Situation

Imagine that your grandmother was born in Mexico. You show her the map on page 599. Your grandmother points to the Toltec sites on the map. "This is near my city," she says. "It is called Mexico City now. Get me a pencil. I'll show you when some big things happened." Then she draws a time line like the one on this page.

Strategies

Both **maps** and **time lines** are graphic ways to present information.

Use a time line to find out when events happened.
- A time line can show any amount of time, from a few days to millions of years.
- On a time line, events are shown in chronological order, with long-ago events at one end and more recent events at the other.

Use a map to find places.
- Most maps show some natural features, such as oceans and bodies of land. Some maps show things that people have made, such as cities and streets.
- The map on page 500 contains a **legend,** or **key,** which tells you what the symbols mean. It also has a **scale,** which compares distance on the map to distance in real life. One-half inch on that map equals one hundred miles.
- You can read a map to see how to get from one place to another. On page 137 you'll find a symbol called a **compass rose,** which shows where north, south, east, and west are located.

Using the Strategies
1. Find the Toltec sites on the map on page 599. In which direction would the Toltecs have had to travel to get to Quetzalcoatl's temple?
2. What large area of land is north of Mexico?
3. Look at the time line on this page. What two big events happened to your grandmother in 1961?
4. Name three countries that had something to do with events shown on the time line.

Extending the Strategies
- Find a recent map of Mexico and southern Texas. What large cities lie between Mexico City and San Antonio, Texas?
- Make a time line that shows important events in your life.

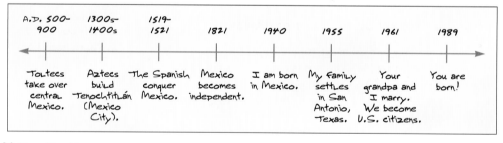

A.D. 500–900 · 1300s–1400s · 1519–1521 · 1821 · 1940 · 1955 · 1961 · 1989

Toltecs take over central Mexico. · Aztecs build Tenochtitlán (Mexico City). · The Spanish conquer Mexico. · Mexico becomes independent. · I am born in Mexico. · My family settles in San Antonio, Texas. · Your grandpa and I marry. We become U.S. citizens. · You are born!

664 TELL ME A TALE

Reaching All Students

Struggling Readers
To help students understand compass directions, have them draw a large compass rose on a sheet of paper and place it on the floor. Then have students stand on the rose, point to something in the classroom that is to the east, and turn their body to face the east and the object they identified. Repeat this procedure with each major direction of the compass rose.

English Language Learners
To help students understand the concept of a time line, guide them in creating a simple time line for the events in a day in their life, beginning with getting up in the morning and including such events as going to school, coming home, eating dinner or supper, doing homework, going to bed, and sleeping. You might also guide students in creating a time line for a one-week period.

Advanced Learners
Guide students in using their mathematics skills to calculate distances between cities, using the map scale. Students may also calculate travel time by car or jet, using average speeds for each (55 mph and 600 mph, respectively). Some students may find it interesting to research and report on time zones.

Learning for Life

Making Oral Presentations: The Storyteller's Art

OBJECTIVES
1. Research oral storytelling, select a story to share, analyze it, and practice telling it in a dramatic manner
2. Present the story to the class as part of a storytelling festival, reader's theater, or song

Problem

Many cultures have a rich tradition of oral storytelling. In Africa, for example, storytellers called *griots* memorize and recite traditional stories.

What makes a good oral story? How can we preserve our own family stories so that others can enjoy them?

Project

Study the techniques of oral storytelling, and use them to pass on tales about your own background and culture.

Preparation

1. Go to the library, and look up *oral storytelling*. Your librarian may be able to help you find information on the topic.
2. Read several folk tales that have been told by storytellers, or listen to tapes if you can. Write notes on why the stories are powerful and entertaining. Look for
   - memorable characters
   - clever dialogue
   - reflection
   - rhythm
   - humor

Procedure

1. Pick a story that you grew up with, and tell it as an oral storyteller would. Write down the story, keeping in mind that you will be presenting it orally. Try to include vivid language and interesting dialogue.
2. Practice your story by telling it to a friend or family member or in front of a mirror. Vary the tone of your voice, and use hand and body gestures to help dramatize the story.

Presentation

Present your tale in one of the following ways:

1. Storytelling Festival

Arrange a storytelling festival for your class. Decide which stories will be told and in what order. If possible, include stories that represent a number of different cultures or topics. If you can, arrange to make an audiotape or videotape of the performances. Afterward, discuss as a class what you learned about the cultures represented.

2. Reader's Theater

Team up with three or four students and create a dramatic reading based on one of your stories, with each person taking the part of a different character or the narrator. Rehearse the reading, and then perform it for a local elementary school or nursing home.

3. Song

Write a folk song about your story. The song should consist of several verses and a chorus. Record the song on audiotape. If possible, make a class tape including songs by other students. Submit it to your school or local library.

Processing

Discuss this question with your classmates:
- Why do people enjoy hearing and telling stories?

LEARNING FOR LIFE **665**

Resources

Viewing and Representing
HRW Multimedia Presentation Maker
Students may wish to use the *Multimedia Presentation Maker* to create the script for their story

Grading Timesaver

Rubrics for this Learning for Life project appear on p. 186 of the *Portfolio Management System*.

Developing Workplace Competencies

Preparation	Procedure	Presentation
• Acquiring data • Evaluating data • Making decisions	• Thinking creatively • Monitoring performance • Processing information • Demonstrating individual responsibility	• Working in teams • Selecting equipment • Communicating ideas and information • Exhibiting self-esteem • Reasoning

RESOURCE CENTER

HANDBOOK OF LITERARY TERMS 667

COMMUNICATIONS HANDBOOK 677

Putting Together a Multimedia Presentation 677
    Scanning, Clipping, and Creating 678
    Making an Interactive Program 678
    Word Processing 679

Research Strategies 680
    Using a Media Center or Library 680
    Using the Internet 680
    Evaluating Web Sources 681
    Listing Sources and Taking Notes 682

Reading Strategies 684
    Using Word Parts 684
    Summarizing, Paraphrasing, and
      Outlining 685

Study Skills 685
    Using a Thesaurus 685
    Using a Dictionary 686
    Reading Maps, Charts, and Graphs 687

Strategies for Taking Tests 688

Writing for Life 691
    Writing Business Letters 691
    Filling Out Forms 692

Proofreaders' Marks 692

LANGUAGE HANDBOOK 693

The Parts of Speech 693

Agreement 703

Using Verbs 706

Using Pronouns 713

Using Modifiers 717

The Prepositional Phrase 721

Sentences 724

Complements 729

Kinds of Sentences 733

Writing Effective Sentences 736

Capital Letters 743

Punctuation 748, 754, 758

Spelling 761

Glossary of Usage 766

GLOSSARY 773

HANDBOOK OF LITERARY TERMS

For more information about a topic, turn to the page(s) in this book indicated on a separate line at the end of the entries. To learn more about *Alliteration,* for example, turn to pages 178–179.

On another line are cross-references to entries in this Handbook that provide closely related information. For instance, *Autobiography* contains a cross-reference to *Biography*.

ALLITERATION **The repetition of the same or very similar consonant sounds in words that are close together.** Alliteration usually occurs at the beginning of words, as in the phrase "*busy* as a *bee*." It can also occur within or at the end of words. The following poem repeats the sounds of *s* and *p*:

> **January**
> In January
> it's so nice
> while slipping
> on the sliding ice
> to sip hot chicken soup
> with rice.
> Sipping once
> sipping twice
> sipping chicken soup
> with rice.
>
> —Maurice Sendak

Alliteration can establish a mood, emphasize words, and serve as a memory aid. If you ever twisted your tongue around a line like "She sells seashells by the seashore" or "How much wood could a woodchuck chuck if a woodchuck could chuck wood," you have already had some fun with alliteration.

See pages 178–179.

ALLUSION **A reference to a statement, a person, a place, or an event from literature, history, religion, mythology, politics, sports, or science.** Writers expect readers to recognize an allusion and to think, almost at the same time, about the literary work, person, place, or event that it refers to. The cartoon below makes an allusion you will recognize right away.

"Someone's been sleeping in my bed, too, and there she is on Screen Nine!"

AUTOBIOGRAPHY **The story of a person's life, written or told by that person.** Maya Angelou's account of her childhood experiences, called "Brother" (page 110), is taken from her autobiography *I Know Why the Caged Bird Sings*.

See pages 86–90, 108.
See also *Biography*.

BIOGRAPHY **The story of a real person's life, written or told by another person.** A classic American biography is Carl Sandburg's life of Abraham Lincoln. A biography popular with young adults is Russell Freedman's *The Mysterious Mr. Lincoln* (page 127). Frequent subjects of biographies are movie stars, television personalities, politicians, sports figures, self-made millionaires, and artists. Today biographies are among the most popular forms of literature.

See pages 108, 158–162.
See also *Autobiography*.

CHARACTER **A person or an animal in a story, play, or other literary work.** In some works, such as folk tales, animals are characters (see "How the Snake Got Poison" on page 546). In other works, such as fairy tales, a fantastic creature like a dragon is a character (see "Dragon, Dragon" on page 648). In still other works a character is a god or a hero (see "Quetzalcoatl" on page 600). Most often a character is an ordinary human being, as in "The All-American Slurp" (page 32).

The way in which a writer reveals the personality of a character is called **characterization.** A writer can reveal character in six ways:

1. by describing how the character looks and dresses
2. by letting the reader hear the character speak
3. by showing the reader how the character acts
4. by letting the reader know the character's inner thoughts and feelings
5. by revealing what other people in the story think or say about the character
6. by telling the reader directly what the character's personality is like (cruel, kind, sneaky, brave, and so on)

See pages 79, 96, 105, 147, 247, 288, 326, 366, 406, 462.

CONFLICT **A struggle or clash between opposing characters or opposing forces.** An **external conflict** is a struggle between a character and some outside force. This outside force may be another character, a society as a whole, or a natural force, like bitter-cold weather or a ferocious shark. An **internal conflict,** on the other hand, is a struggle between opposing desires or emotions within a person. A character with an internal conflict may be struggling against fear or loneliness or even being a sore loser.

See pages 2, 14, 15, 66, 79, 288, 326.

CONNOTATION **The feelings and associations that have come to be attached to a word.** For example, the words *inexpensive* and *cheap* are used to describe something that is not costly. The dictionary definitions, or **denotations,** of these words are roughly the same. A manufacturer of VCRs, however, would not use *cheap* in advertising its latest model, since the word *cheap* is associated with something that is not made well. *Inexpensive* would be a better choice. Connotations can be especially important in poetry.

See pages 355, 475.

DESCRIPTION **The kind of writing that creates a clear image of something, usually by using details that appeal to one or more of the senses: sight, hearing, smell, taste, and touch.** Description works through **images,** words that appeal to the five senses. Writers use description in all forms of writing—in fiction, nonfiction, and poetry. Here is a description of a famous character who has found a place in the hearts of readers everywhere. The writer's description appeals to the sense of sight, but it also gives a hint of the girl's character. Viewing this lone figure in a deserted train station, an "ordinary observer" would see

a child of about eleven, garbed in a very short, very tight, very ugly dress of yellowish gray wincey. She wore a faded brown sailor hat and beneath the hat, extending down her back, were two braids of very thick, decidedly red hair. Her face was small, white, and thin, also much freckled; her mouth was large and so were her eyes, that looked green in some lights and moods and gray in others.

—L. M. Montgomery,
from *Anne of Green Gables*

See pages 53, 65, 87, 109, 115.

DIALECT **A way of speaking characteristic of a particular region or of a particular group of people.** A dialect may have a distinct vocabulary, pronunciation system, and grammar. In a sense, we all speak dialects. The dialect that is dominant in a country or culture becomes accepted as the standard way of speaking. Writers often reproduce

HANDBOOK OF LITERARY TERMS

regional dialects or dialects that reveal a person's economic or social class. For example, the characters in the excerpt from *The Adventures of Tom Sawyer* (page 150) speak varieties of a nineteenth-century Missouri dialect. The characters in "How the Snake Got Poison" (page 546) use an African American dialect spoken in the rural South. In the passage below, a spunky young girl gets up the courage to ask her uncle a hard question (she is speaking an African American urban dialect).

> So there I am in the navigator seat. And I turn to him and just plain ole ax him. I mean I come right on out with it. . . . And like my mama say, Hazel—which is my real name and what she remembers to call me when she bein serious—when you got somethin on your mind, speak up and let the chips fall where they may. And if anybody don't like it, tell em to come see your mama. And Daddy look up from the paper and say, You hear your mama good, Hazel. And tell em to come see me first. Like that. That's how I was raised.
> So I turn clear round in the navigator seat and say, "Look here, . . . you gonna marry this girl?"
>
> —Toni Cade Bambara,
> from "Gorilla, My Love"

See page 553.

DIALOGUE **Conversation between two or more characters.** Most plays consist entirely of dialogue. Dialogue is also an important element in most stories and novels. It is very effective in revealing character and can add realism and humor to a story.

In the written form of a play, such as *Blanca Flor* (page 440), dialogue appears without quotation marks. In prose or poetry, however, dialogue is usually enclosed in quotation marks.

DRAMA **A story written to be acted in front of an audience.** A drama, such as *Blanca Flor* (page 440), can also be appreciated and enjoyed in written form. The related events that take place within a drama are often separated into **acts.** Each act is often made up of shorter sections, or **scenes.** Most plays have three acts, but there are many, many variations. The elements of drama are often described as **introduction** or **exposition, complications, conflict, climax,** and **resolution.**

See page 406.
See also *Dialogue.*

ESSAY **A short piece of nonfiction prose.** An essay usually examines a subject from a personal point of view. Most essays are short. The French writer Michel de Montaigne (1533–1592) is credited with creating the essay. Robert Fulghum, a popular essayist, is represented in this book (page 292). "Scanning the Heavens" (page 539) and "Snakes: The Facts and the Folklore" (page 550) are examples of essays on scientific topics.

See pages 291, 296.

FABLE **A very brief story in prose or verse that teaches a moral or a practical lesson about how to succeed in life.** The characters of most fables are animals that behave and speak like human beings. Some of the most popular fables are those thought to have been told by Aesop, who was a slave in ancient Greece. You may be familiar with his fable about the sly fox that praises the crow for her beautiful voice and begs her to sing for him. When the crow opens her mouth to sing, she lets fall from her beak the piece of cheese that the fox had been after the whole time.

See page 69.
See also *Folk Tale, Myth.*

FANTASY **Imaginative writing that carries the reader into an invented world where the laws of nature as we know them do not operate.** In fantasy worlds, fantastic forces are often at play. Characters wave magic wands, cast spells, or appear and disappear at will. These characters may be ordinary human beings—or they may be Martians, elves, giants, or fairies. Some of the oldest fantasy stories, such as "The Nightingale" (page 215), are

HANDBOOK OF LITERARY TERMS 669

T669

called **fairy tales.** A newer type of fantasy, one that deals with a future world changed by science, is called **science fiction.** "All Summer in a Day" (page 313) is Ray Bradbury's science fiction story about life as he imagines it on the planet Venus.

FICTION **A prose account that is made up rather than true.** The term *fiction* usually refers to novels and short stories.

See also *Fantasy, Nonfiction.*

FIGURE OF SPEECH **A word or phrase that describes one thing in terms of something else and is not literally true.** Figures of speech always involve some sort of imaginative comparison between seemingly unlike things. The most common forms are **simile** ("My heart is like a singing bird"), **metaphor** ("The road was a ribbon of moonlight"), and **personification** ("The leaves were whispering to the night").

See pages 183–184, 325, 511.
See also *Metaphor, Personification, Simile.*

FLASHBACK **A scene that breaks the normal time order of the plot to show a past event.** A flashback can be placed anywhere in a story, even at the beginning. There, it usually gives background information. Part of *The Adventure of the Speckled Band* (page 409) is told during a flashback.

See page 418.

FOLK TALE **A story with no known author, originally passed on from one generation to another by word of mouth.** Folk tales generally differ from myths in that they are not about gods and they were never connected with religion or beliefs. There are a number of folk tales in this book, including "How the Snake Got Poison" (page 545), "The Seventh Sister" (page 529), "Why Dogs Chase Cats" (page 554) and "The Emperor's New Clothes" (page 625). Sometimes the same folk tale appears in many cultures. For example, the old European folk tale of Cinderella has turned up in hundreds of other cultures.

See page 608.
See also *Fable, Myth, Oral Tradition.*

FORESHADOWING **The use of clues or hints to suggest events that will occur later in the plot.** Foreshadowing builds suspense or anxiety in the reader or viewer. In a movie, for example, strange, alien creatures glimpsed among the trees may foreshadow danger for the exploring astronauts.

See pages 408, 431.
See also *Suspense.*

FREE VERSE **Poetry that is "free" of a regular meter and rhyme scheme.** Poets writing in free verse try to capture the natural rhythms of ordinary speech. The following poem is written in free verse:

> **The City**
> If flowers want to grow
> right out of the concrete sidewalk cracks
> I'm going to bend down to smell them.
>
> —David Ignatow

See page 179.
See also *Poetry, Rhyme, Rhythm.*

IMAGERY **Language that appeals to the senses—sight, hearing, touch, taste, and smell.** Most images are visual—that is, they create pictures in the mind by appealing to the sense of sight. Images can also appeal to the senses of hearing, touch, taste, and smell. They can appeal to several senses at once. Though imagery is element in all types of writing, it is especially important in poetry. The following poem is full of images about rain:

> **The Storm**
> In fury and terror
> the tempest broke,
> it tore up the pine

and shattered the oak,
yet the hummingbird hovered
within the hour
sipping clear rain
from a trumpet flower.

—Elizabeth Coatsworth

See pages 121, 124, 334.

IRONY **A contrast between what is expected and what really happens.** Irony can create powerful effects, from humor to horror. Here are some examples of situations that would make us feel a sense of irony:

- A shoemaker wears shoes with holes in them.
- The children of a famous dancer trip over their own feet.
- It rains on the day a group of weather forecasters have scheduled a picnic.
- Someone asks "How's my driving?" after going through a stop sign.
- A Great Dane runs away from a mouse.
- Someone living in the desert keeps a boat in her yard.
- A relative of a police officer robs a bank.
- Someone walks out in the midst of a hurricane and says, "Nice day."

See pages 204, 212.

LEGEND **A story, usually based on some historical fact, that has been handed down from one generation to the next.** Legends often grow up around famous figures or events. For example, legend has it that Abraham Lincoln (see page 127) was a simple, ordinary man. Yet Lincoln was, in fact, a complicated man of unusual ability and ambition. The stories about King Arthur and his knights are legends based on the exploits of an actual warrior-king who probably lived in Wales in the 500s. Legends often make use of fantastic details.

LIMERICK **A humorous five-line verse that has a regular meter and the rhyme scheme *aabba*.**

Limericks often have place names in their rhymes. The following limerick was published in Edward Lear's *Book of Nonsense* in 1846, when limericks were at the height of their popularity:

There was an old man of Peru
Who dreamt he was eating a shoe.
    He awoke in the night
    With a terrible fright
And found it was perfectly true!

MAIN IDEA **The most important idea expressed in a piece of writing.** Sometimes the main idea is stated directly by the writer; other times the reader must infer it.

See pages 212, 279, 296.

METAPHOR **A comparison between two unlike things in which one thing becomes another thing.** An **extended metaphor** carries the comparison through an entire work. A metaphor is an important type of figure of speech. Metaphors are used in all forms of writing and are common in ordinary speech. When you say about your grumpy friend "He's such a bear today," you do not mean that he is growing bushy black fur. You mean that he is in a bad mood and ready to attack, just the way a bear might be.

Metaphors differ from **similes,** which use specific words, such as *like, as, than,* and *resembles,* to make their comparisons. "He is behaving like a bear" is a simile.

The following famous poem compares fame to an insect:

Fame is a bee.
It has a song—
It has a sting—
Ah, too, it has a wing.

—Emily Dickinson

See pages 183–184, 185,
192, 325, 334.
See also *Figure of Speech, Personification, Simile.*

HANDBOOK OF LITERARY TERMS 671

MOOD **The overall emotion created by a work of literature.** Mood can often be described in one or two adjectives, such as *eerie, dreamy, mysterious, depressing*. The mood created by the poem below is sad and lonely:

> **Since Hanna Moved Away**
> The tires on my bike are flat.
> The sky is grouchy gray.
> At least it sure feels like that
> Since Hanna moved away.
>
> Chocolate ice cream tastes like prunes.
> December's come to stay.
> They've taken back the Mays and Junes
> Since Hanna moved away.
>
> Flowers smell like halibut.
> Velvet feels like hay.
> Every handsome dog's a mutt
> Since Hanna moved away.
>
> Nothing's fun to laugh about.
> Nothing's fun to play.
> They call me, but I won't come out
> Since Hanna moved away.
>
> —Judith Viorst

MYTH **A story that usually explains something about the world and involves gods and other superhuman beings.** Myths are deeply connected to the traditions and religious beliefs of the cultures that produced them. Myths often explain certain aspects of life, such as what thunder is or where sunlight comes from or why people die. **Origin myths,** or **creation myths,** explain how something in the world began or was created. Most myths are very old and were handed down orally for many centuries before being put in writing. The story of the hero Perseus (page 573) is a famous Greek myth. "Quetzalcoatl" (page 600) is a Mexican myth.

See pages 490, 495, 598, 599, 605, 608.
See also *Fable, Folk Tale, Oral Tradition.*

NARRATION **The kind of writing that relates a series of connected events to tell "what hap-** pened." Narration (also called **narrative**) is the form of writing most used by storytellers. Narration can be used to relate both fictional and true-life events.

See pages 262–263, 288.

NONFICTION **Prose writing that deals with real people, events, and places without changing any facts.** Popular forms of nonfiction are the autobiography, the biography, and the essay. Other examples of nonfiction are newspaper stories, magazine articles, historical writing, travel writing, science reports, and personal diaries and letters.

See also *Fiction.*

NOVEL **A fictional story that is usually between one hundred and five hundred book pages long.** A novel includes all the elements of storytelling—**plot, character, setting, theme,** and **point of view.** Because of its length, a novel usually has a more complex plot and more characters, settings, and themes than a short story.

ONOMATOPOEIA **The use of a word whose sound imitates or suggests its meaning.** Onomatopoeia (än′ō·mat′ō·pē′ə) is so natural to us that we begin to use it at a very early age. *Boom, bang, sniffle, rumble, hush, ding,* and *snort* are all examples of onomatopoeia. Onomatopoeia helps create the music of poetry. The following poem uses onomatopoeia:

> **Our Washing Machine**
> Our washing machine went whisity whirr
> Whisity whisity whisity whirr
> One day at noon it went whisity click
> Whisity whisity whisity click
> click grr click grr click grr click
>   Call the repairman
>   Fix it . . . quick.
>
> —Patricia Hubbell

See pages 181, 182, 192, 198.
See also *Alliteration.*

ORAL TRADITION **A collection of folk tales, songs, and poems that have been passed on orally from generation to generation.**

See pages 545, 551, 608.
See also *Folk Tale*.

PARAPHRASE **A restatement of a written work in which the meaning is expressed in other words.** A paraphrase of a poem should tell what the poem says, line by line, but in the paraphraser's own words. A paraphrase of a work of prose should briefly summarize the major events or ideas. Here is the first stanza of a famous poem, followed by a paraphrase:

> Once upon a midnight dreary, while I
>   pondered, weak and weary,
> Over many a quaint and curious volume of
>   forgotten lore—
> While I nodded, nearly napping, suddenly
>   there came a tapping,
> As of someone gently rapping, rapping at my
>   chamber door.
> "'Tis some visitor," I muttered, "tapping at my
>   chamber door—
>   Only this, and nothing more."
>
>   —Edgar Allan Poe,
>   from "The Raven"

One midnight when I was tired, I was reading an interesting old book that contains knowledge no one learns anymore. As I was dozing off, I suddenly heard what sounded like someone tapping at the door to the room. "It is someone coming to see me," I said to myself, "knocking at the door. That's all it is."

Notice that the paraphrase is neither as eerie nor as elegant as the poem.

PERSONIFICATION **A special kind of metaphor in which a nonhuman thing or quality is talked about as if it were human.** You would be using personification if you said "The leaves danced along the sidewalk." Of course, leaves don't dance— only people do. The poem below personifies the night wind:

> **Rags**
> The night wind
> rips a cloud sheet
> into rags,
> then rubs, rubs
> the October moon
> until it shines
> like a brass doorknob.
>
>   —Judith Thurman

In the cartoon below, history and fame are talked about as though they were human.

"While you were out for lunch, History passed by and Fame came knocking."

See pages 183–184, 325, 511.
See also *Figure of Speech, Metaphor, Simile.*

PLOT **The series of related events that make up a story.** Plot tells "what happens" in a short story, novel, play, or narrative poem. Most plots are built on these bare bones: An **introduction** tells who the characters are and what their **conflict,** or problem, is. **Complications** arise as the characters take steps to resolve the conflict. When the outcome of the conflict is decided one way or another, the plot reaches a **climax,** the most exciting moment in the story. The final part of the story is the **resolution,** when the characters' problems are solved and the story ends.

See pages 250, 326, 356. See also *Conflict.*

HANDBOOK OF LITERARY TERMS 673

POETRY A kind of rhythmic, compressed language that uses figures of speech and imagery to appeal to emotion and imagination. Poetry often has a regular pattern of rhythm, and it may have a regular pattern of rhyme. **Free verse** is poetry that has no regular pattern of rhythm or rhyme.

See pages 178–179, 183–184, 194–195.
See also *Free Verse, Imagery, Refrain, Rhyme, Rhythm, Speaker, Stanza.*

POINT OF VIEW The vantage point from which a story is told. Two common points of view are the omniscient (äm·nish′ənt) and the first person.

1. In the **omniscient,** or all-knowing, **point of view,** the narrator knows everything about the characters and their problems. This all-knowing narrator can tell us about the past, the present, and the future. Below is part of a story told from the omniscient point of view.

   Once upon a time in a small village, there were three houses built by three brother pigs. One house was made of straw, one was made of twigs, and one was made of brick. Each pig thought his house was the best and the strongest. A wolf—a very hungry wolf— lived just outside the town. He was practicing house-destroying techniques and was trying to decide which pig's house was the weakest.

2. In the **first-person point of view,** one of the characters, using the personal pronoun *I,* is telling the story. The reader becomes familiar with this narrator but can know only what he or she knows and can observe only what this character observes. All information about the story must come from this one narrator. In some cases, as in the following example, the information this narrator gives may not be correct:

   As soon as I found out some new pigs had moved into the neighborhood, I started to

practice my house-destroying techniques. I like to blow down houses and eat whoever is inside. The little pigs have built their houses of different materials—but I know I can blow 'em down in no time. That brick house looks especially weak.

See pages 326, 327, 335.

PROSE Any writing that is not poetry. Essays, short stories, novels, news articles, and letters are written in prose.

REFRAIN A repeated word, phrase, line, or group of lines in a poem or song or even in a speech. Refrains are usually associated with songs and poems, but they are also used in speeches and some other forms of literature. Refrains are often used to create rhythm. They are also used for emphasis and emotional effects.

See pages 168, 176.

RHYME The repetition of accented vowel sounds and all sounds following them. *Trouble* and *bubble* are rhymes, as are *clown* and *noun.* Rhymes in poetry help create rhythm and lend a songlike quality to a poem. They can also emphasize ideas, provide humor or delight, and aid memory.

End rhymes are rhymes at the end of lines. **Internal rhymes** are rhymes within lines. Here is an example of a poem with both kinds of rhymes:

In days of *old* when knights caught *cold,*
They were not quickly *cured;*
No aspirin *pill* would check the *ill,*
Which had to be *endured.*

—David Daiches,
from "Thoughts on Progress,"
from *The New Yorker*

Rhyme scheme is the pattern of rhyming sounds at the end of lines in a poem. Notice the pattern of end rhymes in the poem in the cartoon on page 675.

See pages 178, 192, 199, 202, 379, 385.

674 HANDBOOK OF LITERARY TERMS

RHYTHM **A musical quality produced by the repetition of stressed and unstressed syllables or by the repetition of other sound patterns.** Rhythm occurs in all language—written and spoken—but is particularly important in poetry. The most obvious kind of rhythm is the repeated pattern of stressed and unstressed syllables, called **meter.** Finding this pattern is called **scanning.** If you scan or say the following lines aloud, you'll hear a strong, regular rhythm. (Crowns, pounds, and guineas are British currency.)

> When I was one-and-twenty
>   I heard a wise man say,
> "Give crowns and pounds and guineas
>   But not your heart away."
>
>   —A. E. Housman,
>   from "When I Was One-and-Twenty"

See pages 179, 199, 202.
See also *Free Verse, Poetry.*

SETTING **The time and place of a story, a poem, or a play.** The setting can help create mood or atmosphere. Some examples of vivid settings are the gloomy planet where it rains for seven years in "All Summer in a Day" (page 313), the snow-covered countryside in "Zlateh the Goat" (page 241), and Ernie's Riverside restaurant in "Ta-Na-E-Ka" (page 16).

See pages 256, 312.

SHORT STORY **A fictional prose narrative that is from about five to twenty book pages long.** Short stories are usually built on a **plot** that consists of these elements: **introduction, conflict, complications, climax,** and **resolution.** Short stories are more limited than novels. They usually have only one or two major characters and one setting.

See page 326.
See also *Conflict, Fiction, Novel, Plot.*

SIMILE **A comparison between two unlike things using a word such as *like, as, than,* or *resembles.*** The simile (sim'ə·lē') is an important figure of speech. "His voice is as loud as a trumpet" and "Her eyes are like the blue sky" are similes. In the following poem the poet uses a simile to help us see a winter scene in a new way:

> **Scene**
> Little trees like pencil strokes
> black and still
> etched forever in my mind
> on that snowy hill.
>
>   —Charlotte Zolotow

See pages 44, 183, 325.
See also *Figure of Speech, Metaphor.*

SPEAKER **The voice talking to us in a poem.** Sometimes the speaker is identical to the poet, but often the speaker and the poet are not the same. A poet may speak as a child, a woman, a man, an animal, or even an object. In "The Sidewalk Racer" (page 187), the speaker is a skateboarder. The speaker of "Things to Do If You Are a Subway" (page 188) asks the reader to imagine that he or she is a subway train and to act like one.

STANZA **In a poem, a group of lines that form a unit.** A stanza in a poem is something like a paragraph in prose; it often expresses a unit of thought.

SUSPENSE **The anxious curiosity the reader feels about what will happen next in a story.** Any kind of writing that has a plot evokes some degree of suspense. Our sense of suspense is awakened in "The Gold Cadillac" (page 339), for example, when the narrator and her family begin their trip to Mississippi. The anxious and fearful warnings of the family's friends and relatives make us eager to read on to see if the journey will prove dangerous.

See pages 240, 247, 408, 418, 620.
See also *Foreshadowing, Plot.*

SYMBOL **A person, a place, a thing, or an event that has its own meaning *and* stands for something beyond itself as well.** Examples of symbols are all around us—in music, on television, and in everyday conversation. The skull and crossbones, for example, is a symbol of danger; the dove is a symbol of peace; and the red rose stands for true love. In literature, symbols are often more personal. For example, in "The Gold Cadillac," the Cadillac stands for success in the eyes of Wilbert and his family.

TALL TALE **An exaggerated, fanciful story that gets "taller and taller," more and more farfetched, the more it is told and retold.** The tall tale is an American story form. John Henry (page 169) is a famous tall-tale character. Here is a short tall tale:

When the temperature reached 118 degrees a whole field of corn popped. White flakes filled the air and covered the ground six inches deep and drifted across roads and collected on tree limbs.
    A mule that saw all this thought it was snowing and lay down and quietly froze to death.

THEME **An idea about life revealed in a work of literature.** A theme is not the same as a subject. A subject can usually be expressed in a word or two—*love, childhood, death.* A theme is the idea the writer wishes to reveal about that subject. A theme has to be expressed in a full sentence. A work can have more than one theme. A theme is usually not stated directly in the work. Instead, the reader has to think about all the elements of the work and then make an inference, or an educated guess, about what they all mean. One theme of "The Emperor's New Clothes" (page 625) can be stated this way: People are often afraid to speak the truth for fear that others will think them stupid.

See pages 250, 256, 326,
356, 363, 473.

TONE **The attitude a writer takes toward an audience, a subject, or a character.** Tone is conveyed through the writer's choice of words and details. The tone can be light and humorous, serious and sad, friendly or hostile toward a character, and so forth. The poem "The Sneetches" (page 380) is light and humorous in tone. In contrast, Luci Tapahonso's "Yes, It Was My Grandmother" (page 118) has a loving and respectful tone.

See pages 117, 120.

COMMUNICATIONS HANDBOOK ≡

PUTTING TOGETHER A MULTIMEDIA PRESENTATION

When people talk about **media,** they mean both print and nonprint ways of communicating. Newspapers, magazines, advertisements, TV, radio, photographs, music videos, movies, and the World Wide Web are just some of the media you may see and hear every day.

In the computer industry the word **multimedia** refers to a combination of two or more of the following media:

- **text:** words, sentences, paragraphs, numbers

- **sound:** music; speeches; readings of stories, poems, and plays; sound effects, such as thunder

- **graphics:** drawings, paintings, photographs, charts, maps, graphs, posters, patterns, color

- **video:** sections clipped, or copied, from professionally made full-length movies or from videos made with a hand-held camcorder

- **animation:** movement of objects and figures on screen

- **interactivity:** constant exchange of information between the computer and the user

People find new ways of working with media all the time. Don't worry if you don't have the latest software and equipment. You can learn a lot by working on both low-tech and high-tech media and multimedia projects. Follow these steps:

1. **Get together with others.** When several students combine their talents and skills, they can often come up with a better product than a student working alone. You can learn a lot about yourself and other people by working with others. Besides, it's often more fun than working by yourself.

2. **Decide what you want to do.** Keep in mind

    - group members' interests and strengths

    - your equipment, tools, software, and hardware

3. **Design the project.** Use a word processing program to make a plan and a schedule. Keep a record of who is supposed to do what and of when each job has to be done.

4. **Create the content.** If you're doing skits based on Japanese myths, write a script, make costumes, and find props. If you're doing a multimedia presentation, create or find the text, graphics, and

---

High Tech

For a **high-tech presentation** including sound, you'll need a computer with a sound card and speakers. Find out if your school has the software you'll need to

- create and edit graphics, video, and sound
- combine all the media you want to include
- make your presentation interactive

Low Tech

Equipment for a **low-tech presentation** might include the following items:

- recorders
- musical instruments
- a copy machine
- an overhead projector
- cameras
- camcorders
- a VCR

---

sounds you'll need. Check multimedia "galleries" (or graphics archives) of paintings on-line and on CD-ROMs to see if you can find scenes from Japanese myths. You may be able to find a clip from a performance of Japanese music to use as background for your presentation.

5. **Put it all together.** If you're doing a reading of poems about American history with background music, for example, you may need to hold several rehearsals. Try reading the poems in different sequences to see which you like best. Ask another group to give you feedback before you perform in front of the class. If your group would rather not perform live, you could videotape your work. With the right technology, you can turn a live performance into a multimedia presentation. Just add some graphics and text, and make your program interactive.

Scanning, Clipping, and Creating

If you have access to a scanner, you can scan photos, artwork, and maps, as well as handwritten and printed material from books, newspapers, and magazines. A scanner stores images in a digital format so that they can be used on a computer.

You can also find lots of material on the Internet and on CD-ROM disks. Multimedia programs give you access to graphics, video, and sound "galleries" from all over the world. If the program allows you to use as much material as you want, clip whatever you need.

It may be impossible for you to create certain kinds of material, such as nature scenes or news coverage of a historical event. Still, try to create your own text, graphics, sound, and video whenever you can. You can get CD-ROMs of actors reading stories, but why not do your own readings? You can find and download text about Gary Paulsen, for example, but you'll learn more about writing if you read articles about him and write your own text.

Making an Interactive Program

Multimedia or authoring programs show you how to create interactive links. You can set up your presentation in either of these ways:

- The user moves from one screen to the next along a path you've laid out.

- The user has choices about where to go next.

To plan your presentation, try making a flowchart, a map showing what's on each screen. Draw a rectangle for each screen and arrows showing the paths the user can follow.

Presenting Ray Bradbury. Suppose your teacher has assigned the class to do a project on an American writer. Your group decides to do a multimedia presentation on Ray Bradbury. The group chooses to include the information laid out in this flowchart, which shows the paths a user might follow.

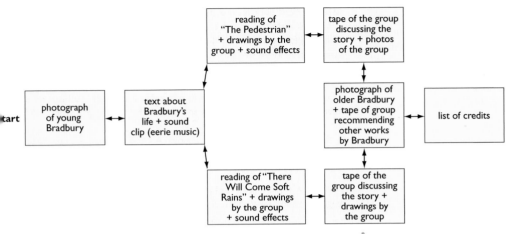

Word Processing

Use word processing programs to

- create schedules and assignment sheets for your project

- type original text, scripts, and programs

- correct errors and revise your writing

There's no substitute for peer editing. Spelling checkers and grammar checkers pick up only certain kinds of errors. Give everyone in the group a chance to edit your writing. Leave room for comments and questions by triple-spacing drafts, and make a copy for each group member. Have everyone put comments on his or her own copy or on screen. Make sure all the group members are in agreement before you create the final text.

Word processing programs offer many formatting options. You can choose from a number of type styles and sizes to create different effects. For example, you may want to use large type for headlines. If you have a drawing program, you can even design your own letters. Word processing programs also let you change the margins for parts of your text. For example, you may want to leave extra space around an important section. You can also use lines, boxes, and bullets (dots) to separate items and make them easier to read.

Giving Credit Where It's Due

It's important to give credit to anyone who contributed in any way to your presentation. Even if the owner of the material gave it to you, you should credit the person who created it. Avoid **plagiarizing** (plā′jə·rīz′ĭn), or passing off others' work as your own.

You may want to print a separate page or screen of credits at the end of your presentation. See pages 682–683 for information on writing credits.

Using a Media Center or Library

To find a book, tape, film, or video in the library, start by looking in the **catalog.** Most libraries use an **on-line,** or computer, **catalog.**

On-line catalogs vary from library to library. With some you begin searching for resources by **title, author,** or **subject.** With others you simply enter **keywords** for the subject you're researching. With either system you enter information into the computer, and a new screen will show you a list of materials or subject headings relating to your request. When you find an item you want, write down the title, author, and **call number,** the code of numbers and letters that shows you where to find the item on the library's shelves.

Some libraries still use card catalogs. A **card catalog** is a collection of index cards arranged in alphabetical order by title and author. Nonfiction is also cataloged by subject.

Periodicals. Most libraries have a collection of current and back issues of magazines and newspapers. To find up-to-date information on a topic, use a computerized index, such as *InfoTrac*. Some indices provide a summary of each article. Others provide the entire text, which you can print out or read on screen. The *Readers' Guide to Periodical Literature* is a print index of articles that have appeared in hundreds of magazines.

Using the Internet

The **Internet** is a huge network of computers. Libraries, news services, government agencies, researchers, and organizations communicate and share information on the Net. The Net also lets you chat on-line with students around the world. For help in using the Internet to do research or to communicate with someone by computer, explore the following options.

The World Wide Web. When you do research on the Internet, you'll use the World Wide Web. There, information is stored in colorful, easy-to-access files called **Web pages.** Web pages usually have text, graphics, images, sound, and even video clips.

Using a Web Browser. You look at Web pages with a **Web browser,** a program for accessing information on the Web. Every page on the Web has its own address, called a **URL,** or Uniform Resource Locator. If you know the address of a Web page you want to go to, just enter it in the location field on your browser.

Hundreds of millions of Web pages are connected by **hyperlinks,** which let you jump from one Web page to another. These links are usually underlined or colored words or images, or both, on your computer screen.

Using a Web Directory. If you're just beginning to look for a research topic, click on a **Web directory,** a list of topics and subtopics created by experts to help users find Web sites. Think of the directory as a giant index. Start by choosing a broad category, such as <u>Literature</u>. Then, work your way down through the subtopics, perhaps from <u>Poetry</u> to <u>Poets</u>. Under <u>Poets</u>, choose a Web page that looks interesting, perhaps one on Ogden Nash.

Using a Search Engine. If you already have a topic, you're ready to use a **search engine,** a software tool that finds information on the Web. Go to an on-line search form and enter a **search term,** or keyword. The search engine will return a list of Web pages containing your search term. A search term such as *Nash* may produce thousands of **hits,** or results, including information about Nashville, Tennessee, and Nashua, New Hampshire. To find useful material, you have to narrow your search.

Refining a Keyword Search. To focus your research, use **search operators,** such as the words AND and NOT, to create a string of keywords. If you were looking for material on Ogden Nash and his poetry, for example, you might enter the following:

Ogden Nash AND poetry

This focused search term yields pages that contain both *Ogden Nash* and *poetry*. The chart below explains how several search operators work.

COMMON SEARCH OPERATORS AND WHAT THEY DO	
AND or +	Demands that both terms appear on the page; narrows search
OR	Yields pages that contain either term; widens search
NOT or −	Excludes a word from consideration; narrows search
NEAR or ADJ	Demands that two words be close together; narrows search
" "	Demands an exact phrase; narrows search

Evaluating Web Sources

Since anyone—even you—can publish a Web page, it's important to evaluate your sources. Use these criteria to evaluate a source.

- **Authority.** Who is the author? What is his or her knowledge or experience? Trust respected sources, such as the Smithsonian Institution, not a person's newsletter or Web page.

You've Got Mail!

E-mail is an electronic message sent over a computer network. On the Internet you can use e-mail to reach institutions, businesses, and individuals. When you e-mail places like museums, you may be able to ask **experts** about a topic you're researching. You can also use e-mail to chat with students around the country and around the world.

Internet forums, or newsgroups, let you discuss and debate subjects with other computer users. You can write and send a question to a forum and get an answer from someone who may (or may not) know something about your topic.

Techno Tip

- If you get too few hits, use a more general word as your search term, or add another keyword or phrase.

- If you get too many hits, use a more specific word as your search term.

COMMUNICATIONS HANDBOOK **681**

T681

Techno Tip

To evaluate a Web source, look at the top-level domain in the URL. Here is a sample URL with the top-level domain—a government agency—labeled.

top-level domain

http://www.loc.gov

COMMON TOP-LEVEL DOMAINS AND WHAT THEY STAND FOR

.edu	Educational institution. Site may publish scholarly work or the work of elementary or high school students.
.gov	Government body. Information is generally reliable.
.org	Usually a nonprofit organization. If the organization promotes culture (as a museum does), information is generally reliable; if it advocates a cause, information may be biased.
.com	Commercial enterprise. Information should be evaluated carefully.
.net	Organization offering Internet services. Information is generally reliable.

Sample Note Card

Bradbury on Education	3

—Teach "tools" of reading & writing at gr. K–2; no Internet till gr. 3

—"Teach students to be in love with life, to love their work, to create at the top of their lungs." p. F1

- **Accuracy.** How trustworthy is the information? Does the author give his or her sources? Check information from one site against information from at least two other sites or print sources.

- **Objectivity.** What is the author's **perspective,** or point of view? Find out whether the information provider has a bias or hidden purpose.

- **Currency.** Is the information up-to-date? For a print source, check the copyright date. For a Web source, look for the date on which the page was created or revised. (This date appears at the bottom of the site's home page.)

- **Coverage.** How well does the source cover the topic? Could you find better information in a book? Compare the source with several others.

Listing Sources and Taking Notes

When you write a research paper, you must **document,** or identify, your sources so that readers will know where you found your material. You must avoid **plagiarism,** or presenting another writer's words or ideas as if they were your own.

How to List Sources

List each source, and give it a number. (You'll use these source numbers later, when you take notes.) Here's where to find the publication information (such as the name of the publisher and the copyright date) you'll need for different types of sources:

- **Print sources.** Look at the title and copyright pages of the book or periodical.

- **On-line sources.** Look at the beginning or end of the document or in a separate electronic file. For a Web page, look for a link containing the word *About.*

- **Portable electronic databases.** Look at the start-up screen, the packaging, or the disc itself.

There are several ways to list sources. The chart on page 683 shows the style created by the Modern Language Association.

How to Take Notes

Here are some tips for taking notes.

- Put notes from different sources on separate index cards, sheets of paper, or computer files. Put the source number in the upper right-hand corner.

- At the top of each card, write a label telling what that note is about. At the bottom, write the numbers of the pages on which you found the information.

- Use short phrases, abbreviations, and lists. You don't have to write in full sentences.

- In general, use your own words. If you do quote an author's exact words, put quotation marks around them.

How to Prepare a Works Cited List

Use your source cards to make a **works cited** list, which should appear at the end of your report. At the top of a sheet of paper, type and center the heading *Works Cited*. Below it, list your sources in alphabetical order. Follow the MLA guidelines for citing sources (see the chart below). The sample works cited list below shows you how to do this.

Works Cited

"Bradbury, Ray." The World Book Encyclopedia. 1998 ed.

Geirland, John. "Interview with Ray Bradbury." The Fresno Bee 3 Jan. 1999: F1.

Mogen, David. Ray Bradbury. New York: Macmillan, 1986.

MLA GUIDELINES FOR CITING SOURCES	
Books	Give the author, title, city of publication, publisher, and copyright year. Mogen, David. Ray Bradbury. New York: Macmillan, 1986.
Magazine and newspaper articles	Give the author, title of article, name of the magazine or newspaper, date, and page numbers. Geirland, John. "Interview with Ray Bradbury." The Fresno Bee 3 Jan. 1999: F1.
Encyclopedia articles	Give the author (if named), title of the article, name of the encyclopedia, and edition (year). "Bradbury, Ray." The World Book Encyclopedia. 1998 ed.
Films, videotapes, and audiotapes	Give the title; producer, director, or developer; medium; distributor; and year of release. Ray Bradbury: Tales of Fantasy. Listening Library Productions. Audiocassette. Filmic Archives, 1992.
On-line sources	Give the author (if named); title; title of project, database, periodical, or site; electronic posting date; access date; and Internet address (if any). Johnson, Richard, and Chris Jepsen. The Ray Bradbury Page. 1997. 20 Dec. 1999. <http://www.brookingsbook.com/bradbury/bradbury/html>.
CD-ROMs	Give the author (if named); title; title of database; type of source; city; publisher; and publication date. "Science Fiction." The Encarta © 98 Desk Encyclopedia. CD-ROM. Redmond: Microsoft Corp., 1996–1997.

Understanding Influences of Other Languages on the Spelling of English

In addition to knowing the meaning of these prefixes, students should understand that their spelling can also often offer clues to meaning and that they should learn to look for **spelling-meaning relationships.** For example, *in–*, a prefix that comes from Latin, means "not." This prefix takes other forms or spellings depending on the consonant that it precedes. However, its meaning remains the same. Explain to students that *in–* becomes *il–* before *l* (*illogical, illegal*), *im–* before *m* and *p* (*immortal, impure*) and *ir–* before *r* (*irregular, irrational*). In each case, regardless of spelling, the meaning is "not." Ask students to check a dictionary for several more words that have absorbed the prefix *in–* into the base word (*illegible, illiterate, immature, improper, irreverence, irreversible*).

Using Word Parts

Many English words can be divided into parts. If you know the meanings of various word parts, you can often determine the meanings of words.

Word Root	Meaning	Examples
–bio–	life	biology, biography
–geo–	earth, ground	geography, geology
–spec–	see, look at	spectacles, spectator

COMMONLY USED PREFIXES

Prefix	Meaning	Examples
bi–	two	bicycle, bimonthly
dis–	away, opposing	disappear, dislike
in–	not	inactive, inappropriate
mis–	badly, not, wrongly	misspell, misconduct
non–	not	nonhuman, nonvoter
pre–	before	precook, preview
re–	back, again	reapply, refill
sub–	under, beneath	subtitle, submerge

A **base word** (like *care*) can stand alone. It is a complete word all by itself, although other word parts may be added to it to make new words (*uncaring, careful*). **Roots** usually can't stand alone; they combine with one or more word parts to form words.

A word part added to the beginning of a word or root is called a **prefix.** A word part added to the end of a word or root is called a **suffix.** Prefixes and suffixes can't stand alone. They must be added to words or other word parts.

COMMONLY USED SUFFIXES

Suffix	Meaning	Examples
–able	able, tending to, worthy of	respectable, reliable
–en	become, cause to be	lengthen, strengthen
–ful	full of, characterized by	cheerful, stressful
–ion	action, condition	inspection, fascination
–less	without	careless, hopeless
–ly	in a certain way	quickly, usually
–ness	quality, state	togetherness, sadness
–ous	characterized by	luxurious, joyous

Summarizing, Paraphrasing, and Outlining

When you finish reading a text, check your understanding by writing a **summary,** a short restatement of the important ideas and details in a work. There are many ways to summarize; use the one that works best for the type of text you've read. For a short story, use a **story map** like the one shown on the right. For nonfiction, **outline** the **main ideas** and **supporting details,** using the form shown on the right.

For a poem, try writing a **paraphrase.** In a paraphrase you express every idea, line by line, in your own words. Here is a paraphrase of a verse from a poem.

Poem	Paraphrase
I was angry with my friend: I told my wrath, my wrath did end. I was angry with my foe: I told it not, my wrath did grow. —William Blake, from "A Poison Tree"	The speaker in the poem was upset with a friend. Telling the friend about the problem made the anger go away. When the speaker was angry with an enemy and kept his feelings inside, he became angrier and angrier.

STUDY SKILLS

Using a Thesaurus

A **thesaurus** is a collection of synonyms. You use a thesaurus when you're looking for a word that expresses a specific meaning. There are two kinds of thesauruses (see the sample entries on this page).

In one kind, developed by Peter Mark Roget, you look in the index for a word that conveys your general meaning. Under *crooked,* for example, you might find the subentries shown at the right. Then you choose the subentry whose meaning is closest to what you have in mind. In this case, suppose you choose *dishonest.* Next, in the body of the text, you find the

Sample Thesaurus Entry

crooked *adj.* **1** askew, awry, not straight; curved, twisted, twisting, winding, meandering, tortuous, sinuous, serpentine, zigzag, spiral; bent, bowed, hooked; distorted, deformed, warped, out of shape. **2** dishonest, corrupt, unscrupulous, dishonorable, criminal, unlawful; deceptive, fraudulent, unethical, underhanded, deceitful, perfidious, nefarious; sneaky, shifty, shady, wily, crafty.
Ant. **1** straight, straight as an arrow; flat. **2** honest, legal, lawful, ethical, scrupulous, honorable, fair, aboveboard, upright.

©1996, 1995 *Random House Roget's Thesaurus.*

STORY MAP

Basic situation:

Setting:

Main character:

His or her problem:

Main events or complications:

Climax:

Resolution:

OUTLINE

I. Main idea
  A. Supporting detail
    1. Supporting detail
      a. Supporting detail

Sample Entry from the Index of Roget's International Thesaurus

crooked angular 251.6
  askew 219.14
  curved 252.8
  dishonest 975.16
  distorted 249.10
  falsehearted 616.31
  zigzag 219.20

Organizing Information

Remind students to use outlining, paraphrasing, and summarizing as a means of organizing and assimilating information. Outlining can help them clarify the relationship between ideas. Paraphrasing can help them break down and organize complicated ideas. Summarizing allows them to condense information and make decisions about what is important.

Have the students turn to the guide to pronunciation symbols that appears at the bottom of p. 773 of the Glossary. Ask them to practice using the guide's phonetic symbols and diacritical marks to sound out several Glossary words they already know how to pronounce. Then, tell them that the guide's words and symbols will help them decode unfamiliar words. Suggest an unfamiliar word, and work with the class to help them sound the word out using the guide's pronunciation symbols.

number that follows the subentry *dishonest* (975.16). Finally you look under this number to find synonyms for *dishonest*.

The other kind of thesaurus is much easier to use: It lists words in alphabetical order, like a dictionary.

Using a Dictionary

You can use a print or electronic dictionary to find the precise meaning and usage of words. The elements of a typical entry are explained below.

1. **Entry word.** The entry word shows how the word is spelled and how it is divided into syllables. It may also show capitalization and alternative spellings.

2. **Pronunciation.** Phonetic symbols and **diacritical marks** (symbols added to letters) show how to pronounce the entry word. A key to these symbols usually appears on every other page.

3. **Part-of-speech label.** This label shows how the entry word is used in a sentence. Some words may function as more than one part of speech. For words like these, a part-of-speech label is provided before each set of definitions.

4. **Word origin.** A word's **etymology** (et′ə·mäl′ə·jē), or derivation, is its history. It tells how the word or its parts entered the English language. In the example shown, the etymology traces the word *respect* to its origins in the Latin (L) prefix *re—* (back) and verb *specere* (to look at). More information can be found in the etymology of the word *spy*.

5. **Examples.** Phrases or sentences show how the word is used.

6. **Definitions.** If a word has more than one meaning, the meanings are numbered or lettered.

7. **Idioms.** The entry may define phrases that include the word and that mean something other than their literal meaning.

8. **Synonyms and antonyms.** Synonyms (words similar in meaning) and antonyms (words opposite in meaning) may appear at the end of an entry. The entry may also tell you where to find a listing of other synonyms (in this case, in the entry for *regard*).

9. **Related word forms.** These are other forms of the entry word, usually created by the addition of suffixes.

Sample Dictionary Entry

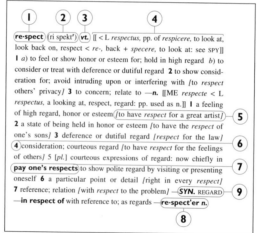

©1997 *Webster's New World College Dictionary,* Third Edition.

Reading Maps, Charts, and Graphs

Types of Maps

Physical maps show the natural landscape of an area. Shading is often used to show physical features, such as mountains, hills, and valleys; colors are often used to show **elevation** (height above or below sea level). **Political maps** show political units, such as states and nations. They usually show borders and capitals. **Special-purpose maps** present information such as the routes of explorers. The map on page 137 showing Harriet Tubman's route to freedom is a special-purpose map.

How to Read a Map

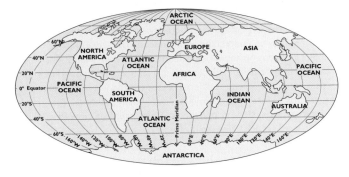

1. **Figure out the focus of the map.** The map's title and labels will tell you its focus—its subject and the geographical area it covers.

2. **Study the map legend.** The **legend,** or **key,** explains any special symbols, lines, colors, and shadings. (The map on page 500 contains a legend.)

3. **Check directions and distances.** Maps often include a **compass rose,** or **directional indicator,** showing north, south, east, and west. (The map on page 137 has a compass rose.) If there is no compass rose, assume that north is at the top, west is to the left, and so on. Many maps also include a **scale** to help you relate distances on the map to actual distances on the earth's surface.

4. **Be aware of the larger context of the area.** The **absolute location** of any place on the earth is given by its **latitude** (number of degrees north or south of the equator) and **longitude** (number of degrees east or west of the prime meridian). Some maps also have **locator maps,** which show the area of focus in relation to surrounding areas or to the entire world.

Compass Rose

```
        N
   W    *    E
        S
```

Scale

```
0    75      150 Miles
0    75   150 Kilometers
```

If students create their own graphs for reports or presentations, remind them that their visual aids will be more legible if they print instead of using cursive writing.

Line Graph

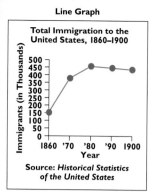

Total Immigration to the United States, 1860–1900

Source: *Historical Statistics of the United States*

Bar Graph

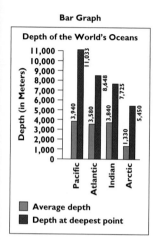

Depth of the World's Oceans

■ Average depth
■ Depth at deepest point

Pie Graph

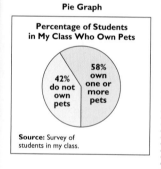

Percentage of Students in My Class Who Own Pets

58% own one or more pets

42% do not own pets

Source: Survey of students in my class.

Types of Charts and Graphs

A **flowchart** shows a **sequence** of events or the steps in a process. Flowcharts are often used to show cause-and-effect relationships. The sequencing chart on page 136 is an example of a flowchart.

A **time line** shows events in **chronological order** (the order in which they happened).

A **table** presents categorized facts arranged in rows and columns to make them easy to understand and compare. The table on page 690, for example, gives tips on answering different kinds of essay questions.

Line graphs usually show changes in quantity over time. In line graphs, dots showing the quantity at different times are connected to create a line. **Bar graphs** generally compare quantities within categories. **Pie graphs,** or **circle graphs,** show proportions. A pie graph is a circle divided into different-sized sections, like slices of a pie.

How to Read a Chart or a Graph

1. **Read the title.** The title tells you the subject and purpose of the chart or graph.

2. **Read the labels.** The labels tell you what type of information is presented.

3. **Analyze the details.** Read numbers carefully. Note increases or decreases. Look for the direction or order of events and for trends and relationships.

STRATEGIES FOR TAKING TESTS

When you begin a test, **scan** it quickly and count the items. Then, decide how to spend your time. Here are some sample test questions and specific strategies for answering five kinds of test questions.

True/false questions ask you to determine whether a given statement is true or false. For example:

1. T F Lensey Namioka was born in China and moved to the United States as a teenager.

HOW TO ANSWER TRUE/FALSE QUESTIONS

- Read the statement carefully. The whole statement is false if any part of it is false.
- Look for words like *always* and *never*. A statement is true only if it is always true.

Multiple-choice questions ask you to select a correct answer from several choices. For example:

1. **Alliteration** is the repetition of

   A meanings   **C** sounds
   B images   **D** parts of speech

HOW TO ANSWER MULTIPLE-CHOICE QUESTIONS

- Make sure you understand the question or statement before you look at the choices.
- Look for words like *not* and *always*, which may help you eliminate some choices.
- Read all the choices before selecting an answer. Eliminate choices that you know are incorrect.
- Think carefully about the remaining choices. Pick the one that makes the most sense.

Matching questions ask you to match the items in one list with the items in another list. For example:

Directions: Match each item in the left-hand column with its definition in the right-hand column.

_____ 1. character   **A** story of a person's life

_____ 2. biography   **B** struggle between opposing characters or opposing forces

_____ 3. plot   **C** person in a literary work

_____ 4. conflict   **D** sequence of events in a story

HOW TO ANSWER MATCHING QUESTIONS

- Read the directions carefully. You may not have to use all the items in one column, and you may use some items more than once.
- Scan the columns. First, match items you are sure of. Then, match items you are less sure of.
- For the rest of the items, make your best guess.

T689

Analogy questions ask you to figure out the relationship between two words and identify a pair with a similar relationship. For example:

Directions: Select the pair of words that best completes the analogy.

HAT : HEAD : : _____

A arm : leg   **C** shoe : foot
B glove : foot   **D** shoe : glove

HOW TO ANSWER ANALOGY QUESTIONS

- Figure out the relationship between the words in the first pair. (A hat is an item of clothing that covers the head, a part of the body.)

- Express the analogy in the form of a statement or question. (In HAT : HEAD the first word is an item of clothing, and the second word is the part of the body it covers. What other pair of words have that relationship?)

- Select the pair of words with the same relationship as the original pair. (A shoe is an item of clothing that covers a foot.)

Essay questions in a test ask you to think critically about things you have learned and to express your understanding in a paragraph or more. Before you begin writing, read the question carefully and identify its **key verbs.** These verbs tell you what kind of response to give.

ESSAY QUESTIONS

Key Verb	Task	Sample Question
analyze	Take something apart to see how it works.	Analyze the character of Manuel in "La Bamba."
compare	Discuss likenesses (Sometimes *compare* means "compare *and* contrast.")	Compare the theme of "What Do Fish Have to Do with Anything?" with the theme of "The Sneetches."
contrast	Discuss differences.	Contrast two myths about the origin of fire.
define	Give specific details that make something unique.	Define the term *foreshadowing*.
describe	Give a picture in words.	Describe the setting of "All Summer in a Day."
discuss	Examine in detail.	Discuss the imagery in "Petals."
explain	Give reasons for something.	Explain why writers use flashbacks.
identify	Discuss specific characteristics.	Identify the rhymes in "Ankylosaurus."
list (*also* outline *or* trace)	Give all steps in order or certain details of a subject.	List three figures of speech, and give an example of each.
summarize	Briefly review the main points.	Summarize the myth of Perseus and Medusa.

Writing Business Letters

To request information from someone who is far away or difficult to reach, write a business letter. Follow these guidelines:

1. **Write in formal English.** Avoid slang. The tone of your letter should be polite and respectful.

2. **Be clear.** Explain why you are writing. Include important information, and be as brief as possible.

3. **Make the letter look professional.** Type, print, or write your letter on unlined 8½- × 11-inch paper. Follow the **block form** (shown below).

Sample Business Letter

> **(1)** 2683 North Elston Avenue
> Petaluma, CA 64952
>
> October 21, 2000
>
> **(2)** Ms. Wanda Rollins
> Home Economics Agent
> Sonoma County Cooperative Extension Center
> 1219 Raritan Street
> Santa Rosa, CA 95402
>
> **(3)** Dear Ms. Rollins:
>
> **(4)** I am writing a proposal to my school principal asking that the school lunchroom add a salad bar. I would like to know the nutritional value of the ingredients in a typical salad bar.
>
> Please send me any information that might help me with my proposal. I have enclosed a self-addressed, stamped envelope.
>
> **(5)** Sincerely,
>
> **(6)** *La Ronda Mitchell*
> La Ronda Mitchell

(1) Heading
Your street address
Your city, state, and ZIP code
The date you write the letter

(2) Inside Address
The name and address of the person you are writing to. Use a title like *Mr., Ms.,* or *Mrs.* or a professional title, such as *Dr.* or *Professor,* before the person's name. Put the person's business title after the name.

(3) Salutation (greeting)
End the salutation with a colon.

Body
(4) Your message. If the body is more than one paragraph long, leave an extra line between paragraphs.

Closing
(5) Use *Yours truly* or *Sincerely,* followed by a comma.

Signature
(6) Type or print your name, leaving space for your signature. Sign your name in ink below the closing.

After students have read about how to fill out forms, ask them to bring a variety of forms to class. For example, they might bring in subscription forms for newspapers and magazines, job applications from a local employment office, or applications for a library or video-store card. Have students work in small groups to fill out the forms. You might also want to have students practice filling out the form below.

```
┌─────────────────────────────────────────────┐
│            INFORMATION FORM                   │
│                                               │
│  NAME    _____    │
│                                               │
│  NICKNAME _____ PHONE _____      │
│                                               │
│  ADDRESS _____      │
│                                               │
│          _____      │
│                                               │
│  PARENT OR GUARDIAN _____       │
│                                               │
└─────────────────────────────────────────────┘
```

Filling Out Forms

When you fill out a form, your purpose is to give clear, complete information. Follow these guidelines whenever you complete forms.

1. Look over the entire form before you begin.

2. Look for and follow special instructions (such as *Type or print* or *Use a pencil*).

3. Read each item carefully.

4. Supply all the information requested. If an item does not apply to you, write *does not apply,* or use a dash or the abbreviation *N/A* (meaning "not applicable").

5. When you're finished, make sure nothing is left blank. Also, check for errors and correct them neatly.

6. Mail the form to the correct address, or give it to the right person.

PROOFREADERS' MARKS

Symbol	Example	Meaning
≡	an african myth	Capitalize lowercase letter.
/	my School	Lowercase capital letter.
∧	the end of May	Insert.
ঽ	How are are you?	Delete.
⌒	a child hood friend	Close up space.
∿	I beleive you.	Change order (of letters or words).
¶	¶"Oh, no!" he cried.	Begin a new paragraph.
⊙	We'll see you later⊙	Add a period.
⋏	Yes, I'll be there.	Add a comma.
◇	Dear Mr. Mills◇	Add a colon.
⋏;	Columbus, Ohio⋏; Dallas, Texas	Add a semicolon.
⋎ ⋎	⋎Are you OK?⋎ he asked.	Add quotation marks.

1 THE PARTS OF SPEECH

THE NOUN

1a. A *noun* is a word used to name a person, a place, a thing, or an idea.

PERSONS	PLACES	THINGS	IDEAS
grandmother	Cascade Range	braids	courage
Maya Angelou	home	tree	freedom
waiter	Bucktown	cat	luck

Compound Nouns

A *compound noun* is two or more words used together as a single noun. The parts of a compound noun may be written as one word, as separate words, or as a hyphenated word.

ONE WORD	Passover, grasshopper, riverbank
SEPARATE WORDS	U.S. Cavalry, Mary Whitebird, "The Fun They Had"
HYPHENATED WORD	Ta-Na-E-Ka, great-grandparents, eleven-year-old

 When you are not sure how to write a compound noun, look in a dictionary.

Common Nouns and Proper Nouns

A *common noun* is a general name for a person, place, thing, or idea. A *proper noun* names a particular person, place, thing, or idea. Proper nouns always begin with a capital letter. Common nouns begin with a capital letter in titles and when they begin sentences.

COMMON NOUNS	PROPER NOUNS
poem	"Things to Do If You Are a Subway"
street	Fifty-first Street
day	Monday

☞ For more about capitalizing proper nouns, see pages 743–748.

 QUICK CHECK 1

Identify the nouns in the sentences on the following page. Classify each noun as *common* or *proper*.

EXAMPLE   1. The eruption of Mount St. Helens destroyed forests.
   1. *eruption—common; Mount St. Helens—proper; forests—common*

Resources ⎯⎯⎯⎯
- *Language Handbook Worksheets, pp. 1–13*
- *Language Workshop CD-ROM, Chapter 1: Parts of Speech*

Quick Check 1: Answers

1. Patricia Lauber—proper, miles—common
2. People—common; plants—common; animals—common; ash—common; heat—common; smoke—common
3. Spirit Lake—proper; beauty—common
4. Darkness—common; Yakima—proper; Washington—proper; noon—common
5. Geologists—common; earthquake—common

Try It Out: Possible Answers

[1] Hot and tired from playing baseball, Jamie wanted some cold orange juice. [2] The teenager went into the cottage and discovered a raccoon in the kitchen. [3] The intruder was sitting on a table and calmly eating an apple. [4] Surprised and puzzled, Jamie didn't move a muscle for a full minute. [5] Then, Jamie picked up another apple and joined the thief at its snack.

Try It Out ✎

In the following paragraph, replace each vague noun with an exact, specific noun.

[1] Hot and tired from playing a game, the boy wanted a drink. [2] The boy went into the house and discovered a wild animal in a room. [3] The animal was sitting on a table and calmly eating a fruit. [4] Surprised and puzzled, the boy didn't move his body for a while. [5] Then, the boy picked up another fruit and joined the animal at its meal.

☞ For more information about pronouns and how they are used, see Part 4: Using Pronouns.

1. According to Patricia Lauber, 230 square miles were involved.
2. People, plants, and animals died in the ash, heat, and smoke.
3. Spirit Lake was gone, its beauty lost forever.
4. Darkness covered Yakima, Washington, until noon.
5. Geologists had predicted the disaster.

Using Specific Nouns

Whenever possible, use specific, exact nouns. Using specific nouns will make your writing more precise as well as more interesting.

EXAMPLE A woman wrote a poem.
Pat Mora wrote "Petals."

THE PRONOUN

1b. A *pronoun* is a word used in place of one or more nouns or pronouns.

EXAMPLE When Bailey heard the elders' unkind words, **he** [Bailey] spoke up.

The word that a pronoun stands for is called its *antecedent.* Avoid the common error of using a pronoun with an unclear antecedent.

UNCLEAR ANTECEDENT Bailey spoke to Uncle Willie. **He** was angry. [Who was angry?]

CLEAR ANTECEDENT Even when **Bailey** behaved badly, **he** was rarely punished.

Personal Pronouns

A *personal pronoun* refers to the one speaking (*first person*), the one spoken to (*second person*), or the one spoken about (*third person*).

PERSONAL PRONOUNS		
	SINGULAR	**PLURAL**
First Person	I, me, my, mine	we, us, our, ours
Second Person	you, your, yours	you, your, yours
Third Person	he, him, his, she, her, hers, it, its	they, them, their, theirs

EXAMPLES **I** enjoy Maya Angelou's forthright style. [first person]
Have **you** ever heard Angelou speak? [second person]
Please give **them** a copy of the interview. [third person]

Possessive Pronouns

Possessive pronouns are personal pronouns that are used to show ownership. Like personal pronouns, possessive pronouns have singular and plural forms.

POSSESSIVE PRONOUNS		
	SINGULAR	**PLURAL**
First Person	my, mine	our, ours
Second Person	your, yours	your, yours
Third Person	her, hers, his, its	their, theirs

EXAMPLES Angelou and **her** family doted on Bailey.
             Is this notebook **yours**?
             The story tells about some of **their** antics.

Reflexive Pronouns

A *reflexive pronoun* refers to the subject and directs the action of the verb back to the subject.

REFLEXIVE PRONOUNS	
First Person	myself, ourselves
Second Person	yourself, yourselves
Third Person	himself, herself, itself, themselves

EXAMPLE Angelou wrote about Bailey and **herself** in "Brother."

Demonstrative Pronouns

A *demonstrative pronoun* (*this, that, these, those*) points out a person, a place, a thing, or an idea.

EXAMPLE **This** is a recent picture of Maya Angelou.

Indefinite Pronouns

An *indefinite pronoun* refers to a person, a place, or a thing that is not specifically named.

Common Indefinite Pronouns			
all	either	many	one
any	everybody	none	several
both	everything	no one	some
each	few	nobody	somebody

EXAMPLE Bailey did **everything** well.

 NOTE Don't confuse the pronoun *its* with the contraction *it's*. The pronoun *its* means "belonging to it." The contraction *it's* means "it is" or "it has."

 NOTE Possessive pronouns are also called *possessive adjectives*.

 NOTE *This, that, these,* and *those* are also used as adjectives.

PRONOUN **That** is an example of dialect.

ADJECTIVE **That** word is a colloquialism.

 NOTE Many indefinite pronouns can also serve as adjectives.

INDEFINITE PRONOUN **Many** of the pickles ended up in his pockets.

ADJECTIVE **Many** pickles ended up in his pockets.

Quick Check 2: Answers
1. this, one, my
2. each, you, your
3. she, I
4. We, her, himself
5. someone, us, they

 **QUICK CHECK 2**

Identify each of the pronouns in the following sentences.

EXAMPLE   1. I have a brother like Bailey, but my brother doesn't like pickles.
   1. *I, my*

1. Actually, this is one of my favorite stories.
2. Did each of you compare your brother or sister to Angelou's?
3. How lucky she and I have been!
4. We wonder if her brother still gets pickle juice on himself.
5. Would someone please let us know if they are still friends?

THE ADJECTIVE

1c.   **An** *adjective* **is a word used to modify a noun or a pronoun.**

To **modify** a word means to describe the word or to make its meaning more definite. An adjective modifies a word by telling *what kind, which one, how much,* or *how many.*

WHAT KIND?	WHICH ONE?	HOW MUCH? or HOW MANY?
tired dog	**first** one	**few** others
parlor stove	**that** year	**only** one
early winter	**another** one	**fifty** people

An adjective may come before or after the word it modifies.

EXAMPLES   **Many** dogs could not survive. [*Many* modifies *dogs.*]
Storm was **tough** and **loyal.** [*Tough* and *loyal* modify *Storm.*]

Articles

The most frequently used adjectives are *a, an,* and *the*. These adjectives are called **articles**. Use *a* before words that begin with a consonant sound. Use *an* before words that begin with a vowel sound.

EXAMPLES   **The** story "Storm" is **a** good example of **an** autobiographical incident.

Proper Adjectives

A **proper adjective** is formed from a proper noun and begins with a capital letter.

☞ For more about adjectives and about using modifiers, see Part 5: Using Modifers.

 Some proper nouns, such as *Klondike* and *Hopi,* do not change spelling when they are used as adjectives.

696 LANGUAGE HANDBOOK

PROPER NOUN	PROPER ADJECTIVE
Alaska	Alaskan crab
Newton	Newtonian physics
Hebrew	Hebraic law
Klondike	Klondike area

Demonstrative Adjectives

This, that, these, and *those* can be used both as adjectives and as pronouns. When these words modify a noun or a pronoun, they are called **demonstrative adjectives.** When they are used alone, they are called **demonstrative pronouns.**

DEMONSTRATIVE ADJECTIVES	Is **this** dog Storm? **Those** dogs are strong.
DEMONSTRATIVE PRONOUNS	**That** is Storm. Are **these** your only boots?

☞ For more information about demonstrative pronouns, see page 695.

 QUICK CHECK 3

Identify each adjective in the following sentences. Then, give the word the adjective modifies. Do not include the articles *a, an,* and *the.*

EXAMPLE 1. Dogs that pull sleds must be hardy.
    1. *hardy—Dogs*

1. Many types of dogs are used for transportation.
2. You may be familiar with the Siberian type of husky.
3. These dogs can survive in the frigid, bleak Arctic regions.
4. However, Storm didn't like running in the pre-Iditarod race.
5. After a rest, he was ready for another run.

☞ For more information about verbs and how to use them, see Part 3: Using Verbs.

THE VERB

1d. **A** *verb* **is a word used to express action or a state of being.**

EXAMPLES   Lois Lowry **wrote** "The Tree House."
        It **is** a story about friendship.

Action Verbs

1e. **An** *action verb* **may express physical action or mental action.**

PHYSICAL ACTION	build, climb, yell, say, wash
MENTAL ACTION	plan, think, feel, imagine, remember

☞ Every sentence must have a verb. The verb says something about the subject. For more about subjects and verbs, see pages 725–728.

Quick Check 3: Answers
1. Many—types
2. familiar—You, Siberian—type
3. These—dogs, frigid—regions, bleak—regions, Arctic—regions
4. pre-Iditarod—race
5. ready—he, another—run

For more information about objects, see pages 730–731.

 NOTE A verb may be transitive in one sentence and intransitive in another.

TRANSITIVE Leah's father **finished** her tree house.

INTRANSITIVE Leah's father **finished** quickly.

 Like intransitive verbs, linking verbs never take direct objects. See page 732 for more information on linking verbs.

NOTE Sometimes the verb phrase is interrupted by other words.

EXAMPLES **Will** Chrissy and Leah **be** friends again?

Chrissy **did** not [*or* didn't] **consider** Leah's feelings.

Transitive and Intransitive Verbs

(1) A *transitive verb* **is an action verb that expresses an action directed toward a person or thing.**

EXAMPLE Chrissy **decorated** the tree house. [The action of *decorated* is directed toward *tree house*.]

With transitive verbs, the action passes from the doer—the subject—to the receiver of the action. Words that receive the action of a transitive verb are called **objects.**

EXAMPLE She made a **sign.** [*Sign* is the object of the verb *made*.]

(2) An *intransitive verb* **expresses action (or tells something about the subject) without passing the action to a receiver.**

EXAMPLE She **climbed** carefully. [The action of *climbed* is not directed toward a receiver.]

Linking Verbs

If. **A** *linking verb* **links, or connects, the subject with a noun, a pronoun, or an adjective in the predicate.**

EXAMPLES One of her best friends **was** Leah.
That day, she **became** an enemy.

Linking Verbs Formed from the Verb *Be*			
am	was being	should be	has been
are	be	would be	was
is	been	must be	were
will be	may be	being	will have been

Other Linking Verbs appear, grow, seem, stay, become, look, smell, taste, feel, remain, sound, turn

Some words may be either linking verbs or action verbs, depending on how they are used.

LINKING Leah **looked** angry.
ACTION Leah **looked** for her father.

Helping Verbs

Ig. **A** *helping verb (auxiliary verb)* **helps the main verb to express an action or a state of being.**

EXAMPLES **could** see   **had been** seen   **will be** seen

A *verb phrase* consists of a main verb and at least one helping verb.

EXAMPLE Chrissy **should have been** nicer. [The main verb is *been*.]

COMMONLY USED HELPING VERBS	
Forms of *Be*	am, are, be, been, being, is, was, were
Forms of *Do*	do, does, did
Forms of *Have*	have, has, had
Other Helping Verbs	can, could, may, might, must, shall, should, will

 QUICK CHECK 4

Identify the italicized verb in each of the following sentences as an *action verb,* a *linking verb,* or a *helping verb.* Then, for each action verb, tell whether the verb is *transitive* or *intransitive.*

EXAMPLE **1.** Grandpa had *made* Chrissy's tree house.
 1. *action verb, transitive*

1. Chrissy's tree house *was* beautiful.
2. Leah *walked* away angrily.
3. Leah *wanted* a tree house, too.
4. Her tree house *seemed* cozy but lonely.
5. What *would* she do?

 Using Vivid Verbs

Using a variety of vivid action verbs can make your writing more interesting. Eliminate dull, vague verbs. Instead, choose vivid verbs that accurately express the specific action you are describing.

DULL, VAGUE Her tree house had many admirers.
VIVID Her tree house attracted many admirers.

THE ADVERB

1h. **An *adverb* is a word used to modify a verb, an adjective, or another adverb.**

EXAMPLES The two brothers quarreled **angrily.**

The Creator became **even** angrier.

Very soon, there would be war.

An adverb tells *where, when, how,* or *to what extent* (*how much* or *how long*).

WHERE?	The Creator took them **away.**
WHEN?	**Then** they released their arrows.
HOW?	**Obediently,** the brothers did as they were told.
TO WHAT EXTENT?	The Creator's plan **almost** worked.

For more information about helping verbs and verb phrases, see pages 703 and 727.

Try It Out ✎

In the following sentences, replace each dull, vague verb with a vivid, specific verb (and helping verbs).

1. Friendship is important in our lives.
2. However, friends may not always be friendly to each other.
3. Conflicts can come between them.
4. Angry words may be said.
5. Yet just as quickly, friends can be forgiven and be friends again.

Quick Check 4: Answers
1. linking verb
2. action verb, intransitive
3. action verb, transitive
4. linking verb
5. helping verb

Try It Out: Possible Answers
1. Friendship plays an important part in our lives.
2. However, friends may fight with each other.
3. Conflicts can drive a wedge between them.
4. Angry words can hurt.
5. Yet just as quickly, forgiveness can heal.

Quick Check 5: Answers
1. badly—needed
2. extremely—hard
3. Then—lived; quite—peacefully; peacefully—lived
4. Unfortunately—had made; too—beautiful
5. Not—surprisingly; surprisingly—quarreled; eventually—quarreled; again—quarreled

Try It Out: Possible Answers
1. Smith's dragon is chrome-plated and wired for electricity.
2. His dragon sits placidly at his side.
3. I was shocked at its name.
4. Can a three-thousand-year-old dragon learn to cook?
5. It can if you believe Smith's hilarious poem in this book.

☞ For more on using adverbs and on using modifiers in general, see Part 5: Using Modifiers.

Adverbs may come before, after, or between the words they modify.

EXAMPLES   They had lived **happily** in the new lands.

They **happily** had lived in the new lands.

They had **happily** lived in the new lands.

✓ *QUICK CHECK 5*

Identify the adverb (or adverbs) in each of the following sentences. Then, give the word (or words) each adverb modifies.

EXAMPLE   1. Have you ever imagined life without fire?
   1. *ever—have imagined*

1. The people badly needed fire.
2. Without fire, their lives were extremely hard.
3. Then the people lived quite peacefully.
4. Unfortunately, the Creator had made Loo-Wit too beautiful.
5. Not surprisingly, the brothers eventually quarreled again.

Try It Out ✎

For each of the following sentences, replace *very* with a more descriptive adverb, or revise the sentence so that other words carry more of the descriptive meaning.

1. Smith's dragon is *very* modern.
2. His dragon is *very* tame.
3. I was *very* surprised at its name.
4. Can a *very* old dragon learn to cook?
5. It can if you believe Smith's *very* humorous poem in this book.

Using Descriptive Adverbs

The adverb *very* is overused. Try to replace *very* with more descriptive adverbs. You may also revise the sentence so that other words carry more of the descriptive meaning.

EXAMPLE   The poem "The Toaster" is very short.
REVISED   The poem "The Toaster" is the shortest poem I've ever read.
         or
The poem "The Toaster" has only four lines.

THE PREPOSITION

1i.   A *preposition* is a word used to show the relationship of a noun or a pronoun to another word in the sentence.

Notice how a change in the preposition changes the relationship between the snake and the chair in each of the following sentences.

A snake is **on** your chair.   A snake is **next to** your chair.
A snake is **under** your chair.   A snake is **near** your chair.

NOTE   The word *but* is a preposition when it means "except."

EXAMPLE   My little brother can be nothing **but** a pest sometimes.

Commonly Used Prepositions			
aboard	before	in	over
about	behind	in addition to	past
above	below	in front of	since
according to	beneath	inside	through
across	beside	like	throughout

The Prepositional Phrase

A preposition is usually followed by a noun or a pronoun. This noun or pronoun is called the **object of the preposition**. All together, the preposition, its object, and any modifiers of the object are called a **prepositional phrase**.

EXAMPLE   Rattlesnakes can be found **in the desert.**

A preposition may have more than one object.

EXAMPLE   Rattlesnakes can be found **in the desert or the forest.**

Adverb or Preposition?

Some words may be used as either prepositions or adverbs. To tell an adverb from a preposition, remember that a preposition always has a noun or a pronoun as its object.

ADVERB   The snake slithered **along.**
PREPOSITION   The snake slithered **along** the path.

☑ *QUICK CHECK 6*

Identify the preposition (or prepositions) in each of the following sentences. Then, give the object of each preposition.

EXAMPLE   1. The rattlesnake rested beside the rocks.
        1. *beside—rocks*

1. The sound of its rattles frightens animals away.
2. Even large animals like buffalo or deer fear it.
3. Without that sound, rattlers might waste their venom.
4. Do not rouse a rattler from its sleep.
5. Like people, rattlers can awake in a bad mood.

THE CONJUNCTION

1j. A *conjunction* is a word used to join words or groups of words.

The most common conjunctions are called *coordinating conjunctions*.

Coordinating Conjunctions

and	but	or	nor	for	so	yet

EXAMPLES   Have you ever heard of Buck Jones, Tom Tyler, **or** Hoot Gibson?
Did you buy the cards **and** get a present for Father?
He was confused, **but** he made a choice.

☞ For more about prepositional phrases, see pages 721–724.

NOTE Do not confuse a prepositional phrase that begins with *to* (*to town*) with a verb form that begins with *to* (*to run*).

☞ For information on using commas in a series of words, see page 750. For information on using commas when joining sentences, see page 750.

Quick Check 6: Answers
1. of—rattles
2. like—buffalo, deer
3. Without—sound
4. from—sleep
5. Like—people; in—mood

NOTE When *for* is used as a conjunction, it connects groups of words that are sentences, and it is preceded by a comma. On all other occasions, *for* is used as a preposition.

THE INTERJECTION

 1k. An *interjection* is a word used to express emotion. An interjection does not have a grammatical relation to other words in the sentence. Usually an interjection is followed by an exclamation point but sometimes may be set off by a comma.

EXAMPLES **Oh!** Is that a President Cleveland card?
Why, this must be your lucky day!

Common Interjections

aha	goodness	hooray	ouch	wow
alas	gosh	oh	well	yikes
aw	hey	oops	whew	yippee

 QUICK CHECK 7

Identify the *conjunctions* and *interjections* in the following sentences.

EXAMPLE 1. Well, Armand did seem kind and thoughtful.
1. *Well—interjection; and—conjunction*

1. Gosh, that family had hard times but stuck together.
2. Hey! Rollie's not your friend, yet you sold him your card.
3. Hooray! I have thirty-five cents, so I can get a new card.
4. Wow! You certainly know a lot about presidents and cowboys.
5. Oh, Rollie or Roger knows just as much about them.

DETERMINING PARTS OF SPEECH

The part of speech of a word is determined by the way the word is used in a sentence. Many words can be used as more than one part of speech.

EXAMPLES The boys were angry at Jerry, **for** he had sold the card. [conjunction]
He had sold the card **for** five dollars. [preposition]

The bucket fell to the bottom of the **well.** [noun]
Well, don't you look nice today! [interjection]
Suddenly, I did not feel **well.** [adjective]
How **well** did you do on the test? [adverb]

His warm jacket was filled with **down.** [noun]
Attendance is **down** at our soccer games. [adjective]
She slowly came **down** the stairs. [preposition]
Don't look **down.** [adverb]
The team will **down** more water in this heat. [verb]

702 LANGUAGE HANDBOOK

✓ QUICK CHECK 8

Identify the part of speech of the italicized word in each sentence.

EXAMPLE   1. His *search* led him to the closet.
               1. *noun*

1. Armand's *need* was more important.
2. *Goodness*! That was a kind thing to do.
3. In confusion, he looked *away.*
4. I'm *so* happy!
5. May I borrow your *baseball* glove?

2 AGREEMENT

NUMBER

Number is the form of a word that indicates whether the word is singular or plural.

2a. **When a word refers to one person, place, thing, or idea, it is *singular* in number. When a word refers to more than one, it is *plural* in number.**

SINGULAR	road	goat	child	he	each
PLURAL	roads	goats	children	they	all

☞ For more about forming plurals, see pages 764–765.

AGREEMENT OF SUBJECT AND VERB

2b. **A verb agrees with its subject in number.**

A subject and verb *agree* when they have the same number.

(1) Singular subjects take singular verbs.

EXAMPLES   **Hanukkah comes** once a year.
               Aaron loves Zlateh the goat.

(2) Plural subjects take plural verbs.

EXAMPLES   Isaac Bashevis Singer's **stories celebrate** ordinary life.
               His **characters seem** real.

The first helping verb in a verb phrase must agree with its subject.

EXAMPLES   **Reuven is** selling the family's beloved goat.
               The **sisters are** crying at the news.
               Does he know the way to the town?
               Do you have a pet?

LANGUAGE HANDBOOK 703

Quick Check 8: Answers
1. noun
2. interjection
3. adverb
4. adverb
5. adjective

Resources ────
- *Language Handbook Worksheets,* pp. 17–23
- *Language Workshop CD-ROM,* Chapter 2: Agreement

QUICK CHECK I

For each of the following items, choose the correct form of the verb in parentheses.

EXAMPLE   I. (*Do, Does*) Aaron have any trouble on his trip?
                I. *Does*

1. A sudden storm (*covers, cover*) the roads with snow.
2. Icicles (*forms, form*) on the goat's beard.
3. (*Has, Have*) Aaron gotten lost?
4. They (*is, are*) seeking shelter from the storm.
5. I (*is, am*) not telling the end of the story.

PROBLEMS IN AGREEMENT

Prepositional Phrases Between Subjects and Verbs

2c. The number of a subject is not changed by a prepositional phrase following the subject.

EXAMPLE   **Drifts** of snow **cover** the roads.

Indefinite Pronouns

Some pronouns do not refer to a definite person, place, thing, or idea and are therefore called *indefinite pronouns.*

2d. The following indefinite pronouns are singular: *anybody, anyone, each, either, everybody, everyone, neither, nobody, no one, one, somebody, someone.*

EXAMPLE   **No one knows** where the boy and the goat are.

2e. The following indefinite pronouns are plural: *both, few, many, several.*

EXAMPLE   **Both** of them **were** safe.

2f. The following indefinite pronouns may be either singular or plural: *all, any, most, none, some.*

The number of the subject *all, any, most, none,* or *some* is often determined by the number of the object in a prepositional phrase following the subject. If the subject refers to a singular object, the subject is singular. If the subject refers to a plural object, the subject is plural.

EXAMPLES   **Some** of the hay **has been eaten.** [*Some* refers to *hay.*]
                  Some of his dreams **were** of warm days. [*Some* refers to *dreams.*]

Compound Subjects

2g. Subjects joined by *and* usually take a plural verb.

EXAMPLE **Aaron** and **Zlateh are sleeping** in the haystack.

2h. When subjects are joined by *or* or *nor*, the verb agrees with the subject nearer the verb.

EXAMPLES Neither **Aaron** nor his **sisters want** to sell Zlateh.
Neither Aaron's **sisters** nor **he wants** to sell Zlateh.

✓ QUICK CHECK 2

Most of the following sentences contain an error in agreement. Correct each error. If a sentence is correct, write *C*.

EXAMPLE **1.** The grass in the meadows were growing at Hanukkah.
1. *was*

1. Furriers like Reuven has no work.
2. Reuven and Leah sends Aaron to the town.
3. A cap and earmuffs keeps Aaron warm.
4. Both of Aaron's younger sisters cry at the news.
5. None of the children wants to see Zlateh go.

2i. When the subject follows the verb, find the subject, and make sure the verb agrees with it. The subject usually follows the verb in sentences beginning with *here* or *there* and in questions.

EXAMPLES There **is food** for Zlateh in the haystack. [food is]
Does Aaron dream of flowers? [Aaron does dream]

The contractions *here's, there's,* and *where's* contain the verb *is* and should be used only with singular subjects.

NONSTANDARD Here's the books.
STANDARD Here **are** the **books.**
STANDARD Here's the **book.**

2j. The contractions *don't* and *doesn't* must agree with their subjects.

Use *don't* with plural subjects and with the pronouns *I* and *you.*

EXAMPLES **They don't** need anything else.
I don't like goat's milk.
Don't you like goat's milk?

Use *doesn't* with other singular subjects.

EXAMPLE **She doesn't** understand his worries.

NOTE When the subject of a sentence follows the verb, the word order is said to be *inverted.* To find the subject of a sentence with inverted order, restate the sentence in normal word order.

INVERTED There **goes Zlateh.**
NORMAL **Zlateh goes** there.
INVERTED **Does Zlateh go** there?
NORMAL **Zlateh does go** there.
INVERTED Into the kitchen **goes Zlateh.**
NORMAL **Zlateh goes** into the kitchen.

☞ For more about contractions, see page 759.

Quick Check 2: Answers
1. have
2. send
3. keep
4. C
5. want

Quick Check 3: Answers

1. Here are several poems about pets. (or Here're)
2. Doesn't he have a pet?
3. His mother doesn't want one for a number of reasons.
4. Don't you and your brothers want a pet?
5. All over the house are dog hairs.

Try It Out: Answers

1. The themes of this story are simple.
2. Have they looked in the glossary?
3. We find some interesting information there.
4. Here are your copies. (or Here're)
5. One of my pencils is broken.

Resources

- *Language Handbook Worksheets,* pp. 25–34
- *Language Workshop CD-ROM,* Chapter 3: Using Verbs Correctly

---

 QUICK CHECK 3

For each of the following sentences, correct each error in agreement.

| EXAMPLE | 1. Poems like "Steam Shovel" ends on a humorous note. |
| | 1. *Poems like "Steam Shovel" end on a humorous note.* |

1. Here's several poems about pets.
2. Don't he have a pet?
3. His mother don't want one for a number of reasons.
4. Doesn't you and your brother want a pet?
5. All over the house is dog hairs.

Try It Out ✎

Revise each of the following sentences. If a subject and verb are plural, change them to singular. If they are singular, change them to plural.

1. The theme of this story is simple.
2. Has she looked in the glossary?
3. I find some interesting information there.
4. Here's your copy.
5. Both my pencils are broken.

 TIPS FOR WRITERS

Using Singular and Plural Forms

Generally, nouns ending in *s* are plural (*candles, ideas, neighbors, horses*), and verbs ending in *s* are singular (*sees, writes, speaks, carries*). However, verbs used with the singular pronouns *I* and *you* often do not end in *s*.

EXAMPLES	**Winter arrives** early there.
	The **seasons change** quickly.
	I like Singer's stories.
	Do you like them, too?

3 USING VERBS

THE PRINCIPAL PARTS OF A VERB

The four basic forms of a verb are called the ***principal parts*** of the verb.

3a. The principal parts of a verb are the *base form,* the *present participle,* the *past,* and the *past participle.*

BASE FORM	PRESENT PARTICIPLE	PAST	PAST PARTICIPLE
work	(is) working	worked	(have) worked
sing	(is) singing	sang	(have) sung

The principal parts of a verb are used to express the time when an action occurs.

PRESENT TIME	Ray Bradbury **writes** science fiction.
	I **am writing** a report on "All Summer in a Day."
PAST TIME	I **wrote** the first paragraph last night.
	I finally **had written** a thesis statement.
FUTURE TIME	I **will write** the rest of it this weekend.
	By Monday, I **will have written** the whole report.

NOTE Present participles and past participles always require helping verbs (forms of *be* and *have*).

706 LANGUAGE HANDBOOK

Regular Verbs

3b. A *regular verb* forms its past and past participle by adding *–d* or *–ed* to the base form.

BASE FORM	PRESENT PARTICIPLE	PAST	PAST PARTICIPLE
use	(is) using	used	(have) used
suppose	(is) supposing	supposed	(have) supposed
attack	(is) attacking	attacked	(have) attacked
drown	(is) drowning	drowned	(have) drowned
rely	(is) relying	relied	(have) relied

One common error in forming the past or past participle of a regular verb is to leave off the *–d* or *–ed* ending.

NONSTANDARD   The sun was suppose to come out.

STANDARD   The sun **was supposed** to come out.

If you are not sure about the principal parts of a verb, look in a dictionary. Entries for irregular verbs give the principal parts of the verb.

☑ QUICK CHECK 1

For each of the following sentences, supply the correct past or past participle form of the verb given in italics.

EXAMPLE   1. *crush*   On Venus, heavy rain _____ all the new plants.
                    1. crushed

1. *watch*   Many of the children have never _____ the sun set.
2. *look*   How they _____ forward to it!
3. *remember*   Only Margot _____ the sun.
4. *live*   However, she has _____ on Venus for many years.
5. *like*   She and the other children have not always _____ each other.

Irregular Verbs

3c. An *irregular verb* forms its past and past participle in some other way than by adding *–d* or *–ed* to the base form.

An irregular verb forms its past and past participle

• by changing vowels or consonants

BASE FORM	PAST	PAST PARTICIPLE
ring	rang	(have) rung
make	made	(have) made
hold	held	(have) held

Quick Check 1: Answers
1. watched
2. looked
3. remembered
4. lived
5. liked

- by changing vowels and consonants

BASE FORM	PAST	PAST PARTICIPLE
eat	ate	(have) eaten
go	went	(have) gone
be	was/were	(have) been

- by making no changes

BASE FORM	PAST	PAST PARTICIPLE
spread	spread	(have) spread
burst	burst	(have) burst
cost	cost	(have) cost

COMMON IRREGULAR VERBS			
BASE FORM	PRESENT PARTICIPLE	PAST	PAST PARTICIPLE
begin	(is) beginning	began	(have) begun
blow	(is) blowing	blew	(have) blown
break	(is) breaking	broke	(have) broken
bring	(is) bringing	brought	(have) brought
choose	(is) choosing	chose	(have) chosen
come	(is) coming	came	(have) come
do	(is) doing	did	(have) done
drink	(is) drinking	drank	(have) drunk
drive	(is) driving	drove	(have) driven
fall	(is) falling	fell	(have) fallen
freeze	(is) freezing	froze	(have) frozen
give	(is) giving	gave	(have) given

✔ QUICK CHECK 2

For each of the following sentences, give the correct past or past participle form of the verb in parentheses.

EXAMPLE   1. Margot had (*come, came*) from Ohio.
          1. *come*

1. Rain had (*fell, fallen*) for years on Venus.
2. Their teacher has (*gave, given*) them a brief recess.
3. Happily, the children (*gone, went*) to see the sun.
4. Sunlight (*burst, bursted*) out of the clouds.
5. What terrible thing have they (*did, done*)?

Quick Check 2: Answers
1. fallen
2. given
3. went
4. burst
5. done

COMMON IRREGULAR VERBS			
BASE FORM	**PRESENT PARTICIPLE**	**PAST**	**PAST PARTICIPLE**
know	(is) knowing	knew	(have) known
ride	(is) riding	rode	(have) ridden
run	(is) running	ran	(have) run
see	(is) seeing	saw	(have) seen
shrink	(is) shrinking	shrank	(have) shrunk
sing	(is) singing	sang	(have) sung
sink	(is) sinking	sank	(have) sunk
speak	(is) speaking	spoke	(have) spoken
steal	(is) stealing	stole	(have) stolen
swim	(is) swimming	swam	(have) swum
take	(is) taking	took	(have) taken
throw	(is) throwing	threw	(have) thrown
wear	(is) wearing	wore	(have) worn
write	(is) writing	wrote	(have) written

 QUICK CHECK 3

For each of the following sentences, give the correct past or past participle form of the verb in parentheses.

EXAMPLE 1. Who (*wrote, written*) this version of Medusa's story?
1. *wrote*

1. The oracle (*knew, known*) the future of King Acrisios.
2. He (*threw, throw*) poor Danae into an underground room alone.
3. Danae and the boy have (*rode, ridden*) inside a chest for days.
4. Dictys the fisherman (*took, taken*) them out.
5. Danae must have (*sing, sung*) many songs to young Perseus.

VERB TENSE

3d. The *tense* of a verb indicates the time of the action or state of being that is expressed by the verb.

This time line shows how the six tenses of every verb are related.

Past	*Present*	*Future*
existing or happening in the past	existing or happening now	existing or happening in the future

Past Perfect	*Present Perfect*	*Future Perfect*
existing or happening before a specific time in the past	existing or happening sometime before now, or starting in the past and continuing now	existing or happening before a specific time in the future

LANGUAGE HANDBOOK 709

Quick Check 3: Answers
1. knew
2. threw
3. ridden
4. took
5. sung

EXAMPLES

present perfect   present

She **has read** "Petals" and **has** a topic for her paper.

past perfect   past

She **had chosen** another poem but **decided** against it.

future perfect   future

She **will have written** it by Friday and **will proofread** it on Monday.

Listing all the forms of a verb in the six tenses is called **_conjugating_** a verb.

<table>
<tr><td colspan="2" align="center">CONJUGATION OF THE VERB WRITE</td></tr>
<tr><td colspan="2" align="center">PRESENT TENSE</td></tr>
<tr><td>SINGULAR
I write
you write
he, she, or it writes</td><td>PLURAL
we write
you write
they write</td></tr>
<tr><td colspan="2" align="center">PAST TENSE</td></tr>
<tr><td>SINGULAR
I wrote
you wrote
he, she, or it wrote</td><td>PLURAL
we wrote
you wrote
they wrote</td></tr>
<tr><td colspan="2" align="center">FUTURE TENSE</td></tr>
<tr><td>SINGULAR
I will write
you will write
he, she, or it will write</td><td>PLURAL
we will write
you will write
they will write</td></tr>
<tr><td colspan="2" align="center">PRESENT PERFECT TENSE</td></tr>
<tr><td>SINGULAR
I have written
you have written
he, she, or it has written</td><td>PLURAL
we have written
you have written
they have written</td></tr>
<tr><td colspan="2" align="center">PAST PERFECT TENSE</td></tr>
<tr><td>SINGULAR
I had written
you had written
he, she, or it had written</td><td>PLURAL
we had written
you had written
they had written</td></tr>
<tr><td colspan="2" align="center">FUTURE PERFECT TENSE</td></tr>
<tr><td>SINGULAR
I will have written
you will have written
he, she, or it will have written</td><td>PLURAL
we will have written
you will have written
they will have written</td></tr>
</table>

NOTE In the future tense and the future perfect tense, the helping verb *shall* is sometimes used in place of *will*.

QUICK CHECK 4

Change the tense of the verb in each of the following sentences to the tense given in italics.

EXAMPLE   1. *past*   In "Petals," Pat Mora writes about an old woman.
       1. *In "Petals," Pat Mora wrote about an old woman.*

1. *future*   The woman sells baskets and paper flowers.
2. *present perfect* Her stall was there for many years.
3. *past perfect*   Straw hats are popular there.
4. *present*   She will remember the days of her youth.
5. *future perfect* By day's end, many people saw her flowers.

SIX CONFUSING VERBS

Sit and Set

(1) The verb *sit* means "to rest in an upright, seated position." *Sit* seldom takes an object.

(2) The verb *set* means "to put (something) in a place." *Set* often takes an object. Notice that *set* has the same form for the base form, the past, and the past participle.

BASE FORM	PRESENT PARTICIPLE	PAST	PAST PARTICIPLE
sit (to rest)	(is) sitting	sat	(have) sat
set (to put)	(is) setting	set	(have) set

EXAMPLES   She **sits** in the market. [no object]
       Sellers **set** their goods on the tables.
          [Set what? *Goods* is the object.]
       The children **sat** quietly. [no object]
       She **set** them there. [Set what? *Them* is the object.]

 QUICK CHECK 5

For each of the following sentences, choose the correct verb in parentheses.

EXAMPLE   1. Tapahonso's grandmother (*sat, set*) on a wild horse.
       1. *sat*

1. Where did she (*sit, set*) her saddle?
2. Was the saddle (*sitting, setting*) on the fence?
3. Her family (*sat, set*) and waited for her.
4. Only then, did she (*sit, set*) down.
5. She (*set, sat*) the place mats on the table.

Quick Check 4: Answers
1. The woman will sell baskets and paper flowers.
2. Her stall has been there for many years.
3. Straw hats had been popular there.
4. She remembers the days of her youth.
5. By day's end, many people will have seen her flowers.

Quick Check 5: Answers
1. set
2. sitting
3. sat
4. sit
5. set

Lie and Lay

(1) **The verb _lie_ means "to rest," "to recline," or "to be in a place." _Lie_ never takes an object.**

(2) **The verb _lay_ means "to put (something) in a place." _Lay_ usually takes an object.**

BASE FORM	PRESENT PARTICIPLE	PAST	PAST PARTICIPLE
lie (to rest)	(is) lying	lay	(have) lain
lay (to put)	(is) laying	laid	(have) laid

EXAMPLES   Puppets **are lying** under the table. [no object]
A girl **is laying** a puppet down. [Is laying what? _Puppet_ is the object.]

One flower **lies** on the ground. [no object]
A child **laid** it there. [Child laid what? _It_ is the object.]

☑ **QUICK CHECK 6**

For each sentence, choose the correct verb in parentheses.

EXAMPLE   1. Her hair (_lay, laid_) neatly against her head.
         1. _lay_

1. The kitchen utensils (_laid, lay_) in their places.
2. Where have you (_lain, laid_) Grandmother's picture?
3. The foals have (_lain, laid_) down for a nap.
4. She (_lay, laid_) the blanket on the pony's back.
5. She was (_lying, laying_) in the dirt where the horse had thrown her.

Rise and Raise

(1) **The verb _rise_ means "to go up" or "to get up." _Rise_ seldom takes an object.**

(2) **The verb _raise_ means "to lift up" or "to cause (something) to rise." _Raise_ usually takes an object.**

BASE FORM	PRESENT PARTICIPLE	PAST	PAST PARTICIPLE
rise (to go up)	(is) rising	rose	(have) risen
raise (to lift up)	(is) raising	raised	(have) raised

EXAMPLES   She **rises** very early on market days. [no object]
She **raises** her eyes to the hills. [She raises what? _Eyes_ is the object.]

COMPUTER NOTE   Most word processors can help you check to be sure that you have used verbs correctly. For example, a spelling checker will highlight misspelled verb forms such as _drownded_ or _costed_. Style-checking software can point out inconsistent verb tense. It may also highlight uses of problem verb pairs such as _lie/lay_ or _rise/raise_. Remember, though, that the computer is just a tool. You still need to make all the style and content choices that affect your writing.

Quick Check 6: Answers
1. lay
2. laid
3. lain
4. laid
5. lying

She **has risen** from her seat. [no object]

A man **has raised** a basket up high. [A man has raised what? *Basket* is the object.]

 QUICK CHECK 7

For each sentence, choose the correct verb in parentheses.

EXAMPLE 1. She must have (*raised, risen*) the saddle carefully.

          1. *raised*

1. The horses' heads (*raised, rose*) at her step.
2. They (*raised, rose*) their heads when she called.
3. She must have (*risen, raised*) early in the morning.
4. The horse's hooves were (*rising, raising*) in the air.
5. She (*raised, rose*) clouds of dust behind her.

 Using Consistent Verb Tense

When writing about events that take place in the present, use verbs in the present tense. Similarly, when writing about events that occurred in the past, use verbs in the past tense. Do not change needlessly from one tense to another.

INCONSISTENT When she read "Petals," she thinks of you. [*Read* is past tense, and *thinks* is present tense.]

PRESENT When she **reads** "Petals," she **thinks** of you.

PAST When she **read** "Petals," she **thought** of you.

4 USING PRONOUNS

THE FORMS OF PERSONAL PRONOUNS

The form of a personal pronoun shows its use in a sentence. Pronouns used as subjects and predicate nominatives are in the **subject form**.

EXAMPLES **I** read "A Glory over Everything." [subject]

The author is **she.** [predicate nominative]

Pronouns used as direct objects and indirect objects of verbs and as objects of prepositions are in the **object form**.

EXAMPLES Harriet Tubman asked **her** for help. [direct object]

Many people gave **her** help. [indirect object]

Have you read about **her**? [object of preposition]

Try It Out 🖉

Read the following paragraph, and decide whether you think it should be rewritten in the present or past tense. Then, change the appropriate verb forms to make the verb tense consistent.

[1] We frequently go to the flea market just outside town. [2] The sellers had some unique merchandise. [3] At lunch, we stop and get a sandwich there. [4] Usually, someone like the woman in Pat Mora's poem "Petals" was there. [5] I enjoyed talking with these interesting people.

Quick Check 7: Answers
1. rose
2. raised
3. risen
4. rising
5. raised

Try It Out: Possible Answers
[1] We frequently go to the flea market just outside town. [2] The sellers have some unique merchandise. [3] At lunch, we stop and get a sandwich there. [4] Usually, someone like the woman in Pat Mora's poem "Petals" is there. [5] I enjoy talking with these interesting people.

Resources ———
- *Language Handbook Worksheets,* pp. 36–41
- *Language Workshop CD-ROM,* Chapter 4: Using Pronouns Correctly

The **possessive form** (*my, your, his, her, its, their, our*) is used to show ownership or relationship.

EXAMPLES   With **her** help, many escaped slavery.
The first report about Harriet Tubman was **ours.**

PERSONAL PRONOUNS		
SINGULAR		
SUBJECT FORM	**OBJECT FORM**	**POSSESSIVE FORM**
I you he, she, it	me you him, her, it	my, mine your, yours his, her, hers, its
PLURAL		
SUBJECT FORM	**OBJECT FORM**	**POSSESSIVE FORM**
we you they	us you them	our, ours your, yours their, theirs

☑ *QUICK CHECK I*

Classify each of the following pronouns as the *subject form* or *object form*. If the pronoun can be the subject form or the object form, write *either*.

EXAMPLE   1. she
1. *subject form*

1. them
2. I
3. us
4. you

5. he
6. him
7. they
8. her

9. me
10. it

The Subject Form

4a. Use the subject form for a pronoun that is the subject of a verb.

EXAMPLES   **She** and **they** set out on their journey. [*She* and *they* are the subjects of *set*.]
Can **we** imagine such a thing? [*We* is the subject of *can imagine*.]

To choose the correct pronoun in a compound subject, try each form of the pronoun separately.

EXAMPLE: Liza or (*me, I*) will play Harriet Tubman.
Me will play Harriet Tubman.
I will play Harriet Tubman.
ANSWER: Liza or **I** will play Harriet Tubman.

Quick Check I: Answers
1. object form
2. subject form
3. object form
4. either
5. subject form
6. object form
7. subject form
8. object form
9. object form
10. either

4b. Use the subject form for a pronoun that is a predicate nominative.

EXAMPLES Her husband was **he.** [*He* identifies the subject *husband.*]

Her betrayers were **they.** [*They* identifies the subject *betrayers.*]

 **QUICK CHECK 2**

For each of the following sentences, choose the correct form of the pronoun in parentheses.

EXAMPLE 1. Did her brothers and (*she, her*) succeed?
1. *she*

1. In the fields, (*them, they*) sang songs with hidden meanings.
2. Harriet Tubman and (*he, him*) did not agree about leaving.
3. (*Her, She*) and many others helped the Underground Railroad.
4. The conductor is (*she, her*).
5. The next reader will be (*him, he*).

The Object Form

4c. Use the object form for a pronoun that is the direct object of a verb.

EXAMPLES Her story amazed **us.** [*Us* tells *who* was amazed.]

Vines were plentiful, but the men did not see **them.**
[*Them* tells *what* the men did not see.]

To choose the correct pronoun in a compound direct object, try each form of the pronoun separately in the sentence.

EXAMPLE Did anyone help (*she, her*) and the others? [Did anyone help *she?* Did anyone help *her? Her* is the correct form.]

4d. Use the object form for a pronoun that is the indirect object of a verb.

EXAMPLE Harriet gave **her** a quilt. [*Her* tells *to whom* Harriet gave a quilt.]

To choose the correct pronoun in a compound indirect object, try each form of the pronoun separately in the sentence.

4e. Use the object form for a pronoun that is the object of a preposition.

EXAMPLES to **them**   in front of **me**   according to **her**

To choose the correct pronoun when the object of a preposition is compound, try each form of the pronoun separately in the sentence.

NOTE When choosing the correct form of a pronoun used as a predicate nominative, remember that the pronoun could just as well be used as the subject in the sentence.

EXAMPLE The one in the wagon was **she.**
or
She was the one in the wagon.

☞ For more about predicate nominatives, see page 732.

☞ For more information about direct objects, see page 730.

☞ For more about indirect objects, see pages 730–731.

☞ For a list of prepositions, see page 700. For more information about prepositional phrases, see pages 721–724.

LANGUAGE HANDBOOK 715

LANGUAGE HANDBOOK

Quick Check 2: Answers
1. they
2. he
3. She
4. she
5. he

☑ QUICK CHECK 3

For each of the following sentences, identify the correct personal pronoun in parentheses.

EXAMPLE   I. At each stop, new directions were given to (*she, her*).
       I. *her*

1. Tubman's journey took (*her, she*) far away from (*them, they*).
2. She would have taken (*they, them*) with (*she, her*).
3. Will you read (*me, I*) these lines for the Reader's Theater?
4. Between you and (*I, me*), Viola should be playing Harriet.
5. Who will play (*he, him*) and (*they, them*)?

Try It Out ✎

Revise the following sentences to show standard, polite usage of pronouns.

1. That was them in the blue sedan.
2. May I and Rhoda ride with you?
3. The one doing the dishes is always me.
4. Call me, and tell me if it was her.
5. Save a seat for me and Larry.

Revising for Polite Usage

Expressions such as *It's me, That's her,* and *It was them* are accepted in everyday speaking. In writing, however, such expressions should generally be avoided.

STANDARD   It is **I.**   That is **she.**   It was **they.**

Additionally, remember that in English it is considered polite to put first-person pronouns (*I, me, mine, we, us, ours*) last in compound constructions.

EXAMPLE   My friends and **I** will design the set.

SPECIAL PRONOUN PROBLEMS

Who and Whom

The pronoun *who* has two different forms. *Who* is the subject form. *Whom* is the object form. When deciding whether to use *who* or *whom* in a question, follow these steps:

STEP 1:   Rephrase the question as a statement.

STEP 2:   Decide how the pronoun is used—as subject, predicate nominative, object of the verb, or object of a preposition.

STEP 3:   Determine whether the subject form or the object form is correct according to the rules of standard English.

STEP 4:   Select the correct form of the pronoun.

EXAMPLE: (*Who, Whom*) did Harriet Tubman tell?

STEP 1:   The statement is *Harriet Tubman did tell* (*who, whom*).

STEP 2:   The subject of the verb is *Harriet Tubman,* the verb is *did tell,* and the pronoun is the direct object.

STEP 3:   A pronoun used as a direct object takes the object form.

STEP 4:   The object form is *whom.*

ANSWER: **Whom** did Harriet Tubman tell?

> **NOTE**   In spoken English, the use of *whom* is becoming less common. In fact, when you are speaking, you may correctly begin any question with *who* regardless of the grammar of the sentence. In written English, however, you should distinguish between *who* and *whom.*

716 LANGUAGE HANDBOOK

Pronouns with Appositives

Sometimes a pronoun is followed directly by an appositive. To decide which pronoun to use before an appositive, omit the appositive, and try each form of the pronoun separately.

EXAMPLE: *(We, Us)* boys will read for the parts. [*Boys* is the appositive identifying the pronoun.]
We will read for the parts.
Us will read for the parts.

ANSWER: **We** boys will read for the parts.

 QUICK CHECK 4

For each of the following sentences, choose the correct pronoun in parentheses.

EXAMPLE 1. Four of *(we, us)* girls want to play Harriet.
1. *us*

1. *(Who, Whom)* is Ann Petry?
2. The behavior of Tubman's brothers angered *(we, us)* girls.
3. For *(who, whom)* did Tubman work?
4. *(Whom, Who)* do you like to read about?
5. The readers will be *(us, we)* boys.

5 USING MODIFIERS

COMPARISON OF MODIFIERS

A **modifier** is a word or a phrase that describes or limits the meaning of another word. Two kinds of modifiers—adjectives and adverbs—may be used to compare things. In making comparisons, adjectives and adverbs take different forms. The form that is used depends on how many syllables the modifier has and how many things are being compared.

5a. The three degrees of comparison of modifiers are *positive*, *comparative*, **and** *superlative*.

The **positive degree** is used when only one thing is being described.

EXAMPLES Perseus's discus flew **high.**
The discus flew **quickly.**

The **comparative degree** is used when two things are being compared.

EXAMPLES Perseus's discus flew **higher** than the course.
The discus flew **more quickly** than the wind.

 For more information about appositives, see page 751.

For more information about appositives, see page 751.

Quick Check 4: Answers
1. Who
2. us
3. whom
4. Whom
5. we

Resources ——————
- *Language Handbook Worksheets,* pp. 46–50
- *Language Workshop CD-ROM,* Chapter 5: Using Modifiers Correctly

The **superlative degree** is used when three or more things are being compared.

EXAMPLES   Which athlete's discus flew **highest** of all?
Which discus flew **most quickly**?

To show decreasing comparisons, all modifiers form their comparative and superlative degrees with *less* and *least*.

POSITIVE	swift	fully
COMPARATIVE	less swift	less fully
SUPERLATIVE	least swift	least fully

Regular Comparison

(1) Most one-syllable modifiers form their comparative and superlative degrees by adding *–er* (*less*) and *–est* (*least*).

POSITIVE	dark	warm	swift
COMPARATIVE	darker	warmer	less swift
SUPERLATIVE	darkest	warmest	least swift

(2) Some two-syllable modifiers form their comparative and superlative degrees by adding *–er* and *–est*. Other two-syllable modifiers form their comparative and superlative degrees by using *more* (*less*) and *most* (*least*).

POSITIVE	angry	helpful	eager
COMPARATIVE	angrier	more helpful	less eager
SUPERLATIVE	angriest	most helpful	least eager

(3) Modifiers that have three or more syllables form their comparative and superlative degrees by using *more* (*less*) and *most* (*least*).

POSITIVE	hideous	fearfully	intelligent
COMPARATIVE	more hideous	more fearfully	less intelligent
SUPERLATIVE	most hideous	most fearfully	least intelligent

✓ QUICK CHECK I

Give the comparative forms and the superlative forms for each of the following modifiers. You may use a dictionary if necessary.

EXAMPLE   I. easy
I. *easier (less easy), easiest (least easy)*

1. furious   6. lucky
2. wise   7. beautifully
3. quickly   8. swiftly
4. helpless   9. handsome
5. poor   10. terrible

LANGUAGE HANDBOOK

For more information about spelling words when adding suffixes, see page 763.

Quick Check I: Answers

1. more (less) furious, most (least) furious
2. wiser (less wise), wisest (least wise)
3. more (less) quickly, most (least) quickly
4. more (less) helpless, most (least) helpless
5. poorer (less poor), poorest (least) poor
6. luckier (less lucky), luckiest (least lucky)
7. more (less) beautifully, most (least) beautifully
8. more (less) swiftly, most (least) swiftly
9. more (less) handsome, most (least) handsome
10. more (less) terrible, most (least) terrible

Irregular Comparison

Some modifiers do not form their comparative and superlative degrees by using the regular methods.

POSITIVE	bad	far	good	well	many	much
COMPARATIVE	worse	farther	better	better	more	more
SUPERLATIVE	worst	farthest	best	best	most	most

You do not need to add anything to an irregular comparison. For example, *worse*, all by itself, is the comparative form of *bad. Worser* and *more (less) worse* are nonstandard forms.

✓ QUICK CHECK 2

For each blank in the following sentences, give the correct form of the italicized modifier.

EXAMPLE **1.** *well*   I liked "Medusa's Head" _____ than "The Fly."

          1. *better*

1. *far*   Perseus threw the discus _____ of all the athletes.
2. *many* Athene helped Perseus through _____ trials than Zeus did.
3. *much* King Polydectes was _____ cruel than Dictys.
4. *good* This drawing of Medusa's head is the _____ in the class.
5. *bad*   Which of the three sisters looked _____?

SPECIAL PROBLEMS WITH MODIFIERS

5b. The modifiers *good* and *well* have different uses.

(1) Use *good* to modify a noun or a pronoun.

EXAMPLE The three old women had only one **good** eye among them.

(2) Use *well* to modify a verb.

EXAMPLE Perseus listened **well** to Athene's advice.

Well can also mean "in good health." When *well* has this meaning, it acts as an adjective.

EXAMPLE In spite of their ordeal, Danae and her son were **well.**

5c. Avoid using double comparisons.

A *double comparison* is the use of both –er and *more (less)* or both –est and *most (least)* to form a comparison. A comparison should be formed in only one of these two ways, not both.

EXAMPLE To Nereus, no one was **lovelier** [*not* more lovelier] than his daughters.

Quick Check 2: Answers
1. farthest
2. more
3. more
4. best
5. worst

Quick Check 3: Answers

1. Who could have been braver than Perseus?
2. He did well on his quest.
3. Medusa's head was the most horrible sight in the world.
4. Perseus became angrier at the king's insult.
5. All of the presents were good, but Perseus had given none.

Quick Check 4: Possible Answers

1. Perseus had rashly made a promise with hardly any thought at all.
2. I could hardly look at Medusa in the movie.
3. There wasn't anybody to help Andromeda.
4. Neither Acrisios nor Perseus could avoid the fate that befell each of them.
5. Didn't anyone there in Larissa know anything about Acrisios?

☑ QUICK CHECK 3

The following sentences contain incorrect forms of comparison. Revise each sentence, using the correct form.

EXAMPLE 1. Andromeda was the most beautifulest person in the land.
    1. *Andromeda was the most beautiful person in the land.*

1. Who could have been more braver than Perseus?
2. He did good on his quest.
3. Medusa's head was the most horriblest sight in the world.
4. Perseus became more angrier at the king's insult.
5. All of the presents were well, but Perseus had given none.

Double Negatives

5d. **Avoid the use of double negatives.**

A **double negative** is the use of two negative words to express one negative idea.

Common Negative Words			
barely	never	none	nothing
hardly	no	no one	nowhere
neither	nobody	not (−n't)	scarcely

NONSTANDARD Polydectes shouldn't never have laughed at Perseus.

STANDARD Polydectes **should never** have laughed at Perseus.

STANDARD Polydectes should**n't** have laughed at Perseus.

☑ QUICK CHECK 4

Revise each of the following sentences to eliminate the double negative. Some double negatives may be corrected in more than one way.

EXAMPLE 1. Without the gods' help, there wasn't no hope for him.
    1. *Without the gods' help, there was no hope for him.*
           or
    1. *Without the gods' help, there wasn't any hope for him.*

1. Perseus had rashly made a promise with hardly no thought at all.
2. I couldn't hardly look at Medusa in the movie.
3. There wasn't nobody to help Andromeda.
4. Neither Acrisios nor Perseus could hardly avoid the fate that befell each of them.
5. Didn't no one there in Larissa know nothing about Acrisios?

6 THE PREPOSITIONAL PHRASE

PHRASES

6a. A *phrase* **is a group of related words that is used as a single part of speech. A phrase does not contain both a verb and its subject.**

Phrases cannot stand alone. They must always be used with other words as part of a sentence.

PHRASE from the Persian culture

SENTENCE "Ali Baba and the Forty Thieves" is a tale that comes **from the Persian culture.**

THE PREPOSITIONAL PHRASE

6b. A *prepositional phrase* **includes a preposition, a noun or a pronoun called the** *object of the preposition,* **and any modifiers of that object.**

EXAMPLES This tale is the story **of a simple woodcutter.** [The noun *woodcutter* is the object of the preposition *of.*]
In the distant past, great things happened **to him.**
[The noun *past* is the object of the preposition *in.* The pronoun *him* is the object of the preposition *to.*]

A preposition may have more than one object.

EXAMPLE The tale is the story **of a man and a treasure.** [The nouns *man* and *treasure* are both objects of the same preposition *of.*]

☞ For a list of commonly used prepositions, see page 700.

☑ **QUICK CHECK I**

Identify the prepositional phrase or phrases in each of the following sentences. Underline each preposition, and circle its object. A preposition may have more than one object.

EXAMPLE 1. In ancient Persia lived two brothers.
   1. *In ancient (Persia)*

1. Cassim was one of the richest merchants in the city.
2. His brother Ali Baba loaded wood onto donkeys.
3. One day in the woods, Ali Baba discovered a great treasure.
4. Inside a cave were heaps of gold and silver.
5. Ali Baba filled some sacks with treasure and returned home.

Quick Check I: Answers
1. of the richest (merchants); in the (city)
2. onto (donkeys)
3. in the (woods)
4. inside a (cave); of (gold) and (silver)
5. with (treasure)

The Adjective Phrase

A prepositional phrase used as an adjective is called an *adjective phrase.*

ADJECTIVE	**Buffalo** herds roamed a few miles away.
ADJECTIVE PHRASE	Herds **of buffalo** roamed a few miles away.

6c. An *adjective phrase* is a prepositional phrase that modifies a noun or a pronoun.

Adjective phrases answer the same questions that single-word adjectives answer: *What kind? Which one? How many?* or *How much?*

EXAMPLES   Long ago, a group **of people** called the Toltecs lived there. [What kind of group?]

The boy **with the headphones** did not hear the news. [Which boy?]

Notice in these examples that an adjective phrase generally follows the word it modifies.

More than one adjective phrase may modify the same noun or pronoun.

EXAMPLE   Huynh Quang Nhuong's journey **from Vietnam to the United States** makes an interesting read. [Both phrases modify the noun *journey.*]

An adjective phrase may modify the object of another adjective phrase.

EXAMPLE   The name **of the hero in this myth** is Quetzalcoatl. [The phrase *in this myth* modifies *hero,* which is the object in the other adjective phrase.]

☑ QUICK CHECK 2

Identify the adjective phrase or phrases in each of the following sentences. Then, give the word that each phrase modifies.

EXAMPLE   1. Quetzalcoatl was an old man with a beard.

1. *with a beard—man*

1. All of the people from the neighboring states were jealous.
2. Quetzalcoatl buried his treasures of gold and silver.
3. The "medicine" in Tezcatlipoca's cup was strong wine.
4. A train of pages and musicians accompanied Quetzalcoatl.
5. The other gods hoped to gain some of his secrets.

The Adverb Phrase

A prepositional phrase used as an adverb is called an *adverb phrase.*

ADVERB	He woke **early.**
ADVERB PHRASE	We woke **in the morning.**

Quick Check 2: Answers
1. of the people—all; from the neighboring states—people
2. of gold and silver—treasures
3. in Tezcatlipoca's cup—"medicine"
4. of pages and musicians—train
5. of his secrets—some

6d. An *adverb phrase* is a prepositional phrase that modifies a verb, an adjective, or an adverb.

An adverb phrase tells *how, when, where, why,* or *to what extent* (that is, *how long, how far,* or *how many*).

EXAMPLES Ali Baba stared **in amazement.** [How?]
In front of him was a heap of gold, silver, and fine silks. [Where?]
His life changed **on that morning.** [When?]
For years, Ali Baba kept his secret. [How long?]
The gold pieces he found numbered **in the thousands.** [How many?]
The thieves traveled together **over many miles.** [How far?]

An adverb phrase may come before or after the word it modifies.

EXAMPLES **In the story "All Summer in a Day,"** children on Venus experience sunshine for the first time.
Children on Venus experience sunshine for the first time **in the story "All Summer in a Day."**

More than one adverb phrase may modify the same word or words.

EXAMPLE **Without any guidance** Richard's Shetland pony can lead him **to the apple orchard.** [Both adverb phrases modify *can lead.*]

An adverb phrase may be followed by an adjective phrase that modifies the object of the preposition in the adverb phrase.

EXAMPLE **In their rush to the door,** the other children forget Margot. [The adverb phrase *in their rush* modifies the verb *forget*. The adjective phrase *to the door* modifies *rush,* which is the object in the adverb phrase.]

 **QUICK CHECK 3**

Identify the prepositional phrase or phrases in each of the following sentences. Then, label each phrase as an *adjective phrase* or an *adverb phrase*. Give the word or words the phrase modifies.

EXAMPLE 1. Forests on Venus had been crushed under the rain.
1. *on Venus—adjective phrase, Forests; under the rain—adverb phrase, had been crushed*

1. In a quiet voice, Margot read her poem.
2. The other children in the class edged away.
3. Margot beat against the closet door.
4. The forest was the color of rubber and ash.
5. The children played in the sun for an hour.

Quick Check 3: Answers
1. In a quiet voice—adverb phrase, read
2. in the class—adjective phrase, children
3. against the closet door—adverb phrase, beat
4. of rubber and ash—adjective phrase, color
5. in the sun—adverb phrase, played; for an hour, adverb phrase, played

Try It Out: Possible Answers

1. The Lins emigrated to the United States from their homeland, China.
2. Mrs. Gleason offered the Lins celery on a relish tray.
3. The celery strings got caught in the Lins' teeth.
4. The Lins dined out at a French restaurant.
5. With his chopsticks, Mr. Gleason chased a pea on his plate.

Resources

- *Language Handbook Worksheets,* pp. 58–64
- *Language Workshop CD-ROM,* Lesson 24: Subject; Lesson 25: Predicate

---

Try It Out

Use prepositional phrases to combine each of the following pairs of choppy sentences into one smooth sentence.

1. The Lins emigrated to the United States. China had been their homeland.
2. Mrs. Gleason offered the Lins celery. The celery was on a relish tray.
3. The celery strings got caught. The strings got caught in the Lins' teeth.
4. The Lins dined out. The restaurant served French food.
5. Mr. Gleason chased a pea on his plate. He chased it with his chopsticks.

NOTE In speech, people often use sentence fragments. Professional writers may use sentence fragments to create specific effects. However, in your writing at school, you will find it best to use complete sentences.

COMPUTER NOTE Some computer programs can help you identify sentence fragments. Such programs are useful, but they aren't perfect. The best way to eliminate fragments from your writing is to make sure that each sentence has a subject and a verb and that it expresses a complete thought.

TIPS FOR WRITERS
Combining Sentences Using Prepositional Phrases

Knowing how to use prepositional phrases can help you improve your writing. For example, you can use prepositional phrases to combine short, choppy sentences. Take a prepositional phrase from one sentence, or turn one sentence into a prepositional phrase. Then, add the phrase to the other sentence.

CHOPPY	The pony was waiting. It was near the hill.
REVISED	The pony was waiting near the hill.
CHOPPY	Rachel and I wanted to swim. The lake was cool and inviting.
REVISED	Rachel and I wanted to swim **in the cool, inviting lake.**

7 SENTENCES

SENTENCE OR SENTENCE FRAGMENT?

7a. A *sentence* is a group of words that has a subject and a verb and expresses a complete thought.

A sentence begins with a capital letter and ends with a period, a question mark, or an exclamation point.

EXAMPLES Vo-Dinh retold the story of "The Fly**.**"
Read it for Monday**.**
Did the ending surprise you**?**
What a clever boy he was**!**

A *sentence fragment* is a group of words that either does not have a subject and verb or does not express a complete thought.

SENTENCE FRAGMENT	The boy's mother and father. [What about the boy's parents?]
SENTENCE	The boy's mother and father were away from the house.
SENTENCE FRAGMENT	With its twist at the end. [What about the twist at the end?]
SENTENCE	With its twist at the end, this story will surprise you.

724 LANGUAGE HANDBOOK

QUICK CHECK 1

Tell whether each group of words is a *sentence* or a *sentence fragment*. If the word group is a sentence, correct it by adding a capital letter and end punctuation. If the word group is a sentence fragment, correct it by adding words (and a capital letter and punctuation) to make a complete sentence.

EXAMPLE   1. in a huge house with a beautiful garden
     1. *sentence fragment—In a huge house with a beautiful garden lived a rich man.*

1. playing in the dirt in the peasant couple's yard
2. a rich man in his fancy clothes
3. the clever boy posed a riddle
4. about the sun and the moon and about living and dead trees
5. could he solve the boy's riddle

☞ For more about sentence fragments, see page 737.

THE SUBJECT AND THE PREDICATE

A sentence consists of two parts: a *subject* and a *predicate*.

The Subject

7b.   A *subject* **tells whom or what the sentence is about. A *complete subject* may be one word or more than one word.**

EXAMPLES   **The fly in the story** has only a small part.
     It has only a small part.

Finding the Subject

The subject does not always come at the beginning of a sentence. The subject may be in the middle or even at the end. To find the subject of a sentence, ask *Who?* or *What?* before the predicate.

EXAMPLES   The **boy** saw the stick. [Who saw it? The boy saw it.]
     In his hand was a **stick.** [What was in his hand? A stick was.]
     Did **you** read this story? [Who did read it? You did.]

 QUICK CHECK 2

Identify the complete subject in each of the following sentences.

EXAMPLE   1. The moneylender in this story was not an honest man.
     1. *The moneylender in this story*

1. He cared only about material things.
2. The welfare of others was not his concern.
3. Didn't the rich moneylender lie to the boy?
4. At the end of the story is a surprise.
5. What a curious story "The Fly" is!

Quick Check 1: Possible Answers
1. sentence fragment—A boy was playing in the dirt in the peasant couple's yard.
2. sentence fragment—A rich man in his fancy clothes came to the house.
3. sentence—The clever boy posed a riddle.
4. sentence fragment—The riddle was about the sun and the moon and about living and dead trees.
5. sentence—Could he solve the boy's riddle?

Quick Check 2: Answers
1. He
2. The welfare of others
3. the rich moneylender
4. a surprise
5. "The Fly"

7c. A *simple subject* is the main word or words in the complete subject.

EXAMPLES The **boy** did not become upset. [The complete subject is *the boy.*]

"**Dragon, Dragon**" by John Gardner is in this book. [The complete subject is *"Dragon, Dragon" by John Gardner.*]

What a clever boy was **he**! [The complete and the simple subject is *he.*]

The simple subject is *never* part of a prepositional phrase.

EXAMPLE **Many** of the students laughed at the ending. [Who laughed? You might be tempted to say *students,* but *students* is part of the prepositional phrase *of the students. Many* laughed. *Many* is the subject.]

✓ QUICK CHECK 3

Identify the simple subject in each of the following sentences.

EXAMPLE 1. The poor son of the peasant couple was playing.
1. *son*

1. His only playthings were stones and sticks.
2. Much of his time must have been spent in thought.
3. In the poor boy's yard were no witnesses for the promise.
4. Even one witness would have been enough.
5. Did they find one?

The Predicate

7d. The *predicate* of a sentence is the part that says something about the subject. A *complete predicate* consists of a verb and all the words that describe the verb and complete its meaning.

In the following examples, the vertical line separates the complete subject from the complete predicate.

EXAMPLES The boy's mother and father | **owed a debt.**

From a traditional story comes | this surprising tale.

Finding the Predicate

The predicate usually comes after the subject. Sometimes, however, the predicate comes before the subject. Part of the predicate may even appear on one side of the subject and the rest on the other side.

EXAMPLES On a bamboo pole near them **was** a fly.

In a few sentences, the boy **solved the riddle.**

Could a fly **be a witness**?

QUICK CHECK 4

Identify the complete predicate in each of the following sentences. Keep in mind that parts of the complete predicate may come both before and after the complete subject.

EXAMPLE   1. His father was planting dead trees.
                1. *was planting dead trees*

1. These trees would be part of a fence.
2. The boy answered with a riddle.
3. Perhaps the boy should have been more polite to the man.
4. Do you think so?
5. I wonder about the future of a boy with such an ability at riddles.

7e. A *simple predicate,* or *verb,* is the main word or group of words in the complete predicate.

A simple predicate may be a one-word verb, or it may be a verb phrase. A *verb phrase* consists of a main verb and its helping verbs.

EXAMPLES   The moneylender **is** angry at the boy.
                 He **should** not **have made** such a promise to the boy.

Notice in the second example that the word *not* is not part of the verb phrase. The words *not* and *never* and the contraction *—n't* are adverbs, not verbs.

 QUICK CHECK 5

Identify the verb in each of the following sentences.

EXAMPLE   1. Such a boy may well get into trouble.
                1. *may get*

1. He might succeed beyond his wildest dreams.
2. Couldn't he become a lawyer?
3. No doubt, he will be wealthy.
4. Surely, the moneylender must not have been thinking clearly.
5. Was the fly really on his nose?

The Compound Subject

7f. A *compound subject* consists of two or more connected subjects that have the same verb.

The usual connecting word between the subjects is the conjunction *and, or,* or *nor.*

EXAMPLES   Neither the **boy** nor the **moneylender** had been honest.
                 Among the people at court were the **boy,** his **parents,** and the **lender.**

> ☞ For more information about helping verbs and verb phrases, see pages 698–699.

Quick Check 4: Answers
1. would be part of a fence
2. answered with a riddle
3. Perhaps . . . should have been more polite to the man
4. Do . . . think so.
5. wonder about the future of a boy with such an ability at riddles

Quick Check 5: Answers
1. might succeed
2. Could . . . become
3. will be
4. must . . . have been thinking
5. Was

The Compound Verb

7g. A *compound verb* consists of two or more verbs that have the same subject.

A connecting word—usually the conjunction *and, or,* or *but*—is used between the verbs.

EXAMPLES   This weekend I **will read** "Baucis and Philemon" or **prepare** my report on Medusa.

The mandarin **listened, asked** questions, and **made** a decision.

Both the subject and the verb of a sentence may be compound.

EXAMPLES   The **mother** and **father laughed** and **went** home. [The mother laughed and went home. The father laughed and went home.]

Jose or **she made** dinner and **set** the table. [Jose made dinner and set the table. She made dinner and set the table.]

 QUICK CHECK 6

Identify the *subjects* and *verbs* in each of the following sentences.

EXAMPLE   1. The poem "Things to Do If You Are a Subway" is short but is also funny.

1. *poem—subject; is—verb; is—verb*

1. Dragons and subways sound alike and have many things in common.
2. They both live underground and roar.
3. Caves and tunnels are their homes and hide them from view.
4. Darkness and speed protect them from danger.
5. Both dragons and modern trains seemingly swallow people and carry them off.

 ### Using Compound Subjects and Verbs

Sometimes you may choose to repeat a subject or a verb for special emphasis. Most of the time, however, you will want to communicate as efficiently as possible. Using compound subjects and verbs, you can combine ideas and reduce wordiness in your writing. Compare the examples below.

WORDY   Under the city are dragons. Subways are there, too.

REVISED   Under the city are dragons and subways.

Try It Out ✎

Use a compound subject or verb to combine each of the following pairs of sentences.

1. A metaphor is a figure of speech. A simile is a figure of speech.
2. Compare the modern world with the ancient world. Contrast the modern world with the ancient world.
3. Motorcycles carry people. Horses carry people.
4. Saddles can express the personality of their owners. Bridles can do so, too.
5. Horses require much care. Horses give joy to their owners.

Quick Check 6: Answers

1. Dragons, subways—subjects; sound, have—verbs
2. They—subject; live, roar—verbs
3. Caves, tunnels—subjects; are, hide—verbs
4. Darkness, speed—subjects; protect—verb
5. dragons, trains—subjects; swallow, carry—verbs

Try It Out: Possible Answers

1. Metaphors and similes are figures of speech.
2. Compare and contrast the modern world with the ancient world.
3. Motorcycles and horses carry people.
4. Saddles and bridles can express the personalities of their owners.
5. Horses require much care but give joy to their owners.

Resources ———

- *Language Handbook Worksheets,* pp. 66–73
- *Language Workshop CD-ROM,* Lessons 26–28: Complements, Direct Objects and Indirect Objects, and Subject Complements

8 COMPLEMENTS

RECOGNIZING COMPLEMENTS

8a. A *complement* **is a word or a group of words that completes the meaning of a verb.**

Every sentence has a subject and a verb. Sometimes the subject and the verb can express a complete thought without a complement.

EXAMPLES   Fish swim.

Each evening my grandfather walks for an hour with his neighbor Mr. Silverstone.

Many verbs, however, need complements. A complement may be a noun, a pronoun, or an adjective. Each of the following subjects and verbs needs a complement to complete the meaning of the verb and create a complete sentence.

	S	V	
INCOMPLETE	John Gardner	became	[*what?*]
	S	V	C
COMPLETE	John Gardner	became	a **writer.**

	S	V	
INCOMPLETE	His stories	are	[*what?*]
	S	V	C
COMPLETE	His stories	are	**wonderful.**

	S	V		
INCOMPLETE	Rachel	will tell	[*whom? what?*]	
	S	V	C	C
COMPLETE	Rachel	will tell	**us** the	**story.**

A complement is never in a prepositional phrase.

COMPLEMENT	A dragon was **loose.**
OBJECT OF A PREPOSITION	A dragon was on the **loose.**

☑ *QUICK CHECK I*

Identify the subjects, verbs, and complements in the sentences in the following paragraph. A sentence may have more than one subject, verb, or complement.

EXAMPLE   [1] Many traditional tales have a foolish son for a hero.
   1. *tales—subject; have—verb; son—complement*

[1] Often, the silly son is the youngest child in the family. [2] Sometimes he appears stupid to everyone. [3] Supernatural or magical helpers give him special powers. [4] With their help, he becomes a hero. [5] Frequently, this character later marries a beautiful princess and becomes a king.

> **NOTE** An adverb is never a complement.
>
> **ADVERB**   He writes **humorously.** [*Humorously* describes how he writes.]
>
> **COMPLEMENT**   His writing is **humorous.** [The adjective *humorous* describes the subject *writing.*]
>
> For more information about adverbs, see pages 699–700.

☞ For more about prepositional phrases, see pages 721–724.

Quick Check I: Answers
1. son—subject; is—verb; child—complement
2. he—subject; appears—verb; stupid—complement
3. helpers—subject; give—verb; him, powers—complements
4. he—subject; becomes—verb; hero—complement
5. character—subject; marries, becomes—verbs; princess, king—complements

8b. A *direct object* is a noun or pronoun that receives the action of the verb or that shows the result of the action. A direct object tells *what* or *whom* after a transitive verb.

EXAMPLES   A fierce dragon threatens **them.** [The pronoun *them* receives the action of the transitive verb *threatens* and tells *whom.*]

The king made a **bargain.** [The noun *bargain* shows the result of the action verb *made* and tells *what.*]

A direct object may be compound.

EXAMPLE   The dragon stole **jewels, treasure,** and the wizard's **book.** [The nouns *jewels, treasure,* and *book* receive the action of the transitive verb *stole* and tell *what.*]

A direct object never follows a linking verb.

LINKING VERB   The king **seems** cowardly. [The verb *seems* does not express action; therefore, it has no direct object.]

A direct object is never part of a prepositional phrase.

DIRECT OBJECT   He needs **volunteers.**
OBJECT OF A PREPOSITION   He calls for **volunteers.**

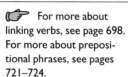 **QUICK CHECK 2**

Identify the direct object (or objects) in each of the following sentences.

EXAMPLE   **1.** The wizard had lost his book of spells.
   1. *book*

1. He could not help the king.
2. The dragon was frightening people and breaking things.
3. Did he take the spark plugs from cars' engines?
4. A cobbler makes shoes and leather goods.
5. This man had a wife and three sons.

8c. An *indirect object* is a noun or a pronoun that comes between the verb and the direct object and tells *to what* or *to whom,* or *for what* or *for whom,* the action of the verb is done.

EXAMPLE   The king gave the young **man** a chance. [The noun *man* tells *to whom* the king gave the chance.]

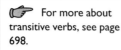 For more about transitive verbs, see page 698.

 For more about linking verbs, see page 698. For more about prepositional phrases, see pages 721–724.

Quick Check 2: Answers
1. king
2. people, things
3. spark plugs
4. shoes, goods
5. wife, sons

NOTE If a sentence has an indirect object, it always has a direct object also.

T730

Linking verbs do not have indirect objects. Also, an indirect object is never in a prepositional phrase.

LINKING VERB	A dragon **is** a fearsome beast.
INDIRECT OBJECT	It causes **people** trouble.
OBJECT OF A PREPOSITION	It causes trouble for many **people**.

An indirect object may be compound.

EXAMPLE The dragon caused the **king** and his **subjects** a great deal of trouble.

 QUICK CHECK 3

Identify the indirect object in each of the following sentences. If a sentence has no indirect object, write *none*.

EXAMPLE 1. The cobbler told each of his sons a special poem.
    1. *each*

1. The first two sons gave little thought to the poem.
2. However, the youngest son always showed his father respect.
3. A friend lent the youngest son a suit of armor.
4. The youngest son got himself a sword from another friend.
5. The cobbler had taught him well.

 Revising to Avoid *Be* Verbs

Overusing the linking verb *be* can make writing dull and lifeless. As you evaluate your writing, you may get the feeling that nothing is *happening*, that nobody is *doing* anything. That feeling is one indication that your writing may contain too many *be* verbs. Wherever possible, replace a dull *be* verb with a verb that expresses action. Remember that most action verbs take direct objects, and some can have indirect objects, too.

BE VERB	His voice **was** loud and confident.
ACTION VERB	He **shouted** loudly and confidently.

SUBJECT COMPLEMENTS

A **subject complement** completes the meaning of a linking verb and identifies or describes the subject.

EXAMPLES The youngest son became a **hero.** [*Hero* identifies the subject *son.*]

    His task was **difficult.** [*Difficult* describes the subject *task.*]

Try It Out ✎

Revise each of the following sentences by substituting an interesting action verb for the dull *be* verb.

1. The queen was a rosebush.
2. The king was not really upset about this transformation.
3. The rosebush is in need of water.
4. The wizard has not been helpful.
5. His book of spells will be in the dragon's cave.

Quick Check 3: Answers
1. none
2. father
3. son
4. himself
5. none

Try It Out: Possible Answers
1. The wizard transformed the queen into a rosebush.
2. The king did not really show any concern for this transformation.
3. The rosebush needs water.
4. The wizard could not help.
5. You can find his book of spells in the dragon's cave.

☞ For information about linking verbs, see page 698.

☞ See page 698 for more about verbs that may be used as either linking verbs or action verbs.

NOTE In conversation, many people say *It's me* and *That was him.* Such nonstandard expressions may one day become acceptable in writing as well as in speech. For now, however, it is best to follow the rules of standard English in your writing.

Quick Check 4: Answers
1. lunch
2. man
3. weakness
4. shoemaker, teacher
5. they

Common Linking Verbs

appear	become	grow	remain	smell	stay
be	feel	look	seem	sound	taste

Some verbs, such as *look, grow,* and *feel,* may be used as either linking verbs or action verbs.

LINKING VERB   The dragon **looked** fierce. [*Looked* links the adjective *fierce* to the subject *dragon.*]

ACTION VERB   The youngest son **looked** in the cave. [*Looked* expresses the youngest son's action.]

The two kinds of subject complements are the *predicate nominative* and the *predicate adjective.*

Predicate Nominatives

8d. **A *predicate nominative* is a noun or a pronoun that follows a linking verb and identifies the subject or refers to it.**

EXAMPLES   The queen became a **rosebush.** [The noun *rosebush* is a predicate nominative that identifies the subject *queen.*]

The son who marries the princess is **he.** [The pronoun *he* is a predicate nominative that refers to the subject *son.*]

Predicate nominatives never appear in prepositional phrases.

EXAMPLE   His father's advice was only two **lines** of poetry. [*Lines* is a predicate nominative that identifies the subject *advice. Poetry* is the object of the preposition *of.*]

Predicate nominatives may be compound.

EXAMPLE   The troublesome dragon was a **thief,** a **vandal,** and a **mischief-maker.**

✓ QUICK CHECK 4

Identify the predicate nominative or predicate nominatives in each of the following sentences.

EXAMPLE   1. In the right situation, a coward may be a hero.
            1. *hero*

1. Did the oldest son and the middle son become the dragon's lunch?
2. The wizard was not a young man.
3. A sense of humor can be a weakness.
4. This cobbler was a shoemaker and wise teacher.
5. It was they in the dragon's belly.

Predicate Adjectives

8e. A *predicate adjective* is an adjective that follows a linking verb and describes the subject.

EXAMPLE   The dragon felt **confident.** [*Confident* is a predicate adjective that describes the subject *dragon.*]

Predicate adjectives may be compound.

EXAMPLE   The youngest son was neither **clever** nor **strong.**
[*Clever* and *strong* are predicate adjectives that describe the subject *son.*]

 QUICK CHECK 5

Identify the *predicate adjective* (or *adjectives*) or *predicate nominative* (or *nominatives*) in each of the following sentences.

EXAMPLE   1. Is "Dragon, Dragon" a true story?
1. *story—predicate nominative*

1. A story may reveal a truth but not be factual.
2. To the dragon, the poem seemed laughable.
3. The youngest son became frustrated and angry at the dragon's laughter.
4. At the end, the queen was all wet and ungrateful.
5. Did the princess become a happy bride?

9   KINDS OF SENTENCES

SIMPLE SENTENCES AND COMPOUND SENTENCES

The Simple Sentence

9a. A *simple sentence* has one subject and one verb. A compound subject has two or more parts, but it is still considered one subject. Likewise, a compound verb or verb phrase is considered one verb.

EXAMPLES
　　　　　S　　　　　V
　"Baucis and Philemon" is an ancient Greek story.
　　[single subject and single verb]

　　S　　　V
　You will be reading it soon. [single subject and verb phrase]

　　S　　　　S　　　V
　Baucis and **Philemon lived** in a cottage near a marsh.
　　[compound subject and single verb]

Quick Check 5: Answers
1. factual—predicate adjective
2. laughable—predicate adjective
3. frustrated, angry—predicate adjectives
4. wet, ungrateful—predicate adjective
5. bribe—predicate nominative

Resources ————
- *Language Handbook Worksheets,* pp. 75–81
- *Language Workshop CD-ROM,* Lessons 29: Simple Sentences and Compound Sentences; Lesson 30: Classifying Sentences According to Purpose

The **cottage was** small and **had been thatched** with dried weeds. [single subject and compound verb]

S   S   V   V

Zeus and **Hermes were visiting** earth and **asking** for food. [compound subject and compound verb]

✓ QUICK CHECK I

Identify the *subject* (or *subjects*) and *verb* (or *verbs*) in each of the following sentences.

EXAMPLE   **1.** Baucis and Philemon were quite poor.
            1. *Baucis—subject; Philemon—subject; were—verb*

1. They did have a few goats and grew their own vegetables.
2. The man and woman welcomed the strangers and asked them in.
3. Their couch and old table had seen their best days years ago.
4. Baucis kept the table clean and scented it with mint.
5. Soon, olives, cherries, and many other fine foods were placed on the table and offered to the strangers.

The Compound Sentence

9b. A *compound sentence* **consists of two or more simple sentences usually joined by a connecting word.**

In a compound sentence, the conjunction *and, but, for, nor, or, so,* or *yet* often connects the simple sentences. A comma usually comes before the conjunction in a compound sentence. The simple sentences in a compound sentence may also be joined by a semicolon.

                                          S   V

EXAMPLES   **Olivia Coolidge wrote** the book *Greek Myths*, **but**
                                S   V
                   Edouard Sandoz illustrated it.

                     S   V   S   V

             It had been a good season; **they had** a good harvest.

Do not confuse a compound sentence with a simple sentence that contains a compound subject, a compound verb, or both.

                                              S   S   V

SIMPLE SENTENCE   **Zeus** and **Hermes ate** and
                                        V
                                  drank heartily.

                                            S   V   S

COMPOUND SENTENCE   **Zeus smiled,** and **Hermes**
                                    V
                                  spoke to the couple.

☞ For more about compound subjects and compound verbs, see pages 727–728.

COMPUTER NOTE

A computer can help you analyze your writing for sentence length and structure. Programs that tell you the average number of words in your sentences are now available. Such programs also tell you how many of each kind of sentence you have used. This information can help you decide whether you need to revise some of your sentences to add variety to your writing.

Quick Check I: Answers

1. they—subject; did, have, grew—verbs
2. man, woman—subjects; welcomed, asked—verbs
3. couch, table—subjects; had seen—verb
4. Baucis—subject; kept, scented—verbs
5. olives, cherries, foods—subjects; were placed, offered—verbs

QUICK CHECK 2

Identify each of the following word groups as either a *simple sentence* or a *compound sentence*.

EXAMPLE **1.** The gods punish the unkind but reward the kind.
 1. *simple sentence*

1. Baucis and Philemon were afraid, but Zeus and Hermes smiled.
2. You gave us shelter and fed us, yet many others did not.
3. What were the requests and desires of the old couple?
4. Did they want money, or did they want splendor?
5. Philemon thought and then answered the gods.

Using Varied Sentence Structure

Variety is the spice of life. It's also the spice of writing. By varying the length and the structure of sentences, you can make your writing clearer and more interesting to read.

Simple sentences with single subjects and verbs are best used to express fairly simple ideas. To present more complicated ideas and to show relationships between them, use compound subjects, compound verbs, and compound sentences.

SIMPLE SENTENCES The bowl was almost empty. He brought the wineskin. He discovered the bowl was full.

COMPOUND SENTENCE The bowl was almost empty, so he brought the wineskin but discovered that the bowl was full again.

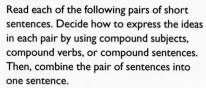

Try It Out ✎

Read each of the following pairs of short sentences. Decide how to express the ideas in each pair by using compound subjects, compound verbs, or compound sentences. Then, combine the pair of sentences into one sentence.

1. Olives lay on the table. Baked eggs lay on the table.
2. The goose cackled. The goose ran away.
3. The guests were hungry. Baucis fed them.
4. Baucis and Philemon loved each other. They would never be parted.
5. Zeus and Hermes rewarded the couple. Baucis and Philemon were together forever.

SENTENCES CLASSIFIED BY PURPOSE

In addition to being classified by structure, a sentence is also classified according to its purpose: *declarative, interrogative, imperative,* or *exclamatory.*

9c. A *declarative sentence* makes a statement. It is followed by a period.

EXAMPLE Their home became a temple**.**

9d. An *interrogative sentence* asks a question. It is followed by a question mark.

EXAMPLE How did the gods reward them**?**

LANGUAGE HANDBOOK 735

Quick Check 2: Answers
1. compound sentence
2. compound sentence
3. simple sentence
4. compound sentence
5. simple sentence

Try It Out: Possible Answers
1. Olives and baked eggs lay on the table.
2. The goose cackled and ran away.
3. The guests were hungry, so Baucis fed them.
4. Baucis and Philemon loved each other and would never be parted.
5. Zeus and Hermes rewarded the couple, and Baucis and Philemon were together forever.

9e. An *imperative sentence* gives a command or makes a request. It is followed by a period. A strong command is followed by an exclamation point.

EXAMPLES　Bring the wine. [command]
　　　　　　Please light the candles, Baucis. [request]
　　　　　　Catch that goose! [strong command]

In an imperative sentence, the "understood" subject is always *you*.

EXAMPLES　**(You)** Watch out!
　　　　　　Rita, **(you)** tell us your opinion.

9f. An *exclamatory sentence* shows excitement or expresses strong feeling. An exclamatory sentence is followed by an exclamation point.

EXAMPLES　Wow, that was fun!
　　　　　　What a fortunate couple they were!

✓ QUICK CHECK 3

Classify each of the following sentences according to its purpose—*declarative, interrogative, imperative,* or *exclamatory.*

EXAMPLE　**1.** Have you read "Baucis and Philemon" yet?
　　　　　　1. *interrogative*

1. Myths sometimes explain natural phenomena.
2. Kyle, does a myth always include a god as a character?
3. What marvelous stories these are!
4. Sharon, please read the next paragraph aloud.
5. Thank goodness!

10 WRITING EFFECTIVE SENTENCES

WRITING CLEAR SENTENCES

A **complete sentence** has both a subject and a verb, and it expresses a complete thought.

EXAMPLES　I often dream of a secret garden.
　　　　　　Do you dream about a garden, too?
　　　　　　What a wonderful dream that was!

Two stumbling blocks to the development of clear sentences are *sentence fragments* and *run-on sentences.*

NOTE
Be careful not to use too many exclamation points. Save exclamation points for sentences that express especially strong emotion. When exclamation points are overused, they lose their impact.

☞ For more information about complete sentences, see pages 724–728.

Quick Check 3: Answers
1. declarative
2. interrogative
3. exclamatory
4. imperative
5. exclamatory

Resources ———
• *Language Handbook Worksheets,* pp. 83–100
• *Language Workshop CD-ROM,* Lessons 31–35: Faulty Sentences and Writing Effective Sentences

Sentence Fragments

10a. Avoid using sentence fragments.

A *sentence fragment* is a part of a sentence that has been capitalized and punctuated as if it were a complete sentence.

FRAGMENT Traveled far away to England. [The subject is missing. *Who* traveled?]

SENTENCE Mary traveled far away to England.

FRAGMENT After the death of her parents, the girl. [The verb is missing. What did the girl *do*?]

SENTENCE After the death of her parents, the girl lived at Misselthwaite Manor.

FRAGMENT As soon as she arrived in England. [*What happened* as soon as she arrived?]

SENTENCE As soon as she arrived in England, she met Mrs. Medlock.

 QUICK CHECK 1

Identify each of the following word groups as either a *complete sentence* or a *sentence fragment*.

EXAMPLE 1. The swift and deadly spread of cholera.
  1. *sentence fragment*

1. Killing Mary's parents with amazing speed.
2. With no family left in India and absolutely alone in the world.
3. In what way did Mary's behavior change?
4. No one knows in advance his or her reaction to shocking events.
5. Although she was only a child.

 ## Revising Sentence Fragments

Usually, a sentence fragment is closely related to the sentence that comes before or after it. In most cases, you can correct the fragment by attaching it to the related sentence.

SENTENCE AND FRAGMENT Mary was often troubled during her days on the estate. Because many strange events occurred.

REVISED Mary was often troubled during her days on the estate **because many strange events occurred.**

For more information about sentence fragments, see page 724.

Try It Out

Each of the following numbered items contains a sentence fragment. Correct each item by connecting the two word groups to create a complete sentence.

1. In mourning after the death of her parents. Mary has no appetite for food in the hotel dining room.
2. The woman was Mrs. Medlock. A tall, thin housekeeper more than sixty years old.
3. According to Mrs. Crawford, Mary's mother did not care for the girl. Because Mary was not beautiful.
4. Because they are strange and unfamiliar to her. Mary apparently dislikes everyone and everything in England.
5. With her attitude of cold, rude, and rejecting silence. Mary offends just about everyone.

Quick Check 1: Answers
1. sentence fragment
2. sentence fragment
3. complete sentence
4. complete sentence
5. sentence fragment

Try It Out: Possible Answers
1. In mourning after the death of her parents, Mary has no appetite for food in the hotel dining room.
2. The woman was Mrs. Medlock, a tall, thin housekeeper more than sixty years old.
3. According to Mrs. Crawford, Mary's mother did not care for the girl because Mary was not beautiful.
4. Because they are strange and unfamiliar to her, Mary apparently dislikes everyone and everything in England.
5. With her attitude of cold, rude, and rejecting silence, Mary offends just about everyone.

Run-on Sentences

10b. Avoid using run-on sentences.

If you run together two complete sentences as if they were one sentence, you create a *run-on sentence.*

RUN-ON   Mr. Craven will be Mary's guardian the girl has no other relatives.

REVISED   Mr. Craven will be Mary's guardian**.** **T**he girl has no other relatives.

REVISED   Mr. Craven will be Mary's guardian**,** **for** the girl has no other relatives.

REVISED   **Because** Mary has no other relatives**,** Mr. Craven will be her guardian.

You also create a run-on sentence if you use only a comma between two complete sentences.

RUN-ON   Mrs. Medlock offers Mary sandwiches**,** Mary refuses them.

REVISED   Mrs. Medlock offers Mary sandwiches**.** **M**ary refuses them.

REVISED   Mrs. Medlock offers Mary sandwiches**,** **but** Mary refuses them.

To spot run-ons, try reading your writing aloud. A natural pause in your voice usually marks the end of one thought and the beginning of another. If you pause at a place where you don't have any end punctuation, you may have found a run-on sentence.

Here are two ways you can revise run-on sentences.

1. You can make two sentences.
2. You can use a comma and a coordinating conjunction, such as *and, but, for,* or *or.*

RUN-ON   The manor had been built long ago it was a beautiful place.

REVISED   The manor had been built long ago**.** **It** was a beautiful place.

REVISED   The manor had been built long ago**,** **and** it was a beautiful place.

☞ For a list of coordinating conjunctions, see page 701.

 QUICK CHECK 2

The following paragraph is confusing because it contains fragments and run-ons. Identify the *fragments* and *run-ons.* Then, revise each fragment and run-on to make the paragraph clearer.

EXAMPLE   [1] The house seems dark to Mary tapestries hang from the walls.

   1. *run-on—The house seems dark to Mary, and tapestries hang from the walls.*

[1] Her first night at the manor. [2] On orders issued by Mrs. Medlock, may not go into the rest of the house. [3] The sound of

crying fills the air Mary cannot sleep. [4] Mary is frightened by the sound, she sits up in bed. [5] The sound may be a ghost it may be something else entirely.

Revising Stringy Sentences

For variety, you'll sometimes want to join sentences and sentence parts with *and*. But if you string too many ideas together with *and*, you create a **stringy sentence**. Stringy sentences ramble on and on. They don't give the reader a chance to pause between ideas.

STRINGY   Dickon is a boy at the manor and he seems nice and he always smiles and there is something magical about him and many animals follow him.

REVISED   Dickon is a boy at the manor**. He** seems nice, **and** he always smiles**. There** is something magical about him**, and** many animals follow him.

In the revised version, only two groups of ideas are linked by *and*. These ideas can be joined in one sentence because they are closely related to each other. Also, notice that a comma has been added before the *and*. The comma is necessary to show a slight pause between the two complete ideas.

> ### Try It Out ✎
>
> The following sentences are stringy. Revise them in any way you choose.
>
> 1. At dawn, Ben sees Dickon on the moors and Dickon has a crow, a lamb, a fox, and a squirrel with him and because Ben and Dickon are good friends, Ben puts his work aside for a while so that Dickon can show him a trick.
> 2. Dickon plays the pipe and walks on his hands and Ben laughs at the sight and then must resume work and Dickon goes off with the animals.

Try It Out: Possible Answers

1. At dawn, Ben sees Dickon on the moors. Dickon has a crow, a lamb, a fox, and a squirrel with him. Because Ben and Dickon are good friends, Ben puts his work aside for a while so that Dickon can show him a trick.
2. Dickon plays the pipe and walks on his hands. Ben laughs at the sight and then must resume work. Dickon goes off with the animals.

COMBINING SENTENCES

10c.   Improve choppy sentences by combining them to make longer, smoother sentences.

Good writers usually use some short sentences, but an entire paragraph of short sentences makes writing sound choppy. Notice how dull and choppy the following paragraph sounds.

> Mary's parents die. She must go to England. She arrives at Misselthwaite Manor. The manor is beautiful but mysterious. She first meets Mrs. Medlock. The woman tries to be friendly. Mary is unhappy at the manor. She hears about the locked garden.

Now, see how the writer has revised the paragraph.

> Mary's parents die, and she must go to England. She arrives at the beautiful but mysterious Misselthwaite Manor, where she first meets Mrs. Medlock. The woman tries to be friendly, but Mary is unhappy at the manor until she hears about the locked garden.

Quick Check 3: Possible Answers

1. Sad and alone, Mary speaks wistfully to Dickon of her desire for a friend.
2. Gentle Dickon will be Mary's friend.
3. Mary proudly hides her tears.
4. Each day, Mary searches for the locked garden.
5. Tucked in her bed, she listens to the howling wind outside.

 TIPS FOR SPELLING When you change the forms of words, you often add endings such as *–ed*, *–ing*, *–ful*, and *–ly* to make adjectives and adverbs. When adding the suffix *–ly* to most words, do not change the spelling of the word itself. However, for words that end in *y*, you usually need to change the *y* to *i* before adding *–ly*.

EXAMPLES slow + ly = slowly

easy + ly = easily

Inserting Words

One way to combine two sentences is to take a key word from one sentence and insert it into the other sentence. Sometimes you can simply add the key word to the other sentence. Other times, you'll need to change the form of the key word before you can insert it.

ORIGINAL	A wind blows across the moors. The wind is mournful.
COMBINED	A **mournful** wind blows across the moors.
COMBINED	A wind blows **mournfully** across the moors.

✓ QUICK CHECK 3

Each of the following items contains two sentences. Combine the sentences by taking the italicized word from the second sentence and inserting it into the first sentence. The directions in parentheses will tell you how to change the form of the italicized word if you need to.

EXAMPLE 1. What was this sound? This sound was *eerie*.

1. *What was this eerie sound?*

1. Sad and alone, Mary speaks to Dickon of her desire for a friend. She speaks *wistfully*.
2. Dickon will be Mary's friend. Dickon is *gentle*.
3. Mary hides her tears. Mary is *proud*. (Add *-ly*.)
4. Each day, Mary searches for the garden. The garden is *locked*.
5. Tucked in her bed, she listens to the wind outside. The wind makes a *howl*. (Add *-ing*.)

Inserting Groups of Words

Often, you can combine two related sentences by taking an entire group of words from one sentence and adding it to the other sentence. In some cases, you will need to add or change a word to make the group of words fit smoothly into the sentence.

ORIGINAL	Dickon eats dinner. He does so on the moors.
COMBINED	Dickon eats dinner **on the moors.**
COMBINED	**On the moors,** Dickon eats dinner.
ORIGINAL	The hidden garden has a wall. The wall goes all the way around it.
COMBINED	The wall goes all the way **around the hidden garden.**
COMBINED	The hidden garden has a wall **that goes all the way around it.**

Sometimes you will need to put commas around the group of words you are inserting. To determine whether a comma is needed, ask yourself whether the group of words renames or explains a noun or pronoun in the sentence. If it does, use a comma or commas to set off the word group from the rest of the sentence.

ORIGINAL   Martha is kind to Mary. Martha is a maid at the manor.

COMBINED   Martha**, a maid at the Manor,** is kind to Mary.

ORIGINAL   Lilias loved the garden. She was the wife of Mr. Craven.

COMBINED   Lilias**, the wife of Mr. Craven,** loved the garden.

✓ QUICK CHECK 4

Combine each of the following pairs of sentences by taking the italicized word or word group from the second sentence and inserting it into the first sentence. Be sure to add commas if they are needed.

EXAMPLE   1. Mary explores the house. Mary is *a curious child.*
              1. *Mary, a curious child, explores the house.*

1. Mary investigates the gallery. It is *a long hall full of portraits.*
2. She discovers a room. The room is *beautifully furnished.*
3. In it are flowers. The flowers are *in bowls and vases.*
4. The scent of the perfume triggers a memory. The perfume has a *familiar* scent.
5. For a moment, a memory takes Mary to Delhi. The memory is *of her mother.*

Using Connecting Words

Another way you can combine sentences is by using connecting words called *conjunctions*. Conjunctions such as *and, but,* and *or* allow you to join closely related sentences and sentence parts.

ORIGINAL   Dead leaves litter the ground. Dead branches do, too.

COMBINED   Dead **leaves and branches** litter the ground.

ORIGINAL   The key was there all along. It was hidden by debris.

COMBINED   The key **was** there all along **but was hidden** by debris.

ORIGINAL   Mary could replace the key. She could find a new hiding place for it.

COMBINED   Mary **could replace** the key **or find** a new hiding place for it.

Combining Sentences

When you connect two sentences by using *and, but,* or *or,* place a comma before the conjunction.

ORIGINAL   The roses are ugly now. They must have been lovely at one time.

COMBINED   The roses are ugly now**, but** they must have been lovely at one time.

☞ For more about using commas to set off phrases, see page 751.

☞ For a list of coordinating conjunctions, see page 701.

☞ For more about using commas with conjunctions, see page 750.

Quick Check 4: Answers

1. Mary investigates the gallery, a long hall full of portraits.
2. She discovers a beautifully furnished room.
3. In it are flowers in bowls and vases.
4. The familiar scent of the perfume triggers a memory.
5. For a moment, a memory of her mother takes Mary to Delhi.

When you are combining sentences, you may find that one sentence helps explain the other sentence by telling *how, where, why,* or *when.* A good way to combine these sentences is to add a connecting word that shows the special relationship. Some connecting words that you can use are *after, although, as, because, before, if, since, so that, until, when, whether,* and *while.* The word that you choose will depend on the relationship between the sentences you are combining.

ORIGINAL	The door was shut. No one could see the entrance.
COMBINED	**When** the door was shut, no one could see the entrance.

✓ QUICK CHECK 5

The following paragraph sounds choppy because it has too many short sentences. Use the methods you've learned in this section to combine some of the sentences.

CHOPPY	A gust of wind reveals the door. The door leads to the garden.
COMBINED	*A gust of wind reveals the garden door.*

Mary is joyful. She places the key in the lock. Layers of dead leaves cover the ground. The leaves are wet and brown. The grass is dead. The plants are dead. High on the walls, ivy climbs. Rose vines climb there, too. Mary explores the garden. Mary sees something green. A small, tender shoot is growing. It is growing in the dead grass. The garden seems dead. There are many tiny plants.

Revising Wordy Sentences

Unnecessary words and phrases tend to make writing sound awkward and unnatural. As you revise your writing, read each of your sentences aloud to check for wordiness. If you run out of breath before the end of a sentence, chances are the sentence is wordy. You can revise wordy sentences by

1. replacing a group of words with one word

WORDY	With great happiness, she began her work.
REVISED	**Happily,** she began her work.

2. replacing a clause with a phrase

WORDY	She always felt happier when she was in the garden.
REVISED	She always felt happier **in the garden.**

3. taking out a whole group of unnecessary words

WORDY	What I mean to say is that *The Secret Garden* was suspenseful.
REVISED	*The Secret Garden* was suspenseful.

Quick Check 5: Possible Answers

Joyfully, Mary places the key in the lock. Layers of wet and brown leaves cover the ground. The grass and plants are dead, too. High on the walls, ivy and rose vines climb. Mary explores the garden and sees something green. A small, tender shoot is growing in the dead grass. The garden seems dead, but there are many tiny plants.

11 CAPITAL LETTERS

11a. Capitalize the first word in every sentence.

EXAMPLE   Have you ever heard the song "John Henry"?

The first word of a sentence that is a direct quotation is capitalized even if the quotation begins within a sentence.

EXAMPLE   At John Henry's grave, passing trains say, "There lies a steel-driving man."

Traditionally, the first word in a line of poetry is capitalized. However, some modern poets do not follow this style. When you are quoting, follow the capitalization used in the source of the quotation.

EXAMPLE   John Henry was about three days old
Sittin' on his papa's knee.
He picked up a hammer and a little piece of steel
Said, "Hammer's gonna be the death of me, Lord, Lord!
Hammer's gonna be the death of me."
—Traditional African American song

11b. Capitalize the pronoun *I*.

EXAMPLE   Mark and **I** made our own music video of "John Henry."

 QUICK CHECK 1

Most of the following sentences contain errors in capitalization. If a sentence is correct, write *C*. If there are errors in the use of capitals, correct the word or words that should be changed.

EXAMPLE   1. Did you see the set i designed for "John Henry"?
                1. *I*

1. who will be designing the costumes?
2. Pearl and Lisa want to do a rap voice-over during the dance.
3. no way, i think we should keep the traditional lyrics.
4. well, couldn't i modernize a few lines?
5. how would you change a line like "his hammer was striking fire"?

11c. Capitalize proper nouns.

A *common noun* is a general name for a person, place, thing, or idea. A *proper noun* names a particular person, place, thing, or idea. A common noun is capitalized only when it begins a sentence or is part of a title. A proper noun is always capitalized. Some proper nouns consist of more than one word. In these names, short prepositions (those of fewer than five letters) and articles (*a, an, the*) are not capitalized.

COMMON NOUNS	statue	man
PROPER NOUNS	Colossus of Rhodes	Attila the Hun

> ☞ For more on using capital letters in quotations, see page 755.

> ☞ For more about proper nouns, see page 693.

Resources
- *Language Handbook Worksheets,* pp. 105–110
- *Language Workshop CD-ROM,* Lessons 46 and 47: Rules for Capitalization

Quick Check 1: Answers
1. Who
2. C
3. No, I
4. Well, I
5. How, His

(1) Capitalize the names of persons and animals.

EXAMPLES   Cindy Chang, Nick de Vries, Black Beauty, Wilbur

(2) Capitalize geographical names.

TYPE OF NAME	EXAMPLES
Towns, Cities	San Jose, New York City
Islands	Isle of Hispaniola, Ellis Island
Counties, States	Polk County, Wyoming
Countries	Nigeria, France
Bodies of Water	San Francisco Bay, Dead Sea
Forests, Parks	Black Forest, Everglades National Park
Streets, Highways	Route 41, Keltner Street
Mountains	Mount St. Helens, Camelback Mountain
Continents	South America, Antarctica
Regions	the Northwest, the Sun Belt

(3) Capitalize the names of planets, stars, and other heavenly bodies.

EXAMPLES   Mercury, Antares, Sagittarius, the Southern Cross

(4) Capitalize the names of teams, organizations, businesses, institutions, and government bodies.

TYPE OF NAME	EXAMPLES
Teams	Baltimore Orioles, Indiana Pacers
Organizations	Glee Club, Home Builders Association
Businesses	Wallpaper World, Kellogg Company
Institutions	Bay Memorial Hospital, Houston High School
Government Bodies	Internal Revenue Service, Department of Health

 **QUICK CHECK 2**

Correct all errors in capitalization in each of the following sentences.

EXAMPLE   1. Life on venus was often dismal for a child from ohio.
              1. *Life on Venus was often dismal for a child from Ohio.*

1. Up early, Mary saw the sun rise over the Missouri river and thought of her grandfather, amos deer leg.
2. She was raised in the salinas valley and had family in mexico.

NOTE   In a hyphenated street number, the second part of the number is not capitalized.

EXAMPLE
West Fifty-fourth Street

NOTE   Words such as *north, east,* and *southwest* are not capitalized when they indicate direction.

EXAMPLES   flying north, south of Boise

NOTE   The word *earth* should not be capitalized unless it is used along with the names of other heavenly bodies. The words *sun* and *moon* are not capitalized.

EXAMPLE   Venus and Mars are the two planets closest to Earth.

Quick Check 2: Answers
1. Up early, Mary saw the sun rise over the Missouri River and thought of her grandfather, Amos Deer Leg.
2. She was raised in the Salinas Valley and had family in Mexico.
3. The baseball cards were at Lemire's Drugstore, next to St. Jude's Parochial School.
4. Rollie Tremaine lived on Laurel Street and wasn't much use to the Frenchtown Tigers during a football game.
5. Didn't you ever pretend you were Robin Hood in Sherwood Forest?

3. The baseball cards were at lemire's drugstore, next to st. jude's parochial school.

4. Rollie Tremaine lived on laurel street and wasn't much use to the frenchtown tigers during a football game.

5. Didn't you ever pretend you were robin hood in sherwood forest?

(5) **Capitalize the names of historical events and periods.**

TYPE OF NAME	EXAMPLES
Historical Events	Battle of Britain, Cold War
Historical Periods	Dark Ages, Industrial Revolution

(6) **Capitalize the names of special events, holidays, and calendar items.**

TYPE OF NAME	EXAMPLES
Special Events	Ohio State Fair, Mardi Gras
Holidays	Memorial Day, Independence Day
Calendar Items	Saturday, December

(7) **Capitalize the names of nationalities, races, and peoples.**

EXAMPLES   Italian, Sudanese, Caucasian, Hispanic, Cherokee

(8) **Capitalize the names of religions and their followers, holy days, sacred writings, and specific deities.**

TYPE OF NAME	EXAMPLES
Religions and Followers	Zen Buddhism, Catholic
Holy Days	Christmas, Ramadan
Sacred Writings	Koran, Torah
Specific Deities	Vishnu, Yahweh

(9) **Capitalize the names of buildings and other structures.**

EXAMPLES   Trump Towers, Golden Gate Bridge, the Pyramids

(10) **Capitalize the names of monuments and awards.**

TYPE OF NAME	EXAMPLES
Monuments	Tomb of the Unknowns, Lincoln Memorial
Awards	Caldecott Medal, Distinguished Flying Cross

NOTE The name of a season is not capitalized unless it is part of a proper name.

EXAMPLES   the first day of summer, the Carson Summer Festival

NOTE The word *god* is not capitalized when it refers to a mythological god. The names of specific gods, however, are capitalized.

EXAMPLE   The god of war in ancient Rome was Mars.

(11) Capitalize the names of trains, ships, airplanes, and spacecraft.

TYPE OF NAME	EXAMPLES
Trains	*Orange Blossom Special, Orient Express*
Ships	**USS** *Saratoga, Yarmouth Castle*
Airplanes	*Glamorous Glennis, Spirit of Columbus*
Spacecraft	*Telstar 1, Eagle*

(12) Capitalize the brand names of business products.

EXAMPLES   **Pilot** pens, **Corvette** convertible, **Lee** jeans [Notice that the names of the types of products are not capitalized.]

☑ *QUICK CHECK 3*

Correct each of the following expressions, using capital letters as needed. If an item is correct, write *C*.

EXAMPLE   1. passages in the bible
               1. *Bible*

1. congressional medal of honor
2. a Mattel toy
3. the friday before easter sunday
4. the last flight of the *hindenburg*
5. the great wall of China
6. Jason's ship, the *argo*
7. a baptist minister
8. the age of chivalry
9. strawberry festival
10. the battle of gettysburg

11d. Capitalize proper adjectives.

A **proper adjective** is formed from a proper noun and is almost always capitalized.

PROPER NOUN	China	Pawnee
PROPER ADJECTIVE	Chinese porcelain	Pawnee customs

11e. Capitalize titles.

(1) Capitalize the title of a person when it comes before a name.

EXAMPLES   **Dr.** Washington, **Governor** Hill wants to talk to you.

(2) Capitalize a title used alone or following a person's name only when you want to emphasize the position of someone holding a high office.

EXAMPLES   Everyone was waiting for the **R**abbi's decision.
              How long have you wanted to become a **r**abbi?

A title used alone in direct address is usually capitalized.

Quick Check 3: Answers
1. Congressional Medal of Honor
2. C
3. the Friday before Easter Sunday
4. the last flight of the *Hindenburg*
5. the Great Wall of China
6. Jason's ship, the *Argo*
7. a Baptist minister
8. the Age of Chivalry
9. Strawberry Festival
10. the Battle of Gettysburg

EXAMPLES May I speak to you for a moment, **D**octor?
What can I do for you, **S**ir [*or* sir]?

(3) Capitalize a word showing a family relationship when the word is used before or in place of a person's name.

EXAMPLES Hey, **M**om, **A**unt Lisa and **U**ncle John are here!

Do not capitalize a word showing a family relationship when a possessive comes before the word.

EXAMPLES Bill's **m**other and my **g**randfather Ned lived in Nigeria.

✓ QUICK CHECK 4

Correct each of the following expressions, using capital letters as needed. If an item is correct, write *C*.

EXAMPLE **1.** a British school
1. *C*

1. my cousin Jane
2. latin
3. Amy's Uncle Joe
4. jewish rye bread
5. senator Daniels
6. the mayor of Seattle
7. a dance with mexican music
8. Grandfather Paul
9. president Clinton
10. a shakespearean sonnet

(4) Capitalize the first and last words and all important words in titles of books, magazines, newspapers, poems, short stories, historical documents, movies, television programs, works of art, and musical compositions.

Unimportant words in titles include

- prepositions of fewer than five letters (such as *at, of, for, from, with*)
- coordinating conjunctions (*and, but, for, nor, or, so, yet*)
- articles (*a, an, the*)

TYPE OF NAME	EXAMPLES
Books	*The Land I Lost, Science in Ancient China*
Magazines	*Horse and Pony, Family Circle*
Newspapers	*Milwaukee Journal, The Miami Herald*
Poems	"Jimmy Jet and His TV Set," "The Sneetches"
Short Stories	"The Southpaw," "The Golden Serpent"
Historical Documents	Magna Carta, Declaration of Independence
Movies	*The Lion King, Roots*
Television Programs	*Home Improvement, Paleoworld*
Works of Art	*Nocturne in Blue and Silver, The Gulf Stream*
Musical Compositions	*West Side Story,* "La Bamba"

☞ For more information about words used in direct address, see rule 12i(2) on page 751.

NOTE The article *the* before a title is not capitalized unless it is the first word of the title.

EXAMPLES Was your picture really in the *New York Post*?
Send your letter to *The Atlantic Monthly.*

☞ For information on when to italicize (underline) a title, see page 754. For information on using quotation marks for titles, see page 757.

Quick Check 4: Answers
1. C
2. Latin
3. Amy's uncle Joe
4. Jewish rye bread
5. Senator Daniels
6. C
7. a dance with Mexican music
8. C
9. President Clinton
10. a Shakespearean sonnet

11f. Do *not* capitalize the names of school subjects, except language courses and course names followed by a number.

EXAMPLES Next semester I am planning to take Spanish, math, and Music II.

 QUICK CHECK 5

The following sentences contain words that should be capitalized. Correct the words requiring capitals.

EXAMPLE 1. Did you read "All summer in a day" yet?
  1. *Summer, Day*

1. I read in the television listing that tonight *Ancient warriors* is about the romans.
2. I am calling the poem that I wrote about Dickon in *the secret garden* "nature's magic."
3. For my project in French class, I wrote a paper about La Fontaine's "The fox and the crow."
4. Wasn't there a photo in *Time* of *Ducks in a stream* and some other paintings of Hokusai's?
5. How about reading *The old man and the sea* for your report?

12 PUNCTUATION

END MARKS

An **end mark** is a mark of punctuation placed at the end of a sentence. The three kinds of end marks are the *period,* the *question mark,* and the *exclamation point.*

12a. Use a period at the end of a statement.

EXAMPLE Huynh Quang Nhuong is a writer**.**

12b. Use a question mark at the end of a question.

EXAMPLE Didn't he write *The Land I Lost***?**

12c. Use an exclamation point at the end of an exclamation.

EXAMPLES Wow**!** What a life he has led**!**

12d. Use a period or an exclamation point at the end of a request or a command.

EXAMPLES Please tell us about it**.** [request]
  Give me a chance**!** [command]

QUICK CHECK 1

Add an appropriate end mark to each of the following sentences.

EXAMPLE 1. Is that story about the crocodile actually true
1. *Is that story about the crocodile actually true?*

1. I thought so
2. Just imagine it
3. Was Lan brave

4. How frightened she must have been
5. Please read me that part again

12e. Use a period after most abbreviations.

TYPES OF ABBREVIATIONS	EXAMPLES
Personal Names	Herbert S. Zim W.E.B. Du Bois
Titles Used with Names	Mr. Ms. Jr. Sr. Dr.
States	N.Y. Fla. Tenn. Calif.
Addresses	St. Rd. Blvd. P.O. Box
Organizations and Companies	Co. Inc. Corp. Assn.
Times	A.M. P.M. B.C. A.D.

When an abbreviation with a period ends a sentence, another period is not needed. However, a question mark or an exclamation point is used as needed.

EXAMPLES   Hello, P.J.
Have you been introduced to Yoshiko, P.J.?

 QUICK CHECK 2

Insert punctuation where it is needed in the following sentences.

EXAMPLE 1. "The Sneetches" is one of my favorite Dr Seuss stories
1. *"The Sneetches" is one of my favorite Dr. Seuss stories.*

1. Did J R tell you about our plans for a play about the Sneetches
2. We need 10 ft of felt to make stars for the Star-Belly Sneetches
3. Write to the Tim P Smith Co, 101 W Sixth Ave, St. Louis, MO 64505
4. The PTA's address is 412 E Oak Rd
5. We'll meet at 10:00 AM on Monday at the Savings and Loan Assoc on Elm Blvd

COMMAS

An end mark is used to separate complete thoughts. A *comma* is used to separate words or groups of words *within* a complete thought.

 NOTE A two-letter state abbreviation without periods is used only when it is followed by a ZIP Code.

EXAMPLE
Atlanta, **GA** 30327

 NOTE Abbreviations for government agencies and some widely used abbreviations are written without periods. Each letter of the abbreviation is capitalized.

EXAMPLES   UN, FBI, PTA, NAACP, PBS, CNN, YMCA, VHF

 NOTE Abbreviations for most units of measure are written without periods.

EXAMPLES   cm, kg, ml, ft, lb, mi, oz, qt

EXCEPTION   in.

Quick Check 1: Possible Answers
1. I thought so.
2. Just imagine it!
3. Was Lan brave?
4. How frightened she must have been!
5. Please read me that part again.

Quick Check 2: Answers
1. Did J. R. tell you about our plans for a play about the Sneetches?
2. We need 10 ft of felt to make stars for the Star-Belly Sneetches.
3. Write to the Tim P. Smith Co., 101 W. Sixth Ave., St. Louis, MO 64505.
4. The PTA's address is 412 E. Oak Rd.
5. We'll meet at 10:00 A.M. on Monday at the Savings and Loan Assoc. on Elm Blvd.

Items in a Series

12f. **Use commas to separate items in a series.**

Make sure that there are three or more items in a series; two items do not need a comma.

EXAMPLES   Joey had been to Hawaii, Venezuela, and Panama. [words in a series]

         We looked for our cat Jeffrey under the beds, in the closets, and under the porch. [phrases in a series]

If all items in a series are joined by *and* or *or,* do not use commas to separate them.

EXAMPLE   I miss him **and** our talks **and** our walks.

12g. **Use a comma to separate two or more adjectives that come before a noun.**

EXAMPLE   He was a good, true friend.

Do not place a comma between an adjective and the noun immediately following it.

INCORRECT   His new, house is far from here.

  CORRECT   His new house is far from here.

Sometimes the last adjective in a series is closely connected in meaning to the noun. In that case, do not use a comma before the last adjective.

EXAMPLE   He was my only best friend.

✔ QUICK CHECK 3

Rewrite each of the following sentences, correcting any comma error. If a sentence is correct, write *C.*

EXAMPLE   1. Lara Joe and Mike admire Langston Hughes's poetry.
          1. *Lara, Joe, and Mike admire Langston Hughes's poetry.*

1. Hughes's poems often have short simple direct lines.
2. Wasn't he one of the modern African American poets?
3. Hughes's career began when he was elected Class Poet wrote a poem about his school and received loud applause when he read it at his graduation.
4. Hughes often memorized his poems and took a walk and recited them aloud.
5. What gives this poem a "soft," end?

12h. **Use a comma before *and, but, or, nor, for, so,* or *yet* when it joins the parts of a compound sentence.**

EXAMPLE   I liked *Owls,* **but** I did my report on *Volcano.*

Quick Check 3: Answers

1. Hughes's poems often have short, simple, direct lines.
2. C.
3. Hughes's career began when he was elected Class Poet, wrote a poem about his school, and received loud applause when he read it at his graduation.
4. C
5. What gives this poem a "soft" end?

Interrupters

12i. Use commas to set off an expression that interrupts a sentence.

Two commas are needed if the expression to be set off is in the middle of a sentence. One comma is needed if the expression comes first or last.

EXAMPLES The author of this story, **Ray Bradbury,** sometimes appears on television.
Yes, he's a science fiction writer.
Isn't one of his stories in our book, **Bess**?

(1) Use commas to set off appositives and appositive phrases that are not needed to understand the meaning of a sentence.

An *appositive* is a noun or pronoun that identifies or explains another noun or pronoun beside it. An *appositive phrase* is an appositive with its modifiers.

EXAMPLE Her illustration, **a sketch of a volcano,** is well drawn.

Do not use commas when an appositive is needed to understand the meaning of a sentence.

EXAMPLES My sister **Paula** drew it. [I have more than one sister and am giving her name to identify which one I mean.]
My sister, **Paula,** drew it. [I have only one sister and am giving her name simply as extra information.]

(2) Use commas to set off words used in direct address.

Using the name of the person to whom you are speaking is using *direct address.*

EXAMPLE **Mona,** tell us about yourself.

(3) Use a comma after such words as *well, yes, no,* and *why* when they begin a sentence.

EXAMPLE **Well,** I have always liked drawing.

Conventional Situations

12j. Use commas in certain conventional situations.

(1) Use commas to separate items in dates and addresses.

EXAMPLES They married on June 1, 1965, in Taos, New Mexico.
The plant opens in Reno, Nevada, next week.
Summer vacation begins on Friday, May 20.
My new address will be 110 Oak Drive, Minneapolis, MN 55424. [Notice that a comma is not used between a two-letter state abbreviation and a ZIP Code.]

Quick Check 4: Answers

1. Nicky, tell us about Bailey, the title character.
2. Yes, Ms. Walsh, I'd be glad to.
3. Isn't your brother's address 12 Linden Road, Atlanta, Georgia?
4. Well, it has been for years, but he may have moved by now.
5. No, he won't move until Monday, October 10.

Quick Check 5: Answers

1. This cat is at home in a drawer; he hides behind the door.
2. No one can stop his antics; this cat makes up his own mind.
3. His eating habits are finicky; yes, even cream may not suit him.
4. Fish may revolt him; cream may disgust him.
5. Perhaps you have a cat like him; perhaps you know of one.

---

(2) Use a comma after the salutation of a friendly letter and after the closing of any letter.

EXAMPLES Dear Uncle Rollo, Sincerely yours, Yours truly,

 **QUICK CHECK 4**

Add commas where they are needed in the following sentences.

EXAMPLE 1. Maya Angelou a major modern poet wrote "Brother."
   1. *Maya Angelou, a major modern poet, wrote "Brother."*

1. Nicky tell us about Bailey the title character.
2. Yes Ms. Walsh I'd be glad to.
3. Isn't your brother's address 12 Linden Road Atlanta Georgia?
4. Well it has been for years but he may have moved by now.
5. No he won't move until Monday October 10.

SEMICOLONS

12k. **Use a semicolon between parts of a compound sentence if they are not joined by *and, but, or, nor, for, so,* or *yet.***

EXAMPLE The Rum Tum Tugger is quite a character; he, not his owner, is the boss.

 QUICK CHECK 5

Write the following sentences, adding semicolons as needed.

EXAMPLE 1. Try to read "The Rum Tum Tugger" soon it's funny.
   1. *Try to read "The Rum Tum Tugger" soon; it's funny.*

1. This cat is at home in a drawer he hides behind the door.
2. No one can stop his antics this cat makes up his own mind.
3. His eating habits are finicky yes, even cream may not suit him.
4. Fish may revolt him cream may disgust him.
5. Perhaps you have a cat like him perhaps you know of one.

COLONS

12l. **Use a colon before a list of items, especially after expressions like *as follows* or *the following.***

EXAMPLES Poets may use the following: rhyme, metaphor, and imagery.
   One poetic device is rhyme: end rhyme and internal rhyme.

752 **LANGUAGE HANDBOOK**

T752

I2m. Use a colon in certain conventional situations.

(1) Use a colon between the hour and the minute.

EXAMPLES 1**:**15 P.M.   6**:**32 A.M.

(2) Use a colon after the salutation of a business letter.

EXAMPLES Dear Ms. Cruz**:**   Dear Sir or Madam**:**

Dear Sales Manager**:**   To Whom It May Concern**:**

(3) Use a colon between a title and a subtitle.

EXAMPLE "Snakes**:** The Facts and Folklore"

 QUICK CHECK 6

The following items contain errors in the use of colons. Rewrite each item, correcting each error.

EXAMPLE 1. The following poets use cats as a subject T. S. Eliot, Gary Soto, and Suki Lehman-Becker.

1. *The following poets use cats as a subject: T. S. Eliot, Gary Soto, and Suki Lehman-Becker.*

1. Poetry may be composed on any subject; common subjects include the following love, grief, special moments.
2. Characteristics of successful poets are as follows love of words, love of sound, dedication to their poetry.
3. Did you ever watch *Star Trek; The Next Generation*?
4. Some writers get up at 5 30 in the morning.
5. Dear Sir or Madam

 Using Semicolons

Semicolons are most effective when they are not overused. Sometimes it is better to separate a compound sentence or a heavily punctuated sentence rather than to use a semicolon.

ACCEPTABLE Like so many pets, the kitten had been abandoned; luckily, Gary Soto found it, just a few weeks old, and carried it to his home, a safe harbor at last for the hungry kitten.

BETTER Like so many pets, the kitten had been abandoned. Luckily, Gary Soto found it, just a few weeks old, and carried it to his home, a safe harbor at last for the hungry kitten.

 NOTE Never use a colon directly after a verb or a preposition. Omit the colon, or reword the sentence.

INCORRECT The devices Eliot uses in the poem are: rhyme, repetition, and alliteration.

CORRECT The devices Eliot uses in the poem are rhyme, repetition, and alliteration.

CORRECT In the poem, Eliot uses the following devices: rhyme, repetition, and alliteration.

Try It Out ✎

Decide how the information in each of the following sentences could be most clearly and effectively expressed. If you think the information can be better presented, revise the sentence.

1. Soto's cat loves the crunchy rattle of dry cat food; equally appetizing are pieces of soft, cold, aromatic cheese taken from the writer's own hand.
2. Some cats hunt mice and small birds; we have a cat.
3. For this skinny kitten, Soto, unlike many cat owners, cooked eggs; eggs, rich in nutrients, helped the kitten back to health.
4. Some cats enjoy a nap on an article of their owners' clothing, in this case, slippers; other cats prefer the privacy and darkness of a closet.
5. Soto's family protected, fed, and cuddled the kitten; in turn, the kitten responded with love and happiness.

Quick Check 6: Answers
1. Poetry may be composed on any subject; common subjects include the following: love, grief, special moments.
2. Characteristics of successful poets are as follows: love of words, love of sound, dedication to their poetry.
3. Did you ever watch *Star Trek: The Next Generation*?
4. Some writers get up at 5:30 in the morning.
5. Dear Sir or Madam:

Try It Out: Possible Answers
1. Soto's cat loves the crunchy rattle of dry cat food. Equally appetizing are pieces of soft, cold, aromatic cheese taken from the writer's own hand.
2. Some cats hunt mice and small birds. We have a cat.
3. For this skinny kitten, Soto, unlike many cat owners, cooked eggs. Eggs, rich in nutrients, helped the kitten back to health.
4. Some cats enjoy a nap on an article of their owners' clothing, in this case, slippers. Other cats prefer the privacy and darkness of a closet.
5. Students may say the sentence is acceptable as is.

• Language Handbook Worksheets, pp. 121–134
• Language Workshop CD-ROM, Lessons 42 and 43: Punctuating Titles and Quotations

If you use a computer, you may be able to set words in italics yourself. Most word-processing software and many printers are capable of producing italic type.

For examples of titles that are not italicized but are enclosed in quotation marks, see page 757.

13 PUNCTUATION

UNDERLINING (ITALICS)

Italics are printed letters that lean to the right, such as *the letters in these words*. In your handwritten or typewritten work, indicate italics by underlining.

HANDWRITTEN *The Land I Lost is an autobiography.*

TYPEWRITTEN The Land I Lost is an autobiography.

13a. Use underlining (italics) for titles of books, plays, periodicals, works of art, films, television programs, recordings, and long musical compositions, and for the names of trains, ships, aircraft, and spacecraft.

TYPE OF TITLE	EXAMPLES	
Books	Hank the Cowdog	Barrio Boy
Plays	The Secret Garden	Brian's Song
Periodicals	TV Guide	Sports Illustrated
Works of Art	The Pietà	View of Toledo
Films	Toy Story	The Land Before Time
Television Programs	Ancient Warriors	The Magic School Bus
Recordings	Unforgettable	Ave Maria
Long Musical Compositions	Don Giovanni / The Mikado	The Four Seasons / Water Music
Ships	Calypso	USS Nimitz
Trains	Orient Express	City of New Orleans
Aircraft	Spruce Goose	Spirit of St. Louis
Spacecraft	Friendship 7	USS Enterprise

QUICK CHECK 1

Write and underline the words that should be italicized in each of the following sentences.

EXAMPLE 1. Who wrote the book Greek Myths?
1. *Greek Myths*

1. How many people did the Mayflower carry?
2. Did the Kansas City Star review the film Pocahontas?
3. My copy of The Stories of Ray Bradbury is overdue.
4. I love the show Where in the World Is Carmen Sandiego?
5. Why are you calling your painting Silver Suite 682?

Quick Check 1: Answers
1. Mayflower
2. Kansas City Star, Pocahontas
3. The Stories of Ray Bradbury
4. Where in the World Is Carmen Sandiego?
5. Silver Suite 682

QUOTATION MARKS

13b. Place quotation marks before and after a *direct quotation*—a person's exact words.

EXAMPLES   "Has everyone read the story?" she asked.
"I read it last night," said Carlos.

Do not use quotation marks for an **indirect quotation**—a rewording of a direct quotation.

DIRECT QUOTATION   Carlos said, "I enjoyed it very much."
INDIRECT QUOTATION   Carlos said that he enjoyed it very much.

13c. A direct quotation begins with a capital letter.

EXAMPLE   Nicole added, "It's based on an Indian folk tale."

13d. When the expression identifying the speaker interrupts a quoted sentence, each part of the quotation is enclosed in quotation marks.

EXAMPLE   "This story by Rudyard Kipling," said Tanya, "is my favorite so far."

Notice in the example above that the second part of the divided sentence begins with a lowercase letter.

When the second part of a divided quotation is a new sentence, it begins with a capital letter.

EXAMPLE   "Rudyard Kipling is famous for this type of story," said Mrs. Perkins. "Have any of you read *The Jungle Book*?"

13e. A direct quotation is set off from the rest of the sentence by a comma, a question mark, or an exclamation point, but not by a period.

If a quotation comes at the beginning of a sentence, a comma follows it. If a quotation comes at the end of a sentence, a comma comes before it. If a quoted sentence is interrupted, a comma follows the first part and comes before the second part.

EXAMPLES   "Well, we could write a fable about how the elephant got its tusks," Alyssa said.
Mark said, "Didn't somebody do that?"
"Maybe somebody did," Alyssa pointed out, "but we could, too."

When a quotation ends with a question mark or with an exclamation point, no comma is needed.

EXAMPLES   "Didn't he write *Just So Stories*?" asked Delia.
"What an imagination!" exclaimed Mark.

Quick Check 2: Possible Answers

1. Sam replied, "Kipling must have been a workaholic."
2. "I don't know about him," Mary said, "but I have lots to do already."
3. "Just doing my homework keeps me busy," Ken interjected. "Doing yardwork and other chores takes up the rest of my time."
4. "Humph! I hate yardwork!" Mary said.
5. "Yeah, and Kipling says that we should work until we sweat! I don't think so," Sam retorted.

 QUICK CHECK 2

Revise the following sentences by adding commas, end marks, and quotation marks where necessary.

EXAMPLE   1. "Hey, what did you think of that poem asked Mary.
               1. *"Hey, what did you think of that poem?" asked Mary.*

1. Sam replied Kipling must have been a workaholic."
2. I don't know about him, Mary said, but I have lots to do already.
3. Just doing my homework keeps me busy Ken interjected. Doing yardwork and other chores takes up the rest of my time.
4. Humph! I hate yardwork Mary said.
5. Yeah, and Kipling says that we should work until we sweat! I don't think so," Sam retorted.

13f. **A period or a comma is always placed inside the closing quotation marks.**

EXAMPLES   Mrs. Alaniz said, "Read this for tomorrow**.**"
                "I'll get started right away**,**" replied Chip.

13g. **A question mark or an exclamation point is placed inside the closing quotation marks when the quotation itself is a question or an exclamation. Otherwise, it is placed outside.**

EXAMPLES   "Why does the camel have such a bad attitude**?**" asked Mario. [The quotation is a question.]
                Did Ms. Johnson say, "All reports are due on Friday"**?**
                [The sentence, not the quotation, is a question.]

13h. **Use single quotation marks to enclose a quotation within a quotation.**

EXAMPLE   "What happened to the **'**steel-driving man**'** John Henry?" Mr. Zinn asked.

13i. **When a quotation consists of several sentences, place quotation marks at the beginning and at the end of the whole quotation.**

EXAMPLE   **"**Read the story by Thursday. Gather your thoughts and make notes. Please be prepared to discuss your idea in class,**"** said Mr. Ellis.

13j. **When you write dialogue (conversation), begin a new paragraph each time you change speakers.**

EXAMPLE   "He says 'Humph!'" said the Dog; "and he won't fetch and carry."
               "Does he say anything else?"

"Only 'Humph!'; and he won't plow," said the
Ox.
     "Very good," said the Djinn.
        —Rudyard Kipling, "How the Camel Got His Hump"

 QUICK CHECK 3

Revise the following sentences by adding commas, end marks, and quotation marks where necessary.

EXAMPLE   1. Ms. Ash asked What, class, is this story's moral?
            1. *Ms. Ash asked, "What, class, is this story's moral?"*

1. Work! yelled Austin.
2. What about work? mused Ms. Ash. Is it good or bad for you?
3. Kipling says that if you're unhappy, work's good for you, Laura said.
4. I wonder why the Djinn called the camel 'Bubbles,' Austin said.
5. Serena Ms. Ash said would you tell us about your ride on a camel?

13k. Use quotation marks to enclose titles of short works such as short stories, poems, articles, songs, episodes of television programs, and chapters and other parts of books.

TYPE OF TITLE	EXAMPLES	
Short Stories	"All Summer in a Day"	"The Fun They Had"
Poems	"The Sidewalk Racer"	"The Lawn Mower"
Articles	"Volcano"	"The Survivors"
Songs	"The Star-Spangled Banner"	"Amazing Grace"
Episodes of TV Programs	"Heart of a Champion"	"The Trouble with Tribbles"
Chapters and Other Parts of Books	"Learning About the Lungs" "Chapter Summary"	"Parts of Speech" "Appendix 1: Maps of the World"

☞ For examples of titles that are italicized, see page 754.

 QUICK CHECK 4

Revise the following sentences by adding commas, end marks, and quotation marks where necessary.

EXAMPLE   1. Will you play John Henry on your guitar for us? asked Ed.
            1. *"Will you play 'John Henry' on your guitar for us?" asked Ed.*

1. Read the next chapter, Food for Health, by Monday, said Mr. Carl.
2. I'm calling my poem Wind at Morning.
3. My sister and she are like the girls in that story The Tree House.
4. I'll be playing So Rare at my recital; it's an old tune.
5. Wow! Read this review titled Too Little, Too Late exclaimed Paul.

Quick Check 3: Answers
1. "Work!" yelled Austin.
2. "What about work?" mused Ms. Ash. "Is it good or bad for you?"
3. "Kipling says that if you're unhappy, work's good for you," Laura said.
4. "I wonder why the Djinn called the camel 'Bubbles,'" Austin said.
5. "Serena," Ms. Ash said, "would you tell us about your ride on a camel?"

Quick Check 4: Answers
1. "Read the next chapter, 'Food for Health,' by Monday," said Mr. Carl.
2. I'm calling my poem "Wind at Morning."
3. My sister and she are like the girls in the story "The Tree House."
4. I'll be playing "So Rare" at my recital; it's an old tune.
5. "Wow! Read this review titled 'Too Little, Too Late,'" exclaimed Paul.

Resources ————

- *Language Handbook Worksheets,* pp. 127–132
- *Language Workshop CD-ROM,* Lessons 40, 41, and 45: Punctuating Possessives, Contractions, and Plurals (Apostrophe); Colons and Hyphens

APOSTROPHES

Possessive Case

The ***possessive case*** of a noun or a pronoun shows ownership (**Harriet's** courage) or relationship (**her** brother).

14a. To form the possessive case of a singular noun, add an apostrophe and an *s.*

> **EXAMPLES** a person**'**s best friend   a day**'**s time

> A proper name ending in *s* may take only an apostrophe to form the possessive case if the addition of *'s* would make the name awkward to pronounce.

> **EXAMPLES** Marjorie Kinnan Rawlings**'** novels
> Hercules**'** feats

Do not use an apostrophe to form the *plural* of a noun. Remember that the apostrophe shows ownership or relationship.

14b. To form the possessive case of a plural noun ending in *s,* add only the apostrophe.

> **EXAMPLES** dreams**'** meanings   wolves**'** caves

14c. To form the possessive case of a plural noun that does not end in *s,* add an apostrophe and an *s.*

> **EXAMPLES** people**'**s habits   mice**'**s holes

14d. Do *not* use an apostrophe with possessive personal pronouns.

> **EXAMPLES** The cat was **hers.**   That is **his** dog.

14e. To form the possessive case of some indefinite pronouns, add an apostrophe and an *s.*

> **EXAMPLES** anyone**'**s guess   no one**'**s report

 QUICK CHECK 1

Add an apostrophe to any word that needs one in the following sentences.

> **EXAMPLE** 1. Cat would go to Adams house.
> 1. *Adam's*

1. Dog heard a gorillas footsteps and barked his loudest.
2. According to Cats thinking, his promise was most important.
3. Cats have always been mices enemies.
4. In most cases, cats enemies are dogs.
5. Somebodys cat was scratching loudly at the back door; I think it must have been hers.

Quick Check 1: Answers
1. gorilla's
2. Cat's
3. mice's
4. cats'
5. Somebody's

Contractions

14f. **To form a contraction, use an apostrophe to show where letters have been left out.**

A *contraction* is a shortened form of a word, a number, or a group of words. The apostrophe in a contraction shows where letters, numerals, or words have been left out.

EXAMPLES   I am .... I'm   1997 .... '97
where is .... where's   of the clock .... o'clock

The word *not* can be shortened to *n't* and added to a verb, usually without changing the spelling of the verb.

EXAMPLES   has not ...... has**n't**   are not ..... are**n't**
had not ...... had**n't**   do not ...... do**n't**
should not ... should**n't** were not ... were**n't**

EXCEPTIONS will not ...... wo**n't**   cannot ..... ca**n't**

Do not confuse contractions with possessive pronouns.

CONTRACTIONS	POSSESSIVE PRONOUNS
It's an African fable. [*It is*]	**Its** explanation of dogs and cats amuses me.
Who's Eve's favorite? [*Who is*]	**Whose** home was the cave?
There's not much food. [*There is*]	This home was **theirs.**
They're not home. [*They are*]	**Their** dog warned them.

Plurals

14g. **Use an apostrophe and an *s* to form the plurals of letters, numerals, and signs, and of words referred to as words.**

EXAMPLES   Your *T*'s look like *F*'s.
He always crosses his 7's with a horizontal line.
Don't use so many *!*'s and *oh*'s.

 QUICK CHECK 2

Write the correct form of each item that requires an apostrophe in the following sentences.

EXAMPLE   **1.** Cat wouldnt come to an agreement.
       1. *wouldn't*

1. Were reading "The Fun They Had" next.
2. Its not right to break a promise.
3. Do #s mean "pounds"?
4. Lets ask him if hes going there, too.
5. "Whos its owner?" I asked.

Quick Check 2: Answers
1. We're
2. It's
3. #'s
4. Let's, he's
5. Who's

14h. Use a hyphen to divide a word at the end of a line.

When dividing a word at the end of a line, remember the following rules:

(1) Divide a word only between syllables.

INCORRECT	Both Dog and Cat had agreed that they would, unfort-unately, separate, and Cat went to Adam's house.
CORRECT	Both Dog and Cat had agreed that they would, unfor-tunately, separate, and Cat went to Adam's house.

(2) Do not divide a one-syllable word.

INCORRECT	Without any warning, Gorilla reached down and pick-ed Dog up angrily.
CORRECT	Without any warning, Gorilla reached down and picked Dog up angrily.

(3) Do not divide a word so that one letter stands alone.

INCORRECT	After some discussion with his friend, Dog set out a-lone on his search for food.
CORRECT	After some discussion with his friend, Dog set out alone on his search for food.

14i. Use a hyphen with compound numbers from *twenty-one* to *ninety-nine* and with fractions used as adjectives.

EXAMPLES **twenty-two** verbs, **one-half** pint, **fifty-first** state

QUICK CHECK 3

Proofread each of the following sentences for errors in the use of hyphens. Correct each error.

COMPUTER NOTE Some word-processing programs will automatically break a word at the end of a line and insert a hyphen. Occasionally, such a break will violate one of the rules given under rule 14h. Always check a printout of your writing to see how the computer has hyphenated words at the ends of lines. If a hyphen is used incorrectly, revise the line by moving the word or by rebreaking the word and inserting a "hard" hyphen (one that the computer cannot move).

EXAMPLE 1. Have you read the poem on page thirty nine yet?
1. *Have you read the poem on page thirty-nine yet?*

1. Unhappy at first, Dog and Cat did not like being a-part from each other.
2. However, after several days of being apart had pass-ed, Cat was quite content.
3. They sat together and thought, and Dog and Cat scr-atched fleas.
4. Do you remember, Elizabeth, which animal's loud fo-otsteps Dog heard?
5. Is your report actually twenty three pages long?

Quick Check 3: Answers

1. Unhappy at first, Dog and Cat did not like being apart [not divided] from each other.
2. However, after several days of being apart had passed [not divided], Cat was quite content.
3. They sat together and thought, and Dog and Cat scratched [not divided] fleas.
4. Do you remember, Elizabeth, which animal's loud footsteps [not divided; or foot-steps, if divided] Dog heard?
5. Is your report actually twenty-three pages long?

USING WORD PARTS

Many English words are made up of various word parts. Learning to spell frequently used parts can help you spell many words correctly.

Resources
- *Language Handbook Worksheets,* pp. 134–140
- *Language Workshop CD-ROM,* Lessons 48 and 49: Rules of Spelling

Roots

15a. The *root* of a word is the part that carries the word's core meaning.

COMMONLY USED ROOTS		
WORD ROOT	**MEANING**	**EXAMPLES**
–ped–	foot	pedal, pedestrian
–port–	carry	porter, portable
–vid–, –vis–	see	video, visual

> **NOTE** When you are not sure about the spelling of a word, look it up in a dictionary. A dictionary will also tell you the correct pronunciation and syllable divisions of a word.

Prefixes

15b. A *prefix* is one or more letters or syllables added to the beginning of a word or word part to create a new word.

COMMONLY USED PREFIXES		
PREFIX	**MEANING**	**EXAMPLES**
dis–	away, opposing	disarm, disagree
il–, im–, in–, ir–	not	illegal, incomplete
semi–	half	semicircle

Suffixes

15c. A *suffix* is one or more letters or syllables added to the end of a word or word part to create a new word.

COMMONLY USED SUFFIXES		
SUFFIX	**MEANING**	**EXAMPLES**
–en	made of, become	wooden, broaden
–ful	full of	joyful, hopeful
–ness	quality	kindness, goodness

LANGUAGE HANDBOOK

ie and *ei*

15d. Except after *c*, write *ie* when the sound is long e.

EXAMPLES	ceiling	receive	piece	believe	chief	field
EXCEPTIONS	either	sheik	protein	seize	weird	

15e. Write *ei* when the sound is not long e, especially when the sound is long *a*.

EXAMPLES	eighteen	sleigh	neigh	vein	their
EXCEPTIONS	ancient	mischief	pie	friend	conscience

This time-tested verse may help you remember when to use *ie* and when to use *ei*.

I before *e*
Except after *c*
Or when sounded like *a*,
As in *neighbor* and *weigh*.

 NOTE Rules 15d and 15e and the rhyme following rule 15e apply only when the *i* and the *e* are in the same syllable.

✓ QUICK CHECK 1

Add the letters *ie* or *ei* to spell each of the following words correctly.

EXAMPLE   1. bel . . . ve
          1. *believe*

1. f . . . rce
2. conc . . . t
3. perc . . . ve
4. h . . . r
5. . . . ght
6. h . . . ght
7. pr . . . st
8. rel . . . f
9. rev . . . w
10. fr . . . nd

–cede, *–ceed*, and *–sede*

15f. The only word ending in *–sede* is *supersede*. The only words ending in *–ceed* are *exceed, proceed,* and *succeed*. Most other words with this sound end in *–cede*.

EXAMPLES   concede   intercede   precede   recede   secede

Adding Prefixes

15g. When adding a prefix to a word, do not change the spelling of the word itself.

EXAMPLES	pre + view = **pre**view	post + script = **post**script
	mis + spell = **mis**spell	im + mature = **im**mature

Adding Suffixes

15h. When adding the suffix *–ly* or *–ness* to a word, do not change the spelling of the word itself.

    EXAMPLES   quick + ly = quick**ly**   near + ness = near**ness**

    EXCEPTIONS   For words that end in *y* and have more than one sylla-
ble, change the *y* to *i* before adding *–ly* or *–ness*.
tardy + ly = tard**ily**   ready + ly = read**ily**

15i. Drop the final silent e before a suffix beginning with a vowel.

    EXAMPLES   strange + er = strang**er**   close + ing = clos**ing**

    EXCEPTIONS   Keep the final silent *e* in a word ending in *ce* or *ge*
before a suffix beginning with *a* or *o*.
change + able = chang**eable**
service + able = servic**eable**

15j. Keep the final silent e before a suffix beginning with a consonant.

    EXAMPLES   false + ly = false**ly**   pride + ful = pride**ful**

    EXCEPTIONS   nine + th = nin**th**   argue + ment = argu**ment**

15k. For words ending in y preceded by a consonant, change the y to i before any suffix that does not begin with i.

    EXAMPLES   empty + ness = empt**iness**   dry + ed = dr**ied**

15l. For words ending in y preceded by a vowel, keep the y when adding a suffix.

    EXAMPLES   stay + ing = staying   pay + ment = pay**ment**

    EXCEPTIONS   day—da**ily**   lay—la**id**   pay—pa**id**   say—sa**id**

15m. Double the final consonant before a suffix beginning with a vowel if the word

(1) has only one syllable or has the accent on the last syllable
        and
(2) ends in a single consonant preceded by a single vowel.

    EXAMPLES   wed + ing = we**dd**ing   begin + er = begin**ner**

Do not double the final consonant in words ending in *w* or *x*.

    EXAMPLES   bow + ing = bo**w**ing   tax + ed = ta**x**ed

Also, the final consonant is usually not doubled before a suffix beginning with a vowel.

    EXAMPLES   send + er = send**er**   final + ist = final**ist**

NOTE **Vowels** are the letters *a, e, i, o, u*, and sometimes *y*. All other letters of the alphabet are **consonants.**

NOTE When adding *–ing* to words that end in *ie*, drop the e and change the *i* to *y*.

    EXAMPLES
    tie + ing = **tying**
    lie + ing = **lying**

NOTE In some cases, the final consonant either may or may not be doubled.

    EXAMPLE   travel + ed =
    trave**l**ed *or* trave**ll**ed

Quick Check 2: Answers

1. immobile
2. reset
3. unlucky
4. happily
5. semiprecious
6. forceable
7. shopper
8. dirtiness
9. hurried
10. outrageous

✓ **QUICK CHECK 2**

Spell each of the following words, adding the prefix or suffix given.

EXAMPLE   1. display + ed
                1. *displayed*

1. im + mobile   6. force + able
2. re + set   7. shop + er
3. un + lucky   8. dirty + ness
4. happy + ly   9. hurry + ed
5. semi + precious   10. outrage + ous

Forming the Plurals of Nouns

15n. For most nouns, add *–s.*

SINGULAR	log	thought	pen	hoe	soda	Baker
PLURAL	logs	thoughts	pens	hoes	sodas	Bakers

15o. For nouns ending in *s, x, z, ch,* or *sh,* add *–es.*

SINGULAR	lass	box	waltz	pinch	blush	Ruíz
PLURAL	lasses	boxes	waltzes	pinches	blushes	Ruízes

15p. For nouns ending in *y* preceded by a consonant, change the *y* to *i* and add *–es.*

SINGULAR	fly	puppy	cry	lady
	enemy	remedy		
PLURAL	flies	puppies	cries	ladies
	enemies	remedies		

EXCEPTIONS   For proper nouns ending in *y*, just add *–s.*

Nicky—Nickys   Kelly—Kellys

However, for nouns ending in *y* preceded by a vowel, add *–s.*

SINGULAR	joy	replay	key	Wiley
PLURAL	joys	replays	keys	Wileys

15q. For some nouns ending in *f* or *fe*, add *–s.* For others, change the *f* or *fe* to *v* and add *–es.*

SINGULAR	belief	wife	tariff	life	giraffe
PLURAL	beliefs	wives	tariffs	lives	giraffes

15r. For nouns ending in *o* preceded by a vowel, add *–s.*

SINGULAR	radio	patio	stereo	cameo	Nunzio
PLURAL	radios	patios	stereos	cameos	Nunzios

15s. For nouns ending in o preceded by a consonant, add *–es*.

SINGULAR	torpedo	potato	echo	hero
PLURAL	torpedo**es**	potato**es**	echo**es**	hero**es**

EXCEPTIONS For musical terms and proper nouns, add *-s*.
　　　　　　alto—altos　　　　　　soprano—sopranos
　　　　　　Palombo—Palombos　　Soto—Sotos

15t. A few nouns form their plurals in irregular ways.

SINGULAR	ox	child	foot	tooth	man
PLURAL	ox**en**	child**ren**	feet	teeth	men

15u. For some nouns, the singular and the plural forms are the same.

SINGULAR AND PLURAL Sioux　Japanese　salmon　deer　moose

15v. For numbers, letters, symbols, and words used as words, add an apostrophe and *–s*.

EXAMPLES *3*'s　*z*'s　*!*'s　*or*'s

✓ *QUICK CHECK 3*

Spell the plural form of each of the following items.

EXAMPLE **1.** $
　　　　　1. $'s

1. rodeo　**3.** Gómez　**5.** child　**7.** shelf　**9.** *L*
2. dairy　**4.** toy　　**6.** push　**8.** Chinese　**10.** 200

Writing Numbers

15w. Spell out a number that begins a sentence.

EXAMPLE **Thirteen** people helped stage *The Secret Garden*.

　Within a sentence, spell out numbers that can be written in one or two words.

EXAMPLE More than **sixty-five** people came for the opening performance.

15x. If you use several numbers, some short and some long, write them all the same way. Usually, it is better to write them all as numerals.

EXAMPLE In all, we spent **23** days rehearsing and sold **250** tickets.

15y. Spell out numbers used to indicate order.

EXAMPLE This was our **third** stage play of the year.

Quick Check 3: Answers
　1. rodeos
　2. dairies
　3. Gómezes
　4. toys
　5. children
　6. pushes
　7. shelves
　8. Chinese
　9. *L*'s
　10. *200*'s

16 GLOSSARY OF USAGE

The Glossary of Usage is an alphabetical list of words and expressions with definitions, explanations, and examples. Some examples are labeled *Standard* or *Formal*. These labels identify language that is appropriate in serious writing or speaking, such as in compositions for school or in speeches. Expressions labeled *Informal* are acceptable in conversation and in everyday writing. *Nonstandard* expressions do not follow the guidelines of standard English.

---

a, an   Use *a* before words or expressions that begin with consonant sounds. Use *an* before words or expressions that begin with vowel sounds.

EXAMPLES   Tom Sawyer was **a** friend of Huckleberry Finn.
The two boys had quite **an** adventure.
Mark Twain certainly created **a** unique character.
Was Tom **an** honest person?

Notice in the last two examples that a word may begin with a vowel that has a consonant sound or with a consonant that has a vowel sound.

accept, except   *Accept* is a verb that means "receive." *Except* may be either a verb or a preposition. As a verb, *except* means "leave out" or "exclude." As a preposition, *except* means "other than" or "excluding."

EXAMPLES   The Lins **accept** a dinner invitation from the Gleasons.
No guest was **excepted** from the Gleasons' hospitality.
No one **except** the Lins zipped the strings from the celery.

affect, effect   *Affect* is a verb meaning "influence." As a noun, *effect* means "the result of some action."

EXAMPLES   One error will not greatly **affect** your score on the test.
What **effect** did Rosa Parks's action have on the civil rights movement?

ain't   Avoid this word in speaking and writing. It is nonstandard English.

all ready, already   *All ready* means "completely prepared." *Already* means "before a certain point in time."

EXAMPLES   Mary was **all ready** for the test of endurance.
Her grandfather had **already** passed the test.

all right   Used as an adjective, *all right* means "unhurt" or "satisfactory." Used as an adverb, *all right* means "well enough." *All right* should always be written as two words.

EXAMPLES   Mary wondered if she would be **all right.** [adjective]
She did **all right** during her time away from home. [adverb]

a lot   *A lot* should always be written as two words.

EXAMPLE   She certainly learned **a lot** during those few days.

among   See **between, among.**

anywheres, everywheres, nowheres, somewheres   Use these words without the final *s.*

EXAMPLE   She didn't want to go **anywhere** [*not* anywheres].

at   Do not use *at* after *where.*

EXAMPLE   Where was Roger? [*not* Where was Roger at?]

bad, badly   *Bad* is an adjective. *Badly* is an adverb.

EXAMPLES   The berries taste **bad.** [*Bad* modifies the noun *berries.*]
Roger's eyes had swollen **badly.** [*Badly* modifies the verb *had swollen.*]

between, among   Use *between* when referring to two things at a time, even though they may be part of a group containing more than two.

EXAMPLES   A deal was made **between** Ernie and Mary.
Between explorations in the forest, lessons in cooking, and hearty meals, Mary told Ernie about Kaw legends. [The storytelling occurs only *between* any two of these activities.]

Use *among* when referring to a group rather than to the separate individuals in the group.

EXAMPLE   She walked **among** the many flowers.

bring, take   *Bring* means "come carrying something." *Take* means "go carrying something." Think of *bring* as related to *come.* Think of *take* as related to *go.*

EXAMPLES   Please **bring** your new puzzle when you come over.
Take your bathing suit when you go to the beach.

bust, busted   Avoid using these words as verbs. Use a form of either *burst* or *break.*

EXAMPLES   The dam **burst** [*not* busted], causing a flood.
Did you **break** [*not* bust] that window?
If you **break** [*not* bust] anything, you have to pay for it.

choose, chose   *Choose* is the present tense form of the verb *choose.* It rhymes with *whose* and means "select." *Chose* is the past tense form of *choose.* It rhymes with *grows* and means "selected."

EXAMPLES   What story did you **choose** for your report?
I **chose** a Greek myth.

 NOTE   Many writers overuse *a lot.* Whenever you run across *a lot* as you revise your own writing, try to replace it with a more exact word or phrase.

EXAMPLE   The dinner guests ate a lot.
REVISED   The dinner guests piled their plates with food.

could of   Do not write *of* with the helping verb *could*. Write *could have*. Also avoid using *ought to of*, *should of*, *would of*, *might of*, and *must of*.

EXAMPLE   Roger **could have** [*not* could of] done as Mary did.

   Of is also unnecessary with *had*.

EXAMPLE   If he **had** [*not* had of] done so, he would have had a better time.

doesn't, don't   *Doesn't* is the contraction of *does not*. *Don't* is the contraction of *do not*. Use *doesn't* with most singular subjects and *don't* with plural subjects and with *I* and *you*.

EXAMPLES   He **doesn't** look well.
Mary's feet **don't** have very many cuts.
I **don't** think so.

double subject   See **he, she, they.**

effect   See **affect, effect.**

everywheres   See **anywheres,** etc.

except   See **accept, except.**

fewer, less   *Fewer* is used with plural words. *Less* is used with singular words. *Fewer* tells "how many"; *less* tells "how much."

EXAMPLES   My family has **fewer** traditions than Mary's family.
Next time, use **less** chili powder.

good, well   *Good* is always an adjective. Never use *good* as an adverb. Instead, use *well*.

EXAMPLE   Mary did **well** [*not* good] on her endurance ritual.

   Although *well* is usually an adverb, *well* may also be used as an adjective to mean "healthy."

EXAMPLE   She looked **well** after her test.

had of   See **could of.**

had ought, hadn't ought   Unlike other verbs, *ought* is not used with *had*.

EXAMPLE   Mary **ought to** [*not* had ought to] tell the truth.

hardly, scarcely   The words *hardly* and *scarcely* are negative words. They should never be used with other negative words.

EXAMPLES   Grandfather **could** [*not* couldn't] **hardly** believe it.
He **had** [*not* hadn't] **scarcely** begun his Ta-Na-E-Ka when he found a dead deer.

> **NOTE**   *Feel good* and *feel well* mean different things. *Feel good* means "feel happy or pleased." *Feel well* means "feel healthy."
>
> **EXAMPLES**   She felt **good** [*happy*] about her Ta-Na-E-Ka.
> But Roger didn't feel **well** [*healthy*] at all and had lost weight.

he, she, they   Avoid using a pronoun along with its antecedent as the subject of a verb. This error is called the ***double subject.***

NONSTANDARD   Ray Bradbury he wrote "All Summer in a Day."

STANDARD   Ray Bradbury wrote "All Summer in a Day."

hisself   *Hisself* is nonstandard English. Use *himself*.

EXAMPLE   He fed **himself** [*not* hisself] on that deer the whole time.

how come   In informal situations, *how come* is often used instead of *why*. In formal situations, *why* should always be used.

INFORMAL   I don't know how come Roger didn't think of it.

FORMAL   I don't know **why** Roger didn't think of it.

its, it's   *Its* is a personal pronoun in the possessive form. *It's* is a contraction of *it is* or *it has*. See page 759.

EXAMPLES   **Its** purpose is to build confidence. [possessive pronoun]
It's called Ta-Na-E-Ka. [contraction of *it is*]
It's been practiced for many years. [contraction of *it has*]

kind, sort, type   The words *this, that, these,* and *those* should agree in number with the words *kind, sort,* and *type*.

EXAMPLES   Have you ever read **that kind** of story before?
Have you ever read **those kinds** of stories before?

kind of, sort of   In informal situations, *kind of* and *sort of* are often used to mean "somewhat" or "rather." In formal English, *somewhat* or *rather* is preferred.

INFORMAL   Mary seemed kind of upset about the ritual.

FORMAL   Mary seemed **somewhat** upset about the ritual.

learn, teach   *Learn* means "gain knowledge." *Teach* means "instruct" or "show how."

EXAMPLES   The young people **learned** how to survive in the wilderness.
Their parents **taught** them what foods to eat.

less   See **fewer, less.**

lie, lay   See page 712.

might of, must of   See **could of.**

nowheres   See **anywheres,** etc.

of   Do not use *of* with other prepositions such as *inside, off,* and *outside*.

EXAMPLES   She waited **outside** [*not* outside of] the restaurant.
Jesse dared me to jump **off** [*not* off of] the dock.

Quick Check 1: Answers

1. A ritual marks time and personal changes, and its tradition holds a society together.
2. Perhaps, you have already participated in a ritual and found it was quite an exciting experience.
3. A ritual doesn't always involve danger, though.
4. However, a lot of rituals can be dangerous.
5. I wonder if I could have done as well as Mary.

QUICK CHECK 1

Revise each of the following sentences to correct any error in usage. A sentence may contain more than one error.

EXAMPLE 1. How come cultures need rituals?
　　　　　　 1. *Why do cultures need rituals?*

1. A ritual marks time and personal changes, and it's tradition holds a society together.
2. Perhaps you have all ready participated in a ritual and found it was quite a exciting experience.
3. A ritual don't always involve danger, though.
4. However, alot of rituals can be dangerous.
5. I wonder if I could of done as good as Mary.

ought to of See **could of.**

rise, raise See pages 712–713.

scarcely See **hardly, scarcely.**

should of See **could of.**

sit, set See page 711.

somewheres See **anywheres,** etc.

sort See **kind, sort, type.**

sort of See **kind of, sort of.**

take See **bring, take.**

teach See **learn, teach.**

than, then *Than* is a conjunction used in making comparisons. *Then* is an adverb that means "at that time."

EXAMPLES Are dogs friendlier **than** cats?
　　　　　　 Back **then,** Dog and Cat were best friends.

that See **who, which, that.**

that there See **this here, that there.**

their, there, they're *Their* is used to show ownership. *There* is used to mean "at that place" or to begin a sentence. *They're* is a contraction of *they are.* See page 759.

EXAMPLES Won't **their** parents be pleased?
　　　　　　 They will go into the woods over **there.**
　　　　　　 There are many ways to gain self-confidence.
　　　　　　 They're leaving today for their Ta-Na-E-Ka.

theirself, theirselves   *Theirself* and *theirselves* are nonstandard English. Use *themselves.*

EXAMPLE   Dog and Cat found **themselves** [*not* theirself *or* theirselves] a home with Adam and Eve.

them   *Them* should not be used as an adjective. Use *those.*

EXAMPLE   Have you read all **those** [*not* them] poems about machines?

this here, that there   *Here* and *there* are not necessary after *this* and *that.*

EXAMPLES   **This** [*not* this here] cricket doesn't taste much worse than **that** [*not* that there] berry.

this kind, sort, type   See **kind, sort, type.**

use to, used to   Be sure to add the *–d* to *use. Used to* is in the past tense.

EXAMPLE   Kaw young **used to** [*not* use to] paint themselves white before their journey.

way, ways   Use *way,* not *ways,* in referring to a distance.

EXAMPLE   They were quite a **way** [*not* ways] from home.

well   See **good, well.**

when, where   Do not use *when* or *where* incorrectly in writing a definition.

NONSTANDARD   The ritual Ta-Na-E-Ka is when young men and women journey alone into the wilderness for several days.

STANDARD   The ritual Ta-Na-E-Ka is a journey taken by young men and women, who go alone into the wilderness for several days.

where   Do not use *where* for *that.*

EXAMPLE   I read **that** [*not* where] Ta-Na-E-Ka is still practiced today.

who, which, that   The relative pronoun *who* refers to people only; *which* refers to things only; *that* refers to either people or things.

EXAMPLES   The man and woman **who** were sitting next to us cheered.
The player dropped the ball, **which** was wet from the rain.
He made an error **that** allowed the other team to score.

would of   See **could of.**

Quick Check 2: Answers

1. The Kaw people treated one another well.
2. Take the time to research your own culture's past.
3. Perhaps you're a member of more than one culture.
4. Your family's traditions can teach you about yourself.
5. My family used to celebrate births and christenings in special ways.

Try It Out: Possible Answers

1. In Grandfather's time, Ta-Na-E-Ka was quite dangerous.
2. Life alone in the wilderness was very hard.
3. However, the endurance trial was very exciting, too.
4. These traditions have survived an extremely long time.
5. Ernie doesn't understand that people must learn self-sufficiency quite young.

---

your, you're   *Your* shows possession. *You're* is the contraction of *you are.*

EXAMPLES   **Your** story was very interesting.
You're part of a long tradition.

 QUICK CHECK 2

Revise each of the following sentences to correct any error in usage. A sentence may contain more than one error.

EXAMPLE   1. This here story tells about a Kaw ritual.
1. *This story tells about a Kaw ritual.*

1. The Kaw people treated one another good.
2. Take the time to research you're own culture's past.
3. Perhaps your a member of more then one culture.
4. Your family's traditions can learn you about yourself.
5. My family use to celebrate births and christenings in special ways.

 Using a Variety of Adverbs

In informal situations, the adjective *real* is often used as an adverb meaning "very" or "extremely." In formal situations, *very, extremely,* or another adverb is preferred.

INFORMAL   Ta-Na-E-Ka is a real important event in the Kaw culture.

FORMAL   Ta-Na-E-Ka is an **extremely** important event in the Kaw culture.

Try It Out

Revise each of the following sentences by substituting an adverb for the word *real.*

1. In Grandfather's time, Ta-Na-E-Ka was *real* dangerous.
2. Life alone in the wilderness was *real* hard.
3. However, the endurance trial was *real* exciting, too.
4. These traditions have survived a *real* long time.
5. Ernie doesn't understand that people must learn self-sufficiency *real* young.

GLOSSARY

The glossary below is an alphabetical list of words found in the selections in this book. Use this glossary just as you use a dictionary—to find out the meanings of unfamiliar words. (Some technical, foreign, and more obscure words in this book are not listed here but instead are defined for you in the footnotes that accompany many of the selections.)

Many words in the English language have more than one meaning. This glossary gives the meanings that apply to the words as they are used in the selections in this book. Words closely related in form and meaning are usually listed together in one entry (for instance, *compassion* and *compassionate*), and the definition is given for the first form.

The following abbreviations are used:

adj.	adjective
adv.	adverb
n.	noun
pl.	plural
v.	verb

Each word's pronunciation is given in parentheses. A guide to the pronunciation symbols appears at the bottom of this page.

For more information about the words in this glossary or for information about words not listed here, consult a dictionary.

abundance (ə·bun′dəns) *n.*: great plenty.

accumulate (ə·kyo͞om′yo͞o·lāt′) *v.*: gather; save.

accustom (ə·kus′təm) *v.*: make familiar by habit or use.

acquaint (ə·kwānt′) *v.*: cause to know personally.

acquaintance (ə·kwānt′′ns) *n.*: person whom one knows, but not closely.

adapt (ə·dapt′) *v.*: adjust in order to suit new conditions; get used to.

adhere (ad·hir′) *v.*: **1.** stick tight. **2.** stay firm in supporting or following.

adjacent (ə·jā′sənt) *adj.*: near or close; adjoining.

ado (ə·do͞o′) *n.*: fuss; trouble; excitement.

advocate (ad′və·kit) *n.*: supporter; person in favor of something.

aghast (ə·gast′) *adj.*: shocked or horrified.

agitated (aj′i·tāt′id) *adj.*: upset; excited; disturbed.

ajar (ə·jär′) *adj.*: slightly open.

alien (āl′yən) *n.*: foreigner.

alight (ə·līt′) *v.*: come down after flight; land.

allot (ə·lät′) *v.*: distribute to; give as a share. —**allotted**

ambitious (am·bish′əs) *adj.*: eager to succeed or to achieve something.

anguish (aŋ′gwish) *n.*: great suffering from worry, grief, or pain.

angular (aŋ′gyo͞o·lər) *adj.*: **1.** having angles or sharp corners. **2.** with bones that jut out.

animation (an′i·mā′shən) *n.*: liveliness; life.

annoyance (ə·noi′əns) *n.*: irritation; something that bothers.

anonymous (ə·nän′ə·məs) *adj.*: nameless; done by an unidentified person.

anticipate (an·tis′ə·pāt′) *v.*: consider ahead of time; expect.

anticipation (an·tis′ə·pā′shən) *n.*: expectation; feeling or condition of looking forward to something.

appalling (ə·pôl′iŋ) *adj.*: causing horror or shock.

apparatus (ap′ə·rat′əs) *n.*: complicated device or machine for a specific purpose. —**apparatus** or **apparatuses** *pl.*

apparel (ə·per′əl) *n.*: clothing.

appease (ə·pēz′) *v.*: satisfy, relieve, or quiet.

appendage (ə·pen′dij) *n.*: additional or extended part of an animal, such as a tail.

apply (ə·plī′) *v.*: concentrate one's energies on; work hard at something.

apt (apt) *adj.*: quick to learn or understand.

arrogance (ar′ə·gəns) *n.*: behavior showing too much pride and too little regard for others.

ascend (ə·send′) *v.*: go up; rise.

associate (ə·sōsh′it) *n.*: friend, partner, or companion.

astonishment (ə·stän′ish·mənt) *n.*: great surprise; amazement.

astound (ə·stound′) *v.*: amaze; greatly surprise. —**astounded** *v.* used as *adj.*

---

at, āte, cär; ten, ēve, is, īce; gō, hôrn, look, to͞ol; oil, out; up, fur; ə *for unstressed vowels, as* a *in* ago, u *in* focus; ′ *as in* Latin (lat′′n); chin; she; zh *as in* azure (azh′ər); thin, *the*; ŋ *as in* ring (riŋ)

---

attribute (ə·trib′yo͞ot) v.: assume as a quality of something.

audacity (ô·das′ə·tē) n.: bold courage; daring.

aught (ôt) n.: anything.

automatic (ôt′ə·mat′ik) adj.: operating on its or their own. **—automatically** adv.

avail (ə·vāl′) n.: good use or help; advantage.

avenge (ə·venj′) v.: get revenge for some kind of injury; get even.

awe (ô) v.: fill with wonder, fear, or admiration. **—awed** v. used as adj.

banish (ban′ish) v.: send away; get rid of.

bay (bā) v.: bark or howl.

bayonet (bā′ə·net′) n.: daggerlike blade on the end of a rifle.

beacon (bē′kən) n.: any light for warning or guiding.

bear (ber) v.: 1. have or show. 2. carry. **—bore** (bôr), **borne** (bôrn)

befall (bē·fôl′) v.: come to pass; happen to. **—befell, befallen**

belabor (bē·lā′bər) v.: 1. beat severely. 2. spend too much time and effort on.

bellow (bel′ō) v.: roar with a powerful sound.

besiege (bē·sēj′) v.: crowd around; overwhelm.

bestow (bē·stō′) v.: give or present as a gift (usually used with on or upon).

betray (bē·trā′) v.: deceive.

bewildered (bē·wil′dərd) adj.: confused; puzzled.

billow (bil′ō) v.: swell and rise. **—billowing** v. used as adj.

blasé (blä·zā′) adj.: having done something so much as to be bored by it.

blissful (blis′fəl) adj.: full of great joy or happiness. **—blissfully** adv.

boggle (bäg′əl) v.: confuse or overwhelm (the mind or imagination).

bore, borne v.: See bear.

bow (bō) v.: bend or curve in the shape of a bow. **—bowed** v. used as adj.

burnish (bʉr′nish) v.: make or become shiny by rubbing; polish.

cajole (kə·jōl′) v.: convince with flattery or false talk. **—cajoling** v. used as adj.

captivate (kap′tə·vāt′) v.: capture the attention or affection of.

carcass (kär′kəs) n.: dead body of an animal.

cascade (kas·kād′) v.: fall or drop in a rushing way, like a waterfall.

cast (kast) v.: send out; project (as cast a shadow). **—cast**

catalog or **catalogue** (kat′ə·lôg) v.: list.

celestial (sə·les′chəl) adj.: of or in the sky or universe, as planets, stars, and so on.

chamber (chām′bər) n.: room; any enclosed space or compartment.

chaos (kā′äs′) n.: extreme confusion.

characteristic (kar′ək·tər·is′tik) adj.: typical.

chastise (chas·tīz′) v.: punish; scold sharply.

churn (chʉrn) v.: move violently.

circumstance (sʉr′kəm·stans′) n.: fact or event; condition.

cleave (klēv) v.: split. **—cleaved** v. used as adj.

cleft (kleft) adj.: formed with a partial split.

coax (kōks) v.: gently urge or try to persuade. **—coaxed**

compassion (kəm·pash′ən) n.: sorrow for the suffering of others; pity. **—compassionate** (kəm·pash′ən·it) adj.: sympathetic.

compound (käm·pound′) v.: increase or become stronger by adding things.

comrade (käm′rad′) n.: friend; close companion.

concealment (kən·sēl′mənt) n.: hiding; putting out of sight to keep secret.

condemn (kən·dem′) v.: declare guilty of wrongdoing; sentence to an unhappy future.

confirm (kən·fʉrm′) v.: prove the truth of.

confiscate (kän′fis·kāt′) v.: take away as punishment.

confrontation (kän′frən·tā′shən) n.: bold, face-to-face disagreement.

consent (kən·sent′) v.: agree; give permission.

consultation (kän′səl·tā′shən) n.: meeting to discuss, decide, or plan something.

consumption (kən·sump′shən) n.: the eating or drinking up of something.

contemplate (kän′təm·plāt′) v.: study carefully.

contempt (kən·tempt′) n.: scorn; feeling that someone or something is low or unworthy. **—contemptuous** (kən·temp′cho͞o·əs) adj.: full of scorn.

contented (kən·tent′id) adj.: satisfied. **—contentedly** adv.

contraption (kən·trap′shən) n.: machine thought of as strange; gadget.

converse (kən·vʉrs′) v.: talk; hold a conversation.

cosmos (käz′məs) n.: the universe viewed as an orderly system.

costly (kôst′lē) adj.: showing great effort or sacrifice; magnificent.

countenance (koun′tə·nəns) n.: facial expression or the way one holds oneself.

crusade (krōō·sād') *n.*: struggle for a cause or belief.

cudgel (kuj'əl) *n.*: short, thick stick or club.

curt (kʉrt) *adj.*: brief to the point of rudeness; blunt.

debut (dā·byōō') *n.*: first performance before the public.

decisive (dē·sī'siv) *adj.*: deciding; showing firmness.

dedicate (ded'i·kāt) *v.*: set apart seriously for a special purpose; devote. —**dedicated** *v.* used as *adj.*

deduce (dē·dōōs') *v.*: reason out; conclude from known facts or evidence. —**deduced**

defiant (dē·fī'ənt) *adj.*: openly and boldly resisting.

defy (dē·fī') *v.*: resist completely.

dejection (dē·jek'shən) *n.*: depression; sadness.

delve (delv) *v.*: 1. dig. 2. search.

depart (dē·pärt') *v.*: go away; leave.

deprive (dē·prīv') *v.*: keep from having or using.

descend (dē·send') *v.*: move from a high place to a lower one; come down.

descendant (dē·sen'dənt) *n.*: person who is an offspring of a family or group.

desolation (des'ə·lā'shən) *n.*: lonely grief; misery.

despair (di·sper') *n.*: hopelessness.

desperation (des'pər·ā'shən) *n.*: extreme need.

despondent (di·spän'dənt) *adj.*: hopeless; discouraged; very sad.

devastate (dev'əs·tāt) *v.*: cause great damage or destruction. —**devastating** *v.* used as *adj.*

devise (di·vīz') *v.*: create; invent.

devote (di·vōt') *v.*: give (time or energy) to a special purpose.

dignity (dig'nə·tē) *n.*: proper pride and self-respect.

discard (dis·kärd') *v.*: throw away; treat as no longer useful.

disclose (dis·klōz') *v.*: make known; uncover.

disconsolate (dis·kän'sə·lit) *adj.*: very unhappy. —**disconsolately** *adv.*

disdain (dis·dān') *n.*: the feeling or expression that someone or something is unworthy; scorn.

disembodied (dis'im·bäd'ēd) *adj.*: not of the body.

disengage (dis'in·gāj') *v.*: unfasten.

disheveled (di·shev'əld) *adj.*: untidy (said of hair or clothing).

dismal (diz'məl) *adj.*: gloomy; depressing.

dismantle (dis·mant''l) *v.*: take apart. —**dismantled** *v.* used as *adj.*

dismay (dis·mā') *v.*: disturb; alarm. —**dismayed** *v.* used as *adj.*

dispute (di·spyōōt') *v.*: argue; debate.

distort (di·stôrt') *v.*: twist out of shape; change the usual appearance of.

distressed (di·strest') *adj.*: anxious and troubled; suffering.

divine (də·vīn') *adj.*: of or like God or a god; sacred.

divulge (də·vulj') *v.*: reveal.

docile (däs'əl) *adj.*: easy to manage or discipline; obedient.

domain (dō·mān') *n.*: territory under one ruler or government.

dominant (däm'ə·nənt) *adj.*: ruling; having power.

double take (dub'əl tāk') *n.*: delayed reaction where something goes unnoticed and then is noticed with great surprise (often used for comedy in acting).

dour (dour) *adj.*: stern; harsh; severe.

dreadful (dred'fəl) *adj.*: very bad; disagreeable.

dumbfound (dum'found') *v.*: make speechless by shocking; amaze. —**dumbfounded** *v.* used as *adj.*

dwell (dwel) *v.*: live; make one's home. —**dwelt** or **dwelled**

dwindle (dwin'dəl) *v.*: steadily shrink; become less and less or smaller and smaller.

eavesdrop (ēvs'dräp') *v.*: listen secretly to a private conversation of others.

ebb (eb) *n.*: flow of water back toward the sea; lowering of the tide.

eddy (ed'ē) *n.*: current moving in a circular motion; whirlpool.

effective (e·fek'tiv) *adj.*: having a desired result; efficient.

elate (ē·lāt') *v.*: make proud, happy, or joyful. —**elated** *v.* used as *adj.*

elegant (el'ə·gənt) *adj.*: rich in style, dress, or design.

eloquent (el'ə·kwənt) *adj.*: smooth, clear, and persuasive in writing or speech.

elude (ē·lōōd') *v.*: escape notice of.

emerge (ē·mʉrj') *v.*: come forth or come out; become visible or known.

emit (ē·mit') *v.*: give off. —**emitted**

encounter (en·koun'tər) *n.*: battle; conflict.

endurance (en·door'əns) *n.*: ability to last, especially through pain or tiredness.

enfold (en·fōld') *v.*: hug; embrace.

engage (en·gāj') *v.*: attract and hold the attention of.

ensue (en·sōō') *v.*: come afterward; follow.

entreaty (en·trēt'ē) *n.*: serious request; prayer.

etiquette (et'i·kit) *n.*: manners and ceremonies that are acceptable to a society.

evacuate (ē·vak′yoo·āt′) *v.*: remove from the area.

evident (ev′ə·dənt) *adj.*: easily seen or understood; obvious.

evolutionary (ev′ə·loo′shən·er·ē) *adj.*: showing gradual change.

exasperate (eg·zas′pər·āt′) *v.*: annoy very much. **—exasperated** *v.* used as *adj.*

exertion (eg·zʉr′shən) *n.*: effort; use of strength or power.

exorbitant (eg·zôr′bi·tənt) *adj.*: beyond fair in price or charge.

expire (ek·spīr′) *v.*: come to an end.

exquisite (eks′kwi·zit) *adj.*: carefully done or beautifully made.

extraordinary (ek·strôd′′n·er′ē) *adj.*: far beyond ordinary; exceptional.

exude (eg·zyood′) *v.*: give off.

fallow (fal′ō) *adj.*: left unplanted.

famine (fam′in) *n.*: widespread shortage of food.

feeble (fē′bəl) *adj.*: weak; without force.

flabbergast (flab′ər·gast′) *v.*: make speechless with amazement. **—flabbergasted** *v.* used as *adj.*

flail (flāl) *v.*: move (usually the arms) in a swinging motion.

flippant (flip′ənt) *adj.*: saucy; disrespectful.

flirtation (flʉr·tā′shən) *n.*: playing at love, without serious intention.

fluster (flus′tər) *v.*: make or become confused or nervous. **—flustered** *v.* used as *adj.*

foretell (fôr·tel′) *v.*: predict; announce beforehand. **—foretold** (fôr·tōld′)

forlorn (fôr·lôrn′) *adj.*: sad; pitiful; hopeless.

formulate (fôr′myoo·lāt′) *v.*: work out or form in one's mind.

forsaken (fər·sā′kən) *adj.*: abandoned; deserted.

frantic (frant′ik) *adj.*: wild with emotion. **—frantically** *adv.*

fraud (frôd) *n.*: person who is not what she or he pretends to be; impostor.

frazzle (fraz′əl) *v.*: make or become physically or emotionally exhausted. **—frazzled** *v.* used as *adj.*

fugitive (fyoo′ji·tiv) *n.*: person who escapes from danger or justice.

gaggle (gag′əl) *n.*: flock or cluster.

gape (gāp) *v.*: stare with the mouth open, as in wonder or surprise.

gaunt (gônt) *adj.*: thin and bony as from hunger, sickness, or age.

gawky (gô′kē) *adj.*: awkward; lacking grace or elegance.

glaring (gler′iŋ) *adj.*: staring in a fierce, angry way.

gnarled (närld) *adj.*: knotty and twisted.

gorge (gôrj) *n.*: deep, narrow pass between steep heights.

gorge (gôrj) *v.*: fill up; stuff.

gratify (grat′i·fī) *v.*: give pleasure or satisfaction to.

grating (grāt′iŋ) *adj.*: irritating or annoying.

grim (grim) *adj.*: fierce; cruel; savage.

grimace (grim′is) *v.*: twist the face to express pain, anger, or disgust.

grudge (gruj) *v.*: give with reluctance. **—grudging** *v.* used as *adj.* **—grudgingly** *adv.*

guff (guf) *n.*: rude talk.

hallucination (hə·loo′si·nā′shən) *n.*: dreamlike vision of sights, sounds, and so on, that are not actually present.

harass (hə·ras′) *v.*: trouble or worry; pester. **—harassed** *v.* used as *adj.*

hasty (hās′tē) *adj.*: 1. quick; hurried. 2. too quick; rash. **—hastily** *adv.*

haughty (hôt′ē) *adj.*: proud.

heart-rending (härt′ren′diŋ) *adj.*: causing extreme grief or mental suffering.

heed (hēd) *n.*: close attention; careful notice. **—heedful** (hēd′fəl) *adj.*: paying close attention.

heritage (her′i·tij′) *n.*: something handed down from ancestors or from the past.

hideous (hid′ē·əs) *adj.*: horrible; very ugly.

hobble (häb′əl) *v.*: walk awkwardly; limp.

homage (häm′ij) *n.*: anything done to show honor or respect.

hospitality (häs′pi·tal′ə·tē) *n.*: friendliness and kindness toward guests.

hover (huv′ər) *v.*: stay suspended in the air.

humiliation (hyoo·mil′ē·ā′shən) *n.*: act of hurting someone's pride by making him or her seem foolish.

idle (īd′′l) *adj.*: inactive; not in use.

ignorance (ig′nər·əns) *n.*: lack of knowledge.

illuminate (i·loo′mə·nāt′) *v.*: light up; give light to.

immense (im·mens′) *adj.*: very large; huge.

immensity (im·men′si·tē) *n.*: limitless space.

immigrate (im′ə·grāt′) v.: come to a new country to settle there.

immobilize (im·mō′bə·līz′) v.: prevent movement of; keep in place. **—immobilized** v. used as adj.

imperious (im·pir′ē·əs) adj.: proud and haughty.

imply (im·plī′) v.: express by hint; suggest.

imposing (im·pō′ziŋ) adj.: impressive; grand.

incessant (in·ses′ənt) adj.: never-ending; constant. **—incessantly** adv.

inconsolable (in·kən·sōl′ə·bəl) adj.: brokenhearted; sad beyond comforting.

incredulous (in·krej′oo·ləs) adj.: unbelieving.

indifferent (in·dif′ər·ənt) adj.: having or showing no interest. **—indifferently** adv.

indignant (in·dig′nənt) adj.: angry because of something thought to be not right or unfair.

induce (in·doos′) v.: 1. bring on or bring about; cause. 2. persuade.

inedible (in·ed′ə·bəl) adj.: not fit to be eaten.

inexplicable (in′ek·splik′ə·bəl) adj.: not explainable.

infest (in·fest′) v.: inhabit in large numbers; swarm.

inseparable (in·sep′ə·rə·bəl) adj.: that can't be separated or parted.

insidious (in·sid′ē·əs) adj.: working or spreading in a hidden but dangerous way.

insolent (in′sə·lənt) adj.: rude; disrespectful.

integrate (in′tə·grāt′) v.: put or bring together into a whole.

intensity (in·ten′sə·tē) n.: extreme degree; great energy.

intent (in·tent′) adj.: having attention firmly directed. **—intently** adv.

intern (in·turn′) v.: detain or confine.

intervene (in·tər·vēn′) v.: come or lie between. **—intervening** v. used as adj.

intoxication (in·täks′i·kā′shən) n.: act of making or becoming drunk; drunkenness.

intrigue (in·trēg′) v.: excite interest or curiosity. **—intrigued** v. used as adj.

intrusion (in·troo′zhən) n.: unwelcome entering or visit by someone or something.

irritation (ir′i·tā′shən) n.: soreness, as from increased activity or the presence of a foreign substance.

jargon (jär′gən) n.: speech full of long and unfamiliar words.

jostle (jäs′əl) v.: bump or shove roughly.

jubilation (joo′bə·lā′shən) n.: rejoicing; great joy.

laborious (lə·bôr′ē·əs) adj.: involving a lot of hard work; difficult.

lair (ler) n.: resting place of a wild animal; den.

lament (lə·ment′) v.: feel or express deep sorrow for; regret deeply.

laud (lôd) v.: praise.

lavender (lav′ən·dər) adj.: pale-purple color.

lavish (lav′ish) adj.: abundant; plentiful. **—lavishly** adv.

legitimate (lə·jit′ə·mət) adj.: reasonable; logically correct.

lethargy (leth′ər·jē) n.: feeling of dullness and tiredness.

linger (liŋ′gər) v.: be unnecessarily slow in doing something; continue to stay.

listless (list′lis) adj.: lacking energy or interest in anything.

lobby (läb′ē) v.: try to influence. **—lobbied**

lofty (lôf′tē) adj.: noble or very high.

lumber (lum′bər) v.: move heavily, clumsily, and often noisily.

magnitude (mag′nə·tood′) n.: size or amount; largeness.

maintain (mān·tān′) v.: support by providing necessary things.

makeshift (māk′shift′) adj.: capable of doing for a while as a substitute.

maneuver (mə·noo′vər) v.: move by a strategy or plan.

marvel (mär′vəl) v.: become filled with admiring surprise; be amazed.

meander (mē·an′dər) v.: take a winding or twisted course.

melancholy (mel′ən·käl′ē) adj.: sad and depressed; gloomy.

membrane (mem′brān) n.: thin, flexible layer of tissue covering an organ.

menace (men′əs) v.: threaten; endanger. **—menacing** v. used as adj.

menagerie (mə·naj′ər·ē) n.: collection of wild animals for exhibition.

merchant (mur′chənt) n.: person who sells goods for profit; businessperson.

metallic (mə·tal′ik) adj.: made of or seeming like metal.

minimal (min′i·məl) adj.: smallest or least possible.

mire (mīr) v.: sink or stick, as if in mud.

moderate (mäd′ər·it) adj.: within reasonable limits; avoiding extremes.

molt (mōlt) v.: shed outer skin, horns, or feathers.

mortify (môrt'ə·fī') v.: cause to feel shame or embarrassment. —**mortified** v. used as adj.

mournful (môrn'fəl) adj.: sad; sorrowful.

muddle (mud''l) v.: mix up in a confused way. —**muddled** v. used as adj.

murky (murk'ē) adj.: dark; gloomy.

murmur (mur'mər) v.: mumble or mutter a complaint.

mutual (myōō'chōō·əl) adj.: shared; present on both sides.

mystical (mis'ti·kəl) adj.: 1. spiritual. 2. mysterious.

neigh (nā) v.: make a loud, horselike cry.

nonchalant (nän'shə·länt') adj.: showing cool lack of concern. —**nonchalantly** adv.

numerous (nōō'mər·əs) adj.: very many.

nurture (nur'chər) v.: promote the growth of; nourish.

oblige (ə·blīj') v.: force.

obliging (ə·blī'jiŋ) adj.: ready to do favors; helpful. —**obligingly** adv.

oblivious (ə·bliv'ē·əs) adj.: not conscious; unaware.

obsess (əb·ses') v.: occupy the thoughts of; take up the full attention of. —**obsessed** v. used as adj.

obtain (əb·tān') v.: get possession of.

omen (ō'mən) n.: event, object, or situation that supposedly tells what will happen in the future.

omnipotent (äm·nip'ə·tənt) adj.: having unlimited power; all-powerful.

oracle (ôr'ə·kəl) n.: place where the ancient Greeks and Romans asked the gods things.

orator (ôr'ət·ər) n.: talented public speaker.

originate (ə·rij'i·nāt) v.: come into being; begin.

outrage (out'rāj') v.: offend; insult. —**outraged** v. used as adj.

pantomime (pan'tə·mīm') n.: actions or gestures without words.

paramount (par'ə·mount') adj.: most important.

patronize (pā'trən·īz') v.: be a regular customer of.

penetrate (pen'i·trāt') v.: make its or one's way through.

periodic (pir·ē·äd'ik) adj.: happening from time to time. —**periodically** adv.

permeate (pur'mē·āt') v.: pass into or through; penetrate.

perpetual (pər·pech'ōō·əl) adj.: continual; constant.

perplexity (pər·pleks'ə·tē) n.: bewilderment; confusion.

persecution (pur'si·kyōō'shən) n.: constant bothering; unfair treatment.

petulant (pech'ə·lənt) adj.: impatient with a minor matter.

phenomenon (fə·näm'ə·nən) n.: 1. something that can be scientifically described. 2. very unusual or extraordinary thing. —**phenomena** pl.

placate (plā'kāt') v.: calm.

plight (plīt) n.: bad situation.

poise (poiz) v.: balance; keep steady. —**poised** v. used as adj.

ponder (pän'dər) v.: think deeply about.

pooh-pooh (pōō'pōō') v.: make light of; treat scornfully.

precision (prē·sizh'ən) n.: correctness; accuracy.

predator (pred'ə·tər) n.: animal that lives by capturing and feeding on other animals.

primary (prī'mer'ē) adj.: main. —**primarily** adv.

procession (prō·sesh'ən) n.: people or things moving forward in an orderly way, as in a parade.

proclaim (prō·klām') v.: announce officially.

profusion (prō·fyōō'zhən) n.: rich or abundant supply.

prompt (prämpt) adj.: quick to act or do what is required.

pronounce (prō·nouns') v.: say or declare officially.

prophecy (präf'ə·sē) n.: prediction of the future guided by God or a god.

propose (prō·pōz') v.: put forth for consideration or acceptance.

prospective (prō·spek'tiv) adj.: expected; future.

prosperity (prä·sper'ə·tē) n.: wealth.

prosperous (präs'pər·əs) adj.: having continued success; well-off.

protrude (prō·trōōd') v.: jut or stick out; project.

proverb (präv'urb') n.: well-known traditional saying that expresses a truth.

query (kwir'ē) n.: question.

quest (kwest) n.: journey in search of adventure.

radiant (rā'dē·ənt) adj.: shining brightly; showing well-being. —**radiantly** adv.

ravage (rav'ij) v.: destroy violently; ruin.

ravine (rə·vēn') n.: long, deep hollow in the earth's surface, especially one worn by a stream.

reassurance (rē'ə·shoor'əns) n.: the act of giving confidence; the act of making safe or secure.

recess (rē'ses) n.: hollow place.

reckless (rek′lis) *adj.*: careless; irresponsible. **—recklessly** *adv.*

reflect (ri·flekt′) *v.*: think seriously; consider.

refuge (ref′yōōj) *n.*: shelter or protection from danger.

regain (ri·gān′) *v.*: recover.

regalia (ri·gāl′yə) *n.*: the symbols and decorations of any group or society.

regard (ri·gärd′) *v.*: think of in a certain way; take into account.

register (rej′is·tər) *v.*: show on a scale or other measuring device.

reign (rān) *v.*: rule as king or queen.

rejoice (ri·jois′) *v.*: feel or make glad; delight.

reluctant (ri·luk′tənt) *adj.*: unwilling; not eager.

remedy (rem′ə·dē) *n.*: medicine; something that cures or corrects.

repercussion (rē′pər·kush′ən) *n.*: reflection of light or sound.

repose (ri·pōz′) *n.*: restful state.

repulsive (ri·pul′siv) *adj.*: disgusting; horrifying.

resent (ri·zent′) *v.*: feel or show displeasure at (something).

reservation (rez′ər·vā′shən) *n.*: doubt.

resilient (ri·zil′yənt) *adj.*: springy.

resolve (ri·zälv′) *v.*: decide.

resort (ri·zôrt′) *v.*: turn (to) for use, help, or support.

resplendent (ri·splen′dənt) *adj.*: dazzling; splendid.

reticent (ret′ə·sənt) *adj.*: reserved; choosing not to talk about what one thinks or feels.

retort (ri·tôrt′) *v.*: answer in a sharp, quick, or witty way.

reveal (ri·vēl′) *v.*: make known something that was hidden; expose.

revelation (rev′ə·lā′shən) *n.*: something realized.

revive (ri·vīv′) *v.*: bring back to life or to a waking state.

revolting (ri·vōlt′iŋ) *adj.*: disgusting.

revolution (rev′ə·lōō′shən) *n.*: time taken for an object in space, such as a star or planet, to go around another object and return to its original position.

rigorous (rig′ər·əs) *adj.*: very strict; harsh.

ritual (rich′ōō·əl) *n.*: a formal act, usually religious; a ceremony.

rollick (räl′ik) *v.*: behave in a lively, carefree way. **—rollicking** *v.* used as *adj.*

rue (rōō) *v.*: feel sorrow or regret for.

rural (roor′əl) *adj.*: having to do with country life.

salve (sav) *n.*: something that soothes or heals.

saunter (sôn′tər) *v.*: walk slowly and casually.

savor (sā′vər) *v.*: delight in; taste or smell.

scald (skôld) *v.*: burn with hot liquid or steam. **—scalding** *v.* used as *adj.*

scarcity (sker′sə·tē) *n.*: lack, especially of goods or services.

scenario (sə·ner′ē·ō) *n.*: outline for a series of events.

scornful (skôrn′fəl) *adj.*: showing extreme dislike or contempt.

scour (skour) *v.*: remove as if by cleaning and scraping; sweep away.

secure (si·kyoor′) *v.*: get possession of; acquire.

seethe (sēth) *v.*: bubble, foam, or rise, as if boiling. **—seething** *v.* used as *adj.*

segment (seg′mənt) *n.*: section.

segregation (seg′rə·gā′shən) *n.*: separation of racial groups.

shimmer (shim′ər) *v.*: shine with unsteady light. **—shimmering** *v.* used as *adj.*

shrewd (shrōōd) *adj.*: clever; sharp.

shroud (shroud) *v.*: cover; hide from view. **—shrouded** *v.* used as *adj.*

silhouette (sil′ōō·et′) *v.*: show or project a dark shape or figure against a light background. **—silhouetted** *v.* used as *adj.*

sinewy (sin′yōō·ē) *adj.*: strong; firm; tough.

sinister (sin′is·tər) *adj.*: threatening harm or evil; wicked.

skirmish (skur′mish) *n.*: slight, unimportant fight or disagreement.

slacken (slak′ən) *v.*: fall off; lessen. **—slackening** *v.* used as *adj.*

smug (smug) *adj.*: self-satisfied to an annoying degree. **—smugly** *adv.*

snicker (snik′ər) *v.*: laugh in a sly or insulting way.

spectacle (spek′tə·kəl) *n.*: strange or remarkable sight.

splendor (splen′dər) *n.*: great brightness; magnificence.

sprawl (sprôl) *v.*: spread the limbs in a relaxed way. **—sprawled** *v.* used as *adj.*

spur (spur) *v.*: urge to greater effort.

stalemate (stāl′māt′) *n.*: situation in which no side can win; a draw.

stamina (stam′ə·nə) *n.*: endurance; ability to stand hard work, pain, or hardship.

stationary (stā′shə·ner′ē) *adj.*: not moving; set or still.

straggly (strag′lē) *adj.*: hanging in a messy way (said of hair or clothes).

strife (strīf) *n.*: fighting or quarreling.

subsequent (sub′si·kwent) *adj.:* coming after. —**subsequently** *adv.*

subtle (sut″l) *adj.:* not obvious.

sultry (sul′trē) *adj.:* 1. sexy. 2. hot and humid (said of weather).

superficial (soo′pər·fish′əl) *adj.:* shallow; not going past the surface.

surge (sʉrj) *v.:* swell or push violently.

systematic (sis′tə·mat′ik) *adj.:* having a good system or orderly method.

tart (tärt) *adj.:* sharp in meaning; mean. —**tartly** *adv.*

tentative (ten′tə·tiv) *adj.:* unsure; hesitant.

testify (tes′tə·fī′) *v.:* be a witness or give evidence under oath in court.

testy (tes′tē) *adj.:* touchy; easily annoyed.

thistle (this′əl) *n.:* plant with prickly leaves and pink or purple flowers.

thwart (thwôrt) *v.:* frustrate or defeat; block.

tinge (tinj) *v.:* color slightly.

tolerant (täl′ər·ənt) *adj.:* patient; showing acceptance of others.

torment (tôr·ment′) *v.:* cause great mental or physical pain in. —**tormented** *v.* used as *adj.*

totter (tät′ər) *v.:* rock or shake as if about to fall.

transcend (tran·send′) *v.:* go beyond the limits of.

transparent (trans·per′ənt) *adj.:* capable of being seen through; clear.

transpire (tran·spīr′) *v.:* come to pass; happen.

tread (tred) *v.:* walk on. —**trod** (träd), **trodden** (träd″n)

tremor (trem′ər) *n.:* a trembling or shaking.

trivial (triv′ē·əl) *adj.:* unimportant; insignificant.

trundle (trun′dəl) *v.:* roll along.

uncanny (un·kan′ē) *adj.:* strange or weird; so unusual as to seem fantastic.

uppity (up′ə·tē) *adj.:* snobbish.

urgency (ʉr′jən·sē) *n.:* insistence; need for fast action.

vague (vāg) *adj.:* not clear; uncertain. —**vaguely** *adv.*

vain (vān) *adj.:* having no success; worthless. —**vainly** *adv.*

vengeance (ven′jəns) *n.:* revenge.

venomous (ven′əm·əs) *adj.:* poisonous; containing venom.

vicinity (və·sin′ə·tē) *n.:* area nearby.

visible (viz′ə·bəl) *adj.:* capable of being seen; observable.

visualize (vizh′oo·əl·īz′) *v.:* form a mental image of; see in the mind. —**visualizing** *v.* used as *adj.*

waver (wā′vər) *v.:* change in brightness; flicker. —**wavering** *v.* used as *adj.*

weave (wēv) *v.:* make a fabric by interlacing threads. —**wove** (wōv), **woven** (wō′vən)

wench (wench) *n.:* old term for "country girl; female servant."

wily (wīl′ē) *adj.:* sly.

wistful (wist′fəl) *adj.:* longing; wishful. —**wistfully** *adv.*

withdrawn (with·drôn′) *adj.:* shy; tending to keep to oneself.

wove *v.:* See *weave.*

wretch (rech) *n.:* miserable person; person who is hated and scorned.

wring (riŋ) *v.:* twist or wrench; twist forcefully to get liquid out of. —**wrung** (ruŋ)

writhe (rīth) *v.:* make twisting movements; squirm. —**writhing** *v.* used as *adj.*

wrung *v.* See *wring.*

wry (rī) *adj.:* ironic; sarcastic.

yield (yēld) *v.:* give up under pressure; surrender.

ACKNOWLEDGMENTS

For permission to use copyrighted material, grateful acknowledgment is made to the following sources:

Andrews McMeel Publishing: From "Star Wars" from *Roger Ebert's Video Companion,* 1991 Edition. Copyright © 1992 by Roger Ebert. All rights reserved.

Arte Público Press: "Petals" and translation "Los pétalos" from *Chants* by Pat Mora. Copyright © 1984 by Pat Mora. Published by Arte Público Press–University of Houston, Houston, TX, 1985.

Atheneum Books for Young Readers, an imprint of Simon & Schuster Children's Publishing Division: "Mother Doesn't Want a Dog," "Since Hanna Moved Away," and "WEIRD!" from *If I Were in Charge of the World and Other Worries* by Judith Viorst. Copyright © 1981 by Judith Viorst.

Bancroft Library, University of California, Berkeley: From *Desert Exile: The Uprooting of a Japanese American Family* by Yoshiko Uchida. Copyright © 1982 by Yoshiko Uchida.

Bantam Doubleday Dell Books for Young Readers, a division of Random House, Inc.: "Just Once" by Thomas Dygard from *Ultimate Sports,* edited by Donald R. Gallo. Copyright © 1995 by Donald R. Gallo.

Catherine Beston Barnes: "The Storm" by Elizabeth Coatsworth.

Susan Bergholz Literary Services, New York: "Once" (translation of "Eleven") from *El arroyo de la Llorona* by Sandra Cisneros. Copyright © 1991 by Sandra Cisneros. Translation copyright © 1996 by Liliana Valenzuela. Published by Vintage Español, a division of Random House, Inc. All rights reserved. "Eleven" from *Woman Hollering Creek* by Sandra Cisneros. Copyright © 1991 by Sandra Cisneros. Published by Vintage Books, a division of Random House, Inc., New York, and originally in hardcover by Random House, Inc. All rights reserved.

Georges Borchardt, Inc., for the Estate of John Gardner: "Dragon, Dragon" from *Dragon, Dragon and Other Tales* by John Gardner. Copyright © 1975 by Boskydell Artists Ltd.

Candlewick Press, Cambridge, MA: "What Do Fish Have to Do with Anything?" from *What Do Fish Have to Do With Anything?* by Avi, illustrated by Tracy Mitchell. Copyright © 1997 by Avi.

Centre Daily Times: From "Star Struck: Drama Camp Teaches Youngsters Basics of Theatre" by Chris Krewson from *Centre Daily Times,* August 4, 1998. Copyright © 1998 by Centre Daily Times.

James Cheung: "Coming to America" by James Cheung from *Young Writers Literary Magazine,* June 1993. Copyright © 1993 by James Cheung. Published by Atlantic Middle School, North Quincy, MA.

Children's Literature, 7513 Shadywood Road, Bethesda, MD 20817-2065, (800) 469-2070, www.childrenslit.com: From review by Uma Krishnaswami of *The Well* by Mildred D. Taylor from "Themed Reviews" from *Children's Literature.* Copyright © 1999 by Children's Literature. Available April 26, 1999, http://www.childrenslit.com/f_midl.htm.

Christopher-Gordon Publishers, Inc.: From "Prospects and Perils: A Final Word: The Good, the True, and the Beautiful" by Julius Lester from *Children's Literature: Resource for the Classroom,* edited by Masha Kabakow Rudman. Copyright © 1989 by Christopher-Gordon Publishers, Inc.

Clarion Books/Houghton Mifflin Company: Text and illustration from "The Heimlich Maneuver" from "What to Do in an Emergency" from *The New Complete Babysitter's Handbook* by Carol Barkin and Elizabeth James, illustrated by Martha Weston. Text copyright © 1995 by Carol Barkin and Elizabeth James; illustrations copyright © 1995 by Martha Weston. All rights reserved. "The Mysterious Mr. Lincoln" from *Lincoln: A Photobiography* by Russell Freedman. Copyright © 1987 by Russell Freedman. All rights reserved.

Cobblestone Publishing Company, 30 Grove Street, Suite C, Peterborough, NH 03458: "Working on the Railroad" by Gloria A. Harris from *Cobblestone: African American Inventors,* February 1992. Copyright © 1992 by Cobblestone Publishing Company.

Don Congdon Associates, Inc.: "All Summer in a Day" by Ray Bradbury. Copyright © 1954 and renewed © 1982 by Ray Bradbury. Quote by Ray Bradbury from "Ray Bradbury: A Biographical Sketch" by William F. Nolan from *The Martian Chronicles* by Ray Bradbury. Copyright © 1973 by William F. Nolan. Quote by Ray Bradbury from *Something About the Author,* vol. 40. Copyright © 1976 by Gale Research Company Inc.

Bruce Coville c/o Ashley Grayson Literary Agency: "Duffy's Jacket" from *Oddly Enough: Stories by Bruce Coville.* Copyright © 1989 by Bruce Coville.

Creative Arts Book Company: From "The Magic Mortar" from *The Magic Listening Cap: More Folk Tales from Japan,* retold by Yoshiko Uchida. Copyright © 1955 and renewed © 1983 by Yoshiko Uchida.

CRICKET Magazine: From "Hungry Reader" by Lloyd Alexander from *CRICKET* Magazine, vol. 1, no. 1, September 1973. Copyright © 1973 by Carus Publishing Company. "Apples in the Snow" by Jane Caflisch from *CRICKET* Magazine, vol. 21, no. 9, May 1994. Copyright © 1994 by Carus Publishing Company.

Richard Curtis Associates, Inc.: From "The Flood" from *The Beauty of the Beasts* by Ralph Helfer. Copyright © 1990 by Ralph Helfer.

Dial Books for Young Readers, a division of Penguin Putnam Inc.: From *The Gold Cadillac* by Mildred D. Taylor. Copyright © 1987 by Mildred D. Taylor.

Doubleday, a division of Random House, Inc.: "The Fun They Had" from *Earth Is Room Enough* by Isaac Asimov. Copyright © 1957 by Isaac Asimov.

Farrar, Straus & Giroux, Inc.: From *A Day of Pleasure: Stories of a Boy Growing Up in Warsaw* by Isaac Bashevis Singer. Copyright © 1969 by Isaac Bashevis Singer. "The Toaster" from *Laughing Time: Collected Nonsense* by William Jay Smith. Copyright © 1990 by William Jay Smith.

Jennifer Flannery Literary Agency: From "Gary Paulsen" from *Authors and Artists for Young Adults,* vol. 2, edited by Agnes Garrett and Helga P. McCue. Copyright © 1989 by Gary Paulsen.

Abigail S. Friedman: "Myself" by Abigail S. Friedman. Copyright © 1997 by Abigail S. Friedman.

Fulcrum Publishing, 350 Indiana St., #350, Golden, CO 80401, (800) 992-2908: "Loo-Wit, the Fire-Keeper" from *Keepers of the Earth: Native American Stories and Environmental Activities for Children* by Michael J. Caduto and Joseph Bruchac. Copyright © 1988 by Joseph Bruchac.

The Gainesville Sun: Text and photo from "Suit Helps Girl Enjoy Daylight" by Lise Fisher from *The Gainesville Sun,* January 31, 1999. Copyright © 1999 by The Gainesville Sun.

The Gale Group: From "Huynh Quang Nhuong" from *Contemporary Authors,* vol. 107, edited by Hal May. Copyright © 1983 by Gale Research Company. All rights reserved. From "Olivia Coolidge" from *Something About the Author,* vol. 1, edited by Anne Commire. Copyright © 1971 by Gale Research Company. All rights reserved. From "Virginia Hamilton" from *Something About the Author,* vol. 4, edited by Anne Commire. Copyright © 1976 by Gale Research Company. All rights reserved. From "Bobbi Katz" from *Something About the Author,* vol. 12, edited by Anne Commire. Copyright © 1977 by Gale Research Company. From "Ogden Nash" from *Something About the Author,* vol. 46, edited by Anne Commire. Copyright © 1987 by Gale Research Company. From "Cynthia Rylant" from *Something About the Author,* vol. 50, edited by Anne Commire. Copyright © 1988 by Gale Research Company.

Greenwillow Books, a division of William Morrow & Company, Inc.: "Ankylosaurus" from *Tyrannosaurus Was a Beast* by Jack Prelutsky. Copyright © 1988 by Jack Prelutsky.

ACKNOWLEDGMENTS 781

Grolier International, Inc.: From "Scanning the Heavens" from *Science in Ancient China* by George Beshore. Copyright © 1988 by George Beshore. Published by Franklin Watts.

Harcourt, Inc.: "Macavity: The Mystery Cat" and illustration from *Old Possum's Book of Practical Cats* by T. S. Eliot, illustrated by Edward Gorey. Copyright 1939 by T. S. Eliot; copyright renewed © 1967 by Esme Valerie Eliot. Illustrations copyright © 1982 by Edward Gorey. From "Words from the Author" by Russell Freedman from *HBJ Treasury of Literature: Beyond Expectations* by Roger C. Farr and Dorothy S. Strickland. Copyright © 1993 by Harcourt Brace & Company. "The Hummingbird," "The Hill Mynah," and illustrations from *On the Wing* by Douglas Florian. Copyright © 1996 by Douglas Florian. "Theater Words" from *Onstage & Backstage: At the Night Owl Theater* by Ann Hayes, illustrated by Karmen Thompson. Text copyright © 1997 by Ann Hayes. From Poem #50 from *The People, Yes* by Carl Sandburg. Copyright 1936 by Harcourt Brace & Company; copyright renewed © 1964 by Carl Sandburg. From *In the Forest with the Elephants* by Roland Smith and Michael J. Schmidt. Copyright © 1998 by Roland Smith and Michael J. Schmidt. "La Bamba" from *Baseball in April and Other Stories* by Gary Soto. Copyright © 1990 by Gary Soto. "Ode to Mi Gato" from *Neighborhood Odes* by Gary Soto. Copyright © 1992 by Gary Soto. From a Letter to Kids by Gary Soto from *Promotional for Local News* by Gary Soto. Text and illustrations from *King Long Shanks* by Jane Yolen, illustrated by Victoria Chess. Text copyright © 1998 by Jane Yolen; illustrations copyright © 1998 by Victoria Chess.

HarperCollins Publishers: "Cynthia in the Snow" from *Bronzeville Boys and Girls* by Gwendolyn Brooks. Copyright © 1956 by Gwendolyn Brooks Blakely. Excerpt (retitled "How the Snake Got Poison") adapted from *Mules and Men* by Zora Neale Hurston. Copyright 1935 by Zora Neale Hurston; copyright renewed © 1963 by John C. Hurston and Joel Hurston. From *The Land I Lost* by Huynh Quang Nhuong. Copyright © 1982 by Huynh Quang Nhuong. "January" from *Chicken Soup with Rice: A Book of Months* by Maurice Sendak. Copyright © 1962 by Maurice Sendak. "Jimmy Jet and His TV Set" from *Where the Sidewalk Ends* by Shel Silverstein. Copyright © 1974 by Evil Eye Music, Inc. From "Zlateh the Goat" from *Zlateh the Goat and Other Stories* by Isaac Bashevis Singer, illustrated by Maurice Sendak. Text copyright © 1966 by Isaac Bashevis Singer. From *Whoppers: Tall Tales and Other Lies* by Alvin Schwartz. Text copyright © 1975 by Alvin Schwartz.

Highlights for Children, Inc., Columbus, OH: From "Who's the New Kid?" by Lois Lowry from *Highlights for Children*, January 1994. Copyright © 1994 by Highlights for Children, Inc.

Henry Holt and Company, Inc.: "The Stone" from *The Foundling and Other Tales of Prydain* by Lloyd Alexander. Copyright © 1973 by Lloyd Alexander. "The Emperor's New Clothes" by Hans Christian Andersen from *Michael Hague's Favorite Hans Christian Andersen Fairy Tales* by Michael Hague. Copyright © 1981 by Henry Holt and Company. "Steam Shovel" from *Upper Pasture* by Charles Malam. Copyright 1930, © 1958 by Charles Malam. From *Out of My Life and Thought* by Albert Schweitzer, translated by C. T. Campion. Copyright 1933, 1949 by Henry Holt and Company, Inc.; copyright © 1990 by Rhena Schweitzer Miller; translation copyright © 1990 by Antje Bultmann Lemke.

The Horn Book, Inc.: From "The Common Ground" by Ann Petry from *The Horn Book Magazine*, April 1965.

Houghton Mifflin Company: "Baucis and Philemon" and "Medusa's Head" from *Greek Myths* by Olivia Coolidge. Copyright © 1949 and renewed © 1977 by Olivia E. Coolidge. All rights reserved.

Bobbi Katz: "Things to Do If You Are a Subway" by Bobbi Katz from *Upside Down and Inside Out: Poems for All Your Pockets*. Copyright © 1973 by Bobbi Katz. Bobbi Katz controls all reprint rights.

Alfred A. Knopf, Inc.: Text from "He Lion, Bruh Bear, and Bruh Rabbit" from *The People Could Fly* by Virginia Hamilton. Copyright © 1985 by Virginia Hamilton.

Robert Kyle: From "Crow Poets" by Robert Kyle from *Native*

Peoples, vol. 8, no. 2, Winter 1995. Copyright © 1995 by Robert Kyle.

Michael LaForge, Jr.: "Vision" by Michael LaForge, Jr., from "Crow Poets" by Robert Kyle from *Native Peoples*, vol. 8, no. 2, Winter 1995. Copyright © 1995 by Michael LaForge, Jr.

Brian Lanker: Excerpt (retitled "I Was Not Alone") from *I Dream a World: Portraits of Black Women Who Changed America* by Brian Lanker. Copyright © 1989 by Brian Lanker.

Patricia Lauber: Comment on "Volcano" by Patricia Lauber. Copyright © 1997 by Patricia Lauber.

Suki Lehman-Becker: "Meow" by Suki Lehman-Becker from *Identity: Art and Literary Magazine*, vol. II, 1993. Copyright © 1993 by Suki Lehman-Becker. Published by East Northport Middle School, East Northport, NY.

Lescher & Lescher, Ltd.: Text from "The Southpaw" by Judith Viorst from *Free to Be . . . You and Me* by Marlo Thomas and Associates. Copyright © 1974 by Judith Viorst.

Sara Lesher: "John, Sue, and the Talking Snake" by Sara Lesher from *Webb of Words, 1991–1992*. Copyright © 1991 by Sara Lesher. Published by the Students of the Middle School, Webb School of Knoxville, TN.

Linnet Books/The Shoe String Press, Inc., North Haven, CT: Quote by Floating Eagle Feather from *Peace Tales: World Folktales to Talk About* by Margaret Read MacDonald. Copyright © 1992 by Margaret Read MacDonald.

Little, Brown and Company: "A Caution to Everybody," "The Camel," "The Duck," "The Octopus," and "The Panther" from *Verses from 1929 On* by Ogden Nash. Copyright © 1933, 1936, 1940, 1942, 1950 by Ogden Nash; copyright renewed © 1977 by Frances Nash, Isabel Nash Eberstadt, and Linell Nash Smith. "A Caution to Everybody" first appeared in *Hearst's International Cosmopolitan*. "The Octopus" first appeared in *The New Yorker*. "The Camel," "The Duck," and "The Panther" first appeared in *The Saturday Evening Post*.

Edward Lueders: "Your Poem, Man . . ." by Edward Lueders from *Some Haystacks Don't Even Have Any Needle: And Other Complete Modern Poems*, compiled by Stephen Dunning, Edward Lueders, and Hugh Smith. Copyright © 1969 by Scott, Foresman and Company.

Macmillan General Reference USA, a division of Ahsuog, Inc.: From *Webster's New World Dictionary*, Third College Edition. Copyright © 1988, 1991, 1994, 1996, 1997 by Simon & Schuster, Inc.

Walter McVitty Books: *Ali Baba and the Forty Thieves* with four illustrations, retold by Walter McVitty, illustrated by Margaret Early. Text copyright © 1988 by Walter McVitty Books; illustrations copyright © 1988 by Margaret Early.

Merlyn's Pen: The National Magazines of Student Writing: From "The Earth Is in Your Hands" by Todd Lehne from "Letters to the Pen" from *Merlyn's Pen*, vol. X, no. I, October/November 1994. Copyright © 1994 by Todd Lehne. First appeared in *Merlyn's Pen: The National Magazines of Student Writing*.

Pat Mora: Quote by Pat Mora describing her interest in writing for children.

Lensey Namioka: "The All-American Slurp" by Lensey Namioka from *Visions*, edited by Donald R. Gallo. Copyright © 1987 by Lensey Namioka. All rights reserved by the author.

National Geographic Society: From "What Is It Like to Walk on the Moon?" by David R. Scott from *National Geographic*, September 1973. Copyright © 1973 by National Geographic Society. From "Earth Almanac: Scores of Serengeti's Lions Perish from a Virus" from *National Geographic*, January 1995. Copyright © 1994 by National Geographic Society.

The New Yorker: From "Thoughts on Progress" by David Daiches from *The New Yorker*, August 28, 1954. Copyright © 1954, 1982 by The New Yorker Magazine, Inc. All rights reserved.

The New York Times Company: Text and photos from "Performers at an Early Stage" by Jack Manning from *The New York Times*, January 1, 1999. Copyright © 1999 by The New York Times Company.

Pantheon Books, a division of Random House, Inc.: From Introduction and "President Cleveland, Where Are You?," slightly adapted, from *Eight Plus One: Stories* by Robert Cormier. Copyright © 1965 and renewed © 1993 by Robert Cormier.

People Weekly: From "Talking with . . . Robert Fulghum: Food for Thought," an interview by Jill Rachlin from *People Weekly,* vol. 40, no. 9, August 30, 1993. Copyright © 1993 by Time Inc. From "Seeking Wisdom, Robert Fulghum Went to Kindergarten" from *People Weekly,* vol. 41, no. 9, March 7, 1994. Copyright © 1994 by Time Inc. From "Brave Hearts" (retitled "Trial by Fire") from *People Weekly.* Copyright © 1997 by Time Inc.

Princeton University Press: From "Myth and Dream" from *The Hero with a Thousand Faces* by Joseph Campbell. Copyright 1949 by Bollingen Foundation; copyright renewed © 1976 by Princeton University Press.

The Putnam Publishing Group: From "Lessons" from *Childhood* by Bill Cosby. Copyright © 1991 by William H. Cosby, Jr.

Ramapo Catskill Library System: From "KidsClick!" Web page. Available on-line at http://sunsite.berkeley.edu/KidsClick!/. Copyright © 1998, 1999 by Ramapo Catskill Library System. All rights reserved.

Random House, Inc.: Excerpt (retitled "Brother") from *I Know Why the Caged Bird Sings* by Maya Angelou. Copyright © 1969 and renewed © 1997 by Maya Angelou. From *Gorilla, My Love* by Toni Cade Bambara. Copyright © 1971 by Toni Cade Bambara. From *All I Really Need to Know I Learned in Kindergarten* by Robert L. Fulghum. Copyright © 1986, 1988 by Robert L. Fulghum. "The Sneetches" from *The Sneetches and Other Stories* by Dr. Seuss. TM and copyright © 1961 and renewed © 1989 by Dr. Seuss Enterprises, L. P.

Marian Reiner on behalf of Patricia Hubbell: "Our Washing Machine" from *The Apple Vendor's Fair* by Patricia Hubbell. Copyright © 1963 and renewed © 1991 by Patricia Hubbell.

Marian Reiner for Lillian Morrison: "The Sidewalk Racer or On the Skateboard" from *The Sidewalk Racer and Other Poems of Sports and Motion* by Lillian Morrison. Copyright © 1965, 1967, 1968, 1977 by Lillian Morrison.

Marian Reiner on behalf of Judith Thurman: "Rags" from *Flashlight and Other Poems* by Judith Thurman. Copyright © 1976 by Judith Thurman.

Mara Rockliff: "Rumpelstiltskin" dramatization by Mara Rockliff. Copyright © 2000 by Mara Rockliff.

Russell & Volkening as agents for Ann Petry: "A Glory over Everything" from *Harriet Tubman: Conductor on the Underground Railroad* by Ann Petry. Copyright © 1955 and renewed © 1983 by Ann Petry.

Scholastic Inc.: "Why Dogs Chase Cats" from *How Many Spots Does a Leopard Have? and Other Tales* by Julius Lester. Copyright © 1989 by Julius Lester. "Ta-Na-E-Ka" by Mary Whitebird from *Scholastic Voice,* December 13, 1973. Copyright © 1973 by Scholastic Inc.

Scovil, Chichak, Galen Literary Agency, Inc.: From "Robots in the Nursery" by Arthur C. Clarke from *Holiday Magazine.* Copyright © 1958 by The Curtis Publishing Company.

Loretta Shane: "Grandmother" by Loretta Shane from "Crow Poets" by Robert Kyle from *Native Peoples,* vol. 8, no. 2, Winter 1995. Copyright © 1995 by Loretta Shane.

Robert Silverberg: From "Pompeii" from *Lost Cities and Vanished Civilizations* by Robert Silverberg. Copyright © 1962 and renewed © 1990 by Agberg, Ltd.

Simon & Schuster Books for Young Readers, an imprint of Simon & Schuster Children's Publishing Division: "The Nightingale" from *The Nightingale* by Hans Christian Andersen, translated by Anthea Bell. Copyright © 1984 by Neugebauer Press, Salzburg, Austria; English text copyright © 1988 by Simon & Schuster, Inc. All rights reserved. Quote by Avi from the Avi Bradbury Press Promotional Brochure. Copyright © 1992 by Avi. From *Volcano: The Eruption and Healing of Mount St. Helens* by Patricia Lauber. Copyright © 1986 by Patricia Lauber. Excerpt (retitled "Storm") from *Woodsong* by Gary Paulsen. Copyright © 1990 by Gary Paulsen. "Stray" from *Every Living Thing* by Cynthia Rylant. Copyright © 1985 by Cynthia Rylant.

Laurie Smith: From "If I Could See Tomorrow" by Laurie Smith from *Paw Prints: Simonsen Junior High Literary Magazine,* May 1992. Published by the Pen 'n Ink Club of Simonsen Junior High School, Jefferson City, MO.

Gary Soto: Comment on "Summer School" by Gary Soto. Copyright © 1993 by Gary Soto.

Staniels Associates: Text from *The Seventh Sister: A Chinese Legend,* retold by Cindy Chang. Copyright © 1994 by Troll Associates, Inc.

Stone Soup, the magazine by children: "Weasel" by Chris Brown, 12 years old, from *Stone Soup, the magazine by children,* vol. 8, no. 4, March/April 1980. Copyright © 1980 by the Children's Art Foundation. "The Swim of My Life" by Lacey Clayton, 13 years old, and "The Brother I Never Had" by Gim George, 13 years old, from *Stone Soup, the magazine by children,* vol. 21, no. 5, May/June 1993. Copyright © 1993 by the Children's Art Foundation. "Special Small World" by Casie Anne Smith, 11 years old, from *Stone Soup, the magazine by children,* September/October 1993. Copyright © 1993 by the Children's Art Foundation. From "Book Review: *A Whole New Ball Game* by Sue Macy" by Merenda Garnett-Kranz, 12 years old, from *Stone Soup, the magazine by children,* vol. 23, no. 5, Summer 1995. Copyright © 1995 by the Children's Art Foundation.

Claudia Tate: From "Maya Angelou" from *Black Women Writers at Work,* edited by Claudia Tate. Copyright © 1983 by Claudia Tate.

Mildred D. Taylor: From "Mildred D. Taylor" from *Something About the Author Autobiography Series,* vol. 5, edited by Adele Sarkissian. Copyright © 1988 by Mildred D. Taylor.

Teacher Ideas Press, Englewood, CO, (800) 237-6124: Adapted from "Blanca Flor/White Flower" from *¡Teatro! Hispanic Plays for Young People* by Angel Vigil. Copyright © 1996 by Teacher Ideas Press.

Third Woman Press: "Good Hot Dogs" from *My Wicked, Wicked Ways* by Sandra Cisneros. Copyright © 1989 by Third Woman Press.

Scott Treimel New York for Charlotte Zolotow: "Scene" from *River Winding* by Charlotte Zolotow. Copyright © 1970 by Charlotte Zolotow.

University of Arizona Press: From *Sáanii Dahataal, The Women Are Singing* by Luci Tapahonso. Copyright © 1993 by Luci Tapahonso.

University Press of New England: "The City" from *David Ignatow: Poems 1934–1969* by David Ignatow. Copyright © 1970 by David Ignatow. Published by Wesleyan University Press.

Laurence S. Untermeyer on behalf of the Estate of Louis Untermeyer, Norma Anchin Untermeyer, c/o Professional Publishing Services Company: "The Dog of Pompeii" from *The Donkey of God* by Louis Untermeyer. Copyright 1932 by Harcourt Brace & Company.

Viking Penguin, a division of Penguin Putnam Inc.: From *My Lord, What a Morning* by Marian Anderson. Copyright © 1956 and renewed © 1984 by Marian Anderson. "Rumpelstiltskin" by Rosemarie Künzler, translated by Jack Zipes, from *Spells of Enchantment,* edited by Jack Zipes. Copyright © 1991 by Jack Zipes. From *Snakes: The Facts and the Folklore* by Hilda Simon. Copyright © 1973 by Hilda Simon.

Vocal Point: From "Rainforest Rights" by Aviv Gazit from *Vocal Point,* October 1998. Available on-line at http://bvsd.k12.co.us/cent/ Newspaper/oct98/stories/rain.html. Copyright © 1998 by Vocal Point. Published by the students of Centennial Middle School, Boulder, CO.

Weekly Reader Corporation: "Foul Shot" by Edwin A. Hoey from *READ® Magazine.* Copyright © 1962 and renewed © 1989 by Weekly Reader Corporation. All rights reserved.

West End Press: "Yes, It Was My Grandmother" from *A Breeze Swept Through* by Luci Tapahonso. Copyright © 1987 by Luci Tapahonso.

John Wiley & Sons, Inc.: Adapted from *Online Kids: A Young Surfer's Guide to Cyberspace* by Preston Gralla. Copyright © 1996 by Preston Gralla.

Young Voices Magazine, subscriptions, guidelines, and sample copies, P.O. Box 2321, Olympia, WA 98507, (206) 943-3711: "The Lawn Mower" by Taunya Woo from *Young Voices,* September/October, 1993. Copyright © 1993 by Taunya Woo.

SOURCES CITED
Quote by Tom Stoppard from *The Observer,* August 30, 1981.

PICTURE CREDITS

The illustrations on the Contents pages are picked up from pages in the textbook. Credits for those illustrations can be found either on the textbook page on which they appear or in the listing below.

Pages xx–1, Reuters/Mike Segar/Archive Photos; 2, (left) ©PhotoDisc, Inc. 1998; 2–3, Tony Stone Images; 5, 6, ©PhotoDisc, Inc. 1998; 7, 8 (top), Tony Stone Images; 8, (bottom) ©1997 Radlund & Associates for Artville; 9, ©PhotoDisc, Inc. 1998; 12, David Young-Wolff/PhotoEdit; 18, Carson Baldwin Jr./Earth Scenes; 19, John Gerlach/Animals Animals; 23, ©PhotoDisc, Inc. 1998; 39, Lensey Namioka; 49, Carolyn Soto; 53, Collection of David J. and Janice L. Frent; 54, (top and right) National Baseball Hall of Fame; 54 (bottom left), 56 (top, center, and bottom), Collection of David J. and Janice L. Frent; 56, (right and left) National Baseball Hall of Fame; 63, (bottom) The Atlanta Journal, (background) ©PhotoDisc, Inc. 1998; 65, Richard Howard Photography; 78, Henry Holt and Company; 82, (top) Mark MacLaren/Retna LTD, (bottom) Globe Photos, Inc.; 83, NBC Photo by R. M. Lewis Jr./Globe Photos, Inc.; 84, Bill Davila/Retna LTD; 93, F. Cruz/© SuperStock Inc.; 94–95, © Vesey/Vanderburg-International Stock; 103, Dr. E. R. Degginger; 104, (background) Paul Souders/Tony Stone Images, (inset) Gary Paulsen; 113, Paul Fetters/Matrix International, Inc.; 117, Michal Heron/Woodfin Camp & Associates; 123, Arte Público Press/University of Houston; 126–127, Lawrence Migdale/Stock Boston, Inc.; 128, National Archives, Photo No. 111-B-6135; 130, Culver Pictures, Inc.; 131, Clarion Books; 146, AP/Wide World Photos; 151, The Eaton Press and the Mark Twain Home Foundation, Hannibal, MO; 165, F. Cruz/© SuperStock Inc.; 172, Culver Pictures, Inc.; 174–175 (background), 176, Lester Lefkowitz/FPG International; 177, Dean Siracusa/FPG International; 179, ©Ken Karp; 185, Lester Lefkowitz/FPG International; 187, Bardinet/Photo Researchers, Inc.; 189, The New York City Transit Authority; 190, ©91 Paul Steel/The Stock Market; 191, (top) Dorothy Alexander, (center) Elizabeth Gilliland, (bottom) Bobbi Katz, (background) Lester Lefkowitz/FPG International; 199, William Day/Photo Researchers, Inc.; 201, HarperCollins; 204–205, (background—clouds) Chris Bell/FPG International, (inset) Tom and Dee Ann McCarthy/The Stock Market, (background—books) Lightscapes/The Stock Market; 208, Zefa, Germany/The Stock Market; 209, (background) Lightscapes/The Stock Market, (inset) D. Kirkland/Sygma; 212, Tom and Dee Ann McCarthy/The Stock Market; 215, (background) Keren Su/Tony Stone Images, (inset) Jos Korenremp/Animals Animals; 226, Michal Heron/The Stock Market; 237, F. Cruz/© SuperStock Inc.; 238, Lee Boltin Picture Library; 246, (inset) Susan Greenwood/Gamma Liaison, (background) Sygma; 251, Vince Streano/Tony Stone Images; 254, Orchard Books; 255, J. P. Thomas/Jacana/Photo Researchers, Inc.; 256, Chip Henderson/Tony Stone Images; 260, 261, Courtesy of Julie Koenig/HRW; 264, M. Antman/The Image Works; 265, ©PhotoDisc, Inc. 1998; 266, (left) Richard R. Hewett/Shooting Star; 266 (right), 267, 268 (left), ©PhotoDisc, Inc. 1998; 268, (right) Richard R. Hewett/Shooting Star; 269, ©PhotoDisc, Inc. 1998; 270, Richard R. Hewett/Shooting Star; 271, ©PhotoDisc, Inc. 1998; 272, Richard R. Hewett/Shooting Star; 273, ©PhotoDisc, Inc. 1998; 275, (top) AP/Wide World Photos/Chris Kasson, (bottom) North Shore Animal League; 280, John Darling/Tony Stone Images; 281, E. Boubat/Photo Researchers, Inc.; 282, 283, Ruth Massey/Photo Researchers, Inc.; 284–285, Alain Evrard/Photo Reseachers, Inc.; 286, (inset) Ken Ross 1992/FPG International; 286–287, (background) Belinda Wright/DRK Photo; 287, (bottom right) Roger Jones; 288, Mitch Reardon/Tony Stone Images; 291, Duncan Wherrett/Tony Stone Images; 292–293, E. R. Degginger/Photo Researchers, Inc.; 295, (background) Dr. E. R. Degginger, (inset) Villard Books, a division of Random House; 296, Corbis; 299, (bottom left) Menny Borovski; 300, (top) UPI/Corbis; 309, F. Cruz/© SuperStock Inc.; 310–311, Fotopic/Omni–Photo Communications; 312–313, Peter Gridley 1988/FPG International; 320, AP/Wide World Photos; 321, © Jon Fletcher/The Gainesville Sun; 322, Ron Thomas/FPG International; 323, Frank Whitney/The Image Bank;

329, Omni–Photo Communications; 333, Skylab; 335, Bob Daemmrick/Stock Boston, Inc.; 337, Courtesy of Judy Fowler and Joan Burditt/HRW; 338–339, 343, Nicky Wright Photography; 346, Laurance B. Aiuppy 1992/FPG International; 348, Penguin, USA; 351, UPI/Corbis; 352, AP Photo/Michael Caulfield; 362, Courtesy of The Bancroft Library, University of California, Berkeley; 377, Tony Freeman/PhotoEdit; 387, ©PhotoDisc, Inc. 1998; 388, (inset) David Stoecklein/The Stock Market; 388–389, (background) © PhotoDisc, Inc. 1998; 389, (inset) Frank Cezus/FPG International; 390–391, (background) Jim Cummins/FPG International; 391, (inset) David Young-Wolff/PhotoEdit; 392, Judith Viorst; 397, Tony Freeman/PhotoEdit; 403, F. Cruz/© SuperStock Inc.; 404–405, (inset) Bob Lambert, (background) Hiroyuki Matsumoto/Tony Stone Images; 418, Photofest; 424, (top) ©1994 Zefa, Germany/The Stock Market, (right) Culver Pictures, Inc.; 434–435, (top border) © Bob Lambert, (background) ©PhotoDisc, Inc. 1998; 435 (inset), 436, 437, 438, InterActive Theater Company, @ Houston, TX; 444, 445, ©94 Mendola/Jeff Mangiat/The Stock Market; 456, Photo courtesy Angel Vigil; 457, Courtesy of Catherine Goodridge/HRW; 476–478, Jack Manning/New York Times Pictures; 479, (left) *Jennifer Murdley's Toad* by Bruce Coville. © Harcourt Brace & Company, (top right) *Oddly Enough* by Bruce Coville. © Harcourt Brace & Company, (bottom right) From *Sherlock Holmes: The Complete Novels and Stories*, volume II (jacket cover), by Sir Arthur Conan Doyle. Copyright. Used by permission of Bantam Books, a division of Random House, Inc.; 486, F. Cruz/© SuperStock Inc.; 490, Randy Wells/Tony Stone Images; 494, Greenfield Press Review; 498, PhotoCraft; 499, Austin Post/U.S. Geological Survey; 500, PhotoCraft; 501, 502, 503, Pat and Tom Leeson/Photo Researchers, Inc.; 504, Lyn Toponka/U.S. Geological Survey; 505, PhotoCraft; 506, (top) Thomas Casadevall/U.S. Geological Survey, (bottom) U.S. Geological Survey; 507, Gary Braasch/Woodfin Camp & Associates; 508, (background) PhotoCraft, (inset) HarperCollins; 513, Scala/Art Resource, New York; 515, 516, 518, 522, Photography by John Hauser; 523, Archive Photos; 524–525, © Photograph by Erich Lessing/Art Resource, New York; 531, Allan Morton/Dennis Milan/Photo Researchers, Inc.; 534, ©PhotoDisc, Inc., 1998; 538, (left) Derke/ O'Hara/Tony Stone Images, (right) Kristin Finnegan/Tony Stone Images; 539, Ronald Royer/Science Photo Library/Photo Researchers, Inc.; 550, (inset) Tom Ulrich/Tony Stone Images, (background) Tony Stone Images; 558, (top) Scholastic Inc.; 568, F. Cruz/© SuperStock Inc.; 581, Michelle L. Smith; 589, Charlie Waite/Tony Stone Images; 594, Dr. E. R. Degginger; 617, Chris Michaels 1992/FPG International; 643, AP/Wide World Photos; 656, UPI/Corbis.

Borders for Speaking and Listening Workshops and for Sentence Workshops, Troy Vis; borders for Elements of Literature features and for Writer's Workshops, Paul Kazmercyk.

In Writer's Workshops, Macintosh windows elements and icons © 1984 Apple Computer, Inc. All rights reserved. Used with the permission of Apple Computer, Inc.

Portions copyright Netscape Communications Corporation, 1998. All rights reserved. Netscape, Netscape navigator, and the Netscape N logo are registered trademarks of Netscape in the United States and other countries.

Border for Reading Skills and Strategies, (background) Art Montes De Oca/FPG International, (left) Copyright 1998, USA TODAY. Reprinted with permission, (right) Copyright 1998 Netscape Communications Corp. Used with permission. All rights reserved. This electronic file or page may not be reprinted or copied without the express written permission of Netscape. Netscape Communications Corporation has not authorized, sponsored, or endorsed or approved this publication and is not responsible for its content. Netscape and Netscape Communications corporate logos are trademarks and trade names of Netscape Communications Corporation. All other product names and/or logos are trademarks of their respective owners.

INDEX OF SKILLS

LITERARY TERMS

The boldface page numbers indicate an extensive treatment of the topic.

Actors 436
Acts, drama 406, 669
Administrative staff, for a play 437
Aesthetic language. See Figurative language.
Alliteration 178, 192, 198, **667**
Allusion **667**
Analogy. See Metaphor; Simile.
Anecdote 106, 296
Argument, logical 486.
Autobiography 86, **108,** 280, **667**
Basic situation, drama 406
Biography **108,** 136, 158, **667**
Cause and effect 204, 439, 448, 498
Character 79, **96,** 105, 164, 247, 288, 326, **366,** 376, 406, 537, 587, 606, 608, 637, 659, **668**
  traits 96, 106, 134, 147
  types **462,** 473
Characterization 668
Chronological order 88, 90, 161, 232, 236, 304, 366, 418, 564, 566, 662, 664, 688
Climax 326, 406, 660, 669, 673
Comparison and contrast 51, 513, 551
Complications 406, 669, 673
Conflict 2, 11, 12, **14,** 15, 27, 41, 66, 79, 288, 326, 487, 495, 606, 660, **668,** 669, 673
  external 14, **15,** 27, 668
  internal 14, **15,** 27, 668
Connotation 355, 475, **668**
Costume designer 437
Creation myth 672
Denotation 475, 668
Description 28, 50, 53, 67, 88, 106, **109,** 115, 120, 121, 124, 134, 148, 181, 198, 305, 353, 356, 363, 376, 378, 490, 495, 496, 510, 511, 512, 526, 527, 535, 543, 552, 553, 605, 606, 607, **668**
  of mental images 192, 198
Details, sensory 44, **53,** 67, 87, 88, 109, 121, 124, 278, 527, 543, 562-566, 662
Dialect 552, 553, **668-669**
Dialogue 88, 336, 365, 435, 474, **669,** 756-757
Director, of a play 435
Direct quotations 378
Drama **406,** 435, **669**
  acts 406, 669
  basic situation 406
  climax 406, 669, 673
  complications 406, 669, 673
  conflict 669, 673
  exposition 669
  introduction 669, 673
  resolution 406, 669, 673
  scenes 406, 669
End rhyme 178, 674

Essay **291,** 296, 512, **669**
Exaggeration 298, 486
Exposition, in drama 669
Extended metaphor **185**
External conflict 14, **15,** 27, 668
Fable **669**
Fairy tale 69, 670
Fantasy 620, **669-670**
Fiction 14, 326, 513, 526, **670**
Figurative language (figures of speech) **183-184,** 325, 498, 511, **670**
  metaphor 183, **185,** 192, 325, 334, 670, **671**
  personification 183-184, 325, 511, 670, **673**
  simile **44,** 50, 183, 325, 670, 671, **675**
First-person point of view 326, 335, 674
Flashback 263, 418, **670**
Folk hero 176
Folk tale 439, 462, 496, 545, **608,** 639, 665, **670,** 673
Foreshadowing **408,** 431, **670**
Free verse 179, **670,** 674
Golden Age **599,** 605
Hero 177, 288, 572, 586, 587
Historical fiction **513,** 526
How-and-why tale **528,** 535
Humor 41, 50
Idiom 638, 686
Imagery **121,** 124, 334, 668, **670-671**
Indirect quotations 378
Informative writing 498, 509, 537, 538
Internal conflict 14, **15,** 27, 668
Internal rhyme 178, 674
Introduction
  of drama 669
  of plot 673
Irony **204,** 212, **671**
Legend 286, **671**
Lighting designer 436
Limerick **671**
Loaded words 402
Main events 79, 80, 247, 262, 263, 280, 473
Main idea 109, 115, 212, 262, **279,** 291, 296, 303, 402, 537, 538, 543, **671,** 685. See also Theme.
Mental images, description of 192, 198
Message 41, 147, 596, 623, 636. See also Theme.
Metamorphosis 495, 496, **589,** 595, 596
Metaphor 183, **185,** 192, 325, 334, 670, **671**
  extended **185**
Meter 179, **199,** 202, 675
Mood 431, 432, **672**
Moral lesson **69,** 79, 80, 385
Motif **439,** 448, 460, 473
Motive 431
Myth 490, 495, 509, 569, 587, **598,** 599, 605, **672**
Mythic hero **572,** 586
Narration **672**
Narrative 262, 263, 288, 672
Narrator 327

Nonfiction 108, 279, 498, 512, 513, 545, **672**
  autobiography 86, **108,** 280, **667**
  biography **108,** 136, 158, **667**
  essay **291,** 296, 512, **669**
  informative writing 498, 509, 537, 538
  objective writing **512**
  persuasive writing 324, 335, 354, 364, 377, 386, 396-400, 432, 460, 474, 480-484
  subjective writing **512**
Novel 537, **672**
Objective writing **512**
Ode 258
Omniscient point of view 326, 674
Onomatopoeia **181,** 182, 192, 198, **672**
Oral tradition **545,** 551, **673**
Origin myth **490,** 495, 672
Outcome. See Resolution.
Personification 183-184, 325, 511, 670, **673**
Plays 435. See also Drama.
Playwright 434, 435
Plot 250, 326, 356, 537, 621, 623, 660, **673,** 675
  climax 326, 406, 660, 669, 673
  complications 406, 669, 673
  conflict 2, 11, 12, **14,** 15, 27, 41, 66, 79, 288, 326, 487, 495, 606, 660, **668,** 669, 673
  flashback 263, 418, **670**
  foreshadowing **408**
  resolution 288, 326, 406, 551, 660, 669, 673
  suspense **240,** 247, **408,** 509, 620, **676**
Poetry **178-179,** **183-184,** 194, 195, **674**
  alliteration 178, 192, 198, **667**
  end rhyme 178, 674
  figurative language (figures of speech) **183-184,** 670
  free verse 179, **670,** 674
  imagery **121,** 124, **670-671**
  internal rhyme 178, 674
  mental images 192, 198
  metaphor 183, **185,** 192, **671**
  meter 179, **199,** 202, 675
  onomatopoeia **181,** 182, 192, 198, **672**
  personification 183-184, 670, **673**
  rhyme 178, 192, 198, 199, 202, **379,** 385, 551, **674**
  rhythm 182, 194
  scanning **199,** 202, 675
  simile **44,** 183, 670, 671, **675**
Point of view 326, 402, **674**
  author's, how it affects the text, 147, 212
  first-person 326, 335, 674
  omniscient 326, 674
Problem resolution. See Plot.
Production staff, for a play 437
Prose **674**
Quest 586
Red herring 431
Refrain **168,** 176, **674**
Resolution 288, 406, 660, 669, 673
Rhyme 178, 192, 198, 199, 202, **379,** 385,

551, **674**
  end 178, 674
  internal 178, 674
Rhyme scheme **199,** 202, 674
Rhythm 182, 194, **675**
Scanning **199,** 202, 675
Scenes, drama 406, 669
Scenic designer 436
Sensory details 44, **53,** 67, 87, 88, 109, 121, 124, 278, 527, 543, 562-566, 662
Setting 256, **312,** 432, 436-437, 537, 637, 660, **675**
Short story 14, **326,** 537, **675**
  character 79, **96,** 105, 164, 247, 326, **366,** 376, 537, 587, 606, 608, 637, 659, **668**
  climax 326, 660, 673
  conflict **2,** 11, 12, **14,** 15, 27, 41, 66, 79, 288, 326, 495, 606, 660, **668,** 673
  flashback 263, 418, **670**
  introduction 673
  plot 250, 326, 356, 537, 621, 623, 660, **673,** 675
  point of view 326, 335, **674**
  setting 256, **312,** 432, 436-437, 637, 660, **675**
  theme **250,** 256, 326, **356,** 363, 596, **623,** 636, **676**
Simile **44,** 50, 183, 325, 670, 671, **675**
Sound designer 436
Speaker **675-676**
Stanza **676**
Story 608, 623. *See also* Short story.
Style 298, 355
Subjective writing **512**
Summary 289
Suspense **240,** 247, 408, 509, 620, **676**
Symbol 353
Tall tale 286, 288, **676**
Theater 434
Theme **250,** 256, 326, **356,** 363, 596, **623,** 636, **676.** *See also* Main idea.
Time order. *See* Chronological order.
Title 11, 323, 376, 495, 620
Tone **117,** 120, 198, **676**
Topic 279
Trickster 608, **639,** 646

READING AND CRITICAL THINKING

Active reading 2
  assignments (Dialogue with the Text) 2, 4, 11, 96, 97, 105, 168, 169-170, 176, 240, 241, 247, 312, 314, 323, 490, 491, 495, 572, 575, 586
  student models 4, 89, 97, 162, 169-170, 233, 241, 305, 314, 399, 483–484, 491, 565, 575, 661
Analogies, word 433, 690
Analysis questions (Shaping Interpretations) 11, 27, 41, 50, 66, 79, 105, 115, 120, 124, 133, 147, 176, 182, 192, 198, 202, 212, 247, 256, 261, 276, 288, 296, 323, 334, 353, 363, 376, 385, 418, 431, 448, 460, 473, 495, 509, 526, 535, 543, 551, 586, 595, 605, 620, 636, 646

Anticipation/response survey 15, 27, 250
Author's point of view, analyzing 147, 212
Brainstorming 168, 182, 185, 193, 203, 303, 324, 397, 481, 498, 538, 599, 606, 659, 660
Captions 498, 510, 568
Cause and effect 212, 262, 439, 448, 498, 646
Charts 27, 30, 79, 81, 92, 96, 105, 107, 125, 159, 168, 182, 199, 203, 232, 236, 240, 257, 262, 324, 398, 434, 462, 481, 498, 509, 510, 551, 565, 568, 569, 595, 597, 606, 609, 659, 688
  how to read 688
  types of 688
Chronological order 88, 90, 161, 232, 236, 304, 366, 418, 564, 566, 662, 664, 688
Chronology, using 263
Cluster diagram 87, 185, 262, 263, 276, 280, 288, 290, 291, 297, 398, 544
Comparison and contrast 15, 27, 51, 79, 90, 105, 124, 147, 161, 192, 194, 195, 247, 261, 304, 325, 432, 474, 482, 509, 510, 513, 526, 527, 543, 545, 551, 552, 605, 636, 663
Comprehension, monitoring 2, 312
Comprehension questions (Reading Check) 11, 27, 41, 50, 66, 79, 105, 115, 133, 147, 212, 247, 256, 276, 288, 296, 323, 334, 353, 363, 376, 385, 418, 431, 448, 473, 495, 509, 526, 535, 543, 551, 586, 595, 605, 620, 636, 646
Conclusions, drawing 125, 407
Connections, recognizing 589
Connotation 355, 475, 668
Context clues 13, 30, 31, 43, 79, 105, 194, 236, 250, 498, 638
Criteria 432, 481
Critical reader 512
Decision making 93
Definition of word 30, 686
Denotation 475, 668
Diacritical marks 686
Dialogue with the Text 2, 4, 11, 96, 97, 105, 168, 169-170, 176, 240, 241, 247, 312, 314, 323, 490, 491, 495, 572, 575, 586
Dictionary, using a 686
Double-entry journal 363
Drama 406, 435, 669
Evaluation 432, 460, 474, 480-484
Evaluation questions (Challenging the Text) 11, 66, 79, 105, 133, 147, 202, 212, 276, 288, 323, 334, 363, 376, 460, 473, 495, 509, 526, 586, 620
Evidence 69, 125, 250, 356, 398, 402, 418, 432, 460, 482
Fact and opinion 407, 431, 486, 512
Fiction 14, 326, 513, 526, 670
Fish-bone organizer 262
Flowcharts 678-679, 688
Folk tale 439, 462, 496, 545, 608, 639, 665, 670, 673
Generalizations 69, 356, 363
Glossary, using a 647
Graphic aids 498, 510
Graphic features in a book, using 92

Graphic organizers 27, 30, 41, 51, 79, 81, 87, 88, 90, 92, 96, 105, 107, 115, 117, 120, 125, 134, 136, 147, 159, 160, 168, 182, 185, 199, 203, 231, 233, 236, 240, 257, 262, 263, 276, 279, 280, 288, 290, 291, 297, 303, 312, 323, 324, 325, 337, 353, 363, 366, 376, 398, 434, 462, 481, 498, 509, 510, 543, 544, 551, 565, 568, 569, 595, 596, 597, 606, 609, 620, 622, 646, 659, 660, 664, 678-679, 685, 688
Graphs
  how to read 688
  types of 688
Hand organizer 262, 279
Index, searching an 680
Inferences 109, 125, 133, 147, 164, 250, 262, 327, 334, 407
Information, locating specific 92
Informative texts, how to read 498, 537, 538
Judgment 480-484
Knowledge questions (Reading Check) 11, 27, 41, 50, 66, 79, 105, 115, 133, 147, 212, 247, 256, 276, 288, 296, 323, 334, 353, 363, 376, 385, 418, 431, 448, 460, 473, 495, 509, 526, 535, 543, 551, 586, 595, 605, 620, 636, 646
KWL chart 127, 133
Language structure, applying knowledge of 609, 610, 622, 684
Main events
  recapping 473
  sequence of 646
Main idea 109, 212, 279, 296, 303, 402, 537, 538, 543, 671, 685
  finding supporting details for 279
  identifying the 109, 115, 262, 291
Maps
  cluster 262, 263, 276, 280, 288
  geographic 15, 92, 137, 280, 498, 500, 503, 510, 568, 569, 574, 599, 664, 687
  how to read 510
Matching purpose to text 528
Meanings, building 609
Media literacy 165, 403
Memorizing poetry 194
Narrative texts, how to read 262, 263, 537, 538
Nonfiction 108, 279, 498, 512, 513, 545, 672
Note taking 2, 31, 42, 51, 80, 87, 88, 93, 96, 124, 134, 148, 159, 165, 168, 176, 193, 237, 240, 304, 309, 474, 490, 496, 510, 527, 553, 637, 665, 682–683
Opinion 11, 15, 27, 29, 41, 50, 66, 79, 105, 109, 133, 134, 147, 192, 202, 203, 212, 250, 276, 327, 353, 354, 366, 376, 385, 396–400, 402, 407, 408, 418, 432, 460, 462, 473, 480, 481, 482, 486, 512, 538, 620, 636
Organizers 262, 276, 280. *See also* Graphic organizers.
Outline 304, 685
Paraphrasing 685
Personal response (including First Thoughts and Connecting with the Text) 2, 11, 15, 27, 31, 41, 44, 50, 53, 66, 69, 79, 96, 105,

109, 115, 117, 120, 121, 124, 126, 133,
136, 147, 168, 176, 180, 182, 185, 192,
195, 198, 199, 202, 204, 212, 240, 247,
250, 256, 258, 261, 263, 276, 280, 288,
291, 296, 312, 323, 327, 334, 338, 353,
356, 363, 366, 376, 379, 385, 408, 418,
431, 439, 448, 460, 462, 473, 490, 495,
498, 509, 513, 526, 528, 535, 538, 543,
545, 551, 572, 586, 589, 595, 599, 605,
610, 620, 623, 636, 639, 646

Persuasion 335, 354, 364, 377, 386, 396-400,
480-484
  evaluating 402
Poetry 178-179, 183-184, 194, 195, 674
  strategies for reading 194, 195
Predictions 2, 41, 44, 50, 79, 147, 164, 176,
204, 213, 258, 261, 312, 337, 338, 353,
363, 376, 408, 418, 431, 448, 513, 538,
572, 589, 599, 605, 610, 620, 636, 639
  making and adjusting 337
  tracking 338, 340, 344, 345, 347, 348
Prediction trail 337, 353
Prefixes 107, 609, 610, 622, 684, 762
Previewing 126, 408, 498, 538
Prior experience 2, 12, 15, 28, 42, 44, 53,
80, 96, 105, 106, 109, 117, 121, 125, 126,
168, 180, 185, 192, 194, 195, 199, 212,
240, 250, 256, 258, 312, 327, 338, 353,
356, 366, 377, 379, 398, 432, 482, 490,
498, 526, 561, 563, 564, 599, 659
Prior knowledge 27, 28, 30, 44, 125,
126-127, 263, 280, 288, 291, 337, 461,
599, 623
Problem solving 93, 165, 237, 309, 324, 335,
354, 364, 377, 386, 396-400, 403, 487,
569, 665
Purposes for reading, establishing 528, 535,
537, 538
Reading
  a manual 236
  poetry 194, 195
  for varied purposes 537, 538
Reading for Life
  evaluating persuasion 402
  independent reading situation 164
  induction/deduction 486
  reading a manual 236
  reading a map and a time line 664
  reading a science book 568
  searching the Internet 308
  using text organizers 92
Reading for varied purposes 537, 538
Reading rate 164, 537, 538
Reading skills, using 164
Recognizing connections 589
Recording text information 2, 126, 168, 572
Red herring 431
Reflecting 93, 165, 237, 309, 395, 403, 487,
569, 665
Rereading 161, 228, 306, 537, 551, 566, 662
Restating important events 53
Reviewing 27, 41, 50, 67, 79, 80, 105, 115,
133, 147, 247, 256, 276, 288, 303, 334,
353, 363, 376, 385, 481, 495, 496, 509,
535, 543, 551, 563, 586, 595, 605, 620,
636, 646

Roots 684
Science book, reading a 568
Semantic map 325, 622
Sequence chart 136, 147, 262, 263, 276, 366,
376, 646
Sequence, reading in 136, 147
Setting a purpose (Before You Read) 2, 15,
31, 44, 53, 69, 96, 109, 117, 121, 126, 136,
168, 180, 185, 195, 199, 204, 240, 250,
258, 263, 280, 291, 312, 327, 338, 356,
366, 379, 408, 439, 462, 490, 498, 513,
528, 538, 545, 572, 589, 599, 610, 623,
639
Similarities and differences, finding 51, 513,
551
Skimming 67, 105, 481, 498, 538
Stage directions 474
Story map 596, 685
Study skills 685-688
Suffixes 336, 609, 610, 622, 684, 761, 763
Summarizing 41, 52, 53, 58, 62, 64, 67, 115,
120, 136, 148, 157, 250, 280, 289, 376,
418, 565, 685
Supporting details 160, 232, 262, 279, 280,
291, 482, 483, 537, 662, 685
Synonym map 290
Synthesis (including Extending the Text) 27,
41, 50, 105, 124, 133, 147, 176, 192, 202,
247, 323, 353, 363, 376, 385, 431, 460,
473, 495, 509, 526, 586, 595, 605, 620
Test taking 688–690
Text organizers, using 92
Text structure, finding 262
Think-pair-share 96, 180, 240, 528
Think tank 379
Time line 664, 688
Time order. See Chronological order.
Time-order words 136
Venn diagram 51
Word parts, using 609, 610, 622
Word web 291, 297
Writer's perspective, analyzing 402

LANGUAGE (GRAMMAR, USAGE, AND MECHANICS)

A, an 696, 766
Abbreviations 236, 749
Accent marks in names 764
Accept, except 766
Action verbs 697
Adjective phrases 722
Adjectives 696-697
  commas separating two or more 536, 750
  comparing 135
  defined 696
  demonstrative 697
  phrase 722
  possessive 695, 714
  predicate 733
  proper 696-697, 746
Adverb phrases 722-723
Adverbs 699-700
  are never complements 729
  defined 699
  phrase 722-723

or prepositions 701
Affect, effect 607, 766
Affixes 622
Agreement 703-706
  problems in 704-706
  subject-verb 29, 43, 703-704
Ain't, avoiding 766
All ready, already 766
All right 766
A lot 767
Among, between 767
An, a 696, 766
And, using 567
Antecedents 278, 694
  with pronouns 249, 278
Anywheres 767
Apostrophes 758-759
  with contractions 257, 759
  not used with plurals 758
Appositives 751
  phrases 751
  pronouns with 717
Articles 696
At, avoiding after where 767
Auxiliary verbs 698
Bad, badly 149, 767
Base words 684
Between, among 767
Bring, take 767
Bust, busted 767
But, using 567
Capitalization 743-748
  of brand names 746
  of buildings and other structures 745
  of calendar items 745
  of first word in every sentence 743
  of geographical names 744
  of historical events and periods 745
  of monuments and awards 745
  of names of persons and animals 744
  of nationalities, races, and peoples 745
  of new quotations 336
  of planets, stars, and other heavenly bodies
    744
  of pronoun I 743
  of proper adjectives 746
  of proper nouns 743-746
  of religions, holy days, sacred writings, and
    deities 745
  of school subjects 748
  of teams, organizations, businesses, and
    government bodies 744
  of titles of persons 746-747
  of titles of works 747
  of trains, ships, airplanes, and spacecraft
    746
  of words showing family relationships 747
Choose, chose 767
Choppy sentences 485, 739
Chose, choose 767
Colloquial expressions 638
Colons 752-753
Combining sentences 401, 485, 663, 739-742
  by inserting words 740-741
  using connecting words 567
  using prepositional phrases 724

Commas 749-752
  in addresses 751
  with adjectives 536, 750
  in conventional situations 751-752
  correcting run-on sentences 163
  direct quotations set off by 755
  with interrupters 751
  with items in a series 544, 750
  in letters (salutations and closings) 752
  with quotation marks 756
  with speaker tags 336
Common nouns 743
Comparative and superlative forms 135, 717-718
Comparison
  with adjectives 135
  double 719
  irregular 719
  of modifiers 717-719
  regular 718
Complements 729-733
  direct objects 730
  indirect objects 730-731
  predicate adjectives 733
  predicate nominatives 732
  subject complements 731-733
Complex sentences 663
Compound nouns 693
Compound sentences 663, 734-735
Computer
  grammar checker 679
  hyphens and 760
  identifying sentence fragments 724
  italic type and 754
  spelling checker 236, 679, 712
Conjunctions 567, 701, 741
Connecting words, combining sentences using 567
Contractions 257, 638, 660, 759
Coordinating conjunctions 701
Could of 768
Declarative sentences 735
Demonstrative adjectives 697
Demonstrative pronouns 695, 697
Dialect 552, 553, 668-669
Dialogue 88, 336, 365, 435, 474, 669, 756-757
Direct objects 730
Direct quotations 378
Don't, doesn't 81, 705, 768
Double comparisons 719
Double negatives 720
Effect, affect 607, 766
End marks 214, 336, 735-736, 748-749, 755-756
Everyone 249
Everywheres, avoiding 768
Except, accept 766
Exclamation points 214, 336, 736, 748-749, 755-756
Exclamatory sentences 736
Fewer, less 768
Formal English 638, 691
Formal and informal English 638
Fragments, sentence 724, 737
Good, well 107, 719, 768
Grammar checker, computer 679

Greek roots 182, 214
Had ought, hadn't ought 768
Hardly, scarcely 768
Helping verbs 698-699, 706
Hisself 769
How come 769
Hyphens 298, 760
I, capitalization of 743
Imperative sentences 736
Indefinite pronouns 695, 704
Indirect objects 730-731
Indirect quotations 378
Interjections 702
Interrogative sentences 735
Interrupters, commas setting off 751
Intransitive verbs 698
Inverted word order, in sentences 705
Irregular comparison 719
Irregular verbs 13, 707-709
Italics (underlining) 484, 754
Its, it's 257, 695, 759, 769
Kind, sort, type 769
Kind of, sort of 769
Lay, lie 712
Learn, teach 769
Less, fewer 768
Lie, lay 712
Linking verbs 698, 730
Might of 768
Modifiers 717-720
  comparison of 717-719
  defined 717
  general and specific 116
  special problems with 107, 135, 719-720
  using 717-720
Must of 768
Nobody 249
Nouns 693-694
  capitalization of 743-748
  common 743
  compound 693
  defined 693
  as objects of prepositions 721
  plurals of, forming 764-765
  possessive 758
  proper 693, 743-746
  specific 694
Nowheres 767
Numbers 759, 760, 765
Objects 698
  direct 730
  indirect 730-731
  of prepositions 290, 701, 721
Or, using 567
Ought to of 768
Parts of speech 693-703
  adjectives 696-697
  adverbs 699-700
  conjunctions 567, 701, 741
  determining 702-703
  interjections 702
  nouns 693-694
  prepositions 700-701
  pronouns 694-696
  verbs 697-699, 727
Past participles of verbs 13, 706-709
Periods 214, 748

after abbreviations 749
correcting run-on sentences 163
ending declarative sentences 735
with quotation marks 336, 755-756
Personal pronouns 257, 694
Phrases 721
  adjective 722
  adverb 722-723
  appositive 751
  prepositional 290, 701, 704, 721-724
  verb 727
Plural nouns 758, 759, 764-765
Possessive adjectives 695, 714
Possessive nouns 758
Possessive pronouns 257, 695, 758
Predicate adjectives 733
Predicate nominatives 715, 732
Predicates 726-727
Prefixes 107, 609, 610, 622, 684, 761-762
Prepositional phrases 290, 701, 721-724
  adjective phrase 722
  adverb phrase 722-723
  combining sentences using 724
  between subjects and verbs 704
Prepositions 700-701
  or adverbs 701
  objects of 290, 701, 721
Present participles of verbs 706-709
Pronouns 694-696
  agreement of antecedents and 249, 278
  with appositives 717
  demonstrative 695, 697
  first-person 716
  indefinite 695, 704
  as objects of prepositions 290
  personal 257, 694, 713-714
  possessive 257, 695
  reflexive 695
  using 713-717
Proper adjectives 696-697, 746
Proper nouns 693, 743-746
Punctuation 336, 748-760
  apostrophes 257, 758-759
  colons 752-753
  commas 163, 336, 536, 544, 749-752, 755-756
  end marks 214, 336, 735-736, 748-749, 755-756
  exclamation points 214, 336, 736, 748-749, 755-756
  hyphens 298, 760
  italics (underlining) 484, 754
  periods 163, 214, 336, 735, 748-749, 755-756
  in poetry 194
  question marks 43, 214, 735, 748-749, 755-756
  quotation marks 304, 336, 378, 474, 484, 755-757
  semicolons 752, 753
  in Spanish 214
  underlining (italics) 484, 754
Question marks 43, 214, 735, 748-749, 755-756
Quotation marks 304, 336, 378, 474, 484, 755-757
Quotations 336, 378, 482, 755-757

Raise, rise 712-713
Reflexive pronouns 695
Regular verbs 707
Rise, raise 712-713
Roots 684
Run-on sentences 163, 738
Salutations, of letters 752-753
Scarcely, hardly 768
Semicolons 752, 753
Sentence fragments 724, 737
Sentences 91, 724-728
  choppy 485, 739
  classified by purpose 735-736
  combining 401, 485, 567, 663, 724, 739-742
  complete 736
  complex 663
  compound 663, 734-735
  declarative 735
  defined 724
  exclamatory 736
  fragments 724, 737
  imperative 736
  interrogative 735
  inverted word order in 705
  kinds of 733-736
  run-on 163, 738
  simple 733-734
  stringy 235, 739
  subjects of 43
  using varied 735
  verbs in 697
  wordy 307, 742
  writing clear 736-739
  writing effective 736-742
Series 544
Set, sit 711
Should of 768
Simple sentences 733-734
Sit, set 711
Slang 638, 660
Somewheres 767
Sort, type, kind 769
Sort of, kind of 769
Spanish
  punctuation in 214
  translation of 327
Speaker tags 336
Speech, parts of. *See* Parts of speech.
Spelling 761-765
  -cede, -ceed, -sede 762
  computer spelling checker 236, 679, 712
  doubling final consonants 257, 763
  ie, ei 762
  nouns ending in s 764
  numbers 765
  plural nouns 764-765
  prefixes 761, 762
  suffixes 336, 761, 763
  word roots 761
Spelling checker, computer 236, 679, 712
Stringy sentences 235, 739
Subject complements 731-732
  predicate adjectives 733
  predicate nominatives 732
Subject form of pronouns 713-715
Subjects 725-726

  agreement of verbs and 29, 43, 703-704
  compound 29, 43, 567, 705, 727, 728
  defined 725
  of sentences 43
  simple 726
Suffixes 336, 609, 610, 622, 684, 761, 763
Take, bring 767
Teach, learn 769
Tenses of verbs 709-713
  consistency of 52, 713
  defined 709
  future 709-710
  future perfect 709-710
  past 13, 52, 706-710
  past perfect 709-710
  present 52, 709-710
  present perfect 709-710
Than, then 770
That, who, which 771
That there 771
Their, they're 257, 759
Their, they're, there 597, 770
Theirs, there's 759
Theirself, theirselves 771
Then, than 770
There, they're, their 597, 770
There's, theirs 759
They're, their 257, 759
They're, their, there 597, 770
This here 771
Titles
  of persons 746-747
  of works 747, 754, 757
To, too, two 647
Transitive verbs 698
Translation, Spanish 327
Two, to, too 647
Type, kind, sort 769
Underlining (italics) 484, 754
Use to, used to 771
Verb phrases 727
Verbs 697-699, 727
  action 697
  agreement of subjects and 29, 43, 703-704
  auxiliary 698
  compound 567, 728
  helping 698-699, 706
  intransitive 698
  irregular 13, 707-709
  linking 698, 730
  principal parts of 706-709
  regular 707
  tenses of. *See* Tenses of verbs.
  transitive 698
  using 706-713
  vivid 68, 565, 699
Way, ways 771
Well, good 107, 719, 768
When, where 771
Where, avoiding, for *that* 771
Where, when 771
Which, that, who 771
Who, which, that 771
Who, whom 716
Who's, whose 257, 759
Word parts 107, 336, 609, 610, 622, 684
Wordy sentences 307, 742

Would of 768
Your, you're 257, 772
ZIP Codes 749

VOCABULARY AND SPELLING

Abbreviations 236, 749
Abstract words 278
Accent marks in names 764
Acquisition exercises (How to Own a Word) 13, 29, 43, 52, 68, 81, 107, 116, 135, 149, 214, 249, 257, 278, 290, 298, 325, 336, 355, 365, 378, 433, 448, 461, 475, 497, 511, 527, 536, 544, 553, 588, 597, 607, 622, 638, 647
Affixes 107, 336, 609, 610, 622, 684, 762-764
American Indian names 497
Analogies, word 433, 690
Antonyms 686
Base words 684
Borrowed words 448, 461
-cede, -ceed, -sede 762
Colloquial expressions 638
Compound words 298
Computer grammar checker 679
Computer spelling checker 236, 679, 712
Concrete words 278
Connotation 355, 475, 668
Consonants 763
  doubling final 257, 763
  silent 536
Context clues 13, 30, 31, 43, 79, 105, 194, 236, 250, 498, 638
Definition of word 30, 686
Denotation 668
Diacritical marks 686
Dialect 552, 553, 668–669
Dictionary 116, 135, 194, 213, 214, 298, 448, 461, 497, 536, 588, 606, 622, 647, 680, 686, 693, 707, 761, 773
English words, sources of 448, 461
Etymology 497, 588, 606, 622, 686
Formal and informal English 638
Glossary, using a 647
Glossary of usage 766–772
Greek roots 182, 214
Homonyms 553
Homophones 193, 597
Idiom 638, 686
ie, ei 762
Language structure, applying knowledge of 609, 610, 622, 684
Letters, silent, words with 336, 536, 597
Nouns, plurals of, forming 497, 764–765
Numbers, spelling 759, 760, 765
Plurals of nouns, forming 497, 764–765
Prefixes 107, 609, 610, 622, 684, 761–762
Pronunciation 686
Rhyming words 198
Roots 684
Scientific terms 498
Semantic mapping 325, 622
Silent letters 336, 536, 597
Slang 638, 660
Spanish roots 461
Spelling rules 762–765

Study skills 685-688
Suffixes 336, 609, 610, 622, 684, 763
Synonym map 290
Synonyms 81, 116, 135, 290, 325, 355, 686
Thesaurus 116, 135, 355, 685-686
Usage glossary 766-772
Word origins 461
Word parts 107, 336, 609, 610, 622, 684
Word roots 214, 622, 761
Words from world languages 497, 588, 606, 622
Word web 291, 297
Workplace vocabulary 149, 511

WRITING

Advertisement, writing an 487
Advice manual, writing an 93, 487
Analogies, word, writing 433
Anecdote, writing an 106, 400
Animal dialogue, writing an 248
Animal tales, writing 240
Anthology, collecting an 386
Arguments, listing 460
Article, writing an
  on astronomy 543
  for a magazine 256
  for a travel guide 289
Audience for writing 86, 158, 230, 231, 233, 234, 302, 304, 396, 398, 400, 480, 482, 562, 564, 566, 658
Autobiographical incident, writing an 12, 28, 42, 51, 67, 80, 86–90
Biographical sketch, writing a 106, 115, 120, 124, 134, 148, 158–162
Body
  drafting the 304
  writing the 161, 303, 482
Brochure, writing a 51, 309
Business letter, writing a 691
Captions, writing 134, 403, 510
Cause-and-effect matching game, making a 448, 460
Character
  describing a 134, 606
  profile, writing a 659
  traits, describing 134
Choosing a topic 87–88, 156, 159, 231, 289, 303, 398, 481, 560, 564, 569, 659–660
Clustering, using 398
Comic strip, making a 79, 552
Comparing and contrasting 90, 161, 304, 305, 474, 511
Computer dictionary, compiling a 213
Conclusion, writing a 88, 161, 233, 234, 303, 305, 398, 400, 481, 483, 564, 662
Concrete poem, writing a 277
Conversation, writing a 377
Criteria, writing 432, 482
Data sheet, filling out a 324
Description (descriptive writing) 28, 50, 53, 67, 88, 106, 109, 120, 121, 124, 134, 148, 181, 198, 304, 353, 356, 363, 376, 490, 495, 496, 510, 511, 512, 526, 527, 535, 543, 552, 553, 562–566, 605, 606, 668
Details, writing 12, 109, 115
  sensory details 53, 67, 87, 88, 109, 121,

124, 278, 527, 543, 562–566, 662
  supporting details 160, 232, 262, 279, 280, 291, 482, 483, 537, 662, 685
Dialect, writing 553
Dialogue, writing 42, 257, 336, 364, 365, 377, 403, 527, 552, 660, 662, 665
Dialogue bubbles, writing 473
Diary entry, writing a 27, 256, 636
Dictionary, compiling a 606
Documenting sources 304, 305, 682
Double-entry journal, writing in a 363
Drafting 88–90, 160–161, 232–234, 304–305, 398–400, 482–484, 564–565, 662
Elaboration strategies for writing 87, 232, 304, 399, 400, 482, 565, 660
E-mail, writing 681
Ending of a play, changing the 473
Evaluating and revising 13, 90, 161, 234, 306, 400, 484, 565–566, 567, 662
Evaluation, writing an 432, 460, 474, 480–484
Evaluation criteria 90, 162, 234, 306, 400, 484, 566, 662
Examples, writing 482
Expository writing 117, 158–162, 182, 193, 198, 203, 213, 230–234, 248, 256, 261, 277, 289, 302–306, 511, 535
Facts, as support in writing 304
Features, describing 161
Figures of speech, writing 325
5W-How? questions, answering 12, 147, 498, 509
Flowcharts, making 678–679
Formal and informal English, writing 638
Forms, filling out 692
Frameworks for writing 88, 161, 232, 303, 398, 481, 564, 659
Freewriting 28, 80, 87, 159, 256, 377, 462, 589, 610, 646, 659
Gift diagram, making a 117, 120
Glossary entry, writing a 647
Greeting card, writing a 335
How-and-why story, writing a 535, 552
How-to essay, writing a 177, 182, 193, 198, 203, 213, 230–234
Humorous essay or poem, writing a 297
Informative report, writing an 248, 256, 261, 277, 289, 302–306
Instruction manual, writing an 237
Introduction, writing an 88, 161, 234, 303, 398, 481, 482, 564, 662
Journal entry, writing a 213
Key words, listing 109
Legend, continuing a 177
Letter, writing a 354, 363, 403, 691
Literary magazine, compiling a 662
Main events, writing down 263, 276, 289, 662
Main idea, writing the 109, 279, 671
Map, making a 42
Memorial, making a 364
Menu, writing a 289
Message, writing to teach a 637
Movie proposal, writing a 587
Multimedia presentation, preparing a 677–679
Music commentary, writing 148
Myth, writing a 496

Narrative writing 12, 28, 42, 51, 67, 80, 86–90, 108, 587, 596, 606, 621, 637, 646, 658–662
Narrowing a topic 303, 569
Newscast, writing a 165
News story, writing a 147, 149
Note cards
  sample 682
  for speeches 561
  writing on 682
Note taking 2, 31, 42, 51, 80, 87, 88, 93, 96, 124, 134, 148, 159, 165, 168, 176, 193, 237, 240, 304, 309, 474, 490, 496, 510, 527, 553, 637, 665, 682–683
Obituary, writing an 148
Objective writing 512
Observational writing 161, 496, 510, 527, 535, 543, 552, 562–566, 662
Ode, writing an 261
On-line sources, listing 682
Order of events. See Organizing by chronological order.
Order of importance, organizing by 304, 482, 564, 566
Organizing
  by chronological order 88, 90, 161, 232, 236, 304, 418, 564, 566, 662, 688
  by comparison and contrast 90, 161
  by features 161
  by order of importance 304, 482, 564, 566
  by spatial order 564, 566
  using graphic organizers 51. See also Graphic organizers.
Outline, writing an 304, 685
Paragraphs
  writing 12, 51, 474, 596, 606, 637
  in written conversations 365
Paraphrasing 685
Pawbook, writing a 106
Peer review/editing 90, 234, 306, 400, 484, 566, 679
Personification, using 511
Persuasive writing 324, 335, 354, 364, 377, 386, 396–400, 432, 460, 474, 480–484
Phrase book, writing a 42
Plagiarism 679, 682
Plot map, making a 660
Poem, writing a 28, 120, 124, 182, 193, 198, 203, 386
Point of view, writing from a 67, 106, 256, 297, 335, 552, 621
Portfolio building 12, 28, 42, 51, 67, 80, 86–90, 91, 106, 115, 120, 124, 134, 148, 156–157, 158–162, 163, 177, 182, 193, 198, 203, 213, 228–229, 230–234, 235, 248, 256, 261, 277, 289, 297, 302–306, 307, 324, 335, 354, 364, 377, 386, 394–395, 396–400, 401, 432, 460, 474, 480–484, 485, 496, 510, 527, 535, 543, 552, 560–561, 562–566, 567, 587, 596, 606, 621, 637, 646, 658–662, 663
Position, supporting a 324, 335, 354, 364, 377, 386, 396–400
Potluck poem, writing a 124
Prediction trail, drawing a 353
Prewriting 87–88, 159–160, 231–232, 303–304, 397–398, 481–482, 563–564,

659–660
Print sources, listing 682
Process, writing instructions for a 230
Proofreaders' marks 692
Proofreading 43, 52, 91, 107, 149, 163, 214, 235, 249, 257, 278, 307, 336, 401, 484, 485, 497, 536, 567, 647, 663, 678
Pros and cons, writing 396
Proverb, writing a 527
Publishing 162, 306, 662
Questions, writing 120, 247, 498, 568
Question sheet, making a 537, 543
Quickwrite 15, 27, 44, 51, 53, 67, 69, 79, 109, 115, 117, 120, 121, 124, 126, 133, 136, 147, 181, 185, 193, 195, 198, 199, 202, 204, 213, 250, 256, 258, 261, 263, 280, 288, 291, 297, 327, 334, 338, 353, 356, 363, 366, 376, 379, 385, 408, 431, 439, 460, 462, 473, 498, 509, 513, 526, 528, 535, 538, 543, 545, 552, 589, 595, 599, 605, 610, 620, 623, 637, 639, 646
Quotations, using 482, 682
Reflection, writing a 93, 165, 237, 309, 395, 403, 487, 569, 665
Report, writing a 302–306, 511, 535, 543
Research and writing 106, 108, 256, 277, 289, 302–306, 377, 496, 527, 543, 606, 680–683
Responses to predictions, writing 204
Revising and evaluating 13, 52, 68, 90, 91, 116, 135, 161, 163, 214, 234, 235, 278, 306, 307, 335, 378, 400, 484, 485, 511, 565–566, 567, 638, 662, 663, 679, 694, 700, 706, 713, 716, 731, 739, 753, 772
Riddles, writing 193
Science writing 511
Script, writing a 42, 165, 248, 646
Self-evaluation 161, 306, 566, 662
Sentences, writing 43, 115, 214, 354, 481, 511, 513, 551, 588, 639
Sequence chart, making a 366, 376
Short short story, writing a 80
Sketch, biographical, writing a 106, 115, 120, 124, 134, 148, 158–162
Skit, writing a 93, 165
Song, writing a 93, 177, 665
Song title, writing a 93
Spatial order, organizing by 564, 566
Sportscast, writing a 12
Story, writing a 67, 106, 309, 527, 587, 596, 606, 621, 637, 646, 658–662, 665
Story ending, writing a new 324, 527
Story extension, writing a 637
Story ideas, writing 528
Story map, making a 596, 685
Style in writing 68, 116, 298, 325, 355, 511, 553, 588, 638
Subjective writing 512
Summarizing 41, 52, 53, 67, 148, 157, 289, 565, 685
Summary, writing a 12, 156, 280, 289, 309, 537, 586, 685
Suspense, using 662
Synonym map, making a 290
Talk, writing a 42
Thank-you note, writing a 237, 309, 377
Time capsule, creating a 213

Time line, making a 87, 182, 509, 543, 620, 664
Time order. See Organizing by chronological order.
Title, writing a 11, 51, 403, 495, 496, 662
Topic statement, writing a 637
Transitional expressions, writing 234, 289
Trickster tale, writing a 646
TV survey, making a 203
Venn diagram, making a 51
Word graph, making a 622
Word map, making a 81
Word web, making a 291, 297
Workplace English
  Learning for Life 93, 165, 237, 309, 403, 487, 569, 665
  vocabulary for the workplace 149, 511
Works cited, listing 305, 306, 683
Writer's Workshop 86–90, 158–162, 230–234, 302–306, 396–400, 480–484, 562–566, 658–662
Writing about theme 596

SPEAKING, LISTENING, AND VIEWING

Acting out 88
Active listening 395
Arguments, supporting 486
Audience 229, 560–561
Audio/video 12, 28, 148, 157, 165, 289, 297, 474, 487, 553, 569, 646, 665, 677, 678
Body language 436
Book review, oral 134
Choral reading 228–229
Class discussion 28, 386, 487
Class vote, taking a 377
Conflict resolution 487
Conversation 335, 394–395
Debate 28, 277, 377
Deductive reasoning 486
Demonstration 115, 237, 569
Dialogue 257, 335
Discussion, group 28, 68, 134, 136, 148, 164, 165, 237, 309, 354, 355, 379, 386, 462, 486, 487, 572, 599, 665
Drama 406, 435, 669
Dramatic reading 474, 621, 665
Facial expressions 120, 248
Gestures, using 229, 378, 665
Group work 28, 31, 42, 51, 68, 93, 105, 106, 120, 124, 134, 136, 148, 164, 185, 231, 248, 261, 277, 297, 303, 306, 309, 312, 324, 334, 354, 377, 379, 386, 394, 397, 403, 432, 437, 474, 481, 487, 496, 509, 538, 552, 572, 599, 637, 646, 665, 677, 678, 679
Inductive reasoning 486
Interactive program 678–679
Interview 50, 51, 88, 93, 108, 120, 148, 156–157, 165, 237, 277, 304, 309, 512
Interviewers, evaluating 157
Introductions 394
Learning for Life
  decision making 93
  machines, using 237

making oral presentations 665
  persuading with editorial cartoons 403
  researching media personalities 165
  scientific research 569
  settling conflicts with friends 487
  teaching people about animals 309
Listening skills 395
Media 134, 157, 165, 203, 309, 356, 379, 386, 480, 481, 487, 512, 526, 552, 569, 586, 677
Movement control 192
Multimedia presentation 677–679
Narrator, using a 134, 248, 496, 621, 637, 646, 665
Newscast 165
Note taking, during an interview 157
Ode presentation 261
Oral interpretation 228–229
Oral presentation 28, 31, 42, 67, 115, 134, 297, 378, 432, 474, 487, 496, 569, 599, 621, 637, 646, 665
Oral reading 105, 552
Oral storytelling 240, 298, 395, 596, 665
Pacing in interviewing 157
Panel discussion 354
Pantomime 248
Partner work 11, 52, 67, 79, 90, 91, 96, 115, 124, 134, 163, 165, 180, 182, 185, 192, 199, 203, 213, 229, 236, 237, 240, 247, 257, 276, 277, 298, 303, 306, 307, 308, 335, 364, 378, 386, 395, 397, 400, 401, 460, 481, 482, 484, 485, 510, 528, 536, 553, 560, 561, 566, 567, 569, 596, 620, 638, 660, 663, 665
Poetry reading 120, 228–229
Practice reading 12
Presentation
  multimedia 677–679
  oral 28, 31, 42, 67, 115, 134, 297, 378, 432, 474, 487, 496, 569, 599, 621, 637, 646, 665
Radio spot 309, 487
Reader's theater 31, 120, 496, 637, 665
Reading aloud 105, 120, 165, 179, 182, 192, 194, 195, 202, 214, 228–229, 235, 261, 386, 485, 551, 552, 646, 660
Reading script 229, 248
Reasoning, inductive and deductive 486
Rehearsal 42, 432, 474, 552, 561, 621, 637, 665, 678
Retelling
  a poem 12
  a story 11, 90, 460, 620
Role-play 11, 15, 27, 28, 31, 50, 51, 67, 69, 106, 115, 133, 134, 135, 136, 147, 148, 149, 185, 193, 202, 213, 248, 256, 277, 288, 289, 297, 334, 335, 362, 364, 365, 376, 408, 418, 436, 437, 448, 474, 487, 495, 510, 511, 512, 513, 535, 589, 595, 620, 621, 636, 637
Round robin 136, 599
Science fair 569
Science show 569
Skit 93, 165
Social interaction 394–395
Sound effects 229, 249, 386, 432
Speaking and Listening Workshop 156–157,

228–229, 394–395, 560–561
Speaking to inform 560–561
Spirituals 148
Storytelling festival 665
Survey 11, 203
Tableaux 134
Team-teaching 364
Think-pair-share 96, 180, 240, 528
Think tank 379
Tone 120
Video/audio 12, 28, 148, 157, 165, 289, 297, 474, 487, 553, 569, 646, 665, 677, 678
Visual aids 51, 237, 306, 510, 569, 606
Voice control 120, 192, 229, 436, 474, 552, 561, 621, 637, 665
Welcoming committee, forming a 42

RESEARCH AND STUDY

Absolute location, on a map 687
Almanac 304, 680
Atlas 680
Bar graphs 688
Bibliographies 680
Boldface words 92
Book, selecting a 164
Business letter, format for a 691
Call number, in a library 680
Card catalog 680
Catalog, in a library 680
  card 680
  on-line 680
CD-ROMs 678, 680
Character graph 134
Charts 27, 30, 79, 81, 92, 96, 105, 107, 125, 159, 168, 182, 199, 203, 232, 236, 240, 257, 262, 324, 398, 434, 462, 481, 498, 509, 510, 551, 565, 568, 569, 595, 597, 606, 609, 659, 688
Circle graphs 688
Compass rose 664, 687
Computers
  with CD-ROMs 678, 680
  databases 543, 680, 682
  design program 487
  dictionary 686
  grammar checker 679
  hyphens and 760
  identifying sentence fragments 724
  Internet 148, 277, 304, 308, 678, 680–682
  italic type and 754
  libraries on 135, 325
  library catalogs on 680
  making lists on 232
  progress in 204
  reference software 135, 325
  spelling checker 236, 679, 712
  style checker 712
  terms 213
  word processing software 236, 677, 679
  writing analysis by 734
Consulting sources 304
Databases, computer 543, 680, 682
Diacritical marks 686
Dictionary 116, 135, 194, 213, 214, 298, 448, 461, 497, 536, 588, 606, 622, 647,

680, 686, 693, 707, 761, 773
Documenting sources 304, 305, 682
Elevation on maps 687
E-mail 681
Encyclopedias 148, 365, 497, 569, 680
Entry words, in a dictionary 686
Footnotes 30
Forms, filling out 692
Glossary 30, 236, 773–780
  using a 647
Graphs 498, 510, 569, 688
  reading 688
  types of 688
Headings in texts 92, 568
Hits on World Wide Web 681
Hyperlinks, Web 680
Index, of a book 236, 568
Indices, in library reference section 680
Information, researching 165, 182, 289, 304, 568, 569, 680–683
Internet 148, 277, 304, 308, 678, 680–682
Key, on map 664
Key verbs, identifying 690
Keywords, on-line 308, 680
Latitude, on a map 687
Legend, on a map 664, 687
Letters, business 691
Libraries 80, 106, 148, 156, 277, 297, 306, 474, 606, 665, 680
Line graphs 688
Listing sources 679, 682, 683
Locator maps 687
Logos 92
Longitude, on a map 687
Maps
  cluster 262, 263, 276, 288
  geographic 15, 92, 137, 280, 498, 500, 503, 510, 568, 574, 599, 664, 687
  how to read 510
Media centers 680
Modem 680
Note card, sample 682
Note taking 2, 31, 42, 51, 80, 87, 88, 93, 96, 124, 134, 148, 159, 165, 168, 176, 193, 237, 240, 304, 309, 474, 490, 496, 510, 527, 553, 637, 665, 682–683
Oral reports 80
Outlines 262, 685
Part-of-speech label in dictionary 686
Periodicals 680
Physical map 687
Pie graph 688
Plagiarism 679, 682
Plot map 660
Political map 687
Portable databases 680, 682
Pronunciation in a dictionary 686
Proofreaders' marks 692
Rating scale 15, 27, 134, 203, 231, 250, 366, 432
Readers' Guide to Periodical Literature 543, 680
Reference software 135, 325
Reference works 680
Research activities 28, 42, 51, 80, 106, 108, 134, 135, 148, 156, 182, 256, 277, 289, 297, 304, 324, 354, 364, 365, 377, 496,

497, 527, 543, 569, 587, 606
Researching information 165, 182, 236, 289, 304, 568, 569, 680–683
Resources, searching for 680
Scale of map 664, 687
Scanning tests 688
Search engine 681
Search terms 308, 681
Sequence chart 136, 147, 262, 263, 276, 366, 376, 646
Sources
  consulting 304
  documenting 304, 305, 682, 683
  evaluating electronic 681–682
  listing 679, 682–683
  MLA guidelines for citing 683
Special-purpose maps 687
Study skills 685–688
Synonym finder 135, 325
Synonyms, books of 685–686
Table of contents 92, 568
Tables of facts 92, 498, 568, 688
Taking notes. See Note taking.
Tests, taking 688–690
  analogy 690
  essay 690
  matching 689
  multiple-choice 689
  true/false 688–689
Thesaurus 116, 135, 355, 685–686
Top-level domains, Web 682
Uniform Resource Locators (URLs) 680
Venn diagram 51
Web browsers 680
Web directories 308, 681
Web sources, evaluating 681–682
Web pages 680
Word map 81
Word origins in a dictionary 686
Word processing software 236, 677, 679
Works cited 305, 306, 683
  guidelines for 683
  sample entries for 683
World Wide Web 308, 680–681

CROSSING THE CURRICULUM

Ads, evaluating 386
Archaeology 513
Art 258
  animation 677
  biographical sketch 134
  birthday card 335
  book cover 496
  cartoon 296, 297, 403, 473, 587
  clay model 80
  collage 124, 165, 193, 261, 364
  comic strip 79, 297, 552
  concrete poem 277
  costumes 432, 437, 621, 646
  cultural objects 606
  diagram 117, 498, 510, 569
  dialogue bubbles 473
  diorama 432
  drawing 12, 42, 80, 106, 117, 180, 182, 193, 198, 213, 214, 237, 261, 276, 296, 297,

309, 325, 335, 354, 364, 403, 460, 527, 596, 606
fabric puppet 80
game design 487
graphics 677
life map 12
map 42, 510, 587
modeling clay 261
multimedia presentation 28, 677–679
mural 148
pawbook 106
photography 28, 134, 261, 297, 309, 496, 498, 510, 552, 568, 569
poster 51, 237
props 42, 248, 432, 646
road map 354
scenery 248, 432
science mural 569
sculpture 193
sketch 148, 249, 334, 403, 496, 596, 621
stage set 432
star map 587

storyboard 67
time capsule 213
Astronomy 531
Book club 164
Commercials, evaluating 386
Community service 42
Culture 15, 27, 28, 42, 598, 608, 617, 665
Dramatic arts 444
E-mail shorthand 211
Folklore 617
Geography 280, 354, 510
Interactivity 677
Legends 286
Literature and . . .
  astronomy 531
  culture 617
  dramatic arts 444
  legends 286
  music 44
  real life 96, 189, 545
  religion 240
  science 63, 103, 424

social studies 2, 15, 53, 121, 136–137, 168, 172, 280, 346, 490, 520, 604
Math 256, 304
Media 134, 157, 165, 203, 309, 356, 379, 386, 480, 481, 487, 512, 526, 552, 569, 586, 677
Multimedia 677
Music 28, 44, 93, 148, 177, 229, 248, 665, 678
Real life 93, 96, 165, 189, 237, 309, 403, 487, 545, 569, 665
Religion 240
Science 63, 103, 182, 237, 277, 289, 309, 324, 510, 511, 531, 543, 569, 587
Social studies 15, 28, 53, 121, 134, 136–137, 168, 172, 280, 289, 346, 356, 364, 490, 520, 543, 569, 604
Songs 297
Sports 96
Technology 176, 199, 212, 213, 237, 543

INDEX OF ART

FINE ART

Alston, Charles, *Family No. 9* 341
American folk art
  pair of parrots 548
  rooster 545
Avery, Milton, *Seated Girl with Dog* 252
Baggett, William, *Reflex* 312–313
Brady, Mathew, photograph of Abraham Lincoln and his son Tad 130
Caravaggio, Michelangelo, *Fruit Basket* 590–591
  Medusa 577
Chagall, Marc, *The Village* 247
Chinese painting of an astronomer (1675) 541
Dulac, Edmund, *The Chamberlain Goes in Search of the Nightingale* 224
  Chinese Man in Bed with Goblin over Him 223
  Chinese Man on Boat 220
  Chinese Man with Two Women with Fans 216
Elsheimer, Adam, *Baucis and Philemon* 592–593
Fabergé, *The Orange Tree Egg* 219
Finn, David, *Large Sun* 319
Greek, *Perseus beheading the Medusa* 579
Greek statue of Gorgon 572–573
Green, Jonathan, *Boy by the Sea* 111
  Fishing on the Trail 112
  Tales 570–571
Hayden, Palmer C., *He Laid Down His Hammer and Cried* 173
  John Henry on the Right, Steam Drill on the Left 171
  When John Henry Was a Baby 169
Hockney, David, *Japanese Rain on Canvas* 315

Hoffman, Martin, *Open Road* 344
Ibarra, Rose, *Girl Seated at Table* 329
Jiménez, Manuel, *Animals* (1960) 238–239
Kane, John, *Across the Strip* 60
Kennedy, Scott, *Eager to Run* 98–99
  Never Alone (detail) 100–101, 102
  Siberian Husky 97, 106
Lawrence, Jacob, *Harriet Tubman Series* No. 7 141
  Harriet Tubman Series No. 10 143
  Harriet Tubman Series No. 11 145
Marin, John, *Sunset, Casco Bay* 316–317
Mazloomi, Carolyn L., *Hoop Dreams* 10
Midgette, Willard, *Sitting Bull Returns at the Drive-In* 16–17
Northwest Coast Indian mask 492, 493
Pious, Robert Savon, *Harriet Tubman* 148
Pompeian mosaic 513
Rivera, Diego, *Flower Day* 122
Rockwell, Norman, *Pinch Bug in Church* 151
  School, This Year Means More Than Ever Before (Boys on Bicycles) 58
Rogers, Sultan, *Crawling Snake* 546–547, 551, 552
Seuss, Dr. (Theodor Geisel), *The Sneetches* 379, 380–381, 382–383, 385, 386
Sioux moccasins 20
Spanish engraving of Montezuma II (c. 1480–1520) 604
Tang dynasty (A.D. 618–906) celestial sphere 542
York, Star Liana, *Minnie Manygoats* 119

ILLUSTRATIONS

Bollinger, Peter 180–181
Borovski, Menny 117, 118–119, 121, 122–123, 240–241, 244–245, 246, 294–295
Britt, Tracy 186, 192

Callanan, Brian 137, 599
Chess, Victoria 630, 631, 632, 633, 634, 635
Chesworth, Michael 366–367, 370, 374–375, 648–649, 651, 652, 653, 654–655
Colby, Gary 210, 211

Davis, Nancy 35, 37, 41
Diagle, Stephan 488–489, 618–619
Diaz, David 138, 139, 146
Duranceau, Suzanne 623, 624, 625, 627, 628, 629

Florian, Douglas 195, 196, 197

Galouchko, Annouchka 610–611, 612–613, 614–615, 616
Gill, Mariano 644, 645

Henderson, David 54, 55

Ingber, Marty 96–97, 102–103, 114

Morris, Burton 554, 555, 556, 557

Newsom, Tom 150, 153, 154

Park, Chang 356–357, 358–359
Pavey, Jerry 639, 640, 642
Prato, Rodica 574

Ross, Bill 299, 300

Sauber, Robert 471, 472
Schrier, Fred 30, 184, 188, 298, 395, 511, 588
Slimfilms/Christie 19, 265, 280, 500, 503
Spector, Joel 514, 516, 518, 522
Stevenson, David 600, 601, 603

Vázquez, Carlos 439, 440, 443, 447, 451, 453, 455
Verougstraete, Randy 425, 426, 427, 428

Wenzel, David 69, 70–71, 72–73, 74, 75, 77, 78
Wiley, Paul 204–205, 207, 208

MAPS

Ancient Greece 574

Cascade Range 500

Destruction Caused by the Eruption of Mount St. Helens 503

Harriet Tubman's Route to Freedom 137

Kaw Homeland 15

Toltec Sites in Mexico 599

Vietnam 280

CARTOONS

The Born Loser 116

Caricature, Long Abraham Lincoln a Little Longer 133

Koren, Edward 673

Schulz, Charles, Peanuts 91, 183, 306, 561
Shanahan, Danny 667
Stevenson 157

Tobey, Barney 563

Watterson, Bill, Calvin and Hobbes 14, 194, 202, 229, 278, 675
Williams, Marcia, Perseus and the Gorgon's Head 582–585
Wilson, Tom, Ziggy 125

INDEX OF AUTHORS AND TITLES

Page numbers in italic type refer to the pages on which author biographies appear.

Adventure of the Speckled Band, The 409
Adventures of Tom Sawyer, The, from 150
Aesop 644, 645
Alexander, Lloyd 71, *78*
Ali Baba and the Forty Thieves 611
All-American Slurp, The 32
All I Really Need to Know I Learned in Kinder-garten, from 292
All Summer in a Day 313
Andersen, Hans Christian 215, 226, 625
Anderson, Marian 158
Angelou, Maya 110, *113*
Ankylosaurus 180
Anonymous African American 169
Asimov, Isaac 205, *209*
Avi 367, *375*

Bambara, Toni Cade 669
Barkin, Carol 231
Baucis and Philemon 590
Beauty of the Beasts, The, from 264
Beshore, George 539, *542*
Blake, William 685
Blanca Flor 440
Book of Nonsense, from 671
Bracelet, The 357
Bradbury, Ray 313, *320*
Brooks, Gwendolyn 178
Brother 110
Browning, Robert 178
Bruchac, Joseph 491, *494*

Camel, The 299
Caution to Everybody, A 299
Chang, Cindy 528
Charles, Dorthi 277
Cisneros, Sandra 179, 328, 331, *333*
City, The 670
Coatsworth, Elizabeth 670
Concrete Cat 277
Coolidge, Olivia 573, *581, 590*
Cormier, Robert 54, *65*
Cosby, Bill 82, *84*
Coville, Bruce 425
Crow Poets 24
Cruse, Amy 600
Cynthia in the Snow 178

Daiches, David 674
Dickinson, Emily 671
Dog of Pompeii, The 514
Doyle, Sir Arthur Conan 409, *424*
Dragon, Dragon 648
Duck, The 299
Duffy's Jacket 425
Dygard, Thomas J. 3, *9*

Eleven 328
Eliot, T. S. 429
Emperor's New Clothes, The 625

Fame Is a Bee 671

Fisher, Lise 321
Flood, The 264
Florian, Douglas *195, 196, 197*
Foul Shot 10
Fox and the Crow, The 644
Freedman, Russell 108, 127, *131*
Fulghum, Robert 292, *295*
Fun They Had, The 205

Gardner, John 649, *656*
Geisel, Theodor Seuss 380, *384*
Get Off the Couch 396
Glory over Everything, A 138
Gold Cadillac, The 339
Good Hot Dogs 179
Gorilla, My Love, from 669
Gralla, Preston 210

Hamilton, Virginia 640, *643*
Harris, Gloria A. 174
Helfer, Ralph 264, *274*
He Lion, Bruh Bear, and Bruh Rabbit 640
Hill Mynah, The 196
Hoey, Edwin A. 10
Housman, A. E. 675
Hovland, Lynn 396
How the Camel Got His Hump 756
How the Snake Got Poison 546
Hubbell, Patricia 672
Hummingbird, The 197
Hurston, Zora Neale 546, *549*
Huynh Quang Nhuong 281, *287*

I Dream a World, from 350
Ignatow, David 670
I Know Why the Caged Bird Sings, from 110
In the Forest with the Elephants, from 302
I Was Not Alone 350

James, Elizabeth 231
January 667
Jimmy Jet and His TV Set 200
John Henry 169
Just Once 3

Katz, Bobbi 188, *191*
King Long Shanks 630
Kipling, Rudyard 756
Koenig, Louis W. 132
Krewson, Chris 457
Krishnaswami, Uma 480
Künzler, Rosemarie 471
Kyle, Robert 24

La Bamba 45
Land I Lost, The, from 281
Lanker, Brian 350
Lauber, Patricia 499, *508*
Lear, Edward 671
Lessons 82
Lester, Julius 554, *558*
Lincoln's Humor 132
Loo-Wit, the Fire-Keeper 491
Los pétalos 123
Lowry, Lois 87
Lueders, Edward 184

Macavity: The Mystery Cat 429
Magic Mortar, The, from 658
Malam, Charles 190, *191*
Manning, Jack 476
McVitty, Walter 611
Medusa's Head 573
Montgomery, L. M. 668
Mora, Pat 123, *123*
Morrison, Lillian 187, *191*
Mother Doesn't Want a Dog 255
Murie, Margaret E. 562
My Lord, What a Morning, from 158
Mysterious Mr. Lincoln, The 127

Namioka, Lensey 32, *39*
Nash, Ogden 299, *300*
Netiquette 210
New Complete Babysitters Handbook, The, from 231
Nightingale, The 215

Octopus, The 299
Ode to Mi Gato 259
Once 331
Our Washing Machine 672

Panther, The 299
Parks, Rosa 350
Paulsen, Gary 97, *104*
Perseus and the Gorgon's Head 582
Petals 123
Petry, Ann 138, *146*
Pied Piper of Hamelin, The, from 178
Poe, Edgar Allan 673
Poison Tree, A, from 685
Pompeii 524
Prelutsky, Jack 180, *181*
President Cleveland, Where Are You? 54

Quetzalcoatl 600

Rags 673
Raven, The, from 673
Rockliff, Mara 463, 644, 645
Rumpelstiltskin (dramatization) 463
Rumpelstiltskin (fairy tale) 471
Rylant, Cynthia 251, *254*

Scanning the Heavens 539
Scene 675
Schmidt, Michel J. 302
Science in Ancient China, from 539
Sendak, Maurice 667
Seuss, Dr. (Theodor Geisel) 380, *384*
Seventh Sister, The 528
Sidewalk Racer, The 187
Silverberg, Robert 524
Silverstein, Shel 200, *201*
Simon, Hilda 550
Since Hanna Moved Away 672
Singer, Isaac Bashevis 241, *246*
Smith, Roland 302
Smith, William Jay 186, *191*

Snakes: The Facts and the Folklore 550
Sneetches, The 380
Soto, Gary 45, 49, 259, 260
Southpaw, The 387
Stars of Stage, Screen . . . and Social Studies
   Class 476
Star Struck 457
Steam Shovel 190
Stone, The 71
Storm 97
Storm, The 670
Stray 251
Suit Helps Girl Enjoy Daylight 321

Ta-Na-E-Ka 16
Tapahonso, Luci 118, 119
Taylor, Mildred D. 339, 348–349
Things to Do If You Are a Subway 188
Thoughts on Progress, from 674
Thurman, Judith 673
Toaster, The 186
Trial by Fire 274
Twain, Mark 150, 154
Two in the Far North, from 562

Uchida, Yoshiko 357, 362, 658
Untermeyer, Louis 514, 523

Vigil, Angel 440, 456
Viorst, Judith 255, 387, 392, 407, 672
Volcano, from 499

Weird! 407
What Do Fish Have to Do with Anything? 367
When I Was One-and-Twenty, from 675
Whitebird, Mary 16
Who's the New Kid?, from 87
Why Dogs Chase Cats 554
Williams, Marcia 582
Wolf and the House Dog, The 645
Woodsong, from 97
Working on the Railroad 174

Yes, It Was My Grandmother 118
Yolen, Jane 630
Your Poem, Man . . . 184

Zlateh the Goat 241
Zolotow, Charlotte 675

STUDENT WRITERS

Ali, Raisa 233
Behee, Paul 314
Boscamp, Jenny 305

Caflisch, Jane 661
Chen, Elena 399
Cheung, James 40
Clayton, Lacey 89
Friedman, Abigail 189
Gaddis, Katharine ("Katie") 575
Garnett-Kranz, Merenda 483
Gazit, Aviv 402
George, Gim 114
Gilner, Meagan 491
Goodridge, Emily 459
Harris, Matt 162
Hernandez, Monique 170
Jaber, Rana 97
Kolar, John 4
LaForge, Mike 26
Lehman-Becker, Suki 260
Lesher, Sara 619
Novak, Morgan Faris 534
Orthey, Sharon 565
Shane, Loretta 26
Sisaleumsak, Bea 241
Smith, Casie Anne 322
Woo, Taunya 192